DAILY LIFE
at the Turn of the Neolithic

DAILY LIFE
at the Turn of the Neolithic

A comparative study of longhouses with
sunken floors at Resengaard and nine other
settlements in the Limfjord region, South Scandinavia

John Simonsen

MUSEUM SALLING

JUTLAND ARCHAEOLOGICAL SOCIETY

DAILY LIFE AT THE NEOLITHIC

A comparative study of longhouses with sunken floors at Resengaard and nine other settlements in the Limfjord region, South Scandinavia

© The author and Jutland Archaeological Society 2017

Layout: Ea Rasmussen and Lars Foged Thomsen
Graphics: Lars Foged Thomsen
Language revision: Elaine Bolton
Printed by Narayana Press
Paper: Luxosatin 130g

Jutland Archaeological Society Publications Vol. 98

ISBN 978-87-93423-14-5
ISSN 0107-2854

Published in cooperation between
Museum Salling and Jutland Archaeological Society

Jysk Arkæologisk Selskab
Moesgaard
Moesgaard Allé 20
DK-8270 Højbjerg

Distribution:
Aarhus Universitetsforlag
Langelandsgade 177
DK-8200 Aarhus N

This book is published with the gracious support of the following Danish private foundations:

Aage og Johanne Louis-Hansens Fond
Beckett-Fonden
Farumgaard-Fonden
Den Hielmstierne-Rosencroneske Stiftelse

Contents

Acknowledgements 11

Introduction: Theme, time and area 15

Chapter 1: Aims, research history and methodological approach 17

    1.1. Characteristics of sunken-floor houses 17

    1.2. Objectives of the present work 18
        Ground plan elements of the houses   18
        Architecture, agriculture and domestic refuse   19
        Artefacts, interior arrangements and activities   19
        Household production, specialization and exchange   20
        Pottery chronology in the shadowy centuries   20

    1.3. Existing interpretations of South Scandinavian house sites 21
        Initial knowledge 1957   21
        A quantum leap in new knowledge 1973   22
        Further knowledge from 1980 onwards   22

    1.4. Field research history in Denmark and beyond 27
        Investigations in the Limfjord region   27
        Investigations elsewhere in Jutland   29
        A glance at neighbouring countries   33
        Some "classic" South Scandinavian house sites   37
        The end of a 900-year era   37

    1.5. Methodological reflections and theoretical inspiration 38
        Sunken-floor formation processes   38
        Field research strategies   39
        Source critique on geographical representativeness   39
        Source critique on physical destruction   41
        Analytical approach   42
        Sources of theoretical inspiration   44

    Notes 46

Chapter 2: Analysis and interpretation of houses with sunken floors 51

    2.1. Establishing the sources 51
        Strategies for methods of excavation   52
        Measuring distances between postholes   58
        Measuring sunken floor depths   59

    Measuring soil features and raw dimensions of houses   60
    Sunken-floor horizon versus secondary fill   61

2.2. Presenting the Resengaard houses ... 62
    The hill, its terraces and the house plots   63
    Occurrence and absence of thick topsoil layers   64
    Presentation of the buildings   64
    Twelve longhouses   66
    Three minor houses with specific traits   93
    Ten other minor houses   95
    A short house   102
    Two uncertain structures   102

2.3. Elements of the Resengaard houses ... 103
    Sunken-floor longhouses in brief   103
    Burned house versus burned house scrap   105
    Two-aisled constructions   105
    Outer wall posts   106
    Interior panel wall stakes and posts   106
    Thick turf walls   108
    Doorways and a remarkable "corridor"   109
    Connecting, east-sloping ramps   109
    Dividing walls and compartments   109
    Long side recesses and cubicles   110
    Bejsebakken, Myrhøj, Fosie and Scord of Brouster   110

2.4. Radiocarbon dating at Resengaard ... 112
    Selecting suitable samples   112
    Dating results on short-life materials   112

2.5. Other "late" houses in the central Limfjord region ... 113
    Gåsemose   114
    Kluborg II   119

2.6. Beaker houses in the central Limfjord region ... 121
    Glattrup I/III   122
    Marienlyst Strand   123
    Granlygård   125
    Hellegård   127
    Glattrup IV   130
    Rosgårde   137
    Tromgade   139

2.7. Lifecycle biographies of longhouse plots ... 142
    Destructive and preserving agents   142
    Twelve lifecycle stages   143

2.8. Further Limfjord region traits of sunken floors ... 146
    Relative lengths of the sunken floors   146
    Sunken-floor areas in special longhouses   148
    The selected house plots   149
    The sunken floor idea   150

Notes ... 153

Chapter 3: Chronology of pottery assemblages ... 155

3.1. Primary chronological objectives ... 155
Aiming for an independent chronology — 156

3.2. Chronological method ... 157
Survey of pottery assemblages — 157
Source-critical aspects — 161
Frame of interpretation — 162
Design of concrete methodological path — 163
Chronological entities — 164
Comparing rim profiles — 164
Further comments on method — 165
Technical remarks — 167

3.3. Provisional chronology of the Resengaard pottery ... 168
Comparison of the four reference assemblages — 168
Affinities of the eight remaining longhouse assemblages — 172
Affinities of assemblages from twelve minor houses and a short house — 176
Affinities of certain pit assemblages — 182
Strong and weak links in the chronological chain — 190
Results of a relative chronology at Resengaard — 190
Comparison with the radiocarbon dating — 194
Ad hoc substantiation and options for further validation — 197
Making use of the provisional Resengaard chronology — 199

3.4. Beaker decoration and pottery shapes ... 199
Beaker ornamentation on early Resengaard pottery — 200
Pottery shapes at Bejsebakken, Stendis, Myrhøj, and Tastum I — 200

3.5. Anchoring certain "classic" sites to the provisional Resengaard chronology? ... 201
Egehøj, Torslev, Vadgård and Vejlby — 201

3.6. Anchoring certain new sites to the provisional Resengaard chronology? ... 203
Gåsemose and Kluborg II — 203

3.7. Relationships of certain new sites to Myrhøj and Tastum I? ... 206
Glattrup I/III and Marienlyst Strand — 207
Granlygård, Hellegård and Glattrup IV — 210
Rosgårde and Tromgade — 212

3.8. Towards a settlement chronology for the Limfjord region? ... 215

Notes ... 216

Chapter 4: Artefacts, pits, patches, and daily life activities ... 219

4.1. Some *a priori* considerations ... 220
Artefacts and soil patches — 220
Core areas and activity spaces — 221
Systematic study of floor horizons — 222
Characterizing the activities — 223

4.2. Interpreting the floors in twelve longhouse sites at Resengaard ... 226

4.3. Interpreting the floors in three special minor house sites at Resengaard ... 258

4.4. Interpreting the floors in ten minor house sites and one short house site at Resengaard 262

4.5. Interpreting the floors in other house sites from the central Limfjord region 272
    Gåsemose   272
    Kluborg II   272
    Glattrup I/III   277
    Marienlyst strand   280
    Granlygård   284
    Hellegård   285
    Glattrup IV   294
    Rosgårde   303
    Tromgade   305

4.6. Further considerations on soil features, plant remainders, and artefacts 309
    Things placed below roofs or above floors?   313
    Presence of floor layers in sunken-floor horizons   314
    Placement of pits and patches   322
    Scorched-stone patches, stones, and fireplaces   326
    Scorched-stone patches and charred plant residues   332
    Scorched-stone patches and emergence of low zones   333
    Scorched-stone patches and artefact placements   334
    Vestiges in further house sites from the Limfjord region   340

4.7. Repeated everyday doings performed in the activity spaces? 341

Notes 344

Chapter 5: Household, livelihood and exchange 345

5.1. Architecture, household and local settlement 345
    Main functions of the eastern and western floor areas?   346
    Longhouse architecture reflecting economic strategies?   346
    Indoor pit arrangements and livelihood strategies   349
    Household composition, social status and architecture   351
    Three alternative outlines of local settlement   352
    Crystallization of a particular place among local settlements?   355

5.2. Living and working conditions indoors 358
    Keeping the longhouse interiors warm?   358
    How did scorched-stone devices work?   360
    Further evidence of heating devices from the Limfjord region   361

5.3. Settlement continuity and short-range relocation 362
    Settlements with strong area continuity   362
    Relocation of dwellings and avoidance of old grounds   364

5.4. Strategic, ritual and votive depositions 367
    Household waste and its handling   367
    Strategies on use of abandoned sunken floors and hollow terrains   372
    Ritually performed re-deposition of house waste?   373
    House abandonment rituals   374
    Votive pit with a set of items and another with an exquisite sickle   375
    Pits with deliberately smashed, deposited pottery   375
    Votive offerings of charred cereals   379

5.5. Fields, pastures and other agricultural aspects 379
   Presenting the "Field/pasture hypothesis"   380
   Long-term cultivation cycles   382
   Growing season and crops   385
   Harvest and further treatment   386
   Storage and use of cereals   389
   Some other ecological facets   391
   Initial ard-ploughing as a ritual doing?   392

5.6. Household production and specialization 393
   Seven cases of presumed specialization   394
   Commodities such as amber, honey and salt   401
   Presenting the "Model of three-level household production"   402
   A-level production in all or most households   404
   B-level production in many households   405
   C-level production in a few households   407
   Further comments on the idea behind model   408

5.7. Household exchange from a regional perspective 410
   Inspiring classic and newer anthropological studies on exchange   410
   Transport of people and commodities in the Limfjord archipelago   416
   Population density, production and exchange   417
   Exchange, maritime travel and ocean gateways   420

Notes 421

Closing remarks 425

Appendix: Further detail on pottery relationships 429
Part A. Resengaard, LN II/emerging Bronze Age 429
Part B. Classic sites, LN I or LN II/emerging Bronze Age 444
Part C. New sites, LN II/emerging Bronze Age 446

Catalogue A: Ceramics at Resengaard 449

Catalogue B: Stone artefacts at Resengaard 499

Catalogue C: Charred plant remains at Resengaard 513

Illustration credits 516

Literature 517

Acknowledgements

In the life of an archaeologist, particular moments in time remain indelibly stamped on one's memory and, even many years later still remain as clear as if they were yesterday. You remember where it took place, how the environment looked and what happened. One such incident occurred in August 1989. Two employees at the museum in Skive, now Museum Salling, returned to the office late in the afternoon. They had spent the day digging a trial excavation near the top of a hill by the fjord because engineer Hans Møller from the municipality, as so often before, had kindly given us a tip off about ongoing sewer work. Their eager reporting that they had observed and cleaned a minor area around two closely placed major soil features containing potsherds of a certain coarsely tempered ware got our minds wondering: was it now that we had, at last, after years of intensive efforts, found house sites with sunken floors several centuries younger than the vestiges of the Beaker houses at Myrhøj and Tastum? The archaeological office was at this time located in the old manor house, Krabbesholm, on the Limfjord coast. Through the small rectangular panes, the late afternoon sun found its way into the dim room. And, with the help of the bright light from its yellow rays, the potsherds were carefully twisted, turned and discussed. It certainly seemed that we had at last found something we had long been seeking. At that crucial moment, however, we had no idea that an investigation of the entire settlement would take many regular campaigns over the next 11 years!

The settlement found was Resengaard and, soon after, the investigation was able to begin. With the assistance of a machine driver from a local contractor, who had so often dug for us before, the topsoil was cautiously removed from an area. After hours of careful excavation on our knees, digging with trowels, the rim of a broken clay pot or a heavily used flint scraper might, for instance, turn up. Such artefacts would probably not usually have called for such great attention but, in fact, they did just that in the months we spent at these two sites of ancient longhouses. Due to their exceptional state of preservation, we realised that we had a unique opportunity to obtain an unusually close insight into the everyday life of people who lived around four millennia ago, at a momentous time of transition between the Stone Age and the Bronze Age. Our expectations were high, as the objects were precisely where they had been left by these residents of the ancient past. Even the smallest discoveries brought joy and enthusiasm to the excavation team, being so close to the authentic remains of the ancient life. And, for me and others, it was not simply the excavations of objects that were of interest but also the possibility of observing old soil features coming to light, telling us yet more about prehistoric life in these longhouses.

I would like to sincerely thank all those volunteers, workers, students and professionals who toiled during the excavations at Resengaard, Kluborg II, Glattrup, I/III & IV, Marienlyst Strand, Granlygård, Hellegård, Rosgårde and Tromgade, often under the harsh North

Jutland weather conditions. I am likewise extremely grateful to all those who took part in the subsequent cleaning, drying, registering, packing and storing of artefacts. Thanks above all to my archaeological colleague, Poul Mikkelsen, for his pleasant cooperation. Also to the late Kurt Glintborg Overgaard, whom we unfortunately lost only recently, all too young. Similar appreciations go to Ole Jensen, Hans Holck and Abdolkarim Torabinejad who all conducted careful and committed work over the years of excavations. Thanks also to Agner Nordby Jensen, being the leader of a group of shifting young helpers for years.

During and after the excavations, many colleagues and volunteers at the museum were helpful in various ways, and my thanks are due not least to Niels Bonnesen, Hans Erik Christensen, Ingelise Faursby, Ole Hansen, Kirsten Jørgensen, Eline Juhl, Lilli Lund, Marianne Mondrup, Niels Mortensen, Knud Nielsen, Malene Nyman, Grethe Skovgaard Sørensen, Charlotte Bunch Thomassen, Turi Thomsen, and Ellen Østergaard.

When preparing the manuscript for publication, it has been a great experience for me to cooperate with very dedicated colleagues in the field of archaeology as well as other disciplines. It has thus been a real pleasure to work with Terkel Brannet, who digitized the analogue fieldwork plan drawings, as well as to cooperate over several years with Henrik Vind Frimurer on the further working of these in GIS, and currently discussing several relevant interdisciplinary topics with him, as he is trained in the history of natural sciences. Likewise I am most grateful to Ivan Andersen, who has produced a wealth of fine studio photos of the artefacts for this book. Last but not least, the friendly support that Inge Kjær Kristensen has given me over many years, as the head of the archaeological department of Museum Salling, has been of essential importance.

I am furthermore very grateful to the many archaeologists at different museum institutions and universities for their friendly information of relevance to this book over the many years of research. In particular, Søren H. Andersen, Jens-Henrik Bech, Niels Axel Boas, Per Borup, Janus Czebreszuk, Erik Drenth, Per Ethelberg, Scott Robert Dollar, Ejvind Hertz, Anja Vegeberg Jensen, Sine Toft Jensen, Jens Jeppesen, Charlotta Lindblom, Przemyslaw Makarowitz, Martin Mikkelsen, Nina Helt Nielsen, Frank Nikulka, Jens N. Nielsen, Vibeke Juul Pedersen, Torben Sarauw, Bo Steen, Lisbeth Wincentz and Sidsel Wåhlin. Sincere thanks to Kristine Stub Precht who kindly took on the rather complex task of creating two distribution maps of Limfjord Region areas from information in the Danish public databases. I am also indebted to Lars Møller Andersen for preserving some of our very fragile objects from the settlements in question. Further, I owe thanks to the staff of the library of Skive and its mobile library, bringing books from distant institutions to the doorstep of my home, so to speak, in a small faraway village by the Limfjord.

I am grateful for the good advice of Aino Kann Rasmussen who, as an archaeologist, together with Jørn Bie, headed the Gåsemose excavation for the National Museum of Denmark. Over the years, it has been a pleasure for me to travel to Copenhagen to the archives of this institution, meeting its staff and, in particular, I am here grateful to Poul Otto Nielsen for friendly help in various cases and for much information relevant to this present work. Also on these occasions, I have experienced the warm hospitality of Marjatta and Svend Nielsen's home. Both being archaeologists, he in Nordic prehistory and beyond, she in classical archaeology and especially Etruscan, many a thoughtful and cheerful discussion would unfold over Italian dinners with them, the red wine miraculously disappearing from the bottles. My wife, Esther Fihl, would often arrive and give her input to the debate from the perspective of Central Asian nomads, South Indian fishermen or other. We have over the years also had inspiringly relevant and joyful dinner conversations with Inge Meldgaard and Ole Høiris, both ethnographers.

I have good reason to be very grateful to colleagues within the natural sciences and related disciplines. Prior to the first radiocarbon determinations, carefully produced by Kaare Lund Rasmussen, the palaeobotanical determinations were carried out at the National Museum by David Earle Robinson who, together with his wife Anne Bloch Jørgensen Robinson, also welcomed me with great hospitality in the Isle of Wight early on in my research, during a tour of English museums and monuments. Peter Steen Henriksen later expertly carried out the bulk of work on our charred plant materials at the National Museum and, likewise, Lis Højlund Pedersen analysed the pollen samples there. At this institution, Irene Skals – together with Michelle Taube – took a preliminary look at some traces from a Beaker site for me, with the support of Ulla Mannering. At Moesgaard Museum, Claus Skriver proficiently carried out micro-wear analysis on numerous flint artefacts from Resengaard. I am also highly grateful to ethnologist Johannes Møllgaard for discussing with me post-medieval the livelihood at farmsteads in North Jutland and to researcher Finn T. Okkels for sharing a fraction of his comprehensive knowledge on plants and nutrition for livestock with me in a most inspirational way. Jesper Olsen and Marie Kanstrup from the Aarhus AMS Centre, Department of Physics and Astronomy, Aarhus University kindly provided the project with many new Oxcals and diagrams. The AMS determinations were originally carried out very carefully by Jan Heinemeier.

Thanks also go to the administrative staff of the Arts Faculty at Aarhus University. The committee members for the assessment for the higher doctoral degree are Helle Vandkilde (Chair of the Committee, Professor, dr.phil., School of Culture & Society, Department of Archaeology & Heritage Studies, Arts, Aarhus University, Denmark), Charlotte Damm (Professor, Dr., Archaeology and Social Anthropology, Arctic University, Norway) and Nick Thorpe (Principal Lecturer, Dr., and Head of Department of Archaeology at the University of Winchester, United Kingdom). I am most thankful for the great efforts made by the committee members and I value their positive comments and frank critical words most highly, written as they were within a productive assessment.

Being a Scandinavian archaeologist writing in English almost inevitably results in frequent language disasters in terms of syntax and other, and hence I am grateful that Elaine Bolton, from her office in Sussex, managed to improve the manuscript in a professional and friendly manner. During many humorous conversations along the way, Lars Foged Thomsen, of the Jutland Archaeological Society, listened patiently to my ideas for the visual layout of the illustrations and he produced the graphics with a magic touch and in a highly proficient way, for which I am most thankful. I sense that the printing of the book is in really good hands at Narayana Press. Behind the activities of bringing the book to market is the general editor at the publishing house, Jesper Laursen, to whom I owe thanks.

All in all, I appreciate most highly the advice and friendly help I have received from so many sides during the years of fieldwork, the years of research, and now regarding the preparations for the book. Nonetheless, errors or omissions of any kind are entirely my responsibility.

Over the many years of research, I am tremendously grateful for the financial support I have received, and without which this project could not have been implemented. First of all, I greatly appreciate the contributions from the Danish royal foundations, Dronning Margrethe II's Arkæologiske Fond as well as Dronning Margrethes og Prins Henriks Fond. I am also most grateful for the immensely generous contributions from the Danish private foundations: VELUX FONDEN, Farumgaard-Fonden, Beckett-Fonden, Augustinus Fonden, Brødrene Hartmanns Fond, and Harboefonden. An early grant from the Ministry of Culture, Denmark, proved to be very important as pilot project money. Moreover, I am thankful for vitally important grants from the Danish Council for Independent Research, Humanities. The museum council of the former Viborg County kindly supported two study trips abroad. As may be obvious, this has been a long-enduring project hosted at the rather small archaeological department which I was in charge of for many years before my present job as a senior researcher there, and I happily acknowledge that, as far back as the 1990s, the museum leaders – being the late Jens Ole Lefèvre, whose humorous approach to things I appreciated, and thereafter notably Gudrun Gormsen – welcomed and aided my initiative and the preparations for it, such as for instance allowing me to ask Henny Lundsdorff, Aarhus, for professional help in preparing the general Resengaard map. Museum Salling thus has supported the project in several ways, for which I am grateful.

The main idea of this book crystallized during a stay on the shores of Lake Orta in Italy in the mid-1990s and the manuscript has now accompanied me many times to Italy and elsewhere, allowing me to work in a kind of "flow" over long periods without much interruption. Writing about traces of ancient everyday life in cold Scandinavia was, however, rather strange while sweating in the hot and tropical climate of an amazing fishing village on the Coromandel Coast of South India, where I stayed on several occasions during my wife's ethnographic fieldwork there.

Knowing that I have sometimes been fairly absent-minded in my *own* daily life due to research and writing, I would like to dedicate this book to Esther and our two, now long grown-up kids, Asger and Ingrid.

Hejlskov, June 2017
John Simonsen

Introduction

Theme, time and area

This thesis will allow unique insights into the local level of everyday life, its organization and its economy due to the presence of an altogether exceptional assemblage of remainders from longhouses and their living floors dating from the Late Neolithic and emerging Bronze Age in a South Scandinavian region. Completely new knowledge is generated by presenting, analysing, and interpreting the comprehensive find materials. Knowledge of this kind is essential for many wider interpretations of this crucial transitional period from the Stone Age to the Bronze Age. In calendar years, this period (LN I, LN II and Older Bronze Age period IA according to Helle Vandkilde's chronological system) corresponds to the time range c. 2350 -1600 calBC (Vandkilde 1996:139pp. & Fig. 134; 2007:75pp. & Fig. 1; 2009.76). Within this author's more newly introduced "Jutish Beaker Group", the longhouses in North Jutland can be considered to belong to a core area of this "Beaker" culture in the first centuries of the Late Neolithic. At the opposite end of the time range, the concern of this present work ceases when the tradition of the sunken-floor longhouses fades out, around the time of the breakthrough of the classic Nordic Bronze Age (Vandkilde 1993b:150; *cf.* Rahbek, Rasmussen & Vandkilde 1996).

Since the early 1950s, vestiges of sunken-floor houses have been found and investigated not least in the Limfjord region (e.g. Jensen, J.A. 1973; Simonsen 1983; 1987; 1993b; Nielsen, P.-O. 1998; Sarauw 2006; 2008). In a Danish context, however, numerous traces of sunken-floor houses have more recently also been excavated in other areas of the Jutland peninsula. Some sunken-floor house sites have also long been known in other South Scandinavian areas, in particular Scania.

Despite the increasing number of archaeological investigations of these structures, regular assumptions concerning their use and their immanent traces of ancient life have only been elaborated on a rather limited scale and, in essence, we have hitherto acquired but little knowledge. Even basic topics relevant to these buildings and everyday life in these sunken-floor longhouses are still fairly obscure. The archaeological mystery of these buildings therefore pertains to questions such as: Why were they supplied with deep floors? Which kinds of interior arrangements and organization of the floor spaces were present? How do the vestiges of human behaviour materialize? Even the question of whether the sunken floors served as human dwellings still needs to be addressed properly.

My study concerns the traces of daily life from many longhouses as well as some minor and short houses with sunken floors found in several selected locations. The study further centres on certain other concrete settlement traits relating to everyday life. The numerous illustrations, including GIS plans, diagrams, tables, photos and hand drawings, have never before been presented. It will hopefully become apparent from the ensuing chapters that the key site, Resengaard, located on the eastern coast of the Salling peninsula, holds fine qualities for analysing the evidence of daily life that is, in my understanding, embraced in building remainders (as physical frames of living), interior arrangements, artefacts, debris, plant remainders, pits, and patches – and further, for interpreting and discussing these in terms of activities, production/service, exchange and other.

Due to the character of the data, some of the topics are fairly complicated to explore. My concrete research questions will be further developed below. The basic materials presented, analysed, interpreted and discussed in this work come from the central Limfjord region but, in terms of the wider perspectives and considerations, often relate to the entire region – and in several respects also to South Scandinavia.

The Limfjord region as understood here is quite clearly delineated to the west and east by the shores of the North Sea and Kattegat, although it has been exposed to constant erosion and other modifications over the millennia (see map Fig. 1.1). To the north it is in part delimited by the shores of Skagerak and in part slips smoothly into the adjacent landscapes. To the south the region cannot be clearly defined by natural geography because it gradually merges into the landscapes of mid-Jutland. Straight lines east-west thus form the northern and southern limits of the region.

Chapter 1

Aims, research history and methodological approach

This chapter presents the objectives of the study, the existing interpretations of sunken-floor houses, the field research history relevant to the house sites, looks at neighbouring countries, some "classic" sites of two-aisled houses in South Scandinavia, offers some methodological considerations, including thoughts on source critique, the analytical approach and, finally, some sources of theoretical inspiration. We start off with a brief portrayal of sunken-floor houses.[1]

1.1. Characteristics of sunken-floor houses

Due to their often deep level below the subsoil surface, the bottoms of these sunken floors have frequently – even in usually ploughed fields – been spared from destruction to this very day. This makes these house sites privileged archaeological material since the sunken floors are often so well preserved that we could consider them "fossil floors" with considerable variations in their traces of activity, tools and charred plant remainders, found exactly at the spots where the residents left them millennia ago.

A few conspicuous traits distinguish the sunken-floor longhouses. From the evidence of reasonably well-preserved sites, it is clear that the sunken floors took up a significant part of the interior of the longhouses of the Limfjord region. So when we talk in the following of "sunken-floor longhouses" this always implies that it concerns partially sunken floors. These were placed to the east, beginning in the area of the eastern gable ends. The majority of the sunken-floor areas were more or less flat-bottomed, though often with a tendency for the lower parts to be central. The combination with unsunken floors to the west must also be considered a characteristic and significant element of these longhouses. At the sites of minor and short sunken-floor houses it appears that the deepened areas took up much of the entire length.

For practical reasons, I use the following metric definition of a longhouse with walls constructed by means of posts: a longhouse has a span of 10 m or more from centre to centre of the outermost postholes in each gable end. In contrast, a minor house simply has a length of minimum 5 m and less than 10 m. A short house has a length of less than 5 m. These short and minor houses are often neglected in the discussion of buildings but may have been of great importance for managing daily life needs, and hence it is vital to our understanding of the period's living conditions that we also have a clear focus on these building remainders.

Some sunken floors were dug only modestly into the subsoil whereas other reached a considerable depth. It is necessary, however, to operate with a certain minimum to distinguish between a sunken and an unsunken floor. As we cannot, in practice during fieldwork, be sure to distinguish this from an unintended or natural lowering of the level, I therefore consider a minimum of an original 15 cm into the subsoil as the criterion. During excavation, the measurable depth after cleaning could well thus be reduced, with the minimum criterion still being met even with a measurable depth of now just 10 cm, of which we have examples (Dollar 2013:43). The sunken-floor longhouses were two-aisled and this constructional trait was also a clear characteristic of longhouses without these deep floors. In contrast to "sunken-floor longhouse", I therefore propose the term "ground-floor longhouse" whereby the latter had floors mainly at ground level, usually being relatively close to that of the surrounding terrain.

1.2. Objectives of the present work

Investigating new house sites and other settlement vestiges from the Late Neolithic and emerging Bronze Age in profound detail is of paramount importance for expanding the empirical body of data on ways in which these people settled and their traces of daily activities. And yet the material that already exists has in no way been explored to its full potential and much remains unpublished. It is frequently just the most interesting or impressive artefacts that have been presented and publications often do not go beyond rather basic levels of presenting the placements, surface contours, depths, widths and cross-sections of pits and other soil structures. One reason why publications have not drawn more on existing excavation material could be that, despite meticulous investigations, the individual sunken floors do not always contain particularly grand or delicate finds. Considered in isolation, these could therefore be taken to be of only little value in a wider perspective.

My thesis will demonstrate that the sites of sunken-floor houses from the Late Neolithic and emerging Bronze Age can together constitute a richly-facetted source of information on certain fields of past human life in which there are huge breaches in our understanding. Beyond presenting the empirical data concerning soil traces, artefacts and other evidence from a selected number of Limfjord region sites, the primary objective of this work is to analyse, interpret and discuss this material in order to significantly broaden our insight and knowledge of daily life, and to put some of that into further perspective.[2]

Thorough analysis of the floors may highlight soil patches that indicate particular spaces where daily life activities have taken place. Systematic analysis of artefact distributions in the floor horizons may evidence spaces for specific activities from everyday life. Even house sites with apparently few qualities may, when considered from a comparative perspective, contribute important data. The presence of carbonized plant materials can contribute information on other aspects of activities performed in the houses. The results of a variety of analyses may, together, facilitate new achievements on other levels of abstraction concerning settlements, households, production, exchange and related themes.[3] As my study takes its starting point in Resengaard, it is also necessary to carry out a fairly detailed chronological analysis of the comprehensive pottery assemblages from this settlement in order to strengthen the interpretations.

The entire study will first and foremost be based on primary source materials from recent, hitherto unpublished, archaeological excavations. In terms of the reading of what are often complex materials, it will in many instances be necessary to clarify that, as the author, these are my interpretations that are being ventured and other excavation directors cannot be considered responsible. In the following, the main themes are expanded in relation to five vital fields of study and important research questions are put forward in this respect.

Ground plan elements of the houses

At most locations dating from the Late Neolithic and emerging Bronze Age in Jutland, only a single or a few of the house sites have so far been recovered but there are some sites where a considerable number have been identified. Up to now, the investigation at Resengaard has revealed by far the highest number of sunken-floor house sites in South Scandinavia.

Resengaard has been chosen as the key site for this work not least because an analysis of the many house remains here, as physical frames for daily life, is able to help elucidate some of the almost unexplored subjects of dwellings and settlement: Can an analysis of the recordings tell us whether we are dealing with relatively uniform layouts of the house ground plans or did great variations exist? How do traces of the exterior and interior wall parts, the roof-bearing constructions, the doorways and the interior arrangements appear? How much of the houses' length did the sunken floors take up within well-preserved ground plans?

As we shall see, some house sites in particular are especially informative regarding questions such as these. The different dimensions of the sunken-floor houses also attract attention, ranging as they do from distinct longhouses to rather small buildings at this settlement. It is my intention to go through the available data on house ground plans fairly systematically and highlight the important elements. I shall, in this process, be much concerned with source critique. As further comparative material, I have selected a number of other settlements which will, together, demonstrate fairly interesting kinds of sunken-floor house sites. It is also of importance that these materials can bring a balance by representing, not least, buildings from the earlier parts of the Late Neolithic.

Traces of buildings from the same time span with unsunken floors have, in recent years, been excavated in relatively high numbers in South Scandinavia. I shall present three of these ground-floor longhouses from the central Limfjord region but not go into details about the buildings and find materials. These houses are considered when discussing the functions of different kinds of longhouses.

Architecture, agriculture and domestic refuse

The basis for considering various aspects of the economy has changed radically since Carl Johan Becker some half century ago complained of the lack of useful finds evidencing husbandry, agriculture, settlement character, dwelling and other essential elements of the economy and society from the Late Neolithic (Becker 1964:21). At that time, the period was believed to have lasted just 200-400 years. Since then, rich new finds have profoundly changed the possibilities for studying economic traits.

The sunken-floor buildings that households had at their disposal for daily living were not always a static physical frame. At Resengaard it appears that marked changes are noted to have taken place in particular concerning three longhouses. This brings us to other relevant research questions: How are we to understand the significant variations in the layouts of the longhouses? Do the evident differences in ground plans and house dimensions, for instance, primarily reflect social disparities or rather some kind of specialization among households? And, further, could a particular location indicate a special significance among the settlements?

At Resengaard, the highly differentiated presence of charred cereals in the sunken floors is particularly provocative and will form the subject of analysis and reflection. Some of the important research questions in this respect are: Why, in some houses, do we find thousands and thousands of charred grains? Did the houses burn down? Or were the grains exposed to a controlled fire? Or did only limited heat cause the carbonization? Might there be certain intentions behind this or is this a product of simple mishap?

I have also chosen to take into consideration some aspects of agricultural production in the younger part of the Late Neolithic and emerging Bronze Age at Resengaard and one research question is: What knowledge can we gain about elements of the annual cycle? Indications of activities connected to the agricultural sequence of cultivation, such as preparation of the soil, sowing of cereals, maintaining of fields, harvesting, cleaning, storing and further treatment shall all be taken into consideration.

The specific handling of waste from the households is rather interesting, too. On the whole, the rubbish produced in connection with activities at Resengaard appears to have been disposed of in numerous areas. One of the important research questions is: Does any strategy appear to be behind the handling of household refuse? I shall take the preserved garbage areas into consideration and discuss the residents' possible strategies regarding domestic refuse.

As we shall see, not only Resengaard but also locations such as Hellegård and Glattrup IV offer fresh, new evidence as a basis for exploring the above research questions and related topics.

Artefacts, interior arrangements and activities

When conducting excavations of sunken floors from the period in question, some of the most immediately remarkable components most frequently observed are stones found more or less cracked by the impact of heat and often spread in the fills. These stones, with their characteristic colours and gritty surface, sometimes appear in high numbers during the excavation of soils directly above the sunken floors, although they may also turn up as singular specimens or in fact be absent. When excavating minor and short sunken-floor houses, the latter is particularly the case. Three of the most immediate research questions are therefore: Where were they heated? Where were they used? What were the main ideas behind these stones?

The artefacts from such houses with sunken floors have, in some instances, been published in fine detail (e.g. Jensen, J.A. 1973; Boas 1983; 1993) but as a whole only a tiny share of the existing finds has been presented in depth. It sometimes seems that only a few expressive or otherwise illustrative artefact examples have been picked out for description.

Apart from pottery from the sunken floors, it is mainly items of flint or other kinds of stone that have been preserved. In handling the finds, however, it is always necessary to be acutely aware that only small fractions of the original variations of artefacts have probably survived in the soils. Things that may have been shaped out of wood, bark, straw, bone, horn, antler, hide, skin, textiles etc. will all have vanished from the known settlements.

Since the possible motivations of the Late Neolithic and emerging Bronze Age people for having sunken floors have puzzled archaeologists for some time now, I shall go deeper into the finds of tools and household utensils. One of the essential research questions is thus: Which kinds of activities are mirrored in the remains of artefacts, soil traits and other observations from the floor horizons? As already noted, the appearance of a sunken floor may, in some fortunate instances, give rise to strong associations with a "fossil floor" since a variety of tools and pottery fragments may be observable *in situ* as they were the very day the residents left the house. In this respect, several excavated floors from the Limfjord region appear quite promising as regards the possibilities of recognizing interesting traces of daily life.

As the artefacts and soil features in the sunken floor horizons and elsewhere in the interior are studied with the aim of identifying the specific spaces in which activities took place, I shall also attempt to pass judgement on whether these may have been repeatedly performed. It is my intention to systematically study the recordings of soil features and artefact remains inside the houses at all the selected sites, wherever possible. Comparisons of some important aspects will also be made with traits from other settlements in the Limfjord region and elsewhere in South Scandinavia.

Household production, specialization and exchange

We do not have any "facts" about the longhouse residents themselves but this topic must obviously be considered and one evident research question is: What might the composition and size of households have been like?

The artefacts, soil traces and other elements of the floor horizons – and sometimes elsewhere in the settlements – provide us with the substance to propose an understanding of the role of household "economics" in the Limfjord region and one really important research question is hence: What role did the households play in the production (and exchange) of goods, commodities and services? And more specifically: To what extent did the individual households take part in ordinary production and how far did they specialize?

To explore these questions, vital results and observations from several locations will be used, including fresh new knowledge on settlements such as Rosgårde, Granlygård, Kluborg II, Hellegård and Resengaard. The well-known settlement at Myrhøj will also be considered in this respect.

At the present level of research, we do not know whether or not the Limfjord region had a socio-political development of its own, diverging significantly from e.g. Zealand. This question is highly interesting, with wide prospects for our understanding of the period. And yet, after some reflection on this aspect, I have come to realize that the issue of social order, hierarchy and political leadership would be better discussed in connection with the presentation of adequate numbers of geographically and typologically representative ground plans of two-aisled, ground-floor longhouses, including all their finds and soil patches. Such a discussion would clearly therefore go beyond the remit of this study. It is also clearly beyond my scope to consider the comprehensive evidence of graves, hoards and other deposits in the landscapes.

Pottery chronology in the shadowy centuries

In terms of the preserved materials, one urgent research question is: What are the daily life ceramics represented by the rather unknown, younger part of the Late Neolithic and emerging Bronze Age like? One of my goals is therefore also to present a wide range of forms and sizes of the ceramics at Resengaard, since the multitude of clay pot fragments from a really large collection of settlement material from that time have never before been presented following their systematic scrutiny.

Ceramics are frequently well represented at the settlements of the Limfjord region. And yet there have been no attempts at all to set up pottery chronologies for the Danish Late Neolithic and this is very unfortunate as chronology forms a backbone for the interpretation of certain topics concerning settlement materials.

Regarding the appearance of the pottery, no researchers have yet demonstrated how the producers and users of pottery changed their preferences from the sophisticated, richly decorated pottery designs of the early Late Neolithic Beaker milieu to the somewhat more coarse and generally undecorated, but often highly expressive, ceramic forms of the later parts of the period and further on into the emerging Bronze Age. All things considered, several matters relating to detailed chronology are at present unclarified. And yet, my chronological study will first and foremost attempt to become instrumental in strengthening these interpretations. The main research question concerning chronology itself can be put rather simply: How do the pottery assemblages from the house sites at Resengaard relate to each other internally?

To answer this research question, my path, tailored to this specific case, is also relatively simple but, in order to try to pursue the aim, a great deal of effort first has to be put in. Based on the comprehensive Resengaard pottery assemblages, comprising many hundreds of clay pot profiles primarily stemming from the sunken floors and fills directly above, it is my intention to suggest the first relative-chronological, provisional outline of pottery transformations during the shadowy latter parts of the Late Neolithic, and bridging also the transition to the Older Bronze Age.

1.3. Existing interpretations of South Scandinavian house sites

Archaeologists from the National Museum of Denmark have, on and off over a long period of time, continued a tradition of interpreting the whole bulk of prehistoric evidence and given their accounts of the prehistory of Denmark. Sophus Müller wrote the monograph "Vor Oldtid" at the end of the 19th century and enclosed considerable new evidence on the later part of the Stone Age (Müller, S. 1898). When Johannes Brøndsted put pen to paper, it resulted in three richly illustrated volumes of "Danmarks Oldtid" which appeared in the 1930s and were later revised to also elucidate in some detail the later part of the Stone Age and emerging Bronze Age, including the Limfjord region (Brøndsted [1957] 1966a; [1957] 1966b. More recently, Jørgen Jensen has given a comprehensive new account, also including the Late Neolithic and beyond (Jensen, J. 2006a; 2006b). I therefore see no need to enter into a broad introduction to the period as an overview of current research into the Late Neolithic in Denmark has also been more recently presented (Vandkilde 2007).

Initial knowledge 1957

The first professional presentation of the site of a Late Neolithic house with sunken floor concerns Gug in the Limfjord region (Brøndsted [1957]1966a:311p; Simonsen 1983, Fig. 8). The traces of the house appeared as a shallow, almost rectangular soil feature of rather modest size, flanked by postholes on all four sides. It was east-west aligned and Brøndsted proposed that the entrance would have been in the western gable end. He further considered two circular, stone-lined fireplaces, somewhat dug down, as well as two other circular pits, as belonging to the floor. It was stated that the floor was fully covered with debris of worked flint and, in his account of the flints, several roughouts for daggers, spear blades and sickles were mentioned. Finds of arrowheads, scrapers and a borer were also referred to. A small clay pot and many potsherds were furthermore found. In one of the postholes, a pressure-flaked spear blade had been deposited in a position alongside the post. Brøndsted considered this to have been a possible votive offering. These finds in the Gug house were understood as belonging to a layer accumulated on top of the floor, and a flat stone observed near the northwest corner of the house was incorporated into his interpretation, describing how he interpreted the flint smith had been sitting, with the wall as the back to his stone seat, while chopping flint items (Brøndsted 1966a:312). This emblematic reading long stood as the sole clearly expressed interpretation of a Late Neolithic house floor. More recently, the flint knapping techniques concerned with the production of bifacial flint at Gug have been studied and differences in skills observed (Olausson 2000:128p).

In other parts of South Scandinavia, some house sites were made public very early on. These concern, in particular, three finds from Sweden. The observations from a large pit, site 2 at Furulund in Scania, were associated with a kind of dwelling (Tilander 1963:123pp). The cautious considerations reflected in this article are rather interesting, bearing in mind that these were presented some 10 years before the publication of Myrhøj: "There is little to hold on to when it comes to deciding the use of the pit, especially as there is no equivalent from the same period either in Scania or Denmark. It seems too regular and too large to have been a refuse pit. A few circumstances point to its having been used as a dwelling. There are no remains of a hearth in the pit itself but right at the edge, in the west corner. The stone layer at the bottom may have served to drain the pit or as a firm basis for a more even flooring. The soot stratum at the bottom and toward the edges indicated that the site contained a good deal of combustible material. The posthole at the west short side may have something to do with a superstructure. As the pit is comparatively deep a superstructure need not have been especially strong. That may be the reason why no more post-holes have been found. Also, they may have been removed or lie just outside the excavated ground, the boundaries of which were very narrow. If it is at all a question of a dwelling-place it must have been of so primitive a construction that it is quite useless to try to find material for comparison from other archaeological or ethnological spheres" (Tilander 1963:133p). Among other things, pottery dating the structure to the Late Neolithic was found. Some years later, Stockholmsgården in Valleberga near Ystad in southern Scania, and Norrvidinge in western Scania were published (Strömberg 1968; 1971; Calmer 1972). For further discussion of house sites from Scania and beyond, see Sarauw 2006:46pp.

A quantum leap in new knowledge 1973

With his prompt publication of three sunken-floor houses (D, GAB, & EAB) from Myrhøj almost immediately after the excavation, Jens Aarup Jensen made it possible for the first time to gain more insight into the character of settlements with such houses and this really represented a major step forward in our knowledge of several aspects (Jensen, J.A. 1973). The importance of the findings was substantiated yet more by the observation that the sunken floors were found in sealed layers, chiefly without disturbance or mix up with other material. Four aspects of the Myrhøj site were particularly important for increasing our knowledge of the houses and the settlements.

Firstly, a number of constructive features became evident. It was clear that these buildings had been regular longhouses and consisted of a sunken and an unsunken part. It was also obvious that the houses had been two-aisled and that the centre-post constructions were observable in the sunken areas of the houses as well as in the western unsunken part, albeit exemplified by only one of the buildings. Wall construction traits, contours and depths of the sunken floors were, furthermore, elucidated.

Secondly, light was thrown on several elements of the economy. The kinds of flint and other stone tools from the house contexts were unsurprising, as these were commonly known, but the abundance of flints, in particular, in these dwelling contexts was naturally very important and these flint items or their fragmented pieces included axes, adzes, chisels, scrapers, flakes with retouch, burins, as well as arrowheads and transverse points. Stone implements such as hammers and querns were also found. Pottery was furthermore exceedingly well represented, both decorated and undecorated. Singular specimens in other materials such as a button and disk of amber, a stone bracer and a loom weight fragment of burned clay illuminated the picture yet more. In addition to this, agriculture was documented at the site through observations of ard-furrows and grain impressions in the ceramics. A few teeth from young oxen were also found.

Thirdly, it was very important for our understanding that the house contexts appeared not only with coarse daily ceramics but also with pottery clearly affiliated to late Beaker milieus, and often richly decorated.

Lastly, the chronological position within the frame of the Late Neolithic was indicated by flint items and by the ornamentation of pottery, as well as radiocarbon dating on pieces of charred oak tree (K 2067) from a layer (8b) in House D. The deeper floor was not dated by radiocarbon determination.

Almost contemporaneously with the Myrhøj investigation, a settlement at Stendis was excavated. It was published somewhat later and revealed an almost similar pottery milieu (Skov 1978; 1982). Among other things it was evident that the Myrhøj settlement did not comprise a unique combination of sunken-floor longhouses and richly ornamented pottery with obvious late Beaker affinities. In my interpretation, a sunken floor from the Late Neolithic was partly investigated at Nygaard in 1976 but, by then, recognized as a culture layer (Nielsen, S. 1977:81p).

Further knowledge from 1980 onwards

We now enter a period of more growth in the presentations of new settlements, beginning with Niels Axel Boas' publication of the very important Older Bronze Age site Egehøj, enclosing comprehensive finds from three two-aisled houses with sunken floors (Boas 1980; 1983). This was accompanied by considerations of the interior pits and activity areas and this publication has long stood as a cornerstone of the research. Interestingly, it seems that these houses, with their substantial post settings and special placements of the sunken areas, appear to represent a tradition at Djursland that is somewhat different from, for instance, the Myrhøj houses within the Limfjord region.

Anders Jæger and Jesper Laursen next published the Older Bronze Age site Lindebjerg at northern Funen (Jæger & Laursen 1983). The house site, though not fully preserved, gave fine evidence of interesting traits. The longhouse at Tastum I was published in the same year, and a number of comparative topics such as dimension, construction and function of the houses from Gug and Myrhøj were brought up (Simonsen 1983). And yet it was not, at that point, realistic to begin a detailed interpretation of activity-spaces and specific uses of the interior as this clearly demands substantial *a priori* method development. The Stendis site was, however, discussed and a new understanding proposed, namely that it concerns one sunken-floor house partly covering the site of a foregoing one. This would explain the irregular surface feature of the sunken area and the alignments of postholes (Simonsen 1983:88). In other words, at Stendis we saw the first example of a site with two houses that could not have existed simultaneously, while the three Myrhøj houses could not, in terms of internal stratification, be shown to have succeeded each other. In the following year, Jens Jeppesen presented a sunken-floor house site from Vejlby belonging to the Late Neolithic/Older Bronze Age transition (Jeppesen 1984). That same year, new evidence about a partially preserved, sunken-floor house from the early half of the Late Neolithic at Hovergårde was published, too (Jensen, J.A. 1984). In 1985 Per Ethelberg presented the Højgård settlement briefly, later publishing the site in more detail (Ethelberg 1987; 1993b). Three minor/short sunken-floor house sites, considered to belong to the younger part of LN II, were recovered. In addition to this, a site of a two-aisled house with a relatively small sunken area to the west possibly belongs to the period, even though the radiocarbon dating does not support it (Ethelberg 1993b:143; 2000:165pp; Sarauw 2006:47).

Taken together, the publication of the above sites also demonstrated that sunken-floor house sites could further be identified in East Jutland, West Jutland and South Jutland. It was therefore clearly indicated that more finds might show up elsewhere in the Jutland peninsula and nearby parts of Funen and that the Danish sunken-floor houses were thus not confined to the Limfjord region and its immediate vicinity. Evidently, the development of finds since then has confirmed this.

In 1987, an unusual house site from Povlstrupgård was grouped with the sunken-floor houses and dated to a time contemporaneous to House II at Egehøj on a typological basis (Jespersen 1987:260pp; Boas 1983:92). The wall posts had been dug relatively deep into the subsoil.

When publishing Diverhøj in 1988, Pauline Asingh demonstrated a relatively early pottery milieu with rich ornamentations somewhat resembling those from Myrhøj, with the finds stemming from the substantial remains of two sunken-floor houses preserved beneath a grave barrow (Asingh 1988:130pp).

Five years later, a two-aisled longhouse with sunken floor from Hemmed Plantage ("Hemmed Plantation") was published (Boas 1993; 1997). This site, appearing relatively well preserved in the excavated part, also belonged to the early half of the Late Neolithic and the publication included detailed observations. That same year, Marianne Rasmussen, in connection with her writing on Danish settlement pottery from the Older Bronze Age, dealt with the question of how the sunken floors came into existence when considering the interpretation of a sunken-floor house site at Vadgård (Rasmussen 1993a; Rasmussen & Adamsen 1993:136pp). The prior and existing understanding of this Vadgård house (CB) was that the sunken area had come about through wear and tear, through use of the floor. However, she posited that the deep floors at other sites were intentional parts of the construction, with reference to Egehøj and Højgård (Rasmussen 1993a:31). I would here add that if the first interpretation of the Vadgård building was what actually happened then the users of this house would have experienced the house becoming more and more sunken over time, which is in direct contrast with the originally proposed interpretation of the Myrhøj houses, in which the house floors became less and less sunken, as can be rationalized from the publication. Some years earlier, one of the sunken-floored buildings at Højgård (House IX) had already been understood as "regularly dug into the subsoil" (Ethelberg 1987:153).

The Egehøj houses offered an idea of the general outer wall contours of houses in the Djursland area, whereas the outlines of the sunken-floor longhouses had long remained somewhat uncertain in the Limfjord areas because the houses at Myrhøj, Tastum and Stendis gave little indication of the entire buildings. In this respect, the excavation at Resengaard presented the first relatively clear wall lines in the Limfjord region. In 1993, at an early stage in the investigation, a single ground plan from this site was presented as a congress paper (Simonsen 1993b. See also Mikkelsen, P. & Simonsen, J. 2000; Simonsen, J. 2001).

Questions regarding the use of the sunken-floor houses have not been the subject of broad debate, probably largely due to the fact that comprehensive

Aims, research history and methodological approach

details of the floors had hitherto not been presented. In the Myrhøj publication, the floors as such were not the direct focus and succeeding articles dealing with the sunken-floor houses have only sporadically presented and discussed details relevant to the functional aspects of the sunken floors. Jens Aarup Jensen early on suggested that the houses may have been used for a rather permanent kind of occupation (Jensen, J.A. 1973:119). This view seems to be implicitly held by several archaeologists. Correspondingly, with regard to the Tastum I house, it was argued that sunken-floor longhouses must first of all be seen as human habitations and that the finds substantiate this view (Simonsen 1983:88). In this respect, it was further argued that the careful selection of the topographical location was also an important factor and that the prevailing east-west direction of the sunken-floor obviously makes an argument in this respect. Climatically, many longhouses would gain much benefit from the sun about its most southerly position and would, in this position, enjoy significant shielding from cooling by westerly winds.

One of the propositions later put forward deserves attention as an element of the research history. It concerns the opinion that the sunken floors could represent stables and we shall later return to this view. Of the more conspicuous functions of the houses, two in particular have been elucidated. The notion of particular arrangements for drying or roasting cereals in parts of the sunken floors has been cautiously put forward (Boas 1983:97). The Petersborg site in the eastern part of central Jutland attracts attention in this respect. Per Borup, who directed the investigation of the site, has suggested that a small flat-bottomed sunken area with blackish soil and heat-cracked stones was an arrangement for drying or roasting cereals (AUD 1998, no.443; Vandkilde 2007:92). The presence of several kilos of charred grains of pure wheat led to this interpretation. Borup stated that no traces of posts were observed outside the pit area but that the layer with blackish soil was sharply delimited, indicating that the arrangement had been surrounded by some kind of construction. The possibility that it concerns the remainders of a sunken-floor house seems worth considering. On flint working, the publication of Egehøj also delivered some important observations which might serve as an example of the studies that are clearly needed into the floor areas: "One of the biggest concentrations is in the gable end region of House I; this consists almost entirely of arrowhead roughouts. Just inside the end of the house is a corresponding scatter of small fine waste flakes. A group of large, coarse flakes can also be seen a couple of m further east inside the house. This, therefore, seems to be an example of specialised arrowhead production, with rough shaping taking place near the first roof-bearing post, finer working between this post and the gable wall, and the apparently rejected examples of roughouts being disposed of against the wall itself. To this may be added the high frequency of completed arrowheads in this whole part of the site" (Boas 1983:97). Among other things, he further provided information on special flint dagger and sickle production in House II (Boas 1983:98).

In 1995, Poul Mikkelsen presented the quite extensive settlement traces at Trængsel situated near the western boundary of the central Limfjord region and, at this location, the many recovered sunken-floor house sites, being mainly from around the emerging Bronze Age, were heavily threatened by destructive factors (Mikkelsen, P. 1995:21pp).

In 2006, Torben Sarauw published the Bejsebakken settlement, representing the first Danish results from a large-scale excavation enclosing numerous Late Neolithic house sites (Sarauw 2006). Many of the recovered house sites had been provided with sunken floors, while others had only ground floors. The buildings date to LN I, and richly decorated Beaker ceramics were found in many contexts at the settlement. The investigation at Bejsebakken took place in 1998-99 and was thus carried out in parallel with the closing period at the Resengaard settlement, investigated from 1989 to1999. The initial digging of a long trial trench system, mostly with equal internal distances, was a common method at both settlements. Because the publication of Bejsebakken plays a significant role in the discussion of functions of the sunken-floor houses and traces of everyday activities, applied methods of excavation must obviously come into focus.

Methodologically, the excavation of the sunken-floor houses at Bejsebakken is stated to have taken place as follows: "The sunken part was typically divided into square metre squares. If a stratified fill was observed, the fill layers were as far as possible excavated separately, and the finds were attributed to the individual layers. Especially the lowest 5 cm of the fill layer was carefully excavated, as it was expected that possible floor layers would be situated here. In cases where special tools, flint concentrations, vessel sides, etc. were found during the excavation, these were individually measured" and, further: "In most cases, the entire fill from presumed Neolithic pits and postholes from roof posts in Neolithic houses were hand-sieved through a net with 5 x 5 mm mesh size. Similarly, the entire fill from houses with sunken features was hand-sieved using mainly a 5 x 5 mm mesh. In addition, flotation samples were taken of almost all structure types, including postholes …" (Sarauw 2006:12).

One of the resulting outcomes at Bejsebakken is that the investigation evidenced the existence of a very large concentration of longhouses from LN I compared to several minor settlements hitherto presented. This site has subsequently provided input to the discussion of single versus several longhouses existing contemporaneously at Late Neolithic settlements. The Bejsebakken publication furthermore presents a comparative analysis in which the two-aisled ground-floor houses in South Scandinavia are also in focus.

Theoretically, it is worth noting that Sarauw is in line with my interpretation of sunken areas from 1983 as regards the main division into floors and above fills. Moreover, it is broadly reassuring in the research on everyday life in the longhouses that he also considers these floors were used for human habitation and that he actually presents further evidence in the form of phosphate analyses, thus supporting the notion that sunken-floor longhouses at Bejsebakken had not been used as stables for livestock (Sarauw 2006:59, with further references). In his own words "…the sunken features seems to have been used mainly as some sort of dwelling or activity area, as indicated by the presence of fireplaces, weaving pits, loom weights etc. Small pits or depressions on the bottom of many sunken areas indicate that special activities also took place" (Sarauw 2006:61). And here, his work accelerates the basis for discussion of several elements of the evidence that may concern everyday life at the settlements. Furthermore, in relation to sunken-floor house sites and beyond, the article "On the Outskirts of the European Bell Beaker Phenomenon. The settlement of Bejsebakken and the social organization of Late Neolithic societies" offers topics of considerable interest for new research on such themes (Sarauw 2008). In all, a great many observations and considerations concerning Bejsebakken are of importance for this work and will appear repeatedly in the following chapters (Sarauw, T. 2006; 2007a; 2007b; 2007c; 2008; 2009).

It is also of great significance for the research that northern Jutland has been argued to have played a regular gateway role for South Scandinavia in relation to the spread of Late Neolithic Culture and to have played a major role in the intensive contacts and exchanges with Beaker communities (Vandkilde 2001:338; 2009:76p; Sarauw 2007c:258; 2009:39).

The publication, one year later, of Enkehøj (including some aspects of Gilmosevej and Sjællandsvej V) brought new evidence of sunken-floor houses and some other two-aisled houses to light, in addition to important pits and charred plant remainders relating to the topic of daily life (Møbjerg, T., Jensen P. M., & Mikkelsen, P. H. 2007:9pp). Among other things, Beaker pottery was found, as well as – not least – large amounts of carbonized cereals. At Gilmosevej, two sunken-floor house sites were recovered, as well as a pit with many charred cereals and acorns that could represent a votive offering. Numerous charred cereals were found in a sunken-floor house at Sjællandsvej V.

In 1998, the first survey of the general development of houses from the Early Neolithic to the Older Bronze Age in Swedish, Norwegian and Danish areas appeared and, besides considerations of some sunken-floor houses, many interesting observations on the sectioning of the two-aisled ground-floor longhouses were made (Nielsen, P.-O. 1998:16pp; See also Artursson 2005a; 2005c; Sarauw 2006).

Certain Swedish sites with sunken-floor houses relate to the current discussions in different ways, like the above-mentioned site at Furulund (see map below, Fig. 1.1). Of importance are, not least, the publications of Norrvidinge (Callmer 1973), Fosie IV (Björhem & Säfvestad 1989; 1993), Karaby (Petterson 2000; Artursson 2005a:90; 2005c; 2009), Dösemarken (Brink 2013), and Almhov. At this last-mentioned settlement Almhov in Scania, remainders of a total of 38 buildings, of which most were longhouses, have been published and several radiocarbon dates may indicate their chronological positions (Gidlöf, Dehman & Johansson 2006:100pp; Artursson 2005b:90 & 102; 2005c; 2009; 2010; Brink 2013). Only one of the longhouses had a sunken floor to the east, being of moderate dimensions (Gidlöf, Dehman & Johansson 2006:125p). However, discussing the classification of South Scandinavian buildings into detailed categories is also clearly beyond the scope of this present work (cf. Björhem & Säfvestad 1989:78pp; Artursson 2000:17p). More recently, a survey of the development of longhouses in Scania 2300-1500 BC has been presented (Artursson 2009, in: Bygnadstradition, Fig. 2). Further works also provide information on many different house traditions (Göthberg, Kyhlberg & Vinberg (eds.) 1995; Artursson 2005a; 2005b). However, some houses from Hagestad in southeast Scania

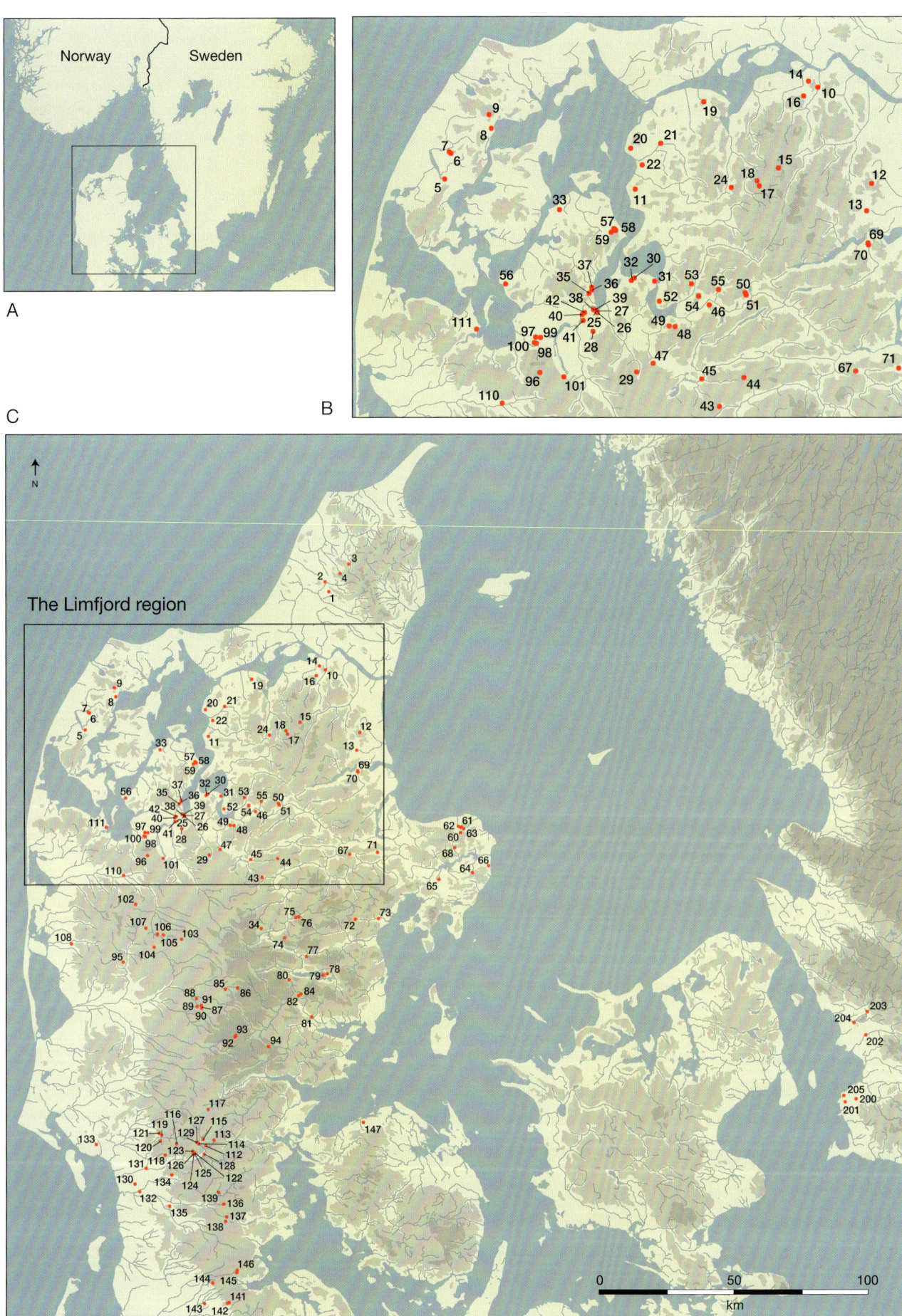

26 Chapter 1

seem to represent quite another tradition of houses with deep floors and are not considered relevant to the present work (Strömberg 1992; Artursson 2005c).

The history of the interpretation of sunken-floor houses is, of course, longer and presents more details from various geographical areas than I have brought in here. However, the public knowledge generated in the last 60 years contrasts starkly with the amount of detailed information available – more or less explicitly – through excavation reports. The establishment of public knowledge is clearly out of step and has therefore not been available for suitable feedback on the current excavations in order to optimize the scope of field investigations and direct it in various ways. Clearly, more focussed, precise and detailed observations during fieldwork concerning the themes for which we have only sparse information may henceforward play a decisive role in improving the interpretations.

The field research has partly lived a life of its own, without continuous build-up of knowledge through presentation, analysis, interpretation and discussion in publications of the sunken-floor houses. We now turn to a brief account of the field research history.

1.4. Field research history in Denmark and beyond

Not least, archaeological excavations could have previously taken place at sites of sunken-floor buildings without any recognition of these as house plots and that the observations could represent human dwellings. In particular, before the publication of Myrhøj, the sunken floors may, in several cases, have been taken as simple culture layers. Existing museum recordings therefore may, in some cases, include observations related to sunken floors without acknowledging their significance.

An account some years ago estimated that at least 280 Late Neolithic house sites of different kinds were known in Denmark (Sarauw 2006:46). This number has increased greatly in recent years (pers. comm. Poul-Otto Nielsen).

Investigations in the Limfjord region

The research history begins with the excavation at Gug (Beatesminde) in 1952 but it was not until 15 years later that significant progress in field research came about. One year before the Myrhøj excavation campaigns, an excavation at Gåsemose had thus already been initiated in 1967. However, it has hitherto remained unpublished. It was located just across the Limfjord in the eastern part of Salling and, as the crow flies, only a few kilometres separated these two locations. The interpretation of the results was in some respects left open but it was written in the excavation report that the observations could be perceived as a large flat pit, either a waste pit or an original habitation area. And yet the meticulous investigation at Gåsemose has now made it possible to recognize that the examined area evidently has the qualities of a house with a sunken floor. Interestingly, it has also become clear that the finds from the fills disclosed a pottery assemblage from a much later time than the finely ornamented ceramics from Myrhøj. At the same time, an investigation at Solbjerg III also revealed the remains of a Late Neolithic sunken-floor house. During excavation campaigns at Vadgård 1970-76, a single sunken-floor house was recovered to the north together with prominent traces of five turf-walled buildings without deep floors. At Vadgård further to the south, a presumed sunken-floor house site was found.

This was the beginning of Danish field research into the enigmatic sunken-floor houses and it all took place within a narrow area of the Limfjord region. I shall not go further into the history of field research as maps and a table with the investigations speaks for itself and indicate that these usually E-W lying houses with sunken floors were rather common in the landscape (Fig. 1.1, 1.2, & 1.3).

An investigation of the settlement at Bjergene II (THY 2756) concerned a rather lengthy, shallow soil feature and must briefly be considered here. The sunken area was 0.2 m deep and included pottery with Beaker decoration. Timothy Earle and Paul Treherne interpreted the structure as the strongly ploughed down remainders of a N-S aligned sunk-

◀ *Fig. 1.1. A-C. Sunken-floor house sites in South Scandinavia from the Late Neolithic/emerging Bronze Age. The grey-tone shading on the map denotes heights of 30 m, 80 m, and 150 m. Many locations are more or less newly found and unpublished. See Fig. 1.3. The six selected settlements from western Scania are Fosie (200), Almhow (201), Furulund (202), Norrvidinge (203), Karaby (204) and Dösemarken (205), see references in the text. Sources for sites in Denmark: Danish museums/Fig.1.3, the database Fund og Fortidsminder, & Wikimedia Commons.*

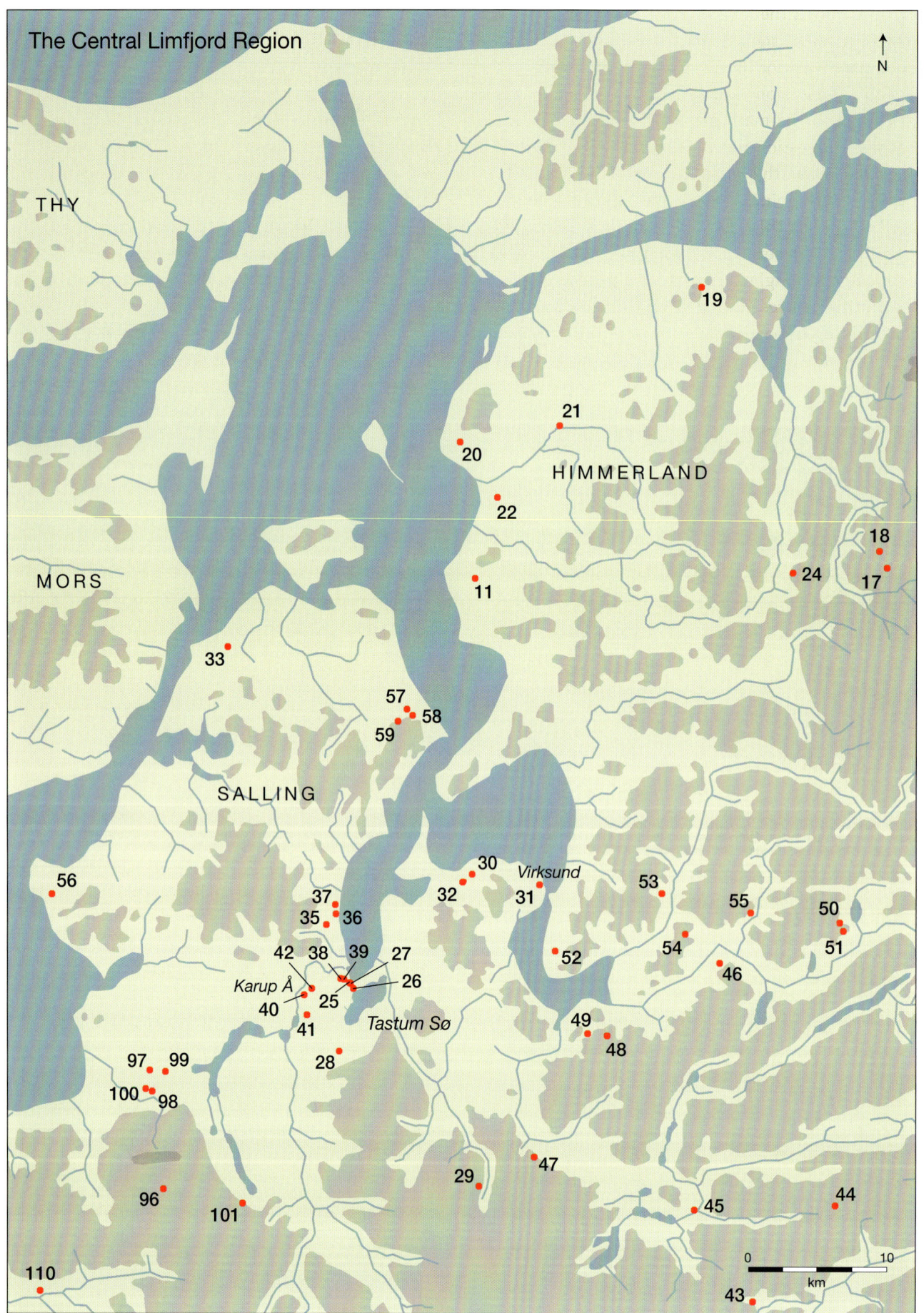

en-floor house, the length being 36 m and the width up to 6 m (AUD 1992, no.186). A substantial ground-floor part was not found, however, and due to the sizeable dimensions it may not immediately appear to belong to the main group of sunken-floor longhouses in question here. More recently, it has been suggested that the structure could represent two partly overlapping house sites (Prieto-Martinez 2008:125). With this new interpretation, it could be significantly closer to the dimensions of the bulk of sunken-floor longhouses from the Limfjord region than initially presented although the alignment of the building in particular is still in striking contrast to the usual.

In this respect, House 1 at Bjergene VI (THY 2758) also requires attention due to its direction, again N-S (Thorpe 1997; 2000:75 & Fig. 5.2; Prieto-Martinez 2008, Fig. 6). The length of the sunken area is stated as 13.7 m with no ground-floor part reported. Numerous potsherds have been found in this house site and many with ornamentation that is fairly close to some of the Myrhøj ceramics (Prieto-Martinez 2008, Fig. 11 & 13).

It is beyond the scope of this work to consider the sites of minor three-aisled houses presented as likely belonging to a very early group with this kind of construction and found at several locations in the central Limfjord region, and so they shall not be considered (Terkildsen & Mikkelsen 2011).

Investigations elsewhere in Jutland

Before the early 1980s, very few sunken-floor house sites from the Late Neolithic and emerging Bronze Age had been recognized in other parts of Denmark. This is remarkable as the subsequent advances in field research clearly provide evidence that such buildings were used in considerable numbers outside the Limfjord region as well, albeit particularly in Jutland. Several new sites thus emerged in Jutland, not least Vejlby, Hovergårde, Diverhøj, Højgård, Brdr. Gram, Vorgod, Troldbjerg, Hemmed Plantage and Grønnegård. From around 1990 on, the progress in field research resulted in numerous new sunken-floor house sites in Jutland.

Really promising and fast growing amounts of evidence on sunken-floor houses in particular areas of mid- and south Jutland are now coming to light due to the very dedicated efforts of many excavation directors. The new information on finds of Beaker materials, as well as the new evidence on placements of numerous settlements with sunken-floor houses and other buildings in Jutlandic areas south of the Limfjord region, may in my reading open up the possibility that some communities in LN I had their own more or less direct contacts with northwest European Beaker communities such as the Dutch. It is rather unclear for the moment but it is possible that the Limfjord region did not play a major gateway role in terms of communicating Beaker Culture for these communities. Their contacts and exchanges may, perhaps not least, have taken place by transportation along extensive waterways such as Storå, Skjern Å, Holsted Å, Kongeå, Ribe Å and Vidå and the more minor streams feeding these from higher grounds in their easterly

◄▲ *Fig. 1.2. Zooming into the area of the southwest part of the central Limfjord region, the placements of the ten particularly studied settlements with sunken-floor houses are shown. The entire central Limfjord region, as understood in this work, is indicated in Fig. 5.20. Sources: See Fig.1.1.*

Nr	Location	Sted-nr	SB-nr	Field directors	Some basic archaological sources
				Hjørring County	
1	Thorsmark Sønder Fald	100101	143	Marlena Haue	
2	Lille Thorup	100113	126	Lone Andersen & Torben Nilsson	AUD 1996, no. 200.
3	Vestervang	100116	135	Anne Louise Haack Olsen	
4	Søndergård	100116	158	Lone Andersen	
	Thisted County				
5	Ingersminde	110104	98	Bjarne Henning Nielsen	AUD 1999, no. 293.
6	Bjergene VI	110112	259	Timothy Earle	AUD 1992, no. 18;. Thorpe, I.J.N. 1997; 2000; Apel, J. 2001; Prieto-Martinez, M.P. 2008.
7	Bjergene II	110112	262	Paul Treherne	Apel, J. 2001.
8	Nr. Nordentoft	110305	263	Martin Mikkelsen	AUD 1993, no. 247; 1994, no. 288.
9	Høghs Høj II	110310	70	Jens-Henrik Bech	AUD 2000, no. 284.
				Aalborg County	
10	Gug	120113	21	Christen Leif Vebæk	Brønsted, J. 1966a:311p; Simonsen, J. 1983:86; Olausson, D. 2000:128p; Apel, J. 2001
11	Myrhøj	120212	105	Jens Aarup Jensen	Jensen, J. Aa. 1973; Apel, J. 2001.
12	Solbjerg III	120311	104	Oscar Marseen	Johansen 1986:289pp; Jensen, J.Aa. 1973:108p.
13	Mølledalsgård	120311	118	Karen Povlsen	Poulsen, K. 2014.
14	Bejsebakken	120506	51	Torben Sarauw & Jens N. Nielsen	Sarauw, T. 2006; 2007b; 2007c; 2008; 2009.
15	Povlstrupgård	120509	129	Jørgen Seit Jespersen	Jespersen, J.S. 1987:260p.
16	Leere Gård	120510	84	Lars Egholm Nielsen	Nielsen, L.E. 2010.
17	Sønderup	120512	53	Karen Povlsen	
18	Hylkekær	120512	65	Karen Povlsen	
19	Riisgård	120701	79	Lisbeth Christensen & Jens N. Nielsen	Nielsen, J.N. 2004.
20	Rønbjerggård	120710	117	Niels Terkildsen	Terkildsen, N. 2006.
21	Vadgård	120714	30	Ebbe Lomborg	Lomborg, E. 1976; 1980; Rasmussen, M. 1993:26pp
22	Borregård 5	120809	118	Thomas Nielsen	
23	Mosegården	120814	248	Susanne Klingenberg	AUD 1987, no. 211.
24	Tandrupgaard	120814	248	Charlotta Lindblom	Andreasen 2009:36p.
				Viborg County	
25	Glattrup IV	130102	86	K.G. Overgaard	AUD 1999, no. 359; Simonsen, J. present work.
26	Glattrup VI - øst	130102	97	Kurt Glintborg Overgaard	
27	Glattrup V	130102	117	Kurt Glintborg Overgaard	
28	Tastum I	130107	264	John Simonsen	Simonsen 1983:81pp; Apel, J. 2001.
29	Rosgårde	130110	111	K.G. Overgaard	AUD 2000, no. 337; 2001, no. 306; Simonsen, J., present work.
30	Hejlskov Hede	130117	224	K.G. Overgaard	Simonsen, J. present work.
31	Virksund I	130117	243	Peter Birkedal	
32	Lærkenborg II	130117	248	Inge Kjær Kristensen	
33	Hellegård	130208	48	Kurt Glintborg Overgaard	AUD 1998:321; Hornstrup et al. 2005; Simonsen, J. present work.
34	Balle Nørremark I	130301	161	Kurt Glintborg Overgaard & Kaj F. Rasmussen	
35	Nygård	130408	22	Svend Nielsen	Nielsen, S. 1977; Simonsen, J. present work.
36	Resengaard	130408	69	Poul Mikkelsen & John Simonsen	Simonsen, J. 1993b; Mikkelsen, P. & Simonsen, J 2000. Simonsen, J. present work.
37	Marienlyst Strand	130408	2	Poul Mikkelsen	AUD 1992, no. 248; Simonsen, J. present work.
38	Glattrup I	130410	141	John Simonsen	Simonsen 1996c; Simonsen, J. present work.
39	Glattrup III	130410	134	Poul Mikkelsen	AUD 1990, no. 223; Simonsen, J. 1996c; Simonsen, J. present work.
40	Granlygård	130410	139	Poul Mikkelsen	AUD 1994, no. 352; 1995, no. 271; Simonsen, J. present work.
41	Kluborg II	130410	146	Kurt Glintborg Overgaard	AUD 2000, no. 349; Simonsen, J. present work.
42	Bilstrup I	130410	158	Malene Nyman	
43	Vindelsbæk I	130602	31	Martin Mikkelsen	AUD 2000 no. 352.
44	Mammen Porsbjerg	130709	43	Mads Ravn & Martin Mikkelsen	AUD 2000, no. 353.
45	Randrup Mølle	130716	75	Sidsel Wåhlin	Wåhlin, S. & Mikkelsen, M. 2008.

Fig. 1.3 (Pages 30-32). Table of Danish locations with sites of sunken-floor houses from the Late Neolithic/emerging Bronze Age. For map, see Fig. 1.1. Sources: Danish museums and the database Fund og Fortidsminder.

Nr	Location	Sted-nr	SB-nr	Field directors	Some basic archaeological sources
46	Nordmandshede B	130809	65	Astrid Skou Hansen	Boddum, S., Kieldsen, M., Larsen, L.A., & Terkildsen, K.F. 2015:93p.
47	Bruunshåb	130810	106	Inge Kjær Kristensen	AUD 2000, no. 356.
48	Kølsen Gårde	130816	147	Mikael Holdgaard Nielsen	
49	Løgstrup Nord	130816	166	Mikkel Kieldsen	Kieldsen, M. 2010.
50	Klejtrup Syd	130906	105	Marianne Høyem Andreasen	AUD 2005, no.342.
51	Møllegård	130906	129	Sanne Boddum	Boddum, S. 2010.
52	Skrubben	130907	72	Mikael Holdgaard Nielsen	
53	Bygdalgård	130908	89	Sidsel Wåhlin	Kieldsen, M. & Wåhlin, S. 2012.
54	Skringstrup	130911	92	Kurt Glintborg Overgaard	AUD 2002, no. 337.
55	Abildal	130914	85	Lars Agersnap Larsen	Larsen, L.A. 2012.
56	Kås Hovedgård II	131005	162	Inge Kjær Kristensen	AUD 2002, no. 341.
57	Gåsemose	131108	59	Aino Kann Rasmussen	Simonsen, J. present work.
58	Tromgade	131108	65	Kurt Glintborg Overgaard	AUD 2001, no. 387. Simonsen, J. present work.
59	Havbakker	131108	66	Inge Kjær Kristensen	AUD 2001, no. 386. Simonsen, J. present work.
Randers County					
60	Glesborg Lyng	140107	130	Niels Axel Boas	AUD 2002, no. 351.
61	Egehøj	140110	2	Niels Axel Boas	Boas 1980:pp. 102-120; 1983:pp. 90-101; Apel, J. 2001.
62	Hemmed Kær	140110	145	Hans Runge Christoffersen	Rasmussen 1993:88.
63	Hemmed plantage	140110	161	Niels Axel Boas	Boas 1993:128pp; Apel, J. 2001.
64	Diverhøj	140206	18	Pauline Asingh & Niels Axel Boas	Asingh 1988:145pp; Apel, J. 2001.
65	Mårup	140210	235	Niels Axel Boas	AUD 2001, no. 411.
66	Ramskovgaard	140214	33	Niels Axel Boas	AUD 1998, no. 375.
67	Frederiksdal	140304	19	Søren Bertelsen & Niels T. Sterum	AUD 1987, no. 286.
68	Ørum Øst	140119	264	Thomas B. Nielsen & Niels Axel Boas	Nielsen, B.T. & Rasmussen, L.W. 2013.
69	Å Mølle, Green 10	140410	158	Birgitte Ribert & Ernst Stidsing	
70	Å Mølle, Green 16	140410	160	Birgitte Ribert & Ernst Stidsing	
71	Kongsager	141006	54	Reno Fiedel	AUD1994, no. 414; 1996, no. 305.
Aarhus County					
72	Geding	150308	39	Jens Jeppesen	AUD 1991, no. 286.
73	Vejlby	150309	30	Jens Jeppesen	Jeppesen, J. 1984:99pp. Apel, J. 2001.
Skanderborg County					
74	Hårup Østergård	160105	279	Kaj F. Rasmussen	
75	Troldbjerg	160109	60	Knud Bjerring Jensen	Aud 1988, no. 323.
76	Søhøjlandets Golfbane	160109	74	Knud Bjerring Jensen	
77	Kildebjerg I/III	160203	263	Rikke Isler & Merethe Schifter Bagge	
78	Heathaven Skanderborg	160207	36	Anja Vegeberg Jensen	
79	Vrold	160208	145	Merethe Schifter Bagge	
80	Vilholtgård	160400	192	Per Borup	Aud 1998, no. 440.
81	Egebjerg Kær	160502	137	Per Borup	
82	Petersborg	160515	170	Per Borup	AUD 1997, no. 360; 1998, no. 443.
83	Petersborg vest	160515	83	Per Borup	AUD 1999, no. 485; 2000, no. 506; 2002 no. 484.
84	Birkholmvej	160515	83	Per Borup	AUD 2000, no.506; 2001, no. 504; 2002, no. 483.
85	Birkevej	160601	14	Per Borup	AUD 1997, no. 362.
86	Arildskov	160605	584	Constanze Rassmann	
Vejle County					
87	Sjællandsvej-Lillebælt	170802	129	Hans Rostholm & Tinna Møbjerg	
88	Søvej I	170802	283	Hans Rostholm	
89	Enkehøj	170802	303	Tinna Møbjerg	Møbjerg, T., Jensen, P. M. & Mikkelsen, P. H. 2007.
90	Sjællandsvej VII	170802	315	Søren Timm Meltvedt Christensen	
91	Sjællandsvej V	170802	336	Vibeke Juul Pedersen	Møbjerg, T., Jensen, P. M. & Mikkelsen, P. H. 2007.
92	Dalsgård II	170805	309	Aase Gyldion	AUD 2000, no. 569; 2001, no. 530; 2002, no. 507.
93	Dalsgård III	170805	327	Peter Deichmann	
94	Skjelborg	170811	65	Per Borup	
Ringkøbing County					
95	Vorgod	180113	122	Hans Rostholm	Rostholm 1986: 36pp; 1987:362.
96	Stendis	180206	46	Torben Skov	Skov 1978; 1982:39pp; Apel, J. 2001.

Nr	Location	Sted-nr	SB-nr	Field directors	Some basic archaeological sources
97	Bjørnkærgård	180208	13	Poul Mikkelsen	AUD 1993, no. 384.
98	Trængsel	180208	125	Poul Mikkelsen	AUD 1993, no. 386.
99	Gulfælgård	180208	152	Poul Mikkelsen	AUD 1995, no. 397; 1996 no. 373.
100	Hasselholtvej	180208	149	Bo Steen	AUD 1998:487.
101	Skank	180209	691	Poul Mikkelsen & Lis Helles Olesen	AUD 1994, no. 478.
102	Hedegård	180303	149	Rikke Isler	
103	Kirkebakke	180305	56	Hans Rostholm	AUD 1994, no. 480.
104	Krogstrup V	180314	50	Vibeke Juul Pedersen	
105	Gilmosevej	180318	57	Vibeke Juul Pedersen	Møbjerg
106	Trindtoft	180318	77	Søren Timm Meltvedt Christensen	
107	Nøvling Plantage	180320	51	Hans Rostholm	AUD 1999, no. 562; 2000, no. 632.
108	Hovergårde	180405	95	Jens Aarup Jensen	Jensen, J. Aa. 1984:59pp.
109	Mejrup Syd	180510	119	Bo Steen	AUD 1999, no. 517
110	Katrinesminde	180510	119	Bo Steen	AUD 1999, no. 517; 2001, no. 587.
111	Drosselvej	180706	90	Bo Steen	AUD 1999, no. 586
Ribe County					
112	Langkærgård	190101	130	Janne Krøtel	Dollar, S.R. 2013.
113	Havgårdslund	190101	137	Lars Grundvad	
114	Vestervang VII	190103	93	Steffen Terp Laursen	Dollar, S.R. 2013.
115	Revsinggård	190103	94	Thomas Rune Knudsen	Dollar, S.R. 2013.
116	Tuesbøl	190103	228	Nanna Kirkeby	Dollar, S.R. 2013.
117	Margrethenborg	190110	63	Ejvind Hertz	AUD 2000, no. 653; 2001, no. 603; Dollar, S.R. 2013.
118	Følvling I	190303	162	Maria Walther	AUD 1997, no. 441; Dollar, S.R. 2013
119	Guldagergård	190304	78	Per Ole Rindel	AUD 1992, no. 364; Dollar, S.R. 2013.
120	Sønder Holsted	190304	83	Ejvind Hertz	
121	Nørregård VIII/IX	190304	105	Lars Grundvad	Dollar, S.R. 2013.
122	Mannehøjgård I/IV	190307	192	Steffen Terp Laursen & Martin Egelund Poulsen	Dollar, S.R. 2013.
123	Øster Skibelund I	190307	204	Britt Petersen	
124	Kongehøj II	190307	208	Martin Egelund Poulsen	Poulsen, M.E. 2008.
125	Kongehøj III	190307	212	Martin Egelund Poulsen	Dollar, S.R. 2013.
126	Kongeengen	190307	225	Martin Egelund Poulsen	
127	Stavnsbjerg III	190308	119	Per Ole Rindel	AUD 1992, no. 373; Dollar, S.R. 2013.
128	Lundgård III	190308	174	Stig Grummegaard-Nielsen	Dollar, S.R. 2013.
129	Mariasminde III	190308	177	Steffen Terp Laursen	Dollar, S.R. 2013.
130	Nygårdstoft	190401	45	Jens G. Lauridsen & Claus Feveile	AUD 2003, no. 533.
131	Karmdal Banke	190402	39	Claus Feveile	AUD 1994, no. 547; Ethelberg, P. 2000:165.
132	Klostermarken IV	190409	115	Claus Feveile	AUD 2002, no. 564.
133	Grønnegård	190503	176	Palle Siemen	AUD 1989, no. 371; 1993, no. 465; Siemen, P. 1993:63p.
Haderslev County					
134	Lille Tornumgård	201003	249	Martin Egelund Poulsen	Poulsen, M.E. 2015.
135	Højgård	200201	170	Per Ethelberg	Ethelberg, P. 1985:13-21; 1987:153pp.; 1993:136pp; 2000:165pp.
136	Grønvang	200203	194	André Bendix Matthissen	
137	Søndermose	200203	195	Katrine Moberg Riis	
138	Brdr. Gram	200208	18	Per Ethelberg	Ethelberg, P. 2000:165, & Fig. 15, 35 & 37.
139	Grimballe	200209	59	Lisbeth Christensen & Tenna Reinholt Kristensen	AUD 2000, no. 688.
140	Gammelbrovej	200311	186	Silke Eisenschmidt	AUD 1996, no. 495; Ethelberg, P. 2000:165.
Åbenrå County					
141	Johannesminde	220110	83	Hans Chr. H. Andersen & Per Ethelberg	AUD 1999, no. 674.
142	Møllehøje	220110	19	Frauke Witte	AUD 2002, no. 611.
143	Smedeager	220201	140	Frauke Witte	AUD 2003, no.604.
144	Stamplund	220202	127	Erling Madsen	
145	Brunde	220204	161	Per Ethelberg	AUD 1992, no. 407; Ethelberg, P. 2000:165.
146	Egelund 2	220204	195	Lene Heidemann Lutz	
Odense County					
147	Lindebjerg	080608	53	Anders Jæger & Jesper Laursen	Jæger, A. & Laursen, J. 1983:102pp, Apel, J. 2001.

hinterlands. These six streams all flow into the North Sea (Vesterhavet) or the fjords leading to it (Storå into Nissum Fjord and Skjern Å into Ringkøbing Fjord), and there is now rapidly growing evidence of settlements with sunken-floor houses located close to the upper parts of these waterways (Fig. 1.1 & 1.3, with literature references).

Near Storå, in its upper water systems that reach into central areas of Jutland, this concerns sites such as Hedegård, Kirkebakke, Krogstrup, Gilmosevej, Trindtoft and Nøvling Plantage. Similarly, in the area of the upper water systems of Skjern Å to the east, in particular, it relates to sites such as Birkevej, Arildskov, Sjællandsvej-Lillebælt, Søvej 1, Enkehøj, Sjællandsvej VII, and Sjællandsvej V. Near Holsted Å, not as long as the two previous, it relates to sites such as Føvling I, Guldagergård, Sønder Holsted and Nørregård VIII/IX around its upper water systems.

Close to Kongeå, and especially in the vicinity of the upper water systems feeding it from eastern parts of Jutland, numerous settlements with sunken-floor houses have more recently become known from the period in question and this concerns sites such as Langkærgård, Havgårdslund, Vestervang VII, Margrethenborg, Mannehøjgård I/IV, Øster Skibelund I, Kongehøj II, Kongehøj III, Lundgård III, Mariasminde III and Karmdal Banke. Near Ribe Å, and not least along its upper water systems far to the east, it relates to sites such as Nygårdstoft, Klostermarken IV, Lille Tornumgård, Højgård, Grønvang, Søndermose, Brdr. Gram and Grimballe. Finally, also far to the east in the upper water systems of Vidå in Jutland, it concerns sites such as Johannesminde, Møllehøje, Smedeager, Stamplund, Brunde and Egelund 2.

Many of the Jutlandic settlements with sunken floors near the above mentioned six major water systems belong to the Danish "Zone II", being the ancient central area of the Single Grave Culture (Lomborg 1973a:96). In terms of more of the new locations with ornamented ceramics south of the Limfjord region, a detailed and clear picture of the extent to which Beaker pottery and affiliated items belong to the individual settlements is still awaited, and hence absolutely needs to be clarified. A large-scale survey project, initiated by the Kroppedal Museum and the National Museum of Denmark, is currently also focusing on two-aisled houses from the Late Neolithic and emerging Bronze Age. It intends to embrace all Danish areas and a great deal of new, interesting information on local and regional building traditions and find materials are likely to emerge.

One conspicuous trait of House 1 at Egehøj was the presence of a sunken floor in the western third of the interior, given that this placement appears to be rather atypical for such longhouses in Jutland. It could, of course, be specific to the local area but, in my view, it can perhaps be seen as related to certain buildings in eastern parts of South Scandinavia. I am not, however, convinced that the more recently investigated House 1 at Margrethenborg and House K35 Mannehøjgård to the south of Jutland offer other examples of sunken floors to the west (Dollar, 2013:42p). In the case of Margrethenborg it would instead be worth considering the evident possibility that the row of four quite sizeable postholes east of the sunken floor belongs to a separate two-aisled ground-floor house. The apparent oblique direction in relation to the sunken floor might support that understanding.

A glance at neighbouring countries

In the following, we shall first turn to some of the excavated house sites from the British Isles, and then to remainders from the northern lowlands of the European continent from Holland to Poland and, finally, to some house sites from Finland and parts of Scandinavia not yet considered. First and foremost, this concerns some prominent examples of buildings from the period before or contemporaneous with the South Scandinavian Late Neolithic. Some of the literature referred to takes into consideration other houses or traditions from adjacent periods and further references can be found in the bibliographies of these publications. My main interest, however, is to look for the existence of early building traits that may somehow relate to those of the sunken-floor longhouses in the Limfjord region.

Concerning the Late Neolithic in England and Wales, more or less substantial traces of post-framed buildings, post and wall-slot buildings, stone and turf-walled buildings, and stake-walled buildings have been found (Darvill 1996:92-93). Some agreement seems to exist that Neolithic dwellings may over time have changed from predominantly rectangular ground plans to round or oval ones (Darvill 1996:83pp; Malone 2001:57). Some of the houses had floors in a sunken position.

At Ronaldsway, on the Isle of Man, a house with an almost rectangular ground plan was built in such a way that it had a naturally sunken floor because it incorporated a natural hollowing in the ground (Burgess 1980; Thomas 1996:12; Darvill 1996:98 & Fig. 6.8

& Appendix 1, no. 64. Topping 1996:166p & table 11.1). It had a length of c. 7.5 m and a width of 4.1 m and was supplied with a hearth in the centre. Whether this house was an exceptional building, based on the old tradition of a sub-rectangular layout or possibly a local tradition for such houses is not clear (Burgess 1980:61). Different tools and several clay pots were so well preserved and lacking evident traces of use that it has been questioned as to whether this house had a primarily domestic function (Topping 1996:166).

At Skara Brae on Mainland, Orkney, the Late Neolithic settlement also left interesting traits because the often sub-rectangular stone houses were, in several instances, placed in a semi-subterranean position (Clarke, D.V. 1976; Burgess 1980:220; Clarke, D.V. & Sharples, N. 1990; Malone 2001). Central hearths built with kerbs and beds, benches, shelves and cupboards also constructed from stone materials were some of the featured characteristics (Malone 2001:58). The houses had often been rebuilt and the duration of the residence in each house can be difficult to estimate (Barclay 1996:67). One of the houses with later occupation is Building 7, which had an almost square ground plan with c. 9 m long outer sides and northerly entrance. Particular features of this house were beds and other floor arrangements but evidence of tools that might have given clues to what went on in the uniquely preserved houses was more or less absent (Barclay 1996:67).

The comprehensive new evidence from Barnhouse, likewise on Mainland, contributes much to the basic understanding of the building traditions, the artefacts, the daily life, and the way of organizing activities within and also outside the sub-circular sandstone houses (Richards 2005:7pp; Jones & Richards 2005:25pp). Some of the houses even showed evidence of several phases of occupation and House 3 and House 5, for instance, had a sequence of several re-building phases with only minor displacements traceable (Downes & Richards 2005:61pp). The radiocarbon determinations place the settlement, within a few centuries, around 3000 calBC (Ashmore 2005:385pp). Interestingly, both these Orcadian traditions of extremely long usage are – as we shall see – in stark contrast with the many sunken-floor longhouses in the Limfjord region.

According to Mike Parker Pearson, the Stonehenge Riverside Project has revealed several house sites with quite well-preserved floors in the area of Durrington Walls.[4] The buildings belong to the Late Neolithic and seem to be earlier than the ditches and banks of the henge monument. One example is the rectangular House 851 with thick walls consisting of crushed chalk, of which some traces were still preserved. The interior appears to have been very well organized. The floor measured 5.2 x 4.8 m, with a doorway to the south, hearth at the centre, and traces of beds to the east and west, while storage took place to the south and to the north.

It has been suggested that a fair question for reconsideration relates to whether certain large, shallow pits could represent sunken floors (Darvill 1996:111, note 9). In general, it seems that the British house building traditions incorporated a wide variety of concrete forms. And yet Julian Thomas may possibly be right when he suggested that the known house sites represent mainly atypical examples (Thomas 1996:7). He further argued that several soil features and clusters of possible postholes have also uncritically been claimed to represent traces of houses once used for dwellings because the traces appear rather different in character and because it is often difficult to clearly perceive the structure.

Although deep floors and other relevant traits exist from the British Isles, it must be acknowledged that traces of dwellings with significant affiliations to the Limfjord region house tradition have so far, to my knowledge, not been published. From the present material, it therefore does not seem that it was from this corner of the world that the idea of the longhouses with sunken floors came to the South Scandinavian Late Neolithic.

When we turn to the Netherlands and Germany in the Early Bronze Age and the time immediately before that, several settlement sites have, not least in recent years, been recovered, clearly evidencing a massive tradition of regular longhouses with two-aisled constructions of varying character in this extensive northwest part of continental Europe.

From the Netherlands, the ground plan of the two-aisled, E-W aligned longhouse from Molenaarsgraaf forms a classic case (Harrison 1980:28p). This house seems to belong to the Early Bronze Age but remainders from two-aisled houses of the Dutch Bell Beaker Culture also appear to be present at this site (Hogestijn & Drenth 2001:66pp). The building remainders from Noordwijk offer another example of a two-aisled longhouse construction (Hogestijn and Drenth 2001:72pp; Fokkens 2003, Fig. 2.). According to Erik Drenth (pers. comm.) the two-aisled house building tradition known from the Barbed Wire Culture (Noordwijk) in the Dutch Early Bronze Age appears to go back to the Bell Beaker Culture and even further (*cf.* Hogestijn & Drenth 2001:56p; Anscher 2000:80pp). Other examples of ground plans exist from the Bell Beaker Culture, while the sites Zeewijk-Oost and Mienakker are dated to the Dutch Single Grave Culture (Hogestijn, Koudijs, & Bulten 1994:24pp; Hogestijn & Drenth 2001:61pp; Drenth 2005:353pp, Fig. 16-18. See also Hogestijn & Drenth 2000).

Of all of these, not least the Haamstede-Brabers building remainders, considered to belong to the Vlaardingen Culture, are interesting and, in particular, "Cluster 1" attracts attention (Verhart 1992:82pp; Sarauw 2006:46). This house site has a number of traits with resemblances to certain sunken-floor longhouses in Jutland. First and foremost, it was clearly two-aisled and supplied with a relatively large sunken area which appears to have been separated into two parts, as also depicted in a reconstruction drawing. Rather densely placed stake- and postholes were present within and just outside the sunken parts. Many stake-and postholes in rows also indicated interior walls. The postholes of the outer walls were more sizeable and largely preserved in the long sides as well as the gable ends. The house dimensions were quite moderate, however, a mere 9.1m long by 3.8 m wide.

Substantial evidence of longhouses belonging to the Early Bronze Age now exists widely in many of the German Länder.[5] From Schleswig-Holstein, the eastern parts of an E-W aligned, two-aisled longhouse were investigated at Flintbek. No sunken floor was found and the entire length was not recognizable (Zich 1994:20pp; 2000. See also Ethelberg 2000b). The house is considered to belong to the transition to the Bronze Age. A SW-NE aligned longhouse was recovered from Mecklenburg-Vorpommern, at Neuenkirchen, with interesting tool finds associated with bronze casting (Szczesiak 1999:110pp).

From Brandenburg, at the Dyrotz and Wustermark sites in Havelland, ground plans of almost E-W aligned, partly preserved two-aisled houses have been recorded (Beran 2000:53pp). From Niedersachsen, at Esbech in the Helmstedt area, a ground plan of a two-aisled well-preserved house site has been recorded, as well as another partly preserved example. Both buildings were E-W aligned (Thieme & Maier 1995:166pp). From the lower Elbe area, four ground plans of E-W aligned, partly preserved two-aisled longhouses have been recorded at Daerstorf but it appears difficult to narrow down the chronological position of these buildings (Thieme 1997:29pp).

From Sachsen-Thüringen, rather interesting investigations at the Zwenkau site near Leipzig have revealed many, more or less E-W aligned longhouses (Stäuble 1997:133pp; Huth & Stäuble 1998:188pp). Two-aisled as well as three-aisled constructions are represented among the total of 26 ground plans recovered and a series of radiocarbon determinations on reasonable short-lived wood pieces from wells exists (Stäuble 1997, Fig. 9).

A significant tradition of using two-aisled longhouses also existed in Bavaria and some of these were extremely long and divided into sections. Fine examples are from Straubing-Öberau, Eching in the southern parts of Bavaria, dating from the final Neolithic or Early Bronze Age (Nadler 1997:161pp, Nadler 2000:39pp). Remains of other Early Bronze Age houses are from Bophingen and Zuchering (Nadler 1997:168. Krause 1997:150pp; Schefzik 1995; 2001:87pp). One of the particular traits from Niederbayern is that the buildings were almost N-S aligned, thereby contrasting with examples of two-aisled longhouses mentioned from the more northerly areas of Germany and also diverging from those in Brezno, Postoloprty and other sites in northwest Bohemia and Franzhausen in Moravia (Krause 1997:160pp). Longhouses at Bophingen were, for instance, approximately N-S aligned.

We must, however, acknowledge that the steadily increasing evidence of two-aisled traditions from the different German Länder does not point to combinations with substantial sunken floors in the longhouses (*cf.* Nielsen, P.-O. 1998; Jensen 2006b).

When turning to Poland, the vestiges of houses have gradually come more and more into focus as regards the Early Bronze Age but the cultural and chronological situation still appears rather complex.[6] However, settlements with sizeable, more or less flat-bottomed pits, often with pottery remainders, became known early in Poland (Krzak 1976:62pp). In later years, the research efforts, not least in Kujawy areas and beyond, have borne fruits.

One of the more recent investigations of a possible sunken area took place in Kujawy at Smarglin, stan. 22 (Czebreszuk 1996; Makarowicz 2005). The pottery from the sunken area is considered to date it to the Iwno Culture (Czebreszuk 1996, Fig. 34-35). The sunken area tended towards a partly rectangular shape on the surface. It was almost E-W aligned with the length reaching c. 6 m and the width c. 4 m (Czebreszuk 1996, Fig. 32; Makarowicz 2005, Fig. 1). The sunken area was fairly flat-bottomed and had a depth of c. 0.6 m below the old surface (Czebreszuk 1996, Fig. 33). Another interesting settlement with a sunken area is Rybiny, Kujawy-Pomorze province, stan. 17, dated through a series of radiocarbon determinations to about 1800-1700 BC (Makarowicz & Milecka 1999; Makarowicz 2000:124 & Fig. 48-54. Due to the traits of the pottery, Makarowicz considers it to belong to the Trzciniec Cultural Circle, specifically its classic phase, although it is also considered to include certain late Iwno Culture traits (Makarowicz 2000:124). The sunken area had a sub-circular outline, being a little more than 11 m in diameter. The depth of the flat-bottomed area reached about 0.8 m into the subsoil (Makarowicz 2000, Fig. 7-8). Two hearths were located centrally in the flattest part, while a third was recorded to the north. Some minor sunken floors are also known, being dated to the Trzciniec Cultural Circle. This concerns, for instance, the Zurawce, stan and Kaczórki, stan sites (Makarowicz 2010:439 & Fig. 2.61).

In conclusion, evidence of a tradition of dwelling structures that included sunken areas does exist in certain parts of Poland. This concerns not least Kujawy (*cf.* Czebreszuk 2001:194p). However, the diagnostic traits are thus far too few to make a direct comparison with the remainders of South Scandinavian sunken-floor houses or, in particular, those from the Limfjord region. To note clear affinities with the South Scandinavian sunken-floor houses would require the presence of a number of more specific building traits.

When turning to Finland, it is interesting that longstanding and widespread traditions of using markedly deepened floors have been recognized. The archaeological efforts of the last decades have, not least, documented many such vestiges. Two of the remarkable NE-SW aligned house remainders were investigated at Kauvonkangas, but are fairly old and considered to belong to a time closer to 3000 BC (Kankaanpää 2002). These houses had an oval ground plan, appear to have been much smaller than the longhouses of the Limfjord region and it is not thought that they included regular ground-floor parts. A number of house pits were found at the settlement and the discussion of the observations has involved analogies with certain Indian winter houses. Quartz assemblages from both house sites have been studied in much detail (Rankama 2002).

Other interesting semi-subterranean houses are found at sites such as Peurasuo, Madeneva, Rusavierto, Kärmelahti and Martinniemi (Ojanlatva & Alakärpi 2002; Miettinen 2002; Leskinen 2002; Katiskoski 2002; Halinen et al.2002). At Rusavierto, a dating of the semi-subterranean house to 2300-1900 calBC is considered most probable but it appears that repeated use may have taken place according to the interpretation of the radiocarbon determinations. Among other things, it has turned out that the five stone hearths found in the deepened area cannot be dated to the same period as the house structure (Leskinen 2002:151pp).

Even though some of the above sites of huts and houses belong to the Early Metal Age in Finland, it has been suggested that the majority of the semi-subterranean huts and houses can be placed within the three millennia preceding 2000 BC, and some might even be earlier (Pesonen 2002:9). There is no reason here to go through the many interesting details of these kinds of buildings and, evidently, the buildings did not have sizeable ground-floor parts.

Judging from the above settlements with house sites, it does not seem that the Finnish traditions for semi-subterranean buildings were closely related specifically to the sunken-floor houses of the Limfjord region. As we also did not find any obvious relationship with sunken-floor house traditions in Britain, Germany or Poland, it seems reasonable to conclude from the now available material that the South Scandinavian houses with deepened floor parts may have developed fairly independently. However, in my reading, relationships between building traditions in Holland and Jutland are not excluded, given not least the more recently excavated vestiges from Haamstede-Brabers, with some resonance in certain sunken-floor longhouses in Jutland.

From Norway, indications of Late Neolithic settlements were found early on rather sporadically to the south and west (e.g. Bakka 1976). The most northerly known location with Beaker-related items so far has been investigated at Slettabø (Skjølsvold 1977; Østmo 2005:61; Prieto-Martinez 2008). Here, besides five lobed and tanged flint arrowheads, the remainders of a Beaker decorated with horizontal zones were found (Skjølsvold 1977, Fig. 54). Yet, sunken-floor house sites have neither been discovered here nor at the locations of many other lobed and tanged arrowheads at Jæren and Lista (*cf.* Løken 1998a, on building remainders in western Norway). It is interesting, however, that far north of the polar circle, houses with sunken floors are known from a period corresponding to the South Scandinavian Late Neolithic and emerging Bronze Age. At Slettness, many houses with deepened floors are thus recorded from the early metal period, c. 2000-1500 BC. The buildings were rectangular with rather small floor areas. Some examples ranged from c. 17-30 m², and some had a small annex, presumably for storing (Hesjedal, Damm, Olsen & Storli 1996:214). The entrances formed sunken corridors in the wall banks of stone and soil. Hearths were placed within the interior. Not all house sites at this settlement have been investigated. In terms of two-aisled ground-floor houses, it seems that sites are gradually beginning to come to light in south Norway.[7]

From a period corresponding to the South Scandinavian Late Neolithic and Bronze Age some finds of thick stone walls as well as artefacts and other settlement remainders are known from Norrland in Sweden but sunken floors, to my knowledge, have not been recovered in these contexts (Liedgren 1995:121p).

As we have seen, within South Scandinavia, the sunken-floor houses have been recovered first and foremost from Jutland and southwest Sweden. Yet it cannot be ruled out that intensified field research on Zealand, Funen and nearby islands may lead to further sites of houses with sunken floors from the period in question. Henceforward, it would not be very surprising if vestiges of sunken-floor longhouses with more direct affinities to the South Scandinavian traditions were recovered in Schleswig-Holstein and Mecklenburg-Vorpommern.

Some "classic" South Scandinavian house sites

In this part, we shall briefly look at some more or less "classic" house examples from South Scandinavia as these sites with relics of dwellings and architectural expressions have sketched out the initial point of departure for my study of sunken-floor house sites. Besides sites of two-aisled longhouses with ground floors and with sunken floors, a few remnants of minor sunken-floor houses are also included.

Regarding Jutland, it is sometimes not possible to be specific about the chronological positions of the "classic" sites because even some of the relatively clear house ground plans do not have reliable radiocarbon determinations of short-life organic materials from relevant contexts or detailed chronology on ceramics or other. It is reasonable to have the longhouses in just two main groupings, i.e. an early and a late group within the Late Neolithic/emerging Bronze Age. It is necessary to point out that the methods of measuring the dimensions are not known in all instances. With regard to the early group of two-aisled, ground-floor longhouses, seven sites are seen as relatively classic examples from their geographical areas.[8] When it comes to the late group of two-aisled, ground-floor longhouses, the more sizeable buildings in particular are selected, as the state of publication of the minor and middle-sized houses seems somewhat lagging, although some examples are known (e.g. Lord 2000:64pp; Artursson 2000; 2009). Ten sites have been selected as classic examples from their geographical areas.[9] In the early group of two-aisled sunken-floor longhouses, five sites have been selected as classic examples.[10] When it comes to the late group of two-aisled longhouses with sunken floors, just two sites have been considered classic examples.[11] Four house sites from the period in question may be representative of the group of minor buildings with sunken floors.[12]

Other kinds of house remains have also long been known, e.g. some of those represented at Vadgård (Lomborg 1973b; 1976; 1980; Rasmussen, M. 1993; 1995; Simonsen 1996c) or other, rather special, buildings like the Nautrup house in the central Limfjord region (Simonsen 1982a:52pp), or buildings such as House 92 at Fosie IV, which had a limited sunken area in its middle (Björhem & Säfvestad 1989:52pp; *cf.* Larsson, M. 1995:38p; Säfvestad 1997).

The end of a 900-year era

In my understanding, longhouses with partially sunken floors and those with solely ground floors existed in parallel to each other throughout the entire period of the Late Neolithic and emerging Bronze Age. While the two-aisled, ground-floor longhouses in particular already had a very long history in South Scandinavia at the beginning of the Late Neolithic, it is still more interesting that both categories appear to have gone out of use more or less simultaneously.

Even though the sunken-floor longhouses can be considered a rather special branch within South Scandinavian house building, the tradition for such deep floors should also be considered longstanding because, instead of strong foreign influences, it must have mainly had its roots back in the Single Grave Culture. And as this building tradition even continued for some time after the transition to the Bronze Age, the finds as a whole evidence a South Scandinavian practise of using sunken-floor houses for at least 900 years.

Now we shall just briefly consider what happened after the abandonment of sunken-floor houses at three settlements in the central Limfjord region. At Glattrup I/III, we have two examples of traces showing how, in each case, a three-aisled Older Bronze Age longhouse partly covered the plots of a sunken-floor longhouse from LN I. Several hundred years must therefore have passed between these settlements because no traces of settling were found from the interim period at these two plots.

At Resengaard, we have an example of one three-aisled Older Bronze Age longhouse partly covering the plots of two minor, sunken-floor houses. Another example shows how a three-aisled Older Bronze Age longhouse was overlapping the site of the gable end of a sunken-floor longhouse. All three sunken-floor houses belonged to LN II/the emerging Bronze Age. There could thus have been some time between the occupation of these individual plots and no vestiges were found from any intermediate settlement.

At Kluborg II, a three-aisled Older Bronze Age house was placed so that its western gable end overlapped with the eastern gable end of the plot of a longhouse with sunken floor. In this case, no vestiges of intermediate settling were observed and there may not have been much time between these longhouses.

The construction of these new three-aisled buildings on the plots of the old sunken-floor house sites may indicate that these lands, at that time, were again regarded as rather attractive for building new dwellings. However, the three-aisled longhouses that were placed on top of the plots of former sunken-floor longhouses symbolize, more than anything else, that the era of the sunken-floor longhouses had come to an end.[13]

1.5. Methodological reflections and theoretical inspiration

Having gone through the existing interpretations of the sunken-floor houses and an outline of the field research history, including a look at North European countries, we shall now turn to considerations of formation processes, field research strategies, source critique, analytical approach and theoretical inspiration concerning the present work.

Sunken-floor formation processes

Focusing on the sunken-floor formation processes involves being clearly aware of the phases of construction and deconstruction. The history of a dwelling plot can be quite long and include several steps. Many factors can affect its preservation and, in any case, every sunken floor has a history of its own in the details. In order to provide a solid basis for analyses and interpretations, it is vital to try to understand the stages in the development of the sunken floors, in particular from construction and use through destruction and preservation to their recovery as sites. During fieldwork, consideration of the formation processes therefore needs to be carried out thoroughly. If not, it could lead to unpleasant surprises, when e.g. radiocarbon determinations come up. Even though such considerations can be time-consuming, in my view it is really important not to try to cut corners in this respect. Kristian Kristiansen presented the first systematic views of formation processes and representativeness in Danish contexts (Kristiansen 1974; 1978; 1985).

From the period of construction, particular traits regarding the placing of the house often need to be recorded: What was the position like in relation to plane and sloping areas of the site terrain? What was the soil composition like beneath and around the chosen spot? Did it seem that the sunken floor had originally been dug deeper into the subsoil than was immediately apparent? With the last research question, in particular, I am aiming to ascertain the scale of damage caused by recent ploughing.

From the period of residence, it would for example be interesting to know more about the process of floor deepening. What factors might have caused it, e.g. specific activities in certain areas? Or could it be the result of removing thin layers of subsoil over time? From the period of use once it is no longer used as a residence, would it at least not be of great importance to seek to identify for what purposes the longhouse may now have been secondarily used?

From the period following last use and abandonment of the longhouse and subsequent demolition, it might for instance be interesting to know more about how the sunken-floor hollow had been filled in: What were the details of the contents? How was the domestic refuse treated? How deliberate does the process of filling in appear to have been? Did agricultural activities and ploughing with the ard take place before, in between and after completing this process? After sinking due to natural compression, what kind of new fills came on top of the old? And, later on, what happened further to the house site and the plot?

Field research strategies

In Danish contexts, the excavation methods had already improved significantly from about the mid-1960s on with the introduction of machines for the removal of most of the topsoil at the intended excavation area, thus often surprisingly bringing many different soil features to light. Ideally today, after scrutinizing the area by means of aerial survey/aerial photos, modern geophysical methods and other, the sequence of field research activities can advantageously, when possible, begin with reconnaissance followed by trial excavations and regular excavations. When using appropriate machines for this purpose, it will usually be possible to quickly look over large areas at the same time, while the soils still maintain their fresh colours.

Even though several new techniques are now available for surveying prior to excavation, the sunken-floor house sites are repeatedly located through the results of trial excavations. During such surveys, sunken-floor parts may simply appear in a trench where machines have removed the topsoil. Their direction, their considerable surface dimensions and their relatively flat bottoms are frequently three of the immediate indicators. Various artefacts such as potsherds, worked flint and heat-affected stones spread in the fills may help to further qualify the indication of the presence of a sunken-floor house site.

A regular excavation can be favourably carried out through the gradual removal of the topsoil. For practical reasons, one area could thus be excavated to a certain level before removing the topsoil in a new area, thereby maintaining the possibility of obtaining a complete section for observations of stratification in a selected position. In practice, however, what often happens is that all the topsoil over the entire house site is removed soon after commencement because the above-mentioned strategy can become costly.

Further excavation processes are ideally carried out using traditional tools such as hand shovels and diverse trowels. Habitually, tasks like measuring, drawing, describing and basic interpretation are undertaken continuously for the report. New techniques using GPS, GIS and other kinds of IT-based equipment are now widely employed. And yet, when the excavations at Resengaard and the other nine settlements considered in the following chapters commenced, such means were not locally available to us.

In terms of strategies for future excavations of sunken-floor house sites, I would strongly advocate that the field directors should as far as possible focus on addressing the unsolved questions pertaining to this field of settlement research. It is thus of crucial importance that attempts are made to establish excavation strategies with clear potential for helping to narrow down the gaps in our current knowledge. It may consequently be necessary to make some hard priorities in terms of the available time and resources. Such strategies might of course lead to an unavoidable downgrading of other "normal" tasks – and hence perhaps be met with criticism.

In a debate article, Torsten Madsen has pointed out the evident need to always direct the archaeological excavations towards current problems rather than just undertaking a minute registration of trivial details (Madsen 1988:24pp). This is an extremely important statement and I can only agree with this view.

Source critique on geographical representativeness

It is hardly possible to state with absolute certainty that a given archaeological distribution of a find group, in our case the sites of sunken-floor houses, is representative geographically but, through comparison with other groups of finds or monuments, it can be possible to establish reasonable assumptions (cf. Simonsen 1982b). For instance, comparison with distributions of datable flint artefacts from different geographical areas can, in certain respects, be an obvious possibility for the period in question.

Yet the dagger distributions, in particular, can reveal a paradox compared with the spread of sunken-floor house sites because the production of these pressure-flaked flint items throughout the entire Late Neolithic and emerging Bronze Age corresponds to the time of the sunken-floor longhouses.

Certain early as well as late daggers noticeably point to a relatively dense population in the inner parts of Himmerland (Lomborg 1973a:32pp) but the paradox is that only modest evidence of relevant sunken-floor houses has come to our attention in large parts of that landscape. The possibility that sunken-floor houses were not used in these parts is unlikely given that such building remainders are well documented in the peripheries of Himmerland:

they are found to the north at Gug (Beatesminde), Bejsebakken, Leere Gård, Riisgård, and Vadgård; to the east at Solbjerg III, Mølledalsgård, Å Mølle Green 10, and Å Mølle Green 16; to the southeast at Frederiksdal and Kongsager; to the west at Myrhøj, Rønbjerg, and Borregård; and, finally, to the southwest at Møllegård, Skrubben, Bygdalgård, Skringstrup, Abildal and Nordmandshede B. In contrast, in the vast interior areas of Himmerland (with prevailing sandy subsoil) so far only the sites of Povlstrupgård, Sønderup, Hylkekær, Mosegården and Tandrupgaard can be placed on the map. In addition to the mentioned locations there may, however, be some where the character of the building or the dating has not yet been adequately clarified.

In Salling, no sunken-floor house remains have yet come to light in the interior (with a prevailing clayey subsoil) but settlements have been documented in areas more or less near the coast. This relates first of all to Resengaard but also to the sites at Marienlyst Strand, Nygård, Gåsemose, Tromgade, Havbakker III, Hellegård and Kås II. On the island of Mors, no settlements with Late Neolithic and emerging Bronze Age sunken-floor houses have as yet been presented, despite the flint dagger indication of some level of population. Likewise, to my knowledge no such house sites have become known from the area between Nissum Bredning and Nissum Fjord, even though we can note the presence of some population at that time, judging by the distribution of flint daggers, many of which stem from barrows (Lomborg 1973a, Fig. 71).

It must be concluded that vast areas with little or no representation of sunken-floor houses exist, although some presence is expected from comparison with other distributions. This concerns areas with prevailing moraine sand as well as clay-dominated areas. It is therefore reasonable to propose that the present distribution of sites of houses with sunken floors cannot be considered representative geographically in relation to any of the three prevailing soil types in the Limfjord region. One consequently has to be rather careful when dealing with this find group in geographical respects. We need to explore why the original distribution is not proportionately represented.

Some of the activities that affect our knowledge of sites with sunken-floor houses are quite conspicuous. First of all, we can identify several factors that tend to destroy house remainders. Recent ploughing has clearly, and to a high degree, affected the preservation of sunken-floor house sites, even though the deep parts may long survive. Secondly, the raising of new forest and building of new houses and roads are likewise important factors in this respect. And yet, the obligatory requirement to inform museums about such undertakings will likely continue to lead to the recognition of many new house sites. Thirdly, the archaeological level of activity, the economic possibilities and the priorities of the local museums within the current decentralized Danish structure are really important factors. When weighing up these factors, it seems to me that some of the explanation for the distribution of known sites of sunken-floor houses must in particular be sought in the differences in the early and continuing interest shown by certain museums and excavation directors.

Irrespective of the disparity in geographical representation, it is still in the Limfjord region that really many sites have been found although, as I proposed earlier, it is probably incidental that sunken-floor house sites were first found particularly in this area, and that future excavations are likely to reveal that the distribution is not actually limited in this way (Simonsen 1983:88). Since then, the vestiges of many sunken-floor houses have been found widely elsewhere in Jutland, and the prospect is that the museums here will continue to bring to light numerous other sites of this kind.

The assumption that very many sunken-floor remains are still to be found beneath the topsoil in cultivated land can be substantiated by the observation that when farmland changes status to an area where new forest is planned and trial excavations can be financed, this frequently leads to interesting results. Thus in the Limfjord region, the trial excavations that have been carried out before deep ploughing prior to the raising of new forest and other activities leading to deep soil treatment have, in a number of cases, unearthed the remains of sunken-floor house sites.[14]

The above can be further substantiated by considering areas where cultivated land is accidentally exposed to building, digging or other activities of different kinds (*cf.* Dollar 2013:48, on heavy building activities north of Kongeå). Such undertakings have overall led to a considerable number of house sites.[15] Road building has also contributed several new sites.[16] In my opinion, these data clearly indicate that sunken-floor house sites are still preserved in amazingly high numbers beneath the topsoil but threatened heavily by the action of modern agricultural methods, as we shall consider below.

Source critique on physical destruction

An extremely large number of Danish grave monuments have been more or less destroyed over the last hundred years or so. One major factor in this process has been physical destruction by agriculture. As a rough estimate, it can be assumed that three out of four barrows are now ploughed over or otherwise more or less destroyed in the Limfjord region. An overview of graves from the Late Neolithic and preceding period in Denmark is available (Hansen & Rostholm 1993:116pp).

When one of the potentially most devastating factors for house sites is clearly recent ploughing, it is thus interesting that the sunken-floor houses hold a rather exceptional position. If we, as a hypothetical case, compare the possible influence on the traces of three important constructional longhouse elements, namely the traces of postholes of roof-bearing posts, traces of holes from wall posts and the remains of the floors, the effects of ploughing immediately become apparent (Fig. 1.4). As far as I can see, numerous house sites with sunken floors and shallow wall postholes in the Limfjord region may go through a gradual development as outlined in the hypothetical example, if exposed to recent ploughing. Many are certainly already found in a condition comparable to stage 2 or stage 3. Known longhouses with sunken floors in the region can thus be suggested as belonging to different stages of destruction.

Stage 1- house sites, which do not appear to have been influenced in their preservation by recent ploughing, are quite rare. From the Limfjord region, two house sites (1 & 41) at Resengaard are among the best preserved and, even in these cases, the wall posthole lines were not fully observable. From Resengaard, the wall postholes flanking the sunken floor of another house (2) were also rather few, although it entirely avoided any impact from recent ploughing. In my opinion, the explanation can only be that the posts did not go adequately deep into the subsoil and hence could not be recorded. When postholes are apparently missing, it is therefore not necessarily due to ploughing but may well be a consequence of the building methods and techniques. Presumably all three house sites at Myrhøj likewise belonged to stage 1 but, in two cases, the western floor parts were not excavated (GAB & EAB). From the early part of the Late Neolithic at Bejsebakken, another house (A896) seems to be a stage 1 example, despite some minimal effects of later ploughing. A number of house sites may be considered as being between stages 1 and 2 (e.g. House 3 & 5 at Glattrup IV, House 1 at Rosgårde, besides House 13 & 128 at Resengaard). At Bejsebakken, house sites such as A170, A556 and A896 could also belong here.

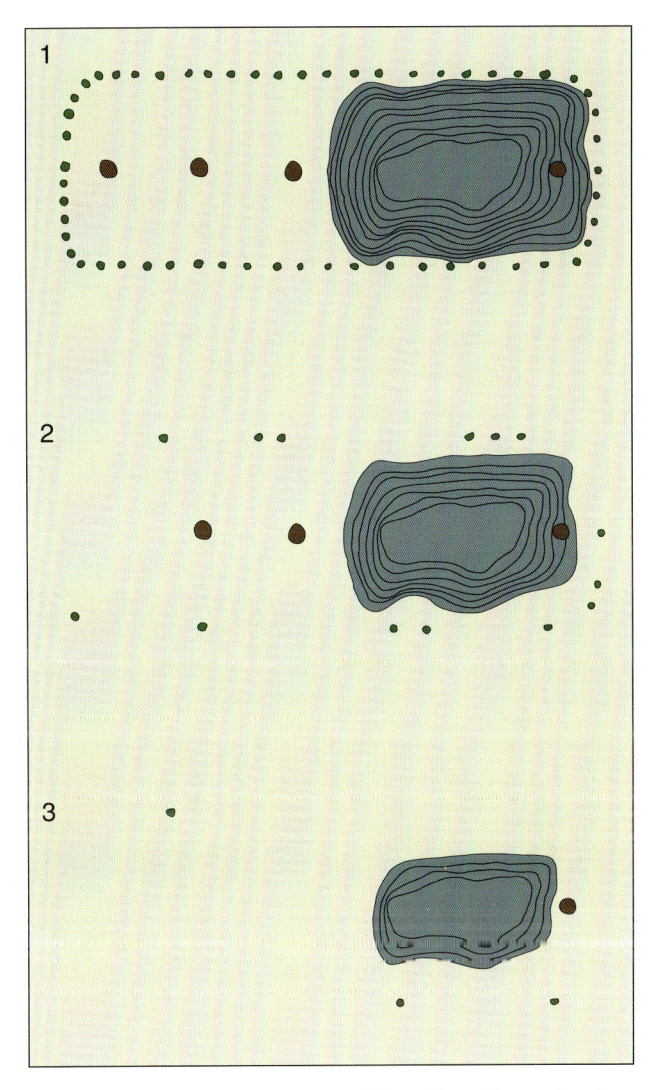

Fig. 1.4. Three stages of the impact of ploughing, illustrating the formation of a hypothetical sunken-floor longhouse site. This building would originally have been characterized by posts set at only a little depth into the subsoil. Two holes of roof-bearing posts in the middle of the sunken floor had already disappeared for other reasons during occupation. Stage 1 corresponds to the house site before the effects of recent ploughing and the depth of the sunken floor is 45 cm. Stage 2 corresponds to 15 cm ploughed off. Many of the wall postholes exist no more, whereas the postholes along the central axis are still observable. The surface dimensions of the sunken floor are diminished. Stage 3 corresponds to 30 cm ploughed off. Most wall postholes have now been removed. The surface dimensions of the sunken floor have diminished yet further. The next steps after stage 3 would gradually lead to the complete destruction of the house site.

The remains of houses originally with sunken floors and shallow postholes that can be considered as belonging to stage 2 are known from a number of locations in the Limfjord region and likewise several much-destroyed sites with stage 3 houses. Yet, it is important to note that house sites in stage 2 and even stage 3 can be very informative as regards the vestiges of activity in the sunken floors. Their fills of artefact remainders are also often quite valuable.

Some house sites in the region diverge more or less from this scheme. Lundvej 19 from Roum parish is an example (Fig. 1.5). If the sub-circular shallow pit to the east were perceived as a sunken floor like those in the longhouses at Myrhøj and the house was hence considered to belong to the main group of the Limfjord region longhouses in question, it would be somewhat conspicuous if recent ploughing had reduced its area while leaving the lines of wall postholes well-preserved.[17] In my view, the house belongs to a somewhat different tradition that may, instead, point towards house building traditions more to the south and east, such as at Djursland.

A final remark on source critique relates to the general representation of the material from the selected sites. We cannot know the extent to which the house remains to be presented are representative in various fields, such as, for instance, the layout of the sunken floors, the presence and placement of soil features or the presence and distribution of artefacts. However, it is my understanding, from working with the sum of the data, that the sunken-floor houses selected for this present study as a whole offer detailed and varied material and that they represent relevant examples of some of the variations found among the preserved sites in the Limfjord region.

Analytical approach

To some extent, many South Scandinavian archaeologists appear to have long favoured research based on the traditional methods of dealing with find materials and have thus not been much occupied with abstract discussions, even though theoretical issues may lie just beneath these habits. In particular, among those of us working in museums, handling sizeable find materials on a daily basis, a solid consensus has long existed about the proper way of approaching data without explicit positioning. This also appears to have been the case elsewhere, as noted by Colin Renfrew "…there is a considerable disparity between the forms of explanation advocated by the partisans of the various isms and those actually employed and found effective by working archaeologists. As a result, the theorists lack credibility, and their formulations sometimes seem irrelevant to the actual development of contemporary archaeological theory. But, on the other hand, that theory, as it is developed by those working first-hand with the data and with a real sense of problem, often seems lacking both in logical form and in any clear awareness of what would (if found valid, after further investigation in relation to the data) constitute a good explanation" (Renfrew 1982:20).

The establishment of fieldwork data is certainly a process deserving of more focus. When dealing with recognition and interpretation regarding excavations in Orkney, Jane Downes and Colin Richards proposed that "… archaeological fieldwork is not simply a technical exercise in data collection but an interpretative or hermeneutic endeavour… Part of the interpretative process involves the preconceptions which are drawn on to facilitate understanding and perhaps nowhere is this more strongly apparent than in the context of fieldwork. Consequently, the construction of field data is based upon the recognition and attribution of meaning to artefacts, layers, walls, etc." (Downes & Richards 2000:159).

My study of complex archaeological observations and find materials from the house sites and settlements is first and foremost based upon a long tradition of analytical approaches deeply rooted in Scandinavian, prehistoric archaeological research. Although

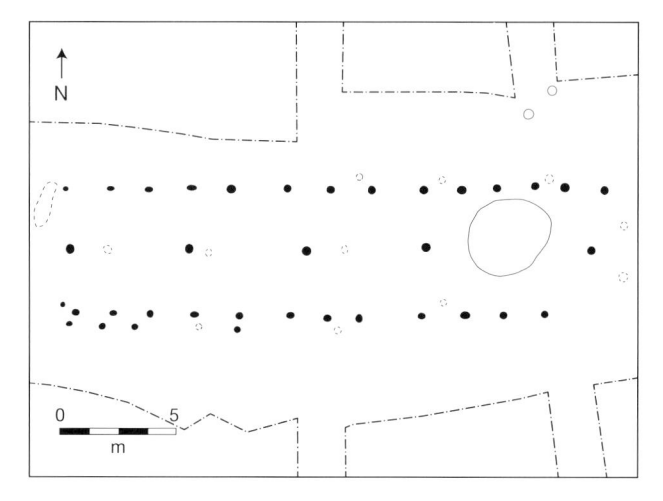

Fig. 1.5. A site of another character is the interesting two-aisled House 1 at Lundvej 19, which was recovered in the southern part of the Limfjord region. No artefacts were found in the large pit to the east. For further detail, see text.

it is often not made explicit within this tradition, it is considered a navigable route to move from a given set of data to a more abstract, general explanation. This explanation may concern relations between data or relations between relations. We have to be conscious of these and try to explain them because relations obviously cannot be excavated. Scandinavian archaeology has often ignored that the empirical data or finds are already theoretically informed, because these data are first collected and then selected for analysis on the basis of some more or less conscious assumptions and ideas.

My empirical data, collected mainly from more recent excavations, are theoretically informed as they are met with research questions which, from the start, are instrumental in defining my field or my empirical object of study, in this case artefacts, soil patches, sunken floors etc. My analytical object of study consists of relations between the various data. These relations cannot be seen, measured or weighed – for instance the household activities performed – and hence are constructions. The explanations of these relations are answers to research questions, for instance in my case on the role of household production in the wider community. It is thus these different aspects of the object of study which, to a high degree, set the direction of my research. This move towards the material allows for a progression of new questions that might be considered relevant to the analytical process.

Research questions may be generated on inspiration from various sources and could, for instance, arise from former studies or otherwise from the given scholarly environment. If an evident clarification of the structure between the data is reached, the researcher may consider it as his or her hypothesis in relation to the particular field of research. In this way, the analytical approach will be characterized by a process of seeking logical explanations for how the data are connected and how relations between relations are connected.

My approach involves two contextual perspectives, the empirical context of finds as well as the analytical context of the archaeologist trying to find explanations. According to the anthropologist Roy Dilley the "… act of interpreting has been described as the act of creating connections; that to interpret is to make a connection … Contexts too involves making connections and, by implication, disconnections. A phenomenon is connected to its surroundings: contexts are sets of connections construed as relevant to someone, to something or to a particular problem, and this process yields an explanation, a sense, an interpretation for the object to be connected. The context or frame also creates a disjunction between the object of interest and its surroundings on the one hand, and those features which are excluded and deemed as irrelevant on the other…" (Dilley 1999:2). Other discussions of the meanings of the term "context" in archaeological research have also been conducted (e.g. Hodder 1991:121pp).

As I am now embarking on a course of research in which I shall focus on the archaeological significance of some physical remains from a human culture so long ago, I need to start from scratch in several respects. Viewed from above, doing this may sometimes seem a rather tiresome process, trying to ask questions or structuralize recordings from different angles, and to embark on possible directions in order to conduct analyses that may lead to significant results.

And yet there may be a fear that some of the outcome could be seriously marked by the current way of thinking. It is hard to avoid the questions being asked and the answers given reflecting at least to a certain extent the time, the place and the person writing. It is therefore necessary to at least be aware of this when addressing the complexity of archaeological research questions. I am certainly aware that the analyses and reflections will, not least, be conducted against a backdrop of general experiences, on the one hand, as a member of a modern society, and of course against my varied and concrete experiences in the fields of study on the other. My research questions are thus positioned according to these experiences.

I find it vitally important to strive to take into consideration the whole range of probable source-critical factors in order to evaluate the floors, patches and finds as base for further analysis. Some of the sunken floor areas have lain almost undisturbed by human activity since prehistory, while others have been exposed to disturbances of various kinds. It is thus necessary, as far as possible, to ensure that all the occurring intrusions from later periods are carefully accounted for. The ancient interruptions that sometimes affected the floors, such as ard-ploughing and digging of pits, should also be taken into consideration.

From a theoretical point of view, it must be acknowledged that fills are not just fills. For the analyses and interpretations of the house sites, it is in my understanding vitally important to strive to separate fills from the time of residence from those of later activities. It is thus crucial to make a distinction between primary fills and secondary fills. Primary fills of house sites refer to the time when the houses still existed and people used them for various purposes, whereas secondary fills refer to the time after they were torn down.

It is still difficult to ascribe definite cultural content to all the centuries of the Late Neolithic and emerging Bronze Age, even though – as may have appeared from the above – the museums as a whole now possess a fairly large body of unpublished materials on sunken-floor houses. It would certainly be ideal if the whole range of artefacts and soil patches from the existing bulk of houses both with and without sunken floors could be analysed and interpreted in relation to the current research frontier.

This present work embraces the first really large body of settlement material from Denmark, bridging the younger Late Neolithic and emerging Bronze Age.[18] Because it is now to be presented in detail, it has been important to attempt to select or develop concrete ways and methods of handling this material. However, the task of trying to understand how different finds and observations relate internally may often seem a laborious, uphill struggle. Only through an intensive and systematic way of working does it seem possible to wrest at least some of the "secrets" from the sunken floors. It is therefore often necessary to be completely explicit about the observations and understandings.

On the other hand, the presentation of particulars ought not be too excessive because the details of the excavations should not overshadow the further intentions of the study and I should perhaps state right away that it is not intended as a work about unbearable numbers of postholes or pits for their own sake. Yet it is the intention as far as possible to deal systematically with all relevant soil features and artefacts from the house interiors at Resengaard and likewise from the many other selected settlements that hold important characteristics.

Sources of theoretical inspiration

I can sympathise with John C. Barrett's statement when in *Defining Domestic Space in the Bronze Age of Southern Britain* he makes it clear that "… material culture in itself means nothing until it is situated within a regime of interpretation" (Barrett 1997:89). He further states that if we want to elucidate how the records have come into being, the activities originally performed have to be acknowledged.

Before analysing and interpreting archaeological source materials, we must accept that traces of soil features, structures and artefacts do not necessarily articulate much more than the kinds of material, the kinds of shaping and other very basic traits. The possible relations between these can often not be observed directly but have to be inferred analytically and theoretically from other sources, in other words constructed.

It has long been rather axiomatic among archaeologists to turn to ethnographical analogies when it comes to fabrication and use of material objects. Archaeological suggestions on the production and use of an item have, for years, been generated by taking their point of departure in ethnographic knowledge of certain presumably alike items, their fabrication, use and meaning. This happens when these items are considered to have evidently strong similarities with certain archaeological items. Yet, as was pointed out back in 1896 by Franz Boas, we must be aware that the meaning of an item in the concrete ethnographic context may be quite different for a similar item in another concrete context (Boas 1982:270pp). Meaning and use are generated in the concrete cultural context.

More complicated, however, are procedures of searching for analogies when we seek to achieve knowledge about internal relations among items, people and space, for instance, in a concrete household of the Limfjord region at the turn of the Neolithic. Or, even more complicated, when searching for relations between relations, i.e. households' relationships to one another and to other material and non-material phenomena. These kinds of analogy cannot be expected to be applicable at the concrete empirical level but may give inspiration on the level of analysis and interpretation within the numerous, perhaps inexhaustible, human variations possible.

On the whole, I see ethnographical analogies as food for thought, indicating boundless variations in practice and theory, some of which nourish my reflections. In this present work, archaeological analogies are also sought and used for reflecting on finds. Some main sources of theoretical inspiration are presented in the following.

When I was considering how to analyse the sunken-floor patches and artefacts as remainders from human doings, the first really inspiring source was reading D. W. Bailey's *The life, times and works of House 59, Tell Ovcharovo, Bulgaria* (Bailey 1996). In particular, it concerned his ideas on how to present possible indications of extinct working processes and, from this point of departure, I have attempted to develop a method and procedure for our South Scandinavian context. At Resengaard and other selected Limfjord region settlements, the multitude of sunken-floor traits – which in my understanding mostly reflect traces of daily life – mainly concern a number of varying soil patches and pits, many different artefacts, charred macrofossils and the recognized gradual development of lower zones in the floors. My analysis of finds and soil traits will, not least, be directed towards indications of traits of everyday life and household economy. And yet I cannot ignore the possibility that the settlement material in question could also incorporate other interesting traces, for instance of symbolic character, and that through analyses and reflections on traces, for instance those done by Ian Hodder, as presented in *Çatalhöyük. The Leopard's Tale – Revealing the Mysteries of Turkey's ancient 'town'* (Hodder 2006; cf. Hodder 2005), it would be possible to obtain other results of value for our knowledge of people's lives in certain settlements at the turn of the Neolithic. However, in the main, that is beyond the scope of this present work.

My considerations on the material shall also look at the complex of topics relating to the handling of discarded objects in the concrete prehistoric context. The research questions stated above in relation to domestic refuse and sunken-floor formation processes are mainly directed towards certain rather factual steps and occurrences but do not, of course, embrace all aspects. A further objective could be to consider how domestic refuse may have been looked at by prehistoric households. Were the discarded objects considered simply as rubbish or given some kind of further significance or meaning? Were all kinds of waste treated exactly alike or were some discarded things treated differently or even with particular concern? From social anthropological contexts, we learn that the handling of waste may sometimes demand special care or may even be considered dangerous to individuals or society. Parts of Mary Douglas' work *Purity and danger. An analysis of concept of pollution and taboo*, from (Douglas 2008) and *Implicit meanings. Essays in Anthropology* (Douglas 1984) are especially inspiring in terms of interpreting possible attitudes towards domestic refuse. These seminal studies as well as the classic anthropological studies mentioned below still serve as great theoretical inspiration in archaeology.

When I consider the performance of rituals in connection to alterations in the use of house plots, some ideas are, in certain respects, generated from consulting two studies. These are Arnold van Gennep's publication *The Rites of Passage* (1975) and, further, Victor Turner's *The Forest of Symbols: aspects of Ndembu Ritual* (Turner 2005).

Biographies on "life-cycles" of the house plots at Resengaard will be considered against a backdrop of this present study's intense focus on formation processes. The significance of studying life-cycles in relation to this work is, not least, to evoke an awareness of the individual house site history. Awareness of how the plots changed character and added to their record step by step over the millennia is of major importance because, with these steps, the relationship to their surroundings were altered simultaneously. The major shifts may have been from an area with natural vegetation to a place of human occupation, to an ard-ploughed field and, further on, to an area with natural vegetation and, finally, to an object of archaeological investigation and study. A focus on these shifts may form the basis for portraying a more nuanced picture of house plots, not least as concerns the longhouses. My procedure is not inspired directly by certain writers but I would rather point to reflections on such issues becoming topical.

Some of my research questions relate to the central notion of "household". What do we *a priori* know about such units in the Late Neolithic and emerging Bronze Age? The study of topics related to this subject is, in many ways, at a rather incipient stage. It seems fairly difficult to identify anything clearly about the social compositions, age, gender or kinship constellations of the households, and we are merely left to discuss a number of possibilities. Sources of thoughts on certain aspects are, however, available. When asking: "What is a household?", Richard Hingley in *Domestic Organisation and Gender Relations in Iron Age and Romano-British Households* offers some answers (Hingley 1990). Further, in characterizing what might then be "household archaeology", G. Coupland and E.B. Banning in *The Archaeology of Big Houses* suggest that as the main analytical entities we must use the household concept closely connected to its physical frames (Coupland & Banning 1996). When it comes to the connection between the dwelling and the household, Colin Richards provides an interesting view on the relationship between the architecture and its residents (Richards 1990).

For my considerations on exchange at the turn of the Neolithic in the Limfjord region, ethnographic research offers a great deal of inspiration in terms of different theoretical views on its organization. One source of inspiration is Bronislaw Malinowski's classic study of the comprehensive exchange systems on the Trobriand Islands in the early 20th century, as described in his book, presented in 1922, *Argonauts of the Western Pacific* (Malinowski 1984). It is a study that constantly seems to inform and provoke new economic considerations. He argued that the exchange of daily as well as high-status items works for the social integration of vast areas in the archipelago, where he saw exchange as taking place between self-centred individuals concerned with gaining pride and prestige. The idea that exchange might even work to prevent war has, however, recently been challenged by some researchers, e.g. Jürg Helbling in *War and Peace in Societies without Central Power: Theories and Perspectives* (Helbling 2006).

On dealing with exchange, an ever inspiring source is Marcel Mauss' comparative study on the practice of gift giving presented in his seminal book, presented in 1924, *The Gift. The form and reason for exchange in archaic societies* (Mauss1997). Among other things, he argued that there is nothing such as a free and innocent gift between a giver and a receiver. A gift is always spun in webs of expectation, power, status, and the obligation to give, receive and repay in appropriate behaviour, such that the object given will always bear the identity of the giver (the 'spirit of the gift'). Another source of inspiration is Poul Bohannan's classic study of the economic spheres practised among pastoralist peasants in the mid-20th century in the Nigerian savannah, *Some principles of Exchange and Investment among the Tiv* (1953). He describes how the exchange system in society was stratified but he also deals with the possibilities under certain circumstances of converting items from one economic sphere to another. A further source of inspiration is Fredrik Barth's seminal study *Economic Spheres in Darfur* (1967). In his view, different actors are continuously negotiating and challenging cultural traditions, rules, and the obligation to exchange with certain individuals or groups. His perspective remains based on individuals and their possibilities for entrepreneurship.

Finally Tim Ingold's essay *The temporality of the landscape* should be mentioned as a source of inspiration (Ingold 2000). He develops the concept of "place" and thus helps to understand and imagine the possible atmosphere of a particular place that I propose as representing an outstanding location for meetings and gatherings in the central Limfjord region in the early Late Neolithic Beaker context.

Notes

1. My process of scrutinizing the basic materials, followed by analysis, interpretation and discussion, took place over the 1999-2006 and 2009-2016 periods. The gathering of literature for the many topics in the sub-chapters was thus finalized at different points in time as was, correspondingly, the writing.

2. In cooperation with many local museums, the archaeological department at Arts, Aarhus University, carried out a large-scale project during 1989-98 concerning the Limfjord region. The aims of the project were to document and discuss the cultural unity and variations from the earliest up to modern times from the perspectives of both the humanities and natural sciences. The prehistory and history was in focus in a number of thematic seminars, and resulted in eight reports. For further reference, see Lund, J. & Ringtved, J. (eds.) 1998. The geographical region is moderately different from the delimitation of the Limfjord region of the present work.

3. In the course of analysing and interpreting, I have built on my personal fieldwork experiences from a number of excavations of sunken-floor house sites from the Single Grave Culture, the Late Neolithic and the Older Bronze Age in the central Limfjord region. Though the interest came about somewhat earlier, my first real familiarity with the excavation of a longhouse site of this kind was in 1981, when directing the investigation of the Tastum I house (Simonsen 1983). Very many years of personal focus on this kind of building remainders are thus behind the present writing.

4. The University of Sheffield, for further reference,: https://www.sheffield.ac.uk/archaeology/research/2.4329 (Accessed 28.03.2017).

5. In Schleswig-Holstein and Mecklenburg-Vorpommern, this concerns houses from the Late Neolithic/Early Bronze Age and the documentation is growing (e.g. Holsten et al.1991, Nikulka 1991, Schauer 1996, Assendorph 1997, Bönisch 2001, and Kuhlmann & Segschneider 2004:71pp). Earlier houses are also known and one example is the site from Randau, Brandenburg, which has been ascribed to Schönfelder Kultur (Wetzel 1979:83pp).

6. In relation to the house sites, it is not my intention to deal with the rather complex and multifaceted cultural and chronological situation in Poland, although references can be given to a number of publications. As concerns Beakers, see Kamienska & Kulczycka-Leciejewiczowa 1970; Czebreszuk 1998; Makarowicz 1998; 2003; Czebreszuk & Szmyt 2003. Regarding the Iwno Culture, found in certain areas of Poland, see Machnik 1977. As regards the Trzciniec Cultural Circle, see Makarowicz 1999. In essence, the Iwno Culture primarily belonged to the first part of the Early Bronze Age and was associated with certain Beaker traits (*cf.* Czebreszuk 1996:283pp). The Trzciniec Cultural Circle, which embraced a much larger area than the Iwno Culture, developed during the Early Bronze Age.

7. From southwest Norway, a house site at Voll in Rennesøy has traits in common with the Fosie IV houses (Nielsen, P.-O. 1998:19; Mydland 1996; Løken 1998b; Artursson 2005c, Bilaga 1:44). Further house sites exist from Stokkset in the Sande area (Johnson, T. & Prescott, C. 1993:79pp; Nielsen, P.-O. 1998:22). This also concerns Talgje in Rogaland (Hemdorff 1993; Nielsen, P.-O. 1998:24; Artursson 2005c, Fig. 39).

8. Early group of two-aisled, ground-floor longhouses: the site of the Øster Nibstrup house from Northern Jutland was well-preserved (Michaelsen 1989:77pp; Nielsen, P.-O. 1998:18; 1999:156pp; Artursson 2005c). The dimensions were c. 19.5 x 7.0 m. Six postholes were observed in the central longitudinal axis. In the long sides was found a single row of postholes to the south, whereas to north it had a double row. The eastern gable end was nearly straight. The western gable end appeared not placed fully at right angles to the parallel long sides. Interestingly, a seventh posthole was recorded, by and large, in line with the central longitudinal axis just west of what is considered the western gable end. It has been suggested that repairs might have been done to the western end of the house. The site of House 210 at Bejsebakken is a fine example of a ground-floor longhouse (Sarauw 2006:23p). It was supplied with an oval pit to the west. The dimensions are stated as c. 15.5 x 5.6-6 m. In the central longitudinal axis five postholes were observed, and in the long side to the south a single row of postholes, whereas to the north two rows were recorded. The eastern gable end postholes show that it may have been relatively straight, while to the west postholes were absent. It seems to have become slightly broader towards the west. The site of House VI at Hemmed Kirke at Djursland also shows a rather well preserved house site, but its dating might alternatively be very late Single Grave culture (Boas 1993:126pp; Nielsen, P.-O. 1998:16; Artursson 2005c). Its dimensions were c. 16 x 6 m and five postholes were found in the central longitudinal axis, including two in the gable end. Single rows of postholes were observed in the long sides. The gable end to the east appears to have been straight with rounded corners, whereas the western gable apparently was more rounded on the whole. The site of House 3 at Nymarksgård at south Zealand had dimensions of c. 22.5 x 5 m (Hansen & Christiansen 1997:60pp). In the central longitudinal axis, seven postholes were recorded and among the particular traits were the supporting stones around the centre posts. Single rows of postholes were observed in the long sides. The site of House 11 at Fosie IV in the Malmö area was rather well-preserved (Björhem & Säfvestad, 1989:32pp; Artursson 2005a:28pp; 2005c; 2009). Its dimensions were c. 17.5 x 6.15 m. In the central longitudinal axis five postholes were observed. Three in the middle were deeper than those at the ends. In the long sides were found extra "drawn in" postholes. The site of House 22 at Stångby north of Lund was likewise rather well-preserved (Artursson 2000:21pp; 2005a:28pp; 2005c; 2009). The dimensions were c. 17 x 6 m. In the central longitudinal axis five postholes were recorded. In the long sides a few "drawn in" postholes were likewise found. House 10 at Stångby was c. 28.6 m long and the ground plan shows that the width to the west was significantly less than to the east, being 5.6-6.6 m respectively (Artursson 2000:23; 2005a:28pp; 2005c.2009). Altogether 9 postholes were found in the central longitudinal axis. In the eastern half a repair post or extra post had apparently been placed. In the long sides single rows of postholes were found and some "drawn in" postholes were found in about the middle of the building.

9. Late group of two-aisled ground-floor longhouses: House IV at Lundbro was c. 29.5 m long, while the width was c. 7.4 m to the east and c. 7.0 m to the west (Overgaard 2003: 126). In the central longitudinal axis 9 postholes were observed including two slightly "drawn in" postholes in the gable ends. Some of the postholes in the interior were quite sizable. In the long sides single rows of postholes were observed but, in one area to the southeast particularly, the row of postholes was relatively dense which might indicate repair posts or extra supports. The gable end to the east was almost straight with rounded corners, whereas to the west it was more rounded. The site of House 1 at Lundvej 19 is stated as at least 23 m long (possibly 26 m) and c. 5.3 m wide. It had two rows of postholes in the long sides and in the gable ends it appears to have some similarity with the following site. To the east it had a deepened area (3.5 x 3.2 m), depth 27 cm (Fig. 1.5). We shall return to this building further below. The site of House 1 at Hemmed Plantage ("Hemmed Plantation") at Djursland somewhat resembles the rather long buildings at Bornholm and in Scania (Boas 1993:130p; Artursson 2005c). The dimensions of the two-aisled house were c. 45 x 8 m. Eight substantial postholes after the roof-bearing post, including the two outermost postholes in the gables, were found in the central longitudinal axis. In both long sides a single row of postholes was recorded in combination with regularly placed, "drawn in" postholes near the four centre posts in the middle of the house. In the western and eastern ends three marked postholes were observed, as known also from other longhouses. The building had a limited deepened area about its middle. The site of House III at Hemmed Kirke had dimensions of c. 43 x 7 m (Boas 1993:125). Nine postholes made out traces of roof-bearing posts in the central longitudinal axis, excluding the posthole in the middle of the western gable end. On both long sides were found a single, marked row of postholes combined with some postholes after "drawn in" posts near several of the centre posts. The western gable end was rounded, whereas to the east it had three marked postholes and two "drawn in". The interesting wall construction of the long sides was made of horizontal wooden planks combined with interior clay sealing. About the middle of the building was a flat-bottomed, deepened area. The house site at Stuvehøj mark was among the longest, reaching c. 47 m (AUD 1990, no.36; Nielsen, P.-O. 1998, note 66; Artursson 2005c, Fig. 23). Altogether 11 postholes after roof-bearing posts were found in the

central longitudinal axis. In both long sides a single row of postholes was mostly observed but, in some parts, it seems to have been double. The longhouse had a special marking at the eastern gable end. The site of House S at Limensgård at Bornholm was likewise very long, being c. 40 x 7.5-8 m, having been broadest at the ends (Nielsen & Nielsen 1985:108p; Nielsen, P.-O. 1998:21; Artursson 2005a:34pp; Artursson 2005c; 2009). Nine sizable postholes belonged to traces of roof-bearing posts in the central longitudinal axis. A tenth posthole in the eastern half a little north of the axis could represent a repair post or an extra post for some other purpose. In this part of the building a small deepened area was also investigated. In both long sides were found single rows of wall postholes in combination with some "drawn in" near several of the centre posts. The site of House AM at Limensgård was likewise well-preserved (Nielsen & Nielsen 1985:108p; 1986; Nielsen, P.-O. 1998:21p; Artursson 2005a:34pp; Artursson 2005c; 2009). The dimensions appear to have been c. 28 x 6.6 m. Five postholes were recorded in the central longitudinal axis. Single rows of postholes were observed in the long sides and some "drawn in" were again found near the centre posts in the interior. Both gable ends were moderately rounded. The site of House 1 at Piledal near Ystad was relatively well preserved (Larsson, L. 1992; Nielsen, P.-O. 1998:22. Larsson, M.1995:39; Göthberg, Kyhlberg & Vinberg (eds.) 1995:81. Artursson 2005a:34pp; 2005c; 2009). The dimensions were c. 30 x 7 m. Four postholes in the central longitudinal axis were recorded and single rows of postholes were observed in the long sides combined with a few clusters of soil features which apparently might indicate extra posts or repairs. The gable end to the east had been rounded, and maybe also the west, judging by the few postholes. The site of House 95 at Fosie IV had a relatively clear ground plan and was not one of the longest (Björhem & Säfvestad 1989:57pp; Nielsen, P.-O. 1998:21; Larsson, M.1995:38p; Göthberg, Kyhlberg & Vinberg (eds.) 1995:62; Artursson 2005c). The dimensions were c. 26.3 x 7.25 m. A number of postholes were recorded in the central longitudinal axis. However, it appears that several might stem from either repair posts or extra, supporting post. In the long sides were locally observed double rows of postholes in the middle and eastern part. It has been proposed that the house had been prolonged towards west. The site of House V at Kvarteret Anten in Scania had dimensions of c. 28.65 x 5.9-6.3 m (Larsson, M. 1995:39; Nielsen, P.-O. 1998:20p; Göthberg, Kyhlberg & Vinberg (eds.) 1995:33). At least nine postholes, of which most had substantial dimensions, marked out the traces of centre posts. In the long sides were found single rows of postholes combined with some "drawn in" posts near some postholes after centre posts.

10. Early group of two-aisled sunken-floor longhouses: the site of House 896 at Bejsebakken was among the relatively well-preserved. It had dimensions of c. 17.5 x 5.0 m, while the sunken floor had a length of c. 9.6 m (Sarauw 2006:42p & Fig. 45). In the sunken floor, four postholes after roof-bearing posts were preserved in the central longitudinal axis, whereas to the west none were found. In the long sides west of the sunken floor double rows of wall postholes were recorded, while in the gable ends it only concerns single rows, indicating a nearly straight course. The site of House GAB at Myrhøj had a well-preserved eastern half and makes out a very important classic house site in when combining with the knowledge on the western ground-floor from House D (Jensen, J.A. 1973:73pp; Artursson 2005c; 2009). The sunken floor was c. 12.5 m long. Traces of two centre posts were found. Single rows of postholes, showing parallel long sides were observed. The width of the building had been c. 6 m. The site of House 1 at Vilholtgård was also rather well preserved (AUD 1998, no.440). It had dimensions of c. 12 x 5.5-6.5 m and three postholes were present in the central longitudinal axis, besides one in line with this to the east and to the west. On the long sides, double rows of postholes were recorded. Whereas the course of the eastern gable is uncertain, the western appears to have been rounded. The site of House III at Hemmed Plantage showed a rather well preserved eastern half (Boas 1993:131p; Artursson 2005c). The total length of the building is uncertain. It presumably had parallel long sides and the width was c. 6 m. In the central longitudinal axis three postholes were recorded. A double row of postholes appears to have been present on the long side to the north, whereas to the south only a single row was found. The gable end to the east was rounded. The house site at Grønnegård gives some idea of the building layout, though it did not have its full outline preserved (Siemen 1993:63p). The dimensions were at least c. 12 x 5 m. Four postholes with relatively small intervals were present west of the sunken floor on the central longitudinal axis. To the east it seems possible that a posthole in line with the central axis might belong to the gable end. On the long sides, single rows of postholes were observed at regular intervals in the western part of the house and the long sides were parallel. The outlines of the gable ends cannot be stated.

11. Late group of two-aisled sunken-floor longhouses: the site of House 1 at Egehøj had dimensions of c. 21 x 6 m and concerned a rather late sunken-floor building (Boas 1980; 1983; Nielsen, P.-O. 1998:23p; Artursson 2005c). Four posts were placed in the interior in the central longitudinal axis. On the long sides were observed single rows of postholes and some "drawn in" too. The postholes of the gable ends documented gables with rounded corners, not least being fairly clear to the east. The site of House 12 at Karaby had dimensions of 27 x 5.3 m including the westernmost area, interpreted as an entrance shaft (Petterson 2000:16pp; Artursson 2005c; 2009). Seven posts were placed on the central longitudinal axis but, in the sunken area to the west, no postholes after centre posts were observed. On the long sides, single rows of wall postholes were recorded. A few postholes seem to indicate an almost straight gable end to the east, whereas none was found to the west. The sunken area has been interpreted as the remainders of a cellar (Petterson 2000:17p, & Fig. 10a & 10b).

12. Group of minor buildings with sunken floors: the site of House VIII at Højgård had dimensions of c. 8.5 x 4.45 m (Ethelberg 1987:153 & Fig. 3; Artursson 2005c; 2009). It had no centre-posts and the long sides were presumably parallel. The gable end to the west appears to have been straight and at right angles to the south side. The eastern gable end may have been slightly oblique in its course. The preserved sunken area had a length of c. 6.15 m. The site of House XII at Højgård was a little larger and had the dimensions of c. 8.85 x 5.7 m (Ethelberg 1993b:137 & Fig. 2 & 3; Artursson 2005c; 2009). It had no centre posts and it seems that the long sides converged towards the west. The western gable end was straight, whereas the course of the eastern is uncertain. The preserved length of the sunken floor was c. 6.7 m. Structure 339 at Norrvidinge in Scania is here grouped with the minor houses (Calmer 1972). Yet, it has been argued that the building was presumably larger than originally presented and should belong among longer houses (Petterson 2000:20p). It thus seems possible that the house continued somewhat in eastern direction, as the row of postholes north of the sunken area seems to indicate. The length of this row was about 9.3 m and it went nearly 1.5 m more to the east. The length of the sunken floor reached c. 8.8 m. The site of House XI at Karaby was relatively well preserved, even though traces of the eastern gable end were not found (Petterson 2000:22p; Artursson 2005c; 2009). Its dimensions were c. 6.3 x 4.8 m. It had no centre-posts and the building appears to have had parallel long sides.

13. Jytte Nielsen and the present author headed a survey project (1989-1996) focussing on the investigated remainders of three-aisled longhouses from the Bronze Age in Mid- and Northwest Jutland. This embraced investigations primarily within the areas of four museums with archaeological responsibility areas (Simonsen 1996a). The project thereby covered central and western parts of the Limfjord region. The main topics were the house topographies (Simonsen 1996b), the layout of the houses (Mikkelsen, M.1996a), the pottery (Nielsen, J. 1996), aspects of the economy (Mikkelsen, P. 1996), micro-wear analyses of flint tools (Christensen 1996), and settlement patterns (Bertelsen 1996, Mikkelsen, M. 1996b and Simonsen 1996c). The project also intended to establish a backdrop for future investigations of three-aisled Bronze Age house sites (Mikkelsen & Simonsen 1998; Simonsen 1998). In the course of this Bronze Age project, pottery and other finds from several Late Neolithic settlements were also inspected and discussed within the group of researchers and it thereby has also indirectly formed a basis for a minor part of this present work.

14. In the Limfjord region, raising of new forests relates to sites such as Ryderne I, Bjørnkærgård, Trængsel, Kongsager, Gulfælgård, Mammen Porsbjerg, Rosgårde, Tromgade, Havbakker III, and Hejlskov Hede. Elsewhere in Jutland these activities have led to more or less corresponding finds at Grønnegård, Hemmed Plantage, Vilholtgård, Ramskovgaard, Margrethenborg, and Mårup.

15. In the Limfjord region, digging and building activities relates to sites such as Glattrup III, Frederiksdal, Resengaard, Bjergene VI, Marienlyst Strand, Bejsebakken, Ingersminde, Glattrup IV, Mejrup Syd, Drosselvej, Katrinesminde, Bruunshåb, Kluborg II, Skringstrup Øst, Kås Hovedgård II and Skrubben. Similarly, elsewhere in Jutland it has led to the recovery of the sites at Vorgod, Gården, Størsbøl Ø I, Kirkebakke, Karmdal Banke, Lille Torup, Gammelbrovej, Føvling, Birkevej, Askov Seniorby, Vindelsbæk 1, Petersborg Vest, Klostermarken IV, Møllehøje, Nygårdstoft and Smedeager.

16. In the Limfjord region, road building concerns Granlygård but, elsewhere in Jutland where these activities are more intense, it has resulted in sites such as Geding, Stavnsbjerg, Guldagergård, Nøvling Plantage, Birkholmvej, Glesborg Lyng and Dalsgård II.

17. I am grateful to Martin Mikkelsen and Malene R. Beck, who headed the excavation (VSM 232G), for permission to briefly present the unpublished house ground plan from Lundvej 19.

18. Many years ago, Henrik Thrane had already posited that. "There is a strong need at the present time for careful selection of sites for total excavation. The basis for this selection should ideally be a knowledge of the situation in a given region, so that the structure of the individual settlement may be seen in the context of local settlement patterns known from survey and sampled by excavation" (Thrane 1985, note 5).

Chapter 2

Analysis and interpretation of houses with sunken floors

Imagine just for a moment the numerous cultural traits embedded in a habitation used by a modern average household in South Scandinavia: the general arrangement of spaces and the overall furnishings, equipment and other traits would be so abundantly informative of cultural and social factors that the house could only belong within a very definite cultural and chronological context. Even a single house would thus be an excellent key to very many aspects of current culture.

Correspondingly, it is my understanding that longhouses with sunken floors from the Late Neolithic and emerging Bronze Age would, to some extent, have had the same degree of excellence and I presume that some of these, even as ancient building remainders, may still hold at least a fraction of their former qualities. As we try to analyse and interpret different elements and structures from an assortment of relatively well-preserved house sites – as significant frames of daily life – we may thus also have begun a process of improving our knowledge of various relevant fields within this ancient culture and society.

It is considered vital for the study that the selected settlements derive from a rather limited area within the Limfjord region so that the observed variation could not *a priori* be explained in terms of different geography. Furthermore, it is seen as essential that the selected new investigations (apart from Gåsemose) have in common that a main objective during the field investigations was to give the highest priority to the recording of soil patches and artefacts belonging to the floor horizons, which is crucial for research into evidence of daily life in the longhouses. These building relics thereby provide opportunities for thematic and comparative analyses of observations from the floors. Besides Resengaard, the nine other selected settlements include the "late" settlements at Gåsemose and Kluborg II, and the somewhat earlier Beaker settlements at Glattrup I/III, Marienlyst Strand, Granlygård, Hellegård, Glattup IV, Rosgårde and Tromgade.

The vestiges of sunken-floor houses from Resengaard and the other selected new settlement finds will firstly be subject to presentation, analyses, evaluations and interpretations in relation to the chosen grounds, post-habitation disturbances, house dimensions, sunken-floor proportions and other facets. Several radiocarbon determinations conducted on short-life, charred materials from Resengaard help set a timeframe for the duration of the settlement in absolute years and open up the possibility of further analyses of chronology and phases. Resengaard and the other aforementioned sites taken together offer multifaceted research material comprising 43 sites of sunken-floor houses.[1] The best preserved houses in particular yield much fresh, new data on the two-aisled longhouse constructions and some of the smaller ones as well. Certain observations offer suggestions as to the wall materials used, as well as the wall construction, doorways and other characteristics of the longhouses.

Finally, biographies on the lifecycles of the house plots are established, and some further traits of the sunken floors from elsewhere in the Limfjord region are presented, and the sunken floor idea discussed.

2.1. Establishing the sources

The importance of methodological reflections has already been emphasized and it naturally also includes strategies of using specific excavation methods for the house sites, as well as ways of measuring.

Strategies for methods of excavation

The path outlined in the following first and foremost concerns the method used in the excavation campaigns at Resengaard (Fig. 2.1 & 2.2). It has also largely been applied when investigating the new settlement finds selected from the central Limfjord region.

The longhouses from Myrhøj, Stendis and Tastum I were largely placed E-W, all with sunken-floor lengths exceeding eight metres. The strategy set in 1989 and followed thereafter to maximize the recovery of sunken-floor longhouses at Resengaard was hence that most trial trenches should be set up N-S and that the internal distances between the sides of the trial trenches could be eight metres. Such placement of trial trenches did not, of course, fully guarantee that every sunken-floor house site would be recognized. In particular, if a minor or short house happened to be located exactly in between two trial trenches, it could be missed. A further source-critical factor chiefly concerns the uninvestigated strip north of Houses 13 and 42, where a short road track had been built prior to the archaeological excavation. Nearby pits with rather early pottery might thus indicate the former presence of a relatively old dwelling. With this reservation, however, I am convinced that all sites of sunken-floor longhouses, and a relatively high proportion of sites of other kinds of sunken-floor buildings, have been found at the Resengaard hill.

The first rough removal of topsoil was carried out by means of a machine that was fitted with a two-metre broad iron bucket with straight edges and no teeth. In order to obtain a relatively clean surface for conducting the archaeological observations of the house ground plans, it was generally necessary to scrape off some centimetres of their uppermost soil.

On the whole, the ground floors to the west were fairly even. Level measurements showed, for instance, that in relation to House I it gradually rose just c. 10 cm towards the west. This floor part could usually be investigated rather quickly, as frequently only very little could be recorded.

Ideally then, just a few cm would also have to be removed from the upper fills before the outlines of the sunken floors stood clear. Yet due to old animal activity, we often had to remove a somewhat thicker layer, especially in the peripheries, until the sunken floor fills appeared fairly clear in contrast to the light subsoil. This strategy often left the inner parts over the sunken floors slightly dome-shaped. The reason

Fig. 2.1. Resengaard. After investigating a limited area (House 1 & House 2), a large-scale system of N-S trial trenches were dug by machine in order to locate more Late Neolithic/Emerging Bronze Age house sites. Numerous traces were observed in the two-metre-wide trenches. Poul Mikkelsen and Ole Jensen are here looking at the surface appearance of certain soil features.

we tried to avoid removing these central soil layers by machine was that they often contained artefacts and also sometimes vestiges of what happened later at the spot. The soil benches with cross-sections over the floors therefore often displayed a low dome-shaped top in the middle.

The consequence of the above excavation strategy was that this initial scraping off already influenced the house sites as sources to different degrees. In my estimate, between 5 to10 cm of the top-fill layers in the periphery of the sunken area were generally removed by machine during the initial excavation at Resengaard (see Fig. 4.68). Some 10-15 cm had to be removed at the sites of a single longhouse and two minor houses (138, 143, & 268).

After digging by means of machine, the following step was to excavate the sunken areas according to stratification by means of hand shovels and trowels. The planned procedure was, as far as possible, to excavate the secondary fills first and then proceed to concentrate on the floor horizons with great attention to stratification, i.e. investigation of floor layers, floor patches, pits of different kinds, as well as artefacts in their precise contexts. Finally, the constructional remainders such as postholes, small grooves and other different relics were to be investigated (Fig. 2.8).

As the investigation of a sunken floor proceeded, it was ideally part of the scheme that the excavation teams would repeatedly clean the floor horizon to obtain an overview of the transformations in the appearance of different soil features, besides further monitoring the soil contexts of the artefacts. Details of the floor were discussed on these occasions. It must, however, be noted that the budgets for certain house site excavations were quite small and so they had to be excavated in a somewhat simpler way and with less supervision. This concerns, in particular, the sites of minor houses (143, 158, 198 & 289) as well as those of longhouses (42 & 138).

It was clearly within the field work strategy to endeavour to be aware of possible inconsistencies, even if they appeared only of minor importance. For example, now and then during the excavation campaigns, it was realized that soil features present on the actual floor surfaces appeared less clear or even invisible in the cross-sections and therefore unrecordable when making drawings of these. This could, for instance, relate to vague traces of ard-ploughing. In contrast, it also happened that soil features, vaguely visible in the vertical cross-sections, were not documented sat isfactorily on the horizontal surface. Such instances represented challenges which, in the most important cases, were discussed. There was generally no time during the intermediate stages of digging the sunken floors to make sketches of cross-sections. This would have become too costly and could therefore only be done once. The drawing of the cross-sections and sections of postholes thus usually took place as one of the last tasks, when most horizontal structures had already been destroyed through investigation. At this stage, comparison with plan drawings was often the only possibility.

The strategy of establishing soil benches for vertical profiles was rather straightforward. In most instances a single cross-section of a sunken floor was considered sufficiently informative as a "tool" for the excavators to help evaluate how to proceed with the further excavation and to document the main stratification. To establish further cross-sections during the work would increase the cost and seldom provides proportionately more information. In many cases, the

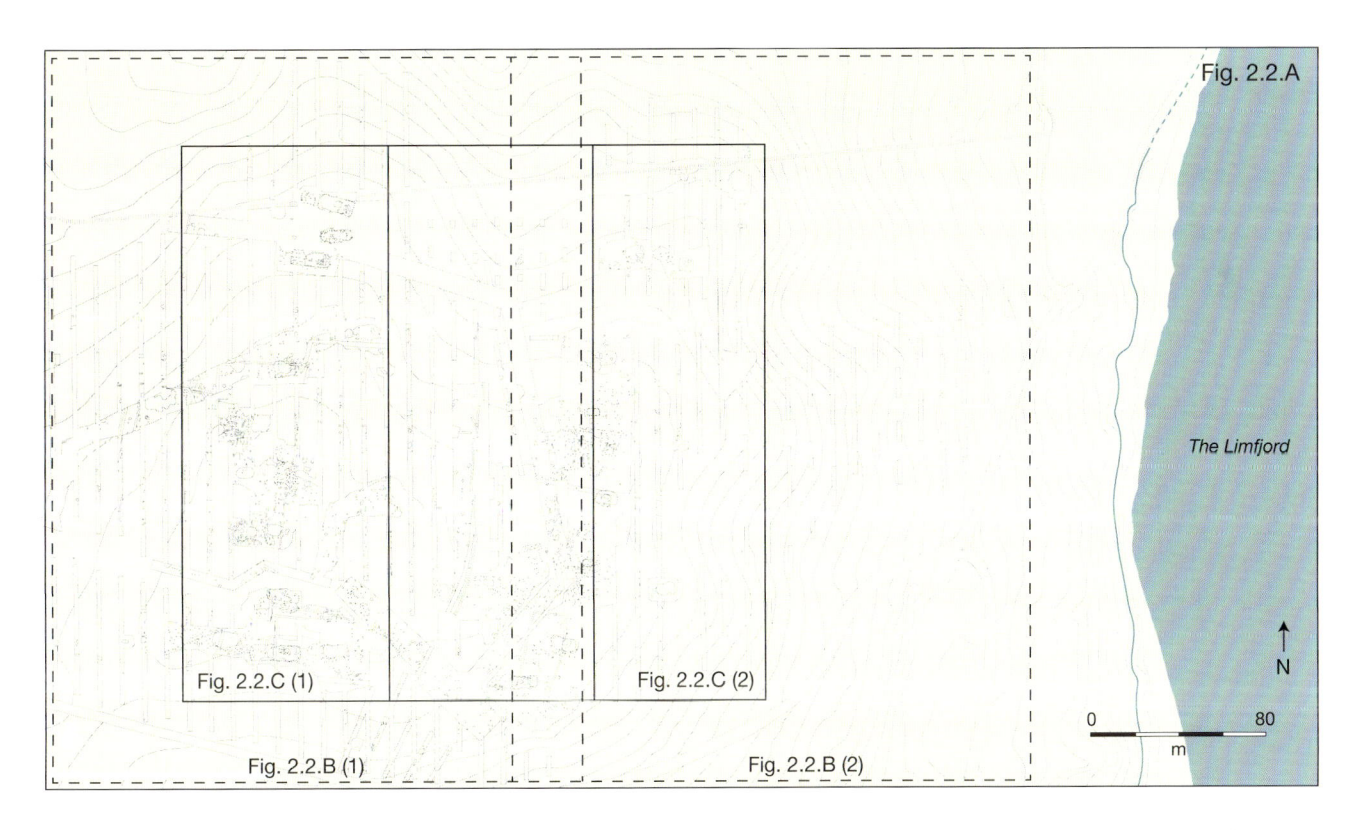

Fig. 2.2 (Pages 53-57). Resengaard. A. The settlement was placed on the upper part of the hill, adjacent to the Limfjord coast. The boundaries of the following maps are indicated. B. Some significant culture traces (other than the sunken-floor houses) are noted. C. In all 26 sites of sunken-floor houses as well as numerous pits from the Late Neolithic/emerging Bronze Age (plus the possible house sites 156 and 160) were recovered. For the distribution of domestic refuse areas see Fig. 5.7. Most pits and postholes found are visible on the map, except some found in particular south of the site of House 1.

Fig. 2.2.B (1)

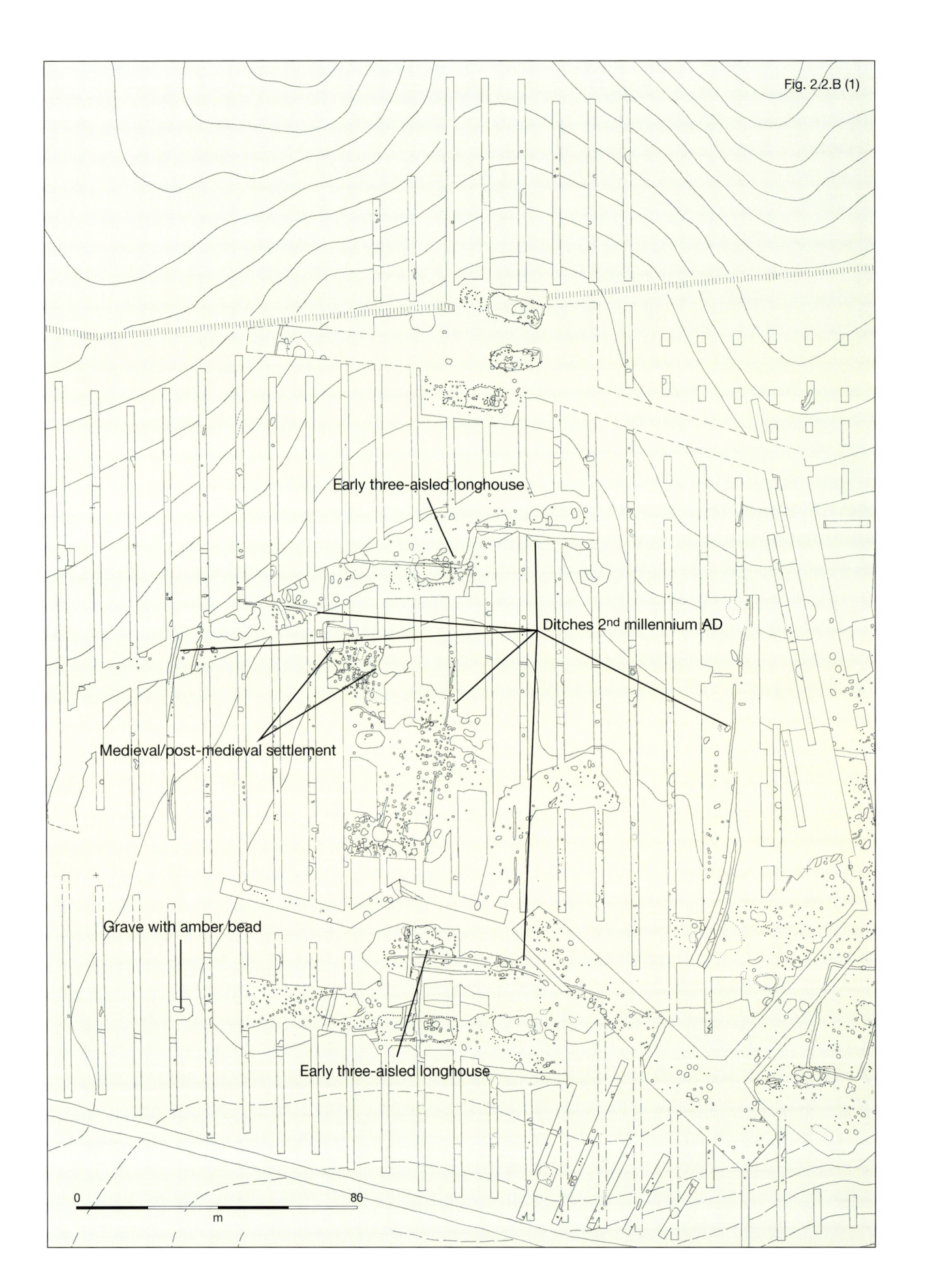

Early three-aisled longhouse

Ditches 2nd millennium AD

Medieval/post-medieval settlement

Grave with amber bead

Early three-aisled longhouse

0 — 80 m

Fig. 2.2.B (2)

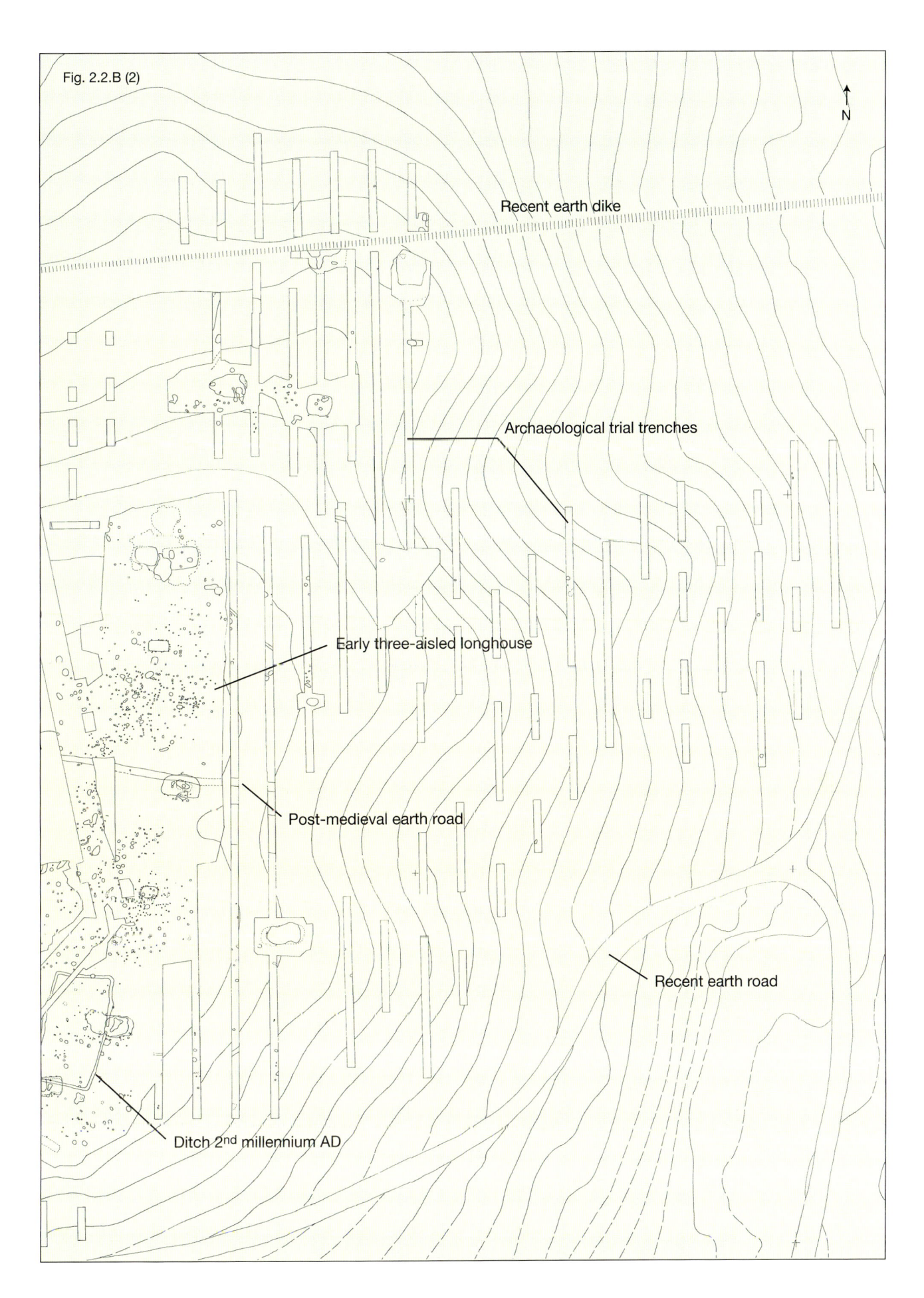

Recent earth dike

Archaeological trial trenches

Early three-aisled longhouse

Post-medieval earth road

Recent earth road

Ditch 2nd millennium AD

Analysis and interpretation of houses with sunken floors

Fig. 2.2.C (1)

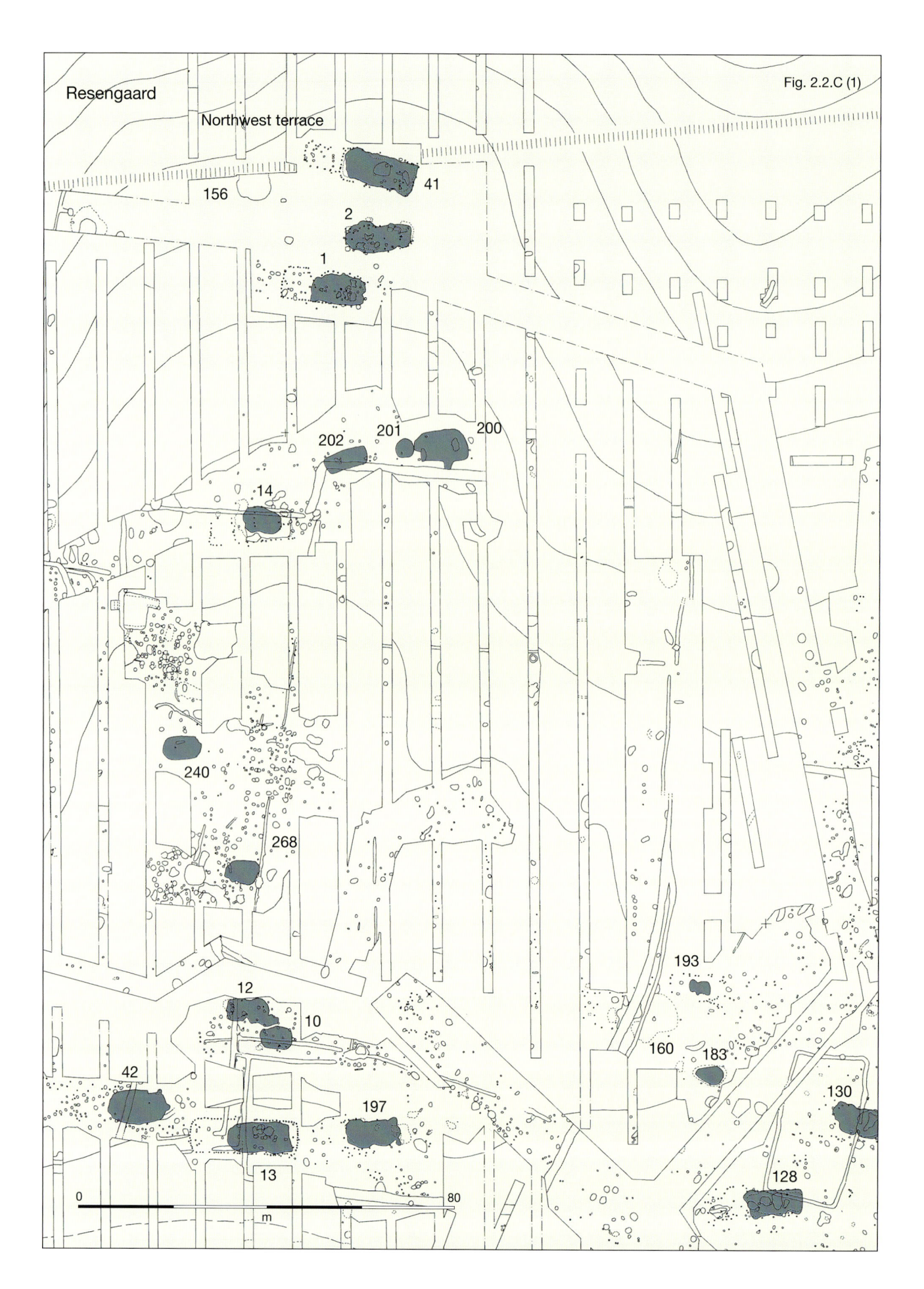

Resengaard
Northwest terrace

56 Chapter 2

Fig. 2.2.C (2)

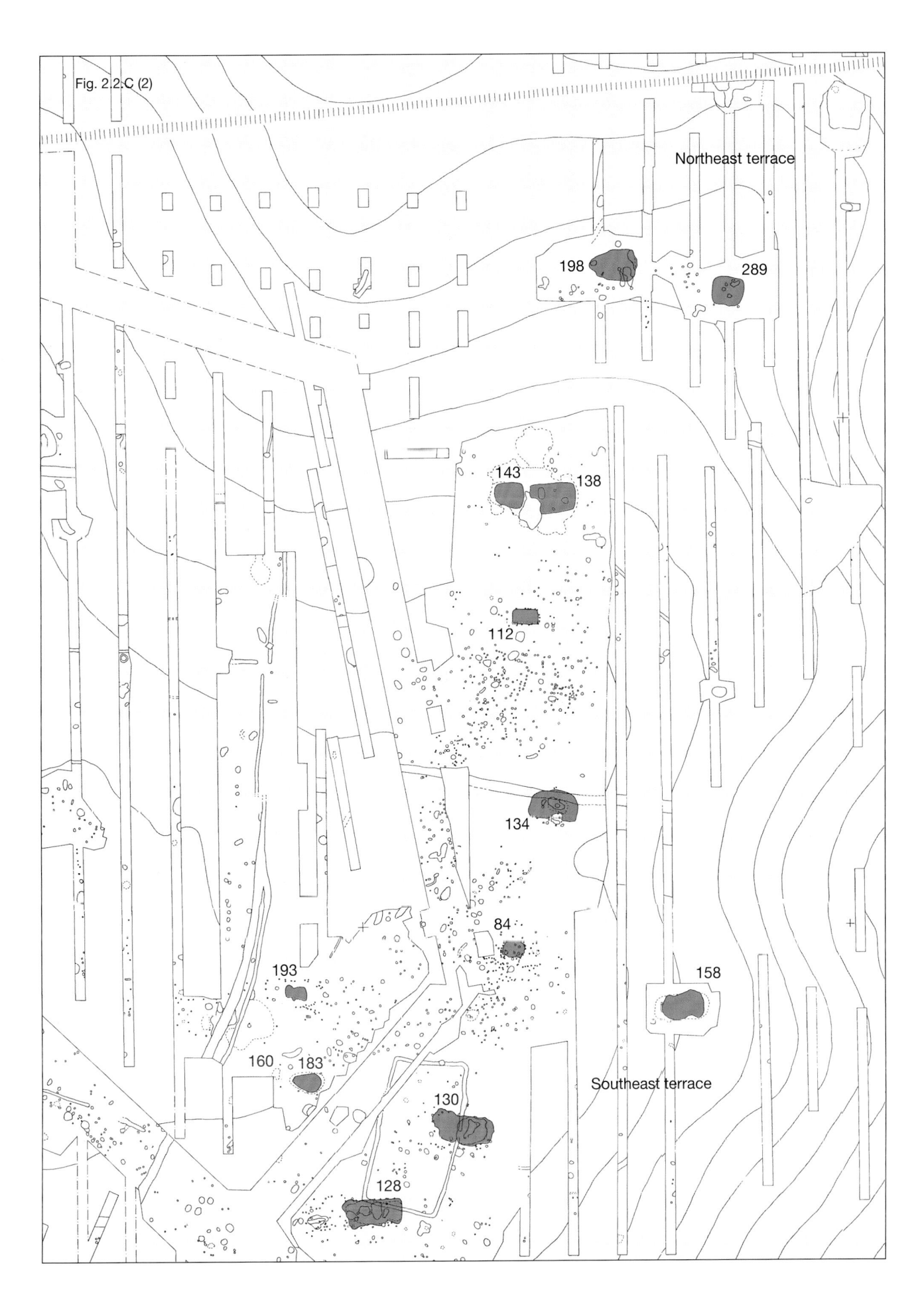

Northeast terrace

Southeast terrace

Analysis and interpretation of houses with sunken floors

presence of two or more soil benches would actually have been an obstacle to achieving safe knowledge of the soil features on the horizontal level.

On the other hand, it was considered worth the effort in a few instances to establish longitudinal sections instead of cross-sections. It was therefore decided a couple of times to make crossing soil benches (House 1 & 2) or solely longitudinal soil benches (House 41 & 42). Longitudinal sections thereby exist from four longhouses (1, 2, 41, & 42). No sketches of the cross-sections are available from much ploughed down building remainders (House 10, 12, 193, & 198). The effects of recent ploughing are evident, as this has often removed a considerable part of the topsoil from the fills (*cf.* Fig. 2.5). The cross-sections were normally studied and interpreted by a senior participant and carried out by means of the technique of incising lines directly on the cleaned vertical soil bench at the transitions of the layers. The different layers and their basic interpretation were discussed as often as possible prior to drawing.

To make it clear, our priorities were foremost given to the investigation and documentation of the horizontal floor surfaces. Contrary sketches of the cross-sections, the drawings of the ground plans concerning the outer edge of the sunken floors and other floor patches may thus have been adjusted or redrawn more than once or even several times as the investigations went on.[2] For the recording, a system of co-ordinates was set up with the Y-axis pointing north, determined by means of a compass. The levels of artefacts and things of interest were measured many times during the time-consuming excavations of the sunken floors. Then, once the excavation of every sunken floor was complete, measuring of their bottom levels took place in order to be able to produce detailed contour lines.

In this present work, I have chosen also to represent information from early readings of sunken floor contours that may indicate something more about the original extension. Such kinds of existing recording could, for example, be when repeated cleaning of the soils for photographing or for discussing the layers had the effect of removing the remaining thin layer of soil in an area so that the sunken floor surface appeared significantly smaller than before. Another example could be an instance where an observed part of the sunken floor was accidentally dug away by a machine. A third example could be when vague, diffuse soil features are not convincingly seen as directly parts of the sunken floors but do need to be represented because it is not impossible that these areas do belong to them. We have more instances where such soil features bordered the sunken floors. These "floor shadows" are introduced in the house ground plans digitized for this present work in relation not least to Resengaard. I have chosen to let these "floor shadows" be represented because they also display some of the important challenges we are facing in the study of the houses and they might thus help to avoid simplification of the basic research material and instead hopefully contribute to a more nuanced approach.

The policy for photo documentation was that mainly colour slides in relatively large formats should be taken at Resengaard to ensure as much detail as possible, and only seldom black and white ones which, elsewhere, were still widely used for photo documentation in the 1980s and 1990s. As a rule, the preferred scale size for drawing of house ground plans was 1:20 but, for various reasons, other scales have been chosen in some cases. Water-resistant, transparent plastic paper was always used in order to avoid spoiling of the drawings from precipitation during fieldwork. In the 2010-2016 period, all relevant plan drawings of the sites of 43 sunken-floor houses and three ground-floor longhouses were digitized and further processed in a GIS system in preparation for this work. This process also facilitated the incorporation of a great deal of detail into the plans and even helped improve the analyses and interpretation of certain particulars.

In reflecting on some of the early soil features that were drawn but which soon disappeared during repeated cleaning of certain house sites, the question arises as to how these should be represented. This concerns, for instance, our recording of traces belonging to a likely doorway to the south in House 2 at Resengaard. Simply to omit the earlier observations of such an important element from the presentation of the house would hardly be satisfactory. In such cases it is therefore my attitude that we should be explicit as to our actual observations during fieldwork and include the early notes or drawings when valuable.

Measuring distances between postholes

In clayey ground, it is frequently the experience that posthole diameters tend to be smaller than comparable ancient structures and, in some instances, even far smaller than holes dug into very sandy subsoil. This difference is likely often due to the extra effort and energy needed to dig holes in clayey grounds. It so happens that the subsoil changes considerably from sandy to clayey from spot to spot within the area of a house site and this could have the consequence that postholes for equal purposes tend to vary significantly in surface dimensions. I thus believe it makes little sense to measure distances between the edges of the postholes because measurements of house sites from different kinds of soil could give incomparable results. Instead, measuring from centre to centre of stake- and postholes is a preferable method. When presenting the 43 sunken-floor house sites this is the method I have sought to apply.

Many postholes tend to be circular or sub-circular and it is usually no problem to establish the centres with reasonable precision so that the intervals between them can be stated accurately. The width of a posthole can be measured as the largest surface dimension. It is not always possible to apply this "centre to centre" method argued for here, e.g. when the distance needs to be measured between a posthole and an irregular pit. In such cases, it seems reasonable to take the measurement from where it seems most appropriate in the given instance and then be explicit as to the method applied. Whether postholes belong together and mark out traces of the same construction is subject to interpretation. This is a basic condition of fieldwork and subsequent analyses, as I have already touched upon.

It was often the experience with sunken floors that some postholes from the roof-carrying construction along the central longitudinal axis were apparently missing, and therefore to state distances between postholes in these instances would hardly have much meaning. Shallow postholes could easily have disappeared when the sunken floors were further deepened during residence. A wooden slab or stone slab used to provide the necessary basis for a centre post could perhaps in some instances have been installed (cf. Strömberg 1971:239p; Calmer 1973:126; Simonsen 1983:88).

From Rosgårde, the wall postholes of the sunken-floor longhouse (House 1) as well as the ground-floor longhouse (House 2) are to be presented in a forthcoming publication, in which I show detailed drawings of the posthole depths as an exemplary case (Simonsen, J., im manus.).

Measuring sunken floor depths

The level measuring was usually done in a grid for every half metre and it often extended beyond the sunken floor limits. It encompassed more than two hundred level measurements for the largest in order to provide a solid basis for studies of the floors. One example concerns the levels of the sunken floor of House 2 at Resengaard (Fig. 2.9). For the present work, these measurements mainly form a basis for pointing out the low zones in the longhouses and for describing the floor levels.

Level differences from the lowest floor spots to the highest sides become quite remarkable when the E-W aligned houses in particular were placed on distinctly east- or west-sloping terrains. For instance, in the markedly deepened floor of House 200, the depth from the lowest point when measured to the eastern subsoil edge comes close to one metre. Instead, the southern or northern edge around the middle gives a more reasonable measure of the sunken-floor depth. Furthermore, from the detailed study of the sunken floors it has emerged that the lowest parts were mostly created by local activities during the period of residence and these do not therefore necessarily represent the more general sunken floor depths.

As the initial scraping off by machine was usually done quite minimally in the middle of the sunken-floor fills at Resengaard and at the other new settlements in question, I have chosen to take my point of departure in the measurable depths of cross-sections or longitudinal sections, where present. This method will mirror the maximum floor depths at the time of final occupancy. In some instances, when sections are absent, the depths will be stated from the above-mentioned level measurements in the central areas of the sunken floors in relation to the preserved top levels of the immediately surrounding subsoil, whether to the south or north. The old surface soil thickness is not taken into consideration here. Sunken-floor depths that may represent a larger area are provided in a table (Fig. 4.69).

At its full width, a ramp marks out the east-sloping western part of the sunken floor, leading from the generally lowest part of it to the limit of the western end. In some instances, there are locally even deeper, minor areas to the east of the ramps and, in particular, this concerns the low zones (see Ch. 4). The beginning of the ramp is usually slight on reaching the low end to the east. In cases where recent ploughing has reduced the depth of a sunken area, the length and height of the ramp may have diminished to the west. Two examples of ramps are documented in Fig. 4.68.

Measuring soil features and raw dimensions of houses

The edges of the soil features were prepared for drawing by incising the lines of interpretation directly onto the soil surfaces. The observations of soil patches on the floors and beyond were normally done by a senior participant and usually discussed and considered before and after by other team members. The recently completed digitization of the manually-drawn house ground plans and processing in a geographical information system (GIS), in cooperation with Henrik Vind Frimurer, facilitated a review of my perception of certain postholes as regards their placements, while it generally helped to confirm the interpretations of the post settings.

Concerning house lengths, it is the aim as far as possible to present the longitudinal measurements of the entire houses, i.e. along the central longitudinal axis. The widths ought to be measured at right angles to this. Yet, in certain cases, when postholes are more or less absent as guidelines for the task, the direction of a sunken floor can be fairly difficult to assess precisely. In such cases, the length of a sunken floor is measured simply as a soil feature where the maximum extension decides the length. The width should then be measured at right angles to that (Fig. 2.3). In most cases, postholes were available to guide the house directions and lengths at Resengaard. However, it is important to realize that the basic lengths and widths are just "raw" dimensions because they do not include the thickness of the walls. If we want to find out the actual house lengths and widths we would therefore have to consider wall thickness in every case. Raw dimensions and areas can be calculated in a GIS system but, in the sunken-floor longhouses, we may in addition expect panel walls to have often existed and the actual floor areas would thus have been significantly reduced.

Within the Late Neolithic and emerging Bronze Age, the South Scandinavian buildings range from short ones of less than five metres in length to really big houses. A division of these into five groups according to raw lengths is suggested for both sunken-floor houses and ground-floor houses (Fig. 2.4). This division is intended for practical use at the present stage of research. For example, among rectangular buildings, a short house of 4.5 x 3.5 m would represent just c. 16 m², whereas a minor house of 9.5 x 4.8 m would amount to c. 46 m², thus being a significantly larger construction and giving good reason for making a distinction. Likewise, a small longhouse of, for instance, 17 x 5.5 m (c. 94 m²) would evidently belong to a different group from a medium longhouse of say 33 x 6.5 m (c. 215 m²). Finally, the big buildings stand out as an extraordinary group and a length of 35 m or more is suggested to denote a big longhouse (*cf.* Poulsen 2009:157pp, for a grouping of longhouses based on square metres). When, at some point in time, numerous sunken-floor house sites of all kinds have been investigated

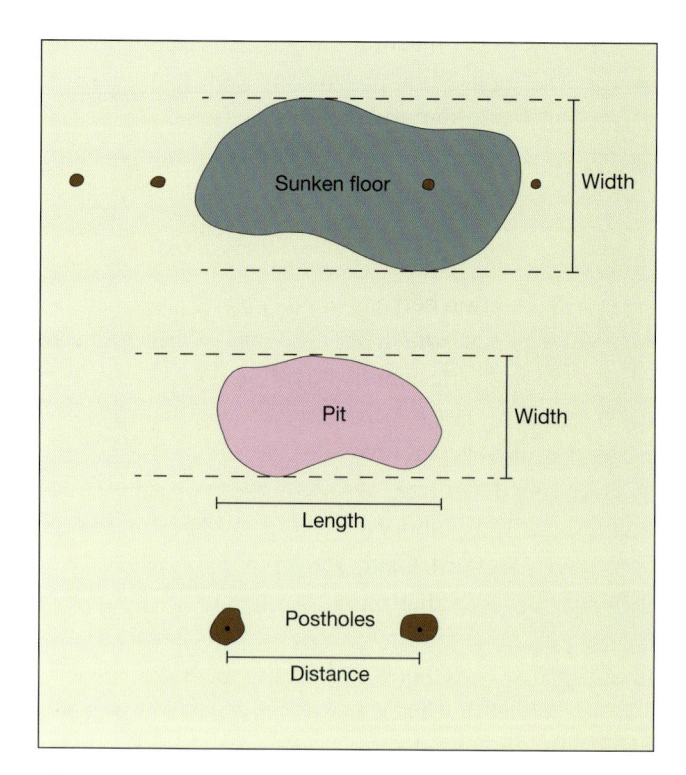

Fig. 2.3. Measuring principles for soil features. The width is measured at right angles to the direction of length.

House dimensions

House term	Length range
Short house	length < 5m
Minor house	5m ≤ length < 10m
Small longhouse	10m ≤ length < 25m
Medium longhouse	25m ≤ length < 35m
Big longhouse	35m ≤ length

Fig. 2.4. Suggested division of houses from the period in question into five groups according to their raw lengths.

and hence a representative picture of variations likely exists, it will be possible to generate a grouping statistically, something which in my view is not realistic right now.

Sunken-floor horizon versus secondary fill

A clear distinction between layers, patches and others belonging to horizons from the use of buildings versus higher layers resulting from the placing of different domestic refuse is crucial for the understanding of the house sites. When investigating the Late Neolithic and emerging Bronze Age sunken-floor house sites at Resengaard, Kluborg II, Glattrup I/III, Marienlyst Strand, Granlygård, Glattrup IV, Rosgårde and Tromgade, the idea of distinguishing between floors belonging to the dwelling and secondarily accumulated strata had already been established. We shall briefly look at this, going back to the classic publication of Myrhøj versus the observations and interpretation of the Tastum I house.

In the Myrhøj publication, certain strata over the bottom of the hollow area were considered to have been "occupation layers" (Jensen, J.A. 1973, Fig. 1, 2 & 11b). As concerns House D specifically, the profile section was interpreted as evidencing three occupation layers (8a, 8b & 8d). In House EAB the profile was understood as showing two occupation layers (8a & 8c). Against these, only one occupation layer (b) over the bottom of House GAB was considered observable (Jensen, J.A. 1973, Fig. 12b). The arguments implied that all three houses had a bottom layer of brownish sand with some charcoal, that two of the houses (house D & House EAB) had another occupation layer over a sterile layer (Jensen, J.A. 1973:63) and that the last-mentioned layer in House D could be separated into two occupational strata.

When reflecting on these statements, it appears that a certain interpretation of the main development of the house floors is involved. If we take Myrhøj House D as an example, the description presented implies that once the sunken floor area had been hollowed out to the lowest depth, which in this case was about 0.50 m below the topsoil (Jensen, J.A. 1973:65), the first evidenced occupation phase of the house residents took place. After the accumulation of a sterile sand layer, the second occupation phase came into existence higher up. Finally then, the possible third habitation phase took place without a sterile layer in between. The artefacts found in these layers were considered as belonging to the occupations. According to this understanding, the residents would have experienced the floor of house D becoming less and less sunken. But why then first dig out the entire sunken area to the full depth and subsequently accept that it gradually lost its sunken-floor qualities?

The house construction was imagined as having been "… a light wooden framework covered with mats of some kind." (Jensen, J.A. 1973:119). We might ask, however, whether the supposed character of the building remainders would allow it to stand strong during three occupational phases in the much wind-affected northern Jutland?

Turning to the publication of the Tastum I house, investigated in 1981, I also wanted to address the formation processes of the layers accumulated over the large, relatively flat bottom in the sunken area, because this was one of the most urgent, unsolved research issues relating to such sites.

In major parts of the sunken area of the Tastum I house, interestingly, a sterile layer (3) was also observed on top of the first occupation layer but this layer was not observable in the western cross-section (Simonsen 1983:82 & Fig. 4-5). Above this sterile layer could be seen dark, almost black sandy soil (3) which appeared to be present over most of the preserved sunken area. It could represent a fire layer stemming from the burning down of the house but it is also possible that it was an occupation layer for some time. Above this, a layer divided into a lower part (2b) and an upper part (2a) had accumulated. Regarding the interpretation of this subdivided layer, I argued that it represented secondary filling up-activities of the sunken area with different kinds of waste (Simonsen 1983:83p & 88).

The suite of layers of House D at Myrhøj and the house at Tastum I thus had much in common. Both had a bottom layer with artefacts, then a sterile layer above, then a second layer with artefacts and succeeding covering layers above. With regard to the latter site, however, the interpretation diverged from the one given for Myrhøj. At Tastum I the understanding reached regarding the upper layer was not that it represented occupation but secondary fills. This new interpretation thus distinguished between layers with traces of human use of the building and secondary fills of domestic refuse of different kinds, placed in the open hollow areas after abandonment and removal of the construction.

Regarding the house at Gug, the notion of it having been a flint-worker's hut was also questioned (Simonsen 1983:88). Based on analysis of the excavation details, I instead preferred an understanding that considered a large part of the remains to be secondary fills placed in the sunken area. This would, of course, not exclude the possibility of flint-working having taken place inside the building but the suggested meaning was that we should reject the consideration that all or most of the flint debris stemmed from *in situ* activities on the floor while the house still stood.

Jan Apel has since discussed the interpretation of the Gug house and seems to endorse my understanding of this specific house as well as the general idea: "In 1982, Simonsen pointed out that the flint debitage filling up the depression probably represented a secondary filling of the pit …From the ethnographical point of view this interpretation makes sense, since it has been demonstrated that natural depressions, abandoned structures and pits often became disposal locations in all types of settlements" (Apel 2001:159, with reference to Schiffer 1987:58pp). The need to distinguish between floors and secondary fills when making interpretations of the sunken-floor houses now seems broadly accepted (e.g. Thorpe 2000:75).

With its many sunken floors, there was ample opportunity at Resengaard to observe the nuances and differences between the house sites. However, the complete absence of observable vegetation horizons beneath or within the secondary fills is common. This trait supports the understanding that the secondary fills accumulated in the period immediately following the tearing down of the houses. Relatively thick layers of secondary fills are observed in all 43 house sites with sunken areas that are the focus of this study. However the amount of flint waste, potsherds and other can vary considerably.

Outside the context of regular floor layers or soil patches at the level of the upper part of the subsoil, the artefacts are ascribed to the floor horizons only after exceedingly cautious investigation that makes it clear they do not belong to the soil of the secondary fills. As we shall see, a prominent example of an artefact disqualified as belonging to the sunken floor horizon is the fishtail flint dagger from House 2 (Fig. 4.10) which, despite its very close proximity to the floor, had to be ascribed to the secondary fills.

Traits relating to the three-dimensional sunken areas of the 43 house sites are richly illustrated and documented in the following. Numerous photographs of the sunken floors before and during excavation, as well as the final stages of excavation, are thus offered, also embracing several find situations, and many soil benches used for clarifying the stratifications are displayed (Ch. 2 & 4). The lowest, local areas of the sunken floors (low zones) are shown on detailed plan drawings for all longhouses (except Gåsemose), as well as a gradually deepening contour of an unusual disposition (House 2 at Resengaard) of a sunken floor (Ch. 4.2-4.5. & Fig. 2.9). Hand drawings of selected parts of a considerable number of cross- and longitudinal sections of soil benches are displayed (Fig. 2.40 & Fig. 4.68, highlighting the secondary fills). Depths representing the central area of each sunken floor, as well as accounts of important patches, the presence of floor layers, shallow patches with heat-affected/cracked stones, ordinary open fireplaces, deep pits and other features of the horizons of the sunken floors are indicated in a table (Fig. 4.69). The method of measuring the sunken floors, as well as the actual dimensions and ground plan traits, has already been explained (Fig. 2.3 & 2.6). Statistics concerning the above-mentioned patches with heat-affected/cracked stones in the sunken floors are given (Fig. 4.70). Accounts of the numerous suggested activities (Ch. 4) are set out in a table (Fig. 4.73) and in diagrams, likewise the charred plant remainders (Fig. 5.16). Horizontal bar charts show the quantities of potsherds, burned flint and worked flint in the secondary fills covering sunken floors (Fig. 5.8, 5.9 & 5.10).

From a majority of the house sites in question, drawings of cross-sections or longitudinal sections of the sunken floors exist in the archives (scale 1:10 or 1:20). Besides the many examples illustrated in this present work, further sections of sunken floors from House 5 at Glattrup IV, House 5 at Kluborg II, and House 1 at Resengaard are planned to be documented in forthcoming thematic articles. The same goes for House 1 at Rosgårde (Simonsen, im manus.).

2.2. Presenting the Resengaard houses

Resengaard is located in Resen parish, Hindborg district, Viborg county. The settlement, with its numerous sunken-floor house remains, was situated on a moraine hill adjacent to the Limfjord on the eastern coast of the present day Salling peninsula. In the following, the local setting and 26 house sites, as well as two uncertain structures, will be presented.

When Poul Mikkelsen and this author together headed the investigations at Resengaard, our roles were different. In the main, my colleague was director of the daily excavations of the house sites, culture layers, pits and other structures. He was largely present during all the regular campaigns and took many of the tactical decisions needed for the investigation, ensured that recordings and plan drawings were properly carried out and made sketches of the cross-sections. I was responsible for the economic and strategic decisions for the investigation of the settlement and participated as often as possible in the manual work related, in particular, to many of the house sites from the period in question. I mostly participated during the essential excavation phases, including not least at the beginning and completion of the investigations of the individual house sites. Besides discussing necessary activities in these situations with members of the excavation teams, I carried out all of the necessary photo documentation and also focused on the recording of plan drawings in particular. The following presentation (together with that of Chs. 3 and 4) is comprehensive and detailed in order also to help researchers who might have other goals and different approaches to mine.

The hill, its terraces and the house plots

The sunken-floor houses were all located on the upper part of the hill, which formed a kind of plateau at the top and sloped softly down onto terraces towards the northwest, northeast and southeast. To the west and south, the plateau faded gradually into the surrounding landscape. Recent ploughing has moderated the character of the hill when compared with information from older mapping. Covered with recently ploughed topsoil, the uppermost part of the hill stands little more than 33 m above today's sea level. The 32 m height contour embraces a sub-triangular area approx. 230 m E-W and 170 m N-S. I term this uppermost part the "hill plateau". With reference to the extensive system of trial trenches, it appears that no traces of sunken-floor houses were located below a height of 27 m on the hill. In relation to the modern contour map, the settlement traces of the sunken-floor houses were restricted to a height of between 33 down to 29 m, with the exception of two minor houses that were located down at about 27 m. This is, in particular, documented through the 12 easternmost lines of trial trenches, dug in a N-S direction and stretching c. 150 metres east of the site of the easternmost longhouse. The total system of trial trenches extended c. 430 m E-W and c. 320 m N-S.

The edge of the northwest terrace largely followed the 29 m contour, as the terrain below is steeper. The edge of the northeast terrace is about three metres lower, marking out a characteristic north-eastern tongue below the hill plateau. The edge for the most part followed the 26 m contour as, again, the terrain below becomes markedly steeper. The southeast terrace appeared broader and the edge largely followed the 31 m contour. This topography was used for varying placements of sunken-floor houses at the turn of the Neolithic. The three terraces attracted a number of these buildings, and the hill plateau and other areas also gave plenty of room for settling.

Three longhouses (1, 2, & 41) were located on the northwest terrace. An uncertain structure (156) was also found here. Just two minor houses (198 & 289) were placed on the northeast terrace. No building remainders were observed in the terrain hollowing between these two terraces.

On the southeast terrace, two longhouses (128 & 130) were located along with three minor buildings (183, 193 & 84) further back from the edge, whereas a minor house (158) was positioned nearer to the coast. In the area between the northeast and southeast terraces, a further two longhouses (134 & 138) and two minor houses (112 & 143) were sited.

On the hill plateau, sunken-floor houses were located to the south, to the east, to the west and centrally. To the south, three longhouses (13, 42 & 197) were located in the border zone towards the somewhat lower terrains. Two minor houses were also placed to the south (10 & 12). To the east, a further two minor houses were sited (183 & 193). An uncertain structure (160) was also found here. To the west and centrally at the plateau, two minor houses (240 & 268) were located. To the north at the hill plateau, two longhouses (14 & 200) were located. A short house and a minor one (201 & 202) were placed in this area, too.

Ten out of twelve longhouses were built on pronouncedly sandy and well-drained grounds. Yet the area selected for constructing House 2 was mostly rather clayey albeit with some sand content. Outside this house were mainly sandy, well-drained areas, so it is puzzling as to why the building was located exactly at this point. The nearby House 1 was built on partly clayey ground too. Could the firmer ground have been preferred for certain reasons related to the function of the house or maybe just to ensure a robust sunken floor? Or might there have been some obstacle to placing the house elsewhere? Three minor houses (202, 240 & 289) were all placed on well-drained sandy grounds and, as we shall see, had the soil features of heat-affected/cracked stones in common with the longhouses. All the remaining minor buildings and a short one were likewise situated on sandy grounds and therefore well drained.

In regard to the observed placements of the longhouses and other buildings, it is worth keeping in mind that the directions were probably carefully chosen. Factors such as the possible impact of the wind and sun would presumably have been of importance (Simonsen 1983:88).

Yet there might have been more than just technical considerations involved in the placement. Local obstacles of a natural, ideological or socio-cultural nature could have played a role in the decisions on placements. There might, for instance, be a certain tree of some significance in the way of the new building. Would it be admissible to cut it down? If not, the placement would have to be changed. Another instance could have been plots where forefathers' longhouses stood. Ought these to be avoided as the ground for a new house? We shall return to this question later.

Occurrence and absence of thick topsoil layers

Varying states of preservation of the individual house sites at Resengaard are observable and the capacity for the covering topsoil layers to offer protection from destruction caused by recent ploughing is of paramount importance. Let us take a look at the Resengaard settlement from north to south (Fig. 2.5).

Thick soil layers had accumulated in the area of more house sites to the north. This concerns all three sites of the longhouses (1, 2, & 41) on the northwest terrace. A modern, ploughed layer of topsoil of a normal thickness, above a thick soil layer, covered Houses 1 and 2. On top of the site of House 2, in particular, the soil layer was unusually substantial. A fairly thick soil layer was also observed over the site of House 41 and, in addition, it was partially covered by a well-preserved earthen dike, probably several hundred years old. The protection from recent ploughing was optimal for these three house sites.

More to the south, the soil thickness declined markedly. Now, over a large area, direct contact between the modern, ploughed layer and the underlying house sites was in many instances observed. Actually, the plough had often consumed the upper parts of the house sites, leaving them more or less damaged. However, even on the hill plateau (following the 32 m contour) the surface was not quite even and the house sites placed on the relatively higher grounds were therefore the most exposed and vulnerable. Only exceptionally have house sites survived here with relatively modest damage from recent ploughing. The best example of this is House 14, placed as it was in a slight, natural lowering on the hill plateau. However, as regards the question of destruction, even a few cm can be decisive, whether the bottoms of shallow postholes belonging to the sunken-floor houses were preserved or not.

Further south we again have a topsoil situation like at the northwest terrace. A good example is the thick soil covering the site of House 197 but we also observed at least some of this quality in the area of the sites of Houses 13 and 42.

When we turn to an overview of the settled area at Resengaard, it generally appears that, on the hill plateau and in some of the immediately surrounding areas, recent ploughing had severely damaged the house sites due to the absence of adequately thick topsoil. In contrast, on the northwest terrace and far south, thick soil had accumulated on top of the house sites. Ploughing out soil from the hill plateau as well as wind depositing probably played a major role here.

Presentation of the buildings

Resengaard is a location where there has been surprisingly little settlement disturbance from later periods, as no really massive settling subsequently took place at any time before the archaeological investigation. Several of the sunken-floor houses at the site may thus look relatively undisturbed in this respect. Yet when the disturbances, even at a settlement with this unusual *a priori* character, are systematically scrutinized, a number of factors and possible effects on the source value come to light. It therefore seems appropriate to include close and systematic considerations of possible disordering and disturbance of the house remains one by one. This will be done briefly by stating certain important aspects of the house site formations.

Irrespective of the quality of the relics of a house, it must be emphasized that all sites at Resengaard and the other individual settlements contribute strongly to our knowledge of each as a whole. Beyond that, my view on the research values of the artefact remainders and the soil observations of the individual house sites will also be presented, being implicitly set against the backdrop of my general impression of sunken-floor house sites from the Limfjord region.

All house sites – and the longhouses in particular – have been minimally or moderately disturbed by animal activities. These galleries and other traces not least most likely stem from mice. Other mostly minimal disturbances may have been caused by tree

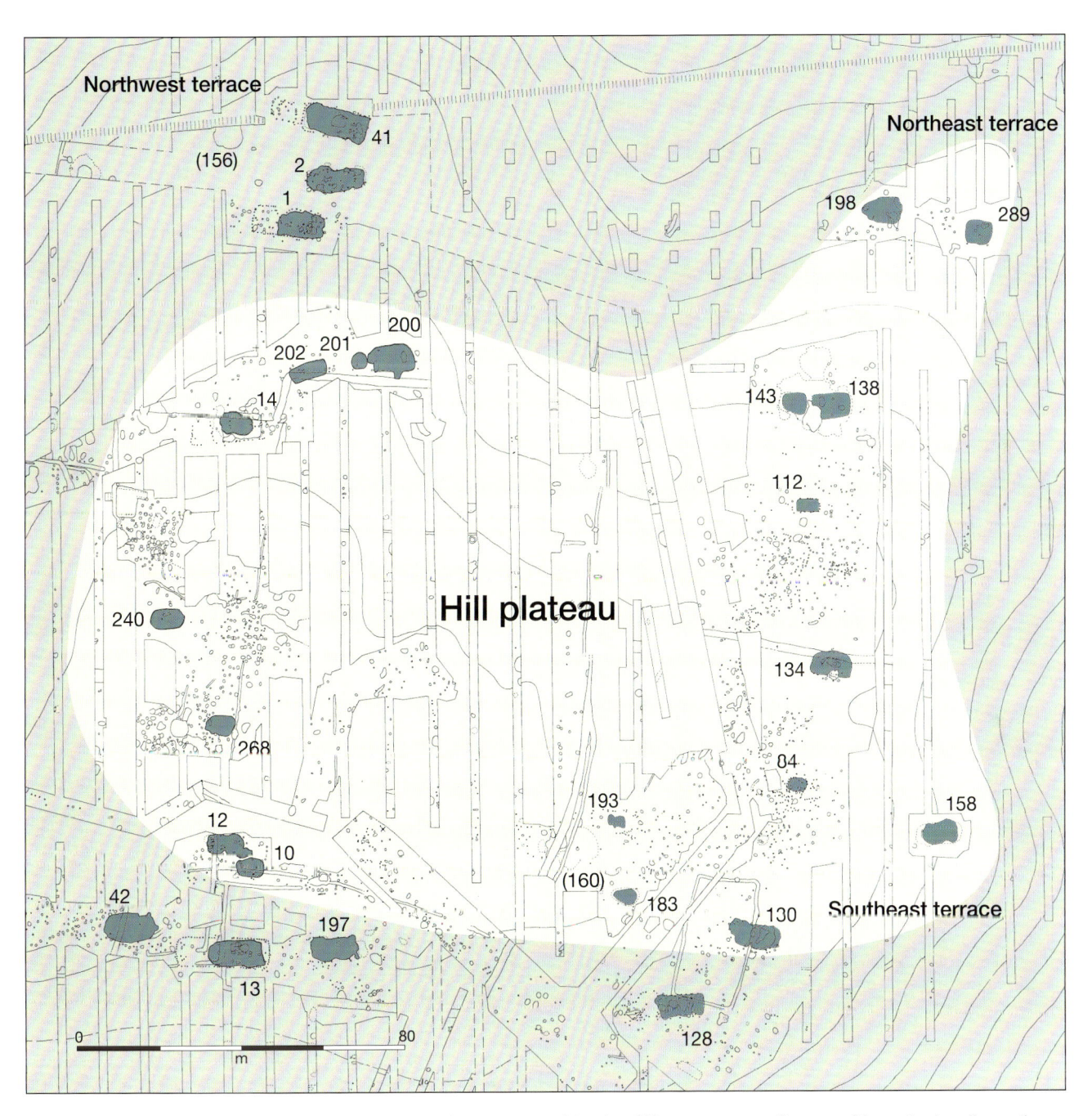

Fig. 2.5. Resengaard. Major protecting and destroying influence. Parts of the site of House 41 were well protected beneath a lengthy earthen dike but relatively thick layers of soil protected many house sites in the hill periphery. The shaded area illustrating this is based on numerous observations and measuring of soil sections around the house sites and at other spots. Conversely, two major source-critical factors were active at central parts of the hill in particular, namely the digging of comprehensive ditch systems (Fig. 2.2.B), largely from the medieval/post-medieval period and recent ploughing, both affecting the house sites. Recent ploughing did not, however, have a severe impact where a moderate terrain hollowing occurred at the plot of House 14. In certain instances, settlements from the classic Bronze Age disturbed those of the Late Neolithic and emerging Bronze Age (e.g. by the sites of House 10, 12 & 14).

Analysis and interpretation of houses with sunken floors   65

roots. Neither kinds of disturbance will be further accounted for, apart from in a few instances.

In the following, the 26 sites of sunken-floor houses will all be presented, divided into four groups and accompanied by detailed ground plans distinguishing many elements. This relates firstly to the group of 12 longhouses, secondly the group of three minor houses with specific traits, thirdly the group of 10 other minor houses and lastly a single short house. In the cases where it was chiefly only a sunken floor that was preserved, certain other qualities are important in order to judge which group the individual site belongs to. These qualities are primarily certain physical traits such as the surface shape, the surface dimensions, the depth, the profile and steepness of the sunken area sides, and the presence or absence of relevant postholes along the central longitudinal axis. Other traits such as the presence or absence of certain soil features, not least patches with heat-affected/cracked stones in the sunken floors, are also seen as important indicators.

Among the Resengaard buildings, it becomes immediately evident that nine house sites are the remainders of longhouses. Furthermore, three house sites in all probability belong to this group. The presence of sizable soil features containing heat-affected or heat-cracked stones in the sunken floors is one of the really conspicuous elements of these longhouse sites, while such traits have not been observed in the ground floors to the west. We shall later return in detail to these soil features, which I term "scorched-stone patches" and in relation to which I shall also account for the presence or absence of floor layers and many other floor traits.

Among the minor houses, three of the sunken floors were also supplied with well-defined soil features containing heat-cracked stones that may indicate some functional similarity with the longhouses. Of the remaining house sites, in all ten of them had minor sunken floors and one had a short sunken floor. In addition to these 26 house sites, two large flat-bottomed pits (156 & 160) that cannot be interpreted with any certainty shall be dealt with. The latter could perhaps represent the disturbed remainders of a sunken-floor longhouse. No vestiges of two-aisled longhouses with only ground floors were found on the hill.

The "raw" house lengths, widths etc. are given in a table (Fig. 2.6). The pits and soil patches in the floor horizons are already shown on the general house plans in order to give a visual impression of their placement in relation to the main construction (Fig. 2.8-2.34). However, the detailed presentations, analysis and interpretations of these follow later (Ch. 4). A common explanation of signs and symbols used for all house sites throughout the present work (Fig. 2.7) is also provided.

Twelve longhouses

The remains of twelve longhouses, all supplied with scorched-stone patches in the sunken floors, are presented in the following. The site of House 1 was the first to be investigated at Resengaard and, during fieldwork, the excavation team was well aware from the very beginning that we had a really unusual opportunity here to explore the finds and soil features of a house site from around the transition to the Bronze Age. It was the first time such an undisturbed, late sunken-floor longhouse had been recognized in the Limfjord region and the excavating team were naturally extra careful insofar as our economic resources allowed. This has already been referred to above as House 1 and the following presentation of this house site is quite extensive because it can hopefully serve as an initial insight into this kind of building. Traces of elements such as the doorway, panel wall, dividing wall are all thus described more explicitly here. It follows naturally that an oblique ramp between the sunken and unsunken floor parts was always present in the sunken-floor longhouses but this will only be described explicitly in relation to House 1. Thereafter, House 2, a regular site of fire that was investigated partly parallel to the site of House 1, will also be presented extensively.

House 1 (Fig. 2.8)

West of the sunken floor, a number of pits were recorded and these generally offered no finds. Some may likely have been dug just in order to obtain some clean subsoil. Most or all may belong to the pit area recorded east, south and west of the house and probably stem from a time before House 1. A posthole belonging to the western gable end of the house thus cut through an older small pit. Unfortunately, it was not possible to observe any postholes cutting across a presumably likewise older pit placed in the area of the southern wall to the west.

The alignment of the building, judging by traces of roof-bearing posts and postholes of the outer walls, was E-W with the length axis turned a few degrees towards

Resengaard longhouses (Fig. 2.6A)

Settlement	Longhouses	Minor houses	Minor houses	Short houses	Longhouses
	Sunken floor				Ground floor
	Scorched-stone patches				
Resengaard	12	3	10	1	
Gåsemose	1				
Kluborg II	1				
Glattrup I/III	2				
Marienlyst Strand	1				
Granlygård	0		2	1	
Hellegård	1			1	2
Glattrup IV	3				1
Rosgårde	1				
Tromgade	3				
(46)	25	3	12	3	3

Resengaard longhouses (Fig. 2.6B)

Location	House number	Raw house length	Sunken area length	Raw house width	Sunken area width	Course of long sides	Site of fire	Remarks
Resengaard	1	17.6	11.4	6.5	6.5	Trapezoid	Limited	Width east gable end 6.1 m
	2		13.8		6.4	Likely trapezoid	Total	Length concerns phase 2
	13	22.4	13.4	6.9	6.5	Parallel	No	
	14	18.7	9.8	7.0	6.4	Likely trapezoid	No	
	41	24.0	15.6	6.8	6.7	Parallel	No	Length concerns phase 1
	42	20.6	13.2	6.9	7.2		No	Raw house length min. 20.6 m
	128	18.4	11.0	5.6	5.8	Trapezoid	No	Raw house length min. 18.5 m
	130		12.9		7.1	Likely parallel	No	Raw house length min. 19.3 m
	134		9.8	6.6	5.7		No	
	138		9.3		5.9	(Possibly trapezoid)	No	
	197	18.3	11.3	6.2	5.8	Parallel	Limited	Raw house length min. 18.3 m
	200		11.4		6.4	(Possibly trapezoid)	No	

Fig. 2.6. Grouping of the houses at the ten studied settlements from the central Limfjord region according to raw dimensions. A: Remarkably, none of the settlements have hitherto indicated the presence of sunken-floor longhouses of the two larger categories, Fig. 2.4. House 5 from Kluborg II was a special sunken-floor longhouse in that it did not have a ground floor to the west. B-D: The "raw" dimensions of buildings. The length of House 41 relates to the phase before reduction. Due to wall thickness House 84 had been more than 5 m long. The "floor shadows" are not included in the accounts, except House 5 at Glattrup IV where it was evidently a part of the sunken floor. There is some uncertainty as to the ground plan dimensions of House 5 at Glattrup I/III.

Resengaard minor and short houses (Fig. 2.6C)

Location		House number	Raw house length	Sunken area length	Raw house width	Sunken area width	Course of long sides	Site of fire
Resengaard	Minor houses With scorched-stone patches	202		9.1		3.9	(Possibly parallel)	No
		240		8.1		4.7		No
		289		6.4		5.7		No
	Minor houses	10		6.5		3.7	(Possibly parallel)	No
		12		8.8		5.0	(Possibly parallel)	No
		84	4.9	4.6	3.6	3.1	Parallel	No
		112	6.7	5.4	3.2	2.9	Likely trapezoid	No
		143		6.3		5.0	(Possibly parallel)	No
		158		8.7		5.9	(Possibly parallel)	No
		183		5.7		3.8		No
		193	9.8	4.4	5.2	3.1	Parallel	No
		198		9.2		6.2		No
		268		7.1		4.8		No
	Short house	201		3.7		3.7		No

Limfjord Region, nine other locations (Fig. 2.6D)

Location		House number	Raw house length	Sunken area length	Raw house width	Sunken area width	Course of long sides	Site of fire	Remarks
Gåsemose	Longhouses	1		10.2		6.2		No	
Kluborg II		5	12.1	10.0	5.5	5.2	Trapezoid	No	
Glattrup I/III		5	17.1	6.0		3.8		No	
		6		6.5		4.6		No	
Marienlyst strand		1		9.3		5.0	(Possibly trapezoid)	No	
Hellegård		122		10.3		5.2		No	
Glattrup IV		3	16.5	7.5	5.6	4.5	Trapezoid	No	Width east gable end 5.0 m
		5	16.0	7.7	7.1	6.1	Trapezoid	No	Width west gable end 5.1 m
		7		6.9		5.0	(Possibly trapezoid)	No	
Rosgårde		1	20.3	9.0	6.3	4.9	Trapezoid	No	Width east gable end 5.3 m
Tromgade		1		6.4		4.4		No	
		2		7.1		5.3		No	
		414		9.6		4.8		No	
Granlygård	Minor houses	2		6.1		5.7		No	
		3		5.7		4.5		No	
Granlygård	Short houses	6		3.2		3.0		No	
Hellegård		35		3.3		2.8		No	

■	Sunken floor/sunken area	■	Roof posthole (centre post)
■	Floor shadow	■	Roof posthole, supplementary
○	Low zone		
┌┄┐	Disturbance, superficially	■	Wall posthole
┌┄┐	Disturbance, comprehensively	■	Panel wall groove
		■	Panel wall, posthole/stake-hole
■	Scorched-stone patch	■	Dividing wall, posthole/stake-hole
■	Fireplace	■	Wall posthole, early removed
■	Reddish-burned subsoil		
‖‖‖	Fire traces, posthole/stake-hole	■	Stone anvil
		■	Stone
■	Significant patch	■	Stone deposit
■	Mosaic patch	□	Flat-sided stone
■	Simple patch		
		■	Culture layer
■	Pit		
■	Cubicle-pit	→	Entrance
■	Deep pit		Ard-furrow
	Excavation area limit		Ard-furrow, lower

Fig. 2.7. The signatures concern house plan drawings (Ch. 2, Ch. 4 & Ch. 5). The term "sunken area" relates to the entire deepened part while "sunken floor" denotes only the part that functioned as a floor in a house. It is necessary to make this distinction in some instances. It is generally the surface appearance of soil patches, pits, and postholes that is depicted. Some patches can represent pits.

the SE-NW. The general slope of the ground in the area was faintly towards the north. The local slope of the ground had a moderate fall towards the north and east. By the time of the investigation, a central sunken floor area lay at a depth of 26 cm below the subsoil surface but the original depth beneath the top of the old surface must have been significantly greater.

Following the excavation of this house site, my immediate impression was that the use of wooden posts along the central longitudinal axis had not been consistent (Simonsen 1993b:109). Actually, only a single posthole to the west appeared fairly regular, while other had greatly rounded cross-sections; some of these even displayed colouring, probably from charcoal dust, and thereby appeared without the obvious posthole character expected of roof-bearing centre posts. On the other hand, I could not exclude the possibility that posts had been standing in these holes and might have had some kind of role in the roof-bearing construction. Subsequently, in the course of the new systematic sifting through of the evidence of soil features at this house site, and the experience gained from many other sunken-floor house sites dug out later, I now have to recognize that deep postholes from aisle posts with reasonably strict vertical sides are not generally to be expected in this group of longhouses in the central Limfjord region. Consequently, I have thus revised my view on the postholes and accepted that a total of six soil features mark out postholes from roof-bearing posts along the central longitudinal axis, and further that others in a line south of these can be considered the traces of extra supporting posts.

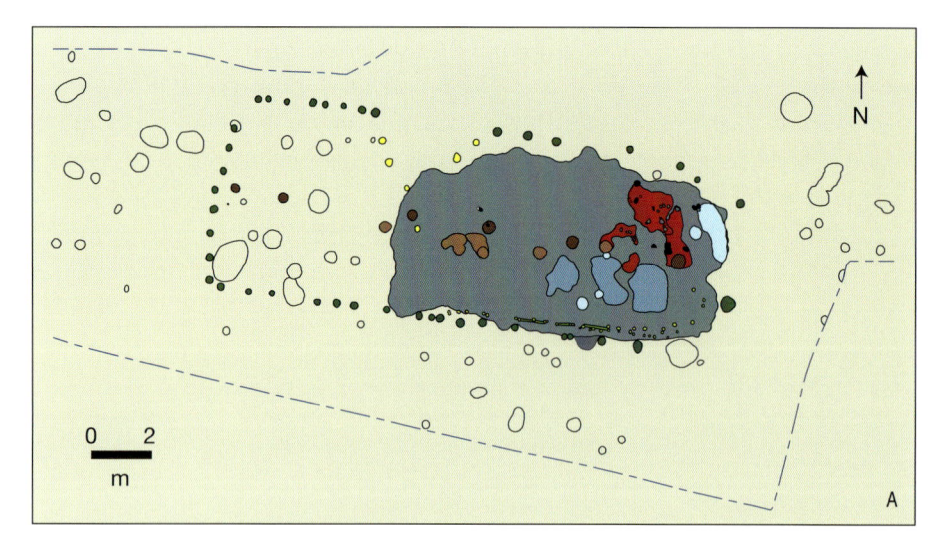

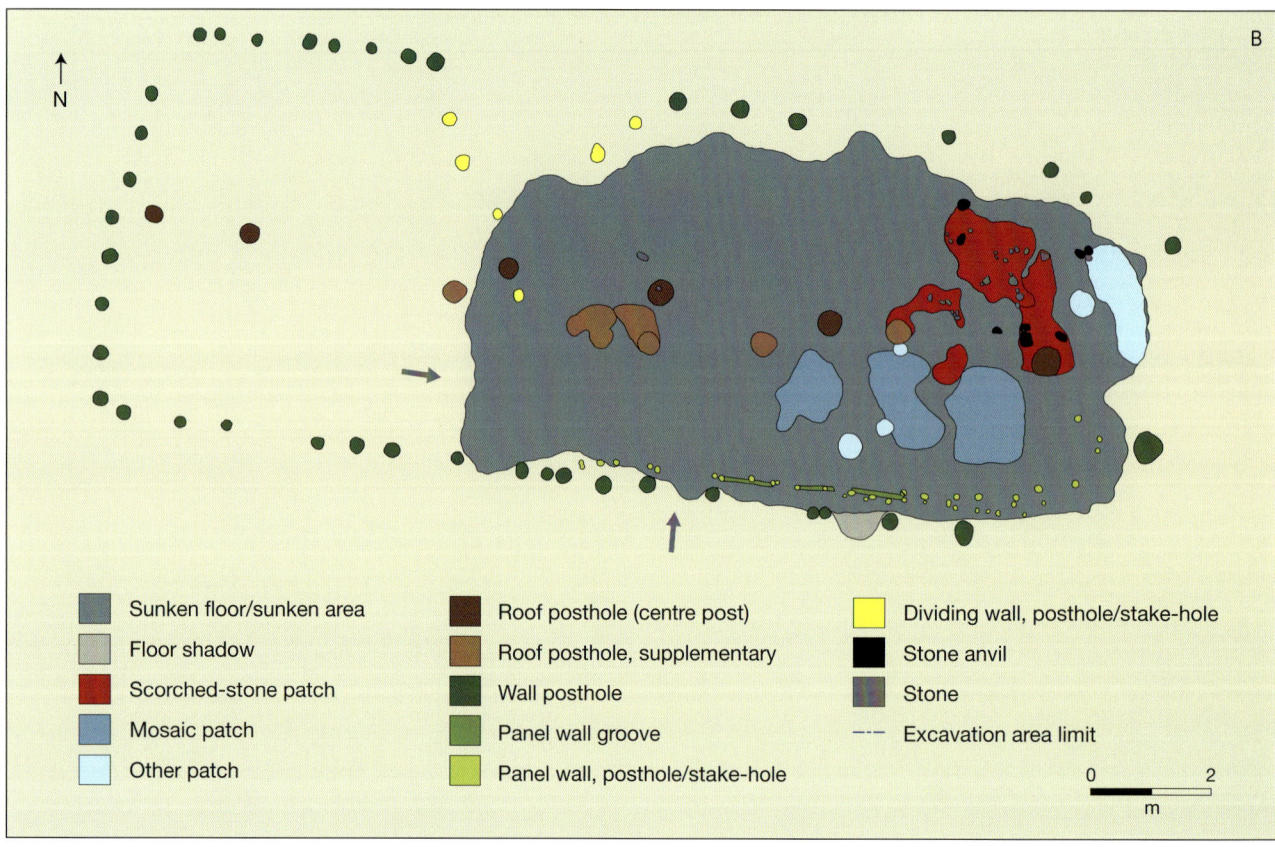

Fig. 2.8. Resengaard, House 1. A: Ground plan, older/younger soil features and nearby excavation limits when investigating the site (N-S trial trenches were dug nearby later on). For further soil features and excavation limits in the surroundings, see Fig. 2.2.C. For two soil section drawings, see Fig. 4.68.A & B. It appears that the house site was free of later digging affecting the construction traces. B: Ground plan, cleaned. The house site was exceptionally well-preserved and clearly evidences a building with a trapezoidal outline. To the west, by the southern limit of the sunken floor, the bottoms of a further four likely stake- and postholes disappeared during a subsequent cleaning and are not represented here. Traces were found to the southeast of two phases of a panel wall, the remains of the latter being burned.

In the western part of the house, the posts of the central longitudinal axis must naturally have been the dividers of the floor area and, not least, the one in the middle of the western floor would have delimited the use of it. So even though this part of the house seems quite spacey, this central post could have been an ever-existing obstacle to any demands for a wider, continuous area. The same of course goes for certain posts in the middle and eastern parts of the house.

Three postholes placed between the third centre post from the west and the wall of the northern long side likely formed the vestiges of a dividing wall. It had been placed rather obliquely in relation to the northern long side. Such a construction was probably quite easy to make as it was possible to consolidate the wall by fixing it to the outer wall, to the centre post and, of course, to the roof construction. On the other side of the hole to the centre post was dug another posthole in line with the foregoing and the interior wall may have ended here, being then about 4 m long. I further suggest that the two postholes south of the northern long side, a few metres to the east, also mark out the traces of a dividing wall. It would have been rather short and likewise in an oblique position to the northern long side of the house. It is interesting to see how the contour of the sunken floor more or less followed this suggested dividing wall at a little distance and how the sunken area expanded some-

C: Massive amounts of soil covered the site of House 1 entirely. Here, a soil profile some three metres south of the house site may illustrate a sequence of the preserved old surface covered by a thick soil stratum and, on top of that, the layer of recently-ploughed soil. Seen from the east. D: The sunken floor at a stage in the investigation. Narrow soil benches crossing E-W/N-S were established. After meticulous excavation of a few centimetres, the entire sunken area was always cleaned and observed again. This almost vertical photo shows the third round of that process. Seen from the north. E: Wall postholes sectioned around the whole perimeter of the house site, as well as some in the area of the central longitudinal axis. F: In the clayey subsoil, stake-holes from the panel wall to the southeast are being investigated. Seen from the east.

what towards the northwest, exactly between the two presumed dividing walls. Such expansion could very well have been created by daily wear. In all, the observations can preferably be interpreted as a construction for a kind of post-framed compartment that served some special purpose (or alternatively as a rather large entrance because traces of the northern wall posts were absent in precisely this area). Even though the excavation did not reveal any wall postholes in this part of the northern long side over a distance of about 4 m, it may be that the postholes did not have much depth and therefore disappeared. It should also be noted that the conditions of preservation of the soil features to some extent were better in the southern part of the house with its more clayey subsoil, while to the north in general it was sandier.

The raw length of the building is made up of postholes at both ends and it is clear that it belonged among the shorter longhouses and was likely the shortest.[3] The length of the sunken floor measured in the longitudinal axis of the house was relatively short too. The raw house width, measured at right angles to the longitudinal axis of the sunken part, was about middle of the range for Resengaard longhouses.

The house was distinctly broader to the west than to the east. Because the recorded lines of outer wall postholes in their main courses were fairly straight on the southern and northern long sides, these lines can safely be prolonged in order to calculate the width near the eastern end. Two phases of what is considered to be inner panel walls in the area by and east of the southern doorway have been recorded at some distance from the line of outer wall postholes. We shall return to these below.

The doorway in the southern long side was constructed so that the distance between the outer wall postholes had been dug at a somewhat larger interval. Characteristic intervals between the postholes of the outer wall to the south seem to have been about 0.6-0.8 m, while this distance was apparently wider in the wall to the north. The distance between the opposite postholes of the doorway was c. 1.15 m. The diameter of these two postholes was c. 0.26 and 0.22 m, and their surface dimensions were thereby about the same as the other of the outer wall line. The doorway postholes do not follow the line of the wall, however, but are drawn a few centimetres back towards the interior. Correspondingly, the traces of inner panel wall stop by the entrance. At each side, two stake-holes were dug close to each other, probably to strengthen the doorway at the transition to the panel wall. The distance between the two opposite stake-holes was 1.00 m so this must have been the width of the entrance. No other postholes were found inside the house near the doorway.

Inside the entrance, the floor was not deepened as much as the eastern parts of the sunken floor. The reason was obviously that this floor area constituted a broad ramp leading from the doorway to the deeper parts of the floor. In this way, the floor level gradually lowered. The subsoil inside the entrance was clayey and it must have been relatively resistant to wear from humans passing in and out. No apparent holes were observable in spite of the very many times the ramp must have been crossed during the lifetime of the house and no signs of repairs of any kind were found either. Under dry conditions, this clayey ground would thus have been quite hard and, unlike the sandy subsoil, the surface parts of it would not have easily disintegrated. A slightly concave part was in a less clayey ramp area, measuring c. 2.5 x 0.5 m and leading from the doorway to the northeast. The presence of this requires explanation and it is tempting to view this dip in the ramp as an indication of wear from humans coming and going.

The ramp connected significant differences in floor level. About 6-8 cm of soil was removed over the house site during the initial excavation and in the ancient past the builders of the longhouse had removed many centimetres of the old surface soil over the ground floor. So from the outside terrain (and thus from the doorway), the ramp appears to have connected a difference of about half a metre down towards the middle of the sunken floor. Even deeper floor areas, which I term "low zones" (see Ch. 4), were observable in the northern part. The ramp was about 3.50 m long, and was relatively steep in its eastern c. 1.8 m long part.

A large number of charred cereals belong to the sunken-floor horizon. The presence of this blackish material in the floor layer and soil patches, often with sandy soil, some coal dust and other things could give the impression of localized fire in areas of the more dense cereal concentrations. Based on evidence of the amounts of charred grains, it has been suggested that the house burned down (report S2001a).

Clearly, the grains had been exposed to considerable heat but we need to ask whether the house actually burned down. If this was the case, it might be expected that pieces of charcoal would be found in some number. And yet there was only a very modest presence of charcoal collected in the floor horizon, despite minute investigation by means of trowels and finer tools. The question therefore arises as to how thousands and thousands of cereal grains would survive in a charred state following a fire that left practically no charcoal? The fire could hardly have burned almost all the wood but left the grains in just a charred state. Other expected traces of fire were largely absent as well. No substantial red burning of the subsoil could be observed in any part of the house as was the case in House 2, which I consider a regular site of fire, see below. Furthermore, a covering layer of charcoal dust or ashes was not observable above the floor. In relation to an undisturbed sunken floor, in particular, I find it hard to accept that a layer of ash and charcoal, as well as comprehensive red burning of clayey or sandy floor, would not be preserved since such evidence is generally not destroyed or broken down by nature.

No "permanent", ordinary fireplace was observed in the well-preserved floors of the longhouse, while several patches with heat-affected/cracked stones were recorded and we shall later return to these. Burning down of the house or an influence from an ordinary fireplace to account for the finds of the large amount of charred grains is thus not an acceptable rationalization. It is therefore necessary to look for other explanations that are functionally compatible with the finds and observations. If live coal and flames from a regular fire did not directly cause carbonizing of the grains, at least an adequate heat must have been present locally to have had this impact.

In my view, no kind of clear evidence of temporary, open fireplaces is available to support such an assumption. Instead, I suggest that the carbonization in all probability took place in connection with the above-mentioned patches of heat-affected/cracked stones, which will be discussed in much greater detail later in this work.

Yet we cannot yet leave the topic of fire because the panel wall vestiges to the south showed some kind of fire impact. This observation does not necessarily prove that the house itself burned down and it is clear that the charred cereals were concentrated more to the north than in the areas of former panel walls. The interior panel wall had two phases in my reading. The second phase had burned down, as evidenced by traces of charcoal in the top of the stake-holes.

Further below, I argue that this kind of buildings at Resengaard had thick turf walls and, in this respect,

it would be understandable if wooden posts in the wall itself, surrounded by such a wall material, did not burn down to the ground even during an intense fire. If other parts of the house, including the wooden construction, also burned down, however, the lack of substantial numbers of charcoal pieces is remarkable.

In conclusion, I suggest the interpretation that, after abandonment, the house was torn down and good timber and other wood, besides utensils etc., were removed. Then the remaining panel wall, and perhaps sporadic organic leftovers in the sunken area, were set on fire. To my mind, the house relics do not represent a regular site of fire but a plot where remaining, unusable scrap was destroyed by fire before further new utilization.

In all, I rate the research value of this longhouse site to be remarkably high as concerns traces of the dwelling structure and, as we shall see, the artefact remainders and soil features emphasize its research value.

House 2 (Fig. 2.9)

Unfortunately, during the removal of topsoil prior to some sewer work in 1989, nearly all traces of the western, ground-floor part of the house were cut by contractor machines and thereby destroyed. The sunken floor part, which still happened to be protected by a massive layer of soil, was however easily recognized and well-preserved when the archaeological investigations subsequently began. That no gable end postholes were observable immediately west of the sunken floor also underlines the former existence of a ground floor west of the limits of the sunken floor. Only a short part of this ground-floor was preserved and a pit immediately inside the southern long side wall was shallow but had sizeable surface dimensions.

In the area of House 2 some postholes from structures in the upper strata of the covering soil did not reach down into the level of the sunken-floor house remainders. In our judgment, these postholes were mainly from the medieval or post-medieval period. Recent ploughing did not cause any disordering of the longhouse site, likewise due to the thick protective layers of soil.

Judging by the traces of roof-bearing posts, the alignment of the building was almost E-W. Locally the ground, as observable in the N-S soil bench, was somewhat north-facing, and the altitude difference between the long sides of the sunken floor was c. 0.30 m. The general slope of the ground in the area was

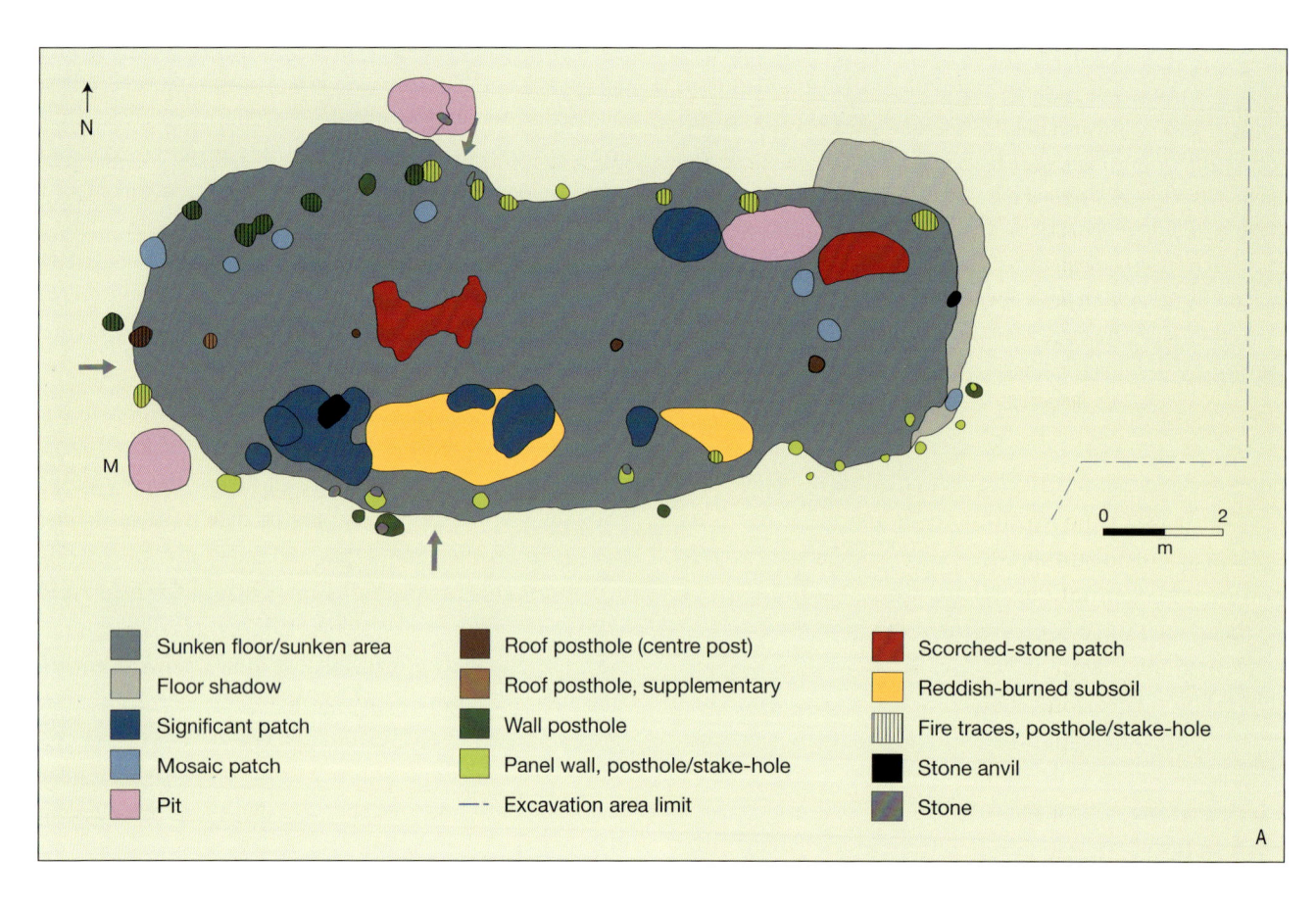

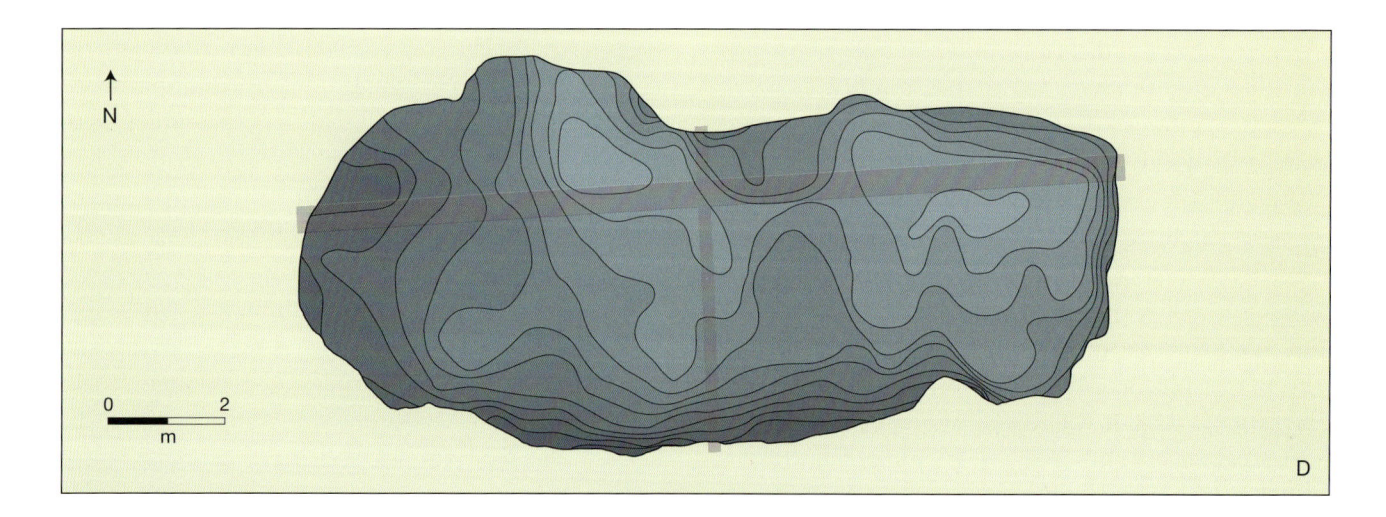

▨ Sunken floor/sunken area	■ Roof posthole (centre post)	■ Scorched-stone patch
▨ Floor shadow	■ Roof posthole, supplementary	■ Reddish-burned subsoil
■ Significant patch	■ Wall posthole	▥ Fire traces, posthole/stake-hole
● Mosaic patch	● Panel wall, posthole/stake-hole	■ Stone anvil
● Pit	-- Excavation area limit	▨ Stone

74 Chapter 2

◀ *Fig. 2.9. Resengaard, House 2. A: Ground plan. For house sites, soil features and excavation limits in the surroundings, see Fig. 2.2.C. For two soil section drawings from this site, see Fig. 4.68.C & D. Most traces of the western ground floor were unfortunately removed prior to the archaeological investigation. Apart from that, the entire sunken floor was preserved due to the presence of thick soil layers. After demolition, the house site was exposed to deliberate burning. B: Below a massive amount of soil, the sunken floor gradually comes to light after a second cleaning. Soil benches are established across the house site and in a longitudinal direction. On the south slope of the hill, in the background, Marienlyst Strand, the early Late Neolithic house site as well as other traces were found many years later. Seen from the south. C: The easternmost part of the E-W section. Before building the longhouse, the old surface soil was removed also east of the sunken floor. An extensive and substantial stratum of dark soil with fire traces is present. Seen from the south. D: Contour lines indicating the gradual deepening of the sunken floor. The level measurements took place after removing several centimetres more subsoil from the floor bottom in search of possible artefacts trodden down or overlooked soil features. As this process was carried out all over the floor, however, the relative level differences are considered reliable.*

faintly towards the north. By the time of the investigation, a central sunken floor area lay at a depth of 34 cm but the original depth beneath the top of the old surface must have been significantly greater.

Immediately west of the sunken floor, a posthole in the ground floor could belong to an extra supporting post or be a later repair for the roof-bearing construction of the central longitudinal axis. The preserved raw length of the house was only a little more than the sunken floor. The raw house width, based on traces of a few posts and the doorways, appears to have been one of the narrowest of the Resengaard longhouses but it might have broadened somewhat towards the west. The long sides of the house converged towards the west, giving the house a trapezoid ground plan.

The sunken floor was the second longest found at the site. Unlike most other Resengaard houses, it had a predominantly clayey bottom and thus a fairly hard floor surface. Four postholes with rather small diameters are considered to represent traces of the roof-bearing construction along the central longitudinal axis. In particular the third posthole from the east seems extremely small and I wonder whether we might have overlooked a faint soil feature of a somewhat bigger diameter here? The wooden post was probably removed before the house was burned down, see below.

During residence, the sunken floor level became gradually deeper, even though it was dominated by clayey soil. Some building changes were apparently carried out during residence. Thus, in my reading, the house including the sunken floor was, at some point in time, extended up to c. 3 metres extra to the east and this extension gives a more irregular character to the ground plan. It was very likely designed to meet certain, quite specific needs, and we shall later return to the traces in this part of the house.

During our field work, it was concluded that the house had burned down. In my understanding, three main reasons drew us to this conclusion. Firstly, many of the aforementioned interior postholes contained pieces of charcoal with charcoal dust on the top. Such traits were found in 14 postholes, all of which were only a few cm deep. They may all have burned down at the same time, judging by the general stratification, and none of them were younger than the sunken floor itself. Secondly, the presence of a sandy layer with abundant traces of charcoal dust may confirm this interpretation (Fig. 4.68). This layer covered a large part of the sunken floor. Thirdly, areas in the clayey subsoil below the sunken floor were evidently burned reddish and, locally, even really red.

In my judgment, the building was deliberately burned down after abandonment. The main reason for this view is that the central wooden posts must have been removed and saved before the house was burned, whereas many minor walls posts appear to have been consumed by the fire. Mainly fragmented artefacts were left on the floor, which is contrary to what might be expected if the house had suddenly burned down. Likewise larger, charred wooden items were not found.

Certain postholes form a unique opportunity to gain an instant picture of the constructional elements present at the time of burning. It is proposed that these postholes with traces of charcoal belong to a compartment, a panel wall, and an entrance. In the sunken floor, five postholes to the northwest were thus found in a line and I suggest that they stem from a compartment wall. Four of these showed evident traces of burning at the top.

Immediately to the east, the western posthole of a doorway, in my reading, appears to represent the end of the compartment. A stone flanked the eastern posthole from the doorway. By and large, this northern entrance was placed just opposite the southern.

East of the doorway, four postholes are, in my interpretation, traces of a panel wall. These were mostly rounded on the surface with diameters of c. 24-44 cm, and thus much bigger than those for the panel wall in House 1. Their internal distance was also much larger although two postholes seem to be missing from the line, likely because they did not go adequately deep into the subsoil. It should be noted that these dimensions are also strange in relation to those for the centre posts of House 2 but rather clayey conditions in the area of the centre post might help to explain this.

To the west in the sunken floor we have two further postholes which, in my reading, belong to a doorway leading to and from the ground floor of the longhouse. Both were rather shallow (10 cm & 7 cm) so it must have been absolutely necessary that the posts were fixed to other parts of the construction, for instance a transverse beam, to consolidate them. A passage near the central longitudinal axis towards the west could be expected since the roof near the sides would presumably not have given adequate height for upright walking.

The south entrance to the house was placed somewhat to the west in the area of the sunken floor. In the doorway, both postholes to the west were recorded during the first cleaning with trowels but, during repeated cleaning, the bottom of the postholes disappeared because they were quite shallow. A stone with a diameter of around 15 cm flanked the posts in each hole, likely for stabilizing the construction. To the east, only the inner posthole was observable. The missing eastern posthole could likely be explained by the same assumption, namely too little depth. Our initial removal of topsoil by means of machines may have taken away several soil features, including postholes of modest dimensions in the western and southwest part of the preserved part of the site.

In the southeast part of the floor, just one posthole from the panel wall had a fill with traces of burning. In area, it was about the same size as some of those to the north and only 7 cm deep. On the remaining southern long side, the postholes that are interpreted as belonging to a panel wall were likewise rather shallow.

In the area of the southern wall to the east, a remarkable structure was found. In my reading, these postholes belong to a kind of recess in the wall. On the ground plan, it was rectangular and framed an area of up to c. 1.98 m in length and c. 0.55 m in width. The edge of the sunken floor extended to the posts in the middle of the back wall of this recess, where the postholes generally had relatively small diameters of c. 10-18 cm, and only little depth.

Altogether, I consider the research value of this house site to be exceptionally high as concerns preserved traces of the sunken floor, while we lack further information on the ground floor. Besides the pits and patches, the remainders of tools, pottery from the floor horizon and the secondary fills are likewise highly valuable.

House 13 (Fig. 2.10)

Some of the pits recorded within the western part of the house site possibly stem from interior activities and arrangements during the lifetime of House 13. Yet, on the other hand, it is difficult to pass judgment on possible relationships to other pits a little to the west of the western gable end. It can be assumed that some of those in the area of the ground floor could have been present quite early on, i.e. before the house was built.

Regarding disturbances, some ditch systems cut across the western part of the sunken area and some of the unsunken part too. They went down into the subsoil and left no traces of the original floor in the area affected. A preliminary assumption suggests the ditches are of medieval or post-medieval origin. Recent ploughing probably did not cause any damage to the house site due to the presence of thick soil layers on top of it and the wall lines were exceptionally well preserved in the sense that it was possible to note the presence almost all around the house of the postholes, though again – despite the fine preservation conditions – most of them being rather shallow.

The alignment of the building, judging by traces of roof-bearing posts and postholes from the outer walls, was E-W with the longitudinal axis turned a very few degrees towards the SE-NW. The local as well as the general slope of the ground in the area was towards the southeast. The long sides were built fairly parallel and the raw length of the house makes it the second longest found at the settlement. Also, due to the considerable raw width, its area correspondingly belongs among the most sizeable at Resengaard. By the time of the investigation, a central sunken floor area lay at a depth of 26 cm but the original depth beneath the top of the old surface must have been greater.

The constructional traces of the western part of the house were well preserved and its row of postholes for the outer walls appears to be almost complete. In the western gable end 16 postholes, including

Fig. 2.10. Resengaard, House 13. A: Ground plan, shown with a part of a larger ditch system creating a deep disturbance. For further house sites, soil features and excavation limits in the surroundings, see Fig. 2.2.C. B: Ground plan, cleaned. With relatively few exceptions, vestiges of the outer wall postholes were preserved around the perimeter, especially evidencing the characteristic rounding of the corners and the regularity of the wall post placements. C: As a preparation for plan drawing, the area of wall postholes belonging to the northeast corner is being cleaned by Hans Holck, who took part in many excavation campaigns. The wall postholes were mostly rather shallow. Seen from the southeast.

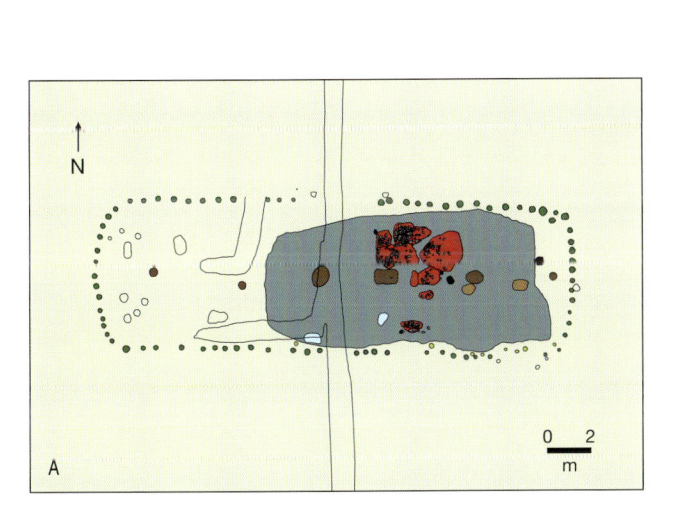

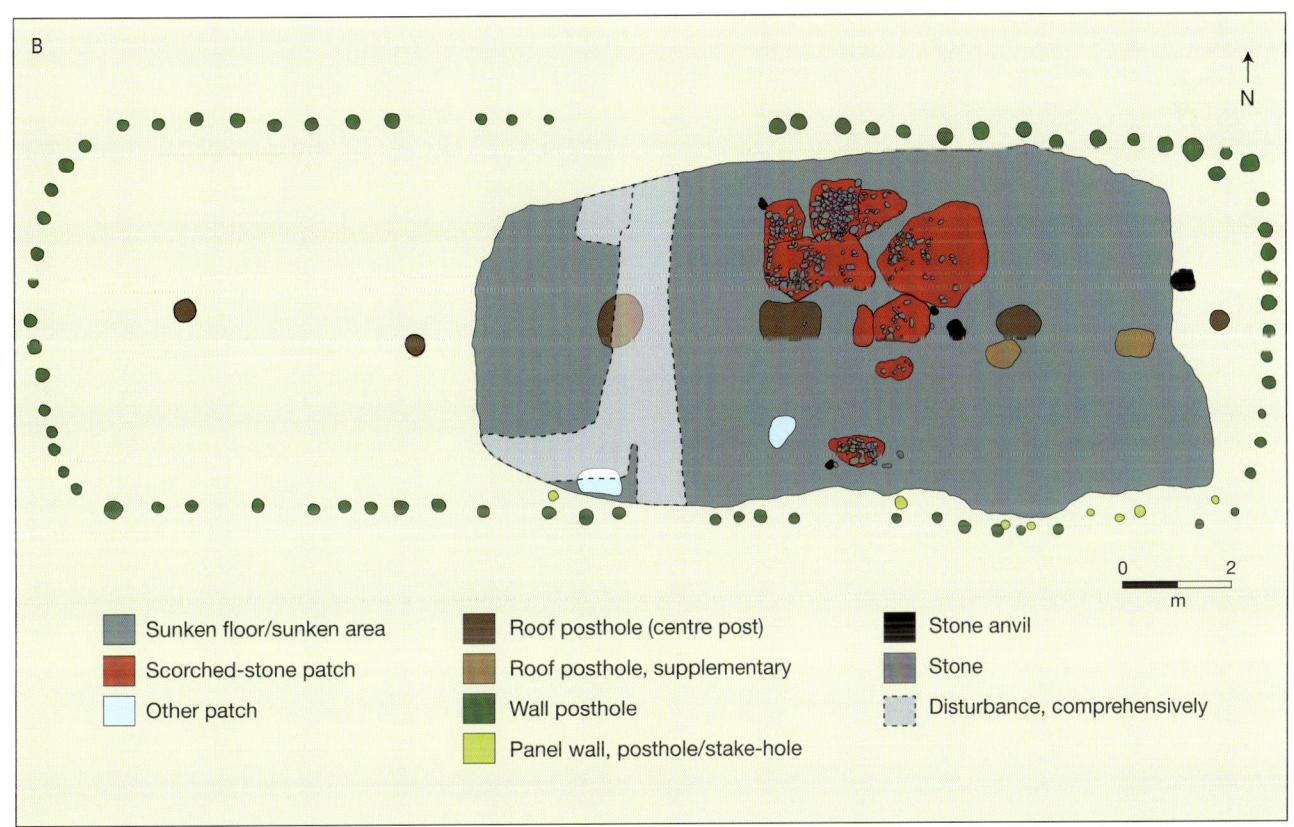

Sunken floor/sunken area	Roof posthole (centre post)	Stone anvil
Scorched-stone patch	Roof posthole, supplementary	Stone
Other patch	Wall posthole	Disturbance, comprehensively
	Panel wall, posthole/stake-hole	

Analysis and interpretation of houses with sunken floors

the posthole shared with the northern and southern long side, mark out a complete row. The characteristically curved line of the gable end had posts on average every half metre, and about the same seems to be the case for the likewise well-preserved eastern gable end. A standard interval for the gable ends of this house thus appears to have been about 0.50 m. The eastern gable end was straighter than the western.

On the long sides, a few postholes are missing from the outer walls even where no disturbances could be recorded. This is probably again due to the general shallowness of the postholes. In the western part of the northern long side, 8 postholes on a course of c. 4.9 m had an average interval of c. 0.70 m, and they thereby stood less dense than at the gable ends.

Two postholes from centre posts were preserved west of the sunken floor. The westernmost of these had a much diffuse character, but this could well be the case if the post was removed during abandonment and the new fill was subsoil. The other was only a few cm deep and placed a little out of line.

Except for the later disturbing ditches to the west, the entire sunken floor appeared quite well preserved. Traces of the roof-bearing posts along the central longitudinal axis continued with three more postholes within the sunken floor. These were all shallow. The westernmost was cut by the later N-S running ditch and its area is tentatively presented on the cleaned ground plan. The preserved remains had a length of at least 0.88 m N-S and thus indicates some size. The next posthole was, during excavation, considered to mark out a large soil feature of c. 1.1 x 0.7 m but, after reconsideration, this sandy, almost rectangular soil patch (though including a few heat-cracked stones and charcoal remainders in its fill) is considered to belong to an aisle post due to its placement and its character, deviating from the neighbouring scorched-stone patches. The next posthole in the sunken floor had dimensions of c. 0.8 x 0.6 m. Two other soil features in the central longitudinal axis possibly stemmed from supporting posts or repairs added later. East of the sunken floor, a shallow posthole is also regarded as belonging to traces of the roof-bearing construction.

No particular divisions were indicated by traces of interior walls. South of the sunken floor, the presence of an interior panel wall in the southern long side was, in my reading, indicated by one stake-hole to the west and 7 stake- and postholes to the east, while several others in the row must have disappeared. As in House 1, some postholes were drawn out towards the line of postholes in the outer wall. In combination with the significant extension of the sunken floor towards the south in the same area, I suggest that we can here see traces of a recess, and that it could have had almost the same dimensions as in House 1.

Unfortunately, later ditches had disturbed the area around the middle of the southern long side where a doorway would be expected, judging by the placement in House 1 and House 2.

No traces indicate that this house had been burned. Due to the rather complete line of outer wall postholes from House 13, the complete row of postholes for centre posts, and also the presence of an unusual number of well-preserved patches with heat-affected/cracked stones, the house site is remarkable and quite unique among the finds from the Limfjord region. In contrast, however, the remainders of artefacts, including those of the secondary fills, are of only moderate research value.

House 14 (Fig. 2.11)

Several disturbances date back to the time after this house was abandoned and demolished. Ard-ploughing of the sunken floor was among the first to take place. The feature of the sunken floor to the northwest had thus been ploughed out, whereas the western end of it was reasonably intact. Later postholes of considerable diameters penetrated the easternmost part. These belonged to the western gable end of a three-aisled building (House 25) from the Older Bronze Age. Three pits, which also appear to belong to this period, disturbed areas near the former walls of the sunken-floor house. A ditch which, in my preliminary judgment, is of medieval or post-medieval origin, crossed the house site in the longitudinal direction. Long after, recent ploughing in all probability removed some of the topsoil over the sunken area although the house was not situated in the higher part of the local terrain and a number of wall postholes were likely therefore spared from destruction.

The alignment of the building, judging by traces of roof-bearing posts and postholes from the outer walls to the south was E-W with the longitudinal axis turned a very few degrees towards the NE-SW. Locally, the ground was somewhat north-facing. The general slope of the area was just slightly north-facing. The altitude difference between the long sides of the sunken floor was c. 0.24 m. By the time of the investigation, a central sunken floor area lay at a depth of 36

Fig. 2.11. Resengaard, House 14. A: Ground plan, older/younger soil features and nearby excavation limits. For further house sites, soil features and excavation limits in the surroundings, see Fig. 2.2.B & C. After demolition of the building, the sunken floor had been significantly disturbed by ard-ploughing. The house site was furthermore exposed to several later intrusions, see Fig. 2.62. B: Ground plan, cleaned. Traces of dividing walls were found in the area of the ground floor. C: Despite disturbances of many kinds, the house site enclosed rather valuable information and significant finds. In the foreground, a stone deposit (24). Seen from the north. D: Ard-furrows, marked for plan drawing, in the sunken floor. Seen from the north.

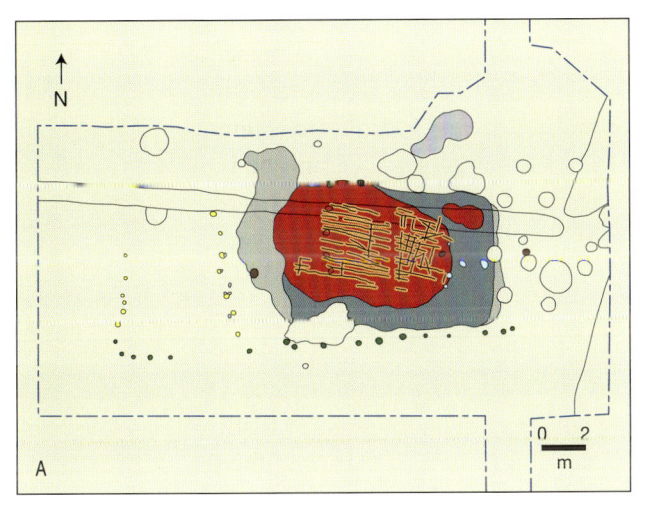

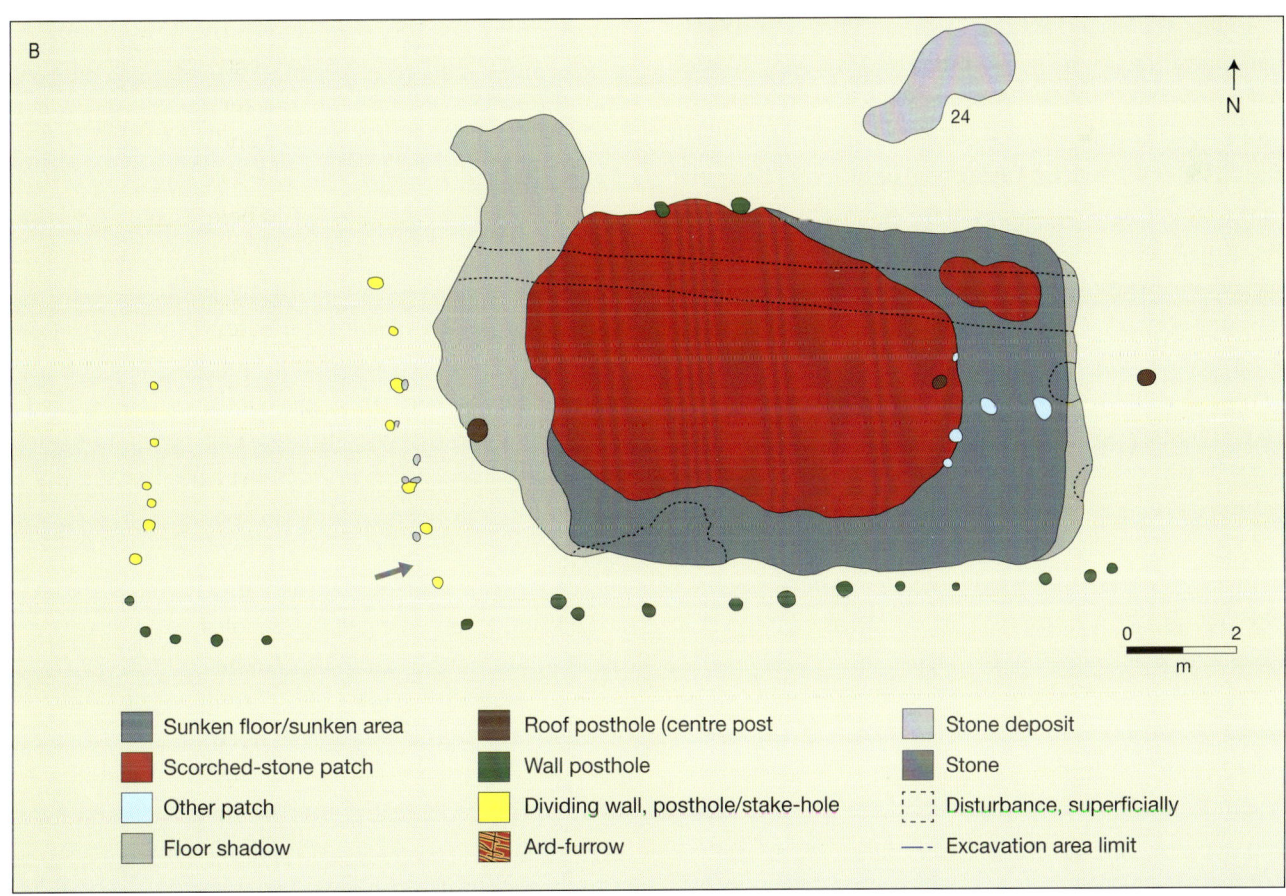

Analysis and interpretation of houses with sunken floors

cm but the original depth beneath the top of the old surface must have been significantly greater.

Judging in particular by the combined indication of postholes for the outer wall to the south and the eastern outer wall posthole, the raw length of the house appear to have been below medium compared to other houses at the settlement. Many postholes belonging to the outer wall of the southern long side were preserved and, in the southwest area, five postholes marked out the vestiges of the corner construction, while in the northern long side only two were found. By and large, the long sides seem to have been parallel. The raw width of the house appears to have been the biggest among Resengaard longhouses.

Altogether 6 stake- and postholes indicate a panel wall to the west. The western ground-floor area seems to have been separated physically from the sunken floor because a line of 6 stake- or postholes together with a post in the central longitudinal axis likely mark out the traces of a dividing wall. It is suggested that an area between two postholes in this wall gave access to and from the room relatively close to a possible doorway on the southern long side. The raw length of the western room would have been about 5 m.

The raw length of the sunken floor was almost 10 m, but it would have been significantly longer if the area of "floor shadows" were included. It would very likely have been even longer towards the west because, in my understanding, the presence of the aforementioned dividing wall could also indicate that the sunken floor from the eastern gable end had more or less reached this wall. Altogether, an original raw length of up to about 13 m would have been possible. No traces of inner panel walls were recorded near the sunken floor.

Along the central longitudinal axis, only two postholes from the roof-bearing construction were found in the sunken floor. A posthole almost in line with these belongs in my reading to the supposed east gable end. What the tongue of the "floor shadow" to the north may indicate is difficult to judge but it could be a northern entrance. However, we have no other vestiges to support such an assumption and hence it is not my suggestion. West of the middle of the southern long side wall, three posts could indicate the placement of a doorway.

No traces indicate that this house burned down. In all, I consider the research value of this longhouse site, despite the disturbances, to be relatively high as concerns the preserved traces of the dwelling structure. The remains of tools and pottery from the floor horizon and, not least, those from the secondary fills are very valuable study objects. The soil features of the floor are of modest to moderate research value.

House 41 (Fig. 2.12)

In the area of House 41, some postholes from structures higher up in the covering soil were present. During fieldwork it was considered that these mainly stemmed from about the mid-second millennium AC and did not disturb deep down into the level of the house remainders in question, due to the thick soil layers accumulated. A massive earth dike that separated two recent agricultural fields and was partly covering the house site came into being later in the 2nd millennium AD. Together with the thick soil layers, it offered considerable house-protecting effects. Likewise due to the thick, covering soil layers, recent plough-

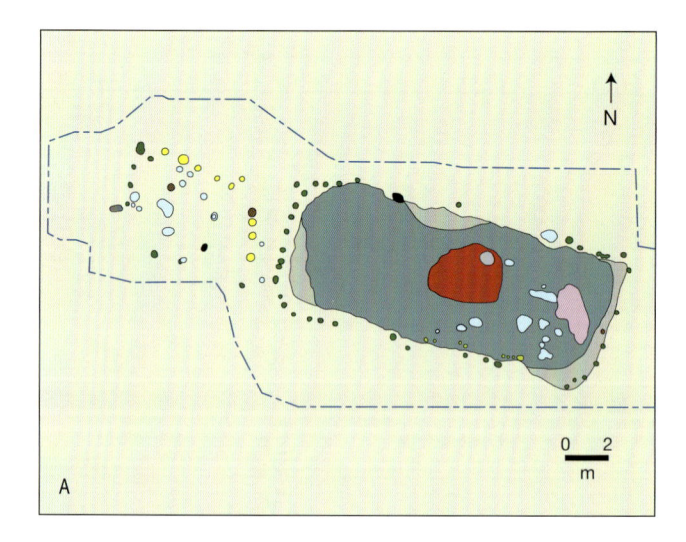

Fig. 2.12. Resengaard, House 41. A: Ground plan. The area of the house site was generally free of older/younger soil features. For further house sites, soil features and excavation limits in the surroundings, see Fig. 2.2.C. B: Ground plan, cleaned. The ground-floor part was later torn down, while the sunken-floor part remained in use and was supplied with a new western gable end. C: Note, in particular, the presumed stake- and postholes that were early on recorded in the plan drawing but which disappeared during the subsequent cleaning, and in this case not represented in Fig. 2.12.B. D: An earthen dike of more recent origin covered parts of the house site which, moreover, was covered in its entirety by a relatively thick layer of soil. For a soil section drawing from this site, see Fig. 4.68.E. The sunken floor turned out to be the largest at the settlement, and in its first phase, this house was also the longest. Seen from the southeast. E: In the foreground, stake- and postholes belonging to the new gable end that was established immediately west of the sunken floor. Seen from the west.

80 Chapter 2

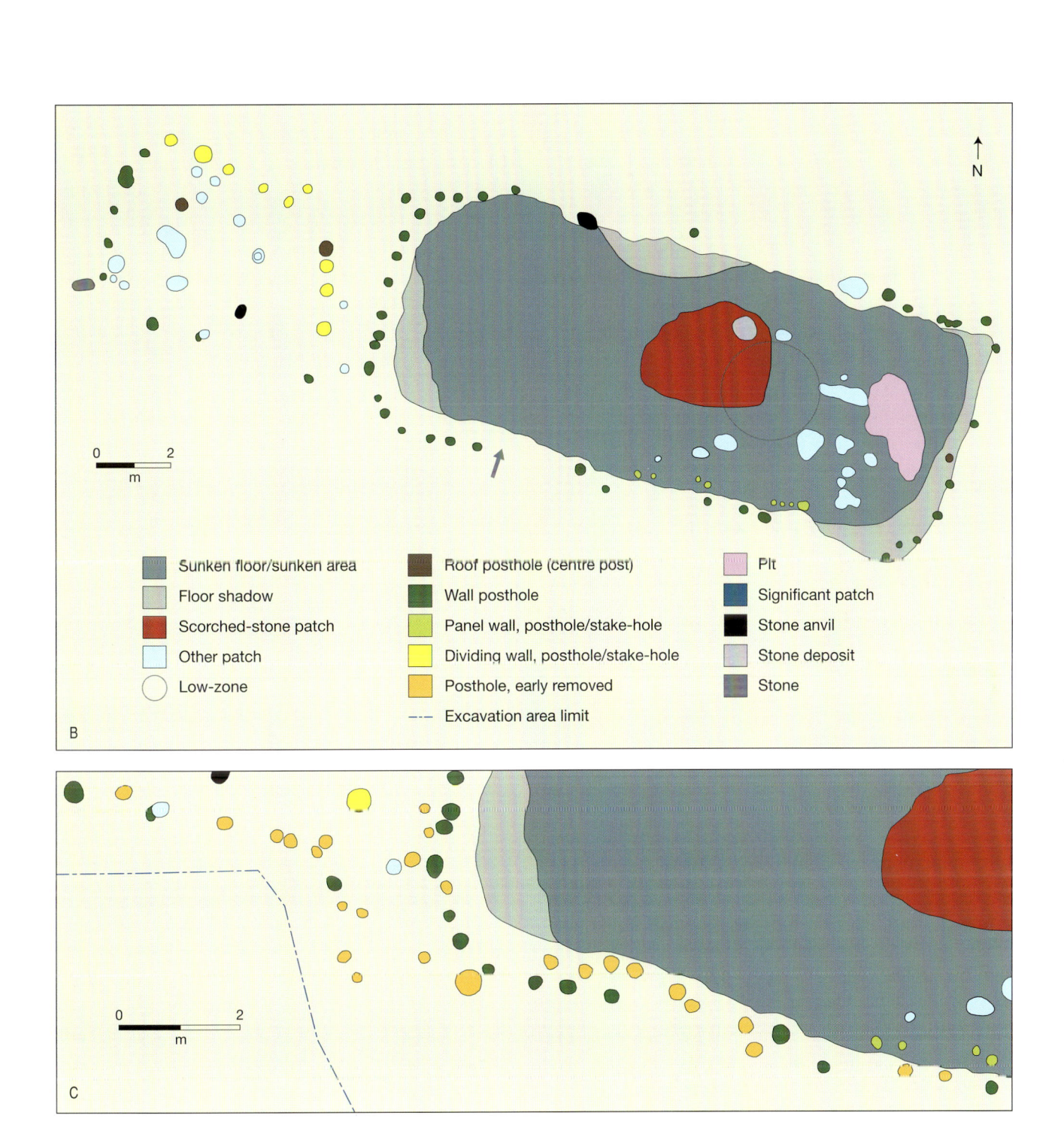

Sunken floor/sunken area	Roof posthole (centre post)	Plt
Floor shadow	Wall posthole	Significant patch
Scorched-stone patch	Panel wall, posthole/stake-hole	Stone anvil
Other patch	Dividing wall, posthole/stake-hole	Stone deposit
Low-zone	Posthole, early removed	Stone
	--- Excavation area limit	

Analysis and interpretation of houses with sunken floors 81

ing had not caused any disordering of the house site. Consistent with this, no disturbances at all were observed, apart from some animal activity and roots. The careful manual cleaning of the house site showed very many soil features outside the southwest part of the sunken floor, the majority of which probably represented posthole bottoms. However, after our first total cleaning and surface recording of the soil features, we had to recognize that it was necessary to conduct a thorough second cleaning using trowels, whereby many of these rather shallow patches vanished. In my estimate, c. 2-5 cm soil/subsoil was removed by this second cleaning.

Judging by the long sides of the sunken floor, traces of roof-bearing posts and postholes from the outer walls, the alignment of the building was almost SSE-NNW. The local and general slope of the ground in the area was towards the north. By the time of the investigation, a central sunken floor area lay at a depth of 26 cm but the original depth beneath the top of the old surface must have been greater.

The ground plan of the house is unusual. On the face of it, the western part of the house could seem to have been narrower than the sunken-floor part house. A closer analysis reveals that the original length of the house instead appears to have been reduced at some point in time, in such a way that the house merely comprised the sunken floor area. According to this view, the house was thus initially built in full length and then, at a later stage, reduced to about two-thirds of its original length. In this process, a new western gable end was built, seemingly in a relatively stronger construction with many posts. The west corner of the southern long side wall towards the west was then reinforced, as the additional postholes indicate. The raw area of the western ground floor would have been about 50 m² or more before it was torn down.

In the first phase, the raw length of the house was c. 24.0 m and thus the longest at the settlement. The long sides were parallel. The raw width is also among the broader. When the western part was removed in the second phase, the raw length of the house was then reduced to c. 16.2 m. No other major building changes during residence were observed.

The traces of the western, ground-floor part of the house site were relatively well preserved at the gable end and along the south side. Two postholes from the construction were observed along the central longitudinal axis. Despite the protection from any major disturbances, the centre post nearest to the sunken floor was merely 11 cm deep and, before the beginning of excavation, probably went only about 20 cm into the subsoil. It seems that a posthole by the middle of the western gable may represent a reinforcing post almost in line with the central longitudinal axis. The postholes of the gable ends and the long sides were often only a few cm deep, and this observation is of course underlined by the disappearance of many during the second cleaning.

In the western part of the house, some lines of postholes likely indicate the existence of a compartment to the north and towards the sunken-floor part. The northern wall of this seems to have an obtuse bend at the eastern end. The method of constructing the dividing wall could possibly have been more or less as suggested for House 1.

Two postholes at the northwest corner of the second-phase gable end wall may point to the presence of a panel wall. Apart from this, no stake- or postholes along the northern long side or the western gable end indicated an interior panel wall. A single, shallow posthole for the eastern gable is suggested to be an indication of a panel wall. Yet a post placed exactly here could also have served a constructional purpose being on the central longitudinal axis. Along the southern long side of the sunken floor, 8 stake- and postholes, in my reading, belong to a panel wall. The recorded depths of these ranged from 6-24 cm into the subsoil.

Even though four in-drawn soil features/postholes among those that vanished during the second cleaning of the site might indicate a doorway in the south side of the sunken floor to the west, it must be strongly emphasized that no certain observations are available. In the first phase of the house, a doorway here would have been about the middle of the southern long side.

Finally it must be stated that no traces indicate that this house was burned. In all, I rate the research value of this longhouse site to be really high as concerns preserved traces of the dwelling structure. The artefact remains, also including those from the secondary fills, are rather valuable, likewise the soil features in the floors.

House 42 (Fig. 2.13)

As suggested for House 13, it is possible that some of the pits in the area were present quite early on, i.e. in this case before House 42. Adequate resources were not, however, available for the investigation team to try to clarify the extent to which the pits and postholes south and west of the sunken floor marked out older or later traits in relation to the longhouse. Correspondingly, the chronological relations between the pits within the ground-floor part of the house have not been explored in detail.

A distinct, rather straight row of large postholes traversing the ground-floor from east-northeast to west-southwest was of fairly recent date, judging by the appearance of their fills. A broad ditch system of presumed medieval or post-medieval dating was present to the east and also crossed almost N-S. It penetrated the fills of the sunken area and went slightly into the subsoil. Recent ploughing had hardly removed any topsoil over the sunken area. Where postholes of the wall lines seem missing it is my understanding that many of the posts were probably not dug significantly deep into the subsoil.

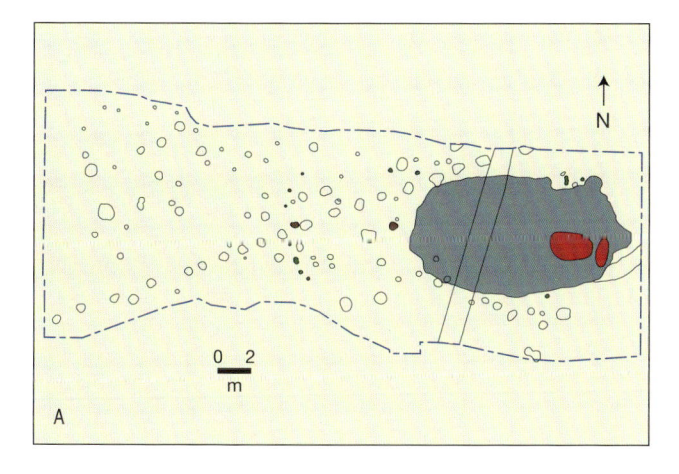

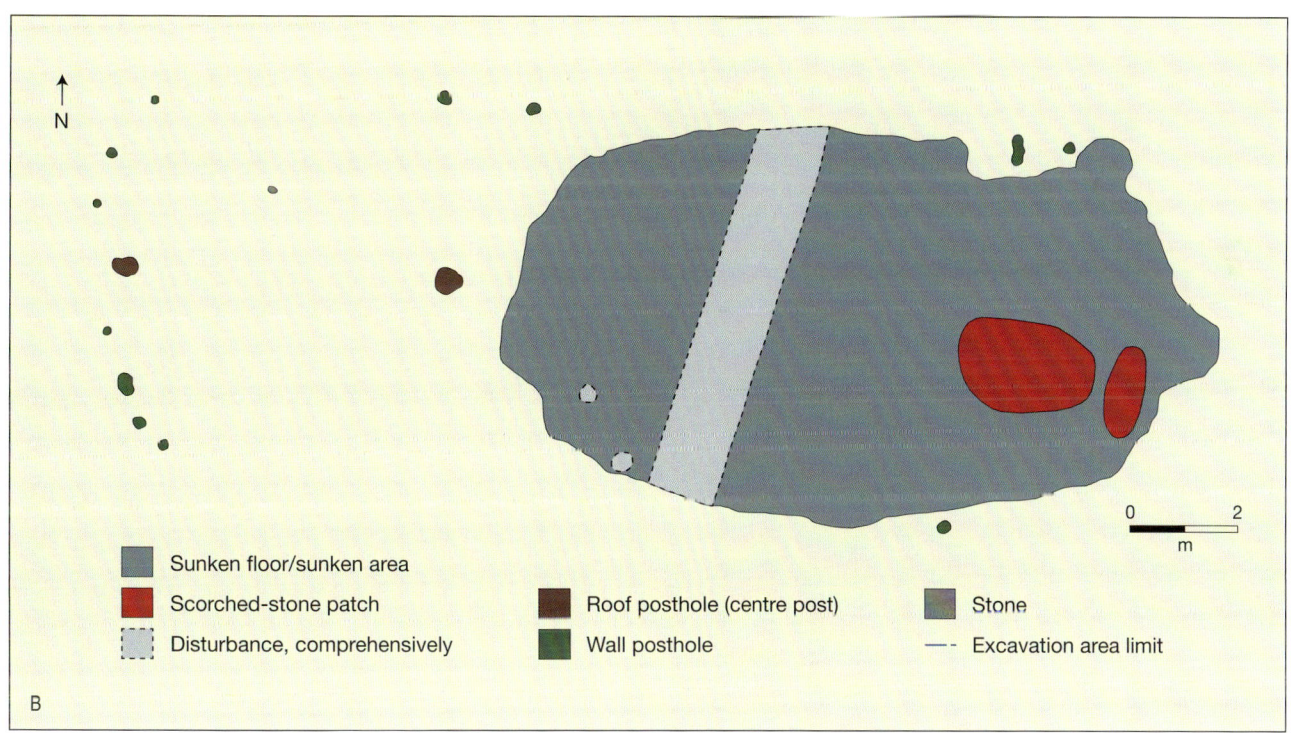

Fig. 2.13. Resengaard, House 42. A: Ground plan, older/younger soil features and nearby excavation limits. For further house sites, soil features and excavation limits in the surroundings, see Fig. 2.2.B & C. A straight row of postholes from a relatively recent period forms a significant disturbance in the area of the ground floor and a ditch from the medieval/post-medieval period crosses the sunken floor. B: Ground plan, cleaned. Only few soil patches were recorded in the sunken floor. C: Unfortunately, it took a long time before the recovered site could be excavated. The trial trenches and our piles of removed soil thus became more or less covered with vegetation. The medieval/post-medieval ditch cutting across the sunken floor had a fill of characteristic greyish soil and could be easily distinguished. Seen from the north. For a soil section drawing, see Fig. 4.68.F.

Analysis and interpretation of houses with sunken floors

The alignment of the building was E-W with the longitudinal axis turned only a very few degrees towards the SE-NW, judging by traces of roof-bearing posts and a sparse number of postholes from the outer walls, The local and general slope of the ground in the area was towards the south and southeast. By the time of the investigation, a central sunken floor area lay at a depth of 36 cm but the original depth beneath the top of the old surface must have been greater.

No postholes were preserved in the eastern gable and the length of the house is therefore proposed with a small margin, since the distance to the gable was likely but little. The raw length was around medium for Resengaard longhouses but the width

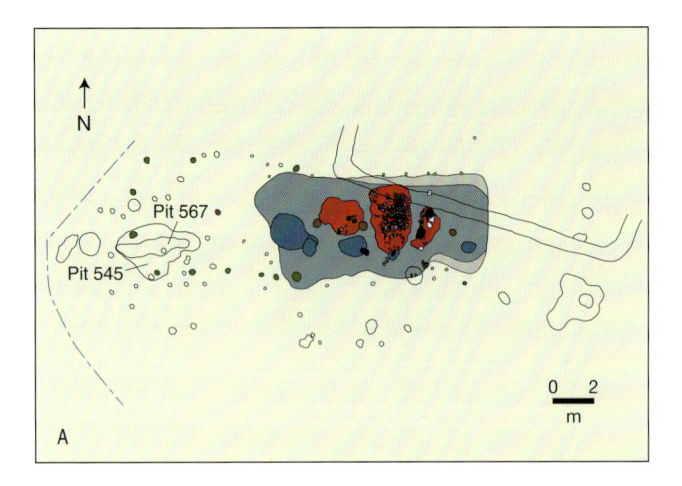

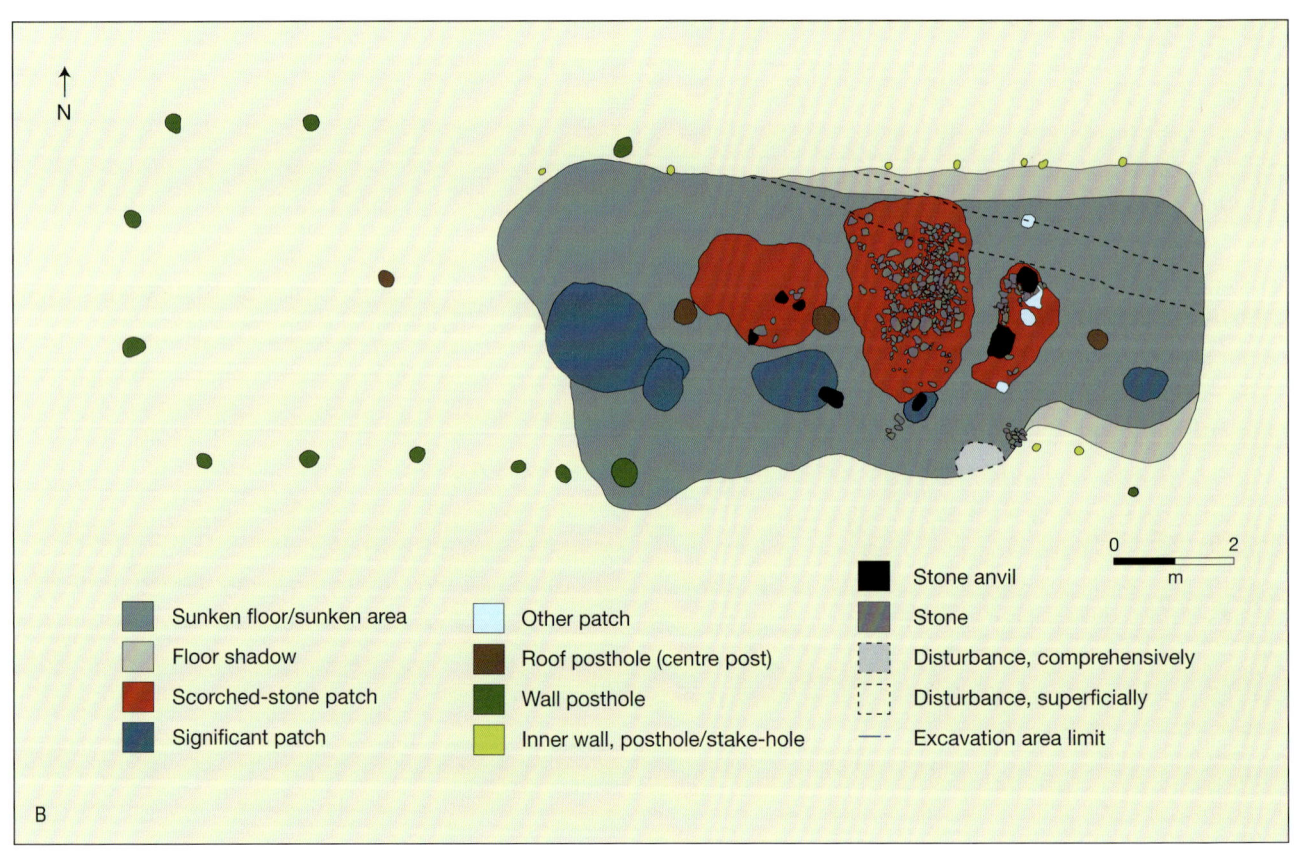

Fig. 2.14. Resengaard, House 128. A: Ground plan, older/younger soil features. For further house sites, soil features as well as excavation limits in the surroundings, see Fig. 2.2.B & C. Later disturbance of the sunken floor relates, not least, to a medieval/post-medieval ditch. B: Ground plan, cleaned. The house site was fairly well-preserved and clearly evidences a building with a trapezoidal outline. C: A soil bench is established across the sunken floor. Scorched-stone patches, stone anvils and other elements are visible in the cleaned floor. Almost vertical photo, seen from the south.

was broader than most. The long sides of the house may very well have been parallel but it cannot be stated from the available evidence. The length of the sunken floor was fairly large compared to the house length but data on doorways, panel walls, compartments, dividing walls, and other interior arrangements are lacking. Apart from the gable end, traces of the western part of the house were only modestly preserved.

No traces indicate that the building was burned. I consider the research value of this longhouse site as less than average as concerns preserved traces of the dwelling structure. The tool and pottery remainders, including those of the secondary fills, are altogether of moderate research value. The soil features in floors I rate as being of only modest research value.

House 128 (Fig. 2.14)

It appears that at least some of the pits and postholes in the area of the ground floor were present quite early on, i.e. before the house. One of these is the large pit 567 that contained some artefacts, and the proposed outline of the western gable end of the house also suggests that it did not belong to the house.

To the southeast, a later sub-circular pit cut into the edge of the sunken floor. A ditch system presumably from the medieval or post-medieval period crossed the northeast part of the sunken floor but it caused generally only superficial damage. Despite the observation that recent ploughing appears to have removed some of the uppermost soil over the sunken area and perhaps destroyed some wall postholes, it is clear that many are preserved.

Judging by stake- and postholes from outer walls as well as panel walls and, in particular, the centre posts, the house was aligned almost precisely E-W. The general slope of the ground was towards the southeast, although locally in the area of the house slightly north-facing. The altitude difference between the long sides of the sunken floor was thus c. 8 cm. By the time of the investigation, a central sunken floor area lay at a depth of 32 cm but the original depth beneath the top of the old surface must have been significantly greater.

The raw length of the house, measured from the western gable end posthole to the preserved edge of the sunken floor to the east, groups it among the more minor houses at the settlement. The long sides were not parallel but diverged significantly towards the west. The raw width was c. 5.6 to the east and c. 6.2 m to the west. It thus broadened by some 0.6 m and, combined with its slenderness and its main dimensions, the longhouse shows obvious affinities with House 1, while – as we shall see later – the use and arrangement of the sunken floor was quite different. In the sunken floor three postholes, considered traces of centre posts, were all merely a few cm deep. A fourth posthole was recorded in the ground floor to the west. The outer wall postholes were especially well-preserved to the west, whereas to the east a long course of panel wall was recorded to the north, in addition to a couple to the south. It is conceivable that the longhouse was actually built of a stronger construction in the western half so that it could withstand greater pressure. No doorways, compartments, dividing walls or other features were identified.

No traces indicate that this house was burned. In all, I rate the research value of this longhouse site as quite high as concerns preserved traces of the dwelling, and the artefact remainders, including those from the secondary fills, may support this view. The soil features and stone placements of the interior are of high research value.

House 130 (Fig. 2.15)

Some of the pits in the area were possibly present quite early on, i.e. before the house was built. Two minor pits and a posthole had cut the southwest part of the sunken floor but with only little damage. Furthermore, the same ditch system that crossed the site of House 128 also passed this house 130 through the middle of the sunken floor. No severe damage was recorded, however, partly because the ditch was mainly superficial and also because a break in the course of the ditch was placed exactly over this floor. Another disturbing factor is recent ploughing and this must have removed some soil from the fills above the sunken floor and presumably destroyed a number of wall postholes.

The alignment of the building, judging by postholes from the outer wall to the south, was E-W with the longitudinal axis turned a few degrees towards the SE-NW. The general slope in the area was towards the southeast and, locally, the ground was slightly south-facing. The altitude difference between the long sides of the sunken floor was c. 10 cm. By the time of the investigation, a central sunken floor area lay at a depth of 42 cm but the original depth beneath the top of the old surface must have been greater.

Fig. 2.15. Resengaard, House 130. A: Ground plan and older/younger soil features. No excavation limits nearby. A ditch and recent ploughing, not least, affected this house site. For further house sites, soil features as well as excavation limits in the surroundings, see Fig. 2.2.C. B: Ground plan, cleaned. C: A medieval/post-medieval ditch had cut across the site of House 128 in the foreground and House 130 further behind to the left. Seen from the west-southwest.

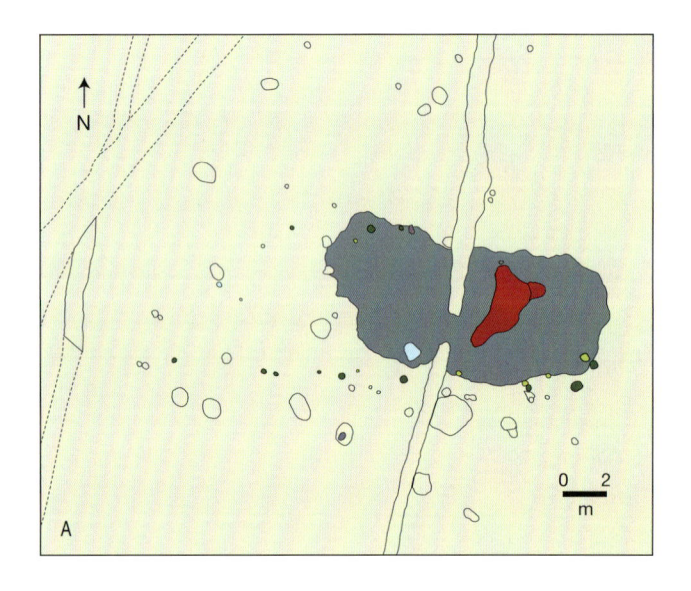

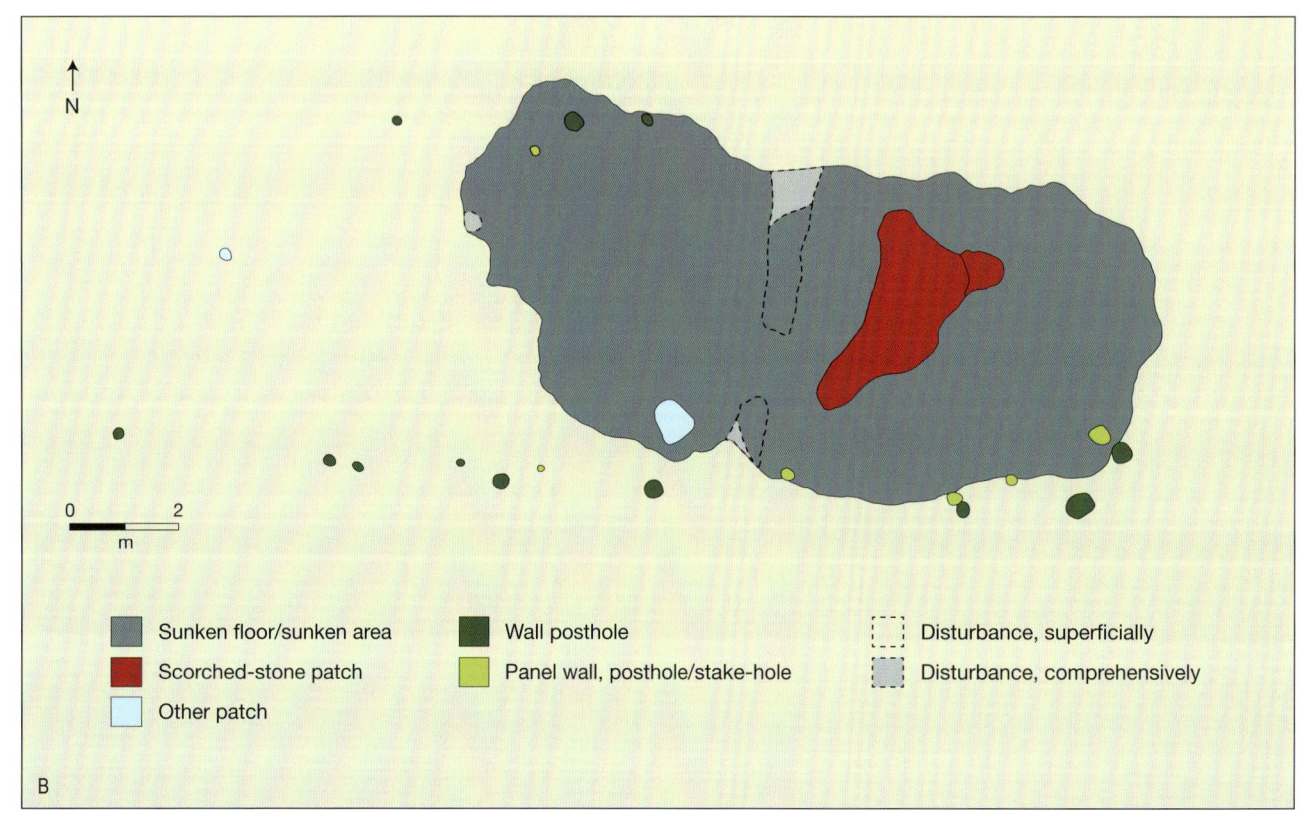

▬ Sunken floor/sunken area	▬ Wall posthole
▬ Scorched-stone patch	▬ Panel wall, posthole/stake-hole
▬ Other patch	
▭ Disturbance, superficially	
▭ Disturbance, comprehensively	

86   Chapter 2

Postholes from the wall construction were only sporadically present in the northern part of the house site. The raw house length is measured from the westernmost posthole of the southern long side to the eastern edge of the sunken floor but it probably extended a little further to the east. The northern outer wall postholes were scanty but the long sides were presumably parallel. The raw length of the house was below average for Resengaard longhouses, whereas the raw width was about middle of the range for these. No postholes from roof-bearing posts were recorded. Some stake- or postholes, in my reading, belong to traces of a panel wall to the southeast, and one posthole to the north. Vestiges of doorways, compartments, dividing walls and other traits were not found.

No traces indicate that this house was burned. I rate the research value of this longhouse site as modest to moderate as concerns preserved traces of the dwelling structure. The remains of artefacts, and especially those from the secondary fills, are rather valuable. The soil features of the floor are of modest research value.

House 134 (Fig. 2.16)

A track, presumably from the post-medieval period, crossed the northern part of the house but hardly damaged the preserved areas of the sunken floor. Recent ploughing, however, had severely affected the state of preservation because it must have diminished the sunken floor significantly and likewise probably removed many wall postholes and maybe some of those of the centre posts, too. Only a few postholes belonging to traces of the construction of this house have thus survived. It seems that recent ploughing also caused comprehensive damage to the immediate surroundings of the house site, due to the prevailing absence of other settlement traces.

The alignment of the building, judging by the southern edge of the sunken floor and three postholes of the outer wall to the south, was largely E-W. The general slope of the terrain in the area was faintly towards the east and, locally, it was slightly south-facing. The altitude difference between the long sides of the sunken floor was c. 6 cm. By the time of investigation, a central sunken floor area lay at a depth of 45 cm but the original depth beneath the top of the old surface must have been significantly greater.

The site is considered to constitute the eastern part of a longhouse and the preserved, raw length of the building is identical to that of the sunken floor. It is not

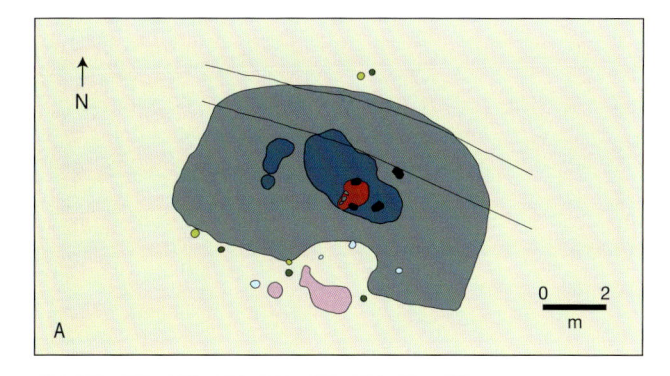

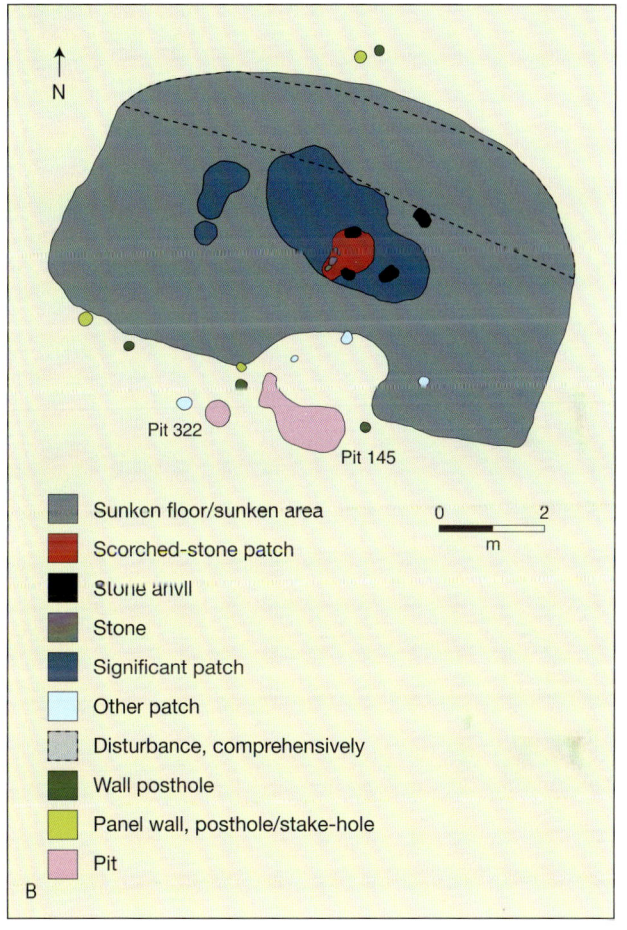

Fig. 2.16. Resengaard, House 134. A: Ground plan, older/younger soil features. For further house sites, soil features and excavation limits in the surrounding area, see Fig. 2.2.B & C. The house site had suffered greatly from recent ploughing and an earth road disturbance. No excavation limits nearby. B: Ground plan, cleaned. The pits placed immediately to the south in front of the middle of the sunken floor may functionally have belonged to the building.

possible to state whether the long sides were parallel or not. The raw house width at the middle of the preserved sunken floor was about middle of the range for Resengaard longhouses. The length of the sunken floor immediately appears to have been relatively short but, when taking into consideration the ploughing damage,

Analysis and interpretation of houses with sunken floors **87**

Fig. 2.17. Resengaard, House 138. A: Ground plan of House 138 and 143. Both show significant impact from recent ploughing and, in particular, the western end of the sunken floor site of House 138 from the disturbances of a large, irregular Bronze Age pit. The time of the culture layer versus that of the house sites could not be defined clearly. For further soil features and excavation limits in the surroundings, see Fig. 2.2.B & C. B: Ground plans, cleaned. C: The topsoil was removed by machine over a larger area. After some rains, the surfaces of the sites and beyond were cleaned manually under harsh weather conditions for the excavation team. Seen from the southeast. D: The same area in a late stage of the investigation. The relatively deep sunken floors and disturbing pits now appear as marked holes with soil benches crossing. In the background, the Limfjord. Seen from the southwest.

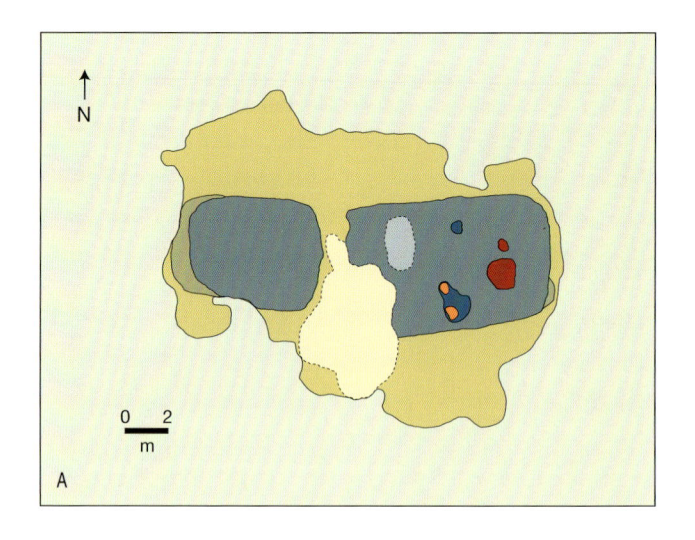

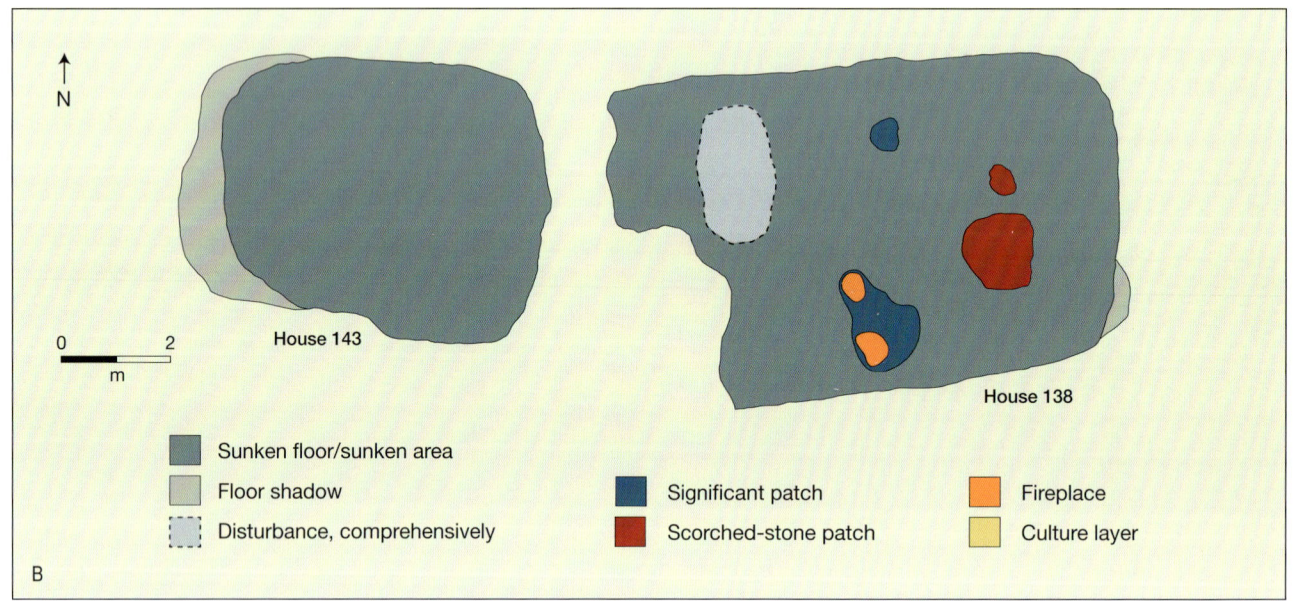

I presume it could originally have been significantly longer. No postholes belonging to the roof-bearing construction were found. Traces of doorways, compartments or dividing walls were not found.

No hints of burning of the house were found. I consider the research value of this house site to be modest as concerns the dwelling structure. The artefact remains are, however, quite valuable if you also include those from the secondary fills. The soil features and stone anvils are of moderate research value.

House 138 (Fig. 2.17)

Immediately west of the sunken area of House 138 another sunken floor was recorded, House 143. Adequate resources for the fieldwork were not available to fully clarify the complex stratification in the area, where an accumulated culture layer was also present.

However, it is my assumption that the construction of House 143, in particular, more or less destroyed the ground floor part of House 138. No other disturbances were observed from the time immediately after the abandonment of House 138 but a really large Bronze Age pit, in addition to another oval pit to the east of it, later caused the destruction of western parts of the sunken floor. Recent ploughing has probably eliminated postholes belonging to the walls of House 138 and 143. In all, several source-critical factors were thus active in relation to House 138.

The alignment of the building was E-W. The general terrain slope in the area was slightly towards the north, whereas locally the ground, as observable in a N-S soil bench, was markedly north-facing. The altitude difference between the long sides of the sunken floor was c. 22 cm. By the time of the investigation, a central sunken floor area lay at a depth of 38 cm but the original depth beneath the top of the old surface must have been significantly greater.

The preserved raw length of the house was identical to that of the sunken floor, which was likely a little longer. Due to the steepness of the sides, recent ploughing had probably not reduced its surface dimensions to the north, east and south. Its outline appears to indicate that the long sides of the house were parallel.

No postholes belonging to traces of the roof-bearing construction or stake- and postholes from the walls were found. Likewise no vestiges of doorways, compartments, dividing walls or other arrangements were observed.

No traces of burning of the house were observed. I rate the research value of this house site rather low as regards the dwelling structure. The artefact remainders and floor soil features are generally few but quite valuable in certain specific respects.

House 197 (Fig. 2.18)

Some or most of the pits in the area around the western ground-floor part were likely dug before House 197 was built but no postholes from its construction had cut through these. A large part of the sunken floor was ard-ploughed so deeply that the furrows could still be seen in the subsoil. This ploughing presumably disturbed the floor more than the relatively few directly observed ard-marks showed. Repeated ard-ploughing had probably intensified this disordering. In contrast, recent ploughing did not reach down into the sunken-floor horizon and hence did not cause any damage.

Judging in particular by certain postholes from the outer walls, the alignment of the building was E-W with the longitudinal axis turned a few degrees towards the NE-SW. The general slope of the ground in the area was towards the south and locally the ground, as observable in the N-S soil bench, was slightly south-facing too. The altitude difference between the long sides of the sunken floor was c. 10 cm. By the time of the investigation, a central sunken floor area lay at a depth of 19 cm but the original depth beneath the top of the old surface must have been greater.

In the western part of the house the traces of posts were only very sporadically preserved. A single posthole close to another posthole (or small pit) is considered to stem from the wall in the western gable end. Some postholes were found on each of the long sides, whereas none were observed in the eastern gable end. The raw length of the house was at least 18.3 m (presumably around 19 m), and the raw width about middle of the range for Resengaard Longhouses. The long sides appear to have been built fairly parallel.

A single posthole, considered to stem from a centre post, was found in the eastern half. Having traces of burned organic material, the postholes placed immediately west of the sunken floor away from the outer walls are, in my opinion, traces of a dividing wall. No obvious vestiges of doorways leading from outside to inside were found but it is my assumption that an area to the south had likely functioned as the interior access to the ground floor part to the west.

Another interesting trait is the spur towards the south in the eastern end. In my interpretation, it concerns a kind of "cubicle" placed within the turf

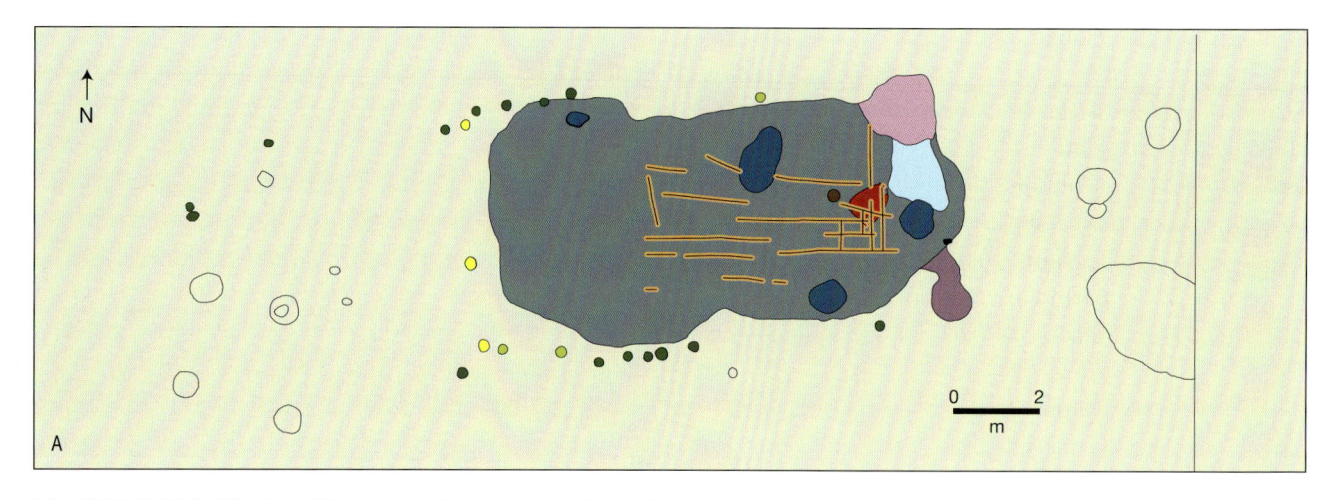

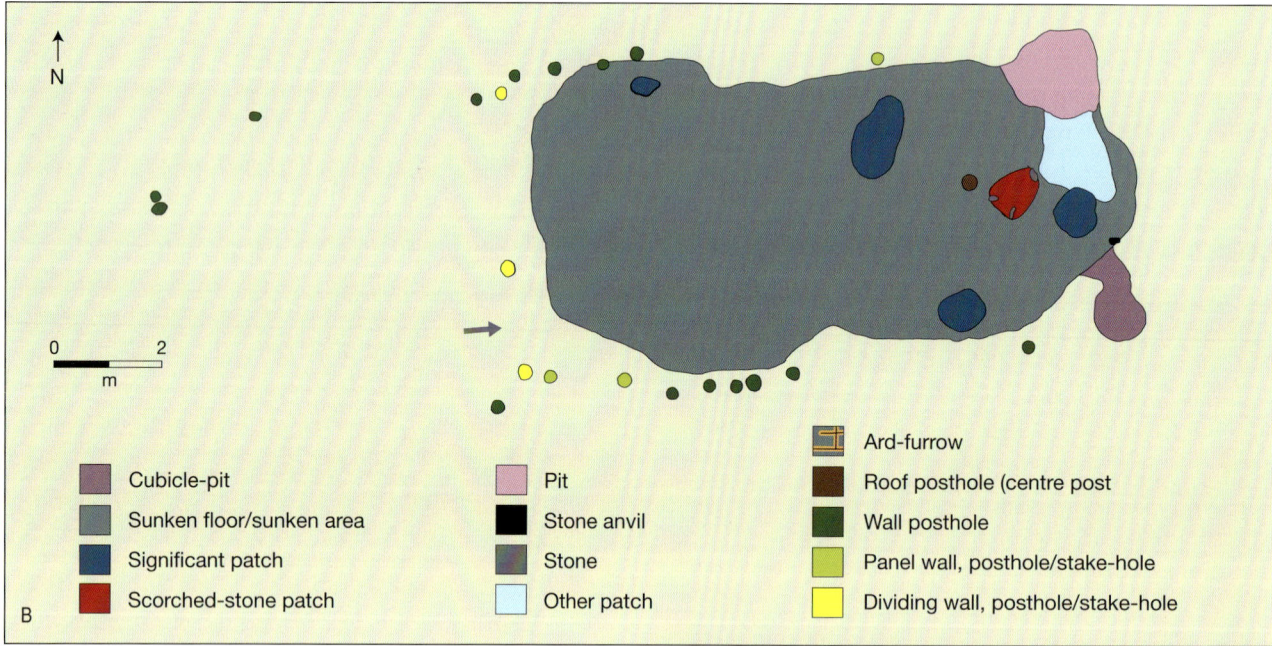

Fig. 2.18. Resengaard, House 197. A: Ground plan and older/younger soil features, including some pits to the west with interesting content (Fig. 3.30, 5.12 & 5.13). For further soil features and excavation limits in the surroundings, see Fig. 2.2.C. After demolition of the building, the sunken floor and beyond was affected by ard-ploughing. B: Ground plan, cleaned. The limit between the cubicle-pit to the southeast and the sunken floor does not represent a soil difference but is a line of interpretation. C: The house site after removing thick protecting soil as evidenced by the profile bench. For a soil section drawing, see Fig. 4.68.G. The second cleaning of the house site is being carried out. The way in which the ard-furrows extend beyond the sunken area to the west can be faintly seen. Seen from the west-northwest.

wall available in this southeast corner of the building. No clear-cut separation could be observed in relation to the sunken floor soil although this is tentatively suggested. Its horizontal dimensions were at least c. 1.4 x 0.9 m but the cubicle could well have been broader and more regular than indicated by the limits of its moderately sunken bottom. We shall later return to the pit in the northeast corner. Panel walls appear to have been present to the north as well as to the south.

90   Chapter 2

In relation to House 1, the question was earlier posed as to whether evidence was present for an extensive burning of the house. This question should also be asked in relation to House 197. During the investigation, it was understood that the house could be a candidate for the site of a fire. The dispersion of abundant charred grains was obviously due to ard-ploughing in the period after demolition of the house. The dark, almost black colour of the ploughed, sandy layer in the sunken area was likely coloured mainly by dust from these grains. We shall later return to these cereals. A few tiny pieces of charcoal were observed in the ard-ploughed floor horizon and this would be remarkable if the house had burned down. It is thus conspicuous that all wood from the house construction had completely disappeared without leaving substantial traces of charcoal or layers of ash.

As with House 1, no evidence of fire or heat impact was observed in the western part of the house site, which is interesting since House 197 was actually covered by a relatively thick, protective layer of soil. If the western end had burned down in an extensive fire, it would be expected that multiple traces of, for example, ash and charcoal from the construction would survive from such a fire. No reddish burning of the subsoil was recorded, either.

However, certain indications of fire were actually observed. That some of the postholes on both long sides showed traces of burned organic material in the top may surely support the notion that some kind of burning took place. As with the site of House 1, however, it concerned a limited number of stake- or postholes and was not a widely found feature of the soil. In my understanding, it is of crucial importance for the interpretation in this instance that postholes with indications of fire were completely absent from the central longitudinal axis of the house. In all, it has become my view that the building remainders are not to be considered a regular site of fire. The traces of fire on top of a few stake- and postholes thus likely represent a limited, deliberate burning of the remaining wooden scraps before ard-ploughing, when preparing the future field for agriculture.

Only a few soil patches in the floor contribute to our understanding of this longhouse site, but I consider the research value of it to be high in certain respects. Not least, the protective, thick soil accumulated above the house helps to limit the possible disturbances of the vestiges of posts. Regarding finds, the pottery in a pit to the northeast in particular is quite a valuable aspect of the site, and we shall return to this later on.

House 200 (Fig. 2.19)

No earlier occurrences such as pits and postholes were identified in the immediate surroundings of the site. A large granite stone placed a little above the sunken floor to the north stems from the time after the house was abandoned. Ard-ploughing also took place shortly after but only minor floor areas suffered moderate damage from this.

Immediately to the west was placed a minor sunken-floor building, House 201. It could not be directly ascertained from stratification as to whether it was later than House 200 or not. However, it is my hunch it was younger than House 200, as this latter building did not appear to have disturbed House 201. It would presumably have left traces if centre posts had been dug down into an only modestly deepened floor. Another argument is that the ard-ploughing into the sunken area of House 200 was not correspondingly present in the sunken area of House 201. Thirdly, the sunken floor of House 201 had clear boundaries and was not directly connected to the sunken area of House 200. Fourthly, the floor level was much higher than the rather deep level in House 200.

It therefore seems most probable that the construction of House 201 disturbed the supposed western ground floor of the site of House 200. No other prehistoric disturbances have been recorded. A broad, presumably medieval/post-medieval ditch cut across the narrow south part of the house site. However, it seems that recent ploughing has done a great deal of damage to the house site and removed postholes belonging to the walls.

The alignment of the building, judged solely by the sunken floor, was approx. E-W. The general slope of the ground was towards the northeast. Locally, as observable in a N-S soil bench, the ground was faintly north-facing. The altitude difference between the long sides of the sunken floor was only c. 4 cm. By the time of investigation, a central sunken floor area lay at a depth of 54 cm but the original depth beneath the top of the old surface must have been significantly greater.

It cannot safely be stated whether the long sides converged towards the west. However, I favour this assumption as the preserved sunken floor itself was trapezoidal. The raw length of the house site was only a little more than the raw length of the sunken floor, given the presence of the wall posthole to the east. The sunken floor was likely only slightly reduced in surface dimensions by recent ploughing, due to the

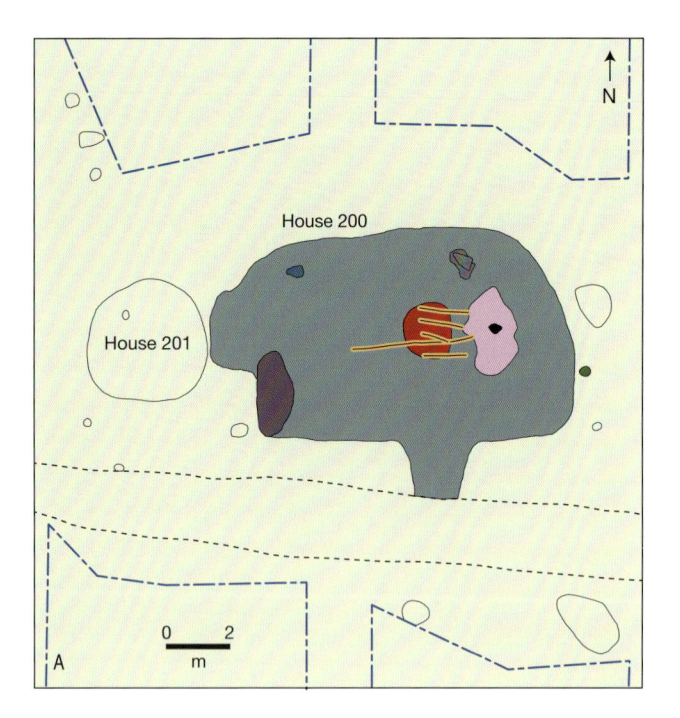

Fig. 2.19. Resengaard, House 200. A: Ground plan, older/younger soil features and nearby excavation limits. After demolition of the building, a minor area of the sunken floor had been disturbed by ard-ploughing. The house site showed significant impact from recent ploughing. From near the middle of the south side, a distinct shallow soil feature, interpreted as traces of a "corridor", was present. However, a later disturbing ditch had cut across its southernmost part. The short House 201 was found west of House 200. B: Ground plan, cleaned. C: The house site at a late stage of the investigation. The large stone was placed after abandonment and demolition of the building. Seen from the west-southwest. D: At a final stage of the excavation, a broad ditch was dug in front of the established N-S soil bench, whereby relationships between the soil and subsoil became clear. The N-S outline of the sunken floor is characteristic of many longhouses at the settlement. Seen from the east. E: This close up shows the characteristic rounding near the northern edge of the sunken floor in the N-S soil bench. Seen from the east.

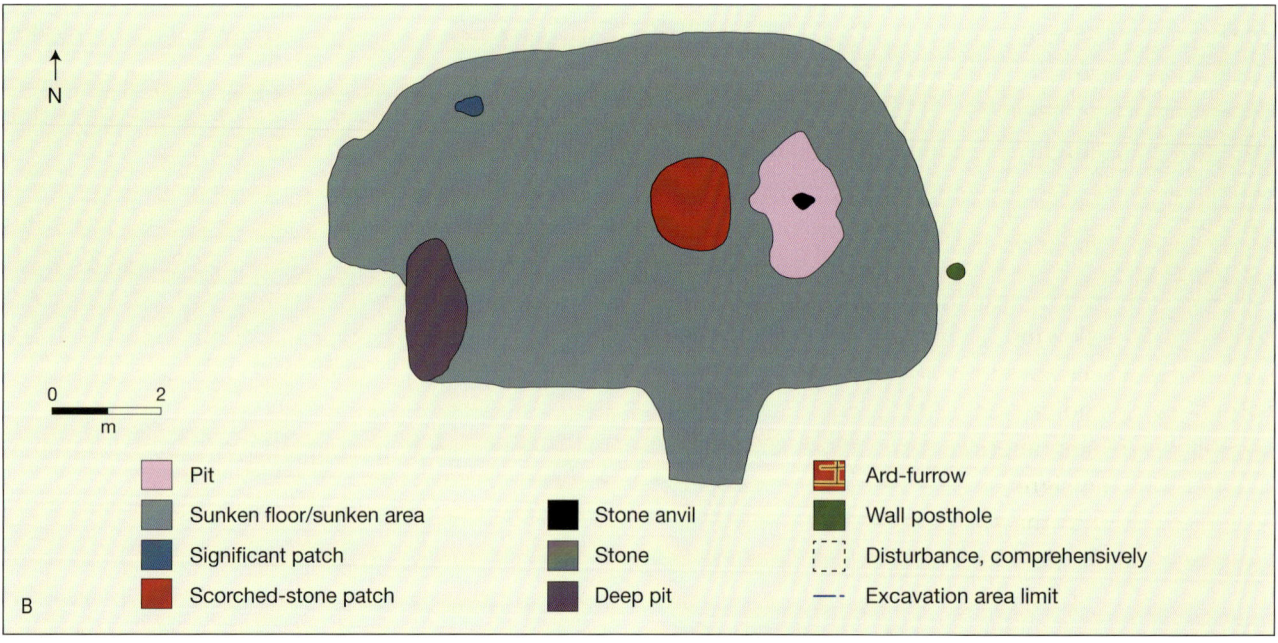

Pit	Stone anvil	Ard-furrow
Sunken floor/sunken area	Stone	Wall posthole
Significant patch		Disturbance, comprehensively
Scorched-stone patch	Deep pit	Excavation area limit

92 Chapter 2

relatively steep sides to the north, east and south. Not including the remarkable soil spur to the south, the raw width of the sunken floor was about middle of the range for longhouses at the settlement.

No postholes were preserved in the sunken part of the floor to guide an evaluation of the interior area. No traces of interior dividing walls or panel walls were thus observed. As to the question of entrances, I think it is unlikely that the extension of the sunken area a little east of the middle of the southern long side represents traces of an ordinary entrance to the house although this cannot be totally excluded. Instead I consider it marks out the traces of a gradually narrowing "corridor", c. 2.4-1.4 m wide, presumably leading to some kind of arrangement just outside the south wall but, unfortunately, we have no evidence of this physical detail.

No vestiges indicate that the house was burned. I rate the research value of this longhouse site to be relatively low as concerns traces of the dwelling structure. In contrast, the soil patches and artefact remainders of the sunken floor, including those from the secondary fills, are highly valuable.

Three minor houses with specific traits

Three sites of minor sunken-floor houses are presented in the following and a scorched-stone patch was found in each. Even though all three lack many of the features indicating their concrete construction and likewise their interior arrangements, they are actually of some significance in the sense that their presence points to the existence of such a group of buildings which, despite their limited dimensions, were supplied with a heating arrangement.

House 202 (Fig. 2.20)

The pits in the immediate vicinity are considered to mainly represent later disturbances and one of these had cut through the sunken floor to the east. A ditch of presumed medieval/post-medieval date crossed the southern and western part of the site and disturbed the fills above the sunken floor. Recent ploughing had probably removed the upper part of the sunken area and likely many postholes of the construction.

The alignment of the building, judging solely by the sunken floor, was E-W with the longitudinal axis turned somewhat to the NE-SW. The general as well as local slope of the ground was slightly towards the north. The altitude difference between the long sides

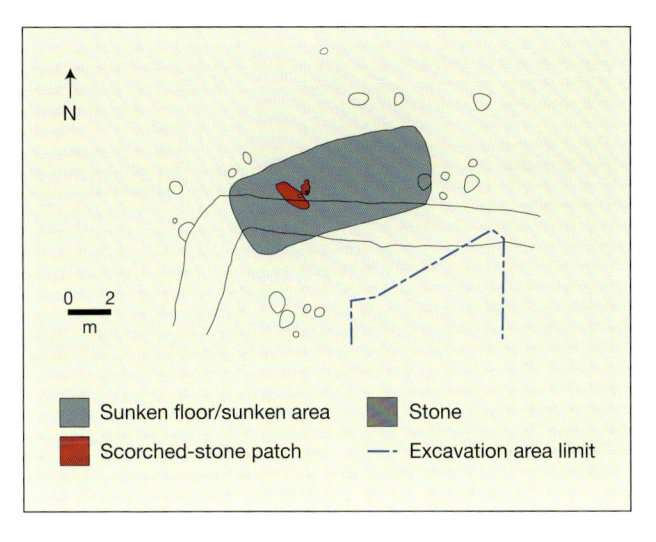

Fig. 2.20. Resengaard, House 202. Ground plan, older/younger soil features and nearby excavation limits. A medieval/post-medieval ditch as well as recent ploughing had had an impact on the house site. For further soil features and excavation limits in the surroundings, see Fig. 2.2.C. For a soil section drawing, see Fig. 4.68.H.

of the sunken floor was c. 6 cm. By the time of investigation, a central sunken floor area lay at a depth of 22 cm but the original depth beneath the top of the old surface could have been significantly greater.

The preserved raw length of the house is identical to that of the sunken floor. It is uncertain whether the house might also have had a ground-floor part to the west but it must be emphasized that no indications of such were observed. The width of the sunken floor was less than half its length and, judging by its outline, the long sides were presumably parallel. No traces of centre posts were found and likewise no wall postholes, dividing walls, traces of entrances or interior arrangements apart from patches with heat-affected/cracked stones.

No vestiges indicated that the house was burned. Apart from the presence of the aforementioned patches, I rate the research value of this house site to be rather low as concerns traces of the building structure and the artefact remainders, including the secondary fills, are only of modest research value.

House 240 (Fig. 2.21)

A large pit was present in the sunken floor to the north. It was c. 0.3 m deep but, unfortunately, it is not recorded in the plan drawing of the sunken-floor surface although it is documented in a sketch of the N-S cross-section. This later digging had disturbed the

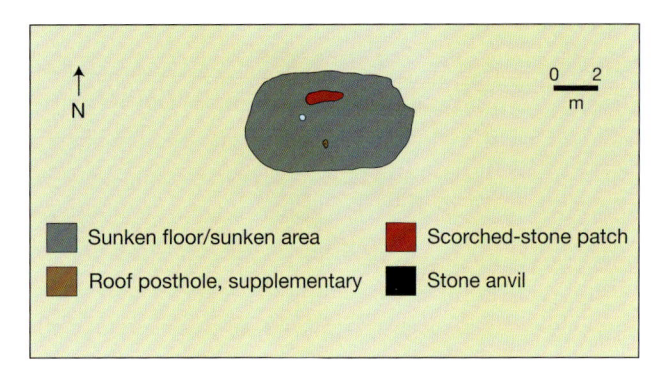

Fig. 2.21. Resengaard, House 240. Ground plan, cleaned. For house sites, soil features and excavation limits in the surroundings, see Fig. 2.2.C. For a cleaned ground plan with find spots, see Fig. 4.31.

uppermost part of a lengthy patch of soil with many heat-affected/cracked stones belonging to the sunken floor horizon. Apart from the disturbing pit, no ancient disturbances were observed in the sunken floor. It appears that recent agricultural activities had had a severe impact on the state of preservation because they had probably removed many postholes and reduced the depth of the sunken area.

The alignment of the building, judging solely by the sunken floor, was E-W. Generally and locally, the ground was almost horizontal, just slightly north-facing. The altitude difference between the long sides of the sunken floor was c. 6 cm. By the time of investigation, a central sunken floor area lay at a depth of 21 cm but the original depth beneath the top of the old surface must have been significantly greater.

The preserved raw length of the house was identical to that of the sunken floor. It is uncertain whether the house had also been supplied with a ground floor to the west. It should nonetheless be pointed out that no indications of such an area were found. Its width was a little more than half its length. Judging by the outline of the sunken floor the sides were presumably parallel.

In the sunken floor near the central longitudinal axis was found a single patch. It might represent a posthole that stems from a roof-bearing post although the depth of it was only few cm. It could concern the placement of an extra support for the roof because the construction might not originally have been two-aisled in this minor building. No traces of wall posts were found. The sunken floor was hardly any larger in surface dimensions, judging by the rather steep sides observed. No vestiges of interior panel walls, dividing walls or entrances were observed.

No traces indicate that the house was burned. I rate the research value of this house site to be rather low when it comes to traces of the building structure. The observable patches and not least the artefacts from the house site are, however, of considerable research value.

House 289 (Fig. 2.22)

The pits and postholes present in the immediate vicinity of the house site may, in some instances, have been contemporaneous, whereas others may be older as well as newer. Two postholes are considered to stem from the house construction. Yet, interestingly, it seems that no ancient factors damaged the sunken floor. In contrast, it appears that recent agricultural activities have done much damage, as they have probably removed many postholes and reduced the depth.

The alignment of the building, judging by the edges of the sunken floor and the placement of two postholes, was E-W. The general slope of the ground in the area was faintly towards the northeast. Locally, the ground, as observable in a N-S soil bench, was slightly north-facing. The altitude difference between the long sides of the sunken floor was c. 5 cm. By the time of investigation, a central sunken floor area lay at a depth of 39 cm but the original depth beneath the top of the old surface must have been significantly greater. From the outline of the sunken floor, it is possible that the sides were parallel although this cannot be stated with any certainty.

It is hardly excludable that some of the postholes may have belonged to a gable end in the area 4-6 m west of the sunken floor but, in my reading, these do not seem to be convincing traces of a western ground floor. In line with this view, the preserved raw length of the house only corresponded to the extent of the sunken floor. The raw width was just moderately less than the length.

No postholes from a roof-bearing construction were found in the sunken floor. Traces of doorways, panel walls, compartments, dividing walls, and other interior arrangements were absent, except the patch with heat-affected/cracked stones.

No relics indicated that the house was burned. Overall, I rate the research value of this house site to be low regarding traces of the building structure. The remainders of artefacts, including those from the secondary fills, are of moderate research value but interesting in certain respects.

Ten other minor houses

Minor house sites without the specific scorched-stone patches are presented in the following. Their minor sunken floors were, in some instances, severely marked by impact from source-critical factors. Some sites were flanked by wall postholes, evidencing houses of moderate width. This observation supports the assumption that these relics do not represent ploughed down longhouses. Due to the, by and large, general distance of 8 m between the trial trenches, it is likely that some minor or short sunken-floor house sites could have avoided recognition.

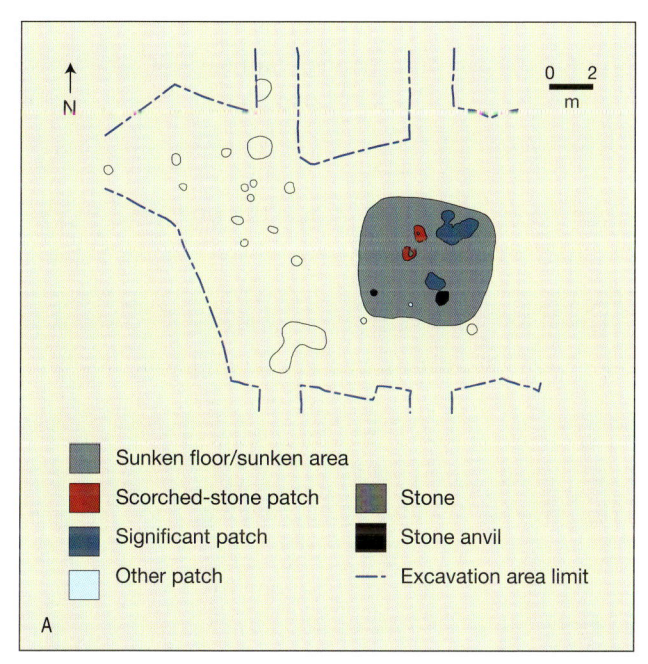

Fig. 2.22. Resengaard, House 289. A: Ground plan, older/younger soil features and nearby excavation limits. For further soil features and excavation limits in the surroundings, see Fig. 2.2.C. B: The eastern part of the sunken floor is visible in front of the established soil bench at a late stage of the investigation. Seen from the east.

House 10 (Fig. 2.23)

Some postholes of a three-aisled Bronze Age house penetrated the sunken area and went into the subsoil. To the southwest, a shallow pit had cut across the "floor shadow" and likewise another pit. An E-W running ditch of presumed medieval/post-medieval origin disturbed the southern part of the sunken floor. Later again, recent ploughing likely affected the house site by reducing the sunken floor surface dimensions and not least its depth.

The alignment of the building, judged solely by the sunken floor, was by and large E-W. Generally as well as locally, the ground was slightly south-facing. By the time of investigation, a central sunken floor area lay at a depth of 31 cm but the original depth beneath the top of the old surface must have been significantly greater.

It is unclear whether the house may also have had a more or less limited ground-floor part but no indications of such an area were found. The raw, preserved length of the house is thus identical to that of the sunken floor. The raw width was more than half the length. Yet, if the "floor shadow" to the south were included it would have resulted in a width of c. 4.8 m and would thus have come close to two-thirds of its length. From the outline of the sunken floor, it is possible that the long sides were parallel although this cannot be stated with any certainty. No postholes belonging to centre posts were found in the sunken

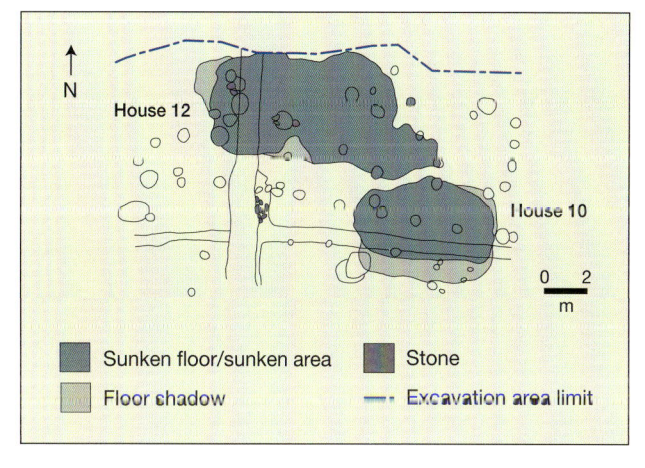

Fig. 2.23. Resengaard, House 10. A: Ground plan, older/younger soil features and nearby excavation limits. House 12 was excavated simultaneously. Disturbances on both sites caused by a three-aisled Bronze Age longhouse and medieval/post-medieval ditches. For further house sites, soil features and excavation limits in the surroundings, see Fig. 2.2.B & C. For a cleaned ground plan of House 10 with find spots, see Fig. 4.33.

Analysis and interpretation of houses with sunken floors **95** area. Traces of posts belonging to outer walls, panel walls, dividing walls or entrances were not observed.

No observations indicated that the house was burned. I rate the research value of the house site to be low as regards the building structure. On the other hand, the remainders of pottery from the floor, including those from the secondary fills, are highly valuable.

House 12 (Fig. 2.24)

Many postholes had been dug into the sunken area and subsoil, causing disturbance. In the western half of the sunken floor, several pits with heat-cracked stones and relatively dark soils had also caused some disturbance. These pits, and probably more or less all postholes, stem from a three-aisled house belonging to the Older Bronze Age. Crossing the house site N-S was, furthermore, a ditch system of medieval/post-medieval origin. Most severe, however, were the effects of recent ploughing, which had probably destroyed many postholes belonging to the house site. It is my estimate that up to a further c. 10 cm of the top-fill over the sunken floor on average had to be removed by means of machine during the initial excavation because the limits of the sunken floor were difficult to clarify.

The alignment of the building, judging in particular by the course of the sunken-floor edges, appears to have been approx. E-W. Generally and locally, the ground was slightly south-sloping. By the time of investigation, a central sunken floor area lay at a depth of 14 cm but the original depth beneath the top of the old surface must have been significantly greater. From the outline of the main part of the sunken floor, it is possible that the long sides were parallel. The preserved length of the house was identical only to that of the sunken floor. It is uncertain as to whether it also had a ground-floor part. No indications of such an area were found.

If the whole length of the sunken area were included it would reach some 10.5 m. However, I am not convinced that the southeast tongue of the entire soil patch actually belonged to the sunken floor. I presume that it did not mark out a sunken-floor part originally but, during fieldwork, it was not possible to observe any clear differences between the soils. When this tongue is ignored, the raw length of the sunken floor was almost 9 m. The width was more than half this length. No postholes from centre posts, outer walls, dividing walls or entrances were found.

No indications were observed as to burning of the house. I rate the research value of this site as low concerning preserved traces of the building structure and likewise the artefact remainders from secondary fills.

House 84 (Fig. 2.25)

Some ancient postholes and pits were present in the area of the house site. Six pits were dug into the sunken floor and contained compact concentrations of heat-affected stones; they likely belong to the classic Bronze Age. Recent agricultural activities may also have caused some disturbance but many wall postholes were still preserved.

Judging by the outline of the sunken floor and the wall postholes, the alignment of the building was approx. E-W. The general slope of the ground in the area was faintly towards the east. Locally, the ground was also slightly south-facing. The altitude difference between the long sides of the sunken floor was c. 5 cm. By the time of investigation, a central sunken floor area lay at a depth of 13 cm but the original depth beneath the top of the old surface could have been significantly greater.

The preserved raw length of the house was only moderately longer than the width and it was almost rectangular with nearly parallel long sides. The entrance area to the southeast appears to have been flanked to the east by some wooden posts, presumably the construction for a short wall. This element may have been established with the intention of creating shelter for some activities but other purposes cannot, of course, be excluded.

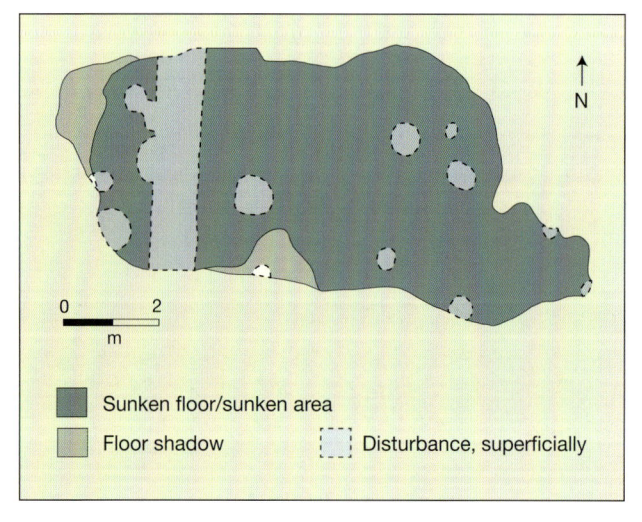

Fig. 2.24. Resengaard, House 12. A: Ground plan, cleaned. See also Fig. 2.23.

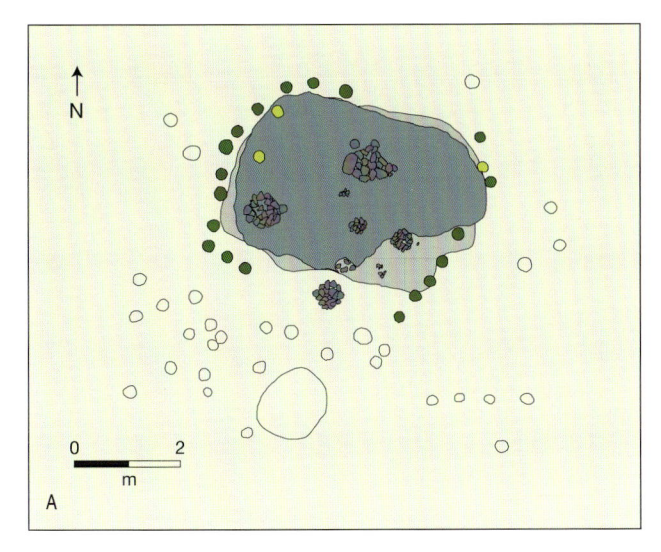

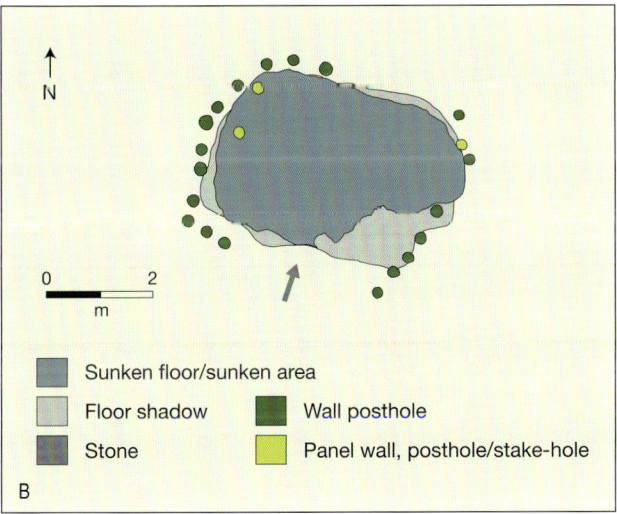

Fig. 2.25. Resengaard, House 84. A: Ground plan and older/younger soil features. For house sites, soil features and excavation limits in the surroundings, see Fig. 2.2.C. B: Ground plan, cleaned.

In particular, the western gable end seems complete as regards the preservation of postholes. The distance between the postholes was on average c. 0.47 m. The eastern gable end appears almost complete, presumably missing two postholes. The line of the northern side is indicated by three postholes, with four in the southern. Generally, the postholes were only a few cm deep but would, of course, have been deeper before impact from recent ploughing and cleaning at the beginning of the excavation. From the evidence of the surrounding wall postholes, the sunken floor took up all or practically all the floor area when including the "floor shadows". When it comes to the roof-bearing construction, no traces of centre posts were found. Vestiges of panel walls, dividing walls, and compartments were absent.

No traces indicated that the house was burned. I rate the research value of this house site to be relatively high with regard to traces of the building structure, whereas the artefact remainders are of very modest research value and no significant soil features belong to the sunken floor.

House 112 (Fig. 2.26)

Some pits and postholes were present in the area of the house site. A single pit with stone concentrations disturbed the middle of the sunken floor superficially and it likely belonged to the Bronze Age. Hence it is possible that some of the surrounding soil features could stem from this period too. Recent ploughing may have disturbed the upper part of the fills in the sunken area but many postholes were still more or less preserved. It thus seems that the house site was largely spared.

The alignment of the building, judging by the sunken area as well as the placement of wall postholes, was E-W with the longitudinal axis turned a few degrees towards the SE-NW. The general slope of the ground in the area was faintly towards the east. However, locally the ground was slightly north-facing. The altitude difference between the long sides of the sunken floor was c. 4 cm. By the time of investigation, a central sunken floor area lay at a depth of 22 cm but the original depth beneath the top of the old surface could have been significantly greater. The raw width of the house was about half its length. The long sides were parallel.

From the appearance, it is possible that it was supplied with a short ground floor to the west. The western edge of the sunken floor was extraordinarily regular and, in the main, parallel to the gable end row of postholes. It is therefore not unlikely that the house farthest to the west had a short ground-floor part. This interpretation seems favourable because even the western edge of the "floor shadow" formed a continuation of the western sunken-floor edge to the south.

The walls probably carried all the weight of the roof since no postholes belonging to centre posts were found. Concerning the walls, the rows of western and eastern gable end postholes were almost complete. The row of postholes in the eastern part of the northern side seems complete, while to the west only a single, somewhat diffuse posthole was observable. Two postholes in the middle of the south wall appear to have been drawn a little back towards the interior and

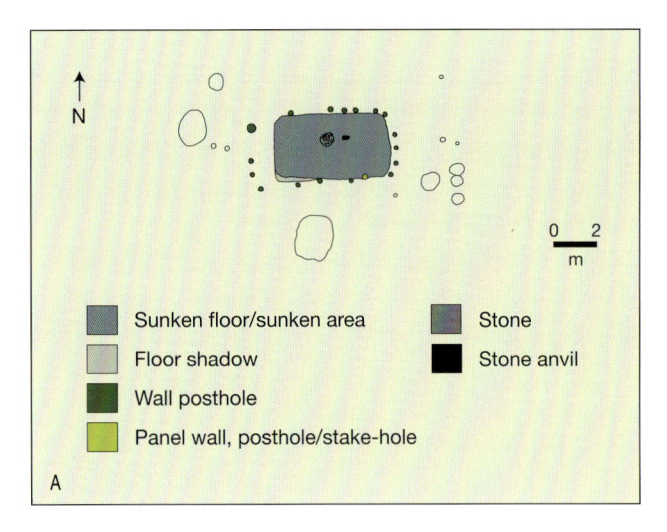

Fig. 2.26. Resengaard, House 112. A: Ground plan and older/younger soil features. Only very limited disturbances affected this house site. For house sites, soil features and excavation limits in the surroundings, see Fig. 2.2. B & C. For a cleaned ground plan with find spots, see Fig. 4.35. B: After removal of the topsoil, the surface of the sunken floor and its flanking postholes are being cleaned by Poul Mikkelsen and Ole Jensen prior to plan drawing. Seen from the east.

likely mark out the traces of an entrance. The postholes of the house site were generally only a few cm deep. No traces of panel walls, dividing walls, or compartments were found.

I rate the research value of this house site to be fairly high as concerns preserved traces of the building structure. The artefact remainders, including those from the secondary fills, are of more modest research value.

House 143 (Fig. 2.27)

According to the above considerations, the ground-floor part of House 138 must have previously been placed here and traces from its construction were very likely destroyed when building House 143. Recent ploughing had probably destroyed the upper parts of the sunken area, as well as many postholes.

Judging solely by the sunken floor, including the "floor shadow", the alignment of the building, was approx. E-W. The general and local slope of the ground in the area was slightly towards the north. The altitude difference between the long sides of the sunken floor was c. 10 cm. By the time of investigation, a central sunken floor area lay at a depth of 36 cm but the original depth beneath the top of the old surface must have been significantly greater.

The preserved length of the house was identical to the length of the sunken floor and no direct traces of any ground floor have been found. However, it is possible that it had a ground floor, perhaps short, due to the presence of the "floor shadow". The long sides were possibly parallel.

The sunken floor width was more than two-thirds the length. Due to the relatively steep sides, it is not presumed that the surface dimensions were much larger. No postholes belonging to traces of the construction were found and it was likely built without centre posts. Vestiges of panel walls, dividing walls, compartments and entrances were absent.

No traces indicated that the house was burned. I rate the research value of this house site very low as concerns traces of the building structure. The absence of artefacts from the sunken floor and the secondary fills prevents much discussion of this house.

House 158 (Fig. 2.28)

Apart from a minor pit containing some stones, only rather dispersed, undated soil features in the areas immediately surrounding the house were observed and none of these disturbed it. Recent ploughing appears to have affected the house site severely because it probably removed many wall postholes and minimized the depth of the sunken floor. The extent of it could also have been larger originally.

The alignment of the building, judging solely by the outline of the sunken floor, was approx. E-W. The house is unusual in its placement on markedly sloping terrain but the plot was presumably quite deliberately chosen. Generally and locally, the ground was thus largely east facing but moderately to the south, too. The altitude difference between the long sides of the sunken floor was c. 14 cm. By the time of investigation, a central sunken floor area lay at a depth of 44 cm but the original depth beneath the top of the old surface could have been significantly greater. When comparing the sunken floor depth with the west end, it could even have been markedly deeper, due to the marked terrain sloping to the east.

The preserved length of the house was identical to that of the sunken floor. Vague and uncertain traces of soil such as that of the sunken floor came to light during the initial cleaning of the ground, indicating that the building might perhaps have been longer. If these "floor shadows" are also taken into consideration, it can be assumed that the sides were parallel although of course this cannot be stated with any certainty.

It is unclear whether the house could also have had a western ground-floor part and no indications of that were observed. I find the existence of a substantial such floor part unlikely.

Judging by the sunken floor, the raw width was around two-thirds its raw length. Postholes from centre posts, outer walls, panel walls, dividing walls, compartments or doorways were not found.

No vestiges indicated that the house was burned. I rate the research value of this house site to be low as concerns preserved traces of the building structure but its placement outermost to the southeast, as well as a few interesting artefacts belonging to the sunken floor and secondary fills, might indicate that the building had an interestingly special function.

House 183 (Fig. 2.29)

Much uncertainty surrounds the traits of this structure. During excavation the question even initially arose as to whether it was a house site at all. The discussion came about due to finds in the upper part. A stone concentration, including relatively small stones, was thus found in the central sunken part along with a granite grinder and brownish sandy soil. The surface dimensions of the stone concentration (not illustrated) were c. 2.65 x 1.35 m. The stones did not seem affected by heat. In the bottom of the sunken area below this concentration was found 2-4 cm soil of another character. In my opinion, this relates to an undated, secondarily deposited stone concentration that was placed on top of the sunken area without any connection to the functional phase of the house. Near the site were found some dispersed pits and postholes without significant finds.

No other ancient disturbances of the sunken area were recorded. Recent ploughing had probably reduced the dimensions of the sunken floor and re-

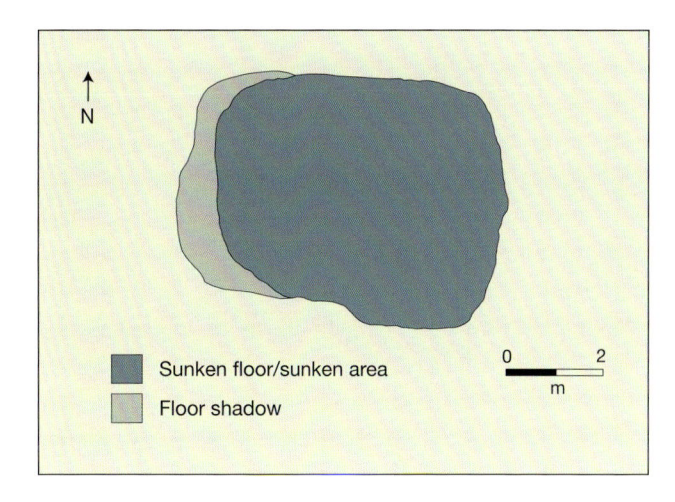

Fig. 2.27. Resengaard, House 143. Ground plan, cleaned. For house sites, soil features and excavation limits in the surroundings, see Fig. 2.2.B & C as well as Fig. 2.17.

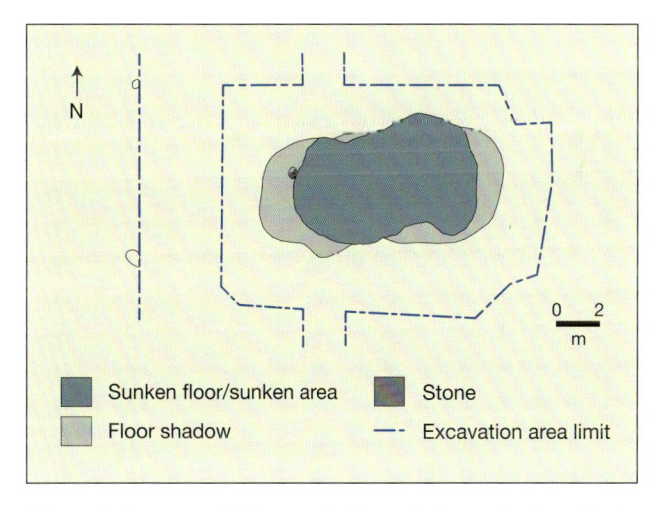

Fig. 2.28. Resengaard, House 158. Ground plan and a few older/younger soil features as well as nearby excavation limits. Though highly uncertain, the "floor shadows" could perhaps indicate that the house had been longer than revealed by the preserved sunken area. For further house sites, soil features and excavation limits in the surroundings, see Fig. 2.2.C. For a soil section drawing, see Fig. 4.68.I.

moved several wall postholes. This annual agricultural activity could easily have removed upper parts of the stone concentration too.

The alignment of the structure, judging by the course particularly of the row of postholes south of the sunken floor, was approx. E-W. The general and local slope of the ground in the area was slightly towards the south. By the time of investigation, a central sunken floor area lay at a depth of 37 cm but the original depth beneath the top of the old surface could have been significantly greater.

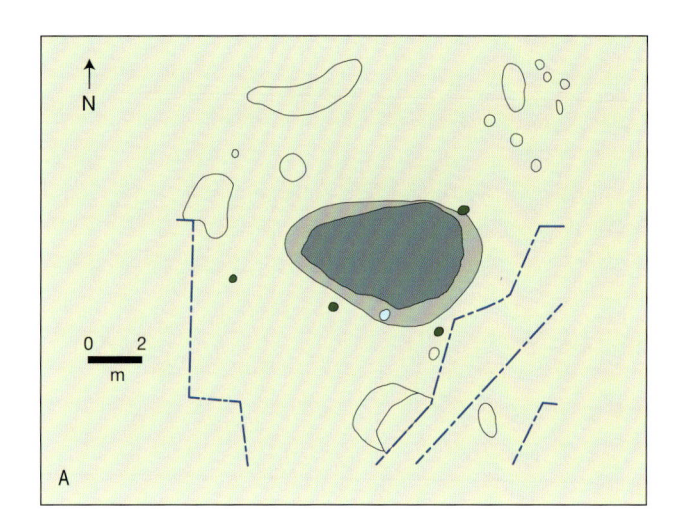

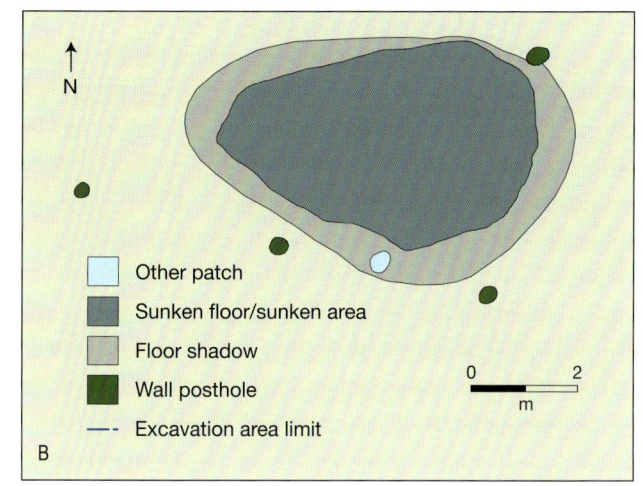

Fig. 2.29. Resengaard, House 183. A: Ground plan, older/younger soil features and nearby excavation limits. A secondarily placed stone concentration covering central parts of the house site is not shown on this plan drawing. For further house sites, soil features and excavation limits in the surroundings, see Fig. 2.2.C. B: Ground plan, cleaned.

Based also on the southern row of postholes, the preserved raw length of the building could have been at least c. 7.6 m. Whether the long sides were parallel or not cannot be estimated. The "floor shadow" indicates a somewhat larger sunken floor. No traces of centre posts, panel walls, dividing walls, compartments or entrances were observed.

No vestiges indicated that the house was burned. In all, I rate the research value of this house site to be very low as concerns traces of the building structure. Soil patches were absent from the sunken floor and the artefact remainders are of modest research value.

House 193 (Fig. 2.30)

Some pits and postholes, mostly undated, were found to the east and southeast in the immediate surroundings of the house site without disturbing it. To the west were observed some ditches, presumably from the medieval or post-medieval period and these did not disturb the house site either. Nearby, to the southwest, were found more pits, not least structure 160, see further on. Recent ploughing must have removed a number of postholes in the wall lines and, in all probability, also diminished the sunken floor area greatly. The sides of the sunken floor were thus only slightly risen towards the sides and even minor ploughing of the top would have reduced its length and width considerably. I presume that the sunken floor originally occupied at least some two-thirds of the interior house length, or maybe even all of it.

The alignment of the building, judging particularly by the postholes of the long sides, was almost E-W. The general and local slope of the ground in the area was slightly towards the southeast. By the time of the investigation, a central sunken floor area lay at a depth of 8 cm but the original depth beneath the top of the old surface must have been significantly greater.

The outer wall postholes were preserved to such a degree that the raw dimensions of the house can be stated. Generally, the postholes were only a few cm deep. The raw width of the house corresponds to more than half the raw length of the house. The long sides appear to have been fairly parallel.

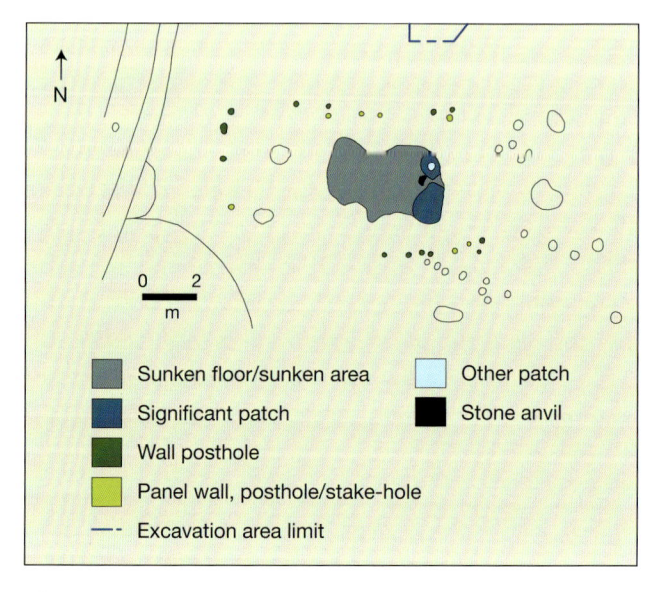

Fig. 2.30. Resengaard, House 193. Ground plan and older/younger soil features. For further house sites, soil features and excavation limits in the surroundings, see Fig. 2.2.C & 4.38.

No traces of centre posts were found in the interior and the walls likely carried all the weight of the roof. Interestingly, it appears that sporadic vestiges of panel walls have been preserved to the north, southeast, and also to the west, although there is only one posthole. Vestiges of dividing walls, compartments, or doorways were not observed.

No traces indicate that the house was burned. I rate the research value of this house site to be relatively high as concerns traces of the building. Interestingly, in the site of this minor building, some significant soil patches were recorded in the eastern part of the sunken floor and this adds to the research value of the site. The few artefacts, including those of the secondary fills, are of moderate research value.

House 198 (Fig. 2.31)

To the south and southwest of the sunken floor in particular, the presence of several undated pits and postholes were recorded. In the eastern part of the sunken floor three later pits had cut across the secondary fills and all went into the subsoil. In the western end, a single later pit also cut across the floor as did also a few postholes elsewhere. Recent ploughing had probably removed many postholes belonging to traces of the construction and may have reduced the dimensions of the sunken floor as well.

The alignment of the building, judging solely by the sunken floor, was E-W. Generally, the ground in the area was sloping towards the northeast but, locally, the ground was somewhat south-facing. The altitude difference between the long sides of the sunken floor was c. 20 cm. By the time of investigation, a central sunken floor area lay at a depth of 17 cm but the original depth beneath the top of the old surface must have been significantly greater.

The preserved length of the house was identical to that of the sunken floor. It is unclear as to whether it might also have had a ground floor although no indications of this were observed. The raw width of it appears to have been about two-thirds of its length. Whether the long sides were parallel cannot be stated from the outline of the sunken floor. No postholes belonging to centre posts, outer walls, panel walls, dividing walls, compartments or entrances were observed.

No traces indicate that the house was burned. I rate the research value of this house site to be rather low as concerns traces of the building structure. The artefact remainders, being mostly from the secondary fills, are of moderate research value.

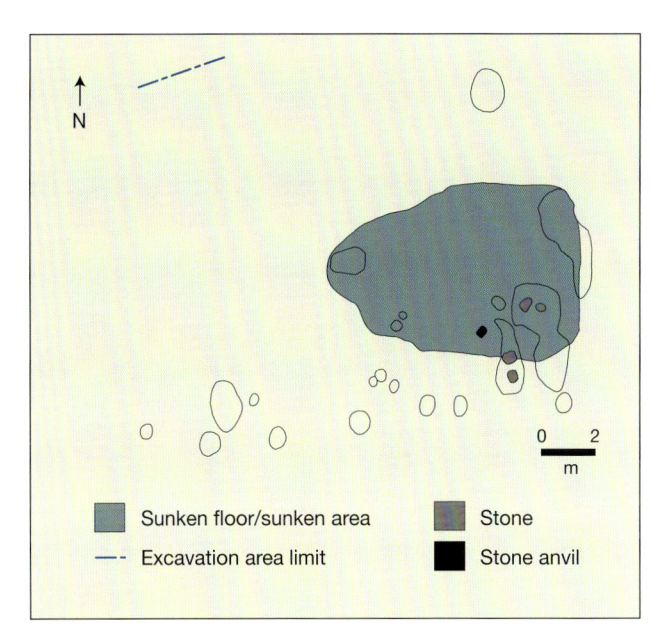

Fig. 2.31. Resengaard, House 198. Ground plan, older/younger soil features. The house site suffered somewhat from the digging of later pits and recent ploughing. For further house sites, soil features and excavation limits in the surroundings, see Fig. 2.2.C.

House 268 (Fig. 2.32)

Much digging of pits (undated, some even rather large, along with a number of postholes from prehistory and perhaps later on) has spoiled the area around, and not least west of, the sunken floor. A later, irregular pit has cut through the northwest floor part. To the east, a N-S aligned ditch, presumably of medieval/post-medieval origin, may have destroyed postholes at the gable end. Recent ploughing has likely reduced the surface dimensions and removed many wall postholes.

Judging by the sunken floor alone, the alignment of the house was approx. E-W. Generally and locally, the ground in the area was almost flat. By the time of investigation, a central sunken floor area lay at a depth of 18 cm but the original depth beneath the top of the old surface must have been significantly greater.

Any indications of a ground floor to the west were not identified. The raw width of the sunken floor corresponded to about two-thirds of its raw length. Based on the outline of the sunken floor, it is not possible to state whether the long sides of the house were parallel or not. Postholes belonging to centre posts, panel walls, dividing walls, compartments or entrances were not found.

No observations indicated that the house was burned. With regard to traces of the building struc-

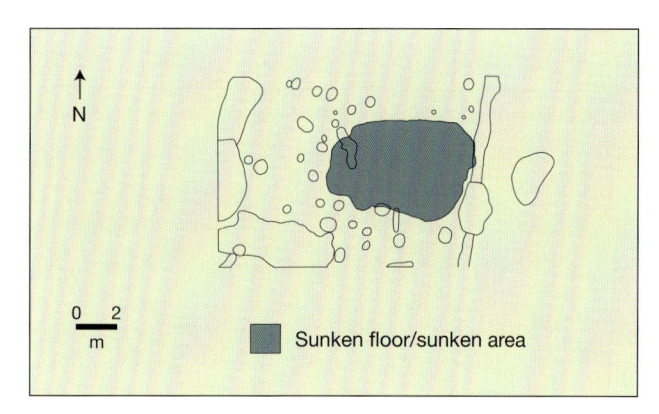

Fig. 2.32. Resengaard, House 268. Ground plan and older/younger soil features. For further house sites, soil features and excavation limits in the surroundings, see Fig. 2.2.C.

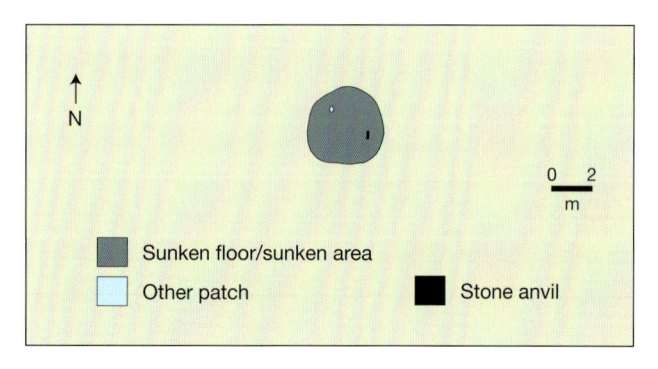

Fig. 2.33. Resengaard, House 201. Ground plan, cleaned. The house site had suffered greatly from recent ploughing. For a ground plan also showing older/younger soil features and nearby excavation limits, see Fig. 2.19. A. For further house sites, soil features and excavation limits in the surroundings, see Fig. 2.2.C. For a soil section drawing from this site, see Fig. 4.68.J.

ture, I rate the research value of this house site as rather low. The absence of significant soil patches in the sunken floor substantiate the low grading although the artefact remainders, in particular those from the secondary fills, are of fine research value.

A short house

Like the foregoing, this house site had no scorched-stone patches in the sunken-floor horizon. It marks out the only site of a short house found at the Resengaard hill although, compared with the above group of buildings, it is even more likely that several short house sites may have been missed, due to their limited dimensions. Such building remainders, of less than five metres in length, may thus well have avoided recognition given the eight metres between the trial trenches.

House 201 (Fig. 2.33)

No pits, postholes or ditches disturbed the house site. Recent ploughing had probably removed the top of the sunken area and some wall postholes but had hardly reduced the surface dimensions of the sunken floor.

The general slope of the ground in the area was towards the northeast. Locally, the ground was somewhat north-facing. The altitude difference of the sunken floor between the northern and southern edge was c. 11 cm. By the time of investigation, a central sunken floor area lay at a depth of 15 cm but the original depth beneath the top of the old surface must have been significantly greater.

No traces of any ground-floor part were found. The sunken floor was sub-circular in area, albeit with a short, straight side to the south. The site had a length E-W of c. 3.74 m and a width of c. 3.66 m. No postholes belonging to vestiges of centre posts, outer walls, panel walls, compartments or entrances were observed.

A relationship to House 200 above was considered and argued for. It might be added that, in contrast to this longhouse – with its many remainders of pottery and other things on the floor horizon – no artefacts were recovered from the context of the sunken floor of House 201, except a semi-buried stone, considered to be an anvil (see Ch. 4).

Nothing indicated that the house was burned. I rate the research value of this house site to be rather low as concerns traces of the building structure. The artefact remains, when also including the few belongings from secondary fills, are only of modest research value.

Two uncertain structures

North of house sites 13, 42 and 197, it seems likely that Late Neolithic settlement left its traces in the course of a local street built somewhat before the archaeological excavation. Some finds in a private collection allegedly stem from there but whether any house sites were present we do not know. Further, it cannot be fully excluded that a culture layer not far from House 143, investigated only with a limited trial trench, could represent the remains of a larger sunken floor but, in my judgment, this was not the case and I shall not take it into further consideration. However, after finalizing the investigations at Resengaard, I have reconsidered two areas in particular. The question is whether the findings are to be regarded as leftovers from house sites? This relates to pit 156 at the northwest terrace and pit 160 (together with nearby pits) at the hill plateau.

Pit 156 – remainders of a minor house? (Fig. 2.34)

It is obvious to reconsider whether the quite sizeable pit 156, placed west of House 41 and near the edge of the northwest terrace, could represent a minor sunken-floor house because it possessed some of the relevant marks, even though it cannot be dated from artefact finds.

The length of the E-W aligned pit was c. 7.0 m and its observable width 5.4 m. To the north a small part of it was not excavated but the width of the pit was presumably c. 6 m. It was relatively flat-bottomed but levels of the pit bottom were not recorded because, during fieldwork, the excavation team agreed that the "clean" fill, the bottom without artefacts, and the absence of soil patches did not support the possibility that it might represent a house site. The investigated area may just represent a raw material pit for digging up sand but, in any case, I prefer to keep open the possibility that the sizeable pit could form the relics of a minor house site.

Pit 160 – remainders of a longhouse? (Fig. 2.35)

It is also obvious to reconsider whether pit 160, together with certain nearby pits, represents the remains of an E-W aligned longhouse with a sunken floor to the east.

The possible sunken floor could have had a length of around 12.80 m when including feature 196. It is conceivable that the nearby pit 161 also marked out remains that could have belonged to this. However, pit 161 was very wide N-S, while its depth was only a few cm. It can hardly be excluded that some postholes to the west might indicate a ground floor with a raw length of some 6.80 m (or perhaps more). No special soil patches of the possible sunken floor were recorded. It was flat-bottomed but levels were not recorded because it was not acknowledged as a possible sunken floor. Unfortunately, the investigation was carried out over several seasons and the disturbances from, in particular, the presumed medieval/post-medieval ditches also impeded a proper interpretation. A longitudinal E-W soil bench with covering top soils would, in this case, have been very useful.

As a matter of precaution, I have chosen to treat structure 160 and nearby pits as representing pits with accumulations of rubbish, albeit without discarding the idea that it could represent a house site. No postholes for centre posts were found, no indications of burning were recorded and no traces of ard-ploughing were observed in the bottom. Potsherds, flint waste and stones were found in the pit.

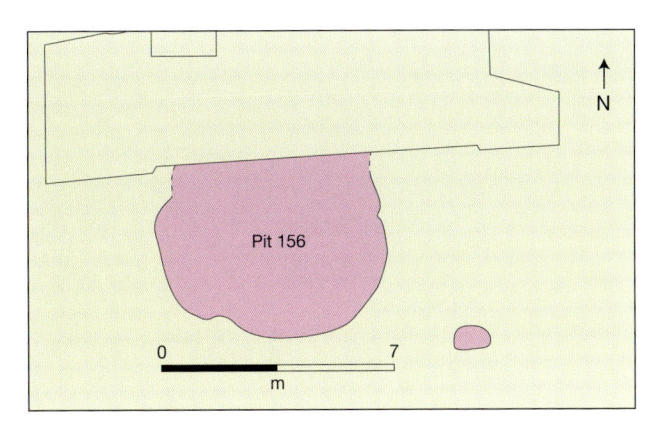

Fig. 2.34. Resengaard, pit 156, possibly the site of a minor house. Found near the sites of Houses 1, 2 and 41. For house sites, soil features and excavation limits in the surroundings, see Fig. 2.2.C.

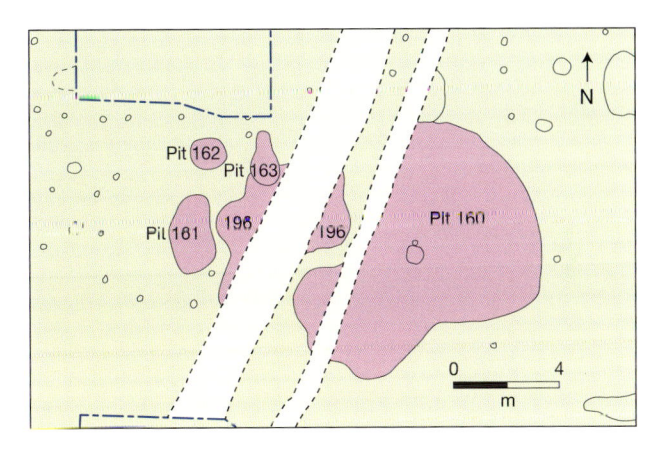

Fig. 2.35. Resengaard, pit 160 (plus 196, 161 and 162), a possible house site. For house sites, soil features and excavation limits in the surroundings, see Fig. 2.2.C.

2.3. Elements of the Resengaard houses

We shall now turn to some of the significant elements of the sunken-floor houses at Resengaard, in particular, but begin by clarifying some characteristic dimensions and physical traits of the main group of sunken-floor longhouses in the Late Neolithic and emerging Bronze Age in the central Limfjord region and beyond (Fig. 2.36). This overview will offer a better platform for observing the similarities and differences between the many new settlements presented further below.

Sunken-floor longhouses in brief

Small sunken-floor longhouses of a maximum 25 m length appear to have prevailed in the Limfjord region. In brief, these buildings appear to have had rather sig-

Construction details

Location		House	Two building phases	Repair phase	Supplementary centre post	Panel wall	Dividing wall	Compartment	Entrance	Interior doorway	Recess	Corridor	Cubicle
Resengaard	Longhouses	1		x	x	x		x	x	(x)			
		2	x			x		x	x	x	x		
		13			x	x					x		
		14					x			(x)			
		41	x			x		x	(x)				
		42											
		128				x							
		130											
		134				(x)							
		138											
		197					x			(x)			x
		200										x	
	Minor houses with scorched-stone patches	202											
		240											
		289											
	Minor houses	10											
		12											
		84							(x)				
		112							x				
		143											
		158											
		183											
		193				x							
		198											
		268											
	Short house	201											
Gåsemose		1											
Kluborg II		5			x				(x)				
Glattrup I/III		5											
		6											
Marienlyst Strand		1											
Granlygård		2											
		3											
		6											
Hellegård		122											
		35											
Glattrup IV		3			x	x							
		5				x			x				x
		7											x
Rosgårde		1				x			x				
Tromgade		1											
		2											
		414											

104 Chapter 2

◀ *Fig. 2.36. Evidence of building elements from ten settlements, the central Limfjord region. Traces of panel walls, compartments, recesses, entrances, and some other traits were seldom found despite the relatively fine preservation of many house sites. An "x" designates presence, while an "(x)" indicates some uncertainty of presence. The well-preserved sites of longhouses on the northwest terrace at Resengaard particularly stand out, with relatively broad representation of elements as well as evidence of building phases. The vestiges of an entrance south of the ground floor in the site of House 5 at Glattrup IV are very unusual.*

nificant common traits as regards certain constructional features and dimensions. In addition to this, the variations as to construction seem to have been chiefly within certain frames. When speaking of buildings belonging to the main group of longhouses in the Late Neolithic and emerging Bronze Age in the region, they were usually aligned in an E-W direction with the sunken floors placed to the east. Including the ramp, these sunken floors in the longhouses would usually have embraced between c. 40-70% of the original raw house length. In the longhouses, the sunken floors generally appear to have included the entire interior width along most of their length.

At Resengaard, the sunken floor of house 200 was one of the deepest. On the whole, the sunken floors of the longhouses in the region appear to have had depths of between 0.15 – 0.95 m into the subsoil, depending also on the method of measurement. Many sunken floors would, however, have originally come close to a depth of half a metre below the subsoil surface.

The outer wall posts were not usually deeply dug down, and we often find them quite shallow during excavation. The long side walls were, in some cases, parallel or nearly parallel but, in other cases, markedly diverging from each other. The longhouse constructions were generally two-aisled whereas examples of sites of minor and short sunken-floor houses with traces of centre posts are by and large absent from the central Limfjord region.

The favoured ground plan proportions appear to have been within certain frames. The average width of the individual longhouses did not exceed half their length, judging by the well-preserved house sites. In the minor houses, i.e. those buildings of 5 m or more in length but less than 10 m, the width often ranged from about half to two-thirds of its length. The sunken floor in the only site of a short house from Resengaard was of almost equal length and width. In two well-preserved sites of minor houses (84 & 112) at Resengaard, the sunken floors took up most of the interior length.

Regular clay floors have never been found in the Resengaard houses or any of the other house sites studied from the central Limfjord region. The existing sand and, in a few instances, clayey subsoil simply mark out the basic floor bottoms.

Burned house versus burned house scrap

Sites of longhouses that caught fire by accident are often among the most valuable sources of information from the past. Sites of such buildings deliberately set on fire can also be very informative (*cf.* Chapman, J. 1999). These will often, unsurprisingly, be of relatively lower research value, however, because the residents may have had time to remove valuable belongings.

In my view, we have no evident traces at Resengaard of the former, i.e. buildings that burned down accidentally. In the above house presentations I proposed in three instances that evidence of burning was available. I consider the fires in all three longhouse as having been deliberately ignited after abandonment. In two instances, the available traces merely indicated limited burning of various scrap. I thus suggest the interpretation that only in one case did it concern a regular site of fire, namely the site of House 2, where residues of coal dust over the sunken floor showed extensive traces of fire. It is my understanding that the fires could very well have been of a ritual nature.

As regards the two other house sites (1 & 197), we saw vestiges of burning only in certain limited areas. Yet these two sites still offer a kind of "snapshot" of the stakes and posts that actually appear to have burned down on one and the same occasion. These traces of fire can thus testify to the simultaneous functioning of certain house elements. In a few instances, these qualities have now provided concrete input into our understanding of longhouse elements such as doorways, panel walls, and dividing walls.

Two-aisled constructions

The postholes from the roof-bearing construction along the central longitudinal axis were placed at varying intervals in the longhouses and, to some degree, likely mirrored the expected use of the floor areas and interior arrangements. In the vicinity of the central longitudinal axis, we have in some instances found soil features that I have interpreted as vestiges of extra supporting posts or repair posts, presumably placed later during the functional use of the building when the original construction became weaker.

Taking House 1 at Resengaard as an example, the postholes in the ground floor to the west, as well as in the bottom of the sunken floor, were circular or sub-circular (Fig. 2.8). The diameters were around 30-45 cm, and the depths from the cleaned surface approx. 12 -38 cm. The eastern postholes would have lost some of their depth when the sunken floor gradually deepened during habitation. In this house, in all 6 roof-bearing posts were placed along the central longitudinal axis. In my interpretation, an extra set of 4 supporting posts would then later have been placed south of the central longitudinal axis after the building had been in use for some time.

In the site of House 13, with its extraordinarily well-preserved traces of wall postholes, 6 centre posts were also placed in the same manner. In other cases, the numbers of preserved and observable postholes for centre posts were fewer. In the ground-floor parts, this would often be due to the impact of recent ploughing and other destructive factors while, in my understanding, in the sunken floors it could frequently stem from the residents´ activities as these gradually lowered parts of the floors so much that the post ends became less and less buried, until they finally stood free.

Interestingly, the situation in the site of House 2 indicates that the centre posts were removed before the longhouse was deliberately set on fire. It would seem reasonable to want to save these strong wooden posts. If we presume this was a usual action before deliberate burning, it clearly implies that these posts were not used for the construction of the new longhouse if the old longhouse was still in use for a period thereafter. Yet these posts would presumably have been kept for later purposes instead.

Outer wall posts

The postholes of the outer wall likely belonged directly to the house construction as opposed to the traces of panel walls facing the interior. In order to present an outline of these postholes, House 1 can again serve as an example (Fig. 2.8). The surface diameters of the outer wall postholes were mostly 16-28 cm and the soil mainly brownish-grey. Many postholes were preserved in the long sides as well as in the western gable end but, evidently, some holes were not deep enough to be recorded during excavation. The depths into the subsoil were mostly 8-12 cm but some of the above soil was removed during the initial excavation and the postholes were therefore somewhat deeper originally. The corner-postholes preserved to the west were placed a little closer than on the long sides. Just like the centre posts, the shallow outer wall holes would not have lent the wooden posts much stability to pressure from the sides. Another example of shallow postholes from the outer walls concerns House 13 (Fig. 2.10). The wall postholes of the minor sunken-floor houses were also shallow, as exemplified by those of House 193 at Resengaard (Fig. 2.30).

At Resengaard, we have no evident examples of double rows of postholes, whereby two posts were repeatedly placed relatively close together, one inner and one outer. Instead, outer wall posts formed one constructional system, while panel wall stake- or postholes formed another system facing the interior.

Interior panel wall stakes and posts

I argue that in the longhouses at Resengaard panel walls probably often bounded the interior spaces. This is not least likely to have been the case of the walls surrounding the sunken areas, but we also have some evidence of stake- and postholes indicating the existence of such walls flanking ground floors to the west. That preserved, observable vestiges of such walls are generally sporadic is probably also due to the prevalence of sandy grounds around most house plots. Now and then during the investigations, some uncertain stake-hole-like changes in the soil were seen at some house sites but discarded because it was not, in these instances, convincing that the observations actually did represent stake-holes.

The most illustrating case of traces of constructions, interpreted as stake-holes belonging to two successive panel walls, was recovered from the site of House 1, with a partly clayey subsoil floor. This concerns 38 stake-holes in all, of which two were placed quite close together and could not be separated. The panel wall posts were recorded to the east along the southern long side and a few by the eastern gable end to the south. In the older panel wall, the surface dimensions of the holes and the internal distances were less than in the newer, whereas only the newer was marked by fire. I shall now describe vestiges of these two-stake systems (Fig. 2.8).

Most northerly to the east, a row of 7 slightly larger stake-holes was found in a row, being the main part of the younger system. The most eastern had a diffuse edge. The stake-hole diameters were c. 7-8 cm and appeared with a relative dark soil coloured by tiny pieces of charcoal and dust from carbonized material. Probably thin stakes, hammered down into the subsoil, had burned to a low level where our first observations were done during the excavation. The stake-holes were recorded at c. 36-64 cm distance but, in the longer intervals, I do not exclude that additional stakes were originally placed in between, albeit unrecordable for us. A single stake-hole considered to belong to this panel wall phase was found more to the north in the gable end.

The older row of panel wall stakes had been positioned closer to those of the outer wall and the traces consisted of very many stake-holes, 30 in all, and their diameters were c. 5-8 cm. They appeared with a greyish, sandy soil and some had been placed at almost equidistant intervals. As the subsoil here was also clayey, the stakes in my reading had been hammered down without the digging of holes.

This would imply that the diameters of the stakes by and large were like those of the observable holes. Slightly thinner stakes had been used in the older panel wall compared to the newer. Two stake-holes seemingly of the same character near the southern area of the eastern gable end are considered part of this system. To the west, the row of stake-holes stopped exactly where the doorway was placed.

When investigating most of the stake-holes in both systems it was decided to empty out the soil instead of making cross-sections. Due to the presence of traces of animal activities it was, in some instances, difficult to state the depth of the holes precisely. The depths were mostly c. 5-15 cm into the cleaned subsoil.

Three straight courses of a narrow, shallow groove with greyish soil also came to light in the border area of the sunken floor and the stake-holes of the older southern row. It was very difficult to distinguish the minute differences in its soil compared to the thin layer of soil on both sides. It was not therefore possible to make a safe drawing of its probable full length. This soil feature must have been at least 3 m long and probably longer. Its width was c. 6-8 cm. Judging by the location of the narrow groove, I am convinced that it represents traces of the bottom of the wall, mounted on stakes and facing the interior. It seems that the groove had been dug into the hard clayey subsoil to make room for the bottom of this inner wall itself.

The sequence appears to be as follows. The outer wall postholes south of the sunken floor were not replaced during the functional period of the sunken-floor house. The southern row of stake-holes for the panel wall was established during the building of the house. These stakes must have served as a vertical construction element for a relatively thin inner walling such as a panel. A new row of stake-holes was later dug north of the first row, likely because the old (which did not burn) had lost its functional qualities. The stakes in this new row must thus have replaced the first row as construction for a partially new inner panel wall. The way in which the northern newer row is aligned towards the west also indicates that only a partial replacement of the older wall took place.

The older, southern row of stake-holes seems to have continued in the gable end, as documented by the presence of two stake holes and also supported by the gradual turning of the southern wall line towards the east. As regards the younger system, only one stake-hole of seemingly the same character as these was found with dust from carbonized organic materials in the soil. When linking the stake-hole here with the younger row of stake-holes, the angle of the wall corner would now appear to be rather sharp.

The northern row of stakes must have burned down at a certain point in time. This fire probably took place after abandonment and could represent a burning of diverse scrap, as argued. It is worth noticing that tiny pieces of burned flint were observed (not recorded) near some of these stake-holes. This might indicate that a fire of considerable heat had occurred. It does not seem that the remaining parts of the older row also burned down on the same occasion. The presence of an added turf wall in between probably prevented the fire from reaching it.

Over time, concepts of the interior walls may have changed. This seems to be evidenced simply by comparing the interior walls posts of House 2 and House 1, which change from strong posts placed at wider intervals to stakes placed fairly close together. No traces of clay plastering have been observed among the remains of the interior walls. Wood may have been used for the panels but other organic materials cannot be excluded.

In my reading, traces of panel walls facing the interior are evidenced in seven of the longhouses at Resengaard. Besides these, there might also be a slight indication at the site of House 134. Such traits were thus observed at a majority of the longhouse sites albeit rather sporadically. Some traces were found to the south, east and north in rows bounding the sunken floors but, occasionally, also in the perimeters of western ground floors. Given that such vestiges were usually quite modest in their appearance and could easily disappear as the excavations progressed, it is assumed that panel walls facing the inside of the longhouses could originally have been present in all twelve longhouses at Resengaard. A panel wall also appears to have been present at the minor House 193.

Thick turf walls

When speaking of turf as a wall material, this implicitly also relates to the heather peat that might have been used as well. Due to its insulating capacity, such kinds of walls would have worked relatively well in the long, cold South Scandinavian seasons. Ample supplies would likely have been available and buildings walls with turf would have reduced the need for long timber. There would thus have been serious reasons for building such walls and I shall later expand on this theme together with a consideration of the idea of the sunken floors. But what evidence is there of turf walls at Resengaard? It must be immediately emphasized that no direct documentation of such material from any walls has been observed here; however, we shall now look at the indirect indications.

Firstly, I consider the lack of safety-stabilizing postholes for the wooden wall constructions to be a rather strong indicator of the presence of other wall elements giving the necessary solidity and weight, lending the necessary firmness against wind pressure combined with a special wooden construction. Heavy turf walls would, in my understanding, play their role in such a construction. The thickness of the walls was probably considerably greater than the rows of postholes belonging to the outer wall construction might immediately indicate, because a turf wall on both sides of the posts would certainly brace the row of posts and explain why it was not necessary to dig down the lower ends of the vertical wooden posts properly. The lower parts of the posts may have been further linked or tied together by constructional arrangements and, in this way, have given strength mutually to the wood construction and the turf construction. I thus presume that the vertical walls would have been composed of simple, interconnected wood constructions flanked by turf on the outer sides as well as the inner. Such kinds of construction would evidently ensure the necessary weight and stability against wind pressure from the sides.

How thick would the turf walls have been? House 1 again makes a good point of departure. In the eastern part of the southern long side, the distance from the postholes of the outer wall to the first built panel wall was about 40 cm. To support the wall posts towards the exterior, it would presumably have been necessary to also add at least a corresponding width outwards. I suggest that about 50 cm could have been added in the long sides, because the outer side might easily have been exposed to some destruction from winds, rains, snow, frost, sun and other weather conditions. The entire wall width on the long side could thus have been some 90 cm or even more.

To the southeast of the sunken floor in House 1 at Resengaard, placement of additional turf presumably hindered the burning of the stakes from the first phase of the panel wall, and this trait is thereby also an indicator of a turf wall. It should be noted that ancient animal activity along an approximately one-metre broad belt was observable in the area of walls, probably largely related to traces of mouse galleries at the bottom level of the turf wall.

If the walls on both long sides were made alike, the width of the house would then have been about one metre broader than the raw dimensions stated. Correspondingly, the stated raw interior width in the area of the sunken floor would have been reduced by the distance from the outer wall postholes to the panel wall, being about 40 cm on each side. This would have represented a marked reduction of the interior and thus overall diminishing the floor area by many square metres in comparison with calculations of raw areas.

There would probably have been more reason for building the above suggested panel walls facing the interior. If not established, the turf walls would presumably have presented a less agreeable surface. Depending on the firmness of the turf, the surfaces might more easily have been destroyed over the years and might gradually have become less suitable as wall material for the dwellings.

From later history, we know of houses with turf walls from many different areas, such as for instance Greenland, Iceland, the Faroe Islands and Norway.

We also have examples from reconstructions of South Scandinavian Late Neolithic houses with turf walls (e.g. Björhem & Säfvestad 1987), from house constructions belonging to the Iron Age in Denmark and Norway (e.g. Hansen 1964; Lund 1977; Binns 1983; Hvass 1985:118pp), from the medieval period in Denmark (e.g. Henningsen 2000), from old historic Island farms (e.g. Bruun 1908; Hermanns-Audardóttir, 1989; Stenberger 1943; Olesen & Kjær 1972; Frederiksen 1976), and from buildings belonging to the more recent past in Denmark (e.g. Strandgaard 1883; Stoklund 1972). The publication by Daniel Bruun on old Icelandic ways of building farmsteads with turf materials, in particular, contains numerous instructive ground plans and cross-sections of turf walls (Bruun 1908:9pp).

People of the later parts of the Neolithic in the region could have gained and maintained considerable experience in turf-building techniques down the centuries, as evidenced from numerous barrows. Turf would likely have been an easily accessibly material and the use of it for house walls is documented also from the central Limfjord region at Vadgård in the Older Bronze Age (Rasmussen, M. 1993a; Rasmussen & Adamsen 1993). Thus, from Vadgård Nord turf was used as a wall material at five house sites (Rasmussen 1993a:26pp). At the site of House 121 at Østbirk, traces of peat have been recovered (Borup, im manus).

Doorways and a remarkable "corridor"

Only few indications of doorways in the outer walls were observed among the traces of the Resengaard houses and most enlightening was the south entrance to House 1. A correlation between five traits makes this doorway exceptionally explicit: the slightly drawn in south entrance, the larger interval between the wall postholes, the traces of double-stakes placed at each side of a free area of the interior panel wall, the ending of the narrow soil strip probably representing the panel wall itself, and finally the sunken floor soil feature showing a bulge southwards. The latter trait could stem from wear. In two other longhouse sites (2 & 41), some vestiges showed more or less certain entrances in the southern long sides.

Northern doorways seem foremost represented in House 2, where several traits point to a presence. Further it cannot be excluded that the dividing wall of House 1 to the north led to a northern doorway although I instead prefer the alternative interpretation that it simply formed a compartment, open to the south.

Interior doorways between the sunken floor and the ground floor, in my reading, are possibly present at the sites of House 1 and House 14, in both cases nearest to the southern long side walls.

With regard to the minor houses at Resengaard, traces of a doorway with drawn in posts were present around the middle of the south side of House 112. In relation to House 84, an entrance is indicated in the south side.

The remarkable spur to the south of the sunken floor in the site of House 200 is the only example of a possible "corridor" at Resengaard and the other settlements particularly studied. Another, possibly to some degree corresponding, arrangement was presented from Egehøj in the area between Houses II and III (Boas 1983:93p & Fig. 3).

Connecting, east-sloping ramps

The sloping sunken-floor areas leading from the sunken floors towards the ground floors and from the interior towards the doorways are in this work referred to as "ramps" (*cf.* Fig. 4.68). Such connecting floor areas were obviously present in all sunken-floor longhouses. The ramp in House 1 was described in some detail above as an example from Resengaard.

Certain areas of these east-sloping floor parts in particular would, in my reading, mainly represent passages for the residents within and towards the doorways. No floor patches or artefacts were generally left there, indicating that they did not usually represent specific activity spaces, an exception being House 2 at Resengaard. Characteristically, the ramps were not particularly steep but, on the contrary, would rise quite gradually towards the western ground floors. Nonetheless, in cases of very deep floors, the ramps would have had to overcome significant differences in level over a distance of quite a few metres.

The ramps are considered as western parts of the sunken floors and thus included within the sunken-floor areas. No clear distinctions were generally observed regarding where the ramps began.

Dividing walls and compartments

Some postholes found in certain positions have, in the above, been interpreted as traces of dividing walls and compartments. In my terminology, a "dividing wall" separates two major areas of a house whereas a "compartment" separates a minor area of a house. Such interpretations are proposed as regards the longhouses numbered 1, 2, 14, 41 and 197 at Resengaard. Three of these thus concern the longhouse that burned down and two that had just limited traces of burning. The establishment of dividing walls and compartments was likely closely connected to the organization of daily life activities in specific areas of the interior.

I presume that there was often a physical separation of the sunken floor spaces from those of the ground floors because it would have been sensible to keep the warmth within the sunken-floor spaces, where the sources of heating were usually placed. Identifiable traces of dividing walls between these two major floor parts are seldom found but appear to have been present in House 14, judging by a row of postholes. At the site of House 197, too, the traces of burned organic material, probably charcoal dust, on top of the stake- and postholes make an interesting case for assuming that a dividing wall had been placed between the two major floor parts. Blankets, mats, hides and similar objects hanging down from transversal beams might have served as further dividers between floor parts.

Long side recesses and cubicles

Of the 43 sunken-floor houses studied, the thickness of the walls appears to have been used for creating some extra room in just a few instances, judging by the sunken floor outlines and some other particular traits. This concerns only longhouses.

Due to interesting correlations between three qualities and elements in the long side to the southeast at the site of House 2, the traits observed in my reading are vestiges of a recess in the turf wall. The first quality was the recognition that postholes frame three sides of a rectangular area of about two metres long and more than half a metre wide. The second was the extension of the sunken floor itself into the same area. The third is the remote placement without any artefacts and soil features in the floor horizon, in contrast to central areas. We also found certain traces which, in my reading, likely indicate a recess in the southern long side of House 13.

The purposes of the recesses are not known from any finds or other attributes. Both arrangements were found in the south sides. These may have been slightly warmer than walls to the north and this factor could have played a role in their intended function. In my interpretation, the recess of e.g. House 2 could very well have formed a regular sleeping area, established for this purpose in the south wall in the area of the extended house part, where such a tranquil expanse could have been much in demand. It would thus have not taken up valuable floor space more centrally.

In a single case at Resengaard, the presence of vestiges of what I term a "cubicle" in my reading were found within the turf wall. This concerns the southeast corner arrangement of House 197. It was evidence from Houses 5 and 7 at Glattrup IV that led me to suggest the existence of such an arrangement at Resengaard too. In the case of House 197, the cubicle had a shallow, rounded bottom, broadest to the south, whereas those at Glattrup IV had much deeper, flat bottoms. Apparently, all three appear to have been supplied with an opening narrower than the interior room. We shall consider the relics of these cubicles at Glattrup IV later on.

Bejsebakken, Myrhøj, Fosie and Scord of Brouster

In relation to the above Resengaard house sites, we shall now consider some specific traits from Bejsebakken and also a few from Myrhøj and Fosie IV for comparison. For one particular observation, we must look outside South Scandinavia for comparable material.

At Bejsebakken, many sunken-floor house sites were affected in different ways by source-critical factors. Unlike some of the Resengaard areas, the Late Neolithic house sites at Bejsebakken were not covered by thick, accumulated layers, e.g. generated through wind activities (Sarauw 2006:46). Certain house sites do, nonetheless, stand out for their fine preservation. In my judgment, four longhouse sites in particular were comparatively well preserved, due to the enlightening presence of centre posts, wall lines, more or less intact sunken floors, and depressions, namely the sites of Houses A896, A170, A556 and A606. Despite disturbances from a much later house pit and some other later diggings, the house (A896) shows several fine elements, i.e. not least the double lines of wall posts, the sunken area, and certain pits.

One particular structure at Bejsebakken, House A66, appeared to have a sunken floor along the whole length, being about 20 m, and it is considered as differing from all other sunken-floor houses at the settlement (Sarauw 2006:13p). In my reading of the plan drawing, however, it may instead indicate that one sunken floor had partly cut across another sunken floor, thus forming the unusual shape of the soil feature taken as a whole. Four arguments in favour of this view can be put forward: it can be seen from the ground plan that the eastern third of the sunken floor is significantly smaller than the remainder of the soil feature. The eastern third is also out of line with the other part. The easternmost posthole of the roof-bearing post is correspondingly out of line with the others in the central longitudinal axis. The easternmost wall posthole is out of line with the others as well. Because the middle and western part seems best preserved, this area could be the younger. The "storing pit" A1136 could then belong to the eastern sunken-floor house.

It is apparent that extensive uninvestigated parts at Bejsebakken were left between the settlement areas A, B, and C, having two preserved grave barrows almost centrally placed in between (Sarauw 2006, Fig. 2). It therefore cannot be excluded that the uninvestigated areas may still contain several Late Neolithic house sites. In particular, certain terrains east of area A, to the south and west of area C catch the eye. Even terrains east and north of area C cannot be ruled out in this respect. Area B and C also comprised three and two sites of ground-floor houses respectively, while the remainder were all sunken-floor houses. When the suggested interpretation is followed as regards House A66, it raises the number of identified and excavated building remains to a total of 24 Late Neolithic houses at the settlement. With the extensive, uninvestigated areas in mind, it seems that Bejsebakken as a whole could be the largest known settlement in Denmark for house sites of the period in question.

A very fine example of wall outlines is found at House A896 at Bejsebakken. On the long sides, an outer as well as an inner row of postholes was recovered, being best preserved to the north in the western half of the house. In terms of their function it is posited that the "…outer row probably held supporting posts for the wall, although there were no signs of slanting posts" (Sarauw 2006:42). In the gable ends, only singular rows of postholes were observed, and both ends were fairly well preserved, giving a clear idea of the post placements. The observed depths of the wall postholes varied from 31 cm down to 3 cm. Several of the sunken-floor houses at Bejsebakken probably had post-built walls (Sarauw 2006:48pp). For a discussion of dividing walls/partitions, see Sarauw 2006:58.

With regard to the observation from many houses at Resengaard that the sunken areas had been present even beyond the panel walls and outer walls, two good examples at Bejsebakken from the house sites A170 and A896 are also available and, in both cases, they show sunken areas extending far beyond the long side walls (Sarauw 2006, Fig. 8 & 45). Torben Sarauw is of the view that the sunken areas had mostly been dug before building the walls and, interestingly, his interpretation is based on quite another argument, namely that "… often, the bottom level was dug so far down across larger areas (up to 83 cm) that this cannot be explained by the repeated removal of dung. In most cases by far, the depression must have been made before the house was built" (Sarauw 2006:60).

Observations of traces of proper doorways are few and far between in the region and other parts of South Scandinavia. For further discussion of entrances, see Sarauw 2006:51.

Regarding the connecting ramps between the sunken- and the ground-floor parts, some traces in the site of House D at Myrhøj have been interpreted as a kind of floor covering (Jensen, J.A. 1973:67; Sarauw 2006:53). Such vestiges have not, to my knowledge, been found elsewhere so far.

At Fosie IV in Scania, where intensive investigations were carried out over an area of c. 40 hectares, this comprised six settlement areas in all (Björhem & Säfvestad 1989:71. Artursson 2005b:94pp). Sites of several longhouses with ground floors from the Late Neolithic and beyond were recovered and some have been radiocarbon dated. Only two sites of sunken-floor longhouses (101 & 92) were found and investigated. The latter was rather well preserved as regards the postholes of the outer walls and certain other traits (Björhem & Säfvestad 1989:52pp). Due to the comprehensive removal of topsoil, all preserved sunken-floor house sites from the period in question have presumably been found. Fosie IV does not thus belong among the larger settlements in terms of sunken-floor houses but valuable observations and interpretations still make it an important settlement in this respect.

Concerning the alterations of the building dimensions at Resengaard, no parallels have to my knowledge been presented from the region. However, at Fosie IV, the two-aisled, 26 m long House 95 with ground floor is considered to have been extended to the west. This interpretation is based on the placement of certain posts (Björhem & Säfvestad 1989:71).

In relation to the suggested turf walls at Resengaard, the reconstruction in Skånes Djurpark of the 14.9 m long building, House 17, found at Fosie IV, is interesting (Björhem & Säfvestad 1987:8pp).[4] Although not supplied with a sunken floor, it still presents a two-aisled house with turf walls. It is also very interesting as concerns the suggested panel walls in the Resengaard longhouses as House 13 at Fosie IV may have had such constructions in the interior. One panel was tested through its physical reconstruction (Björhem & Säfvestad 1989, Fig. 68 & 70).

From the literature, I do not recall observations interpreted as recesses in longhouses from South Scandinavia. However, when looking for evidence in north-western Europe, much interesting knowledge is available on recesses and other interior arrangements. I shall offer only one example of an early milieu in which such recesses are found on the Shetland Isles. It concerns Scord of Brouster, which has traces of a settlement consisting of three small oval/subcircular houses with stonewalls (Whittle et al.1986; Barclay 1996:64-65; Malone 2001:61). The hearths were centrally placed and somewhat lower than the general floor level. One house (3) probably belonged to a period corresponding to a Beaker Phase according to the radiocarbon dating of carbonized grains (Whittle et al.1986:34). The building had an outer diameter of up to c. 8 m and an interior area of about 23 m^2 (Topping 1996, table 11.1) with the entrance facing northeast. The inner and outer wall was preserved up to 0.6-0.8 m height. On the inside, an orthostat about one metre high was placed next to the doorway and minor upright stones made up the facade of the inner and outer sides of the house. It has been suggested that some organic wall material such as peat, turf or timber might have been placed on top of the stone walls, whereby the house inside would have reached a reasonable height (Whittle et al.1986:33). A layer of sandstone pebbles comprised the floor. In an irregular circle around the central hearth were placed a number of large, flat stones. No potsherds and only few other artefacts belonged to the floor. This house, which had such an interesting layout, was supplied with five distinct recesses in the stone walls.

2.4. Radiocarbon dating at Resengaard

A series of radiocarbon determinations enables us to throw light on important chronological issues regarding the sunken-floor houses at the Resengaard settlement. First, however, let us look at the considerations that come into play prior to selecting the materials for radiocarbon determination.

Selecting suitable samples

In order to seek to obtain precise and reliable 14C determinations, the strategy for selecting the most favourable materials was to rule out the risk of obtaining determinations on charcoal with a possible high "own age" of old trees as well as the risk of having charcoal remaining from more ancient reused wood. Instead I preferred to concentrate purely on the charred cereals and other carbonized, short-life remains. The excavation team had a stroke of luck in that the vestiges of the first excavated sunken-floor longhouse, House 1, contained an unexpectedly high number of charred grains of barley and wheat. From the floor contexts of this house, the former Copenhagen Carbon-14 Dating Laboratory at the National Museum dated three samples of cereals with the earlier conventional method (Rasmussen, K.L. 1992:243p). As is well known, this process required comparatively large test materials but, due to the abundant presence of cereals, this was no problem.

When a series of eleven samples from Resengaard were later sent for radiocarbon dating at the present Aarhus AMS Centre, Department of Physics and Astronomy, Aarhus University, the strategy outlined above was followed and, consequently, charred remainders from several sunken-floor houses and one three-aisled longhouse were determined at the laboratory (Heinemeier 2002:283pp). These samples stem from the sunken-floor horizons, i.e. from the sites of four longhouses and a minor house. From these sites, seven grain samples were determined, in addition to two from other short-life plant material. Regarding two determinations from an early three-aisled house, the cereal samples derived from a posthole belonging to the northern long side wall.

Prior to all the radiocarbon datings, palaeobotanical determinations were carried out by David Earle Robinson.

Dating results on short-life materials

Radiocarbon determinations now exist from two of the three well-preserved sunken floors in the longhouses found at the northwest terrace (Fig. 2.2.C). This concerns House 1 (K-5732, K-5733 & K-5734) and House 2 (AAR-6661.A & AAR-6661.B). A little to the south, a dating of the minor sunken-floor House 202 (AAR-6664.A) has been obtained. Determinations are also available from House 13 (AAR-6659.A & AAR-6659.B) and House 197 (AAR-6662.A & AAR-6662.B), both placed southernmost at the upper part of the hill. Further to the southeast, determinations from House 128 (AAR-6663.A & AAR-6663.B) are on hand. Finally, two determinations are offered from the three-aisled House 106, located to the east of the hill. So, altogether the radiocarbon determinations concern six of the sunken-floor houses and one of the early three-aisled houses without a sunken floor (Fig. 2.37).

Despite the high precision and parallelism in the scientific dating of the remaining houses, we cannot, as pointed out by Jan Heinemeier (pers.comm.), avoid the implications of the radiocarbon data. The calibration plot of the probability spread ranges from about 100 to 200 years. According to the statistics, the real age of one in three samples can fall outside the interval of one standard deviation (Fig. 2.37.B).

Of great importance is, not least that five out of twelve sunken-floor longhouses are thus supplied with radiocarbon determinations on material with negligible "own age". As further pointed out by Heinemeier (pers.comm.), the five samples which have been twofold-dated through separate determinations of two single charred grains from each sample have given very fine, almost parallel, results, with the exception of those which concern House 13. In this site we presumably have a later addition of a potsherd (RE272aa) to the secondary fills.

The laboratory in Aarhus has taken the opportunity to weigh the twofold determinations statistically that in each case stem from the same sample and must be of the same age (Fig. 2.38). Also the threefold determinations from House 1 are weighed statistically. The resulting diagram on the calibrated dates thereby narrows the dating intervals down and becomes relatively clear (Fig. 2.38.B).

In rough figures, the earliest calibrated dates from the longhouse contexts may suggest a presence at the settlement sometime after 1900 cal. BC. The latest dates, from a sunken-floor longhouse, may on the other hand suggest a presence as late as about 1600 cal. BC. The spread of the calibrated dates from these house sites thus indicate that the human settlement at the Resengaard site was of long duration. It may denote a presence throughout several centuries.

Significant material changes are to be expected over such a long period, thus inviting a deeper exploration of the chronological relations between, not least, the longhouses. A comprehensive pottery analysis (Ch. 3) will therefore be carried out with the aim of establishing an internal, provisional chronology between the longhouses and certain other houses as well as a number of pits, and the results will finally be related to the calibrated dates.

The calibrated dates obtained also note that the chronological position of the Resengaard settlement was indeed rather late in the Late Neolithic period and that it bridged the transition to the Bronze Age such that some younger sunken-floor longhouses obviously belong to this period.

2.5. Other "late" houses in the central Limfjord region

In the following, a number of further house sites will be presented from nine locations in the central Limfjord region. This concerns the remainders of 13 longhouses, two minor houses and two short. In addition to these, three sites of ground-floor longhouses are also presented, albeit in less detail, and we shall later return to these (Ch. 5).

Above, we considered how the sunken-floor longhouses at Resengaard, judging by radiocarbon determinations, must have existed in the period c. 1900-1600 cal. BC., thus corresponding to existence within LN II and the emerging Bronze Age. Hence the Resengaard settlement is clearly to be considered "late" within our period in question. As we shall see (Ch. 3), the analysis of numerous pottery profiles from its longhouses has resulted in acquaintance with kinds of hitherto more or less unknown ceramics and their transformations over time. On this basis, the pottery from two other house sites at Gåsemose and Kluborg II are also therefore to be considered as "late". Further on, we shall concentrate on house sites from seven other locations which, in contrast to the above, have ceramic assemblages that clearly belong to the LN I Beaker group of settlements, and hence are "early" within our period in question. This relates to Glattrup I/III, Marienlyst Strand, Granlygård, Hellegård, Glattrup IV, Rosgårde, and Tromgade.

As can be seen from the foregoing, in this part I shall present two settlements each with a sunken-floor house site. The first stems from Gåsemose and one of the remarkable features of the site is its richness in pottery and, in particular, the class of its ceramic designs. The second of these sites is Kluborg II which, as we shall see later, may have been almost contemporaneous with the latest sunken-floor longhouse at Resengaard. From the central Limfjord region a third

Resengaard. Basic sample data

House	Lab. Code	Sample type	¹⁴C Age (BP)	δ^{13} (‰) VPDB	Submitter ID
1	K-5732	Charred grain	3400 ± 80	-23.1	SMS449A54
	K-5733	Charred grain	3220 ± 80	-23.0	SMS449A64
	K-5734	Charred grain	3280 ± 80	-22.8	SMS449A77
2	AAR-6661.a	Plant, charred (Hordeum vulgare var.)	3440 ± 35	-22.50	SMS449A8
	AAR-6661.b	Plant, charred (Hordeum vulgare var.)	3375 ± 35	-23.45	SMS449A8
13	AAR-6659.a	Plant, charred (Triticum dicoceum)	3480 ± 30	-23.08	SMS449A631b
	AAR-6659.b	Plant, charred (cf. Hordeum)	3305 ± 35	-20.62	SMS449A631b
106	AAR-6660.a	Plant, charred (Hordeum vulgare var.)	3145 ± 30	-22.34	SMS449A583
	AAR-6660.b	Plant, charred (Hordeum vulgare var.)	3125 ± 35	-22.54	SMS449A583
128	AAR-6663.a	Plant, charred	3330 ± 30	-23.70	SMS449A565a
	AAR-6663.b	Plant, charred	3355 ± 35	-23.65	SMS449A565a
197	AAR-6662.a	Plant, charred (Triticum sp.)	3495 ± 35	-21.61	SMS449A702
	AAR-6662.b	Plant, charred (Triticum sp.)	3490 ± 35	-21.34	SMS449A702
202	AAR-6664	Plant, charred (cf. Hordeum)	3485 ± 40	-22.76	SMS449A816

site, which could favourably have been included here, is Hejlskov Hede with the remains of several sunken-floor houses although these are currently subject to some archaeological analysis and hence not yet ready for presentation.

Gåsemose

The settlement was located in Thise parish, Salling Nørreherred (district), Viborg county. It was partially investigated in 1967 by the National Museum (report U1967a). Aino Kann Rasmussen, who in cooperation with Jørn Bie headed the excavation, did not directly recognize it as a house site, likely because the investigation was carried out several years before the publication of Myrhøj and therefore no fine parallels were at hand. Yet, due to the detailed documentation existing from the field work, I have come to the conclusion that the structure actually represents vital parts of a sunken-floor building, now termed House 1.[5] This interpretation will be accounted for below. My general perception of the chronological relationships between the finds from the Gåsemose excavation can, in brief, be stated as follows: a Late Neolithic culture layer, *inter alia* with Beaker pottery, had already accumulated in the area when the sunken-floor house was built. The finds from the culture layer mirror a period before and simultaneous to the house and perhaps even after the house.

Gåsemose is interesting also in relation to the findings from the neighbouring Tromgade settlement, where several sunken-floor house sites were more recently recovered and some of these have been investigated and are presented below.

House 1 (Fig. 2.39 & 2.40)

The conditions for observations at the location were relatively fine during excavation and, considering that the sunken area had not been markedly exposed to severe source-critical factors, the sunken-area dimensions are interesting. Although the upper parts of the fills, and thereby the outline of the sunken fea-

OxCal v4.2.4 Bronk Ramsey (2013); r:5 IntCal13 atmospheric curve (Reimer et al 2013)

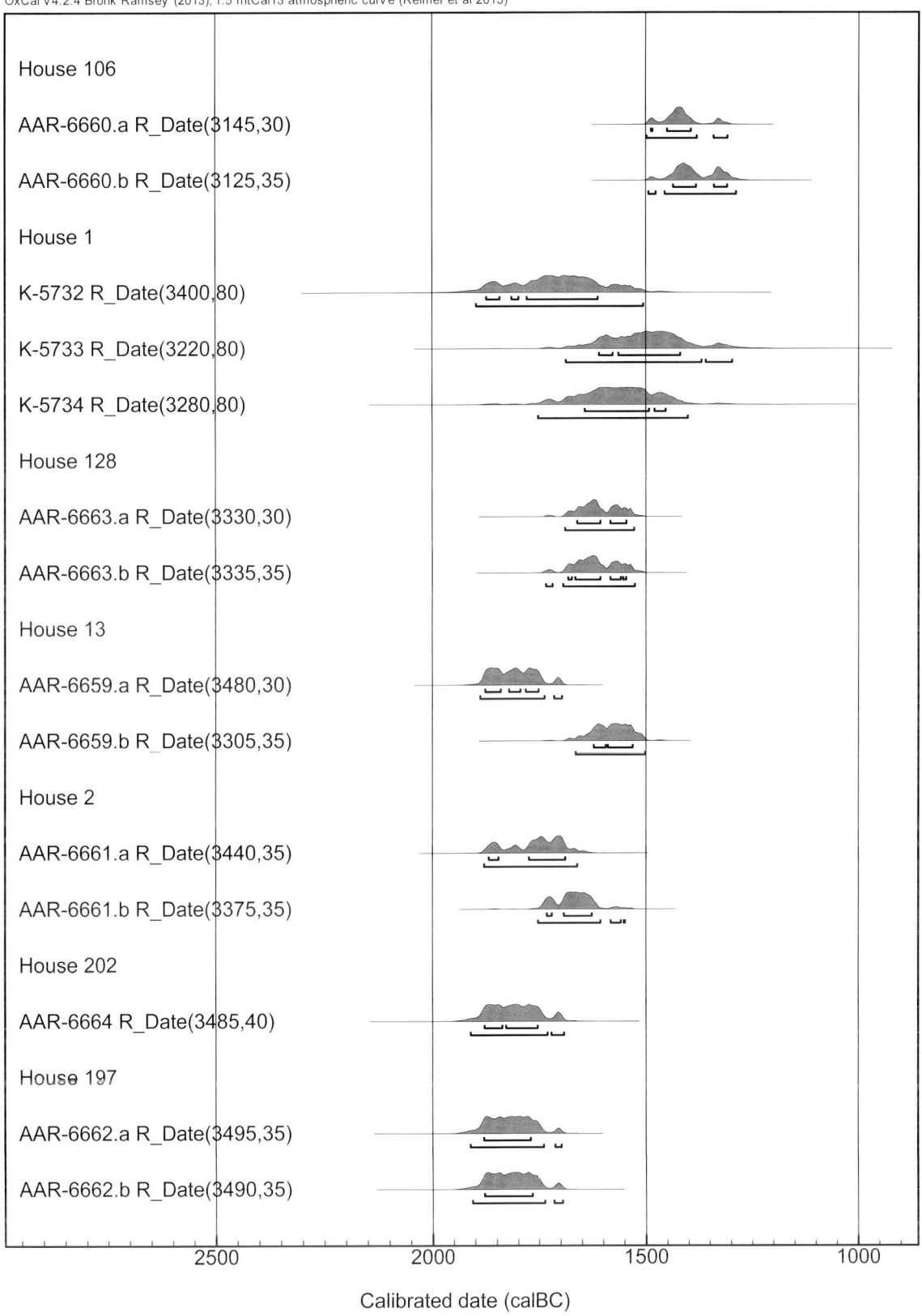

House 106

AAR-6660.a R_Date(3145,30)

AAR-6660.b R_Date(3125,35)

House 1

K-5732 R_Date(3400,80)

K-5733 R_Date(3220,80)

K-5734 R_Date(3280,80)

House 128

AAR-6663.a R_Date(3330,30)

AAR-6663.b R_Date(3335,35)

House 13

AAR-6659.a R_Date(3480,30)

AAR-6659.b R_Date(3305,35)

House 2

AAR-6661.a R_Date(3440,35)

AAR-6661.b R_Date(3375,35)

House 202

AAR-6664 R_Date(3485,40)

House 197

AAR-6662.a R_Date(3495,35)

AAR-6662.b R_Date(3490,35)

Calibrated date (calBC)

◄▲ *Fig. 2.37. Resengaard. A: Fourteen radiocarbon determinations from two laboratories, the former Copenhagen Carbon-14 Dating Laboratory at the National Museum (Rasmussen, K.L. 1992:243p); the present Aarhus AMS Centre, Department of Physics and Astronomy, University of Aarhus (Heinemeier, J. 2002). B: Calibration plot. Diagram: Marie Kanstrup & Jesper Olsen.*

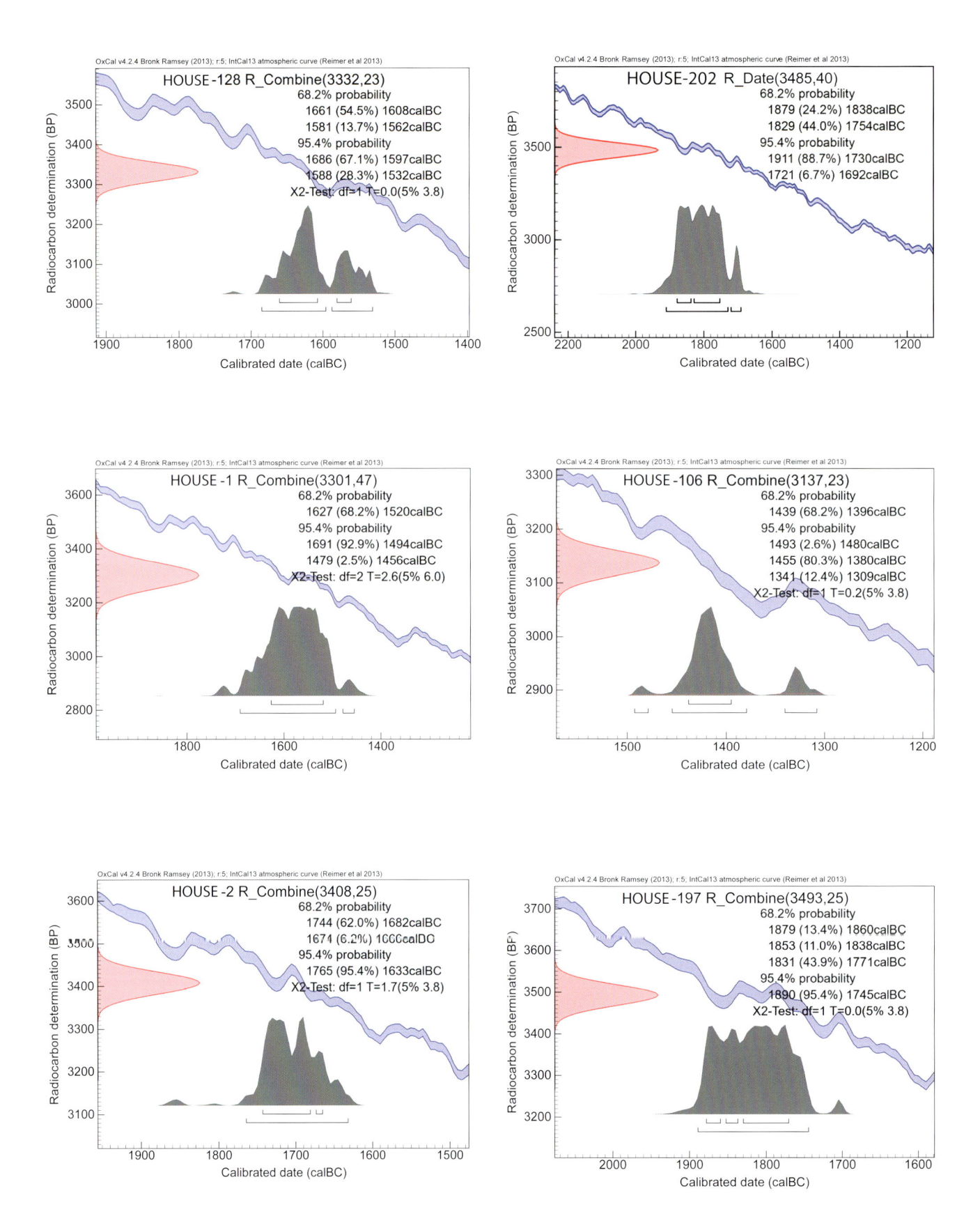

Fig. 2.38. Resengaard. A: Six weighted calibration plots, shown with one and two standard deviations. As regards House 13, combined determinations are inconclusive (see text, Ch. 3.3). B: Diagram of weighted calibration plots from longhouse sites ordered chronologically. House 202 is omitted here. Diagrams: Marie Kanstrup & Jesper Olsen.

OxCal v4.2.4 Bronk Ramsey (2013); r:5 IntCal13 atmospheric curve (Reimer et al 2013)

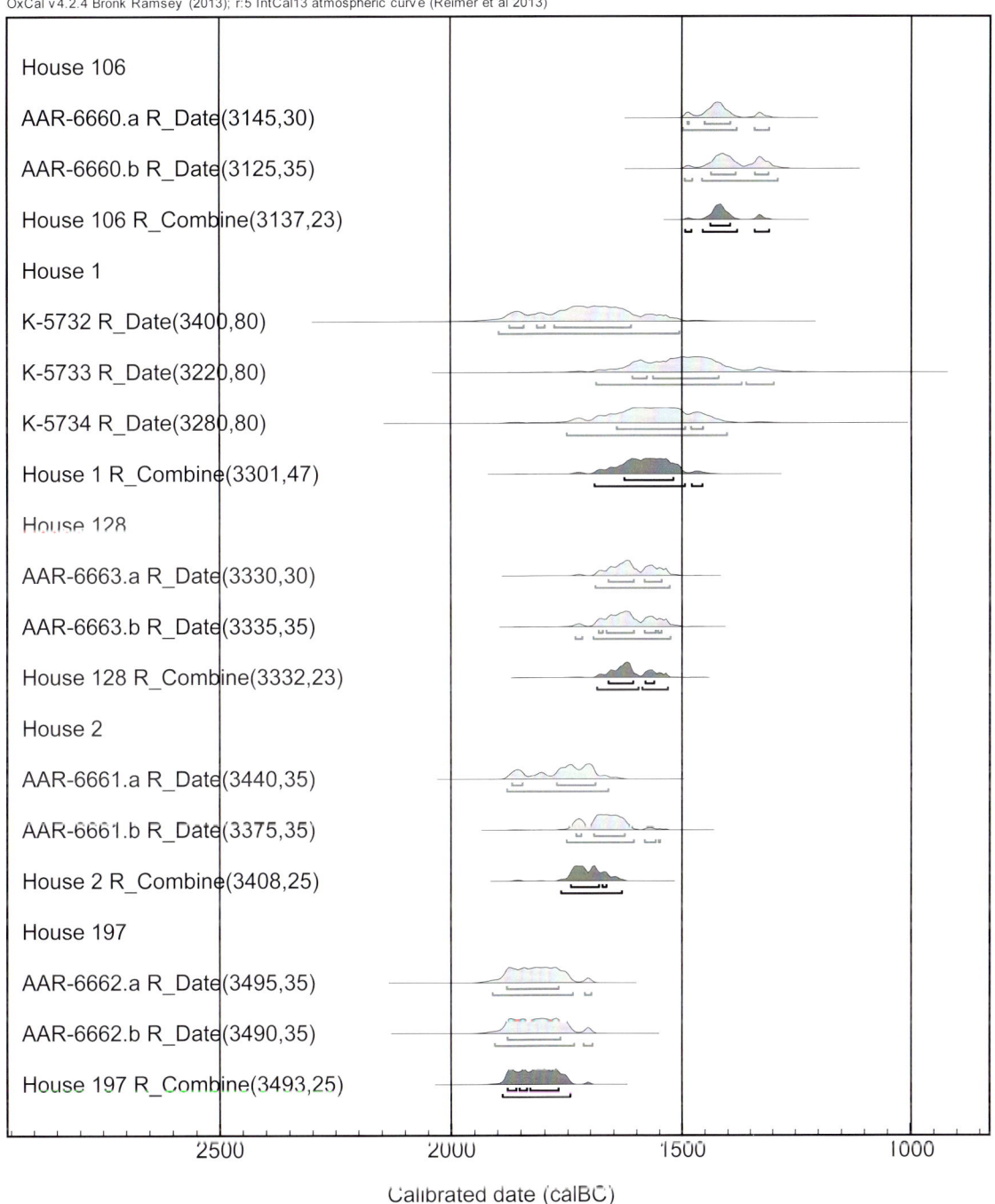

| House 106 |
| AAR-6660.a R_Date(3145,30) |
| AAR-6660.b R_Date(3125,35) |
| House 106 R_Combine(3137,23) |
| House 1 |
| K-5732 R_Date(3400,80) |
| K-5733 R_Date(3220,80) |
| K-5734 R_Date(3280,80) |
| House 1 R_Combine(3301,47) |
| House 128 |
| AAR-6663.a R_Date(3330,30) |
| AAR-6663.b R_Date(3335,35) |
| House 128 R_Combine(3332,23) |
| House 2 |
| AAR-6661.a R_Date(3440,35) |
| AAR-6661.b R_Date(3375,35) |
| House 2 R_Combine(3408,25) |
| House 197 |
| AAR-6662.a R_Date(3495,35) |
| AAR-6662.b R_Date(3490,35) |
| House 197 R_Combine(3493,25) |

Calibrated date (calBC)

ture, may have been affected by recent ploughing, no significant reduction in its horizontal area appears to have taken place. Some disturbances were caused by private digging activities, which mainly affected one of the excavation squares.

It is stated in the report that a large flat pit was present and surrounded by a culture layer in the peripheral parts of the excavation. This culture layer was generally ploughed up and only preserved in minor hollow areas.

The information from Gåsemose closely resembles the knowledge obtained through excavating the sites of many other sunken-floor houses. The descriptions, combined with the documentation from horizontal plans and the cross-sections, convincingly point to the interpretation as a sunken floor. The relatively thick upper layer in the sunken area, which is explicitly described, would thus have been secondary fills with their composition of soil, stones, charcoal and artefacts. The bottom layer, consisting of greyish sand and fewer stones, could perhaps also have been the traces of a secondary fill layer. It could possibly even represent a floor layer but there are no further observations in the report to substantiate and confirm this. Some observations in excavation square III probably had no direct relation to the sunken floor, whereas it seems that this floor was present in excavation square V.

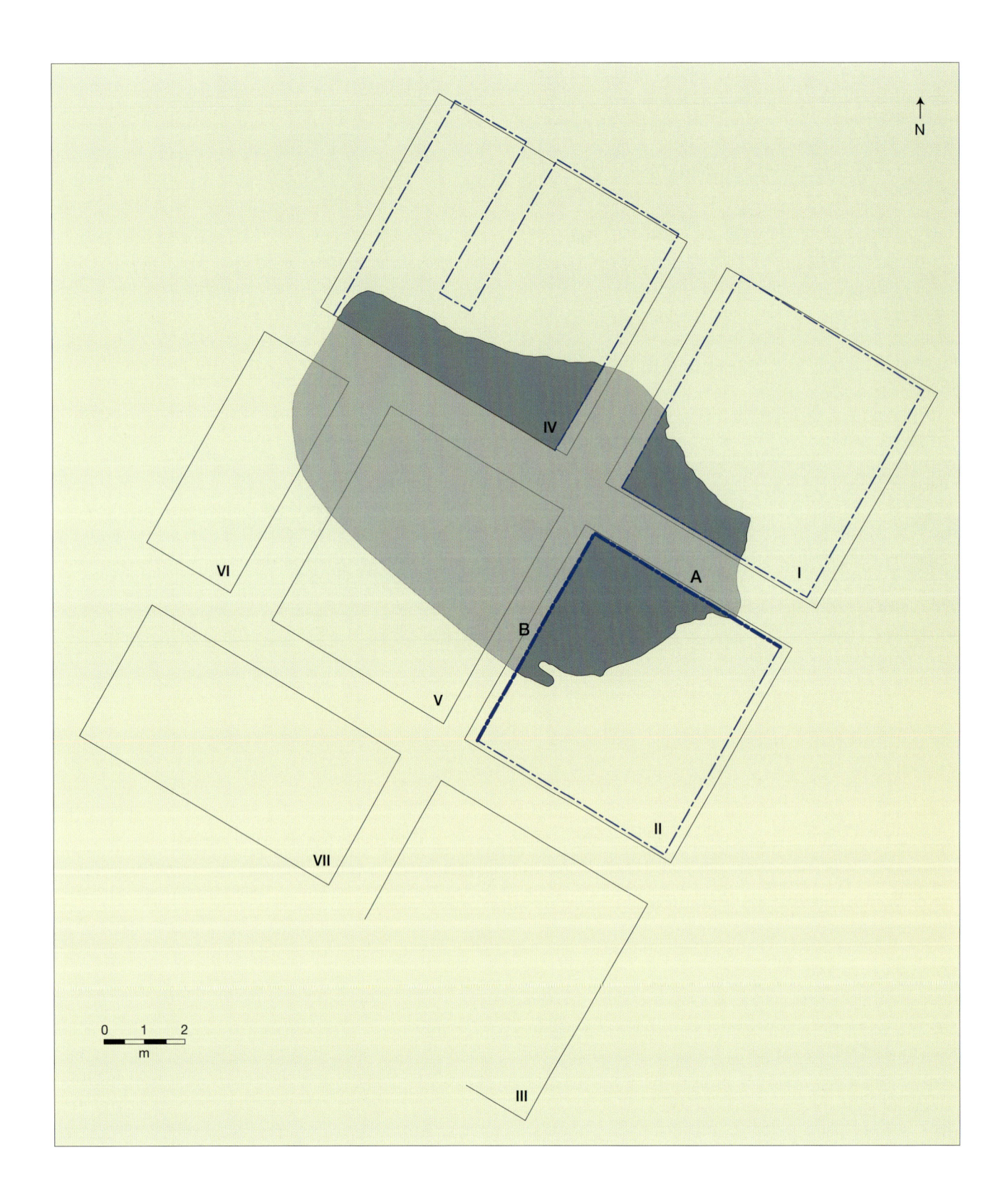

In all, the length of the sunken area from the easternmost part in excavation square II to the most western part in excavation square IV was c. 10.2 m and it is thus close to the size of many other deep floors from longhouse sites at Resengaard. In addition, the numerous artefacts found in fills and the abundant presence of heat-cracked stones in the sunken area may

◀ *Fig. 2.39. Gåsemose. House 1. Sketch of excavation areas with cleaned ground plan. The southwest area of the sunken floor is my tentative suggestion. The house site was affected by recent ploughing and some private digging. At first the excavation was planned to take place within three 5 x 5 metre squares (areas I, II & III) but was later extended with some more areas to be investigated. The placements of these areas were, however, restricted by the limited free space available within the by then cultivated land. One of the new excavation squares (area VII) was opened up mainly to check whether a culture layer was present or not and time did not allow two of the new squares to be investigated. Only the contour of the sunken floor is shown.*

Excavation square I: A brownish-black, sandy soil feature was observed to the southwest. The upper 15-20 cm of this soil feature appeared to have a large content of ash and charcoal. Many heat-cracked stones could be seen in the layer. These were partly fine-grained, partly coarse-grained. The coarse-grained stones were crumbling whereas the fragments of the fine-grained stones had been broken by the heat into many-edged forms. Among the artefacts scattered in the layer were a flat-flaked flint sickle, some flint waste and some potsherds, as well as dispersed pieces of burned bone. The lower 5-7 cm consisted of greyish sand with charcoal pieces. It is presumed in the report that a part of the colouring of this layer was due to rainwater seepage. The boundary between this layer and the ground was diffuse and much disturbed by animal activity. My interpretation is that it concerns a part of the sunken floor with secondary fills above.

Excavation square II: To the northwest a dark soil feature was likewise observed. In the report it is stated that this feature was in all probability connected to the above described soil feature in excavation square I. Spots with more compact occurrences of heat-cracked stone were also observed in this soil feature, as well as charcoal and two concentrations of charcoal. I interpret these observations as a continuation of the sunken floor with secondary fills above.

Excavation square III: The deep soil feature of excavation areas I and II was not present and, instead, another layer was clearly thinner and characterized by several recent disturbances. The trial trench, which was conducted prior to the National Museum's excavation, had cut off the direct link to the soils towards the southwest. The information about the find spot was originally received by Skive Museum and a subsequent trial excavation was conducted by Viborg Stiftsmuseum in 1966.

Excavation square IV: A soil feature with a composition corresponding to the soil feature described in excavation square I was observed in the southern part. The excavation leader explicitly stated in the report that this soil feature had the same characteristics as those of excavation areas I and II, thereby constituting the northern limits of this soil feature.

Excavation square V: This area was dominated by disturbances from a large pit (approx. 3 x 2 metres) dug privately after Viborg Museum had made the initial trial trench across what became part of excavation square V.

support the hypothesis that it concerns a sunken-floor longhouse (see Ch. 4). Various observations from the excavation squares are available that might qualify the traits of the building but it does not seem possible to pinpoint postholes belonging to specific traces of the construction. Judging by the sunken floor, the house was aligned almost SE-NW. The local terrain was slightly sloping towards the north and west. By the time of the investigation, a central sunken floor area lay at a depth of 30 cm but the original depth beneath the top of the old surface must have been significantly greater.

No traces of doorways, outer walls, panel walls, compartments, dividing walls or other interior arrangements were observed.

It cannot be stated whether the building or parts of it had been burned. The research value of this house site is modest as concerns the dwelling structure but extraordinarily detailed and illustrative drawings of vertical sections have been made in connection with the field work. The artefact remainders from the site are quite valuable. Moreover, the massive presence of stones in the secondary fills indicates that the sunken floor – likely the only one of all longhouse sites particularly studied – was not ard-ploughed after being torn down and abandoned.

Kluborg II

The site of a sunken-floor building, House 5, was found at this settlement located in Skive parish, Hindborg herred (district), Viborg county. Kurt Glintborg Overgaard directed the investigation and the site emerged in excavation square II, being about 35 x 22 m (report U2001b). In the surrounding area, altogether many vestiges from the Bronze Age and the Early Iron Age came to light. Thus, several sites of three-aisled longhouses were recovered, but the main thing here is to make clear that despite extensive investigations only this single site of sunken floor house was found. In the following, my interpretations of House 5 differ in some respects from those in the report.

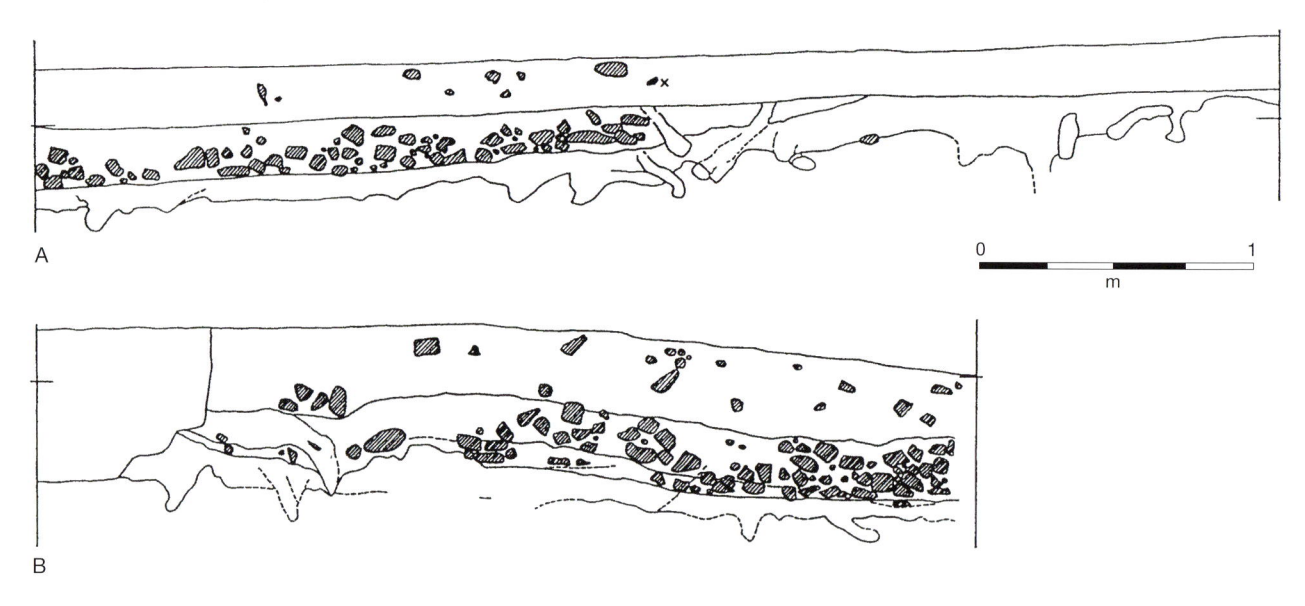

Fig. 2.40. Gåsemose, House 1. Two soil bench sections (A & B) from excavation area II. From the very precise and detailed cross-sections, it could be rather tempting to perceive the lower uneven stratum as largely forming a floor layer but this cannot be stated with any certainty. I am in any case convinced that the above stratum, with its massive presence of stones, constituted secondary fills.

House 5 (Fig. 2.41 & Fig. 2.42)

After abandonment of House 5, certain ard-ploughing activities appear to have disturbed the sunken floor moderately. This concerns minor areas of the middle and western floor parts. Traces of a three-aisled longhouse from the Older Bronze Age were present in the area of the eastern gable end of House 5. The building of this house may have disturbed the sunken-floor house site marginally. A cluster of pits from the western part of the three-aisled longhouse were thus observed just east of the House 5 gable end. Later disturbances caused by recent ploughing have probably diminished the area of the sunken floor.

The terrain in the immediate vicinity of the house was almost flat and the ground markedly sandy. The possibilities for making observations on the site were about average compared to the Resengaard houses. I agree with the excavation director that the house had not, in any case, been supplied with a regular ground floor of some dimensions. By the time of the investigation, a central sunken floor area lay at a depth of 32 cm but the original depth beneath the top of the old surface could have been significantly greater.

In my reading, 14 postholes represent the wall postholes and no traces of an inner panel wall were found. A possible centre post appears to have been placed to the east, whereas other vestiges of centre posts seem absent. Perhaps the roof construction did not need centre posts at first. The possible eastern centre post in the broad end of the building may have been put into position later as an extra support to secure the roof. Some of the wall postholes were of considerable dimensions, whereas it can be assumed that only the bottom of the interior posthole was preserved due to continued deepening of the floor during residence. The width of the house at its widest was about half its length although it was significantly narrower to the west with its roundish gable end, i.e. a largely trapezoidal ground plan.

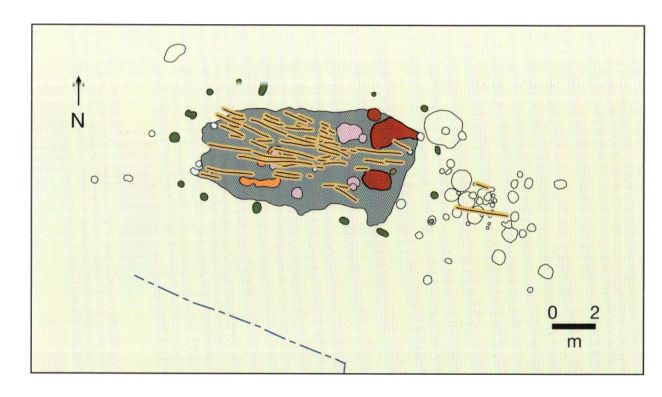

Fig. 2.41. Kluborg II, House 5. Ground plan, nearby older/younger soil features and an excavation limit. For further house sites, soil features and excavation limits in the surroundings, see Kurt G. Overgaard, report U2000a. The disturbing postholes mainly belong to the three-aisled Bronze Age building, House 5a. Ard-ploughing and recent ploughing had also had an impact on the house site.

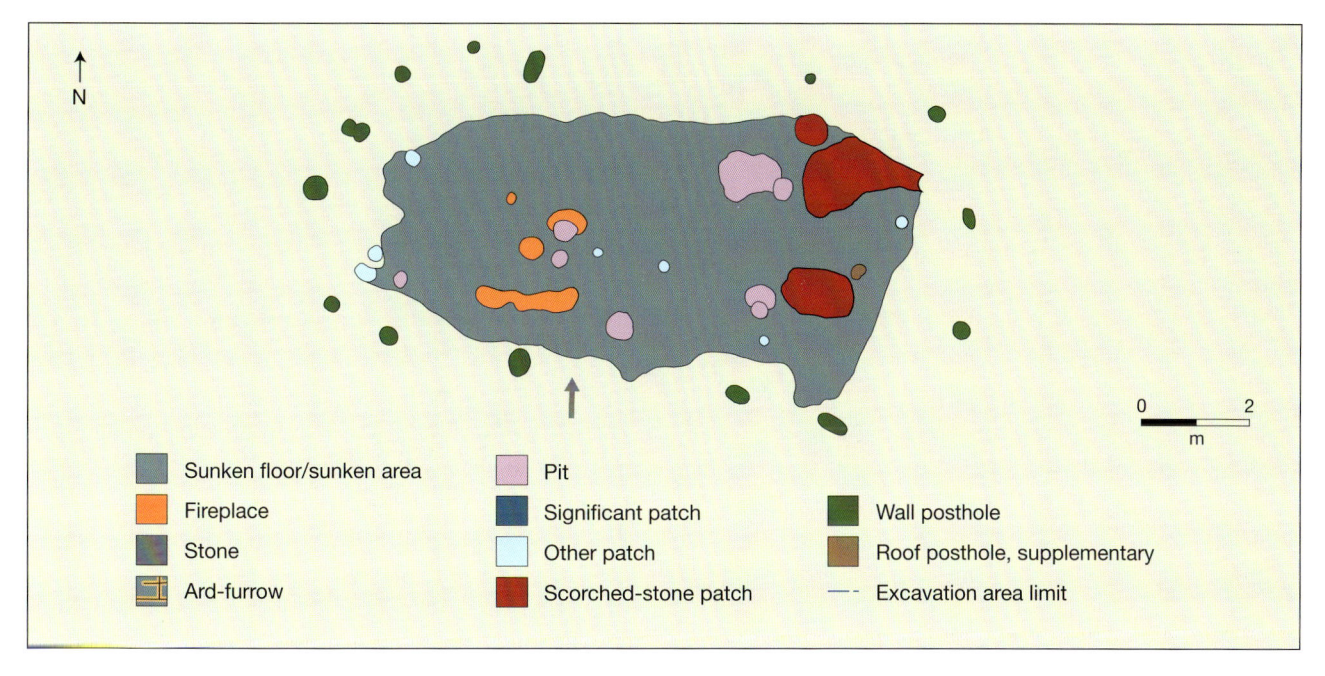

Fig. 2.42. Kluborg II. Ground plan, cleaned. Despite disturbances, the house site was rather well-preserved and indicates a building with a trapezoidal outline, narrowing towards the west.

The evidence from this house site is clearly unusual in several respects. This concerns the size and method of construction and, as we shall see later, also its soil features, its finds and its chronological position. Our attention now, however, is primarily on aspects of the original layout, dimensions and construction of the house. When we include the excavation leader's statement that a ground floor was never a part of the house as point of departure, it is quite remarkable that it had sunken-floor dimensions corresponding to those known from longhouses such as, for instance, at Resengaard, as opposed to the minor variants of sunken-floor houses. And it is further remarkable that the postholes surrounding the sunken floor at the site of House 5 were dimensionally quite substantial and thus contrasting greatly with those at Resengaard.

It is also noteworthy that no postholes were observed, either to the south or to the north in the middle section of the house site. It is hence worth considering that the building here may have been kept more open, perhaps temporarily for light-demanding activities. Another possibility may be that other kinds of walls not needing deeply dug posts were placed here. The absence of regular posts here probably somehow also represents an entrance to the house. Vestiges of compartments or dividing walls were not found.

Much evidence regarding this house seems to indicate that it was intended for rather specific purposes, even though – as we shall see later – some ordinary traces of habitation were found too. In my reading, no vestiges indicate that this special house was burned. I rate the research value of the site to be high as concerns the dwelling structure, the multiple and varied soil patches, and the artefact remainders.

2.6. Beaker houses in the central Limfjord region

Numerous sunken-floor house sites belonging to earlier parts of the Late Neolithic have been recognized in the central Limfjord region. These have, in several cases, also been investigated archaeologically. After scrutinizing many of these materials, I have selected the house sites of seven unpublished settlements for detailed presentation, analysis and interpretation. These concern Glattrup I/III, Marienlyst Strand, Granlygård, Hellegård, Glattrup IV, Rosgårde and Tromgade. These shall be presented here in the order they were investigated. Although some of the individual building remainders do not contain much new information on their own, these settlements taken together offer a relatively broad representation of different qualities, as shall be seen below and in the following chapters, where comparative and thematic analyses of these are provided.

Glattrup I/III

The site was located in Skive parish, Hindborg district, Viborg county. The present author headed the investigation at Glattrup I in 1983 and Poul Mikkelsen was in charge at Glattrup III in 1990 (reports U1983a & U1990a). Both investigations were carried out prior to establishing residential areas and are here treated as one settlement.

House 5 and 6 were situated at some internal distance (*cf.* Simonsen 1996c, Fig. 4, V & VI). Most southerly, House 5 was placed in almost flat terrain, only leaning slightly towards north, while by House 6 the terrain was more markedly sloping towards north.

In the excavation areas, we also investigated a few finds from the Maglemose Culture, Funnel Beaker Culture and Single Grave Culture. Traces of five three-aisled houses and several pits were recovered from the Bronze Age. For an overview of the settlement, see Simonsen 1996c:90pp. One investigated house site belongs to the Iron Age.

House 5 (Fig. 2.43)

Vestiges of ard-ploughing into the sunken floor were observed. Several postholes recorded as disturbances in the area actually belonged to a three-aisled Bronze Age house. Its northern wall postholes passed over the southern part of the sunken floor. In the northern edge of the sunken floor, a sub-circular pit containing heat-cracked stones was likewise clearly a later disturbance, probably from the Bronze Age. Recent ploughing likely diminished the sunken floor greatly and removed many postholes. The sandy soil was

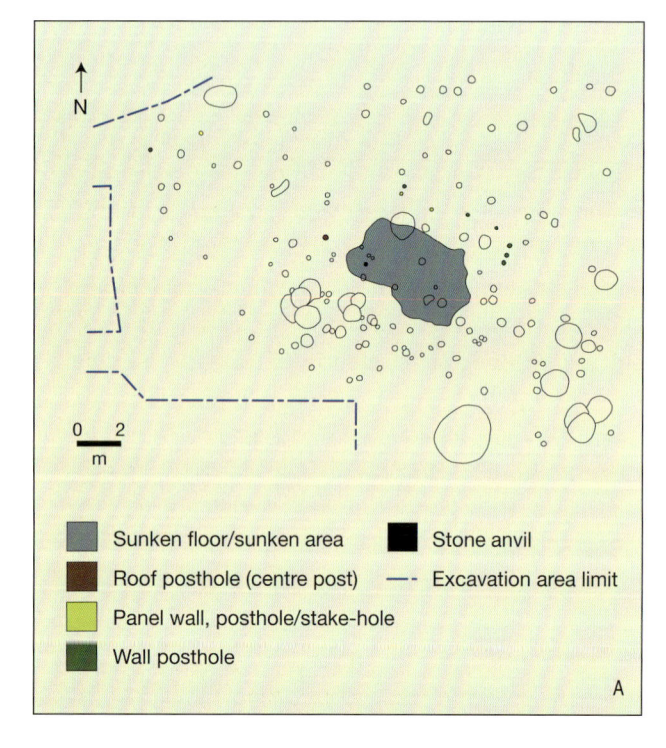

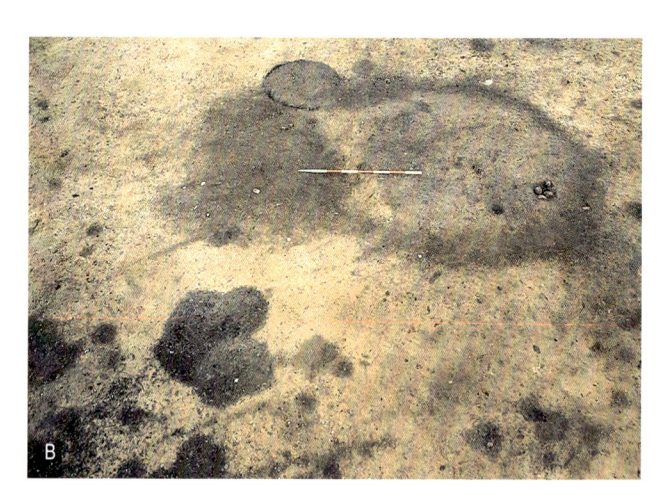

Fig. 2.43. Glattrup I/III. House 5. A: Ground plan, older/younger soil features and nearby excavation limits. For further house sites, soil features and excavation limits in the surroundings, see John Simonsen, report U1983a. Disturbances from a Bronze Age house and recent ploughing are evidenced. B: The sunken area of House 5 and later sub-circular Bronze Age pits after surface cleaning. Seen from the south. C: The sunken area of House 5 and Bronze Age pits at a later stage of excavation. As can be seen, ard-ploughing had evidently taken place in the sunken area as well as beyond it. D: Cross-section of the sunken area. Ard-furrows faintly visible in front of the soil bench. Seen from the west. For a soil section drawing, see Fig. 4.68.K.

very dry in the period of excavation and, because irrigation was not an option, the conditions for observing soil features were not the best. The initial excavation by means of machine went several centimetres deeper along the edges in order to remove disturbances from animal activity before the feature of the sunken floor emerged with a fairly clear contour.

The terrain around the house site was slightly southwest sloping. A sunken floor and some postholes mark out the traces of the house, indicating that it was almost E-W aligned but turned somewhat towards the SE-NW. By the time of investigation, a central sunken floor area lay at a depth of 33 cm. I had earlier estimated the length of the house to have been about 18 m (Simonsen 1996c:95) but, after reconsidering the ground plan and dismissing certain postholes, the raw length of the house is now reduced (Fig. 2.6.D.). A single posthole west of the sunken floor probably belonged to a centre post. Whether the long sides were parallel or not cannot be judged.

Vestiges of doorways, panel walls, compartments and dividing walls were not observed. No traces indicated that the building had been burned. I rate the research value of this longhouse site to be modest as concerns traces of the dwelling structure and likewise the soil traces in the floor. The artefact remainders belonging to the sunken-floor horizon were few but certain potsherds and their ornamentation are clearly interesting.

House 6 (Fig. 2.44)

Traces of ard-ploughing into the floor were not observed. Postholes disturbing the sunken-floor house stem from a three-aisled longhouse from the Bronze Age at the same plot and its wall line was marked by relatively large postholes with three of those of roof-bearing posts cutting through the sunken floor. The area west of the sunken floor was correspondingly greatly affected by postholes dug for the construction of this later building, as well as not least many pits and other soil features deriving from activities performed within this Bronze Age building. Recent ploughing probably also affected the preservation of the site of House 6 and likely diminished the extension and depth of the sunken floor.

The terrain in the immediate vicinity of House 6 was sloping to the north and the soil was sandy. Due to the massive presence of remains after the disturbance of the building, it is rather difficult to pinpoint the postholes that must have belonged to the sunken-floor

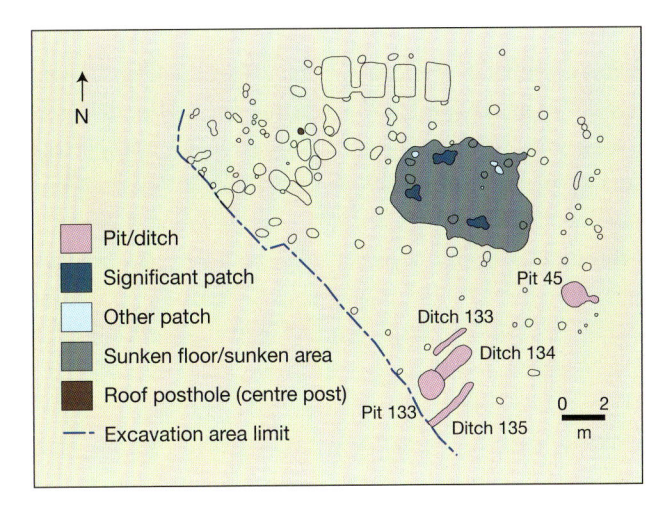

Fig. 2.44. Glattrup I/III. House 6. Ground plan, older/younger soil features and nearby excavation limits. For further house sites, soil features and excavation limits in the surroundings, see Poul Mikkelsen, report U1990a. To the southeast, five pits/ditches considered to belong to the same time as this house. For a cleaned ground plan with find spots, see Fig. 4.48.

house. No postholes can thus be proposed as belonging to the remains of the outer wall construction but, in my reading, a posthole somewhat west of the sunken floor probably represents vestiges of the roof-bearing construction along the central longitudinal axis. From the above it appears first and foremost that the sunken floor evidences the former existence of the house and that the preserved part was only of modest dimensions. By the time of investigation, a central sunken floor area lay at a depth of 16 cm but this was not the original depth beneath the top of the old surface. Whether the building had parallel long sides cannot be stated from the available evidence. Vestiges of inner walls, doorways, compartments, or dividing walls were not observed.

No traits indicate that the building had been burned. I rate the research value of this house site to be modest as concerns preserved traces of the dwelling structure. The remainders of soil patches and artefacts, including those from the secondary fills, are of moderate research value.

Marienlyst Strand

The site was located in Resen parish, Hindborg district, Viborg county (report U1992a). Prior to the establishment of a camping area, Poul Mikkelsen in 1992 directed the investigation in a field, where two currently ploughed grave barrows were *a priori* recorded in the archaeological parish register.

Initially, many N-S trial trenches were dug (not shown) and, at certain spots with interesting observations, these were extended into regular excavation areas. The investigation did not reveal any clear information about the grave barrows which were hence considered demolished. Some settlement traces were recorded in two excavation areas but it is difficult to give a precise date for these; in other areas either nothing or only few quite recent traces were found (Fig. 2.45). In excavation area IV (c. 264 m²), the site of the sunken-floor House 1 and some other settlement traces were uncovered. In excavation area V (c. 90 m²), the irregularly shaped pit 4 was investigated. In excavation area VI (c. 82 m²), culture layer 5 was investigated. See later on for finds from the house site, the pit and the culture layer.

House 1 (Fig. 2.46)

Disordering from ard-ploughing was not observed. It is stated in the report that the entire lower part of the fills above the sunken-floor bottom was highly marked by animal activities. Recent ploughing had damaged the top of the sunken floor and, in all probability, reduced the extension and depth significantly. It also probably destroyed many wall postholes.

The terrain in the immediate surroundings slopes a little to the south but, a few metres to the east and west, it falls somewhat more and, further to the south, it becomes slightly steeper. North of the house, the terrain also slopes a little from the locally highest point of 26 m above modern sea level. The area of the house can be considered a kind of small terrace that was probably more marked before recent ploughing. The ground was distinctly clayey in the area of the house site.

The excavation director considers the remains to belong to a longhouse with sunken floor in the eastern end. I can only agree with this understanding. Yet traces of the construction to the west are difficult to identify. Besides the sunken floor, it is remarked upon in the report that it is uncertain as to whether other soil features in the excavation area belonged to the house site or not. However, I consider a posthole immediately west of the sunken floor to mark out the relics of a centre post placed here. Further, the four small postholes east of the sunken floor were part of the gable end. A posthole observed south of the sunken floor is also suggested to belong to the wall of the house.

The preserved remainders of the longhouse were only of modest dimensions. Judging solely by the outline of the sunken floor, it seems possible that the long sides converged towards the west, giving the ground plan a trapezoidal appearance, although this cannot be supported by any other traces and is therefore somewhat uncertain. By the time of investigation, a central sunken floor area lay at a depth of 22 cm but the original depth beneath the top of the old surface must have been significantly greater.

Judging by comments in the report, no important soil patches belong with certainty to the sunken floor itself. Relics of inner walls, doorways, compartments, and dividing walls were thus absent.

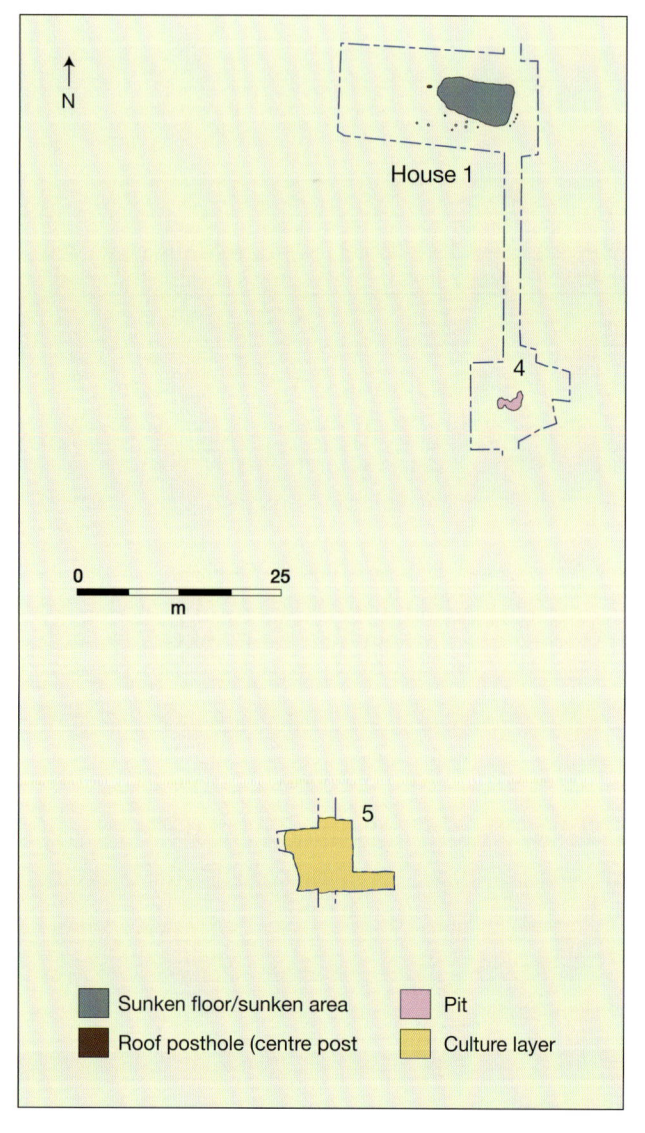

Fig. 2.45. Marienlyst Strand. Settlement sketch of find areas in the south-sloping terrains. The placements of House 1, pit 4 and culture layer 5 are shown with local excavation limits. The system of trial trenches extended far beyond the excavation areas shown. For further soil features and excavation limits in the surroundings, see Poul Mikkelsen, report U1992a.

No vestiges indicated that this house had been burned. I rate the research value of the house site to be very modest as concerns preserved traces of the dwelling structure and, in the excavation report, the artefacts are mainly considered to stem from secondary activities. A strong quality of the settlement is the contents of the above-mentioned pit and culture layer, both found a little distance from the house site.

Granlygård

The settlement was located in Skive parish (Skive landsogn), Hindborg district, Viborg county (report U1995a). The excavation took place in 1994-95 prior to state road works and bridge building across the Karup Å valley. In addition to finds from the Late Neolithic, Poul Mikkelsen directed the investigation of many structures from other prehistoric periods over a long stretch, including numerous postholes and pits in the road track. Some of these were the sites of ten three-aisled longhouses belonging to the Bronze Age and Early Iron Age. A settlement from the Maglemose Culture was also partially investigated. Extensive traces of a medieval field system were observed too. The dimensions of the excavated area were c. 175 x 50 m. A minor area was also opened somewhat as an aside in which a well-preserved site of an Iron Age house was recovered.

The remainders of three sizeable, shallow pits from the Late Neolithic were found near the middle of the road track and all were excavated as the remains of proper sunken-floor houses (Fig. 2.47). Various postholes were present in the area but none of these were considered as obvious house construction traces. Although the excavation director later departed from his first interpretation that these pits (2, 3 & 6) denoted house sites and instead proposed that they merely marked out pits with different fill layers (as proposed in the report), I am convinced that his original view is the most straightforward and probable understanding. In my reading, the surface outlines and the large flat bottoms point to a common interpretation as the ploughed down sites of two minor sunken-floor houses and one short. These houses had hardly any ground floor in addition to their sunken floor.

The distances between these building remainders, found on almost flat, just slightly west-sloping terrain, were modest and this might perhaps indicate that they were not in simultaneous use but instead more or less succeeded each other. Vestiges of outer

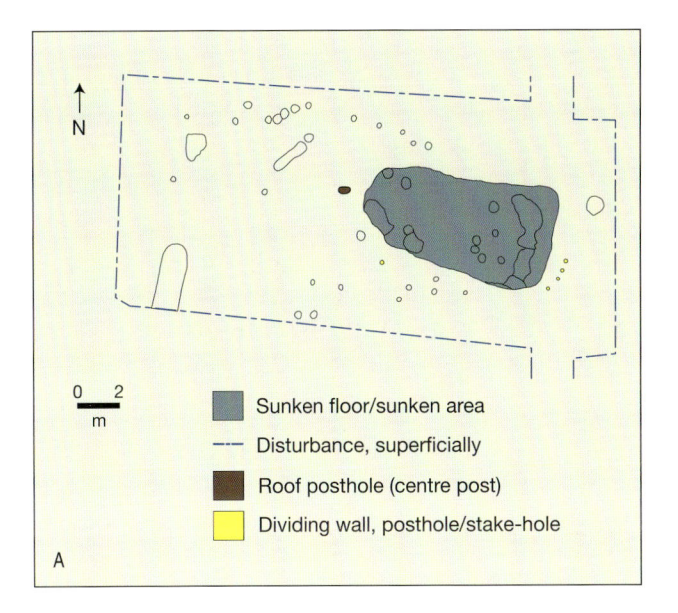

Fig. 2.46. Marienlyst Strand. House 1. A: Ground plan, older/younger soil features and nearby excavation limits. The house site showed significant impact from recent ploughing. For a cleaned ground plan, see Fig. 4.50. For a soil section drawing from this site, see Fig. 4.68.L. B: The sunken floor at a late stage of the investigation. Seen from the east. C: Culture Layer 5, covered by thick soil layers (see Fig. 4.52). Seen from the east.

walls, inner walls, dividing walls, compartments or doorways were not found at any of these sites. Yet, as we shall see later, the contents of a pit a little north of the house sites may shed some light on the settlement.

House 2 (Fig. 2.47)

Disordering from ard-ploughing was not observed. Some later pits had been dug into the fills of the sunken area, causing disturbance. Recent ploughing at the site can explain the missing postholes of the house construction. No remains of the old surface were thus preserved in the area near the sunken floor and recent ploughing must have removed some centimetres of the subsoil beneath. The preserved sunken floor was almost SE-NW aligned. By the time of investigation, a central sunken floor area lay at a depth of 21 cm into the sandy subsoil, but the original depth beneath the top of the old surface must have been significantly greater.

I would like to further substantiate my interpretation of the structure as a house site. First of all, it was a rather large feature which had a raw length of almost 6 m and a width only slightly less. The area was considerable, some 30 m². The building thus belongs to

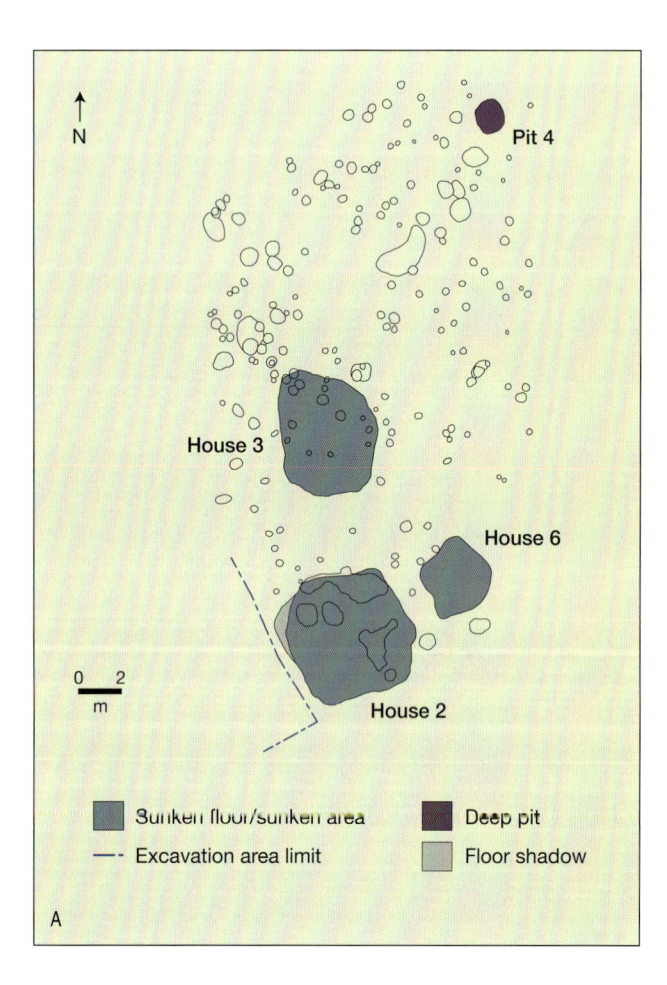

Fig. 2.47. Granlygård. House 2, 3 and 6. A: Settlement plan, older/younger soil features and nearby excavation limits. For further house sites, soil features and excavation limits in the surroundings, see Poul Mikkelsen, report U19995a. The three Late Neolithic house sites showed considerable disturbance from pits, postholes and recent ploughing. B: Cleaned settlement plan. The terrain was slightly west sloping towards the Karup Å valley. C: House 6. After excavating the fills above the sunken floor of this short house, only the established soil bench remained. The shallow floor would have been significantly deeper prior to recent ploughing. Seen from the east.

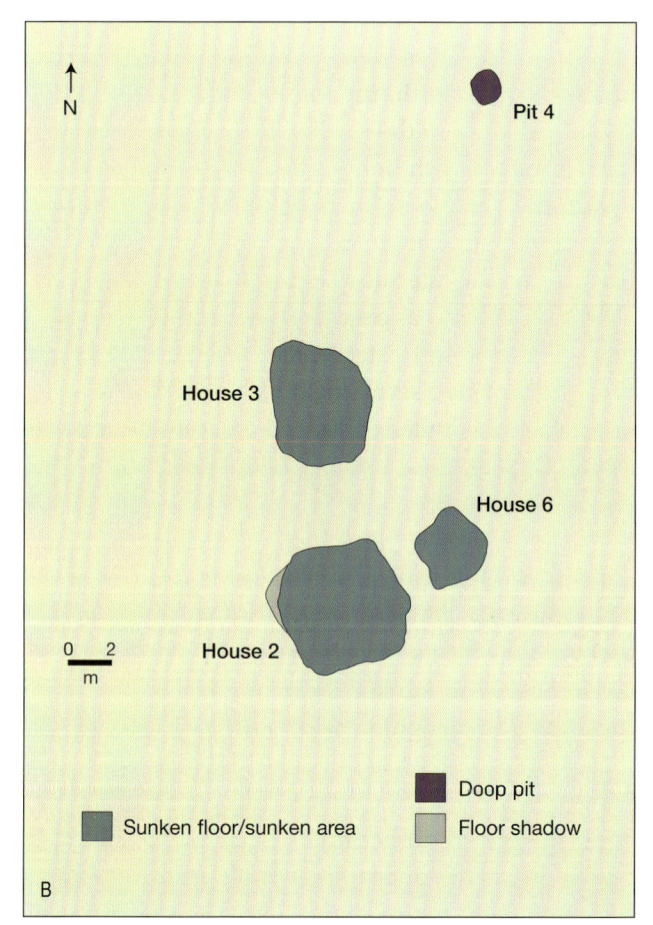

126 Chapter 2

the group of minor houses but might even have been somewhat larger in area before the impact of recent ploughing. Such dimensions far surpass what is generally known from different kinds of Late Neolithic pits in the Central Limfjord region, where these seldom exceed a very few square metres.

Secondly, it appears that the floor itself had a fairly regular outline and became deeper in the middle. The construction of the sunken floor appeared to have cut through some existing pits but. In the N-S section, a large pit appearing some 1.6 m broad and 0.7 m deep as well as some minor digging activities are presumably thus the remainders of activity on the spot before the sunken floor was established. However, this part of the stratification was complex.

Thirdly, the sides were shaped as in other minor houses. To the north, the slope of the side was a little steeper than to the south, in accordance with the local terrain, which only sloped moderately towards the south.

No traces appear to indicate that this house had been burned. I rate the research value of the house site to be quite low as concerns the building structure. No artefacts or soil patches are recorded in the floor horizon. Only the secondary fills enclosed a number of artefact remainders, albeit of generally modest research value.

House 3 (Fig. 2.47)

Some source-critical comments correspond to those stated for the site of House 2 and, likewise, the additional arguments for considering that the sizeable pit represents a sunken-floor house site. Disordering from ard-ploughing was not observed. Some of the disturbing postholes in the area of the house evidently belong to a later three-aisled longhouse.

The preserved sunken floor was almost N-S aligned, which sometimes appears to have been the case with regard to minor sunken-floor houses in the central Limfjord region. In my reading, none of the postholes near the house site belonged to it. The preserved sunken floor was somewhat less in area than the previous. By the time of investigation, a central sunken floor area lay at a depth of 18 cm but the original depth beneath the top of the old surface must have been significantly greater. Numerous level measurements provide evidence that the bottom was reasonably flat, becoming deeper in the centre. Towards the sides, the floor was sloping largely as in the site of House 2. The building belongs to the group of minor houses.

No traces appear to indicate that this minor building was burned. I rate the research value of the house site to be quite low as concerns the building structure and no artefacts or soil patches were recorded in the floor horizon. The secondary fills enclosed a number of artefact remainders, some a little more informative than those in the secondary fills of the previous site.

House 6 (Fig. 2.47)

Disordering from ard-ploughing was not observed. The house site appears to have been severely affected by recent ploughing. The location of this structure in the same limited area as the two previous house sites, in my view, increases the probability that the same interpretation should apply here too. The alignment of the preserved sunken floor is difficult to read but is suggested to have been almost SE-NW. A few postholes were recovered in the area but none of these were considered to belong to the house site.

The preserved sunken floor was much smaller in area than the sites of House 2 and House 3 but it shared with them the important rather flat-bottomed characteristics. By the time of investigation, a central sunken floor area lay at a depth of 10 cm but the original depth beneath the top of the old surface must have been greater. The floor may have been somewhat larger in area and depth before the impact of ploughing but it likely belonged to the group of short houses.

No traces appear to indicate that this short building was burned. I rate the research value of the house site to be quite low as concerns the building structure. No artefacts or soil patches were recorded in the floor horizon. The secondary fills contained pottery of high research value.

Hellegård (Fig. 2.48)

The site was located in Sæby parish, Harre district, Viborg county. The Late Neolithic settlement with two house sites came to light in 1998 when Kurt G. Overgaard was directing an investigation in the immediate vicinity of a grave barrow, where many cremations of different kinds from the Late Bronze Age and the transition to the Early Iron Age were threatened by ploughing (report U1998a). The excavation encompassed the observed graves but not the central parts of the barrow. Furthermore, traces of a row of stones leading from the grave barrow to the west were investigated (Hornstrup et al. 2004:84p, Fig. 2).

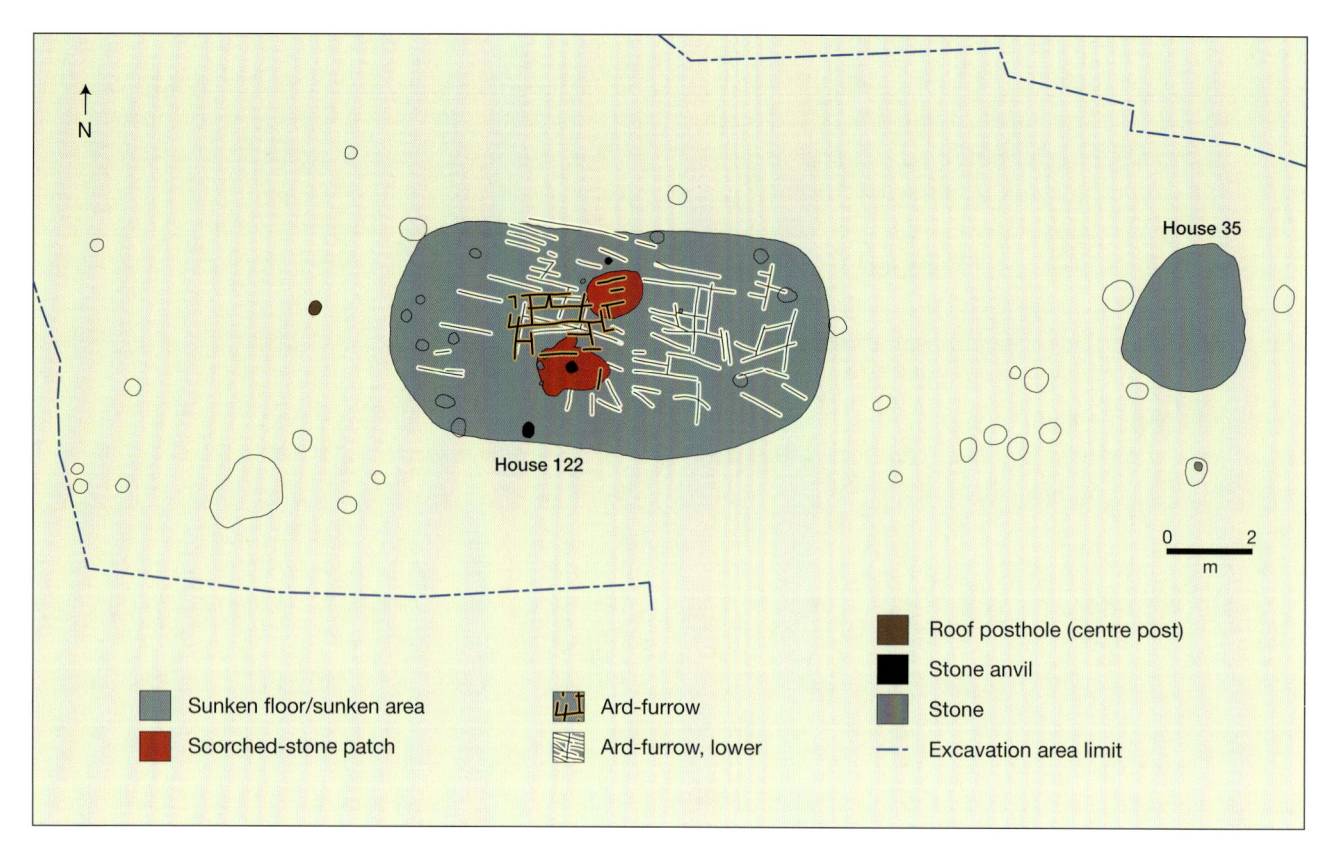

Fig. 2.48. Hellegård. Settlement sketch. Apart from a single posthole from a roof-bearing post, no other traces of the ground-floor area to the west were preserved due to the impact of recent ploughing. In the area of House 122 and House 35 the local terrain was almost flat, sloping just moderately towards the south. To the east and southeast more areas than shown here were investigated but no other house sites were recovered. For further soil features and excavation limits in the surroundings, see Kurt G. Overgaard, report U1998a; Hornstrup et al. 2004). For a cleaned ground plan of House 122 with find spots, see Fig. 4.54.

The sunken floors belonging to a longhouse (122) and a short house (35) were both excavated meticulously. The sunken floors were mainly preserved although it is suggested that a few important postholes in the surroundings belong to the time of these buildings (see Ch. 4). The dimensions of the main excavation area were c. 49 x 26 m. The digging of a few additional trial trenches and some small excavation areas nearby did not result in recognition of further traces of sunken-floor houses.

House 122 (Fig. 2.49 & 2.50)

Several postholes were observable east and west of the sunken floor of this longhouse site, and most probably do not belong to the house site. At least some of these postholes are of later origin, as evidenced for instance by a posthole that cut through the eastern end of the sunken floor. Recent ploughing presumably destroyed many postholes of the wall construction. In the sunken area, the absence of severe disturbances made the conditions for making observations fine because later fills in particular, mainly deposited by winds, protected the sunken floor. In the cross-section, the layers observed during excavation are all thus represented and they evidence the observation that recent ploughing did not reach far down into the sunken floor and therefore had no really destructive effects on it. However, ard-ploughing in the period following abandonment and demolishing of the house intruded onto the floor and the secondary fills although it does not appear to have disturbed the general features of the sunken-floor horizon, the soil traces or artefact remainders significantly.

The terrain in the immediate surroundings was almost flat. The house was nearly E-W aligned, judging solely by the outline of the sunken floor. By the time of investigation, a central sunken floor area lay at a depth of 43 cm but this was not the original depth beneath the top of the old surface. A less steep sunken floor edge near the middle of the south side may perhaps indicate a ramp and entrance area but, because no further supporting traits were observed, this is rather uncertain.

Fig. 2.49. Hellegård. House 122. A: The western half of the sunken floor at a late stage of the investigation after taking up numerous artefacts belonging to the sunken-floor. The established N-S cross-section shows several phases. Seen from the west. B: Close up of the northern part of the N-S cross-section. The limits of the layers and ard-furrows are here incised into the soil prior to drawing (see Fig. 4.68.M). Seen from the west.

Evidently, no vestiges from the presumed western ground floor were preserved, except a single posthole of a centre post. No postholes are proposed as belonging to traces of the wall constructions and no relics of doorways, compartments or dividing walls were found either.

No vestiges were observed to indicate that this house was burned. I rate the research value to be modest as concerns the dwelling structure, whereas the soil patches are quite valuable in this respect. As we shall see later, the artefact remainders are of high research value.

House 35

In contrast to House 122, no traces of ard-ploughing were recorded from the period after demolition of this short house although this apparent absence does not preclude that such activities took place. No later postholes disturbed the sunken floor. The immediate surrounding area of the ground was almost flat and about the same level as that of House 122.

A few nearby postholes cannot be dated, and it is likely that recent ploughing had destroyed postholes after the wall construction. The sunken floor was fairly

Fig. 2.50. Hellegård. House 122. Evidence of repeated ard-ploughing on two levels. A: East of the soil bench, the furrows derive from the first sequences of ploughing into the subsoil of the eastern half of the sunken floor. Seen from the east. B: After wind-depositing of a sterile sand layer, the ard-furrows west of the soil bench thus stem from the second, higher sequence of ploughing in different directions. Seen from the northwest.

Analysis and interpretation of houses with sunken floors

flat. By the time of investigation, a central sunken floor area lay at a depth of 15 cm but the original depth beneath the top of the old surface must have been greater. Vestiges of inner walls, doorways, compartments, dividing walls and other traits were not found either.

No traces indicated that the building was burned. I rate the research value of the house site to be quite low as concerns traces of its structure and no soil patches were observed in the sunken floor. The artefact remainders, when including the secondary fills, are of moderate research value though.

Glattrup IV

The site was located in Skive/Dommerby parish, Hindborg/Fjends district, Viborg county (report U1999a). The excavation took place in 1999, just before the area was to be developed for the building of new family houses. Traces of three two-aisled, sunken-floor longhouses (3, 5 & 7), as well as two two-aisled, ground-floor houses (1 & 4) were recovered, all from the Late Neolithic (Fig. 2.51). The investigation, directed by Kurt G. Overgaard, also included various pits and remains of three-aisled Bronze Age longhouses.

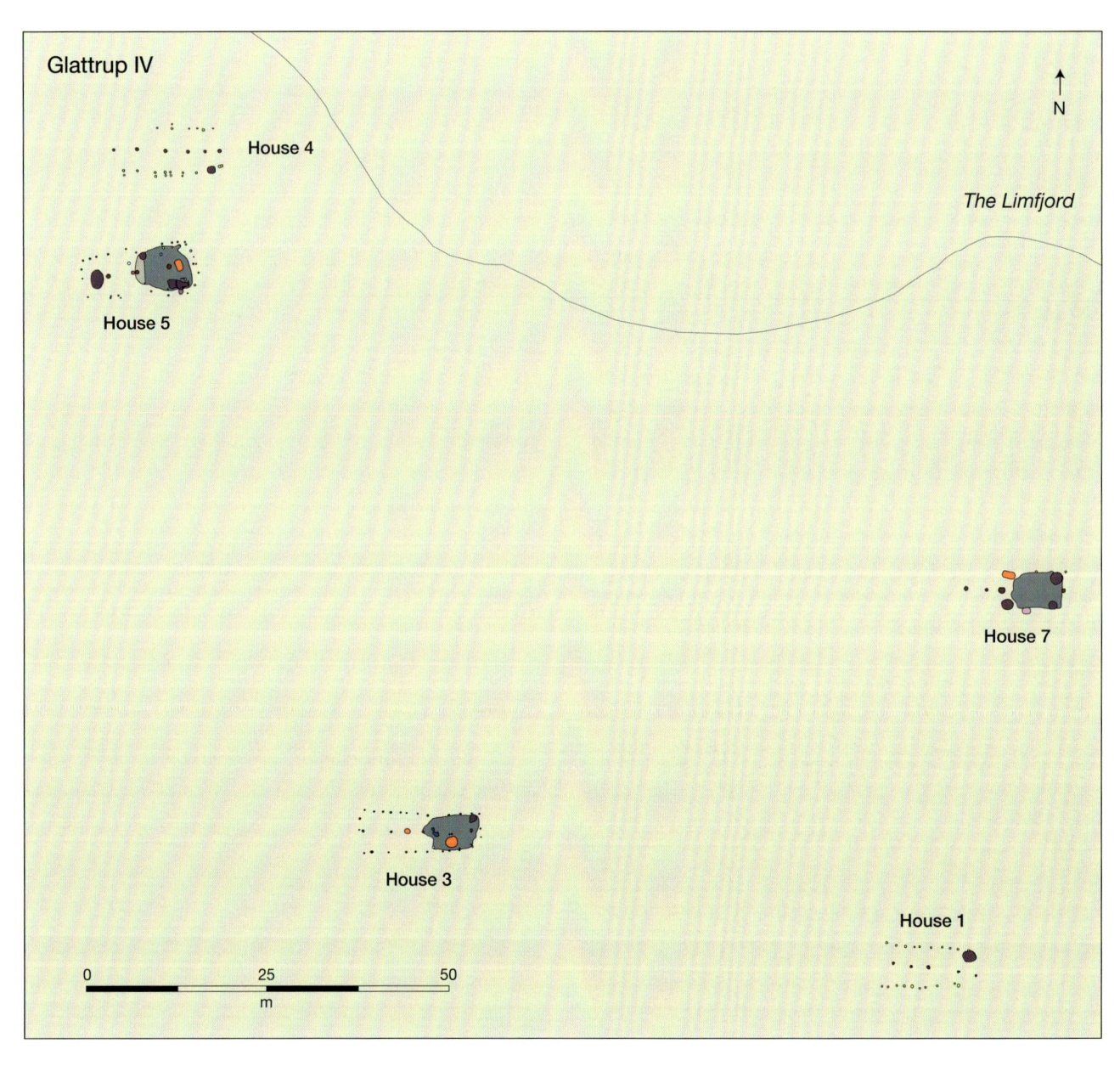

Fig. 2.51. Glattrup IV. Site sketch, cleaned. Adjacent to the Limfjord, the terrain was almost flat, being a few metres high, delimited to the north, east and south by water and wet areas. Houses 1, 3, 4, 5 and 7 were found by digging an extensive net of trial trenches over a large part of the area. For further house sites, soil features and excavation limits in the surroundings, see Kurt G. Overgaard, report U1999a; Simonsen, J., (in prep.).

The site of House 1, a two-aisled ground-floor longhouse, was found somewhat south of House 7 (Fig. 5.5). It was placed on a sandy plot. Its raw length was c. 12.8 m. In my estimate, the raw width to the east was c. 4.4 m and to the west 5.6 m. It thus had a clearly trapezoidal ground plan with a difference of about 1.2 m and it was in the main E-W aligned. In all, 4 holes for centre posts were recovered. It had rows of single postholes along the long sides. To the west, the gable end could have been open or perhaps closed with a different kind of wall construction from the long sides. To the east a single posthole seemed to indicate that a wall had been there. A doorway appears to have been placed in the southern long side wall east of the house middle, where a larger distance was also observed between two of the centre posts. In my reading, the large, deep pit to the northeast belonged to the house, despite the pit appearing to have been cut by a wall posthole to the north. The excavation director nonetheless agreed that the side of the sandy pit may have fallen in (pers.comm.). By the time of the later filling up, the pit could thus seem as if it had been cut by the posthole. To the west it is suggested that two rows of stake- or postholes (not shown), placed symmetrically, belonged to the construction but, presumably, they also functioned as posts for a compartment to the north and south, respectively.

The site of the other two-aisled ground-floor longhouse, House 4, was likewise E-W aligned, and placed a little north of House 5 on sandy grounds (Fig. 5.5). The preserved, raw length was c. 14.7 m and the building was unlikely to have been significantly longer. The raw width was c. 6.7 m. The long sides had double rows of posts, which are not least documented on the southern long side, and they seem to have been parallel. The long sides were apparently rounded slightly inwards towards the ends, as evidenced to the southeast. Entrances cannot be stated with certainty. As in the site of House 1, the large deep pit to the east in my view belonged to the building and, again, its placement was next to the wall, in this instance to the south. Interestingly, the traces of the inner wall to the north and south were more consistently preserved and, on average, had larger surface dimensions.

I shall later present further considerations and ideas on the roles of these ground-floor longhouses for the local settlement (Ch. 5). In the following, I shall focus on presenting the sunken-floor longhouses at the settlement.[6]

House 3 (Fig. 2.52)

Some undated pits and postholes were present in the area of the house and beyond but had apparently not affected the house site. Some disordering from ard-ploughing had mostly affected local areas in the northern half of the sunken floor. Although many postholes from the construction were preserved it is possible that recent ploughing had destroyed a few wall postholes and perhaps also reduced the dimensions of the sunken floor moderately.

The terrain in the vicinity of the house was almost flat. The alignment chosen for the sunken-floor building was almost E-W. By the time of investigation, a central sunken floor area lay at a depth of 24 cm but the original depth beneath the top of the old surface must have been significantly greater. Three postholes along the central longitudinal axis west of the sunken floor clearly belonged to traces of the two-aisled construction. Many wall postholes were preserved on the northern as well as on the southern long side. A few postholes were observed in the eastern and western gable end. The wall outlines of this building are among the best preserved in the Limfjord region. Almost regular posthole intervals appeared, in particular, on the northern long side to the west. The posthole depths and cross-sections varied somewhat as concerns those of wall posts and those of centre posts as well.

The building was clearly broader at the western end, actually nearly one metre more. Regarding the ground plan proportions, the average raw width of the trapezoidal building was significantly less than half its length.

No traces appear to indicate that this building was burned. I rate the research value of the house site to be really high as regards the dwelling structure and also fairly high as concerns the preserved soil patches and artefact remainders. Not least, two sunken fireplaces and sizeable pit are interesting in terms of the activities performed.

House 5 (Fig. 2.53)

Many, more or less undated pits and postholes probably of prehistoric origin were present in the surroundings of the eastern part of the house site, in particular, but did not cause disturbances. A few undated pits or postholes within the boundaries of the house site did not really disturb either. Traces of ard-ploughing into the sunken floor were not observed. Likely recent ploughing had reduced the depth of the sunken floor but seemingly not substantially. The postholes in the wall lines did not apparently go very deep into the ground and would easily have been removed by recent agricultural activity. To the west, a north-south aligned row of easily discernible postholes of recent origin ran across near the gable end but these caused hardly any damage to the house site. In all, several source-critical factors with a possible destructive capacity were present but none of these harmed the house site severely.

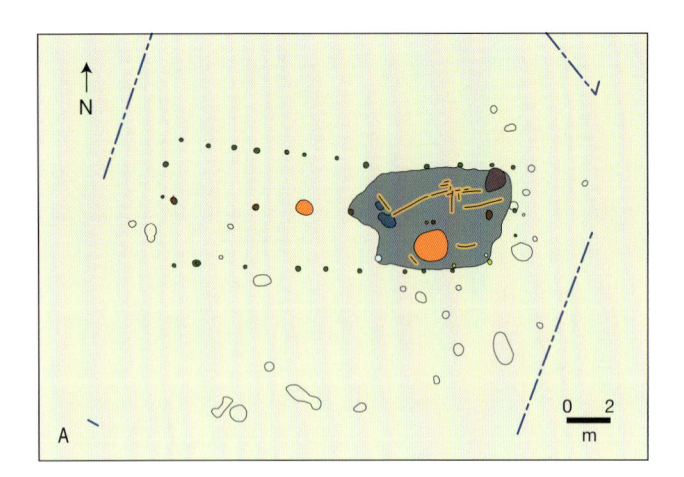

Fig. 2.52. Glattrup IV. House 3. A: Ground plan, older/younger soil features and nearby excavation limits. After demolition of the building, the sunken floor was exposed to ard-ploughing. B: Ground plan, cleaned. The house site was rather well-preserved and evidences a building with a trapezoidal outline becoming gradually broader towards the west. C: The sunken floor and ground floor recovered. Prior to drawing, the limit lines of the soil features are incised into it. Seen from the east. D: The sunken floor and ground floor at a late stage in the excavation, while the large pit and the sunken fireplace were next to be investigated. Seen from the east. For a soil section drawing, see Fig. 4.68.N.

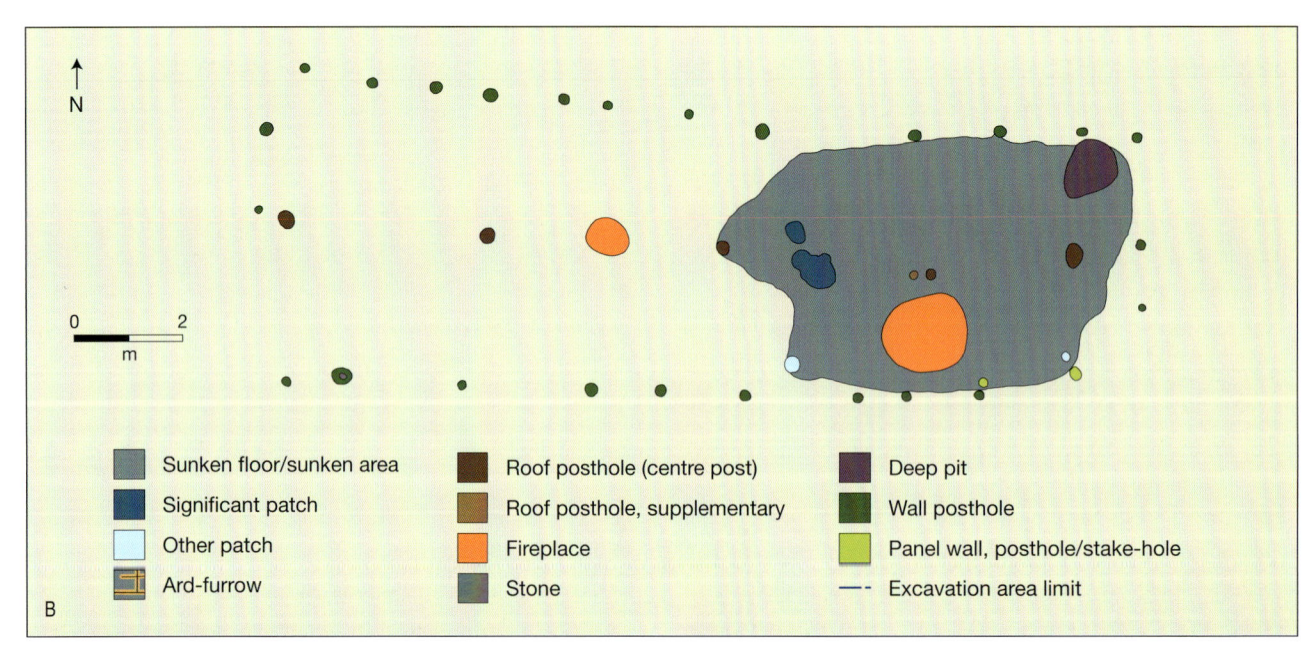

The terrain near the house sloped slightly towards the northeast and the alignment chosen for the sunken-floor building was approx. E-W. By the time of investigation, a central sunken floor area lay at a depth of 20 cm but the original depth beneath the top of the old surface must have been significantly greater. Along the central longitudinal axis, three sizable postholes for roof-bearing posts were recorded. The row of postholes for centre posts was almost in line with one in each gable end. I suggest that the posthole immediately west of the sunken floor represents an extra roof-bearing post.

Several postholes belonged to the outer wall construction to the north, whereas to the south and in the gable end to the west only a few were preserved. It appears that the building was supplied with double rows of posts. In the overall picture, the house had clearly been trapezoidal and, in this case, the western end narrowed markedly. However, the long sides apparently bent slightly outwards. Judging by the northern wall, the construction thus appears to have had two slightly obtuse angles.

Despite the greatly contrasting ground plans, the raw length of the house was nearly the same as House 3, only a little shorter. The house was c. 2.2 m narrower to the west, which is a really marked reduction, giving the ground plan a unique appearance among the longhouses hitherto known in the region.

The western end of the sunken floor cannot be stated definitely because the initial cleaning by means of machine went a little too deep into the area of its western part. However, the continuation of this sunken-floor part was actually observed before that happened and some remnants of soil were still preserved between the middle centre post and the posthole close to the west. While the soil and subsoil still stood fresh in colour, a sketch was therefore made with a contour line guided by the scant traces of the sunken floor in this area.

In my reading, vestiges of an entrance were present in the western part of the outer wall to the south. Two postholes from this wall, together with two from the panel wall, mark the placement of the doorway. The raw outer width of it was c. 1.3 m and the raw inner width c. 1.0 m. This unusual placement to the west in all probability should be seen in relation to the other interior arrangements of the house, but we cannot exclude the possibility that yet another doorway was placed more centrally on the long side towards the east. Traces of compartments and dividing walls were not found.

A really conspicuous quality of the house is the presence of a sunken fireplace and three pits of varying shapes and sizes. A pit with really large surface dimensions was placed centrally in the ground floor to the west, an almost circular pit to the northwest in the sunken floor, and a large, relatively deep pit by its south edge. We shall return in more detail to these pits later but shall merely remark here that it seems that the southernmost part of the latter pit likely formed a "cubicle" in the wall above its subterranean part. However, no clear-cut separation could be observed of the pit fills.

No traces appear to indicate that this house was burned. I rate the research value of the house site to be exceptionally high regarding the dwelling structure, the pits and soil patches, as well as the plant and artefact remainders.

House 7 (Fig. 2.54)

A few dispersed postholes were found to the southeast and southwest of the house site but had caused no disturbances. Ard-ploughing after abandonment and demolition of the building seems to have caused mainly limited disordering of the sunken floor. Later ard-ploughing was even recorded higher up in the secondary fills too. The house site was found under a gravel road track and came to light when contractors removed this road. Due to these circumstances, it is likely that the top filling of the sunken floor and some of its outer wall postholes had thereby disappeared. To the south, an area with deep disturbances from recent activities prevented the possibility of making observations.

The terrain around the house site was almost flat, sloping only faintly to the east. The alignment chosen for the sunken-floor building was approx. E-W. By the time of investigation, a central sunken floor area lay at a depth of 20 cm but the original depth beneath the top of the old surface must have been significantly greater. West of the sunken floor, three postholes along the central longitudinal axis marked out traces of the two-aisled construction. In the sunken floor itself no postholes from this were observable, whereas immediately east of the sunken floor one posthole also likely stems from a roof-bearing post. In the sunken floor, traces of two postholes may thus be missing, presumably due to continued deepening during residence. However, it cannot be excluded that the absence of postholes for centre posts could instead be explained by another trait of the construction.

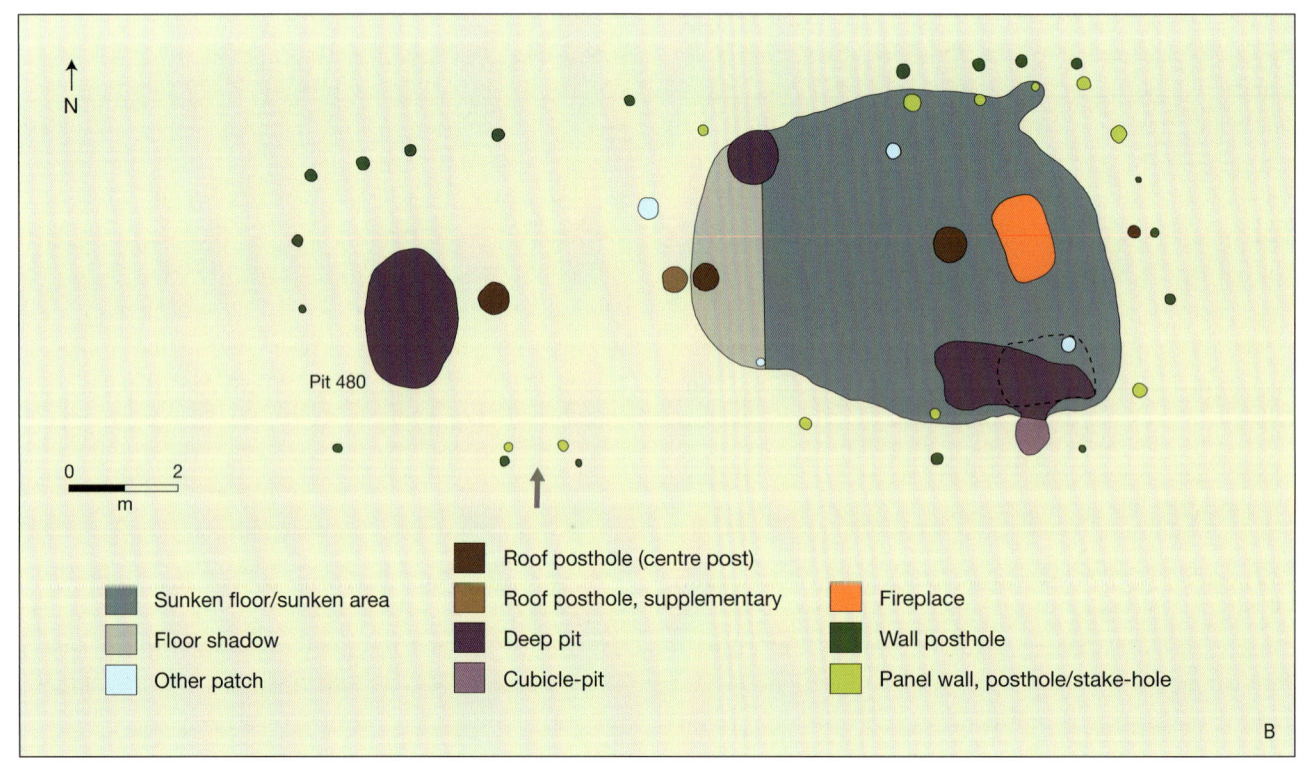

Whereas the two westernmost postholes were about average size, the posthole just west of the sunken floor had an extraordinarily large surface diameter. This hole would easily have provided the basis for a really massive wooden post. Even though the load of the roof itself at the middle could have been large, the capacity to carry the weight of a greater part of the roof in its longitudinal direction may have been quite high. Perhaps a post in the middle of the sunken floor could in this way have been spared. Anyway, east of the sunken floor a post must surely have been necessary to assist carrying the easternmost part of the roof although the posthole was rather shallow. Such a constructional solution would provide a great deal of free, uninterrupted room for specific activities in the sunken floor area.

134   Chapter 2

◂▴ *Fig. 2.53. Glattrup IV. House 5. A: Ground plan and older/younger soil features. No nearby excavation limits. A row of N-S aligned stake-holes to the west is of recent origin. B: Ground plan, cleaned. The house site was rather well-preserved and evidences a building with a trapezoidal outline, being clearly broader to the east. The limit between the cubicle and the deep pit does not represent a soil difference but is a line of interpretation. C: The sunken floor and the ground floor recovered. In the background, the sizable pit 480. Prior to drawing, the limit lines of the soil features are incised into it. Seen from the east. D: The sunken floor excavated, except its large pits, which are next to be investigated. Seen from the east. For a soil section, see Fig. 4.68.O.*

During fieldwork, little could directly be clarified as regards the walls. This was rather unfortunate because the entire ground plan of this particular house, with its noticeable arrangements, certainly calls for archaeological attention. Two postholes are thought to mark out the traces of an inner wall on the northern long side and one of these could have been placed in the corner by the gable end as well. Judging by the placement of these postholes in relation to the course of the sunken floor on the north and south sides it is possible, but not certain, that the house had parallel long side walls due to the very precise sunken-floor outline. While the raw length of the entire building is not measurable, the preserved length was more than 13 m. Judging by the northern wall postholes, the north and south edge of the sunken floor and the line of the centre posts, the raw house width would likely have been come close to 6 m. The cross-section shows an unusually uneven floor to the south but, in the report, it is suggested that the floor was not so uneven originally. No traces of compartments, dividing walls or doorways were observed.

We will look at the contents and other traits of the five remarkable pits surrounding the sunken floor later but for now we shall concentrate on their physical placement. Two pits were located within the contour of the sunken floor although it should be considered that the remaining large pits had also originally been placed within, or partially within, the sunken floor. However, the steepness of the sunken floor side to the south does not indicate that the floor would have been much broader here. It therefore seems plausible that the present relationship between the sunken floor and the pit to the south of it was on the whole as shown on the excavation plan. In other words, this pit was also probably originally located immediately south of the sunken floor and not within it. Furthermore, the unusually regular sunken-floor contour indicates a relatively sharp limit towards the walls but no direct vestiges of any walls were observed. It is precisely here that it is aggravating that the postholes of the southern long side were missing as it would have been highly interesting indeed to know the traces of the construction in this area. Nevertheless, I find good reason to suggest that the pit to the south could have been constructed for placement under the wall, combined with a cubicle within the wall. We shall return later to this arrangement. As regards the two large pits (the northern a sunken fireplace) to the west, it is difficult to assess their original position in relation to the sunken floor. While it is certain that the uppermost top of the soil in the sunken area was removed when initiating the investigation, it is not clear that the floor was much longer. I presume that the sunken floor could perhaps have reached the eastern edges of the pits or a little further to the west.

No traces indicate that this house was burned. I rate the research value of the house site to be a little more than moderate as concerns the dwelling structure and artefact remainders in general. However, the presence of the large pits in combination with the house structure makes it unique.

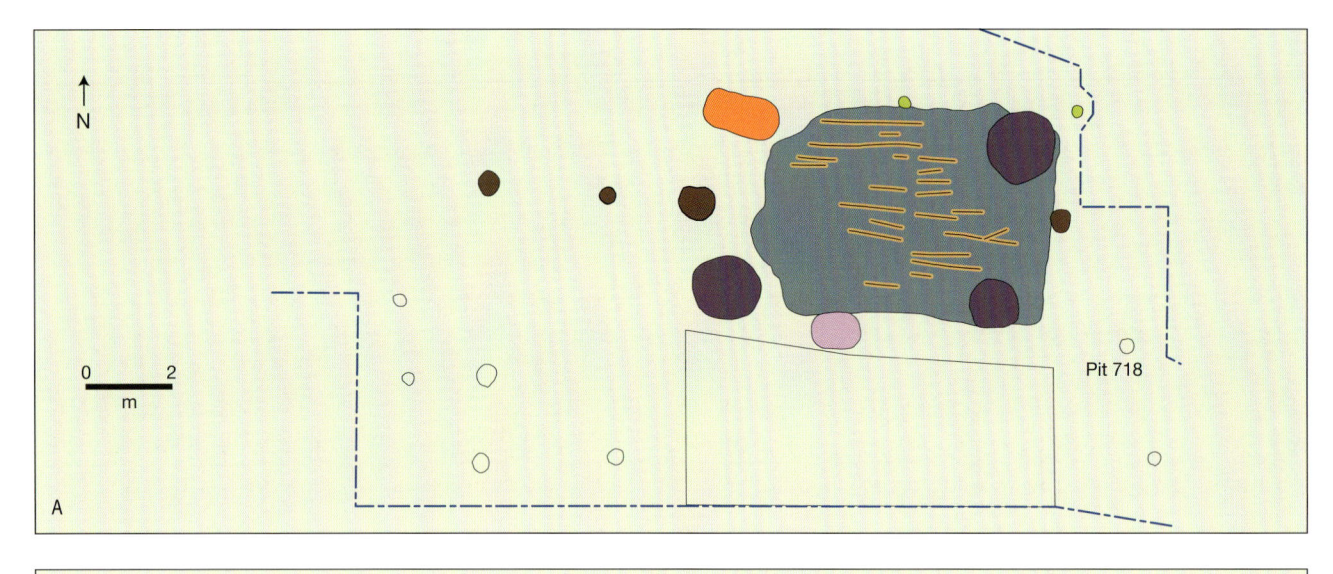

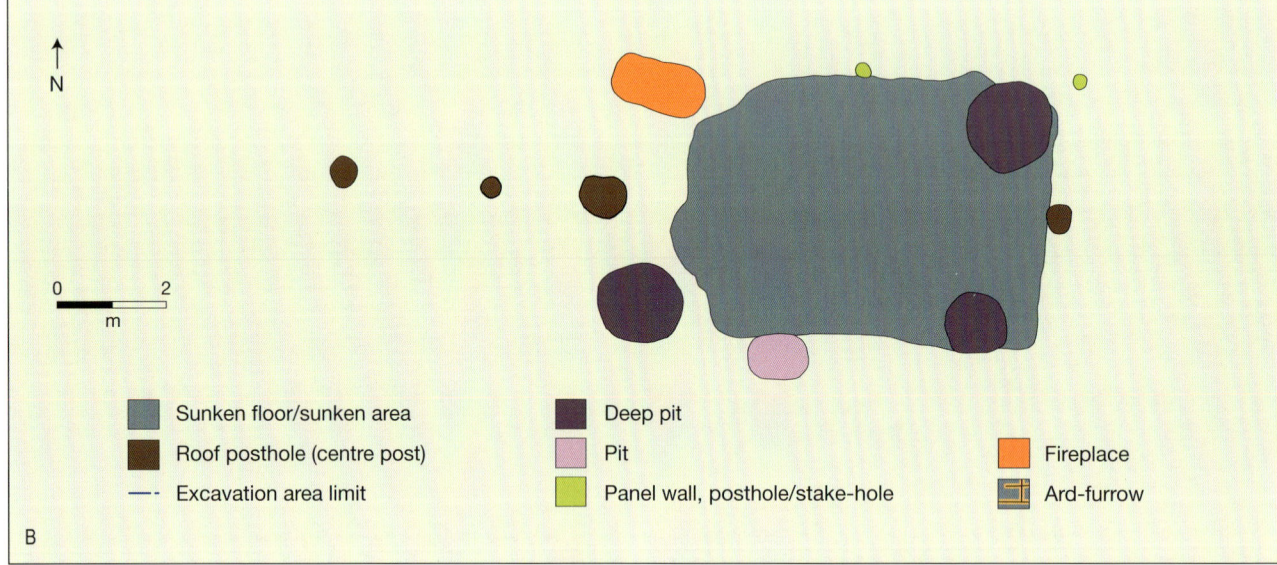

Fig. 2.54. Glattrup IV. House 7. A: Ground plan, older/younger soil features and nearby excavation limits. After demolition of the building, the sunken floor was exposed to repeated ard-ploughing. More recent disturbances such as digging activities and recent ploughing also had an impact on this site. B: Ground plan, cleaned. The house site may have had a trapezoidal outline, becoming gradually broader towards the west. For a soil section drawing from this site, see Fig. 4.68.P. C: Ard-furrows visible on top of the established soil bench as well as beneath it. It evidences repeated ard-ploughing during filling up above the sunken floor. Seen from the east. D: Placed immediately west of the sunken floor, the sizable posthole is here excavated to its bottom. Seen from east.

Rosgårde

The site was located in Mønsted parish, Fjends district, Viborg county (report U2001c). During 2000-2001, the location was investigated in five minor campaigns, all directed by Kurt G. Overgaard (Fig. 2.55). The excavation had to be carried out because former agricultural land was to be transformed into forest by planting trees, a process that would spoil most relics of the prehistoric settlements. In all, the vestiges of a two-aisled longhouse with sunken-floor, a two-aisled longhouse with ground-floor and two pits (23 & 121) belonging to the Late Neolithic were investigated (Simonsen, in press). Besides these finds, traces of three houses with a three-aisled construction from the Older Bronze Age and two three-aisled houses with a preliminary dating to the Late Bronze Age came to light. Some pits, broadly dated to the Bronze Age, were also excavated, as well as a few from the Funnel Beaker Culture.

The ground-floor building (House 2) was found a little to the west of the sunken-floor building (House 1). It was found on sandy grounds and had its longitudinal axis turned slightly towards the SE-NW (Fig. 5.5). Four postholes from roof-bearing posts belong to the central longitudinal axis. An outer and an inner row of postholes mark out the traces of the house walls, which appear to have been rounded near the

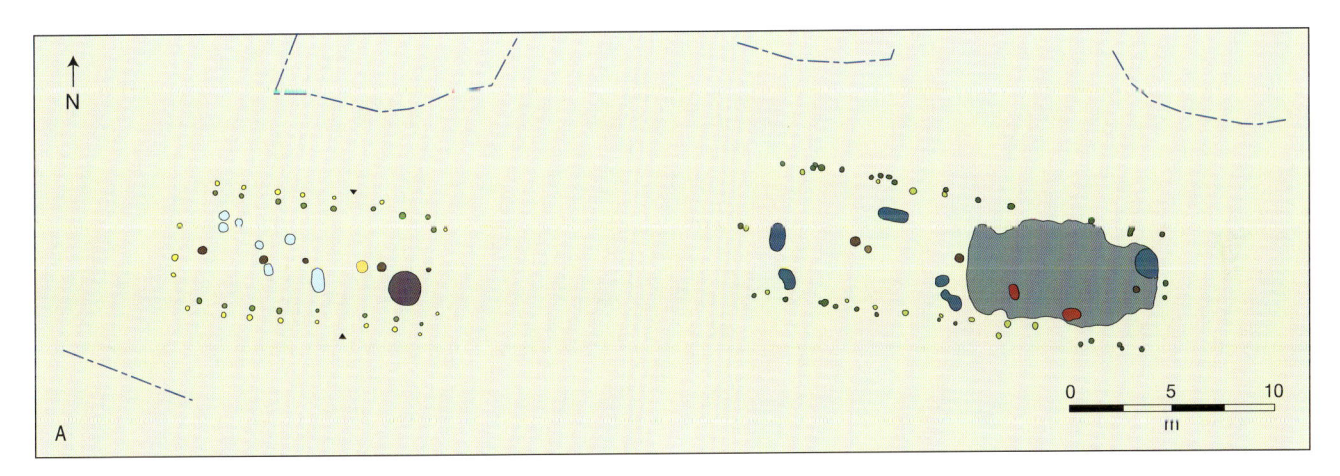

Fig. 2.55. Rosgårde. A: Settlement sketch, cleaned. It shows the placement of House 1 (sunken floor longhouse) and House 2 (ground-floor longhouse, see also Fig. 5.5) and nearby excavation limits. For further house sites, soil features and excavation limits in the surroundings, see Kurt G. Overgaard, report U2001c; Simonsen, J. (im manus.). B: The site of the two-aisled House 2 recovered. Prior to plan drawing, the limit lines of the soil features were incised into it. Seen from the east. C: A deep, circular pit (318) was located in the southeast area of House 2. The pit had rather steep sides and a depth of c. 0.75 m. Altogether 24 flint flakes and 52 potsherds derive from the pit, of which a few bear the remains of Beaker ornamentation. Seen from the east. D: Somewhat more northerly than the two house sites, pit 23 was sub-circular in surface and had a depth of c. 1.15 m. Its sides were markedly oblique all around. It was presumably dug to hold clean subsoil sand. Seen from the north.

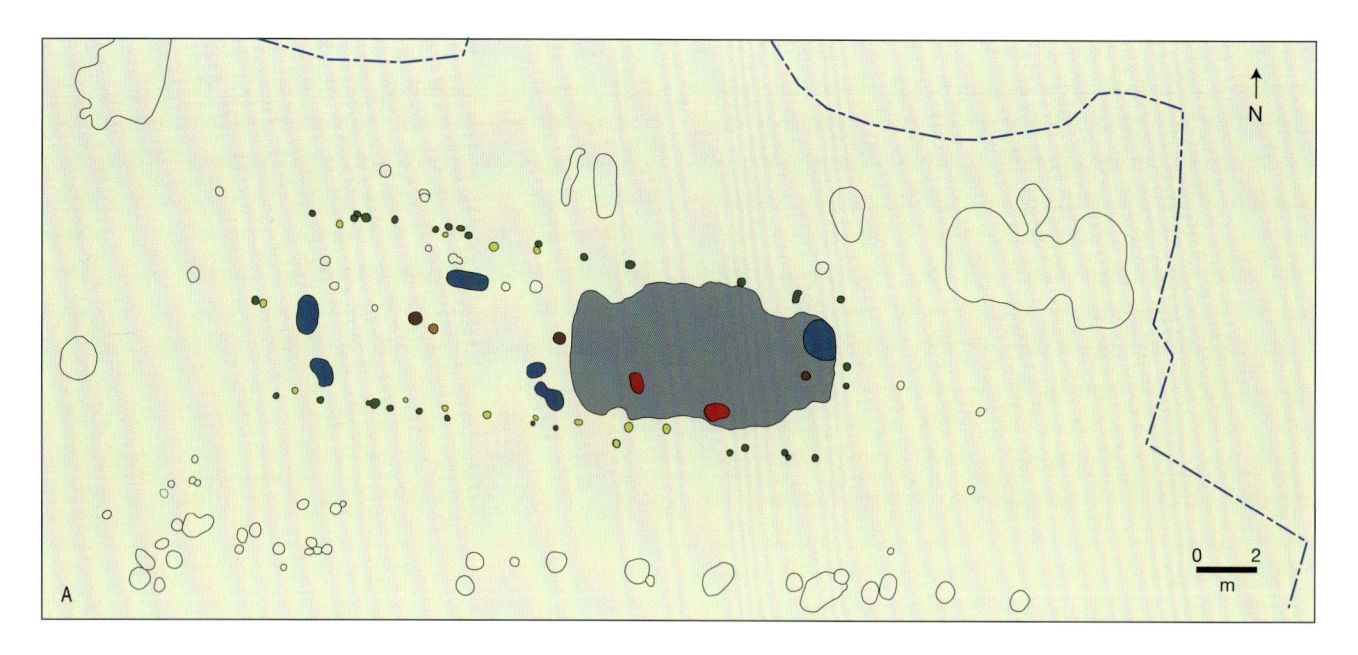

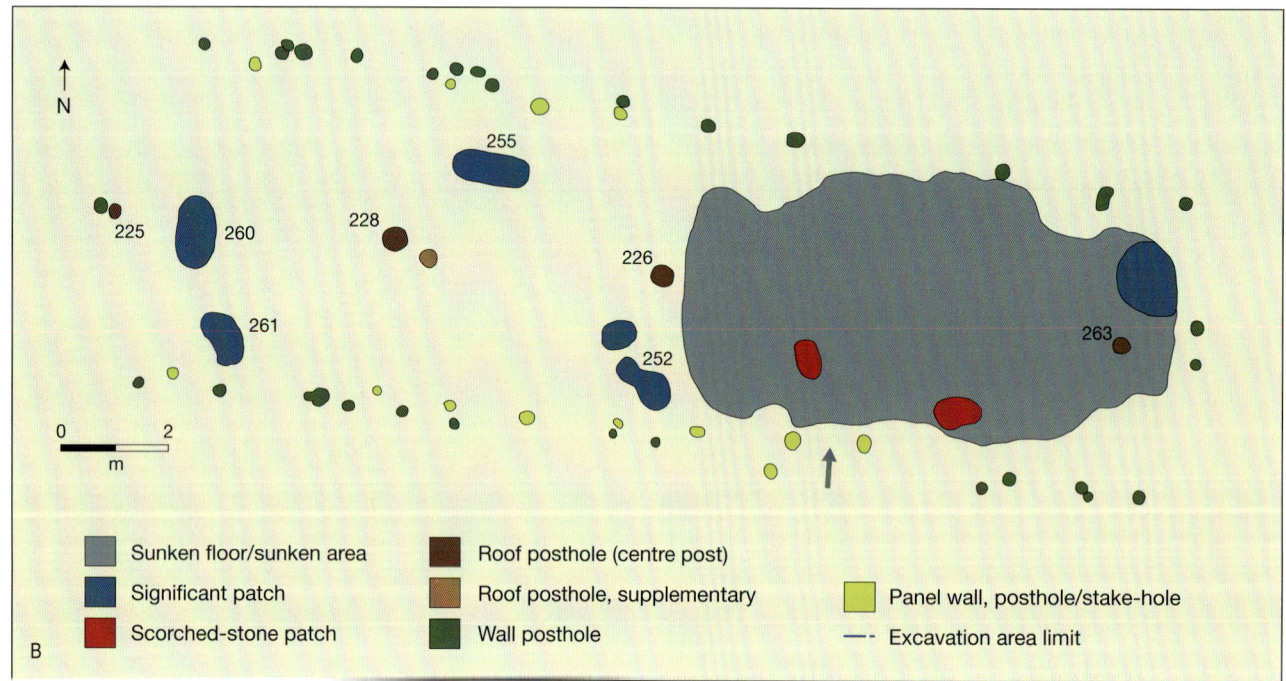

Fig. 2.56. Rosgårde. House 1. A: Ground plan, older/younger soil features and nearby excavation limits. To the south of the site of House 1, an E-W aligned row of postholes belonging to the construction of the northern wall of a three-aisled longhouse from the Bronze Age. B: Ground plan, cleaned. The house site was very well-preserved and evidences a building with a trapezoidal outline, becoming gradually broader towards west. For a drawing of the cross-section of the sunken floor, see Simonsen, J. (im manus.). C: The four centre posts of House 1 at Rosgårde were dug deeply, as shown here. Beginning from the west, the three postholes (225, 228, & 226) had depths of 21, 64, and 44 cm, respectively. The posthole (263) to the east in the sunken floor had a preserved depth of 19 cm. All were likely deeper originally, and thus generally deeper than those of e.g. House 1 at Resengaard. This building also widened significantly towards the west.

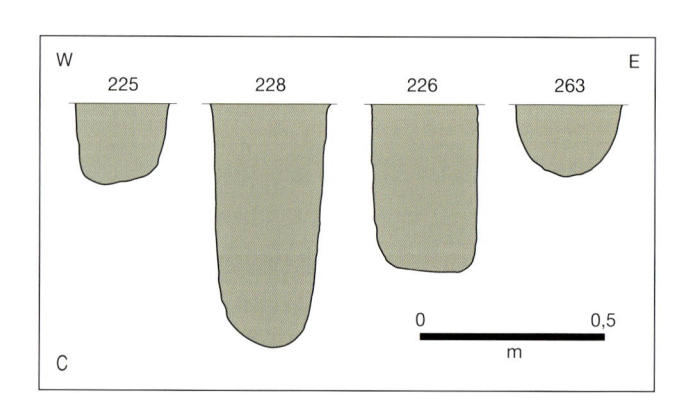

138 Chapter 2

gable ends, as evidenced particularly to the west. The raw house length was c. 12.4 m and the site was preserved by and large in its entire length. The raw house width was c. 5.7 m to the east and c. 6.0 m to the west. The long sides thus diverged moderately, becoming c. 0.3 m broader towards the west. Two doorways were placed just opposite each other in the long sides east of the house middle. In this area, a greater distance was also observed between two of the centre posts although the entrances had been placed closest to the most easterly of these. A large, deep pit to the east was in my view one of the interesting arrangements in the house, and we shall return to this later (Ch. 5).

House 1 (Fig. 2.56)

No traces of ard-ploughing were found at the site of this sunken-floor longhouse. Some animal activity meant that the floor bottom was diffusely delimited downwards in certain areas, but no later pits or postholes were recorded as disturbances. Recent ploughing had probably reduced the surface dimensions and depth of the sunken floor minimally and destroyed some wall postholes. Apart from that, no source-critical factors appear to have affected the house site severely.

Like some other settlement remainders in this excavation area, House 1 was placed on slightly elevated ground. Further east, the terrain fell rather steeply down towards a former lake, Rosborg Sø. The alignment chosen for the house was almost E-W. By the time of investigation, a central sunken floor area lay at a depth of 28 cm but the original depth beneath the top of the old surface must have been significantly greater.

Two postholes for the roof-bearing construction west of the sunken area were relatively deep and far to the west a third minor posthole may also belong to a centre-post. Only one posthole from a centre post was preserved in the sunken floor but another had presumably disappeared due to continued deepening of the floor during habitation. Many postholes from the outer wall construction were preserved on both long sides, whereas in the gable ends only two and one, respectively, were observed. The house appears to have been supplied with double rows of posts but traces of many of these were missing from the inner rows.

The longhouse was clearly trapezoidal, as the building was almost one metre broader to the west. In terms of the ground plan proportions, the average width was close to just a third of the length and it was hence a relatively narrow longhouse. Two postholes south of the western part of the sunken floor were drawn in and likely represent the traces of a doorway. Their internal distance was c. 1.30 m. Vestiges of compartments and dividing walls were not observable. Several pits were recorded within the boundaries of the house site and, in my reading, they belong to its time. We shall return to these pits later.

No traces indicate that the house was burned. I rate the research value of this house site to be very high as concerns preserved traces of the dwelling structure, whereas the value of the soil patches are moderate and the artefact remainders only modest.

Tromgade

The site was located in Thise parish, Salling Nørreherred (district), Viborg county (report U2001a). Kurt G. Overgaard headed the investigation in 2001 and it was carried out just before forest was to be planted in the area. Two sunken-floor house sites and a really large, reasonably flat-bottomed pit were investigated (Fig. 2.57). In my reading, all three represent the sites of longhouses. Several pits rich in pottery from the period were also excavated, and they contribute significantly to the research value of the settlement. Many other soil features were recovered from differ-

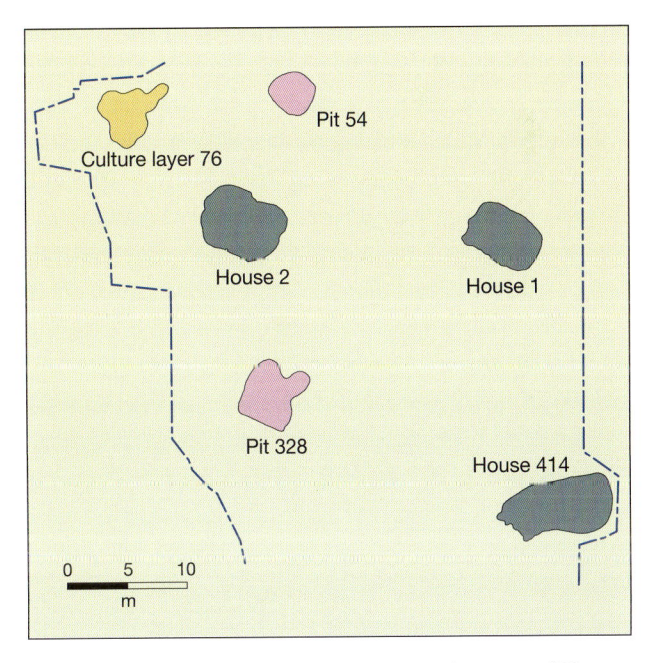

Fig. 2.57. Tromgade. Site sketch, cleaned. The placement of Houses 1, 2, and 414 as well as pit 54, pit 328 and culture layer 76 within nearby excavation limits. For further soil features and excavation limits in the surroundings, see Kurt G. Overgaard, report U2001a. The excavation took place on the higher slopes of a slight hill. The terrain leant faintly to the west in the vicinity of Houses 1 and 2.

ent periods, and among these were observed traces of an almost squared building with two phases, preliminarily dated to the Bronze Age. Relicts of a thus far undated posthole circle were also found, being about 30 m in diameter, as well as a pit from an older part of the Iron Age. The extension of the excavation area was c. 97 x 47 m. Regarding the question of possible area continuity through the centuries, the house sites found here could be early predecessors of the nearby House 1 at Gåsemose.

East of the investigated house remains, some remainders of a further four presumed sunken-floor house sites were observed in a system of parallel trial trenches. A culture layer was also recovered and, according to the excavation director (pers.comm.), it is even possible that this could represent a further one or two sites of sunken-floor houses.

House 1 (Fig. 2.58)

A number of pits and also some postholes were observed to the north and southeast but did not disturb the sunken floor. In contrast, it appears that recent ploughing had certainly had a large impact on the state of preservation of the house site. In my reading, the sunken floor was markedly diminished and traces of the unsunken part had presumably been removed in this way.

The house was situated on sandy ground in the middle part of the excavation area to the east and on slightly south-sloping terrain. It was almost east southeast-west northwest aligned. By the time of investigation, a central sunken floor area lay at a depth of 20 cm but the original depth beneath the top of the old surface must have been significantly greater.

Despite the obvious lack of postholes attributed to the building, I can only agree with the excavation leader that the large, flat-bottomed pit has to be the remains of a sunken-floor house. No postholes were noted in the report as being part of the leftovers from the construction. I suggest that a single posthole belonged to the wall. Other vestiges of walls, doorways, compartments and dividing walls were not found.

No observations indicate that this house was burned. I rate the research value of the house site to be quite modest as concerns the dwelling structure and the artefact remainders. As we shall see later, one of the soil patches early on showed an interesting outline.

House 2 (Fig. 2.59)

The sunken floor had cut across the western part of an earlier, irregular pit, according to the excavation report. In contrast a sub-circular pit has to represent a later digging into the floor. So earlier as well as later settlement traces are present in this local area of the house site. Other later pits and postholes were likewise dug into sunken floor. Recent ploughing appears to have had a severe impact on the house remainders because it likely removed postholes from the construction as well as minimizing the extension and depth of the sunken floor.

The building was placed somewhat west of House 1 and the alignment chosen was almost E-W albeit turned slightly SE-NW. The spot chosen was sandy and the terrain slightly south-sloping. By the time of investigation, a central sunken floor area lay at a depth of 21 cm but the original depth beneath the top of the old surface must have been significantly greater.

Like the previous sites, the lack of postholes attributed to the house site is quite conspicuous. To the west and northwest, only a very few postholes were observed and it is questionable as to whether any could derive from the house construction. Overall, no traces of outer walls, inner walls, doorways, compartments, or dividing walls were observed.

No traces indicate that this house was burned. I rate the research value of the house site to be modest as concerns the dwelling structure and the soil patches, but moderately informative as regards the artefact remainders.

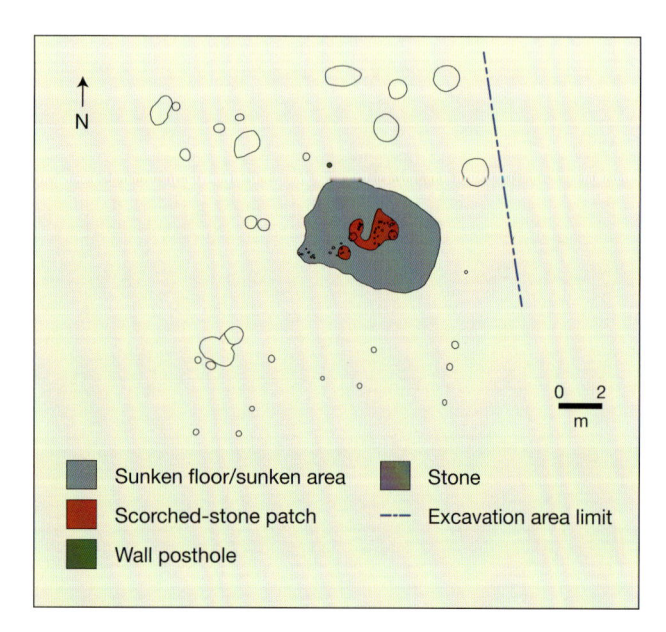

Fig. 2.58. Tromgade. House 1. Ground plan, older/younger soil features and a nearby excavation limit. For a cleaned ground plan with find spots, see Fig. 4.63.

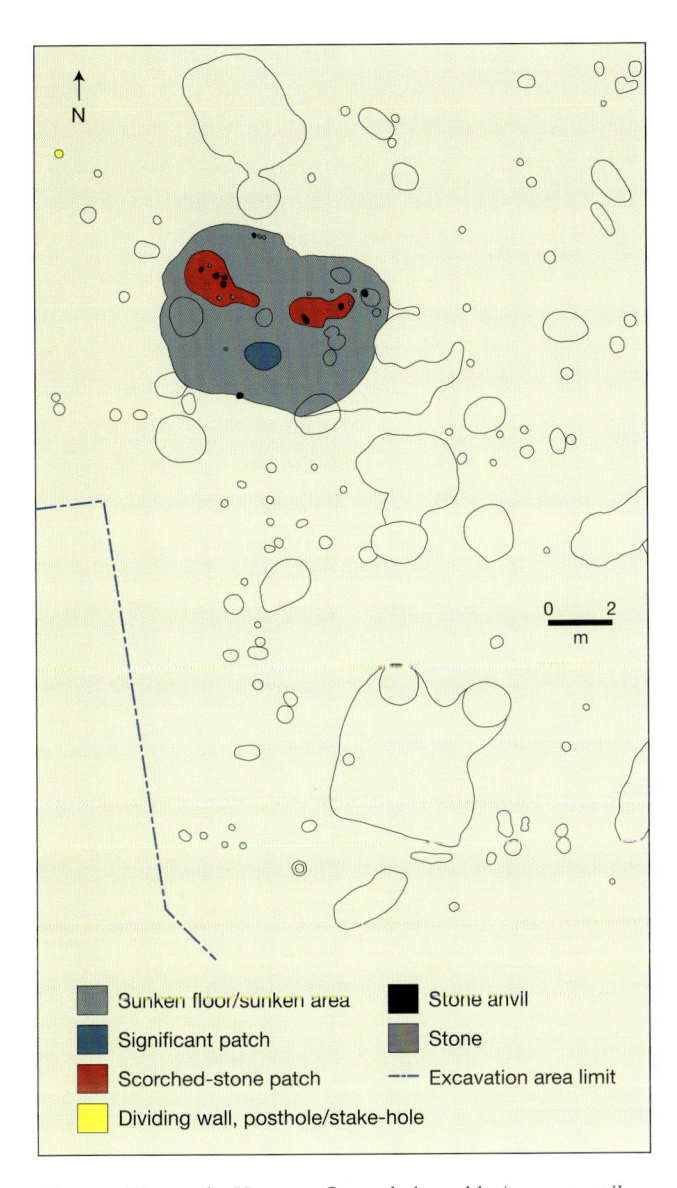

Fig. 2.59. Tromgade. House 2. Ground plan, older/younger soil features and a nearby excavation limit. For a cleaned ground plan with find spots, see Fig. 4.65.

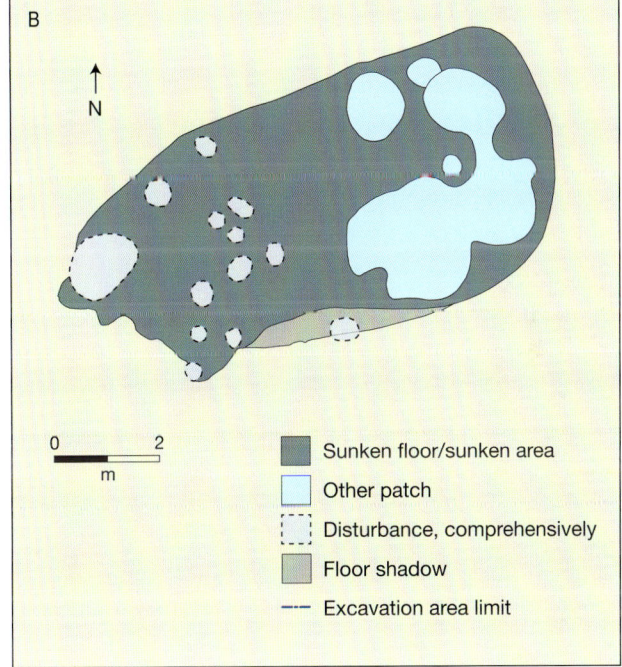

Fig. 2.60. Tromgade. House 414. A: Ground plan, older/younger soil features and a nearby excavation limit. B: Ground plan, cleaned.

House 414 (Fig. 2.60)

In the area west, northwest and southwest of the sunken floor many, more or less undated pits and postholes were recovered although several were likely of later origin. Within the boundaries of the sunken floor, the rows and concentrations of postholes to the west are clearly later than the sunken floor and denote severe disturbances. The large irregular feature to the east is also presumed to represent later digging. Furthermore, recent ploughing has likely affected the house site greatly and probably reduced its extension and depth.

This feature, consisting of mainly brownish-grey soil, was interpreted in the report as a lowering of the terrain and it is argued that, particularly to the west, a gradual transition to the subsoil surface was observable and that the longitudinal direction does not support an interpretation of the feature as the remains of a house. However, in my view it is necessary to reconsider this understanding because I find an interpretation of this as being the relic of a sunken-floor building highly probable. The few finds from the fills do not speak against this view. A cross-section brought in the report shows a depth of 12 cm but the original depth beneath the top of the old surface must have been significantly greater.

The outline of the sunken floor was relatively regular. Some other known sites of houses from the central Limfjord region also show a corresponding alignment. Various obstacles in the terrain, such as big trees for example, may have been present and thereby preventing the most common alignment. Like House 2 at Tromgade, no postholes clearly belong to traces of the construction and no traces of a ground floor are evidenced. The preserved dimensions of the house are thus identical to those of the sunken floor and overall it concerns a feature with a very flat bottom. By the time of investigation, a central sunken floor area lay at a depth of 10 cm albeit not the original depth beneath the top of the old surface. No traces of outer walls, inner walls, compartments, dividing walls and doorways were found.

No vestiges indicate that the house was burned. I rate the research value of the house site to be low as concerns the dwelling structure, the soil patches and artefact remainders.

2.7. Lifecycle biographies of longhouse plots

Having presented more than forty sites of Late Neolithic and emerging Bronze Age house sites, not least with particular attention to the factors that impact on these, it is evident that the formation processes of the individual longhouse plots are all different (*cf.* Schiffer 1987). The overall picture tends to have certain similarities, however, and I shall now try to systematize observations from the twelve Resengaard longhouses by looking for more or less common traits. The resulting portrait, here considered the lifecycle biography of a house plot, can of course also be established to embrace the details of its ecological transformations although I shall refrain from this.

Firstly, a couple of comments on the Resengaard hill over time. The vestiges of use of the hill prior to the sunken-floor houses are actually rather limited. Some presumably Mesolithic pieces of worked flint, a Neolithic grave with amber and sporadic pits with ornamented pottery from Funnel Beaker Culture make up some of the oldest direct traces. From the subsequent Single Grave Culture, a few items of stone and flint reveal a modest presence in this period. We know little about some destroyed grave barrows to the north. An earlier, Late Neolithic settlement left traces in the shape of some pits and other soil traces as well as some Beaker pottery. Thereafter, in contrast to the hitherto scanty vestiges of settlement, there followed evidence of a substantial and long-lasting presence in the Late Neolithic and Older Bronze Age. The grounds with sunken-floor longhouses in the upper part of the hill were, in the main, free from traces of earlier kinds of settlement. This is important and worth considering as it largely eliminates the risk of a mix up with soil traces and artefacts from such settlements.

Even more important is that we are able to conclude that settlements from periods after these longhouses were not really comprehensive. This relates foremost to a small number of three-aisled longhouses. Many pits preliminarily dated to middle or later parts of the Bronze Age were found placed in concentrations. Certain clusters of undated postholes could presumably partly belong to this period too. The Iron Age seems sparsely represented at the Resengaard hill. Provisionally dated to the medieval or post-medieval period, some settlements comprising a few houses and including two cellars and comprehensive systems of ditches came up and disturbed the sunken-floor longhouse sites, albeit mainly superficially and these were always easily distinguished from the prehistoric settlements. In the most recent centuries, farm buildings were not situated on the upper parts of the hill and hence caused no disturbance. The farmstead after which the settlement is named was located closer to the Limfjord coast.

And yet the sunken-floor house sites did not remain uninfluenced over time. From a methodological point of view, it is vital to be aware that we have to deal with destructive as well as preserving agents in relation to the formation of the house sites we meet. Both kinds of agents influence what we can finally add to the lifecycle biographies.

Destructive and preserving agents

As is well known, sandy soils exposed to ever shifting weather conditions from very wet to very dry generally work against the preservation of organic materials that have not been exposed to specific processes such as charring. The decay of the organic components is therefore to be considered an important factor in the site formation.

Damages from destructive powers such as strong winds blowing the soil away and leaving stones, artefacts etc. more or less free of their original soil contexts were not observable in longhouse sites at Resengaard. Furthermore, we see different impacts from animal activities appearing not least to stem from the period of habitation. Networks of tiny galleries, mostly considered to have been made by mice, have caused some damage to the wall areas in particular. Another, mostly minimal disturbance, came from the roots of trees and other plants, these not being clearly observed in relation to the twelve longhouse sites.

The concretely localized destructive agents that concern Resengaard are, nonetheless, largely characterized by human activities. Five kinds of post-habitation disturbances, in particular, play a more or less prominent role.

Firstly, it is evident that ancient ploughing exposed at least three sites of sunken-floor longhouses to varying degrees of impact but I find it likely that all sunken areas of longhouses had more or less already been ard-ploughed during the process of filling up. After tearing down the buildings, ancient ard-ploughing would usually have caused varying degree of disordering of some of the sunken-floor bottoms until sufficient addition of new fills into these raised the level of ploughing.

Secondly, ancient pits caused disturbances to the longhouse sites, albeit mostly sporadically and they seldom appear to have done any really serious damage.

Thirdly, the building of new houses could cause damage. However, the placement of new longhouses on the plots of former longhouses did not take place at Resengaard. And yet, apparently, in one instance a minor house and in another a short house were built on longhouse sites, destroying areas of their ground-floor parts. Two Older Bronze Age three-aisled houses were built such that parts of three sunken-floor houses were partially damaged.

Fourthly, more systems of ditches from the medieval period or later happened to cross the areas of several sunken-floor house sites and, similarly, an old track had forced its way down into a single sunken-floor house site. In some cases, these destroyed rather important parts of the longhouse sites while in others the damage was more or less superficial.

Fifthly, recent ploughing has been responsible for having a considerable impact on some of the house sites. Modern agricultural activities have thus caused severe damage to about a third of the longhouse sites at Resengaard.

Certain human activities and natural forces were, on the other hand, among the major preserving agents. One house site was extraordinarily protected due to the presence of an earthen dike. Even recent ploughing may also have had preserving effects, when soil was gradually ploughed out towards the lower areas thus increasing the soil thickness.

The natural forces that tended to preserve the house sites can be seen not least in the wind deposits resulting in the addition of more or less thick layers of soil which also, for instance, protected certain ard-marks and rubbish deposits from the period in question. When some of the sites of sunken-floor longhouses were found beneath thick soil accumulations, it is likely that wind-deposited sand had played a strong role.

Twelve lifecycle stages

With regard to the publication of Bejsebakken, a key illustration shows three important steps in the house site formation process, indicating the habitation phase (with a cross-section of a roofed house construction), the post-abandonment phase (the house torn down and the dumping of fills in progress) and the ploughing phase (Sarauw 2008, Fig. 5).

When looking for the longer lifecycle of a house plot, I consider twelve stages to be relevant in the case of the Resengaard longhouses. The stages can be described briefly as follows:

Stage 1: Natural vegetation prevailing. It is remarkable that the plots chosen for placement of the sunken-floor longhouses were often rather sterile without any substantial traces of former settlement. As may be seen from the source-critical considerations, it was an exception to the rule if settlement traces earlier than the Late Neolithic were found in precisely the same plots. The sporadic soil traces from the Funnel Beaker Culture were thus generally not found in exactly the same plots as the sunken-floor longhouses.

Stage 2: Digging the sunken floor and building the longhouse. The digging of flat-bottomed sunken floors appears to have taken place early on in the house-building processes. Good observations exist to document this, particularly from House 1 at Resengaard. It would certainly also seem rather inconvenient if the many cubic metres of subsoil had to be dug up and carried out after, for instance, completing most of the house. The surplus fill from this activity must have been quite considerable. Where this mostly sterile surplus soil ended up, we do not know. Presumably it was deposited just outside in the immediate surroundings, perhaps used for levelling an area, for instance. The stakes of the panel walls were placed after the sunken floor was dug. If these had been placed before digging, the sunken area would not extend behind the stakes. Vestiges of panel walls are currently in evidence particularly at Resengaard.

Stage 3: Residence and continued hollowing of the floor. Changes and major repairs to the houses are expected to have taken place in most houses during residence. However, we only have some relatively clear indications of this in relation to four longhouses. We have seen how House 41 was reduced in the length by removing the western part, how House 2 was extended towards the east and how, in House 1, a noticeable replacement of the southeast panel wall was carried out and extra supporting posts apparently placed for the roof construction. In addition, it is evident that a large cellar-pit had collapsed in House 5 at Glattrup IV, and was never re-established. During residence, the sunken floors gradually became further lowered, more in some areas of the sunken floors than in others. Very thin layers may have been removed occasionally for cleaning purposes and, in other instances, limited areas of some floor surfaces appear to have been switched around locally, without regular pits dug. Floors which, from the beginning were presumably rather even over the main part were gradually hollowed as time went on such that deeper parts would be created at some distance from the walls (Fig. 2.61). This lowering frequently appeared in certain parts of the floors in particular. The wooden centre posts had likely, in most cases, originally been somewhat dug down into the subsoil but, as the floor level gradually lowered, some of these were little by little freed from their former hole. Such a process of gradual disappearance of the postholes in the sunken areas is difficult to prove but the excavation experiences as regards a lack of holes for centre posts in the sunken floors are becoming substantial. I, for one, am convinced that this is what actually often happened, not only at Resengaard but also elsewhere, when experienced excavation teams are not able to demonstrate traces of centre posts over large spans in the sunken areas. The observation that postholes in the sunken parts are especially missing, in contrast to in the unsunken parts, in my view tends to support this assumption.

Stage 4: Final residence and post-residence life. As we shall later see in more detail, the recorded soil patches must mainly represent the latest period of residence because, as time went on and parts of the floors were cleaned and rubbish removed, these would gradually have lowered and former traces of activity would thereby have been destroyed. Besides artefacts, flint/other stone waste, and various organic rubbish, the components left in the floor horizon after abandonment concerned diverse soil patches, pits and pit-like soil features stemming from different activities. It is usually difficult to pinpoint specific traits belonging to the post-residence life of the house (Ch. 5 & Fig. 5.6). Sometimes, patches were covered with sandy soil at a late stage and this could have been done to level the floor in readiness for new functions in the post-residence life of the longhouse, as in e.g. presumably House 2 at Resengaard and House 122 at Hellegård.

Stage 5: Tearing down the longhouse. In this stage, the roofs, the timber constructions and the walls are all demolished. It seems very likely that strong timber

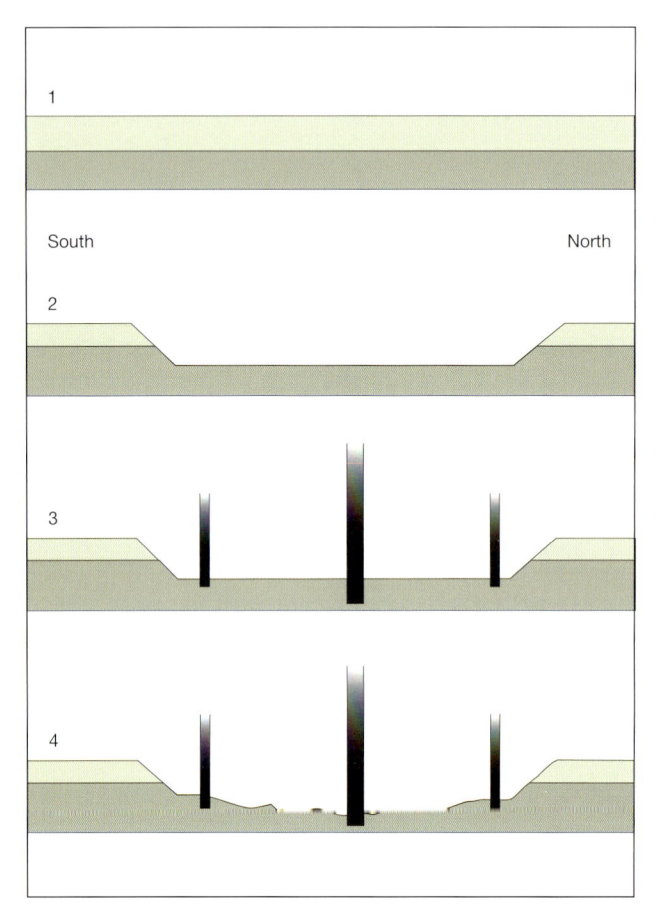

Fig. 2.61 Schematic cross-sections of four stages of a sunken floor. 1: The plot for building the longhouse is selected. A moderate layer of surface soil (light green) covers the subsoil. 2: The sunken area dug to a certain level, being a little broader than the coming sunken floor. 3: Stakes for panel walls facing the interior and a centre post are now put in position (not shown is further topsoil removed, regular wall posts placed, and a broad turf-wall built on the outer side of the panel walls). 4: After long use, the sunken floor has become markedly lower, due to the removal of subsoil during habitation and thereby resulting in the gradual release of the centre posts (cf. Ch. 4). Inspiration for this sketch was drawn particularly from the results of the investigation of the site of House 1 at Resengaard.

and other wood, as well as some other things, were kept to be reused. Only exceptionally were the houses burned. As noted, one longhouse had deliberately become a regular site of fire, whereas in two other house sites it seems that just limited remaining organic scrap from the construction and so on may have been burned. In all three cases, I assume that the burning was carried out on purpose.

Stage 6: Possible use of the open sunken area as an interim activity area. The turf walls would probably have been demolished and spread over the former sunken floor, thereby causing a modest elevation of the bottom. The now open, sheltered space would surely "invite" different activities, such as for instance, having fires and so on. And yet the study of traces in the secondary fills was not given much priority during the Resengaard investigation. In most cases ard-ploughing would likely have spoiled such traces.

Stage 7: Dump site and ard-ploughed field. Several examples from Resengaard and elsewhere have documented that the ard-marks from the initial ploughing activities sometimes reached down into the subsoil below the floor horizons. In my understanding, ploughing would often have been carried on repeatedly between continued dumping activities. Subsequent filling up and ploughing may thus have taken place in a number of steps at Resengaard (as also evidenced in particular as regards Hellegård and Glattrup IV). The placement of different domestic refuse and soil began very soon after the sunken-floor longhouses were abandoned. Artefacts and other things were, in most cases, found in these secondary fills. Vegetation horizons in the abandoned sunken areas have not been observed at Resengaard. The compression and natural "burning" of the organic components would later have given some room for some additional fills in the now shallow sunken areas. This is documented from dateable pottery fragments and other objects in some secondary fills, e.g. in the site of House 6 at Glattrup I/III.

Stage 8: New settling on the plot. A minor house and, in another instance, a short house were apparently built on the former ground-floor areas of sunken-floor longhouses but, usually, the spots of the older buildings were not reused for sunken-floor longhouses at Resengaard. The next houses to be constructed in certain areas after sunken-floor houses were some three-aisled buildings from the Older Bronze Age.

Stage 9: Natural vegetation prevailing. At the hill, sporadic settlement was present periodically and cultivation is not documented from this stage. Between the Late Neolithic/Bronze Age and the medieval period only modest settlement activities are thus traceable. Natural vegetation appears to have prevailed for long periods at the hill.

Stage 10: Medieval or post-medieval activities. Ditches from this time crossed several sunken-floor longhouse sites. In all, the remains of a couple of land houses, two cellars, ditch systems and certain other features characterize this stage. Agricultural activities presumably took place but the balance between these and the natural vegetation is not known.

Stage 11: Recent, cultivated field. Relatively recent ploughing out of soil from the upper hill towards the lower terraces has presumably contributed to the accumulation of relatively thick topsoil layers, in combination with wind deposits. The preservation of certain house sites (such as House 1, 2 & 41) has apparently benefited significantly from this. The mechanization of farming and, in particular, deep ploughing has, however, led to comprehensive disturbances of several house sites. The level of the sunken floors had, in many instances, ensured a rather good resistance to such agricultural activities. Every year, however, the modern plough would almost imperceptibly have reached deeper into the sunken area. Over the decades, this would be measurable. Postholes of the house walls would gradually be difficult to trace and would be the first to disappear, and also often most or all of the traces in the ground-floor part. Gradually, the secondary fills above the sunken floor would be diminished in depth and the plough would eventually become a threat to the sunken floor horizon.

Stage 12: Archaeological investigation and new settlement. Besides recent ploughing, certain activities could have threatened the house sites before the excavation campaigns took place at Resengaard. Some initial roadworks have done harm over a limited area. The initial sewer work was also a damaging factor but, in terms of the longhouse sites, only House 2 was damaged, when thick soil west of the sunken floor was removed. The archaeological investigation campaigns now destroyed the house sites, which have now ended up as objects of archaeological study. The building of detached houses, the making of streets and many other activities now took place.

The plot of the much exposed House 14 is selected as an example as regards the lifecycle transformations, as it is precisely concerning this house that

Life cycle. House 14, Resengaard	
Stage	Activity	Evidence on the plot
1	Prior to any construction	No early traces of cultivation. Natural vegetation prevailed. No observable traces of Funnel Beaker Culture, Single Grave Culture or the early Late Neolithic.
2	**First dwelling period**	Digging to establish the sunken floor and construction of House 14. Postholes of centre- and outer wall posts as well as postholes of dividing walls and the outline of the sunken area indicate the construction and interior arrangements.
3	Residence	No certain soil patches or artefacts from the early and middle part of the occupation.
4	Final time of use during residence & after-residence	A number of finds from the sunken-floor horizon as well as a few soil features.
5	Demolition of the longhouse	No specific observations available. No traces of burning of the construction.
6	Use of the open space	No specific observations on the use of the sunken area after demolition of the longhouse.
7	Subsequent evidence	Agriculture and domestic refuse. Ard-furrows, evidencing a cultivated field on the plot, had cut through the floor horizon into the sandy subsoil. Substantial finds of pottery and other artefacts deposited as secondary fills. Hereafter natural vegetation likely prevailed.
8	**Second dwelling period**	An early three-aisled longhouse, House 25, overlapped with the eastern gable end of the site of House 14. A few pit digging activities had caused damage.
9	Following prehistoric settlement	Natural vegetation prevailed. No specific observations available.
10	Medieval/post-medieval period	A broad E-W ditch had been dug into the upper parts of the secondary fills.
11	Modern times	Effective recent ploughing had taken place but, due to moderate local terrain hollowing, the site of House 14 had avoided heavy impact.
12	**Third dwelling period**	The old house site was destroyed by archaeological excavations before the building of detached family homes took place in the area.

Fig. 2.62. House plot formation. Taking the plot of House 14 at Resengaard as an example, the nature-to-culture-to-nature cycles are at the forefront in the suggested life-cycles, based on my reading of evidence. This plot and its immediate surroundings appear much influenced by several destructive factors but also one factor in particular that was of a preserving nature.

several destructive agents were active over time even though the house site "survived" due, in particular, to one factor (Fig. 2.62).

The above biographic outline clearly demonstrates that the house plots have had somewhat changing formation processes that became almost cyclic. The lifecycles of the house plots thus point to the cyclic nature-to-culture transformations over several millennia at Resengaard, in which nature was prevalent for long periods between more or less short stages of tilling or settlement, the longest period so far embracing the period of sunken-floor longhouses.

This outline also emphasizes the reality that – besides the organic decay – many factors have, over time, endangered the building remainders at Resengaard. It is actually out of the ordinary for a house site to have escaped considerable damage. Yet, in particular as regards a few longhouse sites on the Resengaard northwest terrace, the "struggle" between antagonistic agents actually resulted in extraordinarily good preservation.

2.8. Further Limfjord region traits of sunken floors

Local differences distinguished the longhouse building practices in the Limfjord region through the Late Neolithic and emerging Bronze Age but two main traditions seem to have prevailed, namely two-aisled longhouses with and without sizeable sunken floors, respectively.

The ground floors always took up a good deal of the interior floor area in the sunken-floor longhouses. The relative size and placement of the sunken and unsunken areas can play a major role when considering whether the site of a certain longhouse should be ascribed to the main group of sunken-floor longhouses in the region. Nonetheless, when it comes to sites much disturbed by recent ploughing or other factors, this can be difficult to assess.

Relative lengths of the sunken floors

The sunken-floor house sites from the central Limfjord region have been presented in a late group, including Resengaard, and an early group with several Beaker settlements. We shall now look at examples of the relationships between the raw lengths of these houses and their sunken floors (Fig. 2.63). No suitable

Table of raw dimensions

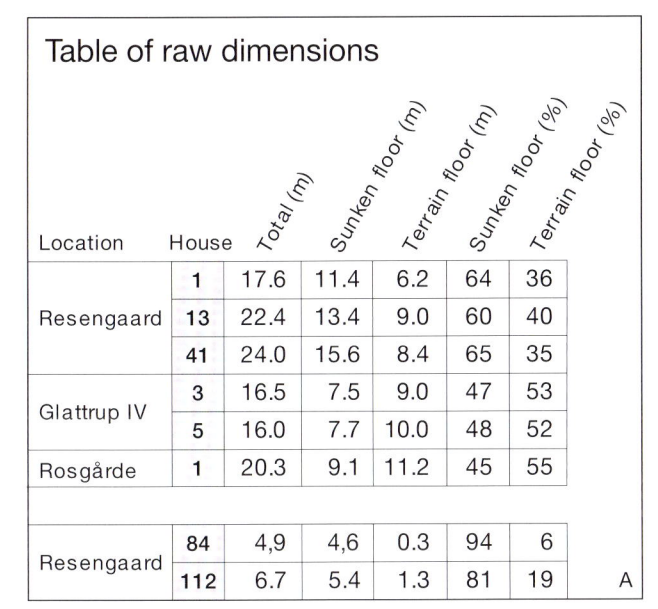

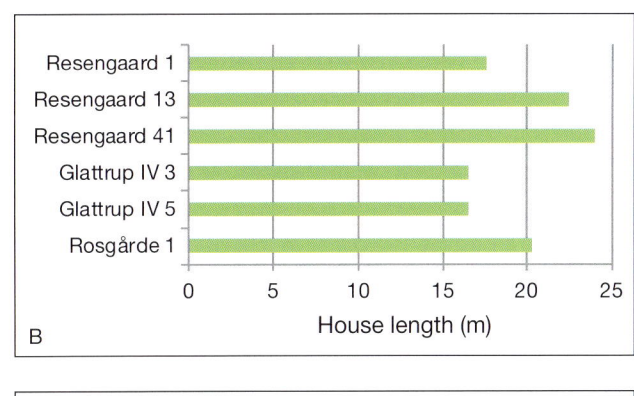

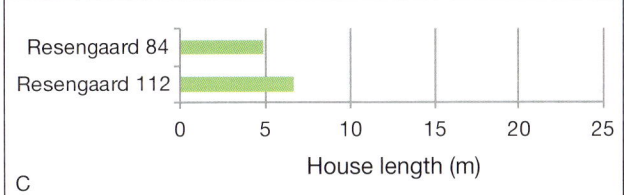

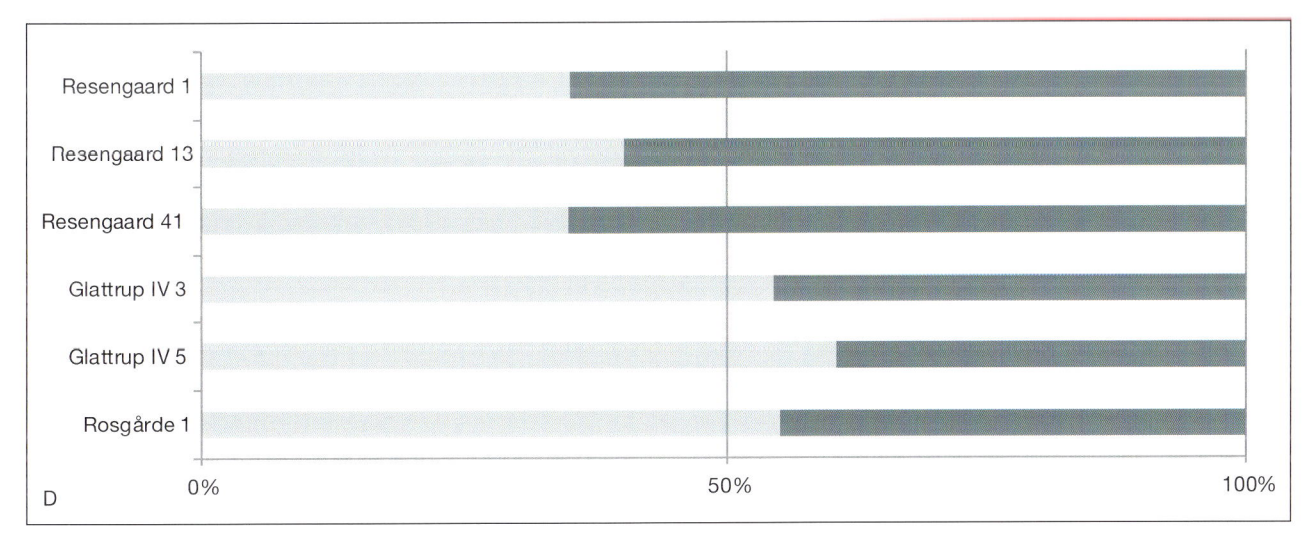

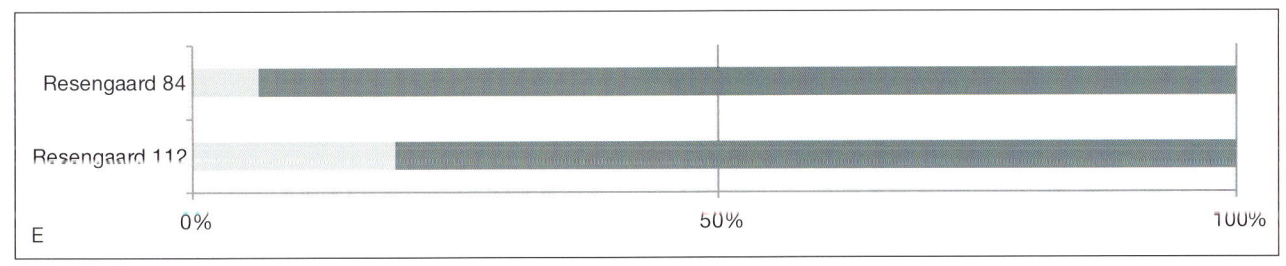

Location	House	Total (m)	Sunken floor (m)	Terrain floor (m)	Sunken floor (%)	Terrain floor (%)
Resengaard	1	17.6	11.4	6.2	64	36
	13	22.4	13.4	9.0	60	40
	41	24.0	15.6	8.4	65	35
Glattrup IV	3	16.5	7.5	9.0	47	53
	5	16.0	7.7	10.0	48	52
Rosgårde	1	20.3	9.1	11.2	45	55
Resengaard	84	4,9	4,6	0.3	94	6
	112	6.7	5.4	1.3	81	19

Fig. 2.63. Floor lengths in well-preserved sites of six longhouses and two minor houses. A-C: The "floor shadow" included in the sunken floor length for House 5 at Glattrup IV. D-E: Relative lengths (left: ground floors; right: sunken floors).

examples of early sites of minor sunken-floor houses are available whereas a few do exist among the late.

From the early part of our period, in particular, the reasonably well-preserved ground plans from Houses 3 and 5 at Glattrup IV and House 1 at Rosgårde show that the sunken floors in these took up just 45-48 % the raw house length. Due to the influence of recent ploughing, it cannot be excluded that the percentage may originally have been slightly higher. The relative lengths of these three longhouses are surprisingly similar despite two of them broadening significantly to the west whereas the third narrows. However, only calculations from many clear ground plans from this period can help to decide whether the stated range of percentages comes close to a norm for sunken floor proportions from this early part of our period or not.

Three rather well-preserved ground plans from Houses 1, 13 and 41 at Resengaard form suitable examples from the late group and show that the sunken floors took up 60-65 % of the raw house lengths. Houses broadening to the west, as well as those with parallel long sides, are both represented. Again, the percentages are quite close but markedly higher than the examples from the early houses.

The mean values indicate a considerable increase, from about 47% to about 63%, in the raw house lengths. From calculations of these six longhouses, the indications are thus that the sunken floors in early houses in the central Limfjord region took up half or just under half the house length while those in late houses took up markedly more than half, approximately two-thirds of the raw house length. Again I must emphasize that a larger number of well-preserved building remainders need to be included in the calculations before we can reach any conclusive statements about the norms for relative sunken-floor dimensions. With the current growth in investigated house sites, however, this may soon be possible.

Very different from the above two-aisled houses were the minor sunken-floor houses without traces of centre posts. Houses from Granlygård, Hellegård and Resengaard are represented in this group but two ground plans from Houses 84 and 112 at Resengaard in particular can give an idea of the relationship between the sunken floors and the raw, entire house lengths. It appears that the preserved sunken floors took up 81-94% of the raw house lengths. However, a larger number of well-preserved building remainders need to be included

Sunken-floor areas in special longhouses

Some special longhouses with sunken-floor areas shall now be considered briefly. Judging by their ground plans, these buildings would have deviated markedly in their layout from the above buildings and thereby also throw into relief the shared traits of the aforementioned groups of early and late longhouses.

Investigations of such sites have seldom taken place. Among the hitherto presented building remains from the central Limfjord region, the only one belonging to such a group is House 5 at Kluborg II. The ground plan revealed that the longhouse was built without a substantial ground floor. It furthermore combined this aspect with otherwise constructed walls. The long sides in particular appear to have been clearly diverging in their outline. The rather regular postholes could presumably also point to the use of other wall materials. The builders of this house may have borrowed elements from turf-walled sunken-floor longhouses as well as from other kinds of buildings.

House 5 at Kluborg II is characterized as having a rather late chronological position. This also appears to be the case of another special house site from Povlstrupgård in the Limfjord region. It is well published and the presentation will therefore only be brief. The house site was found before laying down a gas pipeline near Suldrup in Himmerland (Jespersen 1987:260pp; Rasmussen, M. 1993a:88pp). The dimensions of the two-aisled house were stated as 15.5 x 7 m. The traces of the wall comprised 19 postholes, placed in a single row around. From a source-critical point of view, it would have been ideal to have had a larger uncovered area east and west of the house site, because the limits of the investigated area were just outside the recorded gable ends (Jespersen 1987, no. 838). However, the ground plan appears convincing. As regards the floor, we cannot fully rule out that the three sunken areas near to the three centre posts in the interior may have come into existence from the digging of low pits in the floor or just through wear due to activities. The likeness to one of the Egehøj houses is interesting and, on typological grounds, arguments have been put forward for a chronological position of the Povlstrupgård house in the emerging Bronze Age, based on the similarity with the site of the two-aisled House II at Egehøj (Jespersen 1987; Boas 1980:92). The dimensions of this latter house site were 18 x 6 m. Four postholes marked out traces of the roof-bearing posts in the interior. Around 30 postholes were seen as belonging to the wall construction and these postholes formed a single row all around. House II is considered contemporaneous to House III south of it (Boas 1983:99).

The remains hence represent three longhouses being c. 12.1 m (Kluborg II), 15.5 m (Povlstrupgård) and 18.0 m (Egehøj House II) long. In House 5 at Kluborg II, the question of centre posts to support the roof is unsolved, whereas at Povlstrupgård and House II at Egehøj three and five centre posts supported the roof respectively. All three houses appear to have had a number of other traits more or less in common: the buildings were aligned almost E-W. The ground plans were close to a long oval form with somewhat rounded gables. The sunken parts were not limited to one end of the house but observed along almost the full length (House 5 at Kluborg II), observed covering most of the interior at both ends (House II at Egehøj) or observed in three major areas (Povlstrupgård), also covering most of the interior. All had several sizeable wall postholes compared to the dimensions of many wall postholes belonging to the sunken-floor longhouses of the main tradition in the Limfjord region. As regards the chronological position, at least the house from Kluborg II and Egehøj had a late dating evidenced from the finds. The Povlstrupgård house was also most probably functioning at the same time as House II at Egehøj (Jespersen 1987:262). As regards the interesting structure at Bjergene VI (THY 2758), it seems a possibility that it could be viewed in the light of the above three buildings.

I shall not go into any detail concerning the issue of particular functions but it seems possible that the houses represented rather large workshops for specific purposes. In this respect it ought to be remarked that House 41 at Resengaard in its first phase was built with the usual combination of a sunken floor and a ground floor. The sunken floor was the largest of all those at Resengaard and, interestingly, in its second phase the part with the ground floor was torn down. The house thus became a sunken-floor building in its entire length, like House V at Kluborg II.

The selected house plots

The placement of the longhouses may well reflect thorough consideration with regard to choosing the proper places for the residences. Earlier, when only a relatively small number of sunken-floor houses had been investigated in Jutland, it seemed that terrains sloping southwards were mostly favoured (Simonsen 1983:88). New evidence from recent excavations concerning the positions of the sunken-floor longhouses has clarified that it was not only the horizontal and south-sloping areas that were used. Although it still appears that such terrains were often favoured, it can now be seen from a number of cases that north-sloping grounds were also chosen. Actually, the placements at Resengaard with its twelve longhouses throw up an interesting result when the N-S gradients alone are considered. It shows that while five longhouses (13, 42, 197, 128 & 130) were placed generally on south-sloping terrain, no less than seven longhouses (1, 2, 14, 41, 134, 138 & 200) were situated on more or less north-sloping grounds. The terrains often had a gradient more to the east, for instance.

The quite local gradients of the house grounds just around the buildings in many cases correspond to the general. However, in some instances the local grounds deviate more or less from the general slopes. For instance, as concerns House 128, the local ground was slightly inclining towards the north, whereas the general slope was towards the southeast.

Relatively flat E-W terrain levels appear to have been very important not least for the placement of the longhouses. Regarding, for instance, House 1, the altitude difference of the cleaned subsoil surface between the western gable end and an area 14 m further to the east, measured on the southern side, was c. 0.13 m. In other words, the terrain was falling just c. 1 cm per linear metre towards the east. The longhouse plots were usually reasonably horizontal E-W at Resengaard.

Two minor houses of the kind with sunken-floor patches containing heat-affected/cracked stones were placed on north-sloping terrains and one on northeast sloping. Among the ten minor houses without this kind of soil feature, one house was placed on north-sloping terrain, two on northeast-sloping, three on east-sloping, and four on south-sloping. Again, no west-leaning areas were made use of on the hill. At Resengaard, it therefore seems that north-sloping areas were most preferred for the placing of longhouses as well as for the minor houses with soil features enclosing heat-affected/cracked stones. In each case, the house spot has likely been carefully selected for specific reasons that are not immediately evident but this location pattern, showing interesting preferences, contributes to producing a nuanced knowledge of the settlement.

New investigations focussing on the issue of whether the old surface soils were fully removed before building a longhouse are called for. It stands to reason that the soil had actually been removed before the building activities commenced in the areas of the walls and the ground floors. From Resengaard, one of the most informative observations derives from the site of House 197. We have seen that soil of considerable thickness covered this site and the study of the soil bench across the sunken floor showed that no old surface layer was observable. Obviously, the old surface

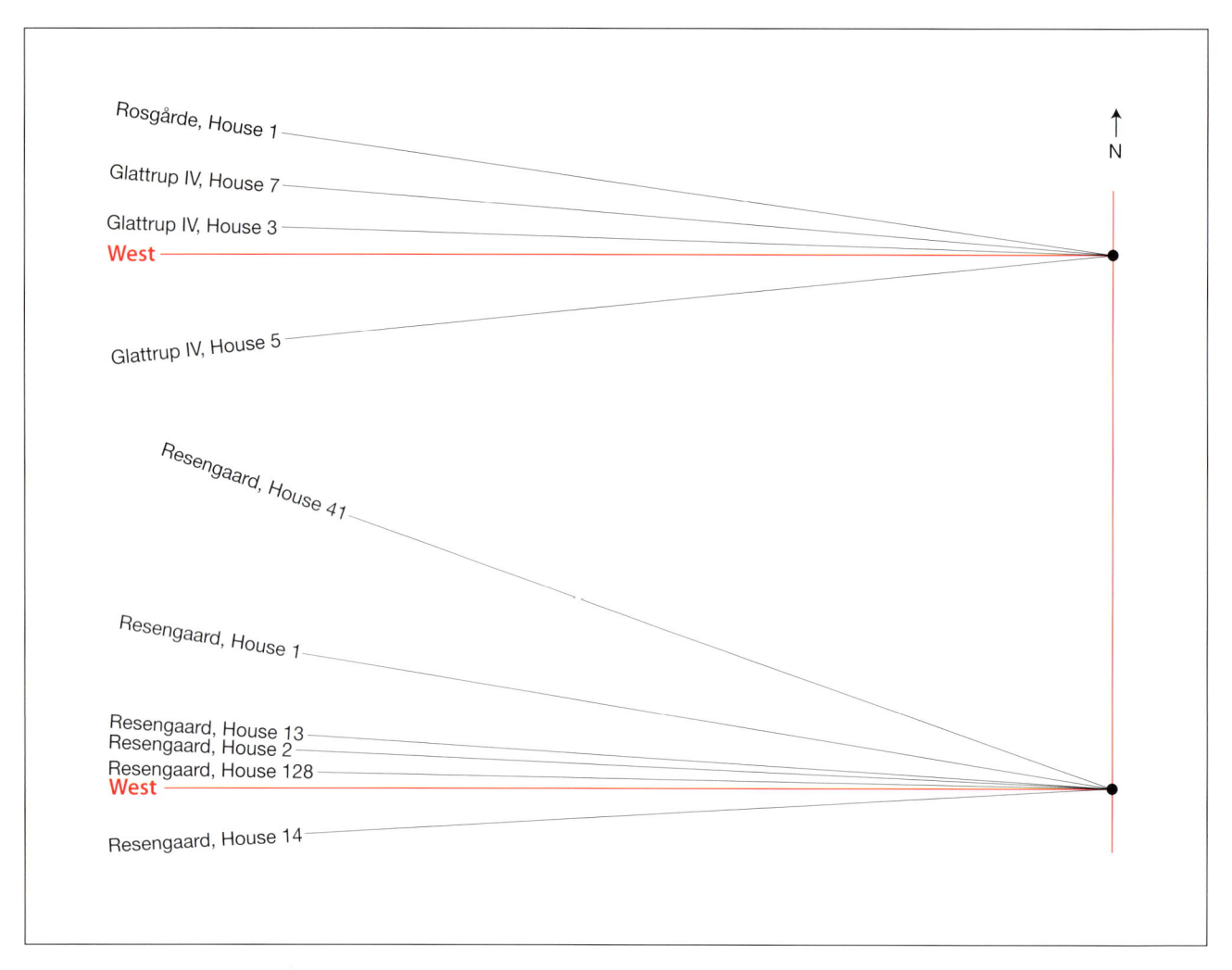

Fig. 2.64. Longhouse alignments. In the central Limfjord region, many sunken-floor longhouses belonging to the main group diverged in their placement from the precise E-W alignment. The examples here only concern the alignment of sites with adequately preserved postholes from centre posts. Many were turned more or less ESE-WNW, while some others were the opposite.

soil had been removed. Likewise House 2, the site of fire, was sealed below thick soil layers and it gave fine opportunities for reading the soil layers (Fig. 4.68). In this case, also, the old surface soil was removed before building the longhouse. However, these few examples from the Limfjord region are not enough because preparation of the building plots may have been carried out differently.

Most of the sunken-floor longhouses belonging to the main group in the Limfjord region diverged in their placement from the precise E-W direction. Many were turned somewhat towards the SE-NW, while certain others diverged oppositely (Fig. 2.64). It appears that several minor and short houses were by and large E-W aligned, whereas other almost N-S, but the number of reasonably well-preserved house sites of these kinds is still quite modest.

The sunken floor idea

Now that we have presented, analysed and interpreted the many new sites of sunken-floor houses, it is reasonable to return to the question of the idea of the sunken floors.

Arguments have been put forward that sunken floors in longhouses from the Late Neolithic could represent stables. One interpretation thus proposed that "… Houses of the central post construction with sunken eastern ends can be traced in Jutland from the late LN until the beginning of the Bronze Age. What was the function of the sunken part of the houses? It could conceivably have been the result of the mucking-out of animal manure. We are thus perhaps dealing with an early stage in the development of the house with the dwelling in the western end and the byre in the eastern end. The two-aisled Late Neolithic houses are of almost the same sizes as the three-aisled houses with the dwelling in the western end and the byre in the eastern end from the Pre-Roman Iron Age. In Holland houses are known from the Roman Iron Age with sunken eastern ends, and there it is clear that the byre was placed in the eastern end" (Nielsen, P.-O. 2000:86). It should be noted that, concerning the topic of sunken stables, phosphate determination has given fine results regarding a Roman Period site at Oosterhout in the Netherlands (Buurman, J.1990; *cf.* Zimmermann 2001).

Sunken stables were also widely used in the central Limfjord region in parts of the Iron Age, for instance at Siggård, a site found some years ago not far from Granlygård. However, the interior arrangements there were quite different from the Late Neolithic sunken floors and evident traces of stalls were preserved at Siggård (AUD 1994, no.336; Aabo 2001:67pp). Due to their method of construction, the three-aisled construction of these longhouses must have been a great deal stronger than the Late Neolithic and emerging Bronze Age longhouses in question. At Siggård, one house was exposed to a comprehensive fire and burned down totally, with livestock among the casualties. Bones from these were to some degree preserved, in addition also to pieces of a rope from around the neck of a cow. So here we have substantial evidence of the sunken area as a stable. Several sites with such sunken Iron Age stables have long been known from other parts of the Limfjord region (Lund 1977:129pp; Lund 1984; *cf.* Hvass 1985:122p. On the early establishment of stables in South Scandinavia, see also Årlin 1999.291pp. *cf.* Barker 1999:273pp).

Actually, when presenting the fresh results from the excavation of the site of a two-aisled longhouse with a minor sunken area at Dalsgaard II from around the transition from the Late Neolithic to the Older Bronze Age, it was proposed that two rows of inner posts to the east could have been intended for tethering the livestock (Gyldion 2004:41p).

In contrast, phosphate analyses rendered it probable that a two-aisled house at Højgård hardly had a stable part (Nielsen 1999:86; Ethelberg 2000a:172). Phosphate analyses have also been carried out on two house sites at Bejsebakken, and it was concluded that none of the sunken floors had been stables (Sarauw 2006:59; On phosphate research methods, see Zimmermann, W.H. 2001:35pp).

The above proposition that the sunken floors might stem from mucking-out was certainly a sensible suggestion to make, since articles concerned with the sunken-floor longhouses seldom actually did document traces of the sunken-floor activities in adequate detail. This also goes for my own writing, although I stated early on that I knew of no observations which might indicate that a separate part of the houses in question could have been set aside for a stable (Simonsen 1983:88). It is hence necessary to clarify here some arguments as to why the sunken floors in longhouses at Resengaard and other settlements in question from the region cannot represent stables.

First and foremost, the multiple traces of human activities make an important point against the use of the sunken floors as stables. Many of these activities did definitely take place in the attractive, comparatively flat areas of the sunken floors. Several of these activities would not have been feasible with cattle simultaneously in the area.

Moreover, it is clear that traces of strong, deeply buried posts, to which cattle could have been tied, actually appear to have been absent from the longhouses considered in the central Limfjord region.

Another argument may refer to the example of the large pits at Glattrup IV. The interior arrangements with, not least, the large pits with different functions in and near the sunken floors in all three longhouses would have been quite incompatible with the keeping of such heavy animals indoors.

It has also been argued in relation to Bejsebakken that the subsoil surfaces normally appeared quite sterile, which would not have been the case if these had been "completely trampled down …" (Sarauw 2006:60; 2008a:11). Correspondingly, if for instance the thousands and thousands of fragile, charred cereals in the sunken-floor horizon of House 1 at Resengaard had been trodden on by cattle, these would likely have been crushed in large numbers.

Against this backdrop of new evidence, it is hardly imaginable that the longhouses in question could have been used as stables. As the traces of human activity in the spaces of the sunken floors will later be presented extensively, I shall just say a few words to point out my understanding that those using the sunken floors of these longhouses would above all have been humans – most likely along with small rodents such as mice, rats, and presumably dogs. But why were such deep floors favoured for human dwellings?

When considering the Resengaard material, I have come to the conclusion that establishing sunken floors in the longhouses must have been closely connected to the choice of materials and the building method, namely that the houses would have been supplied with turf walls and that layout and construction suitable for this had to be employed. In spite of some demerits of such walling techniques, it would have made sunken floors an obvious solution and this view is primarily based on the following considerations.

Turf often comprises a relatively high proportion of non-mineral components. The composition can be somewhat different but roots and other organic materials which tend to more or less decompose may affect the firmness of the turf. It can gradually change structure and lose height. This potential lack of stability would of course influence a high, unprotected turf wall more than a low one. Moreover, a high turf wall would presumably be much more exposed to climatic destruction from wind, rains, frost and sun. Roof eaves might better protect the total height of a low turf wall than a high one. The adequate width of a turf wall is, of course, also an important parameter for stability.

From the reasons given here and earlier, I presume that the turf walls built in the Resengaard longhouses would have been relatively low. Therefore, in principle, two main alternatives may have existed with which to establish adequate free height. One option could have been to establish more free height upwards in some way, while another would have been to sink the floor. If attempts were made to raise the horizontal crossbeam of a roof structure, i.e. based on the construction principles of the triangle, it would become weakened and problems could easily arise in terms of the rafters being able to hold the weight of the roof. It therefore seems plausible that the floors had to be sunken, not least in order to create adequate free height below the crossbeams for the residents to live and work in the eastern areas of the longhouses. The crossbeams might well also have been used for establishing a kind of flat ceiling suitable for storage. The construction would presumably not have allowed much weight there as concerns the Resengaard longhouses although an arrangement like that could, of course, have been established over a part of the sunken floor.

My view may need some further comment. Firstly, the sunken floors did not generally have a drainage problem, which would make deep–floor projects problematic. By far the majority of the known houses were placed on sand, ensuring good drainage, and only a few were placed on part clayey conditions, such as House 1 and House 2 at Resengaard. Moreover, in both these cases, the surrounding terrain would have helped drain the area.

Secondly, it appears that the turf walls were constructed with posts that did not generally go deep into the subsoil, often only a few centimetres. These posts were probably therefore an integral part of a wooden grid stabilizing the turf walls and the entire house construction. Several house sites at Resengaard evidence traces of interior panel walls. Such walls would have helped stabilize the inner front of the turf wall, whereas no traces of any protection of the outer front have been identified. The turf walls would have been rather economical in terms of the requirement for timber and this might actually have been one of the most important additional factors as to why turf walls were chosen and became a house-building tradition of really long duration, i.e. due to the low demand for solid timber.

Thirdly, some further advantages of these walls and the sunken floors would have come along and likely also been decisive. The thick turf would have ensured a more constant interior temperature as opposed to the qualities of thinner walls such as wood and clay plastering. Likewise the digging down of the floor would have tended to minimize temperature fluctuations due to the more constant subsoil temperature and have helped keep the house interior free of frost during the winter. And, further, as low walls and dug down floors would have allowed for lower roofs, the cooling from the wind would have been less. The prevailing wind presumably came from the west, as now, and the E-W alignment of the houses would thus have reduced wind cooling and even optimized the benefits of absorbing the sun's warmth. On the whole, the thick turf wall and the sunken floor would have worked together to create a rather constant interior climate without really severe effects from the extremes in the fluctuating outer conditions. This combination can thus be considered to have been an effective climatic shield. Other researchers have also stressed the insulating value (Nielsen, S. 1999:126p; Sarauw 2006:61).

One of the demerits of thick turf walls and sunken floors would presumably have been that better weather conditions did not easily reach the interiors of these houses. However, the longevity of the tradition for sunken-floor longhouses speaks to their obvious advantages and one of the most important would surely have been the much reduced need for heating. The principal idea of these buildings therefore evidently proved extremely viable.

The above functional explanation may perhaps not have been the only reason for favouring these houses for so long. The tradition of the sunken-floor longhouse may have been due to a kind of cultural "prescription" urging people to build these, but preferences for forefather traditions or ideologies of some kind may also have played a role.

Now we shall briefly turn to sunken-floor houses preceding those of the Late Neolithic and ask what we already know about these. How persistent is the emergence of new evidence of such house sites?

The early, sunken-floor house sites from North Jutland may indicate that those belonging to the main tradition of the Limfjord region had been built right from the beginning of the Late Neolithic. As we have seen, no clear foreign sources for their origin can be demonstrated, and so we must obviously turn our attention to the sunken floors of the previous period, even though no clear counterparts to the Late Neolithic longhouse ground plans have been published. But what do we already know by now?

A substantial number of excavated sunken floors from the Single Grave Culture have come to light and these generally have smaller dimensions than those from the Late Neolithic although, in my reading, the formation processes seem to have been about the same. The sunken floors of the Single Grave Culture house sites also show soil patches and artefact remainders of some resemblance to the Late Neolithic. When searching for sunken floors during fieldwork, an important diagnostic trait is also frequently present from those of the Single Grave Culture, namely the patches with heat-affected/cracked stones. The use of these – and thereby the reasons that the stones became heat affected – were probably more or less the same. On *inter alia* such grounds, I long ago suggested that the Late Neolithic tradition for houses with sunken floors might very likely stem from a house-building practice that dates back to the Single Grave Culture (Schovsbo 1987:144).

Several sunken-floor house sites were found early on in the Limfjord region. Among the longest known sites are Solbjerg, investigated in 1963 (Jensen, J.A. 1973:107; Johansen 1986:280pp), Tofteparken investigated in 1983-84 (Hansen 1986:286pp), and Nr. Lundgaard ("Fur") investigated in 1970 (Jensen, J.A. 1973:109; Simonsen 1987:141p). Some other sunken-floor house sites have also long been known in other parts of Jutland. Among others, this concerns the site at Blegind, investigated in 1963 (Jensen, J.A. 1973:106p) and Sprogøvej near Sædding, investigated in 1966-67 (Ebbesen 1984:128). The Vorbasse site with remainders of two buildings (House XXII, investigated 1974 & House CLVIII, investigated 1977) has also stood for years as an example of the kind of house ground plans to be expected from the Single Grave Culture (Hvass 1977:219pp; 1986:325pp; *cf.* Jensen, J.A. 1986). Since these early finds, many sunken-floor house locations have come to light from the mid-1980s onwards and new sites are still appearing in the region and other parts of Jutland from the Single Grave Culture. The settlement at Strandet Hovedgaard, with two house sites, is just one of those more recently found in the central Limfjord region (Simonsen 2006). In other words, the emergence of evidence of such houses has now persisted for more than half a century. And yet, the recent finds from Single Grave Culture in particular will improve the empirical basis for comparisons and may – when published – strengthen the suggestion that the Late Neolithic idea of the sunken-floor houses primarily derived from these.

Notes

1. The Roman numbers originally given to house sites and certain other structures during excavation at Resengaard and other settlements from the central Limfjord region have in this work generally been transformed to Arabic for the sake of legibility. Regarding systematic practice, some changes have occurred in the labelling of patches from the house sites. Concerning Glattrup I/III both house sites are here numbered differently from in the reports in order to avoid overlapping.

2. The brief reports on excavation areas at Resengaard are not adequate and, to replace these, I am currently preparing a comprehensive report, also including the investigations at intermediate areas, carried out not least on volunteer grounds without the possibility of achieving sufficient economic backing. This final report will include updated lists of artefacts, plan drawings, section drawings, photos, descriptions of structures etc. for the entire settlement.

3. At the 19th Nordic Archaeologist Congress in 1993, a paper was presented on some of the preliminary results from investigating the Resengaard settlement. In particular, I focussed on the new evidence from the site of House 1 belonging to the emerging Bronze Age. In this connection, the length of this building was given in round figures as c. 18.5 m, based on measuring from the outermost parts of the postholes belonging to the house construction in each gable end. The width of the house was also calculated at the western end (Simonsen 1993b:111).

4. Various analyses of the reconstruction of a two-aisled sunken-floor longhouse from the central Limfjord region have been under preparation for some time and the possibility of making a model is currently being considered. However, before this work can be done, a number of details concerning specific house traits still need to be analysed and compared. The reconstruction of a minor sunken-floor house without centre posts has also been considered.

5. Several colleges at the National Museum have been very helpful in enabling me to go through the finds from Gåsemose. It was Karsten Davidsen who first drew my attention to certain qualities of the Gåsemose investigation. Subsequently, in the early 1990s, I had the opportunity to examine the artefacts in the store at the National Museum. In 1993, Poul Otto Nielsen let me loan to the museum in Skive some of the find material in order to carry out a detailed analysis. Helga Schütze undertook much of the paperwork needed for this allocation. Regarding the results, Aino Kann Rasmussen (pers.comm.) has expressed that she finds my interpretation plausible, namely that the large pit represents a sunken floor.

6. The drawings belonging to the reports of the sites of sunken-floor houses at Glattrup IV, Rosgårde and Tromgade are not fully consistent between the general ground plans and the detailed plans of certain house parts. According to the excavation director (pers.comm.), the detailed plans are correct and should be used. It was therefore necessary for me to piece together new house ground plans for this present work. This has not been without its difficulties with regard to some of the elements and I am thankful to the late Kurt G. Overgaard for promptly having met my enquiries in this respect. Concerning House 5 at Kluborg II, it would not have been possible to reach a satisfying result without his personal guidance on certain details, due to the complexity as reflected in the report and its drawings.

Chapter 3

Chronology of pottery assemblages

The first three sections of this chapter focus on establishing a provisional pottery chronology for the longhouse assemblages from Resengaard because it is of paramount importance to try to achieve this kind of knowledge for the settlement at the hill.

After these basic steps, we shall look for possibilities of anchoring other "late" settlement materials within the period in question from the central Limfjord region and beyond to this chronology. Subsequently, in relation to the "early" assemblages from Beaker settlements, the Myrhøj and Tastum I ceramics will be considered when discussing their relationships. The Marienlyst Strand pottery is proposed as representing a Late Neolithic phase earlier than Myrhøj. Finally, the potential for creating a regional settlement chronology is briefly explored as this would be of great importance when conducting research into the richly varied traces of everyday life.

3.1. Primary chronological objectives

It can immediately be seen that chronologies based on some of the most common, widespread and, in some respects, durable items found in settlement contexts of the Late Neolithic and emerging Bronze Age are unfortunately totally lacking here. Apart from for the flint daggers, we thus have no chronologies, either on the flint scrapers, the flint sickles, or many other preserved tools of daily life from this period.

Sophus Müller established the first chronology of the South Scandinavian flint daggers 115 years ago (Müller 1902; *cf.* 1888). It was recognized and used, with a few modifications, by John Elof Forssander in his comprehensive work on eastern Scandinavia during the older metal periods of Europe (Forssander 1936; Lomborg 1973a, Fig. 1). A number of researchers long used, commented on or criticized this chronology and, eventually, Ebbe Lomborg revised the typological sequence (Kaelas 1964; Lomborg 1973a:10pp; 1975a). Several archaeologists commented on this revised chronology, including related matters, and Lomborg replied (Bantelmann 1975; Butler 1975; Ebbesen 1975; Strömberg 1975; Lomborg 1975b). Further comments have, thereafter, been made (e.g. Madsen 1978; Lindman 1988; Wincentz Rasmussen 1990; Vandkilde 1996; Apel 2001). The source of inspiration for the onset of dagger production has been questioned (Butler 1975:15). One critic considered the use of the type concept to be incoherent (Ebbesen 1975:107). Another objection to the system was the lack of precise measurements for the type definitions (Bantelmann 1975:103). A study carried out by Ann Segerberg included a critique on the value of some of the find combinations and statements as regards stratification, brought in to support the flint dagger chronology (Segerberg 1978:178pp; Apel 2001). The problem of the flint dagger typology embracing geographical as well as chronological aspects has also been pointed out and, in particular, types overlapping each other chronologically (Madsen 1978:54pp). Combining chronology and geography in the type descriptions has subsequently been characterized as "two incompatible purposes" (Apel 2001:263).[1]

All in all, the inherent problems of this, now "traditional", dagger chronology have to be considered as rather severe and clearly damaging to its value. It has been concluded that these "…results make the flint dagger typology superfluous as a detailed chronological tool" (Apel 2001:272).[2] Some nonetheless still maintain its value (Ebbesen 2004:101).

These chronological uncertainties can be further seen when we look at the beginning of the Late Neolithic. The entire period is regarded as having lasted c. 650 years (Vandkilde 2007:75pp & Fig. 1). Arguments have been put forward for a long transitional phase without bifacial flint daggers, and an ending of the Single Grave Culture no earlier than c. 2250 calBC (Hübner 2005:660pp). Conversely, a view has thereafter been presented that proposes a one-generational overlap of battle axes and type I daggers, supporting the view that the Beaker phenomenon in Jutland began around 2350 calBC (Sarauw 2007b:37). The calculation of absolute dates in this case relies on more than 50 radiocarbon determinations, mainly on charcoal. These chronological proposals underline the considerable uncertainties in our chronological knowledge of the beginning of the Late Neolithic in Denmark but it is beyond the scope of this present work to enter further into this discussion. I shall simply remind the reader that, in Danish contexts, the beginning of the Late Neolithic is traditionally firmly defined by the first appearance of the bifacial, pressure-flaked flint dagger of type I (Lomborg 1973a:14).

Regarding Resengaard, however, it is evident that this settlement, with its sunken-floor houses, early three-aisled houses and some other structures, chiefly corresponds to the time of the younger flint dagger appearances, as evidenced by the presence of daggers and fragments belonging to types IV, V and VI. Moreover, type III dagger fragments were found in secondary fills over the sunken floors in three house sites (158, 197 & 200). Such fragments would easily survive through changing contexts but their presence might also point to rather long use, maybe latterly as usable fragments. Yet, as recognized, none of these dagger finds would be well-suited to a detailed dating of the buildings. A characteristic dagger can, however, inform us that the find context must be later than the onset of the production of this given type. In certain situations, this can be helpful for dating the context.

A chronology based on pottery variations does not exist for the LN II and Older Bronze Age period IA for the Limfjord region. However, ceramics are on the whole found in fine numbers in many different contexts at Resengaard and shall thus, in the following, form the basis for comprehensive scrutiny in order to seek to establish their chronological order.

Prior to carrying out the analysis and evaluation of the chronological positions of the Resengaard house sites, some impressions and advance observations were gathered concerning the qualities of the ceramics. As an initial undertaking, I examined the materials from the buildings, the pits and the culture layers to determine whether sufficient variations were observable among the pottery profiles. This was carried out firstly as a study of thousands of concrete potsherds and secondly – after making drawings of the clay pot profiles – an initial study not least considering these representations.[3] In this process, the striking differences in terms of quantities of materials from the house sites were also noted. Some of these sites contained abundant pottery materials while others would only be considered adequate. Unfortunately, a few house sites also contained assemblages that I did not find fully suitable for the chronological analysis. On the whole, however, the Resengaard longhouse material appeared quite varied as regards form variation.

In this context, my primary goal is to seek to place the pottery assemblages from the longhouses in their relative chronological order. A further and also fairly important aim is to seek to present some dating of minor houses and other physical remainders at Resengaard. Such a chronology may conceivably have significant wider importance for the Limfjord region settlements in particular, but also for other Danish and South Scandinavian materials. Therefore a value might be that the suggested relative order of assemblages becomes worth considering for other researchers working with find materials from the period in question. However, when the richly varied and comprehensive ceramic material, being quite unique in South Scandinavia, so to speak calls for an attempt to establish a chronological order, it must at the same time be acknowledged that it is a very difficult task.

Aiming for an independent chronology

When designing a method for building up the provisional pottery chronology, I believe a clear precondition is that it must be established quite independently of any other relative chronology. Apart from the oldest and the youngest reference assemblage, there should therefore be no attempts, before the chronology is established, however provisionally that may be, to link it to other chronological points of reference from the region, neighbouring regions or further away. Methodologically, such a decidedly locally-established relative chronology could have the potential for being comparatively strong, as it would not risk confusing, for instance, geographic difference with chronological dissimilarity. Once the chronological order of the assemblages has been established as safely as the material allows, however, an attempt will be made to suggest chronological relationships between different settlement pottery in Jutland and certain Resengaard stages.

It is furthermore my concern to draw on the links between the relative pottery chronology and the absolute chronological sphere. The option to use radiocarbon determinations from short-life materials, in this case, results in a reduced interest in the absolute determinations obtained from charcoal in instances where an own age beyond a few years or reuse of timber might be suspected. We have already seen that a series of AMS-determinations obtained from, in particular, charred cereals is available, as well as a few "traditional" radiocarbon determinations on these short-lived sources.

Only in two instances were house sites at Resengaard (143/138 & 201/200) found in places where the question of internal stratification could arise. However, precisely the two later house sites in both cases (the minor House 143 and the short House 201) contain no apt pottery or other artefacts.

3.2. Chronological method

The following sub-sections focus on consideration of the material, its source-critical factors and consideration of some possible causes for the differences observed in the pottery. The design of the method, the chronological entities, and the actual methodological path and technical procedure to follow are also introduced. First, however, some further observations and comments on the source material prior to chronological analysis.

It is essential to realize that some pottery shapes and elements from Resengaard immediately point towards the Beaker milieus of the early half of the Late Neolithic Period, whereas other shapes and elements display affinities with milieus belonging to the first part of the Older Bronze Age. The reason this point needs to be clarified is simply because the pottery of the middle and late part of the Late Neolithic Period has clearly been poorly analysed and described in the present state of research. The Resengaard pottery assemblages jointly represent the first really substantial material belonging to a settlement from the second half of the Late Neolithic and bridging to the Older Bronze Age in Denmark.

As will emerge from the following analysis, the Resengaard pottery shapes and their attributed elements tend to vary within certain frames. This should be understood insofar as a varied pottery sample with its characteristic rims could hardly be mistaken for belonging to any other time span, despite the hitherto poor description. Actually, much of the pottery is fairly recognizable and a brief glance at such a sample would often be sufficient to make assumptions as to whether the potsherds should be ascribed to this period in general. Tiny potsherds without clear form elements could be more difficult to place, however, although the qualities of the ware, including the surface treatment, can often give hints as to its belonging or not.

It is not my view that the undecorated pottery of the younger part of the Late Neolithic is bad as regards ware, shaping or finish, even though from a cursory inspection of potsherds it might sometimes seem so. The often relatively high content of coarse granite tempering makes the clay pots capable of resisting high temperatures. The shaping frequently seems to reflect a design aimed at practical utility. My basic sense of such pottery from the Limfjord region belonging to the younger part of the Late Neolithic and the emerging Bronze Age is that it very often has a highly characteristic design and is made for functional use, to meet the needs of everyday life. The often rough treatment of the outer surface combined with the characteristic shaping often lends the pottery a noticeably "sculptured" appearance.

Survey of pottery assemblages

It was first necessary to complete a comprehensive inspection of all relevant Resengaard pottery. The ware, the surface treatments, the wall thicknesses, the technical accuracies, the variations of shape and other aspects of significant importance for the perception of the pottery were in this way studied. All relevant rim fragments, bottom fragments and several side fragments from house sites, pits and culture layers were measured and drawings made of their profiles. The only exceptions were rim fragments so tiny that illustrating these would seem meaningless. The aim was to make the drawings quite accurate and this implied, in particular, keeping a strong focus on the observable profile differences, whether slight or marked, and maintaining a rather critical attitude towards my own drawings in order to reach a certain standard. The outcome is, among other things, the presentation of the ceramics in Catalogue A. A further outcome is that these drawings can now facilitate the chronological analysis.

In the case of Resengaard, not a single clay pot from the period in question survived as a complete specimen. It is further remarkable that no complete number of fragments from one clay pot survived in the secondary fills or other dump sites. All ceramics are thus fragmented and some or most parts of every single clay pot have totally disappeared. An aspect thus also relates to the amount of pottery that may not have been found.

Several factors could have influenced the "flow" of clay pots in a longhouse, such as for instance specialized activities, inheritance, gifts, fragility, frequency of use, degree of care in handling, practices of clearing out and waste strategy as a whole. With regard to the Resengaard pottery, no particular clay pot forms related directly to specific kinds of specialized production have been identified.

The prevailing sandy soil and also the sporadically present clayey soil do not appear to attack and destroy the fragments. The potsherds will thus survive in such milieus if no other factors reduce the number of fragments. Besides severe frost, the disturbing factors that actually affected the individual sunken-floor house sites could, of course, also have an impact on the pottery remainders. Yet, apart from this effect, the conditions for ceramics preservation were often extremely good in the sunken areas as compared to the ground floors.

In one pottery sample, many fragments might for instance come from a single clay pot, while the remaining pieces could represent several others. It even seems unrealistic to assume that all pots broken during the lifetime of the buildings would have left at least a single fragment. On the other hand, a number of clay pots could have been undamaged until abandonment of the longhouses and thus could have been used in new contexts.

In the overall picture, it is worth realizing that if the excavation of the undisturbed sunken-floor areas has been meticulously performed then a fairly close relationship will probably exist between what was left and what was found. In other words, the amount of pottery found would be practically the same as that which, for different reasons, was originally left in the prehistoric situation.

I argue that, in a majority of cases, the Resengaard longhouse assemblages from the sunken areas are found mainly with an "inverted" stratification, i.e. strata with older artefacts on top of the younger (Fig. 3.1). In optimal cases, the assemblages may hence correspond to a major part of the functioning time of the buildings when considering the content of the sunken-floor horizon and the above fills as one unit. The finds from the secondary fills on top of the sunken floor may represent much of the functioning time dating back to the early days of the longhouse because the fills, in my understanding, probably derive from heaps of waste consisting of ceramics, flint and other artefacts (besides soil with high organic content from plant materials), all accumulated as middens outside the longhouse during much of the lifetime of

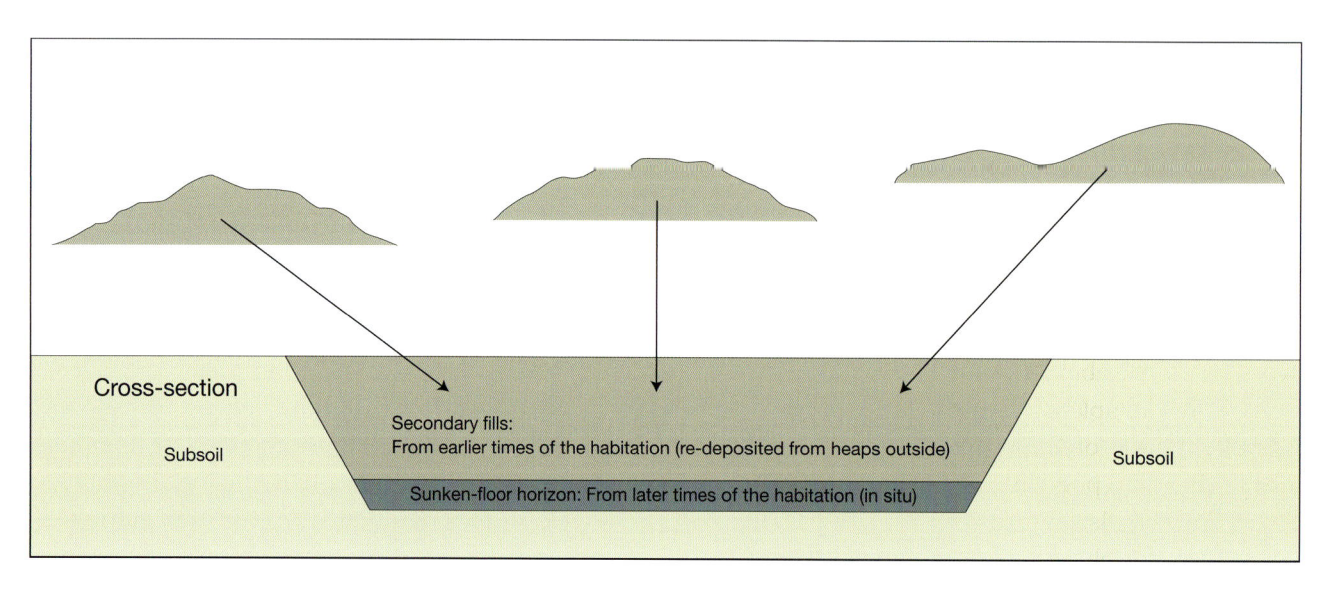

Fig. 3.1. Resengaard. The relative age of finds in sunken areas in the sites of longhouses. At the deepest level, artefacts can be found belonging to the sunken-floor horizon that may primarily represent the later period of residence (and the use of the building thereafter). Above, artefacts can be found in the secondary fills that may primarily represent the time dating back to the early days of residence. As schematically shown here, we can thus speak of inverted stratification in these cases.

the building. On the other hand, the finds *in situ* in sunken-floor horizons at Resengaard, in my interpretation, chiefly stem from later times – and in particular the last time – of residence.

When looking for an expressive concrete example among non-pottery artefacts that would illustrate the assumption of "inverted" stratification, we can turn our attention to the site of House 2 at Resengaard. Being a site of fire, sealed beneath thick soil layers, and with a fine stratification documented in cross-sections with evidence of an extensive floor layer and certain dagger finds, this meets our demands (Fig. 2.8, 2.9, 3.8, 4.7, 4.8, 4.9 & 4.10). From this site we have the exquisite type IV E fishtail flint dagger placed above the sunken floor in secondary fills to the southeast and a type V B flint dagger fragment belonging to the sunken-floor horizon found north of scorched-stone patch A (Fig. 4.10). If the stratification were not inverted, we would instead have expected the typologically younger type V B dagger to be in a context above the type IV dagger (according to the currently-used flint dagger typology, Lomborg 1973a). The 7 cm long type V B dagger fragment (RE90ea) had parts of the handle and blade preserved and the 26 cm long type IV E dagger (RE89ea/175ea) was found in two parts at c. 70 cm internal distance (two minor pieces missing, see Cat. B).

Another expressive example concerns the site of House 200 at Resengaard. Its sunken floor was one of the deepest at the settlement and numerous finds stem from the secondary fills and the sunken-floor horizon (Fig. 2.19, 3.16, 4.8 & 4.29). A type V B flint dagger fragment (RE985ea, Fig. 4.29, see remarks in Cat. B) found in the deep pit D to the west belongs to the sunken-floor horizon. From the above secondary fills we have a type III E flint dagger handle (RE750ei, Fig. 4.29, see remarks in Cat. B). Again, if the stratification were not inverted, we would instead have expected the typologically much younger type V B dagger to be in a context above the type III E dagger handle (again, according to the above-mentioned typology).

A third example of inverted stratification could be from the site of House 42, where a handle fragment (RE405ea), possibly type V A, was present in the secondary fills, whereas another handle fragment (RE430ea), possibly type V B, is ascribed the sunken-floor horizon. However, in this example we have some uncertainty as to dagger types, and it should be recalled that the excavation of this site had to be carried out with rather limited resources.

The longhouse ceramics invoke high interest as they form the essential basics of the chronological analysis that follows. To try to gain an idea of possible numerical representation, we can look at some concrete cases. The ceramics from four longhouse sites (1, 2, 41 & 134), and which shall later be frequently referred to, are here given as examples.

We can begin with House 41. The assemblage contains a relatively large number of clay pot profiles, one part of which stems from the sunken floor itself and another from the secondary fills. The fragments from the secondary fills as described presumably stem from heaps of rubbish accumulated outside. When the ground was cleared for tillage after abandonment, piles of waste would likely have been used as fills in the sunken area. The fully observed representation from the sunken-floor horizon and secondary fills is 55 clay pots if none of the bottoms belong together with the rim profiles or side fragments drawn. To this figure could be added a few tiny fragments that presumably come from separate, unidentified clay pots. If we assume that these, for instance, equate to 10 clay pots then we would have a total representation of 65 clay pots from House 41. I would rate that number as fairly high, considering that it comes directly from a sunken floor and its fills.

House 41 gave strong evidence of a second phase of building. According to my interpretation, the western part with unsunken floor was removed by the end of the main phase and, thereafter, the sunken-floor part alone functioned for some time. There is a question as to whether the evidence of a second phase implies longer use of this house than normal and perhaps further accumulation of heaps outside, with broken clay pots and similar scrap. All else being equal, it does not seem unlikely that the second phase might indicate at least a short prolonged use for habitation. It seems possible that prolonged use of House 41 could have coincided with a reduction in the number of residents and in the economic activities performed by the household. The "rate" of clay pots being broken and replaced might therefore also have been slower. The building likely subsequently had an after-residence life.

When turning to House 2, its pottery assemblage likewise contained a relatively large number of potsherds from the sunken-floor horizon and the secondary fills. The number of clay pots altogether comes to 57, if none of the drawn bottoms belong to the rims or side fragments drawn. Apart from this, a few unidentified clay pots could be represented among the tiny

Pottery representation				
Resengaard assemblages		Recorded	Usable for the analysis	Percentage
Sunken-floor longhouses	1	45	11	24%
	2	57	20	35%
	13	10	6	60%
	14	52	37	71%
	41	55	30	55%
	42	21	19	90%
	128	22	18	82%
	130	24	17	71%
	134	25	13	52%
	138	2	2	100%
	197	38	29	76%
	200	56	44	79%
Minor/short sunken-floor houses	10	25	17	68%
	12	7	5	71%
	84	1	1	100%
	112	1	1	100%
	158	3	3	100%
	183	9	6	67%
	193	2	2	100%
	198	14	11	79%
	201	2	1	50%
	202	4	2	50%
	240	38	29	76%
	268	27	25	93%
	289	22	18	82%
Pits	77 (RE469)	1	1	100%
	312 (RE225)	1	1	100%
	314 (RE469)	4	1	25%
	80 (RE478)	1	1	100%
	89 (RE484)	3	3	100%
	85 (RE486)	1	1	100%
	100 (RE504)	1	1	100%
	111 (RE520)	1	1	100%
	160 (RE632)	3	1	33%
	161 (RE636)	22	16	73%
	313 (RE231)	2	1	50%
	315 (RE673)	1	1	100%
	310 (RE692)	3	3	100%
	311 (RE196)	4	3	75%
	319 (RE693)	6	6	100%
	316 (RE694)	7	6	86%
	317 (RE695)	10	8	80%
	278 (RE880)	3	3	100%
	320 (RE81/85)	4	4	100%
Culture layers	203	62	45	73%
	293	30	25	83%
	302	2	2	100%
	318	1	1	100%

Fig. 3.2. Resengaard. Representation of clay pots from house sites as well as selected pits and culture layers. House 2 and House 41 may both possibly have had a prolonged phase of residence. When including pit 161 into the account of pit 160 (the possible "House 160") a total of 25 clay pots are represented.

or insignificant fragments. If we again assume that these equate to 10 clay pots, it might represent a total of 67 clay pots. At House 2, there is evidence that the sunken floor was extended towards east during its lifetime. As I presume this extension was due to a moderately increased number of residents, prolonged residence seems a reasonable understanding of the circumstances of this longhouse and might account for the relatively high number of clay pots represented.

House 41 and House 2 are the only Resengaard longhouses for which we have reason to suggest a second phase of residence. Only from one building more, House 1, do we have observations on the renewal of a part of the wall and indications on the placing of extra roof-bearing posts along the central longitudinal axis although, in my view, such details do not necessarily indicate a prolonged use of the building.

If we continue to the assemblage of House 1, a good number of clay pots is also represented here, although not as many as in the two previous. Again, some derive from the sunken-floor horizon while others stem from the secondary fills. The representation of clay pots from the sunken floor and secondary fills altogether comes to 45 clay pots, if none of the drawn bottoms belong to the rims or side fragments drawn. In addition, a few unidentified clay pots could be represented among the tiny or insignificant fragments.

Finally, the assemblage of House 134 has a somewhat minor but important representation of clay pots. A few stem from the sunken floor, several others from the secondary fills and, in all, these come to a mere 25 clay pots. Again, a few unidentified clay pots could be present among the tiny or insignificant fragments.

The ceramics of Houses 41 and 2 appear highly varied and many different profiles and variations are characteristic of both assemblages. It does not seem unlikely that a really broad representation of the forms used during the lifetime of these buildings is represented. In part contrast to this, the forms of the pottery from House 134 and House 1 are less varied and their representation therefore immediately seems less optimal.

The degree of variation of clay pot profiles from the remaining eight longhouse assemblages appears to fluctuate greatly. For instance, the relatively large assemblages of House 200 and House 14 have a fine variety of pottery forms, even though several short, uncharacteristic profiles are also seen. On the other hand, the pottery profiles from House 13 offer very few variations, and some rather insignificant specimens are also among them. Only two rim profiles are found in the assemblage of House 138 but both have exceptionally characteristic outlines.

The assemblages from these two latter buildings are likely far from adequate as regards representation of forms but an average of c. 34 clay pots in the twelve longhouse assemblages provides on the general level a fine number of profiles for the chronological study. On this basis, I find the Resengaard material relatively well-suited to the chronological pottery analysis.

The high number of pottery profiles totally derives from sunken floors, secondary fills, certain pits and culture layers. However, dating pottery from the culture layers is not a direct goal of the chronological analysis. In my understanding, the culture layers were apparently supplied with new domestic refuse over a longer period and do not really seem to have value in relation to establishing the chronology.

Besides a few significant side profiles, all preserved rim profiles have been picked out for the analysis, with the exception of specimens that were too tiny (Fig. 3.2). Many less characteristic profiles are thereby also included in order to represent the assemblages as broadly as possible. From the house sites a few, rather dispersed, finds from postholes of the walls and so on are generally left out of the analysis, as these cannot contribute to our chronological topic with any certainty, the only exception being the site of House 193 in which the potsherds stem from a posthole.

Between 2 and 44 clay pot profiles have been selected to represent the longhouses in the chronological analysis. Pit 160 representing the possible longhouse is included in the analysis.

Source-critical aspects

From a source-critical perspective, it is interesting that the degree of pottery fragmentation seems to be different depending on the context of the deposition. Potsherds from certain pits and culture layers thus appear to be relatively larger and have a better chance of survival without risk of much further fragmentation. The clay pot remainders from sunken-floor horizons of longhouses may have been exposed to secondary, partial disintegration caused by human activities. The main explanation, however, could be that the bigger potsherds, easily catching the eye, have been removed, in some instances leaving the minor pieces in the often more or less sandy floors. Unlike sharp flint, these would do hardly any harm to anyone.

From the sunken-floor horizons, we have some instances of sherds from different find spots belonging to the same clay pot e.g. from House 1 (RE24aa/RE35aa), House 2 (RE119aa/RE121aa & RE140aa/RE146aa), and House 41 (RE403aa/RE411ab). Yet direct evidence of pottery from a sunken-floor horizon belonging together with certain others from the above secondary fills is scarce. One example relates to House 128, where some belong to the same clay pot (RE561aa, sunken-floor horizon conjoining RE540aa, secondary fills). However, for reasons of caution, the latter were ascribed to the secondary fills, found, as they were, during our cleaning of the floor surface. Another possible example concerns House 268 (RE846aa, sunken-floor horizon together with RE843aa from the secondary fills). Yet in this case, too, the latter, for reasons of caution, is ascribed to secondary fills. It cannot, however, be ruled out that better examples of potsherds from sunken-floor horizons conjoining those of secondary fills could be identified by time-consuming, systematic scrutinizing of the comprehensive materials.

There are nonetheless reasons why such a procedure would frequently not succeed. Let us take the hypothetical example of a single vessel that had broken indoors and, in the main, been removed from the sunken floor, while a minor fragment was overlooked and left *in situ*. Would it then still be overlooked during repeated floor cleaning and other activities? In my view, it might well have come to light in this way and been thrown out. Actually, when cleaning it could have been removed along with much other material from the subsoil floor, causing a lowering of the floor levels (see Ch. 4.6). Let us say that the minor fragment accidentally still managed to avoid being thrown out. At the same time, most of the vessel's sherds were dumped in a pile of domestic refuse in the surrounding area and if, by good fortune, they were not destroyed by frost and precipitation over many winters (during the continued occupation of the longhouse, as well as during the period of after-residence and tearing down of the longhouse, *cf.* Ch. 2.7, Ch. 4.5, & Ch. 5.3), they might be re-deposited in the sunken areas together with other domestic refuse. In such a hypothetical case, we would have a chance of matching the single potsherd with the surviving potsherds from the pile. In other words, if conditions were favourable for preservation inside as well as outside the longhouse, we would have a chance of identifying potsherds from the sunken floors conjoining those of the secondary fills.

We shall now consider important source-critical issues that might possibly be involved when dealing with pottery changes over time, namely the period of production and period of use.

One aspect of production that could create problems for the chronological analysis relates to long-living traditions in the making of a definite clay pot form. If a characteristic form remains in production practically unchanged over a relatively long period, it could contribute to a wrong understanding of a close time relationship between assemblages when compared. Furthermore, a revival of the production of a characteristic old form could lead to a wrong understanding of a close time relationship, although this situation is considered exceptional.

The length of period of use is also crucial for the chronological analysis. The use of a certain clay pot form parallel to the time of production would not cause problems beyond what might possibly be caused by the length of the period of production itself. A period of use once production has stopped is often to be expected. A very long period of use after ceasing to manufacture a certain kind of clay pot could cause severe problems to the chronological analysis and perhaps lead to a wrong understanding of contemporaneity. For example, this might be the case if two practically uniform clay pots were compared and one of them derives from use in the early time of production while the other stems from long after production was stopped.

Considerable troubles for the chronological analysis could also arise when the use of clay pots was prolonged extraordinarily, for instance when inherited down the generations, causing unexpected long-lasting utilization.

When it comes to the topic of time of production and use in settlement contexts of the Late Neolithic and the emerging Bronze Age, it seems *a priori* of importance to decide whether the goal of the chronological analysis should be at the level of decades, centuries or somewhere in between. If the aim is to set up a relatively coarse pottery chronology, operating with phase lengths of more than a hundred years, a prolonged production or extra long-lasting use would hardly be expected to cause severe problems. In contrast, if the objective is a relatively fine, detailed chronology, operating with phases or intervals embracing only a few decades, the analysis might, in the worst scenario, be greatly influenced.

We now turn to another important issue that touches on the question of whether certain ceramics belong to the same context. When the analysis of the settlement pottery is not based on single potsherds but refers to assemblages, it is vital that it is clarified during the excavation that the concrete potsherds actually belong to the same entity. If such coherence is not considered certain, the results of the chronological analysis will be weakened correspondingly. During fieldwork, establishing knowledge of relationships between potsherds often occurs through evidence of the soil. If the potsherds can be demonstrated to belong clearly to the same soil feature without intrusions of any art capable of threatening this unit, the soil connects the fragments. A chronological position confirmed for some represented clay pots is thereby valid for all others belonging to the same context.

Frequently, though, the situation can be far more complex. The person investigating – and later the analytical researcher – has to be convinced that not only do the fragments belong together through the individual soil feature but also that several other soil features belong to the same time and thereby lend these the same chronological position as the former. Only meticulous excavation with a reasonable level of documentation, combined with solid experience on the part of those excavating, can help to ensure that such a connection can be considered reliable. In many cases, this chronological coherence can only be inferred from incorporating a systemic view of the soil features. For instance, it might be the case when assuming that postholes in a row belong together. Or it might be a number of pits in a floor linked together, for instance, by evidence of stratification and possibly supported by other observations such as other details of soil texture. In such cases, the pits do not necessarily derive from the same act but from a series of activities and, from stratification, it could be presumed that they were dug within a relatively short period.

Frame of interpretation

Disparities between ceramic materials can be subject to interpretations in various directions. It is therefore necessary to seek to explore the range of possible interpretations. Looking at the entire ceramic material from Resengaard, it must be realized that really broad variations can be seen within the forms, sizes and thickness of wares. To make interpretations of these differences is not a simple and straightforward thing. However, it can immediately be firmly excluded that geographic differences between find places could have played a role since all assemblages have been found in house contexts on the same hill. The geographical factor can thus likely be ruled out immediately, as we have no indication that the pottery originated from different, very distant sources (although exceptions cannot be excluded).

Not least the generally high standards of pottery-making exclude the possibility that each and every household could have made their own range of pottery. In my understanding, it must have been a specialized activity (see Ch. 5). Only thus could the skills of preparing and tempering the clay, forming the pots, treating the surfaces, drying and burning the pots correctly, be developed to the high level we witness in the preserved pottery. At Resengaard, fragments of ceramics have only exceptionally turned up that were so simple that one might suspect that an inexperienced "potter" had been behind the product. In this light, it seems unlikely that any of the households at Resengaard were producing real clay pots and we do not have any evidence of traces of pottery-making at this large site. I do not therefore see household pottery traditions at Resengaard as a possible interpretation of the differences between the assemblages. Instead I assume that ceramics were brought to the hill from settlements not very far away and that it seems reasonable to presume that most of the pottery would have been reasonably locally produced. It might have been largely manufactured in the surrounding parts of the central Limfjord region.

Activities of a specialized character (see Ch. 5) would have been performed in the individual households and we might therefore perhaps expect that some clay pots in the assemblages would mirror a deliberate selection of those needed for some of the special undertakings, although this would hardly concern the bulk of the pottery assemblages because the general household need for ceramics in daily life would presumably by and large have been much the same in the central Limfjord region. I have been unable to identify any clay pot forms from Resengaard that might relate to specialized activities and the traditional forms could possibly also have been very useful in such respects.

Time must be the main frame for explaining for disparities between the ceramic assemblages from the longhouses at Resengaard. Successive replacement of clay pot forms and gradual changes in clay pot shapes and rim designs very likely took place down the centuries of occupation at the settlement. In my understanding, this is chiefly what we see in the differences between the assemblages.

In some instances, the conditions for a number of activities in which clay pots were habitually used could have changed over time and modifications to the usual pottery or the introduction of new forms may perhaps have been a necessary response. In other instances, certain clay pot forms might fully serve the functional needs of definite purposes over a long period and consequently remain relatively unchanged. Certain clay pot forms could also have been exposed to new "fashions" and therefore undergone changes without any real functional requirement for them. Influencing factors such as these might have been behind the ceramics that were actually used in the longhouses over time.

Design of concrete methodological path

Actually, many paths could be followed when seeking the main thread in the chronology of the pottery assemblages. Thus, the variations in detail might presumably allow various ways of tackling this challenge. Some would presumably turn to the modern multivariate analyses that have demonstrated results in a number of cases.[4] However, the choice of method is, naturally, completely free and I have decided to approach the question of chronology from a quite simple angle, albeit making a strong effort to implement it in a rather structured and systematic manner. The method is simple in the sense that it will be based on a direct visual comparison of forms; the specific structure of it as regards the path to follow, however, will be tailored precisely to cope with the concrete material from the Resengaard settlement, as it would also probably be possible to do when new excavations bring comprehensive ceramic materials to light.

In designing the method, it shall be implemented in two steps. The first step, corresponding to the sorting of what I term "reference assemblages" ("reference houses" and "reference phases"), will be to bring four important longhouse assemblages, which initially do not seem to succeed each other immediately, into relative chronological order.

The assumption of internal time distance between the four reference assemblages may help to prevent much of the risk that could be caused by possible long-living production or prolonged use. It even seems possible to take further precautions against these possible source-critical factors by involving numerous clay pot profiles. If only a few of the clay pots stem, for instance, from very long use then the presence of rim profiles from many other clay pots not affected by this weakness in terms of our chronological purpose might compensate for that risk.

Methodologically, the second step, which is far more laborious, will be to attempt to relate all the assemblages from the remaining longhouses foremost to these four reference assemblages. In this process, I believe that an effect of long-lasting production and long-time use of the pottery cannot be avoided. The second step shall present more details but, on the other hand, may end up as a less precise order than the first.

Chronological entities

The ceramics from the sunken floor horizons are our main focus and include, in particular, contexts of soil patches, pits, floor surfaces and floor layers. The finds from the secondary fills were usually not split during excavation and these fills worked as a proper sealing layer to the sunken-floor horizons because their accumulation usually began soon after demolishing of the house constructions. This notion is rather important for the chronological aims. I am convinced that most of the finds from the secondary fills were closely linked with those from the sunken floors and so it is scarcely necessary to treat the characteristic pottery from these secondary fills differently in chronological respect. Although I do not believe that possible negative influences from source-critical factors are serious as regards pottery from the secondary fills, it is still, as a precaution, necessary to be aware in every single case of the extent to which a chronological position is established via its relationship with pottery profiles from sunken floors or secondary fills. The sunken floors were investigated in very strict order to avoid finds with uncertain relationships to these horizons being recorded as belonging to them.

Actually, the secondary fills do, in many instances, contain rather characteristic pottery profiles that, alone, could sometimes contribute to a proper relative dating or, in many instances, may add a great deal to a narrowing down of the chronological position. The analysis and considerations in the following also indirectly confirm the close connection between pottery from the sunken floors and secondary fills because the same kinds of relationship come up with reference to both parts again and again. The find material from a sunken floor and its covering fill is then combined in our chronological entity and it can in this way – naturally with caution and observing all relevant source-critical factors – be treated like those belonging to the group of closed, accumulated finds (*cf.* Madsen1978:57p). Rim sherds stemming from later intrusions into the secondary fills or accumulations on top of these belonging to the time span embracing the later prehistoric periods up to the post-medieval can usually quite easily be left out and thus do not affect the source value as regards our chronological task.

Comparing rim profiles

When a clay pot is produced traditionally in a certain area at a certain time of the period in question, it may somehow "contain" its chronological position through its ware, tempering, form, surface treatment, firing or other traits within the ever-changing history of local pottery-making. But how can we decode this time when a preserved rim fragment from it has no clearly describable elements and no ornamentation? This question poses one of the central challenges faced in this approach to the chronology of clay pots at Resengaard.

When turning to the concrete implementation of the method, the path to follow will be a systematic and direct visual comparison of the shapes of clay pot rims from each assemblage with foremost the specimens of the reference assemblages as well as in many cases to some of those of other units. Two notions become central to this approach, namely the concept of "relationship" and that of "likeness" (affinities). Relationships between find materials such as pottery, via the evidence of soil structures, have been considered in the foregoing, whereas reflections on the exploration of relationships through likeness are still to be presented.

Of course, when implementing the concept of likeness it does not necessarily result in fully objective statements but relates to evaluations based on focussed observations. The degree of likeness between rim profiles may vary from very weak to very strong. This implies that the concrete analysis has to seek to identify not only probable relationships with pottery from other assemblages but also to weigh up the nature of the closeness. This evaluation of the degree of likeness must be carried out quite meticulously. I therefore find it necessary in every single case to be explicit as regards profile similarities and how strongly they match. When a given rim profile from an assemblage to be dated shows some kind of likeness to specimens from one of the reference assemblages, the evaluation will usually be described in full. For example, the outline of a clay pot profile may show clearly observable relationships to three profiles from one assemblage, two profiles from a second and one from a third. To give an overview, illustrations of every selected clay pot profile will be shown together with the other selected profiles of the assemblage, and in larger scale than in Catalogue A.

The scope of my analysis is to point out important affinities but, of course, not all more or less distant relationships. When dealing with assemblages that are relatively rich in pottery shape variations, I shall seek to give priority to identifying the most characteristic affinities. The profiles belonging to the reference assemblages will not be described, as the most relevant will be portrayed indirectly through numerous comparisons throughout the analysis.

Besides the rim, the transition to the body will also often be focussed on because much of the clay pot character can be concentrated in this zone, relating it to other vessels or separating it from these. The body may often contribute to the "reading" of the profiles and thereby indirectly become part of the analysis but I shall mostly renounce from describing it.

The example of House 200 presented further below may illustrate how the chronological method builds on relationships of a qualitative as well as a quantitative nature and thereby makes use of the fine variations and strengths of the find combinations (Fig. 3.3).

Further comments on method

To study the chronological transformations of the ceramics over time for Resengaard while refraining from setting up types is certainly not a traditional approach. Actually, I do not know of any comparable pottery chronologies that work without types or defined elements.

The concept of types has already been discussed in several contexts in Scandinavia decades ago. For instance, in Sweden, Mats P. Malmer underlined the notion that artefacts are certainly real whereas "types" do not exist *a priori* and Bo Gräslund noted the subjective element in any type classification (Malmer 1963.19, Gräslund 1974.64p). In relation to Danish finds, a discussion of types has been presented some time ago (Koch 1998:63pp).

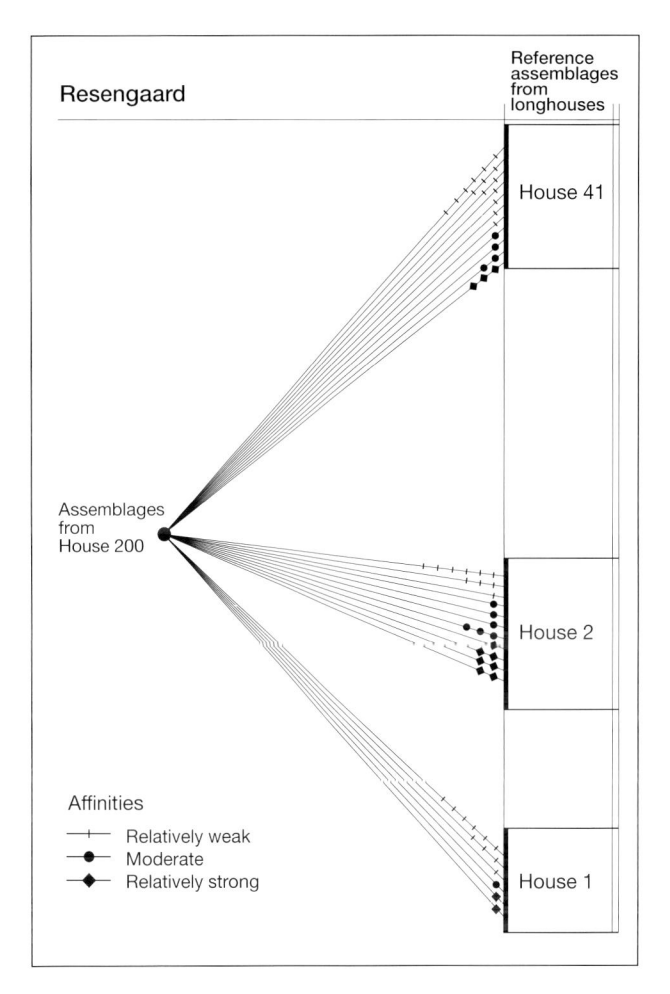

Fig. 3.3. Resengaard. Chronology from rim profile combinations. This figure will attempt to illustrate that the weighting of internal relationships between the individual ceramic assemblages is carried out with regard to their quantitative range as well as their qualitative strength. The example centres on the profiles belonging to the assemblage of House 200. The number of lines indicates the essence of the suggested range of different affinities to the reference assemblages. The number of symbols at the ends of these lines shows the proposed number of rim profiles involved in each case from the site of House 200. Three kinds of symbol suggest their relative strengths. It appears that many of the House 200 pottery affinities relate to the assemblages of House 41 and House 2, and with the latter not least there was a relatively strong relationship in several instances. The weighting of all considered affinities in this case results in a suggestion that the chronological position of House 200 was immediately prior to the time of House 2.

If we look at periods adjoining the Late Neolithic, it can be seen how the use of types is central to the chronological works, albeit established in different ways. As regards the Older Bronze Age, a study of the chronology of ceramics from settlements in Jutland and at Funen focuses much on the presence and placement of "specially modelled points" on the clay pot profiles (Rasmussen, M. 1993a:18pp; 1995:87p.). The type descriptions take these as their starting points along with other elements of the profile curves. The established types as regards profiles for the upper part, belly and lower part in several instances show wide variation of the profiles within each of these types, e.g. of the upper part, type 2 and 6 (Rasmussen, M. 1993a:94p). In the resulting chronology, selected type-examples of profiles from concrete settlements represent transformations over time (Rasmussen, M. 1993a, Fig. 133; 1995, Fig. 2).

As regards the Single Grave Culture, a comprehensive study of ceramics in graves from grave barrows in Jutland focuses on the pottery profiles and these are separated into several form groups (Hübner 2005:166pp). One of the advantages of this material is that the clay pots are often preserved from top to bottom and another is that ornaments are frequently present. In the resulting chronology with seven phases of the Single Grave Culture, the ceramics contribute with types established through detailed combinations of clay pot forms and ornamental motives.

With regard to the Funnel Beaker Culture, an approach to the bog pots – originally deposited in lakes and streams on Zealand and the islands to the south of it – has set up new types not merely for reasons of chronology but also as a contribution to our knowledge of ritual depositions (Koch 1998:172pp). The types are basically, but not purely, based on the bog pot profiles because the presence of simple or complex ornamentation, the latter being surface-covering, is also included in the definitions. The considerations and analyses of the clay pot curves with manually-defined "shape modes" have been exposed to multivariate tests in cooperation with Torsten Madsen (Koch 1998:67pp). Her types are turned into a chronological tool through use of closed finds and radiocarbon determinations.

As concerns this present task of exploring the Resengaard pottery in terms of chronology, it seems *a priori* that the more or less expressed variations of certain clay pot forms in different assemblages may indicate a very gradual development. If types were to be established in such a way that they could embrace several pots, I consider it unlikely that such types would be instrumental in a chronological analysis of the Resengaard pottery. The chronological development could, so to speak, happen within the type definitions and we would not be able catch it. We would thus presumably risk overlooking stages in the transformation of details. At the present state of research at least, therefore, types would not make sense when we are targeting a relatively detailed chronology. Instead, I consider every single representation of a profile as referring only to a separate clay pot in the sense that it is impossible to identify two clay pots as being fully alike. From this position, I shall attempt to carry out the chronological analysis and strive to order the time relationships between pottery assemblages.

I have already commented on the two main steps in the analysis that first intends to place four selected longhouse assemblages in chronological order. This order shall then, as a second stage, be referred to as the standard of reference. The four reference assemblages, which will have some time distance between them, might thus be considered four benchmarks with which all other assemblages of profiles should be compared. In the second step, which will be fairly comprehensive, the analysis will concentrate on placing pottery assemblages from other houses and pits in relation to these reference assemblages.

However, we only seldom have finds or observations linking the pits at the settlement to their primary function. For instance, a pit just dug to take subsoil sand is an activity which would leave hardly any pottery or other artefacts. In such instances, finds of pottery in the pits would be comparable to the secondary fills above the sunken floors. Because no indications of vegetative surfaces have been observed in the lower levels, most of the pits were probably filled up soon after their exploitation ceased. In such instances, the placing or dumping of pottery and other artefacts into the pits probably often mirrors the time of use of the pit quite closely.

When a comparative analysis of the profiles from an individual assemblage has been carried out, the relative chronological positions will be suggested through a careful weighing up of the strength of the relationships to different assemblages. In this evaluation, I find it reasonable to weigh affinities with very characteristic profiles higher than some affinities with less characteristic profiles. Further, I will weigh a single strong qualitative resemblance higher than a number of weaker or more general resemblances. Thus, in practice, I am inclined to let the strong, qualitative relationships between profiles be the prime determinants for placement in the weighing process while, in some instances, a number of less strong relationships might lead to a minor adjustment of the dating towards an older or younger reference assemblage.

The dating achieved can be transferred to further artefacts and to the sunken-floor houses. The suggested relative chronological position can thus, in principle, be transferred to complete clay pot profiles, bottoms, ornaments, wares, surfaces and beyond. Furthermore, through sunken-floor contexts, it can be passed on to a number of more or less complete flint artefacts such as daggers, knives and arrowheads and as well as it can also be passed on to a number of stone artefacts such as hammers, smoothening stones and whetstones. The relative dating can also be passed on to a wide variety of charred macrofossils such as weeds, straw and cereals, some of which also possess a radiocarbon determination.

Structurally, the chronological approach outlined above might be regarded as a kind of "benchmark method". It implies the use of a few find combinations consisting of varied assemblages as benchmarks that are put into chronological order by means of internal, visual comparison. In this case, we need to know from external sources which reference assemblages are likely to be the oldest and youngest, respectively.

Approaches along this line may offer an alternative path when trying to order assemblages chronologically. Although the method is fairly simple, it requires substantial work to carry it out. In the case of unornamented pottery assemblages, the comparisons in my view should not be narrowed down to comparing a few elements that are present but should consider every rim profile as a whole in order to embrace as many nuances in the shaping as possible. A real strength of the method is thus obviously that it does not leave out any features as regards shape and does not limit itself only to a narrow selection of traits.

Technical remarks

To carry out the analysis naturally necessitated some considerations on the technical aspects. As the task is not part of a study of form or style but centres on chronological results, it seems unnecessary to make very detailed divisions of the clay pots (Fig. 3.4). The neck is seldom present as a distinct element in the material and hence it appears irrational to apply the term. It seems adequate in most cases to deal with the terms "rim" and "body" and in some cases also "transition to the body" or "shoulder". It seems ideal that the drawings of the sides, whenever they are preserved adequately, should extend somewhat below the rims in order to present a reasonable "set off" for the rims. However, the preservation of rims and adjoining parts of the sides varies considerably.

The actual museum numbers of the concrete items are often rather long and impractical for use in relation to the present work and would take up too much space when referred to hundreds of times. In addition, it has been necessary to add special letters for handling items which, in the excavation reports, are not numbered separately. The museum numbers for Resengaard have been abbreviated markedly, as described in the introduction to Catalogue A. Corresponding abbreviations cover the nine other settlements in focus.[5]

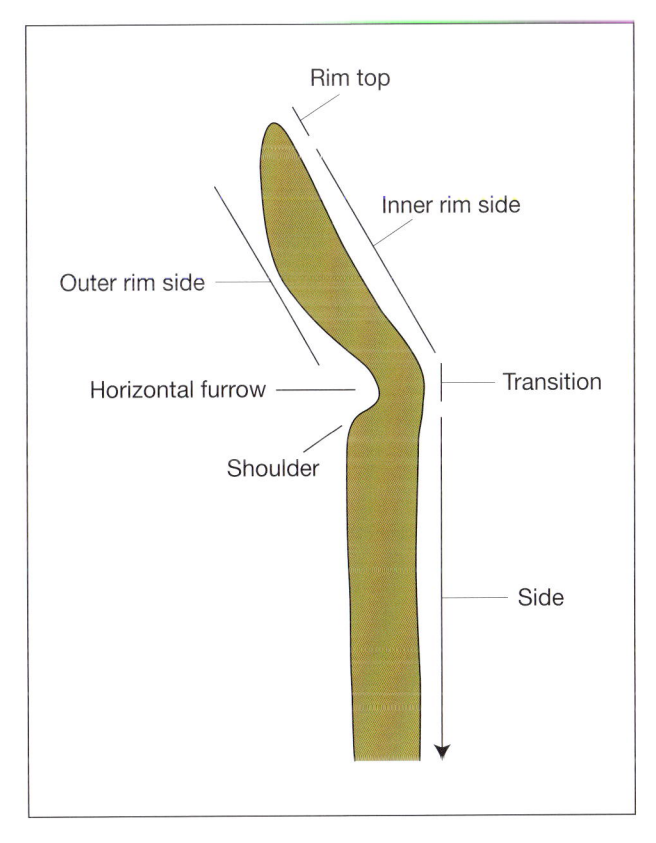

Fig. 3.4. Clay pot terms. The uppermost parts of certain clay pots in LNII/emerging Bronze Age of the Limfjord region are often naturally bound to the body via a more or less pronounced bend. In many instances, a horizontal narrowing or furrow has even been made all around the outer side at the transition between rim and body. With regard to this trait, the term "furrow" has been used in cases where there is a clearly marked upper and lower furrow edge as well as in instances with a less clear furrow-like marking. However, certain other clay pot forms display no natural rim limits and, for these cases, it is proposed that the uppermost three centimetres are considered as being the rim.

3.3. Provisional chronology of the Resengaard pottery

None of the assemblages of the twelve longhouses match each other internally and hence they cannot be considered to have been contemporaneous in the proper sense of the word. The pottery from Houses 1, 2, 41, and 134 has been selected as reference assemblages, because these together appear to best meet the criteria put forward above. Relatively early as well as middle and relatively late assemblages appear to be present. Having been protected by thick soil layers, the ceramics stemming from the sunken-floor horizons and secondary fills from Houses 1, 2 and 41, according to stratification, were undisturbed by recent actions.

Comparison of the four reference assemblages

The contrasts and likenesses between the reference assemblages shall now be considered. The four entities concern richly faceted assemblages, especially those of Houses 1, 2 and 41, whereas that from House 134 is more limited but by no means insignificant. And yet, as regards House 1, it must be remarked that it is rich in many aspects even though the pottery is less varied than the ceramics from House 2 and House 41. The first step involves comparing the clay pot profiles from Houses 1 and 134, each with their pottery forms showing obvious similarities with a "late" milieu (about NBA I) and an "early" milieu (Beaker) respectively.

Houses 1 and 134 pottery assemblages: in all, 6 rim profiles and 2 side profiles belonging to the floor represent the House 1 assemblage along with 2 rim profiles and 1 side profile from the secondary fills (Fig. 3.5). A rim ascribed to the secondary fills (RE73aa) is part of a classical open bowl with fairly straight sides. It possibly belongs to the time of House 1 but, on the other hand, I am not convinced that it does and it is therefore not included in the pottery analysis.

Just 4 rim profiles belonging to the sunken-floor horizon represent the House 134 assemblage together with 4 rim profiles from the secondary fills (Fig. 3.6).

Specimens comparable to the RE31aa profile, with its characteristic, horizontal furrow below the rim, which was found in House 1, are not represented in the House 134 assemblage. Neither are parallels to the RE60aa profile or the RE39aa profile noticeable. The very special profile fragment RE24aa/RE35aa also has no counterparts in the 134 assemblage.

In contrast, the characteristic upper clay pot parts from House 134 with horizontal cordons of RE596ab from the floor, as well as RE564aa and RE564bb from the secondary fills, have no comparable profiles in the House 1 assemblage. The almost similar profiles, albeit without horizontal cordons, RE564ab and RE564ab, likewise find no parallels.

As evident from this short comparison, these two longhouse assemblages do not have any characteristic

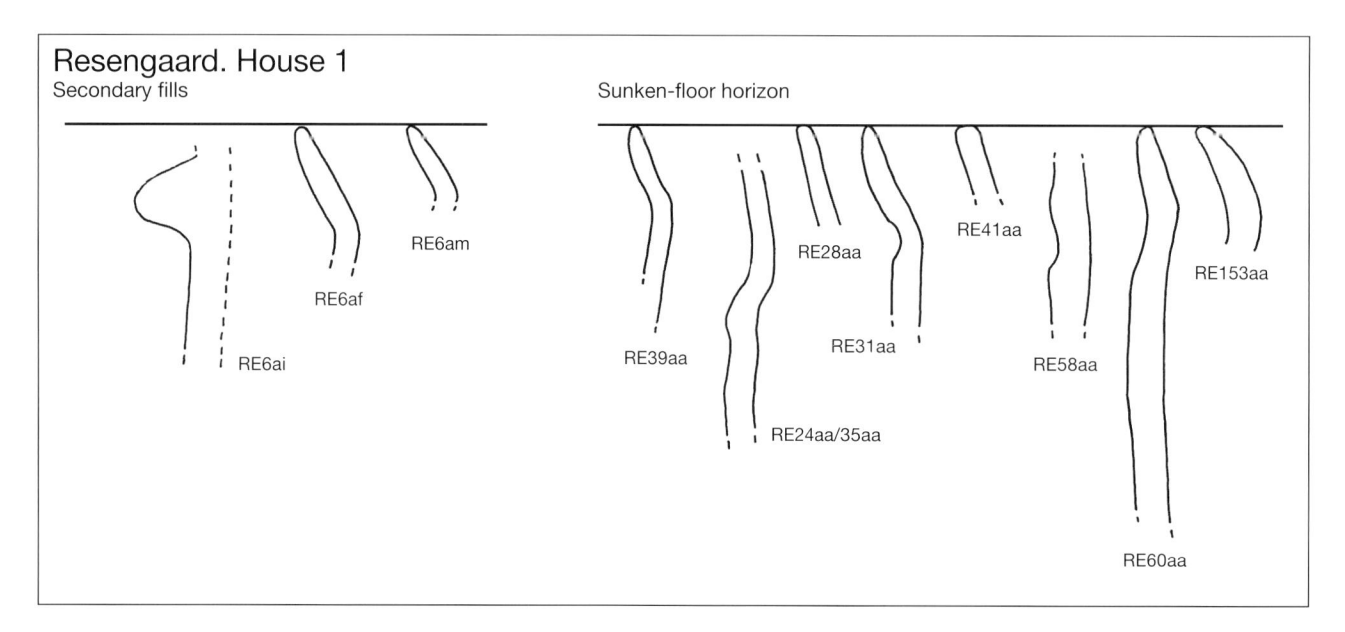

Fig. 3.5. Resengaard, House 1. It relates to one of the four "reference assemblages". Selected pottery profiles from the sunken-floor horizon and the above secondary fills. Scale: 1:2.

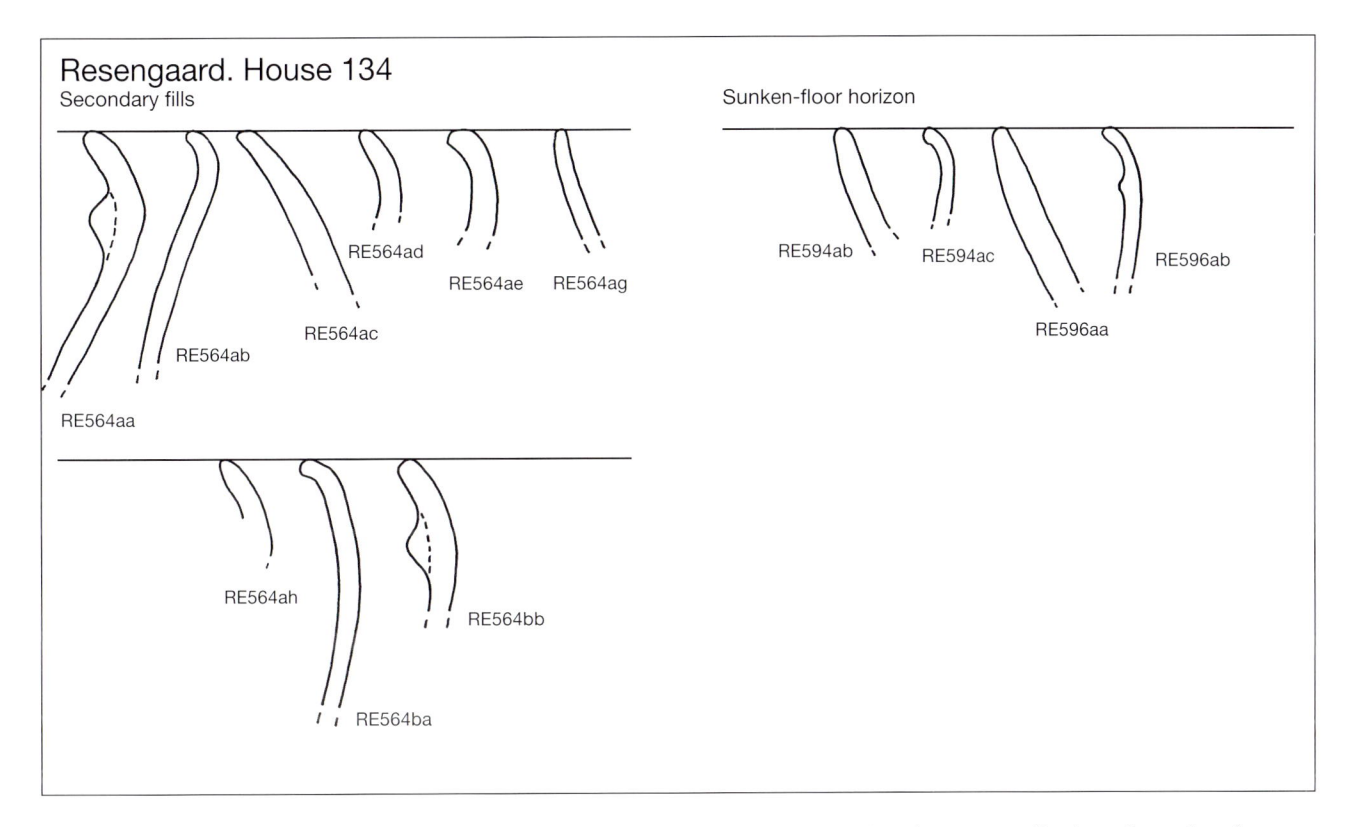

Fig. 3.6. Resengaard, House 134. It relates to one of the four "reference assemblages". Selected pottery profiles from the sunken-floor horizon and the above secondary fills. Scale: 1:2.

profiles in common. It will appear from the considerations below that the House 1 pottery assemblage is the very youngest among those of the 12 sunken-floor longhouses at Resengaard. In contrast, the House 134 pottery assemblage is the very oldest.

House 2 and House 41 pottery assemblages: a total of 8 rim profiles belonging to the sunken floor represent the House 41 assemblage together with 18 rim profiles and 4 side profiles from the secondary fills (Fig. 3.7). In all, 10 rim profiles belonging to the sunken floor horizon represent the House 2 assemblage together with 10 rim profiles from the secondary fills (Fig. 3.8).

The RE135aa profile from the sunken floor horizon of House 2 has no direct counterparts in the House 41 assemblage but it should be noted that a relatively near parallel (RE81bb/85aa), with the whole vessel profile preserved, exists from a pit immediately north of House 2 and, in my understanding, this belonged to the functioning time of this house. Vessel profiles with some points of resemblance were, however, present in the secondary fills of House 41. This relates to the profile RE406cb, with a somewhat shorter, more "abrupt" rim and possibly also RE406ai.

A rim shape with some affinity with the previous is RE134aa, from the sunken floor horizon of House 2, although this tends to have a somewhat more rounded belly. The shape is quite close to RE412aa and, possibly, to a lesser degree, to RE313aa from House 41.

The RE119aa/121aa profile from the sunken floor horizon of House 2 is without clear marking of the transition between rim and the upper parts of the vessel. The profile tends to be somewhat S-curved. From the secondary fills of House 41 stems an almost similar upper profile, RE406 ab. RE420aa also has some resembling traits. The profile of RE404aa also resembles RE119aa/121aa to some degree. Profile RE7ag from the secondary fills of House 2 likewise shows some of the same features as the other House 2 profile.

Also belonging to the sunken floor horizon of House 2 is the dramatically designed upper profile of RE176aa. It is characterized on the outer rim by a convex area above a horizontal furrow. The inner rim is correspondingly concave above a marked section of the profile just opposite the horizontal furrow on the outer side. A profile, RE416aa, with some affinity comes from the sunken floor horizon of House 41 although it is somewhat thicker-walled. A distant

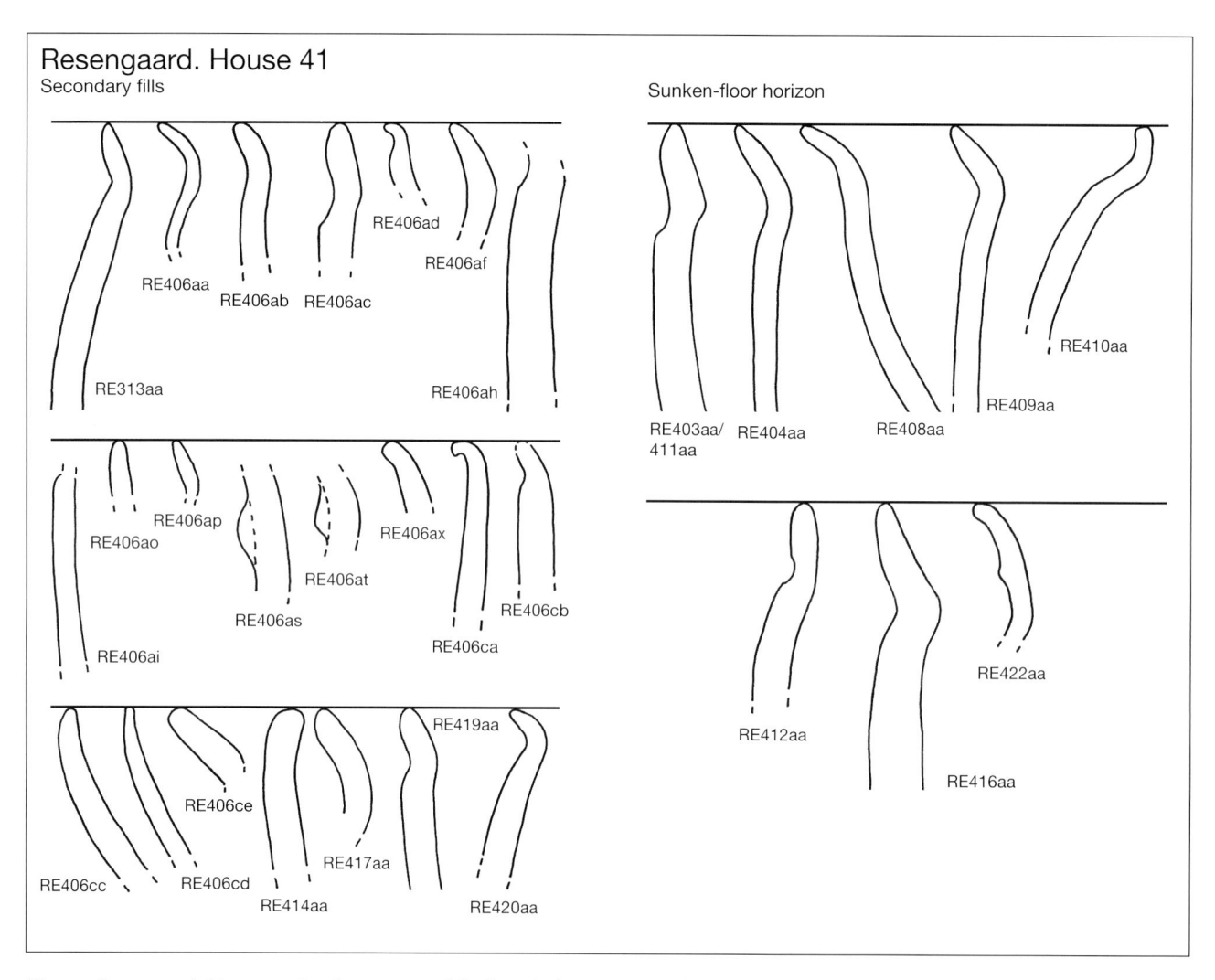

Fig. 3.7. Resengaard, House 41. It relates to one of the four "reference assemblages". Selected pottery profiles from the sunken-floor horizon and the above secondary fills. Scale: 1:2.

relationship to it seems to be present in the profiles RE403aa/411aa of House 41.

A simple bowl shape is represented in the profile 7ah from the secondary fills of House 2. Corresponding forms are present in the profiles RE406ad and the somewhat thicker-walled 406cc from the secondary fills of House 41.

The thick-walled RE92aa profile belongs to the sunken floor horizon of House 2 and does not have direct counterparts in the House 41 assemblage. However, two less distinct specimens, with rims merely a little bent out, RE7ab and RE7ae from the secondary fills, as well as RE179aa and 161aa from the sunken floor horizon of House 2, correspond somewhat to profile RE409, and also possibly to RE406af and 406ce from the sunken floor horizon of House 41.

The bellied outline of profile RE133aa from the sunken floor horizon of House 2 has clear affinities with profile RE410aa from the sunken floor horizon of House 41.

The open form indicated by profile RE93aa from the sunken floor of House 2 might – though very thick-walled – possibly have some affinities with forms such as RE408aa from the sunken floor horizon of House 41.

Profile RE102aa from the sunken floor horizon of House 2 does not exhibit a close relationship to any forms in House 41.

Apart from this last statement, it is really striking that so many individual profiles from House 2 can be demonstrated to possess a kind of relationship and some even a relatively close affinity to pottery profiles from House 41. Some of the characteristic pottery profiles from the House 41 assemblage were not, however, comparable to any forms from House 2. First and foremost this goes for vessels with horizontal cor-

170 Chapter 3

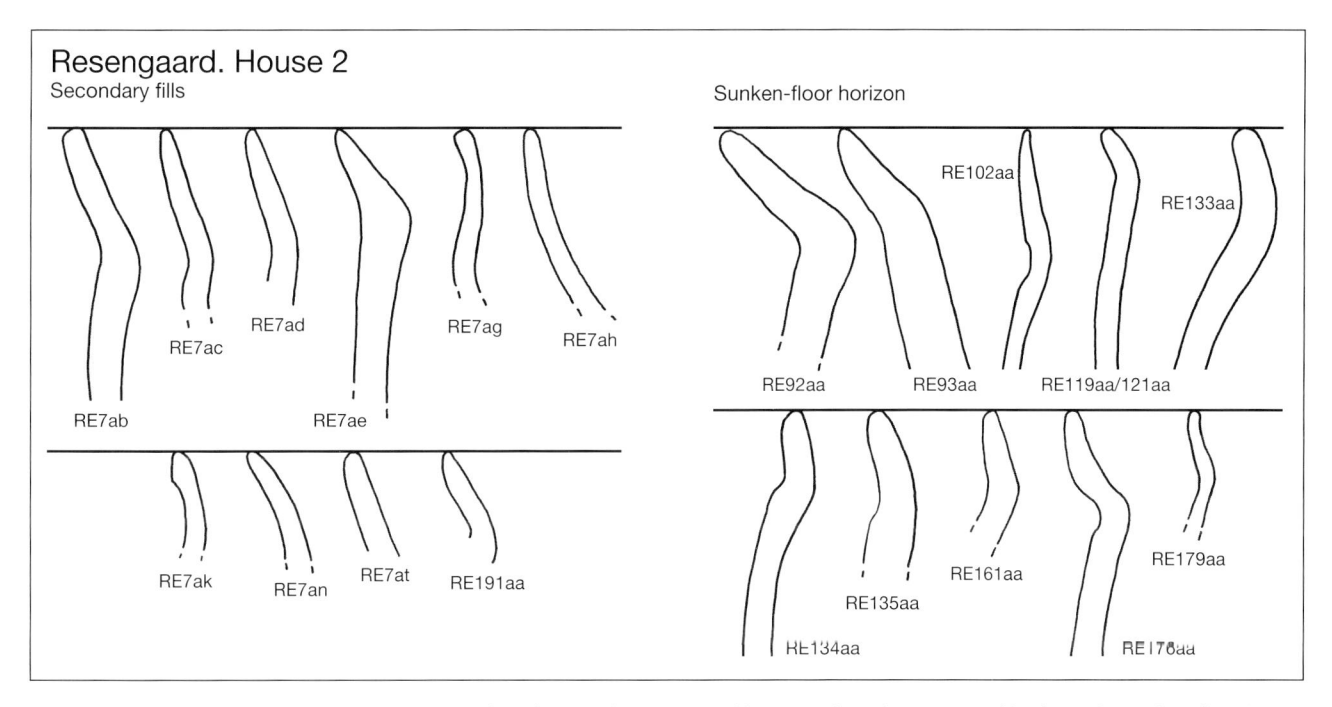

Fig. 3.8. Resengaard, House 2. It relates to one of the four "reference assemblages". Selected pottery profiles from the sunken-floor horizon and the above secondary fills. Scale: 1:2.

dons, RE422aa from the sunken floor horizon as well as the side profiles RE406aa and RE406at. The rim profile 406ca being thin and bent out quite dramatically from the side belongs to the secondary fills of House 41 and does not have any counterparts in the House 2 assemblage. Neither does the almost upright rim profile RE414aa.

The next point to be clearly made is that in between the House 134 and House 1 assemblages – which did not have any characteristic profiles in common – the assemblage of House 41 is the older, and consequently that of House 2 the younger. This is substantiated as follows.

Simple bowls with slightly convex outer sides are represented in the assemblages of Houses 41 and 134 but these only generally lend some support to the idea of a relationship between the two assemblages. From the secondary fills of House 41, this relates to profiles RE406cc and RE406cd. From the sunken floor horizon of House 134 this relates to profiles RE594ab and RE596aa, as well as RE564ac and RE564ag from its secondary fills.

More significant and particularly noteworthy is the presence of horizontal cordons below the rims in the assemblages of both Houses 134 and 41 but, in contrast, these do not exist in those from Houses 2 and 1. From House 41, the horizontal cordons are evidenced in profile RE422aa from the sunken floor horizon and RE406as as well as RE406at from the secondary fills. From House 134 they are present in profile RE596ab from the sunken floor horizon and in profiles RE564aa and RE564bb from the secondary fills. Having other features in common further confirms the relationship between the two assemblages.

The indications of common traits in the general shapes of the cordoned vessels can be visualized by comparing, for instance, profiles RE422aa and RE564aa. The profiles from the House 41 assemblages tend to be slightly "breached" compared to the more smoothly designed pottery profiles of the House 134 assemblage. Furthermore, the tendency to finish the rims in a very slender, somewhat "bent out" fashion seems to be a common trait among some of the clay pots. Compare, for instance, two profiles such as RE406ca from the secondary fills of House 41 and RE594ac from the sunken floor horizon of House 134. These resemble each other in the general shape and both have an unusually slender finish at the top of the rim.

The degree of likeness between the House 41 and 134 assemblages in broad outline settles the question as to which material has the affiliation to older milieus. What remains to be substantiated, then, is the degree of similarity between the House 2 and House 1 assemblages.

Chronology of pottery assemblages 171

The differences between the pottery assemblages of Houses 2 and 1 are relatively obvious. Some side profiles, RE24aa/35aa & RE58aa, that are present from the sunken floor horizon of House 1 do not have any counterparts in the House 2 context. A side profile, RE6ai, with a horizontally-projecting lug, has no counterparts either. Furthermore, from the sunken floor horizon of House 1 no profiles resembling the profile RE60aa, which is not particularly marked, are found in House 2 context. It would have been interesting to see a House 2 version of this profile since a very much marked and elaborated profile, RE403aa/411aa from the sunken floor horizon of House 41, might be an early predecessor of the relatively slack profile, RE60aa, from House 1.

Some of the notable differences which seem to exist between House 2 and House 1 may correspond to the beginnings of the manufacture of less elaborate rims and thereby also less careful pottery designs some time after the beginning of the Older Bronze Age.

The relationship between the two assemblages cannot really be substantiated by referring to only a slight likeness of character, such as the resemblance between e.g. the smoothly bent out profile RE7an from the secondary fills of House 2 and RE153aa from the sunken floor horizon of House 1.

The resemblance between several angular profiles from, on the one hand House 2 (RE179aa & RE161aa from the sunken floor horizon, besides RE7ab & RE7ae from the secondary fills), and on the other House 1 (RE39aa from the sunken floor horizon besides RE6af and RE6am from the secondary fills) lend moderate support to the assumption of a relationship between House 2 and House 1.

However, two other comparable profiles are more significant for a closer relationship, namely RE176aa, with the rather dramatic rim design belonging to the sunken floor of House 2 and the profile RE31aa from the sunken floor horizon of House 1. In this latter profile, the inner side of the rim is straight and the inner area behind the outside furrow is straightened. Profile RE31aa also gives the impression of a powerfully created profile and it is precisely these profiles that point to a comparatively close relationship.

The complete absence of horizontal cordons below the rims in both House 1 and House 2 could also be significant for a close chronological relationship. Yet, as mentioned, the assemblage of House 1 is not large. In my reading, the assemblage of House 1 is clearly younger than the assemblage of House 2. Overall, from the above analysis, I am convinced that the internal chronological positions of the four assemblages, beginning with that of the oldest house, are 134 – 41 – 2 – 1. To my knowledge, this result is not contradicted by other artefacts or observations from the four reference assemblages.

Affinities of the eight remaining longhouse assemblages

We shall now turn to the relative chronological positions of the other sunken-floor longhouses. The outcome as concerns all eight house assemblages is based on the evidence of the find combinations from contexts of sunken floor horizons and secondary fills combined with the suggested relationships of the pottery profiles to reference assemblages and other. For further details of the arguments, see Appendix A. A scheme of suggested relative chronological positions of the 12 longhouses follows later (Fig. 3.55).

House 13: no rim profiles were found in the sunken floor horizon and thus just 6 rim profiles from the secondary fills represent the assemblage (Fig. 3.9). This house site is rather important due to its relatively clear traces of walls and other traits but the pottery from the floor and secondary fills is unfortunately quite scant as regards the shapes represented. In my judgment, the assemblage derives from a time between House 41 and the later House 2. The link to the House 41 pottery seems slightly stronger and hence its chronological position was presumably correspondingly near to this assemblage.

House 14: a total of 7 rim profiles and a single side profile coming from the sunken floor horizon represent the House 14 assemblage together with 29 rim profiles from the secondary fills (Fig. 3.10). The rela-

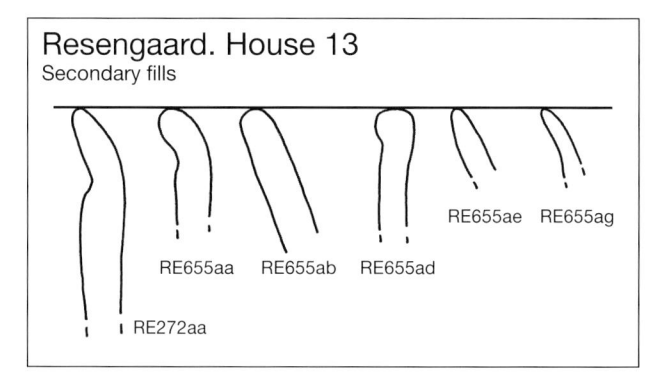

Fig. 3.9. Resengaard, House 13. Selected pottery profiles from the secondary fills. Scale: 1:2.

Resengaard. House 14
Secondary fills   Sunken-floor horizon

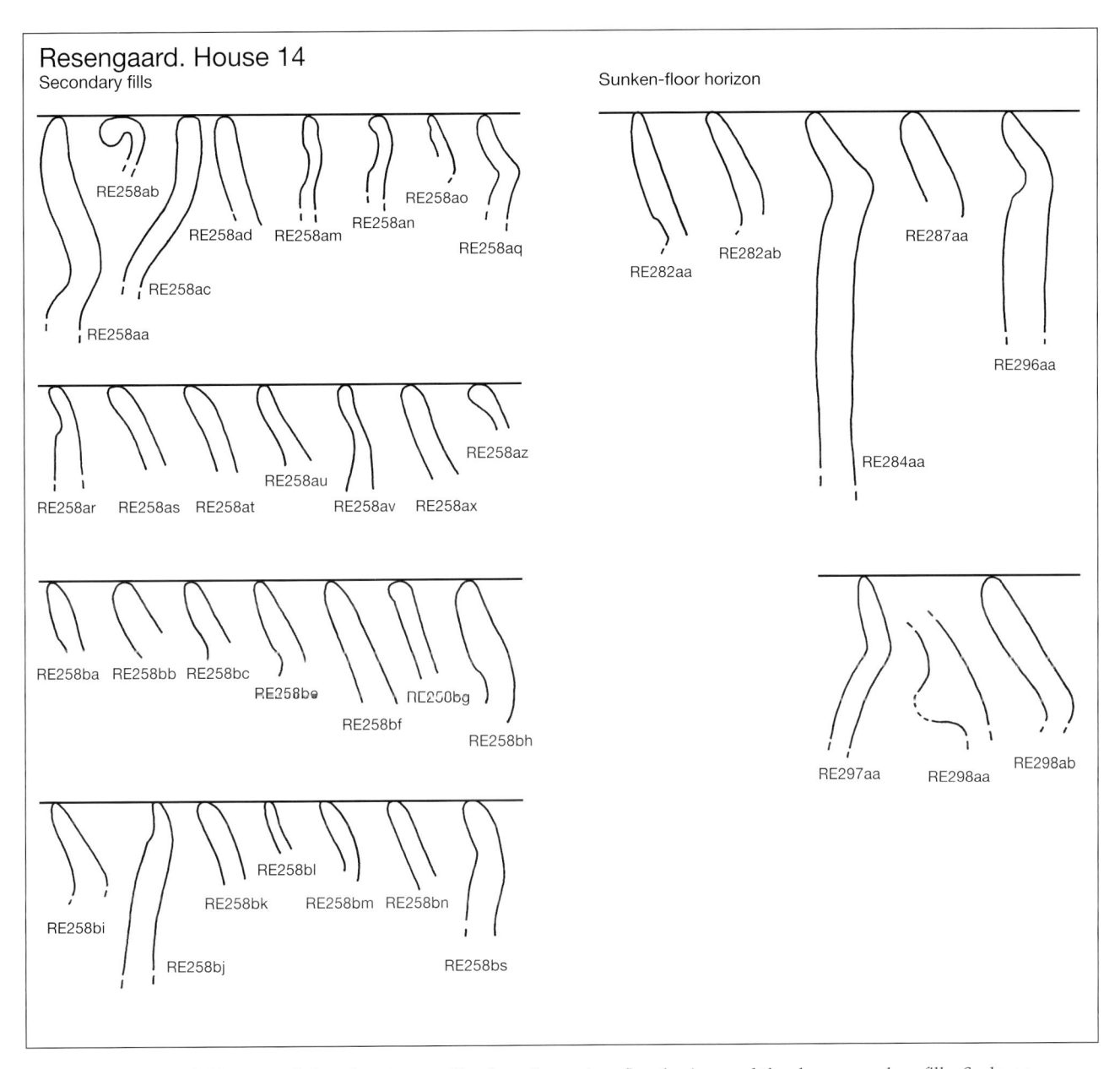

Fig. 3.10. Resengaard, House 14. Selected pottery profiles from the sunken-floor horizon and the above secondary fills. Scale: 1:2.

tive chronological placement of the assemblage can be based on fairly safe grounds because a large number of pottery profiles of broad variation are present. Only the most important relationships between the pottery profiles will be suggested.[6] These exhibit some traits more or less in common with the assemblages of House 41, House 2 and House 1. I put much weight particularly on the closeness to the House 2 pottery, whereas the affiliations with the House 41 pottery tend to be of a more general character and might presumably simply indicate ordinary elements belonging to the same tradition. Taking House 2 as a benchmark for the chronological position of House 14, the special traits shared with House 1 seem quite relevant. Between House 1 and House 2, these elements likely lead to the suggestion of a relative dating to the time nearest to the latter.

House 42: just 4 rim profiles belonging to the sunken floor horizon represent the House 42 assemblage together with 14 rim profiles and 1 side profile from the secondary fills (Fig. 3.11). The ceramics seem relatively homogeneous and only a few characteristic profiles are represented although these are adequate to suggest a dating. The pottery shows relationships to assemblages from Houses 134 and 41 through the presence not least of a cordoned rim. However, the design is much less pronounced than in the early assemblages and this indicates in my reading a somewhat later chronological

Chronology of pottery assemblages   173

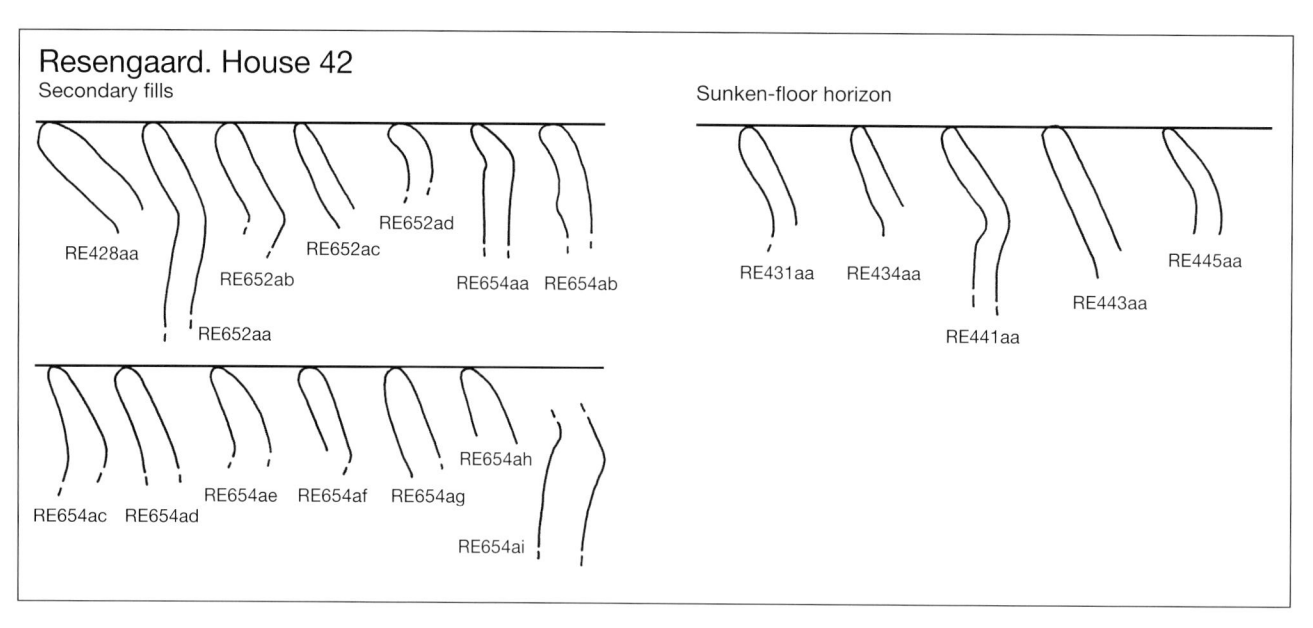

Fig. 3.11. Resengaard, House 42. Selected pottery profiles from the sunken-floor horizon and the above secondary fills. Scale: 1:2.

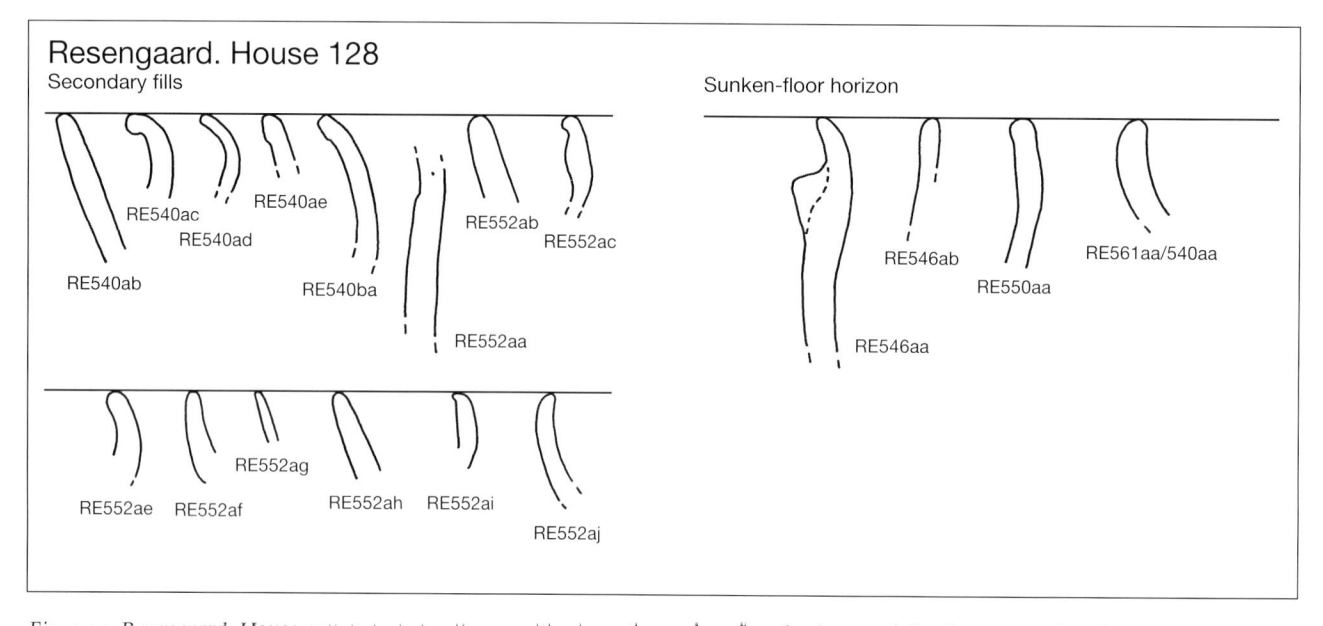

Fig. 3.12. Resengaard, House 128. Selected pottery profiles from the sunken-floor horizon and the above secondary fills. Scale: 1:2.

position. Apart from this, no important traits in common with the early assemblages are observable. The evidence seems to point to a chronological position between the assemblages of House 41 and House 2, presumably a little closer to House 41 than House 2.

House 128: a total of 4 rim profiles from the sunken floor horizon represent the assemblage together with 13 rim profiles and 1 side profile from the secondary fills (Fig. 3.12). The pottery is fairly varied despite the somewhat fragmentary state of many of the potsherds. Broadly speaking, it is evident that the House 128 assemblage must stem from the time between House 41

and House 1, while a more specific date based on the rim profiles in particular can be based on just one element. This relates to the use of a horizontally-projecting lug that could not be demonstrated in the reference assemblages of House 134, House 41 or House 2, whereas it is present in the House 14 assemblage with a suggested dating to shortly after House 2. It therefore seems reasonable to propose a chronological placement between the assemblages of Houses 2 and 1, as this feature was likewise present in the latter assemblage, even though more slight affiliations to the House 41 material exist.

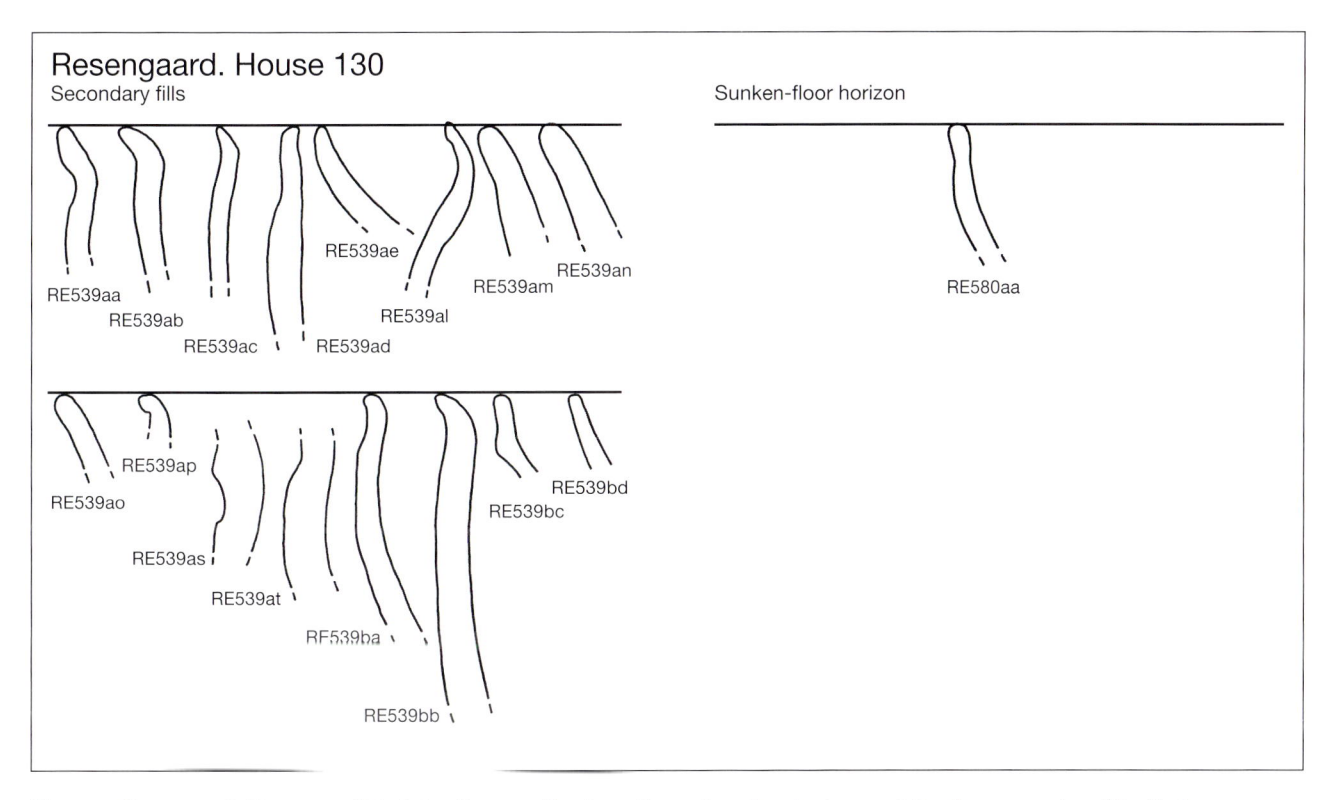

Fig. 3.13. Resengaard, House 130. Selected pottery profiles from the sunken-floor horizon and the above secondary fills. Scale: 1:2.

House 130: just one rim profile belonging to the sunken floor horizon makes up this assemblage together with 14 rim profiles and 2 side profiles from the secondary fills (Fig. 3.13). The pottery is reasonably varied as concerns that from the secondary fills and this creates a basis for suggesting a dating of the assemblage. When weighing up the varying affinities with other assemblages, it must first be realized that many links can actually be demonstrated. In the main, the pottery profiles show strong affiliations to the assemblages of House 134 and, in particular, House 41. They also show some affinities with profiles from the House 2 assemblage. Although the pottery differs from the House 41 assemblage in several details, it seems relatively clear that the time of the House 130 assemblage is close to it. Evaluating the relative chronological position, it seems most likely that it was slightly older than the pottery of House 41.

House 138: just 2 rim profiles from the sunken floor horizon represent the House 138 assemblage (Fig. 3.14) and yet the ceramics allow for a suggestion of the chronological position because the profiles have prominent designs. A close affiliation with the House 2 material seems clear. When weighing up the sketched out relationships to the other assemblages, a chronological position between the assemblages of House 41 and House 2 seems fairly evident. The position is most likely closest to that of House 2.

House 197: as a matter of precaution, pit 1, placed to the northeast, and its find material was first considered as possibly belonging to the sunken floor of House 197. After a review of the outline of the building and its patches, I reached the conclusion that pit 1 must be part of the sunken-floor horizon. The preceding separate chronological analysis has shown that its content

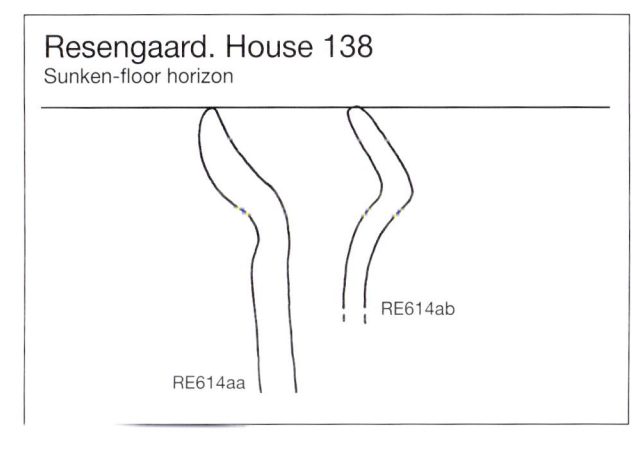

Fig. 3.14. Resengaard, House 138. Selected pottery profiles from the sunken-floor horizon. Scale: 1:2.

Chronology of pottery assemblages 175

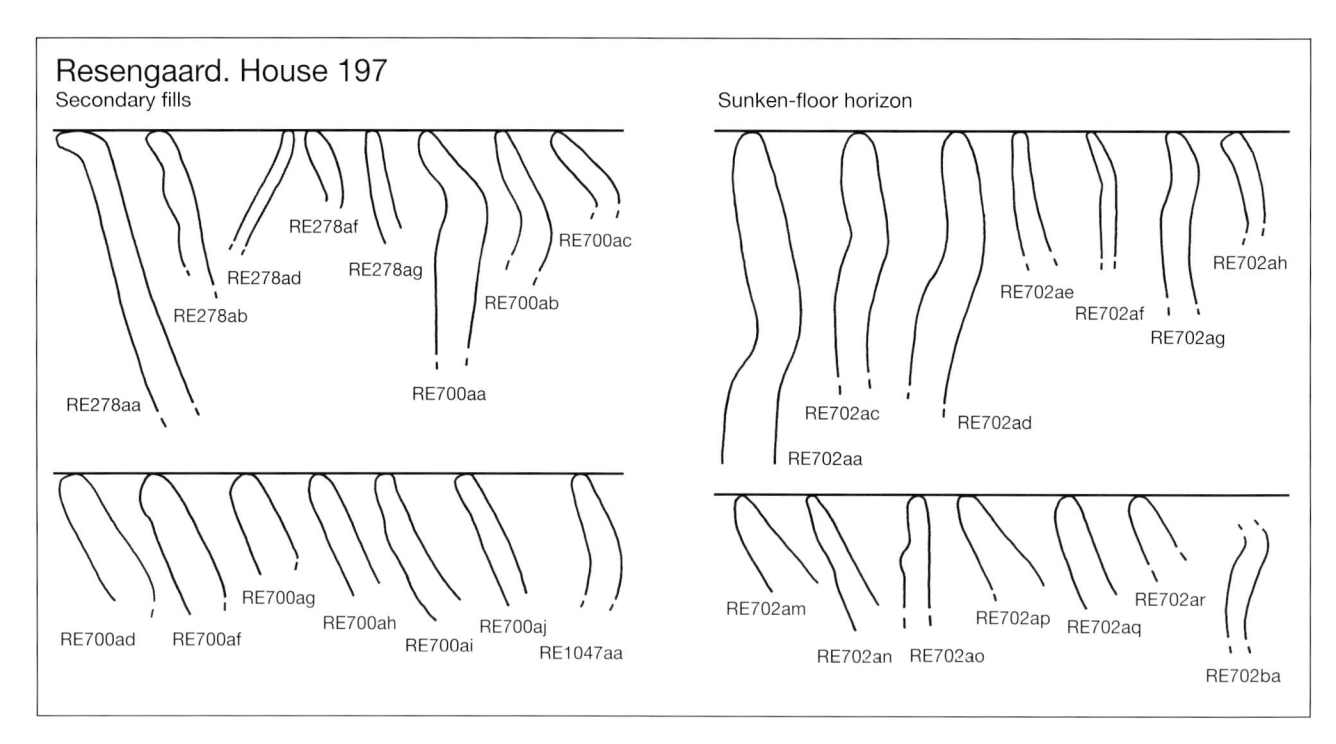

Fig. 3.15. Resengaard, House 197. Selected pottery profiles from the sunken-floor horizon and the above secondary fills. Scale: 1:2.

of potsherds also appears to be well in accordance with the other ceramics from the house site. The number of clay pot profiles deriving from it totals 21, and thus the highest number found in a small pit belonging to the period in question at the settlement. A total of 13 rim profiles and 1 side profile have been selected to represent the pit, and thereby the sunken-floor horizon (Fig. 3.15). A further 15 rim profiles belonging to the secondary fills represent the assemblage of House 197. Considering the affiliations to the reference assemblages, it is possible to observe relationships first and foremost to those of Houses 41 and 2. The chronological position of the assemblage is most probably in the middle of these two assemblages.

House 200: in all, 12 rim profiles stemming from the sunken floor horizon represent the assemblage of House 200 together with 31 rim profiles and 1 side profile from the secondary fills (Fig. 3.16). The ceramics are among the most varied and, in number, they form one of the largest pottery representations from the settlement. Very many profiles are thus available for grading the assemblage into the relative order but it should first be stated that, as in the foregoing, no close match on a general level has been found with any of the other house assemblages. In turn, there are numerous and evidently strong relationships with the materials of Houses 41 and 2. Weighing up the different affiliations, we must also take into consideration the observation that no specimens with horizontal cordons are present in the assemblage. Furthermore, the presence of a profile with a horizontally-projecting lug draws the date towards the younger materials. Seen in isolation, the evidence of this feature would make it temping to suggest a slightly later date but, considering the many relationships also with the House 41 materials, it seems most balanced to suggest a dating just before that of House 2.

Affinities of assemblages from twelve minor houses and a short house

The materials from the sites of three minor sunken-floor houses with scorched-stone patches are considered first.

House 202: just 2 rim profiles from the secondary fills represent the House 202 assemblage (Fig. 3.17). These rim profiles are not particularly characteristic and do not allow for a more precise relative dating. A chronological position with wide frames between the assemblages of House 41 and House 1 seems reasonable but no further dating can be suggested on the basis of the pottery.

House 240: just 4 rim profiles from the sunken floor represent the House 240 assemblage together with 20 rim profiles and 5 side profiles from the secondary fills (Fig. 3.18). Several are quite characteristic and an accom-

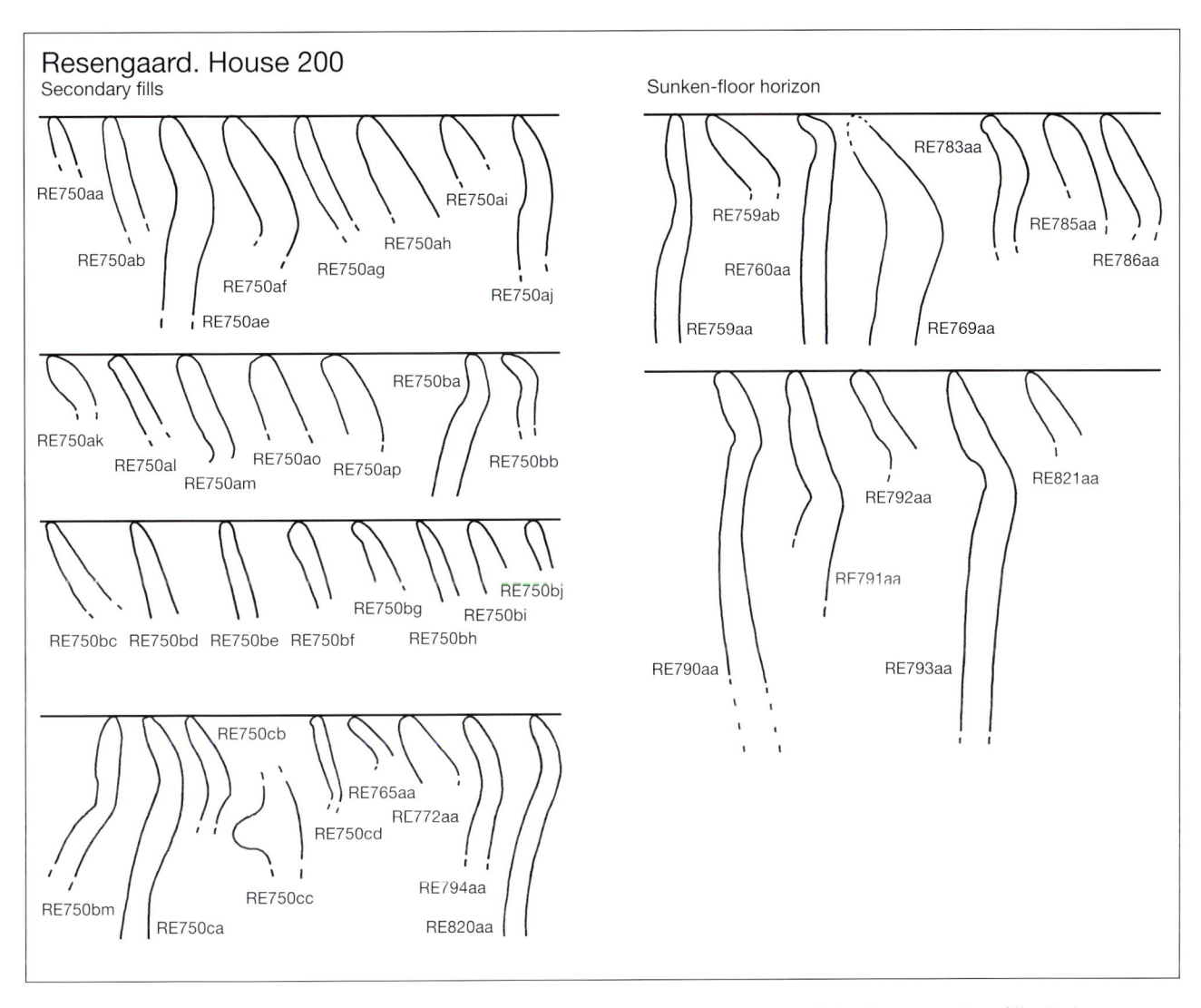

Fig. 3.16. Resengaard, House 200. Selected pottery profiles from the sunken-floor horizon and the above secondary fills. Scale: 1:2.

modation of the assemblage can be based on many observations. The numerous profiles prove to have several affinities with the reference assemblages. Only a few show affiliations to the House 134 assemblage, whereas many are certainly related to those of House 2 and a number even appear to have a very close relationship in this regard. Several profiles also show relationships to the pottery of House 1 and some of these may evidently indicate a strong relationship. Some rim profiles show close relationships to the assemblages of House 1 and House 2. It is, however, interesting that quite a number of the profiles also seem to have affiliations to the assemblage of House 41, although generally not of a close nature. Weighing up these many links to the different pottery samples, it seems most balanced to centre the dating on the House 2 reference assemblage. It is worth noticing that some rims also show a close affinity with the House 14 material. A chronological position close to House 2 and, not least, that of House 14, is suggested. However, even a later dating forward in time to House 1 cannot be excluded.

House 289: in all, 18 rim profiles belonging to the secondary fills represent the assemblage, whereas none derive from the sunken floor (Fig. 3.19). The

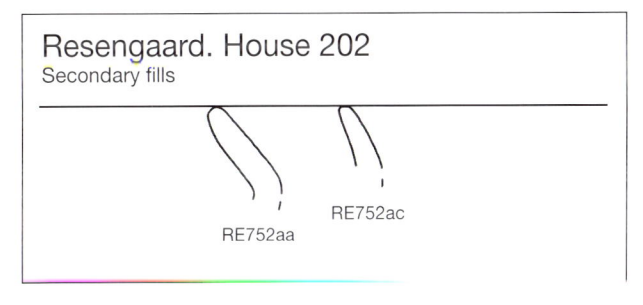

Fig. 3.17. Resengaard, House 202. Selected pottery profiles from the secondary fills. Scale: 1:2.

Chronology of pottery assemblages 177

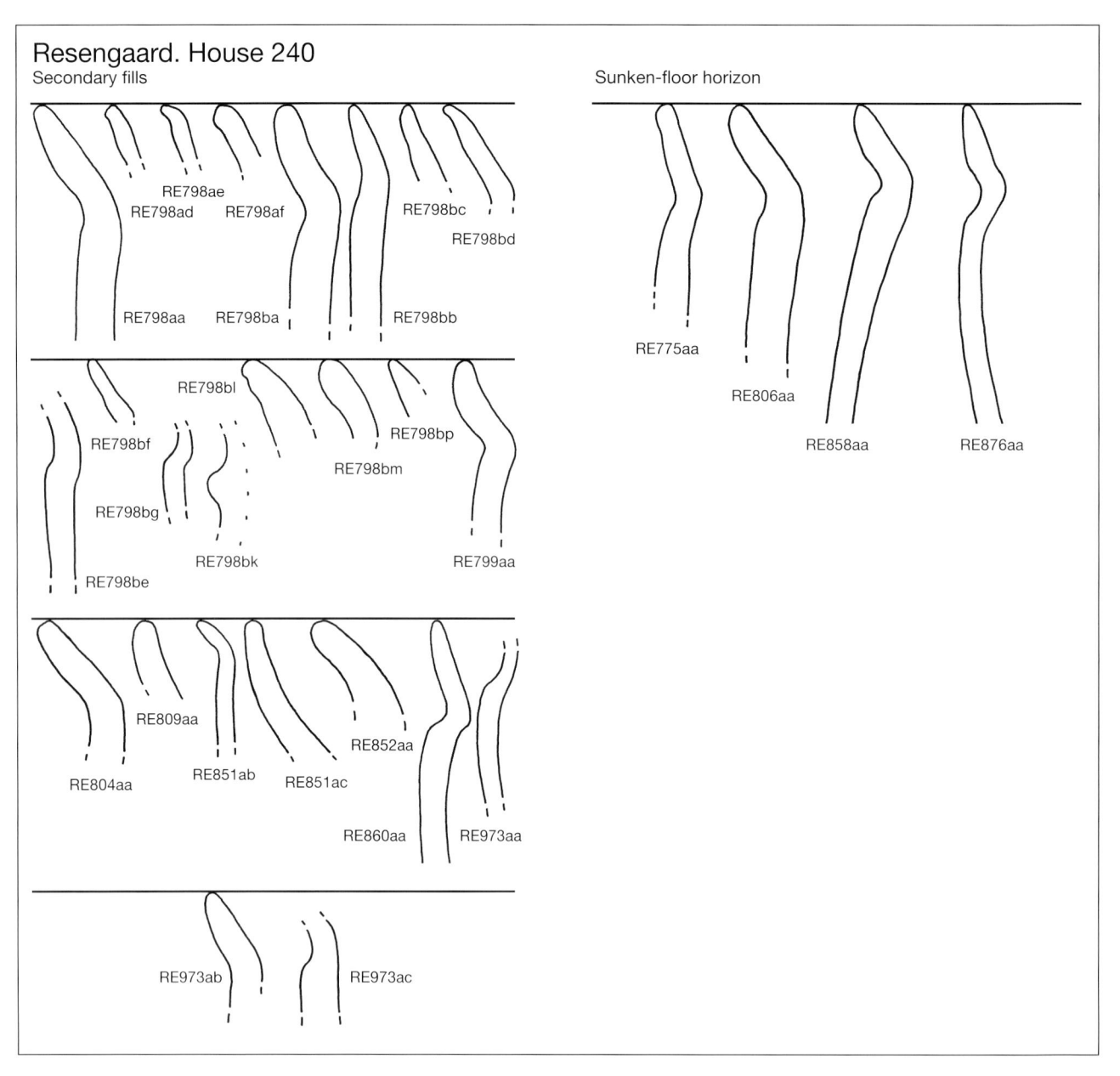

Fig. 3.18. Resengaard, House 240. Selected pottery profiles from the sunken-floor horizon and the above secondary fills. Scale: 1:2.

many profiles only have a few elements of characteristic form. Weighing up the different affinities, it could at first be suggested that several show weak relationships to the assemblages of House 41 and House 2, whereas others may indicate similarly weak relationships to the assemblages of House 134 and House 1. A few of the apparent links to the assemblage of House 41 seem relatively strong, albeit without any striking resemblance, and some of the very characteristic profiles of this assemblage are not present in the House 289 assemblage. Somewhat more specific relationships to the assemblages of House 130 (and House 198, see below) might furnish a clue as to the relative dating and lead to a proposed dating close to their time. As it seems that the affinities with the assemblage of House 2 on the other hand might suggest drawing the dating a little forward in time, a chronological placement of the 289 assemblage around the time of House 41 can be suggested.

We now turn to the 12 minor sunken-floor houses without scorched-stone patches. The minor House 143 is left out because no rim profiles exist from it.

House 10: in all, 5 rim profiles belonging to the sunken floor horizon represent the assemblage together with 11 rim profiles from the secondary fills (Fig. 3.20). One of the latter has no preserved top. The material from this house is fairly important due to finds of relatively large clusters of potsherds on the floor. Weighing up the relative importance of the House 10 affinities, it can be said that several relationships are observed with the assemblages of House 41, House 2 and House 1. The resemblance to the House 134 assemblage, through the tradition of the open bowl, in my reading has no important significance in this case, as stronger affinities are at play. Among the three other reference assemblages, the best match appears to be with House 2. Regarding a more detailed placement in the relative order, it should be noted that several of the affiliations we saw in the above concerning the assemblages of House 200 and, to some degree, House 14, may also concern House 10. A placement around about the lifetime of these assemblages seems obvious. A chronological position contemporaneous to House 200 is hence suggested.

House 12: a mere 5 rim profiles belonging to the secondary fills represent the assemblage (Fig. 3.21). The pottery is scant and fairly one-sided. The few and fragmented profiles do not make closer dating of the assemblage an easy task. However, judging by the presence of three almost uniform profiles which might stem from simple, open bowls, a nearer relationship could be suggested to the assemblages of Houses 134 or 41. A dating near these therefore does not seem unreasonable, although a later dating cannot be excluded.

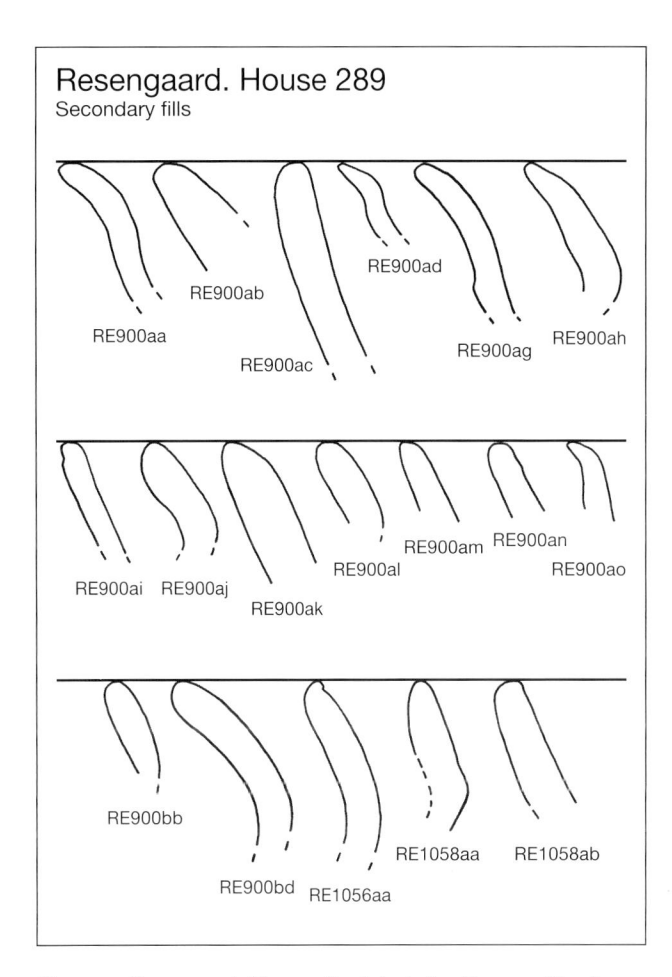

Fig. 3.19. Resengaard, House 289. Selected pottery profiles from the secondary fills. Scale: 1:2.

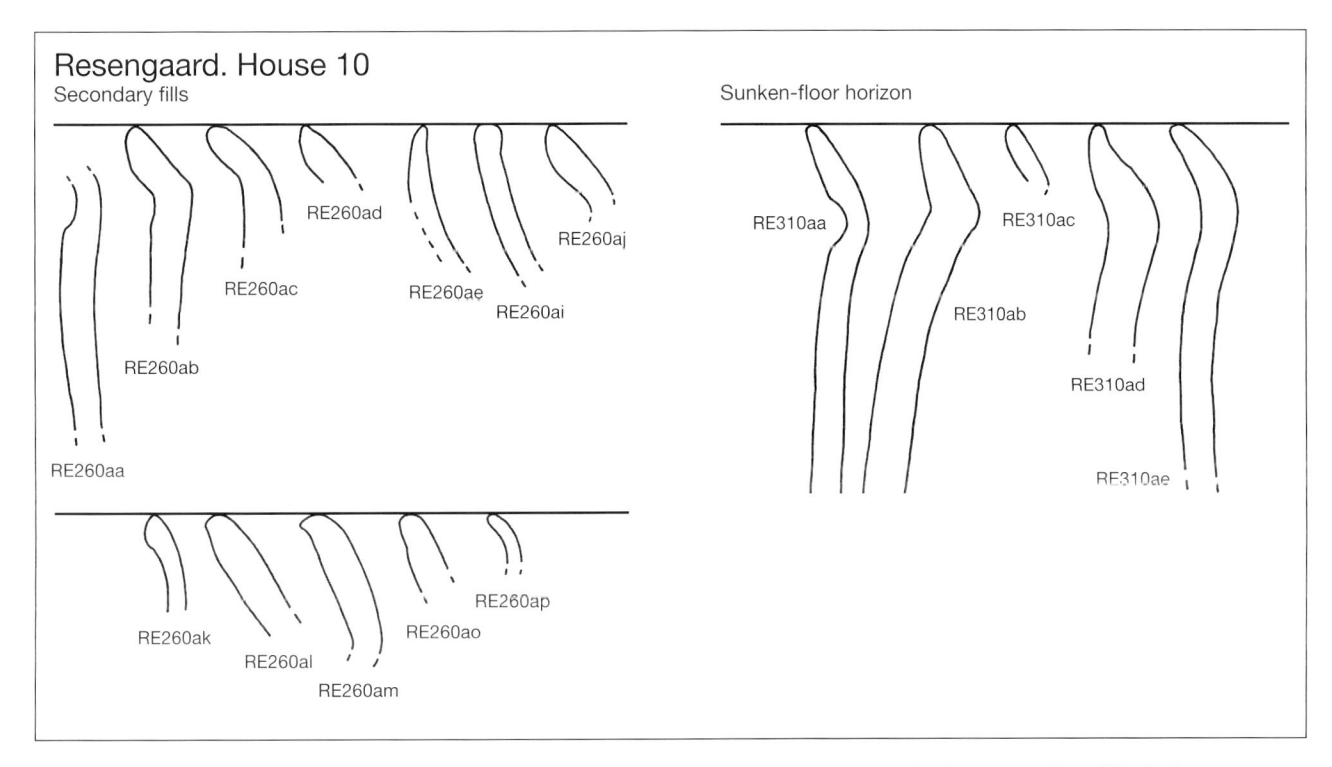

Fig. 3.20. Resengaard, House 10. Selected pottery profiles from the sunken-floor horizon and the above secondary fills. Scale: 1:2.

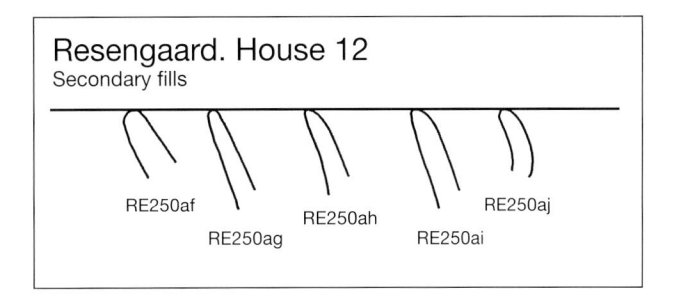

Fig. 3.21. Resengaard, House 12. Selected pottery profiles from the secondary fills. Scale: 1:2.

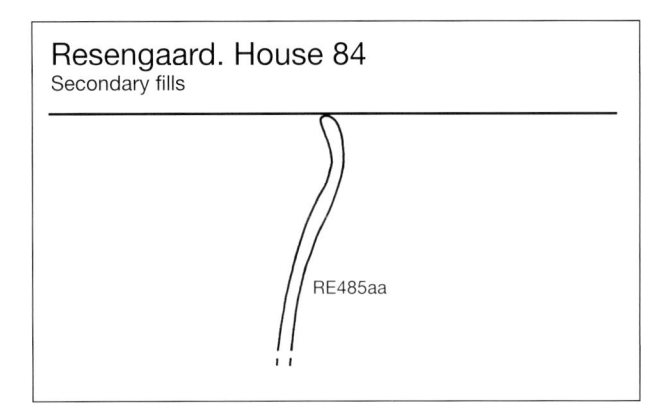

Fig. 3.22. Resengaard, House 84. Clay pot profile from the secondary fills. Scale: 1:2.

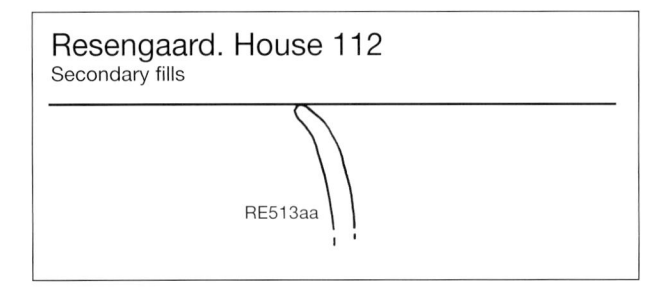

Fig. 3.23. Resengaard, House 112. Clay pot profile from the secondary fills. Scale: 1:2.

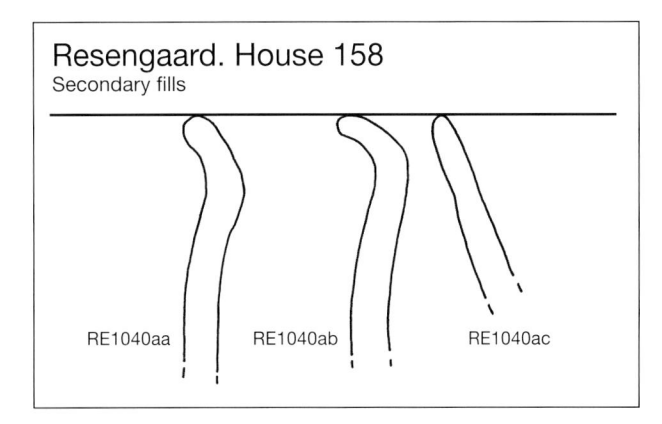

Fig. 3.24. Resengaard, House 158. Selected pottery profiles from the secondary fills. Scale: 1:2.

House 84: just 1 profile belonging to the secondary fills makes up this assemblage. It is fairly characteristic, however (Fig. 3.22). This kind of profiling does not clearly resemble any profiles from the reference assemblages from Houses 41, 2 or 1. And yet it has some traits in common with a specimen known from the House 130 assemblage. The form might suggest contemporaneity to the 134 material, or a little before or soon after. Bearing in mind that a single clay pot profile as in this case hardly gives sufficient grounds for a strong dating, I tentatively suggest a dating contemporaneous with the House 134 assemblage.

House 112: likewise only 1 clay pot profile belonging to the secondary fills makes up this assemblage (Fig. 3.23). As above, this rim profile, with only a few characteristics, in no way provides a regular basis for dating. However, as it exhibits some of the same characteristics observed in a rim profile from the House 13 material, it might stem from about the same time, although the time of House 41 also seems an option. A chronological position between the assemblages of House 41 and House 2 is proposed, albeit with a strong reservation due to the scant evidence.

House 158: just 3 rim profiles belonging to the secondary fills represent the assemblage (Fig. 3.24). Two with some traits in common and a third rim with only a few characteristic elements do not provide a solid point of departure for dating. Based on the two former profiles, an early chronological position near to the House 134 and 41 assemblages seems possible. This chronological position can be considered as faintly supported by the third clay pot profile. Although directly comparable profiles cannot be referred to, the dating suggested is around or parallel to the chronological position of the House 130 assemblage.

House 183: in all, 6 rim profiles from the secondary fills represent the assemblage (Fig. 3.25). Despite the few pottery profiles, some significant relationships can be highlighted. The observable affinities indicate closer relationships to the House 134 and House 41 assemblages. In my judgment, it seems that more relationships can be observed with the House 134 material. A chronological position of House 183 more or less parallel to that of House 134 can therefore cautiously be suggested.

House 193: no clay pot profiles are available from the sunken floor of House 193, whereas 2 rim profiles exist from a posthole in the northern wall line and their likely dating corresponds to that of the building (Fig. 3.26). These allow us to suggest the chronological position and show affinities with more assemblages in general. A time range beginning before the House 134 assemblage to around the time of the House 2 assemblage seems the maximum. However, as a foot ring is represented in secondary fills from two other, relatively early houses, it seems reasonable to put some weight on this in chronological terms because such traits have not been observed in any later assemblages at Resengaard. I therefore favour proposing a rather early dating, i.e. before the assemblage of House 134. A chronological position of about the time of pit 160/161 (the possible house relics) can thus be suggested.

House 198: in all, 11 rim profiles belonging to the secondary fills represent the assemblage (Fig. 3.27). These have qualities that make it possible to suggest a dating. The resemblance with, in particular, certain profiles from the House 41 assemblage as well as, to a lesser extent, with those of Houses 134 and 2, provide the basis for suggesting a time parallel to that of House 41, although a dating to some time before or after cannot be excluded.[7]

House 268: in all, 6 rim profiles belonging to the sunken floor represent the assemblage together with 17 rim profiles and 2 side profiles from the secondary fills (Fig. 3.28). The pottery in this assemblage is fairly varied and a dating can therefore be suggested on a relatively broad basis. Weighing up the affinities with the reference assemblages as well as other longhouse materials from the site, it appears that the affinities with the later materials, in particular, are reasonably obvious. Some of the relationships to the assemblages of Houses 1 and 2 might place the House 268 material chronologically in this interval. Additionally, several affiliations with the assemblages of House 14 and House 200 also point to a chronological position near the time of these houses. In my judgment, certain strong affinities with the House 1 material may suggest a dating more or less parallel to this house assemblage.

As we have seen, only a single short sunken-floor house was found at the Resengaard settlement and its date is now considered.

House 201: just 1 rim profile belonging to the secondary fills makes up the assemblage of this building (Fig. 3.29). It is not particularly characteristic and hence only allows for a broad suggested dating within the time range from the assemblage of House 41 to that of House 1. It might, however, be recalled that consideration of the relationship to the nearby site of House 200 ended in the understanding that House 201 was the younger. In this case, the dating could be narrowed down to after House 200 until about the time of House 1.

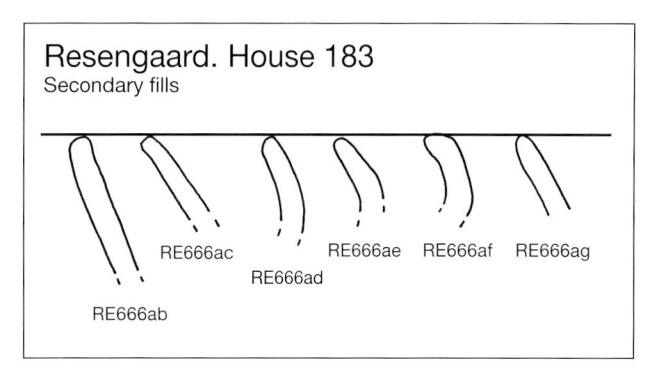

Fig. 3.25. Resengaard, House 183. Selected pottery profiles from the secondary fills. Scale: 1:2.

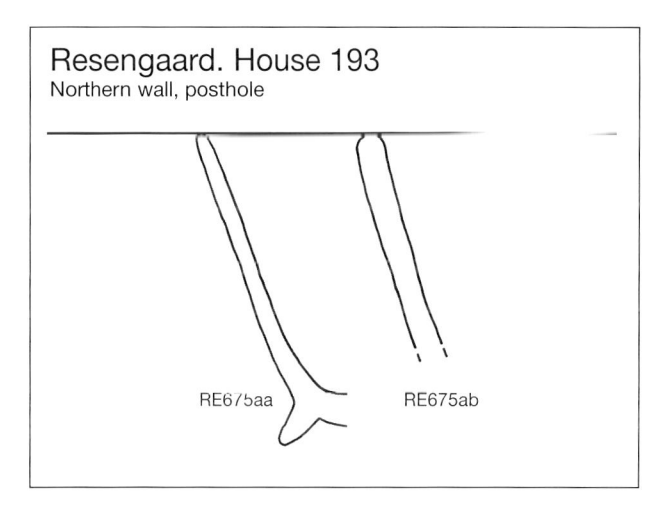

Fig. 3.26. Resengaard, House 193. Two clay pot profiles from a northern wall posthole. Scale: 1:2.

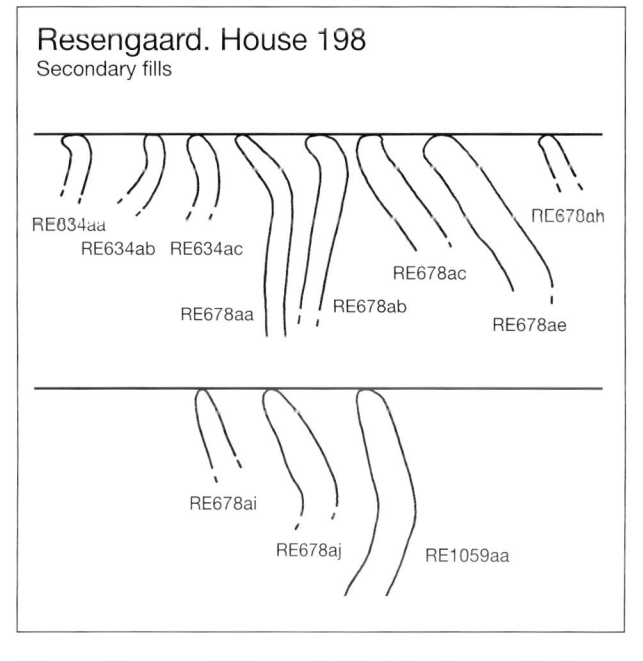

Fig. 3.27. Resengaard, House 198. Selected pottery profiles from the secondary fills. Scale: 1:2.

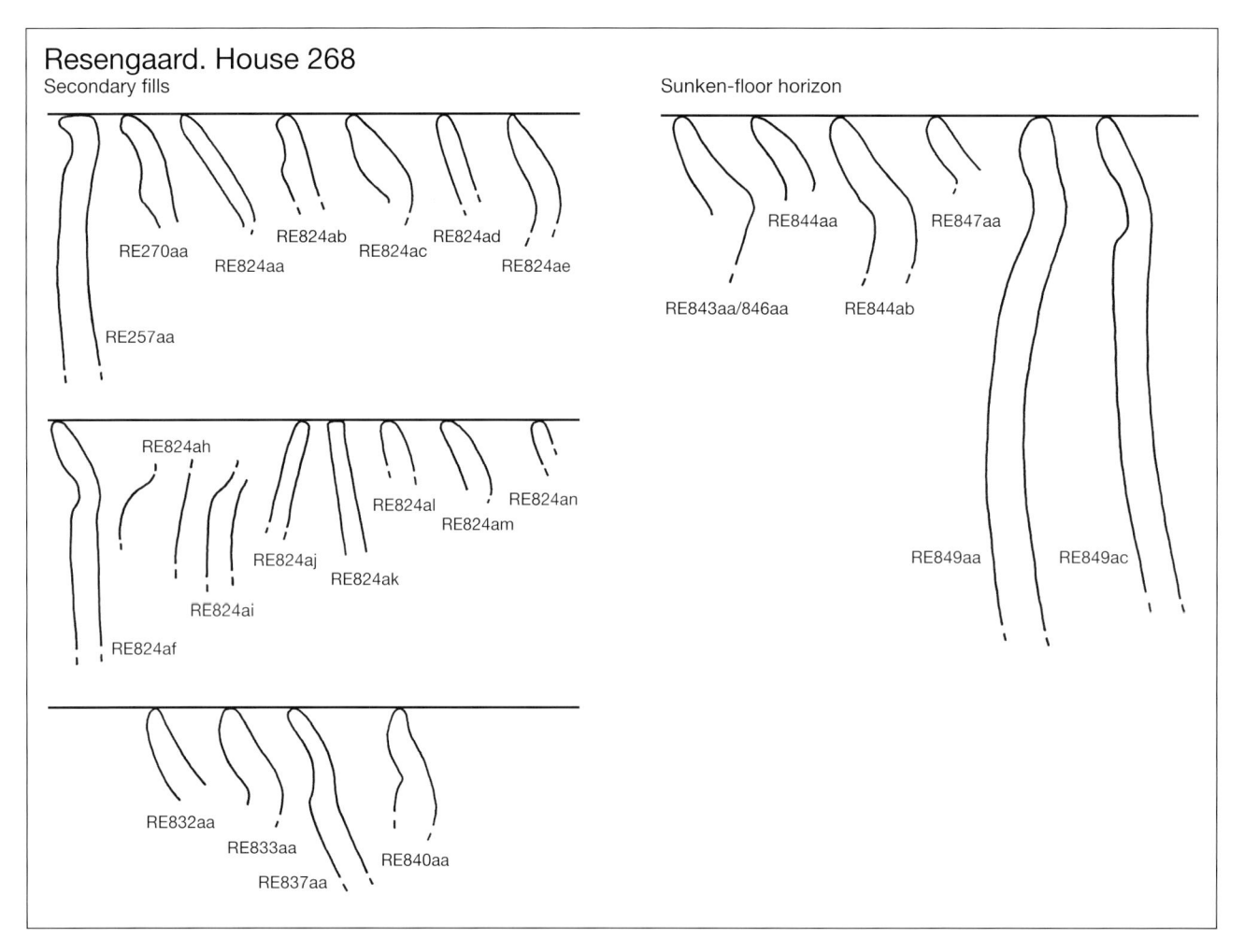

Fig. 3.28. Resengaard, House 268. Selected pottery profiles from the sunken-floor horizon and the above secondary fills. Scale: 1:2.

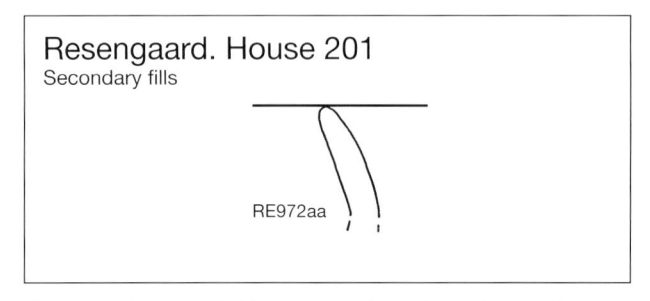

Fig. 3.29. Resengaard, House 201. Clay pot profile from the secondary fills. Scale: 1:2.

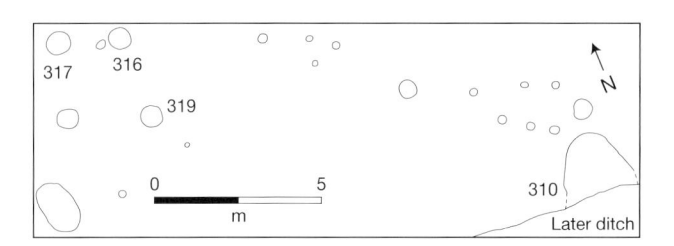

Fig. 3.30. Resengaard. The internal position of four pits containing interesting ceramics chronologically and otherwise. Found in the area west and south of the sunken floor of House 197.

Affinities of certain pit assemblages

We shall now look at a number of pits of chronological interest due to their ceramic contents (Fig. 3.30). As considered earlier, pit 160 might perhaps comprise the remainders of a sunken-floor house (in combination with pit 161 and other soil features).

Pit 160: the preserved profile seems to have a relatively strong relationship to the early assemblages (Fig. 3.31). Judging by its general shaping, the chronological position of the rim could be within the span ranging from somewhat before the time of House 134 until near the time of House 41. In my reading a very early dating is preferable, not least due to the gradual thickening of the rim upwards, a trait that may have relations further back in time.

Pit 161: in all 15 rim profiles and 1 side profile represent the pit assemblage (Fig. 3.32). These show some varying clay pot outlines that first and foremost repeatedly show relationships to the assemblage of House 134 but also may indicate affinities with those of House 41 and House 2. The chronological position can be in the span ranging from somewhat before the House 134 assemblage until maybe near the time of House 41. However, my preference is clearly for a rather early dating and a chronological position before the House 134 assemblage is suggested. In my understanding, the existence of a gap backwards in time between House 134 and pit 160-161 is likely.

When we consider the relationships between clay pot profiles from certain pits of interest in the following, it is noticeable that many other pits from the Resengaard settlement did not contain any artefacts at all. Firstly, the relationships between pits with six or more profiles are considered. This concerns four pit assemblages.[8]

Pit 319: found immediately south of the site of House 197. A total of 6 rims represent the assemblage (Fig. 3.33 & 5.12). The profiles belong to open bowls and only little variation can be observed. The rim-top finish exhibits several minor variations but none of these have the kind of thin and tapering rim top as in the case of both specimens from the House 41 assemblage. The open bowl profile from the secondary fills of House 2 is very slender and without any special rim-top finish. Possibly, the dating of the open bowls from this pit could be from before the assemblage of House 134 to about the time of House 41. Weighing up the affinities, but with very few specific details to take into consideration, I suggest a chronological position close to the House 134 assemblage, ranging from somewhat before to somewhat after.

Pit 316: found west of the sunken floor of House 197. In all 6 rims represent the assemblage (Fig. 3.34 & 5.12). There are only slight variations among the rim profiles belonging to the open bowls. The profiles exhibit relationships on a general level to the assemblages of House 134 and House 2. Yet, a dating about that of the House 134 assemblage, ranging from somewhat before to somewhat after, is proposed.

Pit 317: found west of the sunken floor of House 197. In all, 8 rims represent the assemblage (Fig. 3.35 & 5.13). The profiles, representing only two forms other than the open bowl, show affiliations in general to not least the early materials but possibly also to the assemblage of House 2. In one instance, the thin rim top seems to have some affinities the House 41 assemblage but only a broad dating can be proposed from the evidence as a whole. The time span could range from before the House 134 assemblage to that of House 2. However, the prevalence of the open bowls could again lean towards

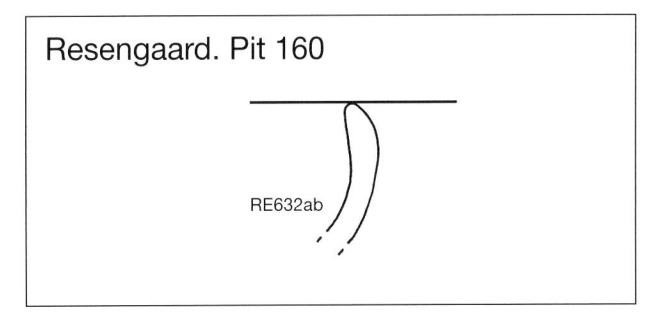

Fig. 3.31. Resengaard, pit 160. Selected clay pot profile from the pit. Main number RE632. Scale: 1:2.

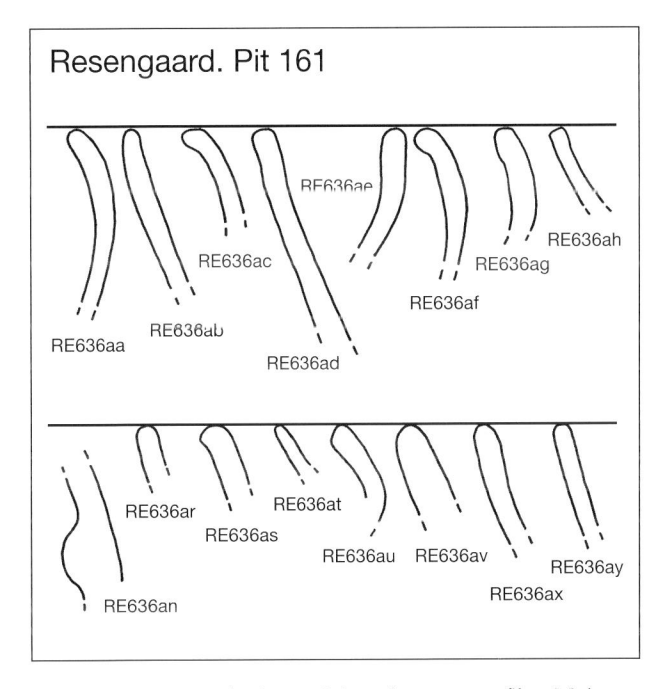

Fig. 3.32. Resengaard, pit 161. Selected pottery profiles. Main number RE636. Scale: 1:2.

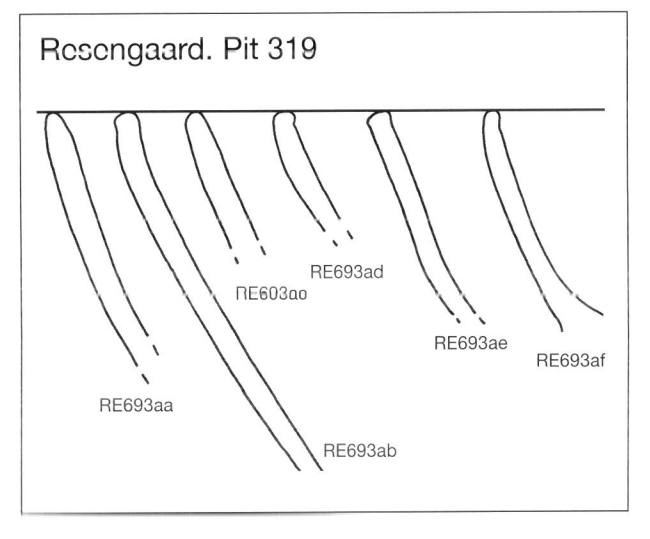

Fig. 3.33. Resengaard, pit 319. Selected pottery profiles. Main number RE693. Scale: 1:2.

Chronology of pottery assemblages **183**

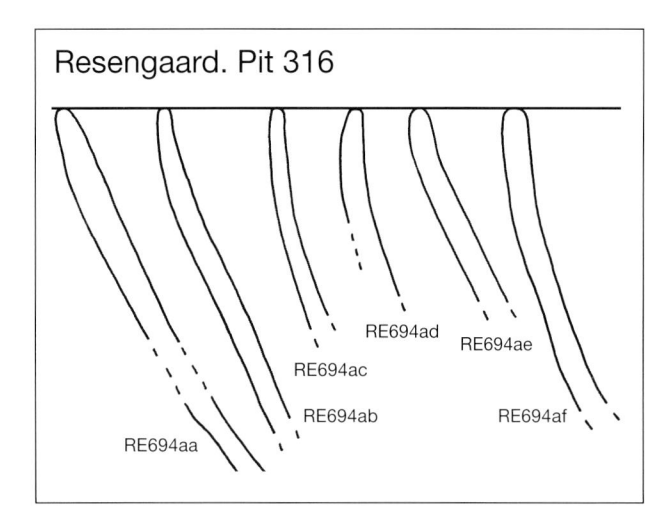

Fig. 3.34. Resengaard, pit 316. Selected pottery profiles. Main number RE 694. Scale: 1:2.

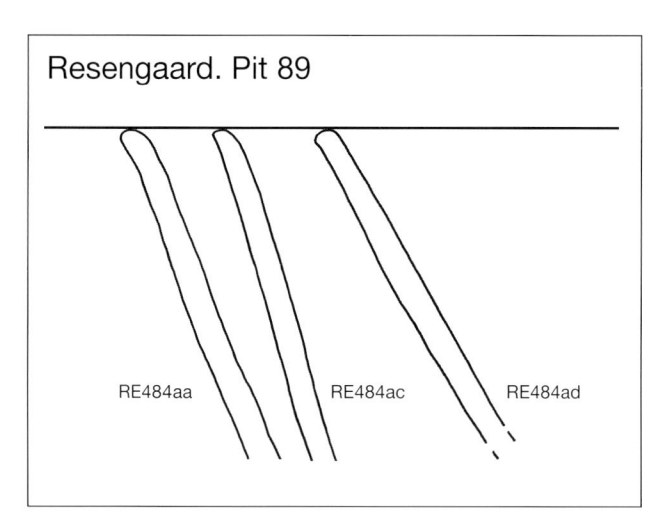

Fig. 3.36. Resengaard, pit 89. Selected pottery profiles. Main number RE484. Scale: 1:2.

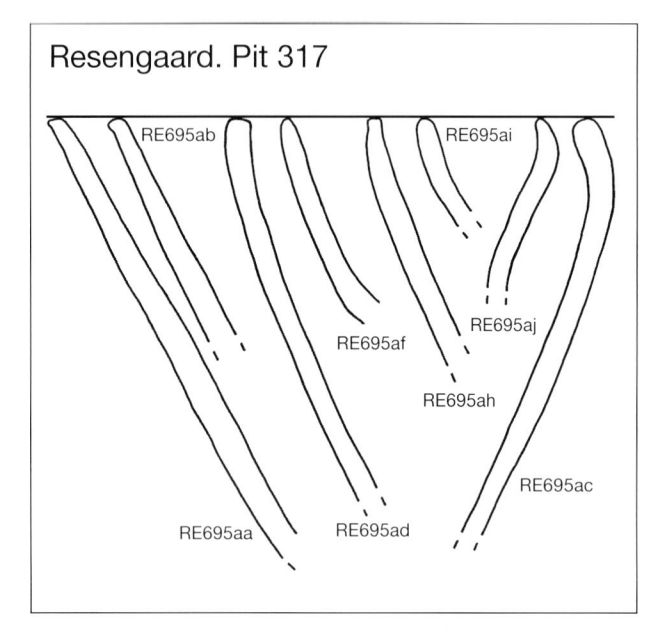

Fig. 3.35. Resengaard, pit 317. Selected pottery profiles. Main number RE695. Scale: 1:2.

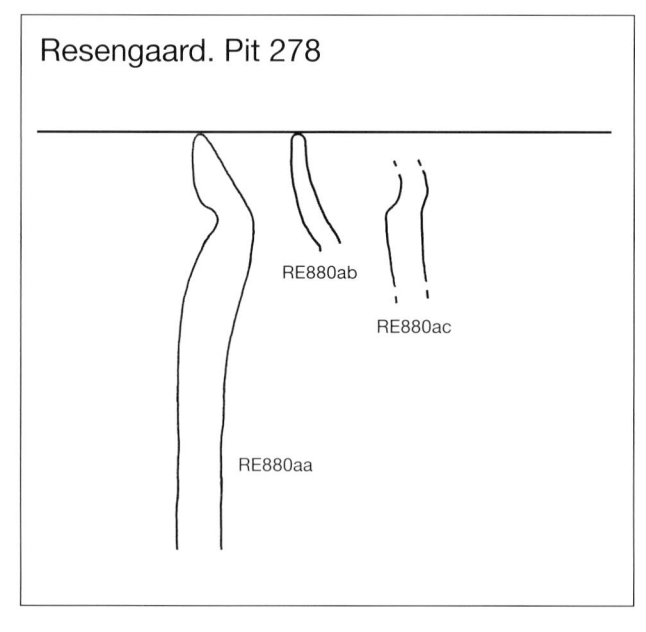

Fig. 3.37. Resengaard, pit 278. Selected pottery profiles. Main number RE880. Scale: 1:2.

the rather early materials. I suggest a chronological position by and large parallel to pit 319.

Turning then to pits with few clay pot profiles, the relationships between five pits with only 4, 3, and 2 pottery profiles, respectively, are considered in the following.

Pit 89: the pit was found somewhat southwest of the site of House 134. To the west-northwest it was closer to the site of House 84. On the whole, it appears that 4 clay pots are represented of which three rim profiles could be illustrated (Fig. 3.36 & 5.11). These have much in common, and do not provide a basis for a specific dating. On a general level, the profiles display some relationship to the reference assemblage of House 134. Although of minor significance, the profiles also have a relationship to the assemblage of House 2. The dating could, therefore, well be from before the time of House 134 to around the time of House 2. However, as only open bowls with an almost identical "touch" of the rims are present, I would again advocate an early pottery dating, due to the prevalence of such bowls early on in the settlement. The chronological position is suggested as being within the span ranging from somewhat before to a little after the assemblage of House 134.

184 Chapter 3

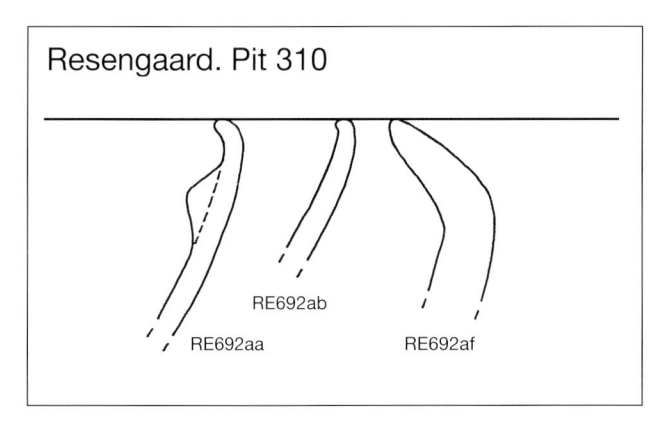

Fig. 3.38. Resengaard, pit 310. Selected pottery profiles. Main number RE692. Scale: 1:2.

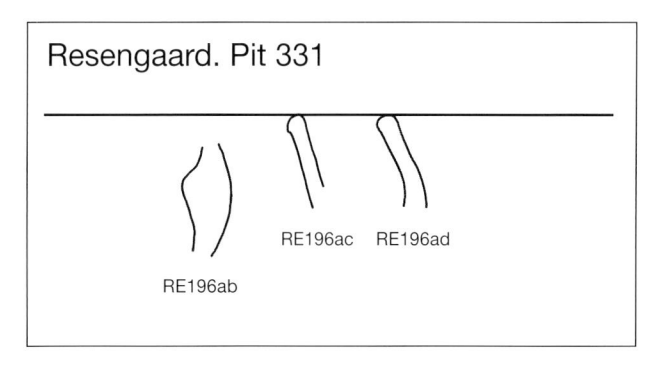

Fig. 3.39. Resengaard, pit 331. Selected pottery profiles. Main number RE196. Scale: 1:2.

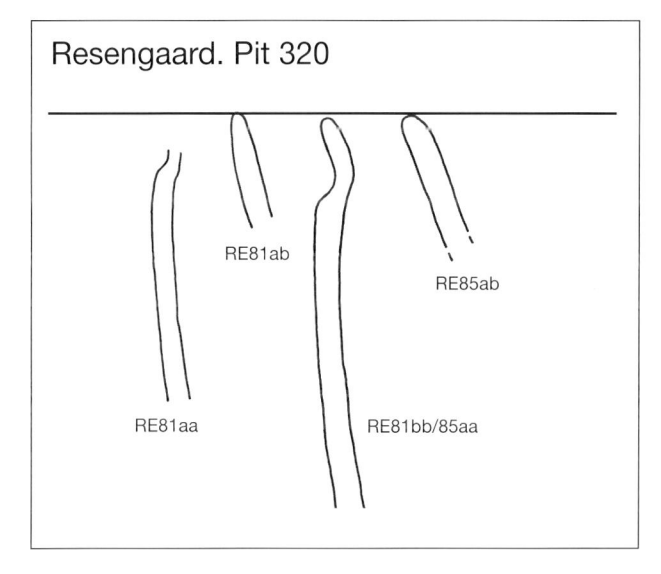

Fig. 3.40. Resengaard, pit 320. Selected pottery profiles. Main numbers RE81& RE85. Scale: 1:2.

Pit 278: found east-northeast of the site of House 240. Just 2 rim profiles and 1 side profile represent the assemblage (Fig. 3.37). Despite the modest number, a rather narrow dating can be suggested due to the characteristic profile outlines. *A priori*, it seems that a dating within the time span from around that of the House 41 assemblage to around that of House 1 might be possible. However, weighing up the relationships between the different assemblages, it appears there are really strong links with that of House 2 and in particular thereafter, i.e. the assemblage of House 14. I hence propose a dating contemporaneous to the assemblage of House 14. The pit 278 assemblage also accords fairly well with that of House 240.

Pit 310: found south of the site of House 197. Just 3 rim profiles represent this pit (Fig. 3.38 & 5.12). The rim profile traits all appear to point to some of the early assemblages, having strong relationships with the House 134 material and also some with that of House 41. A dating within the span ranging from somewhat before the time of House 134 to around the time of House 41 is possible. As for pit 319, I suggest a chronological position ranging from somewhat before to somewhat after the House 134 assemblage.

Pit 311: found a few metres east of the site of House 183. Just 2 rim profiles and 1 side profile represent the assemblage (Fig. 3.39). The profiles are different in outline and it seems probable that the pit assemblage is rather early, evidenced not least by the profile supplied with a horizontal cordon. The faintly thickened rims also point towards comparatively early assemblages. The profiles may position the pit chronologically to somewhere around the assemblages of House 134 and 41. I favour a dating close to that of House 134.

Pit 320: found immediately north of the site of House 2. In all, 4 rims represent the assemblage (Fig. 3.40). One of the profiles, and to a lesser degree a second, is characteristic and a chronological position within the span ranging from around the time of House 41 to around the time of House 1 is not excludable. However, I strongly favour a dating contemporaneous to House 2, and I consider the ceramics of the pit associated with the pottery of that house site.

Only a single rim profile from each of the following pits is available. Their chronological indications are considered in the following.

Pit 77: it was found somewhat northwest of the site of House 84. Its single clay pot profile can only support a broad dating (Fig. 3.41). It has affinities with the early assemblages from before and about the time of House 134 ranging to about the time of House 2. However,

Chronology of pottery assemblages 185

most relationships are observed with the early assemblages. A chronological position from somewhat before the House 134 assemblage to about that of House 41 is hence suggested and, even within this range, a comparatively early dating is preferable.

Pit 80: the pit was found somewhat east of the site of House 112. Despite the presence of just a single profile, a relatively narrow dating can be suggested due to its characteristic shaping (Fig. 3.42). The chronological position of the profile seems to be within the time span ranging from somewhat before the time of House 41 to somewhat after that of House 2. In my judgment, the relationship with the assemblage of House 41 is so strong that a chronological position relatively close to its time appears to be most favourable. Its dating is therefore proposed as ranging from somewhat before to somewhat after the time of the House 41 assemblage.

Pit 85: the pit was found somewhat south of the site of House 84 (Fig. 3.43). The profile has relationships to the reference assemblages of House 41 and House 2 but in particular strong affinities with the assemblage of House 130. Taking these into consideration, a chronological position ranging from somewhat before the time of House 41 until the time of House 2 seems possible, but a dating near the assemblage of House 130 is preferable.

Pit 100: found somewhat northwest of the site of House 134. A single profile stems from this pit, which has affinities with the assemblage of this building and that of House 2 (Fig. 3.44). In my reading of the profile, an early placement within this time span is preferable and, based on the affinities with those of pits 316, 317 and 319, I propose a corresponding chronological position, i.e. close to the House 134 assemblage, ranging from somewhat before to somewhat after.

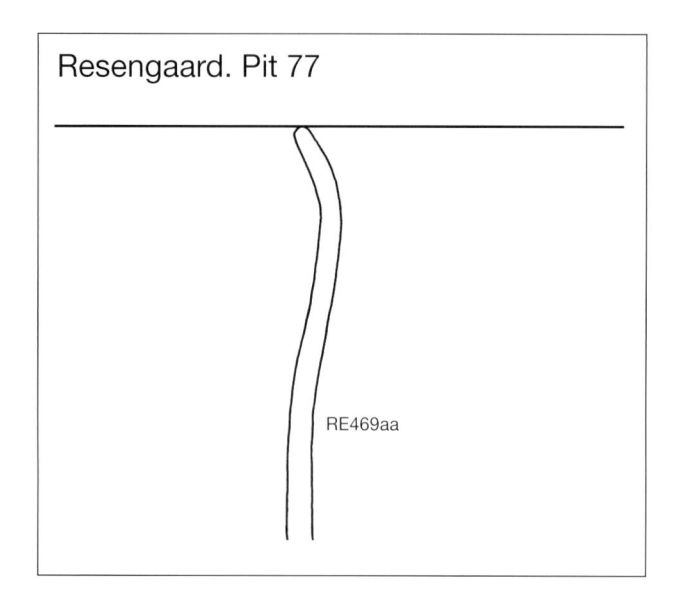

Fig. 3.41. Resengaard, pit 77. Clay pot profile. Main number RE469. Scale: 1:2.

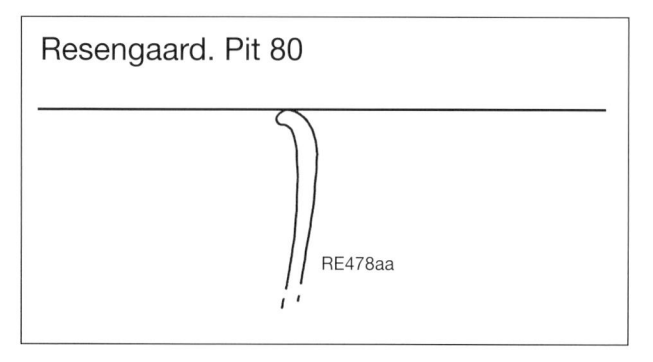

Fig. 3.42. Resengaard, pit 80. Clay pot profile. Main number RE478. Scale: 1:2.

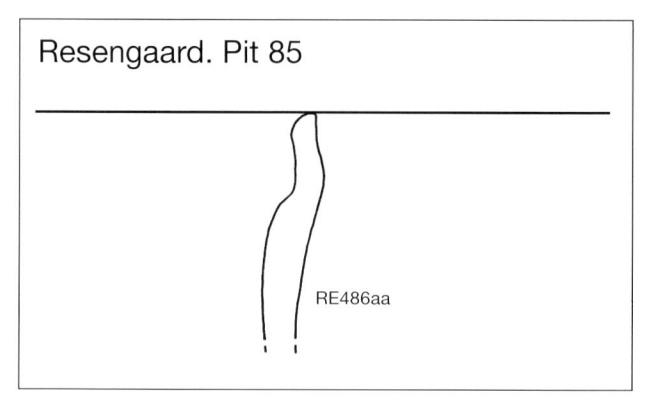

Fig. 3.43. Resengaard, pit 85. Clay pot profile. Main number RE486. Scale: 1:2.

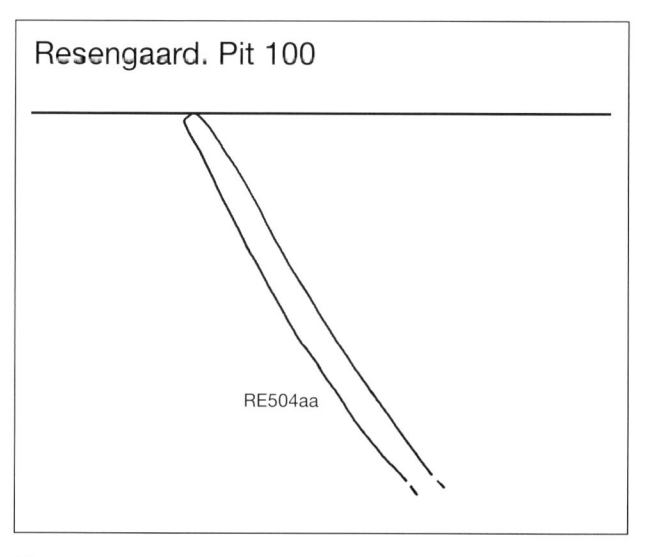

Fig. 3.44. Resengaard, pit 100. Clay pot profile. Main number RE504. Scale: 1:2.

Pit 111: this pit was found south of the site of House 112. It contained a single profile without preserved rim (Fig. 3.45). The few details of the profile limit the possibility of narrowing down the affinities with other find materials and I can only propose a dating within the time span from around that of House 41 to around that of House 1.

Pit 312: from this pit, placed somewhat west of the site of House 183, derives a single rim that seems to have some relationship in general to the assemblages of Houses 134, 41 and 2 (Fig. 3.46). A specific dating cannot be proposed and the suggestion of the chronological position is in the range from somewhat before the assemblage of House 134 to about the time of House 2.

Pit 313: found somewhat west of the site of House 84. A single profile without specific traits derives from this pit which can, likewise, only support a broad dating (Fig. 3.47). The chronological position is proposed as ranging from somewhat before the time of House 134 to about the time of House 2.

Pit 315: the pit was placed somewhat west of the site of House 84 (Fig. 3.48). No clear parallels to the House 134 assemblage or other reference assemblages are observable but relationships to the profiles of House 183 may give some indication. A broad dating ranging from somewhat before the time of the assemblage of House 134 to around that of House 41 is suggested.

We shall now consider the affinities of some clay pots from culture layers. Although the chronology of the culture layer assemblages is not our focus, relationships between a number of clay pot profiles will be proposed because this could serve to obtain at least some idea of the depositional periods of the culture layers against the background of the dating of the houses. The culture layers were excavated in the same way as the secondary fills in the sunken areas of the house sites.

Culture layer 203: this was accumulated in the eastern area of the settlement and the pottery assemblage includes 39 rim profiles and 2 side profiles (Fig. 3.49 & Fig. 3.50). In addition, 4 rim profiles (RE653) stemming from the north-south ditch to the west, where the culture layer faded out, are included. A total of 45 profiles thus represent the pottery and a number of these help to estimate the approximate time of at least part of the depositions in the culture layer. The different affinities with the materials of the sunken-floor houses indicate possible relationships to all four reference assemblages and may thereby point to a chronological

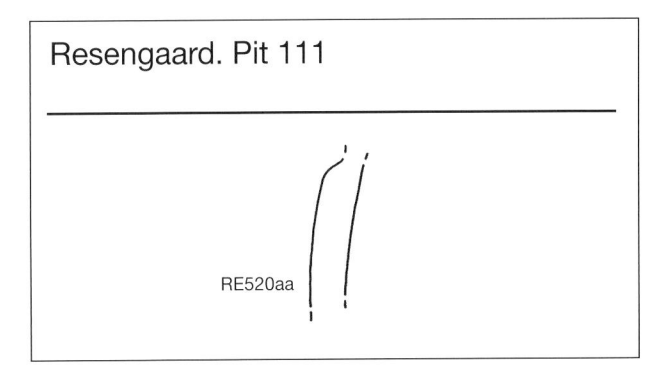

Fig. 3.45. Resengaard, pit 111. Clay pot profile. Main number RE520. Scale: 1:2.

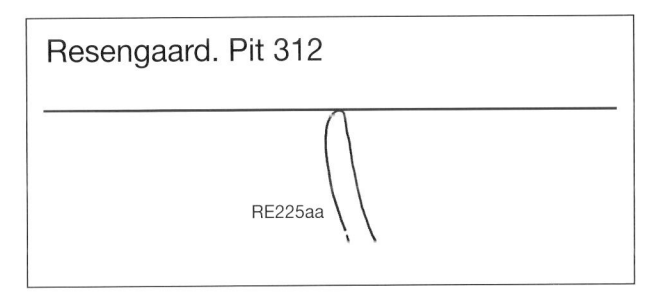

Fig. 3.46. Resengaard, pit 312. Clay pot profile. Main number RE225. Scale: 1:2.

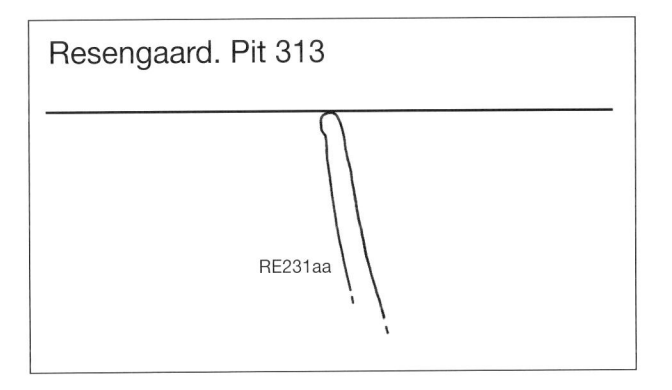

Fig. 3.47. Resengaard, pit 313. Clay pot profile. Main number RE231. Scale: 1:2.

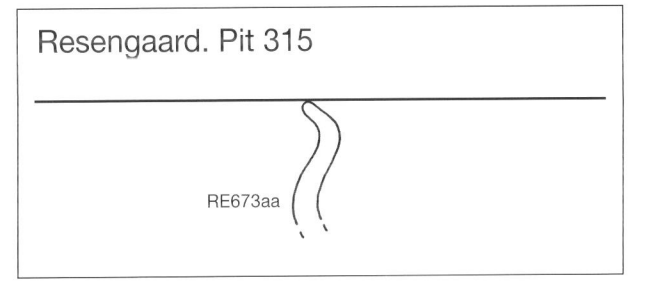

Fig. 3.48. Resengaard, pit 315. Clay pot profile. Main number RE673. Scale: 1:2.

position of the clay pot profiles from before or around the time of the House 134 assemblage to around or after the time of the House 1 assemblage. Whether that frame for dating should be extended some way forward into the period of the three-aisled houses, I cannot judge because some of the profiles are relatively uncharacteristic and a later dating of some potsherds should thus not be excluded. Two profiles (RE653ac & RE751bh) could perhaps point to such a subsequent time. It should be noted that sporadic potsherds in the area of the culture layer show that material of much younger date had also been left there.

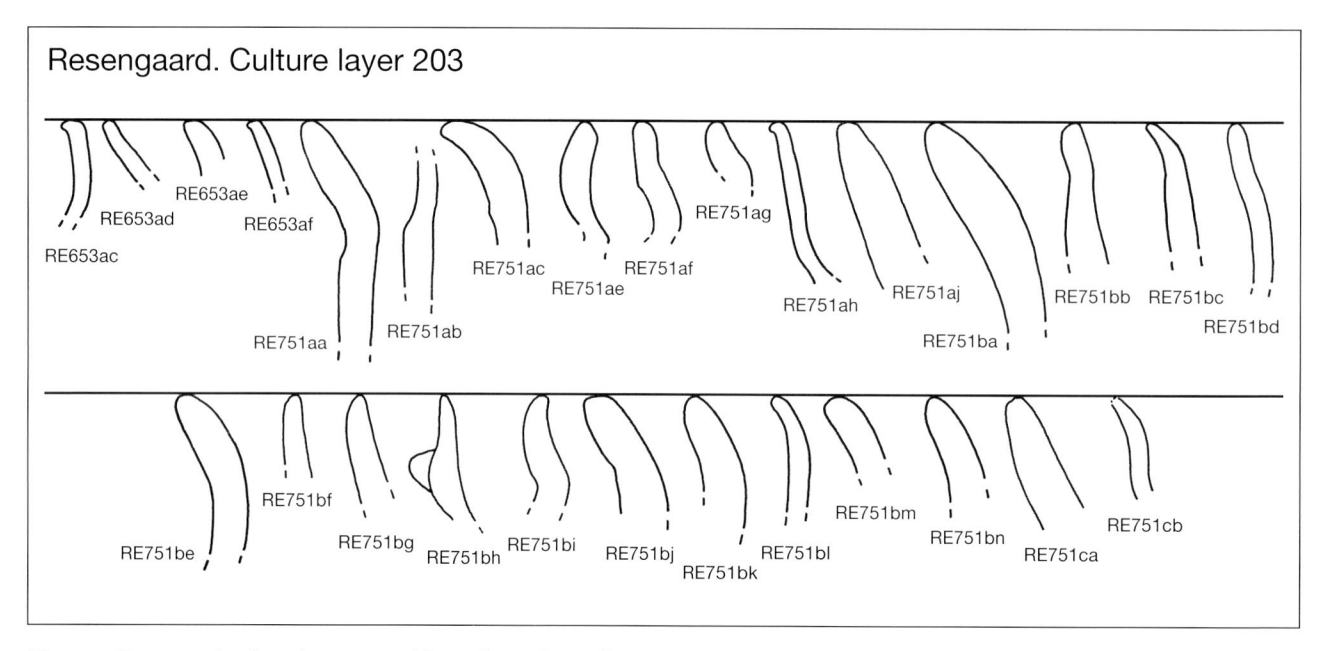

Fig. 3.49. Resengaard, culture layer 203, without observed stratification. Selected pottery profiles. Main numbers RE653 & RE751. Scale: 1:2.

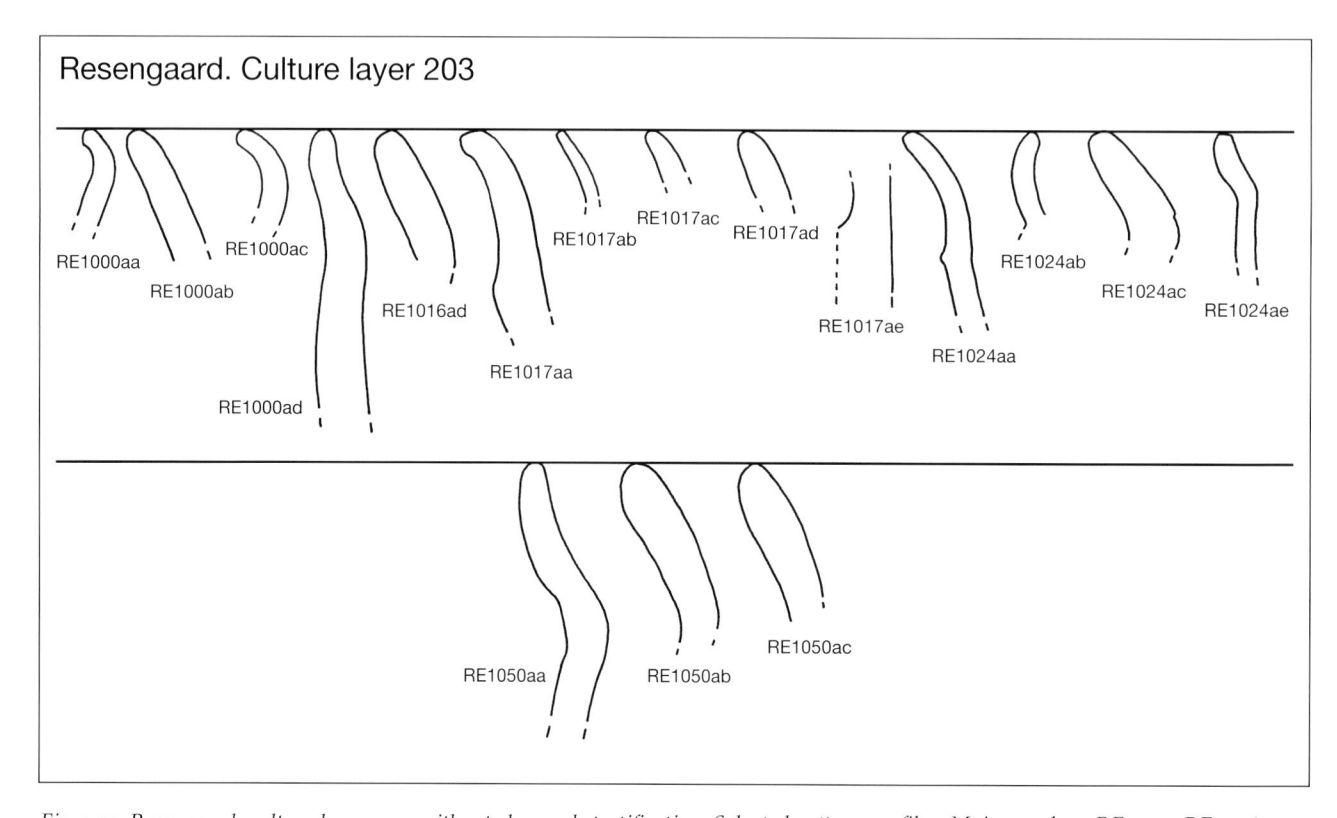

Fig. 3.50. Resengaard, culture layer 203, without observed stratification. Selected pottery profiles. Main numbers RE1000, RE1016, RE1017, RE1024, & RE1050. Scale: 1:2.

Resengaard. Culture layer 293

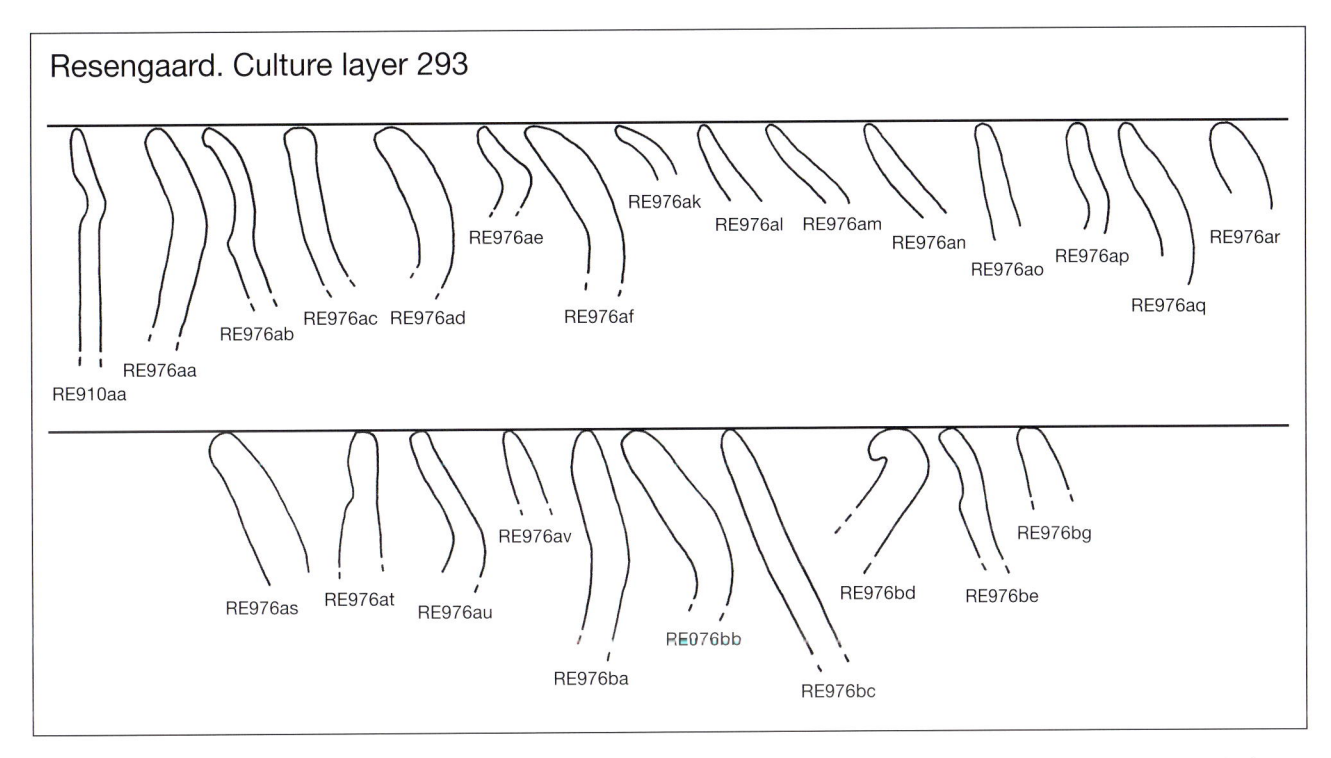

Fig. 3.51. Resengaard, culture layer 293, without observed stratification. Selected pottery profiles. Main number RE910 and RE976. Scale. 1:2.

Culture layer 293: this was accumulated in the western area of the settlement. The assemblage includes 25 rim profiles that show possible affiliations with all four reference assemblages (Fig. 3.51). The chronological position may range from around the time of the House 134 assemblage to around the time of the House 1 assemblage.[9] No clay pot profiles are identified as referring to an immediately following period. It cannot, however, be excluded that a few potsherds could indicate the presence of far later material and, conversely, that there are a few fragments from a much older period.

Culture layer 302: this was accumulated in the northeast area of the settlement. The find material includes just 2 rim profiles that do not really allow for a specific estimate of the timeframe (Fig. 3.52). Both rims appear to have affinities more or less slightly in agreement with the two early reference assemblages. With reservations, the dating could therefore be from somewhat before the time of the House 134 assemblage to around that of House 41.

Culture layer 318: this was accumulated in the northwest area of the settlement (Fig. 3.53). The assemblage includes just 1 rim profile and this only provides the possibility of a rather uncertain dating. This could, however, be tentatively suggested as ranging from about the time of the House 41 assemblage to about that of House 2.

Resengaard. Culture layer 302

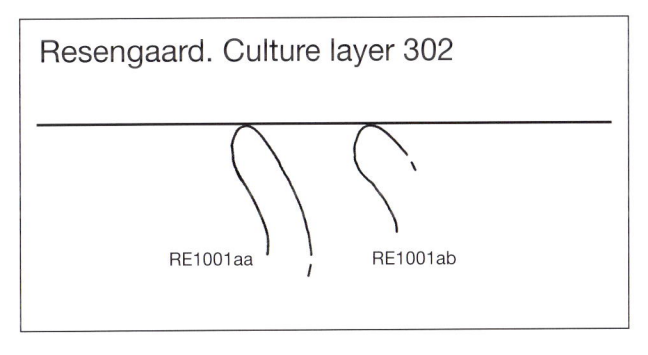

Fig. 3.52. Resengaard, culture layer 302, without observed stratification. Two selected clay pot profiles. Main number RE1001. Scale: 1:2.

Resengaard. Culture layer 318

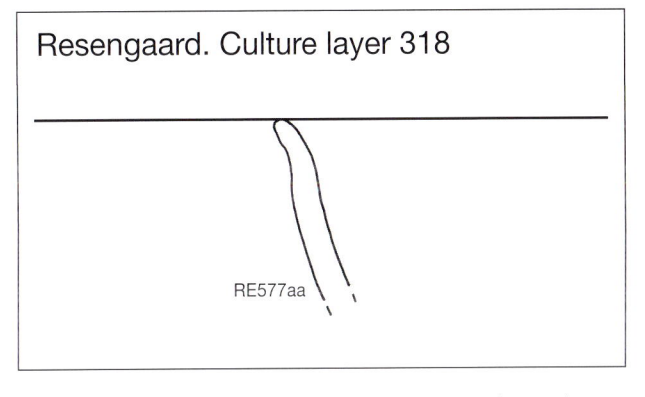

Fig. 3.53. Resengaard, culture layer 318, without observed stratification. A selected clay pot profile. Main number RE577. Scale: 1:2.

Chronology of pottery assemblages 189

Strong and weak links in the chronological chain

A critical evaluation of the strength of the suggested continuity and chronological order of pottery assemblages from the Resengaard longhouses is necessary. A break in our finds appears to exist between the material from the possible "House 160" and the first house assemblage in the provisional Resengaard chronology. What then might the risk be of an interruption during the period covered by this chronology?

A very short break in the long-term settlement at the site would perhaps be difficult to detect but much importance must be attached to the evident presence of the secondary fills covering all sunken floors of the twelve longhouse sites. We could therefore ask why anyone would undertake the laborious task of shovelling or otherwise filling back in many cubic metres of soil and other things if the residence was to move away from the Resengaard hill? No evidence in any of the longhouse sites indicates the existence of a vegetation horizon before the fill came on top, such that a sunken area might have been left for some period and just filled up thereafter. In any case, we have found no indication that the settlement left the hill for even a short time during the long settlement period.

When turning to the strength of the suggested chain of assemblages, we could also ask whether future finds of settlement materials from other locations might have the capacity to lead to necessary changes in the suggested internal order?

Of course only assemblages investigated through detailed, serious fieldwork with full awareness of the source-critical factors would be of interest in this respect. To try to answer the question it must first be said that, in my judgment, the internal order between the four reference assemblages from Resengaard (House 134 – 41 – 2 – 1) would not be affected.

Yet it is also immediately required to acknowledge that some of the pottery assemblages from in between the four reference assemblages are more strongly placed in the relative order than others. Three assemblages in particular are worth discussing in this respect, as the weakest links in the chain would be, not least, those with a more or less slack shaping of the rim profiles combined with the absence of rims with any really characteristic outlines. Such a situation relates to the House 13 pottery assemblage, containing relatively few rim profiles and only one of which appears reasonably characteristic. Correspondingly, as regards House 42, the assemblage is represented by several profiles but the shaping of these is, in most instances, not very marked and hence the relative dating is difficult to state with any accuracy. If we pose the question of whether the relative dating of these two assemblages internally could have been the opposite of that proposed, I would have no strong argument against such an inversion. From the pottery evidence, I thus cannot exclude the possibility that House 42 might have been earlier than House 13. Besides these two relatively "weak" pottery assemblages, we must also focus on that of House 138. It is *a priori* clearly difficult to propose its chronological position in the relative order since only two rim profiles represent the assemblage. And yet it appears that it is more strongly placed in this order than the materials from Houses 13 and 42 due to the powerful and characteristic outlines of the profiles, both stemming from the sunken-floor horizon.

In contrast to House 138, the case of assemblages from Houses 13 and 42 further exemplifies the approach I have strived to follow in the analysis and evaluation. In my understanding, the strength of a relative dating is thus enhanced when it relies on qualitative details as compared to a quantity of traits that only show more or less general affinities. It is thus not necessarily the number of rim profiles contained in the assemblages that decides the strength of the relationships with other pottery materials.

The position of the House 128 assemblage has already been discussed in the above and, of course, there could be a discussion similar to that of Houses 13 and 42, for instance, in relation to Houses 128 and 14 although I put much weight on the presence of the horizontally-projecting lug in each of the assemblages from Houses 14, 128 and 1.

In conclusion, it can be said that even though the assemblages of longhouses 13, 42, and 138 raise the greatest challenge in terms of establishing a relative chronology, the problem is after all of a rather limited nature because, in my view, their individual positions in the relative order cannot have been either much earlier or much later.

Results of a relative chronology at Resengaard

Some of the main results concerning the chronology of assemblages from the sunken-floor houses and pits will here be presented along with some indications concerning the culture layers. We shall first, however, take as our point of departure five cases of prominent clay pots and consider how some affiliated clay pot profiles appear in preceding or later longhouse phases.

The first case relates to an early clay pot profile with a characteristic outline, namely RE564aa from the sunken floor of House 134 (Fig. 3.6). It is supplied with a horizontal cordon and, as we have seen, the profile belongs to a longhouse considered to be the oldest of the twelve phases. Looking back in time, however, we still have the uncertain but possible "House 160" (including pit 161 and other) and an affiliated clay pot profile belongs to this assemblage. Here, we also find a number of ceramics with ornaments pointing back in time towards other Beaker pottery. This concerns, for instance, different clay pots with cordoned rims and richly-decorated ceramics present at Tastum I (Simonsen 1983, Fig. 6). Looking ahead in time, some profiles affiliated to the House 134 profile are present in the assemblages of Houses 130 and 41. Thereafter, corresponding clay pot profiles were not generally present in the longhouse assemblages. The tradition for such forms thus appears to have vanished by then.

The second case concerns a clay pot profile with a horizontally-projecting lug (RE750cc) from House 200, where two of these had probably been placed symmetrically at opposite sides (Fig. 3.16). Ceramics with such features do not seem to appear before about the time of this building and are just found sporadically in later house sites at Resengaard, namely House 1 (RE6ai) and House 14 (RE298aa). This presumably also concerns House 240 (RE798bk), whereas a clay pot with a somewhat diverging feature of that kind is present in the assemblage of House 128 (RE546aa).

The third case relates to a form that has a fairly slender appearance with a "swayed" profile and smoothly out-turned rim (RE119aa/121aa) from House 2 (Fig. 3.8). Affiliated ceramics were found as far back as in the assemblages of Houses 134, 130, 41 and 197, whereas forward in time it is difficult to identify pottery with close affinities, although a profile from House 1 (RE39aa) appears to have some of the same "touch" in its design (Fig. 3.5). This relates generally to a long-living tradition for this kind of clay pot profile, having thus been apparently present from the beginning and throughout most of the period of the sunken-floor longhouse settlement at Resengaard.

The fourth case concerns a profile with more or less roundish belly and marked transition to the nearly upright rims which appeared, at its earliest, in the assemblage of House 41 (RE412aa). It apparently went out of use at about the time of House 14. This form seems rather functional for several purposes and the likeness between those from e.g. House 41 and House 2 shows that there are only slight differences between them (Fig. 3.54.A).

The fifth case relates to a profile (RE176aa) from House 2. A horizontal furrow – or a furrow-like marking – between rim and body marks the outer edge whereas the inner rim side is concave above a pronounced "knee" at the transition to the body. Looking backwards in time, clay pot profiles with more or less close affinities are recognizable in the assemblages of e.g. Houses 41, 42, 138 and 200 and, ahead in time, in those of House 14 and House 1. Clay pots with close affiliations to RE176aa do not thus appear to have been present from the very first phases at Resengaard but must instead represent quite a new form in household equipment which was thereafter favoured more or less until the end of the settlement with sunken-floor longhouses. An illustration shows how these and related rims appear in several longhouse sites (Fig. 3.54.B).

As we saw in the above five cases, the individual clay pot forms appeared rather differently from time to time. In the overall picture of the ceramics at Resengaard, it appears that during the twelve phases of residence at the hill, certain old clay pot forms fade away and fresh forms come into existence but, apart from the more or less straight-sided open bowl, no characteristic forms persisted across all the centuries. In the latest dwelling (House 1) at the settlement, the pottery forms had thus almost completely changed since the early residence (House 134).

We have not yet dealt with the internal time difference between the reference assemblages. It is my understanding from the chronological clarification that, for most of the time during the settlement period in question, only a single sunken-floor longhouse was functioning as a residence at Resengaard. It hence seems possible to specify the internal time difference roughly.

Interestingly, it emerges that the time differences between the reference assemblages were not at all equal (Fig. 3.55). Based on the analysis and evaluations of the pottery, the number of sunken-floor longhouses between those with reference assemblages can be proposed as follows: between Houses 134 and 41 there was one longhouse phase, between Houses 41 and 2 there were five longhouse phases and, finally, between Houses 2 and 1 there were two longhouse phases. Thus, the intervals between the longhouses would have been 1 : 5 : 2, proportionately.

Chronology of pottery assemblages 191

A number of assemblages belonging to other sunken-floor houses and different pits were also suggested as being positioned chronologically before, between or simultaneous to the reference assemblages (Fig. 3.56)

The earliest pottery materials could, without contradiction, be placed simultaneously to or after the first possible longhouse. None of the pottery assemblages belonging to the late minor or short houses with sunken floors or from pits seem to clearly point to a dating any later than that of House 1.

Pottery development in a broader sense through the Late Neolithic and emerging Bronze Age is not a direct objective of this present work. I shall therefore not attempt, from the foregoing, to describe the pottery development represented in the Resengaard pottery over the centuries beyond what has been done already. And yet from the descriptions, analysis and comparisons of the individual assemblages, it should be possible to gain an idea of it.

Some of the significant pottery shapes from the four reference assemblages are now displayed in one table, along with some selected profiles from the assemblage of House 197 (Fig. 3.57). This last phase is interposed to illustrate a step in the relatively long development between House 41 and House 2.

The chronological study of the pottery assemblages has provisionally demonstrated that the settlement concerns a long row of longhouses at Resengaard. Given that, in the main, only one longhouse for residence stood at a time at Resengaard, this is in stark

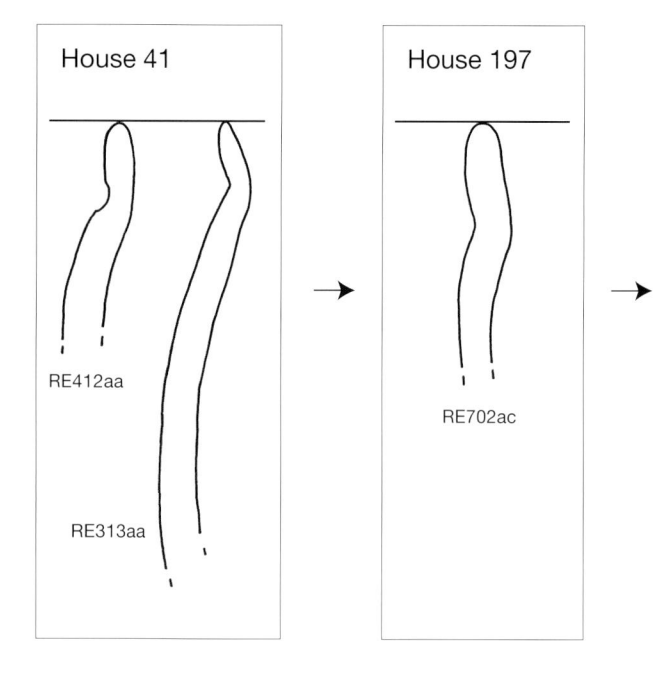

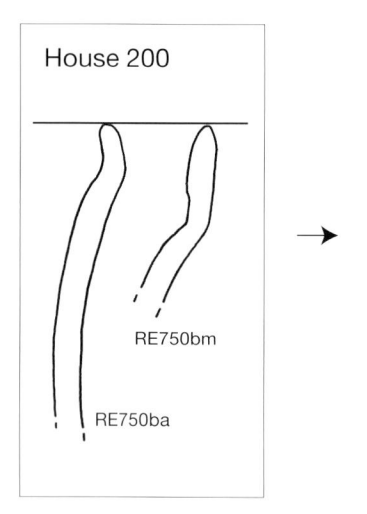

Fig. 3.54. Resengaard. Two groups of apparently much appreciated clay pot forms. A (this page): Selected examples of a group of those with markedly rounded belly and a more or less vertical rim (two with a horizontal furrow) from five longhouse assemblages. B (opposite page): Selected examples of clay pot profiles from nine longhouse assemblages covering a longer period. This group of more or less cylindrical forms, being easy to hold due to the markedly bent out rims, often combined with a horizontal furrow or furrow-like shaping at the transition to the body, likely facilitating the functionality of these jars, thus seems to have been much valued and was characteristic over a relatively long period. It appears that related forms are found again and again, probably due to their high functionality. Many different potters, each following their own favourite versions, must have produced these clay pots. When not much damaged during everyday use, inheritance from generation to generation may also have played a significant role in their broad presence. Scale 1:2.

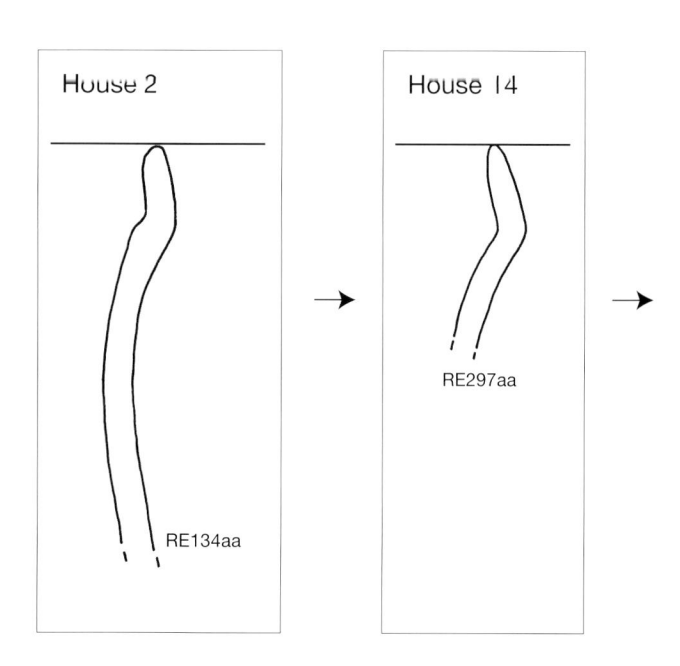

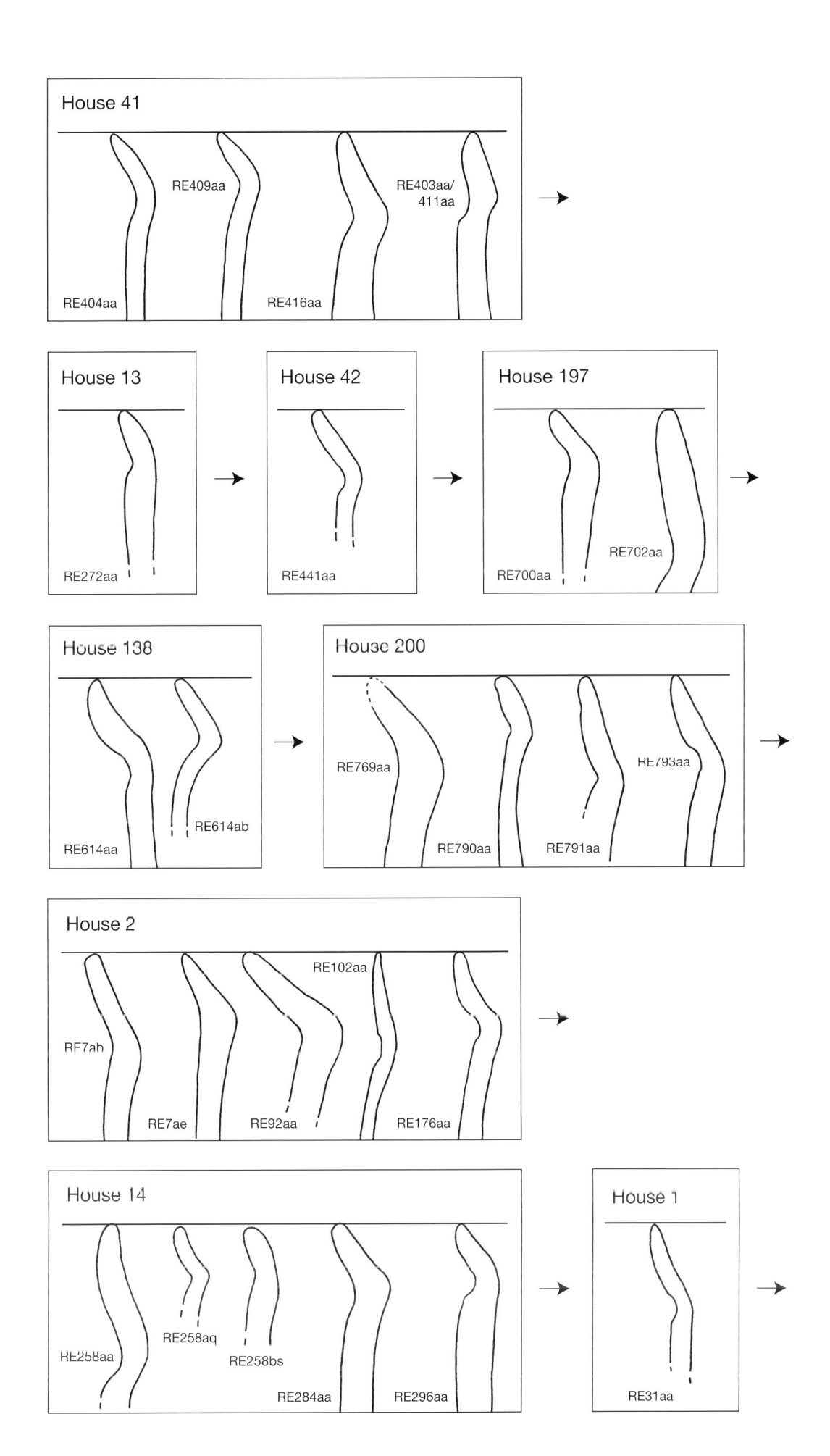

Chronology of pottery assemblages 193

Sequence of longhouses

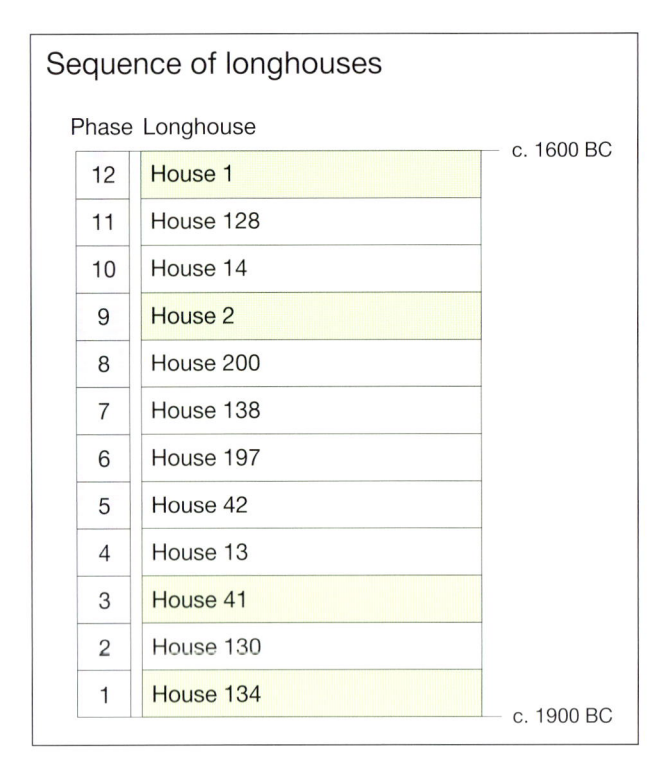

Phase	Longhouse
12	House 1
11	House 128
10	House 14
9	House 2
8	House 200
7	House 138
6	House 197
5	House 42
4	House 13
3	House 41
2	House 130
1	House 134

c. 1600 BC (top) — c. 1900 BC (bottom)

Fig. 3.55. The provisional Resengaard chronology. Based on pottery, the suggested sequence of twelve longhouses is shown with a darker green marking for the four reference assemblages that are used as benchmarks.

contrast to the interpretation of certain other South Scandinavian settlements such as, not least, Almhov in Scania (Gidlöf, Dehman & Johansson 2006:100pp; Arthursson 2010:91p).

Comparison with the radiocarbon dating

We shall now return to the individual houses and their dating. First, we can use as a starting point the simple mean value of radiocarbon determinations BP in order to establish some chronological order among the houses from which radiocarbon determinations have been obtained (Fig. 2.37.A).

If we concentrate on the four regular sunken-floor longhouses, their chronological order can be proposed from these radiocarbon determinations. Beginning with the oldest, the order is 197 – 2 – 128 – 1, whereas the relative chronological position of House 13 (3480 ± 30 & 3305 ± 35 BP) is up for discussion. In comparison, the pottery analysis in the foregoing suggested a chronological order of 13 – 197 – 2 – 128 – 1 for these five houses. From the radiocarbon determinations, it also appears that the three-aisled House 106 was clearly younger than House 1.

Unfortunately, the position of the House 13 assemblage in the suggested relative order of the pottery analysis is comparatively weak, as we have seen above. On the other hand, the radiocarbon dating of House 13 relates to two divergent determinations, one being based on wheat and one on barley. In respect to this delicate problem, contact was again made with Jan Heinemeier at the Radiocarbon Facility in Aarhus and he considers the dating material for this particular settlement to be qualified and of very high quality. There are no critical notes from the preparation procedure of the specific samples. Apart from in one case, the radiocarbon determinations from Resengaard display very parallel results (Fig. 2.37 & 2.38), and the exception relates to those from House 13 (sample AAR-6659.a & AAR-6659.b, combined), which has a Chi Square value: $\chi^2=14.3$. This is almost 4 times higher than the statistical limit value of 3.8 (pers. comm. Henrik Vind Frimurer). Even though the older of the two calibrated dates might accord reasonably well with the chronological result of the pottery analysis, it must therefore be recognized that these two determinations combined are inconclusive as to the dating of the cereals and hence the longhouse. When reflecting on the cause of the difference between the determinations, it seems that it can be narrowed down to the fate of one of the charred cereal seeds. If the younger of these two had, at some point in time, been transported e.g. by some tiny insect, a few centimetres deeper away from upper fills and into the sunken-floor horizon, we would have had practically no chance of observing traces of this, despite our keen interest in any possible disturbances during fieldwork.

The remaining four strong radiocarbon determinations, with almost parallel results for the sunken-floor longhouses, are however in close harmony with the pottery analysis, where the relative positions of the assemblages of Houses 197 and 2 are particularly based on many powerful traits. House 1 is also reasonably well placed in the pottery analysis, being based on fewer but relatively strong features. When based on the pottery analysis, it is therefore suggested that House 197 is older than House 2 which, in turn, is older than House 128 and thereafter House 1. It is my view that the radiocarbon determinations do not appear to contradict this proposed order.

Based on the pottery analysis, it was suggested that House 1 was actually the last sunken-floor longhouse to be used at Resengaard. The weighted, calibrated determinations of this House (Fig. 2.38.B) present a

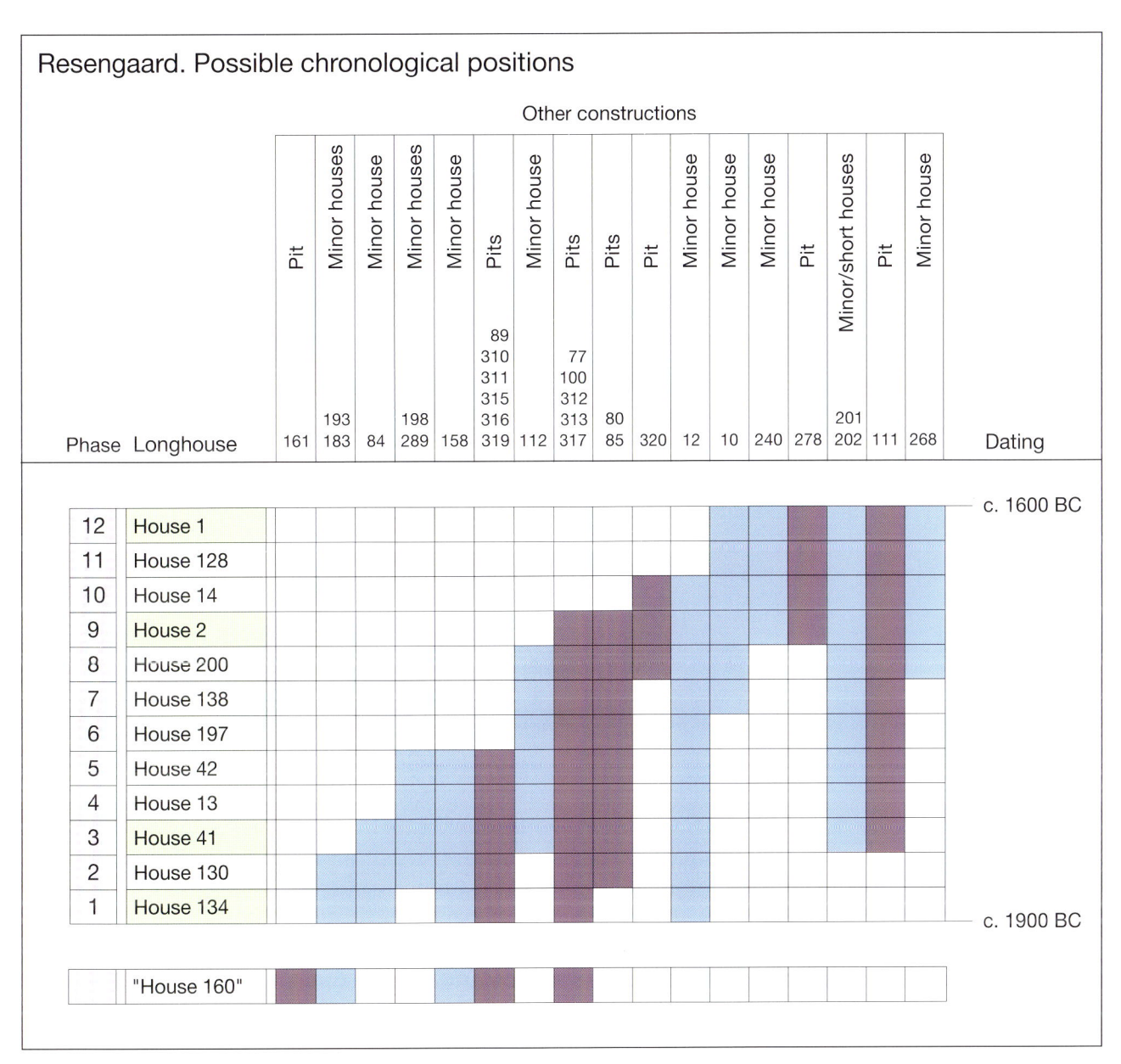

Fig. 3.56. Resengaard. Based solely on pottery profiles, some further suggestions are tentatively given of possible chronological positions of certain pits and the short/minor houses in relation to the suggested order of the longhouses. It seems that these could have been broadly present during the time covered by the provisional Resengaard chronology. The wide possibilities for the chronological positions of the pits are indicated in the table but, in my view, a relatively early dating is preferable not least for pits such as 77, 89, 100, 310, 311, 315, 316, 317 and 319 (see text). The chronological position of pits 161 and 160 (the possible "House 160") appears to have been somewhat earlier than the time covered by the provisional Resengaard chronology.

diagram peak beginning a little before 1600 calBC and continuing somewhat after this date. I am inclined to propose the ending of the time of sunken-floor houses at the Resengaard settlement as about 1600 calBC but acknowledge that the terminal year of House 1 could have been later.

The beginning of the settlement with sunken-floor houses in calendar years is somewhat more difficult to judge. The weighted dates of House 2 peak in the diagram from c. 1750 to c. 1670 calBC. If the building had been functioning around the middle of this period, it could have been there in the years around c. 1700 calBC. The pottery analysis indicated that two phases followed House 2 before House 1 was built. In other words, from the start of House 2 to the end of House 1, four phases may by and large have covered a hundred years. As these four phases out of twelve could correspond to about a third of the entire length of continu-

House 1

Radiocarbon dating available

House 2

Radiocarbon dating available

House 197

Radiocarbon dating available

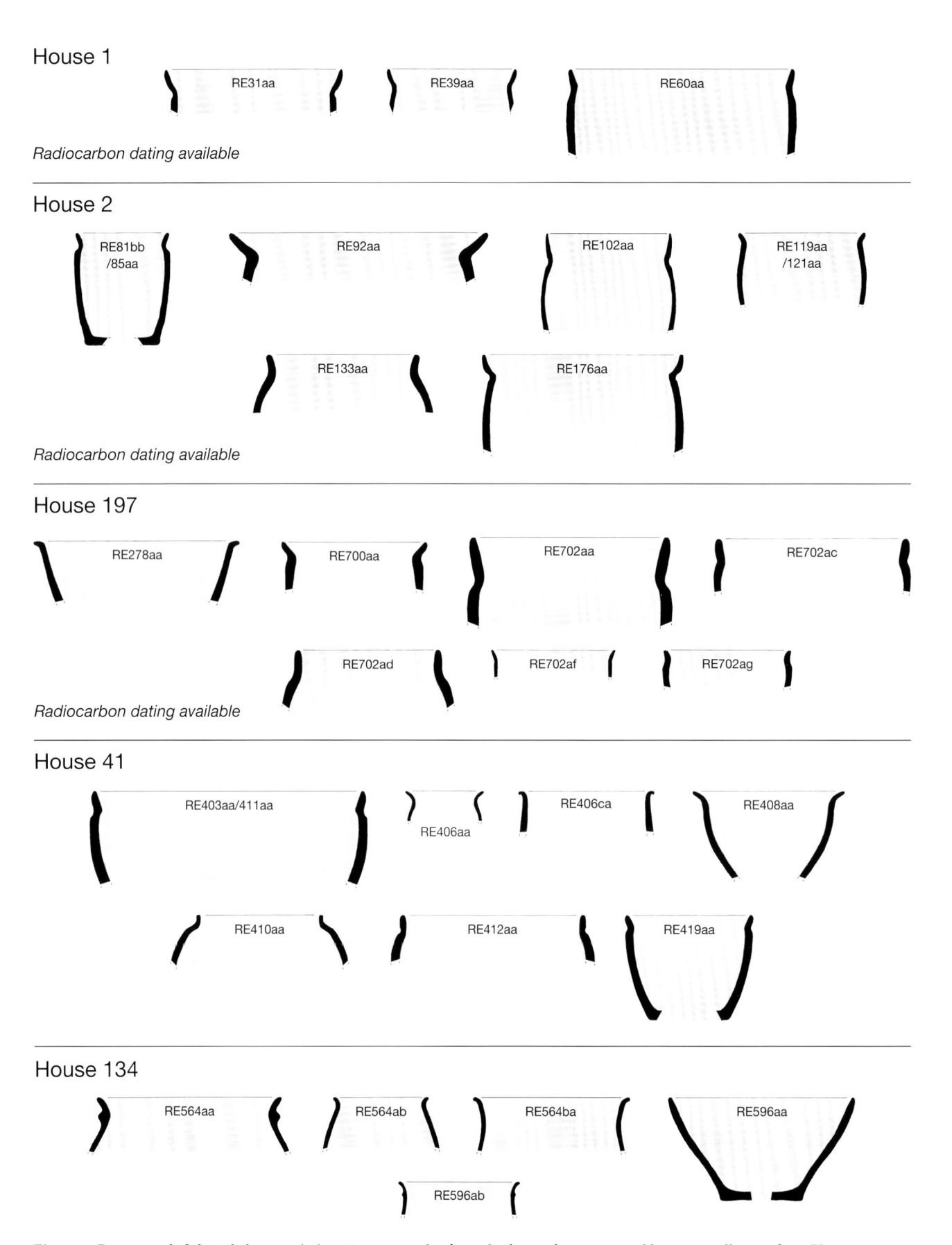

House 41

House 134

Fig. 3.57. Resengaard. Selected characteristic pottery examples from the four reference assemblages as well some from House 197 (proposed dating to around the middle of the long interval between House 41 and House 2) are represented. Included in the House 2 ceramics are fragments of a jar (RE81bb/85aa) from pit 320 just outside the northern entrance. For existing radiocarbon dating of the house sites, see Fig 2.37 & 2.38. Not to scale.

ous settlement with sunken-floor longhouses at Resengaard, this would suggest a period as long as 300 years with these longhouses at the hill.

We still have the question of a possible earliest "House 160" but, based on the pottery dating, there could well have been a break before the beginning of the continuous sunken-floor house settlement at Resengaard. Although it can hardly be excluded that the Resengaard chronology began, for instance, 50 or 75 years before 1900 calBC, I suggest the understanding that the settlement of the twelve sunken-floor longhouses at Resengaard continued by and large 300 years from c. 1900 to 1600 calBC.

This timeframe would have the implication that a new sunken-floor longhouse was built, on average c. every 25 years during the twelve phases. Most probably, there were usually transitional periods when the old longhouse of residence still stood and functioned during the building of the new longhouse and, in my view, probably often much longer, but now for other purposes (see later, Ch. 5 & Fig. 5.6).

The calibrated radiocarbon dating of a minor house site, House 202, places it by and large contemporaneous to the radiocarbon dating of House 197. It might have belonged together with that longhouse, as the radiocarbon dating is not contradicted by the pottery analysis.

After the long suite of the two-aisled, sunken-floor longhouses, some three-aisled houses existed for a period at Resengaard. It cannot be documented clearly but it is possible that settlement continued after the cease of the sunken-floor longhouses at the hill. The three-aisled House 25 belongs to an early kind and had a wall posthole containing an offering of a flint dagger and two flint sickles. The radiocarbon dating of the three-aisled House 106 may indicate residence before or about 1400 calBC.

Ad hoc substantiation and options for further validation

The pottery chronology is labelled "provisional" due to the weakness of certain assemblages in the relative order which hence need validation from independent sources. After a brief recapitulation, we shall look at essential traits regarding *ad hoc* substantiation of the provisional Resengaard chronology and discuss some options for further validation.

At the Resengaard hill, each longhouse appears to be part of a long-term cycle of settlement that has been going on through twelve phases, with in the main one single residential longhouse unit at a time. It points strongly to continuity when every sunken floor has been filled up after use, with the residents' heaps of old waste soil left in the surrounding area outside. Considerable similarities can often be observed between these secondary fills and those of the sunken-floor horizon and, by consequently including the former in the chronological unit of the longhouse, the number of pottery profiles accessible for the analysis is increased hugely, giving a statistically much broader basis.

The pottery and other artefacts found *in situ* in the sunken-floor horizon of the longhouses at Resengaard are highly privileged materials for archaeological dating, belonging as they do to the context of the living floor in a kind of "fossilized" state and sealed as they often are below thick soils layers.

The combined ceramics from the sunken-floor horizons and secondary fills in individual longhouse assemblages in most cases contain relics of several or even many fine and characteristic pots, represented here by profile drawings. Due to the often high quality of these ceramics, their variations and their unusually high numbers, a purely pottery-based relative chronology has been suggested.

Let us briefly recapitulate some essential Resengaard pottery relationships to other specific settlements. In the oldest longhouse unit from the period covered by the Resengaard chronology (House 134, Fig. 3.6), we can observe very strong affinities with the younger Beaker milieus of, for instance, that of Tastum I (Simonsen 1983, Fig. 6). From the House 134 unit, the cordoned rims (RE564aa, RE564bb, & RE596ab), the largely corresponding profiles without cordons (RE564ab, RE564ae, RE564ba) and the open bowls with more or less straight rims (RE564ac, RE564ag,& RE596aa) all thus have some obvious affinities with the Tastum I assemblage. It might be put in that certain kinds of Swedish cordoned ceramics have, for instance, more recently been placed in an interval of c. 1950-1800 BC in Östra Mellansverige (Holm, Olsson & Weiler 1997:220; Vandkilde 2007:83; *cf.* Magnusson 1949).

Conversely, in some of the youngest longhouse units covered by the Resengaard chronology (House 14, Fig. 3.10 & House 128, Fig. 3.12), we can detect rather more solid numbers of affinities with, for instance, the early milieu of the Older Bronze Age at Egehøj (Boas 1983, Fig. 7 & 10). From the House 14 unit, several rims (e.g. RE258aa, RE258aq, RE258ar) thus have evident affinities with the Egehøj material in their outline (for further relationships, see Appendix A). Other pottery units, such as that of House 2, which is a little older according to the provisional Resengaard chronology, have less strong affinities with the Egehøj material. Overall, both outer poles of the chronology are clearly well linked to Beaker milieus or Older Bronze Age milieus, respectively.

Certain main trends provide important support for the chronological results. The cordoned rims relating to the Beaker milieus are thus present in the pottery units of House 134, House 130, House 41, House 42 and, rather noteworthily, seems to disappear thereafter. As at the other end of the chronology, the horizontally-projecting lugs are present in the units of House 1 (RE6ai), House 128 (RE546aa), House 14 (RE298aa) and House 200 (RE750cc). It thus looks like a new introduction of precisely that trait at the time of House 200. These observations are of great importance since certain features are only found in the few oldest units of the chronology and certain others only in the few youngest units. On a general level, these groupings in my view therefore offer a significant check on the suggested chronology and hence mark out elements of substantiation.

Flint daggers may provide some additional substantiation to the later part of the suggested longhouse order. The dagger fragment of type V (RE985ea) belonging to the sunken-floor horizon of House 200 is matched by a type V dagger (RE90ea) from the sunken-floor horizon of House 2 (both proposed as belonging to sub-type V B, see remarks in Cat. B). This could be considered an indication of the two being close to each other in time, and this is also the case in the suggested pottery-based relative order whereby House 2 follows immediately after House 200. The typologically younger type VI dagger from the sunken-floor horizon of House 128 (RE547ea) was completely preserved (proposed as belonging to sub-type VI B, see remarks in Cat. B). It matches the late position of House 128 in the suggested pottery-based relative order well. In each case, the placement in the sunken-floor horizon could obviously not have taken place any time before the beginning of the production of the concrete dagger type. Hence, here we have three dagger datings of sunken-floor horizons that do not speak against the pottery chronology.

As dealt with earlier (Ch. 3.2), further daggers are represented in the secondary fills of House 200, being type III E (RE750ei) and House 2, being type IV E (RE89ea/175ea, see remarks in Cat. B). Moreover, a type III B/C handle fragment (RE265ea) was found in the secondary fills of House 197 and its presence does not speak against the pottery chronology. It should also be noted that a type III (presumably III A) handle fragment (RE1040ea) was found in the secondary fills of the minor House 158. From the site of House 42 we have two dagger handle fragments (RE405ea & RE430ea), possible type V A and type V B, respectively (for further on these daggers, see Cat. B).

Based on the pottery analysis, the suggested sequence of the seven youngest assemblages of the longhouses is 197 – 138 – 200 – 2 – 14 – 128 – 1. The flint daggers we just considered from the floor-horizons concern longhouses 200 – 2 – 128 and may tend to support – or at least not contradict – the proposed pottery sequence, supplying us with evidence of dagger types V B – V B – VI B from the sunken-floor horizons, respectively.

Based on the radiocarbon datings, I earlier presented a longhouse order and, in my view, the pottery sequence corresponds well without contradiction arising (see comments in chapters 2.4 & 3.3). The order of House 197 – 2 – 128 – 1 thus is not contradicted by use of the mean values of the combined radiocarbon results, being 3493, 3408, 3332, 3301 BP, respectively.

Finally, I would like to put forward that in my perception the order of the five pottery assemblages, represented by profiles of selected clay pots in Fig. 3.57, is not at risk of being altered by any future studies of serious character.

The above may outline the current major kinds of substantiation. And yet what might the nature of future options for validation of the provisional Resengaard chronology?

There are hardly any direct possibilities for substantiating the proposed sequence through multivariate analysis or by setting up a matrix because no adequate numbers of particular profile elements of the clay pots can be referred to. Likewise, it will hardly be possible in the near future to set up a convincing typology due to the nature of the settlement materials. Further, in the present case I do not immediately find it possible to produce conclusive profile overlays of the varying ceramic forms to describe the pottery changes during settlement at the Resengaard hill.

We have no evidence as to stratification between sites of two sunken-floor longhouses at Resengaard, as none of these cut across each other. However, I actually consider the consequent quest for pristine soils for building longhouses at that settlement a great advantage for the chronological analysis because contamination of the pottery assemblages can clearly be ruled out in this regard.

I trust that some of the most convincing acts of substantiation will come from studying new find combinations that can relate directly to the Resengaard pottery. From settlements, graves and deposits belonging to LN II and the emerging Bronze Age, such possibilities will probably repeatedly come to light in the central Limfjord region and beyond. This could concern multiple combinations of pottery, flint daggers, flint arrowheads and other artefacts of significance. Presumably, some of such finds will also supply us with possibilities for strong radiocarbon determinations.

However, the first evident option is to search carefully for further possibilities for radiocarbon dating of those of the Resengaard longhouse sites that at present have none. For House 1 will AMS-determinations be needed, and plenty charred cereals are available for that. Thereafter, a Baysian analysis should obviously be considered.

Making use of the provisional Resengaard chronology

It is not my intention here to state how this chronology should be applied. Some guidance might perhaps be sought later on, however, and so I shall take just a few words to present my view regarding two hypothetical cases.

One situation might be when working with a settlement assemblage with many clay pot profiles. In such a case, I would advocate a procedure of the same kind as followed above, comparing and weighing up individually the strengths of every rim profile as regards affinities with assemblages of the provisional Resengaard chronology. It might, in some instances, be practical and time-saving to compare them first with the profiles of the four reference assemblages. Thereafter, other assemblages of the chronology could be included in the analysis and weighing up process. In evaluating the affinities of the rim profiles, it is often an advantage if many profiles are present. It should once again be emphasized, however, that in my concept of the working of the method, it is not primarily a question of the quantity of profiles contained in the assemblages but rather the presence of highly characteristic profiles that can make it very decisive. Further below I make use of the provisional Resengaard chronology when the chronological positions of five settlements from Egehøj, Torslev, Vadgård Nord, Vadgård Syd and Vejlby are discussed.

Another case might be when, for instance, searching for the chronological position of one single clay pot profile. In this case it would, in my view, be necessary for the profile in question to be highly elaborate as opposed to a simple, uncharacteristic rim. An example could be the vessel from an investigated grave barrow at Stårupvej, Dommerby Parish (Aner & Kersten 2008:7p, Tafel 2, no. 5574 B). A comparison with the rims in the provisional Resengaard chronology immediately shows affiliations to several rim contours. It is thus a very characteristic profile that evidently has affinities with House 14 (RE284aa), House 41 (RE416aa), House 138 (RE614aa), House 200 (RE791aa) and House 240 (RE 798ba). Moreover, it even shows strong relationships to certain clay pot profiles, namely from House 2 (RE176aa), House 14 again (RE258aq) and House 240 (RE799aa) again. Most of these concern profiles from sunken-floor horizons. In my reading, the chronological position of the Stårupvej vessel could well correspond to the time of the assemblage of House 14, which I immediately see as the best match in the provisional Resengaard chronology. Alternatively, it could be contemporaneous with House 2 or 200. Even the time of House 138 can hardly be excluded.

3.4. Beaker decoration and pottery shapes

The absence of pottery ornamentation in the younger parts of the Late Neolithic may indicate that the people of the Limfjord region lost their former focus on this in favour of other things, maybe not least the bronzes. However, to be fair, the often elaborate profiles and the highly expressive surface finishes, in my view, would still have been highly demanding for potters to make.

With regard to Resengaard, Beaker decoration is found on some of the ceramics from pit 161 and pit 160 representing the possible "House 160", which is not covered by the provisional Resengaard chronology. These potsherds belong to some of the oldest traces of Late Neolithic settlement investigated archaeologically at Resengaard. However, we also meet late Beaker decoration in some of the early pottery assemblages covered by this chronology and we shall briefly consider these here.

Furthermore, it raises the question of how far the Bejsebakken, Myrhøj, Stendis and Tastum I pottery materials are, in terms of shape, from the early Resengaard assemblages? I shall touch only slightly on these topics, as it is beyond the scope of this work.

Beaker ornamentation on early Resengaard pottery

Beaker decorations on Resengaard pottery mainly derive from assemblages in contexts of rather early house sites and pits. Cardium impressions are present in the assemblages of pit 77 (RE469ad), pit 160 (RE632ac) and pit 161(RE636ac, RE636af, RE636bb, RE636bc, 636be & RE636ba, this latter seemingly as part of a metope decoration with a triangle pattern, edged and covered by oblique cardium impressions). Cardium decoration is also found on a potsherd from pit 325 (RE633ae, north of House 198), as well as on a potsherd (RE264ab) in pit 23 east of the site of House 12..

A second kind of ornamentation is the impression of notch-stamped lines. These are found in the assemblages of House 41 (RE406be), House 158 (RE1042aj) and pit 161 (RE636az). A third kind is the parallel horizontal lines observed on pottery in pit 319 (RE693ae). A fourth kind relates to more or less horizontal rows of vertical spatula incisions ("barbed wire"). This is found in the assemblages of pit 77 (RE469ab & RE469ac, Fig. 4.43) and pit 80 (RE478ac).

From a source-critical point of view, we have to realize that we cannot exclude the possibility that some of the small ornamented clay pot fragments at this large settlement may have come into the above contexts accidentally. In the prehistoric situation this might, for instance, have taken place in relation to the transportation of soil and other materials. As it concerns ornamented potsherds in the context of two of the older sites of houses (41 & 158), I would actually prefer to keep open the possibility that some fragments could represent ceramics that were inherited down the generations until the functioning time of these buildings. These fragments might thus be potsherds representing, for instance, rather functional or venerated clay pots. In the case of the important House 41, they only account for a very modest part of the finds.

Apart from these ornamentations, it is also worth considering the presence of "early" horizontal cordons. These were attached to pottery from House 41 (RE406as, RE406at & RE422aa), House 134 (RE564bb), pit 161 (RE636an), pit 310 (RE692aa), and pit 331, southeast of House 183 (RE196ab). Regarding the assemblage of House 128, a thickening of a profile (RE552ac) could also appear slightly cordon-like but represents a later trait. A potsherd (RE270aa) found in top of the secondary fills of House 268 has an almost similar feature.

Pottery shapes at Bejsebakken, Stendis, Myrhøj, and Tastum I

Regarding the Bejsebakken settlement and its chronological units, it has been said that "…only a very limited part of the artefacts may be ascribed to the habitation phase, and often they cannot be separated from the ones secondarily deposited …so it may be concluded that such former house pits were reused as refuse areas by nearby houses" (Sarauw 2007b:12). However, the experiment of pottery refitting from the fills of House A173 leads to the conclusion that the sunken-floor fills seem "to be a contemporary inter-related unit" (Sarauw 2008a:13pp). Experiments pointing towards the same conclusion were conducted on materials from other sunken floor fills at Bejsebakken.

In terms of stratification and chronology, it has been stated that one house site overlapped another but the internal succession could not be clarified (Sarauw 2007b:11). This relates to a sunken-floor longhouse and a ground-floor longhouse. In addition to this, I have further argued above that another house site (A66) may very well represent partly overlapping sunken floors.

The comprehensive Bejsebakken pottery assemblages as a whole may henceforward form an important contribution to the knowledge of Beaker ceramics in the region, and they have been given a broad dating to LN I, having affinities with the Myrhøj pottery (Sarauw 2006). Yet, as regards a comparison of pottery shapes, only a few, regular profile outlines have been presented. No detailed comments on the similarities between the pottery assemblages in terms of shape shall therefore be posited here. When dealing with profile outlines, it is my impression that some distance in time must have occurred between the youngest Bejsebakken assemblages from sunken-floor houses and the oldest house assemblage (134) covered by the provisional Resengaard chronology. The geographical distance, in a direct line, can be estimated as c. 72 km to Resengaard.

We now turn to the Stendis, Myrhøj and Tastum I pottery. Regarding Stendis, it is evident from the use of ornamental elements and from the metope decoration that it must have been quite close to the time of the Myrhøj houses (Skov 1982, Fig. 1, 5 & 6).

The Myrhøj settlement contained relatively large pottery assemblages (Jensen, J.A. 1973, Fig. 26-66). In a direct line, it is estimated as being located c. 25 km from Resengaard. An evaluation of the relationship clarifies that most of the affinities with the Resengaard material are on a rather general level. Some main forms of the pottery are present at both sites but these concern very long-living forms. The beakers with oblique straight-walls in particular form a significant part of the Myrhøj assemblages. The open bowl is present at both sites, but it is indeed a classical and long-living form. Compared to many of the Resengaard house assemblages, the frequently ornamented Myrhøj material is characterized by few, rather simple forms without much designing of the rims. And yet it is precisely in this respect that the earliest but unornamented Resengaard assemblage (House 134), covered by the provisional Resengaard chronology, have some affinities of a more or less general nature with the Myrhøj material.

The published pottery profiles at Tastum I derive from the sunken-floor house site and some of them are richly decorated (Simonsen 1983, Fig. 6-7). The geographical distance in a direct line from Resengaard can be estimated at c. 10 km. An analysis of the relationship to the Resengaard assemblage demonstrates that a number of relationships with the House 134 assemblage can be observed as well as some affinities with the assemblages of House 41 and House 2, albeit less so. This hardly relates to really strong affinities, even with the early House 134 assemblage. As a very tentative and preliminary assumption, I regard the Tastum I assemblage to be in a chronological position between the pottery of Myrhøj and the earliest Resengaard assemblages covered by the provisional Resengaard chronology (House 134, House 130, & House 41).

3.5. Anchoring certain "classic" sites to the provisional Resengaard chronology?

In the following, the possibilities for implementing the chronological results from Resengaard within wider contexts will be considered. In particular, links to published pottery assemblages from settlements shall be sought. The question is whether or not some of the "classical" sites can be closely related to the provisional Resengaard chronology.

Several publications provide valuable information on relevant ceramics and, interestingly, many of these derive from North Jutland. In terms of some of these selected works, I shall to attempt to evaluate the possible relationships. For further details of the arguments for pottery relationships, see Appendix 1.

Egehøj, Torslev, Vadgård and Vejlby

In her book on settlement pottery, Marianne Rasmussen looked at 23 locations from the western part of Denmark, thereby entering a new field of research with her focus on certain stages of the Older Bronze Age (Rasmussen, M. 1993a. Randsborg 1996:66). No fewer than 20 of these have been found in the northern half of Jutland and some were rather late as they do not belong to the emerging Bronze Age and can therefore be excluded immediately. This concerns the settlements from Oxholm Skov (syd), Stenmarken, Fragtrup, Brøndumgårdand Ertebølle, along with other settlements of minor interest here as regards ceramic assemblages, being Gundestrup Østergård, Mosegården, Bredkær, Vollersgård II, and Skals (Rasmussen, M. 1993a:88; Draiby 1986). The sites Nygård and Povlstrupgård are taken into consideration in other respects in this present work (Nielsen, S. 1977; Jespersen 1987). That leaves us with following localities of concern for the chronological considerations: Egehøj, Torslev, Vadgård Nord, Vadgård Syd and Vejlby (Rasmussen, M. 1993a:87-89). Sunken-floor houses are not known from all these sites but the importance of the pottery assemblages makes it relevant to include these (Fig. 3.58).

Besides its building remainders, Egehøj has long been a cornerstone in terms of its pottery (Boas 1980; 1983; Rasmussen, M. 1993a). The affinities with certain Resengaard assemblages are many in number. These points of similarity are rather amazing, as the distance in a direct line can be estimated at c. 105 km, which was not, after all, a short distance in a Late Neolithic/emerging Bronze Age context. No close affinities with the reference material of the Resengaard House 1 assemblage can be demonstrated, although several relationships with that of House 2 can be suggested. Even more evident are the affinities with the assemblage of House 14 and House 128 because some of the relevant ceramic details seem relatively short-lived, e.g. the somewhat abrupt rim top in the Egehøj material that is present in the assemblage of House 128 (RE-540ae). Further, the affinities with House 240 accentuate the relationship to rather late pottery within the provisional Resengaard chronology. It can hence be suggested that the Egehøj material indicates a chronological parallel with some later Resengaard materials and, among longhouses in particular, obvious closeness to the assemblages of Houses 14 and 128.[10]

The ceramics from Torslev are likewise long known (Johansen 1985; Rasmussen, M. 1993, Fig. 49-53). In contrast to Egehøj, the affinities with the pottery assem-

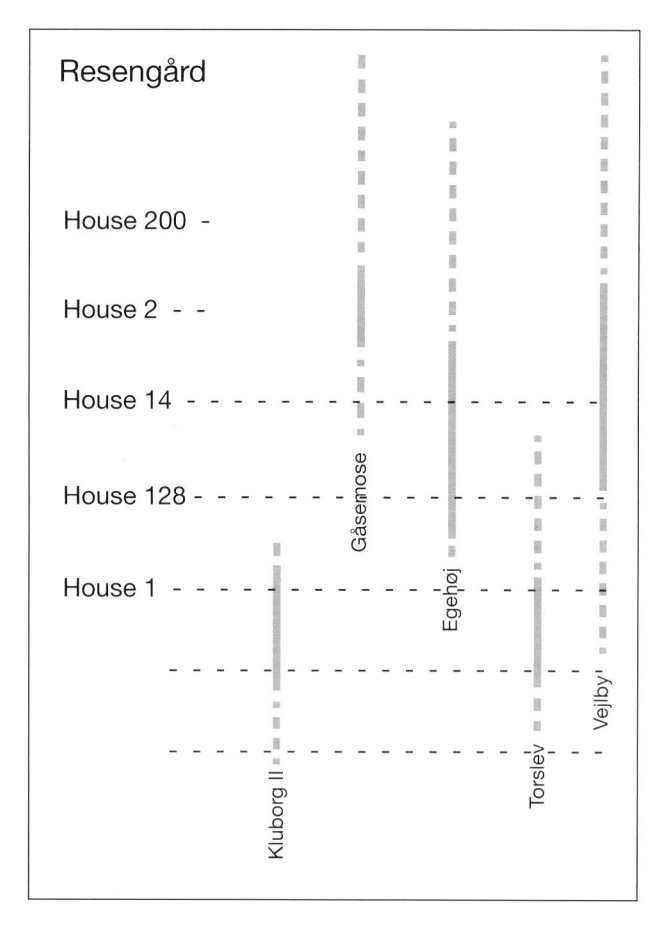

Fig. 3.58. Tentative results of comparisons of pottery profiles at five settlements with the provisional Resengaard chronology. The firm lines show the suggested likely relative-chronological positions, while the dotted lines indicate weaker relationships.

blages from Resengaard appear to be relatively few. As the geographical range in a direct line can be estimated as c. 55 km from Resengaard, it cannot be due to an increase in distance. Some clearly interesting relationships are, however, present. Two of the profiles (Rasmussen, M. 1993a, Fig. 49.b & e) show several affinities with some of the later assemblages and, when considered in isolation, would suggest a dating back to the House 200 assemblage and forward in time to the House 1 assemblage. Furthermore, two different profiles (Rasmussen, M. 1993a, Fig. 51.k & i) have some affinities back to the House 14 assemblage. Together with the previously mentioned affinities, it seems reasonable to assume that the dating of the Torslev material should not be very far on in time from the House 14 material. How it relates directly to the House 1 material is difficult to evaluate since only a few links can be observed. It should be mentioned that the presence of clay pot profiles such as those with a marked shoulder (Rasmussen, M. 1993, Fig. 51.d & m) may point to a slightly later dating, and I see this as a reasonably weighty argument. Some links back in time to traditions from House 200 and House 14 should not be considered an obstacle for a slightly later dating and it could be remarked that some affinities of the profiles with a marked transition to the body can be seen in the rather late House 268 assemblage. One profile thus had a closer relationship to the two aforementioned clay pot profiles with an accentuated transition to the body. On this basis, when purely considering the shaping of the ceramics, it can be suggested that the pottery in question from the Torslev midden had a position chronologically within the span ranging from somewhat before House 1 to somewhat after.

The important Vadgård settlements with their different kinds of house remainders also contained pottery of interest (Lomborg 1973b; 1976; 1980; Becker 1982:54pp; Rasmussen, M. 1993a, Fig. 26-31). In a direct line, the locations can be estimated at a distance of c. 48 km from Resengaard. Some of the pottery profiles at Vadgård Nord show affinities with, not least, the House 200 assemblage. An ear fragment (and its context) is not taken into consideration. Regarded as a whole, the affinities with the Resengaard assemblages are few and mostly of a general character or presumed relatively weak such as e.g. the affinities with a profile from the House 268 assemblage. The only Vadgård Nord relationship notably of some strength relates to a profile belonging to the House 14 assemblage. When weighing up the relationships, it appears evident that the most characteristic designs at Vadgård Nord may indicate a time somewhat after the end of the provisional Resengaard chronology.

The pottery from Vadgård Syd has a character of its own and diverges from the ceramics of Vadgård Nord (Lomborg 1973b; 1976; 1980; Becker 1982:54pp; Rasmussen, M. 1993a, Fig. 38-40 & 42). No clear affinities with the Resengaard sunken-floor house assemblages can be demonstrated. A parallel in time is thus unlikely to be the case and the Vadgård Syd site presumably had a chronological position later than that of House 1 at Resengaard. According to M. Rasmussen, it should be placed in the time of her Torslev phase, which is seen as phase 2 in the suite of settlement pottery finds, ordered by means of multivariate methods (Rasmussen, M. 1993a, Fig. 141).

The sunken-floor longhouse at Vejlby has been proposed as belonging to the transition from the Late Neolithic to the Older Bronze Age (Jeppesen 1984, Fig. 3; Rasmussen, M. 1993a). The geographical distance to

Resengaard is estimated as c. 75 km in a direct line. The pottery represented is rather modest and only two distinct profiles show affinities with the Resengaard material. Broadly considered, the designs of these two rim profiles indicate a chronological frame from about House 41 to about House 128. One of the profiles shows relatively strong affinities to several specimens in the assemblage of House 2, House 14, House 240 and House 268. A dating from about the time of House 2 to House 128 seems hence likely.

The results of the analysis and evaluation concerning a possible anchoring of well-known pottery assemblages to the provisional Resengaard chronology can now be briefly summarized. The pottery from the Egehøj site is suggested as being parallel or close to the time of the House 14 and 128 assemblages. The Torslev pottery is somewhat later but still close to the House 1 assemblage. Still younger seems the Vadgård Nord material. Weak links to the time of some of the latest Resengaard assemblages do also appear to be traceable, however. Against this, the Resengaard chronology seems out of reach for the Vadgård Syd material. The limited assemblage from Vejlby may, with some reservations, point to a chronological position nearer to several assemblages around the assemblages of House 2 and House 128. Henceforward, new radiocarbon determinations may perhaps help to enlighten the chronological positions of certain pottery assemblages.

3.6. Anchoring certain new sites to the provisional Resengaard chronology?

The pottery assemblages of Gåsemose and Kluborg II are both found not very far from Resengaard. Geography as a source-critical factor in terms of pottery differences would presumably have had little influence. The Gåsemose site is new in the sense that it has hitherto remained unpublished.

Gåsemose and Kluborg II

Regarding House 1 at Gåsemose, most of the artefacts from excavation areas I, II and IV may well derive from what I consider to be secondary fills above the sunken floor (Fig. 2.39 & 2.40). Many finds from excavation area V must also stem from these fills although some disturbances make the question of context somewhat uncertain. From House 1, a rich material of clay pot profiles from in particular the excavation squares I, II, and V exists and many shall be taken into consideration (Fig. 3.59). For details of arguments for pottery relationships, see Appendix 1. The distance in a straight line to Resengaard is c. 15 km.

Before weighing up the strength of the affinities with the different Resengaard assemblages, it is first necessary to mention that certain profiles with horizontal cordon, from a culture layer (not illustrated) south of the house site, can hardly belong to the time of House 1. In my understanding, these profiles must be earlier. We shall return to the cordoned rims below.

Some affinities observed with regard to several clay pot profiles (GÅ108, GÅ111, GÅ113 & other) could indicate a chronological position somewhere within the span ranging from around the time of House 41 to around the time of House 2 at Resengaard. Another profile (GÅ65) may also point to the reference assemblages of Houses 41 and 2 (and the time span in between). And yet clay pot profiles supplied with more specific design elements also make it evident that the affinities point not least to these two reference assemblages, and relationships – in particular with further Resengaard house assemblages – serve to support this. Two profiles (GÅ67 & GÅ64) thus point to the time of the reference assemblages of Houses 2 and 41, as well as those of House 14, House 138, House 200, and, in particular, House 240.

It is thereby possible, through certain strong resemblances, to narrow down the suggested frame of dating. Two rim profiles (GÅ19 & GÅ104, the latter not illustrated) point first and foremost to around the time of the assemblage of House 2 although they also have affinities, to some degree, with not least the assemblages of Houses 1, 14, 41,138, 200 and 240.

Weighing up the affinities referred to above, as well as details referred to in the Appendix, I see the time of the Resengaard House 2 reference assemblage as central to the chronological placement of the Gåsemose House 1 assemblage and, judging by some of the rather special profiles mentioned above, I advocate a dating close to that of House 2. I consider it most likely that it is contemporaneous with the assemblage of House 14, House 2, or House 200.

Artefacts from the culture layer are, not least, represented in excavation area III and we shall therefore briefly deal with the dating of such finds although none of these are illustrated here. It is apparent that some of the rim fragments could be contemporaneous with those accounted for immediately above, i.e.

Chronology of pottery assemblages 203

GÅ108

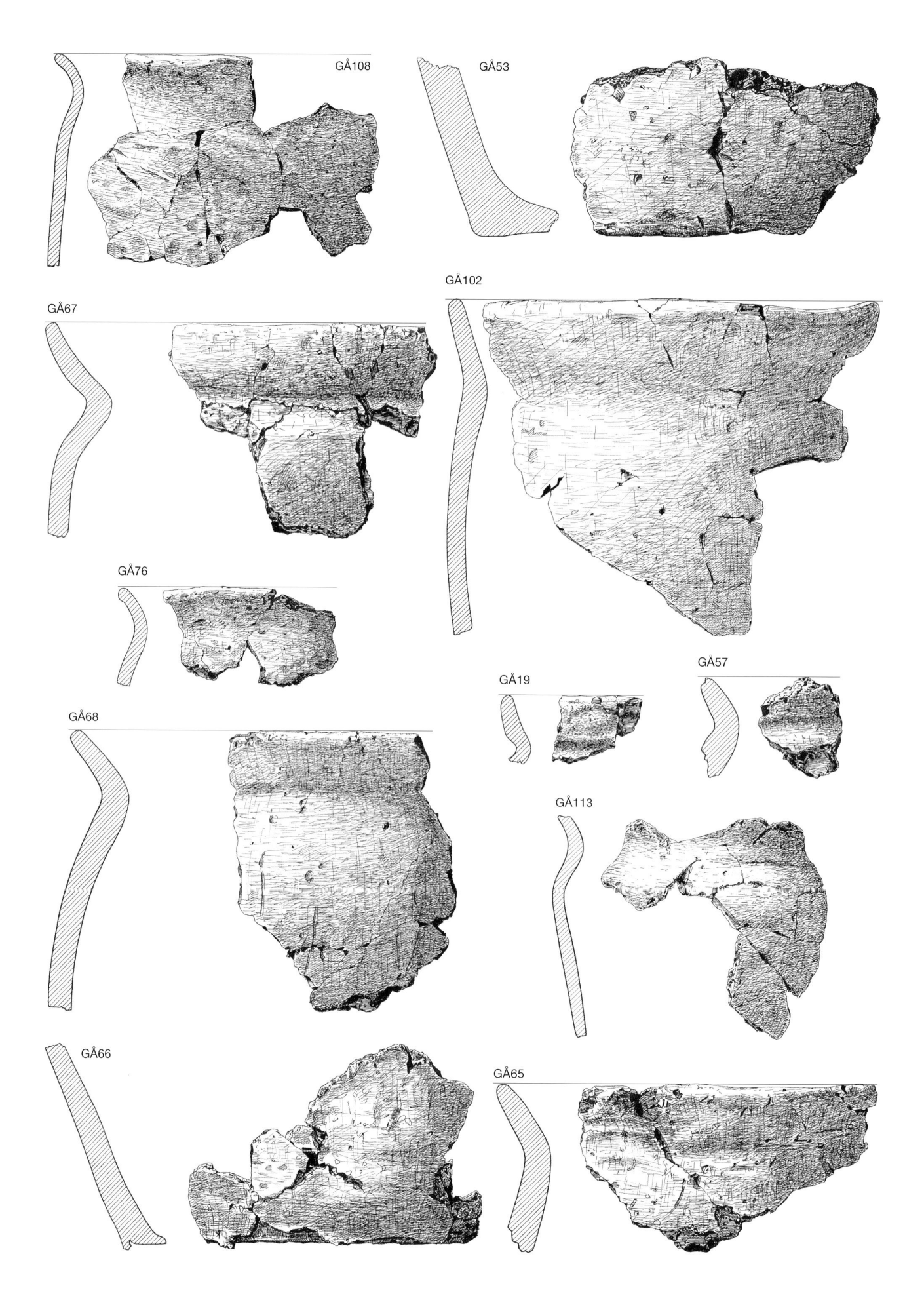

GÅ53

GÅ67

GÅ102

GÅ76

GÅ19

GÅ57

GÅ68

GÅ113

GÅ66

GÅ65

204   Chapter 3

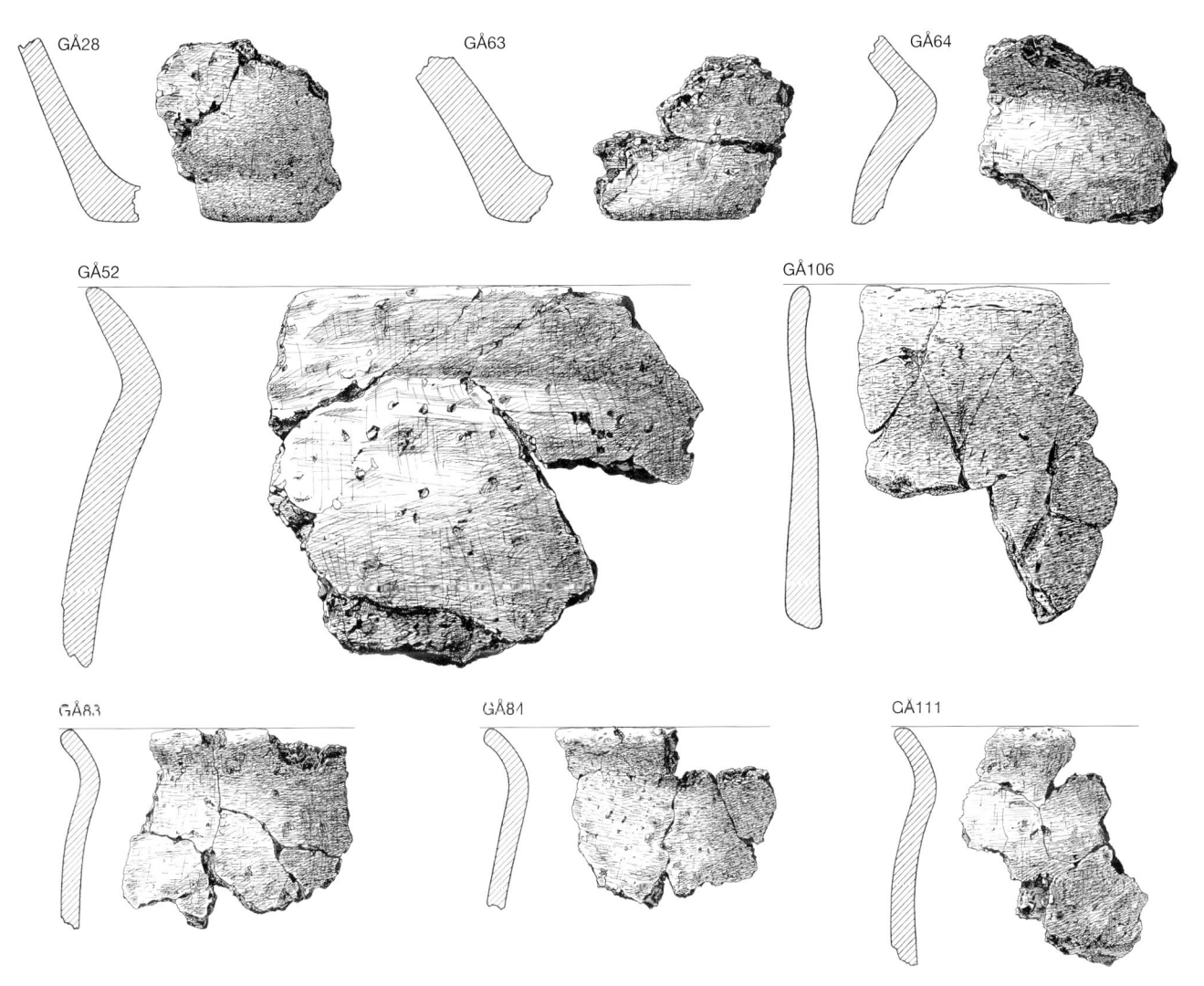

◂▴ *Fig. 3.59. Gåsemose. Selected pottery profiles from the sunken area of House 1 and beyond. As presumably the only longhouse site among those settlements studied in particular, the very dense presence of stones in the secondary fills (evidenced in the sections) may indicate that it was not exposed to comprehensive ard-ploughing after demolition of the building. Moreover, the relatively large preserved sides of the vessels could support this idea because ard-ploughing would presumably have splintered these into smaller pieces. Scale 1:3.*

around the time of House 2 at Resengaard. And yet ornamented pottery is present on a small scale. A rim fragment (GÅ71) with horizontally-incised lines somewhat below the rim and three side fragments (GÅ3, GÅ16, & GÅ70) with horizontally-incised lines belong to the finds from this area. A side fragment (GÅ69) also has a row of circular incisions. Four rim fragments and one side fragment are supplied with horizontal cordons below the rim (GÅ5, GÅ23, GÅ25, GÅ26, & GÅ27). In my understanding, these features evidence a time somewhat before House 1 at Gåsemose. Furthermore, a simple and fairly coarse decoration with a row of notch stamped incisions (GÅ50) and a minor piece of an incised line (GÅ12) stem from excavation area II. A side fragment with horizontal cordon (GÅ88) and a side fragment with horizontally-incised lines were found in excavation area IV. A bottom fragment with notch-stamped lines (GÅ10) was found in excavation area I. The above decorations point to the time of the Late Neolithic Beaker pottery.

Many flint artefacts, such as an axe, a number of scrapers, some sickles and possibly some arrowheads and pieces of daggers may also represent this earlier period. Certain fragments of late flint daggers do exist, for instance GÅ164 (type V) and GÅ165 (type IV or V), both of which were ploughed up into the modern cultivation layer. These flint daggers, in my understanding, are in accordance with the pottery finds dating House 1 at Gåsemose.

We now turn to the pottery of House 5 at Kluborg II (Fig. 3.60). The combinations of the ware and shape of rim fragments do not induce associations to Late Neolithic pottery. Unfortunately, very few rims belonging to the floor itself were preserved and none have been found in the context of the secondary fills. None of the side fragments from the floor or secondary fills have qualities that are suitable for a specific dating. Actually, it has only been possible to reconstruct the uppermost part of three vessels in the drawings. The wares of these are predominantly greyish-brown and, like all other fragments from the excavation area, completely without ornamentation. A vessel, from which fragments were found at three different spots in the sunken-floor horizon seems to have had an almost barrel-shaped profile (KL28aa/40aa/47aa). The preserved fragments show that it was evenly turned inwards from the belly upwards and became gradually thinner towards the top. The outer side towards the rim is characteristically convex, and the inner side correspondingly concave. If we take this clay pot from House 5 as a starting point, it is clear that a comparison with the younger pottery material from the sunken-floor houses of Resengaard, in particular the assemblages of Houses 14, 10, 240, 268 and 1, reveals that no direct counterparts exist in these assemblages. It does seem, however, that profile KL38aa/25aa has some traits in common with RE31aa from House 1, the latest sunken-floor longhouse at Resengaard. That the ceramics from the House 5 assemblage at Kluborg II have no strong affinities with the youngest sunken-floored House at Resengaard is interesting also because the distance to Resengaard is a mere c. 6 km in a direct line and it can therefore hardly be a question of geographical distance.

Turning to some of the North Jutland assemblages of relatively young date, some interesting affinities can be mentioned. From Marianne Rasmussens' phases 2 and 3a, certain profiles have affinities with the profile KL28aa/40aa/47aa from Kluborg II and, more specifically, this concerns a specimen from Torslev and likewise one from Vadgård Nord (Rasmussen, M. 1993a:42 & 55, Fig. 27 & 50). It appears that the best affiliations to the profile KL30aa/35aa again concerns profiles of phases 2 and 3a (Rasmussen, M. 1993a, Fig. 143). And yet no really close relationships are observable. Common to the House 5 specimens and a vessel from Torslev is the broad marking of the rims, which have straight inner sides (Rasmussen, M. 1993a:55-57, Fig. 51g). As regards the last of the three rim profiles (KL25aa/38aa), no clear affiliations are observable from phase 3a whereas profiles from phase 2 suggest a possible connection. The lower part of the rim in particular might point to affinities with a profile from Torslev (Rasmussen, M. 1993a:57, Fig. 51i). Overall, pottery dating of the House 5 assemblage can only be based on a very small amount of material, and it must therefore be underlined that the suggestion below is given with clear reservations. However, affinities with the pottery from Torslev and, in one case, also Vadgård Nord, do not seem to be contradicted by other traits of the ceramics. As the resemblances to the Torslev assemblage may be noted with regard to three profiles from House 5, I suggest that the Kluborg II assemblage may have been contemporaneous with or close to the time of the Torslev assemblage and, through this affinity, thereby presumably not far from the Resengaard House I assemblage, perhaps just slightly later.

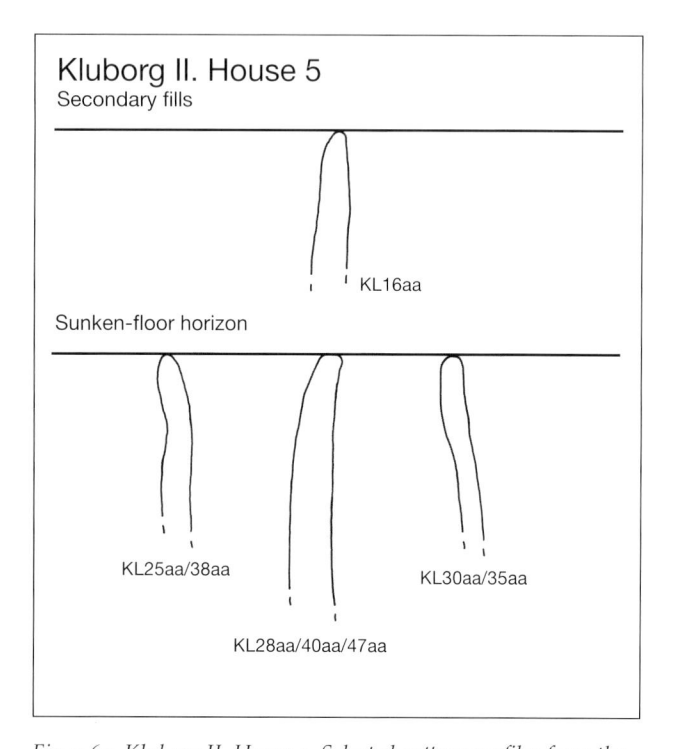

Fig. 3.60. Kluborg II. House 5. Selected pottery profiles from the sunken-floor horizon and the above secondary fills. Scale: 1:2.

3.7. Relationships of certain new sites to Myrhøj and Tastum I?

For further exploring of relationships of the many new finds of pottery and other artefacts from not least the sunken floors we will in particular need a considerable series of radiocarbon determinations to have a chance to set more precise time frames. However, in this part I will present a preliminary and very tentative view on internal relationships of some LN I ceramics from the central Limfjord region.

The Beaker pottery from Resengaard concerns ornamentation with cardium impressions, notch-stamped lines, parallel horizontal lines, and more or less horizontal rows of vertical spatula incisions ("barbed wire"). These finds (Fig. 4.43) point broadly towards the Myrhøj assemblages and later stylistic use of Beaker ornamentation. Judging by the preserved material from the possible "House 160" (i.e. pit 160, pit 161 and other), cardium impression was favoured but, as a single sherd with notch-stamped lines shows, it was not exclusively that decoration. One with cardium impressions (RE636ba) indicates the presence of a metope with a triangular pattern, and hence a relationship to the Myrhøj styles or a derivate thereof.

The other new "early" assemblages include ceramics from eight sites found within a distance of a few hundred metres up to c. 22 km from Resengaard and c. 10-42 km from Myrhøj. This concerns pottery from Gåsemose, Glattrup I/III, Marienlyst Strand, Granlygård, Hellegård, Glattrup IV, Rosgårde, and Tromgade. Examples of some of these ceramics, including some from Resengaard, are illustrated later (Ch. 4). Before considering these new Beaker materials, the pottery shapes in the comprehensive Myrhøj ceramics will first shortly be considered and then, subsequently, the rich decoration. Thereafter, some of the relationships will be considered although no conclusion will be reached on the internal chronology of these new Beaker assemblages, except that a new very early Beaker phase. Marienlyst Strand, of the Late Neolithic in an area of the Limfjord region will be proposed.

Five main form groups of pottery from Myrhøj have been presented (Jensen, J.A. 1973:96-103, 118). Only a single vessel at the settlement was supplied with a cordoned rim, while many clay pots were characterized with otherwise richly-decorated outer sides. The techniques employed for the design of the motives are finely accounted for in the original publication but comparison with several of the new assemblages in the following may necessitate a short account of the ornamentation.

Technically, incised lines and furrows, impressions with the edge of cardium shells, and notch-stamps are relatively common in the preserved Myrhøj pottery, whereas circle stamps are seldom found. Such patterns would likely have given favourable appearances when whitish fills, "incrustation", were rubbed in (e.g.

Jensen 1973:95 & 104; Boas 1986:322; Sarauw 2007b:21; Sarauw 2008a:99). Incrustation or other fill material has not been observed on any of the few, early decorated potsherds from Resengaard. It cannot, however be ruled out that tiny remainders of incrustation might be detected on ceramics from some of the seven new "early" settlements in question.

An important feature of the Myrhøj styles is that the decorated zones and geometrical figures usually alternate with blank areas in between, giving the ornamentation its particular character. Looking at techniques and motives together, the styles of the Myrhøj decorations in particular are characterized by: 1. areas below the rim with horizontally-incised lines, cardium lines or furrows. 2. horizontal zones with oblique notch-stamped lines, cardium impressions and cross-hatching. Horizontal zone of parallel lines (seldom) and horizontal zones with bow-lines (seldom) are also represented. 3. metope-like areas with lozenges covered with cardium impressions or notch-stamps, triangles covered with cross-hatching or notch-stamps, and vertical or oblique zones with cross-hatching or obliquely-incised lines.

The comparative materials from the site of House 1 at Tastum I and from some early Resengaard assemblages with ornamented pottery are also taken into consideration in the following. We first consider the ceramic forms for each house site and then the ornamented pottery.

Glattrup I/III and Marienlyst Strand

Besides the ceramics from the assemblages of longhouses 5 and 6 at Glattrup I/III, a few finds from the nearby ditch 135, pit 133 and pit 45 may help to indicate the dating of the last-mentioned house. In a direct line, the distance is c. 29 km to Myrhøj, c. 4 km to Tastum I, and c. 4 km to Resengaard.

When it comes to House 5 at Glattrup I/III, a clay pot with ornamentation (GL522aa) from the sunken-floor horizon indicate a rather low, barrel-like shape (Fig. 3.61). This form is not known from Myrhøj but a simple rim not much different is present at Tastum I (Simonsen, 1983, Fig. 6, lower row, second profile from right). No clear barrel-like forms are to be found among the Resengaard ceramics but a few convex outlines may, to some degree, be reminiscent of these.

Regarding House 6 at Glattrup I/III, a total of nine rims derive from the top of the secondary fills above the sunken floor of this longhouse (GL1331aa, GL1331ab,

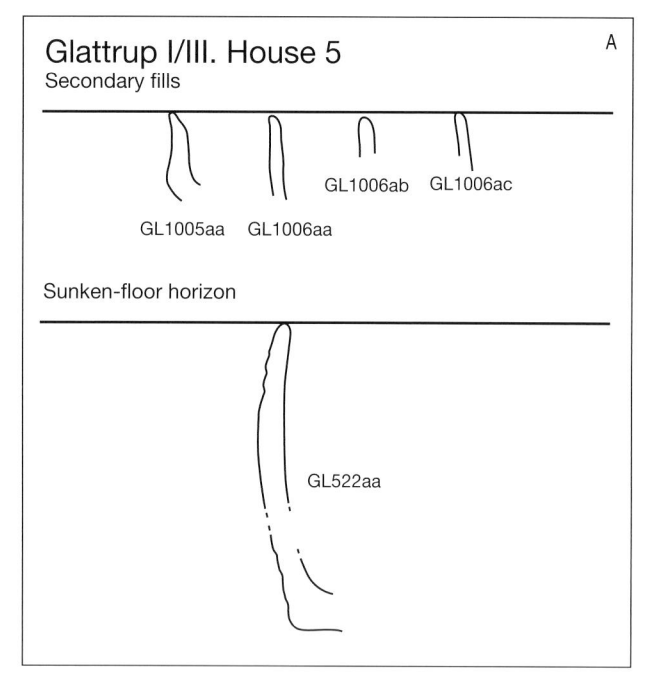

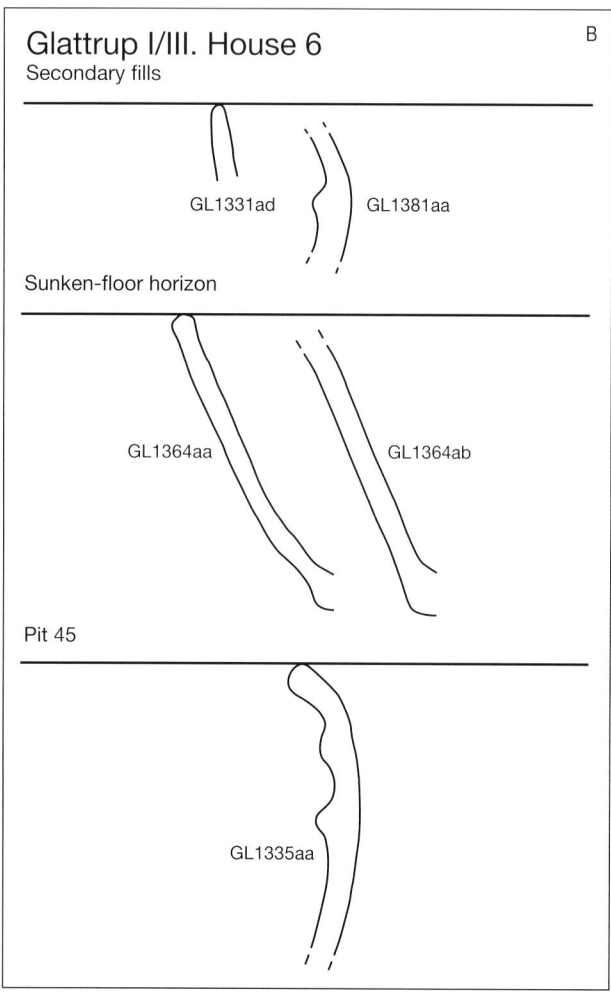

Fig. 3.61. Glattrup I/III. Selected clay pot profiles. A: From the sunken-floor horizon and the above secondary fills of the site of House 5. B: From the sunken-floor horizon and the above secondary fills of the site of House 6, as well as from nearby pit 45 (see Fig. 2.44). Scale: 1:2.

GL1331ac, GL1331ad, GL1331ae, GL1331af, GL1331ag, GL1331ah, & GL1331ai). Some of these may belong to simple, open bowls. In addition, two simple rim profiles belong to these fills (GL1346ab & GL1346ac, not illustrated). Another profile (GL1331aa) has significant affinities with the shaping of a profile from House 41 (RE403aa/411aa). This concerns the quite straight inner rim above the very marked "knee".

Ditch 135, pit 133 and pit 45: the ditch and two pits near the sunken-floor part of the building were presumably contemporary with it (Fig. 3.61). The finds concern fragments of two simple, open bowls (GL1364aa & GL1364ab) from ditch 135. Besides a flint borer, pit 133 contained 6 small potsherds (GL1367aa & GL1367ab). Pit 45 contained a clay pot profile with two horizontal cordons (GL1335aa) which may indicate a relationship of a purely general nature to Myrhøj, Tastum I and early Resengaard assemblages.

The decoration with horizontal notch-stamped lines and horizontally-incised lines from House 5 immediately points to certain Myrhøj pottery and others (Fig. 4.48). Rows of vertical spatula incisions ("barbed wire") are present on the above-mentioned barrel-like clay pot but this decoration is absent from the Myrhøj assemblages, whereas it was found in the assemblage of pit 77 at Resengaard (RE469ab & RE469ac, Fig. 4.43). None of the more complex decorations are present in the House 5 assemblage, and this might of course be due to the small number of potsherds, although another reason could well be that the chronological position is some distance from Myrhøj.

Several clay pot profiles represent the House 6 assemblage (Fig. 3.61). A rather late date was previously seen as possible (Simonsen 1996c:93pp). After reviewing the find material, I prefer to put weight on the presence of a potsherd with ornaments from the secondary fills above the sunken floor (Fig. 4.49). It shows the remainders of three horizontal furrows. When further, somewhat slapdash, ornamented sherds from pit 133 are also considered, it appears that horizontally-incised lines and, in particular, a lozenge decoration may indicate at least some relationship to Myrhøj pottery. A side fragment with a horizontal cordon (GL1381aa) derives from the soil bench across the sunken floor, and I ascribe it to the secondary fills. Cordoned rims are also integrated but apparently rare elements at Myrhøj, while these play a more conspicuous role in the earliest assemblages at Resengaard and at Tastum I (Simonsen 1983, Fig. 6).

When turning to Marienlyst Strand, pottery from the assemblage of House 1, as well that of pit 4 and culture layer 5, will be considered (Fig. 3.62). In a direct line, the distance is c. 25 km to Myrhøj, while to Resengaard it is a matter of just a few hundred metres.

Regarding House 1, a total of 64 potsherds, including 1 rim fragment and 4 bottom fragments, stem from the excavation of the secondary fills of this longhouse. In addition, 6 fragments datable to much later times are present and they are considered to have been ploughed down into the top of the fills. The pottery is generally dominated by coarse tempering and some potsherds are relatively thick-walled. Unfortunately, none of them provide a basis for a precise dating from their appearance. In the report, the building is dated to the Older Bronze Age, whereas I suggest a much earlier dating as indicated by the markedly reddish surface colour of many of the above-mentioned potsherds, as opposed to the often more brownish surface colour of later domestic pottery as at nearby Resengaard. Secondly, the suggestion is based on some rim fragments, supplied with fine and medium grain size tempering and exposed to secondary burning. In my reading, the smooth shaping with turned out rim of the upper part of another vessel (MA19aa) indicates a dating to the early part of the Late Neolithic. And yet the relatively low marking of the belly has no counterpart in the Myrhøj assemblage. The vessel derives from a soil patch (8) which was expressly stated by the excavation director as being later than the floor.

A single ornamented potsherd (MA22aa) was found in a soil patch otherwise devoid of artefacts. It was placed in the eastern part of the sunken area and, in the report, it is specifically stated that this soil feature was later than the floor. The fragment stems from the belly marking, which resembles the shaping of the zone-ornamented vessel from pit 4 (MA4aa, see below). Lowest is a horizontal line of horizontal spatula incisions and, above this, some parallel, oblique rows of vertical spatula incisions. This ornamentation was likely made around the whole perimeter of the upper belly part and seems without clear parallels in the other materials focussed on.

In both cases, these fragments (MA19aa & MA22aa) therefore represent a *terminus ante quem* dating for the longhouse, if we go along with the excavator's statements concerning the soil features being later than the sunken floor. Yet it is remarkable that several large soil patches should later have been made exactly within the

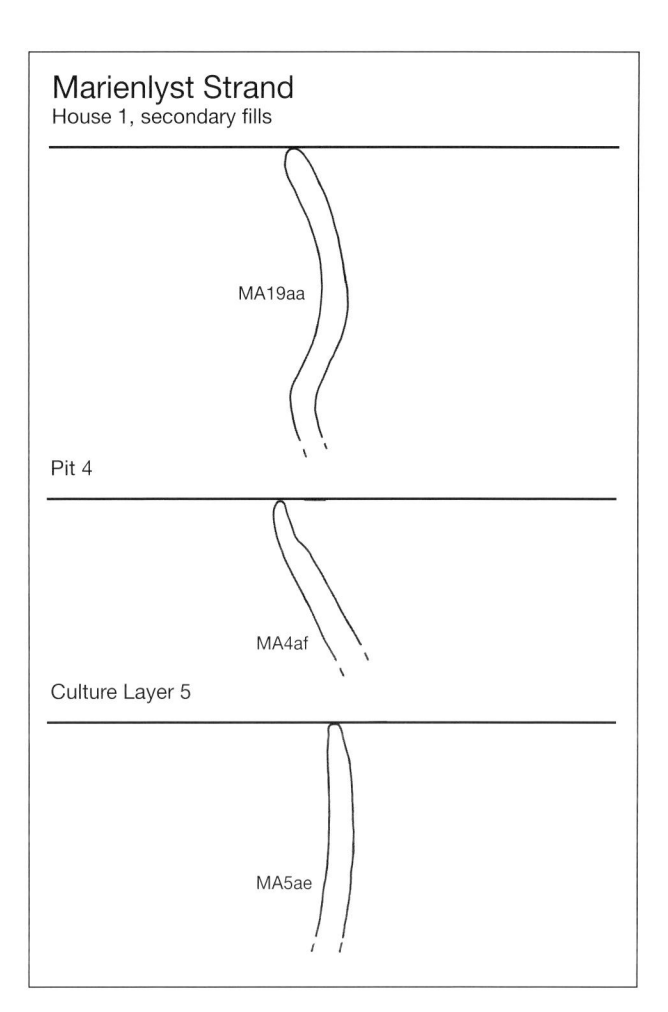

Fig. 3.62. Marienlyst Strand. Selected clay pot profiles from the secondary fills of the sunken area of House 1, as well as from pit 4 and culture layer 5. Scale: 1:2.

contours of the sunken floor, whereas no substantial soil features of a similar kind appeared outside in the remaining part of the excavation area of 264 m².

The premise for dating the house assemblage can, however, be considered from a broader perspective involving the settlement in general. The system of many trial trenches revealed very few relevant settlement remainders from the Late Neolithic. Hence, in my reading, it seems highly plausible that the sunken-floor house belongs together with these, i.e. the large pit 4 and culture layer 5. Both of these contained richly-ornamented pottery. It is my understanding that these traces (including House 1), on the whole, relate to a one-phase settlement at this south-sloping hill side.

The observations from a soil bench in the natural depression in which culture layer 5 had accumulated also showed that only one settlement period left finds of pottery, flint and charcoal there. Judging by the stratification, these finds may belong to a distinctly short period of the Late Neolithic. A number of potsherds from five clay pots without decoration (MA5af, MA5ag, MA5ah, & MA5ai, not illustrated) contribute hardly anything else to a more specific dating but, in its concave upper part contour, another specimen (MA5ae) is reminiscent of the zone-ornamented clay pot (MA4aa, see below) from pit 4 (Fig. 4.50 & 4.51). Some rim fragments decorated with horizontal lines and another with notch-stamped lines were also found in the culture layer (see Ch. 4). The appearance of the pottery from culture layer 5 thus resembles that of pit 4, which we shall now consider.

Concerning pit 4, a number of rim fragments belonging to four unornamented clay pots contribute little (MA4ae, MA4af, MA4ag, & MA4ah, not illustrated). Many decorated potsherds belong to this pit, however, and it is particularly interesting that both lozenge decoration and metope areas are absent.

The chronological position of the assemblage from pit 4, culture layer 5 and House 1 may be relatively close to the Myrhøj assemblages, with its high degree of ornamentation but, in my reading, not contemporary with it. I argue that these ceramics belong to a rather early, richly-ornamented pottery milieu nearer to the beginning of the Late Neolithic than any of the pottery assemblages presented from Myrhøj (Jensen, J.A. 1973). Not least the partly preserved clay pot with maritime Beaker decoration from pit 4 (MA4aa) leads me to suggest such an early Marienlyst Strand phase. Its outer side shaping is convex beneath the belly marking and concave above, thus bearing some Beaker traits that are seldom found among Limfjord region find materials, being also delicately thin-walled. Below the belly turn point, the clay pot is without decoration, whereas the ornamentation begins immediately above. The decoration is composed of three broad, horizontal zones consisting of 7, 8 and 7 parallel notch-stamped lines respectively, interchanging with two broad, blank zones and a blank outer rim side. Neither this ornamentation nor the shaping of the vessel links it to the Myrhøj pottery. As mentioned, a vessel (MA5ae) from culture layer 5 appears to have about the same shaping, judging by its preserved upper parts (Fig. 4.51). Above the relative low belly marking, another clay pot (MA19aa) from the site of House 1 has an evenly concave upper part ending in the out-turned rim. It is without decoration but a shaping like this may perhaps represent a prior form of the later "form 3" from Myrhøj (Jensen, 1973, Fig. 37). Potsherds from two vessels (MA5aa & MA5ac) from culture layer 5 are supplied with horizontally incised lines and may, given the above, also represent a specimen earlier than those of numerous Myrhøj ceramics (Fig. 4.51). The above-mentioned ceramics from pit 4, culture layer 5 and House 1 thus represent this Marienlyst Strand phase of settlement pottery. I assume that this phase was present in areas of the central Limfjord region but it would not be surprising if it had a wider geography.

Granlygård, Hellegård and Glattrup IV

Ceramics from the assemblages of Houses 2, 3, 6 and pit 4 form the basis for the evaluation of the chronological position of the settlement at Granlygård. The distance in a direct line is c. 30 km to Myrhøj and c. 6 km to Resengaard.

No finds are attributed to the sunken floor of House 2. From the secondary fills of this minor house derived 52 potsherds and 180 pieces of worked flint.

No finds belong to the sunken floor of House 3. From the secondary fills rim fragments without ornamentation are recorded (Fig. 3.63). One is from a vessel with out-turned rim (GR10ag, not illustrated). Three belong to clay pots with simple rims (GR10ah, GR10ai & GR10aj, the two last-mentioned not illustrated). The latter rim has close affinities with rim fragments from pit 4, considered below. In the upper part of the sunken floor fills a fragment with horizontal furrows was found (GR3aa, two furrows preserved and vestiges of two more).

No finds stem from the sunken floor of House 6. Besides other artefact remainders, various potsherds stem from the secondary fills. Among these, a potsherd from a low, open bowl is supplied with a hole in the side below the rim. The hole is somewhat like that of the colander from pit 4 (GR61af).

The finds from pit 4 are more informative as regards chronology. An open bowl with a thin, relatively simple rim (GR11ad) does not, however, provide the basis for proposing a more precise relationship. A loom weight (GR11ab) and complete clay colander (GR11aa) likewise cannot contribute to clarifying the dating of the pit. It may, however, be possible to date these items from their decorated ceramics.

Ceramics from the secondary fills of House 2 are scarce but the characteristics of the wares such as tempering, surface treatment and burning point to the Late Neolithic and are reminiscent of potsherds belonging to the assemblages of Houses 3 and 6. Only a single side fragment from the assemblage of House

2 was ornamented. This concerns a potsherd with a horizontal line and, seemingly, indications of two more (GR7aa).

As regards the House 3 assemblage, the decoration of ceramics (Fig. 4.53) with horizontal lines, horizontal furrows, horizontal cardium lines, notch-stamped lines and not least the metope decoration with lozenges clearly points to a relationship with the Myrhøj assemblages.

When it comes to the House 6 assemblage (Fig. 4.53), pottery ornaments with horizontal furrows, horizontal lines with cardium impressions, horizontal zones with short oblique incised lines (edged with incised lines), a horizontal zone with oblique notch-stamped lines (edged with notch-stamped lines) and horizontal furrows also points to a relationship with the Myrhøj assemblages.

Fairly varied kinds of decoration were observed from pit 4 (Fig. 4.53) and the ceramics include ornamentation with horizontally-incised lines and horizontal lines of cardium impressions. It could therefore also point to a time close to Houses 3 and 6.

Together, House 3, House 6 and pit 4 do not seem far from each other in time, whereas sufficient ornamented pottery was not present in the assemblage of House 2. And yet the mere fact of its close placement, with no other Late Neolithic house sites in the investigated areas, presumably points to a chronological connection. In my view it seems plausible that the short houses succeeded one another although simultaneous functioning can also not be excluded. Based on the ornamental evidence from the pottery assemblages, it seems clear that Granlygård has relatively close affinities with the Myrhøj ceramics.

From Hellegård, we shall first consider the assemblage of House 122 and then that of House 35. In a direct line, the distance is c. 19 km to Myrhøj and c. 21 km to Resengaard. From House 122, a potsherd from the secondary fills seems to belong to the same clay pot as another (HE550aa & HE 520aa, not illustrated) from the sunken floor. The assemblage of this longhouse only contained a few rims (Fig. 3.64 & 4.55). Reconstructions of three rims make some comparisons possible but the few forms may perhaps not be adequately representative. Some affiliation with the early pottery from the assemblage of House 134 at Resengaard cannot be *a priori* excluded. Two rims are out-turned albeit one of these (HE550ac) only slightly. The other out-turned rim (HE550ad) could point to a relationship to, for instance, a rim (RE564ae) from the assemblage of House 134. And yet as a whole the rims do not speak strongly in favour of very close affinities with any Resengaard assemblages.

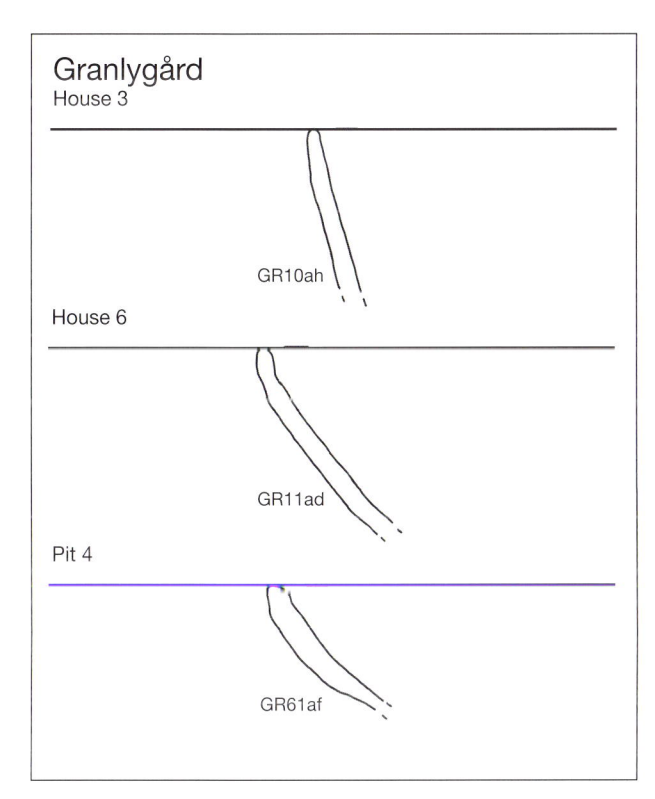

Fig. 3.63. Granlygård. Selected clay pot profiles from the secondary fills of the sunken area of House 3 and House 6, as well as from pit 4. Scale: 1:2.

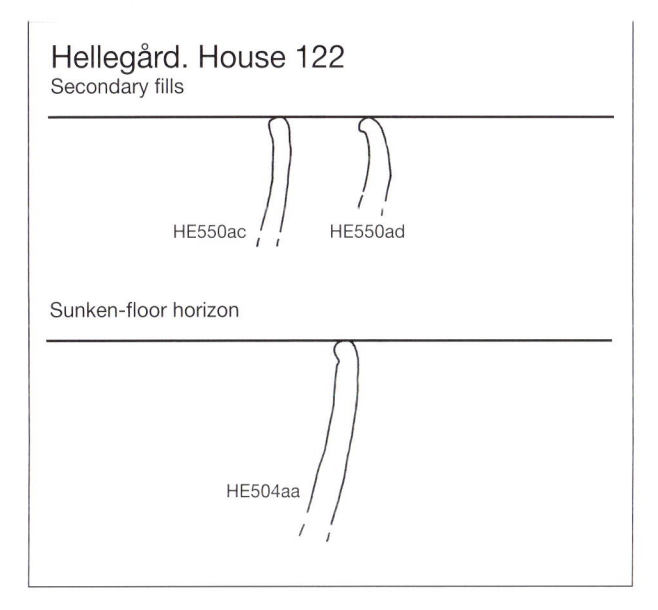

Fig. 3.64. Hellegård. Selected clay pot profiles from the sunken-floor horizon and the above secondary fills of the site of House 122. Scale: 1:2.

On the other hand, close shape affinities with the Myrhøj assemblages cannot be stated on the grounds of the few short rims, although they have some affiliation with several of the rim shapes from Myrhøj (Jensen, J.A. 1973, Fig. 38-40). The rim with an inwards inclination (HE504aa) from the sunken floor has no clear counterpart in the published Myrhøj material.

Regarding House 35, it has not been possible to make an even partial reconstruction of any clay pots from the assemblage of this short house but it includes a few potsherds of about the same appearance as those from House 122, indicating that their chronological positions were presumably the same.

Some ornamentation was present on the ceramics from these two house sites (Fig. 4.53 & 4.54). This concerns the presence of decoration with parallel horizontal lines (HE550aa). This ornamentation is relatively frequent at Myrhøj (Jensen, J.A. 1973, Fig. 54). Further, a plastic decoration reminiscent of horizontal fluting (HE535ab) from the assemblage of House 35 has some relationship to the pottery from Myrhøj (Jensen, J.A. 1973, Fig. 40-41). As this kind of ornamentation appears to have been very rare, this trait might indicate a chronological position fairly close to Myrhøj. Finally, a lozenge decoration, apparently as part of a metope (HE535aa), is also an ornamental pattern known from Myrhøj (Jensen, J.A. 1973, Fig. 47). Connections to the Myrhøj ceramics are thus notable although the absence of decoration characterized by notch-stamp techniques is remarkable and attracts some attention as this is often a prominent element of early Late Neolithic decorative patterns. The pottery assemblages at Hellegård are as a whole rather small, however, and this could more or less explain the absence of that decoration and of cardium impressions. While the rim (HE504aa) without counterparts in the Myrhøj material has some resonance in the Marienlyst Strand assemblages, it is on the other hand not excludable that the generally low frequency of ornamentation and the somewhat slapdash workmanship of the ornamentation at Hellegård might perhaps point to a slightly later time when the interest in highly skilled pottery decoration had decreased.

Concerning Glattrup IV, the ceramics from the assemblages of longhouses 3, 5 and 7 will be considered in the following (Fig. 3.65). The profiles from this settlement are characterized by simple and cordoned rims. Several potsherds with ornamentation belong to two of these longhouse assemblages. The distance in a direct line is c. 30 km to Myrhøj, c. 3 km to Tastum I and c. 5 km to Resengaard.

From the sunken floor and secondary fills of House 3 derives a profile supplied with a horizontal, rather low cordon below the rim (GT145as/GT310aa). A profile with two horizontal cordons below the rim (GT145ad) belongs to the secondary fills. Its upper cordon is relatively low.

Most of the rim profiles from the assemblage of House 5 do not help to suggest relationships although a cordoned rim (GT509aa) from the sunken-floor horizon and one (GT469ad) from the secondary fills both have some affinities with the profiles from House 1 at Tastum I (Simonsen, 1983, Fig. 6, upper row, the first from right). Ceramics with decoration have been found in the sunken-floor horizon, from a minor pit to the west, from a large pit near the gable end and, finally, from the secondary fills above the sunken floor.

In the assemblage of House 7 likewise none of the rim profiles help to date it more precisely. Decorated pottery was found in a large pit and also as part of the secondary fills.

No pottery with incised decoration stems from the assemblage of House 3. As regards such ceramics with decoration from House 5, a weak affinity with the earliest ornamented ceramics covered by the provisional Resengaard chronology is present, although it is immediately clear that certain relationships to the pottery of Myrhøj are much more evident (Fig. 4.58). The use of complex metope decoration (presumably with lozenges) is, not least, important but also the observation that the assemblage includes potsherds with relatively simple decoration such as zones with short oblique notch-stamped lines, a row of vertical bow stamps and areas with parallel horizontal lines, which may support this understanding.

I find it plausible that Houses 3, 5 and 7, in the main, could have succeeded each other but that their chronological order internally are not clarified as yet.

Rosgårde and Tromgade

From Rosgårde, the ceramics belonging to the assemblage of House 1, as well as pits 23 and 121, now come into focus when seeking a dating of the settlement. The distance in a direct line is c. 42 km to Myrhøj, c. 14 km to Tastum I, and c. 22 km to Resengaard.

From House 1, two undecorated rim fragments derive from the secondary fills (Fig. 3.66). One of these (RO201aa) belongs to an open bowl with almost upright rim. The shape resembles some open bowls from Myrhøj (Jensen, J.A. 1973, Fig. 66.1). It also shows a

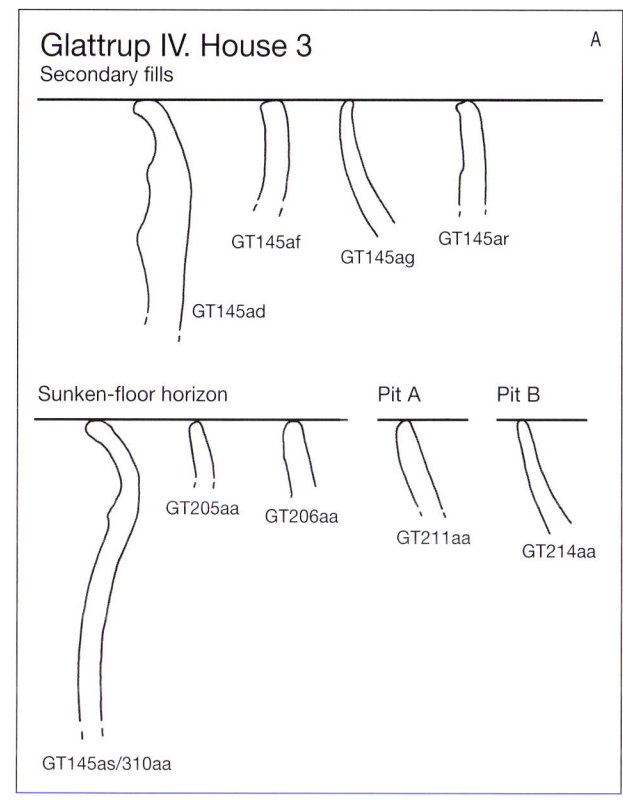

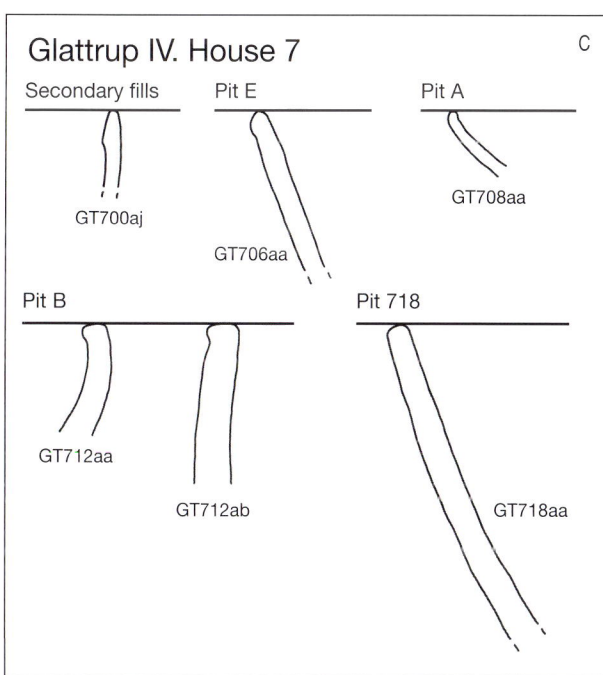

Fig. 3.65. Glattrup IV. Selected clay pot profiles. A: From the site of House 3, the secondary fills and the sunken-floor horizon, including pit A and the sunken fireplace B. The potsherds belonging to clay pot profile GT145as/310aa stem from the secondary fills and the sunken-floor horizon, respectively. B: From the site of House 5, the secondary fills and the sunken-floor horizon as well as pit 480 in the ground floor. C: From the site of House 7, the secondary fills and the sunken-floor horizon (pit A, pit E, and the sunken fireplace B), as well as pit 718 immediately east of the house site (Fig. 2.54.A). Scale: 1:2.

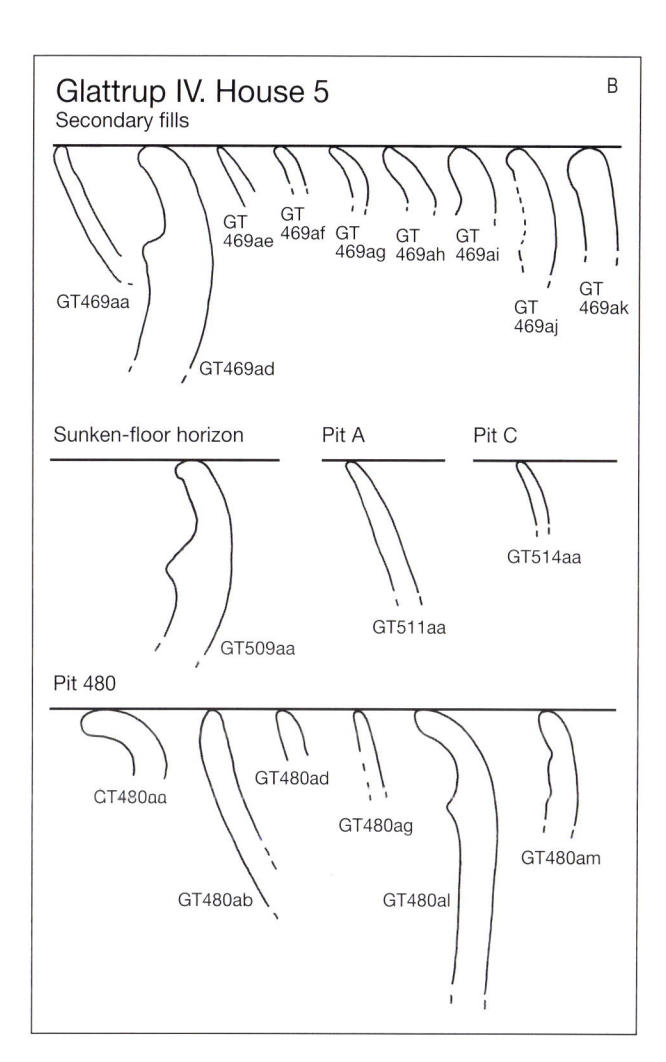

limited likeness to early Resengaard assemblages, e.g. an open bowl (RE695ai) from pit 317, where the rim is turned somewhat towards an upright position. The second rim fragment is very small (RO201ab) and appears fairly irregular. It has a short, turned out rim and represents a minor clay pot. Small clay pots with bent out rim precisely like this are not known from Myrhøj but a single specimen seems relatively close (Jensen, J.A. 1973, Fig. 29). It is difficult to point out clear counterparts from the early Resengaard assemblages.

Pit 23 somewhat north of House 1 contained six profiles among the undecorated ceramics. One of these (RO23aa) represents an open bowl with simple rim. It has a fairly straight side, and corresponds in general to bowls of form group 5 from Myrhøj (Jensen, J.A. 1973:102-103 & Fig. 62-64) and also in general to early assemblages at Resengaard, e.g. from pit 317 (RE695aa). Another profile (RO23ab) is an open bowl with simple rim and convex outer side. It does not have clear counterparts among the published bowls from Myrhøj. It resembles, for instance, specimens from

Chronology of pottery assemblages 213

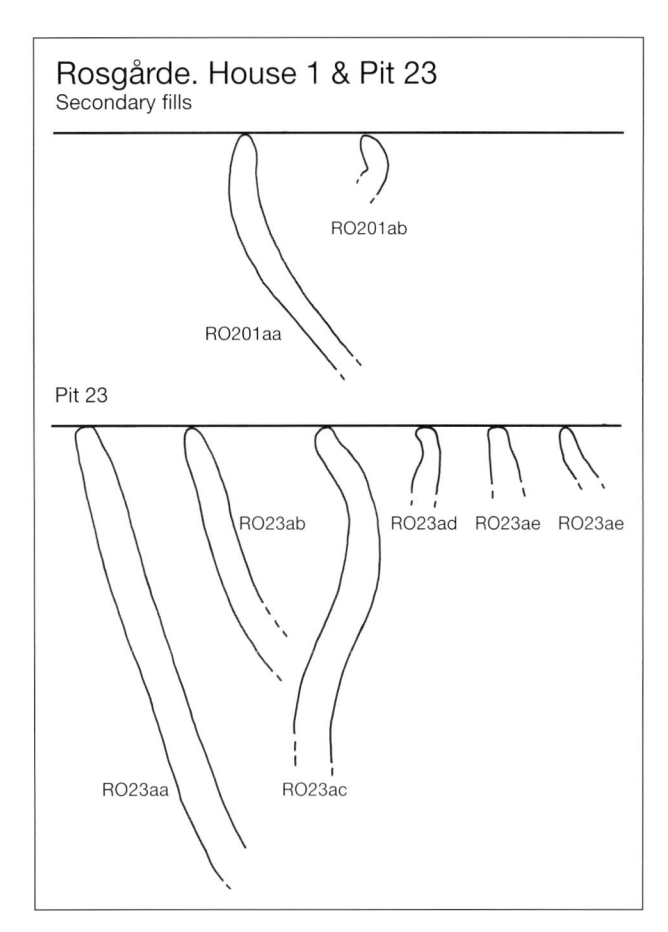

Fig. 3.66. Rosgårde. Selected clay pot profiles from the secondary fills of the site of House 1 and pit 23 somewhat north of the house site. Scale: 1:2.

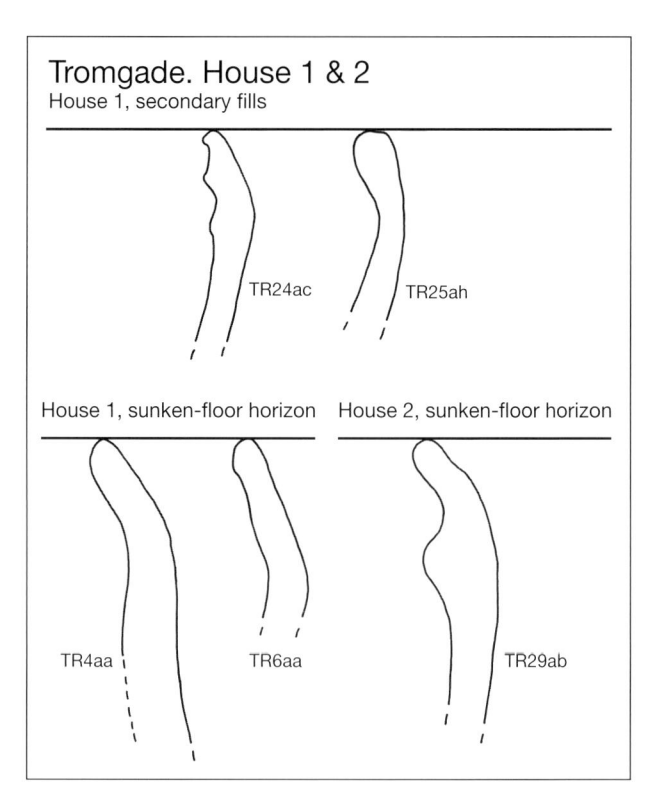

Fig. 3.67. Tromgade. Clay pot profiles from the secondary fills and the sunken-floor horizon of the site of House 2. Scale: 1:2.

Glattrup IV (GT214aa & GT480ab). However, in the early Resengaard assemblages it has affinities with e.g. pit 316 (RE694ad & RE694af). A third profile (RO23ac) with smoothly waving side and out-turned rim has affinities with the Myrhøj material in form group 1 (Jensen, J.A. 1973:96 & Fig. 38-42). It shows some resemblances to the earliest Resengaard assemblages as well, e.g. from pit 161 (RE636aa) and to the secondary fills of House 134 (RE564aa & RE564 bb, ignoring the cordons) and to House 41 (RE406aa). Two other simple rims may represent open bowls (RO23ae & RO23af). A rim (RO23ad) with a concave hollowing just beneath the rim top on the outer side lends the rim top a more marked appearance. It has no clear affinities with any specimen in the Myrhøj material but appears to have some affinity with the reference assemblage of House 41 (RE406ad). Relics of a horizontal cordon are visible on a minor potsherd (RO23an, not illustrated).

Pit 121 was likewise found somewhat north of House 1 but more westerly than pit 23. A single rim fragment represents a piece of undecorated pottery and it proba-bly had an out-turned rim. Little is preserved, however, and clear affinities cannot be noted (RO121aa).

No ornamented ceramics were found in the sunken-floor horizon or the secondary fills of House 1, apart from a tiny potsherd with notch-stamped ornamentation in combination with oblique lines (not illustrated), found in pit 252 (Fig. 4.61). It is greatly reminiscent of elements from the Myrhøj styles (Jensen, J.A. 1973). From a posthole in House 2 south of the ground-floor derives a tiny potsherd with horizontally and obliquely-incised lines, again with resemblances to these styles.

Among the ceramics from pit 121, a single side sherd (RO121ad) was supplied with more parallel, horizontal, notch-stamped lines (Fig. 4.61-4.62). As regards pit 23, only a few ornamented fragments were found and these are – with one exception – of a rather thin ware. Parallel, horizontally-incised furrows mark out the ornamentation on two different sherds (RO23ai & RO23ak), as well as a small fragment with horizontal, parallel lines (RO23am, not illustrated). These decorations only have a relationship in general to the other Beaker ceramics in question.[11]

The extensive system of trial trenches combined with three regular excavation areas merely revealed the site of this single sunken-floor house together with the presumably contemporaneous ground-floor building (House 2). I find it plausible that the above pits with pottery of similar ware also reflect the time of House 1.

When now finally turning to the Tromgade settlement, ceramics from the assemblages of Houses 1, 2, and 414, as well as examples of richly-ornamented pottery from pit 54, are considered in the following. In a direct line, the geographical distance is c. 10 km to Myrhøj and c. 15 km to Resengaard.

Several undecorated rim fragments and side fragments have been found from House 1 and House 2 (Fig. 3.67). Several parts of relatively large vessels have been found at this settlement. Two of these (TR4aa & TR6aa) are represented in the assemblage of House 1 as well as three (TR24ac, TR25ah & TR29ab) from the assemblage of House 2. And yet the profiles of these do not immediately indicate a very specific relationship to other settlement pottery among the locations in focus. However, cordoned rims are present not least in assemblages at Tastum I, Resengaard, Glattrup IV, but also at Myrhøj. There are no rim profiles representing the assemblage of House 414.

Pit 54: this pit 54 was situated near House 2. The ceramics show a rather high degree of ornamentation. Many examples of the ware are fairly thin and fine but a medium thickness and relatively thick-walled pottery without decoration were also found there. This pottery also has coarse tempering as a component.

The ornamented potsherds from House 1 and House 2 are mostly quite small whereas pit 54 had larger fragments preserved (Fig. 4.63-4.66). Only four fragments from House 414 are ornamented, being supplied with notch-stamped lines, cardium impressions and horizontal lines. The chronological position of this building is presumably close to that of Houses 1 and 2. As concerns these houses and pit 54, a slight affinity with the Beaker pottery from Resengaard could perhaps be claimed though the presence of notch-stamped ornaments, spatula incisions, horizontally incised lines and cardium stamps. However, the absence of complex decorative patterns at Resengaard makes it evident that the chronological connection to this settlement is more distant. Against this, it is obvious that the ornamentation of the pottery evidenced not least by that of pit 54 is indeed much closer in design and techniques to the richly-decorated ceramics from Myrhøj, albeit hardly quite contemporaneous with these.

3.8. Towards a settlement chronology for the Limfjord region?

While the Gåsemose ceramics from House 1 first and foremost may point towards the time of House 2 at Resengaard, it is interesting that a mere 5 km or so away in a direct line from the last-mentioned site we also have a further house assemblage with a close chronological relationship to it. This concerns certain ceramics at Hejlskov Hede where several house sites generally appear to have had a late chronological position in the period in question. Not far from this, the Lærkenborg II site is not dated in detail whereas the investigated Virksund I house site is considered by the excavation director to have a late dating in the period in question here, and might thus have been more or less contemporaneous with the Hejlskov Hede settlement. On the whole, however, settlements with "late" pottery are still not presented as frequently as those with the richly-ornamented Beaker pottery of the early Late Neolithic. In this respect, Torben Sarauw has rightly pointed out that the majority of the Beaker pottery from Denmark stems from house site contexts and is hence associated with the domestic sphere (Sarauw 2007b:11 & 44). Concerning the Limfjord region, the percentage is even increasing now because a comparatively large number of new settlement finds have been investigated in recent years. And, moreover, it is not only the sunken floors that contain Beaker fragments but there are also new finds from more or less sizable settlement pits that contain significant numbers of such ceramics. Henceforward, this will reinforce the possibilities for detailed chronological studies based on richly-ornamented settlement pottery.

It is beyond the scope of this work to go deeper into the discussion of the pottery styles but some of the more recent studies should be mentioned as concerns chronological topics. The Late Neolithic Beaker ceramics have more recently been suggested as being confined to the years c. 2350-2000 BC (Vandkilde 2009:74pp). Based on certain radiocarbon determinations, it has conversely been proposed that the "Bell Beaker Culture" even extended far into the second millennium (Prieto-Martinez 2008:159). Further, the chronological position of the Maritime Beakers in Denmark has likewise especially been considered recently (Sarauw 2007b:30pp; 2008:96pp). A three-step chronological sequence of Danish Bell Beaker styles preceding the Late Neolithic has previously been put forward (Liversage 2003:39pp; Prieto-Martinez 2008:117). The existence or not of a Late Neolithic phase with degenerated Beakers has also more recently been discussed (Sarauw 2007b:16p; *cf.* Lomborg 1977). Objects from other find groups might also support the chronological endeavours. For instance, in south-west Jutland, rather interesting early burial contexts have been presented from Solbakkegård IV regarding items such as lobed and tanged flint arrowheads, amber, Beakers and so on (Vandkilde 2007: 92; Siemen 2009:426pp; Sarauw 2008a:108, Fig. 24). In this respect, foreign studies like that of the tiny details of early tanged and barbed flint arrowheads in Brittany might also offer inspiration in terms of chronology (Nicolas 2011). Recordings of valuable find combinations of flint daggers and arrowheads are not only present from grave contexts such as the archery burials and other depositions but also from settlement contexts such as the cellar pit in House 200 at Resengaard.

In my view, the possibilities for establishing a settlement chronology based not least on pottery from the Limfjord region has gradually become more realistic and it would be of paramount importance as a tool to help strengthen cultural and social interpretations of everyday life. Presumably, such a regional chronology could also be useful for other areas of South Scandinavia.

After the methodological considerations (Ch. 1), the interpretations of the sunken-floor houses as physical frames of everyday life (Ch. 2), and the above chronological analysis being of great importance for certain interpretations, we are now well-prepared to zoom in on the sites of the longhouse interiors and explore the manifold vestiges of the residents' activities (Ch. 4).

Notes

1. It has also early been argued that the geographical aspects may impose problems on dagger type determinations in areas far from production centres because re-sharpening would tend to be performed to relatively high degrees (Kaelas 1964).

2. In the main, I can relate to Apel's statement but it seems possible that elements of the form varieties concerning dagger types III and IV might become usable in a slightly more detailed chronology because some of their traits could have been produced for a quite limited period.

3. In preparing for the chronological analysis, it has been extremely important to become acquainted with the entire material, its ware, its form details and variations in order to be convinced that the pottery found at the settlement of Resengaard was well suited to a comprehensive analysis and evaluation of the relative chronology. It was therefore vital to make the original profile drawings personally. This also goes for profile drawings of the other new finds of ceramics from the central Limfjord region.

4. Madsen 1989:17pp; Rasmussen, M. 1993a:103pp. I am also aware that e.g. from Germany and Poland results from a variety of materials from different areas have been presented with the use of multivariate analyses, such as Müller, A.1997, Zimmermann, A.1997, Bartelheim 1997, and Kadrow 1997.

5. Abbreviations for the museum identifications of finds from these settlements are introduced for use in Ch. 3, 4 and 5: RE (Resengaard, SMS 449A), KL (Kluborg II, SMS 722A), GL (Glattrup I/III, SMS 270A), MA (Marienlyst Strand, SMS 519A), GR (Granlygård, SMS 560A), HE (Hellegård, SMS 654A), GT (Glattrup IV, SMS 695A), RO (Rosgårde, SMS 731A), and TR (Tromgade, SMS 746A). Regarding finds from Gåsemose, the abbreviation GÅ (applied by the National Museum) is maintained.

6. A clay pot profile (RE290aa), was found at the edge of a later pit disturbing the sunken floor of House 14. This position creates reservations regarding this specimen as concerns its context and hence it is not included in the account of the House 14 assemblage. The profile has a broad, turned out rim with slightly concave outer rim side above the distinct "shoulder" and a slightly convex inner rim side. It is not possible to point to a clear relationship to any of the four reference assemblages. I presume that the profile belongs to the pit. Perhaps it might stem from about the time of the three-aisled House 25 to the east of it.

7. A number of potsherds (Pit 325) found in a trial trench just north of House 198 at Resengaard possibly belong to about the same time. Among these were four clay pot profiles (Cat. A): RE633ab: having a chamfered rim top, it shows no closer affinities with profiles from the four reference assemblages. RE633ac: the rim top might have a slight relationship to the assemblage of House 2 (RE7ak from the secondary fills). RE633aa: with a faintly curving side, it represents a simple, open bowl which in general might have affinities with the assemblages of House 134, House 41 and House 2. RE633ad: might also represent a bowl, like the foregoing. As earlier mentioned, a potsherd (RE633ae) had decoration of cardium impressions (Fig.4.39).

8. As regards two small pottery assemblages, both likely deriving from pit contexts, it has not been possible to track a recording of the exact find spots at Resengaard. The find area was probably closer to House 240, possibly to the east of it. One of these assemblages (281) consists of 7 rim profiles (RE890aa, RE890ab, RE890ac, RE890ad, RE890ae, RE890af & RE890ag, see Cat. A). These profiles will not be evaluated as regards affinities with other materials. The

other assemblage (318) consists of 6 rim profiles (RE1070ab, RE1070ac, RE1070 ad, RE1070ae, RE1070af, & RE1070ag). It is immediately evident that some of the profiles in particular resemble assemblages of an early date at the settlement but these shall not be analysed and evaluated either.

9. A rim derived from a posthole (54) immediately east of culture layer 293. No obvious remainders of buildings were found in the area. Its almost upright rim above a marked transition to the body combined with a smoothly shaped inner side shows some affiliation to, not least, the assemblage of House 41 (RE412aa, from the sunken floor) and House 2 (RE135aa, from the sunken floor).

10. The question of the proper chronological position of the Egehøj material especially concerns the fact that the archaeological dating of the pottery and other items challenges the somewhat later ^{14}C dating (Rasmussen 1993a, Fig. 76a; Boas 1983:99pp). In my perception, Niels Axel Boas' suggestion of a very early dating of the Egehøj material is now substantiated by the affinities to certain Resengaard ceramics. For more about the incongruity between the archaeological dating and the radiocarbon determination, see Rasmussen 1995:94.

11. A flint dagger fragment of the handle (RO201ea) with lenticular cross-section found in the secondary fills seems to belong to a type II dagger but helps little to refine the dating.

Chapter 4

Artefacts, pits, patches, and daily life activities

Exploring the soil patches, pits, artefacts and plant residues found in the floor horizons in order to find evidence of the residents' everyday doings is the central topic of this chapter. Deepening our knowledge of the activities performed and of the specific kinds of use to which the available interior spaces of the longhouses were put essentially relies on these physical remainders. In a broader sense, improved acquaintance with these activities will widen our understanding of the conditions for existence and living in our regional context of South Scandinavia during the Late Neolithic and emerging Bronze Age.

When writing on the domestic space in Southern Britain's Bronze Age, John C. Barrett expressed an important view that also reaches to the core of this present work: "Archaeologists take the object of their study to be the material residues of the human past. These residues appear to derive from, and to thus represent a record of a number of complex and extinct processes. As a consequence it appears that archaeologists must identify those extinct processes if they are to explain how the record was formed" and further that "…material culture in itself means nothing until it is situated within a regime of interpretation" (Barrett 1997:87pp).

One of the most significant virtues of the sunken-floor house sites is the possibility of obtaining a broad spectrum of knowledge on traces of daily life because recent ploughing in particular, which often tends to destroy the floors of the house sites, has often not yet reached down to these deep floors, meaning that the amazing qualities of the sunken floors can thus be studied in terms of preserving traces of human daily life millennia ago. Numerous artefacts have been found and recorded in these floor areas. This relates first and foremost to tools and utensils made of clay materials, flint and other kinds of stone.

Such items can be recorded *in situ* in the sunken-floor horizons, while the ground-floor parts are, in many instances, found to be comparatively empty of finds and soil traces.

Concerning the late Stone Age, our archaeological assumptions on the use of tools and other items has often been inspired and substantiated from, not least, three kinds of source. One of these is the massive ethnographical and historical recordings acquired over the last centuries from around the globe regarding the use of things and materials (*cf.* Simonsen 1989b:162pp). Another is the many new experiments carried out, for instance, in order to refine and improve our necessary knowledge of the production or use of certain tools. A considerable body of information now exists in this field and I shall not enter into this subject. The third kind of source that needs to be mentioned is the study and analysis of micro-wear on tools, especially flint tools (Jensen, II.J. 1988:131). It should be noted that such micro-wear analysis has also been carried out on tools from Resengaard and other sites, directly for the purpose of this present work.

Some of the tools may have been mounted on organic parts for their functioning but such evidence has long vanished at the settlements in the Limfjord region. However, fortunate finds from other geographical areas have enlightened this area in some respects. With regard, for instance, to the flint dagger from Wiepenkathen in Stade, west of the Elbe, a wooden handle had been fixed onto it by means of a piece of woollen cloth and, in addition to this, the dagger was further supplied with a decorated leather holster with leather straps (Cassau 1935:199pp; Barber 1991:184). In other instances, it might relate to hard materials such as bone, as known for instance from Çatalhöyük (Hodder 2006, Fig. 105). Bone material has hitherto seldom been recovered from the settlements in the Limfjord region but bone finds from five of the eight wells were preserved at Fosie IV (Björhem & Säfvestad 1989:115pp).

The artefacts, plant remainders and soil traces left in the longhouse floor horizons almost always represent some kind of human behaviour and their placement likely often results from varying kinds of human activity connected to these. We need to be acutely aware of these as vestiges of human doings in order to enrich our knowledge of life in the past. I emphasize this point because these people and their activities sometimes appear completely lost in archaeological publications. Concerning this present work, I consider it an essential task to reflect on the possible human doings and hence to suggest certain vestiges as representing concrete activities in particular spaces of the houses.

As we shall see, some soil observations in the surfaces of the sunken floors turn out to consist of low patches that have otherwise come into existence, i.e. patches that must be understood as something other than regular pits. Besides these and other soil observations, numerous artefacts and plant remainders – sometimes plentiful – provide important data. The preserved, charred macrofossils shall be accounted for and we shall see in detail precisely where different kinds of artefacts were left in the floor horizons. A broad variety of ordinary artefacts from daily life will be illustrated. We shall also consider exactly where the pits were placed and where other kinds of patches came into being. All these vital data form the point of departure for our interpretations of where varying, concrete human activities may have taken place.

4.1. Some *a priori* considerations

The longhouse ground plans in question are characterized by being divided along two axes and this may influence the ordering and organization of activities: the east-west division into a sunken floor and a ground floor versus the north-south division formed by the centre-post construction running through the middle of the interior.

The entrance areas are presumably among the very few that can *a priori* be anticipated to have had a specific function. When a doorway in such longhouses allowed humans passage in and out of the building, certain areas just inside could be expected to have functioned as a space for these movements and would thus have given direct access to and from different parts of the interior. These areas were apparently, in all instances, unbounded by walls and nowhere have any traces of something like an "entrance hall" been identified.

Outer walls, together with panel walls, delimited the areas that provided the room for residents' activities. Sometimes, physical dividing walls and internal compartments may also have restricted the possibility of carrying out certain activities. And yet after scrutinizing and analysing all floor recordings, one essential idea has emerged in this present work, namely that the interiors of the houses can be considered as having been separated into a number of habitual spaces for certain activities. With regard to the ground floors to the west, post-built dividing walls only exceptionally seem to have been present. Regarding the sunken floors to the east, no post-built dividing walls usually separated the activities which, for instance, may relate to certain spaces used for cooking or other doings. Yet we cannot exclude the possibility that blankets, hides etc. could have hung down from the roof construction and thus formed some "light" room divisions.

Many different activities seem to have been performed in the deep floors of the longhouses, their specific areas apparently being "reserved" for one or more activities. Some spaces for certain activities may have been "logically" placed, so to speak, in accordance with the general outlines of use of the buildings.

Artefacts and soil patches

When investigating the sunken areas, the principle ideally followed with regard to Resengaard and the other new settlement sites in question was that only when the excavation directors were convinced – after careful consideration of the find context – that a certain artefact belonged to the sunken-floor horizon was it referred to as a floor find. If not, it had to be considered as belonging to the secondary fills.[1] In relation to this statement, we have to identify certain relationships between artefacts and soil features. Before beginning to systematically go through all the floors, we shall look at some of the challenges we may face. While it is not possible to present all practical considerations and concrete arguments for an understanding of the contexts of artefacts and individual soil features from the houses, I shall present three examples that illustrate the kinds of challenge we are facing when investigating the floor areas.

The first example takes its point of departure in a moderately-sized, shallow soil feature consisting of a patchwork of minor diffuse patches. How might this be interpreted? In my reading, the patchwork-like pattern of the soil feature could very well stem from moderate, successive depressions in the floor subsoil without any regular digging being done into the soil. I term such an appearance a "mosaic patch" but, before giving it this label, it is vital to be sure that it does not concern an ordinary soil feature disturbed by mice galleries or the like. Now, in our example only a few flint nodules were found nearby in the floor horizon. Could that observation be what is left from making, for instance, flint tools on the spot? If so, where is the flint waste, including tiny chips? Might tiny sharp pieces have been collected, for instance, by means of some underlay "catching" it during the working process? And the waste then deposited elsewhere outside (*cf.* Schiffer 1987:63)? The mosaic patch might then have come into being during flint working and other doings repeatedly performed there. In my interpretation, however, I would favour being cautious, without involving the mosaic patch, and would hence only suggest that some kind of flint handling or chipping had taken place here, as evidenced by the concrete finds of flint nodules. With regard to this spot, I would therefore note a "mosaic patch" and some artefacts likely connected to flint working.

The second example takes its starting point in a soil feature containing heat-affected/cracked stones within a floor area. A stone hammer is found nearby along with some broken pottery. Could these observations stem from connected activities? The stones with heat impact could have been used for heating up things or substances, the potsherds could stem from pottery used for cooking or heating fluids or other things. The hammer could well have acted as a pestle for crushing, for instance, dried herbs or as a simple nutcracker. Would these traces together indicate the cooking of meals involving, for instance, the crushing of dried plants and boiling of food? I believe that such an understanding is possible. Yet when suggesting actual activities, I would again prefer to remain on the side of caution and – apart from heating – go no further than to see the artefacts as possible traces of hammering/crushing and pottery handling/cooking.

As a third example, we can ask whether remainders from arrow production are actually identified when we find the combination of a flint arrowhead and a notched flint piece within a limited floor area? Might the notched piece have been used for shaping a thin wooden shaft? And a flint arrowhead subsequently mounted on it? Such a process cannot be excluded but I would, in this case, also be reluctant to suggest a specific activity on this basis. A concrete example of this artefact combination derives from Resengaard, House 1 in the area of soil patch C. Notched pieces are much ignored in the literature on the Late Neolithic and emerging Bronze Age but well displayed in the presentation of a settlement from Sør-Jæren in Norway, where it relates to relatively coarse flakes supplied with finely retouched notches (Lindblom 1982, Fig. 10-11).

Core areas and activity spaces

It is my assumption that certain soil features in the sunken-floor horizons may represent some kind of core areas for particular activities. The spread of tools and debris trodden down into the subsoil or on top of it, left in shallow patches or in regular floor layers, in my reading may offer other important indications of the scenes of activity. What I term "activity space" thus relates to evidence of artefacts, plant materials, debris and sometimes one or more pits or patches, all within a more or less limited floor area.

Yet it can be difficult to demonstrate a direct connection between artefact remains and soil patches in the suggested scenes of activity. The ideal situation – that of being able to conclude safely that certain soil features stem from the activities evidenced from certain tools – is relatively seldom present. It is therefore necessary to treat the subject very cautiously. From a source-critical point of view, we must further be aware that it is not impossible that, in some instances, tools that had absolutely nothing to do with the activities carried out in a certain space could have been left there for other reasons, or quite accidentally. On the other hand, certain activities would probably not leave traces in the soil that are identifiable millennia later, whereas artefacts from the activities might have been left there.

The formation of simple-looking soil patches may, in some instances, have been rather complex. I presume that these patches may sometimes stem from multifaceted processes and their presence could have been caused by one or more activities. Such doings may thus have had a direct physical effect on the soil by moving and mixing it with other soils or substances.

My criterion for suggesting activity spaces applies to floor areas where concrete artefacts and/or observed soil features may be left over from former activities. Ideally, such activity spaces could be separated by a relatively broad strip of floor free from finds and soil patches, perhaps indicating a kind of "elbowroom" between working areas. However, such a free space is not always found. In a few instances, it is rather difficult to suggest logical delimitations between activity spaces, due to rather dense finds and soil features covering larger floor areas. As we shall see later, a prominent example of this is the total number of observations and finds in the southern aisle to the west in the sunken floor of House 2 at Resengaard.

The activity spaces could encompass many different activities and some of these may somehow have been connected. Yet, in my understanding, these activity spaces are not to be understood as areas in which the activities necessarily represent all stages in a given process. Some work processes might even have had many steps, of which just one or a number took place in a given activity space. The suggested activity-space delimitations do not thus exclude the possibility that activities in one activity space could have been part of working processes in another. I imagine that some activity spaces could represent areas habitually used by certain persons as their "usual residence" within the longhouses, i.e. for stay, work and maybe eating.

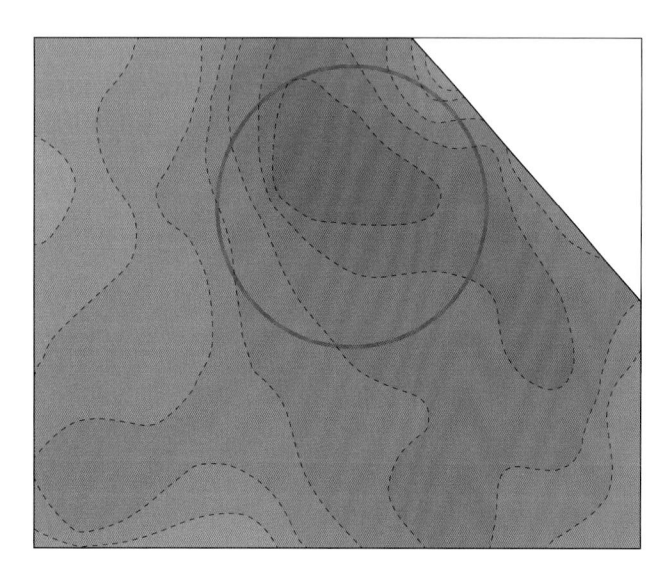

Fig. 4.1. Low zones in the sunken floors. These zones, located by means of numerous depth measurements, are presented as circles with diameters of 2½ metres. The example stems from the western part of the sunken floor at the site of House 2 at Resengaard. Every interval indicates a 5 cm increase in depth.

No activity spaces, or maybe just a single one, can be suggested for some of the floors, whereas in others several activity spaces can be proposed. Furthermore, the position of the lowest area in a sunken floor – which I term the "low zone" – in many instances may indicate a relationship to certain essential activities and so these are worth considering in more detail (Fig. 4.1). In the daily life of this ancient period, there could have been a number of activity spaces other than those proposed in the following relating to activities that left no evident traces at all.

When it comes to my suggestions of "daily life activities" it must be emphasized that the presentation of activity spaces cannot be made entirely objectively but will unavoidably be biased by my personal view of the floors.

Systematic study of floor horizons

It is my overall understanding that complex processes may sometimes have been behind the formation of simple-looking patches, that soil features in many cases indicate "core areas" for certain activities, and that the distribution of artefacts left behind is often an indication of spaces in which certain activities were performed. It is hence my view that studies of the distribution of soil features and artefacts in the floor horizons need to be systematic and focused on the detail in order to work seriously towards an improved knowledge of the activities performed there and thereby the important aspects of the living conditions of the residents. Even with the risk that, now and then, an artefact does not really stem from relevant activities in the area where it is found, it is still vital to carry out systematic studies as I am convinced that the general patterns of distribution present important evidence of the activities.

A find spot indicated on a house ground plan refers to the centre of the item or items recovered. As regards instances where the find contains several pieces, such as for instance a concentration of potsherds, the radius from the marking is ideally set to be up to 15 cm (Fig. 4.2). Concentrations of finds may occasionally exceed this measure and, in every instance, the excavation directors take responsibility for the decision. However, as often as is reasonable and possible, a new find spot is ideally marked on the ground plans where a little free space occurs between the spread of items. A soil patch or pit also, in some instances, marks out the find spot and it may sometimes be of sizeable dimensions.

As regards suggestions concerning indoor activities, the premise I take is that most artefacts found in the floor horizons were generally used or handled near the find spot. The reality that many of the objects are not complete and are sometimes broken into rather small pieces may support this understanding because the fragmentation presumably often resulted from use on the spot. The soil contexts of the finds belonging to the floor horizon are mainly regular pits, various patches resulting from physical activities, floor layers and the subsoil surface, including when objects were trodden or otherwise pressed down into it (Fig. 4.3 & 4.4).

The floor horizons may frequently appear rather poor in terms of tool remainders and other utensils, in contrast to the secondary fills which sometimes had numerous and quite varied artefact remainders. It is, however, necessary to clarify that only in very exceptional circumstances might finds from the secondary fills form the basis for proposing activities in the sunken-floor spaces. No matter how interesting or exciting these objects may be, such finds above the sunken-floor horizons do not provide direct evidence of specific activities in a certain floor area.

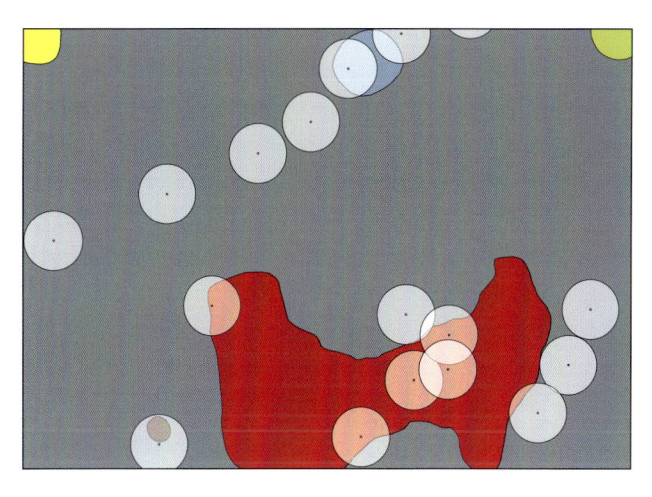

Fig. 4.2. Find spots in the floor horizons. With a few exceptions, the spots normally indicate a find area within a maximum radius of 15 cm as schematically shown here. The example shows finds in the area of patch A from House 2 at Resengaard. When a find spot is marked within a pit (or patch), the find may also belong to that context in general.

Characterizing the activities

Various specific expressions are proposed to designate certain activities. Some of these may need further explanation and shall be elaborated on here. This concerns terms such as drying/roasting/charring, pottery handling/cooking, hammering/crushing, scraping, and knife cutting.

Drying/roasting/charring/cooking/heating: the presence of shallow patches with heat-affected/cracked stones in floor horizons is considered a possible indicator of such activities. The term "roasting" is here understood as the heating of plant material to the point that it achieves a crispy and sometimes brownish appearance. In this present context, I am specifically thinking of the process of treating cereals with heat at some level. In my understanding, the cereals would lose their capacity for germination during a roasting process. When using only low heat, the humidity of the cereals could be more or less reduced but their viability would not necessarily be lost in this way and the term "drying" therefore applies to this. At the other end of the scale, great heat over an even short period can cause comprehensive carbonization of cereals. The heating elements used in such processes could, in these specific

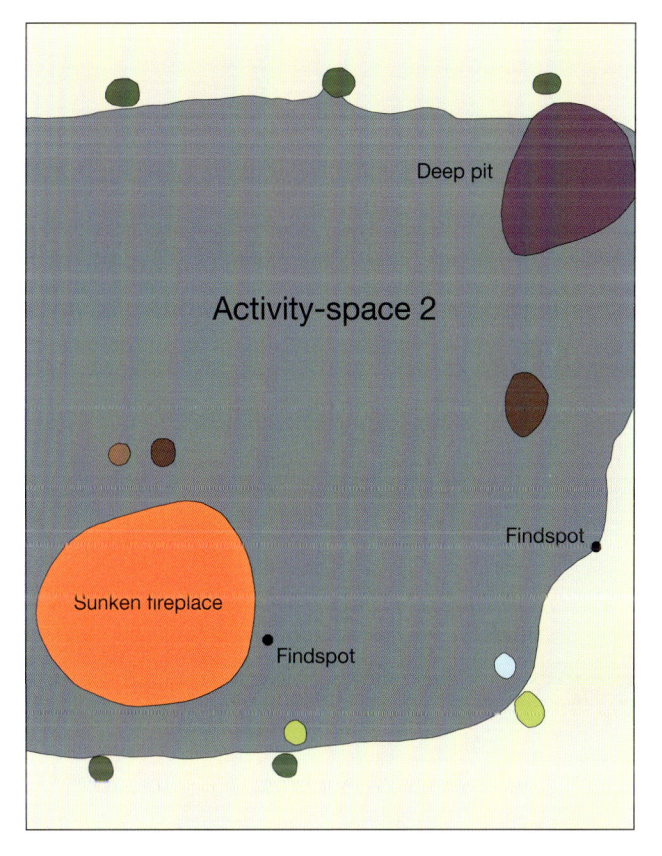

Fig. 4.3. Activity spaces with core areas. Some of the activity spaces are considered to have one or more pits or patches as presumed core areas. The example relates to the sunken floor of House 3 at Glattrup IV, where the large pit to the northeast and the sunken fireplace to the southwest may both have played vital roles in the production and temporary storage of beer, and hence both are considered to belong to the same activity space.

Artefacts, pits, patches, and daily life activities 223

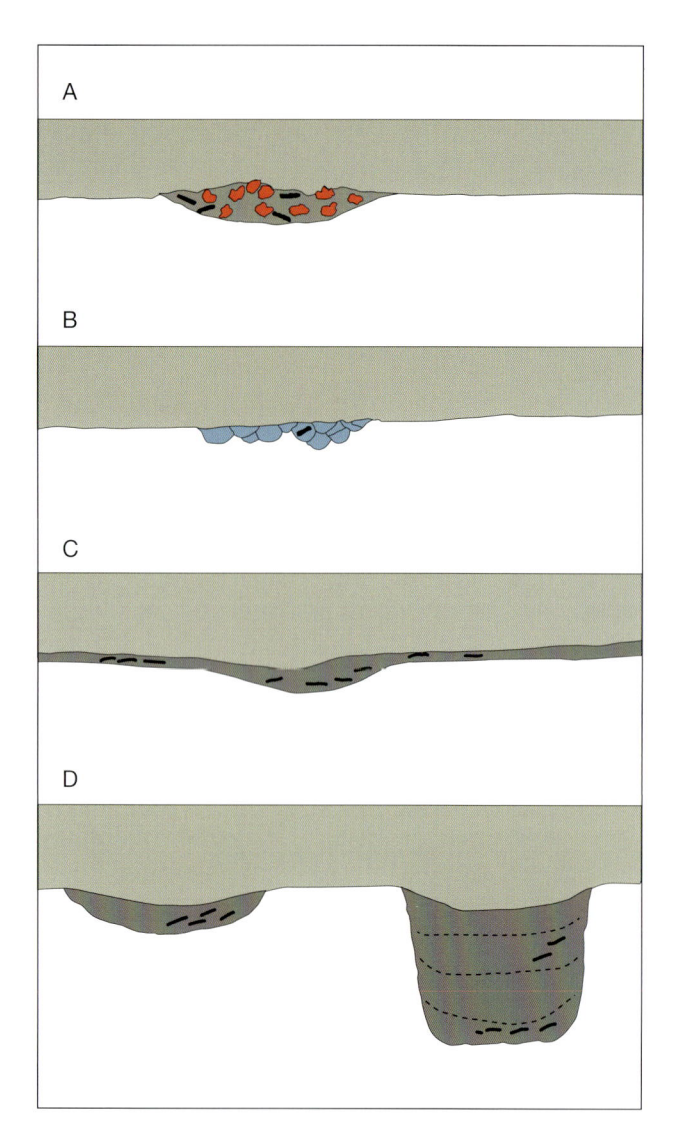

Fig. 4.4. Floor horizon situations. As understood in this work, the sunken-floor horizons (or floor horizons) solely relate to traces of activity left from the period when the building was in use. Four hypothetical fieldwork situations are schematically outlined here as sections, whereby the remains (covered by thick secondary fills, here greyish, topsoil not shown) belong to the sunken-floor horizons. Artefacts are represented by short, flat symbols. A: Shallow soil feature with heat-affected/cracked stones, being a "scorched-stone patch". In my understanding, this kind of a patch gradually came into existence and extended to its later dimensions through repeated removal of the stones for heating, subsequent replacement in the area in their heated state, and the addition of new stones when the old ones crumbled. Unintentionally, diverse soil components and small charcoal pieces would frequently have been brought with them. In instances where a floor layer is present, the horizontal patch boundary may have merged diffusely due to the way the patch was created. B: A pattern of minor diffuse patches, "mosaic patch", which in the present author´s interpretation may derive from moderate, repeated depressions in the floor. In other words, no pit was dug here but the patch may well have formed a core area for some of the activities performed. C: A floor layer accumulated in a shallow hollowing, being thicker than elsewhere. No indication that it forms a special patch or a regular pit. D: A low pit and a large, deep pit. After their functional period, these were filled with diverse soil and waste (i.e. primary fills) that differs more or less significantly from the secondary fills. Due to natural compression of the pit soils, the secondary fills have sunk somewhat into the uppermost parts of these pits.

houses, primarily have been natural stones. Some of these were fine-grained, others more coarse-grained. These could break or crack when exposed to considerable heat. As well as the state of the cereals, the heat-affected/cracked stones might therefore be an indicator of drying-roasting-charring processes. In flaming or glowing fireplaces, the stones could have been heated to the temperatures needed. The stones may thus have reached several hundred degrees Celsius, depending on the needs of the specific purpose. From experience, it was presumably well-known how long stones had to remain in the heat to reach the temperatures required. Various daily cooking activities could have been performed using the stones. Inside the houses, the heating effect of warm stones must, in my view, be considered an important side-effect.

Pottery handling /cooking: potsherds left in the floor horizons are seen as a possible indicator of such activities. By the term "cooking" I here also mean the preparation of foods intended mainly for human consumption, and this also embraces food preparation devoid of any heating, as well as the storage of different foods, herbs, spices etc. Different kinds of pottery were presumably often used for preparing meals and storing foods.

The above shows that I find it necessary to operate two criteria for cooking in relation to the fieldwork observations. On the one hand, a patch with heat-affected/cracked stones placed in the floor horizon is one criterion for suggesting cooking as a possible activity. Different ways of preparing or exposing food to heat are then implied. Such cooking might have involved the use of pottery although this would not necessarily have been the case. On the other hand, the presence of pottery remainders *in situ* in the sunken-floor horizon is the other criterion for suggesting cooking as a possible activity. Various ways of preparing and otherwise handling food with or without exposure to heat are then assumed. Cooking could have involved the use of pottery but not necessarily the use of heat.

Contrary to the deep "cooking pits" of later prehistoric periods, the use of heated stones would have taken place in the level of – or just a little below the level of – the sunken-floor surfaces. The term "cooking pit" would therefore not apply because these stone concentrations in the sunken-floor longhouses (and in certain minor houses) would not have been dug down from the beginning. In my understanding, these just became a little lowered through the gradual removal of material during repeated, daily use. Apart from some soil and often numerous heat-affected/cracked stones, these "scorched-stone patches", as I prefer to call them, often showed some presence of fragile, much crumbled small stone pieces and some parts more or less turned into tiny grains like coarse sand. The presence of these latter fractions is not referred to further in the following descriptions of the patches in the individual house sites. Now and then some seemingly "new" stones with no heat impact and different artefacts were present in these patches.

In order to make just an ordinary meal, some material may for instance have been fetched from storage jars, while other foods may have been collected from outside and brought in, perhaps in different clay pots. Some other earthenware may have been used directly for the heating. So, in all, several ceramics may have been involved and, over time, some clay pots could occasionally have broken apart. Pieces may thereby have been left or trodden down into the floor surface. Other kinds of tools may also have been used in the process of preparing a meal. Aspects of what here, for instance, is termed knife cutting, crushing or hammering may well have been an integral part of the cooking activities.

Potsherds in the sunken floors may also be an indicator of other kinds of activity in which pottery was involved. No obvious way of distinguishing between potsherds for cooking activities and other pottery handling exists. It cannot even be ruled out that certain kinds of pot may have been used for several different purposes. However, the expression "pottery handling" is meant to designate any function other than cooking. It may thus include a broad variety of doings.

Hammering/crushing: stone hammers left in the floor horizons are seen as possible indicators of activities involving hammering or crushing. The term "hammering" is taken to mean the beating of an object, for instance in order to change its form or position. The outcome would have depended on factors such as the weight and strength of the hammer, the force involved, the qualities of the object, and the underlay. The objects may, of course, have been organic as well as inorganic. By "crushing", in the present context, I mean the working of organic and other objects in order to split them or create finer particles. This could, for instance, have included the crushing of herbs, spices, nuts etc. inside the house and, of course, a wide variety of activities concerned with the powdering of other materials. I term the tools "stone hammers" without the possibility of distinguishing between the functions of hammering or crushing, i.e. used, for instance, as pestles or nutcrackers. The hammers usually show clear traces of wear on their hard surface (Cat. B). The hammers of fine-grained stone in particular seem very strong and most probably would not splinter unless massive force was applied. The special flint hammers with coarsely crushed surfaces, in some contrast to other stone hammers, are considered later.

Scraping: flint scrapers left in the floor horizons are seen as indicators of scraping activities. The term "scraping" is here taken to mean the reduction or removal of an object's surface. Many different items of organic origin may have been exposed to scraping processes but some kinds of relatively smooth surfaces from inorganic materials could also have been worked on by scraping. The scraping tools can often be expected to have been harder and have greater power of resistance than the surface of the objects to be worked. It seems rather plausible, however, that various scraping tools could have been made of relatively soft materials. In actual fact, depending on the nature of the job, I presume that scrapers may have been made from a variety of materials such as, for instance, antler, bone and wood, as well as flint. For example, when cleaning clay pots inside to remove the charred remains of cooking processes, flint scrapers would probably have been too harsh for the inner surfaces. Softer scrapers of organic material would presumably have worked better for such purposes, without damaging the inner sides. Clear scratches that could stem from the inside having been scraped have not been identified in the Resengaard pottery.

Only scraping tools made out of flint have been preserved in the sunken-floor houses and they may have been used for tasks such as treating skin, wood and other organic materials. Several kinds of flint scrapers would presumably have been involved in some processes, and these tools may cover a wide spectrum of dimensions and fineness, ranging from rather heavy scrapers with strong working edges to quite light ones with fine working edges.

Knife cutting: flint knives left in floor horizons are considered possible indicators of such activity, and may include a very broad range of different activities. This could often have involved the reduction of objects and their splitting up into parts but might also just have related to some kind of scratching on the surface. With these sharp flint knives, it would have been possible to cut through many different kinds of organic materials such as stalks and roots or cut through strings and bands, carve slices of meat and cut off meat from bones, cut out hides, cut out grooves in wood or otherwise carve wooden materials. I recognize knives as a flint piece with a sharp edge and blunted back or a flint piece having a corresponding naturally blunt surface, showing retouch from wear.

Several tables, diagrams and others will sum up the data and observations from the 43 house sites. These include a table on find spots (Fig. 4.67), on pits, patches, floor layers, ard-furrows, and depths of sunken floors (Fig. 4.69), on scorched-stone patch areas (Fig. 4.70), and on daily life activities (Fig. 4.73). An example of the weight spread of the heat-affected/cracked stones is also shown as a diagram (Fig. 4.71). Examples of soot/soot-crust placement on pottery (Fig. 4.72) are shown. Numerous illustrations of soil bench sections have been selected and placed together in order to make comparisons as easy as possible (Fig. 4.68).

Concerning the finds from Resengaard, in particular, the three catalogues can be consulted for further information. In the following detailed presentation of each house site, some references will firstly be given to the main numbers of the catalogues concerning artefacts from secondary fills. Thereafter, charred plant remainders, where present, will be referred to from the sunken-floor horizons in particular. In Figs. 5.8, 5.9 and 5.10, the amount of potsherds, worked flint and burned flint in secondary fills and culture layers is accounted for in relation to all the house sites focused on, except Gåsemose. Unless otherwise stated, the artefact photos are full scale or close to full scale. For dimensions and measurements of Resengaard artefacts, see Cataloque A and B.

4.2. Interpreting the floors in twelve longhouse sites at Resengaard

The artefacts, plant materials, floor levels, low zones, pits and soil patches from 12 longhouses are presented and considered in the following. These remainders are further interpreted in terms of certain daily activities. The key to the house ground plans remains the same (Fig. 2.7). As stated above on activity spaces, the latter cannot be produced entirely objectively, and it is therefore preferable that neutral lists of artefacts from the sunken-floor horizons are each presented separately in the following.

House 1 (Fig. 4.5 & 4.6; Fig. 4.68.A & B)

Interesting ceramics (Cat. A: RE6, RE11, RE21, RE39, RE49, RE56, RE73, RE 75, RE159, & RE188) and stone artefacts (Cat. B: RE6, RE143, & RE155) stem from the secondary fills. Numerous charred plant materials (Cat. C: RE25, RE27, RE54, RE64, RE77, RE78, RE79, & RE136) derive from the sunken-floor horizon.

Very many find spots were recorded in the sunken-floor horizon. A flint scraper (RE195ea) found in a wall posthole belonging to the northern long side presumably stems from the time the house was built, although it cannot be excluded that it may be older. A large stone hammer (RE194ea) was found in a pit that was subsequently covered by the wall of the southern long side. The organic materials from the sunken floor primarily consist of a rather large amount of charred cereals, some seeds from weeds and a few tiny pieces of hazelnut shell, although just one number is referred to below (RE136ga). The other macrofossils are not listed among the find spots below because these were taken from larger areas of the floor horizon, as we shall see later. A few potsherds (RE25aa) that belong to the sunken-floor horizon stem from a soil sample for flotation but are not listed among the find spots. A tiny potsherd (RE153aa) with a horizontally incised cardium ornamentation must be an accidentally mixed up "antique" from an older settlement, presumably in the vicinity. A flint axe with "hanging" cutting edge (RE20ea) is likewise an "antique", in this case from the Single Grave Culture. It may have been kept as a raw material, for some ideological reason or just as a kind of curiosity but I favour the idea that it was used for chopping purposes in the area. A presumed stone anvil of moderate size was present in the easternmost scorched-stone patch.

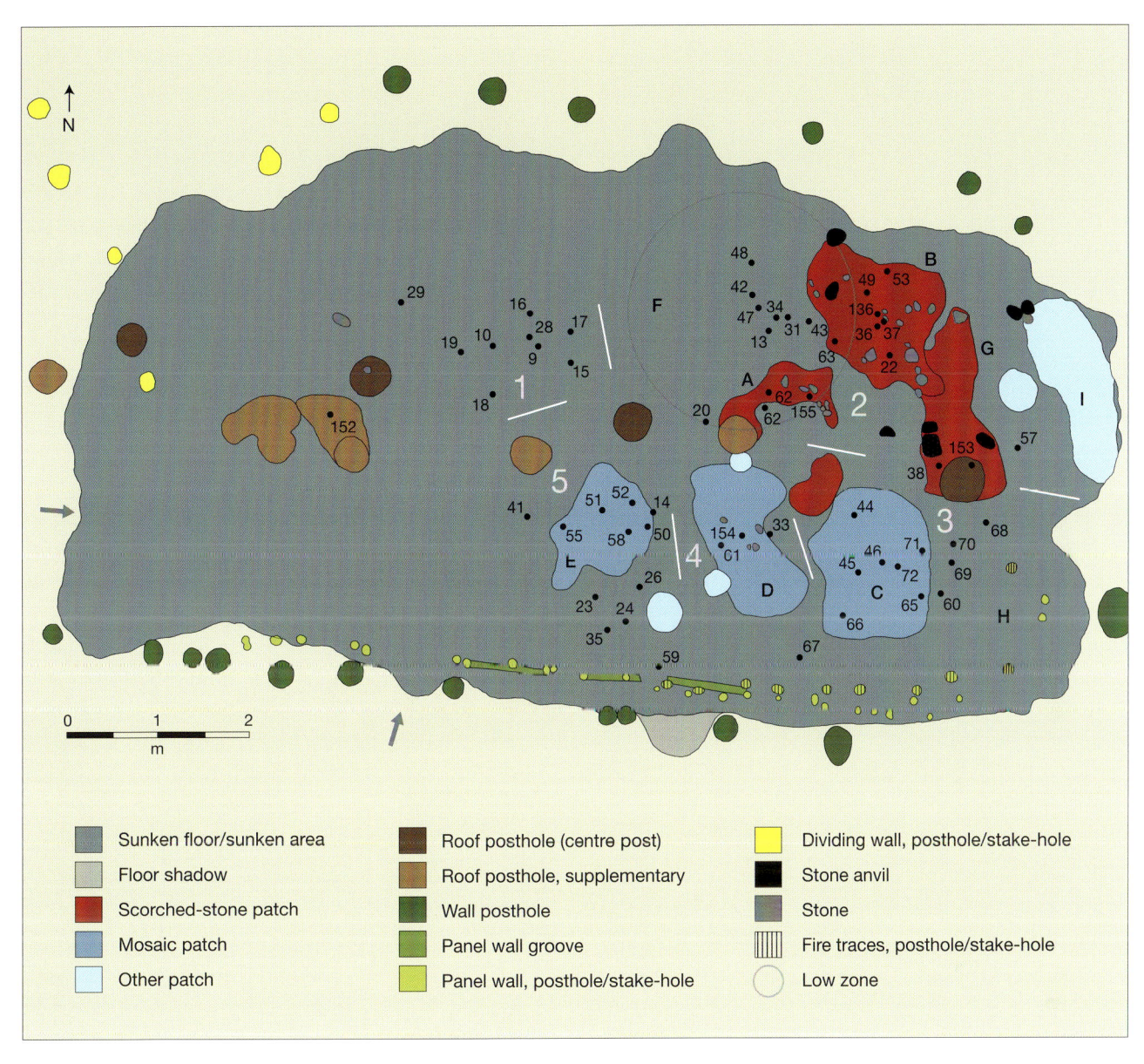

Fig. 4.5. Resengaard, House 1. Ground plan of sunken floor, cleaned. A division into five activity spaces is proposed. Apart from stone anvils and scorched stones, the artefacts found in situ in the sunken-floor horizon overall involve very many find spots: **9**: 2 potsherds (RE9); **10**: 1 flint scraper, retouched sub-circularly (RE10ea).**13**: 1 flint scraper, handle fragment (RE13ea); **14**: 1 flint nodule (RE14ea); **15**: 2 potsherds and a piece of burned flint (RE15); **16**: 1 potsherd (RE16); **17**: 1 potsherd (RE17); **18**: 1 piece of worked flint (RE18); **19**: 1 piece of burned bone (RE19); **20**: 1 flint axe, "antique" (RE20ea); **22**: 1 stone hammer, crushing marks in the ends, presumably also a smoothening tool (RE22ea); **23**: 1 potsherd (RE23); **24**: 1 potsherd (RE24aa, the same vessel as RE35aa); **26**: 1 piece of worked flint, fragment (RE26); **28**: 1 potsherd (RE28aa); **29**: 1 flint scraper (RE29ea); **31**: 1 potsherd (RE31aa); **33**: 1 potsherd (RE33); **34**: 1 bottom fragment (RE34aa); **35**: 1 potsherd (RE35aa, from the same vessel as RE24aa); **36**: 1 clay pot bottom, fragment (RE36aa); **37**: 1 flint nodule, 2 pieces of worked flint & 3 pieces of burned flint (RE37ea & RE37); **38**: 1 flint scraper (RE38ea); **41**: 1 potsherd (RE41aa); **42**: 1 loom weight fragment (RE42aa); **43**: 1 potsherd (RE43aa); **44**: 1 flint nodule (RE44ea); **45**: 1 flint nodule (RE45ea) & 2 potsherds (RE45); **46**: 1 potsherd, bottom-side (RE46aa); **47**: 3 potsherds (RE47); **48**: 4 potsherds (RE48); **50**: 1 potsherd, with soot crust (RE50); **51**: 1 flint nodule (RE51ea); **52**: 1 flint scraper, burned (RE52ea); **53**: 1 flint sickle fragment, burned (RE53ea); **55**: 1 presumed flint nodule, burned (RE55); **57**: 1 clay pot bottom (RE57aa); **58**: 1 potsherd (RE58aa); **59**: 1 potsherd & 2 pieces of worked flint (RE59); **60**: 1 potsherd (RE60aa); **61**: 1 potsherd, bottom-side (RE61aa); **62**: 2 secondarily burned potsherds (with find spots separately, RE62); **63**: 1 flint scraper, burned (RE63ea); **65**: 1 flint arrowhead, tanged & 1 flint nodule (RE65ea; RE65eb); **66**: 1 flint scraper (RE66ea); **67**: 1 piece of worked flint, with retouch (RE67); **68**: 1 potsherd, rim (RE68aa); **69**: 1 flint nodule (RE69ea); **70**: 1 flint nodule (RE70ea); **71**: 1 potsherd (RE71); **72**: 1 flint piece with notch (RE72ea); **136**: Charred macrofossils (RE136gu); **152**: 2 potsherds, rims; **153**: 9 potsherds, 3 pieces of worked flint & 2 pieces of burned flint (RE153aa; RE153); **154**: 2 potsherds, 1 secondarily burned potsherd & 1 piece of worked flint (RE154).

Fig. 4.6. Resengaard, House 1. A: The eastern part of the sunken floor under excavation. Seen from the north, although almost vertically. B: Scorched-stone patch B. Among the dust of charred material, giving it a black colouring, a number of charred cereals are visible. Seen from the west. C: This flint sickle, presumably a little older than House 1, was recovered from the top of a small pit (135) east of House 128.

Compared to certain other longhouses at the settlement, the sunken floor reached a relatively minor depth in the central floor area. A low zone was observable in the northern part of the floor, whereas the highest parts were mainly found to the west and southwest. South of the sunken floor middle, in particular, the observable areas were mostly rather flat-floored. Traces of animal activity, probably from mice, were generally noted in the eastern and central parts of the sunken-floor horizon but these only appear to have been modestly disturbed. The oblique ramp would have given easy access to most sunken-floor areas where several interesting patches, including some minor soil features, were found. This first concerns the five major soil features A, B, C, D, and E, all with relatively firm edges, and four more relatively large but to varying degrees diffuse patches, F,

G, H, and I. All these soil patches were rather shallow, being some 5-15 cm deep apart from the faint "patch F", which cannot be stated. As these patches appeared so relatively distinct from each other, the explanation is likely to be that each one had its own developed area of activity. The soil features of the sunken floor generally consisted of greyish or greyish-brown, sandy clay, unless stated otherwise. The placement of patches C, D, E and H to the south in a row is a particularly remarkable trait and unparalleled in any of the other sunken floors from the Resengaard settlement. To the south, in the western area of the sunken floor, no separate patches were observable. The emptiness of this area must be due to the presence of the entrance and the residents' need for free space there to move around and maybe temporarily unload things. This floor part was thus an area of c. 4.8 m E-W and c. 1.8 m N-S without traces of any special arrangements or patches observable. The significant soil patches in the sunken-floor horizon are briefly characterized as follows:

A: Scorched-stone patch. Sandy, blackish soil with many heat-affected/cracked stones including a relatively large quantity of small pieces. In all, the soil feature was an irregular patch measuring c. 1.44 m x 0.80 m, and a minor patch at its southern end is also regarded as the remains of this.

B: Scorched-stone patch. Sandy, blackish soil coloured by fairly tiny pieces of charcoal and dust from charred organic material. Many heat-affected/cracked stones were present and not least a large quantity of small cracked pieces of such stones. This soil feature formed an irregular patch with surface dimensions of c. 2.08 m x 1.50 m.

C: Mosaic patch. Sandy soil feature with mainly dark, greyish colours. At the surface the patch tended to become almost rectangular with rounded corners. Within the soil feature were several minor patches, probably caused by continued activities and thus, in all, a patch with multiple, simple soil depressions. Dimensions c. 1.56 x 1.36 m.

D: Mosaic patch. Somewhat irregular soil feature with sandy mainly, dark-greyish soil. The edge to the south was relatively darker. A few stones, some of these heat-affected/cracked, were present and hence, in principle, it could also be considered a scorched-stone patch. And yet the whole appearance was very different from the quite distinct scorched-stone patches to the north. Within the soil feature were several minor patches, probably caused by continued activities. Again, this concerns a patch of multiple, simple soil depressions. Surface dimensions c. 1.8 m x 1.04 m. It should be noted that two distinct, minor patches with sandy, greyish soil were found southwest of patch D. These were sub-circular in surface and had diameters of c. 0.26 m and 0.40 m respectively. The former had cut the edge of patch D, and must thus have been later dug although it still belongs to the floor horizon. These patches were both only a few cm deep.

E: Mosaic patch. Sandy patch, with colours varying from greyish to brownish. The patch had a somewhat irregular surface appearance. Within the soil feature were many minor patches, probably again caused by activities and hence, as above, a patch of multiple, simple soil depressions. The dimensions were c. 1.48 x 1.04 m.

F: Shadowy "patch", very thin, diffuse, dimensions not stated. It can be further characterized as sandy with greyish-brown nuances. Scorched stones modestly present in the area but probably did not belong to the patch. Extensive traces of animal activity in the area.

G: Scorched-stone patch, diffusely delimited. Contained sandy, greyish-black soil and a few scattered stones, some of which were heat-affected/cracked. The largest was somewhat rectangular and I suggest that this was a stone anvil. The patch was quite long, and the surface dimensions were approx. 1.92 x 0.92cm, possibly even extending vaguely a little further to the south.

H: Mosaic patch, rather diffuse and shadowy. It was sandy, mainly greyish-black and appeared to some degree to have the same character as patch C. It soon faded out during excavation.

I: Lengthy patch, rather discrete appearance. Light, greyish-brown sandy soil. No particulars observed. Dimensions c. 2.06 x 0.76 m.

In my view, the sunken floor encompasses five main activity spaces in which one or more possible activities may have been concentrated. These are, to some degree, coincidental with the observed soil features. The artefact remains in the sunken floor horizon appear to represent comparatively many and varied doings. The activities proposed include pottery handling/cooking, drying/roasting/charring/cooking/heating, knife cutting, scraping, weaving, hammering/crushing, raw flint handling/chipping and, presumably, also smoothening. Activities involving scorched stones primarily appear to have taken place in activity spaces 1 and 2, while just a few heat-affected/cracked stones were present in patch D. It is quite interesting that no underlying soil feature was recordable in the sunken-floor horizon as regards the suggested activity space 1. Conversely, artefact remainders were found directly in the area of the major part of the diffuse soil feature F. Somewhat corresponding to this, a flint scraper was the only recorded artefact in the area of patch G, and found in the periphery to the south.

As for the suggested compartment to the northwest of the sunken floor, no activities can be ascribed to it but it could well have been a kind of store. Based on the floor traces, the following are suggested as possible doings, separated into five activity spaces:

1. Scraping and pottery handling/cooking. A piece of worked flint and a piece of burned bone present in this area too.

2. Drying/roasting/charring/cooking/heating, pottery handling/cooking, weaving, scraping, raw flint handling/chipping and chopping with the "antique" axe. Besides hammering/crushing, the stone hammer may also have had smoothening purposes. No suggestion is put forward as regards the burned sickle fragment also present in this relatively extensive activity space.

3. Raw flint handling/chipping, pottery handling/cooking, and scraping. The presence of an arrowhead and a flint piece with notch might perhaps indicate some working on arrows and shafts also but this is not directly my suggestion.

4. Pottery handling/cooking and drying/roasting/charring/cooking/heating. Regarding the last activity, it cannot be excluded that the stones do not represent a significant activity here. A piece of worked flint present.

5. Raw flint handling/chipping, pottery handling/cooking, and scraping.

House 2 (Fig. 4.7, 4.8, 4.9, & 4.10; Fig. 4.68.C & D)

From the secondary fills stem interesting ceramics (Cat. A: RE7, RE97, RE104, RE107, RE130, & RE191) and stone artefacts (Cat. B: RE7, RE80, RE89, RE96, RE163, RE164, RE175, RE189, & RE191). From the sunken-floor horizon derive charred plant materials (Cat. C: RE8, RE137, RE198, & RE222).

This sunken floor was exceptionally rich in artefact find spots. These belonged to most floor parts but particularly derived from the western half. In the southern half to the west, a relatively large stone, considered to be an anvil, was found *in situ*, and likewise an anvil was found by the eastern gable end. From a pit (pit M) immediately west of the sunken floor near the south side stem 20 potsherds, along with 5 pieces

▶ *Fig. 4.7. Resengaard, House 2. Ground plan of sunken floor, cleaned. The easternmost part with a stone anvil as well as the westernmost part of the sunken floor (and pit M to the south) is shown on Fig. 2.9. A division into five activity spaces is suggested. Apart from the stone anvil to the east and a number of scorched stones, the artefacts found in situ in the sunken-floor horizon overall belong to very many find spots:* **86**: *1 flint scraper (RE86ea);* **88**: *1 flint scraper (RE88ea);* **90**: *1 flint dagger, handle/blade fragment (RE90ea);* **91**: *1 potsherd (RE91aa);* **92**: *1 potsherd (RE92aa);* **93**: *1 potsherd, fairly thick side (RE93aa);* **95**: *4 potsherds and 1 flint scraper (RE95; RE95ea);* **97**: *1 potsherd, "antique" (RE97aa, ornamented);* **98**: *1 piece of worked flint (RE98);* **100**: *1 flint nodule (RE100ea);* **101**: *1 flint knife (RE101ea) & 1 piece of worked flint (RE101);* **102**: *1 potsherd (RE102aa);* **104**: *11 potsherds (RE104aa; 104ab; 104ac) 4 pieces of worked flint (RE104) & 2 pieces of burned flint (RE104);* **105**: *1 piece of worked flint (RE105);* **108**: *1 flint nodule (RE108ea);* **109**: *2 hammers of granite-like stone (RE109ea, eb) & 3 of quartzite (RE109ec, ed & ee);* **110**: *1 flint nodule (RE110ea);* **111**: *1 flint scraper (RE111ea);* **112**: *1 flint nodule (RE112);* **113**: *6 potsherds & 2 pieces of worked flint (RE113aa, ab; RE113);* **114**: *1 flint nodule (RE114ea);* **115**: *1 potsherd (RE115aa);* **116**: *1 flint scraper (RE116ea);* **117**: *1 flint nodule (117ea);* **118**: *2 potsherds & 2 pieces of worked flint (RE118aa; RE118);* **119**: *1 potsherd (RE119aa, belongs to the same clay pot as RE121aa);* **120**: *1 flint sickle (RE120ea);* **121**: *9 potsherds (RE121aa/RE119; RE121ab; RE121), 1 piece of worked flint & 5 pieces of burned flint;* **122**: *1 potsherd (RE122);* **123**: *12 potsherds (RE123);* **125**: *1 clay tube (RE125aa);* **126**: *1 piece of worked (and burned) flint (RE126);* **128**: *1 potsherd (RE128);* **129**: *1 fossilized sea urchin, fragment, possibly used as a hammer (RE129ea);* **132**: *1 piece of worked flint (RE132);* **133**: *1 potsherd (RE133);* **134**: *2 potsherds, rim & side, soot traces below the rim at the inner side (RE134aa; RE134ab);* **135**: *4 potsherds (RE135aa & RE135) & 1 fossilized sea urchin (RE135);* **138**: *1 flint nodule (RE138ea) & 1 stone hammer (RE138eb);* **139**: *1 flint nodule (RE139ea) & 1 piece of worked flint (RE139);* **140**: *2 potsherds (RE140aa, ab & RE146aa);* **141**: *6 potsherds (RE141);* **142**: *1 potsherd (RE142);* **144**: *1 piece of worked flint, 1 flint nodule (RE144ea);* **145**: *1 presumed flint scraper (145ea);* **146**: *1 potsherd (RE146aa);* **147**: *1 flint nodule (RE147ea);* **148**: *1 quartzite-like smoothening stone (RE148ea);* **150**: *1 piece of worked flint (RE150);* **151**: *2 pieces of worked flint, blades (RE151);* **160**: *2 flint nodules & 3 pieces of worked flint (RE160);* **161**: *1 potsherd (161aa);* **162**: *2 pieces of worked flint, one of these with retouched edge (RE162);* **165**: *4 flint nodules, each with separate find spot (RE165);* **166**: *48 pieces of burned flint (RE166);* **167**: *3 flint nodules (RE167);* **168**: *1 potsherd (RE168);* **170**: *4 potsherds (RE170);* **176**: *7 potsherds & 1 piece of worked flint (RE176aa; RE176);* **177**: *1 potsherd (RE177);* **179**: *1 potsherd (RE179aa);* **193**: *1 flint scraper (RE193ea);* **199**: *1 flint nodule (RE199);* **1064**: *1 stone anvil (RE1064).*

of worked flint and 2 pieces of burned flint (RE87aa & RE87) that belong to the longhouse but are not counted as sunken-floor finds (see Fig. 2.9 for the placement of this pit and the aforementioned anvil to the east). The floor finds are characterized by a fragmented flint dagger, a flint arrowhead, two flint sickles, several flint scrapers, a couple of flint knives, several stone hammers and certain other items. A flint sickle (RE120ea), examined by means of micro wear analysis, shows heavy traces of the harvesting of reeds (Claus Skriver, report S2004a). A relatively high number of different clay pot profiles were also present. In addition, a unique clay tube belongs to the sunken-floor horizon. Among the charred organic materials were a rather limited amount of cereals, seeds from weeds and tiny pieces of hazelnut shells. Two of the pollen samples from the floor layer have been examined, with a positive result (M61387 & M61388) from a soil bench in the site (See Fig. 4.68 for the placement of two other samples likewise taken from the floor layer). Two water-sieved samples (RE137ga & RE222ga) belong to the sunken-floor horizon. The correct sample area has not yet been identified in detail but presumably concerns the area of patch A. A small potsherd RE97aa is of older origin and likely just accidentally present.[2] Some pottery and flint were found immediately outside the house to the north. From pit 320 this concerns 9 potsherds, of which some belong

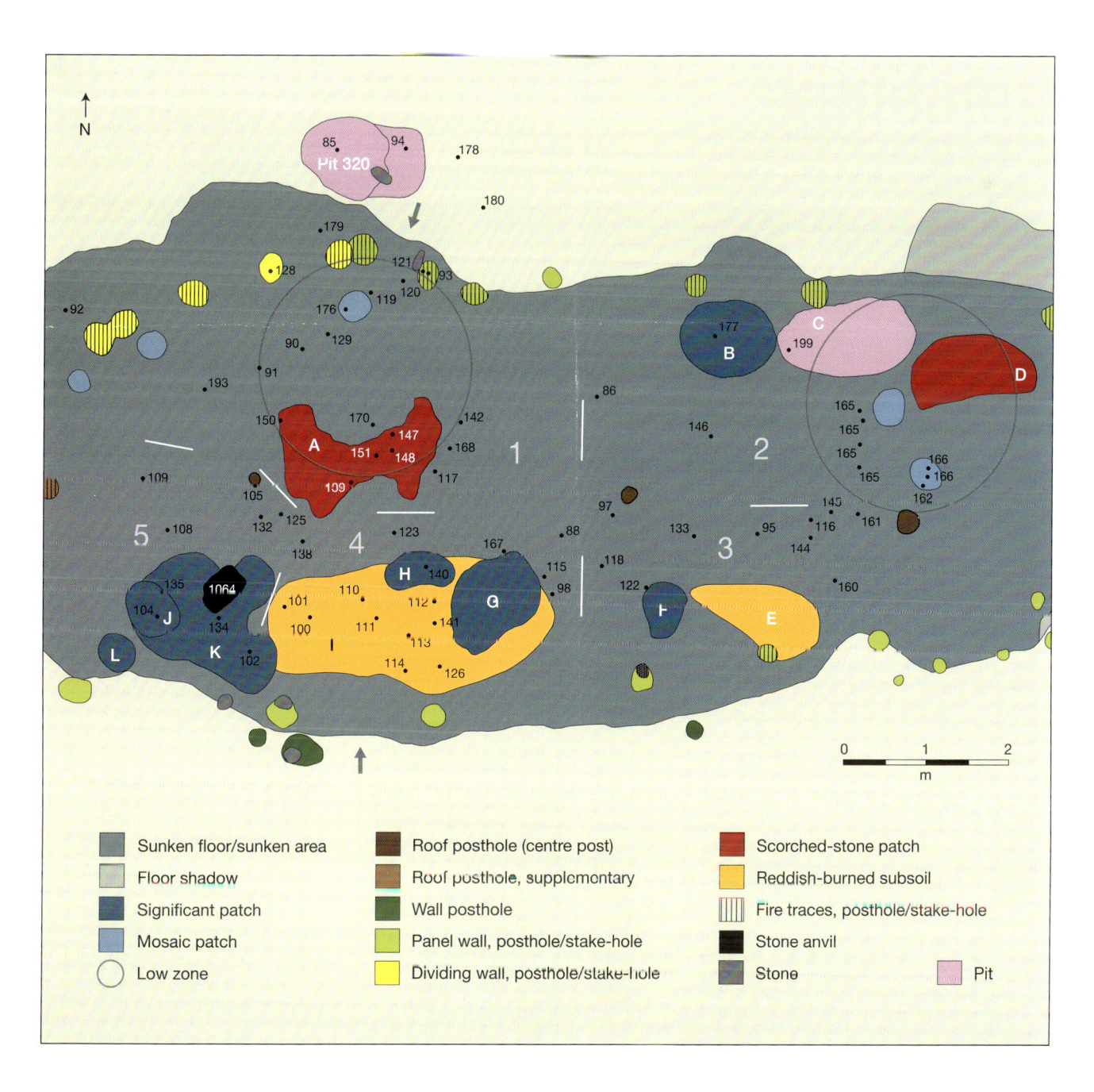

Artefacts, pits, patches, and daily life activities

Fig. 4.8. Resengaard, House 2. A: The south-western area of the sunken floor. Some flint debris was recovered around the large stone. The reddish subsoil in the foreground and the blackish floor layer observed all over, as in the soil benches, evidence that the house site was exposed to a comprehensive fire. B: The scorched-stone patch D visible in the soil bench to the east. Artefacts: Two scrapers (RE116ea & RE193ea) and five minor stone hammers (RE109ea, RE109eb, RE109ec, RE109ed, & RE109ef) found close together on the sunken-floor horizon.

RE125aa

RE125aa

RE93aa 1:2

RE134aa 1:2

RE81bb/85aa 1:2

Fig. 4.9. Resengaard, House 2. Two views of the secondarily burned, coarsely tempered clay tube (RE125aa) and two clay pot sides (RE93aa & RE134aa) belonging to the sunken-floor horizon, as well as rim and side of the fragmented jar (RE81bb/85aa) found in pit 320 immediately outside the northern entrance to House 2.

to different two clay pots (RE85aa & RE85ab) and 9 pieces of worked flint. Nearby, to the east, 4 potsherds (RE94aa) and 1 piece of worked flint (RE94) stem from the other pit. Also nearby were found 1 flint arrowhead roughout (RE178ea) and 1 potsherd (RE180). And further, in a diffuse "culture layer" just north of the house site, was found a triangular arrowhead with two lobes (RE1061ea).

One of two low zones was located in the western part of the sunken floor, being north of the scorched-stone patch, and relatively close to the presumed northern entrance. The other low zone, located in the eastern floor area to the north was correspondingly found mainly south of the eastern scorched-stone patch. The presence of these two low zones appears well in accordance with the sizeable distance

Artefacts, pits, patches, and daily life activities 233

RE89ea/175ea

◀▲ *Fig. 4.10. Resengaard, House 2. Front and backside of the fishtail dagger, found as two major pieces from secondary fills above the sunken floor, as well as a view of the handle end. The missing minor pieces were thoroughly sought but not found among the fills. This may indicate that the dagger broke into pieces elsewhere. These two pieces were found just a little above the floor layer and hence deposited early before much other fill was added. Two flint sickles (RE80ea & RE120ea) are from the secondary fills and the sunken-floor horizon, respectively. An important piece of a broken flint dagger (RE90ea) stems from the sunken-floor horizon.*

in between. The highest parts of the entire floor were mainly observable in the southern half. Relatively flat-floored areas were visible particularly to the west. The evenly north-sloping area inside the southern entrance must have functioned as a ramp for reaching the lower parts of the sunken floor to the east. Here, unless stated otherwise, the soil features consisted of greyish or greyish-brown, sandy clay, including pit M to the west, as well as pit 320 (and the pit it had cut to the east) north of the sunken floor. The two last pits, dug north of the sunken floor, were diffuse and rather shallow. Pit 320 had surface dimensions of c. 1.08 x 0.92 m. The quite conspicuous dark patches J and K, mentioned below, were observable beneath and west of the sizeable stone near the southern long side. Just to the east, a large subsoil area (I) was burned reddish. The significant pits and patches in the sunken-floor horizon, along with those in the immediate periphery, can briefly be characterized as follows:

A: Scorched-stone patch. Shallow, dark-brownish, sandy clay with many heat-affected/cracked stones. Surface dimensions c. 1.92 x 1.44 m.

B: Extensive patch, shallow. Surface dimensions c. 1.16 x 0.88 m.

C: Extensive pit. Surface dimensions c. 1.72 x 0.92 m, depth c. 18 cm.

D: Scorched-stone patch. The upper part consisted of dark-brownish, sandy clay with relatively few heat-affected/cracked stones. To the west, a thin layer of light, yellowy-grey sand. The lower parts of the patch were heavily coloured by carbonized organic dust and hence had a blackish appearance. Covering the bottom to the east was an area of reddish sand that could have been coloured by regular fire or glowing material. Surface dimensions c. 1.52 x 0.80 m (a part of its northern line is interposed).

E: Reddish, sandy subsoil clay area. Colour probably caused by fire. Surface dimensions c. 1.64 x 0.92 m.

F: Shallow patch. Surface dimensions c. 0.66 x 0.54 m.

G: Shallow patch. No clear influence of heat observed on the surface, thus contrasting with the surrounding subsoil. Surface dimensions c. 1.32 x 0.96 m.

H: Shallow patch. No clear influence of heat observed on the soil surface. Surface dimensions c. 0.84 x 0.44 m.

I: Reddish, sandy subsoil clay area. The colour must have been caused by substantial heat. Surface dimensions c. 3.36 x 1.60 m. The feature was only visible in the uppermost part of the subsoil.

J: Shallow patch. Consisting of dark, sandy soil. Surface dimensions c. 0.68 x 0.56 m.

K: Extensive patch, shallow. Contained dark, sandy soil. Surface dimensions c. 1.76 m x 1.56. A granite anvil had been placed here, being 0.56 m long and 0.36 m wide. On the top, it had a minor flat area.

L: Shallow patch. Surface dimensions c. 0.48 x 0.40 m.

M: Shallow pit. Surface dimensions c. 1.12 x 1.08 m (Fig. 2.9).

With the reservation that uncharred artefacts of organic materials would not survive in the soil milieu of the house site, it is remarkable that the area near the south side recess is almost free from such items, and the whole appearance might reflect the prehistoric situation. The recess could possibly have been built as a sleeping compartment.

The artefact remainders in the sunken-floor horizon may represent comparatively many different activities. No activities are directly proposed concerning the presumed compartment but some kind of storage might well have been a function.

The pressure-flaked flint sickle and the flint dagger fragment in activity space 2 need not necessarily have been part of a working process in this area, although it cannot be excluded that the tools we have identified as harvesting implements might also have been used in alternative ways. The observation of worked flint scattered around the large stone in activity space 5, noted below, is interesting.

Fossilized sea urchins were found in two activity spaces. The occurrence of such objects could be accidental. However, I assume they were placed there by residents.

The relatively dense finds and soil features to the southwest in the sunken-floor horizon complicate the delimitation of activity spaces but my suggestion is to set the limits on each side of the reddish-burned floor part in front of the doorway. The presence of this delimited, heavily burned subsoil of long, oval shape might also invite interpretation. It is my hunch that metal handling could have taken place here to the southwest although the enigmatic finds of the floor deposit of five stone hammers and the secondarily burned clay tube of still unidentified function is of course not conclusive and no suggestion of metal-related activities is therefore directly proposed. Based on the floor traces, the following are suggested as possible doings, separated into five activity spaces:

1. Drying/roasting/charring/cooking/heating, pottery handling/cooking, scraping, raw flint handling/chipping and smoothening. No activities are proposed concerning the flint dagger, the flint sickle or the fossilized sea urchin also present in this activity space.

2. Drying/roasting/charring/cooking/heating, pottery handling/cooking, scraping, hammering/crushing, and raw flint handling/chipping. No activities proposed regarding the concentration of burned flint.

3. Raw flint handling/chipping, scraping, and pottery handling/cooking.

4. Raw flint handling/chipping, scraping, knife cutting and pottery handling/cooking. As regards the burned floor, see the above remarks.

5. Raw flint handling/chipping, hammering/crushing and pottery handling/cooking. The raw flint handling/chipping is in this case indicated by the presence of the flint nodule, and additionally by the presence of scattered worked flint around the stone anvil. Other indications in the activity space are the clay tube, and five stone hammers, see the above remarks. The presence of the fossilized sea urchin might possibly have had some kind of significance, e.g. for carrying out certain work processes.

House 13 (Fig. 4.11 & 4.12)

From the secondary fills stem interesting ceramics (Cat. A: RE251, RE272, & RE655) and stone artefacts (Cat. B: RE251 & RE271). From the sunken-floor horizons derive charred plant materials (Cat. C: RE631ga).

A triangular arrowhead with two lobes (RE642ea) belongs to the sunken floor but only the approximate area of the find spot is known. Another very small but complete arrowhead stems from the secondary fills (RE271ea). The organic materials from the sunken-floor horizon consist of a modest number of charred cereals and a few charred seeds from weeds. Two potsherds supplied with cardium ornaments (RE264aa & RE264ab) stem from the southern part of a ditch that disturbed House 13 and are not included in the following account. Many heat-affected/cracked stones were taken as a sample (RE640) from a scorched-stone patch. Five presumed stone anvils were present, but the easternmost seems to have been placed somewhat aside. Charred macrofossils were found in the large scorched-stone patch to the northeast (RE631ga).

A number of soil features are recorded within the area of the western ground floor. It cannot be ruled out that some of these may belong to the house, for

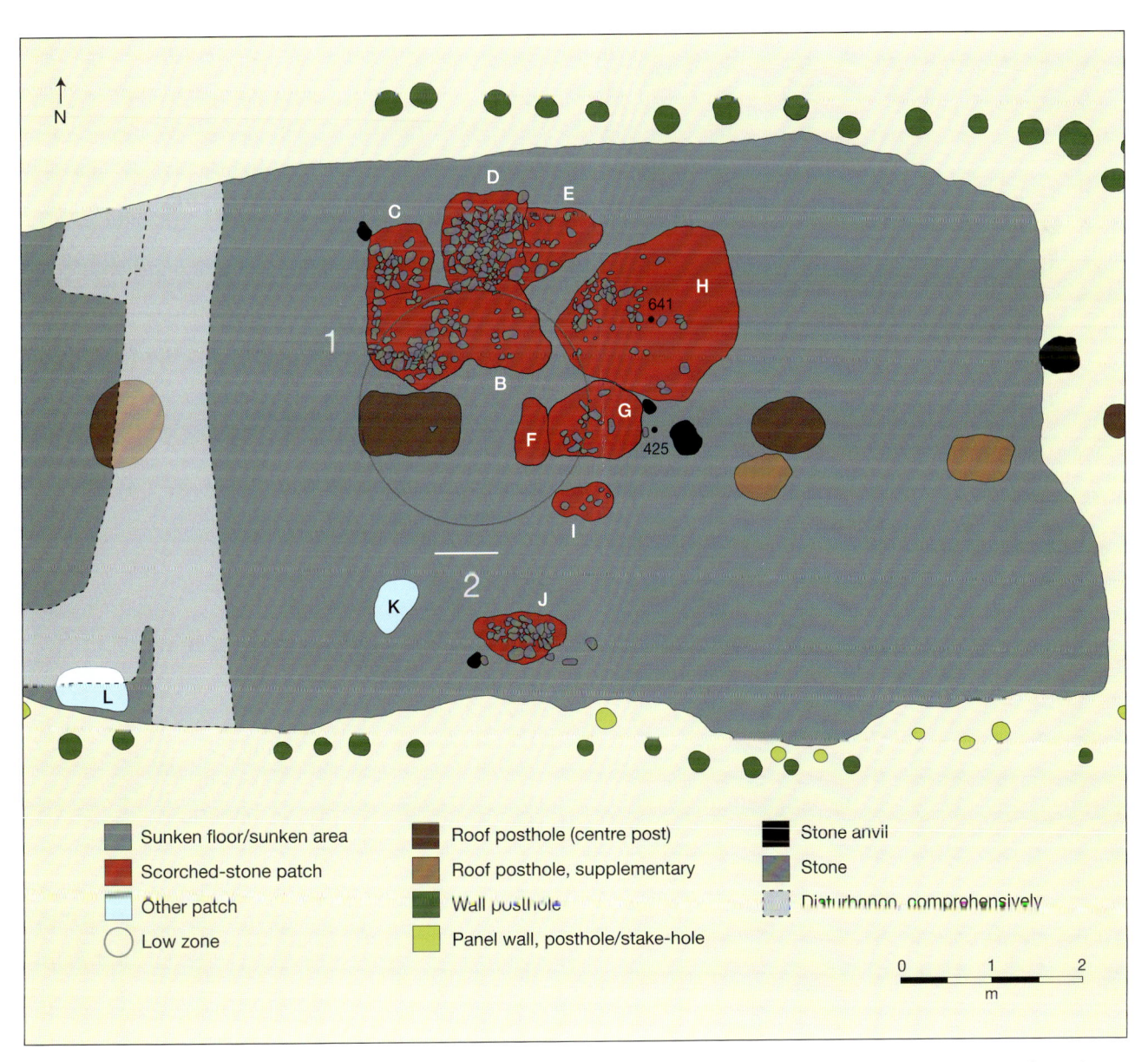

Fig. 4.11. Resengaard, House 13. Ground plan of sunken floor, cleaned. The extensive areas with scorched-stone patches mark out the central parts of the sunken floor. A division into just two activity spaces is suggested. Apart from stone anvils and scorched stones, the artefacts found in situ in the sunken-floor horizon belong to a few find spots: **425:** *1 potsherd and 2 pieces of worked flint (RE425aa; RE425);* **641:** *5 potsherds, 15 pieces of worked flint and 1 piece of burned flint (RE641), all dispersed in the patch.*

Artefacts, pits, patches, and daily life activities 237

instance the two N-S aligned, long oval pits close to the gable end. They are greatly reminiscent of the long oval pits in the ground floor of House 1 at Rosgårde, as we shall see further below. And yet the presence of a number of pits and patches outside the building in the case of House 13 makes it reasonable to presume that the soil features in question might also belong to a time before House 13. Compared to certain other longhouses at the settlement, the sunken floor depth was relatively modest. A low zone was recorded around the middle of the sunken floor. The relatively high-lying floor parts were present to the east. Relatively flat-floored areas were found in the eastern as well as western parts. The eleven significant soil patches of the sunken floor generally had a greyish or greyish-brown soil. All patches were shallow, mainly around 5-15 cm. As noted earlier, the former patch A has to be left out, as it is now considered (the bottom of) a post-hole. The significant pits and patches in the sunken-floor horizon can briefly be characterized as follows:

B: Scorched-stone patch. Sandy soil with several heat-affected/cracked stones. Surface dimensions c. 2.04 x 1.12 m.

C: Scorched-stone patch. Sandy soil with several heat-affected/cracked stones. Surface dimensions c. 0.84 x 0.72 m.

D: Scorched-stone patch. Sandy soil containing a very large number of heat-affected/cracked stones. Surface dimensions c. 1.00 x 0.88 m.

E: Scorched-stone patch. Sandy soil with scattered heat-affected/cracked stones. The soil feature had a diffuse character. Surface dimensions c. 0.88 x 0.84 m.

F: Scorched-stone patch. Sandy soil with and a few heat-affected/cracked stones and traces of charcoal. Surface dimensions c. 0.70 x 0.38 m.

G: Scorched-stone patch. Sandy soil with scattered heat-affected/cracked stones. Surface dimensions c. 1.04 x 0.82 m.

H: Scorched-stone patch. Sandy soil with concentrations of heat-affected/cracked stones. Surface dimensions c. 2.02 x 1.84 m.

I: Scorched-stone patch. Diffuse patch with sandy soil and a few heat-affected/cracked stones. Surface dimensions c. 0.68 x 0.40 m.

J: Scorched-stone patch. Sandy soil with several heat-affected/cracked stones. Surface dimensions c. 1.02 x 0.56 m.

K: Shallow patch. Sandy soil. Surface dimensions c. 0.62 x 0.40 m.

L: Shallow patch. Sandy soil with traces of charcoal. Width c. 0.80 m. A ditch of much later origin disturbed it.

Fig. 4.12. Resengaard, House 13. A: Scorched-stone patches and the western part of a large stone anvil in the foreground. Artefacts: Lobed arrowhead (RE642ea) belonging to the sunken-floor horizon. Flint hammer (RE251ea) from secondary fills.

The pits of the western part of the house (Fig. 2.10.A) may not necessarily belong to the functioning time of the house and no activities will be proposed. The apparent vestiges of a recess in the south side were free of artefact remainders and could possibly have been a sleeping compartment. Despite the exceptionally fine state of preservation of the house site and its sunken floor, it is remarkable that the artefact finds from the floor are so modest. The cluster of scorched-stone patches around the middle of the northern aisle presumably indicates comprehensive activities of some kind but I cannot present any suggestion of its more precise character. It seems reasonable to presume that a part of their massive presence could stem from specialized activities because the scorched-stone patches as a whole number far beyond what is found in most other sunken-floor horizons in longhouses at Resengaard. And yet the activity responsible can hardly have been large-scale roasting or charring of cereals because the remainders of charred grains were quite modest and far more spilled grains would have been expected. Activities such as drying, cooking and heating are possible, and not contradicted by the evidence. Compared with the sunken-floor horizon of House 1, which in spite of its rather moderate quantity of scorched-stone patches contained abundant numbers of charred cereals, it seems evident that the activities related to the scorched-stone patches of House 13 must have somehow been different. No specific activity related to the pit near the wall in the south side of the sunken floor to the west can be proposed. Overall, the following are suggested as possible doings in two activity spaces:

1. Drying/roasting/charring/cooking/heating and pottery handling/cooking related to the patches B, C, D, E, G, F, I, and J.

2. Pottery handling/cooking and raw flint handling/chipping. The latter is suggested due to the number of worked flints present. A stone present.

House 14 (Fig. 4.13 & 4.14)

Interesting ceramics (Cat. A: RE258 & RE282) and stone artefacts (Cat. B: RE258 & RE295) stem from the secondary fills. Charred plant materials derive from the sunken-floor horizon (Cat. C: RE307 & RE308). From Feature 24 (stone concentration) north of House 14 stem plant material (Cat. C: RE293).

Due to ard-ploughing of the floor, the finds need to be presented with the clear reservation that these were seemingly *in situ* but could admittedly have been moved a little. Altogether 12 find spots are recorded.

Compared to certain other longhouses at the settlement, its sunken floor was of around medium depth. A low zone was observable in the middle of the sunken floor. Its relatively high-lying parts were found mostly in the southern area. The relatively flat-floored areas were observable in the eastern as well as in the western end. Only two important soil features were present and one of these was remarkably large. The significant soil patches in the sunken-floor horizon can briefly be characterized as follows:

A: Scorched-stone patch, disturbed. The sandy, greyish to blackish to brownish layer on top contained scorched stones. The bottom layer was light greyish-brown, sandy soil. It contained scattered stones and, unfortunately, the extent to which these were heat-affected/cracked was not recorded. The patch contained a few charred cereals. The surface dimensions were considerable, c. 8.2 x 5.4 m and much of it had been exposed to extensive ard-ploughing. It is possible that it had originally consisted of several minor scorched-stone patches but the excavation team could not segregate such minor areas. The depth of the soil feature was 18 cm at its deepest but mostly about 10 cm.

B: Moderately-sized patch. Consisted of sandy, dark soil, coloured by dust from charred organic material. Surface dimensions c. 0.76 x 0.38 m. Depth only a few cm.

Immediately north of the house site was found a concentration of heat-affected/cracked stones placed in a low pit (Feature 24) When excavating it, the pile of stones with soil in between topped up above the cleaned subsoil surface. My interpretation is that it concerns a deposit of heat-cracked stones presumably from the same time as House 14. A single bottom-side potsherd (RE279aa) was found among the stones. These stones were likely no longer usable for the purpose of heating, but kept nearby because heavily burned, cracking granite might be a resource for some kind of use, e.g. coarse tempering of clay materials. Although the longhouse site showed relatively good preservation in parts, ard-ploughing after abandonment could have reduced the number of artefacts representing different activities. The use of a fossilized sea urchin as a

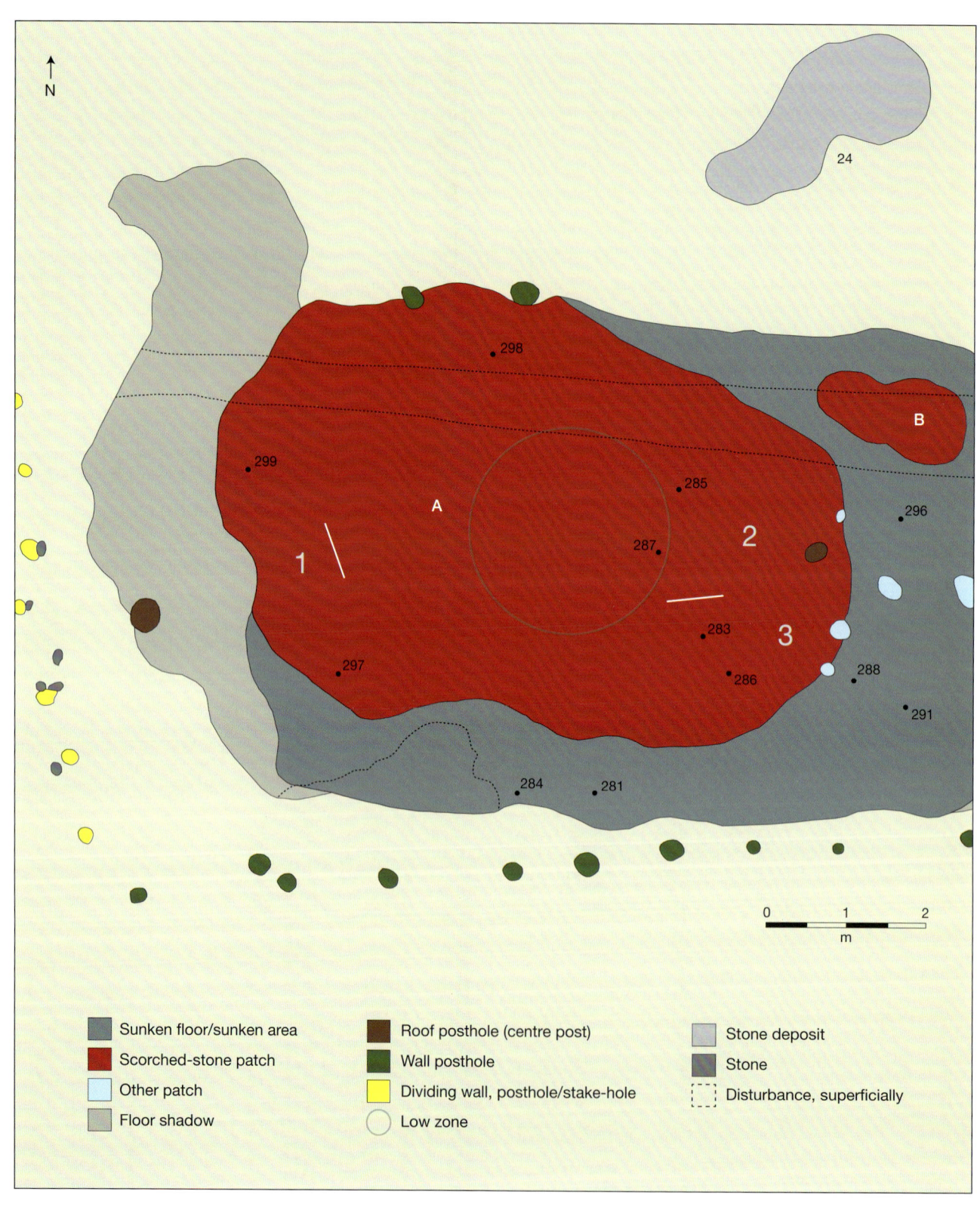

Fig. 4.13. Resengaard, House 14. Ground plan of sunken floor, cleaned. A division into three activity spaces is suggested. The large scorched-stone patch was heavily ard-ploughed, thus probably extending the area, while before abandonment it may have consisted of many such minor patches. Apart from scorched stones, the artefacts found in the sunken-floor horizon overall belong to many find spots: **281:** *1 flint arrowhead (RE281ea);* **283:** *2 flint scrapers (RE283ea; RE283eb);* **284:** *7 potsherds and 1 piece of worked flint (RE284aa; RE284);* **285:** *1 flint piece with pressure-flaking, perhaps a dagger-handle fragment (RE285);* **286:** *1 flint hammer, being a fossilized sea urchin (RE286ea);* **287:** *1 potsherd (RE287aa);* **288:** *1 flint piece with pressure-flaking (RE288);* **291:** *1 flint sickle, fragment (RE291ea);* **296:** *2 potsherds (RE296aa);* **297:** *1 potsherd (RE297aa);* **298:** *10 potsherds (RE298aa; RE298ab; RE298);* **299:** *3 potsherds, 1 flint knife, and 2 pieces of worked flint (RE299ea; RE299).*

Fig. 4.14. Resengaard, House 14. Upper part of clay pot (RE296aa) from the sunken-floor horizon. Notched flint piece (RE258ea) and upper part of a clay pot (RE272aa) from secondary fills.

hammer is rare at the settlement and was possibly used for working other stone material. Based on the floor traces, the following are suggested as possible doings, separated into three activity spaces:

1. Pottery handling/cooking and knife cutting. The placement makes it rather uncertain as to whether activities connected to heat-affected/cracked stones may have taken place far to the west in the ploughed patch.

2. Drying/roasting/charring/cooking/heating and pottery handling/cooking. No suggestions in relation to the pressure-flaked flint piece.

3. Scraping, hammering/crushing, drying/roasting/charring/cooking/heating and pottery handling/cooking. No suggestions on activities related to the flint sickle, the pressure-flaked flint piece or the arrowhead present in this extensive activity space.

House 41 (Fig. 4.15 & 4.16; Fig. 4.68.E)

From the secondary fills stem interesting ceramics (Cat. A: RE313, RE 406, RE414, RE417, RE419, & RE420) and stone artefacts (Cat. B: RE312, RE406, RE415, RE417, & RE418). From the sunken-floor horizon derive charred plant materials (Cat. C: RE433).

When excavating the profile benches, a fragment of a polished flint axe (RE437), a fragment of a pressure-flaked flint sickle (RE438), and a lobed flint arrowhead (RE439) all derived from the sunken-floor horizon. Considering the fine state of preservation of the house site, the number of find spots from the sunken-floor horizon is surprisingly moderate, as it only relates to 16 regular find spots. A potsherd that was found in a posthole just south of the southern long side (RE440) is not listed below. Likewise, a patinated flint sickle with blunted back made on a regular blade (RE1048ea) that presumably belonged to the house site. A sizeable stone was placed near the northern wall of the sunken floor. I interpret it as a stone anvil placed somewhat aside here.

Artefacts, pits, patches, and daily life activities

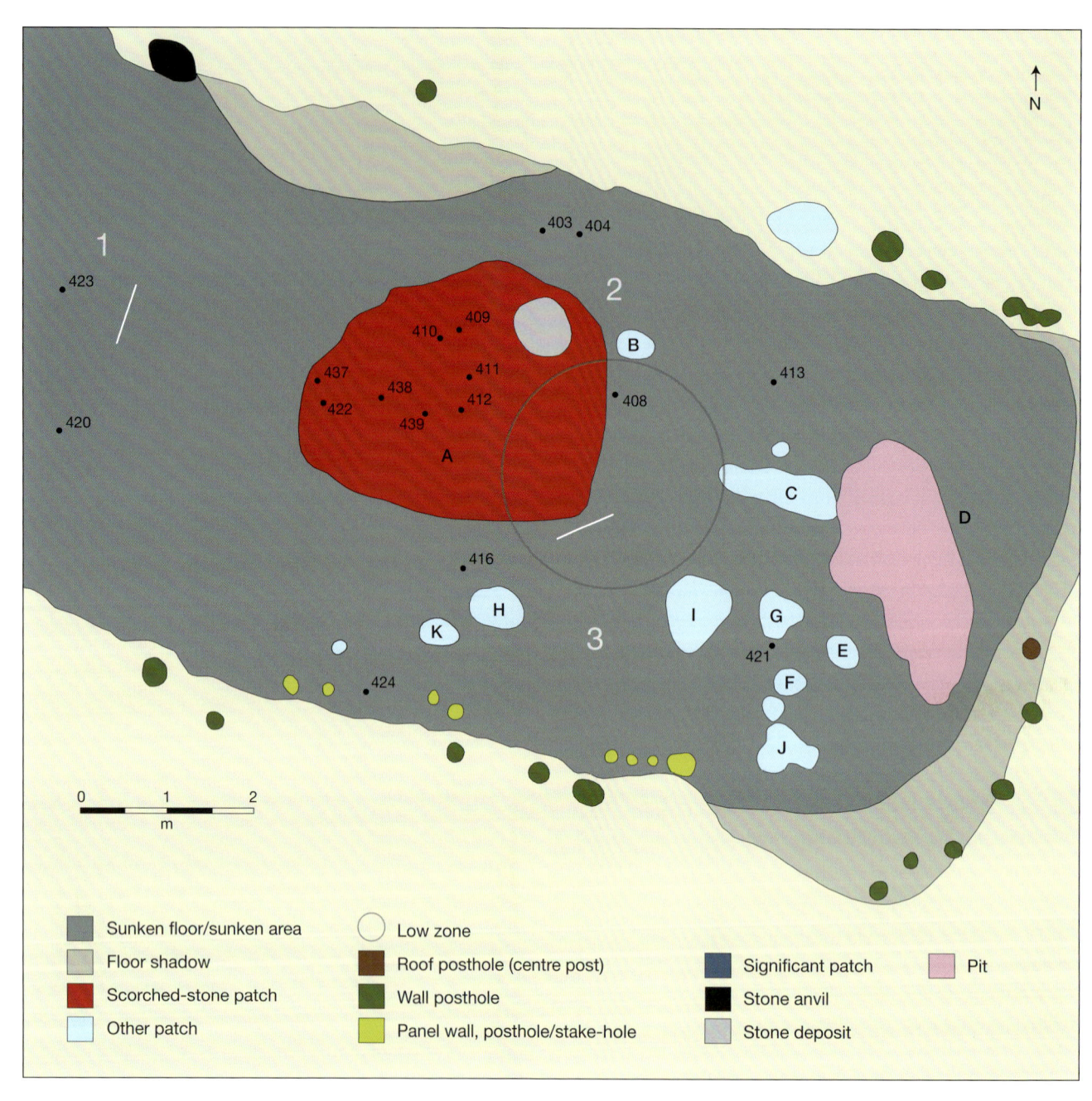

Fig. 4.15. Resengaard, House 41. Ground plan of sunken floor, cleaned. A division into three activity spaces is suggested. Extraordinarily, many small pits were present to the southeast with largely the same kind of soil and their presence may indicate traces of a particular kind of work. Apart from the stone anvil and scorched stones, the artefacts found in situ in the sunken-floor horizon overall involve many find spots: **403**: *7 potsherds (RE403aa);* **404**: *4 potsherds (RE404aa);* **408**: *3 potsherds (RE408aa);* **409**: *1 potsherd (RE409aa);* **410**: *1 potsherd (RE410aa);* **411**: *7 potsherds (RE411aa);* **412**: *2 potsherds & 1 piece of worked flint (RE412aa; RE412);* **413**: *1 flint piece with notches (RE413eh);* **416**: *11 potsherds (RE416aa);* **421**: *1 bone fragment, tubular (RE421);* **422**: *1 potsherd (422aa);* **423**: *1 potsherd (RE423aa);* **424**: *2 potsherds (RE424aa);* **437**: *1 flint axe fragment (RE437);* **438**: *1 flint sickle fragment (RE438);* **439**: *1 flint arrowhead, lobed (RE439).*

Only one relatively distinct low zone in about the middle was observable, with its lowest area immediately east of soil feature A. The relatively higher parts of the floor were found in the southern half of the floor. Relatively flat-floored areas were found particularly in the western part. The soil features of the sunken floor consisted generally of greyish or greyish-brown sandy soil unless otherwise stated. The patches B, C, E, F, G, H, I, J, and K were all shallow, mainly around 5-15 cm. The significant pit and patches in the sunken-floor horizon can briefly be characterized as follows:

RE406aa

RE406eg

RE312ea

RE418ea

RE415ea

RE412aa

RE406ea 1:2

RE409aa

RE416aa 1:2

Fig. 4.16. Resengaard, House 41. A: An example of the mostly small pits, all devoid of artefacts, found to the southeast in the sunken floor. Seen from the west. Artefacts: Borer (point intact, RE418ea), scraper (RE415ea), spearhead (RE312ea), two notched pieces (RE406ea & RE406eg) and the upper part of a clay pot (RE406aa), all from the secondary fills. From the sunken-floor horizon, three upper parts of characteristic clay pots (RE409aa, RE412aa & RE416aa).

Artefacts, pits, patches, and daily life activities 243

A: Extensive scorched-stone patch. Greyish-brown soil and, particularly in the bottom, a thin layer of almost black soil, probably coloured by dust from carbonized organic material. To the northeast, a concentration of scorched stones was observable and, just east of this, by the edge of the patch, a lump of clay being c. 15 cm in surface diameter. Surface dimensions c. 3.50 x 2.80 m and depth c. 0.14 m.

B: Minor patch. Sandy soil. Surface dimensions c. 0.40 x 0.30 m.

C: Minor patch. Sandy soil. Surface dimensions c. 1.40 x 0.45 m.

D: Extensive pit. Sandy soil. Surface dimensions c. 3.00 x 1.58 m. Depth c. 0.13 m. The easternmost part consisted of dark, almost black soil that was likely coloured by charcoal dust. The patch as such was hardly a heating area since only this tiny part contained carbonized organic material. Finally, the soil features E, F, G, H, I, J, and K were all minor patches with sandy soil.

Some interesting vestiges relate to the space of the ground floor. Whereas no artefacts inside the compartment point to specific activities, substantial floor patches in the ground floor were present in the remaining area and these evidently belong to the house because nothing outside might indicate any other relationship. No artefacts give any clues as to a precise explanation for their presence. I cannot therefore present any plausible suggestion as to the kinds of activity that might have created these soil features although it clearly concerns a significant activity space to the west of this longhouse. It probably designates a special activity because we do not see this pattern in the ground floors of any other of the longhouses in question. Interestingly, these many patches are somewhat reminiscent of the cluster of pits in the southeastern area of the sunken floor and it could relate to the same kind of work at both ends of the longhouse. These activities might, of course, have been performed more or less simultaneously in both places but I find a more plausible understanding may be that the activities were moved from the western ground floor when this part of the house was torn down. Concerning the sunken floor part, the artefact remainders only point to a few activities. This is surprising considering that the floor was highly protected from major disturbances due to the thick soils above. Based on the floor traces, the following are suggested as possible doings, separated into three activity spaces:

1. Pottery handling/cooking.

2. Pottery handling/cooking, drying/roasting/charring/cooking/heating, and axe chopping. No activities are directly proposed regarding the flint piece with notches, the arrowhead or the sickle fragment.

3. Pottery handling/cooking. A tiny piece of burned bone was also found here. The unusual concentration of soil patches as considered in the above strongly indicates activities to the southeast and these could very well point to a kind of special activity in this longhouse in particular.

House 42 (Fig. 4.17; Fig. 4.68.F)

From the secondary fills stem interesting ceramics (Cat. A: RE428, RE652, & RE654) and stone artefacts (Cat. B: RE405, Re428, & RE435). From the sunken-floor horizon derive no plant materials. A strike-a-light (RE436ea) presumably belonged to the sunken-floor horizon but the find place does not appear to have been recorded. It is hence grouped with the secondary fills. A possible fireplace with reddish, sandy soil found in the area west of the sunken floor contained six potsherds (RE429) but whether it might belong to the functioning time of the house was not clarified during fieldwork. Several find spots are recorded from the sunken-floor horizon. Included in these is a concentration of flint flakes (RE597) from a minor area (c. 1.0 x 0.6 m, its centre marked) in the north-east part of the sunken floor.

A low zone was observable to the east in the sunken floor. The higher floor parts were located mainly at the western end, where the most flat-floored areas were also found. Two significant soil patches in the sunken-floor horizon can briefly be characterized as follows:

A: Scorched-stone patch. Sandy, greyish soil with many heat-affected/cracked stones.[3] Surface dimensions c. 0.80 x 0.50 m. Depth only a few cm.

B: Scorched-stone patch. Sandy, greyish soil with many heat-affected/cracked stones. Surface dimensions c. 0.50 x 0.20 m. Depth only a few cm.

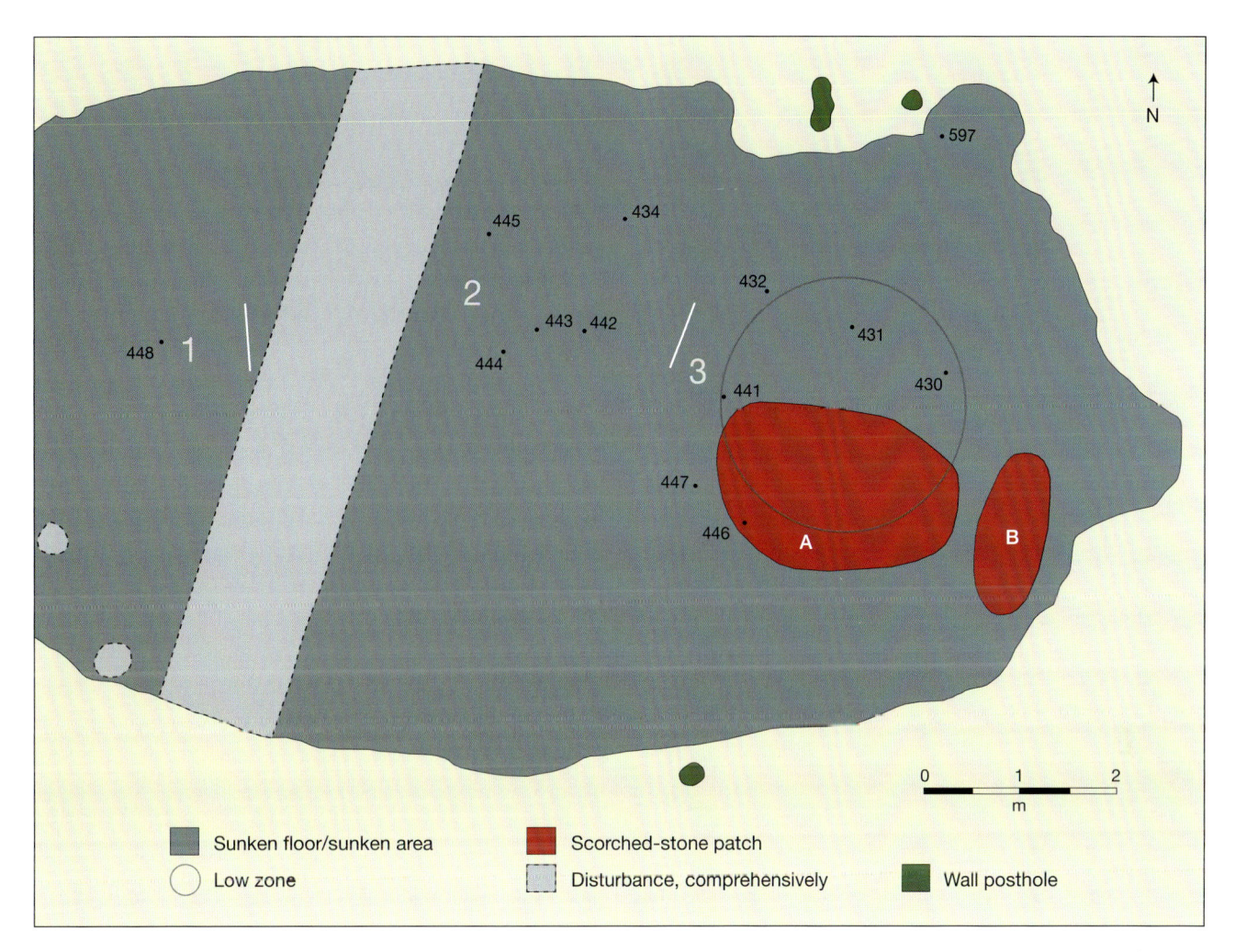

Fig. 4.17. Resengaard, House 42. Ground plan of sunken floor, cleaned. A division into three activity spaces is suggested. Apart from scorched stones, the artefacts found in situ in the sunken-floor horizon overall involve many find spots: **430:** *1 flint dagger fragment (RE430ea);* **431:** *1 potsherd (RE431aa);* **432:** *1 stone hammer (RE432ea);* **434:** *3 pieces of worked flint & 1 piece of burned flint (RE434; RE434);* **441:** *1 potsherd (RE441aa);* **442:** *1 potsherd (RE442aa);* **443:** *2 potsherds (RE443aa);* **444:** *1 flint arrowhead roughout (RE444ea);* **445:** *1 potsherd (RE445aa);* **446:** *1 flint scraper, almost pear-shaped (RE446ea);* **447:** *1 potsherd, secondarily burned (RE447);* **448:** *1 potsherd & 1 flint scraper (RE448; RE448ea);* **597:** *A flint flake concentration (RE597).*

The sunken floor was rather well preserved but the recorded find spots are not numerous. The artefact remainders in this house may represent only a few different doings. Based on the floor traces, the following are suggested as possible activities, separated into three activity spaces:

1. Scraping and pottery handling/cooking.

2. Pottery handling/cooking. No activity proposed regarding the arrowhead roughout.

3. Drying/roasting/charring/cooking/heating, scraping, hammering/crushing, pottery handling/cooking and raw flint handling/chipping.

House 128 (Fig. 4.18 & 4.19)

From the secondary fills stem interesting ceramics (Cat. A: RE540 & RE552) and *inter alia* a flint hammer (Cat. B: RE573). The sizeable pit 545 west of the sunken floor contained some flint items, ceramics and heat-affected/cracked stones, besides a few internodia of emmer from the minor pit 567 in top if it (RE545, RE567 & RE568). These pits are considered to belong to a time before the sunken-floor house. A soil sample from the large pit I in the sunken-floor horizon (RE565ga) contained a few seeds from weeds, a cereal grain and a hazelnut shell (Cat. C: RE565). In the sunken-floor horizon I consider seven significant stones to be anvils. The number of find spots belonging to the floor is moderate. The flint dagger (RE547ea) found by

Artefacts, pits, patches, and daily life activities 245

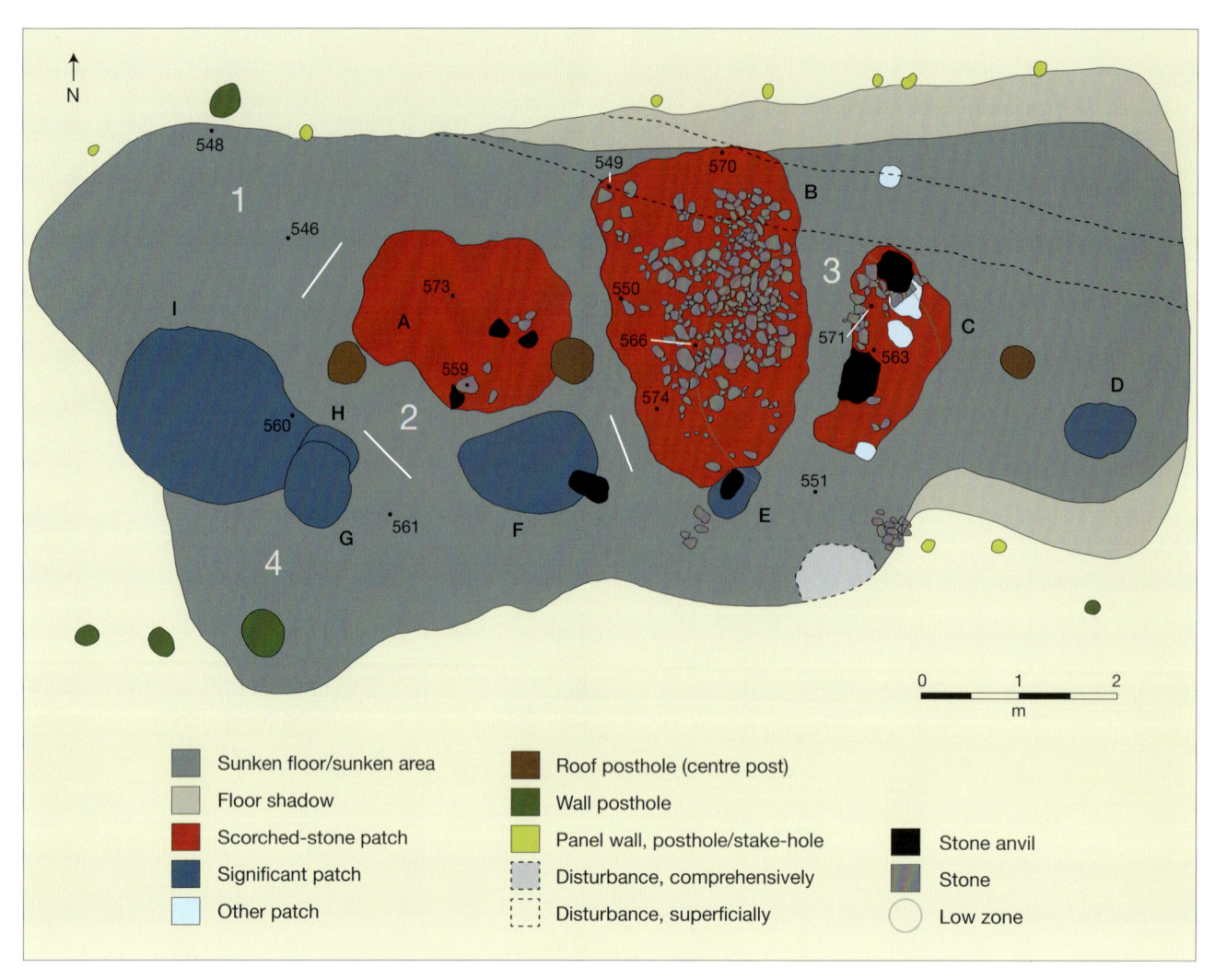

Fig. 4.18. Resengaard, House 128. Ground plan of sunken floor, cleaned. A division into four activity spaces is suggested. Apart from stone anvils and scorched stones, the artefacts found in situ in the sunken-floor horizon overall belong to many find spots: **546:** *6 potsherds (RE546aa; RE546ab);* **547:** *1 flint dagger (RE547ea);* **548:** *1 flint arrowhead, transverse edge (RE548ea);* **549:** *1 flint scraper with notch (RE549ea);* **550:** *1 potsherd, rim (RE550);* **551:** *1 flint knife (RE551ea);* **559:** *1 whetstone (RE559ea);* **560:** *1 potsherd (RE560);* **561:** *12 potsherds, secondarily burned (RE561aa);* **562:** *1 potsherd (RE562aa);* **563:** *1 flint arrowhead roughout (RE563ea);* **566:** *6 potsherds (RE566);* **570:** *4 heat-affected/cracked stones above average size, selected from different parts of patch B (RE570);* **573:** *1 stone hammer (RE573ea);* **574:** *10 potsherds & 4 pieces of worked flint (RE574).*

the eastern gable end is considered to belong to the sunken-floor horizon.

A low zone was observable to the east of the middle of the sunken floor. The relatively high-lying, flat-floored parts were found mostly in the western area of the sunken floor. In all, nine patches were observed and all were shallow, mainly around 5-15 cm. The significant pits and patches in the sunken-floor horizon can briefly be characterized as follows:

A: Extensive scorched-stone patch. Surface dimensions c. 2.36 x 1.98 m. Dark, brownish soil above a 0.6 m long spot of reddish sand, c. 3 cm thickness. A whetstone, three presumed stone anvils and some scattered stones in the surface without visible impact from heat.

B: Extensive scorched-stone patch. Sandy soil with very many heat-affected/cracked stones. Surface dimensions c. 3.36 x 2.12 m.

C: Extensive scorched-stone patch. Sandy soil. Several stones were present and some of these were heat-affected/cracked. Two presumed stone anvils placed at a distance in the patch. Surface dimensions c. 2.12 x 1.16 m.

Fig. 4.19. Resengaard, House 128. A: In the foreground, the scorched-stone patch A with stones, considered to be minor anvils, as well as other dispersed stones. Seen from the east. B: In the foreground, the scorched-stone patch B with numerous stones left in situ and, in the background, one of the sizable stone anvils on top of the scorched-stone patch C. Seen from the west. Artefacts: Stone hammer (RE573ea) and flint knife with traces of wear (RE551ea), as well as a flint dagger, considered to belong to the sunken-floor horizon, although found near the eastern gable end (RE547ea).

D: Sub-circular patch. Sandy soil. Surface dimensions c. 0.72 x 0.56 m.

E: Minor patch. Sandy soil. A presumed stone anvil placed here. Surface dimensions c. 0.65 x 0.40 m.

F: Diffuse, shallow patch, sandy. A presumed stone anvil placed at the southeast edge. Surface dimensions c. 1.48 x 1.04 m.

G: Sub-circular patch. Dark, sandy soil. Surface dimensions c. 0.76 x 0.70 m.

H: Crescent-shaped patch (cut by patch G). Reddish sand, colouring presumably due to burning but no charcoal pieces were found. Surface dimensions c. 0.64 x 0.40 m.

I: Extensive patch. Dark, sandy soil diverging slightly from patch G. Pit I belongs to the sunken-floor horizon

Artefacts, pits, patches, and daily life activities

but according to stratification, older than soil feature G and H. Surface dimensions c. 2.12 x 1.80 m.

The artefact remainders in the sunken-floor horizon may represent many different doings. The main area of pottery handling/cooking was likely activity space 3, which is characterized by the combination of pottery, large patches with heat-affected/heat-cracked stones and the presence of the low zone. House 128 resembles House 1 in certain respects, not least its trapezoidal ground plan and dimensions but, in my reading, the four stone anvils placed in almost a semicircle in the area around the largest scorched-stone patch (B) not least indicate quite another use of the floor areas. The westernmost of the other stone anvils, placed by the southern edge of a patch (A), was flanked by a whetstone (RE559). No activities are proposed for the areas in which the flint arrowhead to the northwest and the flint dagger to the east were found. Based on the floor traces, the following are suggested as possible doings, separated into four activity spaces:

1. Pottery handling/cooking.

2. Hammering/crushing and polishing/sharpening.

3. Drying/roasting/charring/cooking/heating, scraping, knife cutting, pottery, besides pottery handling/cooking. The semicircle of stone anvils might indicate special, rather substantial kinds of activity. An arrowhead roughout present.

4. Pottery handling/cooking.

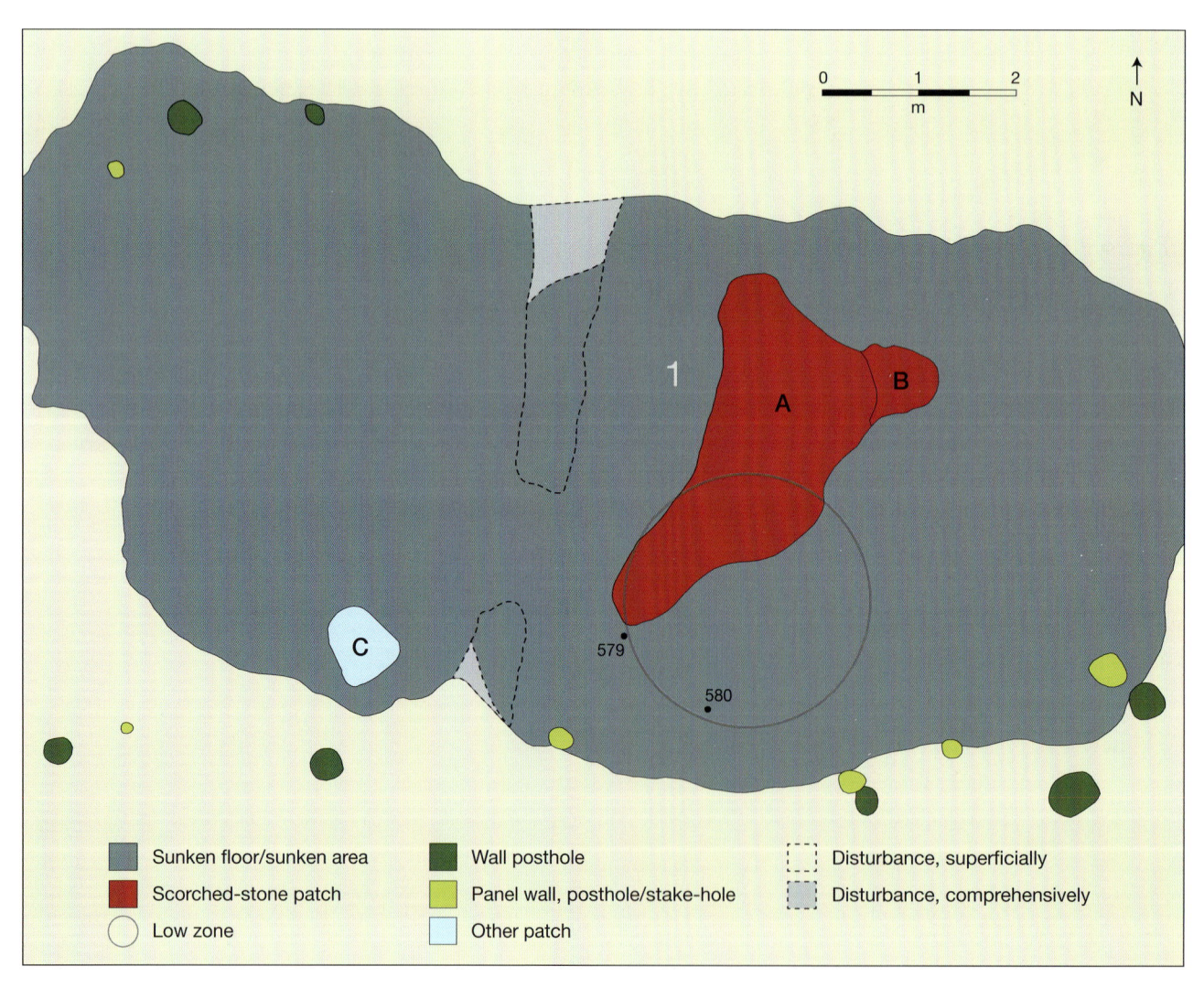

Fig. 4.20. Resengaard, House 130. Ground plan of sunken floor, cleaned. Just a single activity space is suggested. Apart from scorched stones, the artefacts found in situ in the sunken-floor horizon merely come from two find spots: **579:** *1 flint scraper (RE579ea);* **580:** *1 potsherd (RE580aa).*

House 130 (Fig. 4.20 & 4.21)

From the secondary fills stem interesting ceramics (Cat. A: RE539 & RE581) and stone artefacts (Cat. B: RE539). Interestingly, no less than 5 fossilized sea urchins (539ef, eg, eh, ei, & ej) were among the items in the secondary fills. From the sunken-floor horizon derive no plant materials. The house site is not among the best preserved at the settlement and only two regular find spots were recorded from the sunken-floor horizon. I consider a potsherd (RE581aa, from the cross-section) to be part of the secondary fills.

Compared to certain other longhouses at the settlement, the sunken floor was of medium depth. The western half of it was very shallow, being merely a few cm deep and therefore level measurements of these floor parts were not carried out. Only three soil patches were left and all were shallow, mainly 5-15 cm. A relatively deep low zone was observable south of the soil patches A and B. The relatively high-lying and flat-floored areas were observable in the western part. The soil patches in the sunken floor horizon can briefly be characterized as follows:

A: Scorched-stone patch. Sandy, brownish soil with several scattered heat-affected/cracked stones. Surface dimensions c. 3.76 x 1.58 m. NOTE 4.

B: Scorched-stone patch. Sandy, brownish soil with a few heat-affected/cracked stones. Surface dimensions c. 0.68 x 0.64 m. Diffusely limited towards patch A.

C: Sandy soil patch with diffuse edges. Surface dimensions c. 0.72 x 0.54 m.

The artefact remainders in the sunken-floor horizon may represent quite few different doings in this building. Based on the floor traces, the following are suggested as possible doings in one activity space:

1. Drying/roasting/charring/cooking/heating, pottery handling/cooking and scraping.

House 134 (Fig. 4.22 & 4.23)

From the secondary fills stem interesting ceramics (Cat. A: RE564) and stone artefacts (Cat. B: 564). From the sunken-floor horizon derive no plant materials. Immediately to the south of the sunken floor, a large irregular pit and a minor sub-circular pit were placed in front of its middle, presumably contemporaneous with the house. A granite stone was found directly at the bottom

Fig. 4.21. Resengaard, House 130. A: Scorched-stone patches in the foreground and a soil bench behind. Seen from the east. Artefacts: A flint scraper (RE579ea, scraping edge at the distal end) from the sunken-floor horizon. From secondary fills four (out of five) fossilized sea urchins (RE539ef, RE539eh, RE539ei, & RE539er). Why precisely these were present is puzzling.

Artefacts, pits, patches, and daily life activities   249

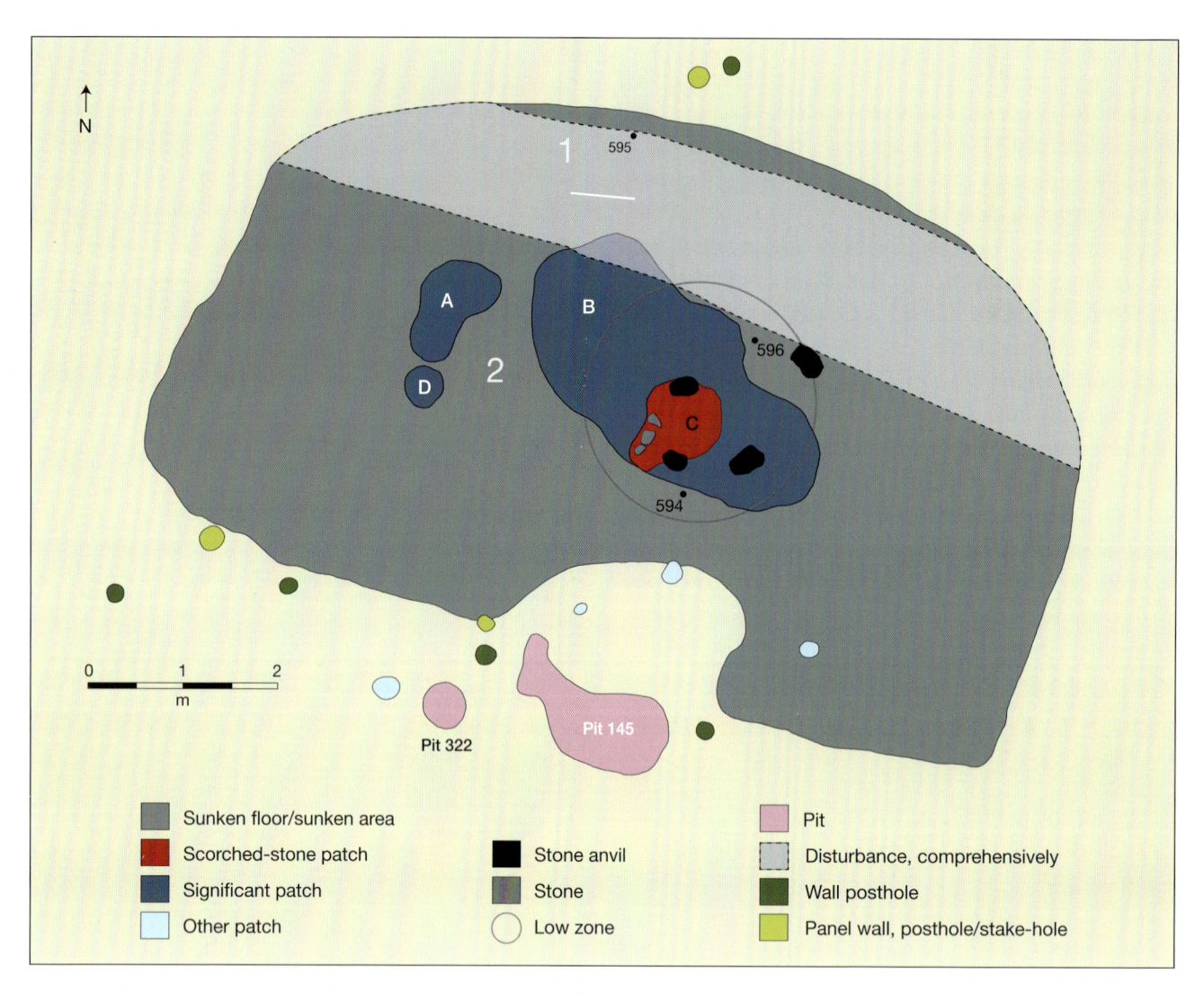

Fig. 4.22. Resengaard, House 134. Ground plan of sunken floor, cleaned. Two activity spaces in the area of the sunken floor are suggested. Apart from stone anvils and scorched stones, the artefacts found in situ in the sunken-floor horizon belong to three find spots: **594**: *13 potsherds (RE594aa, ab, ac);* **595**: *2 potsherds (RE595aa);* **596**: *12 potsherds (RE596aa, ab).*

of the large pit 145 but no other artefacts were found in the fill. From the minor pit 322 west of it stem 13 potsherds (Cat. C: RE591aa) and a tiny piece of burned bone (RE591). Regarding the sunken-floor horizon, I consider four relatively large stones to be anvils. The artefacts from the sunken-floor horizon are rather modest, and only few regular find spots have been recorded.

The sunken floor of this house was severely affected by recent ploughing but, compared to certain other longhouses at the settlement, its sunken floor was still of medium depth although it was probably previously deeper and more extensive. The relatively high-lying parts of the floor were found in the western parts, and the relatively flat-floored areas in the easternmost and, to some degree, in the west. The soil features of the sunken-floor horizon can briefly be characterized as follows:

A: patch, shallow. Greyish-brown sandy soil. Surface dimensions c. 1.20 x 0.72 m.

B: Extensive patch, shallow. Greyish-brown sandy soil. Surface dimensions c. 3.66 x 1.84 m. A stone presumed to be an anvil present to the east, and another north of the pit.

C: Scorched-stone patch, shallow. Placed in area of pit B. Greyish-brown sandy soil. Two presumed stone anvils placed at the edge of patch B. Surface dimensions c. 1.16 x 0.86 m. The soil feature contained several heat-affected/cracked stones.

D: Minor patch, shallow. Greyish-brown sandy soil. Surface dimensions c. 0.44 x 0.42 m.

Fig. 4.23. Resengaard, House 134. A: Stone anvils and a scorched-stone patch in the foreground. Behind that a soil bench across the sunken floor. Seen from the east. Artefacts: A flint borer (RE564ea) and four upper parts of characteristic clay pots RE564aa, RE564ab, RE564ba & RE564bb), all from secondary fills.

In my reading, it would be more than a coincidence if the two pits (145 & 322) and some postholes happened to be present directly in front of the middle of the sunken floor. I therefore presume that the large pit was directly related to the activities of the house although no concrete doings can immediately be proposed in this respect. Based on the floor traces, the following are suggested as possible doings, separated into two activity spaces:

1. Pottery handling/cooking.

2. Drying/roasting/charring/cooking/heating and pottery handling/cooking. Three stone anvils present but no concrete activities can be proposed in connection to these.

Artefacts, pits, patches, and daily life activities 251

House 138 (Fig. 4.24 & 4.25)

From the secondary fills stem interesting ceramics (Cat. A: RE601) and stone artefacts (Cat. B: RE601 & RE602). A large part of the sunken floor was preserved but the finds were rather scant. Those from the sunken-floor horizon are thus characterized by only a few clay pot remainders and a couple of flint items. Charred organic materials from three samples showed that naked barley and fat hen were present (Cat. C: RE616ga, RE617ga & RE1035ga). A few items stem from culture layer 335 around the sunken floors of Houses 138 and 143 (see House 143).

Compared to certain other longhouses at the settlement, the sunken floor of House 138 was of around medium depth and was probably deeper before recent ploughing. A low zone was present in the area of two scorched-stone patches. Relatively high-lying parts of the floor were observable in the eastern and southern parts of the floor. Relatively flat-floored areas were found to the west and northeast. The soil patches A, B, C, D, E, and F were all shallow, mainly having a depth of between 5-15 cm. The significant soil patches in the sunken-floor horizon can briefly be characterized:

A: Minor patch. Sandy soil. Surface dimensions c. 0.58 x 0.48 m. The subsoil to the west of the patch had a slightly darker appearance.

B: Scorched-stone patch. Sandy, blackish soil. Surface dimensions c. 0.60 x 0.50 m.

C: Scorched-stone patch. Sandy, dark, greyish soil containing traces of charcoal and a few heat-affected/cracked stones. Lowest a 2-3 cm thick, sandy, greyish-white layer, presumably influenced by outwash. Surface dimensions c. 1.36 x 1.28 m. Depth c. 0.15 m. A single piece of charred grain was found in a soil sample.

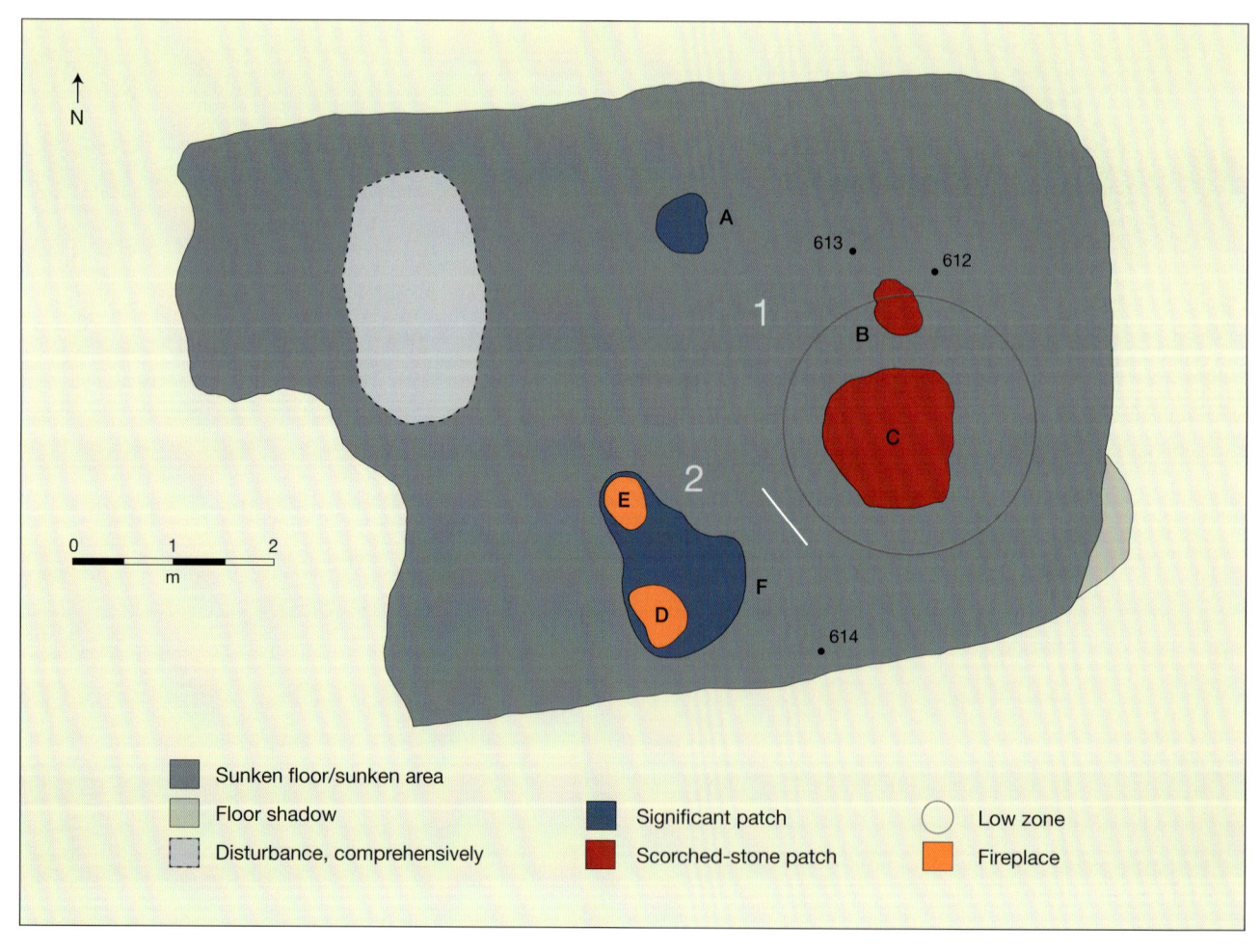

Fig. 4.24. Resengaard, House 138. Ground plan of sunken floor, cleaned. Two activity spaces are proposed. Apart from scorched stones, the artefacts found in situ in the sunken-floor horizon belong to three find spots: **612:** *1 strike-a-light (RE612ea);* **613:** *1 flint dagger (RE613ea);* **614:** *10 potsherds (RE614aa; RE614ab; RE614).*

Fig. 4.25. Resengaard, House 138. A: Strike-a-light (RE612ca) and two characteristic upper parts of clay pots (RE614aa & RE614ab), all from the sunken-floor horizon. From secondary fills above the sunken floor a flint sickle (RE601ca). Lobed flint arrowhead (RE608ea) found in culture layer 335 north of House 143.

D: Fireplace, shallow. Sandy, blackish soil. The modest traces presumably relate to a short-term fireplace. Surface dimensions c. 0.62 x 0.46 m.

E: Fireplace, shallow. Sandy, blackish soil. Here, too, the modest traces presumably relate to a small, short-term fireplace. Surface dimensions c. 0.52 x 0.40 m.

F: Diffuse patch. Sandy, greyish soil. Surface dimensions c. 189 x 130 m.

The artefact remainders from the sunken-floor horizon may represent relatively few activities of different nature in this house. Based on the floor traces, the following are suggested as possible doings in two activity spaces:

1. Drying/roasting/charring/cooking/heating. A strike-a-light and a dagger present.

2. Pottery handling/cooking and heating with stone-free fireplace. Though modest, the two indoor fireplaces observed in this area are unusual at the Resengaard settlement, and the presence of a strike-a-light (more northerly) may support the interpretation.

House 197 (Fig. 4.26 & 4.27; Fig. 4.68.G)

From the secondary fills stem interesting ceramics (Cat. A: RE278 & RE700) and stone artefacts (Cat. B: RE265). An arrowhead (RE699ea) was found immediately north of the cleaned sunken-floor border but the sunken floor area was reduced during the archaeological investigation due to repeated cleaning, and I am convinced that it originally belonged in the periphery of it. Many potsherds were found in the shallow pit F. The placement of this particular pit in the periphery appears to have a possible counterpart in House 2 and House 200, where a pit was likewise placed in each of these by the sunken-floor edge albeit to the west. The number of find spots in the heavily ard-ploughed sunken-floor horizon is very scarce. However, a rather high number of charred cereals derive from it (Cat C: RE294ga, RE309ga, RE627ga, & 705ga) and we also have charred cereals (Cat C: RE702ga) from pit F. The examination of the five samples carried out by Peter Steen Henriksen reveals that

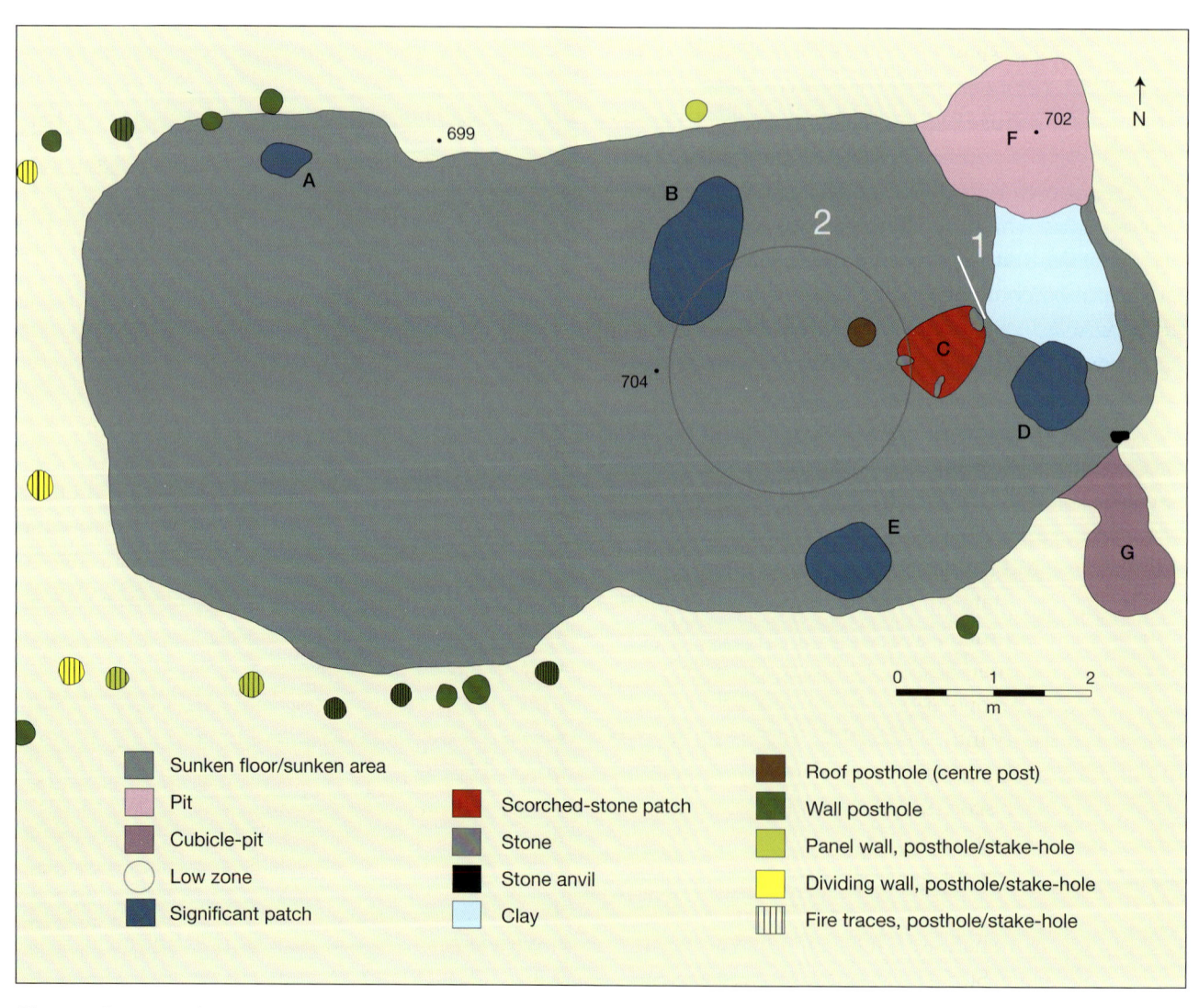

Fig. 4.26. Resengaard, House 197. Ground plan of sunken floor, cleaned. Two activity spaces are suggested. Apart from the anvil and some stones (possibly with heat impact) in situ (patch C) and the lobed flint arrowhead (RE699ea) recorded immediately north of the sunken floor, the artefacts found in the sunken-floor horizon, including its immediate periphery to the north, belong to just two find spots: **702**: *161 potsherds, from several clay pots (RE702aa, ab, ac, ad, ae, af, ag, ah, ai, aj, ak, al, am, an, ao, ap, aq, ar, as, at & ba) & 27 pieces of worked flint (RE702);* **704**: *1 flint arrowhead roughout, very thin at the base, without lobes (RE704ea).*

mainly naked barley and emmer/spelt wheat are present, along with seeds of weeds and hazelnut (For further details, see Cat. C and report S2001a).

The presence of traces of a "cubicle pit" is suggested as an interpretation of the soil feature in the south-east area adjacent to the sunken floor. As no finds are recorded from this area, it is difficult to see a specific meaning to this arrangement, apart from some kind of storage. Compared to certain other longhouses at the settlement, its sunken floor was less than medium deep, and large parts of it were rather shallow with just slight level differences. To the south, in the western part of it, a lower area was also observable but here the depth in relation to the edge of the sunken floor was insignificant. The pits and patches in the sunken-floor horizon can briefly be characterized as follows:

A: Minor patch, shallow. Sandy, blackish soil, probably coloured by a content of carbonized organic material. Rather diffuse edge with surface dimensions c. 54 x 38 cm.

B: Sub-oval patch, shallow. Dark-brownish soil in the upper part and, at the bottom, blackish soil, likely coloured by carbonized organic material. Surface dimensions c. 1.54 x 0.80 m. A soil sample (RE703) stems from this patch.

C: Presumed scorched-stone patch, shallow. Within a minor, sandy area of just 0.75 x 1 m, the few preserved stones in their original position were presumably part of diffuse, not clearly distinguishable, remainders of a patch with ard marks, the outline of which is approximate. The state of these stones does not seem to have been recorded and hence it cannot be said as to whether they had suffered any impact from heat. However, ard-furrows in a larger area went through the floor horizon into the subsoil and some scattered heat-affected/cracked stones were found there. It seems that other scorched-stone patches could have been ploughed out to a degree that made it impossible to make safe observations.

D: Minor patch, shallow. Sandy, blackish soil patch with diffuse edge. Surface dimensions c. 0.88 x 0.84 m. To the north, the patch cut across a presumably natural clay occurrence, measuring an area of c. 1.68 x 1.32 m.

E: Minor pit, shallow. Sandy, blackish soil patch with diffuse edge. Surface dimensions c. 88 x 76 cm.

Fig. 4.27. Resengaard, House 197. From immediately north of the sunken floor, a lobed arrowhead (RE699ea), one lobe missing. From secondary fills, the upper part of a clay pot (RE278aa).

F: Pit. Sandy, dark soil. It is possible that the space above the pit, placed in the northeast corner, formed a kind of small compartment but no postholes support this notion. Surface dimensions c. 1.92 x 1.64 m. Depth of c. 17 cm. To the south, the pit had cut across the above-mentioned clay occurrence.

G: Pit, shallow. Sandy soil. No clear delimitation to the sunken floor was observed. I consider it most likely to represent the vestiges of a small room with hollow bottom, a "cubicle pit" established within the turf wall.

The remainders in the sunken floor horizon only represent limited doings in this house. No activities are suggested in relation to the flint arrowhead to the north or the arrowhead roughout in the centre of the sunken floor. The presence of a great deal of pottery in pit F to the east, in my reading, likely points to storage, maybe also connected to the presence of charred cereals. Pit F to the northeast and pit G to the southeast thereby made use of the remote space of these two corners but no concrete activity is suggested regarding pit G. Concerning other parts of the floor, only activities related to scorched-stone patches are proposed. The following are suggested as possible activities, separated into two activity spaces:

1. Pottery handling/cooking, besides storing (pit F).

2. Drying/roasting/charring/cooking/heating. An arrowhead roughout present.

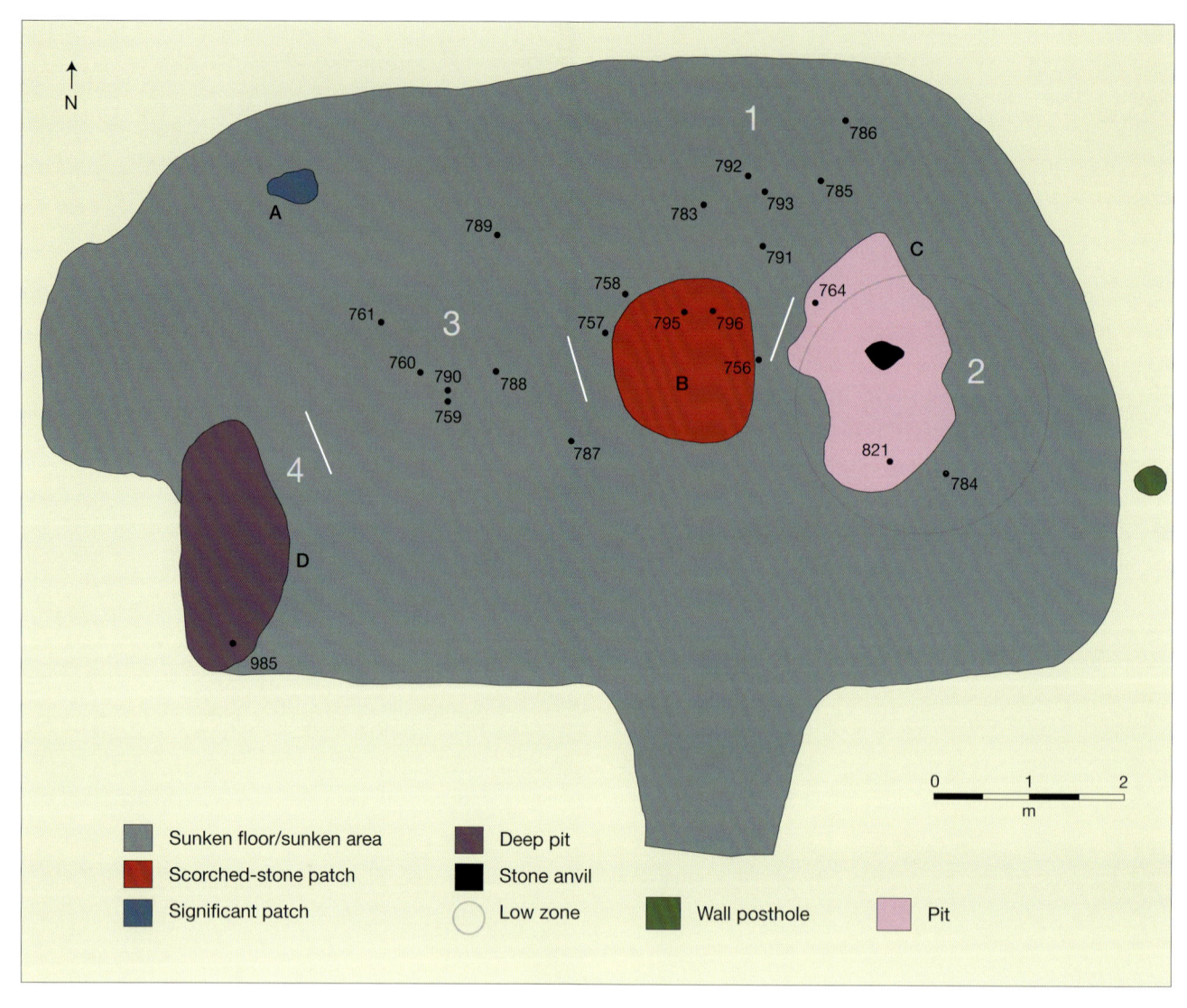

Fig. 4.28. Resengaard, House 200. Ground plan of sunken floor, cleaned. Four activity spaces are proposed. Apart from the stone anvil and the scorched stones, the artefacts found in situ in the sunken-floor horizon overall involve very many find spots: **756:** *1 stone axe with shaft-hole, diameter 30 mm, fragment (RE756ea);* **757:** *1 flint arrowhead (RE757ea);* **758:** *1 flint scraper (RE758ea);* **759:** *19 potsherds & 1 piece of worked flint (RE759aa, ab; RE759);* **760:** *2 potsherds (RE760aa);* **761:** *1 flint arrowhead (RE761ea);* **764:** *1 flint dagger fragment (RE764ea);* **783:** *1 potsherd (RE783aa);* **784:** *1 clay spoon fragment (RE784aa);* **785:** *1 potsherd (RE785aa);* **786:** *1 potsherd (RE786aa);* **787:** *1 flint scraper (RE787ea);* **788:** *1 flint scraper (RE788);* **789:** *1 flint scraper (RE789ea);* **790:** *16 potsherds, all seem from the same clay pot (RE790aa);* **791:** *21 potsherds (RE791aa; RE791);* **792:** *2 potsherds (RE792aa);* **793:** *7 potsherds (RE793; RE793);* **795:** *1 fine-grained whetstone (RE795ea);* **796:** *1 stone hammer (RE796ea), heavily used at both ends, heat-affected;* **821:** *7 potsherds, 2 pieces of worked flint and 1 piece of burned flint (RE821aa; RE821);* **985:** *1 flint dagger fragment & 1 flint arrowhead (RE985ea, eb). From cellar pit D.*

House 200 (Fig. 4.28 & 4.29)

From the secondary fills stem interesting ceramics (Cat. A: RE750, RE765, RE770, RE772, RE773, RE818, RE820, & RE854) and stone artefacts (Cat. B: RE750 & RE763).

Despite the observable influence of ard-ploughing of a certain part of the sunken floor, many finds and important observations were made during excavation. In all, 23 regular find spots are thus recorded from the sunken-floor horizon. A clay pot profile (RE769) probably further derives from the sunken-floor horizon but it has not been possible to identify the precise find spot. Besides some scrapers, flint arrowheads, flint dagger fragments, a whetstone, a shaft-hole axe fragment, some stone hammers and the stone anvil, a relatively high number of different clay pot profiles make up the composition of this house assemblage. Two samples of organic materials contained charred macrofossils (Cat. C: RE904ga & RE962ga).

Fig. 4.29. Resengaard, House 200. A: In front of a soil bench, the ard-ploughed scorched-stone patch C, partly excavated to the right. Likely due to the ard, mainly small heat-cracked stones were left and the patch had a very diffuse boundary. Seen from the east. B: In front of the soil bench, the entire eastern floor at a late stage of its investigation. The anvil was placed semi-buried in the pit. The large stone to the right was placed there after abandonment of the longhouse. Seen from the northeast. Artefacts: Stone axe fragment (RE756ea) with clear traces after drilling the shaft-hole, heavily used and heat-affected stone hammer (RE796ea), part of important flint dagger (RE985ea), and upper parts of two characteristic clay pots, all from the sunken-floor horizon. From secondary fills, a flint dagger handle (RE750ei). Such pieces in fills may have had changing contexts and a long life at the settlements.

Artefacts, pits, patches, and daily life activities

No finds of artefacts or plant materials derive from the "corridor" running from the south side of this sunken floor, being the deepest found at Resengaard. In all probability, recent ploughing had removed the top of the sunken floor so that it was originally even somewhat deeper. The relatively high-lying parts were present in the western half north of pit D. Fairly flat areas were found in the western part, as well as in the middle. The significant pits and patches in the sunken-floor horizon can briefly be characterized as follows:

A: Minor patch, shallow. Sandy, greyish soil. Surface dimensions c. 0.54 x 0.36 m. Depth c. 0.22 m.

B: Scorched-stone patch, shallow. Sandy greyish soil layer, thickness at least 5 cm, containing many minor scattered heat-affected/cracked stones. The boundary of the patch appeared rather diffuse due to impact from ard-ploughing and it is only approximately outlined. Surface dimensions c. 1.45 x 1.65 m. Immediately above, a rather diffusely delimited thin "layer" of sandy soil which, in contrast, was almost free of stones.

C: Sizeable pit. Containing sandy dark, brownish soil, while blackish soil with traces of charcoal was in the periphery. Surface dimensions c. 2.65 x 1.70 m. Depth c. 0.14 m. Besides a few small stones, a large stone partly dug down centrally likely functioned as an anvil, the dimensions being c. 0.40 m x 0.29 m, height c. 0.38 cm. It was recovered *in situ* and did not show any impact from fire.

D: Deep cellar pit. The hole was dug into the sunken-floor periphery and, in my interpretation, this represents an interior cellar pit. Sandy soil. To the north, east and west it had rather steep sides, while to the south it was more unevenly sloping towards the bottom. The surface dimensions were c. 2.52 x 1.12 m, depth c. 0.68 m. Its filling up might have begun simultaneously with the general dumping of soil into the sunken area because its fill corresponded to that of the secondary fills.

When it comes to the rather large stone present towards the northeast in the sunken area, it was concluded that it did not belong to the floor, based on a thorough investigation of the soil beneath. It became clear that the stone was resting on some centimetres of secondary fills and hence it obviously did not belong to the equipment of the house. The two flint arrowheads found more westerly in the sunken floor need not attribute any activity to the find spot but, for instance, mounting of these could of course have been an activity. Many potsherds were found a little north of the scorched-stone patch and somewhat west of it. Some stone tools were present in this patch, presumably indicating various activities. The clay spoon fragment, found to the south, might have been used, for instance, in a cooking process. The sizeable pit D was presumably used for storage of, for instance, foods or liquids. Remarkably, this was the only deep pit in a sunken-floor longhouse at Resengaard. Based on the floor traces, the following are suggested as possible activities, separated into four activity spaces:

1. Drying/roasting/charring/cooking/heating, polishing/sharpening, hammering/crushing, and pottery handling/cooking. An arrowhead and a stone axe fragment also present.

2. Pottery handling/cooking. The sizeable pit and the presumed stone anvil at its centre likely indicate significant activities of unknown character. A dagger fragment stems from the pit.

3. Scraping and pottery handling/cooking.

4. Storing. A dagger and an arrowhead found in the pit.

4.3. Interpreting the floors in three special minor house sites at Resengaard

All three house sites are characterized by the presence of scorched-stone patches and are therefore of a special nature. The artefacts, plant materials, floor levels, low zones and soil patches from these building remainders will be presented and daily life activities suggested.

House 202 (Fig. 4.30; Fig. 4.68.H)

Some potsherds of interest (Cat. A: RE752 & RE974) were remove, together with a sample of heat-affected/cracked stones, without noting their precise location on the plan drawing, and are therefore ascribed only to the secondary fills. Two samples of plant materials from scorched-stone patch A comprised a few charred cereals and seeds from weeds (Cat. C: RE816ga & RE967ga).

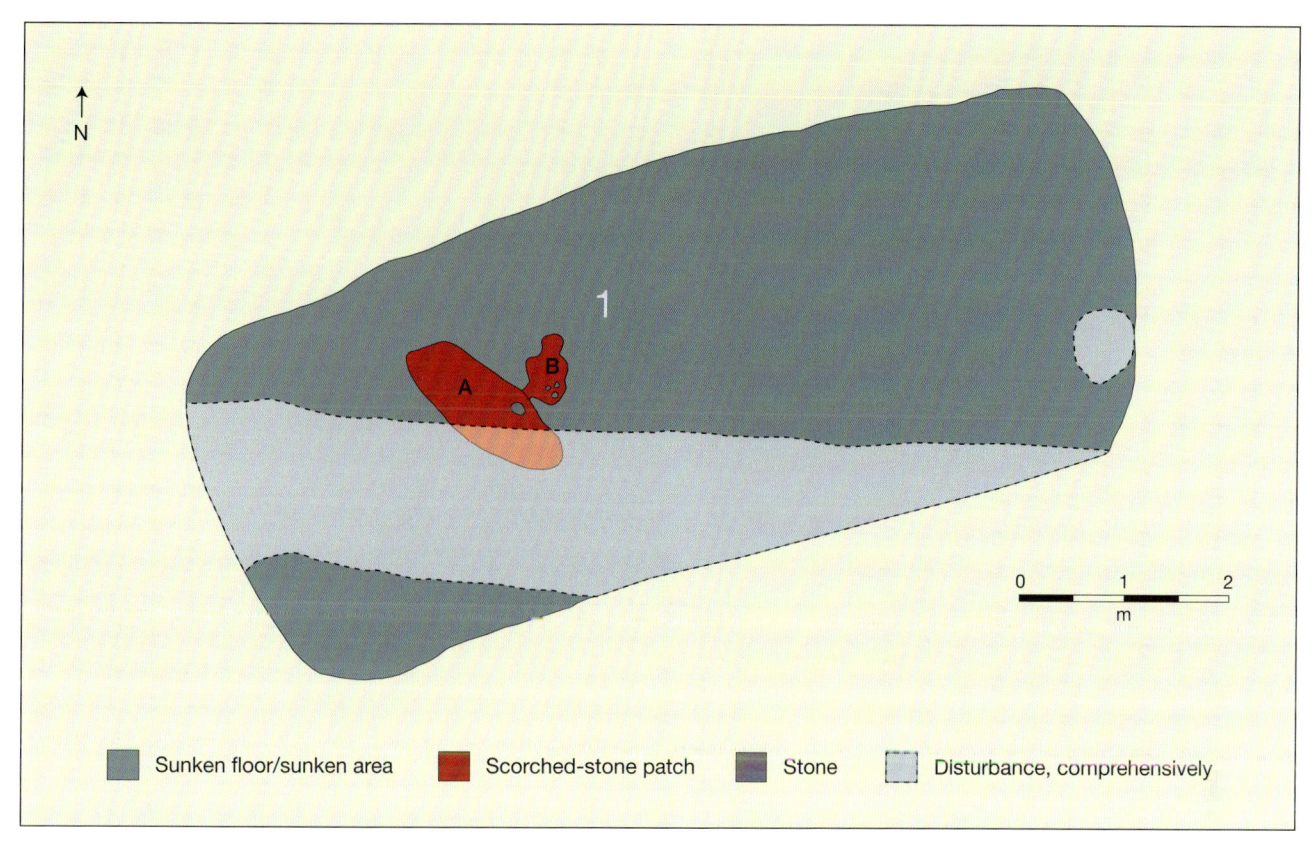

Fig. 4.30. Resengaard, House 202. Ground plan of sunken floor, cleaned. One activity space is suggested.

A low zone (not illustrated) was observable in the area of the soil patches but, compared to the higher parts of the floor to the west, the difference was modest. The significant soil patches in the sunken floor can briefly be characterized as follows:

A: Scorched-stone patch. Sandy, lightish-grey soil in the top with traces of charcoal. To the west and below the top layer, dark greyish-black soil with heat-affected/cracked stones as well as the modest presence of charcoal and dust from charred organic material. Surface dimensions c. 1.74 x 0.64 m, depth c. 0.14 m.

B: Scorched-stone patch, small. Sandy, lightish-grey soil in the top with heat-affected/cracked stones and traces of tiny pieces of presumably reddish-burned clay. Below was observed greyish-black sand with remainders of charcoal and, in the sides, yellow or brownish layers of sand. Surface dimensions c. 0.62 x 0.40 m, depth c. 0.20 m.

The scant traces of charcoal in patches A and B do not provide adequate evidence of a fireplace. Because regular tools and pottery were absent from the sunken-floor horizon, only modest vestiges of activities, connected to the presence of scorched stones and charred plant materials, are available. Heat-affected/cracked stones were often in numbers in the scorched-stone patches but only a few were present here. Based on the floor traces, the following are suggested as possible activities in a single activity space:

1. Drying/roasting/charring/cooking/heating.

House 240 (Fig. 4.31)

From the secondary fills stem interesting ceramics (Cat. A: RE798, RE799, RE804, RE809, RE851, RE858, RE860, RE973, & RE1043) and stone artefacts (Cat. B: RE798, RE805, RE810, RE813, RE814, RE821, & RE853), including also a flint adze (Cat. B: RE801).

From the sunken-floor horizon derive no plant materials. Several finds were recorded just above the floor but only a few artefact remainders from seven regular find spots belong to the sunken-floor horizon, as well as a semi-buried stone that I consider to be a stone anvil (RE1067).

A low zone was observable in the northern part of the sunken floor (not illustrated). Relatively high-

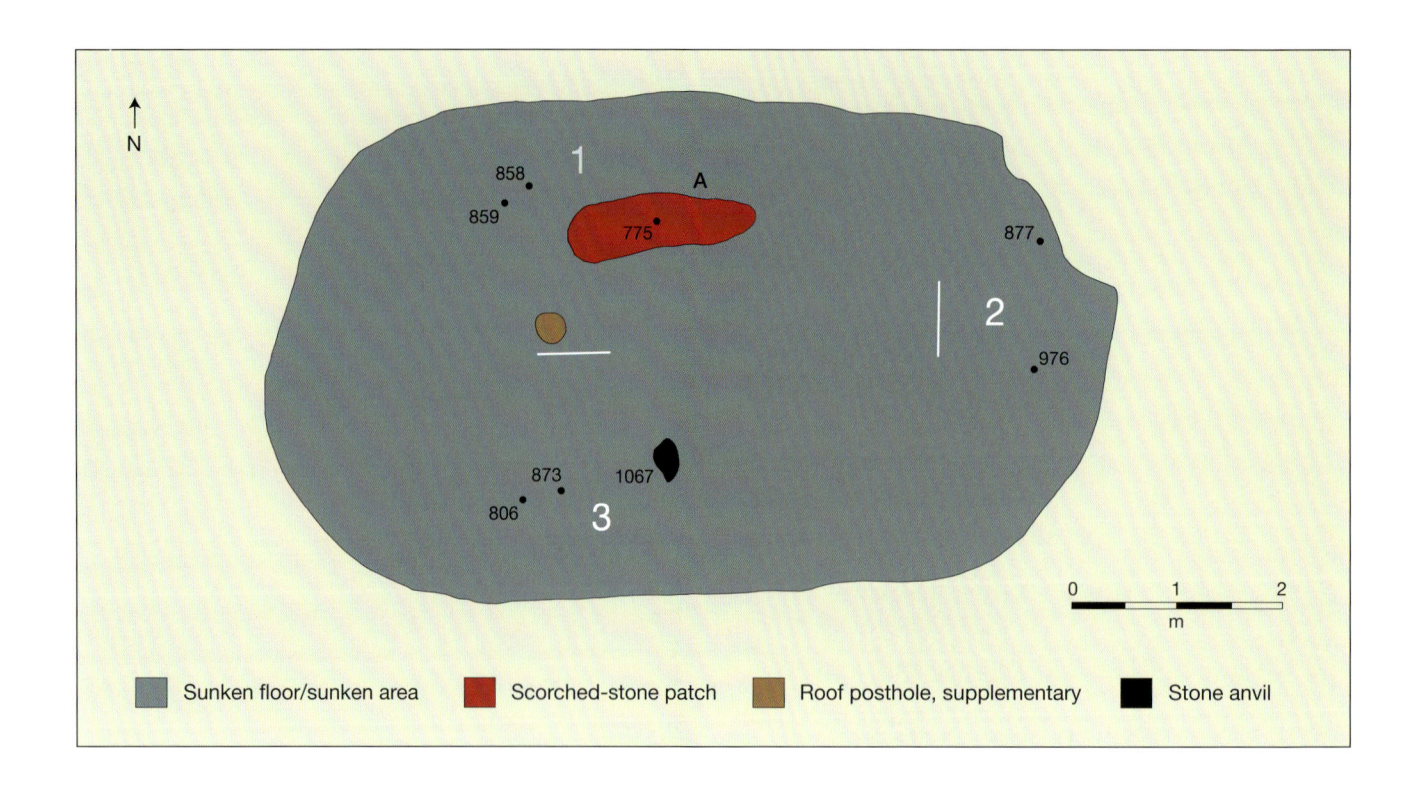

▨ Sunken floor/sunken area	▨ Scorched-stone patch	▨ Roof posthole, supplementary	■ Stone anvil

RE858aa 1:2

RE860aa 1:2

RE806aa 1:2   RE798aq 1:2

260   Chapter 4

◀ *Fig. 4.31. Resengaard, House 240. A: Ground plan of sunken floor, cleaned. Three activity spaces are suggested. B: Besides some artefact remainders, numerous heat-affected/cracked stones (after excavation placed on the soil bench) were found in the lengthy scorched-stone patch A. Apart from these stones and the stone anvil (RE1067), the artefacts found in situ in the sunken-floor horizon belong to a few find spots:* **775:** *6 potsherds & 18 pieces of worked flint scattered in the patch (RE775aa; RE775);* **806:** *1 potsherd (RE806aa);* **858:** *5 potsherds (RE858aa; RE858);* **859:** *1 flint arrowhead roughout (RE859);* **873:** *1 flint hammer (RE873);* **876:** *6 potsherds (RE876aa; RE876);* **877:** *1 flint scraper (RE877ea). Artefact photos: Examples of rather expressive pottery, of which two belong to the sunken-floor horizon (RE858aa & RE806aa) and the other to the secondary fills (RE798aa & RE860aa).*

lying areas of the floor were found to the west and southwest, while relatively flat-floored areas were observable in the western half of the sunken floor. A single soil patch in the sunken floor can briefly be characterized as follows:

A: Scorched-stone patch. Beneath a disturbing pit was observed a lengthy patch with a preserved layer of blackish soil with numerous heat-affected/cracked stones, potsherds and flint. In the bottom, some light-brownish, sandy soil was observed. Surface dimensions c. 1.84 x 0.52 m, depth c. 0.40 m.

The artefact remainders from the sunken-floor horizon could represent several different doings in this building. Considering the representation of potsherds from the floor, it is also remarkable that the secondary fills contained comparatively large amounts of pottery of interest. Based on the floor traces, the following are suggested as possible doings, separated into three activity spaces:

1. Drying/roasting/charring/cooking/heating and pottery handling/cooking. An arrowhead roughout present.

2. Scraping and pottery handling/cooking.

3. Hammering/crushing and pottery handling/cooking. A stone anvil present.

House 289 (Fig. 4.32)

From the secondary fills stem interesting ceramics (Cat. A: RE900, RE1056, & RE1058). From the sunken-floor horizon derive no plant materials. No regular find spots were recorded in the sunken-floor horizon apart from a scorched-stone patch and two presumed stone anvils.

The sunken floor was more square than the two previous and was probably somewhat deeper prior to recent ploughing. Centrally, a low zone was observable (not illustrated), while the relatively high-lying parts of the floor could be seen to the southeast and southwest. Relatively flat-floored areas were present in the northern half of the sunken floor. In all, four patches were recorded and A, C, and D were all shallow, mainly 5-15 cm. The significant soil patches in the sunken floor can briefly be characterized as follows:

A: Scorched-stone patch. Sandy soil with several minor heat-cracked stones. A single larger stone present but, by accident, whether or not it showed traces of heat cracking or other kinds of heat marks was not recorded (although presumably it did not). Surface dimensions of the soil patch were c. 0.76 x 0.52 m.

B: Scorched-stone patch. Sandy, dark soil, likely coloured by carbonized organic material and containing several minor heat-affected/cracked stones. Surface dimensions c. 0.64 x 0.64 m, depth c. 5 cm. It might have been slightly longer N-S than stated because it was not possible to clearly define the end of the soil feature in the area of a cross-section.

C: Irregular patch. Sandy, greyish-brown soil. Surface dimensions c. 2.04 x 1.56 m.

D: Minor patch. Sandy, greyish-brown soil. Surface dimensions c. 0.96 x 0.72 m.

As finds of regular tools and pottery were absent from this sunken floor, only activities relating to the scorched stones can be proposed. Based on the floor traces, the following are suggested as possible doings in a single activity space:

1. Drying/roasting/charring/cooking/heating. Two presumed stone anvils present.

Artefacts, pits, patches, and daily life activities 261

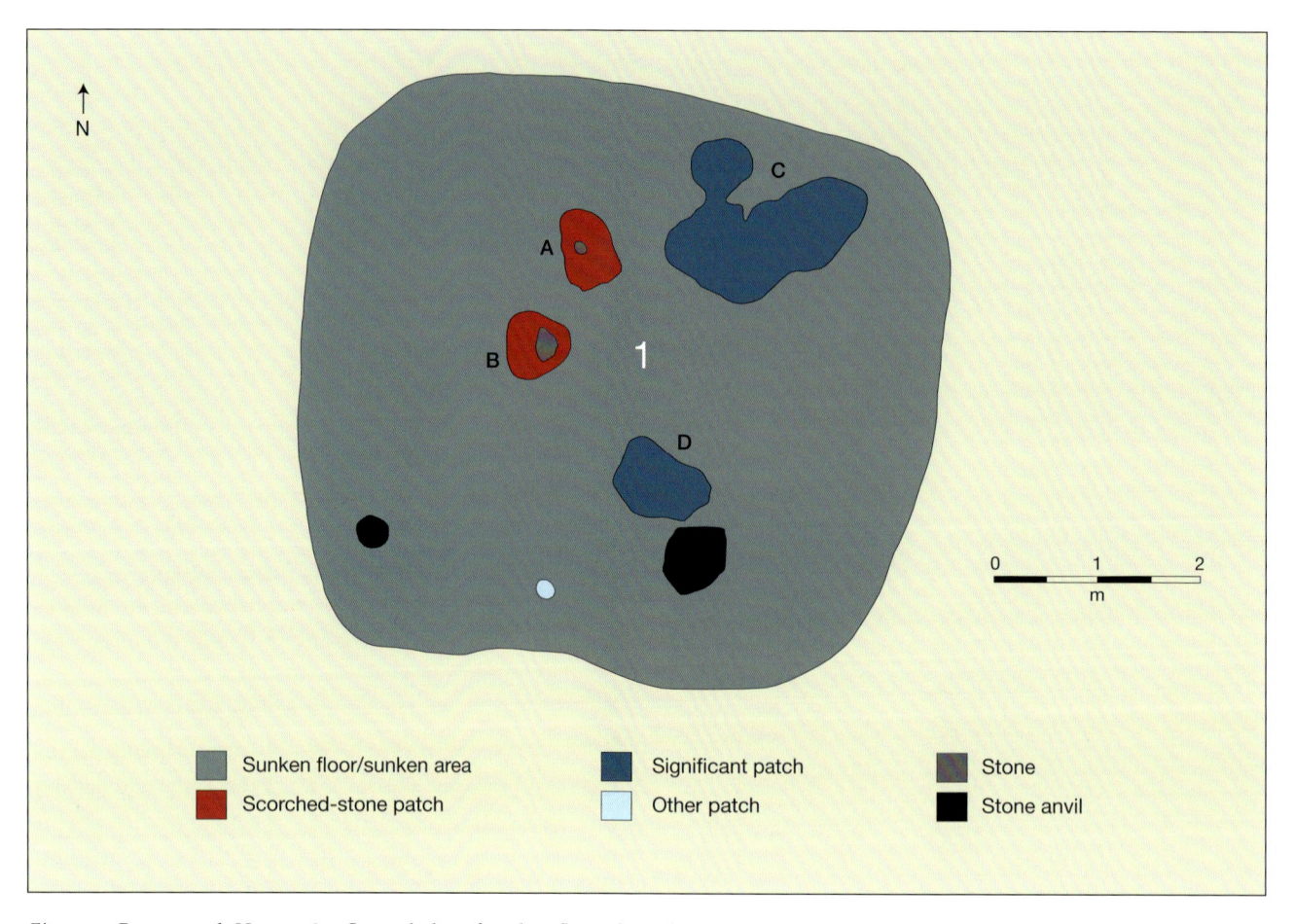

Fig. 4.32. Resengaard, House 289. Ground plan of sunken floor, cleaned. Apart from stone anvils, no find spots exist from the sunken floor. One activity space is proposed.

4.4. Interpreting the floors in ten minor house sites and one short house site at Resengaard

No scorched-stone patches were recovered from the sunken-floor horizons of these building remainders. The artefacts, plant materials, floor levels and soil patches from the sites of ten minor houses and one short house (as well as the possible "House 160") are presented in the following and, where possible, daily life activities are suggested.

House 10 (Fig. 4.33 & 4.34)

From the secondary fills stem interesting ceramics (Cat. A: RE260). The substantial presence of ceramics on the northeast part of the sunken floor presumably evidences a special use of this building. Rims and sides of several clay pots were present and allowed further reconstruction in drawing. In addition, many potsherds were also found in the secondary fills.

Among the organic materials are a few charred cereals and a tiny piece of hazelnut shell (Cat. C: RE305 & RE306). These charred plant materials likely belong to the floor horizon although this cannot be documented.

A lower area was observable to the northeast where the potsherds were also found. The relatively high-lying floor areas were apparent in the western parts of the sunken floor and these were also rather flat-floored. No particular soil patches were present in the sunken-floor horizon.

It is remarkable that the bulk of potsherds were found in the same area, albeit in seven concentrations. I consider these as belonging to one activity space. It is further interesting that the only kind of floor finds were largely the pottery because not even a regular stone tool was found, just two pieces of worked flint. The following is suggested as possible activities in a single activity space:

A. Pottery handling/cooking.

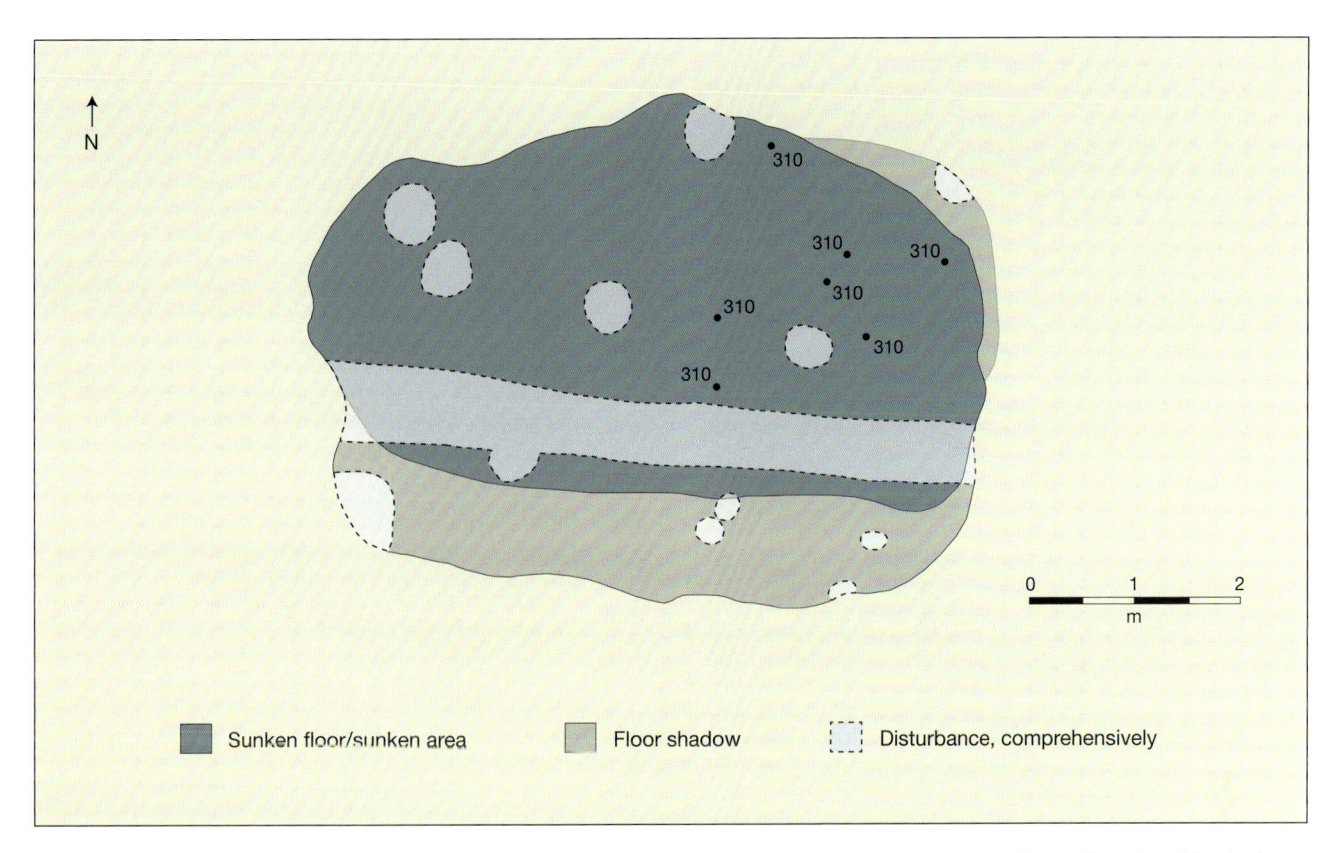

Fig. 4.33. Resengaard, House 10. Ground plan of sunken floor, cleaned. One activity space is suggested. The artefacts found in situ in the sunken floor horizon belong to a potsherd concentration, found as seven minor clusters in the northeast quadrant of the sunken floor: **310:** *RE310aa, ab, ac, ad, ae, & other), as well as 2 pieces of worked flint (RE310).*

House 12 (Fig. 2.23 & 2.24)

From the secondary fills stem interesting ceramics (Cat. A: RE250) and stone artefacts (Cat. B: RE250). From the sunken-floor horizon derive no plant materials. Although many potsherds formed part of the secondary fills, no artefacts or organic materials belonged to the sunken floor. A lower area was observable to the southeast. Relatively high-lying areas of the floor were observable in the northern half of the sunken floor, while rather flat-floored areas were observable in the middle and to the east. No relevant soil patches were observed. No daily life activities can be proposed.

House 84 (Fig. 2.25)

From the sunken-floor horizon stem no plant materials. A clay pot profile (Cat. A: RE485) and other pottery, as well as a strike-a-light and other flint items belong to the secondary fills of this site as does a piece of dark-brownish, semi-transparent amber with original cortex (RE485ga, dimensions c. 3.5 x 2.7 x 2.0 cm, fragmented during excavation).

A lower area was observable in the middle of the northern part of the floor. Relatively high-lying parts were observable to the west and southwest, whereas relatively flat-floored areas were found both in the easternmost and westernmost parts of the sunken floor. No relevant soil patches were observed in the sunken floor. In all, no daily life activities can be suggested.

House 112 (Fig. 4.35)

From the secondary fills stem interesting ceramics (Cat. A: RE513). From the sunken-floor horizon derive no plant materials. Apart from a stone, considered to be an anvil (RE623), only one regular find spot was recorded from the sunken floor. A slightly lower area was observable in the middle and northeast part of the floor. The relatively high-lying parts of the floor were found in the western and southwest part but most of it was rather flat and no particular soil patches were observed.

The following is suggested as a possible activity in a single activity space:

1. Scraping. A stone anvil present.

Artefacts, pits, patches, and daily life activities

Fig. 4.34. Resengaard, House 10. A: Potsherds from several clay pots recovered from the floor. Artefacts: Upper parts of three characteristic clay pots (RE310aa, RE310ab & RE310ae).

House 143 (Fig. 2.17 & 2.27)

A few artefact remainders were found from culture layer 335 near the sites of Houses 143 and 138 (Cat. A: RE603) and two flint scrapers (Cat. B: RE608ea & RE610ea). A flint scraper/borer (Cat. B: RE609) stems from the secondary fills. No artefacts or organic materials belong to the sunken-floor horizon.

A lower area was observable in the eastern part of floor. The relatively high-lying floor parts were observable to the west and southwest, while rather flat-floored areas were found in the northern half of the floor. No significant soil patches were observable. In all, no daily life activities can be proposed.

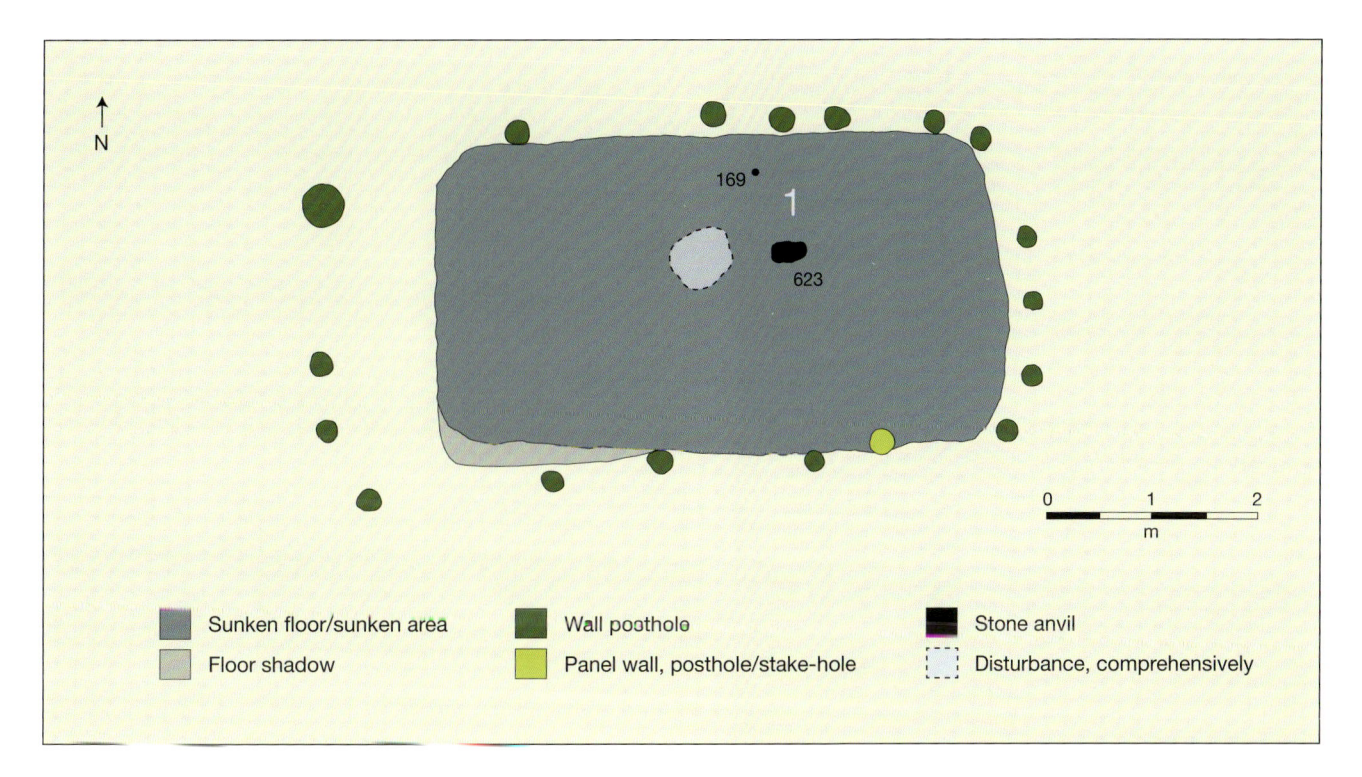

Fig. 4.35. Resengaard, House 112. A: Ground plan, cleaned. One activity space is suggested. B: Semi-buried stone anvil in section, seen from the east. No organic materials belong to the sunken-floor horizon. Apart from the anvil, an artefact found in situ belongs to the sunken-floor horizon and it concerns: **169:** *1 flint scraper (RE169ea).*

House 158 (Fig. 4.36 & 4.37; Fig. 4.68.I)

From the secondary fills stem ceramics (Cat. A: RE1040 & RE1042) and stone artefacts (Cat. B: RE674, 1040, 1041, 1042 & 1045). Among these flint items, a polished axe (RE1045ea), as well as an axe roughout (RE1042ea), could well belong to the sunken-floor horizon but, as a matter of caution, I consider these to belong to the secondary fills. From the sunken-floor horizon derive no plant materials.

The terrain west of the sunken floor was considerably higher than to the east and, due to the terrain differences, the deepest point of the sunken floor would have reached c. 0.85 m if measuring from the highest edge to the lowest to the east. Rather high-lying parts of the floor were thus present in the western parts. Relatively flat-floored areas were observable mostly to the northeast. No particular soil patches were present.

It seems plausible that the house might have been used for a rather special purpose, due to the unusual placing on sloping grounds towards the eastern "edge" of the hill. The small flint axe could have been used for interior purposes for some less demanding tasks. It is the only house with a complete Late Neolithic flint axe found in the floor horizon at Resengaard. The resources available for investigating this house site were too scarce, however, and these conditions have, naturally, significantly influenced our knowledge of it. Based on the floor traces, the following are suggested as a possible activity in the activity space:

1. Axe chopping

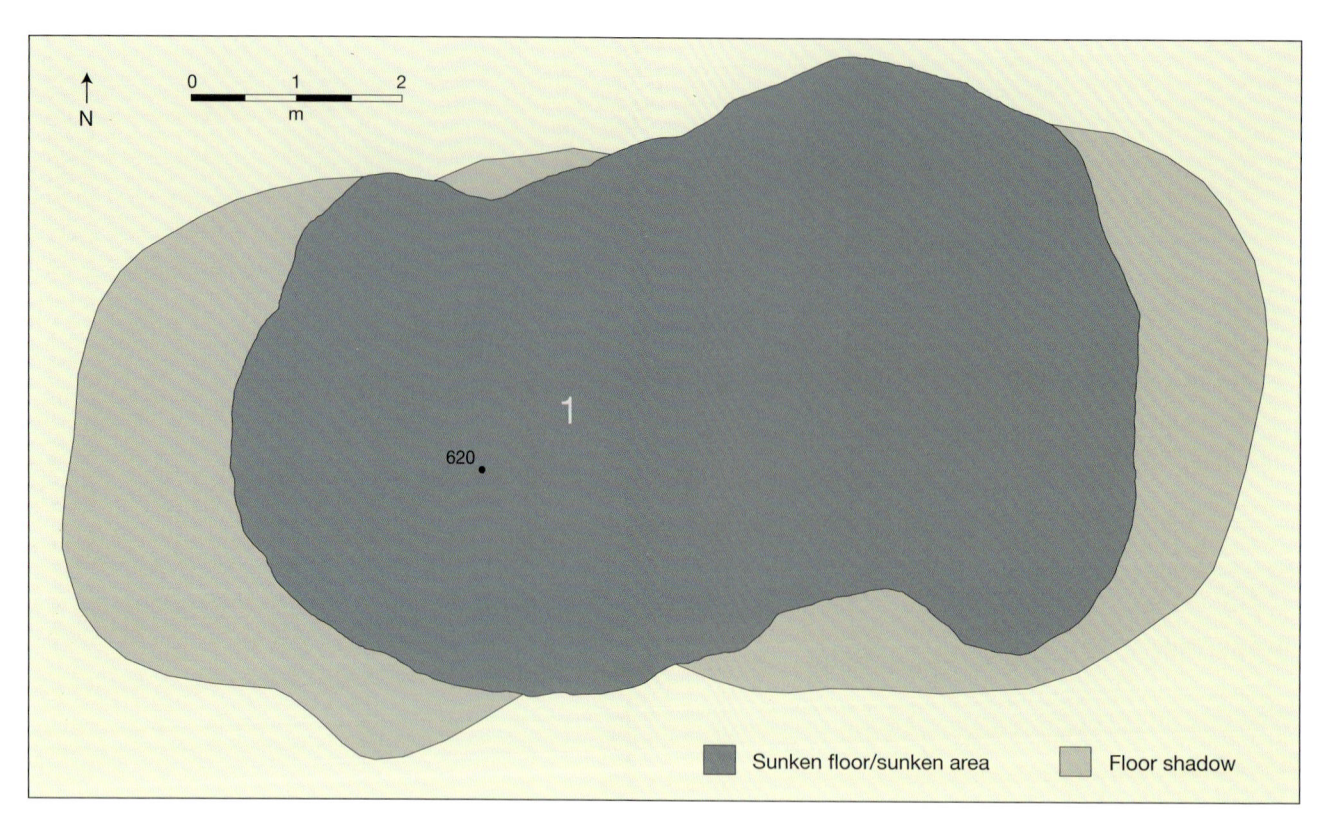

Fig. 4.36. Resengaard, House 158. Ground plan, cleaned. Only a single activity space is suggested. An artefact found in situ stems from the sunken-floor horizon and it concerns: **620:** *1 flint axe, polished (RE620eb).*

Fig. 4.37. Resengaard, House 158. Flint axe belonging to the sunken-floor horizon (RE620eb). Ascribed to the secondary fills is another flint axe (RE1045ea). An axe roughout (RE1042ee) and a lobed flint arrowhead (RE1042ea) belong to these fills.

266 Chapter 4

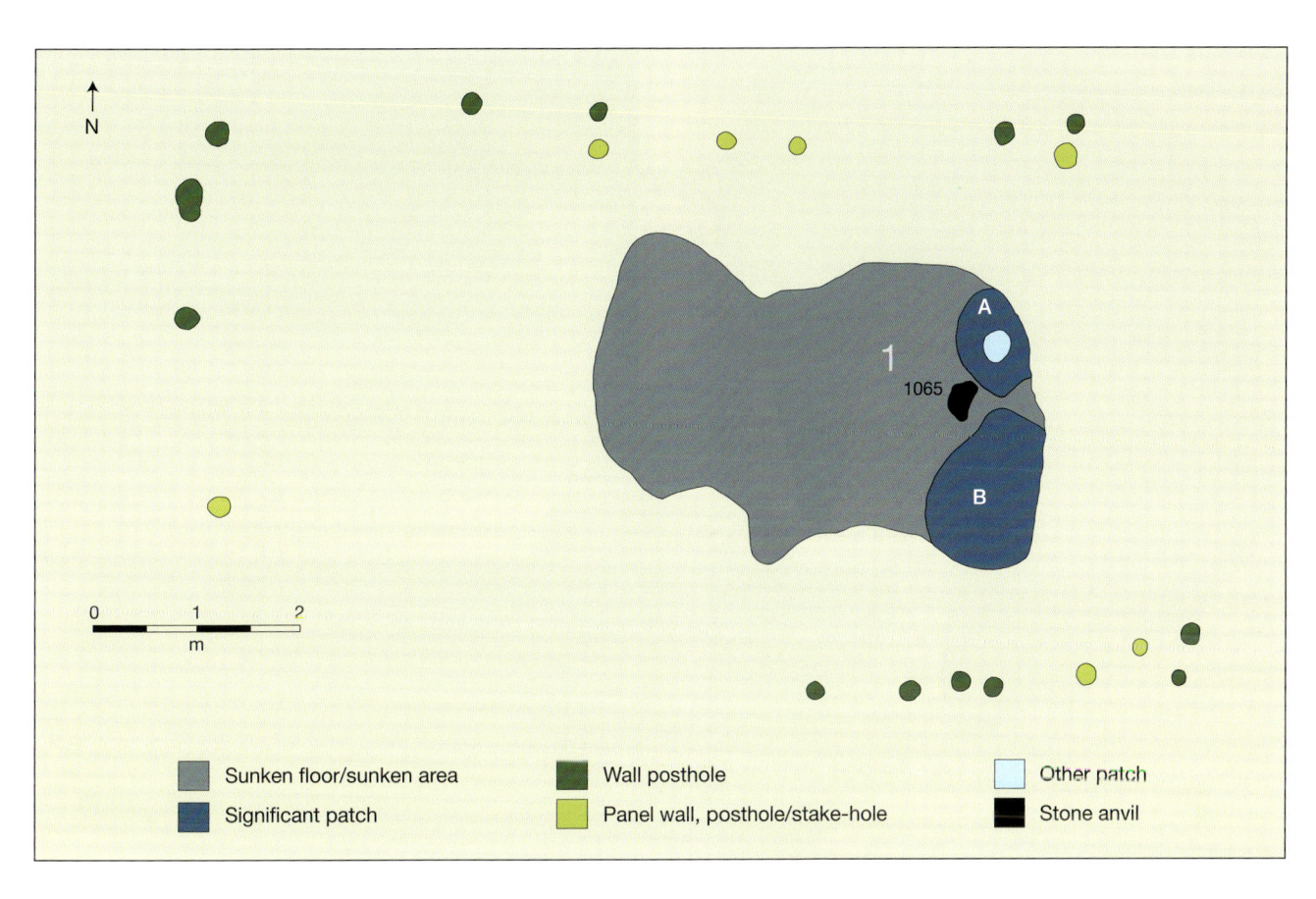

Fig. 4.38. Resengaard, House 193. A: Ground plan, cleaned. Apart from the presence of a stone anvil, no find spots belong to the sunken-floor horizon. One activity space suggested. Artefact photos: Two views of a clay pot side and bottom with an unusual foot ring, not fashioned with the customary craftsmanship. From a posthole, northern wall.

Artefacts, pits, patches, and daily life activities 267

House 183 (Fig. 2.29)

From the secondary fills stem interesting ceramics (Cat. A: RE666). From the sunken-floor horizon derive no plant materials. No artefacts or organic materials belong to the sunken-floor horizon. The sunken floor was relatively deep and a low zone was observable centrally and a little to the north. More high-lying parts were observable to the west. A minor flat area was present to the east. No particular soil patches were observed in the sunken-floor horizon and no daily life activities can be proposed.

House 193 (Fig. 4.38)

A stone that I consider to be an anvil was placed in the eastern part of the sunken-floor horizon and no other artefacts or organic materials belong to the sunken floor. The clay pot with a foot ring stemming from a posthole (Cat. A: RE675) is considered in Ch. 3.

The sunken floor was the shallowest of all those at Resengaard at the time of the investigation although it was probably much deeper and presumably significantly more extensive in length and width prior to the impact from recent ploughing. Compared to the flat-floored parts of the floor in the middle and western parts, a slightly lower area was observable in the eastern part of floor. Two significant soil patches in the sunken floor can briefly be characterized as follows:

A: Sub-oval patch. Sandy, rather dark soil. Surface dimensions c. 1.00 x 0.66 m. Depth only a few cm. A minor sub-circular and shallow soil feature was present in the centre, having a diameter of c. 30 cm. Its soil was not described.

B: Larger patch. Sandy, rather dark soil. Surface dimensions c. 1.48 x 1.08 m. Depth only a few cm.

No specified doings can be suggested in the activity space. And yet it is interesting that this minor house floor comprised a stone anvil and two clear soil patches, presumably stemming from significant doings. The centrally-placed stone anvil could, of course, have been used for various purposes but the remarkable absence of tools and other artefacts may indicate that the activities have made use of now decayed organic objects.

House 198 (Fig. 4.39)

From the secondary fills stem interesting ceramics (Cat. A: RE634, RE678 & RE1059) and stone artefacts (Cat. B: RE634). The fragments of a c. 39 cm high jar (RE1059aa) were taken to the museum without an attached number but, being easily recognizable, the excavator later stated the secondary fills as the proper context. From the sunken-floor horizon derive no plant materials.

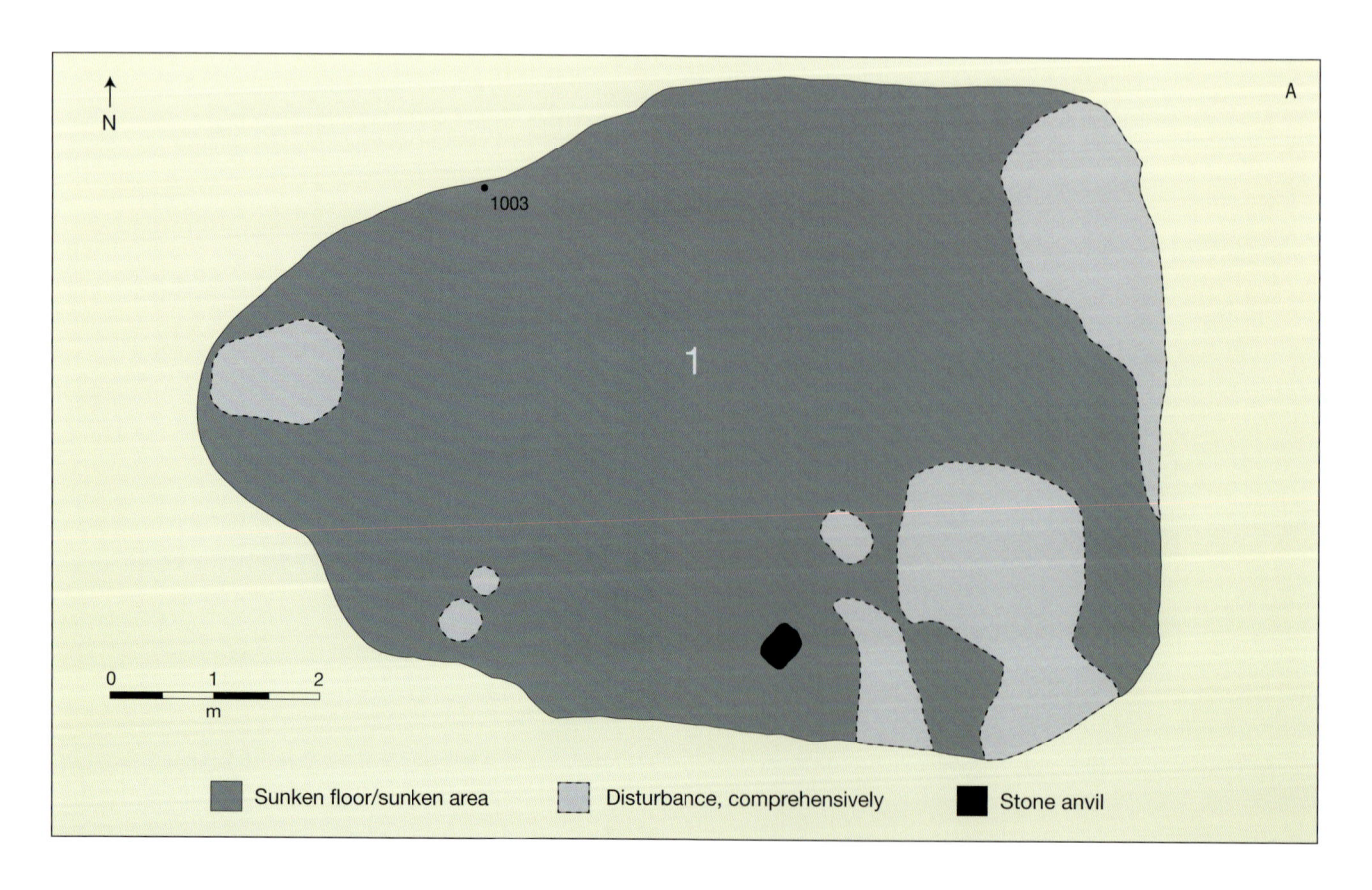

RE1059aa 1:2

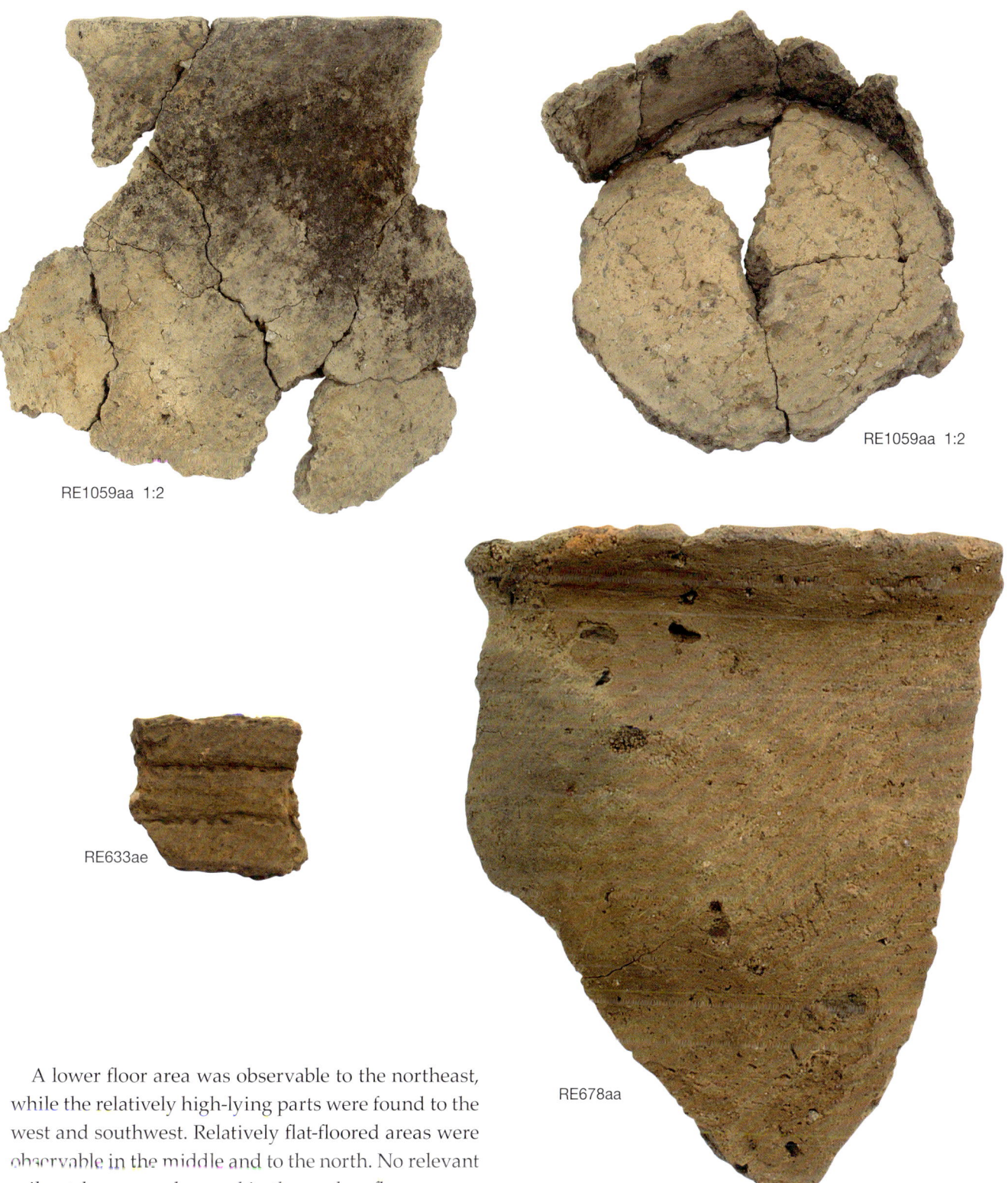

RE1059aa 1:2

RE633ae

RE678aa

A lower floor area was observable to the northeast, while the relatively high-lying parts were found to the west and southwest. Relatively flat-floored areas were observable in the middle and to the north. No relevant soil patches were observed in the sunken floor.

Finds and observations concerning this sunken floor were very meagre. Only a single regular find spot in the periphery of the sunken floor was recorded as well as the presence of a semi-buried stone anvil to the south. The following is suggested as a possible activity in a single activity space:

1. Scraping.

◄▲ *Fig. 4.39. Resengaard, House 198. A: Ground plan, cleaned. One activity space suggested. Apart from the anvil, a single find spot belongs to the sunken-floor horizon:* **1003:** *1 flint scraper (RE1003ea). Artefact photos: Upper and lower part of a vessel (RE1059), secondary fills. Upper part of clay pot (RE678aa), secondary fills. Potsherd with decoration of four horizontal cardium lines (RE633ae), deriving from a pit (325) north of the house site.*

Artefacts, pits, patches, and daily life activities 269

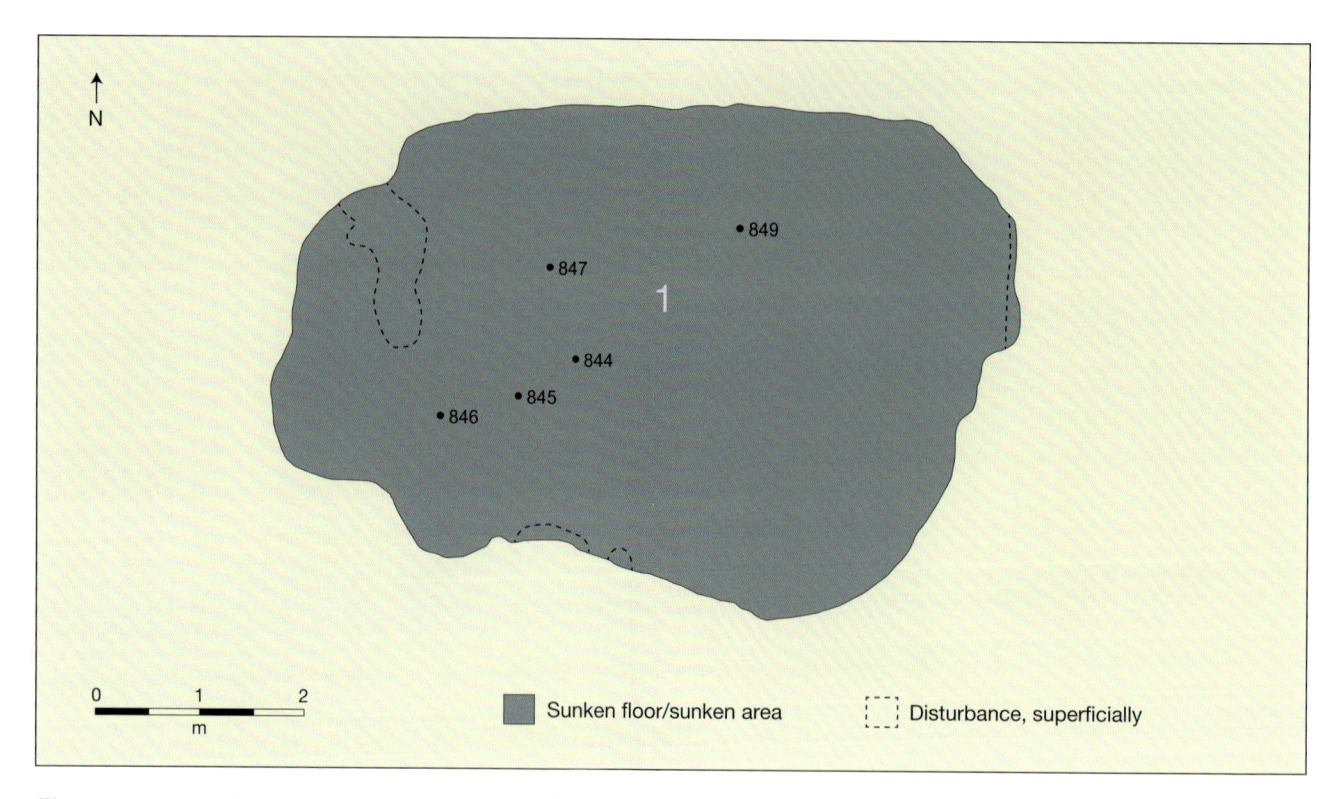

Fig. 4.40. Resengaard, House 268. Ground plan, cleaned. A single activity space is suggested. The artefacts in the sunken-floor horizon involve a few find spots: **844:** *14 potsherds, most apparently from the same vessel, as well as some pieces of burned bone (RE844aa; 844ab; 844);* **845:** *1 piece of worked flint (RE845);* **846:** *1 potsherd (846aa, same clay pot as RE843, ascribed to the secondary fills);* **847:** *1 potsherd (847aa);* **849:** *21 potsherds, including rims from three clay pots (RE849aa; 849ac).*

House 268 (Fig. 4.40 & 4.41)

From the secondary fills stem interesting ceramics (Cat. A: RE257, RE270, RE824, RE832, RE833, RE836, RE837, RE840, & RE843) and a spoon-shaped scraper (Cat. B: RE270). *Inter alia*, a fragmented loom weight (RE836aa) belongs to the secondary fills. From the sunken-floor horizon derive no plant materials. A lower area was observable to the southeast. Relatively high-lying, flat floor parts were observable to the west. No relevant soil patches were found in the sunken floor. Even though the house site was much disturbed and found in an area with many, probably mostly later, settlement elements such as, not least, pits and postholes, a few find spots with ceramics are considered to belong to the sunken floor. The following is suggested as possible doings in a single activity space:

1. Pottery handling/cooking.

House 201 (Fig. 4.42; Fig. 4.68.J)

From the secondary fills stem ceramics of interest (Cat. A: RE972) and a stone hammer (Cat. B: RE753). Apart from a sizeable, semi-buried stone considered to be an anvil (RE1063ea), no regular find spots with artefacts or organic materials belong to this short house. The sunken floor was very shallow but was likely somewhat deeper prior to the impact of recent ploughing. Relatively high-lying parts of the floor were found to the southwest. No significant soil features were found. No doings related to the stone anvil in the eastern half of the sunken can be proposed but some faint traces, apparently from use, were observed on the top of it. No specific activity spaces can be suggested.

"House 160" (Fig. 2.35 & 4.43)

In this pit, which might be a relic of a very early house site (see Ch. 3), was found a single flint item and a moderate number of potsherds (Cat. A: RE632aa, ab & ac; RE621aa) together with those from neighbouring pits to the west, not least pit 161 (Cat. A. RE636aa, ab, ac, ad, ae, af, ag, ah, ai, aj, ak, al, am, an, ao, ap, aq, ar, as, at, au, av, ax, ay, az, ba, bb, bc, bd & be). Pit 196, from which a flint dagger blade fragment (Cat. A: RE639ea) stems, could also have had the same relationship. No organic materials were found in any of these three pits.

RE849ab 1:2

RE849ac

RE836aa

Fig. 4.41. Resengaard, House 268. Upper parts of two clay pots (RE849ab & RE849ac), sunken-floor horizon. A loom weight fragment (RE836aa), secondary fills.

Fig. 4.42. Resengaard, House 201. At a late stage of the excavation, the sunken floor is here cleaned and, to the right, the semi-buried stone anvil is visible as it would have been originally. Seen from the southeast.

Artefacts, pits, patches, and daily life activities 271

Fig. 4.43. Resengaard, pit 161 & pit 77. The possible "House 160" (Fig. 2.35) also includes pit 161, from where the following artefacts stem: with cortex partly preserved, the unusual flint item (RE636ea) is concavely retouched at both ends. Seven examples of ornamentation on Beaker ceramics from this pit, the first being decorated with an indication of horizontal zones with notch-stamped lines (RE636az), and six others (RE636ac, RE636af, RE636ba, RE636bb, RE636be, & RE636bc) being decorated with cardium imprints forming horizontal lines plus, in two instances, indications of metopes with a triangular pattern. The quite varying ways of decorating with cardium incisions may perhaps indicate that the vessels were made by different potters. From pit 77, northwest of House 84, an example of ornamentation with more or less horizontal rows of vertical spatula incisions (RE469ab, "barbed wire").

4.5. Interpreting the floors in other house sites from the central Limfjord region

The settlements at Gåsemose, Kluborg II, Glattrup I/III, Marienlyst Strand, Granlygård, Hellegård, Glattrup IV, Rosgårde and Tromgade are again considered with regard to 17 house sites. I shall present their finds of artefacts, plant materials, soil patches and low zones, and make suggestions as to the daily life activities performed in the house interiors. As before, unless otherwise stated, the artefact photos are full scale or close to full scale.

Gåsemose

Apart from some artefacts deriving from the surrounding culture layer, the find material stems not least from the sunken area of House 1 (Report U1967a).

House 1 (Fig. 2.39, 2.40, 3.59 & 4.44)

Numerous artefacts and other items were found in the excavated areas of this large house pit. A list of artefacts in the report comprises more than four hundred numbers. The fills contained numerous heat-affected/cracked granite stones and other stones as well as the sandy soil, including much charcoal and ashes. Artefacts and burned bone were found spread in this brownish-black fill layer. The artefacts mainly relate to flint items and potsherds. It is possible, but not certain, that some of these might belong to the sunken floor. All finds from the sunken area are therefore here considered part of the secondary fills. The abundant presence of heat-affected/cracked stones is, not least, particularly well-documented from the profile benches. The most low-lying areas of the floor appear to have been in the central parts. Levels of other floor areas are evidenced in the drawn sections. No soil patches are here suggested as belonging to the sunken floor and hence no daily life activities can be proposed.

Kluborg II

From a culture layer above a pit a little to the east of House 5 derives a relatively well-preserved clay spoon (KL29aa), missing part of the handle. However, given its placement it could belong to the later three-aisled building to the east, House 5A.

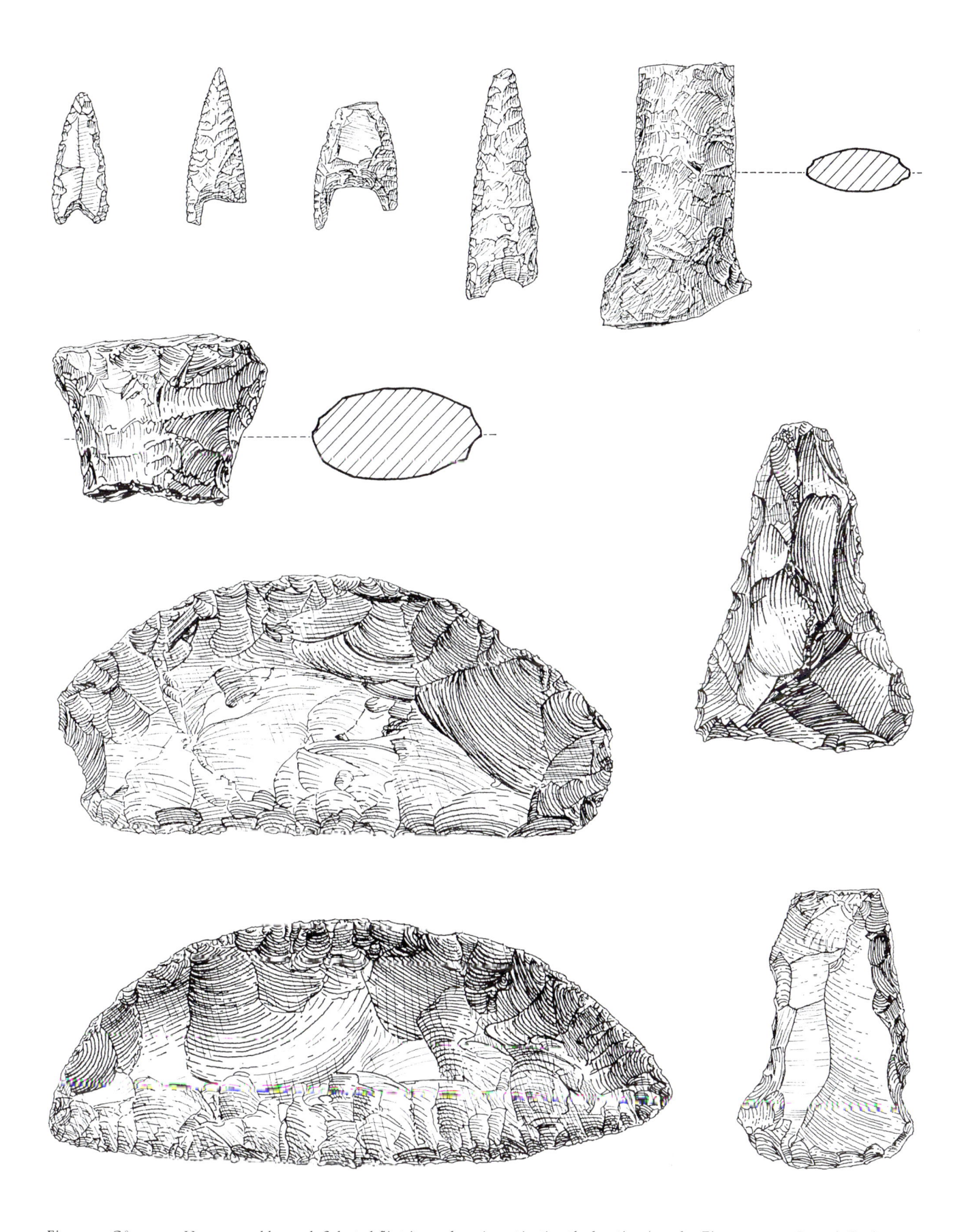

Fig. 4.44. Gåsemose. House 1 and beyond. Selected flint items from investigating the location (see also Fig. 2.39, 2.40 & 3.59). Beginning from the top, it concerns 4 lobed arrowheads, 2 dagger-handle fragments, 2 sickles, 1 scraper roughout and 1 scraper. On the upper sickle (GÅ264), both original ends had been removed and one end shows impact from heat. The dagger fragments seem to belong to type V and VI, respectively. Some relatively early items such as a flint axe also stem from this location. Scale: 1:1.

Artefacts, pits, patches, and daily life activities 273

The find materials belonging to the time of House 5 chiefly stem from the house site itself (report U2000a). This investigated sunken-floor house site with the finds related to metalworking activities is, to my knowledge, unique in South Scandinavia. Metal detectors were currently employed when investigating both house sites.

House 5 (Fig. 4.45 & 4.46)

A whetstone fragment and a number of other finds belong to the secondary fills. Several potsherds stem from the sunken-floor horizon, primarily the remainders of clay pots with simple rims. Two fragments considered to represent a clay mould (KL44aa & KL74aa) also derive from this. These two pieces appear much heat-influenced and seem to fit together. A low edge at the mould could indicate that a thin, narrow metal blade was caste. A clay crucible fragment (KL139aa) was found to the southeast in a posthole from the wall construction of House 5 and therefore is not included in the following list of finds belonging to the sunken-floor horizon. In the western part of the sunken-floor horizon was further recovered a small fragment of burned, tempered clay with only a little area of the surface left (KL31aa). It is described as a bottom fragment from a clay pot in the excavation report but I propose that it alternatively could stem from a loom weight. In this case, it comes from where the flat side meets the rounded edge of the loom weight. Two other, rather small, pieces of the same ware were found at the same spot. Three stone hammers and a modest number of flint items also belong to the sunken-floor horizon. During fieldwork, a tiny piece of bronze (KL23) was considered a part of the secondary fills, presumably as a matter of precaution. It seems possible that it actually may have belonged to the regular floor finds because it could hardly have been placed at the actual spot accidentally. It was found above, but very near, find spots 42 and 36 belonging to the sunken-floor horizon and thereby also in the vicinity of its oval and circular fireplaces. A quern stone fragment was recovered in the context of a gable end posthole to the east, and hence is not listed below. A presumed anvil belonging to the sunken-floor horizon is not listed either but its context is described further on. Patch G and fireplaces H and J contained a few macrofossils, whereas the soil in patch I included a small number of seeds from weeds and relatively many seeds from grasses, besides many buds and a few sprigs (Peter Steen Henriksen, report S2001a). The fills of soil patch N contained several seeds from weeds and a single piece of a spike from spelt. As regards a single potsherd (KL16aa), no context is stated.

A low zone was observable centrally in the western half of the sunken floor, whereas the scorched-stone patches A and B were observed far to the east so, in this case, the major deepening of the floor did not take place in the vicinity of these. Some ard-furrows crossed several of the important features F, J, H, I and N in the middle part of the sunken floor but do not appear to have disturbed these heavily. It is stated in the report and was later confirmed by the excavation director (pers. comm.) that a floor layer covered a large part of the sunken area and that soil features I and F were not observable before the excavation reached down to the level of the subsoil surface. The secondary fills, in turn, covered the entire floor layer. The significant soil patches and pits in the sunken floor can briefly be characterized:

A: Scorched-stone patch. Greyish-black soil with pieces of charcoal and, besides heat-affected/cracked stones, it also contained some flint flakes and potsherds.[4] Surface dimensions c. 2.2 m x 1.1 m. Depth 5-10 cm. To the northwest, a minor patch of a similar nature, which was likely part of patch A but separated due to the cleaning of the floor surface during investigation. Though placed in the corner of the preserved sunken floor, patch A was still some distance from the wall posts.

B: Scorched-stone patch. Brownish, sandy soil with heat-affected/cracked stones and small pieces of charcoal. Surface dimensions c. 1.35 m x 0.85 m. It might originally have been slightly longer. Depth c. 17 cm

C: Sub-circular pit. Yellowish-brown, sandy soil with gravel. Surface diameter of c. 0.19 cm and depth c. 30 cm. A tiny piece of bronze (KL51) was found in the fill 20 cm beneath the pit surface.

D: Oval pit. Greyish-brown, sandy soil with gravel. Surface dimensions c. 0.60 x 0.40 m. Depth c. 25 cm. According to stratification, older than soil feature C.

E: Long-stretched fireplace. Appeared as a rather lengthy, narrow soil feature with greyish-black sandy soil with charcoal pieces that were particularly present in its western part. Surface dimensions c. 1.85 x 0.45 m and depth 5-10 cm. In my understanding, it concerns a fireplace that would have had a rather special function.

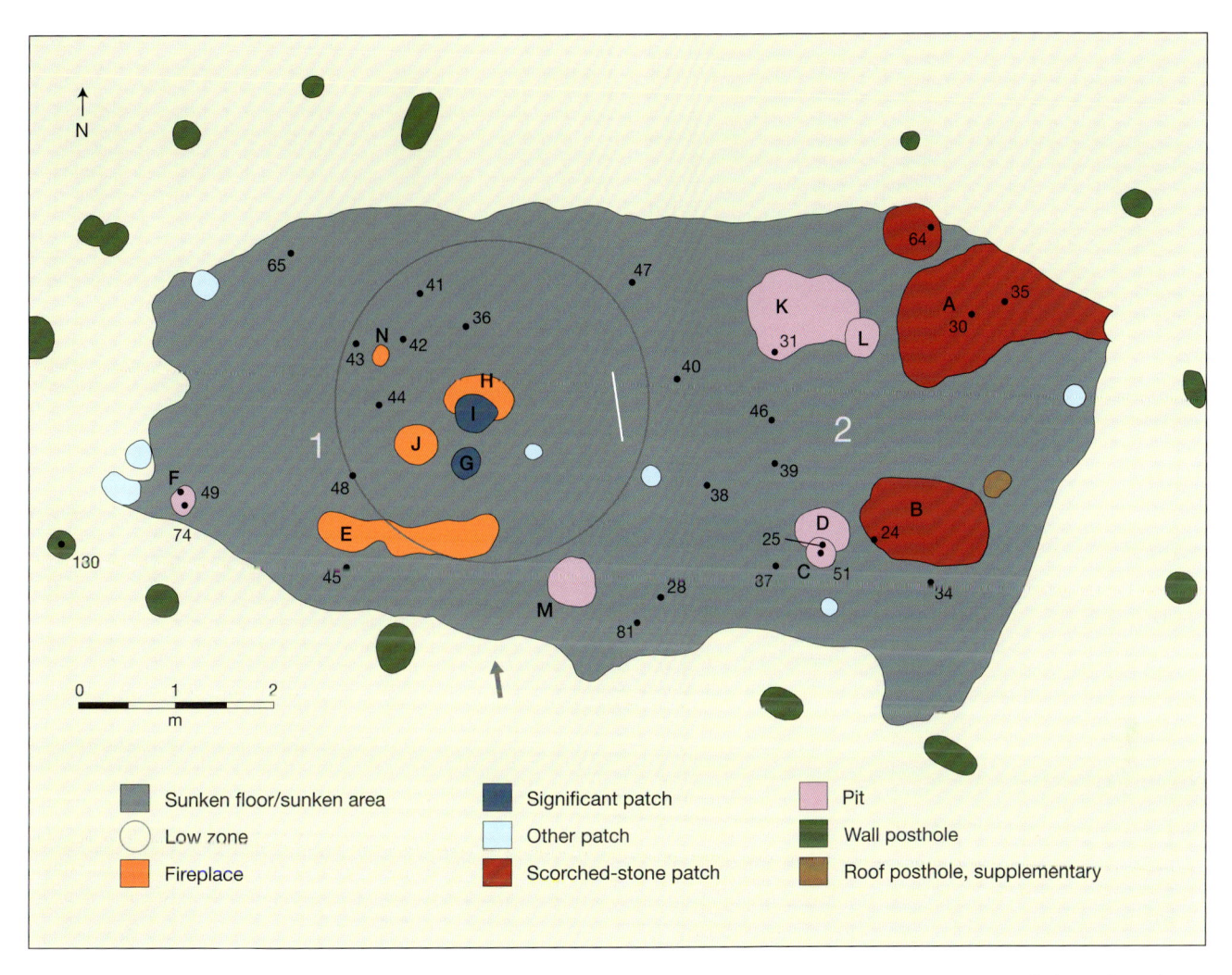

Fig. 4.45. Kluborg II. House 5. Ground plan of sunken floor, cleaned. Merely two major activity spaces are suggested. Apart from the anvil (buried) and the scorched stones, the artefacts found in situ in the sunken-floor horizon overall involve very many find spots: **24:** *1 tiny piece of bronze, length c. 1.1 cm (KL24ma);* **25:** *1 potsherd, rim (KL25aa);* **28:** *1 potsherd, rim (KL28aa);* **30:** *1 potsherd, rim (KL30aa);* **31:** *4 tiny pieces of burned clay, presumably belonging to a loom weight (KL31);* **32:** *9 potsherds, tempering coarse, medium and fine (KL32);* **34:** *1 potsherd, rim and 1 potsherd, side (KL34);* **35:** *1 potsherd, rim (KL35aa, belongs together with KL30aa);* **36:** *1 potsherd, bottom-side (KL36);* **37:** *1 potsherd, rim, tempering coarse, medium & fine (KL37aa);* **38:** *9 potsherds, rim, upper c. 2.5 cm fairly smooth surface (KL38aa);* **39:** *1 potsherd, rim (KL39);* **40:** *1 potsherd, rim (KL40aa);* **41:** *1 potsherd, bottom-side (KL41);* **42:** *1 pressure-flaked, almost complete flint sickle flint, secondarily used as a strike-a-light (KL42ea);* **43:** *1 potsherd, rim (KL43);* **44:** *1 clay fragment, fine tempering, probably belonging to a clay mould (KL44aa);* **45:** *1 stone hammer, specialized, with crushing marks round the edge (KL45ea);* **46:** *1 potsherd, rim & 1 potsherd, side (KL46);* **47:** *1 potsherd, rim (KL47aa, belongs together with KL40aa);* **48:** *1 piece of worked flint (KL48);* **49:** *1 flint scraper, on a curved blade, cortex partly preserved (KL49ea);* **50:** *2 potsherds, 1 piece of worked flint, pieces of charcoal (KL50);* **51:** *1 tiny piece of bronze, length c. 0.7 cm (KL51ma);* **53:** *6 potsherds & 2 pieces of worked flint (KL53);* **54:** *10 potsherds & 1 piece of worked flint (KL54);* **64:** *1 stone hammer (KL64ea);* **65:** *1 piece of worked flint, pressure-flaked, probably a roughout (KL65);* **74:** *1 clay mould fragment (KL74aa);* **81:** *1 stone hammer (KL45ea).*

F: Sub-circular pit. Part clayey soil but not described in general. Diameter up to c. 0.30 m and depth c. 0.26 m.

G: Sub-circular patch with brownish-grey sandy soil containing tiny charcoal pieces. Surface diameter c. 0.25 m, depth only 3 cm.

H: Sunken fireplace, oval, stone-paved at the bottom. Mainly reddish sand in the top and below that blackish, sandy soil with much charcoal and relatively large heat-affected/cracked stones at the bottom. Surface dimensions c. 0.65 x 45 m. Depth c. 0.23 m. Ard-furrows went over a greyish-brown layer of sandy

276　Chapter 4

soil, covering the soil features H and I. According to stratification, patch H is older than patch I.

I: Sub-circular patch with greyish, sandy soil. Diameter c. 0.40 m and depth c. 0.06 m.

J: Circular fireplace, slightly lowered. Blackish sand containing charcoal pieces. In the western side, a layer of reddish sand with charcoal. Diameter c. 40 cm. Depth c. 0.14 m.

K: Extensive pit. Sandy soil. Presumed loom weight fragments (KL31aa) in the soil. Surface dimensions c. 1.15 x 0.9 m. Depth maximum 10 cm.

L: Sub-circular pit with greyish, sandy soil. Diameter c. 0.40 m and depth c. 13 cm. According to stratification, younger than patch K.

M: Sub-circular pit. Greyish-black, sandy soil with a stone at the bottom. Diameter c. 0.42 m and depth c. 0.27 m. I consider this stone to be an anvil, dumped at the bottom of the pit, which became filled up (i.e. primary fills) before the secondary fills over the sunken floor were added.

N: Oval fireplace. Blackish, sandy soil containing charcoal. Surface dimensions c. 0.25 x 20 m, depth c. 10 cm. Likely just used as a short-term fireplace.

In the above, we have seen that the house was built as a construction of a special nature, without a regular ground-floor part. That its function was of a particular kind is further illustrated by the composition of the artefacts and soil features. The presence of clay mould fragments, tiny pieces of raw bronze, a fragmented clay crucible, stone hammers, a strike-a-light made on a sickle, the remainders of a long-stretched fireplace, an oval fireplace and circular fireplaces (some of which were sunken) denote the building as a scene of very special activities, not least metal working. Given these soil features and items, it is remarkable that there is only one stone anvil which, in my interpretation, was buried in a pit. Further such items may have been removed or have been made, for instance, out of hard wood. The most marked low zone had, in this case, developed in a spot other than to be expected compared to the Resengaard observations, namely somewhat at a distance from both scorched-stone patches. Conversely, the presence of fairly ordinary household artefacts such as pottery and a scraper is noteworthy. In some cases, only a single artefact fragment was present, for example just a rim sherd from a clay pot. In a few instances, pieces of the same clay pot were found at some internal distance from each other on the sunken floor, although the significance of this trait is difficult to judge. Based on the floor traces, the following are suggested as possible activities, separated into two activity spaces:

1. Bronze casting/other bronze handling, scraping, hammering/crushing, pottery handling/cooking. Pits with blackish soil and regular fireplaces present in the area. A stone anvil, dumped into a pit before filling up, present in the activity space. It seems possible that clay pots might somehow also have been elements in the processes performed in this activity space.

2. Drying/roasting/charring/cooking/heating, weaving, pottery handling/cooking, and hammering/crushing. Some kind of bronze handling could possibly also have been carried out in this activity space, as a tiny piece of bronze is present.

Glattrup I/III (Fig. 2.42)

First, some remarks on certain finds from the settlement. No find materials clearly belonging to the time of House 5 were found in the pits in its immediate vicinity. It cannot be excluded that one or more of the minor pits to the south might be contemporaneous, however. The few finds from the house site all stem from the sunken area (report U1983a). When it comes to House 6, some pits and ditches (132, 133, 134, & 135) around four metres south of the sunken-floor edge contained a few finds and they were probably contemporaneous with

◄ *Fig. 4.46. Kluborg II. House 5. A: Section of the sunken fireplace (H) with stone-paving in the bottom. On the surface, E-W running ard-furrows are faintly visible. Seen from the west. Artefacts: A flint scraper made on a curved blade (KL49ea), an asymmetrical flint sickle with traces of secondary use as a strike-a-light (KL42ea), a stone hammer with crushing marks in both ends (KL81ea), three clay pot rims (KL25aa, KL28aa, & KL30aa) and two drawings of upper parts of two clay pots (KL30aa/35aa & KL40aa/47aa). Potsherds from each of these stem from two find spots. All belong to the sunken-floor horizon.*

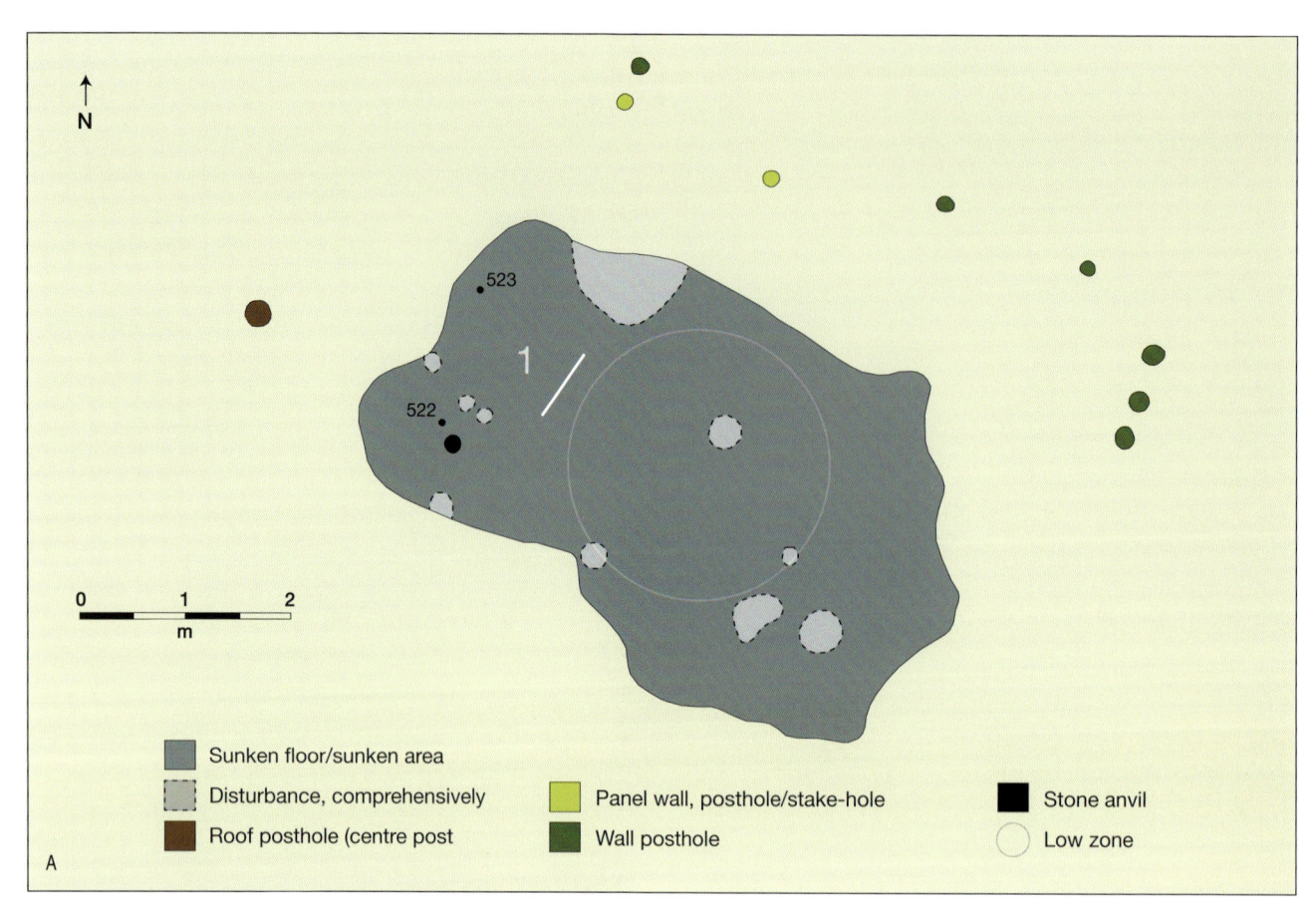

Sunken floor/sunken area	Panel wall, posthole/stake-hole	Stone anvil
Disturbance, comprehensively	Wall posthole	Low zone
Roof posthole (centre post		

GL522aa 1:2

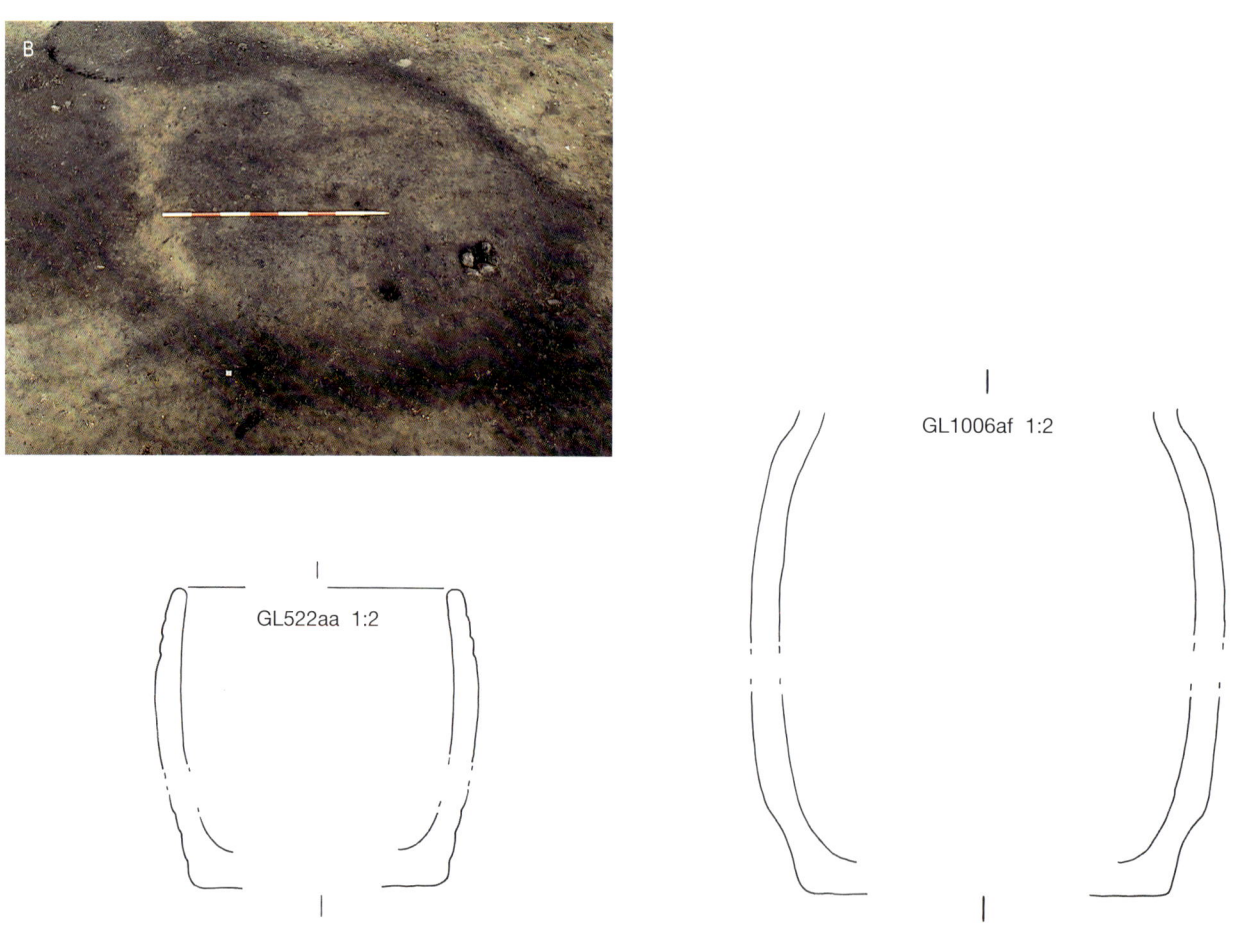

GL1006af 1:2

278 Chapter 4

◀ *Fig. 4.47. Glattrup I/III. House 5. A: Ground plan of sunken floor, cleaned. A single activity space is suggested. The artefacts found in situ in the sunken-floor horizon belong to just two find spots:* **522**: *2 potsherds, side, ornamented (GL522);* **523**: *2 potsherds, of which one is a bottom-side fragment (GL523). B: A close up of the cleaned fills centrally in the sunken area before excavating. Interestingly, the sequence of fills is here observable horizontally. Thin spots of dark greyish (or light brownish) soil at the top may possibly stem from the time of the Classic Bronze Age. These are observed on top of fine-grained yellowish sand, presumably wind-deposited. Appearing in the periphery is secondary fills of greyish-brown sand. It appears that ard-ploughing on top of the secondary fills did not take place. Artefacts: Drawing of barrel-shaped jar (GL522aa) belonging to the sunken-floor horizon. It is decorated with horizontal rows of vertical spatula incisions, "barbed wire". From secondary fills, an almost barrel-shaped jar (GL1000af). For cereal finds, see Fig. 5.17.*

the house (Fig. 2.44). They were placed close together although one cut across another. It is not possible to suggest a certain purpose for their presence. The narrow ditch 132 had a fill of sandy soil. The surface dimensions were c. 1.8 x 0.25 m, but the depth was a mere c. 5 cm. It contained two potsherds and two pieces of worked flint (GL1365). The circular pit 133 with brownish, sandy soil had surface dimensions of c. 1.9 x 0.7 m. The depth was c. 20 cm. In the fill were found six potsherds, of which one had a geometric decoration, likely the remainders of a metope with lozenges, supplied with oblique lines. Another small potsherd was decorated with parallel horizontal lines (GL1367aa & GL1367ab). In addition to this, it also contained a flint borer. The relatively broad ditch 134 was filled with sandy soil. The width was c. 0.7 m and its depth c. 20 cm. Pit 135 also marked out a curved, narrow ditch with sandy soil. The visible surface dimensions were c. 2.6 x 0.3 m but it extended into an unexcavated area. The depth was mostly c. 10 cm but, towards the end, it became deeper, about 30 cm. It contained 24 potsherds belonging to two open bowls (GL1364aa & GL1364ab).

House 5 (Fig. 4.47; Fig. 4.68.K)
Heat-affected/cracked stones were found in some number in the secondary fills but it was not possible to observe any concrete soil features with such stones belonging to the sunken-floor horizon. No artefacts of flint or other stone material belong to the sunken-floor horizon. A relatively high-lying, sloping floor part was observable in the easternmost part of the sunken floor. Rather flat-floored areas were found in the middle and to the west. The low zone was recorded around the sunken-floor centre. Only scant traces of possible activities were left farthest to the west. The following is suggested as possible doings in a single activity space:

1. Pottery handling/cooking. A stone anvil present.

House 6 (Fig. 4.48 & 4.49)
Some pottery, flint objects and a number of heat-affected/cracked stones stem from the upper part of the secondary fills of House 6 in particular, while the deeper fills contained little. When it comes to finds from the sunken-floor horizon, flint tools are scarce and concern a couple of knives and a sickle fragment, as well as some charred cereals and charcoal. Eight regular find spots are recorded in all.

The sunken floor deepened very gradually and was, on the whole, rather shallow. The low zone was observable approximately in its middle. Some areas with carbonized material were recorded to the northeast and southeast but it is not stated as to whether these belonged to the floor horizon or not. These patches are therefore not included below. The significant soil patches in the sunken floor can briefly be characterized as follows:

A: Minor, "three-armed" patch, shallow. Sandy soil. Surface dimensions c. 0.8 x 0.8 m.

B: Minor, irregularly shaped patch, shallow. Sandy soil. Surface dimensions c. 1.2 x 0.6 m.

C: Minor, irregularly shaped patch, shallow. Sandy soil. Surface dimensions c. 1.1 x 0.6 m.

The traces of possible doings appear to concern only a moderate number of possible activities. The following are suggested as possible doings, separated into three activity spaces:

1. Knife cutting and pottery handling/cooking.

2. Pottery handling/cooking. A sickle fragment present.

3. Weaving and pottery handling/cooking.

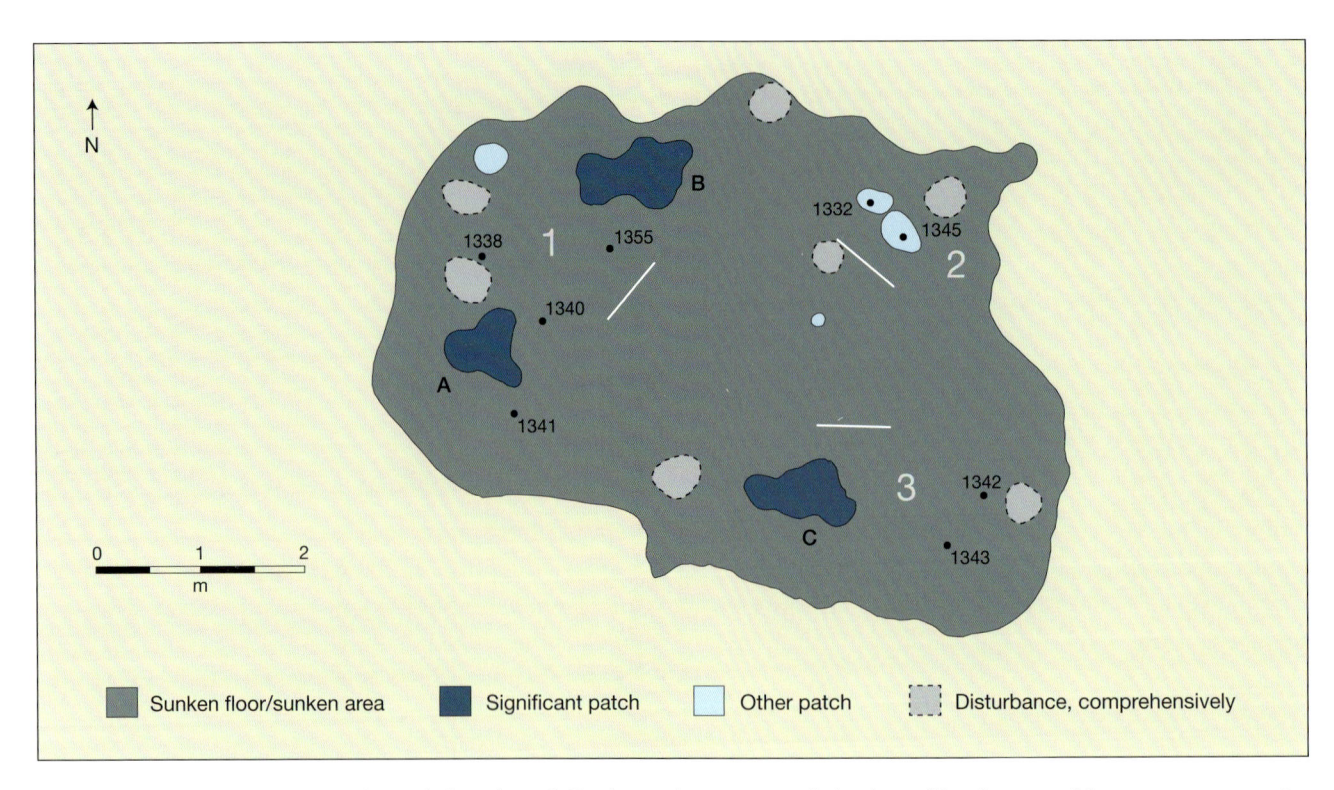

Fig. 4.48. Glattrup I/III. House 6. Ground plan, cleaned. Further to the west, a posthole of a roof-bearing post. A low zone was present centrally in the sunken floor, but not shown here. Three activity spaces are suggested. The artefacts found in situ in the sunken-floor horizon belong to a minor number of find spots: **1332**: *1 flint sickle, fragment (GL1332ea);* **1338**: *1 flint knife (GL1338ea);* **1340**: *1 flint knife (GL1340ea);* **1341**: *1 potsherd, rim (GL1341aa);* **1342**: *3 loom weight fragments (GL1342aa);* **1343**: *1 potsherd, rim (GL1343aa);* **1345**: *2 potsherds, bottom, found in a small patch (GL1345);* **1355**: *1 potsherd, side (GL1355). For cereal finds, see Fig. 5.17.*

Marienlyst strand

The find material is quite modest from the site of the Late Neolithic building (House 1) found on the south-sloping hillside (Report U1992a). Against this, more varied ceramics derive from pit 4 and culture layer 5 (Fig. 2.45, 4.51 & 4.52).

Pit 4 was placed some 30 m south of House 1 and a minor pit with heat-affected/cracked stones had cut pit 4 near its middle. Pit 4 was rather irregular in its area, having a length of c. 3.20 m and a depth of merely 0.20 m. To the east, where the pit was deepest, many fragments of a clay pot with notch-stamped ornamentation (MA4aa) were recovered. In all, 136 potsherds were present. To the southeast was found a minor concentration of worked flint, including 93 pieces. An extraordinarily regular, broad flake with cortex retouched around the perimeter came from the pit, along with a flint axe fragment and two pieces of burned flint.

Culture layer 5 was found around 85 m south of House 1. It had accumulated in a natural sink that was presumably formerly a waterhole (or at least a humid area). Potsherds, flint and a few stones were placed – probably as dump – on a whitish-grey, fine sand layer. The ornamented ceramics appear to be contemporaneous with the pottery found in pit 4. A total of 69 potsherds derive from this culture layer context, along with two fragments of flint axes, a flint dagger fragment, a flint scraper, a flint nodule and 62 pieces of worked flint. Some thick soil layers had subsequently accumulated above this artefact horizon. The history of layer depositing may indicate that only one settlement from the early part of the Late Neolithic left substantial finds at this location.

House 1 (Fig. 4.50, 4.51 & 4.52; Fig. 4.68.L)

More than 50 potsherds of mostly coarse ware belonging to the period in question stem from the secondary fills, besides a few younger potsherds on the top of it. About 150 pieces of worked flint derive from the secondary fills. According to the excavation report, no regular find spots are considered to belong to the sunken-floor horizon. This also includes a rather slim, presumed loom weight fragment (MA20aa) without clear traces of the area around the central

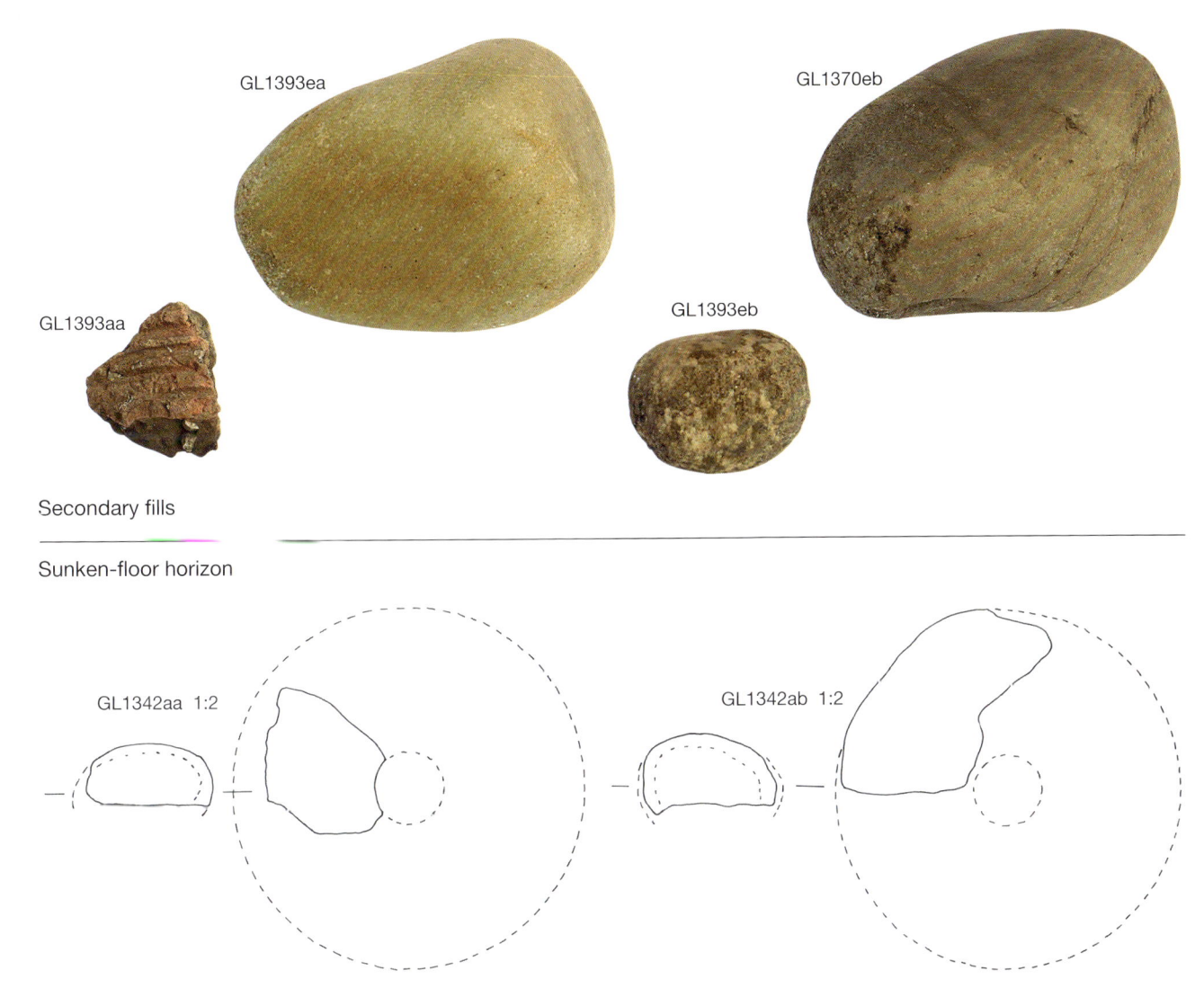

Fig. 4.49. Glattrup I/III. House 6. Artefacts: Two quartzite hammers (GL1393ea & GL1370eb) that have more or less the same characteristic shape, becoming markedly more slender towards their working end. Likewise from secondary fills derive a coarse-grained stone hammer (GL1393eb) and a potsherd with ornamentation of horizontal furrows (GL1393aa). From the sunken-floor horizon stem two pieces of loom weights, here in proposed reconstruction (GL1342aa & GL1342ab).

hole. Tempering of the clay material appears more or less absent. According to the report, it belongs to a patch considered to be secondary in relation to the sunken floor.

The low zone of the sunken floor was located in the eastern part to the south, whereas the remaining parts were fairly plane. The highest floor area was observable to the west. A number of soil features were recovered from the sunken area and some contained heat-cracked stones, one of these being a large patch (1) to the east. According to the stratification, this patch must be older than those to the north (2) and south (9), which had both cut through it. However, it is difficult to give a satisfactory interpretation of the sunken floor. As emerges from the discussion of the chronological position of this house site, it had already been stated during fieldwork that the major patches were considered to be younger than the sunken floor itself. Accordingly, these soil features could not contribute relevant observations when looking for arrangements belonging to the sunken-floor horizon. Other minor patches of little depth might perhaps belong to the floor but are of no real interest for the present work. So, when following the interpretation stated in the excavation report, none of the significant pits or patches are able to provide information about activities in the sunken-floor house. On this basis, no suggestions on everyday doings can be put forward.

Artefacts, pits, patches, and daily life activities **281**

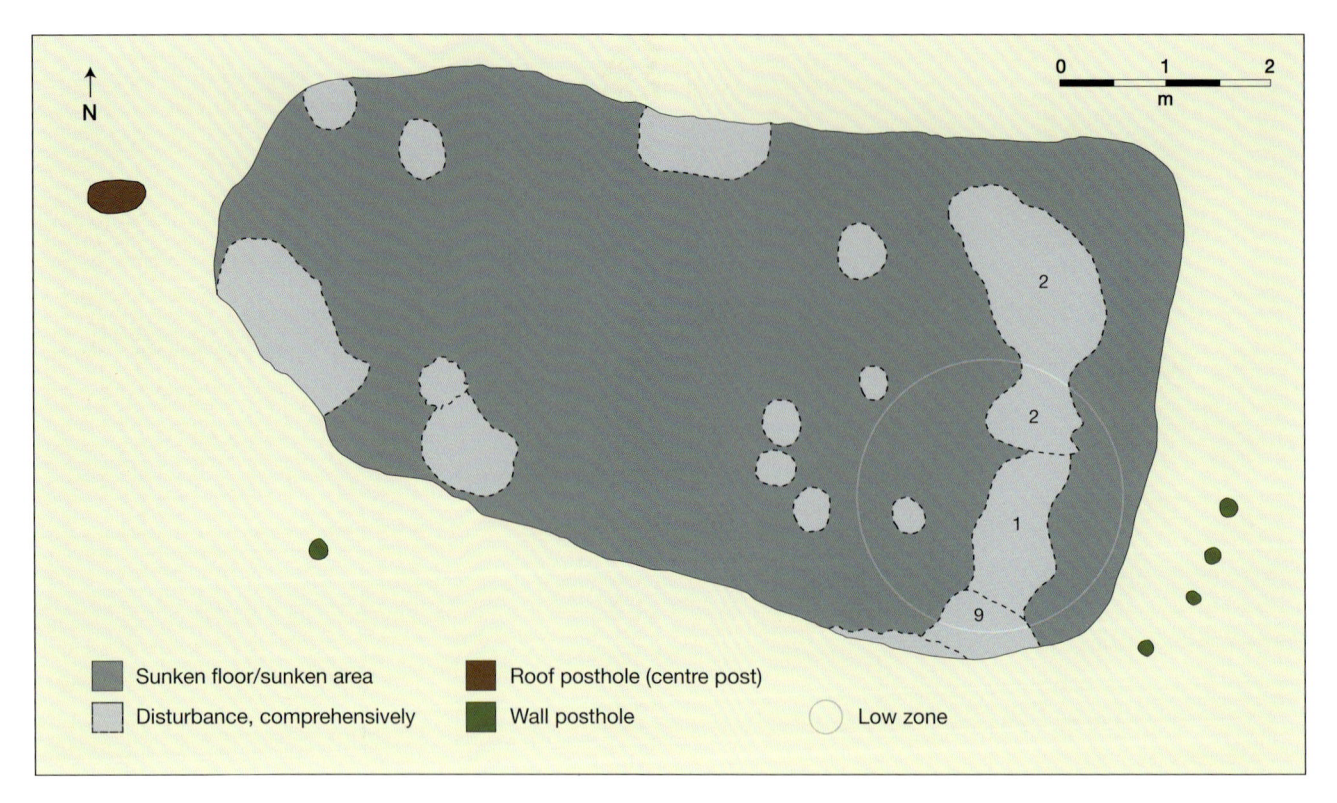

Fig. 4.50. Marienlyst Strand. House 1. Ground plan of sunken floor, cleaned. From the excavation report it appears that the sizable soil features 1, 2, 9, and others were seen as younger than the sunken floor. However, I cannot exclude the possibility that these diffuse patches of mostly greyish sandy soil could alternatively have been interpreted as belonging to the sunken floor and represent traces of indoor activities in its eastern part. A heat-cracked stone was found in soil feature 9.

▲▶ *Fig. 4.51. Marienlyst Strand. House 1. From secondary fills stem a flint scraper (MA3ea), a thin broad flake with cortex and fine retouch of its perimeter (two views, MA3eb), and two presumed arrowhead rough-outs (MA3ed & MA3ee), plus a flint hammer with comprehensive surface crushing marks (MA3ec). From these fills furthermore an unornamented rim and side (MA19aa), a small potsherd with spatula incisions above the belly (MA22aa). Finds from pit 4 south of the house site relate to the side of a zone-ornamented clay pot (MA4aa) and a thin broad flake with cortex and fine retouch of its perimeter (two views, MA4ea). Finds from culture layer 5 relate to potsherds with horizontal lines (MA5aa & MA5ac) and notch-stamped lines (MA5ac).*

MA19aa

MA3ec

MA4ea

MA4aa 1:2

MA5aa

MA5ab

MA5ac

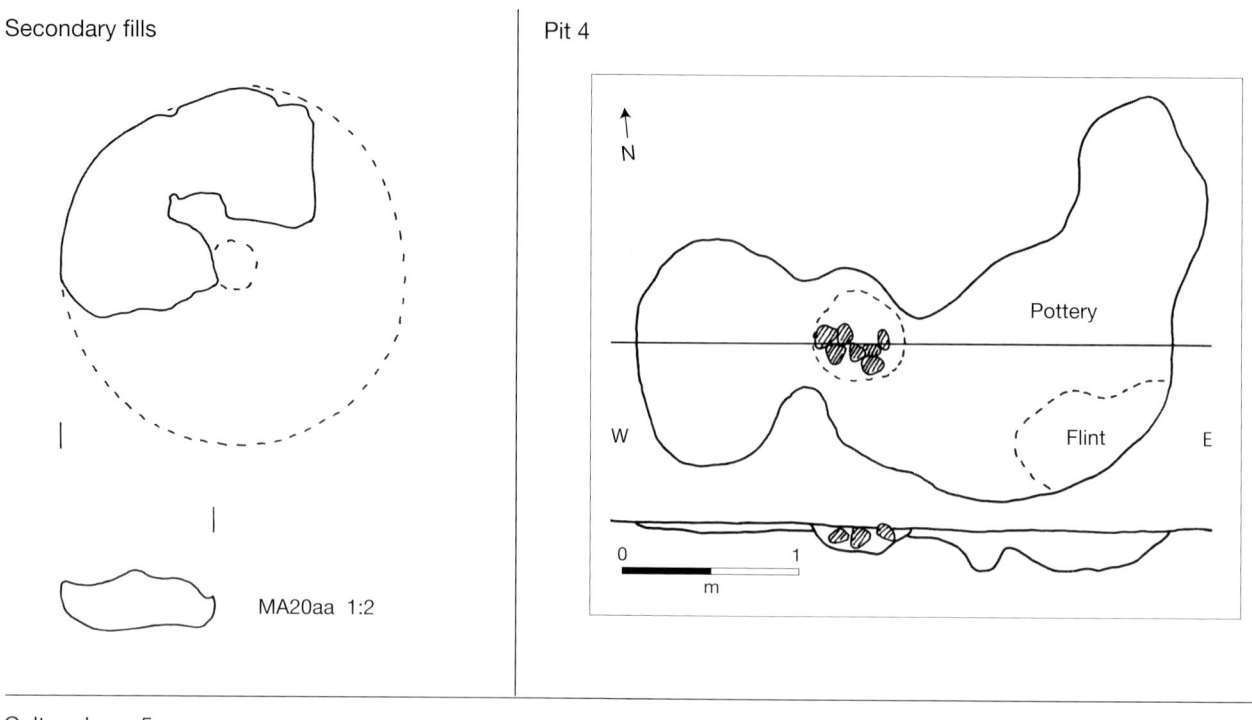

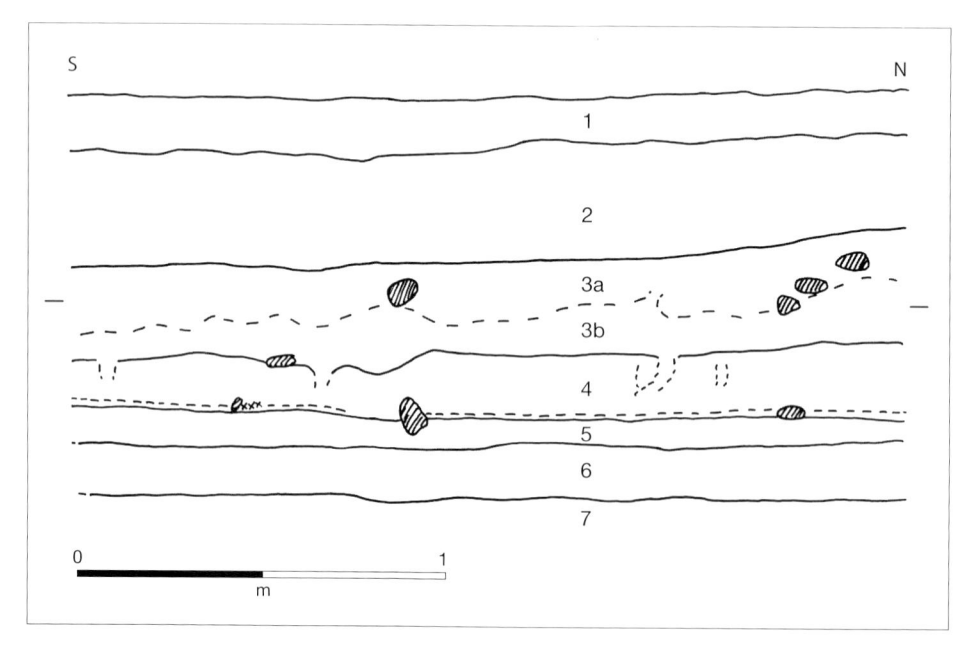

Fig. 4.52. Marienlyst Strand. House 1. Reconstruction drawing of a loom weight. Pit 4 with plan and section. Culture layer 5, N-S section with many layers: the uppermost stratum (1) represents recently-ploughed soil. Beneath that two more or less sterile strata of accumulated soil (2 & 3). Stratum 4 represents the culture layer which, in its upper parts, was marked by traces of animal activities. The layer was dark greyish and sandy, becoming more yellowish towards the north and, at the bottom, it was characterized by scattered pieces of charcoal. Beneath that, two strata of more or less whitish fine sand (5 & 6) and the subsoil of yellowish sand (7).

Granlygård

No vestiges of Late Neolithic longhouses were found at this location but such buildings might possibly have been present more to the south or north and we must therefore accept that this situation gives no clues as to the interpretation of the settlement (Fig. 2.47). And yet a number of artefact remainders were found in the sites of the less sizeable Houses 2, 3 and 6 (report U1995a). Whether these buildings stood more or less simultaneously or in succession is not known.

On the whole, the finds from the secondary fills above the sunken floors of the house sites may indicate some activities concerned with pottery handling/cooking, raw flint handling/chipping and polishing/sharpening in the area. Recovered not far from these sites, the finds from pit 4 are, in my reading, important for our understanding of the place because the pit likely represents activities connected with one or more of these houses. As accounted for below, this pit may indicate an outside activity space concerned with not only weaving/textile handling but, judging by its fills, hammering/crushing, pottery handling/cooking and scraping could also have taken place.

Pit 4 was sub-circular in shape and had a diameter of c. 1.5 m. In section it was evenly rounded and the depth was c. 30 cm. It was likely somewhat deeper before the impact from recent ploughing. Its fill consisted of dark-brownish sand. In the south side was found a complete clay colander and – immediately below it – a loom weight. When a colander is found in the same context as a loom weight, it could suggest its use in connection with textile working although it cannot of course be ruled out that it might have served other purposes. The pit also contained 19 potsherds, of which 4 are rims. Ornamentation is present on 6 potsherds. Apart from these, some badly preserved potsherds were also found. In addition, 1 stone hammer of quartzite, 1 coarsely shaped (presumed) flint scraper, 4 pieces of worked flint, and 3 pieces of burned flint were also present. After filling up, there was again dug into the pit, but just down to a depth of c. 15 cm and no finds stem from the fills after this secondary activity.

House 2 (Fig. 2.47)

During fieldwork three levels of fill were distinguished in the sunken area and these contained many potsherds, some worked flint, some burned flint, a whetstone fragment and stone hammers. No artefacts or organic materials came directly from the sunken-floor horizon.

Soil features with heat-cracked stones were observable on the surface of the sunken area but these patches did not relate to the sunken floor itself and are understood to be remainders from later activities after abandonment and demolition of the house. The sunken floor is comparable to certain minor Resengaard houses. The floor became gradually lower towards the central part. No daily life activities can be suggested.

House 3 (Fig. 2.47 & 4.53)

Some worked flint, some burned flint, some pieces of heat-cracked stones and many potsherds, some of which were supplied with Beaker ornamentation, stem from the secondary fills. Yet no artefacts or organic materials are recorded as belonging to the sunken-floor horizon. The sunken floor was relatively shallow. The lowest part of the floor was in the central area. No soil patches were observable in the sunken floor and no daily life activities can be proposed.

House 6 (Fig. 2.47 & 4.53)

Many potsherds, of which some are supplied with Beaker ornamentation, stem from the secondary fills, which also contained some worked flint, burned flint and a few pieces of charcoal. No artefacts or organic materials belong to the sunken floor. The floor was at its lowest around the middle. No soil patches belong to it and no daily life activities can be suggested.

Hellegård

A relatively large number of find spots belong to the sunken-floor horizon of House 122 whereas this is not the case for the short House 35 (report U1998a). No ordinary Late Neolithic settlement pits apart from these were found (Fig. 2.48). However, two large, stone-lined postholes (49 & 127) south of house 122 and 35 likely belong to the Late Neolithic settlement and we shall return to these below.

House 122 (Fig. 4.54 & 4.55; Fig. 4.68.M)

A chisel fragment polished on all four sides (HE122ea) was found in a pit that was younger than the sunken floor. It has a length of 6.2 cm and the width of the edge is 1.2 cm although ultra-tiny flakes had broken off, probably due to use. Some hundred potsherds, two flint borers, a flint scraper, several hundred pieces of worked flint, a stone hammer and a tiny bead derive from the secondary fills. A flint axe with broad edge partly broken (HE527ea) also belongs to the secondary fills and it was found just a few centimetres above the sunken floor. A fragment of a presumed loom weight (HE550ae) with dimensions c. 3.9 x 2.3 cm also stems from these fills. Turning to finds from the sunken-floor horizon, a few stones without clear traces of heat cracking were observed in the western half. One of these, which I consider to be a stone anvil with minor pieces breaking off (HE547), was found in patch. Another stone that I assume also func-

Granlygård, House 3
Secondary fills

GR10ab GR10ae GR10ad GR10af GR10aa

Pit 4

GR12aa GR12ab

GR11ac

GR12ac

GR11aa

GR11ab 1:2

GR11aa 1:2

286   Chapter 4

GR11ab 1:2

GR11aa 1:2

Granlygård, House 6
Secondary fills

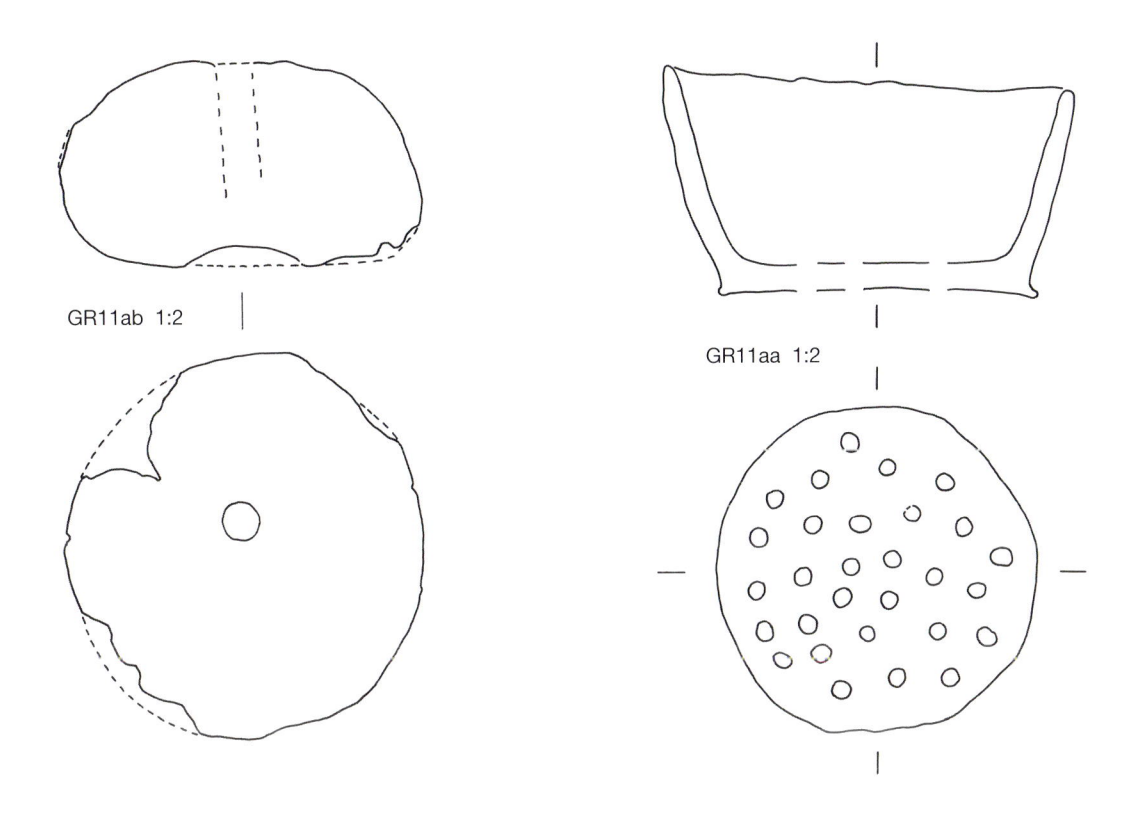

GR61ab

GR61ac

GR61ad

GR61aa 1:2

◄▲ *Fig. 4.53. Granlygård. House 3: Five examples of ornamented pottery, being with horizontal zones of notch-stamped lines (GR10ad & GR10ae), horizontal lines/furrows (GR10aa & GR10ab) and also lozenges, likely part of a metope decoration (GR10af). The varying forms of decoration may indicate that this represents the work of more than one potter. Pit 4: Four examples of ceramics with horizontal zone-ornaments, being incised lines (GR11ac), and lines of cardium imprints (GR12aa, ab & ac). From the south side of this pit also a complete colander (two views, GR11aa). It is 6.1 cm high, 11.2 cm in diameter and supplied with 29 bottom-holes (one blind hole) as well as with two closely placed holes in the side. Immediately below the colander was found a fairly heavy loom weight with vaulted top, damaged underside and a tiny hole almost centrally (GR11ab). It is 10.2 x 9.7 cm in diameter, and 5.4 cm high. Pit 4: Reconstruction drawings of the loom weight and the colander. House 6: Four examples of pottery with ornamentation in horizontal zones, being lines (GR61aa), cardium imprints (GR61ab), short oblique lines within a band of delimiting horizontal lines (GR61ac) and notch-stamps (GR61ad).*

Artefacts, pits, patches, and daily life activities   **287**

288 Chapter 4

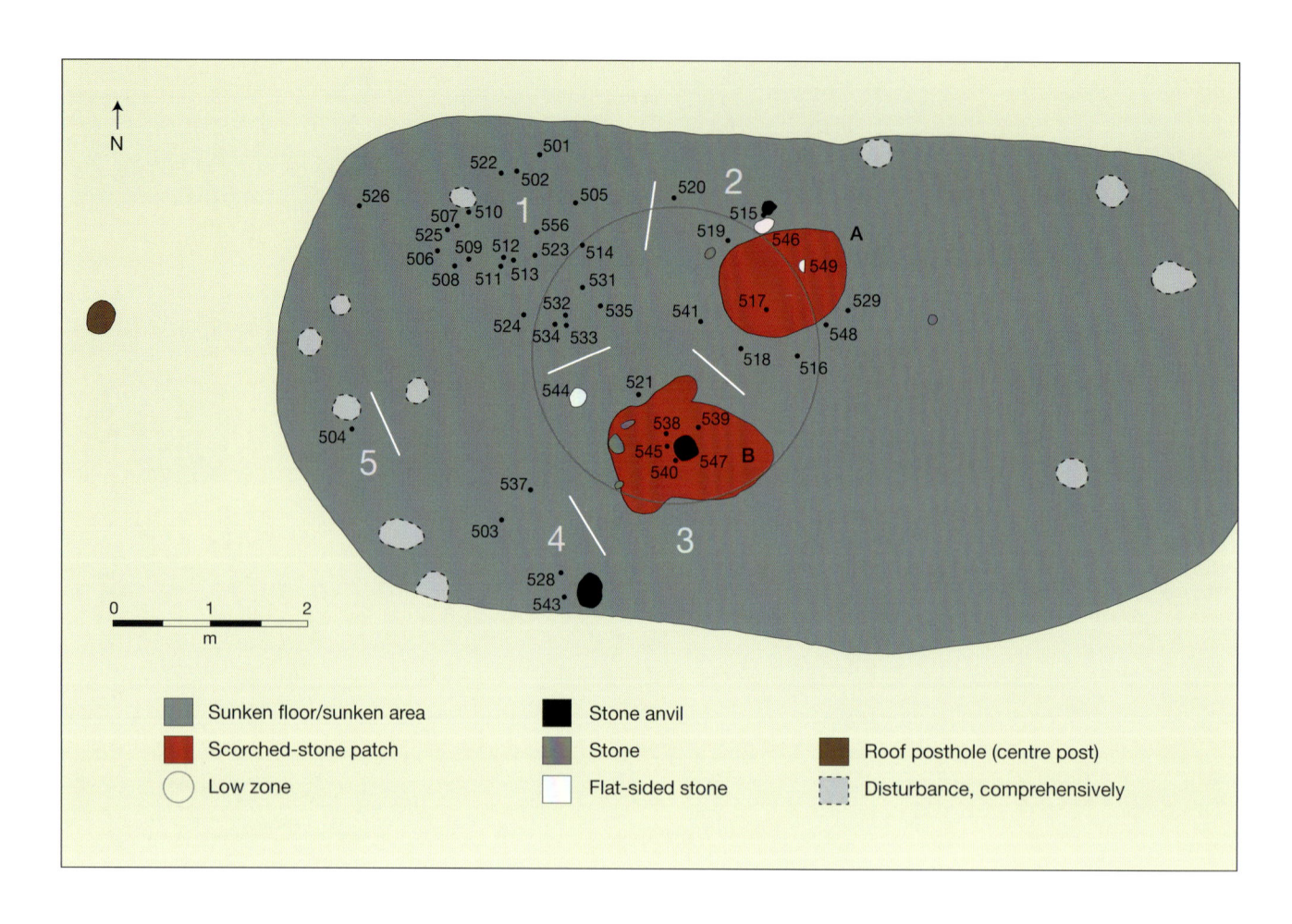

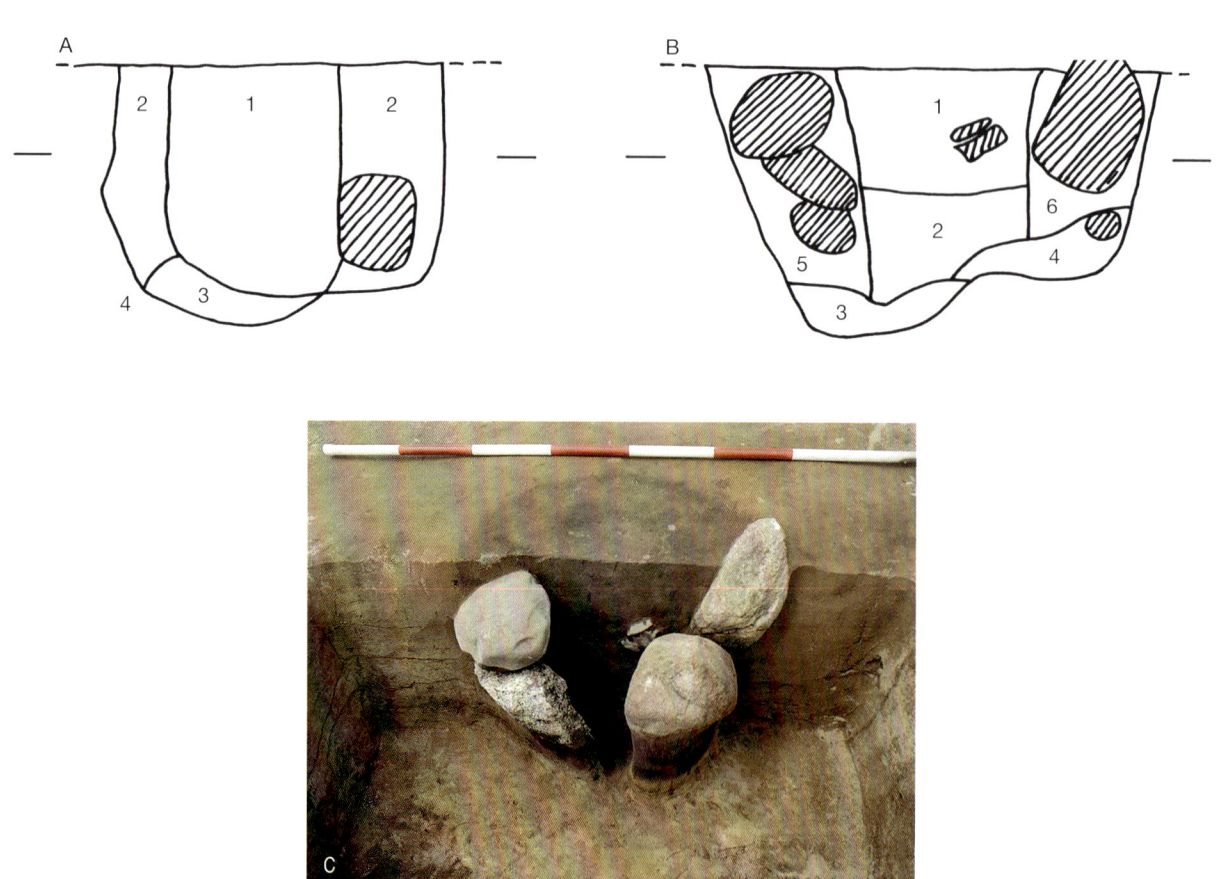

◀ *Fig. 4.54. Hellegård. House 122. Five activity spaces are suggested. A: Ground plan of sunken floor, cleaned. In the north-western area of the sunken floor, the find situation may set a "scene", with many specialized scraper tools present, and it may thus tell of a well-established workshop area. The highly varied assortment of tools may also raise the possibility that, for instance, two or more scrapers of about the same strength and weight could have been used simultaneously during the process by a corresponding number of persons. Moreover, the number of broken scrapers may also give us information about the physical force needed to scrape the hides. This "scene", together with the numerous other remains in the western half of the sunken floor, is the only one among the 43 sunken-floor house sites where such a number of apt and worn-out tools as well as debris, possibly from repairs, was left in this manner. The situation may perhaps indicate an impulsive and abrupt abandonment of the workshop. Apart from stone anvils and scorched stones, the artefacts found in situ in the sunken-floor horizon overall involve very many find spots:* **501:** *1 flint scraper (HE501ea);* **502:** *1 flint scraper (HE502ea);* **503:** *1 flint scraper (HE503ea);* **504:** *1 potsherd, rim (HE504aa);* **505:** *1 flint scraper (HE505ea);* **506:** *1 flint scraper (HE506ea);* **507:** *1 flint scraper (HE507ea);* **508:** *1 flint scraper (HE508ea);* **509:** *1 flint scraper (HE509ea);* **510:** *1 flint scraper (HE510ea);* **511:** *1 flint scraper (HE511ea);* **512:** *1 flint scraper (HE512ea);* **513:** *1 flint scraper (HE513ea);* **514:** *1 flint scraper (HE514ea);* **515:** *1 potsherd, rim (HE515), in the area of a flat-sided stone;* **516:** *1 potsherd, bottom-side (HE516);* **517:** *1 potsherd, bottom (HE517);* **518:** *1 flint scraper (HE518ea);* **519:** *1 flint scraper, fragment (HE519ea);* **520:** *1 potsherd, side, ornamented (HE520);* **521:** *1 flint roughout, possibly for a chisel (HE521ea);* **522:** *1 flint dagger fragment of a blade tip (HE522ea);* **523:** *1 flint scraper (HE523ea);* **524:** *1 flint scraper (HE524ea);* **525:** *1 flint scraper (HE525ea);* **526:** *1 potsherd, rim (HE526);* **528:** *1 potsherd, rim (HE528);* **529:** *1 clay spoon fragment (HE529aa);* **531:** *1 flint scraper (HE531ea);* **532:** *1 flint scraper, fragment (HE532ea);* **533:** *1 flint scraper (HE533ea);* **534:** *1 flint scraper (HE534ea);* **535:** *1 flint scraper (HE545ea);* **537:** *1 flint scraper, fragment (HE537ea);* **538:** *1 potsherd, rim (HE538);* **539:** *5 potsherds, among these a rim (HE539);* **540:** *1 stone, with flat side, fragment (HE540);* **541:** *1 flint scraper (HE541ea),* **543:** *1 stone hammer, sub-quadratic, possibly also smoothening function (HE543);* **544:** *1 stone, flat-sided (HE544);* **545:** *1 flint scraper (HE545eb);* **546:** *1 smoothening stone, flat-sided (HE546ea);* **548:** *1 potsherd, bottom (RE548);* **556:** *About 200 tiny flint flakes (RE556). A & B: Two special postholes (49 & 127) placed a few metres south of House 122 and 35. These were the only stone-lined postholes found in the area and they had strong common traits by their appearance. The internal distance between centres was c. 1.6 m. My suggestion is that they supported strong posts for stretching hides. A: Posthole 49, layer description: Light, brownish-grey soil with reddish spots (1), greyish-brown sand with (darker) soil (2), whitish-grey sand (3) and reddish subsoil sand (4). B: Posthole 127, layer description: Greyish, sandy soil (1), light greyish, sandy soil (2), whitish-grey sand (3), dark brownish-grey, sandy soil (4), brownish, sandy soil (5) and reddish-brown, sandy soil with spots of reddish sand (6). Same subsoil as the foregoing. C: Posthole 127, partly excavated. Seen from the east.*

tioned as a stone anvil was found near the southern edge of the sunken floor. A third, albeit minor stone to the north I likewise consider to be an anvil. In the western part, to the north, a sub-circular area with a flint waste concentration was investigated. Most of the tiny flint waste was found here (RE556). Numerous flint scrapers were also concentrated in about the same floor area. Whether or not much of the small-sized pieces of flint waste from the area derive from e.g. producing or repairing scraper edges has not been clarified. The diameter of this area was c. 1.20-1.40 m, but no particular soil patch was observable. A stone hammer (HE530), a scraper (HE536ea) and a clay pot rim (HE542) also appear to belong to the sunken-floor horizon but the find spot could not be identified beyond the understanding that these objects likely stem from areas in or around the scorched-stone patches. A scraper (HE523ea) was found directly in the soil of an ard furrow and could presumably have been displaced a little. Other disturbances of the finds from ard-ploughing could not be documented. On the whole, therefore, a substantial number of artefact find spots belong to the sunken-floor horizon. A few charred plant remainders were found in a sample (HE551) from the floor layer, while no other organic materials were preserved.

A brownish, sandy layer was considered to be a regular floor layer, mainly having a thickness of c. 4-6 cm. Two scorched-stone patches were excavated in the central part of the sunken floor. From about two hundred level measurements of the whole bottom of the sunken floor, it can be stated that a low zone was present in the area of these two soil features. The two significant soil patches in the sunken floor can briefly be characterized as follows:

A: Scorched-stone patch. Dark, brownish sandy soil with some dust from charred material (likely of charcoal) and containing several heat-affected/cracked stones. Surface dimensions c. 1.32 x 1.02 m and depth c. 5-15 cm.

B: Scorched-stone patch. Somewhat irregular feature with dark, brownish sandy soil coloured by some dust from charred material (likely charcoal) and containing several heat-affected/cracked stones. Surface dimensions c. 1.70 x 1.48 m and depth c. 5-15.

Fig. 4.55. Hellegård. House 122. Pressure-flaked flint piece found between the house sites (HE131ea). From secondary fills, a flint axe with broad edge (HE527ea). From the sunken-floor horizon, a presumed chisel roughout (HE521ea), a sub-quadratic stone hammer, c. 8.9 x 7.3 x 5.4 cm (two views, HE543ea). The latter is slightly reddish, fine-grained with by and large vertical sides, connected by rounded corners. The underside has a large flat area that has possibly become even more so through use, and in this sense could also have worked as a smoothening stone. Concerning the preparation of hides, it is imaginable that this block with steep broad sides may have been used for smoothening and surface finishing. In addition, the corners show marks more or less comparable to those on some stone hammers, and this is therefore also seen as a function of this stone. Likely belonging to the sunken-floor horizon, a stone hammer (HE530ea). From the sunken-floor horizon, a minor scraper (HE502ea) and two relatively large and heavy scrapers (two views, HE506ea & HE545eb).

HE503ea

HE505ea

HE509ea

HE507ea

HE510ea

HE511ea

HE513ea

HE518ea

HE523ea

HE524ea

HE525ea

HE533ea

HE531ea

HE534ea

Fig. 4.55, continued. With the strong focus on cattle and hunting in the period, a lot of hides would likely have needed treatment and, here, a further 14 scrapers from the sunken-floor horizon are displayed, as it is remarkable that none of these are clear examples of the classic Late Neolithic spoon-shaped scrapers.

Hellegård. Scrapers

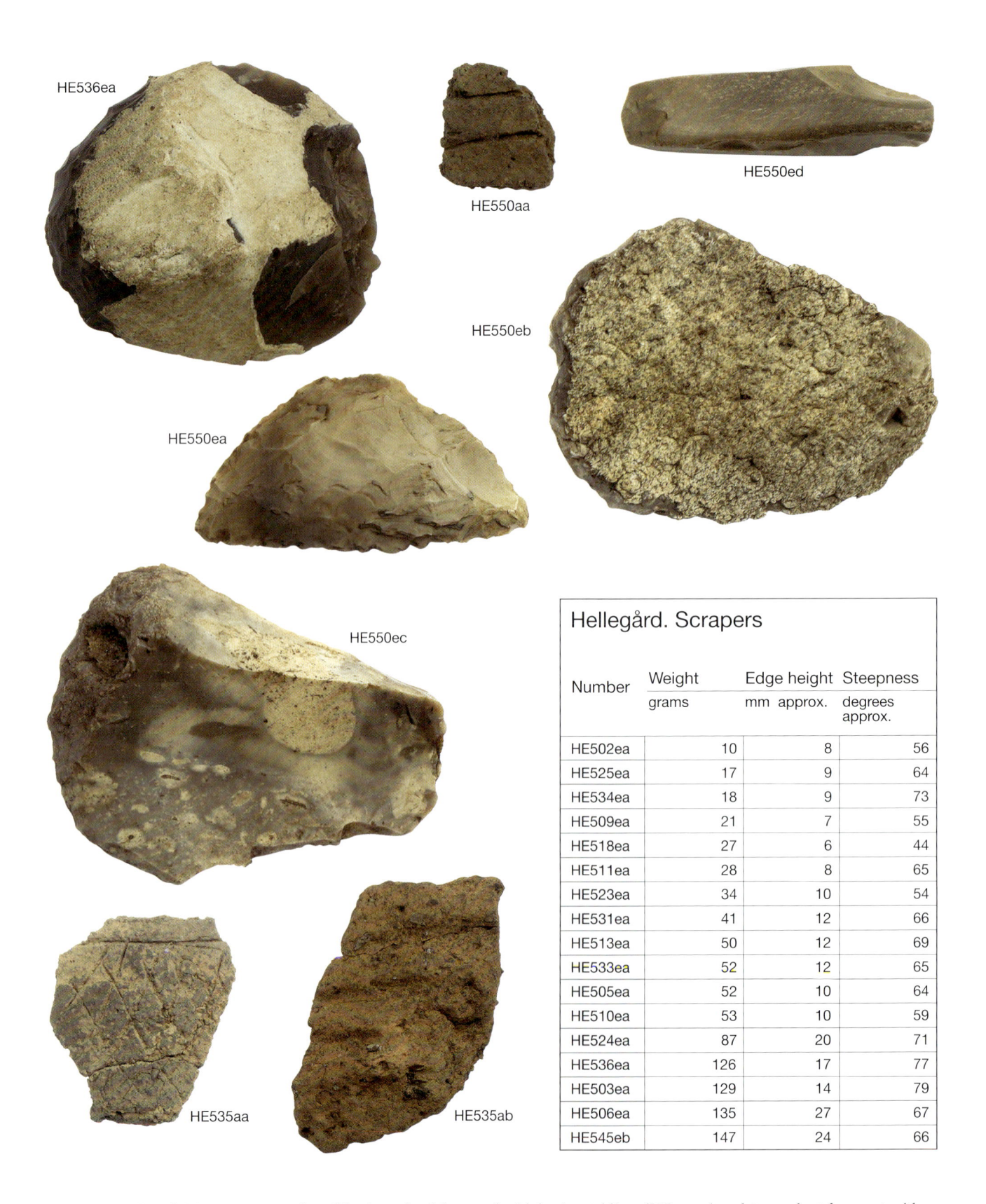

Number	Weight grams	Edge height mm approx.	Steepness degrees approx.
HE502ea	10	8	56
HE525ea	17	9	64
HE534ea	18	9	73
HE509ea	21	7	55
HE518ea	27	6	44
HE511ea	28	8	65
HE523ea	34	10	54
HE531ea	41	12	66
HE513ea	50	12	69
HE533ea	52	12	65
HE505ea	52	10	64
HE510ea	53	10	59
HE524ea	87	20	71
HE536ea	126	17	77
HE503ea	129	14	79
HE506ea	135	27	67
HE545eb	147	24	66

Fig. 4.55, continued. House 122, secondary fills: A potsherd decorated with horizontal lines (HE550aa), a slate pendant fragment with marked wear (HE550ed), a sub-circular scraper (HE536), a crescent-shaped flint sickle (HE550ea), a thin broad flake with cortex and fine retouch of parts of its perimeter (HE550eb), and a pear-shaped scraper (HE550ec). House 35, secondary fills: A potsherd with a kind of horizontal fluting (HE535ab) and a potsherd with a lozenge decoration in the frames of a metope area. House 122, sunken-floor horizon: Table of 17 complete scrapers, ordered according to weight. It shows scraper edge height as well as steepness (360 degree system) of a characteristic area in the front (distal end).

Secondary fills

HE550ac 1:2

HE550ad 1:2

Sunken-floor horizon

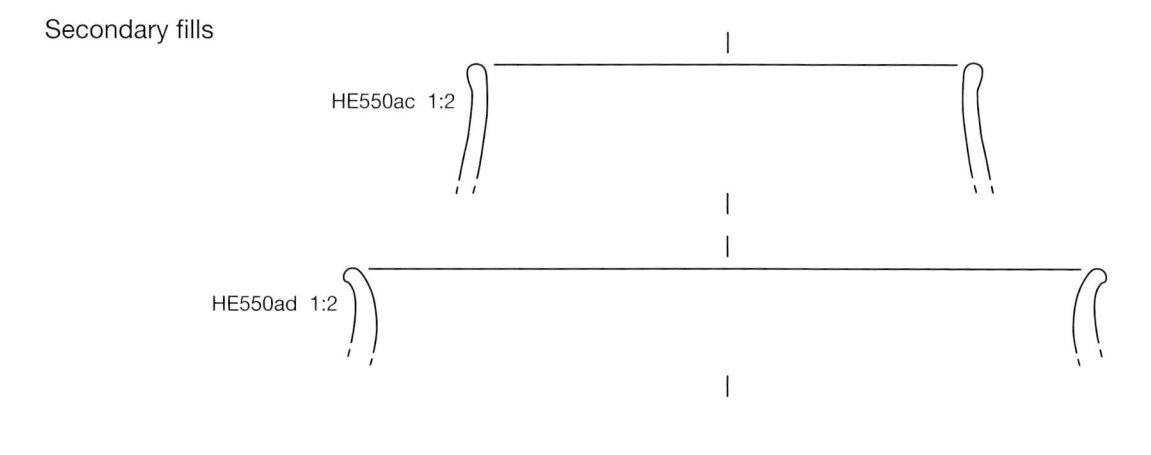

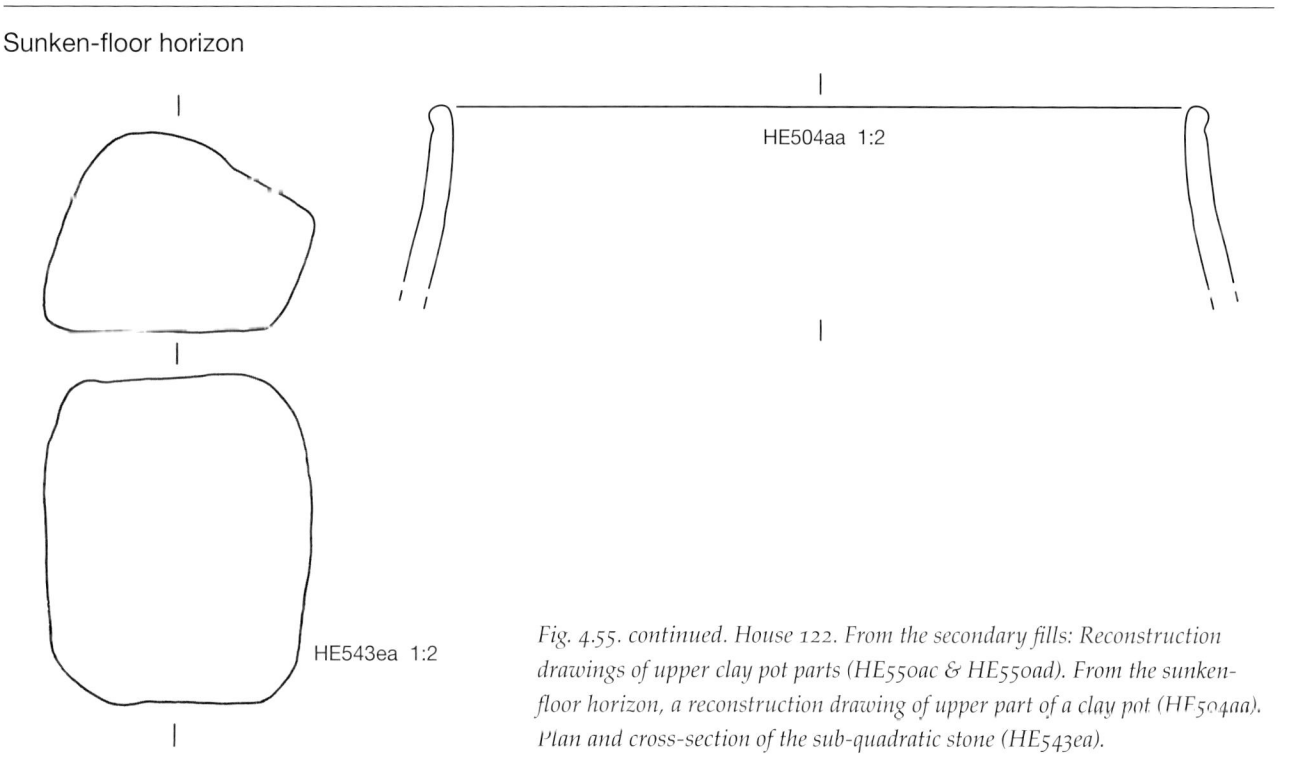

HE504aa 1:2

HE543ea 1:2

Fig. 4.55. continued. House 122. From the secondary fills: Reconstruction drawings of upper clay pot parts (HE550ac & HE550ad). From the sunken-floor horizon, a reconstruction drawing of upper part of a clay pot (HE504aa). Plan and cross-section of the sub-quadratic stone (HE543ea).

It is remarkable that not a single significant artefact, pit or soil patch was left in the sunken-floor horizon to the east. In stark contrast to this, many artefacts and important patches were present in the western half of the sunken floor. The finds from this floor part – and in particular from an area in the northern aisle – were characterized by the presence of numerous tools for one kind of activity, in particular, namely scraping. It is the only known case among all the longhouse sites from the central Limfjord region to have such a concentration of primarily one kind of flint tool in a floor area. In my judgment, it represents the vestiges of a highly-focused workshop and, for this purpose, an unusually broad spectrum of flint scrapers were present. These tools may well have been produced locally and, from their appearance, they comprise scrapers of highly varying qualities. The scrapers range from sizeable and very powerful to extraordinarily fine, combined with varying widths and steepness of edges. Several of these display scraper edges severely damaged from use, bearing scars where pieces had broken off. Some restoration could have taken place in this activity space. Treating bone or other firm, organic material cannot be immediately ruled out although I find it reasonable to suggest that the working of hides and skin was a major and special activity in this longhouse. Some kind of fairly flat underlay may have been necessary for the scraping processes and it is therefore, not least, interesting that it is precisely in this sunken floor that three different stones with flat sides were recorded. The stone anvils could also have been relevant for hide-working processes. As mentioned, a stone hammer also appears to belong to the floor horizon and might thus indicate activities concerned with hammering/crushing. We do not know where the entrance to this longhouse was placed but, in some well-preserved sites at Resengaard, it was established by the southwest part of the sunken floor. The free space nearer to the central scraper area could, for instance, have been used for a stock of raw hides to be exposed to scraping. The massive scraping activities that are suggested to have taken place to the west beg the question as to whether some of the sizeable free space east of the two scorched-stone patches also could have been used for storing finished products, i.e. heaps of ready-made hides, skins and other. At any rate, it is rather conspicuous that no other significant traces of activity were found in this eastern area of the sunken floor which, in many other longhouses was specifically preferred for various household doings. Concerning the treatment of hides, I propose the interpretation that strong wooden posts, placed in the two outdoor holes (49 & 127) south of Houses 122 and 35, served for stretching hides between them (Fig. 4.53). When deeply dug down and reinforced by the presence of stone linings, such posts (presumably connected across at the top and bottom with wooden beams of some kind) would have been capable of resisting substantial pressure from the side. The internal distance between the posthole centres was c. 1.6 m, giving a suitable space to stretch out, for instance, a roe deer skin. Stone-lined postholes of this kind have not been found in connection with any of the other settlements studied from the central Limfjord region. And yet a similar stone lining was used for constructing a Late Neolithic house of special character at Nautrup, likewise located in the northern part of Salling (Simonsen 1982b:39pp & Fig. 11-13).

When we now return to the topic of floor traces, the following are suggested as possible doings, separated into five activity spaces:

1. Scraping, raw flint handling/chipping and pottery handling/cooking. Numerous flint scrapers of varying shapes were found *in situ* in this area, indicating multi-facetted scraping activities. Present were also c. 200 tiny flint flakes, likely not least from repairing tools. A dagger tip also present. Altogether 1,113 tiny flint pieces of flint waste (HE550, lengths mainly ½-3 cm) were further ascribed to the secondary fills above the sunken floor, and many of these derive from archaeological cleaning the area with the concentration of scrapers.

2. Drying/roasting/charring/cooking/heating, scraping and pottery handling/cooking. A flat-sided stone and a clay spoon fragment also present.

3. Drying/roasting/charring/cooking/heating, scraping, and pottery handling/cooking. A flat-sided stone, a stone anvil and an arrowhead roughout present.

4. Scraping and pottery handling/cooking. A stone anvil present.

5. Pottery handling/cooking.

House 35 (Fig. 2.48 & 4.55)

Less than one metre west of the sunken floor was found a 5.3 cm long pressure-flaked flint piece (HE131) on the subsoil surface. The function of this tiny, rather narrow and unique piece is unclear but it could perhaps have been a particular tool in connection with the treatment of hides. A number of artefacts belong to the secondary fills of House 35. This concerns 68 potsherds and includes rim fragments and ornamented specimens. A stone quern, a fine-grained stone with a flat area, a fine-grained stone hammer, a flint scraper and 57 pieces of worked flint also belong to these fills. There is also a tiny wattle-and-daub fragment. And yet no artefacts or plant materials were recorded from the sunken-floor horizon. An ornamented side sherd (HE520aa) from the site of House 122 comes from the same clay pot as an ornamented side sherd from these secondary fills of House 35 and may thereby evidence that these buildings were contemporaneous. The floor was deepest in the central parts. No floor layer, pits or other soil features were observable and therefore no daily life activities can be suggested.

Glattrup IV

One of the truly remarkable traits of the three sunken-floor longhouses at Glattrup IV is the presence of several sizeable pits in the sunken floors and their surrounds (report U1999a). This is so far the only known settlement with such marked traits in the entire Limfjord region. In addition to the daily life activities within the individual longhouses suggested below, certain cereal treatments appear to have taken place indoors at Glattrup IV (report S2001a). The two ground-floor longhouses from this settlement (House 1 & House 4, Fig. 2.51) are considered later on (Fig. 2.51 & 5.3).

It should *a priori* be noted that, with regard to sunken-floor houses 3, 5 and 7, I believe it can be argued that the timespan of these buildings can be divided into two subsequent phases, namely a (likely longer) period of continuing the original activities as outlined below, and a second (possibly shorter) phase when the specific activities related to the large pits were given up. Presumably not before this latter after-residence phase, the large pits were gradually filled up during the longhouses' after-residence life. In House 5, one side of a relatively large cellar had even collapsed at some point in time before filling up. After abandonment and demolishing the longhouse, loading the sunken areas with fills different from those of the primary fills in the indoor pits took place. In this present work, however, I shall go no deeper into the many details of this argument.

House 3 (Fig. 4.56; Fig. 4.68.N)

In the ground-floor area to the west, pit 178 with surface dimensions of c. 0.80 x 0.65 and a depth of c. 27 cm was placed midway between two postholes of the central longitudinal axis. A dagger (GT178ea) was found c. 10 cm beneath the pit surface. It is much re-sharpened and it is difficult to assess its type. This dagger may represent an offering by abandonment of the longhouse. Seven pieces of flint and 2 pieces of burned flint were also recovered from the pit fills. I read the pit as a moderately sunken fireplace that was only used for a short time because no burning reddish of the sides was observed, whereas charcoal and some stones with impact from heat were found. Outside the longhouse in the area of the eastern gable end to the south was placed a shallow pit with sizeable surface appearance (Fig. 2.52.A). It was sub-circular in shape with a diameter of c. 1.05 x 0.80 m. It consisted of yellowish-brown fine sand. Its depth was c. 0.10 m, and the bottom was slightly undulating. No finds are recorded from it. It cannot be excluded that the pit might have had a function in relation to the longhouse but I do not directly suggest this. A stone hammer (GT208) was unearthed from the fill of a posthole south of the sunken floor and it might originally have been placed there as a side support for the wooden post. It is hardly excludable that it could represent a votive deposition. There is only moderate find material from the sunken-floor horizon, whereas many potsherds were contained in the secondary fills above. A potsherd (GT310aa) from the sunken-floor horizon belongs to the same clay pot as one from the secondary fills (GT145as). Some of the finds mentioned below are from the large pit A and the sunken fireplace B that also contained plant materials.

A low zone had developed centrally, as confirmed by many level measurements. In the periphery to the northeast the sunken floor was a little higher than the more southerly areas. No scorched-stone patches were found in this sunken-floor horizon. The significant pits concern:

A: Deep pit. The surface dimensions were c. 1.2 x 0.9 m. Depth c. 0.65 m. Four layers characterized the pit fill (not illustrated). In the top a brownish-yellow, sandy layer (1) containing some potsherds, flint flakes and tiny traces of charcoal. Within that, a somewhat lighter layer (2) but otherwise with the same characteristics. The lower part of the pit had a fill of greyish sandy soil containing worked flint and tiny traces of charcoal (3). From the bottom was recovered a horizontal, slightly undulating layer (4) of brownish, sandy soil with numerous tiny traces of charcoal. A soil sample with cereal remainders derives from the pit.

B: Sunken fireplace, sub-circular. The surface dimensions were c. 1.55 x 1.40 m, depth c. 1.00 m. The sides were almost vertical, although gradually leaning out more as they went upwards. During fieldwork, its strata were described together with the N-S section of the sunken floor, and this pit comprises three layers (not illustrated). Most of the pit fill (3) consisted of light greyish-brown soil closely resembling the surrounding sandy ground and containing scattered potsherds, flint flakes and tiny pieces of charcoal. A limited portion of the fill within stratum 3 comprised yellowish-white, fine-grained sand (4). With its sterile sand, it very likely shows just an intermezzo in the filling up, and no traces of vegetation layers were found. Finally, at the bottom, a c. 5 cm thick layer consisting of greyish-brown sandy soil with a great deal of charcoal was observable (6). In my understanding, the pit bottom had been used as a fireplace. The remainders from the fire had been compressed over time, and blackish soil vestiges were still observable a little up-

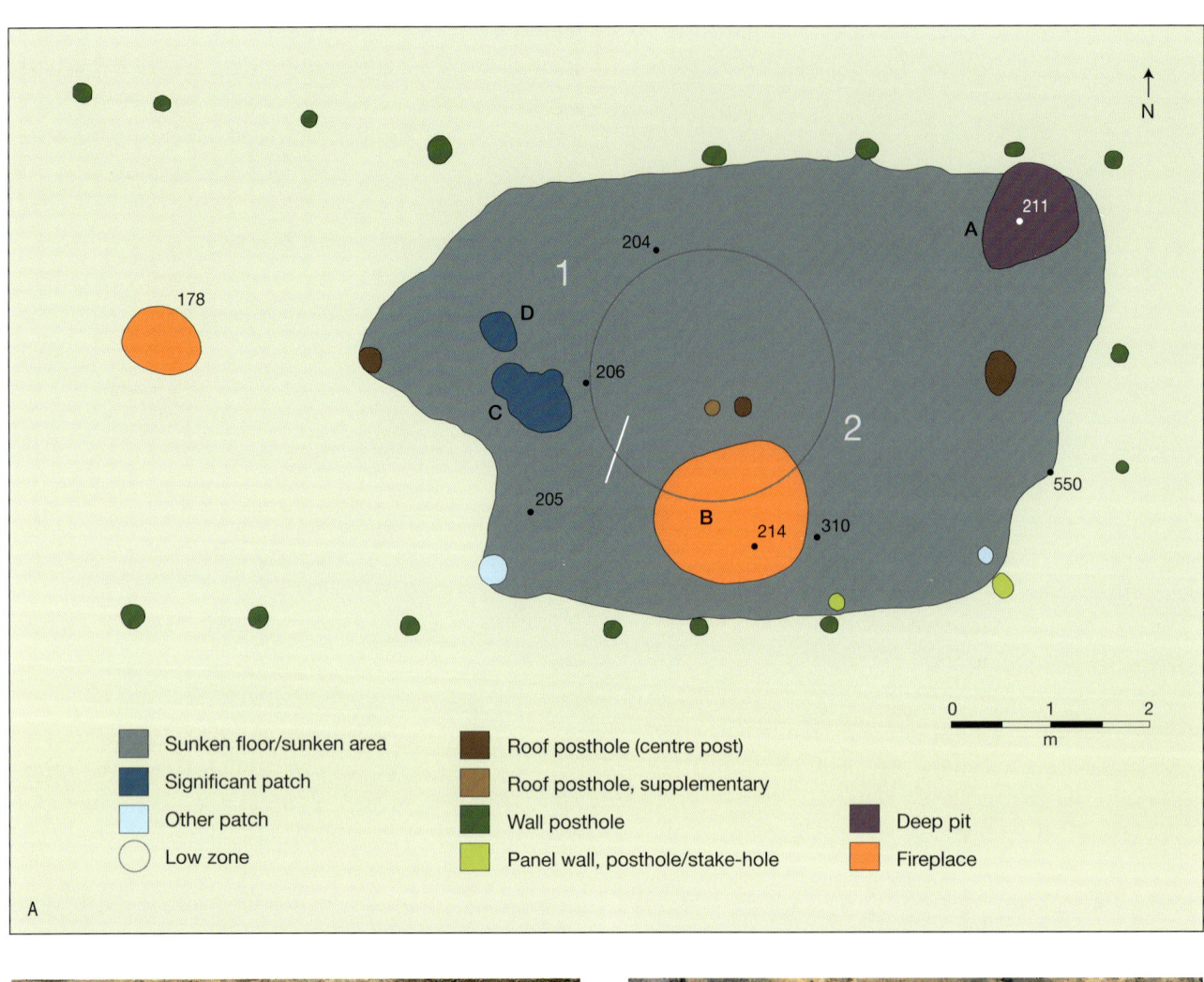

Fig. 4.56. Glattrup IV. House 3. A: Ground plan of sunken floor, cleaned. Two activity spaces are suggested. B: The sunken fireplace, B, excavated to the bottom, where numerous pieces of charcoal are still in situ. Seen from the east. C: The sunken fireplace, 178, seems to have functioned only briefly. A complete flint dagger was later placed there and it likely concerns an offering. The dagger was much retouched and it is difficult to determine the type. The artefacts found in situ in the sunken-floor horizon, including those of the pits, belong to several find spots: **204:** *8 potsherds, among these 2 rims (GT204);* **205:** *1 potsherd, rim (GT205aa);* **206:** *1 potsherd, rim (GT206aa);* **211:** *1 flint sickle fragment, 10 flint nodules, 67 pieces of worked flint, 2 pieces of burned flint, 1 stone hammer, & 1 lump of clay (GT211), from pit A;* **214:** *33 potsherds including a rim, 48 pieces of worked flint, & 2 heat-cracked stones (GT214), from the sunken fireplace B;* **310:** *1 potsherd, rim (GT310aa);* **550:** *1 piece of amber, crumbled into dust, not taken up as a find (GT550). For cereal finds, see Fig. 5.17.*

wards in the sides. Whether reddish colouring of the sides had taken place or not is not mentioned in the excavation report. A soil sample with charred organic material was taken from the bottom layer. Judging by the presence of the layers diverging significantly from the soil of the secondary fills, the sunken fireplace was likely filled up for the after-residence life.

C: Irregularly shaped patch. Sandy soil. Surface dimensions c. 0.9 x 0.6. Depth c. 0.15 m.

D: Small patch. Sandy soil. Surface dimensions 0.4 x 0.3 m. Depth c. 0.10 m.

Judging by the sum of the arrangements, with different sizeable pits marking out the whole of the eastern interior, I find it plausible that the special activities related to beer brewing and storing were more or less the same as in House 5 at Glattrup IV, which will be considered immediately below. The following are suggested as possible doings, separated into two activity spaces:

1. Pottery handling/cooking.

2. Beer brewing/storing, raw flint handling/chipping and heating (sunken fireplaces). An amber piece was found in this activity space. Raw flint handling/chipping was possibly carried out in this activity space due to the presence of 10 flint nodules and 67 pieces of worked flint in the fills of pit A.

House 5 (Fig. 4.57 & 4.58; Fig. 4.68.O)

An extremely large, flat-bottomed pit with almost vertical sides (pit 480) was situated far to the west of the sunken floor area. I argue that this large hole dug into the ground was intended for a special function due to its extraordinary dimensions, its placement in the ground floor and its whole appearance. In shape, the surface appearance was close to an oval although not fully regular. The N-S length was c. 2.44 m, the width c. 1.70 m and the depth c. 1.07 m. The pit was placed very centrally in the ground floor to the west between the gable end and a roof-bearing post. Seven strata are recorded from it and these had been deposited rhythmically over each other and do not immediately appear to represent a complicated formation of the pit fills, although one of the layers may indicate a break in the rhythm of filling up. The bottom was almost flat, being only faintly deeper in the sides than at the middle. Its area was about 3.5 m². During excavation, some of the top centimetres were removed by cleaning of the surface and, prior to that, recent ploughing may also have removed a part of the top. The volume would also depend on how a possible panelling was done. In my opinion, the sides consisting of sand could not have been retained without a panel of some kind. The thickness of such a construction would not necessarily have been more than a few centimetres. I presume that the pit was by and large used during the time of residence. Thereafter, the pit was filled with layers of soil. The excavation director posed the question of whether an upper layer (stratum 2) could represent a vegetation layer or not. In this case, it might point to a pause in the filling up and the layer would presumably have come into existence after tearing down at least the roof of this part of the house. It is not excludable that it could represent a vegetation horizon and the remaining fill would then have been topped up later. The fills of pit 480 at the western end of the house contained a number of artefacts (GT480). This concerns 104 potsherds (among these 2 ornamented rims), 2 cordoned rims, 9 other rims, 5 bottom-side fragments, 2 bottom fragments, and 7 ornamented side fragments. This fill also included 6 flint nodules, 106 pieces of other worked flint and 5 pieces of burned flint, as well as 2 stone hammers. It also contained a piece of amber (GT480-d). In the large posthole immediately to its east was found 1 potsherd and 2 pieces of worked flint (GT523).

When turning to the sunken area, a potsherd with rim and cordon (GT509) stems from the sandy soil just above the large pit C. This potsherd is not considered to belong to the after-residence life of the longhouse. Including the sunken fireplace, four pits contained plant materials (see report S2001a).

Pit A placed in the periphery to the northwest and pit B placed to the southeast along the south side were both a good distance from the low central areas, whereas the third, being a sunken fireplace, was situated more centrally to the east. These three significant pits concern:

A: Large pit, sub-circular. Four layers characterized the pit (not illustrated): uppermost, a greyish-brown, sandy soil with traces of charcoal containing potsherds and flint flakes (1). Below this, a light-greyish, very sandy soil with a few traces of charcoal, potsherds and flint flakes (2). Thereafter follows a layer of greyish-brown sandy soil correspondingly with

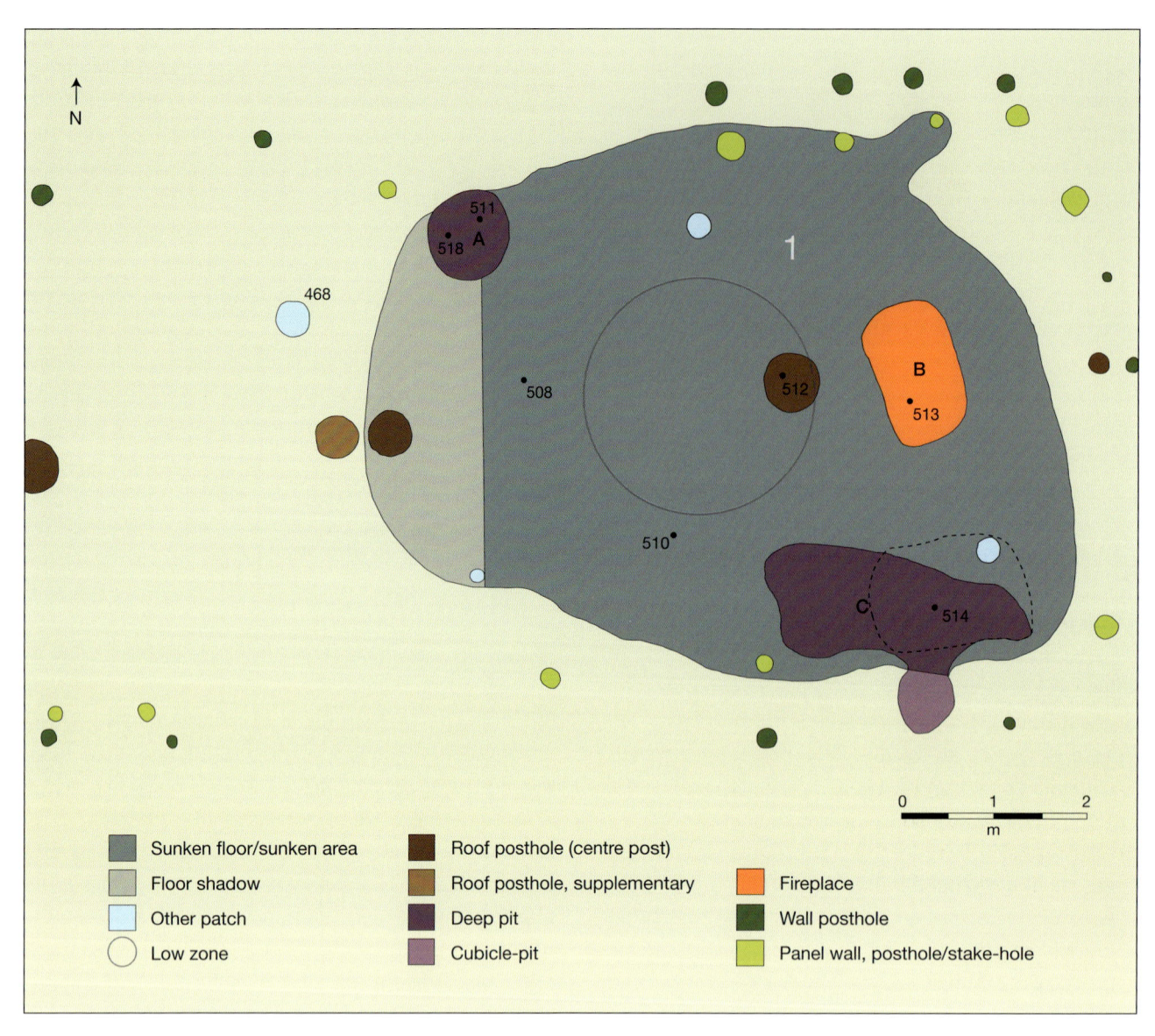

Fig. 4.57. Glattrup IV. House 5. A: Ground plan of sunken floor, cleaned. A single large activity space is suggested. In cellar pit C, the sandy subsoil edge to the northeast collapsed at some point in time but the sub-rectangular stippling indicates the regular bottom observed during excavation. The artefacts found in situ in the sunken-floor horizon, including those of the pits, involve several find spots: **508:** *1 potsherd, bottom (GT508);* **510:** *1 potsherd, rim (GT510);* **511:** *1 potsherd, ornamented, from the bottom layer of pit A (GT511);* **512:** *1 stone hammer (GT512);* **513:** *5 potsherds, among these 1 rim with two cordons, & 9 pieces of worked flint (GT513), from the sunken fireplace B;* **514:** *45 potsherds (among these 2 with rim & 2 with cordoned rim), 1 stone hammer, 1 flint hammer, 11 pieces of worked flint, & 3 pieces of burned flint (GT514), from the large cellar pit C;* **518:** *3 potsherds, among these 1 rim, & 14 pieces of worked flint, as well as charcoal & heat-affected/cracked stones (GT518), all from pit A. For cereal finds, see Fig. 5.17.*

charcoal, potsherds and flint flakes (3). A soil sample from this layer has been examined. At the bottom was found a layer of light-greyish sand, containing potsherds and flint flakes (4). The diameter of the pit was c. 0.90 m and the depth 0.65 m. The upper part had almost vertical sides, whereas the lower part was slanting to the sides. Some heat-affected/cracked stones were also dumped into this large pit.

B: Sunken fireplace. It had an almost sub-rectangular appearance in the surface of the floor but with rounded corners. Surface dimensions c. 1.5 x 1 m. Depth c. 0.35 m. The cross-section had a nearly evenly rounded shape. Some worked flint from the fill showed no clear impact from burning and thus accords well with the understanding that these items stem from later fills. Four layers are recorded: in the top

Fig. 4.58. Glattrup IV. House 5. Artefacts: Flint piece with notches (GT468ea) and a potsherd with oblique notch-stamped decoration in horizontal bands (GT468aa), both from patch 468 west of the sunken floor. From pit A stems a rim sherd with oblique notch-stamped decoration in horizontal bands (GT511aa). From the sizable pit 480 in the ground floor derives a rim sherd with horizontal furrows (GT480aj). A potsherd with horizontal furrows (GT469ae) and another with oblique notch-stamped decoration in a horizontal band (GT469ad) belong to the secondary fills above the sunken floor.

light grey-brownish sandy soil in the central part (1) and to the sides greyish-brown sandy soil (2). In the bottom, black sandy soil with much charcoal (3) and up the side faintly reddish sand (4), where the colouring was likely caused by much heat.

C: Large cellar pit. Its surface length was c. 3.0 m and the width at the western end c. 1.20 m. In my interpretation, the southern extension of the pit represents the lower part of a kind of cubicle established within the south wall. However, during fieldwork the entire pit area was not clearly observable from the sunken floor surface due to some old subsoil slide that took place during the functioning time of the longhouse but which emerged when investigating its sides. At the bottom, the central and eastern parts turned out to have a rather rectangular shape of c. 1.80 x 1.10 m, with evenly rounded corners. The bottom area was thus nearly 2 m². The pit was much deeper in the eastern half than in the western. The depth towards the east was c. 0.77 m, whereas to the west it was only around 0.11-0.18 m. The longitudinal section of the pit is very different from the other pits in the sunken-floor houses at Glattrup IV. The pit fill consisted of six layers. In my understanding, the gradual deepening of the pit from the west, forming a kind of ramp, indicates a way of reaching the flat bottom of the cellar pit.

It seems evident that, not least, the arrangement of the sunken fireplace, the sizeable cellar and the large sub-circular pit, the placement of a doorway (Fig. 2.53), and the entire house ground plan layout shows the remainders of a building and its interior strongly marked by certain special doings. In my reading it is likely that the brewing of beer and all the preparations and subsequent work – including likely short-term storage of the liquids – were decisive factors in the whole ordering of the indoors. When it comes to these activities, the arrangement in the area of the sunken floor, in combination with pit 480 in the area of the ground floor, can be seen as a whole. Besides these doings, pottery handling/cooking is also a focus. In terms of the heat-cracked stones from the fills in pit A, it is possible that limited activities in relation to this could also have taken place, but exactly where we do not know and, naturally, it could also have been outside. Based on the floor traces, the following are suggested as possible doings, considered as a single large activity space:

1. Beer brewing/storing (pits A, B, C, as well as pit 480 to the west), hammering/crushing, and pottery handling/cooking. No activities are suggested concerning the presence of heat-affected/cracked stones in pit A.

House 7 (Fig. 4.59 & 4.60; Fig. 4.68.P)

A moderate number of finds belong to the secondary fills. Other finds all stem from the pit fills and an aisle posthole (707). The fill of this latter contained 3 potsherds, 3 pieces of worked flint and 1 piece of burned flint.

This remarkable house site was investigated as a last-minute excavation beneath a narrow road track, and the recording of the pits and other features is less detailed than the existing data on the two other sunken-floor house sites at Glattrup IV.

The low zone had developed northeast of the central part of the sunken floor. Two of the large pits were found east of the preserved sunken-floor contour and one to the south of it, whereas two other large pits were dug within the areas of the sunken floor to the east. Scorched-stone patches or other low soil features belonging to the functioning time of the house were not observed. The significant pits in the sunken floor, including its immediate periphery, can briefly be characterized as follows:

A: Sunken fireplace. Sub-rectangular, with rounded corners. Surface dimensions c. 1.65 x 0.90 m. Depth c. 0.90 m. The pit bottom was almost flat with only a faint inclination to one side. The sides were almost vertical, albeit slightly curved, and the pit only became slightly broader towards the top. The pit fill consisted of almost horizontal layers of lighter and darker layers of sandy soil with pieces of charcoal. Areas of the vertical sides had a blackish appearance, presumably coloured by charcoal dust (Fig. 4.59.G).

B: Large, sub-circular pit. It is noteworthy that the east side of the sunken-floor surface appeared practically in line with the sunken floor contour to the east. This might indicate that the pit was close to a wall line here. Surface dimensions c. 1.64 x 1.50 m, and depth c. 1.15 m. The bottom was nearly flat. One side was straight and the other slightly curved. Both sides were leaning outwards from the bottom up. The pit fill consisted of almost horizontal layers of lighter and darker sandy soil with pieces of charcoal and dust from carbonized material.

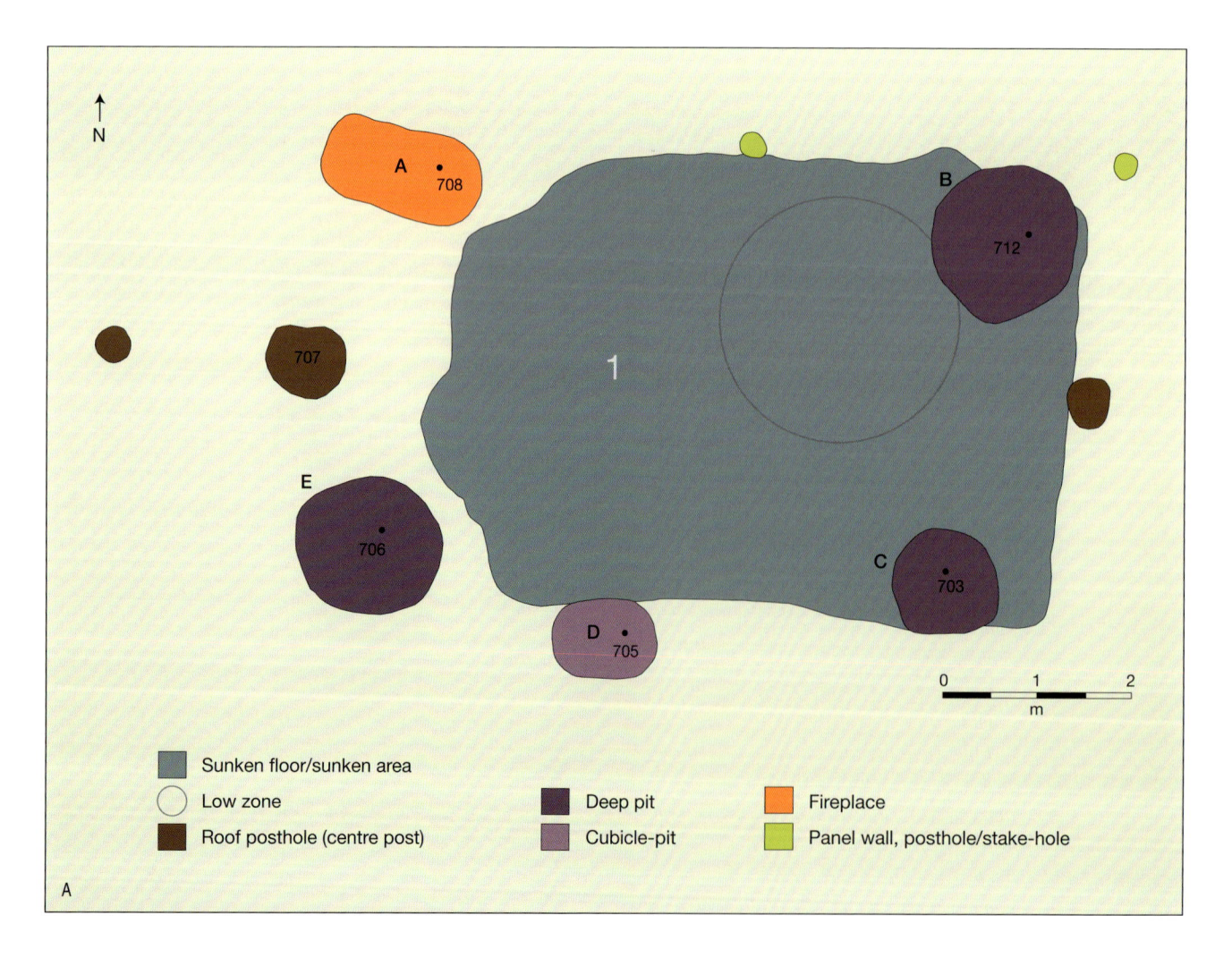

300 Chapter 4

◀▲ *Fig. 4.59. Glattrup IV. House 7. A: Ground plan, cleaned. A single large activity space is suggested. While a number of finds stem from pits in the floor and secondary fills above the sunken floor, no find spots are directly found on this floor surface. The artefacts from pits belonging to the sunken-floor horizon involve:* **703:** *23 potsherds (among these 2 rims), 11 pieces of worked flint, 1 piece of burned flint, 1 presumed stone hammer, some charcoal (GT703), from pit C;* **705:** *10 potsherds and 20 pieces of worked flint (GT705), from pit D;* **706:** *42 potsherds (among these 5 rims & 3 ornamented fragments), 38 pieces of worked flint, & 1 piece of burned flint (GT706), presence of charcoal, from pit E;* **708:** *10 potsherds (including 3 rims & 1 ornamented fragment), 32 pieces of worked flint, 3 pieces of burned flint, heat-affected/cracked stones & charcoal (GT708), from the sunken fireplace, A;* **712:** *56 potsherds (including 2 rims & 1 fragment with cordon). Furthermore, 294 pieces of worked flint (including 74 tiny flint pieces ranging from c. 0.5-3.0 cm in length). It is estimated in the excavation report that some 70 pieces could stem from the same flint nodule (GT712), from pit B. For cereal finds, see Fig. 5.17. B: Abdolkarim Torabinejad excavating Pit B. Seen from the east. C: Pit B in its final stage of excavation. The minor dark patches appearing in the periphery presumably indicate some former construction. Seen from the west-southwest. D: The "cubicle pit", D, during excavation. To the south, a vertical section of its soil fills is still observable. Seen from the north. E: Pit E excavated to the bottom, having spots of charcoal remainders. F: The sub-circular pit C in the final stage of excavation. Seen from the north. G: The sub-rectangular sunken fireplace after completion of the investigation. Blackish traces visible on its vertical sides. Seen from the north-northeast.*

Artefacts, pits, patches, and daily life activities

Fig. 4.60. Glattrup IV. House 7. A flint hammer (GT700ea) from secondary fills above the sunken floor, and a flint knife (GT705ea) from the fills of pit D. From fills in pit B, a piece of tempered burned clay with almost flat underside (GT712aa). From the fills of pit C, a stone hammer (GT703ea) broken during use.

C: Large, sub-circular pit. It is also noteworthy here that, in the sunken-floor surface, this pit appeared as if following a strict wall line, in this case the south side. Surface diameter c. 1.10 m and depth c. 0.50 m. The pit bottom was almost flat with only a slight inclination to the west. The sides were oblique, the western side with a bend, and as it went upwards the pit became significantly broader. The soil consisted of almost horizontal layers of lighter and darker sandy soil with pieces of charcoal and coal dust.

D: Large, oval pit, being interpreted as part of a cubicle. The surface of the sunken floor appears to be in line with the strict wall line but placed conversely to the two aforementioned pits, being outside the sunken floor. As we saw earlier, a modern ditch had cut off its southernmost part but it would probably only have gone a few centimetres further to the south. Its length east/west was c. 1.20 m, and the preserved width c. 0.9 m. Depth c. 0.85 m. By and large, the pit bottom was completely flat. The sides were almost vertical and the pit became just faintly broader as it went upwards. It contained almost horizontal layers of lighter and darker sandy soils with pieces of charcoal and dust of carbonized material. Following my understanding of the pit placements in relation to the walls, my interpretation is that this pit formed the lower part of a cubicle made within the turf wall.

E: Large, sub-circular pit. The diameter was up to c. 1.6 m and the depth c. 0.85 m. The bottom was almost flat with the nearly straight sides leaning slightly outwards towards the top. The fill consisted of nearly horizontal layers of lighter and darker sandy soil with pieces of charcoal and dust from charred material. Areas with traces of charcoal were present in the lower part of the pit. The finds concern the above listed GT706.

In my reading, the finds in many of the five pits do not directly point to the original use of these but merely represent fills. When it comes to the everyday activities of this house site, the presence of the large pits and the entire sum of interior arrangements, I believe, makes it reasonable to presume similar special functions to House 5. With the conspicuous placement of the pits around the sunken-floor periphery, it seems that much of the sunken floor must have been incorporated into one large activity space. No other artefact indications of activity spaces were found in the floor itself, not even pottery remainders. It is presumably accidental that no artefacts from daily life were recovered on the sunken floor. However, clay pot remains were found in fills from four of the five sizeable pits. Numerous tiny flint pieces in pit B could stem from the removal of flint waste from a flint-chipping activity somewhere in the interior, and many might derive from the same greyish flint nodule. The following are suggested as possible doings in the activity space:

1. Beer brewing/storing (pits A, B, C, D, & E), hammering/crushing, and pottery handling/cooking. The presumed stone hammer, numerous pieces of worked flint and some potsherds were present in pit fills.

Rosgårde

A rather limited number of artefacts come from the site of House 1 with sunken floor, and only modest finds from two likely contemporaneous pits (23 & 121) are of interest because, in my reading, they probably belong to the time of that longhouse as elements of a single-phase settlement (Report U2001c). These finds may throw some light on the material side of the settlement, although they are not placed very near the house sites (Fig. 2.55). An archaeo-botanical examination has been carried out on samples from a large, circular pit (318) belonging to House 2 with ground floor (Fig. 5.3).

Pit 23 was found some 60 m to the north of House 1. It was sub-circular in shape with surface dimensions c. 3.0 x 2.4 m. Depth c. 1.15. The bottom was deepest near the middle and, above that, a total of 7 layers were observed. The artefacts stem from the two uppermost strata. Besides heat-affected/cracked stones, this concerns 92 potsherds (including 5 rims and 5 fragments decorated with horizontal furrows), 157 pieces of worked flint, and 2 pieces of burned flint. Soot can be observed on the outside of 1 potsherd and the inner side of 3 potsherds. Some scanty finds of charred cereals representing naked barley, wheat and spelt exist from this pit (Marianne Høyem Andreasen, report S2009a).

Pit 121 was dug some 80 m to the north of House 1. It was almost circular in shape with a diameter c. 2.25 m. Depth c. 0.30 m. To the west, the bottom was fairly flat and towards the east slightly oblique. Two soil strata were observed and the artefact remainders derived from both of these, containing 28 potsherds in all. These included 3 rims and 2 side fragments supplied with horizontal furrows and 1 side fragment with notch-stamped lines. Another potsherd seems to indicate the slight remains of cord-lines.

House 1 (Fig. 4.61 & 4.62)

From the western, unsunken part of the house site stem some pits without finds or with fairly insignificant finds (Fig. 2.56.A & 2.56.B). Pit 255 thus contained 3 pieces of worked flint and 1 burned flint blade. The oval pit 260 contained no finds. Pit 252 contained 5 pieces of worked flint and 4 potsherds (including 1 side sherd with Beaker decoration). Although pits 255 and 260 were of some surface dimension, their volumes were quite limited. The undisturbed pit 260, being almost bathtub-shaped, is calculated to have contained less than 0.1 m³ of fill. Pit 261 consisted of greyish-brown, sandy soil and the depth was c. 0.23 m. A presumed posthole was dug into it to the northwest.

The finds from the secondary fills above the sunken floor consist of 79 potsherds (*inter alia* 2 rims & 2 bottom fragments), 1 strike-a-light based on a flint dagger, 1 flint nodule, and 222 pieces of various worked flint (RO201). Among these is a blade scraper fragment with its working edge almost intact.

The sunken-floor depth was about medium compared to those of the Resengaard longhouses although it was probably deeper before the impact of recent ploughing. It was rather flat over a large area with a low zone to the north although the differences were slight and, in this case, little importance should

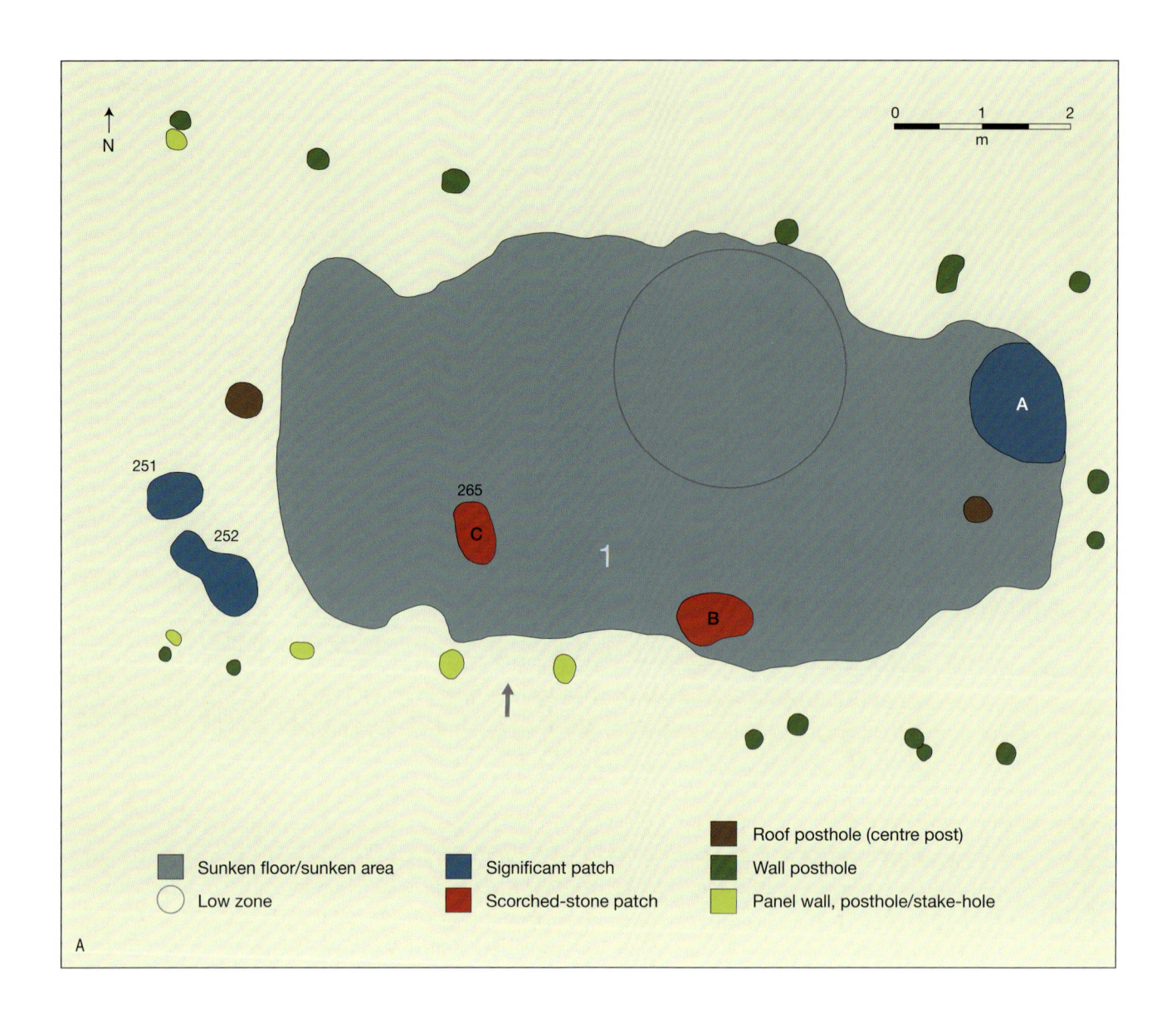

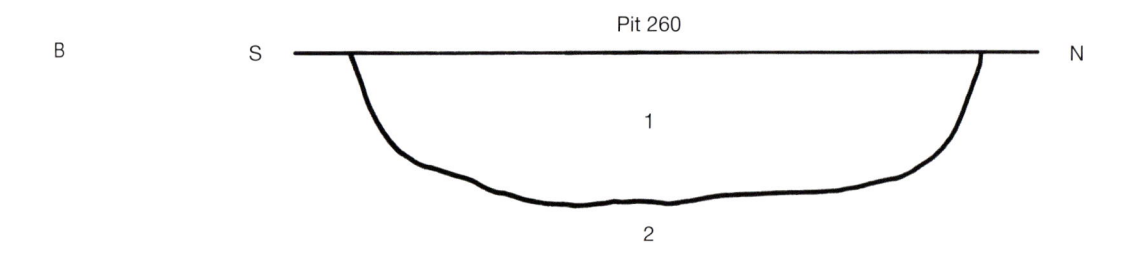

Fig. 4.61. Rosgårde. House 1. A: Ground plan, cleaned. Just a single activity space is suggested. While a number of finds stem from the secondary fills, no find spots are directly found on the floor surface. The artefacts from one patch belonging to the sunken-floor horizon just involve: **265:** *2 potsherds (of which one is a rim), 8 pieces of worked flint & 1 piece of burned flint (RO265), from patch C. B: Two puzzling pits (255 & 260) with almost the same surface appearance were placed in the ground floor (Fig. 2.56). Both were shallow and more or less bathtub-shaped and at present no suggestions can be put forward as to their functions. The depth of the N-S aligned westernmost pit 260 was 20 cm and that of the E-W aligned northernmost pit 255 (not illustrated) was 19 cm. Both were parallel to the nearest wall and a distance of about one metre from it. The westernmost enclosed a brownish to light greyish-brown sandy soil. Two other pits (251 & 252) in the ground floor are also considered to belong to the time of the longhouse and it might even concern further pits.*

Fig. 4.62. Rosgårde. House 1 and two pits. From the secondary fills above the sunken floor stems a stone hammer with crushing marks in both ends (RO201eb). From pit 121 north of the house derives a potsherd with decoration of horizontal notch-stamped lines (RO 121ad) and from pit 23 stem two potsherds with horizontally incised lines/furrows (RO23ai & RO23ak).

probably be attached to its placement. A number of soil features were present in the sunken floor as well as in the ground floor to the west. When also taking into consideration the pits mentioned below, it can be said that the artefact remainders from the pits of the longhouse in all cases appear simply to represent a casual mix-up in the fill. It does not therefore help in terms of indicating the possible purposes of the pits. Some indeterminate, fragmented charred cereals exist from a posthole on the central longitudinal axis to the east (Marianne Høyem Andreasen, report S2009a). The few significant soil patches in the sunken floor can briefly be characterized as follows:

A: Soil patch, following the sunken floor boundary to the east. Light-brownish, sandy soil containing traces of charcoal. The feature was diffusely limited downwards. Surface dimensions c. 1.4 x 1.1 m and fairly shallow, being only c. 5 cm deep.

B: Scorched-stone patch, shallow. Sandy soil with some heat-affected/cracked stones. Surface dimensions c. 0.8 x 0.6 m. It contained a few pieces of worked flint. Some disturbance from animal activity observed.

C: Scorched-stone patch, shallow. The pit consisted of two soil layers. The upper central part was brownish, sandy soil with a few heat-affected/cracked stones, whereas yellowish-brown, sandy soil was present in the sides and at the bottom. The surface dimensions were c. 0.7 x 0.4 m.

Only a few concrete activities can immediately be proposed for the use of this interesting and rather well-preserved longhouse site. It is remarkable that a slight low zone had developed in the northern aisle without any artefacts being found there and, likewise, no artefacts were found in or near patch A. Based on the floor traces, the following are suggested as possible doings in just a single activity space:

1. Drying/roasting/charring/cooking/heating and pottery handling/cooking

Tromgade

Apart from the finds from the sites of three sunken-floor houses (1, 2 & 5), ceramics and other artefacts stem not least from several pits (Fig. 2.57). In particular, interesting pottery derives from two sizeable pits (54 & 328), as well as a culture layer (76). These finds may help characterize this settlement (report U2001a).

Pit 54 was found c. 7 m north of the sunken floor of House 2. This large, sub-circular pit had surface dimensions of approx. 3.5 x 4 m, whereas the depth was only c. 0.42 m. The pit contained much pottery and several sherds are richly ornamented (Fig. 4.66). Fragments of a clay spoon are also present (TR66aa/71aa). Among the worked flint, a strike-a-light can be mentioned. Two stone hammers, a flint hammer, 12 flint nodules, and c. 2000 grams of worked flint were also found.

Pit 328 was found c. 8 m south of the sunken floor of House 2. It was rather large and irregular in surface appearance, with dimensions of about 5 x 4 m. The depth was only c. 0.25 m. It contained some ornamented pottery, as well as a damaged flint arrowhead and c. 1800 grams of worked flint.

Culture layer 76 had accumulated in a lowering c. 7 m northwest of House 2. It was irregular in surface shape and the dimensions were around 6.3 x 4.7 m, including the prolongation towards the northeast. The depth was c. 0.25 m. It included several likewise richly decorated potsherds. In the culture layer were also found an almost complete pressure-flaked flint sickle and a somewhat damaged flint arrowhead. Furthermore, c. 370 grams of minor and tiny flakes from pressure flaking were recovered in a concentration and, from elsewhere in the layer, were found a further c. 3800 grams of worked flint. The culture layer appears to mainly represent a sequence of waste depositions within a limited period.

House 1 (Fig. 4.63 & 4.64)

The secondary fills over the sunken floor contained 101 potsherds (a few with ornamentation), 1 flint scraper, and 378 pieces of worked flint, as well as a fossilized sea urchin, and 9 pieces of burned bone. I propose that two nearly head-size stones were used as anvils. A regular floor layer was not observed.

A low zone was observable near the floor middle. The significant soil patches in the sunken floor can briefly be characterized as follows:

A: Scorched-stone patch. Large, irregular, to some degree horseshoe-shaped patch with sandy soil, containing heat-affected/cracked stones, as well as two small (presumed) stone anvils. Depth merely a few cm.[5]

B: Scorched-stone patch. Grey and greyish-brown, sandy soil with some heat-affected/cracked stones. Surface dimensions c. 0.40 x 0.32 m. Depth only a few cm.

C: Scorched-stone patch. Contained brownish sandy soil with several stones and traces of charcoal. Some of the stones were seemingly not heat-affected/cracked. Disturbed by animal activity, presumably mice. Surface dimensions c. 0.40 x 0.40 m. Depth only a few cm.

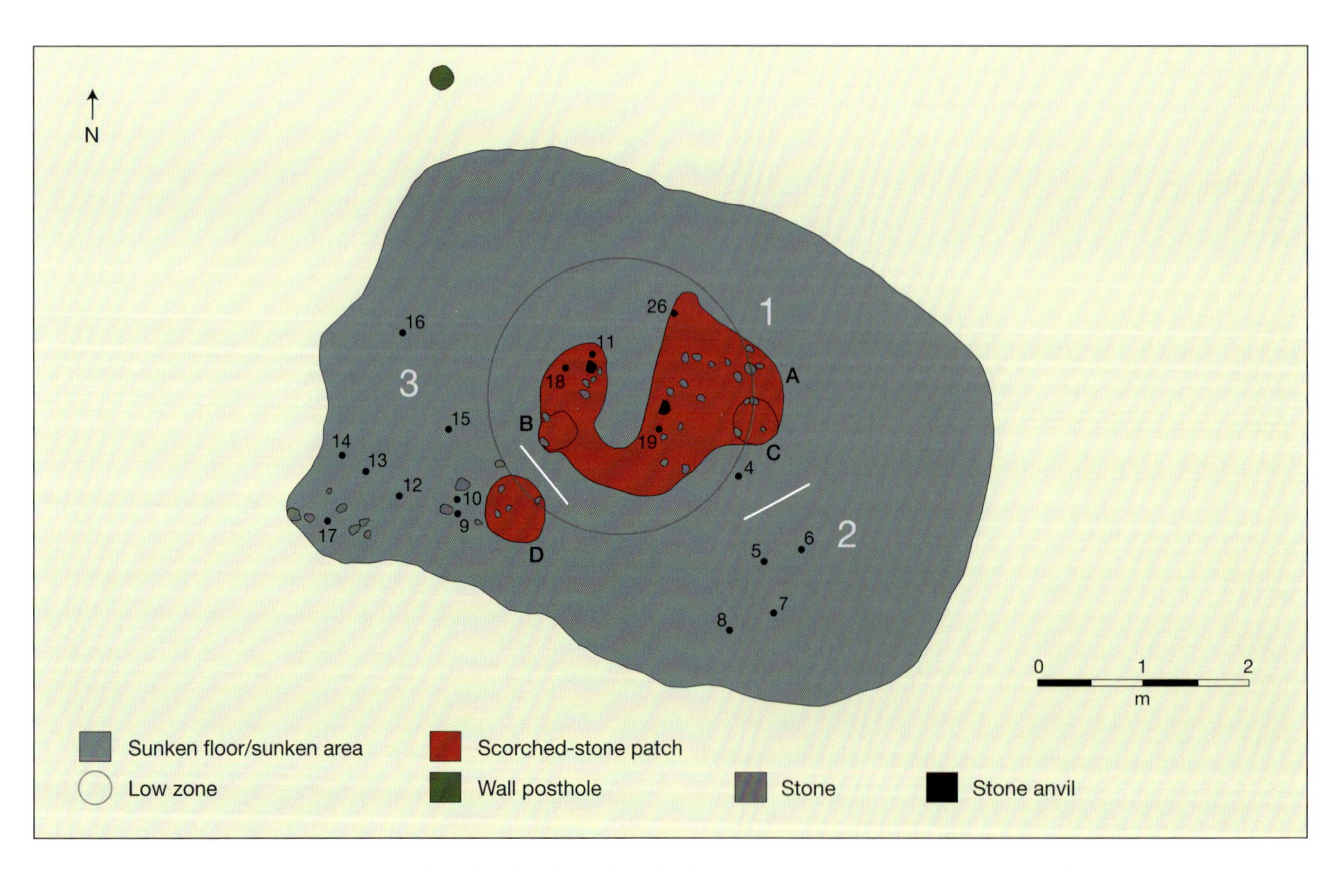

*Fig. 4.63. Tromgade. House 1. A: Ground plan of sunken floor, cleaned. Three activity spaces are suggested. Apart from scorched stones and stone anvils, the artefacts found in situ in the sunken-floor horizon involve many find spots: **4:** 1 potsherd, side (TR4aa); **5:** 14 potsherds, including 1 rim (TR5aa); **6:** 2 potsherds, including 1 rim (TR6aa); **7:** 1 flint nodule (TR7ea); **8:** 1 worked flint (TR8ea); **9:** 1 flint nodule (TR9ea); **10:** 1 flint nodule (TR10ea); **11:** 1 potsherd, rim (TR11aa); **12:** 1 potsherd, rim (TR12aa); **13:** 1 flint sickle, almost complete (TR13ea); **14:** 1 piece of worked flint with retouch (TR14); **15:** 1 potsherd, rim (TR15aa); **16:** 1 flint scraper (TR16ea); **17:** 1 potsherd, rim, notch-stamped lines below the rim (TR17aa); **18:** 1 potsherd, rim (TR18aa); **19:** 1 potsherd, rim (TR19aa); **26:** 1 clay spoon handle (TR26aa).*

Tromgade, House 1
Sunken-floor horizon

TR13ea

TR26aa

TR4aa 1:2

TR6aa 1:2

Tromgade, House 414
Secondary fills

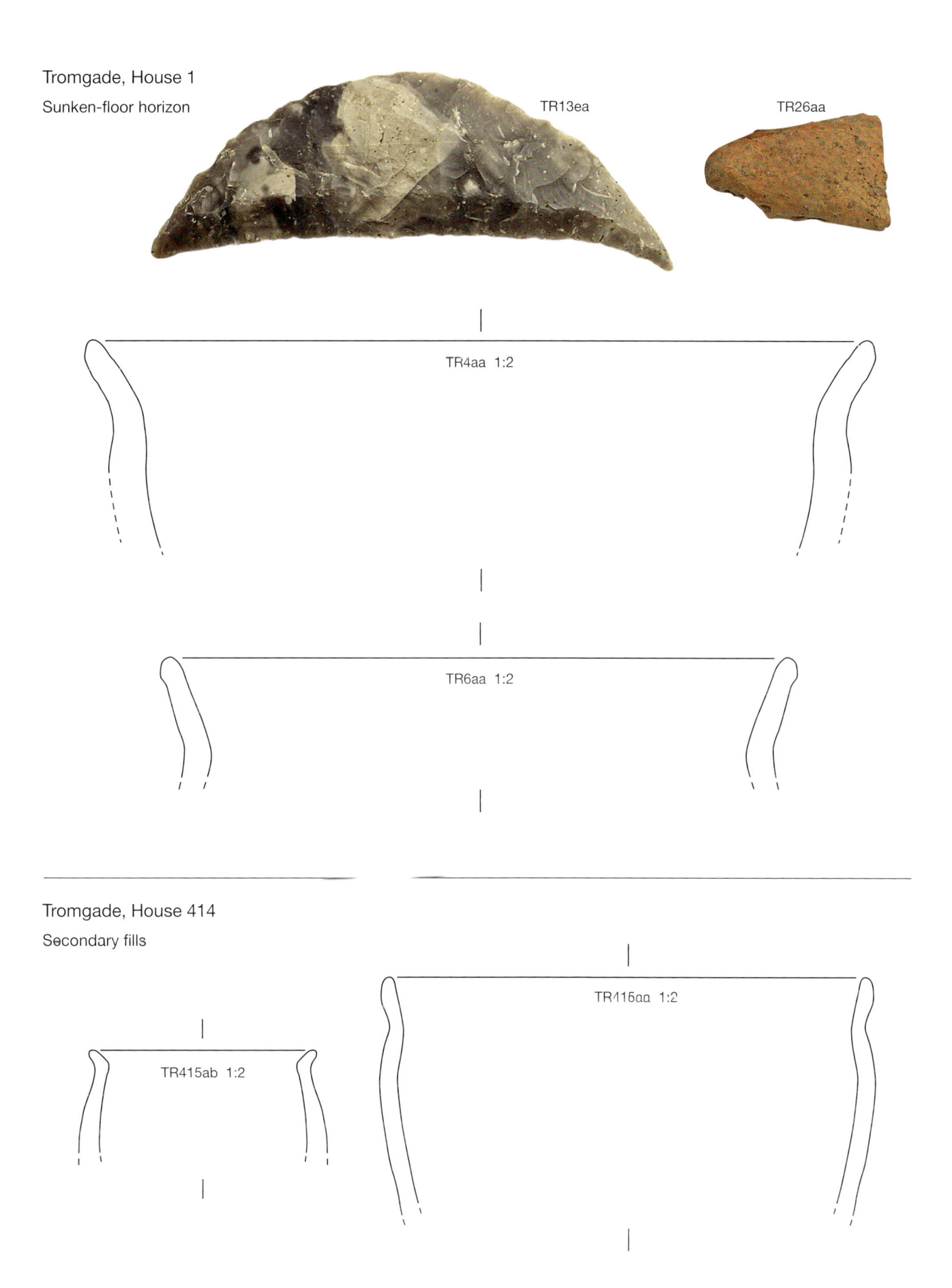

TR415ab 1:2

TR415aa 1:2

Fig. 4.64. Tromgade. House 1, sunken-floor horizon: A flint sickle (TR13ea), a characteristic clay spoon handle (TR26aa), and two reconstruction drawings of pottery (TR4aa & TR6aa). House 414, secondary fills: Two reconstruction drawings of pottery (TR415aa & TR415ab).

D: Scorched-stone patch. Greyish-brown, sandy soil with traces of charcoal and a few heat-affected/cracked stones. Surface dimensions c. 0.65 x 0.60. Depth c. 12 cm.

Based on the floor traces, the following are suggested as possible doings, separated into three activity spaces:

1. Drying/roasting/charring/cooking/heating and pottery handling/cooking. Two stone anvils present.

2. Raw flint handling/chipping and pottery handling/cooking.

3. Scraping, raw flint handling/chipping and pottery handling/cooking. A sickle and a retouched flint piece were also present in this activity space.

House 2 (Fig. 4.65 & 4.66)

From the secondary fills stem 530 potsherds including 27 with ornamentation. Among these are some showing zones with short, oblique, notch-stamped lines, parallel horizontal lines and zones with notch-stamped lines, in addition to a tiny potsherd with relics of a metope decoration. A clay spoon fragment was also present. A total of 875 pieces of worked flint came from these fills, containing *inter alia* a polished axe fragment, a lobed pressure-flaked arrowhead, two scrapers and two scraper edge fragments, as well as 52 pieces of burned flint. A quern stone fragment and two pieces of wattle-and-daub were also found in the fills. As in House 1, no regular floor layer was observed. When it comes to the artefacts from the sunken-floor horizon, a recording of a find spot appears to be missing with regard to a flint blade with retouch (TR28). I suggest that nine relatively large stones, of

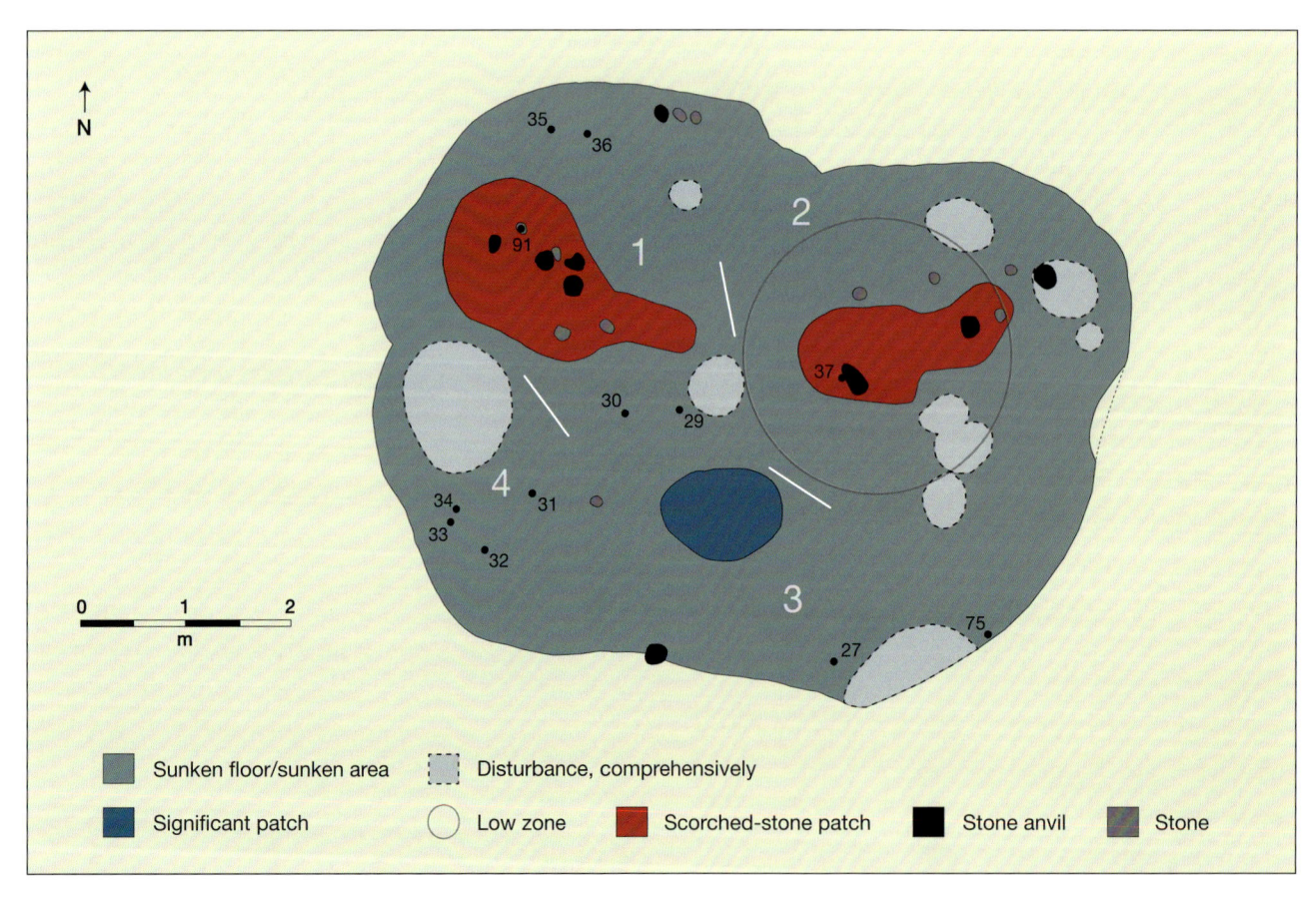

Fig. 4.65. Tromgade. House 2. A: Ground plan of sunken floor, cleaned. Four activity spaces are suggested. Apart from scorched stones and anvils, the artefacts found in situ in the sunken-floor horizon involve many find spots: **27**: *1 potsherd, side, ornamented (TR27aa);* **29**: *1 potsherd, rim with horizontal cordon (TR29aa);* **30**: *1 potsherd, rim (TR30aa) & a cordon fragment (TR30);* **31**: *1 potsherd, rim (TR31aa);* **32**: *1 potsherd, side, ornamented (TR32);* **33**: *1 flint flake, with possible retouch from wear (TR33);* **34**: *1 potsherd, side, ornamented (TR34aa);* **35**: *1 potsherd, bottom-side (TR35);* **36**: *1 potsherd, side sherd with two horizontal cordons (TR36aa);* **37**: *1 potsherd, rim (TR37aa);* **75**: *1 potsherd, rim, ornamented (TR75aa);* **91**: *15 potsherds, 1 stone hammer & 1 piece of worked flint (TR91), all from patch A.*

which eight were without visible impact from heat, were used as anvils. The easternmost was possibly not quite *in situ*, due to some disturbance of the area.

A low zone was observable in the eastern floor part. The significant soil patches in the sunken floor can briefly be characterized as follows:

A: Scorched-stone patch, large, irregular. Light, greyish, sandy soil with heat-affected/cracked stones. Five stone anvils present without traces of impact from heat. Surface dimensions of the patch c. 2.55 x 1.40 m. Depth c. 7 cm.

B: Scorched-stone patch, large, irregular. Greyish, sandy soil with a seemingly "washed out" character. Two stone anvils present, and the eastern was heat-affected. Surface dimensions of the patch c. 2.05 x 0.90 m. Depth c. 7 cm.

C: Sub-oval patch. Greyish-brown, sandy soil. Surface dimensions c. 1.15 x 0.85 m. Depth c. 9 cm.

There was only little variation of the vestiges of possible activities present. Based on the floor traces, the following are suggested as possible doings, separated into four activity spaces:

1. Drying/roasting/charring/cooking/heating, hammering/crushing and pottery handling/cooking. Five stone anvils present in the activity space but one apparently placed a little aside.

2. Drying/roasting/charring/cooking/heating and pottery handling/cooking. Three stone anvils present in the activity space.

3. Pottery handling/cooking. A stone anvil was present in the activity space but seemingly placed a little aside.

4. Pottery handling/cooking. Because only a single heat-affected/cracked stone was present in patch C it is reasonable to presume that activities related to these stones took place primarily in activity spaces 1 and 2. A flake with possible traces from wear present.

House 414

From the secondary fills derive 59 potsherds, 2 flint scrapers, 1 fragment of a burned, pressure flaked flint sickle and 135 pieces of other worked flint as well as some burned flint. No artefacts are considered to belong to the sunken-floor horizon. The floor levels were not measured and a low zone cannot therefore be distinguished. Some soil features had been dug into the subsoil in the eastern half of the sunken floor but were not investigated in a way that allows distinction and presentation of these. No activities are suggested.

4.6. Further considerations on soil features, plant remainders, and artefacts

One of the great surprises to emerge from the systematic analysis of floor traits was the recognition of the variation in use of interior spaces in the sunken-floor longhouses at Resengaard and the other central Limfjord region locations in question, while on the whole these appeared very ordered and organized in certain respects. Moreover, the presence of plant materials such as charred cereals, weeds and others varied substantially in the floor horizons (Fig. 4.67). In the following, the results are considered in broader terms, first regarding the key site of Resengaard, then in relation to the other house sites and, eventually, looking at the wider Limfjord region.

Some parts of most sunken floors in the longhouses were apparently not used for activities that left any observable traces. It also appears from the overall picture that, even in longhouses with many artefact remainders, the finds from certain floor areas represented one kind of material alone, such as for instance potsherds, and therefore only a narrow range of doings could be suggested to have taken place there. And yet such activities of limited variation do not appear to have been the way in which the longhouse floors were generally used. In fact, some of the most interesting discoveries from analysing the placements of artefact remainders and other traits point towards the reverse in many floors. In these instances, the objects left and the patches preserved may indicate several different activities performed in a floor area. The proposed activity spaces may therefore frequently indicate more doings – and even very many.

Further studies than here accomplished would perhaps lead to an understanding that different activities in the same areas, such as cutting with a knife, scraping, hammering or crushing, could have been parts of certain integrated working processes in which the treatment of objects with a variety of tools was

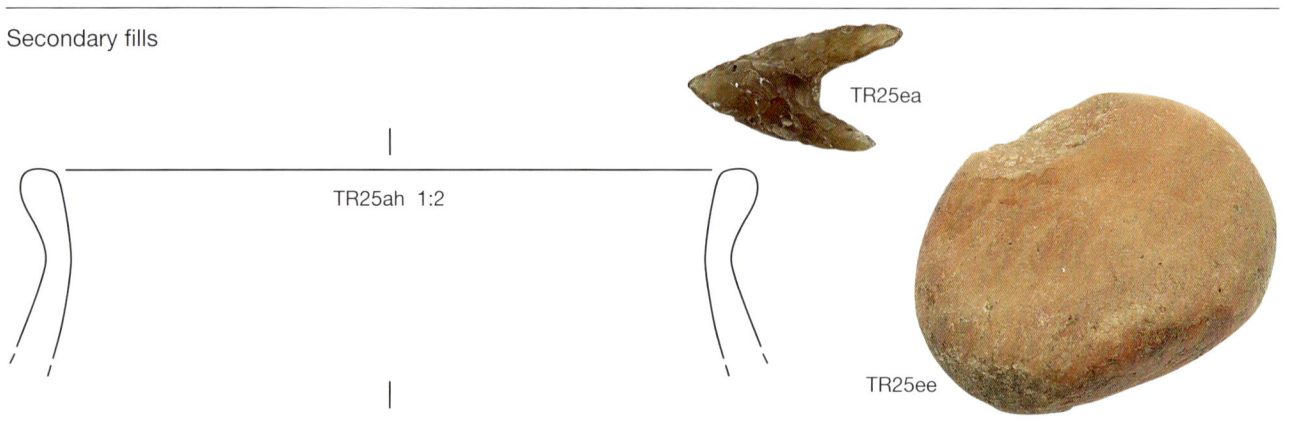

Tromgade, House 2
Sunken-floor horizon
TR29ab 1:2

Secondary fills

TR25ea

TR25ah 1:2

TR25ee

Culture layer 76

TR78ea

Pit 54
TR55eb

TR55ec

TR66aa/71aa 1:2

TR66aa/71aa

TR55ea 1:2

310 Chapter 4

◀▲ *Fig. 4.66. Tromgade. House 2, sunken-floor horizon: Potsherd with cordoned rim (TR29ab). House 2, secondary fills: Reconstruction drawing of upper part of a clay pot (TR25ah), lobed arrowhead (TR25ea) and quartzite hammer with crushing marks in the ends (TR25ee), a part broken off. Culture layer 76: A flint sickle, almost complete (TR78ea). Pit 54. Unusually shaped blade of dark flint (TR55eb), two quartzite hammers (TR55ec & TR55ea) and a clay spoon with a handle ending in beak-like hook (two views, TR66aa/71aa), presumably intended for hanging. Much-decorated clay pot (TR62aa). Below the blank rim are 6 horizontally incised lines (the uppermost and the lowest lines combined with some cardium imprints), and thereunder 10 lines of cardium imprints. Potsherd (TR55ae) with part of a metope having a geometric pattern with interchanging blank and horizontally notch-stamped areas. Lines with a narrow blank band limiting the metope upwards. Potsherd (TR55ac) decorated with a zone of horizontal furrows above a blank area. Potsherd (TR55ad) with five horizontally notch-stamped lines. Rim sherd (TR89aa) having three horizontal bands (and likely traces of a fourth) with oblique notch-stamped lines interchanging with blank areas below the rim.*

necessary. For instance, what kinds of activity would have been performed in the ordinary, daily cooking and food preparation processes?

The clay tube in the sunken floor horizon of House 2 at Resengaard was apparently not a common item and, to my knowledge, is unique in Limfjord region contexts.[6] It is given a rather precise dating as it is identical with the pottery-based chronological position of the longhouse, in addition to AMS determinations on short-lived plant materials. If the clay tube – either as a primary or secondary function – had been used in working processes that required relatively high temperatures, it is interesting to note that it was found very close to the particular area of the sunken floor where the ground showed severe impact from heat, becoming reddish-burned when the longhouse remainders were burned. However, the primary function of the clay tube is difficult to state for the moment. Its very thick wall and the extremely dense, coarse tempering might immediately associate it with processes in which great heat was present. When merely looking at the outer form, it is clear that the clay tube is considerable shorter than, for instance, the tuyere from Evan Rigg in Cumbria (Craddock 1995:185 pp). This specimen, considered to be the only one of its kind found in Britain, belongs to the Bronze Age. On the other hand, the likeness of the clay tube to certain loom weight forms from the Únětice areas is interesting, although these display apparent traces from being hung horizontally, such as for instance specimens from Birmenitz, Lommatzsch and Deila in Sachsen (Billig 1958:160p & 180p, Fig. 97, 112 & 113). Other possible interpretations of its function should also be kept open, but I shall here abstain from further considerations.

Artefacts, pits, patches, and daily life activities **311**

Location		House	Total	Clay tube	Clay spoon	Clay loom weight	Clay pot	Flint scraper	Flint knife	Flint sickle	Flint dagger	Flint strike-a-light	Flint hammer	Flint axe	Flint arrowhead	Flint, notched piece	Flint nodule	Worked flint	Burned flint	Smoothening stone	Stone hammer	Stone anvil	Bronxe piece	Clay mould	Further items	Remarks
Resengaard	Longhouses	1	72			1	31	7		1			1	1	1	9		7	3		8			1	Bone
		2	83	1			28	6	1		1					17		16	4	1	2	2		2	Fossilized sea urchins
		13	15				3											2	1		5			2	Pressure-flaked pieces
		14	13				6	1	1	1		1		1				2							
		41	15				8			1			1	1	1		1				1			1	Bone
		42	15				7	2			1							2	1		1			1	Flint arrowhead roughout
		128	19				7	1	1		1		1		1			1			7			2	Whetstone & arrowhead roughout
		130	2				1	1																	
		134	7				3														4				
		138	3				1					1	1												
		197	4				1							1			1				1				
		200	27		1		10	4		2				3			2	1		1	1			2	Whetstone & stone axe fragment
	Minor houses with scorched-stone patches	202	0																						
		240	9				4	1				1					1				1			1	Flint arrowhead roughout
		289	2																		2				
	Minor houses	10	8				7											1							
		12	0																						
		84	0																						
		112	2					1													1				
		143	0																						
		158	1									1													
		183	0																						
		193	1																		1				
		198	2					1													1				
		268	6				5											1							
	Small house	201	1																		1				
Gåsemose		1	0																						
Kluborg II		5	35			1	18	1			1						5			3	1	2	2	1	Clay crucible fragment in a posthole
Glattrup I/III		5	3				2													1					
		6	8			1	4	2	1																
Marienlyst Strand		1	0																						
Granlygård		2	0																						
		3	0																						
		6	0																						
Hellegård		122	45		1		9	25		1							1			1	3			4	Arrowhead roughout & 3 flat stones
		35	0																						
Glattrup IV		3	11				5				1						2	1	1					1	Piece of amber, crumbled
		5	12				6										3	1	2						
		7	15				5										5	4	1						
Rosgårde		1	3				1										1	1							
Tromgade		1	19		1		9	1		1						3	2			2					Flint flake, retouch possibly from wear
		2	23				11										1			1	9			1	
		414	0																						
Total			481	1	3	3	192	52	5	5	7	2	4	3	8	2	29	57	17	1	13	52	2	2	19	

Fig. 4.67. Find spots representing various artefacts (including fragmented pieces) in sunken-floor horizons and pits adjacent to these. It also involves every anvil and presumed anvil (un-numbered inclusive). Find spots and find areas relating to heat-affected/heat-cracked stones and charred macrofossils are not included. Out of 43 sunken-floor house sites only House 143 is without finds in the sunken-floor horizon. Finds from pits and patches sometimes relate to the whole patch and count as one find spot for each kind of artefact. A find spot with different kinds of artefacts, e.g. some potsherds, a scraper and some worked flint will be marked in three columns. Further items, not accounted for in the columns, are briefly stated on the far right. Strike-a-lights are few, but one more specimen from the site of House 42 presumably also belongs to the floor horizon. In the site of House 128 at Resengaard, a scraper was also supplied with a notch. A stone hammer in the site of House 1 at Resengaard may also have worked as a smoothening stone (RE22ea). In a few cases, more find spots from Resengaard share one inventory number. This concerns House 1 (no. 62 as regards two spots with secondarily burned potsherds), House 2 (no. 165 as regards four find spots with flint nodules and no. 66 as regards two spots each with several pieces of burned flint) and House 10 (RE310 as regards seven spots). Concerning activity space 5 in the site of House 2 at Resengaard, the observation of worked flint scattered around the large stone is interesting but, unfortunately, these were not attached a separate find number during fieldwork. In the site of House 1 at Marienlyst Strand, the large stone to the east in the sunken area could possibly also have been an anvil. Concerning the site of House 122 at Hellegård, it should be remarked that the flint waste concentration (HE556) just counts as one in the account. From this house site, the sub-quadratic stone hammer (HE543) may have worked as a smoothening stone as well but that is not marked in the account.

Certain stone tools were also scarcely present. For instance, a smoothening stone was found in the sunken-floor horizon of House 2 and a whetstone alongside a shaft-hole axe fragment in the area of a soil patch in House 200. Some presumably common flint tools such as strike-a-lights were also relatively seldom found in floor contexts. If considered valuable, they might logically have been removed when the buildings were abandoned and hence seldom left on the floor.

Amber is only exceptionally present in the sunken-floor house contexts at Resengaard or in other house sites from the central Limfjord region. However, a few pieces have occasionally been found during meticulous, manual excavations of pits and house sites, and it cannot therefore be ruled out that if adequate resources had been available for the flotation of large amounts of floor horizon soils, tiny amber pieces or "dust" might have been sorted out (*cf.* Thorpe 2000:75).

The residents presumably used a wide range of gear, vessels and bags etc. made of organic materials in their everyday life. Various sorts of wood might, not least, have been much-appreciated materials for use as tools, shafts and a wide variety of other objects. The fur, skin, horn and bones of animals would also likely have been used widely. From the potter's craft, we know of abundant variations in shapes and sizes but, due to the circumstances of preservation at the sites, we do not know of even a single leather bag. Traces of a great deal of organic materials might thus originally have been left in the floor horizons and since decayed, without offering any information on such material aspects of everyday life.

Despite the fact that various artefacts may point to different activities in many of the sunken-floor areas, the above considerations demonstrate that we are actually left with rather fragmentary sources. And yet, as attempted in the above, this situation should not prevent us from generating ideas about the concrete activities and processes that took place in these longhouses. In the following, further considerations will be presented.

Things placed below roofs or above floors?

We have already briefly touched upon the possibility that blankets, hides etc. might have been hanging down from the roof constructions as "light" room dividers. These constructions could also have been used for keeping a range of other things. Some harvested cereals might obviously have been placed high up in the roof on a kind of platform resting on the cross beams in order to try to avoid damage from mice and other animals although there is absolutely no evidence of this at the concrete sites of the longhouses studied here. In particular, from House 1 at Resengaard, we should have had a chance to observe such traces from the spread of the hundreds of thousands of charred cereals in the sunken floor. We shall later return to further evidence of cereals as well as consider some other options for storage of these and other items (Ch. 5.5). However, no piles of cereals were observed that might point to, for instance, a sack with such content that had fallen down.

And yet various tools, agricultural implements, household utensils, wooden materials, and multiple other things might have been placed above the floors, on the cross beams or hanging down from these. Further items could have been hanging on the panel walls, compartment walls and other walls, besides hanging on centre posts or placed on shelves.

In the above, I have not suggested any activities related to the floor finds of arrowheads, daggers and sickles or broken pieces of these even though, for instance, dagger fragments could occasionally have been used for different kinds of cutting. Producing flint arrowheads and mounting them on shafts could well have taken place indoors in the longhouses, even though we have no evidence of the flint chipping. The tiny chips could, however, have been gathered up in order to get rid of such tiny sharp elements on the floor (see below). It should be noted that direct evidence of the shafts is not available from any of the settlement contexts whereas such knowledge does stem from graves and bogs e.g. Neue Grebs in Mecklenburg and Nybølle Mose at Funen (Petersen 1999:91pp). Most of the pressure-flaked arrowheads from the settlements in question were supplied with double lobes ("barbs") in the sides, giving these an edge that would facilitate firm mounting. In the site of House 14 at Resengaard, one of the arrowheads (RE281ea) was found close to the southern wall. Conceivably, such an arrowhead mounted correspondingly on a shaft could have been kept in a quiver hanging on the southern wall and then fallen down at some later point in time. We have finds of eight flint arrowheads from the sunken-floor horizons in the longhouse sites at Resengaard. Some had a relatively peripheral location in the above sunken floors, while others were found more centrally, and even in the vicinity of the scorched-stone patches.

Flint sickles might well have been placed conveniently a little to the side, for instance on walls, as these are usually rather breakable. We have concrete evidence of sickle fragments from five sunken-floor horizons of the longhouses at Resengaard, Glattrup I/III and Tromgade. However, none of these were found in a position where I would suggest a sickle could have fallen down from a wall.

In all, a single complete and six fragments of flint daggers were found in the sunken-floor horizons of the longhouses at Resengaard and Hellegård. The complete specimen (RE547ea) was found very close to the eastern gable end in the site of House 128 at Resengaard (Fig. 4.19). Together with other gear, it could perhaps have been hanging on the wall and fallen down at a later point in time.

Just two flint axes and a fragment were found in the sunken-floor horizons, all from Resengaard. Of these, I consider it possible that the antique but complete flint axe (RE20ea) could have been kept hanging on the nearby extra, roof-bearing post in the area of the central longitudinal axis of House 1.

Clay pots were probably seldom kept hanging on the walls as none had handles or corresponding features on the sides. For such items, demanding a levelled area for their proper placing with contents, some kind of wooden shelves could have been established. In the northeast corner of the sunken floor in the site of House 197, a large number of pottery remainders were found in a shallow pit. In all, fragments from 21 clay pot were represented here. Being the only example from Resengaard, these could well indicate the presence of some above-floor shelf arrangement that collapsed at some point in time.

It is remarkable that certain special utensils made out of such practically imperishable non-organic clay materials were relatively seldom found in a direct floor context, even though they could supposedly have been kept hanging on posts or walls, for instance. From Resengaard, this relates to objects such as the loom weight fragment (RE42aa) in the sunken-floor horizon of House 1 and the clay spoon fragment (RE784aa) found in a pit in the sunken floor of House 200 but neither of these were found in a position near walls or posts. From Tromgade, the clay spoon found in pit 54 may seem to be shaped for hanging, having an almost zoomorphic design somewhat like a bird's beak (Fig. 4.66).

After use in processes with liquids, a colander would presumably often have been hung up to dry. If a process took place in a central floor area, a roof-bearing post could conveniently have been available to let it dry there. The side of the complete colander from Granlygård is supplied with two holes, likely to incorporate a string for hanging (Fig. 4.53).

Presence of floor layers in sunken-floor horizons

Subsoil and wind-deposited sand together with materials and substances of a different nature, lost or spilt on the floors, could together with elements such as artefact remainders largely have constituted the floor layers. In most cases, sand was the predominant component and it seems likely that windblown sand would have been deposited occasionally and incorporated into the floor layers. Things would presumably have been trodden down into these floor layers and even into the subsoil.

I would *a priori* expect such layers to have gradually come into being in all longhouses at the Resengaard settlement, unless particular circumstances were prevalent in the individual houses. And yet ancient ploughing into the floor horizons has more or less spoiled the possibility of making observations at certain house sites. Besides this, it certainly cannot be excluded that floor layers actually were preserved but were difficult or impossible to discern from the secondary fills in some cases. This could be due to some wash out over four millennia, thereby blurring the boundaries between the strata. The often very slight differences in colour do not enhance the conditions for identifying and separating layers and such rationalization therefore ought to be taken into consideration as well. Against this backdrop, it is a notable discovery that the floor layers were clearly observable above some sunken floors at Resengaard but apparently unrecognizable above others (Fig. 4.68 & 4.69).

I must immediately admit that the precise question of why these divergences appear is rather puzzling and establishes a challenge for future research. Floor layers of a more or less corresponding nature have been observed in some other house sites with deep floors outside the region, e.g. at Lindebjerg in western Funen, where this stratum was characterized by a considerable content of charred cereals (Jæger & Laursen 1983:103p). A floor layer is also recorded from House K23 at Mannehøjgård while several other floors were considered to have been emptied out and cleaned (Dollar 2013:43).

I see the apparent absence of floor layers in certain longhouses as particularly conspicuous considering that many of them may have been used for a rather long time. One explanation might be that the residents' doings and general behaviour did not cause a regular floor layer to accumulate and so no discernible floor layer would be observable during investigation. It cannot be excluded that this might have been the case in some instances but, in my understanding, floor layers would almost inevitably accumulate in houses with various activities. Some rationalizing is, not least therefore, required. In reflecting on the records of the sunken-floor house remainders from a number of other longhouse sites in the region, I have tried to give some possible explanations of the nature of this problem. Where floor layers gradually accumulated, the residents could conceivably have had a different attitude to the question of cleaning the floors. For some, daily cleaning need not have implied much more than removing some organic remains, for instance, along with the main parts of broken pots, a few stones or some sharp flint flakes too annoying to leave on the floor. The build-up of floor layers could, in this way, have been ignored for a long time.

Conversely, where floor layers are absent – and the secondary fills thereby reached more or less down to the subsoil surfaces – this could be explained by the deliberate removal of the floor layer as part of a cleaning regime. This could, in such instances, have been carried out shortly before abandonment. It is possible that thorough floor cleaning could have taken place on a yearly basis, whenever needed or perhaps more regularly, such that the removal of accumulated "dirty" soil on the sunken floors traditionally took place at, for instance, seasonally-determined intervals. This could have been once or twice a year, for example, and could presumably have included removing thin, contaminated layers in relevant areas of the floors, resulting in a gradual lowering of the level. On the whole, the rhythm of major and minor cleanings in the individual longhouses could have had some effect on the number and nature of leftovers in the sunken floors. If a house was abandoned just before a major cleaning, it would likely stay richer as to material remainders and, if cleaning was performed, become rather poor as to artefact remainders.

In all, without ruling out even more possible explanations, I suggest that the reasons for not being able to demonstrate floor layers in the longhouses could, not least, be of four kinds, namely: 1. Spoiled through deep ard-ploughing. 2: Present, but not really discernible. 3: Not accumulated, due to particular behaviours. 4: More or less removed through clean up, regularly or whenever needed.

Stratum 3 in the bottom of House 2 at Resengaard offers an expressive example of a floor layer and, in this case, even from a site of fire. Horizontally, it was extensively observable over the floor and vertically in the longitudinal section, as well as the cross-section, of the sunken floor (Fig. 4.8 & 4.68). It consisted from appearance mainly of dark, brownish sandy soil with tiny pieces of charcoal and some finds of artefacts. It also contained rather spread heat-affected/cracked stones.

When looking at the overall records for Resengaard, many house sites can contribute to our understanding of the floor layers. It appears that extensive or partial floor layers were thus observable in the sites of House 1, House 2, and House 41 but, as regards the latter, it is remarkable that finds were not more plentifully present in the floor horizon. Extensive floor layers may very well have been present in the sites of House 14 and House 197 but the floor bottom in these house sites had been intensively ard-ploughed shortly after abandonment. There was also some damage from ard-ploughing in House 200 but a floor layer was seemingly partially preserved. In reconsideration of House 42, it must be acknowledged that this house site is difficult to evaluate and the information from the investigation is very scarce in this regard; however, it seems that a relatively thick covering stratum of the floor bottom might not be a floor layer (or at least not as a whole). In the relatively well-preserved sites of House 13 and House 128, floor layers seemed to be partially observable. No obvious evidence of floor layers was found in the sites of House 134, House 138, or House 130. And yet, as regards House 134, a thin, presumably accumulated layer of fine-grained, somewhat clayey sand was present. Brownish-yellow sand seems to have been added to certain areas of the floor in House 130.[7] No floor layers were recorded from the minor house sites with scorched-stone patches or from the remaining sites of minor houses or the short house.

The details and relationships concerning the floor layers of certain longhouses are certainly not uncomplicated and can be really difficult to understand and interpret. It appears that the artefacts and patches, as they appear during the archaeological investigation, may often belong to a later part of the habitation.

Fig. 4.68.A-P. In the following, 16 sections of sunken floors are selected with a view to broadly representing the great variation existing in the central Limfjord region. These sections are accompanied by descriptions of soil features such as pit, sunken fireplace, patch, centre post, oblique ramp, and floor layer. For the sake of legibility, the numbering of recorded layers is altered in many instances. Symbols applied to the drawings: Concentration of blackish colouring from charred material or dust of it (vertical hatching), stone (oblique hatching), flint artefact (triangle) and potsherd (lozenge). The secondary fills are generally highlighted with a green colour. As evidenced in the sections, all longhouses were built on sterile subsoil without traces of former prehistoric settlement.

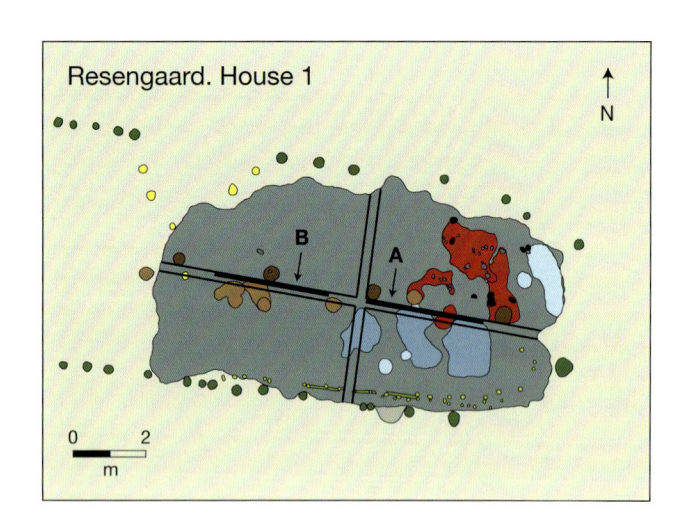

Fig. 4.68.A. Resengaard, House 1, E-W section. Estimated thickness of machine-removed ploughed topsoil (1) and other covering soil (2) during initial excavation is shown. Beneath that, secondary fills of greyish-brown, sandy soil with flint, potsherds and heat-affected stones (3). Thereunder an extensive floor layer of dark-brown to blackish soil with charcoal remainders, flint artefacts and potsherds (4). Many charred cereals were found in this stratum, also contributing to the colouring of the soil. The southern part of the scorched-stone patch A (see Fig. 4.5) appears as dark to blackish sandy soil (5). Clayey subsoil (8) in this section.

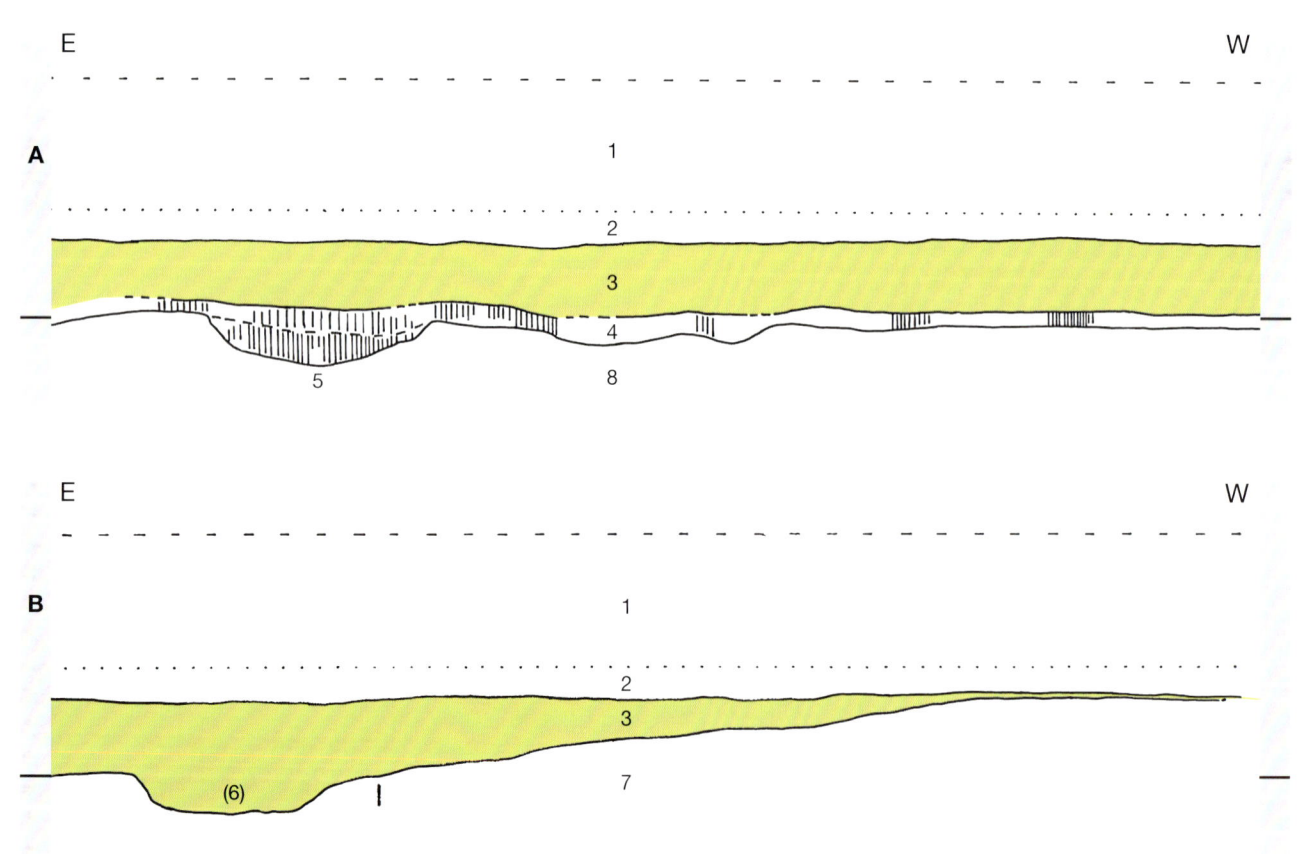

Fig. 4.68.B. Resengaard, House 1, E-W section. For layers 1, 2 and 3 see above. The secondary fills (3) were also present in a locally deeper area (6) and this presumably represents digging (maybe for fresh sand) just before depositing the secondary fills. No floor layer was observed in this section of the floor, where the long oblique ramp leading to the level of the ground floor is the predominant element. Its approximate beginning is marked with a short vertical line. Largely similar oblique ramps were present in all sites of sunken-floor longhouses. Sandy subsoil (7) in this section.

316　Chapter 4

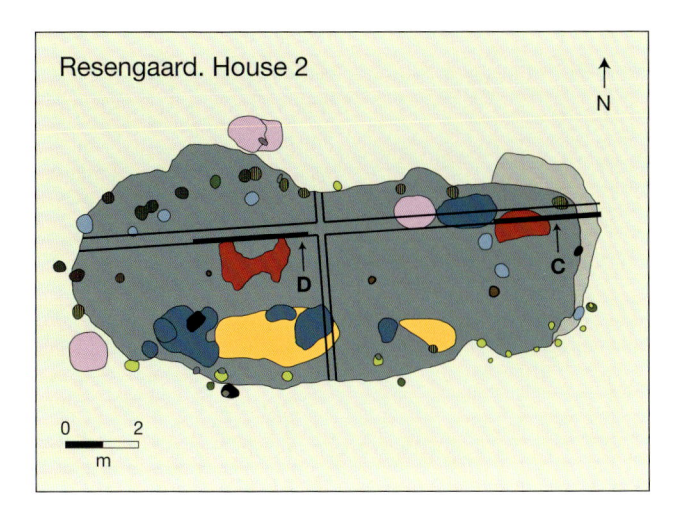

Fig. 4.68.C. Resengaard, House 2, E-W section. Where the sunken floor and its floor layer (4) ends towards the east, it can clearly be seen that the old surface soil had been removed since it does not appear in the profile. This removal must have taken place before building the walls. Beneath the scorched-stone patch D a lens of reddish sand (stratum 5), possibly with heat impact, was observed. The blackish soil at the bottom is not indicated at the drawing, but see photo Fig. 4.8.B. For further soil descriptions, see next text.

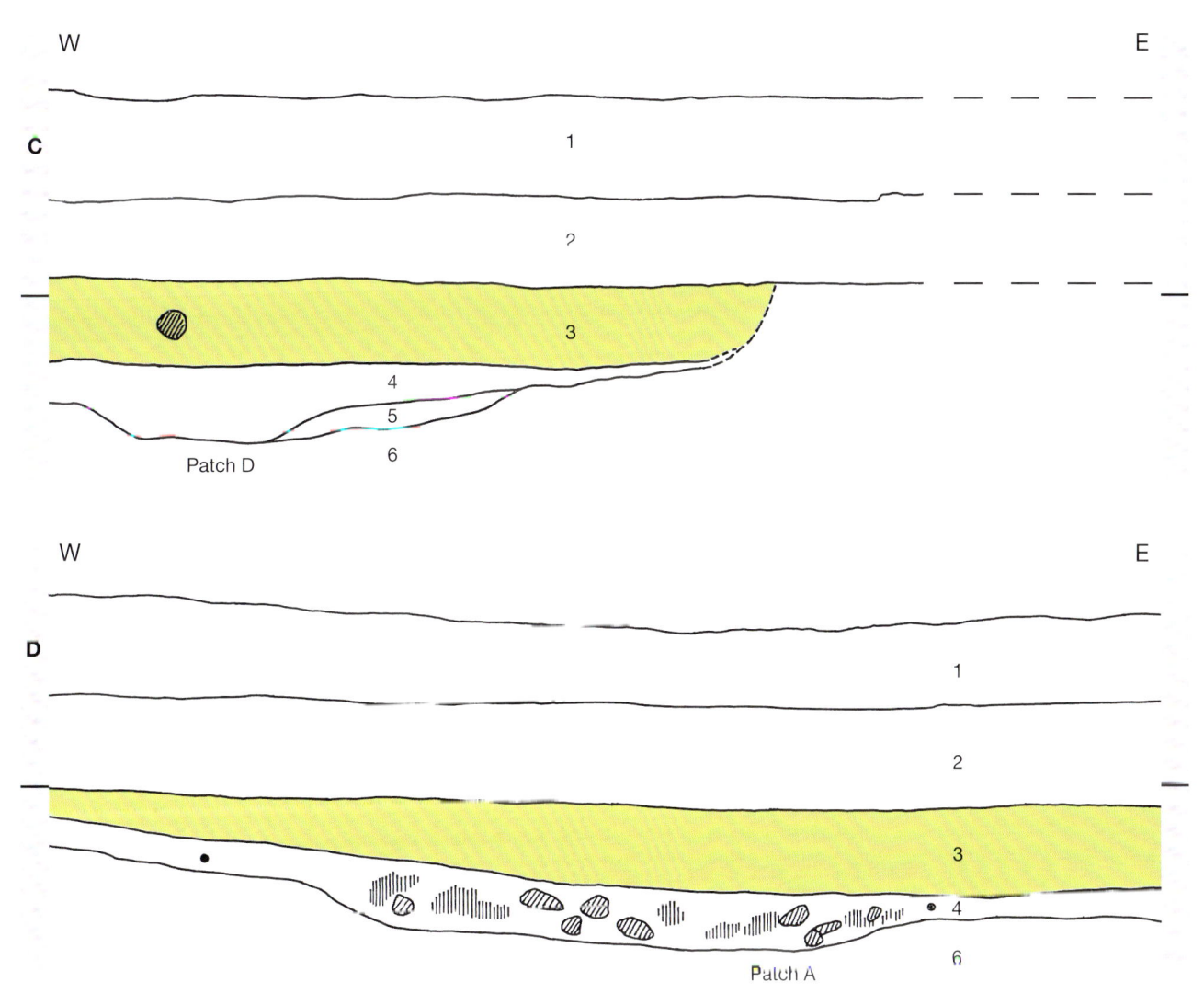

Fig. 4.68.D. Resengaard, House 2, E-W section. From around the northern end of the scorched-stone patch A is shown ploughed topsoil (1), another covering layer of greyish light soil, possibly with a wind-deposited component (2), secondary fills of brownish soil (3), and a floor layer (4) of dark-brownish soil being partially quite blackish with much coal dust due to comprehensive burning of the longhouse. The northernmost remainders of the scorched-stone patch A merges into this layer. On the plan drawing (see also Fig. 4.7), this patch is marked only where it clearly appeared but the profile section may show that it was actually present to the north in an even area broader than shown on the plan drawing. In search of pollen, two samples (round dots) were taken from this layer and the easternmost of these (sample 184) was examined scientifically but it appears that all pollen had vanished in the fire (report A2001a). Clayey/sandy subsoil (6).

Artefacts, pits, patches, and daily life activities

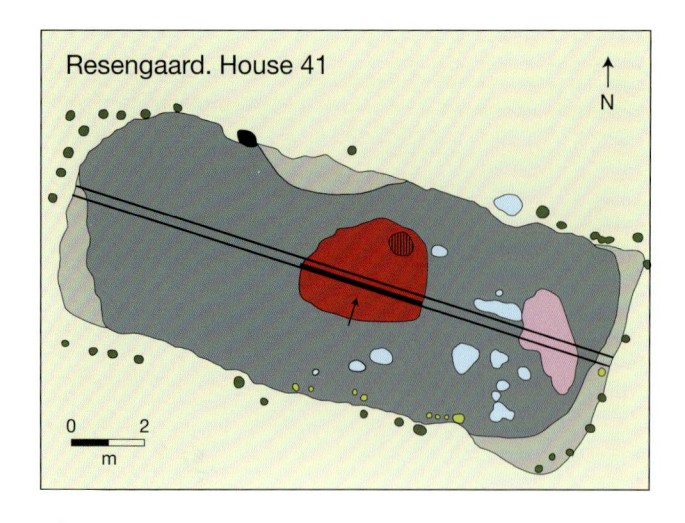

Fig. 4.68.E. Resengaard, House 41, E-W section. Estimated thickness of the machine-removed ploughed topsoil (1) and other covering soil (2) during initial excavation is shown. Beneath that, secondary fills of greyish, sandy soil (3). Further below, a floor layer of greyish-brown soil (4). The scorched-stone patch A (see also Fig. 4.15) had a layer of dark, greyish soil at the bottom (5). Sandy subsoil (6).

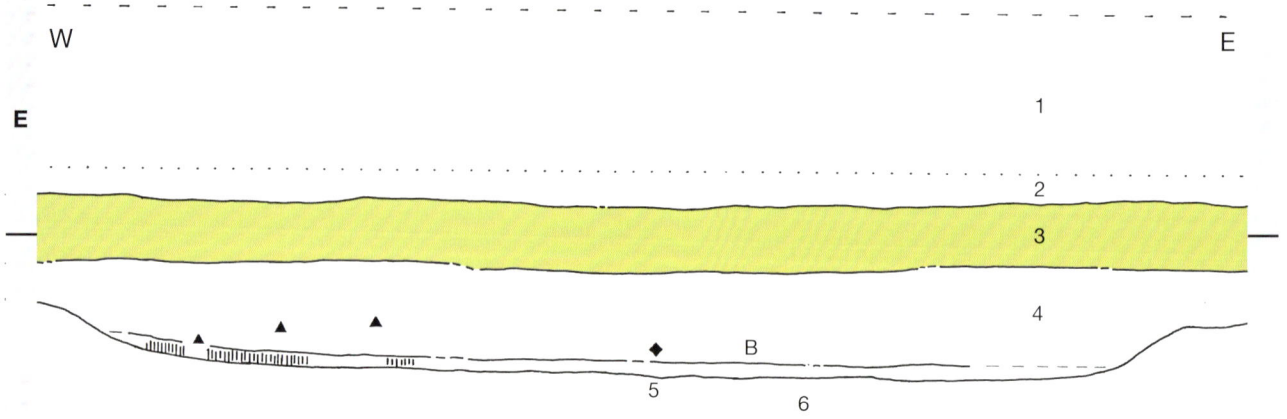

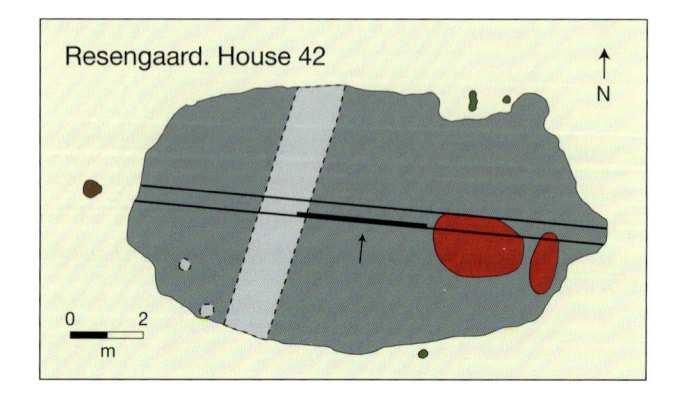

Fig. 4.68.F. Resengaard, House 42, E-W section. Estimated thickness of the machine- removed ploughed topsoil (1) and other soil at the boundary to the sunken area (2) during initial excavation is shown. Beneath that, brownish, sandy soil with a few tiny stones (3). Thereunder, secondary fills of greyish-brown soil, becoming gradually lighter further down (4). No recorded floor layer. To the west, a disturbing medieval/post-medieval ditch (5). Sandy subsoil (6). A short vertical line marks the approximate eastern beginning of the oblique ramp leading to the level of the ground floor.

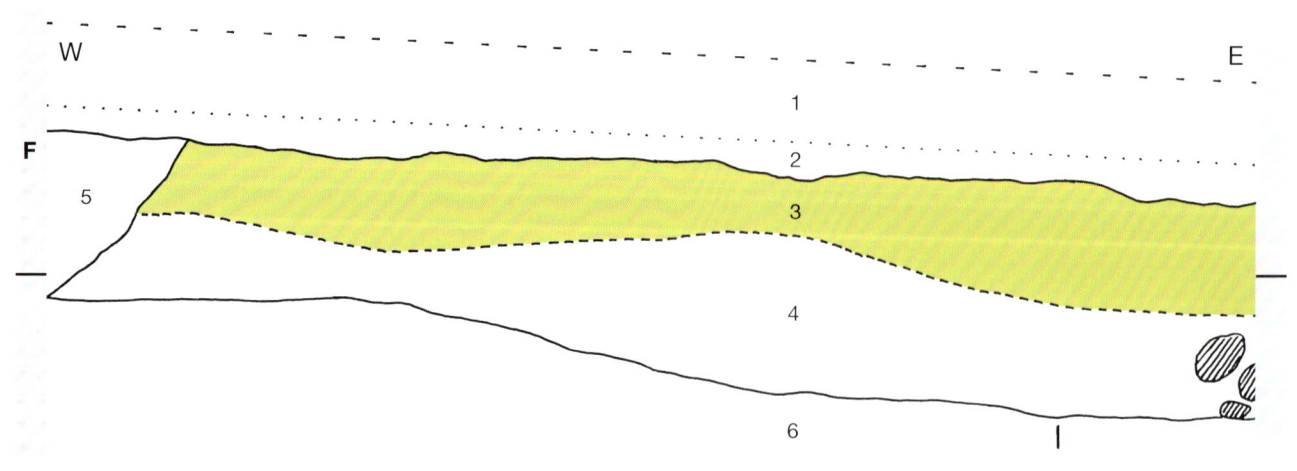

318   Chapter 4

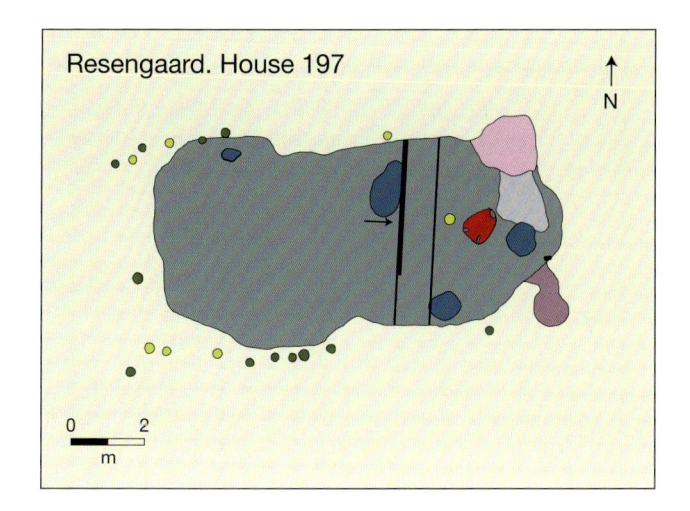

Fig. 4.68.G. Resengaard, House 197, N-S section. The profile shows the recently-ploughed layer (1) and another covering stratum of greyish-brown soil (2). Thereunder, secondary fills of dark-brownish sandy soil with flint artefacts, potsherds and other (3) which had all, as well as the floor surface, been heavily ard-ploughed, but the lower parts of patch B (4) to the north had avoided destruction. Sandy subsoil (5).

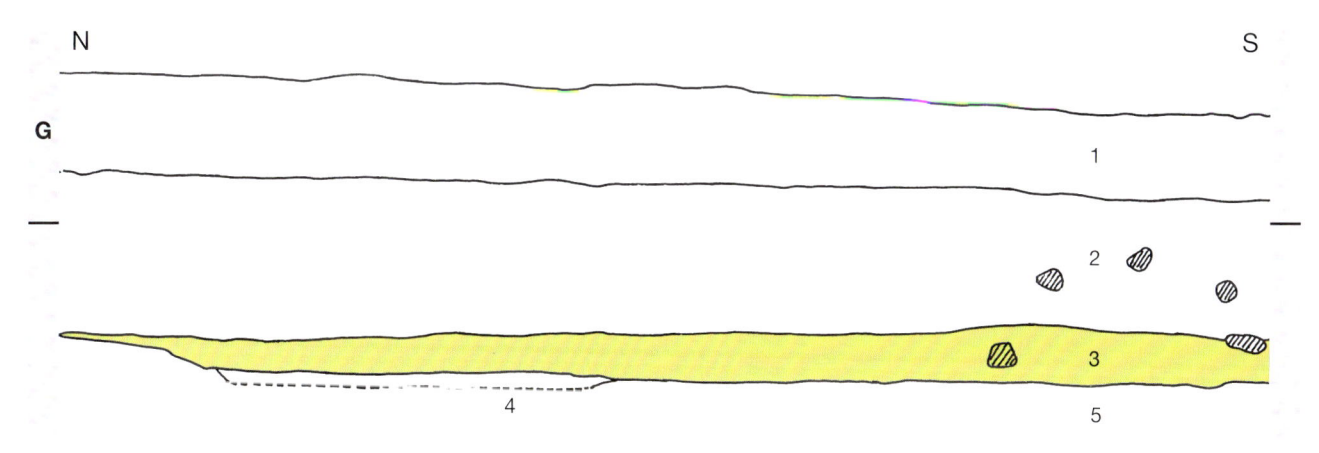

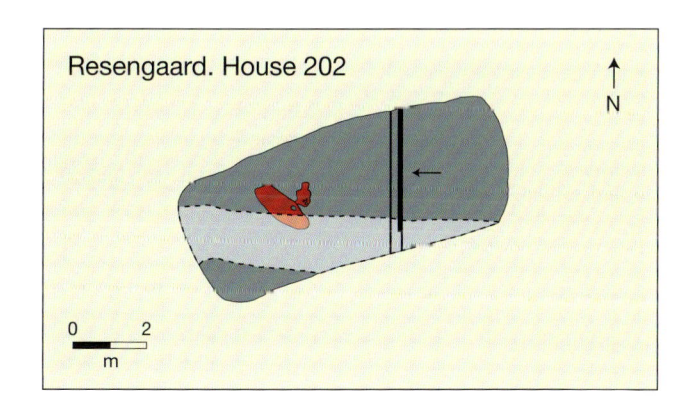

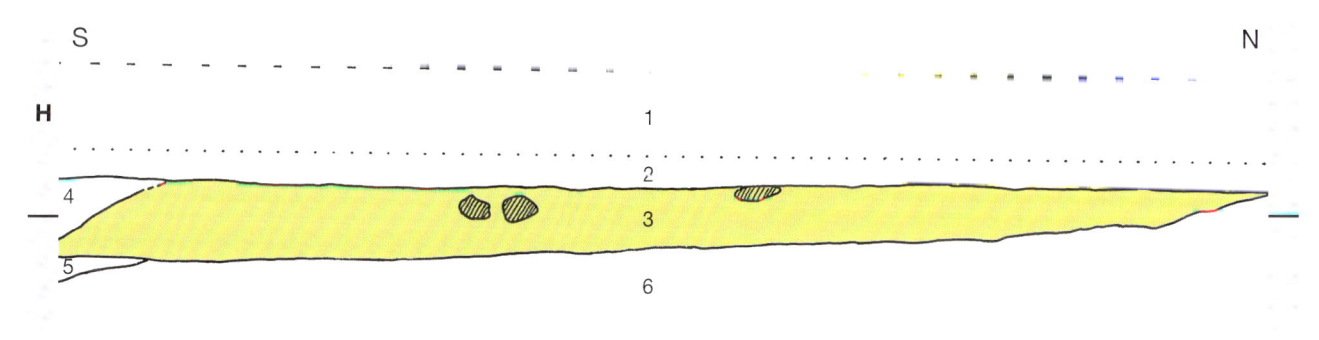

Fig. 4.68.H. Resengaard, House 202, N-S section. Before recent ploughing, the covering soil could have been significantly thicker than indicated here. Estimated thickness of the machine-removed ploughed topsoil (1) and other soil (2) at the boundary to the sunken area during initial excavation is shown. Beneath, secondary fills of sandy, brown to blackish soil (3) that became greyish near the bottom. A medieval/post-medieval ditch with grey-brownish soil (4) had cut through that layer as well as a brownish-yellow sandy layer (5). Sandy subsoil with some stones (6)

Artefacts, pits, patches, and daily life activities 319

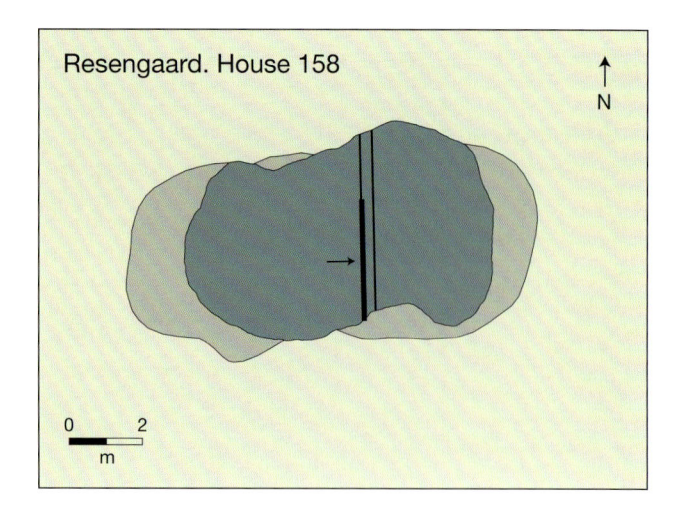

Fig. 4.68.I. Resengaard, House 158, N-S section. Before recent ploughing, the covering soil could have been significantly thicker than indicated here. Estimated thickness of the machine-removed ploughed topsoil (1) and other soil at the boundary to the sunken area (2) is shown. Beneath that, blackish-brown sandy soil (3). Thereunder, yellow-brown, sandy soil (4) and dark-brownish, sandy soil (5), both strata being secondary fills. It cannot, however, be excluded that the latter represents a floor layer. Sandy subsoil (6).

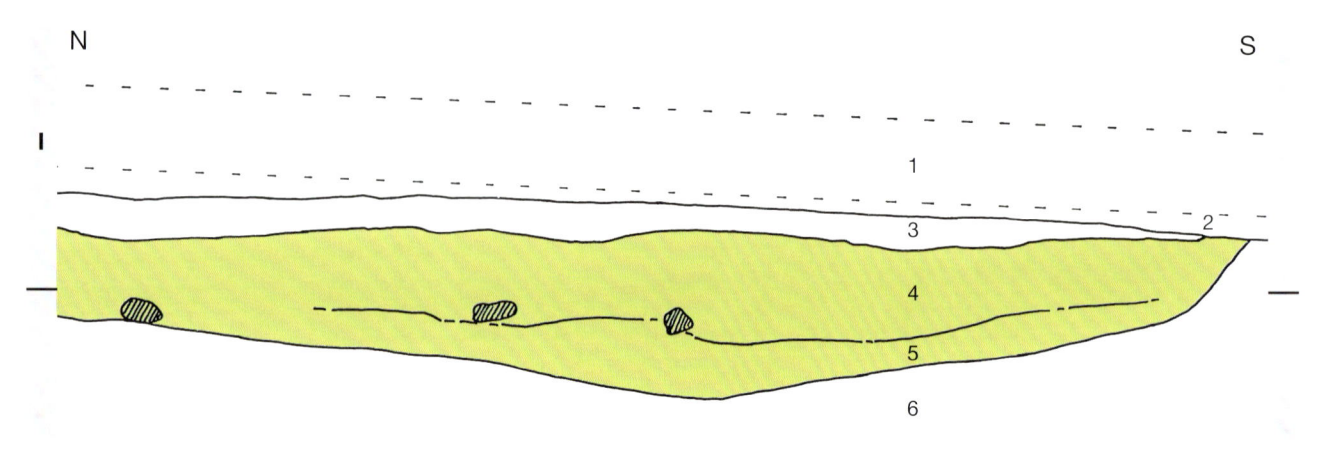

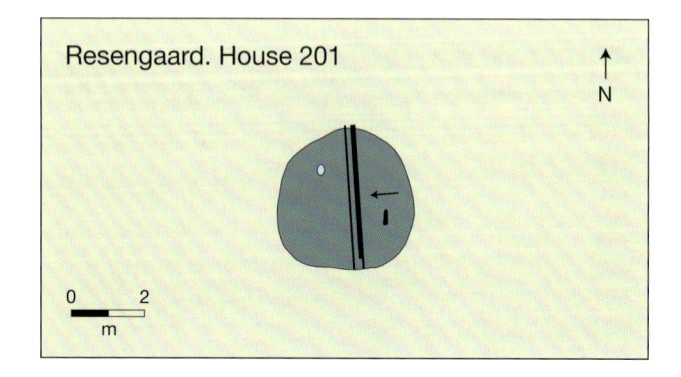

Fig. 4.68.J. Resengaard, House 201, N-S section. Before recent ploughing, the covering soil could have been significantly thicker than indicated here. Estimated thickness of machine-removed ploughed topsoil (1) and other soil (2) at the boundary to the sunken area during initial excavation is shown. Beneath that, secondary fills of blackish-brown soil (3). No recorded floor layer. Coarse-grained, sandy subsoil (4).

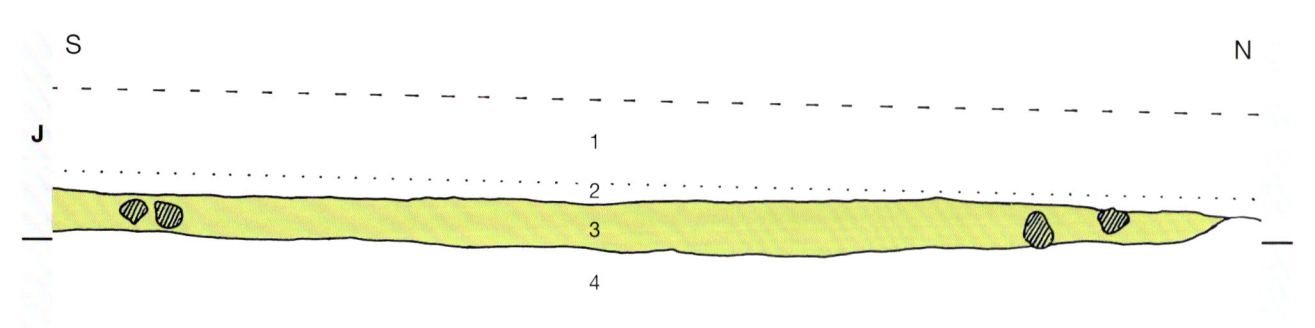

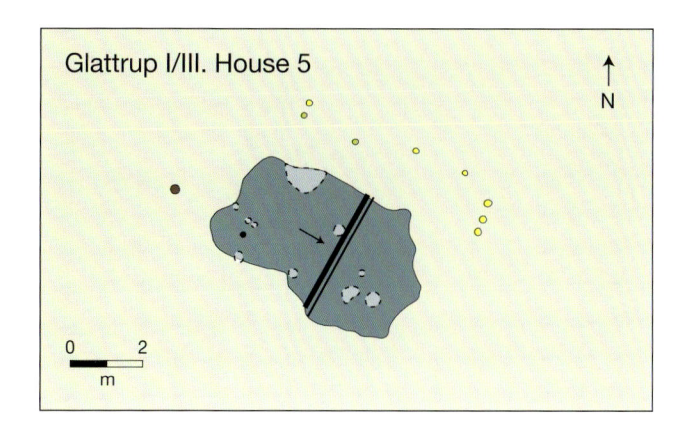

Fig. 4.68.K. Glattrup I/III, House 5, NNE-SSW section. Before recent ploughing, the covering soil could have been thicker than indicated here. Estimated thickness of machine removal of ploughed topsoil (1) and other soil at the boundary to the sunken area (2) during initial excavation is shown. Two lenses of dark greyish, sandy soil (3). Thereunder, fine-grained yellowish sand (4), probably wind-deposited. Beneath that, secondary fills consisting of greyish-brown sandy soil, almost free from natural stones (5). The potsherds indicated (lozenges) were mostly tiny, except the lowest which lay flat on the bottom of the layer. No floor layer recorded. Fine-grained, sandy subsoil, free from stones (6).

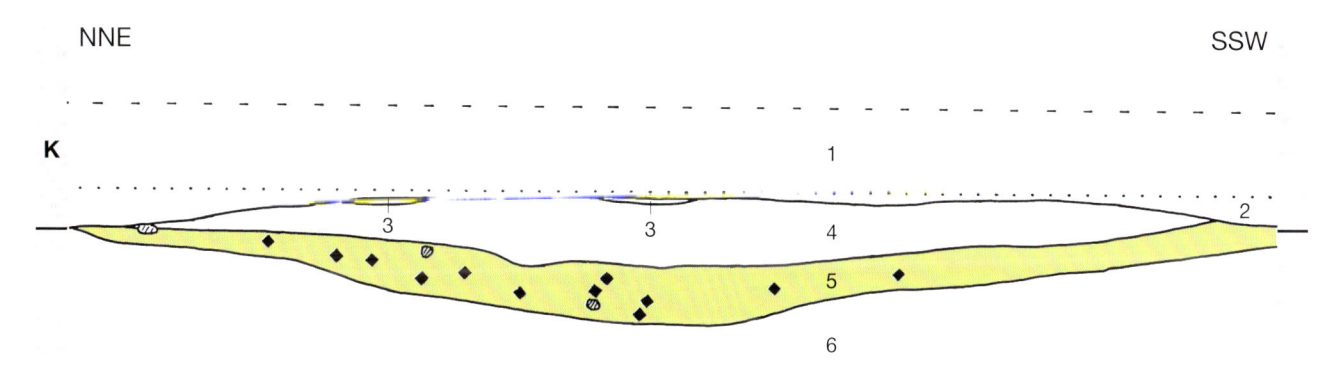

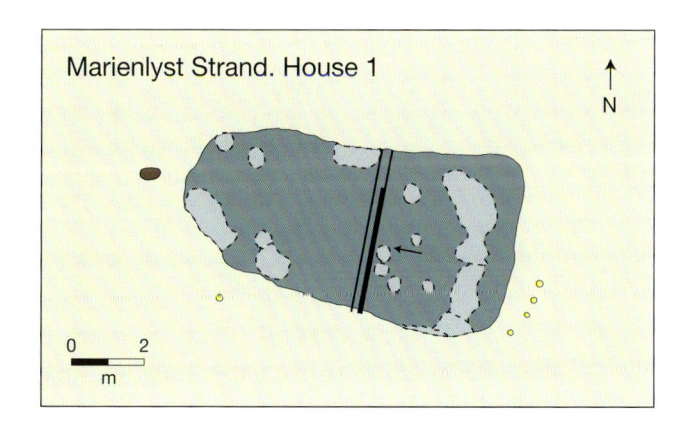

Fig. 4.68.L. Marienlyst Strand, House 1, NNE-SSW section. Before recent ploughing, the covering soil could have been thicker than indicated here. The sunken area was somewhat marked by traces of animal activity. Estimated thickness of machine-removed ploughed topsoil (1) and other soil (2) at the boundary to the sunken area during initial excavation is shown. Beneath, dark-brownish sandy soil (3) and greyish-brown soil with yellowish spots (4), both considered secondary fills. More to the south, an area with yellow clay and greyish spots (5), possibly a natural deposit. No floor layer recorded. Sandy subsoil (6).

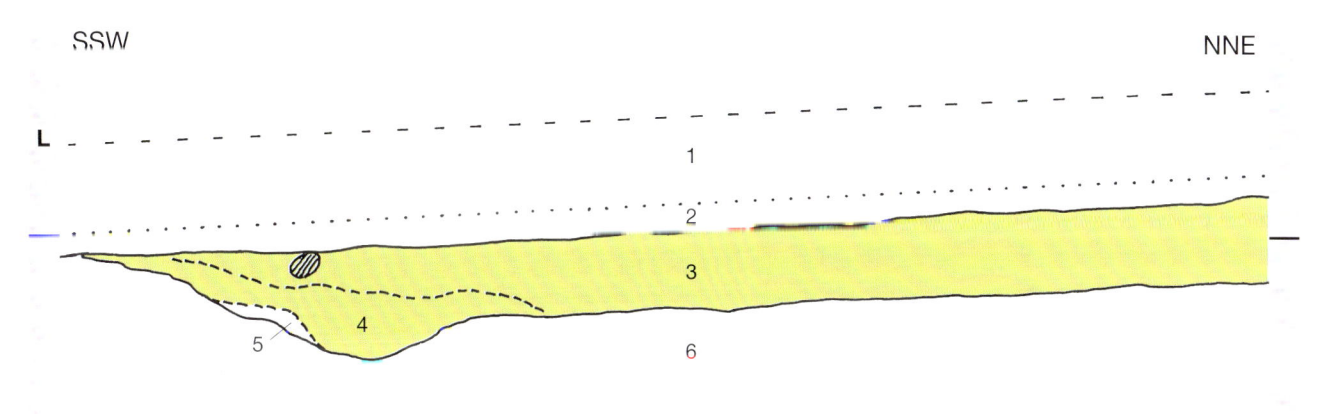

Artefacts, pits, patches, and daily life activities   321

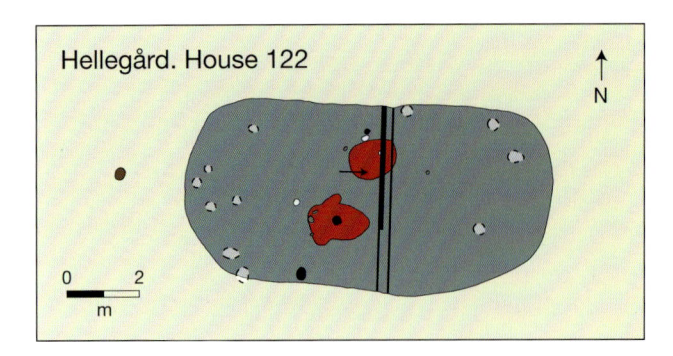

Fig. 4.68.M. Hellegård, House 122, N-S section. Uppermost, ploughed topsoil (1) and sandy, dark-brownish soil (2). Beneath that, secondary fills of sandy, greyish soil (3). Thereunder, an almost sterile layer of fine-grained, homogeneous sand free from natural stones (4), likely wind-deposited but enclosing a few artefacts and therefore also considered to represent secondary fills. This layer had been exposed to ard-ploughing. Beneath that, a floor layer of sandy brownish soil (5), with indication (lozenge) of a potsherd in the profile (RE548). Patch A was located in the lower level of this floor layer, having relatively darker soil (5A). It appeared diffusely delimited in the cross-section but was clearly discernible in the sunken floor surface. Sandy subsoil (6).

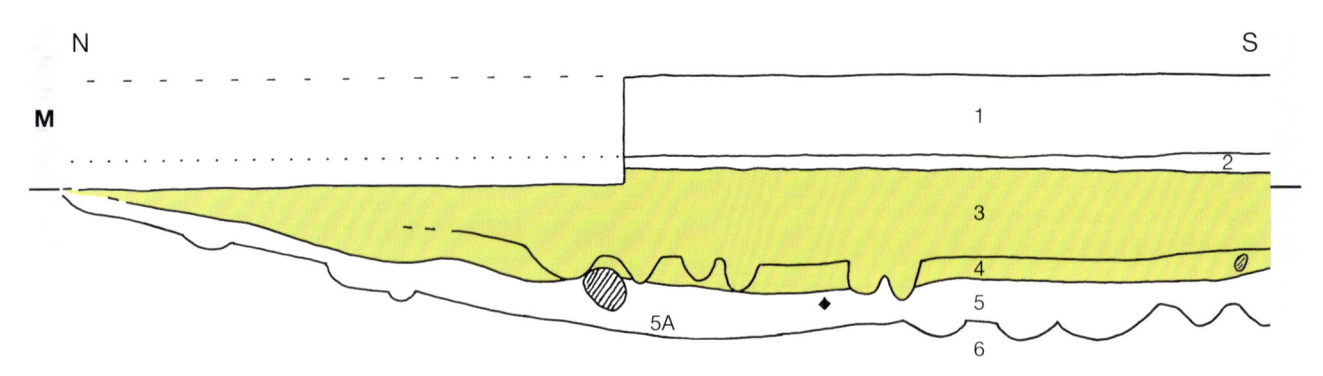

Observations from the site of House 2 at Resengaard show that floor layers without clear limits can merge into and accumulate on top of separate floor patches. I understand this from the way that certain upper parts of the floor layers may belong to a time when the longhouse was used in another manner, when the former patch areas had no function anymore. In other words, these upper floor layers could stem from the after-residence life of the house. Still exposed to human activities, perhaps over many years, any differences between upper and lower floor layer parts could have been erased. In areas where the floor layers appear very thick, a layer of sand could have been added in lower areas for the purpose of levelling the floor for the new use of the building. The after-residence life of longhouses has already been considered in Ch. 2.7 and 4.5, and shall be dealt with further in Ch. 5.3.

Placement of pits and patches

By the time of the investigation at Resengaard, the subsoil in the sunken-floor areas often appeared to have different light yellow colours, albeit always influenced by the degree of dryness, whereas the majority of the soil features were of a darker appearance. Most of the soil features were found in the middle and eastern parts of these, and relatively few were observed in the western ground floors. The first phase of House 41 can be referred to as an example of a site where pits and patches of different dimensions were found in the sunken floor as well as the ground floor.

Pits of varying dimensions and depths had, in a few instances, simply been dug into the peripheries of the sunken floors at Resengaard. This relates, for example, to a deep pit to the southwest in the sunken floor of House 200 and a shallow pit in an almost corresponding position to the southwest in the site of House 2. A shallow pit was placed to the northeast in House 197.

In the sunken floors of six longhouses were found 8-13 significant pits or patches, including those with scorched stones, while in those of the six remaining longhouses, 2-6 of these were present. Intensive ard-ploughing had severely affected two of the sunken floors (House 14 & House 197) and likely minimized the number of preserved patches. A total of 1-4 significant soil features were observed in the three minor house sites with scorched-stone patches (House 202, House 240 & House 289). Just 2 significant patches were found at a minor house site (House 193).

322 Chapter 4

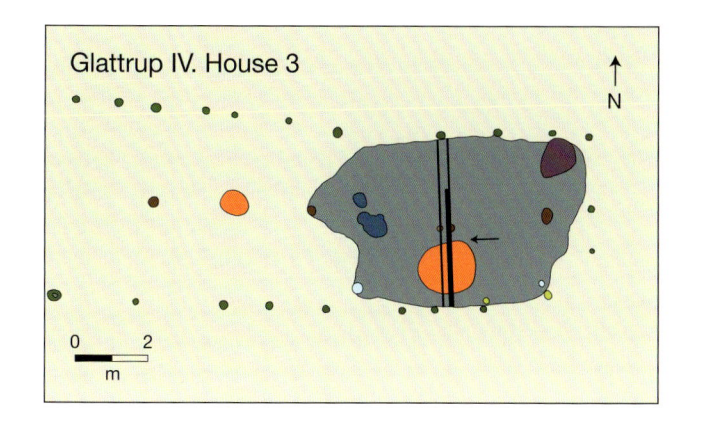

Fig. 4.68.N. Glattrup IV, House 3, N-S Section. Before recent ploughing, the covering soil could have been thicker than indicated here. Estimated thickness of machine-removed ploughed topsoil (1) and other soil (2) at the boundary to the sunken area during the initial excavation is shown. Two layers are considered to represent secondary fills, namely the uppermost brown sandy soil with potsherds, worked flint and a few heat-affected/heat-cracked stones (3) and, beneath that, light greyish-brown sandy soil likewise with potsherds, worked flint and a few heat-affected/heat-cracked stones (4). It cannot, however, be ruled out that the latter could represent a floor layer. The fill in the sunken fireplace (B) consisted of very light greyish-brown sandy soil with tiny flecks of charcoal (5), having an intermezzo of a lens of fine-grained yellow sand (6). At the bottom, a layer of greyish-brown sandy soil containing ample charcoal (8). It appears to have been much compacted over time since its remainders were still present higher up in the sides. The fills of the posthole (centre post) consist of greyish-brown sandy soil with spots of yellow fine sand (7). During fieldwork, the proper surface dimensions of this posthole were not taken (see Fig. 4.56). Fine-grained yellowish-white subsoil sand (9).

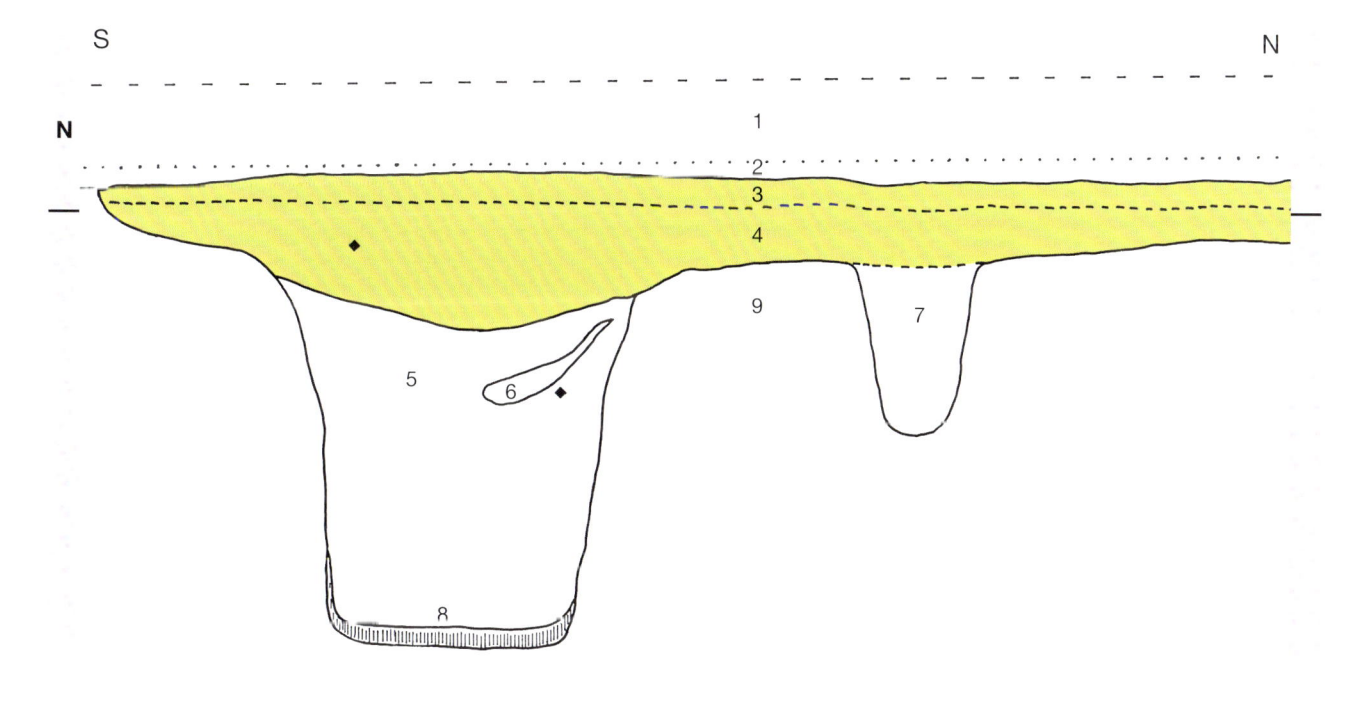

The scorched-stone patches at Resengaard were not placed in a uniform pattern, although certain trends have emerged from systematic analysis. The westernmost and easternmost sunken-floor parts were not used for these activities at Resengaard, although the ard-ploughing of these patches in the sites of House 14 and House 197 offers a slight possibility for exceptions. Consistent with this, a group of houses displayed placements that may come close to a "standard" for the settlement, namely being found in the middle or somewhat east of the middle of the sunken floor and having the majority of the scorched-stone patch areas in the northern aisles. This concerns longhouses 1, 13, 41, 128, 130, and 200. A couple of sunken-floor longhouses, House 42 & House 138, had the scorched-stone areas mostly in the southern half

Artefacts, pits, patches, and daily life activities

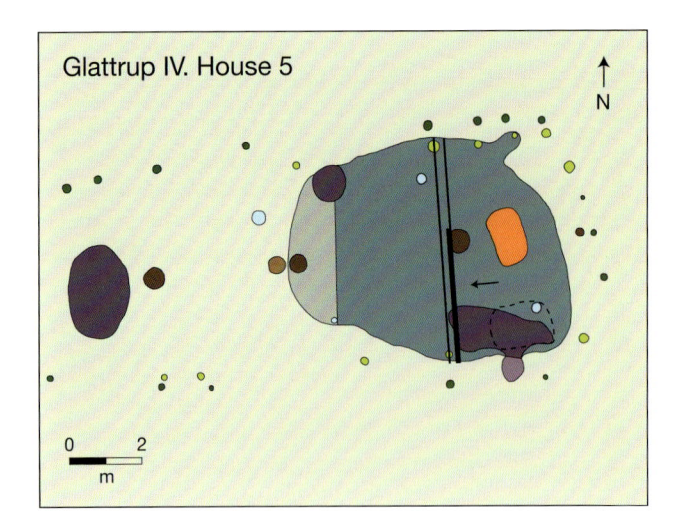

Fig. 4.68.O: Glattrup IV, House 5, N-S Section. Before recent ploughing, the covering soil could have been thicker than indicated here. Estimated thickness of machine-removed ploughed topsoil (1) and other soil (2) at the boundary to the sunken area during the initial excavation is shown. The stratum below is secondary fills (3) of dark, greyish-brown sandy soil with potsherds, worked flint and spread heat-affected/cracked stones. To the south, pit C (4) contained light greyish sandy soil with tiny flecks of charcoal. The fills of the centre post posthole (5) consisted of light greyish sandy soil with tiny flecks of charcoal. Fine-grained, yellow subsoil sand (6).

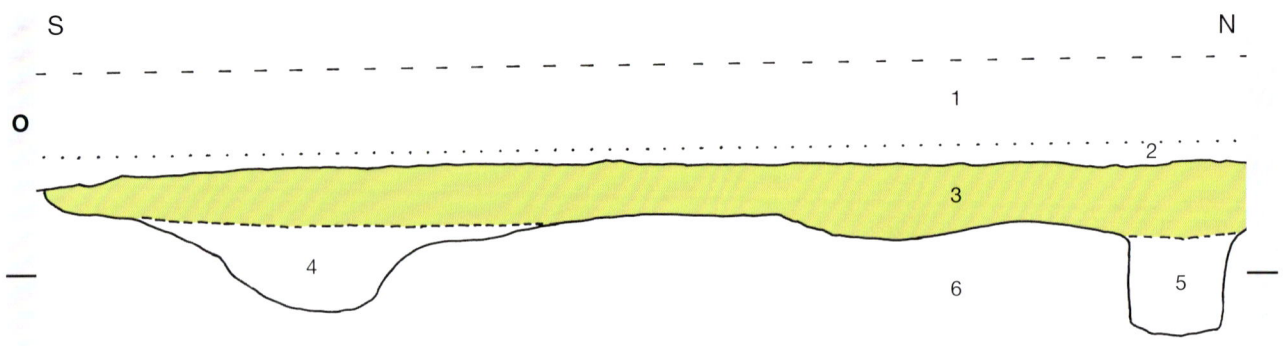

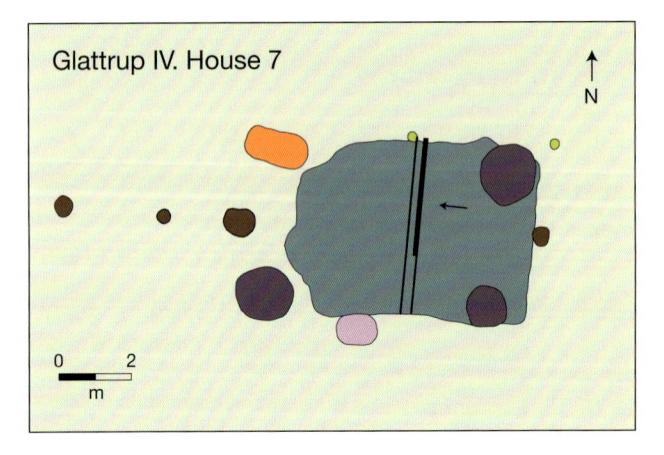

Fig. 4.68.P: Glattrup IV, House 7, N-S Section. On top of this house site, a simple road track level with the field was dug away. The covering soil could possibly have been thicker than indicated here. Estimated thickness of machine-removed topsoil (1) and other soil (2) at the boundary to the sunken area during initial excavation is shown. Thereunder, two ard-furrows with relatively darker soil (3) and secondary fills of brownish-grey sandy soil (4). Five ard-furrows to the north partly vent into the subsoil. To the south, some digging appears to have taken place prior to placing the secondary fills. No floor layer recorded. Fine-grained, greyish-white sandy subsoil (5).

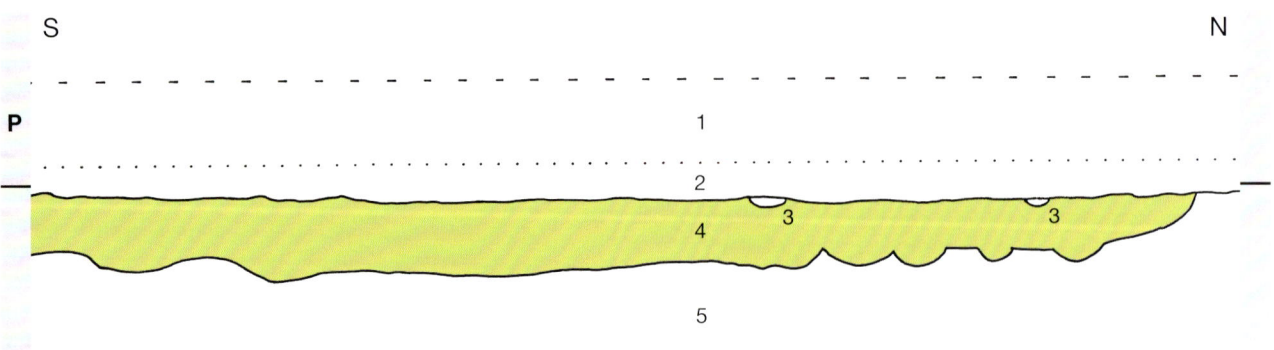

Patches and floor layers

Location		House	Schorched-stone patch	Fireplace, sunken	Fireplace, ground level	Mosaic-patch	Pit, large/deep	Cubicle-pit	Other significant pit/patch	Sunken floor depth	Floor layer observed	Extensive secondary fills	Ard-furrows observed	
Resengård	Longhouses	1	3			3			2	26	Yes	Yes	No	A few heat-affected stones in patch D
		2	2						11	34	Yes	Yes	No	Two areas with burned subsoil in the account
		13	9						2	26	Locally	Yes	No	Floor layer presumably present locally
		14	2							36	No	Yes	Yes	
		41	1						10	26	Yes	Yes	No	
		42	2							36	No	Yes	No	Possible fireplace, un-dated, west of sunken floor
		128	2						7	32	Locally	Yes	No	Floor layer presumably present locally
		130	2						1	42	No	Yes	No	
		134	1						2	45	No	Yes	No	
		138	2		2				2	38	No	Yes	No	Only scanty vestiges of the fireplaces
		197	1					1	5	32	No	Yes	Yes	Evidence of scorched-stone patch inadequate
		200	1				1		2	54	Locally	Yes	Yes	Floor layer presumably present locally
	Minor houses with scorched-stone patches	202	2							22	No	Yes	No	
		240	1							21	No	Yes	No	
		289	2							39	No	Yes	No	
	Minor houses	10								31	Locally	Yes	No	Floor layer present to the northeast
		12								14	No	Yes	No	
		84								13	No	Yes	No	
		112								22	No	Yes	No	
		143								36	No	Yes	No	
		158								44	No	Yes	No	
		183								37	No	Yes	No	
		193							2	8	No	Yes	No	
		198								17	No	Yes	No	
		268								18	No	Yes	No	
	Short house	201								15	No	Yes	No	
Gåsemose		1								30	No	Yes	No	
Kluborg II		5	2	1	2				9	32	Yes	Yes	Yes	Floor layer affected by ard-ploughing
Glattrup I/III		5								33	No	Yes	No	
		6								16	No	Yes	No	
Marienlyst Strand		1								22	No	Yes	No	
Granlygård		2								21	No	Yes	No	
		3								18	No	Yes	No	
		6								10	No	Yes	No	
Hellegård		122	2							43	Yes	Yes	Yes	
		35								15	No	Yes	No	Depth based on the excavation report
Glattrup IV		3		1		1				24	Yes	Yes	No	
		5		1		2	1			20	No	Yes	No	Heat-affected stones in the fills in one deep pit
		7		1		3	1			20	No	Yes	Yes	
Rosgårde		1	2						1	28	No	Yes	No	
Tromgade		1	4							20	No	Yes	No	
		2	3							21	No	Yes	No	
		414								10	No	Yes	No	Depth based on the excavation report
Total (123)			46	4	4	3	7	3	56					

Fig. 4.69. Presence of pits, patches, floor layers, and other. The thickness of the old surface soil as well as some centimetres of soil removed by machine as part of the initial archaeological investigation is in addition to the stated depth of the individual sunken floors. Moreover, in a number of instances, recent ploughing had eradicated parts of the original upper topsoil (cf. Fig. 1.4). In particular, with regard to the sites of House 5 and House 6 at Glattrup I/III, as well as House 5 at Glattrup IV and House 1 at Gåsemose, it is possible that soil on the floors locally represented a preserved floor layer.

and much to the east, although, as pointed out above, never very close to the eastern edge of the preserved sunken floor. In the sites of two minor sunken-floor buildings, House 202 and House 289, the scorched-stone areas were placed west of the middle of the preserved sunken floors.

Scorched-stone patches, stones, and fireplaces

One of the most enigmatic features of the longhouse sites at Resengaard is the presence of the shallow scorched-stone patches. Their surface dimensions varied considerably and thus occupied highly varying shares of the sunken floors. Some were, from appearance, quite large and extensive, while others were of moderate size or rather small. At some house sites, two or more separate patches of these were observable, whereas at others only a single one was recognizable. The individual patches took up between c. 5.8 to 0.2 m² (Fig. 4.70 & 4.71). The ploughed-out and hence large scorched-stone patch in the sunken floor of House 14 covered c. 33.9 m². However, it probably originally consisted of several scorched-stone patches that were later exposed to so much ard-ploughing that the individual patches were no longer discernible. The average area of the patches per longhouse was c. 3.25 m². In this account, the small patch (seen as part of patch A) to the south in the site of House 1, the extremely large ploughed-out patch in the site of House 14 (and the perhaps missing patch area in the site of House 197) are ignored, and this could imply that the average scorched-stone patch area per longhouse would probably originally have been somewhat more, presumably approaching 4 m². The areas of such scorched-stone patches in the three sites of minor sunken-floor buildings (House 202, House 240, and House 289) also varied somewhat.

These differences in surface dimensions of the scorched-stone patches are, on the whole, quite conspicuous. If we try to look for some explanation, it would be reasonable to begin with a sunken floor with just one small scorched-stone area, as representative of the size that might be about the minimum area used in a longhouse at Resengaard, e.g. the well-preserved patch from House 134. It covered as little as 0.6 m². Conversely, when turning to the large well-preserved conglomeration of scorched-stone areas of the site of House 13, we come across a patch area many times larger. In total, nine patches were present,

Scorched-stone patch areas

Location		House	Square metres	Patch	Square metres
Resengaard	Longhouses	1	2,8	A	0,4
				B	1,5
				G	0,9
		2	2,4	A	1,4
				D	1,0
		13	7,7	B	1,7
				C	0,5
				D	0,8
				E	0,5
				F	0,2
				G	0,7
				H	2,7
				I	0,2
				J	0,4
		14	1,4	B	1,4
		41	0,3	A	0,3
		42	4,3	A	3,4
				B	0,9
		128	10,4	A	3,1
				B	5,8
				C	1,5
		130	4,8	A	4,4
				B	0,4
		134	0,6	C	0,6
		138	1,6	B	0,2
				C	1,4
		197	0,6	C	0,6
		200	2,1	B	2,1

together covering an area of 7.7 m². The two smallest scorched-stone patches each covered a mere c. 0.2 m². In my reading, it is likely that a number of smaller areas that could not be discerned during fieldwork actually constituted the larger patches. Viewed in this light, the major scorched-stone areas might each represent numerous such minor areas.

That the scorched-stone areas together became large in some of the houses, as e.g. also in the site of House 13, may perhaps result from a tendency to move the activities a little from time to time, while

Scorched-stone patch areas

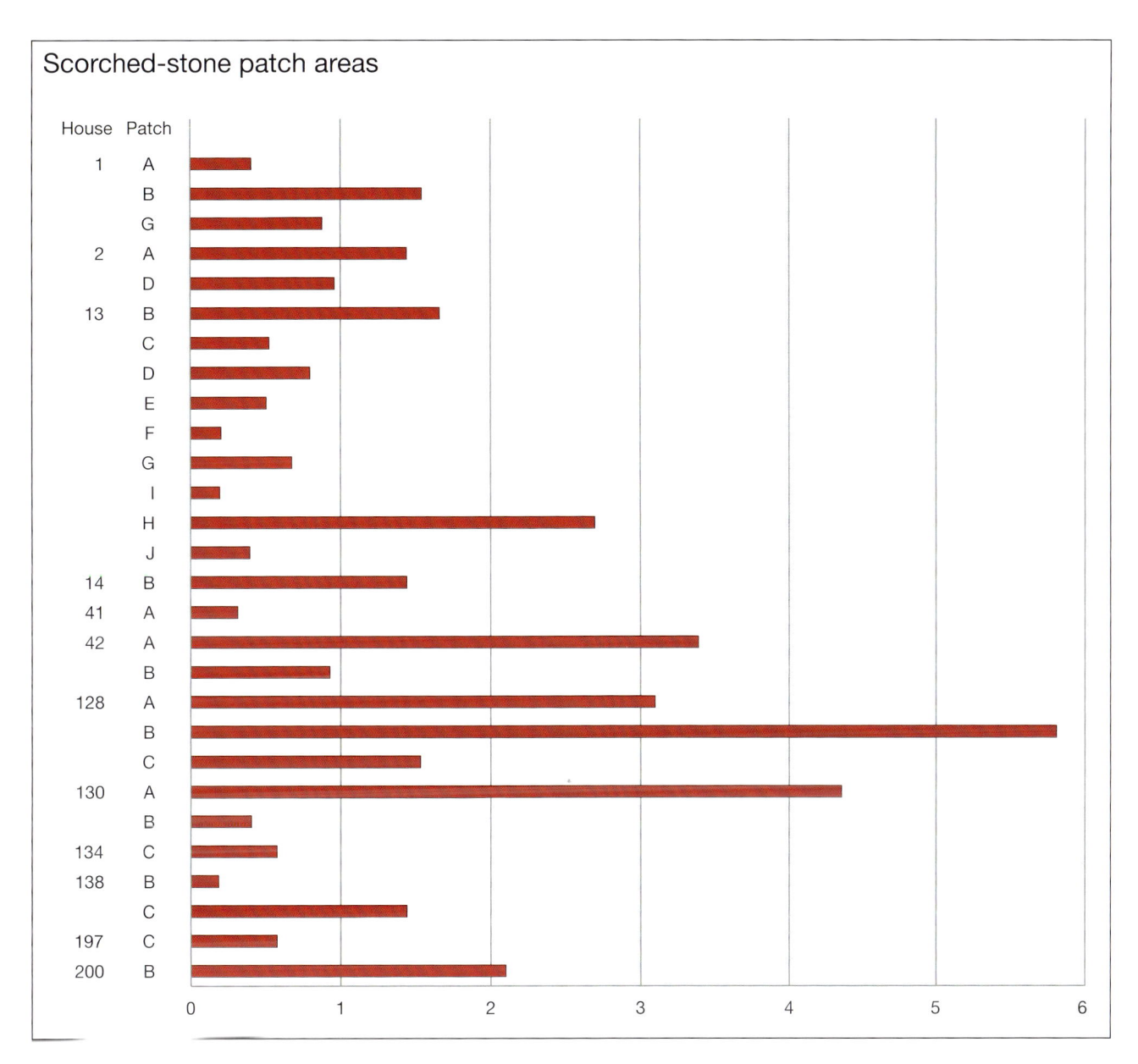

House	Patch	Area
1	A	0.4
	B	1.5
	G	0.9
2	A	1.4
	D	1.0
13	B	1.7
	C	0.5
	D	0.8
	E	0.5
	F	0.2
	G	0.7
	I	0.2
	H	2.7
	J	0.4
14	B	1.4
41	A	0.3
42	A	3.4
	B	0.9
128	A	3.1
	B	5.8
	C	1.5
130	A	4.4
	B	0.4
134	C	0.6
138	B	0.2
	C	1.4
197	C	0.6
200	B	2.1

◀▲ *Fig. 4.70. Resengaard, dimensions of scorched-stone patches. The extremely large, heavily ard-ploughed patch A in the site of House 14 has been omitted. A: Table with areas calculated in GIS. The small part of patch A to the south in the site of House 1 is not included. B: Diagram of areas (square metres). To the left, house number & patch name.*

still maintaining a certain part of the sunken floor as the proper place. With a gradual move of the activities in some direction, it would probably be very difficult to distinguish single features and, during excavation, it might therefore appear as a single large patch. When the moving of the scorched-stone related activities did not take place gradually but moved to new "clean" spots, these can be more easily identified during investigation. On the whole, it thus seems possible that differences in size and number of scorched-stone patches may, to some degree, be explained by a quite simple practice, namely whether these were kept relatively stationary, were moved gradually or located to fresh new spots.

Of course, two or more scorched-stone areas could also have been used simultaneously in a building like House 13. Almost no evidence of internal stratification is available between the recorded scorched-stone patches but the scorched-stone patch D appears to have been younger than patch E (Fig. 4.11). However, these features were so abundantly present in the sunken floor of House 13 that we have to accept

Heat-affected/cracked stones

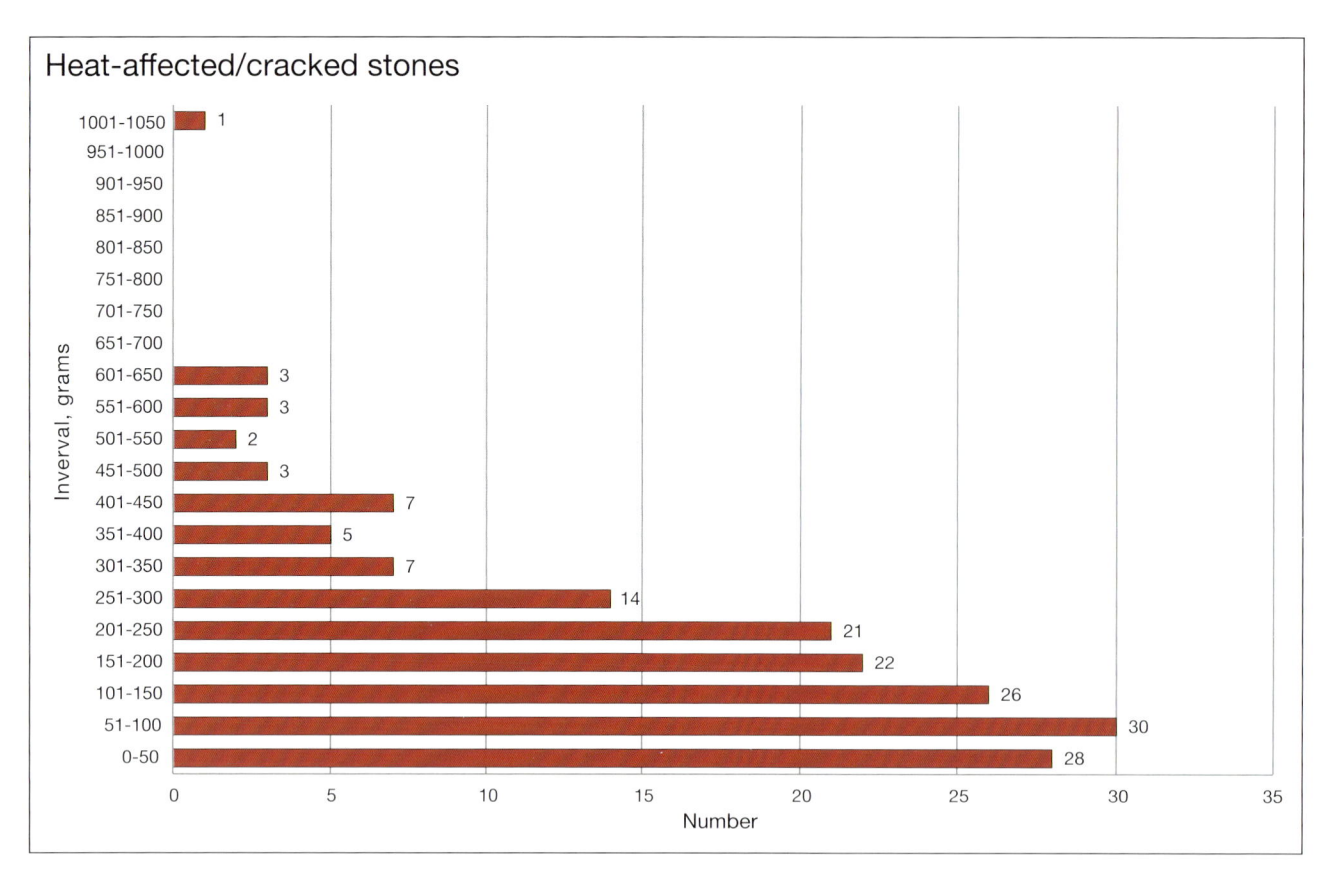

Inverval, grams	Number
1001-1050	1
951-1000	
901-950	
851-900	
801-850	
751-800	
701-750	
651-700	
601-650	3
551-600	3
501-550	2
451-500	3
401-450	7
351-400	5
301-350	7
251-300	14
201-250	21
151-200	22
101-150	26
51-100	30
0-50	28

Fig. 4.71. Resengaard, House 13, heat-affected/cracked stones. Weight spread diagram of a large sample (RE640) from a scorched-stone patch. The lower weight limit in the sample is 15 grams and their lengths range from c. 3 cm to 13 cm. These stones had a mainly reddish appearance. A porphyry was among them.

the possibility that activities concerning these may have taken place on a somewhat larger scale than elsewhere.

An example of an apparent practice relates to House 128 (Fig. 4.18). In the middle part of its sunken floor, the sizeable scorched-stone patch B – being more than 10 m² and thereby the largest at Resengaard – and the somewhat minor patch C were placed relatively close (Fig. 4.70).[8] In the former, the stones were mainly found in the eastern part, whereas in the latter they were mostly to the west. The daily practice appears to have meant that the stones were left closer to the intermediate space between the scorched-stone patches. In this case it is also possible that these two patches originally consisted of several patches that could not be discerned and that a sequence of doings eventually left the stones with the pattern described.

In none of the scorched-stone patches at Resengaard were the stones found densely packed as a horizontal pavement. The stone levels mostly varied greatly and were placed with varying distances horizontally and vertically, although there were no differences as to the degree of heat cracking observed. The stones placed in the uppermost parts of the patches thus did not suffer more heavily from the impact of fire than the others.

It may be clear from the above that we really lack evidence for the assumption that the scorched-stone patches were used as fireplaces. Moreover, some of these were placed somewhat away from the central floor areas, where the roofs must have been significantly lower than along the central longitudinal axis. This observation would also speak against their interpretation as regular fireplaces. In some instances, the soils in the scorched-stone patches were only faintly different from the surrounding soils of the floor. The scorched-stone patch to the east in House 200 is such an example, where it was not clearly visible in cross-section but the floor area in question had been ard-ploughed after abandonment and so the borders between soils could have been blurred.

Being a site of fire, House 2 offered special opportunities for making observations on the working of the scorched-stone patches. The reflections on the house site resulted in an understanding that the building had probably been deliberately burned down. Items of value had therefore most likely been removed beforehand, although this would hardly have concerned the presence of simple stones in floor patches, unless precautions were taken against problems for later ard-ploughing. As we have seen, the special characteristic of this floor was that two scorched-stone patches were recognized at a fairly large internal distance. The patch to the east (D) consisted not least of rather blackish soil, probably coloured by dust from charred organic material, as well as some heat-affected/cracked stones. In the western half of the floor, the scorched-stone patch (A) had many such stones preserved and, in certain parts, the stones were placed quite closely while, in others, they were more spread out. Quite blackish soils were observable between several stones. Dust from burned organic material had probably also coloured these parts. If the scorched-stone patches succeeded each other in House 2 with equal functions, it is remarkable that the number of scorched stones in the western one was very substantial while in the eastern one it was not. A more plausible option is that both were used during the same period, with the western patch having core functions and the eastern some additional ones. Some pieces of the puzzle may fall into place if the western scorched-stone area was used during the entire lifetime of the house and the eastern was later established in combination with the suggested extension towards the east. The eastern end of the longhouse appears a little "unstructured" in the ground plan, and as we have seen a simple *ad hoc* extension caused, for instance, out of social necessity. The remarkable traces of the suggested recess may also have been constructed due to the need to create more space by simple means. The presence of burned red subsoil sand below the eastern scorched-stone patch D may indicate higher temperatures and the plot might have been used as a fireplace for the final ignition of the house remainders and other scrap.

The question of an absence of substantial heat in the scorched-stone patches can also be considered in some further detail. Flint with no visible heat damage exists from the scorched-stone patches and this may also, to some extent, contradict their interpretation as regular fireplaces. An example from the site of House 1 is patch B, where the flint scraper (RE63ea) and the flint sickle fragment (RE53ea) are cracked due to heat, whereas no observed heat damage was done to the flint nodule (RE37ea). Here also, 3 pieces of seemingly undamaged worked flint and 4 pieces of burned flint (RE37) were present. An example from the site of House 2 is patch A, where a flint nodule (RE147) apparently has no heat damage. At another spot in the same patch were found a piece of worked flint (RE139) and a flint nodule (RE139ea) with no observed heat damage. An example from the site of House 13 comes from a spot where 2 pieces of worked flint showed no observable heat damage (RE125), despite their placement close to two scorched-stone patches (G & H). The scattered finds in scorched-stone patch H in the same house site are important, where a total of 5 potsherds, 15 pieces of apparently undamaged worked flint and 1 piece of burned flint (RE641) were found. There are also examples from the sites of House 42 and House 200 and it is, on the whole, thought-provoking that flint items were found without clear heat damage.

The leftovers of burned flint and secondarily burned potsherds from the Resengaard houses are not overwhelming. However, it is possible that the burned flint objects and secondarily burned potsherds mainly represent discarded and forgotten pieces in the sunken-floor horizons. When it comes to the major concentration of burned flint pieces found in House 2, it seems obvious that they were deliberately placed there (Fig.4.7). Judging by their position, it is possible that these flints were heat-affected as a result of the deliberate burning of the building remainders. From Myrhøj, burned flint made up only c. 3 % of all flint and, regarding this site, it is explained that the residents apparently deliberately tried to keep flint out of the fire (Jensen, J.A. 1973:80).

Due to the absence of evidence documenting the use of the scorched-stone patches as fireplaces at Resengaard generally, the topic needs some further attention. One factor in this respect is the presence of spots with reddish colouring of the subsoil sand due to heat impact. In the sunken floor of House 128, reddish sand was observed in patch A but the whetstone, the presumed stone anvils and other stones above did not appear heat-affected/cracked. Reddish sand was also recorded in the lower part of the eastern scorched-stone patch in the site of House 2. The other red-burned floor areas must stem from the deliberate burning of the building remainders.

Stone-free fireplaces were extremely rare in the longhouse interiors at Resengaard. A solitary area with reddish sand was found in the western, ground-floor part of House 42 but no other soils or artefacts were present there. Such placement is the only one of its kind at Resengaard and it cannot be substantiated that it belongs to the time of the longhouse. In the site of House 138, I consider two patches with charcoal remains to be the traces of fire, presumably not strong though, as no reddish-burning of the subsoil was recorded. In the site of the minor House 202, some red-burned clay pieces and scant pieces of charcoal were present in a small scorched-stone patch. As far as I can see, this is the existing evidence of this kind from the investigation at Resengaard, but we will shortly look at the other settlements in question.

Sunken fireplaces were established in some longhouses. Regarding Glattrup IV, my interpretation is that pit B to the south in the sunken floor of House 3, pit B to the east in the sunken floor of the site of House 5 and presumably also pit A immediately west of the sunken floor in the site of House 7 were used as deeply sunken fireplaces (Fig. 4.56, 4.57 & 4.59). Such deep fireplaces were only found in the three houses associated with beer production and were probably functionally necessary. Their sunken position would thus have reduced the danger of igniting fire significantly and hence this construction method made a great deal of sense. Apart from these, pit 178 (placed on the central longitudinal axis of House 3 in the area of the ground floor) in my understanding functioned as a moderately sunken fireplace. Interestingly, scorched-stone patches were not found in any of the three longhouses at Glattrup IV and heat-affected/cracked stones were only sporadically found in their pit fills and secondary fills. On the whole, this may indicate that the technology of the scorched-stone patches was not applied in these three longhouses and this accords well with the presence of the exceptional finds of deeply sunken fireplaces.

At Kluborg II in the site of House 5, we have substantial traces of regular fireplaces and one of these was moderately sunken. As we have seen, it was precisely in this very late sunken-floor house that bronze working took place and the interior arrangements were quite different from all the other longhouses under consideration.

Overall, it must be concluded that reddish-burned patches as well as reddish-burned subsoil are relatively rare, despite our clear focus on such occurrences during fieldwork. When we meet "blackish, sandy soil" and similar descriptions of floor patches, a few of these may perhaps represent casual fires, for instance, needed for a specific purpose at some point in time. However, they could hardly be generally interpreted as regular "permanent" fireplaces.[9] It is worth remembering that even a tiny portion of charred material or charcoal dust may have a strong colouring capacity. And it must be said that the sandy soils described as blackish were seldom really black in the proper sense of the word but often more like a kind of tinting of lighter, sandier soil.

The presence of heat-affected/cracked stones could also, in some instances, have been indicators of activities other than considered above. One of these is the use of warm stones for heating water or other liquids, acting like a kind of immersion heater.[10] One such doing might be just to take the chill off some cold water or in order to make lukewarm water, e.g. for different personal uses. Heating of cold water might have speeded up the stone cracking processes, due to exposure to temperature shocks. It was likely also well-known that moderate temperatures, for instance generated by warm stones, would more easily trigger fermentation processes in liquids and that somewhat higher temperatures would suspend the same processes for a time. It was likewise presumably common knowledge that an adequate amount of significantly heated stones would also have the capacity to produce really hot or even boiling water, needed perhaps for different purposes. It has not been possible to link such use of stones directly to any vessels or other pottery in the present find material from the sunken-floor houses at Resengaard or at the settlements particularly studied.

The recurrent association of scorched-stone patches and sunken-floor longhouses at Resengaard indicates that the stones were vital elements in activities using heat. The capacity of the stones to absorb much warmth compared to other accessible materials was likely much appreciated. The ability of the stones to absorb high temperatures from an energy source and then release the heat gradually may, in particular, have been a key necessary quality. An ordinary fire could burn out and give off its heat relatively swiftly compared to stones, which would have a slower rate under controlled circumstances.

The heat-affected/cracked stones found in the heap of Feature 24 just north of House 14 at Resengaard generally appeared to have the same character as those found in the sunken-floor horizons. Those found in the scorched-stone patches of the longhouses were mostly characterized by a red colour. A "typical" specimen was fragmented, comprising e.g. a quarter of the original stone and it would hence not have had much of the surface preserved. The shape could be something like an irregular, multi-edged polygon. And yet, the granite, quartzite and other stones were not all severely damaged by fire. We can group the stones observed into three according to their appearance: firstly, being heat-cracked and crumbling; secondly, being less affected, with tight cracks and a tendency to a fragile surface; or thirdly being without any clearly visible heat impact. The presence of this latter might indicate that not all the stones in such a patch were used equally or could mean fresh supplies left there. More or less similar soil features are known also from outside the Limfjord region (Boas 1983:92p).

A relatively large sample (RE640) derives from a scorched-stone patch to the north in the sunken floor of the site of House 13 (Fig. 4.71). The sample contains 172 stones weighing a total of c. 33 kilos, the average weight being a little less than 200 grams. The different weights range from a very few grams up to more than 600 grams and one particular stone alone weighs around one kilo. The weights do not seem to show a clear tendency towards any specific weight although there are many stones in the 51-100 gram range. The stones often tended to break further apart during excavation and many may very well have been larger when last used.

For comparison, numerous stones (RE955) were also collected from the scorched-stone patch in the site of the minor House 240. In all, no less than 235 stones were taken as a sample, corresponding to about half the number of stones actually found and this is presumably representative. A large proportion, almost a hundred, was within the 101-200 gram range, while many weighed less than 100 grams. The number of stones weighing more than 200 grams declined gradually as the weight increased. No stones exceeded one kilo.

Many stones with heat impact from other contexts in the Resengaard settlement (Houses 2, 14, 200, 202, & 289) have been weighed and it appears that the predominant weights by and large fall within the above-mentioned results. Some of the samples indicate that when stones in the 101-200 gram range were most frequent, stones below 100 grams came second, and vice versa.

I would *a priori* have expected stones of higher weight to be more prevalent but it is possible that relatively large stones were not better suited for the activities carried out. One quality of the minor stones could have been the ability to give off a more even heat than larger ones, as they could be densely packed with only a little space in between. Minor stones might thus more easily have encircled a solid object and would facilitate the leading and radiation of the heat to the objects. Conversely, larger stones would have absorbed a higher amount of heat but left larger spaces of air in between and the warmth from these might hence have been more uneven. Anyway, the samples considered above indicate that mostly stones of less than 200 grams were used in the time just before the abandonment of the individual houses.

Access to stones with the right qualities would presumably also have influenced how long they were used for. If plentiful in the surroundings of the settlement one might assume that new stones would more easily replace older stones instead of using these until they were markedly diminished.

Gathering numerous tiny stones might presumably have been considered wearisome work and it seems plausible that the sizes used were balanced according to parameters of being effective at warming up the given objects and being manageable as well. Once the stones had given off their heat, they would have been kept until the next heating process. The recurring heating of the stones would gradually lead to cracking. Some stones were more fragile than others and would be damaged sooner and split into minor pieces or the surfaces ever more crumbled. From experience, some of the stones were actually so much affected that even careful handling of them during excavation led to further disintegration. When the dimensions had crumbled below a certain limit, they were probably not considered usable any more.

Some of the crumbling stones may have been collected for pottery tempering with fine, medium and coarse sized grains. The soils in the scorched-stone patches usually contained some tiny crumbled stone and, in several instances, this component seemed to be prevalent next to sandy soil. A rather expressive example could be the scorched-stone patch B in the sunken floor horizon of House 1 (Fig. 4.6).

Naturally, from a source-critical point of view consideration must be given to whether more than a thousand years under the conditions of the site had increased the crumbling of such stones, particularly if water and frost combined might have brought about their disintegration? In my judgment, the conditions of preservation have not usually led significantly to further disintegration of the stones. After demolition of the longhouses, the sunken areas were soon added as fills. The frost would therefore probably seldom have been strong enough to prevail so deeply and would consequently not have caused a severe impact on the preservation of these stones.

Scorched-stone patches and charred plant residues

The scorched-stone patches can now form a starting point for comparing their spatial positions with other traits of the sunken-floor horizons. In line with the other sites at Resengaard, the soils of the sites of longhouses 41, 42, 130, and 134 were searched intensively for charred grains but, despite our best efforts, none were found. When looking at the longhouses placed on the northwest terrace, no charred cereals were found in the site of House 41, more in that of House 2 and very many in that of House 1, but it is rather important that extensive floor layers were preserved in all three cases. On the whole, charred macrofossils were recovered from the sites of eight longhouses, as well as those of House 10 and House 202. The samples of charred organic materials were mainly taken directly from scorched-stone patches and from floor layers.

From sheer appearance, the patches with scorched stones reveal a kind of paradox in relation to the amount of charred cereals in the sunken floors of the sites of House 1 and House 13. In the latter, extensive areas of scorched stones were observed but only a very few charred cereals came to light. In my view, it is most straightforward to presume that the few grains had simply been carbonized accidentally in this case.

Conversely, in the sunken floor of House 1, two regular scorched-stone patches of limited dimensions were found to the north, while the few heat-affected/cracked stones to the south in reality had maybe not been used there. The moderate presence of regular scorched-stone patches in this longhouse strongly contrasts with the presence in the sunken-floor horizon of some 379,000 charred cereals (estimate). The total amount of cereal waste would have represented around 14 kilos of grains before their exposure to the carbonizing process (Peter Steen Henriksen, report S2001a:7).

The state of affairs in the site of House 1 at Resengaard indicates that even though scorched-stone patches were of moderate dimensions, the capacity to handle cereals appears to have been high. Our collection of substantial samples was divided into five areas and included almost all soil belonging to the sunken-floor horizon (Fig. 5.16). From our calculation, the five areas comprised quantities of grain ranging from some 200,000 to a little over 5,000. These differences show that the grains were not found evenly spread. More than three out of every four grains stemmed from the northeast quadrant (sample area A & B). It was my impression during the manual investigation with trowel that the soil closest to the scorched-stone patches contained the most grains, whereas the amount of cereals was relatively modest within the scorched-stone patches. The amount of charred cereals faded out in the southern and western areas of the sunken floor. In no instances can we speak of any heaps of grains found in the sunken-floor horizon. On the contrary, in all find areas, a mixture of charred macrofossils and soils was observed. This spread was also recognizable even in the scorched-stone patches. When investigating the floor layer, the dark grains were frequently observable with a spread which, in my reading, may indicate that they had evidently become mixed little by little. Hundreds of thousands of charred cereals thus mirror heavy activities connected to the areas first and foremost in the vicinities of the scorched-stone patches. In other words, in my reading, the charred grains did not stem from a single event but from numerous repeated activities.

The grains generally derived from the floor layers nearest to the scorched-stone patches. More than 200,000 were thus found in a limited area east of scorched-stone patch B (including patch G). Comparatively fewer but still numerous cereals were also found in a limited area (including scorched-stone patch A) immediately west of patch B. Thus, in essence, the majority of grains were found up to one metre east and two west of patch B. Yet it is remarkable that some 2,000 were contained in patch B itself. It is also noteworthy that charred cereals were present practically all over the sunken floor, albeit gradually decreasing in numbers at a distance from the scorched-stone patches. Most grains were strongly heat-affected.

The quantity of charred cereals from the site of House 197 is also quite high but only little evidence of scorched stones was present and no particular observations as to details could be made. In this case, however, it was more or less due to ard-ploughing. In total some 196,000 charred cereal grains (estimate) were found at this house site (report S2001a).

I ruled out early on the explanation that carbonization of the many cereals could generally have been caused by the burning down of House 1. The strongly heat-affected cereals were present in the upper as well in the lower parts of the floor horizon without any apparent impact from burning of the floor layer or its patches. The carbonization may thus not have taken place in the floor layer outside the scorched-stone patches. A pressing question arises with regard to the kinds of activity all these carbonized plant materials might represent. In my view, processes of drying or roasting must figure highly among the possible explanations. Could the charring be an expression of such processes going wrong? Or might it even relate to deliberate charring for certain purposes? For instance, if intended for sacrifices, might the cereals have been made "eternally" durable on purpose through excessive carbonization? The abundant presence of charred cereals in the sites of Houses 1 and 197 in actual fact might also point to deliberate charring of cereals as a possible primary explanation for their presence. Examples of depositions such as the find from Enkehøj of a total of 3.5 litres of carbonized cereals in a beaker and its surrounding pit might, in particular, support this kind of interpretation (Møbjerg, Jensen & Mikkelsen 2007:17 & 31). Two other pits from this settlement might also further support this.

In trying to understand how and why the charring of the macrofossils came about, it might be fruitful to briefly reflect further on some of the possible reasons for harvested cereals being brought into contact with heat. If a portion of the cereals were harvested in a relatively moist state, I presume that it could have been necessary to carry out a drying process to be able to preserve the cereals during the winter. Repeated mishaps from drying cereals is thus one possible explanation.

We do not know much about the cooking practices of the period and it is therefore an open question as to which kinds of food the residents prepared. As concerns, for instance, cereals such as naked barley, I imagine that one of the options was to mix it with a proportionate amount of liquid and cook it into a kind of porridge. Even if some cooking processes got out of control, it is hardly imaginable that this could account for so many charred cereals.

Another possibility might be the roasting of cereals for immediate or later consumption. During such activities, it is obvious that, through mishap or less careful handling, grains could get spilt and thereby come into contact more directly with temperatures capable of causing carbonization. Roasting after initial germination in connection with the production of fermented beverages could also have been a possibility. However, no direct traces of germinated grains or malt were reported from the scientific examinations.

We must also consider that, prior to possible grinding, the handling of wheat presumably involved hulling it, and the process could likely have been easier when the wheat was roasted immediately before. However, naked barley generally made up the majority of charred cereals in the house and this crop would hardly need roasting. Such a process does not therefore seem to provide the explanation for the amount of charred cereals.

Scorched-stone patches and emergence of low zones

The general layout of the sunken areas was often more or less in broad, bathtub-like forms and the highest areas were usually found in the peripheries, whereas the low zones were not necessarily observed right in the middle of the floor.

The low zones within the boundaries of the sunken floors can be distinguished from the pits by their very smooth deepening and the floor layers, when present, will follow down into the levels of a low zone. In contrast with this, a soil patch will have soil deviating from the floor layers and usually have marked limits. The concrete locations of the low zones in the Resengaard houses are documented by many – between a hundred and two hundred – floor level measurements and their positions compared to the scorched-stone patches are quite interesting.

The development of low zones in most cases took place in relation to certain areas of activity. It thus appears that low zones at Resengaard, in most instances, developed close to or directly in and just around the areas where the activities of the scorched-stone patches were performed. In relation to the low zones, the scorched-stone patches were found mainly in their centres (Houses 134 & 138), close to the south (House 42, House 130, & House 2, the western patch), close to the east (House 1 & House 197), close to the east and north (House 13), and to the west (House 41, House 200 & House 2, the eastern patch). Finally, in the site of House 128, the scorched-stone patches were found east and west of the low zone. When it comes to House 14, it is worth noticing that the low zone probably by and large indicates the real centre of the extremely large, ard-ploughed area with heat-affected/cracked stones.

We can state that the analysis of the sunken floors in the longhouses at Resengaard demonstrates that low zones and scorched-stone patches were mostly linked together spatially. Concerning the three minor houses with scorched-stone patches, it appears that the low zones also developed in the areas near these.

I argue that repeated removals of spilt substances and contaminated subsoil as part of the floor cleaning was a direct activity resulting in the emergence of significant low zones in the sunken floors. The low zones would, in this way, presumably have evolved little by little. And yet it is not possible, on the basis of the existing material, to prove exactly which kinds of activity made the cleaning necessary, although I presume that cooking and other kinds of food management could have been a main cause.

Scorched-stone patches and artefact placements

I have, in the above, suggested that the scorched-stone patches could represent activities of drying, roasting, or deliberate charring, as well as cooking and general interior heating. It appears that a number of other activities may often have been carried out in the vicinity of these patches, judging by the presence of various artefacts left in the sunken-floor horizons. In other words, these soil features, characterized by their contents of heat-affected/cracked stones, often charred organic materials, and usually accompanied by low zones, combined with the presence of various artefacts within and nearby, on the whole point to the multiple functions of these spaces.

As we have seen, no complete clay pots were found at Resengaard and the majority of the potsherds belonged to the secondary fills of the house sites. And yet ceramic remainders were also recorded in all sunken-floor horizons from longhouses and certain minor houses.

The ceramics were spread somewhat differently in the three longhouse sites on the northwest terrace. In the site of House 1, the pottery remainders were found mainly in the eastern half of the sunken floor, although a cluster was found immediately west of the middle, to the north. In the site of House 2, the fragments of pots were found in the eastern as well as the western parts of the sunken floor and thus the distribution is in accordance with the placement of a scorched-stone patch in both floor parts, although remarkably few potsherds were found close to the eastern scorched-stone patch. In the site of House 41, the pottery fragments were recorded almost exclusively in the middle part of the sunken floor, and small potsherd clusters were found north and southwest of the scorched-stone patch.

More to the south, three other house sites also gave fine evidence of the spread of pottery in the sunken-floor horizons. In the site of House 42, the fragments of pots were found mainly north and northwest of the large scorched-stone patch, as well as a single potsherd immediately west of it. In the site of House 128, the fragments of pots were recovered from the middle and western part of the sunken floor. The potsherds appeared chiefly in two clusters in the scorched-stone patch and were more dispersed to the west. In the site of House 200, the potsherds were found mainly in two clusters north and west of the scorched-stone patch. Somewhat to the southeast, a clay spoon fragment was left.

Overall, we repeatedly see a close relationship between ceramics and the scorched-stone patches in the sunken-floor horizons of the Resengaard longhouses. Whether the pottery remainders found directly in and nearby are evidence of traces of cooking activities or other kinds of doings cannot be further qualified from the present analysis but it seems plausible that cooking usually took place here. The spread of ceramics across other parts of the sunken floors could perhaps point to quite varied activities with different kinds of pottery handling but it is difficult to substantiate this further at present.

Many of the functions of the different clay pots will hardly be detectable directly due to clear traces of wear or other alterations to the original surface but ceramics with soot represent interesting remainders in relation to the scorched-stone patches. The black, burned organic material may thus provide evidence that some heating activities took place and continued to the extent that it resulted in carbonization and, in several instances, a regular soot crust (Fig. 4.72). Soot is observable on the upper as well as the lower parts of the vessels. From a source-critical point of view, it is necessary to be aware that soot could also stem from processes after fragmentation of the clay pots. However, in such cases, one might presumably also expect soot on the broken sides and this has not been observed on these particular potsherds. It therefore seems reasonable to understand the presence of the soot on the potsherds as resulting from processes that mainly took place before fragmentation.

From Resengaard, some limited areas with soot are observed on certain clay pot upper inner sides (RE92aa, RE176aa, RE310aa, RE310ab, RE693ab, RE693aa, RE678ae, RE833aa, & RE858aa). Three small areas of soot crust are also noted (RE310ab, RE678ae, & RE858aa). Interestingly there are also a couple of examples of soot on the outer sides of the upper parts (RE833aa, RE692ab, & RE858aa).

On the lower clay pot parts, soot is observed on fragments from 15 clay pots (RE6ab, RE6ac, RE7aa, RE11ac, RE25aa, RE442aa, RE562aa, RE632aa, RE694ag, RE695ae, RE702ai, RE798bh, RE798bj, RE854aa, & RE900ba). The soot on the lower parts is, in several instances, also found as crust, except as regards certain sherds (RE562aa, RE632aa, RE694ag, & RE798bh). A few of these crusts are relatively thick, for instance from House 1 (RE6ab). Yet rather thin crusts are also observed in the assemblage (RE6ac). The charred material could presumably, in many cases, be the remnants of what the vessels contained as of the last time of use and information on the specific contents would, of course, be of great interest for the research. Resources have not, however, been available to launch such scientific examinations as concerns Resengaard. It cannot of course be excluded that some of the soot might even derive from earlier use, considering the relative roughness of the inner sides of much of the pottery. It seems plausible to presume that it would have been a difficult task to fully clean the inner bottoms of the ceramics without damaging the surface. In this respect, the preserved crust on the lower parts of a vessel (RE7aa) from House 1 is interesting. The soot crust is not well preserved on the exposed parts of the inner sides but protected where a recession in the surface appears. This might indicate an attempt to clean the clay pot coarsely.

It is interesting that the soot and soot crusts on the lower part of the vessels are observed on the inner sides, often quite near the lowest part but only exceptionally directly at the bottom. The soot was possibly burned away when the bottoms came into direct contact with relatively high temperatures from below, whereas higher up the sides the warmth would not remove the organic residue. An example of soot crust on the clay pot bottom can be found in one pit (RE695ae).

Contrary to my expectations, the observed soot and soot crust areas on the upper clay pot side is only noted on an open bowl with simple rim (RE693aa) in one instance, whereas in all other recognizable instances it relates to vessels with elaborate rims, of which some (RE310aa, RE310ab & RE1059) were rather high and more or less barrel shaped.

Clay pots used for cooking were presumably heated up time and again. Perhaps the warming was sometimes mild and, in reality, undamaging to the pottery

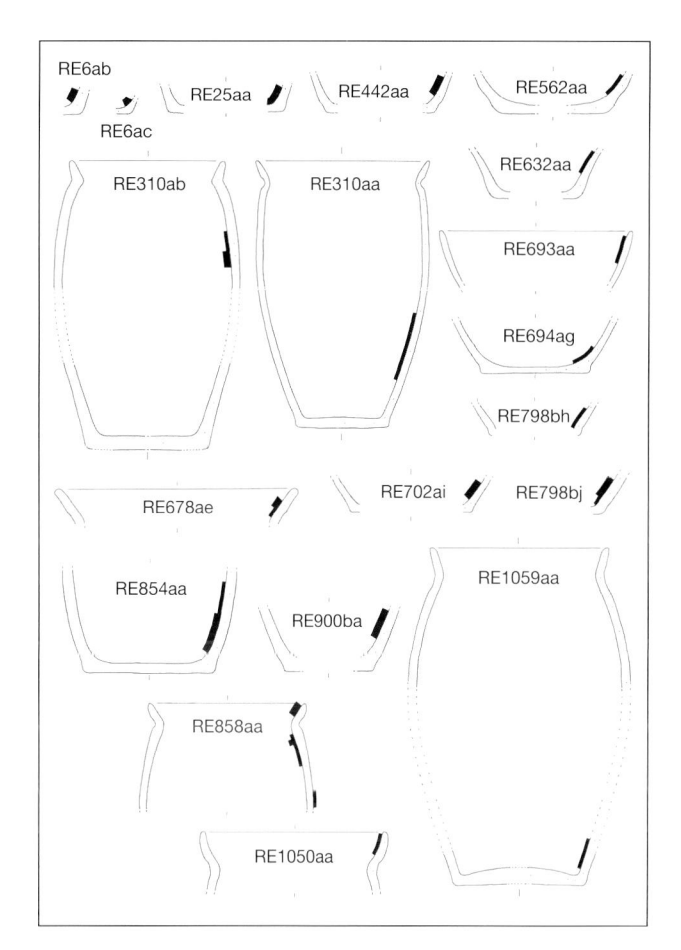

Fig. 4.72. Resengaard. Examples of soot and soot crust on pottery. Around 2-3% of the clay pots appear to have soot traces and, more rarely, soot crust (see Catalogue A). Symbols: The thick marking is soot crust, the thin is soot.

wares. However, having been heated in a regular fire place, secondary burning to a degree that it changed the ware of the vessels seems visible in some instances (e.g. RE655ad, RE695af, & RE695aj). Such damage possibly exists in several instances but the traces are not always safely determinable (such as RE484ac, RE695aa, & RE976ac). I have noted a single example (RE694ag) belonging to a pit to show heavy secondary burning as well as preserved soot on the lower part of the inner side.

It was not always the most robust and strongly built clay pots that were used for heating and cooking. Actually, we have examples from other settlements where finer ware clay pots appear to have been applied for such purposes. From the much earlier Marienlyst Strand, a delicately ornamented and relatively thin-walled vessel (MA4aa), of which many fragments are preserved, in my reading appears to have been greatly exposed to heat.

Location		House	Scraping	Axe chopping	Knife cutting	Polishing/sharpening	Smoothening	Hammering/crushing	Raw flint handling	Cooking/pottery handling	Heating with sunken stone-paved fireplace	Heating with stone-free fireplace	Heating with deep sunken fireplace	Drying/roasting/charring/cooking/heating	Bronze casting/other bronze handling	Beer brewing/storing	Weaving	Supposed anvil activities, unspecified
Resengaard	Longhouses	1	X				X	X	X	X				X			X	X
		2	X		X		X	X	X	X				X				X
		13						X	X					X				X
		14	X		X			X		X				X				
		41								X				X				X
		42	X					X	X					X				
		128	X		X	X		X		X				X				X
		130	X							X				X				
		134								X				X				X
		138								X	X			X				
		197								X				X				
		200	X			X		X		X				X				X
	Minor houses with scorched-stone patches	202												X				
		240	X				X			X				X				X
		289												X				X
	Minor houses	10								X								
		12																
		84																
		112	X															X
		143																
		158		X														
		183																
		193																X
		198	X															X
		268																
	Short house	201																X
Gåsemose		1																
Kluborg II		5	X				X			X	X	X		X	X		X	X
Glattrup I/III		5								X								X
		6			X					X							X	
Marienlyst Strand		1																
Granlygård		2																
		3																
		6																
Hellegård		122	X				X	X		X				X				X
		35																
Glattrup IV		3						X		X			X			X		
		5						X		X			X	X		X		
		7											X			X		
Rosgårde		1								X				X				
Tromgade		1	X					X		X				X				X
		2						X		X				X				X
		414																

One kind of pottery that would likely have been important for storing foods and other items were the large vessels. These would have been rather conspicuous in the house interiors but are now, unfortunately, only found as more or less small fragments in different contexts.

Apart from the suggested beer storage concerning the longhouses at Glattrup IV, we have seen little evidence that could point directly to the use of ceramics for storage but I suggest that some of the pottery in the pit at the northeast corner of the sunken floor in House 197 was used for this purpose. Among the minor houses, particularly interesting is not least House 10, the sunken-floor horizon to the northwest of which held the remainders of several clay pots which might well have involved storage functions. Storage might likewise have been a function of the pottery handling in House 268 and House 240 but this latter also had a scorched-stone patch and therefore the pottery might also have been used for cooking. By filling up these minor sunken areas after use, a great deal of pottery was also present in their fills. Plentiful ceramics were also found in the secondary fills of House 289, whereas no potsherds belonged to the sunken-floor horizon. In these four minor houses storage in pottery could very well have taken place.

When it comes to artefacts of flint and other stone, we know that such items have been recorded in and near the scorched-stone patches, and it seems plausible that some of these were used for cooking activities. We have earlier considered the presence of hammering or crushing tools. Interestingly, stone tools that might indicate polishing activities such that the surfaces of soft materials could be given a smoother appearance are really rare among the floor artefacts.

Unlike stone tools, flint items are much more common in the sunken-floor horizons (Fig. 4.73). Indoors, in a moderate number of longhouses at Resengaard, raw flint handling or chipping of some kind presumably took place, judging by the presence of nodules. It has also been proposed that raw flint handling/chipping was performed in an area with the presence of scrapers and numerous tiny chips in the site of House 122 at Hellegård. Furthermore, I suggested that raw flint handling/chipping was carried out in House 1 and House 2 at Tromgade and presumably also in House 3 and House 5 at Glattrup IV.

The account of worked flint found in the floor horizons has already been presented systematically in the foregoing and it appears that, all in all, we have limited evidence of this. However, it is maybe not so strange that sharp-edged flints did not occur in large numbers on the sunken floors because the edges might have accidentally caused damage to the residents. In line with this, very few, regular flint knives were actually recovered from the sunken-floor horizons of the longhouses. Some pieces of flint daggers and sickles were found and it cannot be excluded that, in an indoor context, these tools might have been used for certain cutting activities.

At Resengaard, in the site of House 2, the large stone to the southwest and the flint within the boundary of soil feature K might more or less belong to related working processes. The flint waste scattered around this stone could hardly have been accidental. In the site of House 1, a little flint waste also came to light (RE153) from the soil of the easternmost posthole of a roof-bearing post but, in general, we have to realize that the traces of flint chippings are scarce despite the fact that the excavation teams gave high priority to excavating the sunken-floor horizons very meticulously during the fieldwork at Resengaard. In the site of House 42, a flint flake concentration (RE597) stems from an area of some ½ m² to the north-east in the sunken-floor horizon. The results of scrutinizing several thousand litres of floor horizon soil, first and foremost from House 1 and House 197, substantiate the general absence of quantities of small flint waste in the sunken-floor horizons. The excavation team performed this work by means of water-sieving through a 2 millimetre net, primarily to catch large amounts of charred cereals although the process would also have caught every

◂ *Fig. 4.73. Numerous indoor activities are proposed for the 43 sunken-floor house sites. Most have indications of at least one activity. At Glattrup IV, the sunken fireplace in the site of House 3 had in the fills a couple of heat-cracked stones which hardly had any direct relevance to the fireplace. The column on drying/roasting/charring/cooking/heating relates to the working of the scorched-stone patches. Activities of an unspecified nature are proposed for the stone anvils. Food storage can, only in a single instance, be suggested, due to the presence of fragments from several clay pots in the northeast corner (pit F) of House 197 at Resengaard. At this settlement, the "antique" flint axe (RE20ea) at the site of House 1 could have been used as such but this is not directly suggested here. At Granlygård, activities related to weaving likely took place in the area of the outdoor pit 4 but this is not indicated in the table.*

tiny piece of flint above that size. Only sporadically did small flint pieces come to light in this way. In my view, this could imply that small-scale flint working for everyday purposes would have taken place mainly outdoors or in some sheds at Resengaard. When the flint chipping took place inside the longhouses, the residents must have had a rather efficient way of collecting flint waste in order to dump it somewhere outside. Interesting in this respect are the many tiny flakes from a large pit in the site of House 7 at Glattrup IV. In the central Limfjord region, this is a rare case of such flint waste being documented from a pit in the periphery of a sunken floor. It could represent the disposal of flint waste from some flint-chipping activity in the house interior. At Marienlyst Strand, flint waste was deposited within a small area in pit 4, placed some distance from the sunken-floor house; likewise in culture layer 76 at Tromgade, many flakes from pressure flaking were found deposited in a concentration. These cases might both represent examples of flint pieces collected from tool production inside or outside a house and then deposited in a dump site, being a pit and a culture layer respectively. In all, it seems that rather careful handling of flint waste took place at Resengaard and the other settlements in question in the central Limfjord region. Likewise, the secondary fills over the former sunken floors or the garbage in the culture layers do not appear to be characterized by quantities of tiny flint waste. It should here be noted as concerns flint-knapping activities that it has recently been proposed that three zones with flint waste might be expected, being the activity area itself, a "toss zone" where waste is casually thrown and a "dump zone" with deliberate deposition (Grøn 2009:157pp). To what extent this might also concern the flint-knapping activities within the longhouses at Resengaard or at the other settlements in question is not clear. As regards Bejsebakken, building A505 is interpreted as having been used for flint knapping and is considered to have been a kind of open shed (Sarauw 2006:30).

At a pinch, many flint flakes could, of course, act as knives but only a small number are here considered to be regular knives. From the secondary fills above the sunken floors and the waste areas on the upper part of the hill at Resengaard, we know in all of several thousand pieces of simple flint waste, also including some knives. The flint waste consists of highly varying shapes and sizes. After abandonment and tearing down of the houses, it cannot be excluded that the sunken areas may have been used for a short period for different flint-working activities. However, priority has not been given to further research into this subject during the fieldwork and repeated ard-ploughing would presumably spoil some such possible traces.

Flint scrapers were found in many sunken-floor horizons at Resengaard. This concerns eight of the longhouse sites (1, 2, 14, 41, 42, 128, 130, & 200) and those of two minor houses (198 & 240). By way of example, from the sunken-floor horizon of House 1, a total of six scrapers belong, respectively, to a scorched-stone patch, a low zone, two patches of simple soil depressions and two more to a floor area without recorded soil features. A seventh scraper was found in the fills of a posthole of a centre post. Evidently, this spread does not point to a particular attachment to the scorched-stone patches in this case.

The placements of the flint hammers appear to be relatively unaccompanied by other items. A function of these tools was presumably the working of stone items in order to shape them, e.g. stone axes and quern stones. It is quite remarkable that we so often find the flint hammers in the form of a neatly roundish or moderately oval shape. The basis would, in many cases, have been ordinary, nearly fist-sized flint nodules that had achieved these shapes not least during long use with moderate hammering, because the flint tool would otherwise burst into pieces. From Resengaard, the ordinary stone hammers of materials such as granite and quartzite have not been geologically examined. I suggest that these could have been used as pestles as well as hammers. The seemingly divergent placements of these tools and the flint hammers might substantiate the idea I earlier put forward that certain stone hammers could belong to cooking processes in the vicinity of the scorched-stone patches.

Surprisingly, quern stones are mostly absent from the sunken-floor longhouse sites at Resengaard and many other locations regionally. This concerns, in particular, their lower parts, such as for instance at Myrhøj (Jensen, J.A. 1973:76). The residents must have removed such items from the longhouses during abandonment and could very well have had some veneration for these functional and durable items, maybe often inherited from earlier generations.

The find spots of the flint arrowheads seem to reveal another pattern, sometimes being placed more at a distance from the scorched-stone patches. The specimen from the sunken floor of House 1 was found c. 2.5 m southeast of the edge of one of the scorched-stone patches. In the site of House 128, an arrowhead was found far to the northwest, c. 4.2 m from the edge of scorched-stone patch B, while a roughout was recovered only 0.7 m from the edge of this patch. An almost complete arrowhead was recorded in the site of House 197 to the northwest, by the edge of the sunken floor but quite far from the scorched-stone patch, and a roughout was recovered c. 2.5 m from it. In the site of House 200, two relatively large, fragmented arrowheads were recovered. One was found 2.5 m west of the edge of the scorched-stone patch but another just 0.1 m from this edge. In the site of House 240, a roughout was found c. 0.6 m west of the edge of the scorched-stone patch.

Two minor axes, both well-shaped and polished, belong to the site of House 158, being from the sunken-floor horizon and ascribed the secondary fills, respectively (RE620eb & RE1045ea). This minor house might very well have had a quite special function because it was also placed on rather east-sloping terrains towards the southeast of the hill. An axe roughout also likely belongs to the secondary fills of this building (RE1042ee). In my reading, it seems plausible that these minor flint axes may have been used for some kind of relatively light axe-chopping activities.

An axe fragment (RE250ec) from the secondary fills of the site of House 12 is polished on the broad sides and missing the cutting edge but the proportions of the preserved part indicate that it belongs to a Late Neolithic, broad-edged axe. Another axe fragment (RE250eb) from the same fills has a "hanging" edge and obviously stems from the Single Grave Culture. It therefore could have been part of a reused axe or a specimen used as a nodule. Some "antique" axes were also found in the contexts of sunken-floor horizons and secondary fills, presumably for special purposes, such as the antique found in the site of the very late House 1 directly on the sunken floor but which could have been hanging on a nearby post, as discussed above. This relates to axes and fragments from Funnel Beaker Culture and Single Grave Culture (RE20ea, RE250eb & RE250ec).

No Late Neolithic flint axes were found in the floor horizons of the longhouses at Resengaard except as regards a fragment in the site of House 41, indicating that flint axes from this time were generally becoming very rare in settlement contexts. Interestingly, the complete flint axes from the youngest Resengaard contexts are of a very modest size (re. the above-mentioned from contexts of House 158 and a tiny specimen from a votive offering in a pit, see later). This might indicate that the relatively heavy flint axes went out of use early on at the settlement. My interpretation is that by the beginning of the time covered by the provisional Resengaard chronology, about 1900 calBC, the flint axes produced in the Late Neolithic were already no longer much in use in the households locally. Anyway, it appears that such axes had by and large been discarded by c. 1800 calBC, judging by the provisional chronological analysis of the Resengaard finds. Metal axes must instead have broadly taken over by then at Resengaard (*cf.* Vandkilde 1996).

A number of activities would presumably have required a kind of firm underlay, for instance when pounding, hammering or scraping. Such underlay could have been wood, stone or other material but, unfortunately, such items would only survive in the actual soils if they were in varying kinds of stone. Scraps of organic materials exposed to such processes would not be preserved. One example of a firm underlay, or as I have termed it a "stone anvil", is the semi-buried stone in the eastern part of the site of the short House 201 at Resengaard. Stone anvils were present at several sites of minor houses. This concerns two of the above-mentioned, namely Houses 240 and 289. It furthermore concerns Houses 112, 193, 198 and the short House 201. The possible function of more or less sizeable stones in the floor contexts has always attracted some attention when carrying out fieldwork at all the new house sites presented here. However, it is regrettable that during the settlement investigations we did not have much time to focus on the functions of stones that might have been used as a support for the different working processes in the houses. These implements which, by their nature, could have had different qualities (such as smooth edges, sharp edges, evenly rounded areas etc.) may have been practical for many different everyday activities and for use in special work processes as well. At Resengaard, between one and eight stone anvils were present in eight of the twelve longhouse sites but none in the four remaining ones. Interestingly, in the site of House 128, the more sizeable stones that I interpret as anvils were placed in a semi-circular row at some distance internally. Contrasting with the absence in some longhouses, I propose that the site of House 2 at Tromgade had a very special floor situation, with nine stone anvils, almost paralleled by the eight in the site of House 1 at Resengaard. Yet, I am not able to suggest any concrete activity in relation to some of these.

No significant finds were usually made on the ramps and near the entrances during excavation and this is hardly to be expected, either. Yet in many other sunken-floor parts of all longhouses, some areas appeared to have no soil patches, pits, artefacts or rubbish. These "free spaces", as I prefer to call them, could however also appear to be relatively close to the sources of heating, i.e. the scorched-stone patches. I find it reasonable to assume that some of these free spaces, not least in cold seasons, would have been attractive as sleeping areas.

Vestiges in further house sites from the Limfjord region

We shall first look at some of the results of the apparent spatial relationships between scorched-stone patches, low zones and artefacts at other settlements from the central Limfjord region. In the site of House 1 at Tromgade, a low zone was observable in the same area as the almost horseshoe-shaped scorched-stone patch, while in the site of House 2, a low zone was present in the area of the eastern scorched-stone patch. At Hellegård, in the site of House 122, a low zone was observed in the central area of the floor together with two scorched-stone patches. At these sites, the close spatial relationship between low zones and heating areas thus corresponds to the observations from Resengaard. At Kluborg II in the site of House 5, two scorched-stone patches were observed in the eastern part of the floor whereas the low zone was observable in its western part. Presumably due to the very special traits and activities of this house, the low zone had exceptionally emerged in quite another floor area to the scorched-stone patches. As considered, the low zone in the site of House 1 at Rosgårde also appeared in an atypical area in relation to the scorched-stone patch. At Gåsemose in the site of House 1, abundant heat-affected/cracked stones may bear witness to the use of such stones, probably in a similar manner to in the longhouses at Resengaard and many other central Limfjord region settlements. The case of Marienlyst Strand was considered above.

When turning to the ceramics in the sunken-floor horizons of the longhouses at Hellegård and Tromgade, it appears that pottery remainders by and large had a corresponding relationship with the scorched-stone patches, as seen at Resengaard, whereas Rosgårde does not contribute relevant data in this regard. At Kluborg II in the site of House 5, a relatively large number of pottery find spots reveals a particular distribution, showing few potsherds directly in or near the scorched-stone patch A. Many find spots, interestingly, were recorded almost in the pattern of an S-curve, beginning from west and north of pit N and H to the east and south of soil feature D, C, and B (Fig. 4.45). This concerns a total of 12 spots which were mostly placed in areas with no patches in the floor, apart from patch C. Such a pattern has not been observed before. When the pottery remainders were not located particularly near to the scorched-stone patches, this may thus indicate that other kinds of pottery handling were predominant in a rather special longhouse.

Just like at Resengaard, flint knives were seldom found in the sunken floor horizons of buildings at the other central Limfjord region settlements (Fig. 4.73). At Glattrup I/III in the site of House 6, two knives were recorded in the western part of the sunken-floor horizon. At Tromgade in the site of House 1, a flint flake with possible traces of retouch from use was found somewhat west of a scorched-stone patch and, in the site of House 2, a flake, presumably worn from use, was found south of a scorched-stone patch.

When it comes to flint scrapers, a single specimen was found somewhat west of a scorched-stone patch at Tromgade in the site of House 1. No scrapers are known from the sunken floors of Kluborg II, Glattrup I/III, Glattrup IV or Rosgårde. In contrast to this scant presence, really strong evidence of scrapers was recorded in the sunken-floor horizon of House 122 at Hellegård, where by far the most scrapers were recovered in a concentration at a marked distance from the scorched-stone patches.

No stone hammers/pestles at Glattrup I/III, Glattrup IV or Rosgårde belonged to the sunken floors, while a few were recorded in the sunken-floor horizons at Kluborg II, Hellegård, and Tromgade. At Kluborg II in the site of House 5, a total of three stone hammers were found in the floor context. One of these (KL45ea) I consider to be a specialized hammer, possibly connected to the activities in the middle of the western half of the floor. Two other stone hammers also seem somewhat specialized. In the site of House 2 at Tromgade, a stone hammer/pestle was found in the northern part of a scorched-stone patch.

We now turn to relevant vestiges in further areas of the region, and we can begin with Myrhøj. Even though the publication of the three house sites makes it difficult to identify the positions of sunken-floor finds or to state a clear distinction between finds from the floors and the secondary fills, it does mark out some basis for considering the activities that probably took place at the settlement (Jensen, J.A. 1973:61pp). First of all, stones with heat impact were abundantly present and this might indicate a use more or less corresponding to what has been proposed for the scorched-stone patches at Resengaard. Large amounts of worked flint, many scrapers, many stone hammers, some flint hammers, a few small pieces of whetstones, many pieces of quern stones, some flint axes, a few borers and burins, a few pieces of loom weights, and comprehensive and varied pottery material derive from the settlement as a whole. It therefore seems plausible that, not least, activities of flint working, scraping, hammering/crushing, sharpening/polishing, grinding, axe-chopping, borer/burin use, weaving, and pottery handling/cooking took place at the settlement.

At Stendis, it is possible that several finds belonged to a floor horizon (Skov 1978; 1982). As proposed earlier, however, it is complicated to clarify this because the sunken area probably represented two sunken floors. Fine pottery and stone artefacts may, in any case, indicate different activities at the site (Skov 1982, Fig. 3, 5, & 6). The remainders of a colander were present (Ebbesen 1978).

At Tastum I, the house is considered to be a regular site of fire and the preserved floor layer was marked by charcoal and dust from charred material (Simonsen 1983:82). The spread of worked flint and potsherds connected to the sunken floor could presumably point to varying activities but these have not yet been rigorously analysed. The fire was presumably started deliberately, as the find material mostly concerns pieces of pottery and simple tools of different kinds. Charred, wooden items were not found and hence it seems that the residents may well have had time to remove such things.

Some finds are still unpublished from the eastern part of the Limfjord region but the presentation of the Bejsebakken settlement is very important. Here, the main method for excavating ceramics was to collect them within a square metre grid, while more important potsherds appearing in concentrations or being supplied with ornamentation were, in many cases, taken up individually (Sarauw 2007b:15, note 5). The Bejsebakken find material primarily stemmed from secondary depositions and the large find material has not been analysed in depth (Sarauw 2006:12).

Yet some of the floor traits concern a number of patches indicating that "special activities sometimes took place here" (Sarauw 2008a:89). Thus, in view of the Resengaard results in particular, certain very important observations were made at this settlement. This concerns the presence of soil features described as "… faint, pit-like depressions which often occur on the bottom of the sunken part. House A643 contains four and A1043 contains six very systematically arranged small pits, whereas in House A556, A606, A827, and A896, all of which contained 3-5 depressions/pits, these were arranged less systematically" (Sarauw 2006:52). Their presence at Bejsebakken confirms that these particular patches are not solely a Resengaard phenomenon, nor a central Limfjord region one. In the site of House 1 at Diverhøj, some floor patches also appear to correspond to those from Resengaard (Asingh 1988:145p & Fig. 19).

Interestingly, some longhouse sites are also characterized by a scarcity of finds. For instance, the site at Drosselvej, from the western part of the region, contained relatively few finds but, judging by the pottery, it stems from the Late Neolithic/Bronze Age transition (Bo Steen, report U1999b). Although the house site seems to have suffered greatly from the impact of recent ploughing, the sunken floor appeared reasonably intact. In Himmerland, such sparse finds also seems to be characteristic of the house site from Skringstrup Øst (Kurt G. Overgaard & Martin Mikkelsen, report U2002b). Its sunken floor was only partly excavated because the artefacts that appeared to be preserved were largely insignificant. The sunken floor from Kås Hovedgård II in the central Limfjord region was also marked by an absence of noteworthy finds although several artefacts belong to the secondary fills (Inge Kjær Kristensen, report U2002a).

4.7. Repeated everyday doings performed in the activity spaces?

In the ongoing discussions of the interpretation of former life in dwellings, Colin Richards put forward – when writing on Late Neolithic Orkney houses – that the "…actual process of building a house and delineating space effectively draws on social and cosmological ideas of order; architecture does not suddenly come into existence but is constructed by people and is therefore defined by their interpretations and intentions. As space has no intrinsic qualities any interpretation of spatial symbolism is dependent on the invocation of meaning through the presence of people. Understanding comes in terms of the social experiences of those who lived within the houses, moved around the settlements, and understood the organization and classification of the world. Since the routines of life incorporate and recreate meaning, a recursive relationship exists in which spatial order may be frequently redefined without any alteration to the physical configuration of the spatial context" (Richards 1990:113).

These words remind us that what we may actually observe concerning the pits, patches, artefacts and plant remainders of the sunken floors does not necessarily represent a state of long duration everywhere but might perhaps, in some instances, rather be the result of changing ideas on the proper use of spaces and dynamic alternating situations, "frozen" at the time of abandonment. Conceivably, some floor situations in the longhouses could have remained relatively static for a long time, others might have been exposed to more or less gradual modifications, and some situations could have been exposed to direct shifts in notions on – and uses of – certain spaces, while in all three instances keeping the material frames, such as outer walls and interior arrangements, unchanged.

When we now turn to the subject of what, from a more holistic viewpoint, we may actually come across when we scrutinize the traces found in the sunken floors longhouses, we could first ask what general picture we obtain from the floor observations?

Again, we can take the opportunity to consult the finds and observations from the site of House 1 at Resengaard and the results generated from its study because it is precisely this house site that has been pivotal with regard to several topics (Fig. 4.4). Let us recapitulate some more general considerations relevant to our interpretations.

Far more objects often derive from the secondary fills than from the floor horizons. In the case of House 1, almost all objects stemming from the secondary fills belong to three inventory numbers (RE6, RE11 & RE12). From these, a total of 414 potsherds, 454 pieces of worked flint, 43 pieces of burned flint and a few other items have come to light, such as for instance two fossilized sea urchins (RE6), in total 914 items. Sometimes, the burned flint in this account had also been worked. On the other hand, only 52 potsherds, 30 flint items (mostly worked flint), 10 pieces of burned flint (including tool fragments), 1 loom weight fragment and a tiny piece of burned bone, in all 94 items, came from the sunken-floor horizon. With a total of 1,008 pieces in all, excluding the numerous macrofossils, it appears that around 90 % derived from secondary fills, even in this case of a well-preserved house site, free from later disturbances.

When not reasonably sure of a clear connection with the sunken-floor horizon, one aspect of the above is that we may, as a precaution, have included some finds in the secondary fills during excavation. Some items that were originally left in the sunken-floor horizons may thus be lacking. And yet, in my judgment, these would be relatively few.

Further, it is my understanding that the finds from the sunken-floor horizon primarily represent the last period of use of the house, although some tools and other items may still remain in the sunken-floor horizons, having been left – unintentionally, I presume – during earlier stages of its lifetime. This might, for instance, concern small flint items or potsherds trodden down into softer parts of the subsoil or objects perhaps left in patches and filled up pits that were not removed by later deepening of the floor surfaces or transformations of the actual use of the floor spaces. This might have been particularly the case in some areas closer to the walls, where continued floor deepening would presumably have been slower. However, such items likely represent only a very small fraction of the finds. Hence, what we see mainly stems from the last period of functioning.

When looking at the overall picture of the sunken-floor spaces, it appears that the roof-bearing posts of the floor were evidently obstacles to the free placement of activities. If we assume that the sunken-floor area between two centre posts would have been organized in such a way as to give priority to an adjoining use north-south, this seems – interestingly – not to have been the case in House 1. The three major patches to the south (C, D, & E) did not cross the middle line of the floor and neither did those to the north really. Instead, it seems that the presence of posts divided the space of the sunken floor into two halves, a northern and a southern aisle. A narrow "passage" thereby appears to have existed east-west immediately south of the roof-bearing posts. It would presumably have been convenient for the residents to move between the different activity spaces of the sunken floor and it would also lead to the entrance area via the oblique ramp. The presumed extra supporting posts placed south of the posts along the central longitudinal axis at some point in time, hardly caused much inconvenience to passage.

On the whole, the ordering of the sunken-floor patches within the prearranged physical frames, in my reading, gives the impression that it was rather well-organized and most likely practical for many everyday activities. A central "passage" such as this might possibly also have been arranged in some of the other longhouses.

When we take a closer look at the differences between the possible activities of the two aisles, some interesting traits appear. It is clear that the dissimilarity in activities was not of an absolute nature between them. Flint objects of varying kinds were found both to the north and to the south. The same goes for pottery of different kinds. However, what we do see are marked differences regarding the relative presence of tools and utensils made out of flint, stone and clay. Recovered around the areas of the southern soil patches C, E and 11 (not a clear patch) were, respectively, three, two, and two flint nodules. Conversely, just a single flint nodule was found to the north in the area of patch B. Correspondingly, five scrapers were found in the northern aisle and only two in the southern.

Most find spots with potsherds were found in the northern aisle. This concerns, not least, two rather significant concentrations. The low zone of the sunken floor was, as we have seen, observed to the north near pottery finds and scorched-stone patches. To this portrait of the interior organization must be added the observation that some objects were exclusively attributed to certain soil features to the north or to the south. Examples are a flint arrowhead and a flint piece with notch found in the southern half and, opposite, a single, fragmented loom weight placed in the northern aisle. Furthermore, the observation that significant soil features with heat-affected/cracked stones were rather conspicuously placed solely in the northern aisle must be noted.

Judging by these artefacts and patches, the aisles seem to have been characterized by different functions. In essence, my interpretation is that the northern aisle may likely have been the scene of weaving, scraping, hammering/crushing, drying/roasting/charring of cereals and cooking/heating. Opposite this, along with pottery handling/cooking, the southern aisle may mainly have been the scene of raw flint handling/chipping and less scraping activities than carried out to the north.

Remarkably, the artefacts and patches are concentrated in the eastern part of the sunken floor, which was the narrowest part of it because the building became significantly broader towards the west. This distribution may indicate that certain areas of the sunken floor were reserved for certain kinds of use that did not leave significant traces. The finds and patches in the house are thus chiefly concentrated within an area of about 25 m². The kind of activities that leave finds of non-organic material in the floor thus occupied only a minor area of the entire interior of the house to the east. Even then, some free spaces appear to have been available relatively near the scorched-stone patches in the immediate vicinity of the walls to the south, east and north, possibly reserved for sleeping.

In the remaining Resengaard longhouses, the placement of patches and artefacts in the floors mostly leave more or less large areas free of which we know nothing directly. It is not to be expected that extensive floor parts were unused, although some activities would presumably leave no evidence, such as for instance places for resting, sleeping, and keeping or storing certain things.

Finally, we shall consider the obviously important question of whether certain activities repeatedly took place at the same floor spots. Of course, varied doings might just occasionally take place here and there in an unplanned manner but the question is specifically whether certain, everyday activities usually took place in the same areas.

In my view, the pattern of activity traces would likely have been completely different if the everyday doings simply took place in shifting floor areas or even at random, i.e. if there were no divided spaces and no spatial organization of doings. And yet, from the placement of soil patches and artefacts, it is evident that certain spaces were preferred for the scorched-stone patches, and that these further played a role in the development of low zones, in the pottery distributions and in the positions of other artefacts and objects. The general division of the houses into a sunken-floor part and a ground-floor part, in addition to specific interior arrangements such as oblique ramps, dividing walls, recesses and doorways, also strongly supports the understanding that many activities were performed within rather organized floor spaces. In the case of House 13 at Resengaard, it appears that new scorched-stone patches were usually placed within a restricted area of the sunken floor. So, overall, it is evident that the placement of these was not spread all over the floor but confined to certain areas, even though no physical walls appear to have been present. The stability of placement of these patches in many other sunken floors was apparently of paramount importance for the positioning of other activities, in addition presumably to resting and sleeping. This can be considered a strong indication of a noticeable "permanence" of the placement.

Regular post-build dividing walls did not usually separate the total floor spaces used for activities. However, the archaeological investigations would not be able to recognize any traces of simple blankets, hides or the like, for instance, hanging down from the transversal beams of the roof construction and thereby forming a kind of physical division of the spaces. Of course, if such separations existed they would probably enhance the stability of performance of everyday routines within certain floor segments.

Based, not least, on the results of the analysis of the better preserved sites, it seems reasonable to state that the sunken floors in the sites of longhouses by and large do not represent a mess of varying soil features, partly eradicating or overlapping each other again and again. On the contrary, the main impression is that the activities in the sunken-floor areas appear well-ordered and organized in all instances where evaluation is possible. This would hardly have been the case if the scene of activity was shifting all the time or even frequently during the lifetime of a longhouse. Repeated everyday doings would therefore have taken place in organized spaces.

Notes

1. It has been necessary to consult the excavation directors as to whether or not certain markings and expressions in the reports mean that these finds belong to the floor horizons. This relates, in particular, to Houses 1 and 2 at Tromgade, House 1 at Marienlyst Strand, House 1 at Rosgårde and House 5 at Kluborg II.

2. On the plan drawing of House 130 at Resengaard, minor displacements of patches A and B – as well as errors in the details of their contours – are possible. This house site was also one of those investigated on a very low budget.

3. Regarding House 42 at Resengaard, minor displacements of the contours of patches A and B on the plan drawings are possible. This house site had to be excavated on a very low budget and it is likely that a more meticulous investigation of the sunken-floor horizon would have resulted in better knowledge of the soil patches and finds belonging to the floor.

4. Concerning patch A in House 5 at Kluborg II, it is expressly noted in the excavation report that it was not a regular fireplace. As concerns patch D, a cross-section sketch shows a length c. 0.50 m. Patch K was very shallow, being only a few cm deep (pers.comm. with the excavation director).

5. Concerning House 1 at Tromgade, the horseshoe shape formed by the scorched-stone patches was recorded early on in the plan drawing. At some later stage during the investigation, this patch gradually vanished due to repeated cleaning. Hereafter, only patches B and C still stood clear, and the horseshoe-shaped soil feature was left out of the final excavation report. However, here I favour showing the way it was originally recorded, albeit with the interpolation of a minor course of the outline covered by a soil bench.

6. To my knowledge, clay tubes of the same dimensions and character have never been published from other South Scandinavian sunken-floor longhouse sites or other settlement contexts.

7. Concerning House 1 at Tastum I, a sandy stratum is interpreted as a possible floor renewal layer although other explanations cannot be excluded (Simonsen 1983:82).

8. Apart from House 13 (RE640), samples of the heat-affected/cracked stones have been taken from e.g. House 128 (RE571) and House 130 (RE578).

9. As regards some of the house sites, such as two of the Glattrup IV longhouses, with fine, well-preserved sunken floors, no scorched-stone patches could be recorded despite meticulous investigations. In some instances during the investigation campaigns at Resengaard, the easy term "fireplace" (ildsted) was used when writing the preliminary fieldwork notes about the patches with the heat-affected/cracked stones (*cf.* Simonsen 1993b, Fig. 1). However, in my later consideration of all these scorched-stone patches, no clearly documented descriptions, drawings or photos point to permanent fireplaces and it would not be correct to use the term in these cases.

10. From a three-aisled Bronze Age house site at Vile in the central Limfjord region, a functional connection is evidenced between a sizeable clay pot partly dug down into the floor and a heap of scorched stones on its well-preserved bottom (Simonsen 1993a). The stones were likely used for heating water or other liquids in the large vessel.

Chapter 5

Household, livelihood and exchange

Numerous vestiges of everyday life in the longhouses have been presented in the foregoing and, in this final chapter, we shall lift our eyes from the ground, look for further evidence and put our findings into perspective. The topics to be considered and reflected upon concern, not least, some basic conditions for the households and their strategies for coping with daily life. We shall draw on examples from any time within the several hundred years of the Late Neolithic and emerging Bronze Age until approx. 1600 BC and we sometimes see significant chronological spans for the longhouses in question, as already dealt with (Ch. 3). When I furthermore put forward a model of household production below, it does not seem reasonable to narrow the timeframe down and I therefore suggest that it should concern the entire period and I realize that, within this, considerable transformations may clearly have taken place, such as reductions, expansions and alterations in production and exchange. However, when presenting three alternative outlines of longhouse functions, the time is set at around 2200 BC. It is correspondingly set at this time when discussing the number of contemporaneously existing households in the landscapes of the Limfjord region.

The chapter starts by discussing longhouse architecture and economic strategies, household compositions, and the proposed establishment of a particular place, followed by reflections on the living and working conditions inside the longhouses. It proceeds to other topics such as settlement continuity versus area continuity, relocation of dwellings, waste handling and agriculture, in which the analysis offers some apparent strategies and also points to certain cyclical aspects. Some considerations on ritual and votive depositions will also be presented. Later, suggestions on common and specialized household production are put forward and a three-level household production model is launched. Overall, these topics will echo the livelihoods of residents of the sunken-floor longhouses. Further, when considering analogies to anthropological research, household exchange becomes the centre of attention. Finally, the chapter reflects on maritime travel within and beyond the archipelagic landscape of the Limfjord region. In Ch. 5 the artefact photos are full scale or close to full scale, unless otherwise stated.

5.1. Architecture, household and local settlement

It has been proposed that architecture might be viewed as "both a container and arena of social action" (Tringham 1995:80). Other researchers have used the metaphor of a body, saying that "… houses are frequently thought of as bodies, sharing with them a common anatomy and a common life history. If people construct houses and make them in their own image, so also do they use these houses and house-images to construct themselves as individuals and as groups. At some level or other, the notion that houses are people is one of the universals of architecture. If the house is an extension of the person, it is also an extension of the self … the space of the house is inhabited not just in daily life but also in the imagination" (Carsten & Hugh-Jones 1995:3).[1]

However, it might also be important to note in this respect that no specific meaning can *a priori* be assigned to houses. Douglass W. Bailey has stated that a house "… denotes a place of worship, eating, drinking, dwelling, entertainment, farming, education, legislation, economic activity, or astral observation. Indeed the presence of numerous variations on the definition of the word inspires one contention of my argument: that any one thing, be it word, artefact, or component of the built environment, has a multitude of meanings dependent on social and material context" (Bailey 1990:22p). With these words in mind, we can begin our consideration of the functions of the sunken-floor longhouses.

Main functions of the eastern and western floor areas?

The idea of the longhouses with major sunken and unsunken floor parts has been a matter of discussion for some time but, given that reasonably broad and detailed fundament has not been brought to light, the discussion has stagnated somewhat. In this respect, the presentation of the finds from Bejsebakken was an important new contribution (Sarauw 2006; 2008a).

The interior main division of the sunken-floor longhouses appears to have been a practical arrangement: the sunken, moderately bathtub-shaped floor to the east and the rather flat ground floor to the west. Supposedly it must have been seen as a very sensible interior division since this kind of house became so characteristic and new longhouses were built again and again in this basic format for centuries.

As we have seen in the above, the core areas for everyday activities in most sunken-floor longhouses in question were the eastern parts, judging by the interior traces, which indicate their use for a wide range of activities. We shall now look at the ground floors to the west and also some suggestions concerning the overall picture of these two opposite floors. Substantial remainders of artefacts have seldom come to light from the ground floors and this also applies to longhouses with no impact from recent ploughing, being sealed below thick soil layers such as Houses 1, 41 and 197 at Resengaard. There is thus no reason to believe that source-critical factors such as modern agricultural activities were generally responsible for the relatively few finds from the ground floors. Traces of activities in these areas of the houses might thus instead be seen as conspicuous by their frequent absence. It is, however, precisely this trait that may become key to our understanding.

As a working hypothesis, I suggest that the ground-floor spaces in sunken-floor longhouses in the central Limfjord region were, in many instances, used for bulk storage of winter fodder of various kinds. This does not relate to all unsunken floors, however. House 5 at Glattrup IV is one of the obvious exceptions because quite another use appears to have predominated in this building. House 41 at Resengaard could have been another exception due to the traces in the ground floor although these could, on the other hand, perhaps simply represent activities from periods when the space was more or less empty anyway. In other words, when it comes to the presumed storage of winter fodder, it seems that at least some of the ground-floor space in some longhouses could have been reserved for regular activities, maybe for a limited season, after which the space could again have been made available for storing winter fodder.

The proposals thus far put forward on the concrete functions of the sunken floors in the longhouses from the Late Neolithic and emerging Bronze Age can be summarized as being: (1) stabling for cattle, (2) habitation and brewing/storage of alcoholic beverages, and (3) habitation and other workshop activities. Correspondingly, the suggested functions of grounds floors in the sunken-floor longhouses are: (1) habitation, (2) barn for different keeping winter fodder plus straw (see below) from the cereal harvest, and (3) brewing/storage of alcoholic beverages.

It should be noted that the use of the ground-floor areas as habitation has not, to my knowledge, been directly posited but seems to be implied in the understanding that the sunken floors of longhouses could represent stables (Gyldion 2004:41p). Brewing in the areas of the sunken floors relates only to Glattrup IV and, in the area of the ground floors, primarily in House 5 at that settlement. The special sunken-floor house without a ground floor at Kluborg II, where traces of bronze working were recovered, is not included above. The idea of the sunken floor as a flint-chipping workshop concerns a minor house at Gug and is hence also not included in the above consideration. Regarding longhouses outside the region, certain suggestions have previously been put forward, e.g. concerning Egehøj (Boas 1983:97pp).

As we have seen, important finds are not characteristic of the transitional ramps between the deeper sunken areas and the ground floors. From the analysis of House 1 at Resengaard, it appears that the area must have, not least, functioned as an intermediary space for human comings and goings.

Longhouse architecture reflecting economic strategies?

Five of the longhouses at Resengaard, in particular, and some at the other central Limfjord region settlements in question give rise to considerations concerning the possible relationship between the architecture and the residents' livelihood strategies. And, although apparently using more or less the same construction techniques, it is rather surprising how different their ground plan designs could be.

House 13 was one of the largest at Resengaard over time and its markedly parallel long sides also seem to have been a characteristic of other houses at this settlement, as well as at locations elsewhere in the Limfjord region, e.g. House GAB at Myrhøj.

Some well-preserved house sites strongly deviate from the buildings with parallel-sided ground plans. This concerns, not least, House 1 at Rosgårde, Houses 3 and 5 at Glattrup IV, as well as Houses 1 and 128 at Resengaard.

At Rosgårde, House 1 gradually became much broader to the west. This implies that the western interior area of the building would have included significantly more square metres than the eastern. The number of cubic metres under the roof to the west would also therefore presumably have been correspondingly higher. In my reading, the western part of this building could very well have been intended for a barn, and the architecture could thus represent an example of a deliberate strategy for storing extra quantities of winter fodder. The sizeable barn would then presumably reflect the fact that the residents tried to keep a comparatively large number of livestock.

In contrast to the above building, House 5 at Glattrup IV became increasingly narrower towards the west. The reduction in width was, indeed, very significant. It was suggested in the above that the residents of this house had predominantly been involved in brewing and short-term storage of beer. The strategy behind this architecture could therefore likely have been that less space towards the west was required when the household was focussing, not least, on this production. Storing a great deal of winter fodder was thus not a major part of the livelihood strategy in this longhouse. Moreover, it seems that the large pit to the west would have taken up so much of the floor space that only limited room was otherwise free in its periphery. House 200 at Resengaard likewise presumably narrowed towards the west, judging by the firm contour lines of the sunken floor and, remarkably, the only deep pit at the settlement was in this building.

Regarding House 3 at Glattrup IV and Houses 1 and 128 at Resengaard, the same arguments of a deliberate strategy for storing winter fodder, as proposed for House 1 at Rosgårde, seem relevant. If we concentrate on House 1 at Resengaard, the building became some-what broader towards the west. This difference does not immediately seem to be much but would presumably have added several cubic metres to the volume of the western part, making it possible to store more winter to feed the livestock. Its compartment to the north could presumably have been used for keeping things other than in the remaining ground-floor spaces. In other words, it seems reasonable to suggest also with regard to this building that the livelihood strategies are mirrored in the architecture.

The thought that the architecture may mirror aspects of the livelihood seems to me to hold some logic. After all, before building a new house, the households must have had some expectations of their future economic doings and likely attempted to build and arrange the houses accordingly. In terms of architecture, I thereby argue that form follows function in these concrete cases.

I earlier presented a scheme concerning the grouping of houses according to lengths (Fig. 2.6) along with many different ground plans for the house sites (Ch. 2). When we look for marked trends in this latter respect in the material in question from the central Limfjord region, we can first state that, in LN I, five Beaker houses can be considered to have been trapezoid (Fig. 5.1). Among the seven selected settlements with Beaker houses, trapezoid ground plans were thus apparently favoured. Three became gradually wider towards the west, while two became gradually wider towards the east. It is, however, necessary to note that, for six of the ground plans in that material, no suggestions can be put forward. When considering LN II and

Longhouse sites	Parallel	Trapezoid	Trapezoid	No suggestion
		Widest to the west	Widest to the east	
Late Neolithic I ("Beaker houses")	0	3	2	6
Late Neolithic II + Emerging Bronze Age	4	5	2	3
Σ 25	4	8	4	9

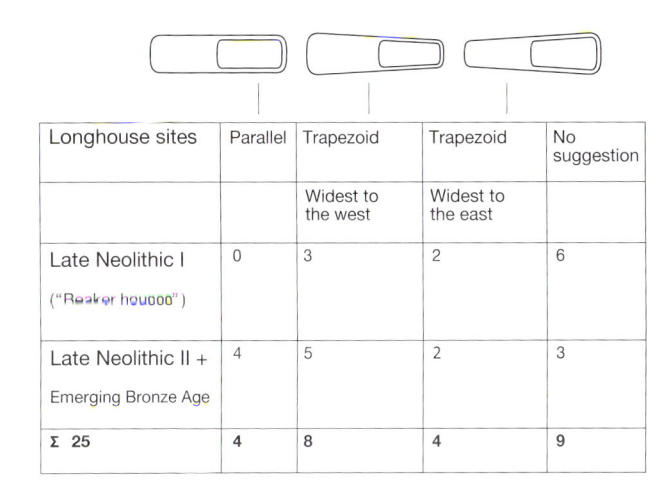

Fig. 5.1. *Parallel and trapezoidal ground plans. The basic forms of many of the longhouse ground plans are suggested, albeit cautiously for some (cf. Fig. 2.6).*

the emerging Bronze Age, four longhouses appear to have had parallel long sides at Resengaard. Yet, at the present stage in research – with an absence of substantial comparative materials – it is not possible to establish, whether sunken-floor longhouses with parallel long sides were actually favoured during a particular period of the younger Late Neolithic. However, some of the relatively late longhouses at Resengaard had markedly trapezoid ground plans that became wider towards the west, while one seems to have been widest to the east. The rather special sunken-floor House 5 at Kluborg II also became wider towards the east. We need more well-preserved sunken-floor house sites to be able to judge whether the apparent shifts in favour of ground-plan layouts – trapezoid to parallel to trapezoid – is more than just accidental.

It appears that the households at Resengaard may have reacted to changing conditions that were somehow likely related to livelihoods. As we have seen, in the site of House 2, the sunken floor area appears extended towards the east and, in the site of House 41, the ground-floor part to the west was later removed. The functions of these buildings may thereby have been reduced or increased, respectively.

The two-aisled construction principle, with a sizeable sunken area to the east, could be considered a kind of "concept house". It is really remarkable how these buildings, in their dimensions, ground plans and interior layout, could be designed for the needs of the individual households while still using the general concept. Every sunken-floor longhouse may thus have had a distinct character of its own.

House 5 at Glattrup IV is an obvious example that shows how this sunken-floor longhouse was individually tailored to a specific purpose. I have no reason to believe that this would not concern the two other sunken-floor longhouses at the settlement as well. And yet use of the spaces in the houses might, of course, have changed at some stage, when new livelihood strategies arose or were otherwise necessary.

Some features of the sunken-floored longhouses clearly document shared traits as regards functions, while other features obviously display differences in this respect. First of all, the general placement of the sunken floors to the east, combined with the frequent use of heating stones in this part of the houses evidences important shared characteristics. In other respects, the longhouses were used rather differently, judging by the deviations in the ground plans, the dimensions of the sunken areas, the traits of the ground-floor areas, the different interior arrangements, the varying number and positions of pits and patches, and the placements of tools. The most well-preserved longhouse sites demonstrate a marked difference, namely that the sunken floors in three of these from the time of the Beaker group took up just 45-48 % of the total house length, whereas three much later sunken floors from Resengaard took up markedly more, some 60-65 % (Fig. 2.63). Although we must state a clear reservation here due to the few really well-preserved sites, these figures are highly interesting and might well indicate that the relative importance of the sunken-floor functions grew over time.

As we shall later consider, these observations raise some important points of departure for ideas about the comprehensive specializations related to the making of products (and carrying out of services).

Regarding the three minor sunken-floor houses with scorched-stone patches at Resengaard, I suggest that these provided shelter for just one or a few people for a more or less limited stay. It might, for instance, relate to individuals who, for some reason, could not live in the longhouses for a certain period. Judging by the finds and their ground plans, with only a few details preserved, none of these directly appear to indicate specific economic aspects, apart from the storage in clay pots or activities connected to stone anvils. Here it should be noted, interestingly, "… at Almhov evidence in the form of indications of hearts suggests that people most likely lived in some of these smaller buildings. Perhaps people lived there on a temporary basis when a main house had been destroyed or was otherwise deemed unfit for living in. The smaller houses may have functioned as living quarters while a new main house was built. They may also reflect permanent residence, indicating that complex social relations existed on these larger farms" (Brink 2013:445p).

Besides a single short house, the other minor sunken-floor houses at Resengaard were likely used for various other purposes. They were hardly used for sheltering cattle because it would have been observable if the sandy floors would have been severely affected by this. Furthermore, and of no less importance, the construction of these minor houses was seemingly all too fragile to shelter large animals.

Minor houses at settlements in Danish contexts have often been termed "economy houses". Against this backdrop, it is remarkable that the majority of traces of "economic activities" are not found in the sites of such buildings at Resengaard but primarily in those of the sunken-floor longhouses.

Indoor pit arrangements and livelihood strategies

Certain livelihood strategies concern brewing and short-term storage of certain beverages, which – as specialized activities – are suggested to have taken place in all three sunken-floor longhouses at Glattrup IV. Certain livelihood strategies and the need to establish sizable deep cellar pits and deep sunken fireplaces in the floor areas have obviously influenced the architecture. And yet what is it about these large pits that leads us to suggest that brewing took place at some scale in all three longhouses?

Establishing deep pits in sunken-floor longhouses took place surprisingly seldom, judging by the published sites from the Limfjord region. Pits are, in this present work, considered "deep" when they exceed 0.50 m depth below the floor surface. Such pits are known neither from Myrhøj nor from Stendis or Tastum I (Jensen, J.A. 1973; Skov 1982; Simonsen 1983). At Bejsebakken, several sizeable pits have been recorded, some of which were deep. House A66 (here suggested to represent two houses) was supplied with two pits (depths 85 & 84 cm), House A214 with two pits (depths 38 & 46 cm), House 170 with one pit (depth 40 cm), and further in area C, pit A732 (depth 100 cm, not found at a house site) and all contained various artefact remainders (Sarauw 2006:16pp). Two of these very regular pits in sunken-floor houses and one in a ground-floor house were placed in the floor peripheries and had the same characteristics of vertical sides and a flat bottom (Sarauw 2006:52). Storage as well as brewing have been suggested as regards their functions and, interestingly, traces of organic material, likely wood lining, were observed in pit A732 (Sarauw 2006, Fig. 22).

Outside the region some deep, steep-sided pits are known from Lindebjerg (Jæger & Laursen 1983). As concerns Fosie IV, it has been suggested that an almost circular pit in one of the two-aisled ground-floor houses, House 92, could have had functions related to brewing (Björhem & Säfvestad 1989:55, 92 & 108; Sarauw 2006:61). At Hemmed Plantation, almost corresponding pits were excavated in the site of House III, supplied with a sunken floor (Boas 1993:131p).

The single deep pit from House 200 at Resengaard did not have vertical sides around the whole perimeter and was not supplied with a large flat bottom. Among the locations considered in this present work, no observations of deep, steep-sided pits exist from the sunken-floor houses at Gåsemose, Hellegård, Tromgade, Marienlyst Strand, Granlygård, Rosgårde, Glattrup I/III or Kluborg II. From this perspective, the massive presence of these pits in the sunken-floor longhouses at Glattrup IV really stands out. All in all, deep steep-sided pits form highly conspicuous elements of the longhouse ground plans and we shall now turn to the specific design traits of the pit walls and bottoms from these buildings (Fig. 4.55, 4.57 & 4.59).

The formation of, for example, the three large, subcircular pits (B, C, & E) in the site of House 7 at Glattrup IV was very carefully done. They were dug so large that they would have had the capacity to store quite considerable volumes. Pit B in the northeast corner, for instance, was thus so voluminous that it would have allowed a person to descend, carry out work there and arrange things. The workmanship of the pit digging was indeed remarkable in more ways than one. The sides were cautiously dug into the sandy subsoil and the leaning of the sides deviated only slightly from the vertical. It would presumably have been possible to keep the walls stable with just moderate panelling of the inner sides. These might have been kept in place by simple transverse construction elements, binding them together. And yet it must be emphasized that, during fieldwork, substantial traces of former construction work in the sides of the many sizeable pits in the sunken-floor houses at Glattrup IV were not observed. In the excavation report, light constructions such as wattle walls are suggested for the pits in Houses 3 and 5. Such walls would probably have been rather open, and dry sand could easily have trickled out if these were not combined with clay plastering or other, perhaps organic material of some kind. However, no traces of clay were observed near the walls in any of the house sites. For this reason, a combination of wickerwork and clay therefore appears less likely, and I instead presume that a wooden panel around the inner sides (packed perhaps with some tightening organic material behind, such as e.g. bark) could have been a reasonable solution. In the case of pit B in House 7, some small, almost regularly occurring darker soil patches were observable on the upper part of the sides (Fig. 4.59.C). These patches possibly represented traces of a by now disappeared wooden construction around the inner perimeter. Pressure from the sides towards the inner area could have been counterbalanced by a circle of well-proportioned stakes. When slightly widening towards the upper parts and densely placed, these stakes would presumably resist the pressure.

The pit bottoms also call for attention. Despite the expected difficulties of establishing level bottoms, the large sub-circular pits in House 7 and some others in these longhouses had rather well-flattened bottoms. The digging tools must have been used with the utmost care to level and finish these without damaging the sides while doing so. The bottoms of the pits in House 7 were possibly covered, for instance, with mats or wooden planks because no major damage to the subsoil sand was observable due to the activities.

No traces of any covering arrangements were found over these large pits and nor could they be expected to have survived in these sandy surroundings. I assume that solid, flat wooden constructions roofed several of the interior pits at Glattrup IV to enable the residents to move about in these floor areas. This would, at the same time, have enabled some of them to function properly as cellars.

The reason for the presence of these steep-sided pits and their extraordinarily fine bottom levelling, in my interpretation, is that the pits were to be used for brewing and storing beer. They were therefore supplied with a large flat bottom so that jars containing fluids could be placed in an upright position, preventing them from toppling over. Indeed, the basic production materials, not least cereals, were present at the settlement, as evidenced by the charred barley and wheat, as well as other different plant materials from the pit fills. The fact that these pits were such dominant traits of the house ground plans at this single settlement, among all presently known from the entire Limfjord region, might further support the notion that the households of this particular area carried out specialized activities of an exceptional character.

The function and working time of the pits can be further illuminated. Among all of them, the large, deep pit C in House 5 appears to be rather special, with its gradual deepening from west to east, placed along the south side of the sunken floor. The available bottom area was somewhat smaller than pit 480 in the ground floor (Fig. 2.53). Storage could have been a particular purpose of pit C. Yet, it did not function until the building was abandoned, due to the collapse of its northern side. This must have happened earlier because the fill did not correspond to the secondary fills. The earlier collapse is also otherwise evidenced because a posthole to the northeast was subsequently established in the top fill (report U1999a). As regards the large pits of House 3 and the three other pits of House 5, it seems that all were contemporaneously in use in each building. When looking at the stratification, no floor layers covered the pits and no other remains were found from using the area over the pits as floors. These observations can be interpreted in that these pits were used until about the time residency of the houses ceased. Regarding House 7, the observation of rather similar fill in the three large sub-circular pits could point to a simultaneous use followed by a coincidental filling up, likely on ceasing residence.

The unusually sizeable, flat-bottomed pit 480 in the western half of House 5 had a much larger bottom area than others at the settlement. It is an obvious possibility that the bottom area could have been used for relatively comprehensive activities connected to brewing. A broad belt of flat ground-level floor around this central pit could have been available for related doings and placing of things (Fig. 2.59). As some deep pits from Houses 3, 5 and 7, in my understanding, were likely supplied with brewing facilities, these would thus represent working pits that might correspond somewhat to the weaving pits, i.e. the idea of using pits as the core areas of "workshops".

When looking at all the sizeable pits, it appears in contrast that only a few small pits/patches were present in these Glattrup IV longhouses. It is also remarkable that no regular scorched-stone patches were present in Houses 3, 5 and 7. Instead, sizeable sunken fireplaces were found in the sites of Houses 3 and 5, and presumably also House 7.

Although other possibilities concerning the predominant specializations of Houses 3, 5 and 7 cannot be entirely excluded, brewing of beer on a relatively large scale was, in my interpretation, a very important aspect of the household's livelihood strategy and hence the digging of such large pits would have had much meaning.

All three longhouses were greatly marked by the residents' livelihood strategies. There is no evidence that these three houses functioned simultaneously, and the varying interior arrangements, in my interpretation, probably represent successive transformations of ideas on how to organize the brewing and storage activities while still leaving reasonable space for other household activities. The positions, designs, dimensions and varying functions of the pits, in combination with the highly varying longhouse architecture, may thus reflect rather different solutions to the same strategy of beer brewing and short-term storage.

Household composition, social status and architecture

The "household" as an analytical entity can form part of a fruitful approach to dwellings and settlements and the study from this angle is described as "… the emerging field of household archaeology" and it "… takes the household and its material correlate, the dwelling, as primary analytical units, and focuses mainly on socioeconomic relations within and among households… Most pre-industrial societies, the kinds that archaeologists study most often, were organized according to the Domestic Mode of Production … in which households were not only social units, responsible for biological reproduction and child-rearing, but also primary producing and consuming units" (Coupland & Banning 1996:1; cf. Tringham 1998). Although such a household approach here is considered an emerging field, it has already been a focus of certain researchers for some time (e.g. Trigger 1968; Wilk & Rathje 1982; Hayden & Cannon 1982; Wilk 1983; cf. Deetz 1982:724. On domestic modes of production, see e.g. Nielsen, S. 1999). More lately, in relation to concrete studies in Northwest Europe, several researchers have also focused on the household as a central term (e.g. Gerritsen 1999; Fokkens 2003; Streifert 2004; Sørensen 2010). It has been proposed that it is difficult to present a general definition of the household, but "… a close correlation between this unit and domestic architecture and arrangements" is understood as part of it (Sørensen 2010:123). As an alternative, other writers have preferred "domestic group" as a reasonably unbiased term (Segalen 1988; cf. Nielsen, S. 1999:45).

Before turning to the subject of the relationship between household and architecture, the challenging question of household size and composition must be considered. If we try to establish some assumptions regarding the people living in the sunken-floor houses, it would clearly not be possible to take for granted something like the often idealized modern, nuclear family with a couple and just a few children in South Scandinavia. Here, the rich variations from the recorded "ethnographic present" around the world extend the imaginable possibilities as regards who might live together. Of course, we cannot know anything for certain about the social compositions or age and gender constellations of households during the period in question.

And yet we can tentatively presume that, when founding a household, the core would have been a young couple, with one of the pair possibly originating from a more or less distant location (cf. Vander Linden 2007:343pp). I believe this might, not least, have happened in the early Late Neolithic of the Limfjord region, with its multifaceted contacts with other areas of South Scandinavia and northwest Europe. The manifold contacts may thus have resulted in spouses from far and near. In any case, a small crowd of offspring would presumably often have gradually become part of this household. In addition, perhaps elderly relatives such as parents, second marital relationships, unmarried kin and other relatives might have been included in the household.[2] Some non-relatives might also have been included due, for instance, to close friendships, specific work competences, or other qualities. The relatively open and flexible household could thus have been exposed to almost constant transformations during its existence, while its members also went through their own biological cycles. Some residents of the longhouses might have lived long lives, while others would presumably have died young or even very young (cf Simonsen 2006). Some could have left the household while others could have joined it. Some changes in composition might have been drastic in character and others gradual. In case of death, or for other reasons, a new spouse might join the household. My assumption is thus that the number of members could have varied considerably from time to time, and its composition as well. A simple, straightforward description that would embrace any variation would correspond to the proposal that "… the household constitutes the group who used or resided within a single house or group of closely related buildings", proposed in connection with considerations of organization and gender in Iron Age Britain households (Hingley 1990:128; cf. Sørensen 2010:125pp, on household size and composition).

It is obviously a complex question to ask whether household characteristics are mirrored in architecture. In the planning of the dimensions of a new longhouse, it seems reasonable to suppose that considerations and expectations of future household size would have been included but hardly trouble-free in foreseeing changes in detail. It is hence doubtful as to whether household sizes actually are mirrored directly in the longhouse dimensions although certain *a priori* attitudes such as, for instance, whether establishing a big or small household would be desirable or foreseeable, may have existed. If a large household were expected to be the outcome within some time, it therefore seems plausible that a relatively big longhouse would be planned and built, if possible. So, in this respect the architecture could have been influenced by household expectations. We have seen how House 41 at Resengaard was reduced during its later stages, maybe indicating a reaction to changes in the household size and economy. Conversely, in the case of House 2 it was extended, likely to create further space, and an additional scorched-stone device was established far to the east, next to the recess to the south (cf. Poulsen 2009:160, on repairs of longhouses).

When attempting to be more specific about the expected household size, House 1 at Resengaard can be taken as an example. Taking into account the interior arrangements and suggested activity spaces, I tentatively suggest an average of 10 persons living in this longhouse. In some periods, therefore, more than 10 persons might have lived there and, in others, fewer. For instance, at times the number of residents, including offspring, might have ranged from 10 to 15 persons or more, while at others perhaps only 5-10 persons or less. Other methods of calculation have also been presented (Hayden et al. 1996). For comparison, the average South Scandinavian household in the Bronze Age has been estimated at 10-15 persons (Sørensen 2010, table 5.2). For Almhov and the Hyllie bog area, it has been proposed that 7-8 adults (besides children) lived in the longhouses (Brink 2013:445). Regarding the Netherlands, the proposal is that the households included 20 or even more persons per longhouse (Fokkens 2003:23).

House 1 was not among the larger houses at Resengaard. Quite the contrary: with some reservations as to the original lengths of Houses 2, 130, 134, 138, and 200, it could very well have been the very shortest of all the sunken-floor longhouses at Resengaard. It is noteworthy that some of the very short buildings, such as House 128, were actually built late at the settlement, while two of the sizeable buildings, Houses 13 and 41, in reality were much earlier. Even though it was not a quite linear development, it thus appears from the more well-preserved ground plans that longhouse length overall possibly may have decreased over time at Resengaard. We are thus now approaching another relevant research question, namely whether or not the building dimensions were rooted in differences in social standing.

It would be tempting to read, for instance the relatively sizeable House 13 as the physical frame of daily life for a household with a relatively high social status. Buildings of comparatively large dimensions are,

in other South Scandinavian contexts from the period in question, considered to mirror higher status when general variations in the dimensions of contemporaneous longhouses/farms are observed (e.g. Artursson 2009:12). I will not reject this possibility regarding e.g. House 13. Concerning Resengaard, however, it must be said that, as the house lengths varied from generation to generation but on the whole appear to have decreased over time, judging by the most well-preserved sites, it would seem that house lengths were not necessarily directly related to social status.[3] Compared with House 13, we see that House 1 was almost five metres shorter in raw dimensions (Fig. 2.6). I do not think this difference necessarily reflects the social standing of the residents but rather that functional differences more or less directly related to changes in the economic activities performed by the households played a significant role. The different kinds of specialized production to be carried out in the future (and perhaps also expected household size) may, not least, have been important parameters when planning the new longhouse. Access to suitable building materials may also have played a very significant role.

Unfortunately, no comparable analyses of long-lasting settlements with sunken-floor longhouses, to my knowledge, exist from South Scandinavia at the turn of the Neolithic. For the moment we cannot therefore seek any indication as to whether or not the decrease in longhouse dimensions was a general trend at the individual settlements from around 1900 to about 1600 calBC. in certain geographical areas.

Three alternative outlines of local settlement

The challenges of dealing with even basic elements of the settlement structure in the Late Neolithic and emerging Bronze Age in the Limfjord region may become apparent through just a few essential statements and three simple research questions concerning what we need to know.

Sites of sunken-floor longhouses are, in some cases, found at the same locations as longhouses with solely ground floors. The settlements at Glattrup IV and Rosgårde can serve as examples. At Glattrup IV, the particular placement of House 4 (with ground floor) opposite House 5, in my reading, likely speaks for the coexistence of these two longhouses. At Rosgårde, the particular placement of House 2 (with ground floor), being only a little distance from House 1 and placed almost in line with it, with no other house sites of that time nearby, may likewise speak for their contemporaneous existence. Against this background, the first research question to be qualified by future research is therefore: to what extent do we have cases of obviously contemporaneous longhouses of both categories present at settlements in the region?

Remainders of several sunken-floor houses have also come to light within extensive excavation areas that were apparently devoid of the sites of ground-floor longhouses: Resengaard offers an example of this (though, in spite of the comprehensive and extensive system of trial trenches and regular excavation areas, it cannot be entirely ruled out that there was a slight presence of ground-floor houses at the settlement). We see many examples of locations in the region where only sunken-floor houses have been recorded, although several of these settlements have not been fully investigated. The second research question to be qualified by future research is therefore: how common were settlements with solely two-aisled, sunken-floor houses?

Vestiges of ground-floor longhouses have come to light within excavation areas apparently devoid of sunken-floor longhouses: the house site at Lundbro appears to be an example (Overgaard 2003). Several other settlements with this kind of longhouse are known from the region but seldom fully investigated and it is consequently difficult to exclude the absence of sunken-floor longhouses. The third research question to be qualified by future research is therefore: how common were settlements with solely two-aisled, ground-floor houses?

Although it is not, for the moment, possible to present sufficient evidence to answer any of these questions, some other information relevant to the issue of settlement patterns is available. First and foremost, we know that both kinds of houses belonged to early as well as late parts of the Late Neolithic and both kinds continued into the Older Bronze Age. Furthermore, it is my impression that no really clear differences concerning topography exist between them.[4]

Regarding the central Limfjord region, one of the really marked dissimilarities in the two categories of houses seems to be the use of raw materials. In my reading, the sunken-floor longhouses at Resengaard would require comparatively few regular timber posts, and these were not even dug deeply down into the subsoil. The construction of their walls mainly needed relatively short timber for the upright posts in combination with comprehensive use of turf. In contrast to this, the construction of at least some ground-floor longhouses would have demanded stronger timber posts for the centre-post construction, where the posts were frequently dug deeply down and could resist considerable side pressure from hefty winds. Moreover, the wall construction would presumably require a great deal of timber. Consequently, terms for the sunken-floor buildings such as "turf-houses", "turf-walled houses" or "turf-longhouses" etc. would be appropriate, whereas the houses with ground floors might be characterized with terms such as "timber-houses" or "timber-longhouses".

I presume that the turf-houses would have been easier to build and imply less work effort but the amount of labour and time needed in such a prehistoric context might not necessarily have been of decisive importance in choosing the kind of longhouse to be built.

The households using the sunken-floor longhouses would presumably often have had minor and short turf-walled houses at their disposal for different purposes and these might perhaps have lasted as long as the longhouses. Traces of small light-construction houses without sunken floors have not been documented at the settlements in question but I assume such constructions were also built and used for diverse activities, such as e.g. livestock sheds or shelters for humans at more or less distant "stations".

From a wide variety of possibilities, I shall now present three alternative outlines of longhouse function in relation to the western part of the central Limfjord region. Let us set the time to around 2200 BC, being that of a well-established Late Neolithic culture with significant Beaker traits. Common to all three outlines is the element that they operate with just one longhouse residence existing at the individual settlement at a time, in addition to a still not demolished old longhouse not being lived in but used for an "after-residence" period of possibly many years for various purposes. The minor and short buildings at the settlements are not taken into consideration in these outlines (Fig. 5.2).

Regarding outline 1, the choice depends largely on the local availability of timber or turf. Houses with turf walls might have been easier to build, although the amount of labour needed is not seen as an important factor in the choice. It could also depend on certain lineage traditions, forefather prescriptions and so on. An interesting case from the central Limfjord region is the fine excavation at Abildal, where sites of eight two-aisled buildings have been identified (Larsen

> **Three dwelling alternatives**
>
> Outline 1, throughout the year: Many households lived in sunken-floor longhouses and many other lived in ground-floor longhouses.
>
> Outline 2, throughout the year: Most households lived in sunken-floor longhouses, while the ground-floor longhouses mostly were used for other purposes.
>
> Outline 3, during seasonal cycles: Most households lived alternately in ground-floor longhouses and sunken-floor longhouses, the last-mentioned being for the cold seasons.

Fig. 5.2. Three alternative outlines of local settlement in the central Limfjord region.

2012:2pp). The excavation director, Lars Agersnap Larsen, states that the main parts of the two-aisled buildings were placed in such a way that they cannot have existed contemporaneously. According to his interpretation, one house (K6) with sunken floor and interior sectioning with dividing walls was much larger than other houses (all with just ground floor) at the location and it is seen as the youngest (Larsen 2012, Fig. 7). However, I would like to suggest a re-interpretation that this part of the plan drawing provides evidence of two overlapping house sites whereby the two "dividing walls" instead represent a western and an eastern gable end respectively. It could therefore concern nine buildings in the same small area. In any case, this settlement very explicitly illustrates how two-aisled ground-floor houses were built again and again in the same area and just one single instance concerns a longhouse with sunken floor. These buildings, all in all, must therefore represent a rather long period. Finds of Beaker pottery belong to some of the houses, including the sunken-floor longhouse.

In relation to outline 3, it should be noted that, based on results from settlement investigations in Thy, it has been proposed that some people used to live near the coast during the summer, whereas winter residences may have been on more elevated grounds (Liversage & Robinson 1995:44p; *cf.* Artursson 2005b:109). The idea of such seasonal movements has been met with counterarguments and it has instead been suggested that …"Perhaps a more general notion of mobility is appropriate, without too strict an emphasis on a sea-sonal round" (Thorpe 2000:76). From Fosie IV it is known that the Late Neolithic non-coastal settlements were actually not placed very high up on the ground compared to the nearby significantly more elevated hills (*cf.* Björhem & Säfvestad 1989, Fig. 1). Yet, as stated, it is not my intention here to delve deeper into the comprehensive topic of settlement patterns.

Outline 2, in my perception, seems to be the most sustainable, judging by the available finds. One important argument is that the sunken-floor house sites display very many different traces of daily activities in the sunken-floor horizons, whereas this is far from the case in the investigated ground-floor longhouses. In my perception, the uses of the timber-houses could have been quite different from those of the turf-houses, and often represent buildings used for local community purposes. Outline 2 therefore forms my working hypothesis with regard to the area of the central Limfjord region.

Yet it is important to underline that the proposed outlines should not be understood too rigorously, as the practices of everyday life could presumably have modified any system. Ample room for individual solutions and human deviations from social and cultural norms could well have existed. It is therefore clear that the known settlements of the period were never absolutely uniform. This is also evidenced in the existence of some other, apparently rare, kinds of dwellings in the region, not least as seen at Vadgård (Rasmussen, M. 1993a; 1995). Nor shall I exclude the possibility that, at some locations, more than one sunken-floor longhouse could have existed for a period longer than needed for the transition, when moving the household from an old longhouse to a new one.

The settlement order proposed by Torben Sarauw is interesting in light of the above. Based on primarily stylistic variations in the pottery and a number of radiocarbon determinations, the duration of the Bejsebakken settlement is presumed to cover 200-400 years, divided into two phases: "Many of the two-aisled houses without a sunken floor seem to belong to an early phase of the habitation (c. 2400-2200 BC…), whereas the major part of the sunken-floor huts have a somewhat later dating (c. 2200-2000 BC)" (Sarauw 2007b:11. See also 2007b:27. For an alternative understanding, see Artursson 2005b:107p). The duration of the entire settlement has also been proposed as 200-300 years (Sarauw 2007c:219). Very briefly expressed, the view is that the LN settlement structure at Bejsebakken concerns 2-3 single farm units over the centuries (Sarauw 2006:64).

An argument put forward in favour of this is that the techniques used for decorating the pottery may relate to "specific potters or to more potters belonging to the same tradition. Consequently, the small concentrations of houses may represent contemporary units using related stylistic expressions or, and perhaps more likely, more generations of potters partly following the same tradition" (Sarauw 2007b:44).

Crystallization of a particular place among local settlements?

It is implied in my working hypothesis that ground-floor longhouses would not necessarily have been built at every place where people were living in sunken-floor longhouses but that, at some locations in the region, several generations of timber-houses could have been built successively. Relatively strong timber dimensions were presumably applied and these buildings might have lasted comparatively longer than the turf-houses due to the quality of the materials, the investment of labour and the presumably often higher focus on proper maintenance. In line with the above, I assume that many were built and used for community purposes and that the appearance of these timber-houses was frequently fairly conspicuous and "monumental" compared to the turf-houses. The most finely accomplished timber-houses may well thus have given the impression of relatively prestigious buildings.

Following this working hypothesis, I suggest that some ground-floor longhouses were built for communal purposes in places where these would have been geographically easily accessible for residents from many settlements scattered in the varied landscapes. They could have been surveyed, maintained, prepared for gatherings etc. by households living nearby. Permanent residential units did not therefore necessarily live in these common timber-houses but maybe instead in sunken-floor longhouses in the neighbourhood. Yet some persons with special abilities and qualifications might well have worked and stayed there under special circumstances.

Further, I propose that the area of the communal timber-houses was used for multiple purposes connected to various fields of human life such as political assemblies, settling of disputes and mediation of conflicts, religious purposes, in forefather cult, for "rites of passage" feasting (such as adulthood, marriages, funerals), and other festivities within or between lineages, and for varying kinds of other occasional meetings, gatherings and arrangements. Moreover, many different kinds of exchange and practical doings related to the economy could have been arranged or carried out during gatherings when people seeking influence and status might have acted openly or more discretely. On the whole, I assume that, in practice, these timber-houses may often have functioned as a kind of "all-purpose community building".

In relation to the above, concrete and thorough studies of the sites of ground-floor longhouses are much needed in the future in order to elucidate vestiges of their functions and their heating facilities as well. In light of the conspicuous absence of burned bone fragments of livestock and other large animals from the sites of sunken-floor longhouses where, exceptionally, just some pieces are present, one kind of function may *a priori* be suggested, namely the consumption of slaughtered oxen and other animals. Inside or out, this could have taken place not least in relation to the timber-houses, perhaps occasionally – or even often –, as ritual meals for large groups and thus conceivably an aspect of exchange.

Two ground-floor longhouses and three sunken-floor longhouses were functioning during a period of LN I at Glattrup IV. I propose that a particular "place" had crystallized here and that it was a site of relatively greater importance than other local Beaker settlements because it was here that people usually met each other for purposes such as above. I am thinking of a particular place where locals and others came, stayed and left. It is imaginable that, on such occasions, for instance during lineage gatherings, a number of other topics and issues may also have been considered and discussed, in addition to the exchange of various goods, commodities and services. The place would have been associated not only with the activities that were going on, and in which the locals and other visitors engaged, but also with the particular atmosphere of sights, sounds and smells that would constitute its specific ambience (Ingold 2000:192). Some planned and well-ordered paths would likely have led to and from this particular place (Ingold 2000:204).

Both ground-floor longhouses at Glattrup IV and the one at Rosgårde all fit into the group of small longhouses (Fig. 5.3; *cf.* Fig. 2.4). They did not have particularly divergent ground plan dimensions and, compared with the sunken-floor longhouses, they could have appeared more hall-like. The interior arrangements of the buildings are conspicuously well-

Rosgårde. House 2

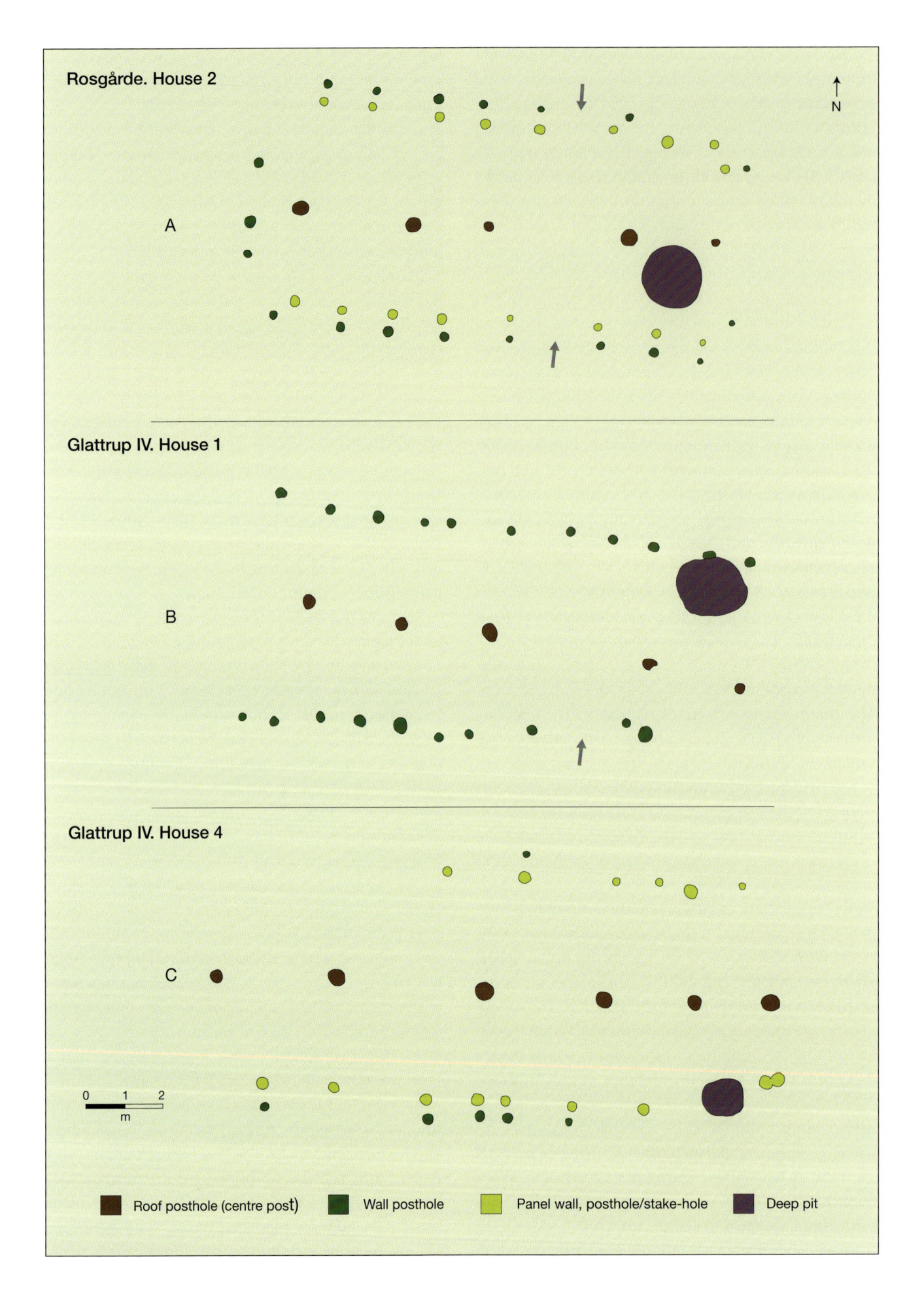

A

Glattrup IV. House 1

B

Glattrup IV. House 4

C

0 1 2 m

■ Roof posthole (centre post) ■ Wall posthole ■ Panel wall, posthole/stake-hole ■ Deep pit

356 Chapter 5

Location	House	Raw length	Raw width	Ground plan	Site of fire	Large sub-circular pit, diameter
Glattrup IV	1	12.4 m	5.7 m	Trapezoid	No	1.8 m
Glattrup IV	4	14.3 m	6.6 m	Parallel	No	1.1 m
Rosgårde	2	12.6 m	6.0 m	Trapezoid	No	1.6 m

◄▲ *Fig. 5.3. Three sites of ground-floor longhouses at Glattrup IV and Rosgårde, cleaned. A-C: Arrows indicate entrances. In all three buildings, a rather sizable, sub-circular pit was established far to the east. In my interpretation, these functioned not least as "beer-cellars". For their placement at the locations, see Fig. 2.51 and 2.55. D (above): Some particulars of these small ground-floor longhouses. The raw dimensions of House 1 at Glattrup IV may have been slightly larger.*

ordered and much alike, each having one sizeable sub-circular pit placed far to the east. I suggest that, when these longhouses were supplied with such pits, it related to a cellar that functioned in connection to the making of beer and thereafter likely cool storage until consumption during an event of this kind took place. No such sub-circular cellars were found in relation to any of the sunken-floor houses at the nine other settlements in question from the central Limfjord region.

I argue that Glattrup IV was, for a period of some 75 years, a place for such gatherings and meetings. The buildings were actually situated in a location presumably easily reached by people coming from settlements in coastal areas around the inner part of the Limfjord and beyond. It would likewise have been easily reached by people travelling along the large Karup Å stream and the distance from its delta to Glattrup IV was only short. Furthermore, the location would have been easy to reach by land transport when using the watershed lines and other dry high grounds in the moraine landscapes. At the place itself, during one of the phases, a ground-floor timber-house (House 4) appears to have been situated opposite and almost parallel to a sunken-floor turf-house (House 5). A moderately-sized "yard" could have existed in between these two buildings. House 4 was supplied with a cellar pit in the southern wall area to the east (Fig. 5.3.C).

Further, I would like to suggest that the household living in the sunken-floor longhouse could have attended to and maintained both buildings, in addition to preparing gatherings etc. in the ground-level longhouse. We have already considered the vestiges in some detail, interpreted as the remainders of the household's great focus on production and short-term storage of alcoholic liquids. We have noted the activities of this household reflected in the architecture, in the conspicuous interior arrangements, in the pottery equipment, and in the samples of charred macrofossils. In my understanding, the brewing of alcoholic beverages was thus carried out in the sunken-floor longhouse in preparation for gatherings, representations, feasts and other communal activities involving people from many other settlements and it would first and foremost have been also within and near the ground-floor longhouse that the alcoholic beverages were consumed on some of these occasions. The ground-floor longhouse would likely have been considered the core building of the "Glattrup IV place". When not used for social events and meetings, it could – occasionally or for a period – have been used for activities such as threshing and sifting of local cereal harvest (as evidenced in the site of House 1 with ground floor at Glattrup IV) and stacking of firewood.

The idea of brewing and storage of beer in House 5 at Glattrup IV would correspond well with the notion of feasts and banquets that may have been held at that time, using the finely ornamented Beaker pottery (Sarauw 2008a:87, with further references; *cf.* Sherratt 1987:92). On the consumption of alcoholic beverages, it has been put forward that "… in societies without institutionalised political power, drinking is a source of inter-individual competition through manipulation of hospitality and reciprocity rules" (Vander Linden 2001:47). What actually did happen at Glattrup IV in this respect we will never know but it is conceivable that alcohol may sometimes have played a major role.

5.2. Living and working conditions indoors

We shall now briefly return to the house interiors and reflect on how certain properties of the sunken-floor longhouses might have contributed to their function as a climatic shield, namely how the houses might have been kept warm and how the scorched-stone devices might have worked. Besides, what do we actually know about open fireplaces in the sunken-floor longhouses of the central Limfjord region?

Keeping the longhouse interiors warm?

The sunken floors must have had rather fine abilities to keep out even the most severe of frosts from the eastern parts of the longhouses compared to houses with just ground floors. The presence of deep floors combined with thick turf walls would have been of paramount importance for ensuring that temperatures did not normally fall too low, even in harsh winter periods when it was severely cold outside, thus providing an effective buffer against regular cold and unkind climatic conditions. It would furthermore presumably have been easy to establish a simple shield, by hanging, for instance, hides or blankets to protect against chilly air from the entrances and elsewhere. As proposed, a kind of flat, wooden ceiling resting on crossbeams might perhaps have been present over a part of the sunken floor, or maybe even a major part of it. Combined with this, hides, blankets, mats etc. could also have been used for reducing the height of the ceiling, shielding the sides, and covering parts of the deep floors. Where people lived, therefore, some reasonable conditions for indoor dwelling could thus have been established without much difficulty.

Despite the obvious insulating qualities of turf walls, sunken floors and presumably further kinds of shielding as described above, it would likely have been considered necessary to add some heat, particularly during the cold seasons. Requirements in this respect could nonetheless have been rather moderate and much less than we would expect inside dwellings today. It would therefore hardly be a good idea to expect something like the modern, South Scandinavian notions of winter comfort temperatures indoors at that time.

The contribution of cooking to interior warming is not easily estimated. The residents' nourishment might have been gained from many sources and some of the foods were probably prepared for eating in ways we can hardly imagine. It seems likely, however, that some kinds of food were cooked in pots, due to the existence of several examples of soot crust on potsherds, and some of these may presumably evidence that a certain need existed for heating in the course of preparing various kinds of meals. The heated stones could often plausibly have been connected to cooking. When cooking was complete, the stones could thereafter slowly have emitted heat for several hours and thus contributed more or less to the comfort of the sunken-floor spaces.

From research concerning dwellings at Keatly Creek on the Interior Plateau of British Colombia, where mid-winter temperatures are quite low, it is quite interesting to learn that, in certain house pits – of dimensions by and large comparable to those of the average sunken floors of the central Limfjord region longhouses – people could live with an extremely scarce addition of heat beyond the warmth from the residents themselves, when living close together (Hayden et. al 1996:151pp & Fig. 10.5).

The use of stones as immersion heaters may very well have been practised for heating water or other liquids but the extent to which this might have been routine is not possible to judge and hence the possible contribution to indoor warming is unknown. Yet I find it likely that the cracking of some of the stones in question could have been caused by the shock of putting heated stones into cold water.

Other activities involving the handling of pottery in heating processes do not seem directly documented through the finds although, for instance, a part of the much affected, secondarily burned pottery could stem from activities other than usual cooking. Even some of the soot crusts could conceivably stem from processes other than the cooking of food.

Storing plant materials as fodder in the western ground-floor spaces would also have contributed to shielding the spaces where people lived from the cold of the westerly winds during the harsh season. Such use of the unsunken floor parts would likely have had a highly insulating effect and may well have reduced the need for heating from other sources. I presume that a critical period in this respect would have been early spring, when most plant fodder would probably have been consumed, while cold weather conditions could still have influenced the buildings.

How much daylight would the sunken-floor buildings have let in? Some light would presumably have entered through doorways and maybe through different openings in the walls. Rays of light might perhaps also have forced their way through even tiny chinks in the roof or small cracks in the walls. Minor openings may have been established in the upper parts of the roofs to let out the smoke. During daytime, some light would thus presumably have lit up the rooms naturally. To carry out the suggested economic activities, of a highly varying nature, indoors would of course have required some minimum of light. Certain processes would perhaps have demanded a relatively large amount of light and might not have been performed well in semi-darkness. Thus, not least if activities had to be carried out in the dark hours, some kind of lighting must have been a necessity. By mid-winter, around 16 in every 24 hours would have been dark at these northern latitudes. I therefore presume that torches, branch snags or other kinds of flammable objects would have been used.

The question of the presence of regular fireplaces giving light and warmth needs some broader consideration. Flaming fires may now and then have been deliberately ignited in the sunken-floor longhouses for some occasional purposes of heating and giving light. At times, maybe some wood that was occasionally placed in the area of the scorched-stone patches could also have begun to flame. Yet it is largely difficult to substantiate more than that from the evidence of the floors. Soil traces that could clearly be interpreted as permanent fireplaces were quite rare at Resengaard. I likewise see no clear documentation of fireplaces from the sunken-floor longhouses at Hellegård, Tromgade, Marienlyst Strand, Glattup I/III, or Rosgårde. Remainders from markedly sunken fireplaces were found in the sites of the unique longhouses at Glattrup IV. At Kluborg II, quite regular fireplaces were present in the special sunken-floor longhouse, where metal casting took place.

If the scorched-stone patches at Resengaard were to be interpreted as "permanent" fireplaces, substantial evidence would be needed. More or less imperishable vestiges, such as significant charcoal remainders, the comprehensive occurrence of reddish-burned subsoil areas and a great deal of ash would be expected to be present. Apart from some ash, however, such vestiges were by and large absent.

At the bottom of a fireplace, one might thus expect the heat to have reached its highest temperatures in the centre and then declined towards the periphery. If not cleaned up, it can be anticipated to leave a fine pattern of practically imperishable traces. In my understanding, a permanent fireplace would be expected to show a concentrated layer of ashes centrally above reddish-burned sand – declining towards the sides – joined with more or less dispersed pieces of charcoal peripherally, representing firewood not totally burned out.

This condition was certainly not observed in, for instance, the sunken floor of House 1 at Resengaard. No such "ideal" fireplace remainders were observed. Even when limiting one's requirements with regard to a possible fireplace and accepting more irregular features, it is not possible to identify any in the areas of the charred macrofossils. Ash was present intermixed with soils in the scorched-stone patches but charcoal was more or less missing there. Moreover, remarkably few pieces of charcoal were found in the entire floor. The notion that a regular fireplace would have been functioning in the sunken floor of this longhouse therefore seems difficult to substantiate. During the gradual deepening of the floor over time, the older traces of a fireplace would surely have been more or less removed. Charcoal and ash are not easily broken down by nature, however, and it is important to bear in mind that the floor of House 1 was undisturbed and a fireplace left from the last period of use would certainly have been observed because this sunken-floor house site was among the most meticulously investigated.

On the whole, it would therefore not be without contradiction to claim that there was a permanent, open fireplace functioning in the sunken floor of House 1, as the minimum requirements to identify this were not observed. Nor has substantial evidence of permanent fireplaces been recorded from the remaining 11 sunken-floor longhouses, of which several were in a rather good state of preservation. And yet, from House 138, two minor patches are suggested to represent short-term fireplaces in the sunken-floor area.

With all their organic materials, the sunken-floor longhouses at Resengaard would have been highly flammable and, in the worst case, could have presented a real fire hazard, as they were presumably built with roofs of wood and reeds as major components and, during long periods of the year, could have been more or less stuffed with dry winter fodder to the west. However, with the exception of the deliberately burned down House 2, as well as the deliberate burning of various waste at the sites of Houses 1 and 197, we have no sites of fire at Resengaard. This means that some 300 years passed at Resengaard without any comprehensive fire accidents in these longhouses. How could the residents have managed to totally avoid any accidental fire, if open fireplaces were used day after day down the many generations of highly flammable longhouses? A plausible answer can be that usually no regular, permanent fireplaces were established in these longhouses.

We have clear evidence from many periods before today about heating arrangements playing a key role for the interior arranging.[5] For cooking and lighting, it appears to have become axiomatic that "permanent", open fireplaces were *a priori* used in the late Stone Age dwellings. And yet could this understanding be a "romantic" notion that is not valid as regards all concrete human dwellings at that time? In my opinion, the idea of ever-present indoor fireplaces does not help us recognise other ways of arranging everyday life.

How did scorched-stone devices work?

The above results also leave us with a great challenge in terms of trying to gain an understanding of the working of the scorched-stone devices, not least concerning where the stones were heated and how they were used.

When it comes to the working of the scorched-stone devices, we can consider two primary alternative scenarios, i.e. that the stones were heated either inside or outside the longhouse. In the first scenario, it is assumed that the stones were heated either directly in the area of the scorched-stone patches or in a fire somewhere else on the floor and subsequently moved to the area of use. In the second scenario, it is assumed that the stones were heated in a fire outside the sunken-floor house, presumably a shielded fireplace, perhaps with some kind of roofing arrangement. Shielding to the sides might, in this case, have been necessary due to the frequent strong winds in Northern Jutland.

Based on the apparent absence of clear evidence of fire and fireplaces in the well-preserved floor horizons, I prefer the second scenario. Additional advantages of heating the stones outside would evidently have been the lack of much smoke stemming from a fireplace in the interior. Most importantly, such a practise might not least have been an intentional precaution against the burning of the longhouses, as the risk of igniting the roofs, built of many organic materials and hence liable to catch fire, would have been reduced significantly. However, performed under shifting weather conditions, it would have had some implications for everyday life through the year.

The surrounding areas of the sunken-floors were often relatively "clean" and usually no concentrations that might represent a stone deposit were found. It is very likely that the area around the longhouses after they were abandoned and torn down was cleared for tillage. At Resengaard, the only find of a stone concentration interpreted as an outside deposit was the heap of heat-affected/cracked stones (Feature 24) with some soil in between, placed north of House 14 (Fig. 5.4). The soil differed greatly and most of it was a sandy, greyish soil, while to the northeast it was very dark, probably coloured heavily by charred organic material. The length of the irregularly shaped feature was 2.44 m and the width 1.16 m. Due to the placement of Feature 24 (as well as House 14) in a slight dip in the terrain, it survived the disturbances of recent ploughing. In my understanding, this stone heap could have belonged functionally to the scorched-stone devices of the sunken floor. In all, 7 potsherds and 18 pieces of worked flint were found in Feature 24 but none of these immediately contribute to dating it more precisely. On the whole, the character of the stones was very similar to that of the scorched-stone patches in many of the sites of sunken-floor longhouses.

From the above considerations, it appears that the general working of the scorched-stone devices could very well could have involved bringing heated stones from outside to the relevant areas inside. When transporting these heated stones, some gloving material

Fig. 5.4. Resengaard. Feature 24 north of House 14. This concerns a low heap of scorched stones, placed outdoors in a shallow pit. Above the sandy subsoil surface it had a height of c. 16 cm, and below it a depth of c. 8 cm. The heap was highest to the northeast, and the stones were placed most densely there, whereas to the southwest they were mostly scattered.

and some ashes could occasionally have been brought in unintentionally and, at times, flames would presumably occur thereafter but such charcoal would likely often have burned more or less out and left just a few pieces of charcoal and some ashes.

In everyday life, the demands for a certain temperature for different purposes could have been combined in a way that took these interests into consideration. The heated stones may thus possibly have been used so that the activities were carried out in a certain sequence, following the gradually declining temperatures of the stones. Reasonably efficient processes could have been run if the most heat-demanding processes used the stones first, then the somewhat less heat-demanding and so forth. During all such activities, the stones would evidently still have given off warmth to the room as a side effect.

Several different processes, in which heating to some level was a necessity, might advantageously have been performed with such a scorched-stone technique instead of heating in an open fire because the warmth could be given off in a relatively even manner without sudden shifts in temperature.[6] A group of heated stones would thus have provided a rather controllable source of heat, where the warmth would remain for a comparatively long time and only gradually decline, contrary to an ordinary open fire which, at its peak, might reach very high temperatures and then, when everything had burned out, would decline faster.

When again turning to House 1 at Resengaard, it is unclear how cereals to be dried, roasted or charred might have been held in the necessary position in relation to the heated stones but the residents likely had long experience of such doings. A kind of device may have been used to keep them some distance from the stones. On the other hand, it can hardly be excluded that the cereals may have been in direct contact with the warm stones. I presume that a fireplace outside at a safe distance from House 1 may have been used for many practical purposes and – besides heating the stones – one of these might, for instance, have been occasional cooking. This would correspond well with the astonishing finding that burned animal bones are by and large absent from the samples from House 1. Fish scales likewise appear to be completely missing from the abundant charred organic materials of this house site, despite its closeness to the Limfjord coast. This kind of absence might further support the idea that an outdoor fireplace was used for cooking near this and the other longhouses.

Scientifically-controlled experiments related to the efficiency of the warmed stones in corresponding surroundings would further enhance a discussion of their functions. The use of scorched-stone devices in all probability dates back to the Single Grave Culture, where heat-affected/cracked stones have been found in patches in the sunken floors as well as often more dispersed in the secondary fills above these. Examples are the sunken-floor houses from Strandet Hovedgaard but the details have not yet been presented (Simonsen 2006:45pp).

Further evidence of heating devices from the Limfjord region

With the exception of observations from Bejsebakken, soil patches with heat-affected/cracked stones in sites of sunken-floor houses have not yet been published in detail from east or west of the central Limfjord region. It is hence, for the time being, unclear to what extent the considerations at Resengaard, Kluborg II, Hellegård, Rosgårde and Tromgade could apply to wider areas of the region.

At Bejsebakken, 6-7 soil features have been interpreted as fireplaces from the sunken-floor houses (House A170, A222, A237, A539, and A643), as well as (House A173) a fireplace that is considered more uncertain (Sarauw 2006:13pp). In light of the observations from Resengaard, it would be interesting to know more about how these fireplaces materialized in terms of the absence or presence of significant layers of ash, substantial remains of charcoal and also areas of reddish-burned subsoil, given the often also sizeable dimensions of these soil features. When it comes to the site of House A222, it is described as "…an oval patch of subsoil coloured red by heat. It measured 1.5 x 0.9 m" (Sarauw 2006:24p). Concerning the site of House A237, the feature concerns "…an oval, 55 x 85 cm large blotch of red burnt subsoil sand" (Sarauw 2006:28p). Regarding the site of House 539, two fireplaces in the central longitudinal axis are described as "slightly red burnt clay" and "red burnt gravel", respectively (Sarauw 2006:33pp). Finally, the fireplace in the site of House A643 is presented as "…an area with red burnt sand mixed with ordinary yellow subsoil sand" (Sarauw 2006:38pp).

In some of the sunken-floor house sites at Bejsebakken, certain features are interpreted as cooking pits. One example is the large, almost rectangular pit 194 placed in between two postholes in the central longitudinal axis of House 170 (Sarauw 2006:15pp). Its dimensions were 1.90 x 1.15 m, with a depth of some 0.26 m. The pit contained large amounts of charcoal and fire-cracked stones dispersed in the fill with reddish sand below. The fireplace 189 from House A170 is considered a sunken fireplace with black colouring from charcoal.

It has also been realized that certain fireplaces may have been destroyed by ard-ploughing of the floors (Sarauw 2006:51). Recent ploughing has also caused damage given that, in spite of "…the relatively fine preservation conditions in the sunken areas, some houses contain neither fireplaces nor special pits. Here, the fireplaces may have been situated in the west end/the not-sunken part of the house and later ploughed over" (Sarauw 2006:57).

Certain patches with fire-cracked stones are presented from Bejsebakken. In the site of House 556, four sizeable patches were thus found in the western half of the sunken floor. Two of these were placed north of the central longitudinal axis and two south of it. In area, the lengths were 1.5-2.75 m and the widths 0.75-1.5 m. The depths were merely 5-10 cm but three of these features contained "large amounts of fire-cracked stones" (Sarauw 2006:36). Three similar observations were also described from the site of House 606, and these were all found north of the central longitudinal axis. The presence of these soil features indicates that particular activities may have been carried out there (Sarauw 2006:61). I find it rather important that both sites clearly belong to regular longhouses. On the whole, the descriptions of these soil features appear to correspond to the observations of scorched-stone patches as presented from the Resengaard longhouses. Their placements in the sunken floors largely correspond to some from Resengaard.

5.3. Settlement continuity and short-range relocation

The topography of the settlements with sunken-floor longhouses reveals that these were often placed on relatively high grounds in the landscapes of the central Limfjord region. This is also true of the Bejsebakken settlement and, judging by the hill contours, it seems that settling on more or less marked terraces on the hill was often preferred (*cf.* Sarauw 2006, Fig. 3).

The sunken-floor longhouses represented a kind of building to which the residents likely assigned much importance in everyday life, although various other kinds of structure may also have been used. On the sloping terrains in the perimeter of the upper hill at Resengaard, diverse scattered postholes were observed and could maybe, in some instances, represent traces of minor structures. Other postholes have often been observed in the vicinity of the sunken-floor houses but the relationships of these are mostly difficult to date and interpret. In certain areas with a number of postholes that apparently do not represent the remainders of regular houses, in particular, it seems possible that some kind of constructions might have existed although their chronological positions are also often unclear. Some pits in these areas were likely dug only to take subsoil sand.[7]

One or more minor sunken-floor houses would often likely have functioned at the same time as the sunken-floor longhouse. The residence at Hellegård is an obvious example of a short sunken-floor house placed close to a sunken-floor longhouse. With regard to Resengaard, however, it is a more complex matter. On the hill, a total of 13 sites of minor sunken-floor houses and one short house were recovered (besides the possible "House 156"). On the face of it, this could be understood such that the residents of each of the 12 longhouses (besides the possible "House 160") had at their disposal at least one smaller building at Resengaard. However, when looking at the chronological indications of the smaller buildings, it seems that in some periods there were perhaps none although, as stated, further sites of minor and short houses at the settlement may well have avoided our recognition. We shall not go further into this topic.

Over the centuries of the Late Neolithic and emerging Bronze Age, the upper part of the Resengaard hill was continuously used for residence, i.e. long settlement continuity. Strong evidence substantiates this view, not least the continual ceramic affinities between the longhouse assemblages, the apparently maintained knowledge of areas with pristine soils for new buildings, the continued filling up of the sunken areas and the likely continued agricultural activities at the old house spots. As we have seen, the radiocarbon determinations of short-lived plant materials have helped to set absolute chronological frames with regard to when all this happened.

Settlements with strong area continuity

The overall use of the landscape of the Late Neolithic and emerging Bronze Age has not yet been greatly elucidated and discussed as concerns the Limfjord region. It seems likely, however, that certain activities usually took place in plots at different distances from the residence and we must expect a number of "stations" to have existed without any traces of contemporaneous longhouses nearby, also largely depending of course on local landscape and resource conditions. The recent finds of flint working areas on slight elevations in rather low, humid areas at Neden Skiden Enge, Djursland, from LN I might be just such an example of a documented element of this kind of terrain use (Nielsen, T.B. 2012:25pp). In some instances, small huts of some kind may have been needed to perform the activities.

A marked spread of the settlements, at some distance from neighbouring households, appears to have prevailed at least in some of the landscapes of the region and also elsewhere in South Scandinavia in the Late Neolithic and beyond (cf. Myhre 1999:126pp). We have some indications of this around the dried out lake, Tastum Sø.[8] From recent history, single farms with rather dispersed locations in the Danish landscape are well known (Schacke 2003:13pp).

It has been said that the settlements became more permanent in LN I and that this change influenced the economy in terms of adjustments towards combined meat and dairy production (Sarauw 2007b:47). And yet how long did the Late Neolithic and the emerging Bronze Age settlements with sunken-floor longhouses last at the individual locations? In several instances, only a single or at most a few sites of such buildings are found in the landscapes of the Limfjord region. It is thus remarkable that four of the new "early" settlements with sunken-floor houses seem to represent a relatively short period of occupation. These settlements are Glattrup I/III, Hellegård, Glattrup IV, and Rosgårde.

In other instances, very many such building remainders evidence or indicate rather long presence at the location. The Resengaard houses, together with the nearby Marienlyst Strand house, could thus well indicate a very long presence in the local area, spanning from soon after the beginning of the Late Neolithic until the end of the Resengaard settlement, which possibly included a few generations of three-aisled Bronze Age longhouses. In this case, we still lack settlement traces to fill out the chronological gap between Marienlyst Strand and the earliest Resengaard houses. We have a single-phase settlement at Nygaard, found a little further to the southwest. Besides the short Marienlyst Strand and Nygaard settlements, our present knowledge of area continuity in this attractive coastal area thus foremost concerns Resengaard, which embraced some 300 years with sunken-floor longhouses, followed by an estimate of 100-200 years with three-aisled longhouses. Whether this last part was fully continuous still awaits further consideration, however.

The investigation at Tromgade evidenced a settlement with a great deal of material from the early Late Neolithic, including three sunken-floor house sites and indications of up to a further six possible remainders of such buildings in the neighbouring area. Even more unknown house sites could conceivably be found in the immediate vicinity and, at a little distance, the Havbakker settlement with a presumed sunken-floor house site was recovered. In addition, we have the evidence of House 1 at Gåse mose, where much settlement material had accumulated and some of the flint was pressure-flaked. It is therefore not unlikely that further house sites might be there, as Beaker pottery was also present at Gåsemose. In all, within a relatively small area, several house sites belong to a time span ranging from an early part of the Late Neolithic at Tromgade to the very late House 1 at Gåsemose. If area continuity had prevailed throughout this time span, we would expect many sunken-floor longhouses to have been built here during the Late Neolithic, even if only a single longhouse was used for residence at a time. Sites of ground-floor houses have so far not been recovered at any of these settlements.

More to the west in the region, seven sunken-floor house sites have been recovered at Trængsel, and it cannot be excluded that even more may have been present (Mikkelsen, P. 1995:21pp). Further exploration in this vicinity might also therefore indicate long area continuity.

More to the east, at Bejsebakken, area continuity may have prevailed for a long time due to the presence of the many sites of sunken-floor and ground-floor buildings and, as we have considered in the above, a settlement period of up to 400 years has been proposed (Sarauw 2006; 2007b:11; Arthursson 2010:91; 2007c:219). An alternative interpretation relates to a settlement of 3-5 farmsteads across maybe 3-4 phases at Bejsebakken (Artursson 2005b:28p). In the same vein, the Myrhøj settlement remainders have been interpreted as representing three contemporaneous farmsteads, albeit with some reservations due to the limited excavation area (Artursson 2005b:108).

Settlements of long duration with ground-floor houses are known elsewhere in South Scandinavia. Many house sites have been recovered at Limensgård, on the island of Bornholm (Nielsen, P.-O. 1998:19; Artursson 2005b:104pp). The finds have been interpreted such that, within the Late Neolithic until c. 1700 BC, one large farmstead existed together with three minor ones for some 350 years (Arthursson 2010:91 & Fig. 4.2). Likewise Fosie IV in Scania is considered an example of long area continuity. It is presumed to concern one or more single farm units moving around within a resource area (Björhem & Säfvestad 1989:124pp; Artursson 2005a:28p; 2005b:94pp).

An even larger cluster of farmsteads has been presented from Almhov in Scania (Gidlöf, Dehman & Johansson 2006). Here, one large farmstead, together with some smaller farmsteads, may have existed throughout the younger part of the Late Neolithic and emerging Bronze Age (Arthursson 2005b:102pp; 2010:91 & Fig. 4.3; 2009). Some smaller buildings were also attached to the longhouses. The settlement is considered to have been continuous, although the presence of ordinary settlement material is very scarce, apart from undated flint pieces (Gidlöf, Dehman & Johansson 2006:173). Kristian Brink proposes that the "… Almhov site has been interpreted in general terms as a village and a chiefly hamlet with one farm having significantly larger longhouses during the whole time of settlement …", and that this "… interpretation is in line with a general view of Late Neolithic leaders being linked to a large chiefly house with one or two smaller farms comprising part of the household …", whereas other authors "… have taken a more careful stance, raising the question of whether Almhov should be seen as indicating either the presence of a collective social organization or the presence of a social elite …" (Brink 2013:434p). In his own study, on the one hand "… the material is interpreted as clearly indicating the presence of a social elite … and therefore the possible presence of chiefs is not contested …", while on the other, he holds that "… collective strategies are regarded as crucial in understanding how the elite was formed and upheld …" (Brink 2013:435). He focuses on these collective sides, taking as his point of departure "… on the size of houses within the farms since this is the main aspect used in research on houses when interpreting the presence of hierarchies during this period …" (Brink 2013:437). Certain strategies are ascribed to the long area continuity and stability, namely that the "… decision at Almhov to locate new houses and farms this close together indicates a strategy of manifesting the importance of the clan or leading lineage as a whole … this further underlines the importance of the group in creating and upholding stability over generations …" and further that the "… general long-lasting stability of settlement within the area clearly suggests that forms of cooperation existed" (Brink 2013:446p). On residents it is suggested that the houses "… seem to represent individual households. Whether this also indicates independent production within each farm at Almhov is not as clear, however …" (Brink 2013:448).

Relocation of dwellings and avoidance of old grounds

Long area continuity in South Scandinavia may have been managed rather differently at the locations in the Late Neolithic and emerging Bronze Age. For instance, the Bejsebakken settlement is considered to have "… moved around within a large resource area …" (Sarauw 2007c:219). As a concrete example in this respect, we shall again look at the evidence from Resengaard, and it is time now to convert the chronological results into an overview divided into three orders of displacement of residences in sunken-floor longhouses down the centuries (Fig. 5.5). It is necessary again to underline the fact that the Resengaard chronology presented in this work is provisional, and I shall also refer in particular to the sub-parts in the foregoing on "Strong and weak links in the chronological chain" and "Options for further validation of the pottery chronology" (Ch. 3.3). The following suggestion on the relocation order is with the reservations stated.

It appears that my suggestion on the building of a new sunken-floor longhouse every c. 25 years on average at Resengaard is well in accordance with recent Dutch research on the durability of wooden house constructions, namely as expressed in the "Wood rot model" (Fokkens 2003:19p; cf. Nielsen, S. 1999:151pp). And yet, in my model, the household at the hill also applied the lengthy building for other purposes during a significant after-residence life (Fig. 5.6). As it certainly seems most likely that the old longhouse would have functioned as a residence until the new one was finished, the building may thereafter have been used for a more or less substantial period, depending also on when proper or adequate maintenance stopped. Thereafter, the building may soon have begun to deteriorate and collapse. After residence, the longhouse may well have been used for keeping agricultural implements, tools, raw materials, products, timber and other wood for construction, as well as firewood. It could also have been used for different indoor work or other activities. However, it seems that such after-residence life of longhouses is often ignored in the literature on settlements. Concerning House 41, which in my reading had two phases of residence, and when also considering its likely after-residence life, the building would have had three phases, each with a different use, namely: first the residence phase with sunken floor and ground floor; then the second residence phase without the ground-floor part; and finally a third after-residence phase. House 2 would likewise have had three phases, where the second phase relates to the time after the sunken floor was extended to the east.

According to the model, two sunken-floor longhouses would have simultaneously stood for longer periods on the upper hill, being the new building for residence/daily indoor work and the old building for keeping things/occasional work, such as for instance chopping and stacking firewood. In addition to these, up to several minor or short buildings would often simultaneously have been there, too.

Fig. 5.5. Resengaard. The suggested order of relocation when building new longhouses at the hill. Judging by the provisional Resengaard chronology, the residences were moved in varying directions on the upper part of the hill in the period from around 1900 to 1600 BC, for practical reasons here divided into three parts. A: The first order of movements involves five plots, beginning with that of House 134 on the eastern part of the hill and ending with that of House 42 to the southwest. House 134 was thus placed on the upper part of the hill nearest the coast. The order implies movement of residence somewhat towards the south southwest, House 130, then far up to the northwest terrace, House 41, then again far to the south, House 13. The next step was merely a modest shift of plot to the neighbouring ground to the west. B: The middle order of movements involves four plots after that of House 42 and ends far to the north. Thus, from House 42, the order implies movement of residence moderately to the west, House 197, then a great deal to the northeast, House 138, then somewhat in a westerly direction to House 200, ending at the northwest terrace, House 2. C: The last order of movements involves only three plots after that of House 2 and again ending far to the north. Thus, after House 2, it implies a movement of residence somewhat to the south, House 14, and from there to the southeast, House 128, finally returning to the northwest terrace, now the plot of House 1. During a period thereafter, three-aisled longhouses were built on at least three plots.

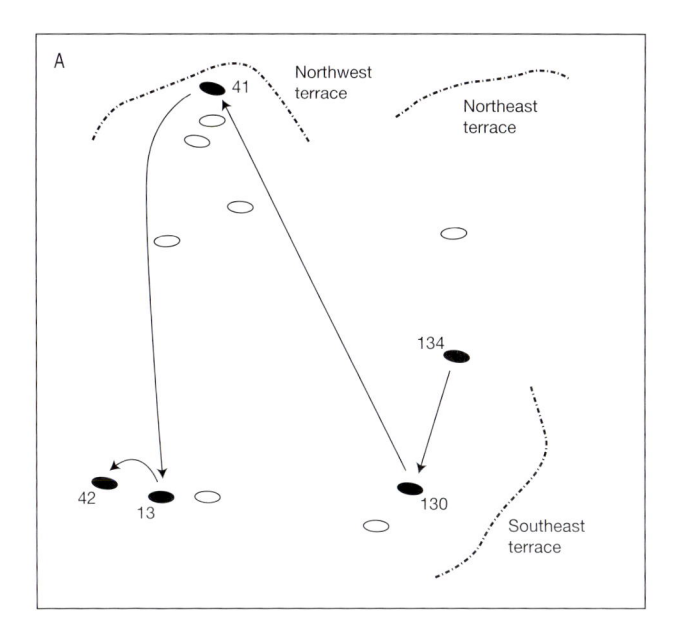

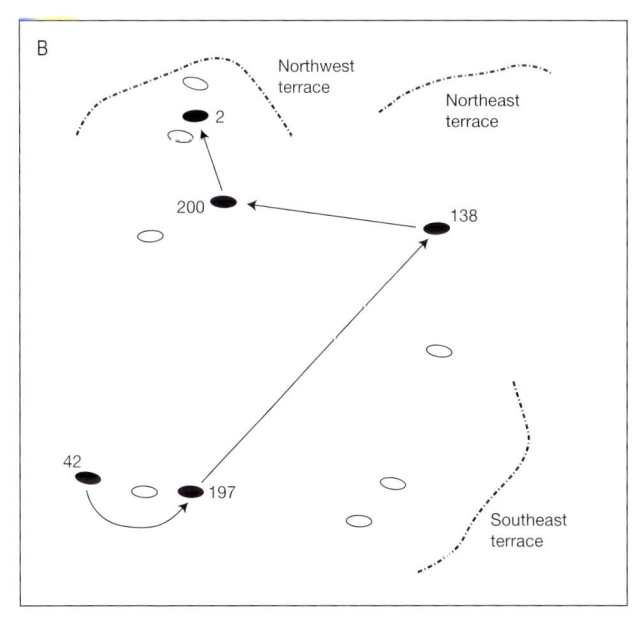

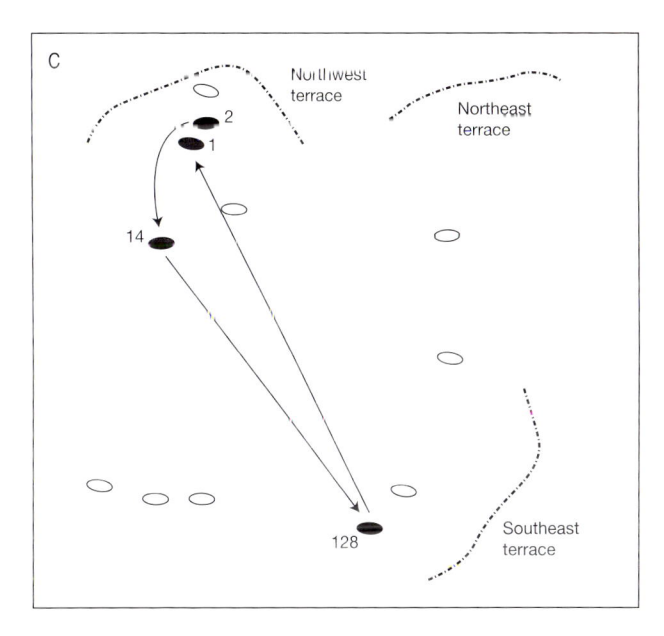

Household, livelihood and exchange

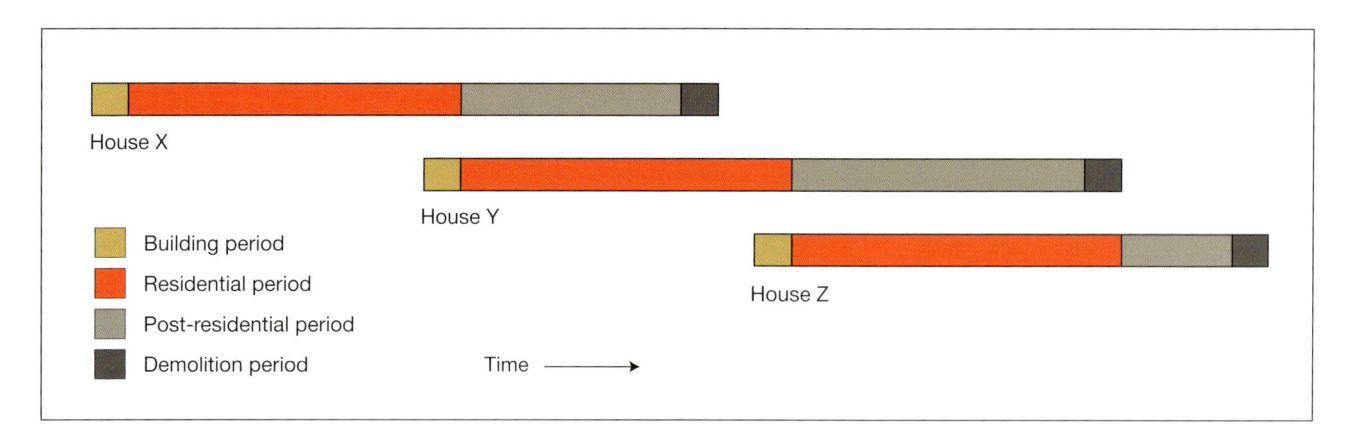

Fig. 5.6. The "after-residence life" of longhouses. Until the building process of a new longhouse had been completed, it seems most plausible that the old one remained in use. This is here illustrated with three hypothetical examples of longhouses with varying duration of after-residence life. After habitation, the former dwellings may often have been used for keeping things (e.g. implements, centre posts, other posts, wall materials, firewood, and winter fodder), and for various working processes. Hence, after residence, the old longhouses may well have stood for a very long period before total abandonment and demolition took place. It might presumably often have been practical to even keep this longhouse as a store for building materials until the next longhouse for residence was to be built.

The physical short-range relocations of the residences across three centuries, from around 1900-1600 calBC, demonstrate orders of displacement in alternating directions on the upper part of the hill. Sometimes only small or minor relocations took place, although it is remarkable that, in several instances, the moves were rather drastic, with marked distances to the old residences. In each of the three orders, one of the longhouses at the northwest terrace was involved.

It is apparent that the spots earlier used for sunken-floor longhouses were seldom selected for the new buildings in the Limfjord region. At Resengaard, no longhouses were built on such old grounds although a short house and a minor one were located on plots used previously for ground floors. In addition to my suggestion regarding overlap at Bejsebakken (House A66), overlapping house sites are found at Stendis and Bjergene II (Simonsen 1983:86; Prieto-Martinez 2008:125). These are exceptional, however, and it appears that normally pristine grounds with sterile subsoil were preferred for the building of new longhouses. The quest for this kind of spot can scarcely be the sole explanation for these movements. If pristine grounds for the placement of the new longhouses had been the only requirement of the Resengaard households, all 12 could for instance have been comfortably located just on the evenly south-sloping terrains in the immediate surroundings of Houses 42, 13 and 197. Hence, we have to think more broadly. I propose that the reasons were, not least, that the forefathers' house spots, including some surrounding living areas, for some reason had to be avoided for the new dwellings. But why might such avoidance have been at play here?

The existence of a kind of taboo due to pollution seems to offer a plausible explanation: "Every human society subscribes to ideas of human purity and pollution in some form. Certain agents, activities, contracts, periods and substances are known to pollute, while others purify. Pollution, as opposed to purity, disturbs equilibrium, destroys or confuses desirable boundaries …" (Khare 2010:437). Further, with reference to *Purity and Danger: an Analysis of Concepts of Pollution and Taboo* published in 1966 by Mary Douglas it is put forward that "…pollution helped explain rules and practices found in 'primitive worlds' as well as complex civilisations." Her explanations concerned the sacred and the secular, the inner and the outer, and the physical and the symbolic. Also, notions of "dirt", hygiene, and uncleanness occupied the centre stage to explain how different peoples treat contaminated foods, bodily fluids, secretions, excretions, remainders, and refuse (Khare 2010:437p). The notion of "taboo" relates to Robertson Smith who "… used the term taboo to describe nonreligious rules of conduct, especially those concerned with pollution, in order to distinguish them from the rules of holiness protecting sanctuaries, priests, and everything pertaining to gods" (Douglas 1984:47).

Regarding the example of Resengaard, the motive for avoiding old plots for new settlement, in my perception, may well have been a kind of "taboo" and we can speculate whether the old sites may have been considered polluted and plagued by the forefathers' spirits or demons, capable of haunting and harming new households that resided on the spot. In that case, the placement of their "polluted" rubbish into the old sunken areas might even have accentuated the meaning and strength of avoidance because it would also have included a multitude of fragments of the forefathers' belongings.

So, on the one hand, long-term settlement on the hill was favoured and the residents thereby lived their daily lives in the vicinity of the sites of their forefathers' houses. On the other, however, it appears that a taboo may have existed for new settlement on the forefathers' plots and in some of the immediate areas. The complex question of how to understand the attitudes towards the house sites is further strengthened because ard-ploughing was apparently not met with a "taboo" and this activity could already take place in the floor bottoms soon after tearing down the longhouses, and thus before substantial filling up with domestic refuse and soil.

We can also ask whether the instances of deliberate burning of abandoned house sites through more or less comprehensive fires should be seen in the light of pollution. Might the flames have been considered to create some kind of purification of the earlier residences? It seems plausible.

Burning the last remainders of the old houses would, at the same time, have been a rather practical activity, i.e. preparing the spot for tillage. As shall be considered below, the use of the old, fertile house grounds for agricultural purposes makes sense and would precisely have been a positive ecological factor that counteracted the gradual deterioration down the centuries of other soils on the upper part of the hill. The use of the earlier longhouse plots for agricultural purposes would thus have been precisely a factor supporting the strategy of long-term settlement on this hill in the neighbourhood of their fathers' and forefathers' plots.

5.4. Strategic, ritual and votive depositions

This part first centres on the domestic refuse placed in different contexts at Resengaard. The discussion focuses on local strategies for rubbish disposal and on possible further ritual meaning of its re-depositing into hollows after demolition of the longhouses. Domestic refuse ("garbage") has been referred to as "…the totality of human discards…" (Rathje & Murphy 2001:9). However, this present work is first and foremost concerned with items that, in practice, will survive down the millennia in the relevant contexts.

Thereafter, we consider offerings of a different character, namely possible abandonment rituals with offerings, votive pits, pits with deliberately smashed and deposited pottery, and cereal offerings.

Household waste and its handling

The condition of our source material from the longhouse sites is highly dependent on multiple factors. Let us take a jar as an example. The time of using the individual specimen may have varied greatly, as some would presumably have a very long "life" and maybe even been passed on to the next household generation, while others may only last a fairly short time. Some jars were solidly made and hence could, in this respect, last a long time, whereas others were of a more fragile nature and might soon be broken. Some could have been handled quite frequently, and hence be more exposed to the risk of breakage, whereas others may have been kept in a more protected place and would tend to have lasted longer. Moreover, some household members could have been rather heavy-handed, while others took better care of things. Overall, this goes to show that a jar in everyday life would have been exposed to various activities that could lead to its destruction but sometimes also its preservation and use over a longer period. We have seen, however, that not a single clay pot was found intact during the fieldwork at the entire Resengaard settlement.

Much waste survived in sunken-floor contexts, terrain hollows and pits at Resengaard, whereas recent ploughing not least likely removed culture layers from the relatively flat top of the hill. The posthole soils also sometimes contained rubbish but are not taken into consideration here.

While a few "antiques" may have come into the secondary fills accidentally, objects of later origin are somewhat more frequent. For instance, while no objects from the secondary fills of House 1 have been dated to a later period, a total of eight potsherds appear to be younger, out of the some 700 objects from the secondary fills of House 14. The secondary fills of House 200 exceeded 2,000 objects, many of them more or less fragmented. Among these, a relatively few rim fragments appear to belong to a later period, as well as some stone hammers. As an average estimate, around 2 % of the material from the secondary fills above the sunken floors at Resengaard stems from later periods although it admittedly cannot be excluded that some flint could be of later origin. On the whole, this is a low percentage and I see no reason generally to consider the impact of younger finds in the secondary fills as worrying, not least because these can usually be isolated.

A noteworthy trait is the presence of fossilized sea urchins. Five specimens were thus found in the secondary fills of House 130, of which two were fragmented. In some instances at Resengaard, it is clear that the fossilized sea urchins were used as hammers. Might there have been some kind of magic strength attached to these?

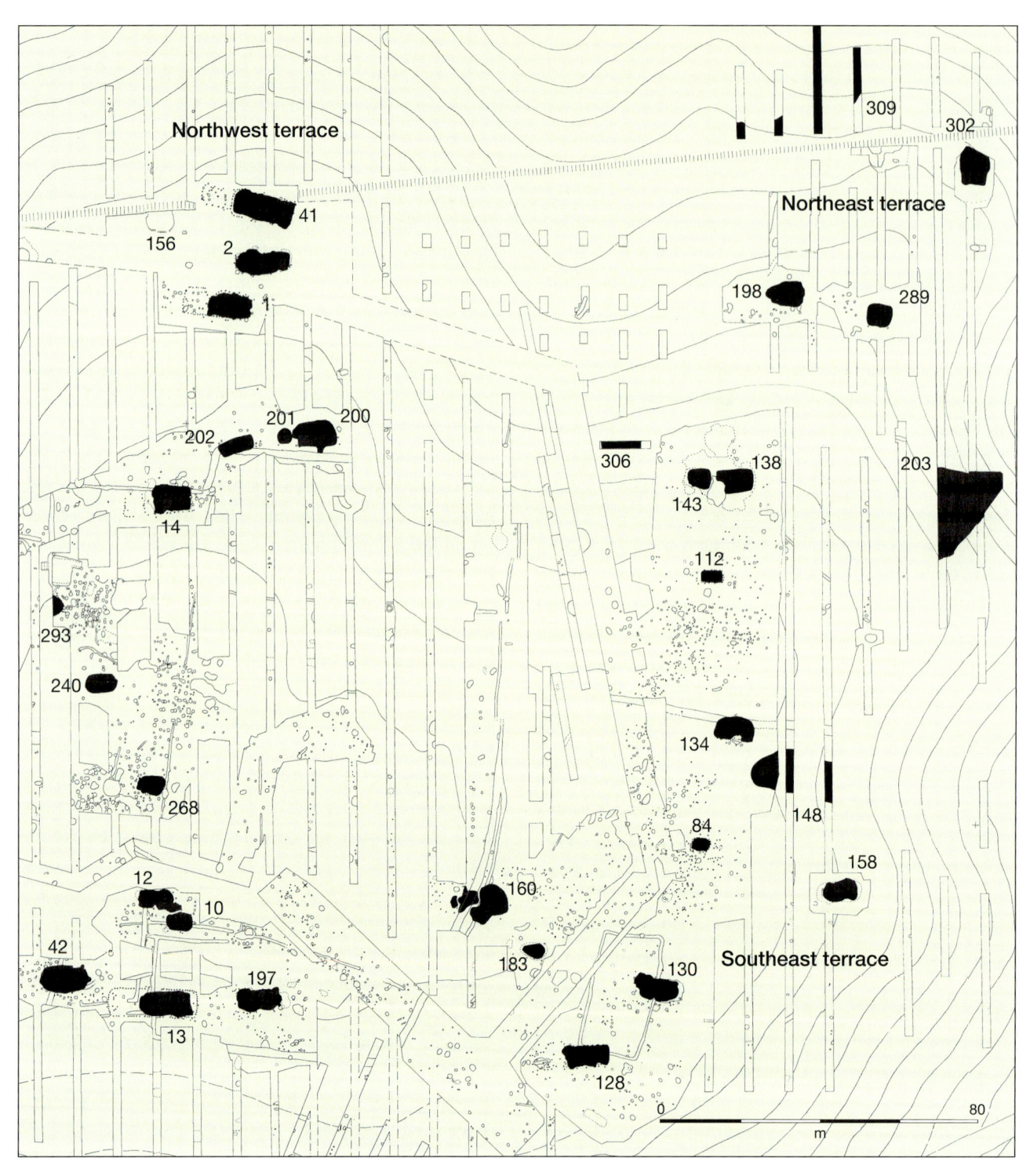

Fig. 5.7. Resengaard. Placing of major waste fills in sunken areas of demolished house sites and in terrain hollows.

The rubbish in the secondary fills above the sunken floors and in the culture layers has several characteristics in common. The presence of different materials indicates that the waste areas were not designated for a particular kind of refuse although, as the conditions of preservation have unfortunately resulted in the complete destruction of all uncharred organic materials, it is impossible to know the extent to which such materials were also deposited in such areas. It seems likely that a substantial volume could have been organic materials, such as discarded remainders of wood, plants, animals etc. From this perspective, the resulting picture of the waste could seem rather poor.

The 32 middens focused on at Resengaard incorporate secondary fills from 12 sunken-floor longhouses, 13 minor sunken-floor houses, 1 short sunken-floor house and 6 culture layers (Fig. 5.7, 5.8, 5.9 & 5.10). The other culture layers contained relatively few finds. Besides these, the possible house site pit 160 also had some rubbish in the soils and this is also included in the accounts. The middens contained varied flint items, ceramics, stone tools and other items but the two former were most prevalent and hence focused on. Worked and burned flint in all amounted to more than 8,600 pieces. Of these, a little more than 7 % were burned. In fills above sunken floors in the longhouse sites, the burned flint on average accounted for 8.6 %, in the sites of minor sunken-floor houses 3.6 %, and in the culture layers 6.0 %. All potsherds and flint (including the burned) in these 32 rubbish areas amount to more than 15,000 pieces, of which the worked flint accounts for some 57 %.

The secondary fills were, on the whole, investigated through careful and meticulous manual excavation at the settlements in focus. A few further finds could, in some instances, be ascribed to the secondary fills. Minor or larger parts of the culture layers were investigated, whereas the secondary fills were in all cases excavated totally and are hence comparable as to numbers of finds. These remarks also concern the secondary fills from sunken-floor houses at Kluborg II, Glattrup I/III, Marienlyst Strand, Granlygård, Hellegård, Glattrup IV, Rosgårde and Tromgade.

The volumes of the secondary fill soils in the sunken areas cannot be calculated exactly but, to give an idea of the find frequency of objects in flint or ceramics per cubic metre, a couple of examples will be presented. In the relatively deep sunken area of House 200, a total of 2,344 objects were found. As the *in situ* volume of the sunken area can loosely be estimated to have been some 30 m³ by the time of excavation, the average content per cubic metre was c. 78 objects. Conversely, 519 objects were found in the comparatively shallow sunken area of House 41. As its volume can loosely be estimated to have been some 12 m³, the average content per cubic metre was c. 43 objects. These two examples are from the sunken areas in which comparatively many artefacts remainders were found. The find frequencies were lower in other secondary fills, and in some even much lower. Yet when the relatively high frequency of flint items from House 200 at Resengaard and House 2 at Tromgade are compared to those of Houses D and EAB at Myrhøj, the massive flint presence from the latter puts the other fills into perspective.

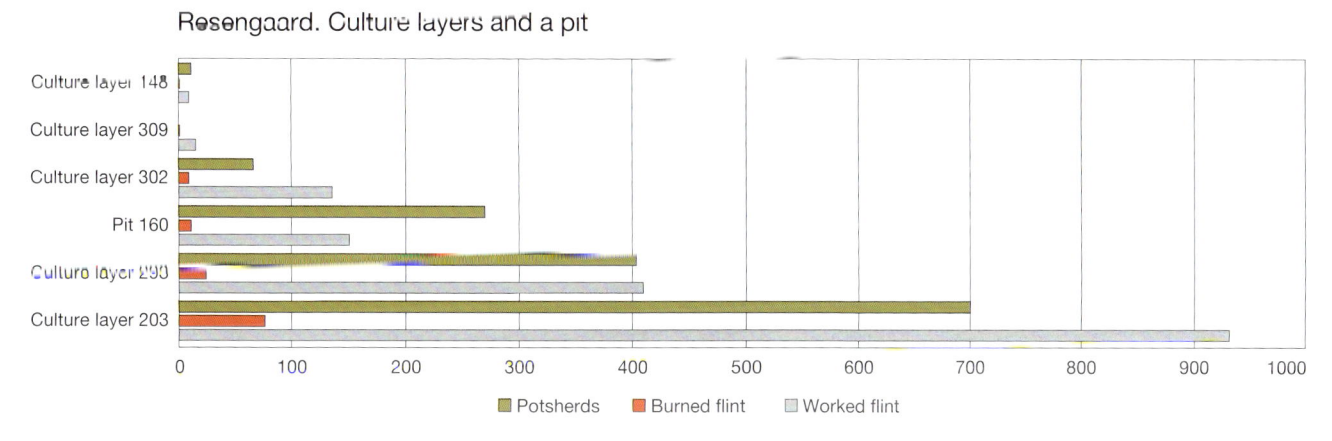

Fig. 5.8. Domestic refuse. Found in 5 culture layers and pit 160, the diagram shows amount of potsherds, worked flint and burned flint (ordered according to the amounts of worked flint). These fills also contained other objects. Worked flint can include tools and fragments thereof. Burned flint can include worked flint.

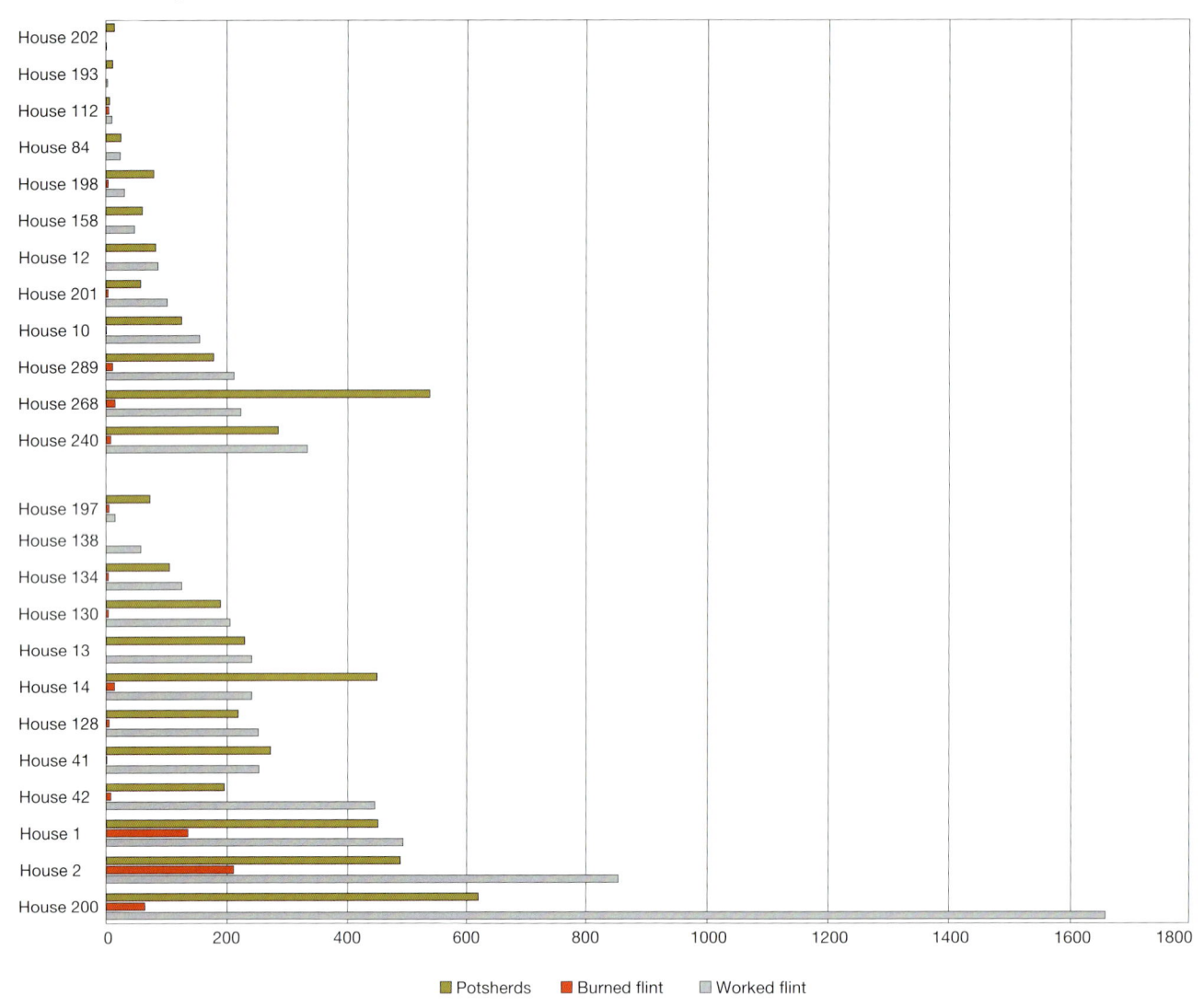

Fig. 5.9. Domestic refuse. Found in 24 secondary fills above sunken floors, the diagram shows amounts of potsherds, worked flint and burned flint (ordered according to the amounts of worked flint). These fills also contained other objects. Worked flint can include tools and fragment thereof. Burned flint can include worked flint. The upper part of the diagram shows those from 11 sites of minor houses and the short House 201.

When considering how the secondary fills could have accumulated, it is obvious that sandy soil was the main component at Resengaard and the other settlements in question. This could stem from external heaps of "old" soil from the original digging of the sunken floor, including some surface soil as well as subsoil. It could also concern surplus soil from various outside activities accumulated nearby over up to several decades. Over a corresponding period, weeds and other plant materials may have been added to such heaps from the immediate surroundings. In removing the weeds from nearby tillage, presumably often pulling them up by the roots, minor lumps of soil would inevitably also have been transferred. Tufts of straw, stalks from various plants, roots etc. would rapidly decay and soon be transformed into soil of high organic content. I suggest the interpretation that, after abandonment and tearing down of the longhouse, such domestic refuse would have been deposited as fills in sunken areas.

More or less daily additions of different rubbish from life in the longhouse interiors would, in my understanding, have been important components of such outside deposits. This might first and foremost have concerned frequent additions of organic leftovers from everyday life. These would, not least, I suppose, derive from cooking activities but, to vary-

A   Limfjord region. Other house sites

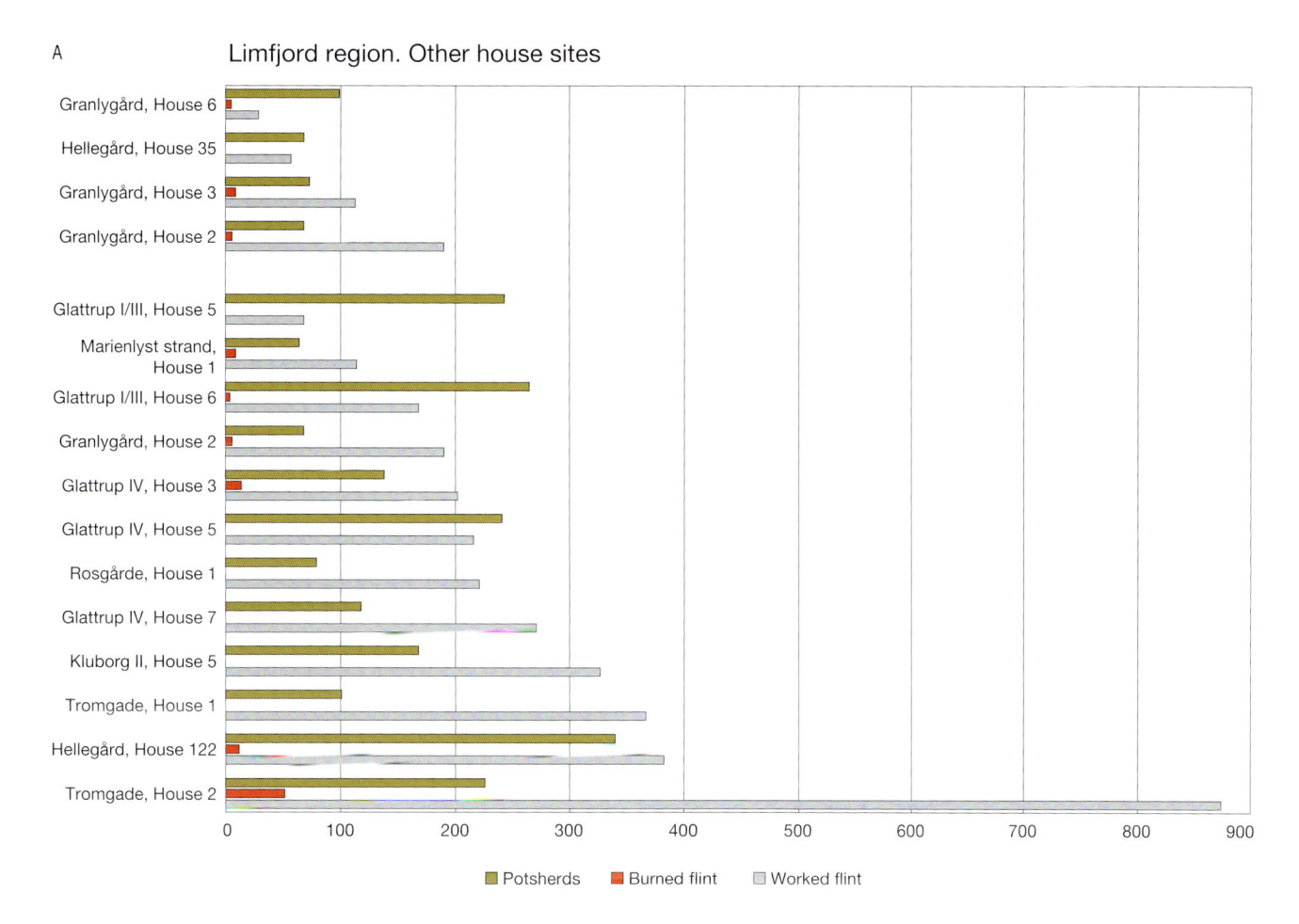

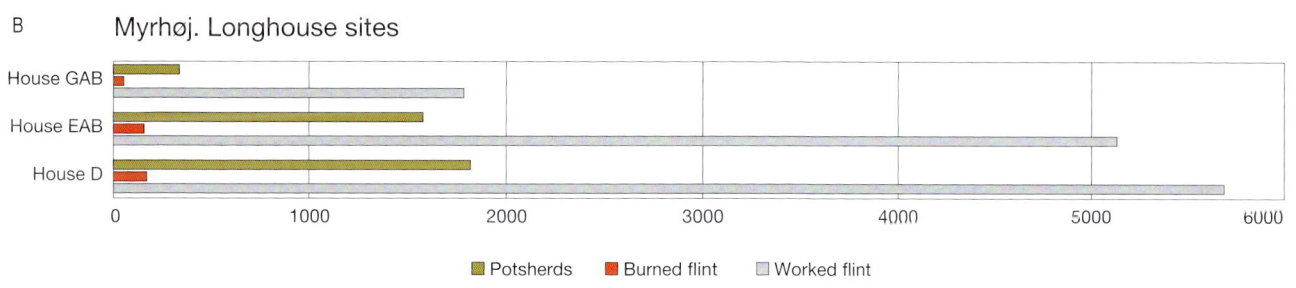

[Bar chart showing Potsherds, Burned flint, and Worked flint counts for houses: Granlygård House 6, Hellegård House 35, Granlygård House 3, Granlygård House 2, Glattrup I/III House 5, Marienlyst strand House 1, Glattrup I/III House 6, Granlygård House 2, Glattrup IV House 3, Glattrup IV House 5, Rosgårde House 1, Glattrup IV House 7, Kluborg II House 5, Tromgade House 1, Hellegård House 122, Tromgade House 2. X-axis: 0 to 900.]

B   Myrhøj. Longhouse sites

[Bar chart showing Potsherds, Burned flint, and Worked flint for House GAB, House EAB, House D. X-axis: 0 to 6000.]

Fig. 5.10. *Domestic refuse. A: Kluborg II, Glattrup I/III, Marienlyst Strand, Granlygård, Hellegård, Glattrup IV, Rosgårde, and Tromgade. Found in 16 secondary fills above sunken floors, the diagram shows amounts of potsherds, worked flint and burned flint. These fills also contained other objects. Worked flint can include tools and fragment thereof. Burned flint can include worked flint. Concerning House 122 at Hellegård, the 1,113 pieces of mostly thin flint waste are not included in the account (RE556). The upper part of the diagram shows those from 4 sites of minor/short houses. B: Myrhøj. Account from three house sites (ordered according to the amounts of worked flint). Based on Jensen, J.A. 1973.*

ing degrees, also wooden items and other organic material from further activities. Now and then, broken pottery, discarded flint objects, and other stone items would have been added.

Another source for secondary fills may have been the remainders of outdoor stone deposits. Some of these could originally have stemmed from the clearing and maintenance of fields, and then used for instance in certain indoor activities and thereafter deposited outside. Stones kept for possible use but not considered worth transporting to the new house plot may have been dumped in this way. Head-size stones or larger stones were unusual in secondary fills.

In individual instances, I assume that the deposition of domestic refuse frequently took place in hollows appearing in limited parts of the sunken are-

Household, livelihood and exchange   371

as. On the whole these fills presumably could have reached substantial volumes in a reasonably short time. The filling up of the sunken floor areas was presumably usually done in such a way that resulted in a level end state.

The secondary fills above the sunken floors may by and large have come into being as sketched out here but, in the cultural and social reality of that time, the practices and methods may have been influenced by several factors that we do not have the slightest chance of recognizing today. In any case, the rubbish and soils were deposited in rapid succession, judging by the already noted absence of vegetation horizons.

Strategies on use of abandoned sunken floors and hollow terrains

On the whole, it is noteworthy that a major share of the total finds from Resengaard was found to have been relocated by the residents, i.e. the abundant material from the fills above former sunken floors and in culture layers. This is rather interesting because this activity appears to form an important element of a deliberate strategy in the agricultural production.

The garbage is found *in situ* or disorganized by ard-ploughing in these contexts. However, the notion of the early ard-ploughing of secondary fills is often difficult to evidence. That it actually took place repeatedly, leading to further disorganization, is even harder to prove, because traces of these activities are usually not directly observable.

The arguments for ard-ploughing of the secondary fills at Resengaard are therefore of an indirect nature. First of all, the soils of these fills were often much more homogeneous than would be expected if many small local dumps of waste soils had just been left without further influence from activities. Accordingly, it is my impression that objects such as potsherds often tended to be found lying in all kinds of directions in the secondary fills, while potsherds were often found lying relatively flat in sunken-floor horizons, such as e.g. on the floor of House 10 at Resengaard (Fig. 4.34). After being relocated as secondary fills over the sunken floors, the explanation must therefore be that the domestic refuse was repeatedly ard-ploughed. In my understanding, a deliberate agricultural strategy was thus followed when relocating waste from the residence into middens in all sunken areas of the former longhouse plots and in a number of terrain hollows.

Significant alterations in the composition of the rubbish relocated to secondary fill areas do not appear to have taken place over the centuries. As far as the preserved material allows, it seems that the residents maintained the same deliberate strategy of rubbish deposition combined with repeated ard-ploughing throughout the period of occupation at the hill. This systematic filling up of the sunken floors at Resengaard is thus in line with this generalized view. After filling up to a markedly higher soil level, we saw earlier that repeated ard-ploughing took place in the sites of House 122 at Hellegård and House 7 at Glattrup IV.

Behind this constancy were, in my interpretation, two main aims. One of these was, of course, to maintain a good practice for the disposal of waste from contexts where it was no longer desirable. The second – and probably main – reason was to increase the agricultural potential of the plot. When a sunken area was gradually filled up with soils and different rubbish, it would have improved the ground for future tillage. It must have long been an established experience of the residents that former sunken floor areas had a rather good capacity for retaining moisture during dry seasons, due to the creation of comparatively thick soils, presumably rich in humus. These waste areas thus became rather attractive for agricultural purposes. We have good reason to presume that the waste strategies at other central Limfjord region sites were largely the same as those at Resengaard.

In actual fact, the only secondary fills in a sunken area that I can think of as not having been ard-ploughed are those of House 1 at Gåsemose. The massive presence of the heat-affected/cracked stones may indicate that the sunken area was hardly exposed to the ard after demolition of the building, perhaps because the Gåsemose settlement suddenly came to an end thereafter (Fig. 2.40).

It is interesting that several artefacts and some rubbish were also dumped into a terrain hollow at Marienlyst Strand, where no evident indications of ancient agriculture have been observed. The horizontal extension of the thus created culture layer cannot be assessed precisely but the area is understood as a little, natural lowering that was formerly wet.

Sites with deposition of domestic refuse are also known from settlements elsewhere in the region (Jensen, J.A. 1973:106pp). At Myrhøj, the average number of waste objects far exceeded the amount of such objects from most other known locations (Jensen,

J.A. 1973:79pp). Comparatively many potsherds were found in two of the three sunken-floor houses (D & EAB) but, as we have seen, not least, the number of worked flints obtained was high. The use of these dump sites for agriculture is not clarified.

Concerning Vadgård, it is stated that rubbish was transported further away from the living house area and deposited in naturally hollow areas. In this respect, it accords well with the Resengaard case (Rasmussen, M. 1995:102).

Ritually performed re-deposition of house waste?

I propose that, after abandonment and demolition of the building, significant meaning would still have been attached to the house plot and its immediate vicinity. In this respect, the following quotation of what a house might have represented is interesting: "The house is an institution, not just a structure, created for a complex set of purposes. Because building a house is a cultural phenomenon, its form and organization are greatly influenced by the cultural milieu to which it belongs. Very early in recorded time the house became more than shelter for primitive man, and almost from the beginning 'function' was much more than a physical or utilitarian concept. Religious ceremonial has almost always preceded and accompanied its foundation, erection, and occupation" (Rapoport 1969:46).

Avoiding the old sites, and hence the quest for fresh grounds for building sunken-floor longhouses, often resulted in quite marked distances between the new plots and the old longhouses. This likely happened in combination with other (to us) unknown factors influencing the relocation of dwellings at Resengaard. Viewed purely from a practical angle, it would actually have been rather laborious to carry rubbish between, for instance, House 128 on the southeast terrace and House 1 on the northwest terrace, a distance of at least 200 m and likely somewhat more, given the possible winding of the path. We must therefore ask why the residents would make such efforts. In my view, it is hardly realistic to assume that the daily waste produced in the new context would have been transported back to the sunken area of the old house. It makes much more sense that the secondary fills above the sunken floors derived from the immediate surroundings of the old house.

Yet, might a deeper meaning not also have existed behind such acts of filling back material from middens near the former buildings? Could fills that likely included the former residents' artefacts, their raw materials, their flint waste, their broken pottery as well as other superfluous soil have possessed some special significance? Might it have been of importance that what came from the old house site and thereby from the households' life that previously took place there was given back to it? Filling back up with the residents' discarded items could well have been perceived as a ritual act. It might even have been regarded as an absolutely necessary procedure. An exception is the possible minor "House 156", where the fills were not of this nature.

Furthermore, as earlier dealt with, we have evidence of three cases of deliberate burning of the house scrap from the sunken areas and beyond at Resengaard. These acts could very well have been fires of a ritual character as their ignition marks the end of residence in each longhouse. These fires preceded the act of filling back the house waste.

The temporary deposition of rubbish in the immediate vicinity of the longhouses likely also pertains to many traits of ordered life at the Resengaard settlement. The many kinds of rubbish from everyday life would, in my reading, hardly have simply been dropped accidentally outside from day to day over the lifetime of a house. On the contrary, I presume that household waste would have been placed in piles at some distance from the house, albeit not inconveniently far away. Out of convenience, this might relate to an accumulation of piles in the periphery of an area around the longhouse and near paths leading from the area. In this way, rubbish middens would hardly have been a problem when accessing the entrances, other areas with good passage or outside activity spaces. When these then had to be redeposited in the sunken area after abandonment and demolition of the longhouse, they could be moved the short distance without much difficulty.

Some domestic refuse may, on some occasions, have been handled differently. It is, for instance, conceivable that waste from certain households or a member of them, having performed particular activities in the community, could possibly have been assigned a special meaning and therefore could possibly be associated with danger. It may therefore have been necessary to carry out unusual rituals when depositing this particular waste. Such stuff might perhaps not even have reached the usual areas for depositing of rubbish because plots with extraordinary virtues may have been required.

The heavy stone placed in the sunken area of House 200 at Resengaard after abandonment does not appear to have any parallels among the published sites of sunken-floor longhouses from the region. It was presumably removed from a former place near the house in order to clear the ground above for tillage. And yet can we be sure that this was a purely practical act? Might the rare stone somehow have been assigned some further importance in relation to the activities of the former residents, perhaps connected to their esteem? I cannot offer any direct suggestion in this respect but it cannot be ruled out that its placement there signified some kind of ritual or sentimental value. It seems plausible that rolling the stone down into the sunken area, where the residents' life formerly took place, could have had some kind of symbolic meaning. This action could represent a ritual in itself. Relocating the stone to the former living area might mark the end of the dwelling and thereby, for the remaining members of the household, possibly be symbolic of that. The house site was finally left and activities concerned with agriculture on the spot could soon begin.

In the secondary fills of House 1 at Resengaard, just a few scattered charred cereals were observed. If many had originally been removed from the sunken floor and carried outside, it was seemingly not necessary to bring these back as fills into the sunken area. We also saw earlier how tiny pieces of sharp flint were only sporadically present in the sunken-floor horizons at Resengaard, and had likely been considered "problematic" rubbish, requiring prompt removal, even to special spots. Pits used for such purposes have not been recovered at Resengaard. It thus appears that tiny flints and charred cereals did not reach the regular dump sites in substantial numbers (*cf.* Schiffer 1987:63).[9]

With regard to certain Iron Age pits in Wessex, it has been observed that the refilling of many, very large pits was structured in certain ways (Hill 1995:95pp). It is hypothesized as to whether or not this should be understood as a kind of ritual depositing. The point of bringing this up now is that it might also be interesting to look at the secondary fills above the sunken floor from this perspective. While at Resengaard we always gave priority to investigating the finds directly connected to the floor horizons of the houses, we never focused systematically on these dumps. And yet we cannot exclude the possibility that ritual episodes or certain sequences of rubbish placement may have taken place. When undertaking new investigations of sunken-floor longhouses where subsequent ancient ploughing for some reason did not spoil the stratification, it might be worth focussing on this topic and also on possible traces of other activities in the sunken areas just after abandonment and tearing down of the buildings. If greater interest in the details of secondary fills and other dumps becomes broadly topical, it will therefore be necessary in future to address rubbish intensively during fieldwork in order to make further considerations and studies of the topic a little more promising. Further below, we shall consider the possible meaning of certain pits.

House abandonment rituals

As dealt with earlier (Ch. 2), we have evidence that some longhouses at Resengaard ended as sites of fire. In one case (House 2), it is obvious that the solid centre posts had been removed prior to the fire and this also seems to have been carried out in another case (House 197). The deliberate burning of the building scrap, in my understanding, could well have had a ritual character. Actions such as igniting the longhouse remainders are therefore seen as abandonment rituals. The subsequent discarding of the delicate fishtail dagger (RE89ea/175ea) into the secondary fills of House 2 could perhaps also have been performed as a ritual act. The dagger may have been complete at the time, although when excavated it was found broken in two, albeit with two tiny pieces apparently missing (for further, see Cat. B).

Two examples of pits containing certain flint items may possibly indicate ritual offerings on abandonment of the longhouses.

In the site of House 200 at Resengaard, we have a single example of what might be the result of rituals carried out on abandonment of the dwelling. This is the possible votive deposition of two items in the only deep pit (cellar pit) from any of the 12 longhouses at the settlement. The deposited items were found near the bottom. This concerns a 7.5 cm long flint dagger fragment of a late type made with the usual pressure-flaking and having a partly preserved cortex (RE985ea). The other item relates to an almost complete 3-cm-long triangular flint arrowhead, just missing one of the lobes (RE985eb). In terms of votive gifts, the dagger might perhaps relate to some idea of *pars pro toto*. No other finds are recorded from this cellar pit.

In the site of House 3 at Glattrup IV, a complete but markedly re-sharpened flint dagger (GT178ea) was deposited in a pit in the ground floor west of the sunken floor. The deposition took place during the filling up of the pit. A stone hammer (GT208) was furthermore placed in a posthole of the same house site. The dagger in particular may indicate a ritual house offering, in this case being on abandonment.

These singular and indeed not very impressive finds are, in my reading, the only ones that might point to votive offerings among the selected house sites from the Late Neolithic and emerging Bronze Age in the central Limfjord region. We cannot therefore speak of evidence of any consistent habit of carrying out ritual offerings in these many house contexts, either when building the longhouses or when abandoning them.

We have evident votive offerings of flint items from two of the early sites of three-aisled longhouses at Resengaard but whether these could also stem from the time of building the houses is not clarified at present.

Votive pit with a set of items and another with an exquisite sickle

Pit 89, with remarkable content, was recovered in the upper part of the hill to the southeast and is the only one of its kind from Resengaard. The pit was covered by two intact soil layers, in all 42 cm, as well as recently-ploughed topsoil. It was relatively shallow and quite ordinary in its shaping, with oblique sides and rounded bottom. It had surface dimensions of c. 85 E-W and 83 cm N-S, and a depth of c. 40 cm. Its eastern side and some ceramics found near the bottom were initially damaged by the machine digging. The content concerns the remainders of four open, more or less straight-sided bowls with some fresh fractures (RE484). A clay spoon and a polished miniature flint axe were also placed at the pit bottom (Fig. 5.11). The last-mentioned indicates that this hardly represented items that were new at the time of deposition, as the just small, axe shows traces of wear on the sides and seems re-sharpened. In my reading, the items had, on the whole, therefore been placed on the bottom maybe on top of some (now vanished) organic material. This position is in stark contrast to the artefacts in a pit cluster near the site of House 197 (see below). It cannot be excluded that only parts of the bowls were present at the time of deposition but, due to the damage from machine digging, this cannot be clarified. This set of items is rather unusual and appears to represent a votive gift, likely part of a ritual communication with deities, higher spirits, or maybe forefathers. It seems to represent the deliberate placing of a tool kit for certain kinds of work. The pit belongs to a rather early settlement at the hill and, conceivably, the deposition could have taken place when, for instance, a nearby longhouse was abandoned.

A finely pressure-flaked crescent-shaped sickle (RE542ea) was found in a shallow pit (135) east of House 128 at Resengaard. The sickle is of relatively dark greyish flint, and its length is 13.9 cm. It is completely preserved, with a cutting edge of 13.5 cm that had probably been re-sharpened at some point in time. The ample gloss on both sides adds to its very delicate appearance. It had been placed flat, horizontally, uppermost in the pit. The fills below contained 24 ordinary potsherds. Taking into consideration the exquisite craftsmanship of this crescent-shaped sickle and its careful flat placement on top of an otherwise ordinary pit leads me to suggest that it was a votive offering, perhaps carried out in relation to the harvesting of cereals.

Some offerings from other South Scandinavian settlement areas can also be referred to. The deposition of two clay pots together with a complete stone quern in a pit was thus found in an area north of Holsted (Grundvad & Poulsen 2013:9pp). At a settlement not far from there, a miniature flint dagger was found in a pit beneath a sunken floor (K37) at Mannehøjgård IV (Dollar 2013:43). There was an unusually illustrative find of six clay pots, placed bottom up on top of each other, in a likely corner posthole of a ground-floor longhouse at Nørregård (Dollar 2013:46, Fig. 6).

Offerings of items such as a flint dagger, a flint axe and other items in dwelling contexts are known from e.g. Øster Nibstrup, Myrhøj, Limensgård and Fosie IV and, from the latter, a bronze axe was also found in the large ground-floor House 95 (Björhem & Säfvestad 1989:107p; Poulsen 2009:162).

Pits with deliberately smashed, deposited pottery

Several pits containing ceramics as the major artefact component and also belonging to an early period of the settlement have been recovered within a narrow area to the south on the upper hill at Resengaard (Fig. 5.12 & 5.13). These pits were observed some two metres east of the eastern gable end of House 13 and fur-

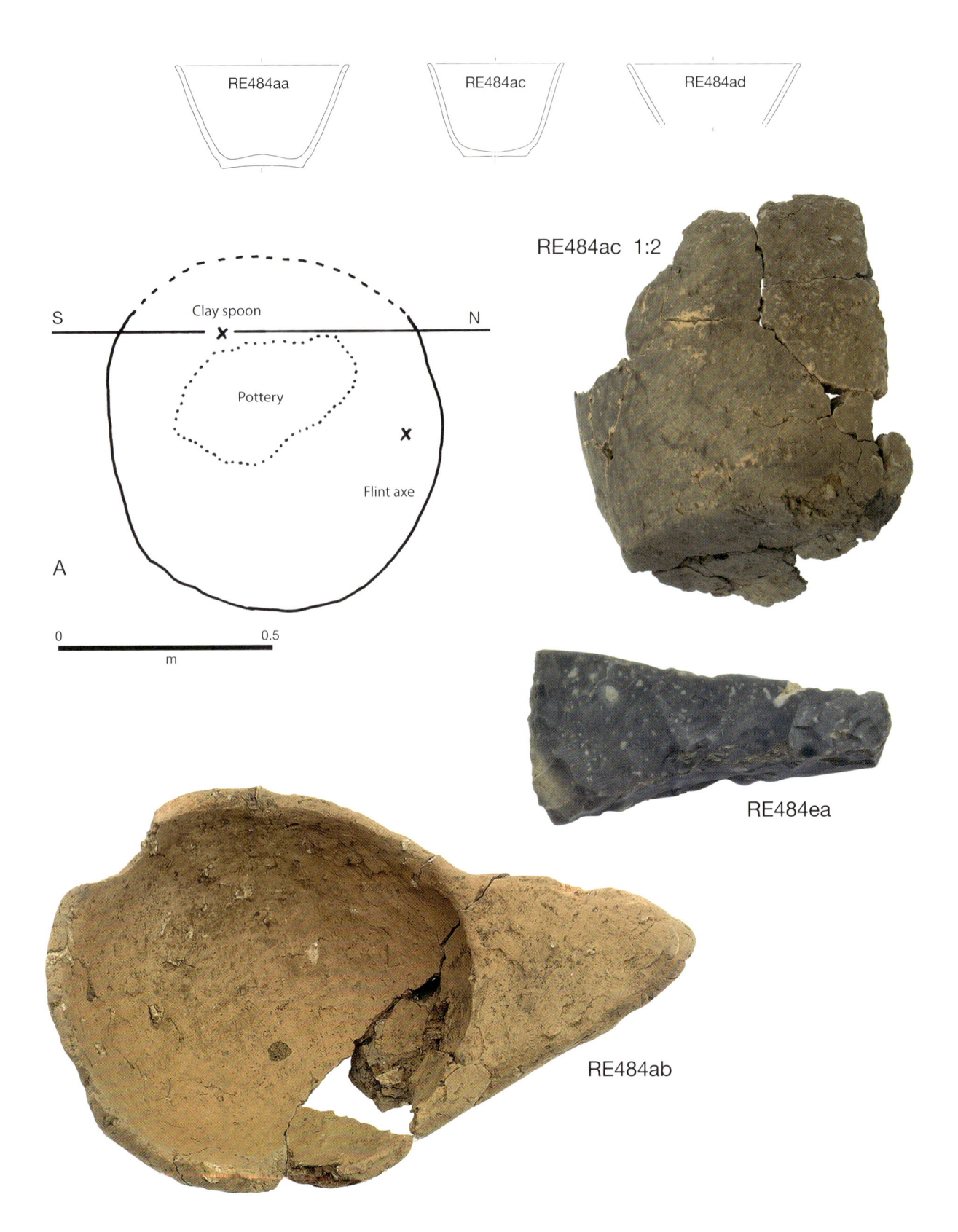

Fig. 5.11. Resengaard. Pit 89. Votive offering of six items, being an axe, a spoon and four bowls (possibly as fragments), all placed in a minor pit. No items of organic material were found but these could well have been present. The set of items may relate to a kit for some kind of household doings. A: Plan drawing of the sub-circular pit. The straight line indicates the position of a profile section. Artefacts: Miniature drawings (not to scale) showing three of the open bowls, see Catalogue A. The flint axe (Cat. B: RE484ea) is 7.0 cm long with broad edge, polished near the edge and partially around its middle. The clay spoon (Cat. A: RE484ab) is made of coarsely tempered clay and burned well. The outer side and bottom of one of the bowls (RE484ac) may indicate that it was burned secondarily but no traces of carbonized content have been observed inside.

Pit 310

RE692aa   RE692ab   RE692af

Pit 319

RE693aa   RE693ab   RE693ac   RE693ad   RE693ae

RE693af

Pit 316

RE694aa   RE694ab   RE694ac   RE694ad   RE694af

RE694ae   RE694ag

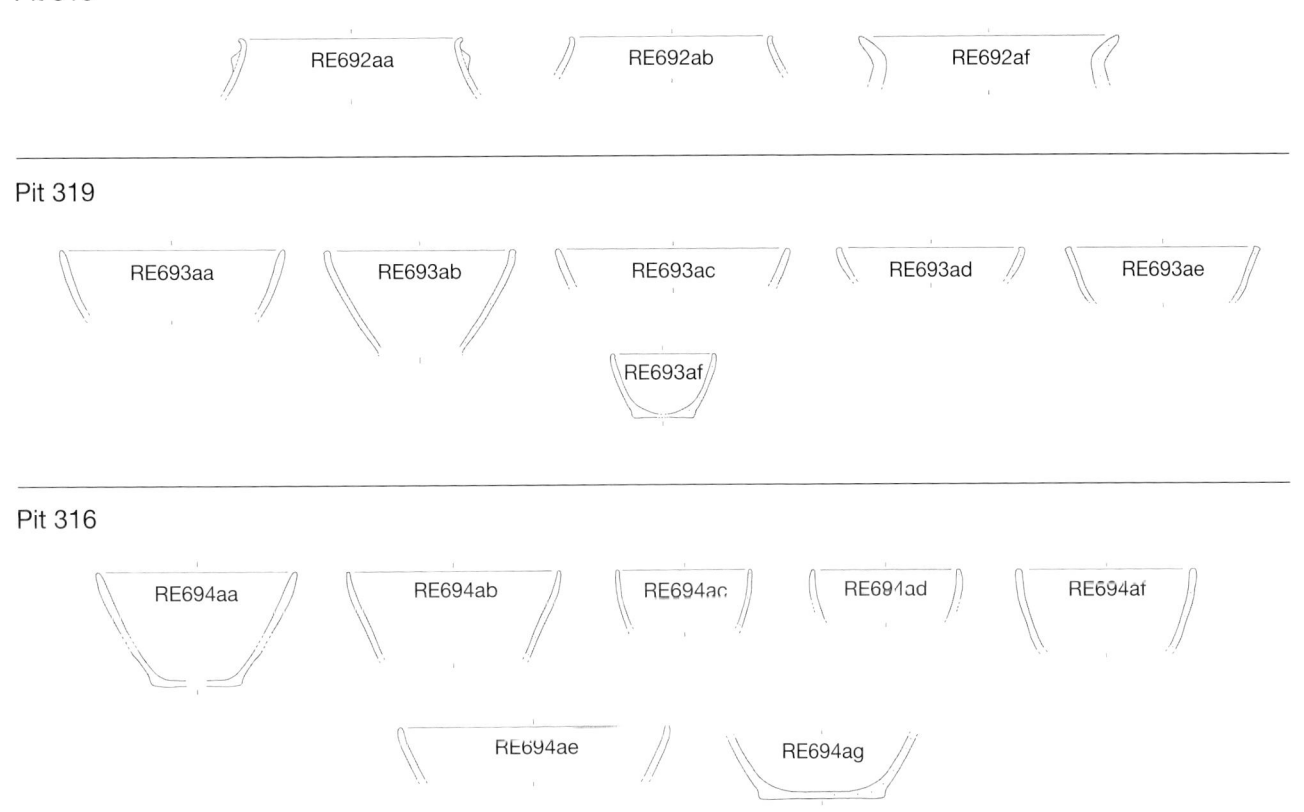

Fig. 5.12. Resengaard. Pit 310, 319 & 316. Selected ceramics (see plan drawing, Fig 3.30 & Catalogue A). The wares, including those of pit 317, have a relatively homogeneous character in common and could represent special activities over a fairly short period. Not to scale.

ther east. The two northernmost pits were found in an area where the southwest part of House 197 was also placed but no preserved wall postholes had cut through them. Stratification cannot therefore help to date these pits but the chronological analysis points to a time long before that building. In all, the presence of three sites of longhouses and two sites of minor houses on this southern part of the hill may well indicate that it was also an attractive spot for everyday living.

Some of the pits were circular or sub-circular in shape. The interesting pottery finds concern, in particular, four pits, namely pit 310 (RE692aa, RE692ab, RE692af & other), pit 319 (RE693ab and other), pit 316 (RE694aa, RE694ab, RE694ac, RE694ad RE694ae, RE694af, RE694aa & other) and pit 317 (RE695aa, RE695ab, RE695ac, RE695ad, RE695aea, RE695af, RE695ag, RE695ah, RE695ai, RE695aj & other). In all, this encompasses fragments from more than 21 clay pots.

Other items in these pits were few and mainly related to a little flint waste. Apart from a piece of bone, pit 319 also contained a piece of dark-brownish, semi-transparent amber with partly preserved cortex (RE-

693ga). Its dimensions were c. 2.9 x 2.0 x 1.1 cm but some amber material had been cut off from three sides in the prehistoric context. Pit 317 also contained a lump of clay (perhaps mildly burned) and a 14.0-cm-long, pressure-flaked flint dagger (RE695ea), having been strongly re-sharpened. In pit 310, a broken-off pointed end of a heavily re-sharpened flint dagger blade (RE692ea) was found.

Interestingly, several other pits in this area were more or less free from finds. This might, of course, mirror the prehistoric situation but it cannot be ruled out that organic material could have been placed in them in some instances.

The ceramics from the four pits appear to have some common "touches" as indicated by the ware tempering, the surface treatment, and the firing. One is supplied with decoration of horizontally incised lines (RE693ga) but most are unornamented open bowls with some variation as to the shaping of the outward-leaning sides and with limited differences in side thicknesses. As a result of the provisional Resengaard chronology, I have suggested a dating of pit

Pit 317

RE695aa RE695ab

RE695ac RE695ad

RE695ae RE695af RE695ah

RE695ai RE695aj RE695ag

RE695ea

Fig. 5.13. Resengaard. Pit 317. Selected ceramics (not to scale). Flint dagger (Cat. B: RE695ea), heavily re-sharpened.

310, pit 316, pit 317 and pit 319 as being close in time to the House 134 assemblage, ranging from somewhat before to somewhat after it. It is my impression that the pottery in all four pits may have been smashed systematically and on purpose. The pieces may have been thrown, hitting some firm material, or been hammered with a heavy item, because they show many relatively "clean" breaks.

The four pits in question may perhaps first have been dug for the removal of fresh, uncontaminated sand. What happened thereafter is open to rather different interpretations as the pottery may, for instance, have been smashed in connection with "public" ceremonies, celebrations, ordinary feasting, incidences of witchcraft (dangerous items) or other.

The destruction of valuables could immediately raise associations with the Potlatch ceremonies of the Kwakiutl Indians, see below (Boas 1982; Mauss 1997). In the present case, however, this would probably be going too far with regard to what happened to the pottery at the four pits. This seems to have been performed on a comparatively small scale and would not necessarily have involved many ritual acts.

In several cases, the pottery had been severely exposed to secondary burning (e.g. RE695aa, RE695af, & RE695aj). In other cases, remaining soot and soot crust were observable on the broken, secondarily burned ceramics (RE692ab, RE694ag & RE695ae). Some of the ceramics belong to a group of large open bowls (e.g. RE694ae & 695aa), which could have contained, for instance, a great deal of food – or liquids. This might support the notion of food consumption on these occasions. Only parts of the ceramics were subsequently buried together with soil in the pits. We have not identified any instances where smashed pieces from the same clay pot ended up in two separate pits. The pits did not stay open long, because no wind deposits or vegetation horizons were observed. On the whole I therefore favour proposing an interpretation of these pits as concerning a row of local occasions for carrying out some ritual, perhaps a celebration, at an early time in the Resengaard settlement, at which plentiful consumption of foods and beverages took place and where pottery was exposed to glowing and flaming fires, destruction and burial in pits – and we can still witness today the presence of some charred organic material, presumably food leftovers, on the sides.

The dating of the above votive pit 89 may be close to the suggested dating of these four pits but, as mentioned, it showed a much more ordered deposition than these four pits. Another find that could well have been close in time to that of the above four pits is pit 311, placed southeast of the site of House 183. In my interpretation it holds more "ordinary" settlement character, containing three pieces of a fine-grained whetstone (RE196ea), three pieces of the upper part of a saddle quern (RE196eb), some potsherds from four clay pots, of which one was supplied with cordoned rim (RE196aa, RE196ab, RE196ac & RE196ad), and a little flint waste. Apart from that, it has not been possible to identify pits with such pottery from any later parts of the Resengaard settlement although examples of pits with potsherds other than in the house sites do exist.

Votive offerings of charred cereals

The votive offerings of intentionally charred cereals also belong in the considerations on the proposed ritually performed re-depositions of the household's waste on top of the former sunken floors, the possible votive offerings carried out on abandonment of the longhouses, the burning of house remainders on abandonment, the votive pits with varying items, and the area of pits containing (presumed) deliberately smashed and deposited ceramics. Such depositions of "eternally" lasting cereals are evidently of high interest in relation to the longhouse sites where comprehensive amounts of charred cereals are observed.

Yet I cannot present any new finds of charred cereal depositions directly at – or in the immediate vicinity of – the selected settlements in the central Limfjord region although I am convinced that these are somewhat ignored in the picture of votive deposition within the period in question. A pit with many charred cereals and acorns at Gilmosevej could well represent a votive offering (Møbjerg, T., Jensen P. M., & Mikkelsen, P. H. 2007:9pp).

At Bjerregrav Enge Nord (Vester Bjerregrav parish), a sizeable, relatively flat-bottomed pit has recently been found containing numerous charred grains of emmer and naked barley considered to belong to LN I (Boddum, S., Kjeldsen, M., Larsen, L.A., & Terkildsen, K.F. 2015:91p). Somewhat to the north, the site of an E-W aligned two-aisled building has been partly investigated. I would favour to consider this cereal pit as representing a votive offering. More evidence exists on this topic (Jæger & Laursen 1983; Møbjerg, Jensen & Mikkelsen 2007; Andreasen 2009). We shall return to these matters further below.

5.5. Fields, pastures and other agricultural aspects

Northern Jutland is a rather windblown part of Denmark and the 57th degree of latitude forms a line that cuts through the northern half of the Limfjord region. Westerly winds are the rule and particularly rough conditions prevail in the western and northern coastal areas, exposed as they are to harsh winds, strong coastal erosion, and very salty sea fog. Temperatures seldom fluctuate particularly high or low, however, due to the moderating influence of the Gulf Stream. The current climate to the west of the region is considered to be sub-oceanic, with January and July mean temperatures of around 0-1 and 15-16 degrees Celsius, generally stretching the growing seasons to around 200 days. Annual precipitation normally ranges from 600 to 800 mm (Odgaard 1994).

It appears that the general climatic conditions in the Late Neolithic and emerging Bronze Age were not very far from this description, although presumably with some fluctuations. The period belongs to the Sub-Boreal, spanning from c. 3000 to 500 BC. The mean temperatures were slightly warmer than today and investigations from Fuglsø Mose have documented increasing air humidity from about the middle of the Danish Neolithic until the late Bronze Age (Andersen, S.T. 1992:90).

It has long been known that considerable changes took place in the vegetation during the period (Iversen 1979). Vegetation development as reflected in sediments from Skånsø can be of relevance to locations in nearby areas from the central Limfjord region. Resengaard was situated some 16 km in a direct line east of this lake. Together with information from two other lakes, pollen examinations have provided a basis for suggesting a regional development (Odgaard 1994). Open forests of oak, ash, birch, alder and hazel were predominant in the landscape earlier but, after 3000 calBC, began to decline, when heath, grazed woods and other grass-fringes began to spread. This development even intensified after 2100 calBC. Indications are that the heath areas were maintained through burning and the presence of sheep. Heather thus played an important economic role in many of these areas of Jutland.

A pollen diagram from the Borremose bog, being some 40 km in a direct line northeast of Resengaard, showed that open grass areas increased gradually over the period (Andersen, S.T. 1977; 1992a:89).

In contrast with western Himmerland and Thy, grasslands progressed slowly in eastern Jutland and the forest is still considered to have been predominant over large areas (Andersen 1992a:89). The landscapes in some south-eastern areas of the region presumably had vegetation more like that of Northern Djursland (Robinson 2003:161).

To the northwest in Thy, the transformations corresponded somewhat to the Borremose results and pollen investigations show an increase in grass areas and also scrub forests. Prior to the beginning of the Bronze Age, the pressure on the growth of trees in Thy areas was so heavy that the forest had more or less disappeared over large areas (Robinson 2003). Considerable knowledge of the transformations of the landscape and its use in Thy and beyond has been established through several more recent studies (Andersen, S.T. 1992b; 1993; 1994; 1995a; 1995b; 1999).

From the literature, cattle appear to have played a particularly major role and, to feed them, the use of extensive grazing grounds in meadows and higher grounds seems to have been common. Pigs, sheep or goats were also kept. Pigs may well have thrived in forest and semi-forest areas, and the very meagre, sandy soils would have favoured sheep or goats. Dogs were kept, possibly also for shepherding (Aaris-Sørensen 1989:213).

Human activities of agriculture and animal husbandry gradually changed the ecological conditions of the settled areas of the region during the Late Neolithic.[10] Direct documentation of the presence of domestic animals at the settlements is unfortunately still rather scant, however, although the finds from the Older Bronze Age midden at Torslev give evidence of cattle, pigs, sheep and goats, as well as dogs. Documentation of red deer is also present (Nyegaard 1995:108pp). In the following, I will sketch out and discuss some ecological aspects concerning Resengaard.

Presenting the "Field/pasture hypothesis"

The modern topsoil at Resengaard is mainly sandy, albeit mixed with some clay, and the old surface layers observed on the relatively flat areas at the upper part of the hill appeared, as expected, primarily sandy.[11] The now drained lower parts of the immediate landscape around the Resengaard settlement do not come close to a real picture of the previous, relatively wet surroundings. Significant wet areas would have marked the environment to the south, west and north.[12]

The situation of the Resengaard settlement, close to the fjord, provided a natural boundary for the residents' tillage or pastures to the east, although it is not known whether their use extended right to the shore. The present fjord formed the inner part of a sea with a level that was about two metres higher than the water level in the area today (see below). The coastline would only have been approx. 10 m closer to the settlement area than now. The easternmost House 158 would have been c. 200 m from the shoreline and the westernmost House 42 c. 400 m from it (Fig. 2.2).

Certain aspects of the agricultural strategy can be illuminated by looking at the N-S trial trench system on the slope towards the coast. The purpose of making these trenches was to discover any traces of further houses or other traits, e.g. furrows from prehistoric ard-ploughing. No such traces were observed although the thickness of the overlaying soil would in many cases likely have protected ard-furrows from being destroyed by recent ploughing. A few trial trenches were also dug north of the settlement. The topsoil layers were reasonably thick and thus protective. The results from this more or less north sloping terrain were negative, too. West of the westernmost sunken-floor houses, seven very long trial trenches stretching some 60 metres to the west revealed many archaeological features but no traces of ard-ploughing, even though potentially shielding soil layers were present. These west and northwest sloping terrains were presumably not used for agricultural land. From the southernmost sunken-floor houses, trial trenches stretched around 20 metres further south. A few archaeological features were recovered but no traces of ard-ploughing were observed even though, again, thick, protective soil layers were present in these slightly south-sloping areas. On the whole, the results from the many trial trenches strongly point to an understanding that the sloping areas around the upper part of the hill had not been used for ard-ploughed fields.

In contrast to the above, clear traces of ard-ploughing were documented in four different areas on the upper hill. In three cases, plough marks were observed directly in the sunken floors of the buildings (14, 197 & 200). The fourth area was in culture layer 203 where the ploughing had been carried out from its surface and down into the subsoil. The observations of a positive and negative nature from the top and sides of the hill may therefore support the following working hypothesis concerning cultivation strategies: the relatively flat top of the hill, including the terraces and some areas in its near perimeter – locally raised with surplus soils and domestic refuse – were in turn used by the residents as fields for growing crops, whereas the sloping sides and relatively low lying areas were chiefly used for pasture.[13]

On the upper part of the hill, it is likely that just a proportion of the potentially arable land was simultaneously cultivated as fields at any given time. Correspondingly, it is reasonable to assume that just a part of the sloping and low lying areas would have been used for pastures at any given time and, in these cases, presumably largely those relatively close to the actual location of the longhouse. After harvest, cattle and other animals might have grazed the fields on the upper part of the hill, presumably also with access to leaves from deciduous trees and bushes. The fields would thereby have been supplied with some manure. Whether accumulated manure may have been spread we do not know. Occasionally some cattle, sheep, goats or pigs needing special care or supervision might have been kept rather close to the dwellings, perhaps in or near simple livestock sheds. During harsh winter periods, some fodder would presumably have been given in these surroundings every day.

For their everyday consumption, the residents may furthermore have exploited the immediate environment in a number ways that had nothing to do with agriculture or livestock keeping.

The relatively flat areas on the upper hill were around 320 m N-S and 300 m E-W. This area was not an ordinary square but had a somewhat irregular, curved shape and, in particular, a lower area to the north made a big dent in it. Worth keeping in mind also was the fact that the residents may have perceived the arable bounds of the area differently from time to time. Having an irregular form, the potentially arable land op the upper hill could have embraced around eight hectares, including the areas improved through the waste depositing strategy.

In my reading, the topographical position of many longhouses may emphasize the idea that the "Field/pasture hypothesis" applies to Resengaard because most were found in the hill top perimeter near the more or less marked edge where the sloping areas started. The terrain began to fall significantly, for instance, a few metres east and south of Houses 128 and 130. This was also the case east of Houses 134 and 138. Three longhouses to the south were placed in a relatively flat area bordering the hill slope beginning immediately to the south. Houses 1, 2 and 41 were placed on the flat, natural terrace extension of the flat top to the north, where the terrain a few metres to the sides began to fall notably. In actual fact, only two of the longhouses (14 & 200) were sited further away from the slopes albeit both still with the possibility of overlooking pastures to the west, where the terrain fell gradually.

Generations of longhouses were placed in a zone near the transition between the flat and the sloping areas. When the longhouse was at any given time positioned between the arable land and the pasture, there would have been good reason for this because it had no stable. Hence, in my understanding an important reason for this location was that it would ease the supervision of cattle and other domestic animals grazing in the pastures below. From this position, it would also have simplified supervision of the fields placed within a close range on the upper hill. In the growing season, these fields would probably have needed protection from, for instance, free-ranging domestic animals, deer and other.

It is, however, important to underline that not all Late Neolithic and emerging Bronze Age settlements in the central Limfjord region had this kind of topography. For instance, Rosgårde was set in a rather plain area with a long-stretched lake a little distance away (Simonsen, J., im manus.). Some other examples are the many Glattrup settlements (cf. Fig.1.2). The settings of some of these relate to another kind of landscape close to the shores of the Limfjord archipelago and not far from the delta of the large stream, Karup Å. It is therefore of interest to explore the varying topographies further (Simonsen, J., in prep.).

One trait of the investigated parts of the settlements in the central Limfjord region is the absence of traceable fences or other physical arrangements with similar functions around the settlements. And yet we cannot exclude the possibility that fencing of some kind may have been established without leaving soil vestiges. In this case, fences could have worked both ways, preventing access on the part of certain animals to the fields or, in contrast, keeping certain animals inside in the grazing areas.

When the sunken-floor houses were placed on the agriculturally preferred flat top of the hill, these buildings and their immediate surroundings occupied valuable agricultural land, and it was apparently of importance that, on abandonment, the sunken areas were given back, adding higher growing capacity.

Overall, through this hypothesis I am seeking to explain that it concerns a well-organized and coherent system that included waste strategies, agricultural strategies, stock keeping strategies, longhouse placements, hill-side use and, probably, a number of other factors working together in cycles. Seen from an ecological perspective, such strategies very likely made it possible for the settlement to subsist and remain at the location over centuries. The system presumably included turning the growing areas into fallow fields for a period (*cf.* Møbjerg, Jensen & Mikkelsen 2007:21). And yet, as regards Resengaard, concrete indications of this are not available. The crops in fields over former sunken areas would often likely have been much better than in areas with just ordinary thin, sandy topsoil and would also have improved abilities to resist longer periods of severe drought. The households might thus have had the repeated experience that their forefathers' house plots yielded relatively well. Fallow periods would perhaps have been relatively short on these plots.

The strategic placement of the longhouses around the perimeter of the upper part of the hill really appears to make sense in such a system. It is even possible that such topographical positions, with a fine overview of the surroundings, may at times have worked as an element of protection.

From a wider perspective, it seems likely that the "Field/pasture hypothesis" could apply to many other situations on the upper parts of hills in the region and beyond in the Late Neolithic and emerging Bronze Age, and likely later in time. In the central Limfjord region, such "hill-edge residency" diverged from the settlement traditions of the Single Grave Culture. When we meet clear examples of this topographical position from subsequent periods, the tradition may therefore date back to the Late Neolithic. The placements of three-aisled longhouses at Jegstrup, dated to the Younger Bronze Age, are an example of hill-edge residency (Davidsen 1982:65pp). One of the main reasons for that is likely to have been very similar, i.e. the possibility not least of overlooking the cattle at pastures below. However, in the Bronze Age at Bjerre, in the northwest part of the region, a quite different topographical position can be seen (Bech 1997:3pp).

Long-term cultivation cycles

The available eight or so hectares on the upper hill at Resengaard include former house plots and the limited arable land would likely imply that the most suitable areas had to be cultivated at closer intervals when also considering that the predominantly sandy soil would hardly yield a reasonable crop after several years of cultivation without a fallow period, even if cattle grazing after harvest left some manure. A vegetation of trees and scrub would presumably have had a chance to regenerate the area before it could again be cultivated. I suppose that fresh new fields would gradually have substituted the old. When former house plots had to be prepared for tillage, including the removal of trees, scrub and other obstacles in the surrounding areas, burning of these regenerated areas (and the remaining organic scrap left in the abandoned plot of the building) may perhaps have taken place. Thereafter, ard-ploughing could begin. Although there are only three instances of clear evidence that the former house sites at Resengaard were ard-ploughed after the period of residence, my understanding is that this was the general practice at Resengaard.[14] The particular tradition of building of more or less circular stone piles in the sunken areas was not practised at any of the 43 house sites in question (Dollar 2013:43p). Such piles would have been a hindrance to ard-ploughing the longhouse sites after abandonment and tearing down. In the site of the minor sunken-floor House 183 at Resengaard, many stones appeared more or less casually dumped into the lower parts of the sunken area.

We have indications from different locations that the fields could also have included areas beyond the former sunken floors, as ard-furrows have been observed that extend these. Some examples relate to the sites of House 197 at Resengaard (Fig. 2.18.C), House 5 at Glattrup I/III (Fig. 2.43.C) and House 5 at Kluborg II (Fig. 5.14). It is noteworthy that we have never, thus far, observed ard-furrows in the sites of minor or short sunken-floor houses.

If the building of new longhouses took place in cultivated areas or formerly cultivated areas, the changes on the upper hill would have tended towards a long-term, cyclical nature: at one plot, a dwelling recently abandoned, demolished and transformed into a field and, at another, a former field becoming the ground for a new longhouse.

In the abandoned house sites with ard-marks, cultivation started before the completion of the filling up process. With regard to Houses 14 and 197 at Resengaard, the ploughing began so early that the ard-furrows went through the former floor down into the light sandy ground beneath the floor. It is immediately apparent that the ard-ploughing had been carried out repeatedly in both sunken floors. When, for instance, traces of the scorched-stone patch in the latter had almost been eradicated, it was obviously due to such repeated ploughing activities. The sunken floor of House 197 was the shallowest belonging to a longhouse, and only a modest fill quantity could therefore be dumped into it. There is also evidence in the site of House 200 that the ard-ploughing began early on.

Filling up and ard-ploughing likely took place alternately in many sunken areas but, as stated, the chances of recording such ploughing with our excavation methods are almost negligible, as the lower part of the furrows did not reach into soil of quite a different colour and character. Correspondingly, as regards Bejsebakken, where ard-ploughing has been observed at three house sites, it is noted that this treatment of the sunken floors made the depositions appear more homogeneous (Sarauw 2007b:13).

Repeated ploughing also took place in culture layer 203, where a later accumulated, thick soil layer protected the ard furrows. During excavation, our cleaning tended to remove the ard-furrows in some parts of culture layer 203 although they were presumably present all over the excavation area and beyond. The directions indicate that the ard-ploughing was carried out at about the same level at least five times since the furrows reached the yellow, sandy subsoil.

Ploughing would presumably have been one of the residents' most significant activities before sowing. The tractive force was likely provided by oxen and so the ard-furrows may furthermore evidence their presence. How they were harnessed we do not know but, for transport purposes, yokes – in principle somewhat like those known from later periods in the central Limfjord region – might have been used (*cf.* Simonsen 1984).

The ard did not turn the soil upside down because it was not equipped with any kind of soil board. Instead it would have worked more like a one-toothed harrow. Hence, the soil in between the furrows after the first ploughing could still be found in their original position at the time of the excavation, making the investigation of the soil traces a straightforward task. The presence of stones, roots and other things may sometimes have caused minor jumps in furrow directions. It is presumed that parallel or almost parallel furrows stem from the same ploughing, considering that two successive ploughings in the same area would hardly make furrows fall exactly in line with the previous system. The intervals between the furrows can be calculated in areas where no furrows seem to be missing. Some examples indicate that the average furrow distances ranged from c. 15 cm to 28 cm, measured from their mid lines. It seems reasonable to presume that the closeness of the furrows was adjusted to the purpose. The ard could scratch a deep furrow into the soil and loosen it but it would hardly have been particularly effective for removing weeds. Evidently, a dense parallel ard-ploughing would be more effective for loosening the soil and more helpful for eradicating weeds. In my understanding, an important purpose of the ard may well have been to create grooves for sowing.

From a source-critical point of view it cannot be completely excluded that, in some instances, the traces of ploughing systems are more fragmentary than one would imagine. Some parallel ploughing in between observed furrows could thus possibly have been performed without leaving clearly observable vestiges. If so, the very narrow intervals recorded in culture layer 203 might have been more common. An example from the sunken area of House 5 at Kluborg II actually shows relatively tight intervals between certain parallel furrows. The shortest internal distances observable need not thus in all cases have been the shortest applied. It is also questionable as to whether an area, cultivated and cleaned for several years, would need as intense ploughing as a newly-established field, if the purpose of the ploughing was to loosen the soil for sowing and removal of weeds. In all, many specific factors may have influenced the method of ploughing, such as the presence of vegetation, character of the soil and subsoil, the slope, precipitation, sowing and so on.

It is now interesting to try to pinpoint how many different ploughing directions the sunken floors might have been exposed to before the gradual filling up with soil and domestic refuse no longer allowed the plough to reach the subsoil. In the sites of Houses 14, 197, and 200, this appears in my reading to relate to five, three and two different directions, respectively (Fig. 5.14).

Ard-ploughing into the sunken area of House 3 at Glattrup IV appears to document at least three directions. Ard-ploughing into the bottom of the sunken area of House 7 seems likewise to comprise at least three directions, while in the upper horizon no more than one is documented.

In my reading at least six ploughing directions are observable in the site of House 5 at Kluborg II and, interestingly, here we have an indication of how late the

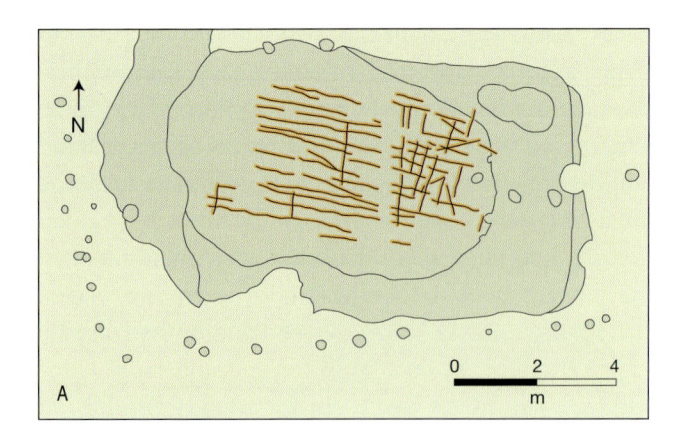

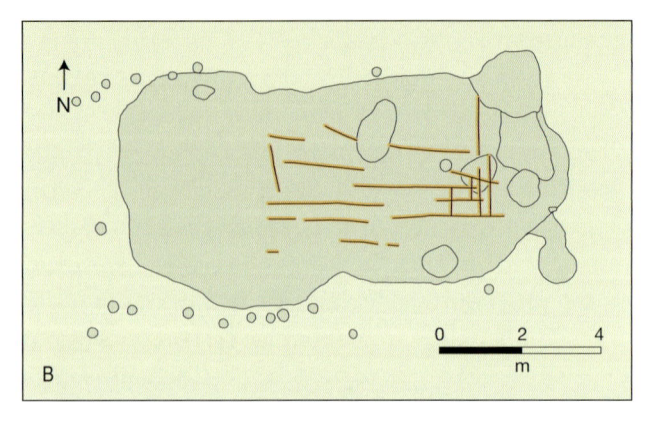

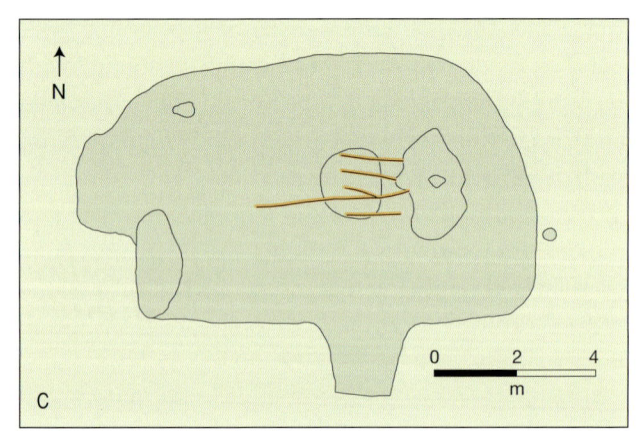

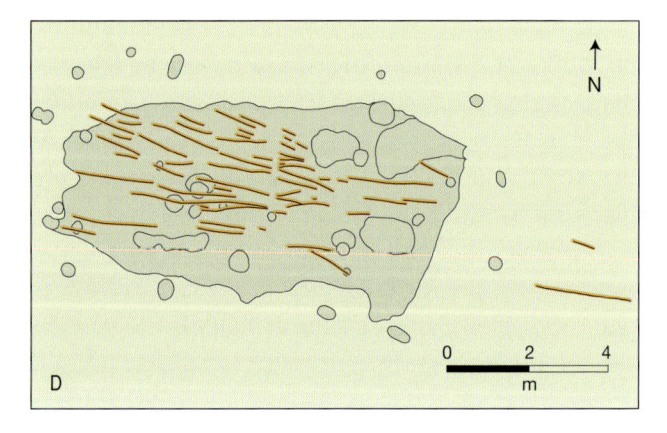

Fig. 5.14.A-C. Ard-furrows. Resengaard. The ard-furrow systems likely demonstrate repeated seasons of growing and harvesting cereals in sunken areas. A: House 14. B: House 197. C: House 197. D: Kluborg II, House 5.

earlier sunken floor was ard-ploughed. Two furrows crossed the cluster of pits placed at the western end of the site of a presumably not much later three-aisled longhouse (*cf.* Fig. 2.41). These furrows appear to be in line with ploughing directions in the sunken area of House 5. In this case, ard-ploughing would have taken place at both house sites at the same time, at a time later than the demolished three-aisled longhouse.

From the central Limfjord region, ard-ploughing has also been discovered at other locations than those considered here, e.g. in the bottom of the sunken area of the house site at Kås Hovedgård II (Inge Kjær Kristensen, report U2002a). At Bygdalgård, too, ard-ploughing took place in the sunken area of House 5 (Kieldsen & Wåhlin 2012:7). As comparative material from the Limfjord region, we have, not least, the comprehensive study of these from the Iron Age at Store Vildmose (Nielsen, V. 1993). Elsewhere in Jutland, ard-ploughing of the sunken floors in the Late Neolithic and the emerging Bronze Age has often been reported, for instance in the Vejen area, where seven instances of traces of such doings have been observed at the four settlements, namely Kongehøj III, Mannehøjgård, Margrethenborg and Vestervang VII (Dollar 2013:44).

The record is highly enlightening from Hellegård, where ard-furrows were present in several directions in the sunken floor of House 122 and were recorded in two horizons above each other, being also evidenced in the cross section (Fig. 5.15). The tale that the c. 0.70 m high profile bench, combined with the horizontal excavation areas, may tell concerns a habitation phase followed by further ard-ploughing phases. After abandonment and demolition of the longhouse, the floor was thus ard-ploughed several times in at least five directions before substantial fills were added to the sunken area. In my understanding, these may each represent a year of growing crops, probably cereals. Thereafter, the sunken area sanded up with a thick layer of wind deposits in the middle, and this may represent a short period of no activity. Then the area was again ploughed repeatedly, likely again for cereal crops. This time at least three ploughing directions are readable. Thereafter it was not possible to trace any further ploughing. However, I presume the plot was ard-ploughed many times again while the sunken area gradually became filled up. Apart from the minor sunken-floor House 35 to the east, nowhere else in the excavated area or in the additional trial trenches have any other house sites been recovered although the amount of ploughing after abandonment of House 122 must imply that the agricultural activities were continued for some time by a household in the neighbourhood.

All in all, it is thought-provoking to observe so many ploughing activities in and above the former sunken floors. Regarding the longhouses at Resengaard, I have argued that the secondary fills were likely also ploughed repeatedly higher up during filling up, without it being possible to document this. It even seems plausible that the household of the first three-aisled longhouse continued ard-ploughing at, not least, the later sunken-floor house sites. Hence, the observations from Hellegård are important because they evidence many ploughing activities in these two horizons, separated only by an intermezzo of wind-deposited sand. In the sunken area of the site of House 7 at Glattrup IV, ard-ploughing was also observed in two horizons during its filling up.

The somewhat diverging tale that the c. 0.33 m high profile bench in the site of House 5 at Glattrup I/III, combined with the horizontal excavation areas, may tell concerns a habitation phase followed by one or more ard-ploughing phases and placement of secondary fills (cf. Fig. 4.47.B & 4.68.K). After abandonment and demolition of the longhouse, the floor was thus ard-ploughed before the sunken area sanded up with a thick layer of wind deposits in the middle. However, in this case we have no further evidence of ard-ploughing and it seems that his activity had ceased.

Growing season and crops

Under changing conditions such as, for instance, when the number of residents in a longhouse increased, the requirement for cereal production may have increased correspondingly. For a household with a fairly constant size and conditions over a period, the crops needed could have been practically the same each year. When sowing was done, likely in the spring, it would presumably have taken place as early as possible, due to the general climatic conditions. As the growing season, like today, would have been rather short and only permitted one harvest, it would certainly have been important to ensure that the cereals had adequate time to grow and ripen before harvest.

Preparation of the fields, changing weather conditions and the sowing activity itself would likely mean that the fields could not all be sowed at once. At Re-

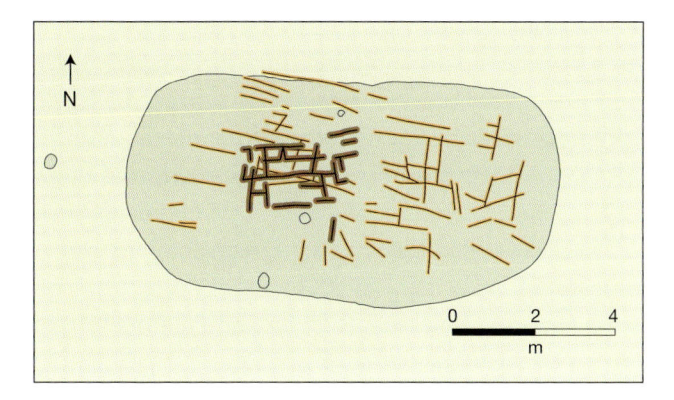

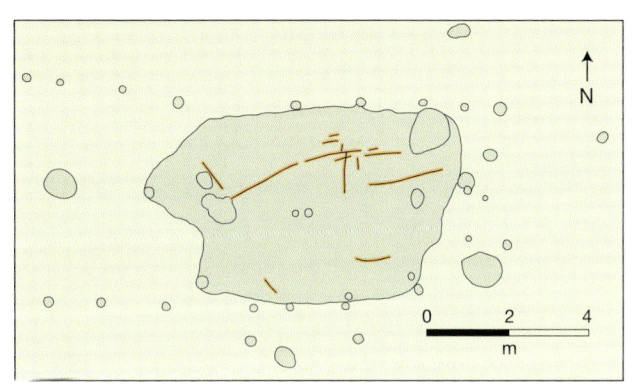

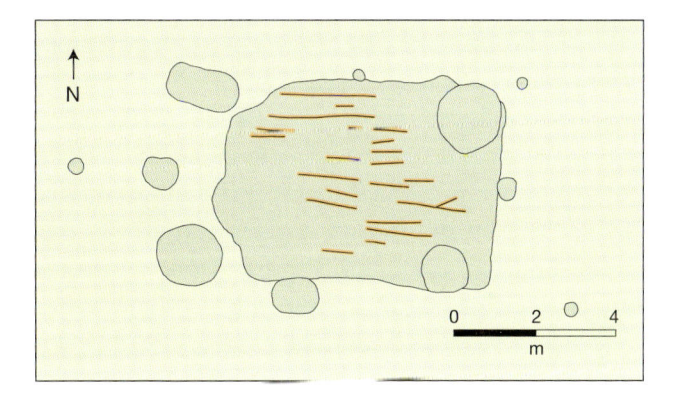

Fig. 5.15. Ard-furrows. A: Hellegård, House 122. B: Glattrup IV, House 3. C. Glattrup IV, House 7.

sengaard, heavy soils were not prevalent on the upper hill but it is likely that some of the soils were ready for sowing sooner than others.

Traditions probably governed the kinds of crops to be grown and, seemingly, no dramatic changes took place in this respect at Resengaard during the middle and later part of the occupational period from which most of the evidence stems. Judging by samples of varying strength from Houses 1, 2, 10, 12, 14, 128, 138, 197, 200, and 202, the most important cereal at Resengaard was naked barley but spelt and emmer were also represented. However, we cannot exclude the possibility that some of the cereals were obtained through exchange.

The total number of grains in the samples from different contexts at Resengaard from the Late Neolithic and emerging Bronze Age is estimated at around 600,000 charred grains (Peter Steen Henriksen, Report S2001a:13). Many were heavily burned and could not be further determined. As underlined in the report, it is the causes of carbonizing processes that determine the kind of organic materials to be found. Indications from the pollen samples confirm the importance of barley.[15] When it comes to spelt, we now know that at Resengaard and Glattrup IV, in particular, it played a more significant role than is known from elsewhere in Jutland and was found in about the same frequency as emmer (Møbjerg, Jensen & Mikkelsen 2007:27).

The activities of maintaining the fields between sowing and harvesting are not sufficiently clear from the evidence at Resengaard. Some manual upkeep likely took place from the spring onwards in order to reduce the occurrence of weeds. By keeping the fields fairly free of unwanted weeds, the nutrients would have been available for the crops instead, and likewise the rainwater. This would have been a sensible strategy for growing cereals in cases where adequate manure was not added to the soil.[16] The few specimens of seed from weeds in the samples could partly be explained by such a strategy. We do not know whether mattocks of some kind were used for maintenance but this seems plausible.

The finds from Glattrup IV add substantially to our records of macrofossils, being fairly enlightening with regard to crops and weeds (Peter Steen Henriksen, Report S2001a). Contrasting noticeably with what we have seen at Resengaard, the cereals from the sunken-floor longhouses were mainly found in the fills of the more or less sizeable pits, mainly considered to relate to brewing and storage of beer. From House 4, with just a ground floor, were found internodia mostly from emmer, whereas those from the sunken-floor House 5 were spelt. It is suggested in the report that einkorn was probably only grown as a mix in the fields with emmer and spelt, judging by the presence of very few spikes. Overall, naked barley was the predominant kind of charred cereal preserved in the material from Glattrup IV. Emmer and spelt were both grown separately, which is evidenced in the finds of two of the longhouses. Most of the samples contained threshed and cleaned cereals with only a few impurities such as carbonized spike fragments and seeds from weeds such as knotgrass and goosefoot. It is made clear in the report that these weeds are often present in samples of cereals even when they are found threshed and cleaned.

On cereals, fields and gathered plant materials, more recent results stem from the settlement at Enkehøj and other nearby sites (Møbjerg, Jensen & Mikkelsen 2007:18pp). With regard to certain Scanian areas during the Late Neolithic, it is posited that in "… most cases in the Hyllie bog area, the general Late Neolithic method of cultivation, with rotating fields with periods of fallow belonging to a single farm, can be expected …" and concretely concerning the largest site of the area that the "… general stability of farms that can be seen, especially at Almhov, also indicates the stability of fields, and thereby possibly manuring …" (Brink 2013:448).

Harvest and further treatment

Most of the fields at Resengaard are unlikely to have been ready for harvest simultaneously, considering not least the different qualities of the thin top soil layers of the old surfaces compared to the thick soils accumulated in the former sunken areas. The different placements of the fields, the different moisture-keeping capacities of the soils and perhaps different exposures to sun and other factors would evidently result in a changing readiness for harvest in the late summer or autumn. It thus seems reasonable to presume that harvesting of the individual areas would not have been carried out at the same time although I suppose such conditions would not have been a disadvantage for the households because it could have been carried out step by step, over some time. In very dry seasons, the sunken-floor areas with their massive soils would probably have given protection from entirely bad yields, and thus helped to ensure the harvest (Fig. 5.16 & 5.17).

Carbonized seeds from weeds were found in samples from Resengaard, Kluborg II, Glattrup I/III and Glattrup IV. It is a common trait of these samples that they represent the last stages of the cereal cleaning processes, whereby most seeds from weeds have already been sorted out and only small numbers are represented (report S2001a:28). Peter Steen Henriksen supposes that certain weeds were predominant in the fields but also draws attention to the possibility that seeds from these species might have had dimensions and weights that, until sifting, would have enabled them to pass through the threshing and cleaning procedures.

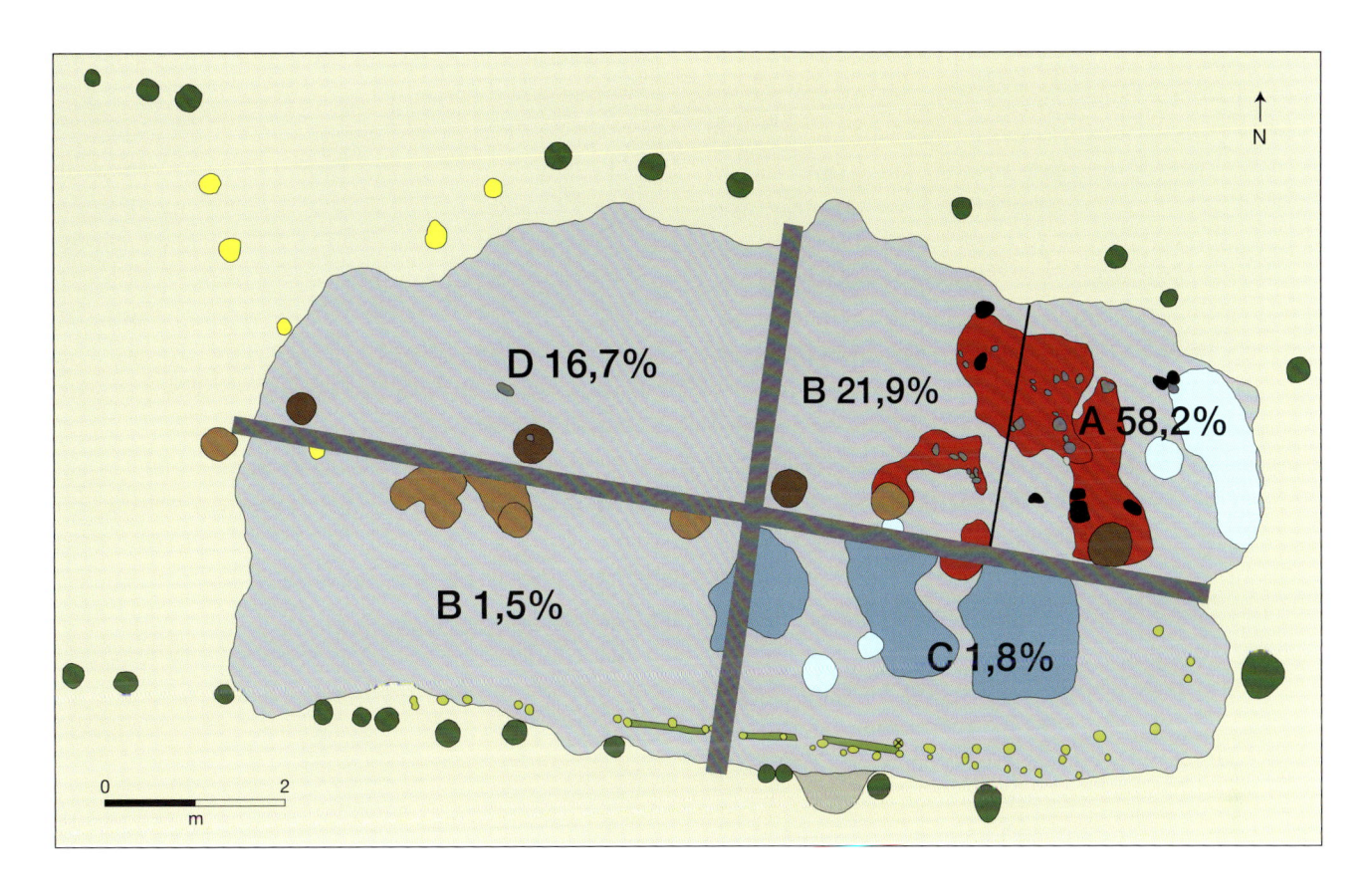

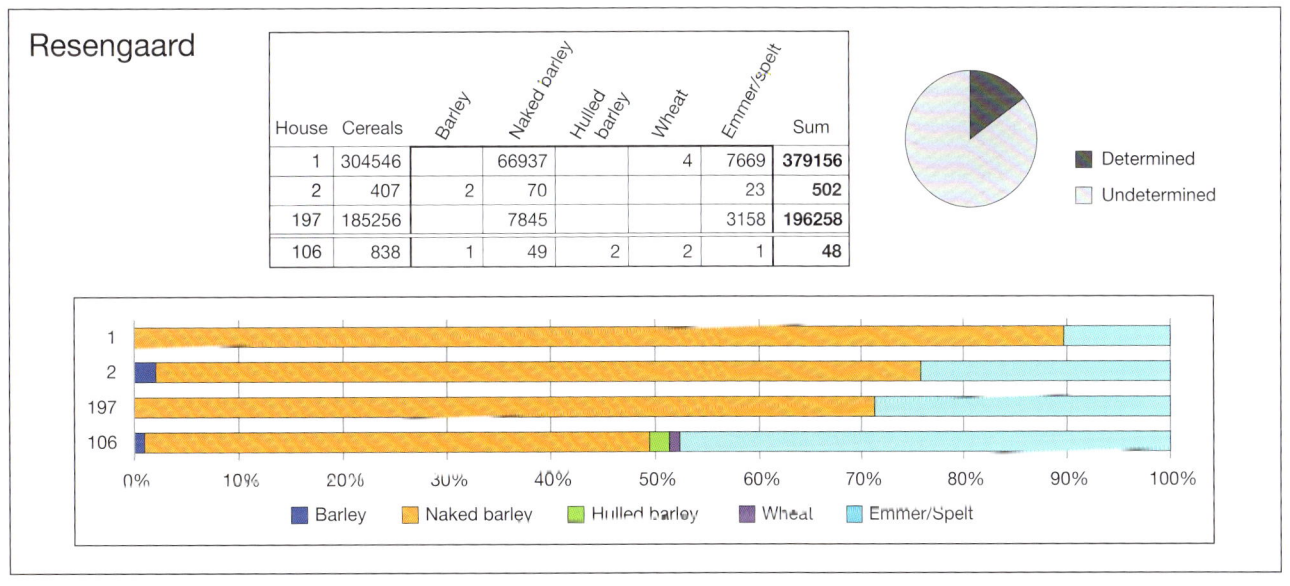

Fig. 5.16. Evidence of charred cereals at Resengaard. A: At the site of House 1 it was intended as far as practically possible to gather all grains. Due to rounding up to 1 decimal point, the sum slightly exceeds 100%. The crossing soil benches formed the primary separations, and the northeast area was further divided into two areas, due to the massive presence of grains. B: Cereals from the sites of House 1, House 2 and House 197 as well as House 106 (early three-aisled). Based on the report by Peter Steen Henriksen (see text).

Crescent-shaped flint sickles would have been used for harvesting. Their general presence is evidenced by many sickles and fragments. How high up the stems were cut cannot be stated directly but some weeds give an indication. It is stated in the report that cutting the stems relatively high can be eliminated as a possibility because nearly all weeds can be avoided by this method.[17] The presence of small weeds thus indicates that the stems were cut correspondingly low. The household would thereby also have procured a great

Glattrup I & III

House	Cereals	Barley	Naked barley	Hulled barley	Wheat	Emmer/spelt	Sum
5	68		78			1	147
6	160		58		4		222
1	1155	24	438		17	6	1640

Glattrup IV

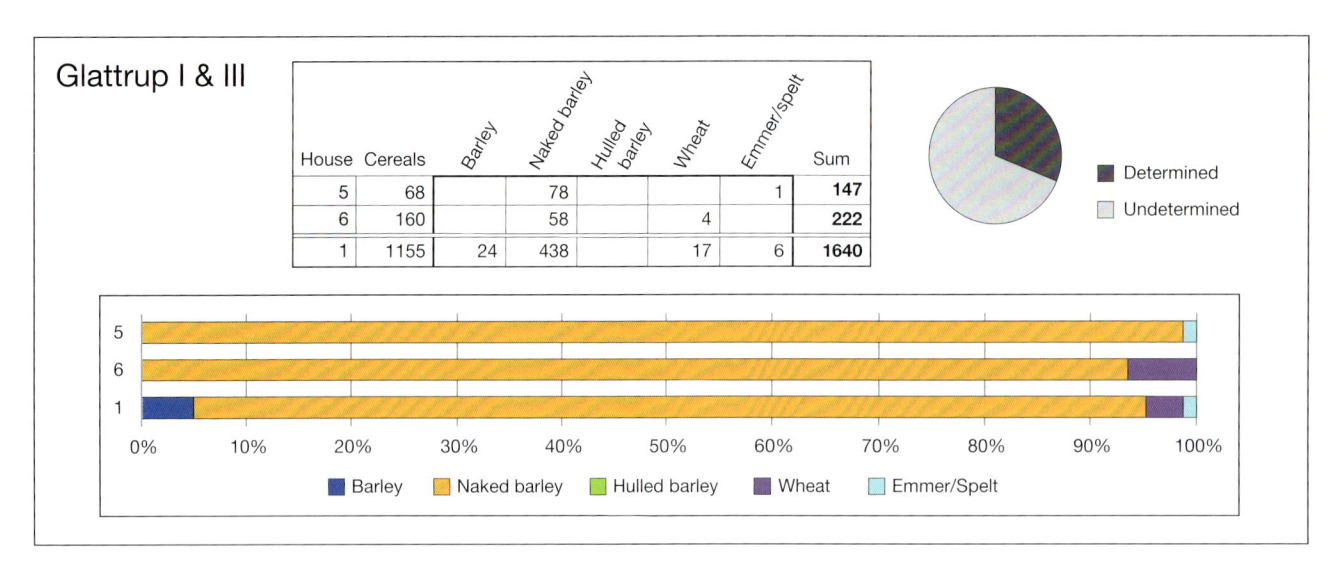

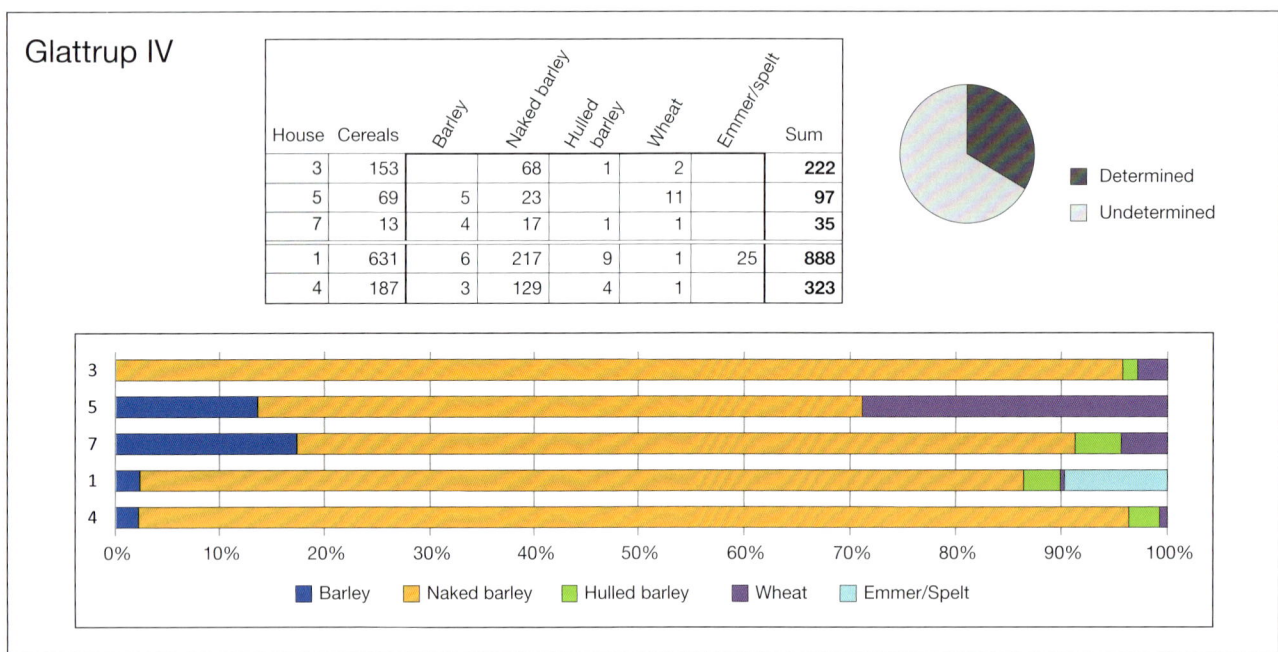

House	Cereals	Barley	Naked barley	Hulled barley	Wheat	Emmer/spelt	Sum
3	153		68	1	2		222
5	69	5	23		11		97
7	13	4	17	1	1		35
1	631	6	217	9	1	25	888
4	187	3	129	4	1		323

Fig. 5.17. Evidence of charred cereals at Glattrup I/III and Glattrup IV. Charred cereals/internodia of einkorn were also modestly represented in four samples from three house sites (Houses 1, 4 & 5 at Glattrup IV). A: Glattrup I/III. Cereals from the sites of House 5 and House 6 as well as House 1 (early three-aisled). B: Glattrup IV. Cereals from the sites of House 3, House 5, and House 7 as well as House 1 and House 4 (both ground-floor houses). Based on the report by Peter Steen Henriksen, see text.

amount of straw that could have been used for placing e.g. in cattle sheds in order to provide insulation from the cold and damp of the ground, as it will be recalled that stabling was not practised at that time.

Further treatment may have involved threshing, as well as the removal of glumes and cleaning of grains. No traces indicate that threshing took place in the sunken-floor areas of the longhouses, and instead such activities might for instance have been performed in the western halves of these, although no traces of cereals were usually found here. Alternatively, the threshing activities could have been performed at some other spot outside the longhouses. The spikes and glumes had to be separated from the grains in this process, although each kind had to be treated differently. In naked barley, the glumes would probably be easily removed from the grains. Conversely for wheat, the glumes would be firmly seated, presumably needing some kind of heating process to remove them (Møbjerg, Jensen & Mikkelsen 2007:25). Traces of such a process could not be identified in the sites of the sunken floor longhouses because what we see in the samples are generally threshed and cleaned grains.[18] If such heating processes took place in order to make the glumes brittle then these must have been carefully removed as almost no evidence of charred pieces was found in the sunken-floor horizons. After separating the glumes from the grains, various sifting processes could have taken place.

The removed glumes ("chaff") were never observed in samples from the Resengaard buildings. However, such waste was found at Glattrup IV, where a sample from the above-mentioned House 1 (with ground floor) shows evidence of cleaning of cereals (Fig. 5.3). Apart from a single specimen of carbonized mouse faeces, a posthole in the central longitudinal axis contained many small underdeveloped barley grains (less than 1.5 mm in diameter) and a few barley spike fragments and some seeds from weeds. In the report it is stated that this is a typical waste composition from the last step in the cereal cleaning process. It thus likely derives from the process of sifting out unwanted small grains, weeds and other possible impurities. Among this waste were also internodia from different kinds of wheat. In the report, Henriksen remarked that the finds of Neolithic barley in Denmark were generally threshed and cleaned and therefore unthreshed cereals were supposedly kept elsewhere, and the processes of threshing and cleaning would also thus have taken place elsewhere. He further pointed out that the find of underdeveloped barley grains from Glattrup IV provides the first Danish observations of this kind, i.e. where the fine sifting took place indoors.

The analysis of cereals from House 5 at Glattrup IV throws light on another treatment. The presence of many charred wheat internodia in two samples is considered to be waste derived from husking the grains and it is noted that this process typically took place inside the houses (Henriksen 2000; NNU Rapport 21.1999).

How grinding or further processing was carried out cannot be directly elucidated by the Resengaard finds as no vestiges of unsifted meal or finer flour have been identified. Moreover, there is a striking lack of grinding stones left behind in the floors or elsewhere at this settlement. It is thus really remarkable that nowhere in the interiors can any space for grinding activities be proposed. This might very well have been due to special attitudes towards grinding stones, meaning these were not usually left at the abandoned house sites. I suspect that after abandonment these implements were taken to the new dwellings or, less likely, otherwise disposed of.

In the above, I have suggested that bulks of winter fodder were kept. In particular, I presume this would concern plant materials used to feed cattle and sheep/goats during periods when grazing did not offer sufficient nutrition. While still green and highly nourishing for cattle, and probably finest before the outermost new thin branches became woody, the harvesting and drying of leaf fodder would have been an evident option, namely the cutting and presumable bundling of the thinner branches with leaves from deciduous trees, for instance elm trees. In that vein, it is interesting to observe how fresh stumps of the now common kind of elm tree in the central Limfjord region usually each produce numbers of upright long thin branches that can simply be cut by means of a minor axe (or other tools), i.e. without climbing up to get hold of the branches with the nutritious foliage. Tending of such coppices in the vicinities of the longhouses seems an ideal activity for the households, thus securing a yearly supply of fodder. In addition to new soft branches from elm (and possibly hazel, poplar, ash, & other), the emerging sugar-containing long stalks and leaves of common reed may have been harvested and dried in the late spring or early summer. Reeds harvested at this stage are very nutritious and may have offered really fine winter fodder, perhaps stored in bundles, for the oxen (pers. comm. Finn T. Okkels).

To make hay from meadows could likewise have been an obvious feeding source, kept for the harsh seasons of the year. Many of the settlements with sunken-floor longhouses in the region were placed in topographical positions where plots bounded by other vegetation within the immediate surroundings could have been set aside for grazing. It seems reasonable to presume that some grass was harvested in the early summer, dried and stored as hay. Storage of heather, cut as winter fodder e.g. for goats, could presumably also have taken place.

Storage and use of cereals

We might ask whether some of the finds of charred grains in the sunken-floor horizons at Resengaard could stem from storage of cereals? Firstly, we have sites where only a few carbonized grains were left and this concerns the longhouses 13, 14, 128, and 138, as well as the minor houses 10 and 202. In my reading, no observations from these seem to evidence traces of storage.

Secondly, we have sites with better representation or even abundant numbers of cereals. The bulk of charred grains in the site of House 1 was found particularly in and near the northern scorched-stone devices and never in crockery or other contexts that might indicate storage. The charred grains from the sunken-floor horizon in House 2 were likewise found mainly in the areas of the scorched-stone devices and no finds appear to indicate storage of cereals. In this respect, it is highly interesting that soil with cereal concentrations were on the whole not observed in the contexts of the many traces of burnt down posts or stakes from the interior at this house site. We thus have no indication of the concentrations that, for instance, sacks of cereals hanging from the posts might represent. In this case, however, this absence might be explained by the deliberate burning of House 2 and valuables such as stored cereals would therefore have been removed. The abundant amount of charred grains from the floor of House 197 cannot directly be related to the area interpreted as leftovers of a scorched-stone device because the stones and the grains were both ploughed out shortly after demolition of the building. And yet the number of carbonized grains belonging to pit 1 in the northwest corner could actually stem from spill connected to the storage of carbonized grains in the area, although no vessels containing cereals were found. Only in this single case at Resengaard can a possible place of cereal storage therefore be noted. It should be noted that the observations from this pit do not help to throw light on whether or not the charring could have taken place in connection with the deliberate burning of scrap after demolition of the building.

A certain portion of quality seed for the coming sowing season was presumably kept separately. It must at any rate have been extremely important that *this seed was stored undamaged and undecimated. If extra precaution was taken regarding this part of the crop, it might for instance have been kept in clay vessels (or perhaps sacks of a kind) that could safely protect the seed from being eaten by mice, attacked by insects and so on. This seeds could furthermore have been placed safely in certain reserved areas of the buildings. Before storing the seed, it must have been necessary to ensure that the grains were at a relatively low percentage of humidity and thereafter kept carefully protected from the impact of moisture. If exposed to humidity above a certain level, they would easily begin to germinate or rot. In other words, too much humidity might cause next year's harvest to fail. Such seed would not tolerate exposure to much heat either.

A part of the grain meant for human consumption would also have to be taken reasonably good care of. Its loss would presumably force the residents to look for other replacement sources or to acquire cereals from other households. Protection from mice could well have been a priority. One of the observations from the excavation of more longhouses at Resengaard was that animal activity in certain areas was intense. Some of this might derive from periods when the abandoned sunken floors functioned as dump sites but many traces of mice galleries were observed in top of the subsoil in the former wall zones. When these walls were torn down, there was nothing to explain the animal activity at this precise location. Therefore, in my understanding, the animal activity is likely to largely stem from the functioning time of the longhouses and the observed traces often appear to represent former mice galleries. Mouse faeces are already known from the Single Grave Culture settlement at Strandet Hovedgaard (David Earle Robinson & Ida Boldsen, report S2000a) and House 1 with ground floor at Glattrup IV from LN I (Peter Steen Henriksen, report S20001a). Rat faeces have been identified from the Late Neolithic at Djursland (by Peter Steen Henriksen, report S2000b). On the whole, I presume that rats were usually present at the Late Neolithic and emerging Bronze Age settlements in question.

The majority of cereals to be stored during the cold seasons are not likely to have been spread out in a lot of minor pots, although it cannot of course be excluded that small portions of cereals, perhaps intended for specific purposes, may have been kept in this way, for instance in the area of pit 1 in House 197. I presume that large clay vessels were generally used and that precisely one of their purposes was the storage of cereals. I have not seen evidence of particularly bad burning of these large clay pots. Many small fragments of such vessels have been found at Resengaard. I have attempted to identify these through the ware thickness and sometimes also through indications of large diameters. It is my impression that several remainders from the settlement belong to vessels of considerable volume, judging by the number of rim fragments. Bottom and side fragments also lend support to this impression. Clay pots with outer rim diameters exceeding 25 cm can be considered to belong to the group of large open bowls (e.g. RE694ae & 695aa). Other sizeable jars may also have been used for storage of cereals and, as examples, two vessels (Cat. A: RE310aa, RE310ab, RE1059aa & RE1050aa; Fig. 4.72) from the site of House 10 and culture layer 203 can be referred to. In the suggested reconstruction drawings of the first three mentioned, in full size they are estimated to reach heights of 31 cm, 34 cm, and 39 cm, respectively. Use of vessels such as these as containers for grain would have provided safe storage from mice and rats, thus keeping cereals and other food supplies intact through the winter. In the site of fire, at the sunken-floor House A120 at Østbirk, almost pure naked barley, emmer and spelt had been kept separately in roundish wooden vessels standing in sub-circular pits dug into the southwest part of the sunken floor (Borup, im manus).

No lids belonging to large vessels were found and, given the amount of potsherds from Resengaard, it thus seems obvious that ceramic lids did not usually exist. Lids might instead have been made of organic materials, not least wood, although it would obviously also have been possible to cover wide openings with some leather or flat stones, for instance. At Resengaard, the quite long period of having the kind of jar with the transition to rim marked by a relatively sharp indrawn angle or furrow-like shaping was probably due to its functionality (see Fig. 3.54.B). Leather or other relatively thin, soft organic material covering the top of such a jar could have been kept in position by means of a string around the furrow. At Resengaard, major parts of one of the better examples of a jar with such a kind of rim were found immediately north of the site of House 2, just outside its doorway (Cat. A: RE81bb/85aa; Fig. 4.8). From this house site, a small planed piece of wood (charred) might perhaps represent a lid.

Henceforward, it may perhaps be possible to obtain detailed information on the use of cereals in the human diet during the Late Neolithic and emerging Bronze Age from the soot crust and other sources. A portion of the cereals could conceivably have been cooked into a porridge of some kind or baked as bread, for instance on flat stones.[19]

The degree to which some of the cereal production was used for animal fodder cannot easily be quantified but it was generally very little. It has been proposed that it is difficult to make a distinction between human food and animal feed, even if it is assumed that there was largely no need to free fodder from weeds and chaff (Jones 1998:95pp). Yet it seems plausible that rubbish from the refinement of cereals might have been used as fodder.

Apart from those needed for seeds, I suggest three main uses of cereals during the Late Neolithic and emerging Bronze Age in the central Limfjord region, namely for human food, for fermented beverages and for offering to deities or spirits. Traditionally, much weight has been placed on explaining the cereal production in the period by the need for human food. Yet the interpretation of evidence from certain longhouses at Resengaard and Glattrup IV may point to idea that we should not underestimate the relative importance of growing cereals for beer and for votive offerings.

Some other ecological facets

The Nygaard settlement, with evidence of a Late Neolithic culture layer below a grave barrow, in my interpretation concerns the remainders of a sunken floor (Nielsen, S. 1977:81p; Rasmussen, M. 1993a:88). The find material contained small piles of common mussel, heat-affected/cracked stones and worked flint. This find highlights the differences in economic activities between settlements because no such mussels were found in the floor horizons of any of the sites of houses at Resengaard, despite its even closer proximity to the coast.

At Resengaard no remainders of any shellfish, fish bones or fish scales were found by means of flotation (with fine mesh size) of samples of charred material from the house sites or through the water sieving of rather comprehensive samples of charred material. Given that no marine residues were recovered from the many trial trenches on the east slope towards the coast either, this might generally support the idea that activities related to marine resources could have primarily taken place directly on the shore. A combination of agrarian settlement at a small distance from the coast and catching stations on the shores has previously been suggested as a possible settlement pattern of the Late Neolithic in the Limfjord areas (Andersen 1998:113).

It is of course also to be expected that the Resengaard households carried out a wide range of activities involving the gathering of firewood, berries, hazelnuts, acorns, nutritious seeds, etc. in the vicinity (cf. Jørgensen, G. 1978, regarding acorns). It seems likely that resources in the naturally fertile habitat would have met many of the residents' daily needs in this respect.

Certain plants and trees are indicated by pollen from Resengaard.[20] The amount of pollen in these samples was rather small and hence the occurrences clearly only represent a minor part of the whole spectrum. Two of the samples stem from the burned down House 2, and both were taken from the floor layer, clearly visible in the profile benches.[21] In both samples, pollen from oak, alder, hazel and poplar were present and, in one of these, also juniper. Tree pollen was also represented in a sample from the somewhat older site of House 138 and related, again, to oak, alder and hazel.[22] I presume that some areas with trees were present, in addition to regenerating fallow land, on the upper part of the hill and that the sloping terrains below were occupied by grazing areas alternating with more or less open forest. Hazelnut shells were present in three samples from the site of House 1, as well as in samples from the sites of Houses 2, 10, 14 and 128. In my view, it cannot be excluded that hazel, possibly as a coppice, could have been tended in order to ensure a stable supply of hazelnuts as well as, presumably, hazel sticks for different household use. The vegetable fat and other nutrient content in the hazelnuts may well have offered valuable nourishment during the cold and harsh winter, and could well have been partly reserved, not least, for a hunger gap in the early spring.

Pollen from plantain and dandelion might indicate relatively open grazing areas.[23] It is furthermore possible that heath vegetation was present relatively close to Resengaard. Charred heather sprigs were found in the floor contexts and also in a couple of other samples.[24] A relatively large amount of heather pollen was observed in some of the samples mentioned. Heather plants may have been used for several purposes such as thatching of the roof ridges, winter feeding, and mattresses for sleeping areas. Heather areas increased around the Limfjord region during the younger part of the Neolithic (Odgård 1994).

Fairly humid areas existed north, south and west of the Resengaard hill until drainage was carried out in modern times. Thus, I presume that wet area vegetation would have existed in the hill periphery to the north, south and west. Small areas of open water presumably also existed elsewhere in this undrained landscape. Pollen from reeds (or plants related to these) was found in two samples.[25] It therefore seems reasonable to presume that such plants grew near the settlement. From a scientific examination of the crescent-shaped flint sickles, it appeared that one of these had, rather surprisingly, been used for cutting reeds (Claus Skriver, report S2004a; Cat. B: RE120ea). This came from the sunken-floor horizon of House 2 (Fig. 4.10).

Initial ard-ploughing as a ritual doing?

When returning to the first ploughing activity in the sunken floors of the longhouses, we might ask whether this could have been ritually performed?

We do not have any evidence from Resengaard, Hellegaard, Glattrup IV or Kluborg II that would indicate that ard-ploughing was done directly into the subsoil of the sunken areas. In all cases, some centimetres of floor layer or other soil was on top of the subsoil before ard-ploughing took place. It is questionable as to whether the ard-marks from the well-preserved site of House 5 at Bygdalgård could form an exception (Kieldsen & Wåhlin 2012:7). The four first-mentioned settlements show that the area ploughed in the former sunken floors was most likely of agricultural potential. And yet the outcome for the households is not quite evident. However, since the crop derived from the old house site, the worth of it might have exceeded that of the ordinary crop, and thus could well have been ascribed an additional and special value.

Whereas the first ploughing into the sunken floor of House 197 at Resengaard would not have needed to force big differences in level, this must surely have been the case in the site of House 200 due to its floor depth. It must have been practically impossible to plough with the ard – likely with oxen providing the tractive power – across the longitudinal direction of that sunken floor and, understandably, there is no evidence of it. It is reasonable to presume that the plough marks in the sunken floor stem from the time after the large stone was placed to the northeast, as these were not observed beneath it. The stone would have formed a hindrance to ploughing until the filling up of the sunken area was almost complete (Fig. 4.28). Due to these two factors, the first ard-ploughing of the sunken floor would have been a challenge but more fill to the west was probably arranged in an oblique layer in order to extend the ramp between the sunken floor and the terrain to the west before the ploughing began. This would explain why the first ploughing did not reach into the subsoil at the western end. In contrast to the efforts needed to prepare the soil by making the oxen repeatedly draw the ard from the east and up the oblique ramp towards the west, the outcome from growing crops here would have been rather modest until the soil level had been markedly raised by more fills. It is overall my understanding that these conditions could support the notion that the agricultural potential in such instances was not necessarily the primary motive for the early ploughing and that it might have instead been a ritual act. It is reasonable to assume that the household members would have been much aware of the significance of the transformation from habitation into field and that it was, not least, precisely this fundamental change that meant a great deal. The plot would now produce cereals for the benefit of the residents living in the new longhouse and, for this – and perhaps other reasons – the awareness of this might well have been so strong that the first ard-ploughing traditionally had to be performed ritually, conceivably accompanied by other kinds of ritual.

Although no observations speak forcefully against this understanding of a purely ritual ploughing of the sunken area, I actually prefer an interpretation that gives room for a practical as well a ritual side to the activity. Ard-ploughing in the prehistoric context might thus very well have been perceived as a necessary ritual, with oxen drawing the first furrows into the former living floors – sometimes so deeply that they would reach into the sterile subsoil – but it would simultaneously have been acknowledged that, after sowing, a harvest of some value would come, albeit perhaps initially more symbolic than real. The ploughing activity could thus very well have served as incorporating both a sacred ritual and a practical function at the same time when transforming the former house area into an agricultural area (*cf*. Mitchell 2002:490pp, with further references). The occasion could, in that case, have been attended and perhaps surveyed or conducted by people who might have lent the act a further sacred or spiritual nature. The broader significance of this might also thus have been to confirm the community itself and the social bonds between the people who took part in it. The site transformation rituals might have had some affinities with "rites of passage"- events of individuals in society, as presented by Arnold van Gennep in *The Rites of Passage* (1975) and Victor Turner in *The Forest of Symbols; aspects of Ndembu Ritual* (2005). One vital trait is that rites of passage events "…do not redefine or restore a lost former status or purify from the effect of contamination, but they define entrance to a new status" (Douglas 1984:56). The "counterpart" to the liminal phase could have been the short period when there was no longer a house but nor yet a well-established field. The ritual ard-ploughing would, in this way, mark the new beginning after the end of this intermediate period.

5.6. Household production and specialization

In many cases it is not a straightforward task to point out areas of concrete household production. Signs of such activity may perhaps be embedded as "information" in the house remainders, without any good opportunity for us to identify these, at least for the time being. Thus, in these instances, neither the artefacts nor the soil patches or other traits relate to particularly specific activities, judging by their appearance.

The case of House 200 (Fig 4.28 & 4.29) may be an example of this from Resengaard. It seems plausible that the pit to the east with the centrally-positioned stone, together with some of the many artefacts, played a significant role with regard to some special doings of the residents. Firstly, the size and placement of the stone and the pit, in the central longitudinal axis far to the east in a sunken floor, is to my knowledge unique among finds in the Limfjord region. Secondly, the sunken floor was unusually deep and ended in a marked c. 2.3 m broad "tongue", being the outermost part of the oblique ramp to the west. Thirdly, to the southwest in the corner of the sunken floor was placed a deep pit containing a dagger fragment and an arrowhead. As we have seen, it was the only deep pit in a longhouse at the Resengaard hill. Fourthly, the afore-mentioned large stone (placed above some secondary fills containing potsherds) might previously have been used by the residents for specific purposes outside the building. Fifthly, to the south, the sunken floor continued into a narrowing area that I interpret as the remainders of a "corridor", i.e. a narrow space leading towards the south. Furthermore, if the long side walls, in the main, followed the northern and southern contours of the sunken floor then the house would have narrowed towards the west, resembling some elements of the ground plan of House 5 at Glattrup IV, i.e. it was therefore presumably trapezoidal (Fig. 2.6). Some or all these traits may have been connected to special doings in the household. I presume that quite reasonable meanings lie behind all these arrangements, beyond what I earlier said concerning affinities with House 5 at Glattrup IV, although I cannot present any plausible interpretation of these elements.

The case of House 13 could be another example from Resengaard where the unusual, large patchwork of a total of nine scorched-stone patches was observed (Fig. 4.11 & 4.12). These evidently provided by far the most predominant kind of soil feature in the sunken-floor horizon and it can be seen that some parts were almost packed with heat-affected/cracked stones while others were more or less free from these. It is tempting to see a pattern with the given activities leaving concentrations of stones to the west and only a few, scattered stones to the east. This might suggest that certain regularities governed the activities. The scorched-stone patches B, C, B, E, G, H, G and F were found quite close to one another without separating floor parts. It thereby marks a very intense area of activities connected to the use of these stones although the scorched-stone devices could not all have been in use at the same time. A single patch of scorched stones placed far to the south might very well indicate a separately functioning area for a period and may, to some degree, remind us of the isolated scorched-stone patch D in House 2 (Fig. 4.7). Whether the southern device in House 13 was used simultaneously with some of the others to the north cannot be deduced from the field observations. In all, it seems difficult to come much closer to narrowing down some of the possible specialized doings, which are likely directly connected to the use of heated stones. Judging by the scant cereal finds in the comparatively well-preserved floor, this can hardly have related to drying, roasting or charring of these but the special activities appear very difficult to identify. The doings connected to the scorched-stone patches were so predominant that only a couple of patches of another nature had been left in the entire sunken floor.

From Rosgårde, a third example of presumably specialized activity, albeit currently of unknown character, may well be reflected in the long oval shallow pits in the site of House 1 investigated in the ground floor west of the sunken floor. This kind of pit has even also been found in the ground-floored House 2 at Rosgårde. Such pits are unusual in the sites of the sunken-floor longhouses of the central Limfjord region.

Together, these three examples underline the fact that, at present, it does not seem possible to read many of the signs found at some house sites. And yet building remainders and other vestiges of a far more readable character do exist.

Seven cases of presumed specialization

In the following, I shall suggest that some households in the central Limfjord region carried out certain kinds of production as part of economic strategies that should be considered on a scale beyond the domestic sphere. In brief, this relates to the specialized household production of cereal treatment, bronze working, skin- and hide preparation, beer brewing, wool textile weaving, cattle breeding and specific flint tool production. By "economic strategies" I am not thinking of economy in the sense of "…the workings and outcomes of market systems – how things get produced, distributed, and exchanged, as well as the effects of regulation and deregulation on these processes" (Browne 2009:3). Instead, my approach attempts to focus on strategies at household level with regard to specialized production, where economic schemes and choices could have been imposed by moral obligations and might have been tightly interwoven into ideological and political relations, including those of the consanguine and affinal relatives, neighbours and others.

Cereal treatment at Resengaard proposed as specialized production: that mishaps taking place during drying or roasting are responsible for the abundant amount of charred cereals present in the site of House 1 at Resengaard is one obvious possibility but, as mentioned earlier, deliberate charring should not be ruled out (Fig. 4.5 & 4.6). This view may also be relevant for the site of House 197. I shall here simply expand a little on the arguments, given that much has already been considered in the foregoing.

Moderate drying of cereals could, of course, have been required in all sunken-floor longhouses now and then. The need for this might supposedly have been about the same over generations of longhouses. Why then do we find huge amounts of cereals at just two house sites if drying processes are to explain their presence? If massive activities had been necessary in this regard due, for instance, to precipitation and high air humidity around the time of harvesting or overly humid conditions during storage, then this situation would likely have affected more or less all households over the three hundred years of residence at the hill.

Although I do not find it possible to present any accurate reason for such ample roasting of cereals beyond my earlier suggestions, one could think of it in connection with, for instance, great events and gatherings. If massive roasting thus had to be carried out on rare occasions it would perhaps not be hard to accept the huge divergence in numbers of charred grains at the longhouse sites. The charred cereals could then represent mishaps.

When it comes to deliberate charring as being responsible for the huge numbers of charred cereals, this would not perhaps immediately seem to be the most straightforward explanation. Yet it is worth remembering that it is precisely barley that has been found in contexts considered to represent ritual food offerings (Andreasen 2009:16pp; Møbjerg, Jensen & Mikkelsen 2007:31pp). A few other house sites elsewhere also included a great deal of charred cereals. At Lindebjerg, a layer with a massive presence of charred cereals was found at the bottom of the sunken floor and, interestingly, no regular fireplace was recovered (Jæger & Laursen 1983:103p). From House A680 at Østbirk, many litres of charred cereals, being predominantly emmer and spelt, were recovered in an almost rectangular arrangement in a sunken floor (Borup, im manus). Although growing of wheat in some areas of Jutland was almost on a par with barley in quantity during the Late Neolithic, it appears that naked barley was still predominant at Resengaard, Glattrup I/III and Glattrup IV.

Intentional charring could thus have been performed for symbolic exchange with or offering to supernatural beings. The charred cereals might have been food offerings that would not decay soon after depositing in the soil context but would last "eternally". Perhaps comprehensive charring activities would only have been necessary in particular periods, when the community was endangered in some way, facing a really big challenge and when exchanges with or offerings to spirits and deities therefore ought to be carried out. The massive charring thus took place in just a few longhouses.

Even though mishaps from drying processes cannot be excluded as an explanation, my suggestion is that, in the sunken floor of House 1 at Resengaard, we see the remainders of specialized production, being the households' deliberate roasting or charring of cereals.

Bronze working at Kluborg II proposed as specialized production: the considerations regarding House 5 at Kluborg II have resulted in an understanding that the house remainders, together with the soil traces and artefacts as a whole, are quite exceptional, being a site of a very early bronze workshop combined with a dwelling (Fig. 4.45 & 4.46). The soil patches – including the fireplaces in particular – are unique in their appearance. Some of the residues in clay materials are also quite unusual in house contexts from the period, namely the crucible piece and the mould fragments. A strike-a-light, tiny scraps of raw bronze, and some stone hammers were also recovered.[26] All in all, within a certain area of the sunken floor, activities concerned with melting, casting, hammering and polishing appear to have taken place.

If the middle part of the building was rather open – or could be largely opened up – then it would presumably have provided reasonable conditions for handling the bronze with adequate ventilation so that the smoke from the fireplaces in the production area could escape into the open air. The activities would in this way have the advantage that a good deal of light could enter the building and that the processes would have been protected from the rain.

It is noteworthy that ordinary traces of living, such as scorched-stone devices and everyday flint and pottery remainders, were also present. Thus, in my reading, the bronze working was carried out in a building where usual household activities also took place. Against the above backdrop, I suggest that different aspects of bronze working were carried out here as specialized household production.

House 5 seems to have had a rather late chronological position within the period in question. While the residents were performing metal working, the production of bronzes in Denmark was already rather well-established. It has been stated that most bronze objects found in Denmark had actually been made locally by the time of the emerging Bronze Age and that spearheads and flanged axes were predominant in the production (Vandkilde 1996:218pp, with further references).

House 5 at Kluborg II is also interesting in relation to the established hypothesis that the early metal smiths, as known from ethnographic records, lived in fixed settlements, and that those interested in obtaining the metal items visited them or alternatively – with this building as point of departure – these people were visited by the metal smiths (Vandkilde 1996:265).

It would be interesting to know whether the production of metal objects might have been attached

Household, livelihood and exchange   395

to nearby ritual sites but no indications of this have been observed with regard to Kluborg II. Such questions must await investigation and analysis of other locations.

Hide and skin preparation at Hellegård proposed as specialized production: numerous flint scrapers were recovered from the western half of the sunken-floor horizon of House 122 and almost all were found to the northwest within a short internal range, apparently just left as if no subsequent clean-up had been done (Fig. 4.54 & 4.55). A total of 26 scrapers came from the sunken-floor horizon and, likely even one more, indicating that massive scraping work took place here (*cf.* Jensen, H.J. 2009:215p).

In addition to a spoon-shaped scraper, large oval scrapers, almost circular scrapers, long oval scrapers with a blade-like character, and scrapers made from thin flakes, some more irregular ones were also found. The diversity of these tools is thus striking, with many different shapes and varying from heavy, very thick, powerful scrapers to light, very thin specimens, presumably used for less demanding purposes. Whereas most are complete or almost complete, a few are much fragmented, probably due to forceful use. Judging by the presence of tiny flint waste, they may have been repaired on the spot. Their edges also display correspondingly great variations. It appears that every one of these tools had qualities of its own, intended for specific tasks. The scrapers may have been used for treating organic materials such as bone, wood, antler, skin and hides. Yet I presume that treatment of grain- and flesh-sides of hides and skin would be the most obvious possibility because this task would likely require such a broad variety of scraper tools, ranging from the forceful to the fine. Judging by the great variations of the preserved scrapers, perhaps also some thickness reduction (somewhat like skiving) of, for instance, oxen leather took place. It might be added that the micro wear analysis of a scraper (RE120ea) from Resengaard points to the scraping of dry hide/skin (Claus Skriver, report S2004a). It seems an obvious possibility that tools corresponding to the flint scrapers in softer materials such as bone or wood might also have been used in the work processes but would not have been preserved due to the soil conditions.

Within the activity space was also found the pointed end of a pressure-flaked dagger. Knives were not found in this floor area and this might perhaps indicate that cutting into the materials was not the main thing here. For the same reason, the initial processes of skinning slaughtered domestic animals such as oxen, pigs, sheep, goats or game of some kind probably took place outside. Skin and hides from other settlements could conceivably have been received for further working at Hellegård.

Might other kinds of knives have been used as tools in the skinning processes of, for instance, oxen? It is imaginable that knives like the "feeding knives" of the leaf-shaped, broad-edged type C, dated to the early part of the Late Neolithic, could have worked well here (Nielsen, P.-O. 1974:109pp). Due to this kind of shaping, they might have cut gently without damaging the hides.

A smoothening stone (HE546) was also present in the workshop area in addition to some more or less flat stones that were likely underlay for the varying processes of working the skin and hide. It cannot be excluded that skin and hides could in this house context have been further processed into various needed leather- or skin-products of different kinds. However, we have no local evidence of tanning within the excavation area at Hellegård. Preparing the skin and hides for removal of hair could have taken place in any waterhole, whereas tanning might have demanded some kind of tighter or otherwise arranged pits. After tanning, total surface scraping of the flesh side could have been performed with the skin or hides stretched out between two posts (see Ch. 4, Hellegård, House 122).

In all, it seems that the many scrapers and other tools are evidence of comprehensive and versatile scraping activities at this sunken-floor longhouse.[27] With the apparently broad focus on cattle and other livestock in the Late Neolithic – and hunting as well – there would likely have been a call for solid experience and high skills when preparing amounts of skin and hides. Some households might well have specialized in different aspects of this. I suggest that skin and hide preparation, not least by means of scraper tools, took place as a specialized production in House 122.

Beer brewing at Glattrup IV proposed as specialized production: the first time this special kind of cylindrical pit was proposed as relating to beer brewing in South Scandinavian contexts was in the presentation of House 92 at Fosie VI (Björhem & Säfvestad 1989:108). Later on, characteristic cylindrical pits were also recorded at Bejsebakken (Sarauw 2006). To my knowledge, however, we have no finds of, for instance, germinated/malted barley grains from such contexts in the South Scandinavian Late Neolithic and this is also the case for Glattrup IV. Yet it is far from certain that we should anticipate such finds because the malting could hardly be expected to have taken place near the sunken fireplaces, and complete short-time germinated waste grains would only have been preserved if carbonization had somehow taken place. An awareness of the processes that might lead to charring and preservation is therefore important. In my understanding, the malting and some further processes would have been commenced and performed in the western areas of the sunken-floor longhouses at Glattrup IV. During the early investigations of the sites of Houses 3 and 5 at Glattrup IV, it was Kurt Overgaard and his excavation team who suggested that brewing had taken place in these buildings.

In my view, the broad presence of charred cereals, the careful digging of the varyingly large cylindrical pits, the presence of cubicle-pits, and the sunken fireplaces in the sites of the sunken-floor longhouses on the whole support the idea that the production of beer took place at Glattrup IV. (Fig. 4.56-4.60). Judging by the dimensions and placements of these arrangements, giving them overall supremacy in the house interiors, it is reasonable to argue that it might relate to occasions of beer production on a relatively large scale. It is noteworthy that while the cereals were mainly found in the contexts of floors layers and, not least, connected to the scorched-stone patches in the site of House 1 at Resengaard, the charred cereals at Glattrup IV instead came to light in the contexts of the sizeable interior arrangements.

As we have seen, the Glattrup IV longhouses belong in the first half of the Late Neolithic, and Beaker pottery is present. The notion that beer drinking was likely associated with the Beaker phenomenon was advanced early on (Burgess & Shennan 1976:309pp). Other interesting reflections concerned with mead, beer or ale in Beaker societies have likewise been put forward (Harrison 1980:104p). The question of alcoholic beverages has subsequently been discussed by several researchers (e.g. Sherratt 1987:96; Vander Linden 2001:47; Sarauw 2008a:87p, with further references).

The documentation of direct residues of beer is still shrouded in some uncertainty in South Scandinavian finds. The presence of beer residues has been argued on the basis of starch grains found in the crust from a clay pot in a grave belonging to an early phase of the Single Grave Culture at Refshøjgård in Jutland (Klassen 2005:39pp). And yet malted or germinated grains from the Danish Neolithic have, to my knowledge, not yet been evidenced. Regarding mead, an oak coffin grave from the Older Bronze Age period II at Bregninge at Zealand documents a crust at the bottom of a clay pot containing a great deal of mead pollen (Nielsen, S. 1978a:32; 1978b:15pp). From the Older Bronze Age, a thick sedimentary layer of a fermented beverage at the bottom of a birch bark bucket was found in the woman's grave in Egtved in Jutland (Brøndsted 1966:59). It seemed to represent something between beer and mead (Dickson 1978:111; Koch 2001:27pp; Klassen 2005:39). I find it plausible that naturally sweet sap from plants and trees could also have been used in brewing processes, such as e.g. birch sap.

Regarding other parts of northern and central Europe, evidence of brewing is much lacking. In relation to discoveries from a south European context several centuries later than the Beaker-period longhouses at Glattrup IV, the excavation director Lindy Crewe considers the finds at Kissonerga-Skalia on Cyprus to represent the vestiges of an early brewery due to the remainders of mud-plastered, dome-shaped kilns presumably used for drying malted cereals, as well as the presence of various artefacts and charred microfossils.[28]

From more recent Danish contexts, the ethnologist Ole Højrup has presented a detailed description of traditional, domestic beer brewing processes in certain parts of Denmark in the second half of the 19th century (Højrup 1980:43pp). The significance of beer production has also been subject to ethnographical study and one of these concerns the Nigerian Mumuye tribe, where beer appears to have resulted in benefits not only for the sociality but also for health, being nutritious and free from bacilli (Bovin 1965:88).

Because evidence has been comprehensively presented in the foregoing, I shall here merely propose that ample beer brewing, including short-term storage in Houses 3, 5, and 7 at Glattrup IV, is suggested as the specialized activity of the households.

Weaving at Granlygård proposed as specialized production: during the early Late Neolithic, sheep wool clothing became favoured, as indicated by finds of loom weights, pins and buttons (Sarauw 2007b:47). Woollen textiles have not yet been evidenced from the Late Neolithic and emerging Bronze Age in Denmark, however, whereas textiles from plant materials have been found from a time as early as about 4200 BC elsewhere (Mannering & Skals 2013:90pp). It is immediately rather strange that so little documentation has been found on loom weights from the individual house sites, namely in each case just a single one

Household, livelihood and exchange 397

from House 1 and House 268 at Resengaard, House 5 at Kluborg II, House 6 at Glattrup I/III as well as presumed loom weights from House 1 at Marienlyst Strand and House 122 at Hellegård. In all cases the specimens were adequately burned. From a source-critical point of view, we can ask whether the few finds from all these sites fully mirror the former weaving activities. Maybe the loom weights were usually removed when abandoning the longhouses and were further handled so carefully that broken pieces would seldom be left in the floor horizons. And yet the loom weights in the above cases seem rather simply made and might therefore perhaps have been of little value. Unfortunately, no sites of fire from the central Limfjord region are able to elucidate this question further.

To my knowledge, this relatively poor presence can also be extended to most sites with sunken-floor houses elsewhere in the Limfjord region. At Myrhøj, a single loom weight was recovered from the House D context (Jensen, J.A. 1973:90). At Bejsebakken, one specimen was found in a pit in House A643 and a loom weight fragment stems from the upper fills in House A539 (Sarauw 2006:35 & 39). A single pit there is considered to be a weaving pit (Sarauw 2006:38p & 57). Two loom weights were found in the context of the site of a large ground-floor longhouse at Nr. Uttrup (Geertz 2007:32pp).

On a European scale, it has been suggested that "... wool is likely to have been a rather rare, elite commodity for many centuries after its first appearance – and perhaps even longer in heavily forested regions" (Sherratt 1987:89). Yet what we see from these first settlements in the Limfjord region, in my reading, points only to ordinary households. The long timeframe for the sporadic finds in the region might indicate that there could have been many, although probably not most, households that performed wool weaving using loom weights.

Against the above background, the complete colander and the loom weight from pit 4 at Granlygård are particularly interesting (Fig. 4.52). It is tempting to see the placement of these two items close together in the pit as a rather deliberate doing, a votive offering. The deposition could well have taken place when the weaving and the related activities were being given up at this particular spot. Perhaps it coincided with the household leaving the settlement.

The loom weight would presumably have been used for weaving on a kind of loom used directly in connection with the pit (*cf.* Nielsen, S. 1987, Fig. 3, left). When weaving took place outdoors, access to adequate light would not have been a problem. As for the colander, it seems reasonable to presume that one of its purposes could have been in relation to preparing to treat the wool, for instance with some kind of plant extract (*cf.* Grierson 1990). No evidence has yet been found of dyeing of the woollen cloth from the Older Bronze Age oak coffins (Ethelberg 2000a:232). However, the weavers of that time evidently paid attention to colours because in some instances the wool had been sorted, e.g. in the way that darker yarn had been applied for edging (pers.comm. Irene Skals). Despite the apparent absence of traces of colouring, it is evident that the woollen textile handling at that time had reached a high level of complexity and perfection (*cf.* Jensen 2006b:164pp). Hence, it is perhaps unlikely that colouring was carried out earlier in Danish contexts, even though the oldest known examples of coloured thread date back to the Neolithic at Çatalhöyük (Barber 1991:223). The European background for using wool is described broadly (e.g. Sherrat 1982:93p; *cf.* Greenfield 1988, as regards the Balkans. Further, concerning South Scandinavia reference can be given to e.g. Jørgensen, L.B. 1992:114pp; On woven dress, see also Ebbesen 2004:102. On bone pins and their mounting, see Hjärthner-Holdar 1977:235pp; Ebbbesen 1995. More broadly on prehistoric textiles, several new publications exist from The Danish National Research Foundation's Centre for Textile Research, University of Copenhagen/The National Museum of Denmark).

Southerly in Jutland, at Nørre Holsted III, the unusually illuminating find in a pit of 17 loom weights of burnt clay together with parts of two clay pots with Beaker ornamentation (including metopes) might perhaps be an example of a site focussing on special weaving activities (Rindel 1993:20p). In a more recent article, however, it is not considered to represent a "special site" (Sarauw 2007b:29p). Traces of 12 two-aisled houses that are presumed to be from about the same period were later found some 200 m to the north (Grundvad & Poulsen 2013:9pp; 2014:16p). At another location, eight loom weights were recovered, namely at Lindebjerg on northwest Funen at a house site that possibly represents a longhouse (Jæger & Laursen 1983:104).

In general, it appears that weaving could have been performed inside the longhouses as well as in connection with the pits in other surroundings. However, it must be noted that the loom weights from the pits at Nørre Holsted III, Bejsebakken, and Granlygård both belong to the early Late Neolithic and that weaving pits, to my knowledge, have not been published from later times within the period in question.

The apparent absence of longhouses nearby at Granlygård but the presence of traces of no less than three buildings of limited size – all closely placed but not necessarily contemporaneous – adds a special touch to the area. Yet it is possible that a longhouse could have existed somewhat to the north or to the south. Against the above background, I suggest that weaving as well as other textile handling was a specialized production at Granlygård.

Cattle breeding at Rosgårde proposed as specialized production: with the great emphasis of that time on grazing livestock, and based on the distinct ground plan of House 1 at Rosgårde, I suggest that the household living here practised cattle breeding on an extended scale, implying that it formed a specialized production (Fig. 2.55 & 2.56). The reason for this proposal is first and foremost that the significant enlargement towards the west was, in my interpretation, intended for storing relatively large amounts of winter fodder. The topic has already been touched upon in the above considerations on the longhouse architecture. Other animal husbandry could, of course, also have been practised simultaneously. The oval pits and other pits in the ground-floor part of the longhouse might indicate occasional other use of the space when empty. Topographically, some of the surrounding land would probably have been well suited to keeping cattle as well as sheep and goats. The soils in these areas were markedly light and sandy, presumably with adequate grazing potential. The sunken-floor longhouse was placed on a slight plateau in the terrain, and the residents would presumably have had reasonable conditions for watching over the cattle when grazing took place in the immediate surroundings, and herding flocks of sheep, goats or stocks of cattle at some distance from the settlement could well have been an option.

Four of the Beaker longhouses had trapezoid ground plans, being broadest to the west (Fig. 5.1). The household living in House 3 at Glattrup IV might likewise have practised cattle breeding as a specialized production alongside the proposed brewing activities. Interestingly, the ground-floored House 1 at Glattrup IV also gradually became notably broader towards the west. Whether this trait may somehow relate to the keeping of extra amounts of winter fodder is difficult to judge.

At Resengaard, the gradually enlarged western part of House 1 is correspondingly suggested to have been used for extra large amounts of winter fodder (Fig. 2.8). It is hence proposed that the household had cattle breeding as another specialized production. For the same reason, I propose that the residents of House 128 at this settlement had cattle breeding as a specialized production. House 2 was also likely gradually broadened significantly towards the west.

At Myrhøj, finds of three teeth probably stemmed from young oxen but no bone fragments of such animals were recovered (Jensen, J.A. 1973:77p). At Resengaard, extremely few, tiny pieces of bone were found in sunken-floor longhouse contexts. These bones have not been examined scientifically. Quite in line with this scantiness – and thus together rather thought-provoking – is the account that no animal bones at all were found at the Late Neolithic settlement at Bejsebakken (Sarauw 2007b:11). The lack of bones from livestock in the longhouses at these two large settlements ought to result in a strong focus on this issue when new locations, including those with ground floors, are to be investigated.

Common to the Late Neolithic and Older Bronze Age is thus the scarcity of finds of bones from domesticated animals and Marianne Rasmussen is right when she states that "… it is a paradox that hardly any period has left so few finds of bones to attest the presence and character of this important stock-breeding" (Rasmussen, M. 1999:281). It has even been suggested that the Late Neolithic, together with the preceding and following period, i.e. around 2800 to 1000 BC, could also be considered "The Age of the Cattle People" (Randsborg 1990:189p; Kristensson, Olson & Welinder 1996).[29]

Although it seems reasonable to presume that some of the traditional routes for the Danish ox trade had ancient roots in driving cattle longer distances between settlements for the purposes of exchange, we have no evidence of this as concerns the Late Neolithic and emerging Bronze Age in the Limfjord region (cf. Enemark 2003:367pp, Ch. XIII; Holst & Rasmussen 2013). And yet cattle might have been exchanged far and near (cf. Glob 1971:114; Jaanusson & Jaanusson 1988:107). Nico Roymans has also pointed to the importance of cattle within exchange (Roymans 1999:294pp; On export of oxen in later prehistory, see Nielsen, S. 2010:188pp).

Advanced flint tool making at Myrhøj proposed as specialized production: a really conspicuous trait of the Myrhøj settlement is the abundant presence of flint objects in the sunken areas, although there is no clear distinction between floors finds and fills presented (Jensen, J.A. 1973:79pp). Yet it is generally evident that the great quantity of flint waste indicates the comprehensive production of flint tools. The number of flint flakes from two of the three sunken-floor houses in particular is very high. From the site of House D, the totally thus comes to 5,856 pieces and from the site of House EAB a total of 5,290 pieces. From the third house, the number only reaches 1,838, which even in comparison with other house sites from the central Limfjord region is also a considerable number. These amounts may support the idea that flint tool making took place on an extraordinary scale in relation to the Myrhøj buildings. If these three longhouses succeeded each other, it seems plausible that flint working skills could have been passed down from generation to generation (*cf.* Apel 2001; Sarauw 2007c).

At Myrhøj, a glossy flint was favoured for making scrapers, daggers and arrowheads, whereas the calcareous, grey flint was preferred for axes and chisels (Jensen, J.A. 1973:80pp). The raw flints used for production were mostly small cores of local flint, often with cortex preserved but, in some instances, this presumably related to mined flint. The flint tools identified from the site are mainly scrapers, awls, burins, borers, chisels, finely retouched flakes, axes, hollow-edged adzes, daggers, lobed arrowheads, transverse points, a strike-a-light and a blade sickle. Pressure-flaked sickles were almost absent but a burin was made on a large piece of one (Jensen, J.A. 1973:82). The excavation director has stated that the arrowheads and, presumably, also the daggers were produced at the settlement. The "broad" flakes form a considerable – and reasonably constant – share of the worked flints and their presumed association with the making of axes, chisels, daggers and other tools as well as blanks has been indicated (Jensen, J.A. 1973:80). These broad flakes and other features of the flint waste therefore hold a key to understanding the characteristics of flint tool production at Myrhøj. The making of axes or adzes thus forms part of the probable specialized production at this settlement. No less than nine axe blanks have been found and they are represented in all house assemblages, albeit least in House GAB (Jensen, J.A. 1973:86). The presence of these axe blanks may indicate some kind of store. Flint tool production in Houses D and EAB could have been an important aspect of their livelihood, and presumably also concerns House GAB. A comparatively high number of flint scrapers from this building might, in turn, point to the fairly heavy use of such tools, as it is, to some degree, evidenced from the many fragmented pieces. The majority of scrapers were more or less round. I suppose that preparing of skin and hides or other scraping activities could have been another specialized production of one or more Myrhøj households. In addition to this, stock keeping and agriculture have been emphasized as activities carried out at Myrhøj (Jensen, J.A. 1973).

I find it evident that the households' specialized flint tool production was not solely intended for the residents' own use. It thus seems that the production of specific flint tools was carried out as a specialized production by the households of House D and EAB first and foremost with the aim of wider exchange. This could also presumably more or less have been the case of House GAB.

Gug and Myrhøj are two examples of settlements which, according to recent studies accomplished by experts on flint working, are considered to have had a finer flint production as well as a more ordinary one (Olausson 1997 and 2000. Apel 2001:199. Vandkilde 2007). Regarding Gug, it has been suggested that "… the lithic debitage indicates that knapping was carried out by individuals of varying skill" (Olausson 2000:129). Production of daggers and thick-butted axes has particularly been proposed to have been carried out at Myrhøj (Apel 2001:199).

When it comes to the making of flint daggers, such production has also been proposed in relation to the settlement at Bjergene VI (THY 2758) and the existence of specialized dagger-producing households has been discussed (Thorpe 2000:75, with further references). It is interesting that when we think of the Bjergene II structure (THY 2756) remainders as presumably representing two longhouses these, together with House 1 at Bjergene VI, would have formed three sunken-floor longhouses with an unusual alignment (Thorpe 1997; 2000:75 & Fig. 5.2; Prieto-Martinez 2008, Fig. 6). Might this particular trait relate to some further kind of production or conditions, favouring the unusual longhouse alignment?

It has been proposed that the dagger production sites, in all, concerned three or more kinds of location (Apel 2001:199pp). From this understanding, the raw flint was obtained from mines and also from spots where the collection of flint nodules was possible due to erosion, e.g. in coastal areas. Then, the initial raw production was carried out at secluded sites not far from the resource area. Finally, the finishing of the items took place at the settlements.

Concerning House 200 at Resengaard, I am inclined to suggest that a little more flint tool production than usual was carried out here but not enough to suggest it as a specialized doing. Many pieces of worked flint were also present in the site of House 2 at Tromgade and House 2 at Resengaard but hardly beyond what might have been needed by the settlement alone, despite the fact that this concerns more than in many other longhouse sites in the central Limfjord region. Diverging local practices for depositing the flint waste may have influenced the accounts of these at the house sites and this is surely a source-critical factor.

Commodities such as amber, honey and salt

In previous Neolithic periods, amber played a very marked role in North Jutland as reflected in graves and hoards; however, it seems that the use of it in such situations declined in the Late Neolithic (Andersen, S H. 1998:105). And yet the precise significance of amber is rather difficult to elucidate from the settlement finds from the Late Neolithic and emerging Bronze Age. So far, amber pieces as raw material or in the shape of artefacts have only exceptionally been found in sunken-floor house contexts in the Limfjord region. At Resengaard, a single amber piece was recovered from the secondary fills of the minor House 84 (Fig. 5.18). At Glattrup IV just one crumbled piece of amber was recovered in the site of House 3. At Myrhøj an amber button, an amber disc and a worked piece were found in the House D milieu (Jensen, J.A. 1973:78). Based on this, it is difficult to estimate the significance of amber collection activities on the coasts of North Jutland, presumably not least after rough winds causing wave erosion. The scale of its further production into beads, buttons, etc. in the Late Neolithic is not easy to judge either but amber workshops have been investigated on the west coast of the region from the time of the Beakers. Some knowledge does thus exist on its shaping and further working (e.g. Hirsch & Liversage 1987:193pp; Vandkilde 1990a). I propose collecting and working of amber as a specialized household production.

Honey extraction was likely carried out on some scale. Bee cakes might also have been consumed. A bronze model of a beehive, found in a rich hoard at Skeldal somewhat more southerly than the Limfjord region and originally stemming from Únětice Culture, could symbolize the general importance of honey (Vandkilde1990:115pp; 1996, Fig. 57; 2010:54pp). The gathering and extraction of honey is proposed to have been a specialized household production. Perhaps it could have been performed through the keeping of bees in forest areas (cf. Sherratt 1987:95).

In northern and central Europe, concentrated salt occurrences appear to have already been exploited in the Neolithic, and importing from the Mediterranean is also suggested (Gräslund 1973:284pp, with further references). An interesting study on salt production and circulation in Spain, Portugal, France, and beyond is currently being carried out by Elisa Guerra Doce (pers.comm.). Concerning western Scandinavia, it has been proposed that salt was procured in the Neolithic and the Bronze Age (Gräslund 1973:290; Jaanusson & Jaanusson 1988:107pp). The procurement of salt is a rather difficult subject to discuss, however. Since some intake of it is a necessity of human life, the residents of the sunken-floor houses must have had their sources for obtaining what they needed. To acquire more or less pure salt from distant sources through exchange could have been a possibility in some instances (cf. Matthias 1976). Yet in ordinary everyday life I believe we should look for other sources. In coastal areas, people might well have used saltwater directly. Concerning production for exchange, the concentration of salt via an evaporation method (taking up crystals by high salt concentration) seems a possibility. Burning or drying of seaweed might also have been an option (cf. Jaanusson & Janusson 1988: 108). The sampling of salty herbs such as samphire on the shores might well have been possibility for the diet, too. However, as salt is a quickly evanescent substance when exposed to water, it is not easy to trace it at the settlements. I tentatively suggest that as a primary source of salt, production took place in the coastal areas of the region, presumably not least in the relatively warm and dry months of the year, during the Late Neolithic and emerging Bronze Age. I see the production (and procurement) of salt as specialized household doing.

All in all, a wide and varied group of commodities can therefore be proposed as specialized household production. The above are taken as examples in the following.

Presenting the "Model of three-level household production"

In the Late Neolithic and emerging Bronze Age, subsistence activities such as basic animal husbandry and agricultural production would have been practised by the households at most settlements. Apart from this understanding as an element of the model, the main characteristic is that highly varying kinds of specialized production contributed significantly to sustaining the economic aspects of life through exchange among households within and beyond the region. The "Model of three-level household production" aims to embrace what is common as well as what is specialized regarding the Limfjord region.

Presumably some kinds of specialized production took place, particularly in certain seasons or shorter periods of the year when activities related to agriculture, stock keeping and other doings did not preoccupy the residents too much. Specialized production could in this way thus have been highly compatible with tillage, animal custody and other.

The ordinary subsistence production of the individual households might usually have yielded only a modest surplus, albeit perhaps sometimes more abundantly than others. Conversely, it might also have been insufficient at times. On the whole, it would hardly have exceeded the everyday needs of a household much, unless special circumstances prevailed in a given period.

The above activities of cereal treatment, bronze working, skin- and hide preparation, beer brewing, woollen textile weaving, cattle breeding and flint tool making relate to seven concrete suggestions of specialized production from particular locations but the model presupposes that multiple other kinds of specialized household production also took place with the intention of exchange. Against the background of numerous pieces of information from fieldwork reports, publications and other sources, my "Model of three-level household production" is introduced essentially as a kind of model to "think with" when considering production, exchange and related aspects of daily life in the period under consideration. In this vein, George Dalton has posited that "one of our tasks…is to invent conceptual models which enable us to extract what is important and not obvious from a welter of diversity…" (Dalton 1981:43).

According to the model, certain kinds of production would have been made by all or almost all households (Fig. 5.18 & 5.19). This is seen as A-level production and concerns some ordinary subsistence products. Consequently, the model proposes that most households in the region would not produce significantly more agricultural or animal output than usable for consumption in the household itself, including for purposes such as, for instance, small-scale ritual offerings. The major part of such production would not have been circulated under "normal" circumstances but some occasional surplus could habitually have been exchanged e.g. among neighbouring households or kin and may have helped ensure that basic subsistence needs were more broadly met for the households.

Besides various services, it is proposed that a lot of things regarded as a necessity or a luxury of daily life were made as B- and C-level production, and then usually exchanged as a commodity, i.e."… an item with use value that also has exchange value" (Kopytoff 1992:64). Most households would have been supplied with specialized products through exchange.

From several up to relatively many households were involved in B-level production, according to the model. Each of these would have carried out one or more different kinds of such production at a given time. It is implied that it would have required additional relevant skills and expertise to undertake many of the B-level doings. Such products would have been needed by the many households that were not producing them and would therefore frequently have been exchanged.

Relatively few households would have engaged in the making of C-level products. Like the foregoing level, it may have required some extra dexterity and capability in certain aspects to make some of the C-

Fig. 5.18. A piece of raw amber (RE485ag) found in secondary fills above the sunken floor of House 84 at Resengaard. Being very fragile after millennia in this soil, it was only faintly touched with a trowel when a side splintered. Scale 2:1.

level products. Likewise, these could have been much in demand and exchanged to a high degree. Whether a given specialized production was at B- or C-level will depend on an estimate of how many households – as a proportion – were considered to have been engaged in producing the given commodities or services.

Some households might possibly have acquired some traditional "rights" to make certain B- and C-level products or services. In this regard, the model also includes the possibility that different kinds of work were exchanged, as in for instance doing different practical services or performing certain ritu-

C-level   (Relatively few households)

* Collecting & working of amber
* Chipping of exquisite flint daggers
* Delicate Beaker pottery making
* Bronze casting & other metal working
* Increased beer brewing
* Sea salt production

Fig. 5.19. In relation to the "model of three-level household production", some examples are here tentatively suggested regarding the Limfjord region. It must be underlined that the three levels are not considered a priori to represent a hierarchy of status but instead to denote the relative number of households engaging in a given kind of production or service. For further, see text.

B level   (Relatively many households)

* Ritual ox-killing
* Cereal roasting or charring
* Hide- & skin preparation
* Small-scale beer brewing
* Wool textile weaving
* Extracting bee honey
* Increased dairy production
* Increased fresh- & saltwater fishing
* Increased cereal growing
* Seaweed gathering
* Shellfish collecting
* Increased hunting
* Increased cattle breeding
* Flint mining & rough flint shaping
* Digging clay for pottery
* Directing & surveying longhouse building
* Advanced stone axe production
* Advanced flint tool making
* Working stones for querns & cists
* Making of pottery in current shapes & styles
* Making bark containers
* Making refined leather- & basketwork

A-level   (Most or all households)

* Broad agricultural activities
* Keeping livestock
* Small-scale hunting
* Small-scale fishing
* Gathering nuts & berries
* Gathering birds' eggs
* Making plain dairy products
* Making soups & porridge
* Everyday cleaning of houses
* Digging clay, sand and turf
* Collecting plant materials for winter fodder
* Collecting firewood & stones
* Procuring easily accessible raw flint
* Procuring flint & making everyday flint tools
* Procuring materials & making plain wooden tools
* Procuring materials & making plain leather- & basketwork
* Broad participation in the process of building longhouses
* Everyday maintenance of houses and other constructions

Household, livelihood and exchange

als. Cooperation among households to create certain products or do certain services would also have taken place but there would also have been some competition in certain respects.

The model is open to the possibility that not all households in the region necessarily made B- and C-level products or services. A few could probably have managed with A-level production, for some reason. Conversely, households that did not carry out all A-level activities could also have existed. It thus seems a possibility that the residents of House 5 at Glattrup IV did not carry out basic animal husbandry, judging by the pit arrangement in the ground-floor part, which here took up much of the floor space and thus indicates that the residents' focus of attention was mainly focused on this. Otherwise, exceptions from doing A-level production might particularly have related to households consisting mainly of people suffering from illness, the disabled, the elderly or people otherwise indisposed and receiving their basic subsistence needs and beyond from neighbouring households, close kin or other.

Through the centuries, frequent changes may have more or less gradually taken place in the kinds of production carried out and just a couple of examples are given to illustrate this: the creation of pottery decorated in the fashion of the Beaker style reached its peak early in the Late Neolithic and then – in my understanding – began to decline until it eventually disappeared completely, while new expressive but undecorated forms were again and again introduced over the coming centuries. The onset of pressure-flaking of flint daggers that defines the beginning of the entire period soon reached an extremely high standard but high quality products in several new dagger forms emerged throughout the Late Neolithic, as the old went out of production. Households may have responded more or less swiftly to such new beginnings, declines and alterations in production. In this way, some kinds of specialized production could relate to the entire Late Neolithic and emerging Bronze Age while others could have had a more limited production period. For a given production (or service), the suggestion of A-level, B-level or C-level relates to the assumed average proportion of households engaging in it during the period it was performed.

In the following, a number of ideas on production at A-, B-, and C-levels will be presented in relation to the model, including arguments, backgrounds and references.

A-level production in all or most households

As proposed, all or most households in the region carried out a wide range of A-level production for their daily subsistence. In now making suggestions as to what A-level production may have encompassed, we can begin with agricultural activities. Preparing the fields, sowing and tending in different ways, as well as harvesting, threshing, cleaning and storage could have been carried out by all or most households. All or most could have kept livestock such as sheep/goats, pigs and cattle that had to be taken care of on a daily basis, possibly including some small-scale herding. Despite the greater focus on cattle, I find it conceivable that sheep and goats actually outnumbered these in many areas. Herding very probably could have been carried out in cooperation among several households, as emphasized for Almhov and other locations by Hyllie bog (Brink 2013:447p, with further references).

The output of the above A-level work was presumably *inter alia* cereals, meat, bone, horn, milk, skin and hides, as well as possibly plain dairy foods with a longer life such as cheese, yoghurt or milk made sour as for junket (*cf.* Jensen 2006:513). The widely found low bowls with oblique straight-walls, might have been used for such dairy production not least in the first half of the Late Neolithic.

Hazel bushes could have been grown and tended partly for their branches, and their nuts were evidently favoured. In addition, hazelnuts, acorns, blackberries, raspberries, apples and some other kinds of useful wild plant food could often have been gathered in the settlement surroundings (Andreasen 2009:34). The collecting of birds' eggs is also evident and it seems obvious that these and other natural resources would have been a part of the usual household subsistence, depending not least on nearby availability. Such activities could have been extended in years with otherwise sparse food production, thereby forming a buffer for subsistence. All or most households are likely to have gathered firewood such as fallen branches and performed small-scale cutting of reeds for thatching, e.g. as repair jobs. Stones would also have been collected for activities such as hammering, drying, roasting, charring, cooking or heating. Cooking may perhaps have included the baking of simple bread, in that case possibly unleavened (Sherratt 1987:93). Making porridge from cereals and various soups seems an obvious possibility.

Small-scale fishing would also have been an A-level activity. Collecting of shellfish would have been carried out by some households. Although only sparse evidence is available on hunting, this probably played an important role for very many households. It may sometimes have been carried out by households in cooperation. Dogs could have taken part in the hunting as well as being used for herding and guarding (*cf.* Aaris-Sørensen 1989:213). The lobed arrowheads would presumably have been suited for hunting certain land and sea mammals. At Resengaard, lobed, triangular arrowheads were thus found in many longhouse contexts and, at Myrhøj, in all three house sites (Jensen, J.A. 1973:88). These arrowheads have been found in their hundreds in settlement contexts, graves and loose finds in the Limfjord region, as evidenced by museum and private collections and these probably only represent a very small percentage of the original numbers. In my understanding, the presence of numerous triangular arrowheads may first and foremost demonstrate a massive interest in hunting and this does not, of course, exclude a possible element of defence. The suggestion that all or most households carried out hunting on a small-scale level is a significant part of the model.

Simple basketwork and leatherwork could well have been A-level production. The model furthermore implies that practically all households made simple implements for own use. Everyday tools like flint knives, flint scrapers, flint borers and simple tools in other materials such as wood, bone, antler and horn would thus have been made or repaired whenever needed. It is also implied in the model that the households maintained their longhouses and other constructions on a day-to-day basis. The building of ordinary sheds, huts and minor houses is also suggested as an A-level doing. It is furthermore proposed that all or most households participated in the building of new longhouses in the local area, or helped provide the materials or provide and make the necessary food during the process. Skilful B-level specialists may often have been the ones leading the comprehensive work of building new longhouses.

B-level production in many households

Five of the seven concrete cases of specialized household production are proposed to have been B-level production. This concerns cereal roasting/charring, skin- and hide preparation, textile weaving, cattle breeding and advanced flint tool making. Beer brewing is also considered B-level production when carried out on a minor scale. A wide range of further B-level activities would, however, have been carried out in the region and a number of suggestions are presented in the following. Some of the households could very well have been engaged in several such kinds of production, while others would have been involved in just a few and some would presumably have stuck to just one. Seen as rather exceptional, however, the model also keeps open the possibility that some households did not have any B-level production.

Flint mining and rough flint shaping is suggested as a B-level doing. Mined flint would still have been in demand late in the period in question, not least as raw material for relatively large items such as daggers, despite the bronzes gaining. In the northern part of the Limfjord region, mining of flint occurrences was carried out to a great extent and these activities began long before the Late Neolithic (Madsen, B. 1993:126pp; Jensen, J. 2006a:514p. Becker 1951a; 1951b; 1993; Vandkilde 1996, Fig. 290; Apel 2001:197pp; Sarauw 2007c). It has been proposed that really good flint was perhaps rarer than thought in the Limfjord region (Becker 1993:121).

Flint mining locations have first and foremost been evidenced from LN I in the region, being rich in natural occurrences of different types of flint (Petersen 1999:21pp). We presumably only know of a low percentage of the locations where flint was taken from regular mines. It has long been known that offerings of flint tools might be an indicator of mining in the neighbourhood (Ebbesen 1981:43p). Regarding the Bejsebakken-Skovbakken-Hasseris Hill area, considerations on flint production, mining and hoards, as well as interpretations of social aspects, have more recently been presented (Sarauw 2007c:217pp). Even though its flint quality was not among the best, it is calculated that at least 800 shafts may have been established for the extraction, giving an idea of the scale of mining at this location (Sarauw 2007c:222).

Mines that could have yielded raw flint for the largest tools still remain to be documented in numbers (*cf.* Jensen 2006:516). Our information on details of flint mines, beyond Skovbakken and Hillerslev, is likewise still rather limited (Becker 1993:112). Despite the occurrence of substantial chalk mining with flint occurrences near the surface from recent periods in areas such as Mønsted and Daugbjerg to the south in the central Limfjord region, no targeted investigations of the possible presence of Late Neolithic flint mines have, to my knowledge, been conducted here. Raw flint could presumably also to some degree have been obtained on the shores of the region, in particular near certain cliff-like chalk formations (*cf.* Sarauw 2007c:236).

Judging by the huge number of daggers and other items of North Jutland origin, many households in the Limfjord region would have been involved in flint mining and I therefore propose that it represents B-level production. More concretely, it seems very plausible that households at Bejsebakken took part in the nearby flint mining activities (Nielsen, J.N. 2000:46p; Sarauw 2006:67p & Fig. 54; 2007c:216). Such flint mining could very well have been undertaken not only by adults. Children from the households might also have carried out important stages in the mining process in the Limfjord region. When considering flint mines in Britain, Miles Russell has pointed out that "…it is unlikely that many of the muscle-bound males depicted in certain modern reconstructions of flint mining would ever have been able to fit with small basal galleries and side chambers of excavated shafts" (Russell 2000:144).

Advanced production of stone axes and other stone items is also suggested as a B-level activity. Shaft-hole axes of various kinds might, in particular, have been in demand. The working of these would have been rather time-consuming (*cf.* Fenton 1984:223pp; Olausson 1997:273). In eastern Jutland, highly interesting remainders from a stone axe-producing workshop have been found in the site of a minor, sunken-floor building (House A5) at Østbirk (Borup, im manus). It is interpreted as belonging to a nearby sunken-floor longhouse (House A4). Concerning repair work on stone axes, it has been argued that most Late Neolithic shaft-hole axes used in certain Swedish areas were originally made in sizes from 20-35 cm and that new, replacement shaft-holes were drilled as the tools became shorter (Lekberg 2000:156pp). Such repairs would then be B-level production as well. Shaping of quern stones could have been quite laborious and is suggested as a B-level doing. I likewise find it conceivable that the procurement and working of stone materials intended for stone coffins might have been performed as a B-level specialization. I thus propose that burial in a sedimentary rock coffin with a type I C flint dagger from Bjergby on the Limfjord island of Mors is an example of this (Ebbesen 2005:61pp).

When it comes to building the dwellings – and not least the longhouses with ground floors – much timber of different strengths and dimensions would have been needed. Stored, reusable timber from earlier buildings would have spared materials and manpower. The removal of wooden posts before deliberately burning House 2 at Resengaard could be an example of this. For the making and further treatment of timbers, a broad variety of flint axes with different qualities would have been at their disposal (Jensen, J. 2006:523). I suggest that timber cutting as well as cutting reeds and thatching beyond a small scale was B-level production. The construction and building of the longhouses is also suggested as a B-level doing on the part of some especially skilled and trained members of certain households.

At Bejsebakken, the residents are considered to have made the pottery used at their settlement themselves, and likewise at Myrhøj (Sarauw 2007b:27p). Based on certain thin section pottery analysis, it has further been suggested that the Danish Beaker pottery "…might never have left the household and apparently did not travel far" (Sarauw 2007b:3). Yet, in my understanding, pottery making would have been a rather demanding activity. Specializing in the tradition of pottery production and keeping up with the fashion of the ceramics, with their very characteristic touch, would thus also imply the use of very definite methods and techniques for mixing the clay, shaping the pots, and treating the surfaces, besides the final firing process. I therefore suggest that the production of Beaker pottery and other ceramics is a B-level doing and would likely have been performed by many households in the Limfjord region. Unfortunately, we still have amazingly little evidence of the accurate spots where the widespread Beaker pottery was produced in the region. Procurement of raw clay, well suited to pottery production, might also have been dug up as a B-level production activity and brought widely into exchange. The future chances of clarifying the provenance of pottery clay seem to be very good due to new methods (Rasmussen, K.L.1998:23pp). Tempering materials such as crushed, sharp granite or the like probably often stemmed from heat-cracked stones (Boas 1983:97; Rasmussen, M. 1993a:39p; Sarauw 2008a:94). Tempering was often probably a by-product of the use of scorched-stone devices and other stone-using heating arrangements, and hence easily accessible for the potter households. Concerning the composition of the clay materials in ceramics from settlements in the Early Bronze Age in Jutland, four types and their relative occurrences have been proposed (Rasmussen 1993:40).

Other kinds of minor jars such as those made of birch bark, known from the Neolithic and Older Bronze Age, are also proposed as B-level production. Complicated basketwork, refined leatherwork and woven textiles are also proposed as representing this level of production.

Further B-level production can be suggested, despite the lack of substantial documentation, for instance, the collecting of honey.[30] Wax is also suggested as having been taken from beehives as a specialized household production. Production of advanced cheese, e.g. processed in a special way that might keep it in good condition for long periods, thus making it suitable for exchange, is also proposed.[31] Shellfish collecting and catching fish beyond a small scale are seen as B-level production. With its small piles of blue common mussel, the Nygaard settlement, placed at some distance from the Limfjord coast, is interesting in this respect (Nielsen, S. 1977:81p).[32] In the omnipresent coastal zones of the region, it furthermore seems likely that gathering of seaweeds might have been performed, also as a B-level doing for different purposes. It cannot be ruled out that nourishing seaweeds in dried form might have been kept, for instance, for a hunger gap in the early spring. In more recent centuries in South Scandinavia, many poor people on the seaboards used seaweeds in their diet (*cf.* Mouritsen 2009:7pp).

Relatively large-scale keeping and herding of cattle and other livestock is also proposed as a B-level doing. It seems to relate to certain households at Rosgårde and Resengaard. I also suggest that hunting was carried out on a relatively extensive scale in the region, using not least bow and arrows, and being performed by very experienced members of many households. In the highly varying Limfjord region landscapes, a correspondingly diversified wildlife presumably existed, giving rich possibilities for gathering, fishing and hunting. With regard to the latter, wild pigs, roe deer and red deer were probably important game (Aaris-Sørensen 1989:216; *cf.* Ethelberg 2000a, Fig. 53). Perhaps aurochs and wild horses were also sporadically present in the region. B-level doings might also concern sea-hunting in the Limfjord archipelago although evidence of this is largely lacking from the period in question.

Numerous other kinds of production might have belonged to the B-level along with several others that are hardly imaginable to us but my suggestion is that all of these products more or less frequently entered into exchange with other households.

C-level production in a few households

Given that relatively few households performed C-level production, according to the model, it is suggested that these households often also engaged in B-level production, as well as the general A-level. Among the seven concrete cases of specialized household production, bronze casting and ample beer brewing are considered C-level production.

Early in the Late Neolithic, some exceptionally delicate pottery was made for a short period by a very few households. Certain highly skilled potters managed to produce extremely thin-walled pots supplied with fine decoration and well fired. This concerns some of the Beaker ceramics, which are seen as C-level production.

It has been discussed as to whether certain graves with archery equipment from the early part of the Late Neolithic represent organized warriors or "some kind of general warrior status related to maleness" (Sarauw 2007a:65; 2007c). However, I prefer to see these archery burials as first and foremost representing people who, as a vital part of their life, took part in bow-and-arrow hunting. Some examples from Langeland provide evidence that the pressure-flaked arrowheads were actually used for hunting (Sarauw 2007a:75). In my interpretation, many of the archery burials of the Limfjord region may belong to exceptionally skilled hunters, represented in graves such as those with the exquisite, parallel-flaked flint daggers of type I C (Lomborg 1973a). When participating in shooting, it might in certain instances have concerned "prestige-hunting" parties (*cf.* Vandkilde 2007:92). It is worth bearing in mind that, in certain foreign contexts, a grave with hunting gear, a beaker, a tanged copper knife, and other items are considered to display a whole set of representational meanings, and it is proposed " that it represents a symbolical hunting equipment – and for the hunting of big game, such as the horse, the wild ox, red deer, the wild pig, mankind and perhaps monsters of the spirit world – the projectiles to wound the quarry and wind it until it dropped, the knife to give the *coup-de-grâce* by cutting its throat, and the Beaker from which to drink its blood" (Case 2004:29). I suggest that participation in the most prestigious hunting parties is to be considered C-level production, as it would concern relatively few people. The slaughtered game might well have been exchanged in prescribed ways, whereby some further prestige would presumably be achieved.

In line with the above quotation, it has recently been argued that an important function of the dagger was not as a weapon but rather as a tool for killing, giving for instance an ox to be slaughtered the *"coup-de-grâce"* (Skak-Nielsen 2009:352pp). This interpretation seems rather plausible and, correspondingly, it seems that the final stab with the dagger might well have been given to some wild game. For prestigious hunting purposes, flint daggers of the most exquisite craftsmanship could well have been much in demand. The making of such daggers is proposed as a C-level production because presumably relatively few, highly skilled members of certain households would have engaged in it. This could have related to a number of specimens among the large, lanceolate daggers with parallel-flaked surfaces, type I C, and some specimens among the daggers with "fishtail" handles supplied with neat seams at the broad blade edges, types IV D and IV E (Lomborg 1973a). Some of the more slender daggers belonging to Lomborg's type III B, which in several cases are produced with rather delicate craftsmanship, could presumably also have been in demand for this reason. However, among these types there are also daggers that do not really appear to fit into the group of greatest excellence.

Bronze casting and other handling of metal items is suggested to have been C-level production and it might have involved more people during certain phases of the processes. Due not least to scarcity, the bronze products were presumably rather valuable commodities in the early Late Neolithic although, gradually, the number of bronze items increased in the region. To my knowledge, the investigation of the site of the early bronze workshop at House 5 at Kluborg II, with its multiple traces, is unique in South Scandinavia and, as considered earlier, it appears to belong at about the end of the period in question.

An unknown number of other kinds of C-level production might have been carried out by members of relatively a few households. In addition, for instance, to the collecting and working of amber, as well as the gathering and extraction of honey, it is suggested this this may have concerned the procurement and production of salt.

Further comments on the idea behind model

The "Model of three-level household production" is, of course, to be considered an abstraction, not a reality. It is based on the idea that, besides the most basic doings, households also carried out various kinds of specialized production, and one essential characteristic here is the way of looking at the production activities as a set of steps where, at one end all or most households were engaged, whereas at the other, only relatively few would have taken part.

We also have to be aware of the time perspective on the levels of production. Each kind of production has its period. The production of certain delicate flint tools and certain extraordinarily fine Beaker pottery, both in superior techniques, was above referred to as cases of C-level production but examples could also have related to quite simple doings, seen to have been carried out by relatively few households. Obviously, the involvement in production of Beaker pottery peaked early in the Late Neolithic. The exquisite flint items each also had their time of production.

Pottery making is seen as B- and C-level doings but not A-level. In contrast, flint working is suggested at all three levels throughout the entire Late Neolithic and emerging Bronze Age. Hunting is also considered an activity at all three levels throughout this long period. Fishing and cattle breeding are both also proposed as having been practised at A-level and B-level throughout this period. The concrete suggestions put forward here may be adjusted or amplified when further new knowledge on different kinds of production is generated.

Cooperation among households likely also took place on a considerable scale. Some households might have worked together in some ways in the manufacturing of certain commodities, or could have cooperated around B-level and C-level services. Various members of a household might have worked at different levels. As well as working at A-level, some household members might even have produced at both B-level and C-level.

From the evidence of concrete settlements, it is a highly interesting trait that some households appear to have ongoing traditions in certain kinds of specialization. With regard to Resengaard, I presume that the residents of two longhouses followed the same practise of specialized cattle breeding (House 128 & House 1). At Glattrup IV the tradition of specialized beer brewing appears to have concerned the households of all three longhouses, presumably succeeding each other. At Myrhøj the practice of specialized flint tool making appears to have been carried out in relation to all three longhouses. Strategies that were originally initiated by a household could thus in some cases have been continued as a tradition for two or more generations, presumably just with some adjustments of different kinds, such as introducing new methods and techniques for their production. Such stable specialization may be a sign of correspondingly steady conditions for household exchange.

All in all, many different kinds of production (and services) would have been exposed to significant changes in conditions over time. Certain challenges, in particular, could have been topical when younger generations were about to take over and establish new households. Quite new strategies for production and exchange might thus have been put in place from generation to generation although, as we have seen, the habitual kinds of production could also simply have continued. The households' considerations may well have been rather closely focused on the possibilities of ensuring long-term viability.[35] If we tentatively take our point of departure in the notion that each century, on average, corresponded to four human generations, then the Late Neolithic and emerging Bronze Age might have approached 30 generations. Again and again, new households in the early stages of establishing themselves may have considered whether to continue the specialization of the former generation or to choose some alternative.

It is even far from certain that plans decided on and carried out for some time were maintained through the entire functional period of a household. Options for the households to revise their current roles within the exchange systems would presumably have been present. Households could also have been unexpectedly forced to alter or adjust their strategies according to sudden changes in the fundamental economic conditions and the emergence of new, alternative options.

Following this model, it would be quite wrong to consider the economies of the households as basically alike, with only moderate differences. The model instead gives room for significant differentiation between household economies not least due to the production in question, with dissimilar kinds of specialized production because of differences in skills and levels of production, due to alterations of production from one household generation to the next, and even due to significant changes during a given generation. The possibilities and resources of the landscape would likely often have been of great importance for the household economies and, as referred to above, significant variations existed among the settlements of the central Limfjord region as regards the landscape settings. In connection with beer production and gatherings of people in the Limfjord archipelago, related topics will be further explored (Simonsen, in prep.).

As the model is meant first and foremost to be an instrument for thinking about household production (and services) in the Late Neolithic and emerging Bronze Age, from a wider perspective it might help to provide a basis for further reflection on exchange among households and its possible organization in the Limfjord region and beyond. In terms of social structure, Torben Sarauw has posited the following: "One could easily imagine a society consisting of different segmentary autonomous groups organised according to kinship and residence, i.e. a non-hierarchical decentralised system without a common leader…" (Sarauw 2007b:44; cf. Sarauw 2007c:258). In all corners of such a society, I presume that people would have been dependent on family relations, neighbourhood and friendship. I consider the notion of a non-hierarchical society in the region to be rather plausible and, in line with this, some reflections on exchange, inspired by anthropology, shall be presented below.

Yet, based on settlement materials, I argue that in terms of further discussion of social organization in the Limfjord region, we have to await a really important key to our understanding of the Late Neolithic and beyond, namely the thorough and comprehensive analyses of available find contexts and other evidence from the regional ground-floor longhouses seen in relation to the knowledge of the sunken-floor longhouses. Chances are that this agenda will present new valuable indications on the topic of social order and hence possibly lead to further ideas on the exchange structure. In the wake of such thorough longhouse analyses, solid considerations of the evidence and organization of elements in the landscape such as burials, deposits (votive and other), road systems, working stations, resource exploitation (flint mines and other) would likely enhance the discussion of social organization significantly and help to produce a nuanced picture.

Although large ground-floor houses such as those known from eastern parts of Denmark and South Scandinavia have not, to my knowledge, been found in the Limfjord region, it is possible that the southeastern parts of it in particular may have been somewhat influenced by, or related culturally and socially to, easterly areas such as, not least, Djursland, where longhouses of that kind existed. In these areas of

South Scandinavia, the ground-floor longhouses began to increase greatly in length from about 2000 calBC (Nielsen, P.-O. 1998:20). The appearance of such sizeable buildings is seen as connected to the increase in metal working, competition over control of bronze production and achieving social status (Nielsen, P.-O. 1998:22 & 26).

My idea as expressed in the "Model of three-level household production" does not refer directly to the social standing of the households.[34] For instance, households engaged in more kinds of B-level production are not proposed to have been more important or to have achieved higher status than those with little or no such production. The relatively few households involved in C-level production would not automatically have been assigned higher status, although it is obviously a possibility, when related to commodities in great demand. Even with an egalitarian ideology prevailing in the region, the households would hardly have been equally strong, and some might have been weakened due to illness, death, or a wide variety of other factors, while others gained strength and became stronger economically over time. The accomplishments or failures of exchange would probably have different outcomes for the individual households. Factors within production and services as well as exchange might thus have opened up a differentiation in the economy and status of households.

On the whole, in relation to the people who lived in the sunken-floor longhouses, I argue that a large number of specialized household products – largely capable of fulfilling the needs for everyday and special foods, beverages, households items, clothing and numerous other commodities and services – were exchanged with other households and occasionally, or maybe even sometimes daily, also with divine powers, spirits or demons.

5.7. Household exchange from a regional perspective

From the evidence of the archaeological investigations, it appears that none of the known settlements in the region were fortified, despite – presumably – the existence of some local territorial endeavours on the part of the households. Moreover, since no direct traces or significant indications of aggressive, warlike confrontations, simple conquests or violent raids have in the main been brought to light, we will have to look for other reasons to account for the widespread similarities in the archaeological remains in the Limfjord region.

In my understanding, the people must thus have had close contacts internally and beyond the region. Communication and exchange of commodities, services and persons may have stimulated a consistent practice of how to behave socially and how to secure sustenance through pertinent production and exchange. This also includes how to build sunken-floor houses and arrange the interiors. I argue that the existence of comprehensive and well-maintained exchange systems in the Late Neolithic and emerging Bronze Age is the main cause of the obvious cultural similarities regionally.

For this reason, an outline of some aspects of classic and more recent anthropological studies of exchange systems from different parts of the world shall now be presented in order to illustrate some of the variety, complexity, and characteristic features that are presumably involved. This will also contribute to exemplifying the scale of some of the social and cultural implications in relation to exchange.

It would hardly have been a simple affair for individuals, households or social groups to navigate in a sociality based on exchange. Any romanticism of social equilibrium can hardly be projected of necessity onto societies of the Late Neolithic and beyond with regard to the area in question. It may at times have been really difficult to obtain the resources, products and services wanted or needed and we have no grounds to believe that compelling demands, unreasonable conditions, massive threats, significant power demonstrations and other strong, complicating factors would have been absent. Disputes and conflicts would inevitably have arisen here and there. However, I find it likely that, through the exchange systems, people managed to take imperative and vital countermeasures against warfare and much other physical violence.

Inspiring classic and newer anthropological studies on exchange

Within economic anthropology, a series of classic studies offers valuable points of reference as they are constant sources of inspiration, though not without having been exposed to scholarly criticism. It is my intention to try to illustrate that these classic studies may still, along with newer views, offer theoretical inspiration for the understanding of archaeological remains. As these studies are likely to be widely known, I shall mainly describe and consider topics that I personally consider inspirational regarding reflections on the possible interpretations of finds from the Late Neolithic and beyond in the Limfjord region.

When warfare breaks out in tribal (stateless) societies, some researchers consider it a consequence of missing or badly performed communication and other facets of exchange (e.g. Mauss 1997; Clastres1998). Conversely, other scholars find it questionable that exchange would prevent war because such doings might, at most, be suitable for gaining allies but cannot prevent war, i.e."…a mode of conflict resolution, namely a planned and organised armed conflict between political units" (Helbling 2006:115pp). War may thus be considered a strategic interaction between groups, despite the fact that it "… has highly detrimental consequences for people, property and resources. Nevertheless, local groups in tribal societies cannot avoid waging war under the prevalent structural conditions. There is no centralised power to prevent war between politically autonomous local groups dependent on locally concentrated resources, and pursuing a unilateral peaceful strategy is too risky and may lead to annihilation of the group" (Helbling 2006:127). And yet other researchers do not perceive warfare as an integral element of tribal societies but see the emergence of colonial empires as responsible, not least due to the strong demand for certain goods, slaves etc. (Ferguson & Whitehead 1992:27p; Helbling 2006:119).

Marilyn Strathern offers another point in the discussion of possible structural tribal warfare and the assumption that comprehensive gift exchange worked to avoid warlike situations when she warns against jumping to hasty conclusions that tribes are *a priori* either aggressive or peace-seeking (Strathern 1985:122; Brandt 2006:80). In the case of certain New Guinean "big men" who wanted people to exchange instead of fight, Strathern observes that they appear to value the power gained through gift exchange above the resulting peace.

Exchange in the anthropological sense "… is the transfer of things between social actors. The things can be human or animal, material or immaterial, words or things. The actors can be individuals, groups, or beings such as gods or spirits" (Carrier 2002:218). Some classic ethnographical studies concerned with the integration of fairly egalitarian communities through gift exchange over extensive geographical areas seem particularly relevant in terms of their significance.

The discussion within anthropology about exchange – and kinship as well – has long shaped social theory and continues to do so today, arguing that gift exchange and the feeling of belonging through kinship integrate communities over a wide geographical range. The habit of giving and receiving gifts thus resonates through human lives because the gift, no matter how small or great it might be, is more than the object. It can, among other things, establish and confirm connectedness and lead to political alliances (Seymour-Smith 1986:106p).

In his anthropological fieldwork on the Trobriand Islands in Melanesia during World War I, Bronislaw Malinowski became familiar with the geographically extensive exchange system, locally called "Kula". Besides ordinary trade, he describes it in 1922 as being centred on giving and receiving prestige objects as gifts (Malinowski 1984). This exchange system, with its circles of exchange, has become central to enhancing our understanding of reciprocity-based (versus market-based, supply/demand) exchange systems and its major economically, politically, and religiously integrating factor in societies or areas without the presence of a state.

Taking part in the Kula exchange network at this time (i.e. about the time of World War I) are people on numerous small islands with internally somewhat different cultures and economies in the area east of Papua New Guinea. The inhabitants participate regularly in major seagoing expeditions in the archipelago between these islands. Although exchange rules – and to a certain extent also language – varies among the islands, the basics are that the network partners appreciate, respect and benefit from each other by exchanging gifts consisting of two sets of prestigious valuables made of sea shells. Necklaces are exchanged clockwise to the north and arm bracelets counter-clockwise to the south around the islands, thereby forming the Kula Ring.

When a person gives a bracelet to his trading partner in the network, the latter is morally obliged to later return a commensurately valued necklace. Upon return, the relationship or partnership created by the initial object may continue or end. Since the fame upon which the esteem is built derives from relationships with the right persons, confirmed by giving and receiving Kula items, the individuals striving for more fame will often struggle to bend basic exchange rules according to their own interests. They may do this by trying to return more than they owe, or by returning items of lesser value, or by delaying returns for as long as possible without losing esteem and maybe offering smaller gifts in a tone of good faith (Malinowski 1984:102. On Trobriand consumption and exchange, see also Keesing & Strathern 1998:152pp).

The regional Kula exchange system of valuables is characterized as being tremendously complex (Appadurai 1992:18). The exchange activities are highly diversified and the strategies at stake multifaceted, deeply involving economy, kinship, politics and religion. To create successful relationships, people engage in all sorts of productive work in their gardens, growing the root vegetable yams to be used in gift exchange with trade partners or as obligatory gifts to kin.

Malinowski claims that the exchange of this root vegetable and of the prestigious Kula items has a socially integrating function over wide geographical areas, since this regular economic pattern will remind the people involved of kinship relations, of existing demands with regard to political loyalty, and moral obligations (Malinowski 1984:64).

Untried young individuals in the Kula network can make ties with equal partners, exchanging easy come/easy go valuables but, as they grow older and become more experienced, they may take the plunge carefully and become involve in ever newer and more esteemed relationships, defined by previous links of fame. What makes certain Kula items more coveted than others are the stories, the names, the magic, and the events associated with the relationships between specific partners, and with the items having confirmed these relationships along their route or line of people in the exchange circle. The field of the Melanesian economy about the time of World War I is founded not least on rights from investments in different persons, as well as secondarily on rights over the gardening of certain land areas.

Over the years, Malinowski's work has been exposed to all sorts of criticism. Among other things, his functionalistic and individualistic approach to the study of exchange has been attacked for being too concerned with social equilibrium and biased by European individualism (Emerson 1976). Malinowski's approach presents individuals as rather self-interested, seeking to acquire better pay back instead of highlighting people's relationships and the sociality. Nonetheless, Malinowski's study stands as a classic example of the empirical complexity of exchange over long distances.

When Marcel Mauss presents the first systematic and comparative study of widespread gift exchange in traditional societies from ancient Rome to American Indian and Melanesian and other societies in 1924, he claims that gift items as well as trade items require counterparts and that there is nothing such as a free gift given out of pure fine moral or sheer love (Mauss 1997). A gift that does nothing to enhance solidarity or moral obligation or to avoid evil is a contradiction. He holds that as far back in human history as we can go, the major transfer of goods and services has been by cycles of obligatory returns of gifts. In this sense, his book is about the matters that establish moral solidarity among individuals, among households, and within and among communities spread over extensive geographical areas. It is thus about the stuff that binds a human society together and what it is made of. His theory is embedded in a French comparative sociological tradition.

Mauss particularly concentrates on the system and the sum of economic services operating among the various sub-groups that make up so-called primitive societies, where gift exchanges are highly extensive and illuminate social life in its entirety: "In these 'total' social phenomena, as we propose calling them, all kinds of institutions are given expression at one and the same time – religious, juridical, and moral, which relate to both politics and the family; likewise economic ones, which suppose special forms of production and consumption, or rather, of performing total services and of distribution" (Mauss1997:3). Every gift is part of a system of reciprocity which involves the honour of the giver as well as the receiver. As a rule, it is rather straightforward, resting on the principle of repayment of kindness, goodwill, invitation, visit, presents and so forth. Yet, to reciprocate must, according to the traditions, be done in a prescribed and regular way and this establishes whole chains of exchange within and between generations, neighbour groups, friends, allies, trade partners, relatives, or in relation to deities, spirits and demons. As Mauss said, gift exchange is a civilized kind of war and of course in practical life, these rules of communication may often have been negotiated in a more or less sophisticated way and bent by certain individuals to suit their own special interests, in some instances leading to peaceful mass destruction of material items or conflicts.[35]

In some societies, the exchange of gift objects and services among equal partners is expected to be of the same value and may, in this way, lead to a rather stable system of status. In other societies, the gift is in certain contexts supposed to surpass or outdo the value of the received gifts and may result in escalating competition over attaining honour. This was characteristic of the social and economic institution known as Potlatch, which was especially followed among the Kwakiutl Indians on the northwest coast of North America and is known not least from empirical fieldwork studies carried out by the geographer and anthropologist Franz Boas late in the 19th century and onwards. Mauss labelled it the "monster child" of gift-giving. Status is based on the ability to offer splendid gifts. The highest-ranking chiefs among the Kwakiutl are thus those who have the most people to produce for them. The competing gift-giving among the aristocratic chieftain families may sometimes culminate in plentiful feasts whereby, in addition to gifts, the guests are entertained with the destruction of material goods by setting fire to tens or hundreds of woven blankets or destroying food or copper items as well as drowning slaves (Boas 1982; Mauss 1997).

Mauss especially explores exchange in societies without markets and states. He takes into consideration the relationship between the individual and his or her community, discussing the possibilities and boundaries of individual manoeuvre within society and the common norms that make the individual perform certain duties and acts. Gift-giving and receiving provides the individual with personal incitement to cooperate and to take part in the system of gift exchange. Special about gifts is observation that they are often given in a context of open drama. They generally become the subject of much more public judgment, opinions and reflections on fairness than goods exchanged in markets. In social systems where the distributions of goods and commodities takes shape without directly setting a price on them, people are often more aware of the social and moral implications embedded in products, services, humans, and words to be exchanged. The gift-giving would often be sanctified as well.

According to Mauss, whether very local or spread over a wide area, a society can be described and understood by listing all transfers, as these will map the prevalent obligations between its members. No gifts are free from obligation of later repayment. Gift chains activate individuals and groups in permanent obligations that constitute the prevailing institutions in society, e.g. matrimony, kinship, neighbourhood, friendship, patron-client relationships, trading partnerships, religious clubs and age groups. These obligations are often manifested during rituals, assemblies, fairs or festivals: "All such festivals presuppose congregations whose duration can exceed one season of social coming together, as do the winter potlatches of the Kwakiutl, or weeks, as do the seafaring expeditions of the Melanesians" (Mauss 1997:79).

The Tiv people on the savannah of Central Nigeria constitute another classic ethnographic example from about the mid-20th century of a peasant society and its exchange system. In Paul Bohannan's view, it is defined by goods and services that can normally only be swapped against certain other things, thus creating a stratified distribution system (Bohannan 1953:60pp). It means that economic resources are exchanged according to different rules in what is considered to represent different spheres. In 1953, Bohannan presents his analysis in relation to three spheres of exchange that are internally ranked, and he describes the mechanism for isolating one area of economic activity from the other. As in many other kinship-based, peasant communities, land is not saleable because it belongs to the forefathers. The Tiv (patrilineal) clan manages it collectively and the land is distributed among the households in the villages. Household production is centred on growing millet, vegetables and fruit, as well as cattle breeding. After meeting own needs in food, the surplus is exchanged in three spheres or spread through gift exchange or, alternatively, simply sold on the market.

Among the three Tiv-spheres of exchange, the everyday foodstuffs sphere ranks lowest and concerns millet products, vegetables, fruit, chickens, spices and kitchen tools, which are all of the same classification and can be exchanged on the market. In the middle and fairly prestigious sphere cattle, costly white textiles, medicines, magic tools, slaves and political posts are circulated. Copper bars function as a means of payment and as a general standard of value for the exchange of these prestige items. The highest-ranking and most restricted level of exchange is called the "bride sphere" and consists of rights in people other than slaves. In addition to women, it also includes men and children. In this sphere, a person can only be exchanged for another person, not necessarily right away but often somewhat later, in the next generation.

No rules exist as to how many subsistence products of a certain character from the first sphere it will be necessary to give to obtain one of the objects from the middle, prestigious sphere, since there are shutters been the spheres. To possess prestige objects gives status but no general standard of value is common to all three spheres. No matter how many sacks of millet one might own, these cannot be measured against a certain amount of copper bars, cattle or brides. It is amoral to sell prestige objects for subsistence goods, whereas the opposite is considered a good transaction. However, it is possible under certain circumstances for the Tiv to convert food into copper bars and brides although it demands a good degree of wealth and entrepreneurship.

While Bohannan is much concerned with the structure and functioning of the economy, in his analysis of exchange in Darfur in Sudan, Fredrik Barth favours an approach to the study of society that emphasizes the individual and his or her possibilities for agency (Barth 1967). His study concerns a population of peasants living in villages on the lower slopes of the Jebel Marra mountain. On the objectives he proposes that "...I try to show in what sense the flow of goods and services is patterned in discrete spheres, and to demonstrate the nature of the unity within, and barriers between, the spheres" (Barth 1967:149pp). For him, as more recently also for other researchers, rules and cultural norms are seen as something to be constantly negotiated by different entrepreneurs or actors in society.

It seems obvious that the economically, culturally, socially, religiously and politically integrating role of exchange should not be underestimated in prehistoric contexts such as the Late Neolithic and emerging Bronze Age. Concretely as regards the region, I find it reasonable to presume that wide-ranging exchange systems created and maintained certain built-in guards that rendered the physical defence of settlements more or less superfluous. It would, in my view, have been of overwhelming importance for households, widely scattered in the landscapes, to have been integrated through comprehensive exchange, thus ensuring life and reproduction. Ample exchange of goods, commodities, services, collaboration, news, ideas, marital partners and other would all in all have brought individual households closer together both socially and culturally.[36]

For considerations on exchange between households in the Limfjord region and beyond, it is useful to bear in mind that while central and eastern Denmark in LN I was particularly culturally linked to the early Únětice and areas influenced by it to the south of the Baltic Sea, Northern Jutland had obvious connections to northwest European Beaker communities. Besides an early North Jutland concentration of metals and ornamented pottery, this is substantiated through finds of pressure-flaked flint arrowheads in varying forms, stone bracers, V-perforated amber buttons, other buttons of amber or bone, and some bone pins (Vandkilde 1996:295pp; 2009:76p). This influence may even have permeated not only life but also the death and the afterlife, as evidenced by the quite early examples of cremation found incidentally in Northern Jutland, such as for instance the three-story burial pit at Fjallerslev, where cremation was the primary burial (Simonsen 1978:33pp). The Limfjord region thus played a very central role in this long distance exchange and "...northern Jutland stands out as an exceptional region with large-scale production and distribution of flint ...and with accumulated wealth of metal items and Beaker symbols, in addition to a relatively complex situation of increased social competition between individuals and groups ..." (Vandkilde 1996:295). South of the Limfjord region, some communities in Jutland may well have had direct contact and exchange with some of the northwest European Beaker communities, as suggested earlier (Ch. 1.3).

Central and eastern parts of Denmark in LN II maintained and intensified their links with the classical phase of Únětice in areas such as central Germany and adjacent Baltic regions, and these were the metal supply regions for local production. It has been proposed that amber, furs, textiles, leather work, wooden articles, alcohol, honey, horses, cattle, sheep and women, to different degrees, could have been exchanged for metals (Vandkilde 1996:306). Northern Jutland, on the other hand, was now considered to have been "outside the mainstream of events" (Vandkilde 1996:298pp; *cf.* Champion 1989). This latter situation may have prevailed contemporaneously with the long-enduring Resengaard settlement.

When we take as our point of departure the above idea of a primarily egalitarian society during the Late Neolithic and emerging Bronze Age in the region and include the notion that exchange systems worked as "total social phenomena" encompassing all politics, morals, economy, aesthetics, ritual and religion, what then might the possibilities of these individual households and groups have been?

Firstly, in my understanding, there appears to have existed considerable room for taking initiatives. The evidence of the highly diverging house forms, varying interior arrangements, multiple traces of different activities in the floor horizons overall supports this interpretation well. It is not unlikely that such possibilities for groups of local households to make separate choices are furthermore mirrored in the intraregional patchwork of highly varying grave forms (*cf.* Vandkilde 2001, Fig. 12).

Secondly, in some ethnographical cases, ample possibilities for agency of varying character existed, letting people engage in numerous trade and gift exchange relations or the converting of value between the spheres. Yet, we cannot, by analogy, impose any concrete exchange systems on the Late Neolithic and emerging Bronze Age of North Jutland. Without institutionalized power, a primarily egalitarian society in the region might have consisted of numerous, relatively independent groupings and it is presumed that household members may have engaged in manifold direct and indirect exchange relations based on reciprocity and gift-giving regarding goods, commodities, services and persons. It can hardly be excluded that some persons or groups could at times have attempted to institutionalize high status, albeit apparently without long-lasting success. The exchange partners could have included lineage members of varying closeness, affinal relatives, neighbours and various others, as well as gods, spirits, demons and other supernatural powers.

I propose an understanding that the households mostly had such traditional exchange partners more or less locally although some would presumably also have carried out exchange beyond the local sphere, i.e. regionally and further away. I presume that everyday exchange between households may have primarily concerned various specialized products and services, whereas high prestige exchange might have had been of a more occasional character. The effects of this comprehensive exchange would have been multifaceted, and plausibly it would have largely met the everyday needs of the households in the Limfjord region. This exchange may have improved and maintained solidarity among households, and could have created cycles of moral obligations, maybe even down the generations. The honour of the households and its members might thus have depended heavily on their ability to reciprocate in every aspect of life.

It is, however, important to underline that an absence of institutionalized power in society does not imply an absence of strong power relations. Exchanges likely had to be performed without neglecting more or less obligatory partners or demands from other powerful domains such as, for instance, relationships based on affection for close kin or religious devotion. They could, for instance, have involved moral pressure from strong lineage members or a display of muscle power from a numerously strong lineage against a weaker one. Further power relations of various unknown kinds might have influenced the exchange between local households. In terms of production and exchange, it seems likely that the influence and power of persons with elderly status might have been secured by their original possession of the agricultural seed and other things which, in turn, might have belonged to still older generations. The elderly simultaneously would have been closer to the forefathers who, in some cases, might even have been living on the same land and maybe somehow still possessed some rights to it. I presume that skills and knowledge in forefather cult might further have reinforced the power of the elderly, defined by age (and maybe also lineage position or status in the community).

In this way, certain kinds of power relations could often have influenced the exchange. Moreover, it cannot be excluded that rather serious acts of power such as threats of beatings, injuries or some even more brutal acts could in certain situations also have been at play. Besides gift exchange, ordinary barter without significant moral implications would likely also have taken place widely.

Household manoeuvres would, according to the presented model, have focused not least on an engagement in different kinds of specialized production. For instance, it seems that initiating specialized bronze working at Kluborg II could have been the scheme of a single household for a period and it was carried out a little after the onset of the South Scandinavian Older Bronze Age. As we have seen, the longhouse had a particular architecture and was presumably built directly with the purpose of bronze casting and other metal handling. Household members could have already been well aware of the demand for different metal objects at that time and thereby the potential for exchange. When the household settled near the large stream, Karup Å, this location may well have facilitated exchange along the waterways. We shall now consider concrete transport options.

Transport of people and commodities in the Limfjord archipelago

The coastline in the Limfjord region differed much from today's landscape because of the post-glacial land rise (Jessen, A.1920; Mertz 1924:16pp; Petersen & Burfelt 1998). Covering vast areas of now raised seabeds, the water level of the Limfjord was significantly higher during the Late Neolithic and emerging Bronze Age than today. Furthermore, the Danish occurrences of salt deep underground from the Perm Period are mostly concentrated in precisely this region and these have locally caused land level changes (*cf.* Madirazza 1974; Petersen 1976; Rasmussen et al. 1979; Rasmussen & Petersen 1980; Møller 1982).

In the central Limfjord region, the current dried out lakes west of Virksund formed a narrow strait of some depth (Rasmussen & Petersen 1980:51). Access to and from Hjarbæk Fjord was broader and, during the Late Neolithic, the Virksund area formed a small island, Thorsholm, in this inner arm of the Limfjord. The open conditions via Hanherred also resulted in influences from the tidal water even into these southernmost arms of the sea.

With a long history involving stages from salty to brackish and thereafter a fresh water lake that was more recently artificially dried out for agricultural purposes, Tastum Sø was connected to the Limfjord via a somewhat narrow strait and it was still salty in the Late Neolithic and emerging Bronze Age (Rasmussen et al.1979:115pp; Rasmussen & Petersen 1980:51; *cf.* Simonsen 1996b:91). These examples demonstrate that the inner parts of the central Limfjord region were connected to the open water areas and further out to Skagerrak and the North Sea, as well as Kattegat to the east (*cf.* Penney 1992).

Topographically, the region provided a rather varied landscape within Denmark. Undulating land formations interrupted by more or less broad valleys and fjords that were deeply carved into the firm land dominated the eastern part, whereas larger and smaller islands were significant elements of its western part (Meesenburg 1992:26). Moraine areas to a great extent marked the region and created a substantial distinction from the southwest area, which was not covered by ice during the last glacial. The heavy clay soils of the large areas of Salling, Mors and Thy in particular diverged considerably from comprehensive areas of light sandy soil in Himmerland and more southerly areas. The abundant presence of open waters in the western part of the region contrasted with the relatively large landmasses of Himmerland and adjacent areas to the south which, in turn, were highly marked by lengthy freshwater streams. These were fed by countless numbers of brooklets in the then undrained landscape.

The ubiquitous water areas, taking the form of wetlands, waterholes, swampy hollow terrains, lakes, brooklets and streams, gave the region a common denominator. The immense waters of the North Sea and Kattegat provided the natural limits of the region to the east and west. In this way, the omnipresence of salty, brackish or fresh water gave the region a common stamp, being unique within South Scandinavia. Hence, at the turn of the Neolithic, a large part of the region would have formed an archipelagic landscape.

Numerous bogs, moors and other more or less impassable wet areas also marked the landmasses of the region. Most of the year, however, major watersheds and other relatively high-lying areas would likely have allowed easier passage. In Himmerland, comparatively long watersheds were accompanied by river systems of almost proportional length. Grave barrows from the period were frequently placed in the vicinity of the watersheds and some distinct lines of grave barrows may in particular be a strong indication of the course of ancient road tracks. This topic has frequently been considered and discussed previously in Danish contexts (*cf.* Olesen & Skov 1989, with further references). As an alternative to land transport along most likely somewhat bumpy road tracks, however, I presume that travel and carriage via the more or less omnipresent waterways, along coastlines and across smaller or larger open water areas was very often favoured, when possible. Regional transport, exchange and communication may thus frequently have been facilitated by these options on and near water.

Ancient connections across the Limfjord archipelago have been demonstrated among areas of the eastern part of the island of Mors and the western part of the Salling peninsula in the Early Neolithic through the evidence of certain groups of grave monuments (Bekmose 1977:58). Traditions of close coastal relations date back to the Ertebølle Culture (Andersen, S.H. 1990; 1998; 2006). At that time, the dense primeval forest behind the coastal settlements would probably have made transport and communication over water preferable. Old traditions therefore appear to have existed in terms of keeping close relationships, despite geographical positions with sometimes considerable waters in between. In many instances, it was perhaps not necessary or desirable to cross along the most direct line between start and end points. Instead, a moderate, more roundabout route along the coast to spots from where the water could be crossed at the shortest point may sometimes have been preferred.

In the overall picture of the archipelagic landscape, this transport, communication and exchange was helped by the prevailing water plains to the west, and the large streams coming from the hinterland to the east. These waters might therefore be viewed as more a factor of gathering than separating the settlements of the region, and the sheltered waters would hardly have required particularly elaborate boats and so were therefore likely navigable by means of plain oak tree dugouts. However, for transport into fully open waters, more regular vessels would most probably have been necessary.

By means of the streams, commodities could have reached deep into the terrain far from the coast, before other ways and means of transportation would have been necessary. However, regular waterways did not begin their course far back in the landscapes of some islands and the regular streams would often have been relatively short.

The coastline around the islands, peninsulas and peripheries of other landscapes in the region would together have offered many hundreds of kilometres of shore and shallow water that might well have been passable most of the year. The shores were mostly rather gentle, although now and then steep cliff-like formations appeared, e.g. Hanklit (c. 60 m high) to the north at Mors and Store Klinthøj (c. 30 m high) east of Thorsholm. These would hardly have hampered passage significantly, however. Locally, some impediment, such as dense vegetation leaning outwards by the water edges or swampy areas, was likely present.

The 10 settlements of particular focus in this present study include four coastal, five at a little distance from the coast and one in the hinterland. I presume that these locations may by and large mirror access in general via water in much of the region. The Hejlskov Hede settlement, with several sunken-floor house sites, was also reachable directly from the Limfjord shore. On the whole, the situation of settlements near the coast on the archipelago and in areas with suitable water courses, would have facilitated an exchange of goods, commodities, services, news, ideas and so on.

Population density, production and exchange

It has been argued that soil types were largely responsible for the settlement distributions because people avoided the lightest and heaviest soils for agricultural reasons (Jensen, J. 1982:139). The potential for growing cereals would, of course, have been an important parameter when settling although suitable soils would have been abundantly present in many Danish areas. In my reading, it is interesting, for instance, when considering the overall distribution of flint daggers in Denmark that it appears that relatively strong population densities to a high degree coincide with large watersheds, significant waterways and certain coastal zones (cf. Lomborg 1973a). These distributions could well thus match important transport routes to a corresponding extent, and thereby also fine possibilities for communication and exchange.

Sustaining the basic livelihood from suitable soils was hardly the primary factor for settling in the Limfjord region in the Late Neolithic. It was attractive for further reasons, namely due to abundant flint occurrences and a favourable geographical placement. Moreover, it has been argued that it was a milieu that experienced significant social competition (Vandkilde 1996:295p). It therefore seems that the distribution of settlements in the central Limfjord region during the early Late Neolithic may, to a certain degree, reflect the notion that people gradually chose to settle more densely where new ideas on life, fashion and prestige flourished, where rich occurrences of certain raw materials were available, where attractive economic possibilities for production and exchange existed, and where well-connected communication took place regionally and beyond. These and other factors – such as e.g. the assumption of relatively open, flexible households lending a particular sociality to the area – may well have worked as a magnet for people and created a continued influx into certain local areas early in the Late Neolithic. With the centrality and accessibility of the Limfjord region from the North Sea, it has been characterized as a "core area" and "gateway community" for South Scandinavia (Vandkilde 2001:338; 2009:76p; Sarauw 2007c:258; 2009:39).

How many people would have been living in the varied landscapes of the region, say around 2200 BC? In relation to the three models of local settlement that we focused on, one option for estimating population density might be that of attempting to calculate from the known distribution of settlements, combined with grave finds and maybe also depositions. This would nonetheless be a fairly comprehensive task although we can assume from the distribution of flint daggers that the Limfjord region was relatively densely populated for Danish areas during the period in question (Lomborg 1973a). If, as a rough estimate, we instead tentatively assume a population of 40,000 inhabitants in the region, and if an average of ten persons lived in each household, as previously proposed, then some 4,000 households would have existed at a given time in the region. The area of the landmass in the region was at that time about 7,000 km^2 (pers. comm. Kristine Stub Precht). This number of people would correspond to an average population density of c. 5.7 per km^2, being apparently higher in certain areas of the central Limfjord region. Apart from the presumably few people that might have lived in minor houses, by and large 4,000 longhouses with residential units would thus contemporaneously have stood in the region. Scattered in the landscape, as much as 1.75 km^2

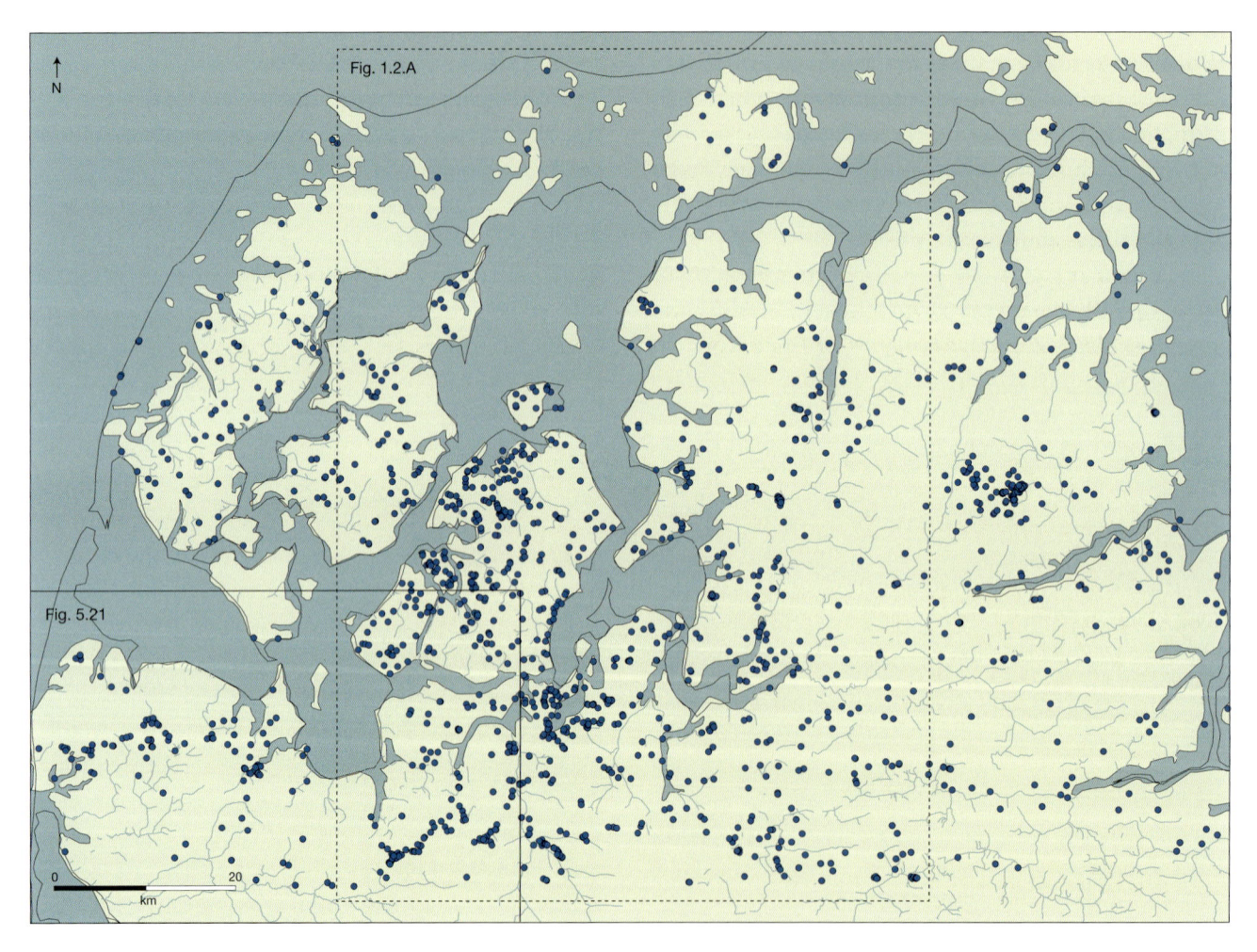

Fig. 5.20. Traces of Late Neolithic settlement and activities in the Limfjord archipelago. A: The stippled rectangular area indicates the central Limfjord region, as understood in this present work. The rectangular area of to the southwest relates to Fig. 5.21. The blue dots may include settlements (counting also a few shell middens with Late Neolithic material), flint mines, cultic structures, stone structures, single/multiple item deposits, graves/barrows (including secondarily used megaliths) and some other registered structures. Not least in the central Limfjord region locations are found so closely in some areas that they appear as merged dots, such as for instance locations at Glattrup and Tastum. The archipelagic landscape had a water level covering vast areas of now raised sea beds that are indicated with a simplified modern coastline. It may thus illustrate the omnipresent possibilities for transport along fjords and streams as well as along the coasts. The geological formation of the Limfjord region is very complex with several strongly influencing factors but, here, the 2.6 m contour (being considered the most relevant for the southern areas of the central Limfjord region) has consequently been used as landwater separation, resulting however in the omission of small areas that actually would have been more or less dry (cf. Fig. 1 in Christensen, Cedhagen, & Hylleberg, 1998). Sources: Streams from maps by the Royal Danish Academy of Sciences. Data from the database Fund og Fortidsminder/The Danish Geodata Agency. Map: Kristine Stub Precht.

of uninhabited lands, corresponding to 1,750 hectares, would on average have been present in the vicinity of each longhouse. Though tentative, this calculation might again bring to mind the notion that keeping in contact through comprehensive exchange would have been of the utmost importance economically, culturally and socially, if only for the sheer existence of people in more or less widely spread out households.

The Tastum Sø project may in the future contribute evidence of high settlement intensity around this former lake, as an example from the younger half of the Single Grave Culture and the Late Neolithic. The numerous excavations in the area of Hagebrogård, Vroue and Koldkur in the southern part of the central Limfjord region are already contributing valuable information in relation to the high Neolithic grave find intensity within a few square kilometres (Jørgensen, E. 1977). Yet, unfortunately, some of this interesting material still remains unpublished.

As might immediately appear from a map based on the public database (SARA), our present recordings of settlements, graves and other finds from the Late Neolithic is far from evidence of the above suggested population density (Fig. 5.20). The geographical representativeness of the regular settlement finds of the Limfjord region was earlier considered but, interestingly, we have other data, based in particular on a comprehensive recording project from private collections regarding a southwest part of the Limfjord region and a little further to the south (Fig. 5.21). This project, headed by Therkel Mathiassen, was carried out by several archaeologists from the National Museum of Denmark in the 1940s (Mathiassen 1948). When comparing with their data, we are faced with indications of a significantly denser settlement in this area. From the evidence of this pilot project, it seems reasonable to presume around the same relative increase in finds if the entire central Limfjord region had been selected for a corresponding pilot project at that time. However, even such intense recording of the southwest part of the region can, after all, only represent a small share of the original settlements when weighed against the suggested 4,000 contemporaneous longhouse residences in the entire region. The map of

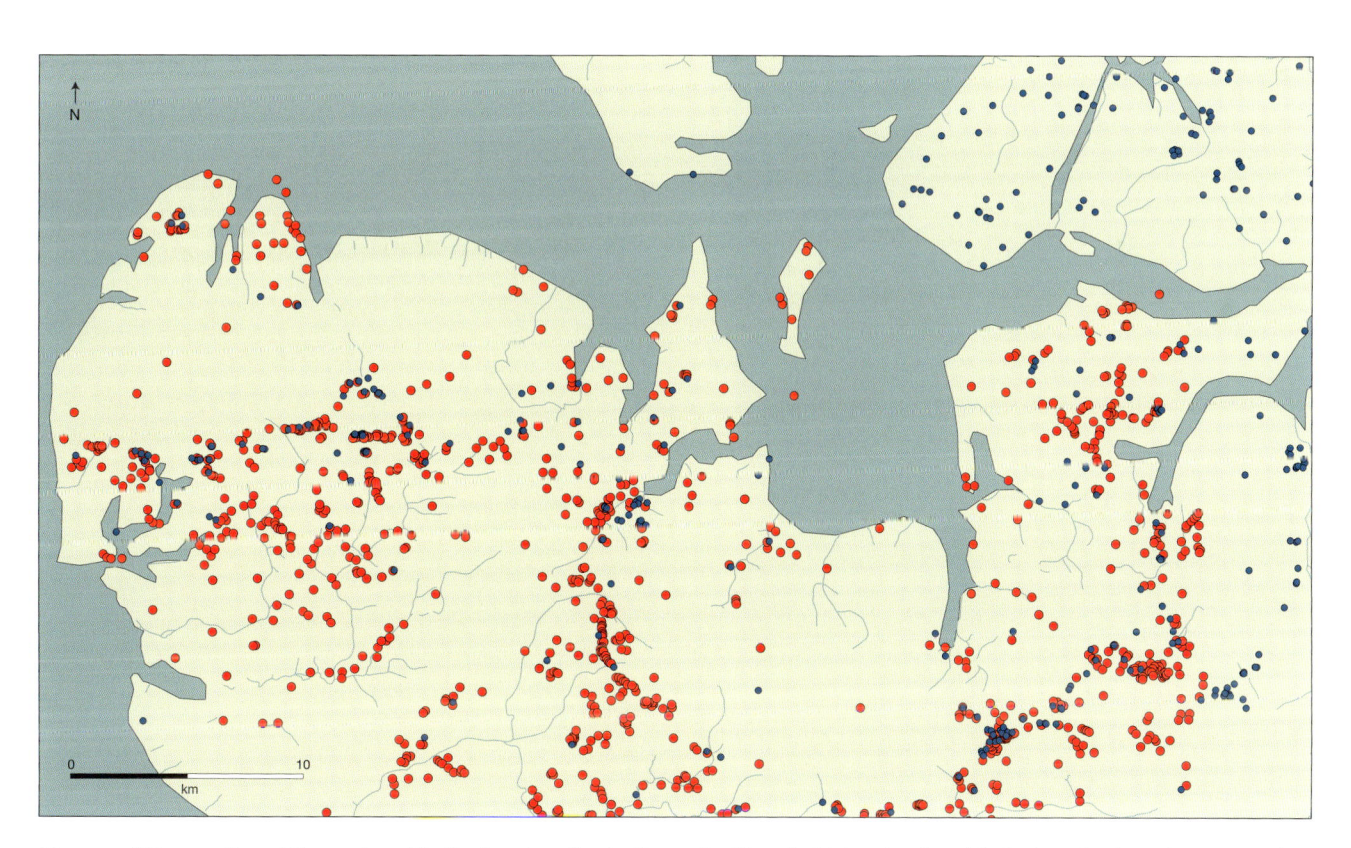

Fig. 5.21. Minor section of the western Limfjord region, illustrating a significantly higher density of finds than the foregoing map, as it is supplemented with finds from the large-scale survey of West Jutland (red dots) carried out as a pilot project during 1942-45 by the National Museum of Denmark (Mathiassen 1948). The sources for these finds are of varying quality. Many are classified as representing single finds in the database, whereby the majority are sorted out from the finds represented by the blue dots. Streams from maps by the Royal Danish Academy of Sciences. Data: see Fig. 5.20. Map: Kristine Stub Precht.

the Limfjord region, including the locations from the pilot project, also indicates that some areas were far more densely populated than others.

When the people of the region, according to the model, carried out a broad spectrum of A-level production, I assume that this concerned more than 98 % of the households. Conversely, at C-level production, I presume this related to less than 2 % of households. It is more challenging to estimate the relative participation in the highly varied kinds of B-level production but it seems plausible that this mostly ranged between 2 % and 10 % of households for each kind of specialization although some kinds of B-level specializations, such as for instance weaving, could probably have been significantly higher.

Against this background, thousands and thousands of transactions concerning commodities and services – first and foremost B-level production – must have taken place every year among households both within the region and beyond.

Exchange, maritime travel and ocean gateways

When household members travelled, for instance, by means of waterways to more remote locations within and beyond the Limfjord region to exchange with trading partners, such possibly seasonal activities would likely have had significant integrating effects. In that vein, it might sometimes have been advantageous to search for a suitable spouse, for instance through personal acquaintances in the economic networks, among lineage members or other, even at some geographical distance.

The presence of slate pendants with "touchstone" qualities may support the assumption of some level of exchange of gold items. And yet, to my knowledge, no scientific analysis has been conducted concerning gold traces on slate pendants found in the region (Ahlberg, Akselsson, Forkman & Rausing 1976:39pp; On pendant types, see Ebbesen 1995. On recent use of touchstones, see Larsen & Nielsen 1987:14p). Some special foreign metal objects reached the region and we do not know what happened to these more or less spectacular items before their deposition. For instance, several gold ornaments with oar-shaped ends dating from LN I are known (Vandkilde 1996:177pp).

Outstanding items such as the gold lunulae have thus far not been discovered within the region but might of course have been present in this South Scandinavian area, being so rich in Beaker materials. We might ask how people locally gained possession of such extraordinary objects in the early Late Neolithic? Did the varying, more or less spectacular, items belong to members of individual households or were some of these specimens one way or another put into some kind of "flow" among certain households? They may not necessarily have been circulated as in the Kula (Malinowski 1984:64; Appadurai 1992:18). Such extraordinary items could maybe otherwise have been conveyed in a manner that gave precise meaning to the people of that time, possibly including the accompanying story of other people having kept them for a period. Such kind of circulation would presumably have supported the feeling of interconnectedness among household peers. When extraordinary items were to be handed over, some kind of expected public performance could have been an integral part of the transaction. And yet objects assigned particularly high value need not, admittedly, always have been those we today would like to imagine and could instead include some of which we have not the slightest idea.

How the massive bulk of B- and C-level products were exchanged is a critical topic if we want to achieve a better understanding of the relationships between people in everyday life in the region and beyond. In the above, I outlined how distribution and exchange took place in different economic spheres (Bohannan 1953:60pp; Barth 1967:149pp). Might the exchange in the region have been structured in a way that had some likeness to these spheres? The idea of such exchange, where the rules may have been different for each one, seems conceivable, although this can hardly be substantiated from the present state of research.

It can be assumed, not least due to the above suggested traits, such as the adoption of new ideas on life and fashion as well as the flexible household economics, that the region strengthened its central position with regard to communication and exchange from the beginning of the Late Neolithic (*cf.* Vandkilde 2001). The tradition of its people for distant contacts was already well-established during the Single Grave Culture (e.g. Simonsen 1986:146pp; Sarauw 2009:39). It has long been recognized that Late Neolithic contacts to the Veluwe and other areas existed (Vandkilde 2001:338p). From the central Limfjord region, several more or less narrow waters connected with the relatively fierce North Sea, as well as Skagerrak and Kattegat in the Late Neolithic and emerging Bronze Age (*cf.* Penney 1992:34pp; Møller 1982:12pp).

The large hoard at Hauske in Norway provides a noticeable example of contact with people from the region. It contains 247 flint items of which the majority are just ordinary flint flakes, while other objects relate to an axe rough-out, a sickle, two feeding knives, four spoon-shaped scrapers, as well as 25 daggers (Magnus & Myhre 1976:91; Jensen, J. 2006a:523). It has been suggested that it was people from Norway who brought the flint items home from North Jutland (Becker 1993:130). However, the South Scandinavian items in Norway have no Norwegian traits and, conversely, no Norwegian artefacts from the Late Neolithic have correspondingly been found in Jutland (Østmo 2005:63). A more recent interpretation of this situation is hence that what we see actually represents a northwards expansion of Bell Beaker Culture, with North Jutland as its point of departure (Østmo 2005:71). The items associated with the Late Neolithic Beakers are considered to have been brought to Norway, thus representing some of the oldest "routes" crossing Skagerak (Østmo 2005:61; 2009:86pp).

Considerations of ship technology are beyond the scope of this present work, and hence I will make just a few remarks here. The kinds of ship used internally in the region are not known at present, and shipwrecks belonging to the Late Neolithic and emerging Bronze Age of South Scandinavia have not yet been identified. The importance of water transport from the period in question is not symbolically mirrored in boat burials in the Limfjord region but, interestingly, such graves have been recovered sporadically from other South Scandinavian areas (Bican 2012:31pp; Brink 2013:452; *cf.* Skårup 1995; Kaul 2004). Some wooden, relatively short dugouts with thick sides and round bottoms from the Danish Late Neolithic have been found in lakes (Christensen 1990:119pp). Yet these are not considered apt for transport between the region and, for instance, Norway. It has instead been attempted to characterize the *a priori* expectations of such ships in these Nordic waters (Rieck & Crumlin-Pedersen 1988:46pp). Besides rock carvings and incised razor knives, the depiction of the bronze sword from Rørby at Zealand has been a source of inspiration (e.g. Brøndsted 1966b:14pp; Østmo 2005:56pp; *cf.* Kaul 2004). It has been pointed out that the technology of building ships suitable for crossing Skagerak between North Jutland and Norway must have been rather new and inventive around the beginning of the Late Neolithic, and was maybe also technically improved through access to metal axes (Østmo 2005:71).

It has been proposed that the boats used for transport across Skagerak could have been built as early specimens of the same tradition, as represented in the much later Hjortspring boat, designed to be paddled by many men (Crumlin-Pedersen 2003:246; Østmo 2005:71; *cf.* McGrail 1998).

By the onset of the Late Neolithic, the Limfjord archipelago was a South Scandinavian area particularly open to contacts, impulses and exchange from far and near. With this in mind, it does not seem difficult to imagine boats leaving the sheltered waters and entering the rough North Sea or Skagerrak while transporting commodities, produced and exchanged by households living, not least, in the sunken-floor longhouses.

Notes

1. James S. Duncan in particular underlines that the significance of houses has a profound impact on the ordering of society (Duncan 1981:40pp). Mike Parker Pearson and Colin Richards, for example, have also presented further insight into the meanings of houses (Pearson & Richards 1997). In western terms, the word "house" now often corresponds to "home" (*cf.* Benjamin 1998).

2. It seems likely that not only would many children often have been born but also that a relatively high proportion would die early compared to modern societies. Numerous graves of minor children from the very late Single Grave Culture and also examples from the Late Neolithic are found in the Limfjord region, as an overview of such graves in short stone cists in North Jutland evidences (Simonsen 2006). At Resengaard, two such short stone cists were found. Other small graves without protecting stones might leave no clearly identifiable vestiges and hence could have been numerous.

3. I do not read the dissimilarities between the lengths and widths of the longhouses e.g. at Resengaard as obvious signs of changing status or "wealth". When considering a much later context (post-medieval England), Matthew Johnson states: "Whether a household will invest its money in architecture is a decision that will vary from culture to culture and from social group to social group. For example, many peasant societies have a strong ethic against reinvesting surplus money back into the household. Rather, there is a strong pressure to dissipate the surplus on feasts, religious celebrations, and similar events, bringing social prestige rather than material wealth back to the family unit" (Johnson 1990:249).

4. I shall not go deeper into the concrete topic of settlement patterns in this present work although sometimes the approaches are based on consideration of the terrain and, in this respect, inspiring publications on the interplay between landscape and settlement are available (e.g. Roberts 1996). Concerning South Scandinavia, it is even likely we still do

not know of all its important components. Besides the settlements, where the longhouses stood and much of daily life probably took place, locations for particular doings should be taken into consideration (e.g. Skousen 1998). In the Limfjord region, it thus seems plausible that coastal stations were frequently used right on the shore. A long tradition of peasants exploiting marine resources existed in the Neolithic (Andersen, S. H. 2005:166). Exploitation of such a nature is also evidenced with regard to southern Norway, where a broad-spectrum economy incorporated agriculture, husbandry, hunting and fishing (Simonsen, Lindblom & Bakkevig 1982). In these areas, much the same landscapes were preferred as in recent periods (Østmo 1977:202). In Danish contexts, Sophus Müller was the first to focus on settlement pattern topics (Thrane 1989:6pp). Not least Henrik Thrane early on advocated the settlement approach and arranged seminars on such themes (Thrane 1976). Apart from Højgård, the settlement patterns of the Late Neolithic in western South Scandinavia have still only been modestly considered but some notions do exist from eastern parts of South Scandinavia, e.g. regarding Limengård, Fosie IV and Almhov (Ethelberg 1987; 1993b; 2000a; Björhem & Säfvestad 1989; Artursson 2010; Brink 2013, with further references). Some projects focussing on long-term development aspects have been carried out, like e.g. the Ystad Project (Berglund 1991 & Larsson, M.1991). Another example is from Ingelstorp (Strömberg 1982).

5. The importance of certain heating sources, namely ovens, in post-medieval contexts is often directly reflected in the ground plans of the farm buildings. In a number of house plans from North Jutland and eastern parts of Denmark, the large ovens thus played a key role among the interior arrangements and these buildings are termed oven-houses ("ovnhuse", Jespersen 1961:83pp).

6. Interestingly, stones heated in a fireplace were used for warming water as part of the cleaning process of barrels used in the traditional process of beer brewing in the second half of the 19th century in Denmark (Højrup 1980:51).

7. Tentative analysis of 30 selected "pit areas" at Resengaard has been carried out regarding their chronological indications and the distances to nearby longhouse sites, though without a clear result.

8. The Tastum Sø settlement project was initiated by the author over the period 1978-1980 (Simonsen 1996c:90pp; 1999:201p). It has continued since then and offers good possibility of considering the situation of several settlements near this lake from the Single Grave Culture and the Late Neolithic in relation to positions of other find groups in the terrain, being not least a substantial number of barrows many of which are more or less aligned (Nielsen & Simonsen 1987:197). Regarding topography, settlement around the lake can be considered a representation at very local scale of the changes that took place over this period. Extensive areas of heath vegetation, present for centuries up to recent times, have helped preserve the prehistoric sites.

9. On handling of rubbish in other South Scandinavian contexts, see for instance Ullén 1994 and Olsson 1999.

10. For a general approach to the landscape and the impact of agriculture and livestock, see Kristiansen 1988:69pp.

11. As a basis for a more precise, objective rating of the composition of top soils, the Danish soil classification ("Den Danske Jordklassificering") was published in 1976 and is divided into six classes range from the lightest soil, coarse sandy soil, to the heaviest soils, heavy clay soil/very heavy clay soil/silt soil. The classification at Resengaard hill is mainly around the middle of this spectrum, being fine sandy soil mixed with clay/coarse sandy soil mixed with clay.

12. The formerly wet landscape of a local area at Zealand has been thoroughly pedologically analysed. It exemplifies the marked differences between a drained and an undrained landscape (Dalsgaard 1985). A recent study on spatial relations between settlements and certain topographical elements in the Viborg area pointed to the vast wet areas in the undrained landscape, being in this case for instance between settlements with two-aisled houses and certain topographical elements (Mikkelsen, M. 2013).

13. Regarding the "Field/pasture hypothesis" I am grateful to ethnologist and former lecturer Johannes Møllgaard for inspiring conversation on farmhouses, topography, agriculture and animal husbandry in post-medieval North Jutland. Regarding recent hamlets (with to some degree corresponding placement), see Hastrup 1964:214pp.

14. Several remains of wooden ards have been found in the Limfjord region (Glob 1942:258pp). For a survey of recorded ard-ploughed fields from the time of the Beakers onwards in Denmark, see Thrane 1991, Fig. 6.

15. Several pollen samples from Resengaard have been examined. Although only three of them contained pollen of an amount worth counting, they tend to support the result that barley played a significant role. Two of the samples stem from the floor layer of the burned down House 2. Cereals, possibly barley, in one of these (M61387) accounted for a total of 13.9 % of the total amount of pollen while in the other sample (M61388) it came to 19.4 %. The third sample stemmed from House 138 and cereal pollen, possibly barley, accounted for 9.7 %.

16. It is remarkable that plants belonging to the cruciferous (brassicaceae), which may appear in grown fields as well as other areas, were represented by 100 pollens corresponding to 57.5 % of the entire sample from House 138, although human activities may have affected samples from indoor areas (pers. comm. Peter Steen Henriksen).

17. For agricultural experiments, see Henriksen 1996:65pp. For harvesting with flint sickles, see Jensen, H.J. 1990:209pp; 1996.

18. Peter Steen Henriksen draws attention to a small sample from House 1 containing only a few seeds from weeds. This presumably concerns threshed and cleaned grains, as well

as two spike fragments (sample RE25, see report S2001a. Sample RE8 belongs to House 2, see Cat. C). We did not have the resources to make systematic soil sampling from the floors horizons during our fieldwork at Resengaard. The samples were mainly taken on spots where charred macrofossils had been observed. Regarding House 1 and 197 we attempted to catch most of the cereals present in the floor horizons and large amounts were thus extracted during fieldwork by means of simple water sieving though a 2 mm certified mesh. This was done in order to achieve comprehensive evidence of their appearance, and to ensure the possibility of making a quantitative analysis of their preservation and of the processes imposed on these plant remainders in the ancient prehistoric situation. As a rough estimate, some 2,500 litres of soil from the floor horizon in the sunken area of House 1 was scrutinized this way, whereas from House 197 it was probably only around 1,500 litres. This procedure would, however, allow small seeds to pass through. When visiting the ongoing Resengaard excavation in the early 1990s, David Earle Robinson recommended the flotation technique. Shortly thereafter we had our own gear constructed for flotation of the dried samples, a technique the museum has used ever since as the standard. Many minor samples have later been examined after flotation and use of a certified 0.5 mm mesh size.

19. On the use of stones for baking, see Lerche and Steensberg 1980:72p. Varying access to energy is seen as one of the main reasons for different baking methods.

20. Lis Højlund Pedersen carried out the pollen examinations (report S2001a, enclosure 3). Thirteen samples were examined in all. In most of these, the acid sandy soil had not preserved the pollen.

21. In one pollen sample (M61387) from the floor layer of House 2 at Resengaard trees make up 17.7 % of the 108 preserved pollens (Fig. 4.68. Peter Steen Henriksen/Lis Højlund Pedersen: Report S2001a). Oak (quercus, 10 pollens, 9.3 %), alder (alnus, 2 pollens, 1.9 %), hazel (corylus, 5 pollens, 4.6 %) and poplar (populous, 2 pollens, 1.9 %) are represented. In the second sample (M61388) 211 pollens are preserved and trees make up 11.5 %. Of these oak (quercus, 18 pollens, 8.5 %), alder (alnus, 2 pollens, 1.0 %), hazel (corylus, 1 pollen, 0.5 %), and poplar (populous, 2 pollens, 1.0 %) are represented. Juniper is also present, though just a single pollen, 0.5 %.

22. The pollen sample (M61390) from patch B in the eastern part of the site of House 138 at Resengaard contains 174 pollens and trees make up 9.7 % (Peter Steen Henriksen/Lis Højlund Pedersen: Report S2001a). Among the 16 preserved tree pollens, oak (quercus, 12 pollens, 6.9 %), alder (alnus, 2 pollens, 1.1 %), hazel (corylus, 2 pollens, 1.1 %) are represented, along with a slight indication of poplar (populous).

23. From the floor layer of House 2 at Resengaard, pollen from plantain (sample M61388) as well as plantago media and plantago major (sample M61387 & M61388), plus dandelion (taraxacum) could represent grazing areas. These pollens possibly reflected what grew just in the immediate surroundings of the building (pers.comm. Peter Steen Henriksen; Report S2001a.). Pollen from plantain, plantago media and plantago major are also represented in the sample from House 138 (M61390).

24. Sprigs of heather were found in two sunken floors at Resengaard, namely at the site of House 1, two samples with two and three sprigs respectively and at the site of House 2, one sample containing 10 sprigs (Peter Steen Henriksen: Report S2001a, with remarks on heather). In addition, stem pollen samples with evidence of the heather family (ericaceae) in one sample (M61387, 24 pollens, 22.2 %) and another sample (M61388, 40 pollens, 19.0 %) are represented from the site of House 2. Relatively few pollens from heather (ericaceae) were found (3 pollens, 1.7 %) in the sample from House 138 (M61390). No sprigs of heather (calluna vulgaris) were found among the charred macrofossils from this house.

25. Poaceae pollens, to which reeds also belong, are found in three samples (Peter Steen Henriksen/Lis Højlund Pedersen: Report S2001a). From the site of House 2, unspecified pollen from the family poaceae was represented through sample M61387 (11 pollens, 10.2 %,) and sample M61388 (40 pollens, 19.0 %). Pollen from the poaceae family came from the site of House 138 (sample M61390, 21 pollens, 12 %).

26. On experiments with prehistoric bronze casting methods, see Rønne 1996.

27. How tanning processes could have taken place in the Late Neolithic and emerging Bronze Age in the Limfjord region needs clarifying. Extracting tannic acids from the bark of oak trees could perhaps have been carried out (Jørgensen, G.1977:237; Tannic acids may also have been available from roasted, crushed acorns using the water extraction method (Wikipedia).

28. http://manchester.academia.edu/LCrewe (accessed 28th April 2017)

29. Some information is available from the Bronze Age settlement at Bjerre, which has comparatively fine preservation conditions (Bech & Mikkelsen, M. 1999:74). The animal bones mostly belonged to cattle and only a few to sheep/goats. Bones from pigs were not found. On evidence of livestock from the Late Neolithic and Older Bronze Age in Sweden, see Kristensson, Olson & Welinder 1996.

30. An article on honey has dealt with the current knowledge of its former production (Koch 2001:7pp).

31. It seems likely that some of the milk would have been processed into products with a relatively long life. Soured milk products are known widely from agricultural societies. Cheese could presumably also have been produced. Some clay colanders may have been instrumental in this processing. And yet, to my knowledge, finds clearly evidencing the production of cheese or soured milk are still lacking from Danish Late Neolithic materials. However, the notion of milk processed into cheese and yoghurt-like products dating

from early in the Late Neolithic in South Scandinavia is well in accordance with the idea of a new wave of using animal products, the so-called "secondary exploitation of animals" (Sherratt 1983:94p).

32. During the Late Neolithic, shellfish collecting (oysters, common mussel and other) took place but seemingly on a comparatively small scale. Later in the developed Bronze Age, shells that predominantly belong to the blue common mussel have been recovered from settlements sometimes situated several kilometres from the coast (*cf.* Mikkelsen, P. 1996).

33. Analysis such as that on pastoral Fulani groups on the Nigerian Savannah carried out by Derrick J. Stenning might inspire one to consider the basic conditions for household viability in contexts such as those of the Late Neolithic (Stenning 1971). On viability, see also Fortes 1971, Freeman 1971 and Goody 1971.

34. When considering craft specialization, Deborah Olausson underlines the fact that "…we must look at how production was organized in those contexts we wish to study" and she considers four ways of organizing production, being household production, household industry, attached specialist production and workshop production for trade (Olausson 2000:123p). Household production concerns only that which is required by its members, whereas household industry is also aimed at exchange/trade.

35. To Mauss, the gift exchange is the solution to Hobbes' assumptions of a war of all against all (Carrier 2005:218). This idea of power taking the place of law very easily came to minds when speaking of the Stone Age in the 19th century but early in the 20th century Malinowski demonstrated that the Melanesians had rather complicated canons about politics, kinship and exchange in their reasonably well-functioning societies.

36. In terms of exchange, knowledge of peasants who also acted as middlemen and sold products from other households exists from later historical periods in Denmark, including the Limfjord region (Møllgaard 1997:55 & 69).

Closing remarks

In carrying out this study and interpreting the new research materials, it is fair to say that I have not been faced with an excessive body of existing interpretation with which to agree or disagree. Indeed, it would be more appropriate to say that, in several respects, this work has been undertaken in fields within which analyses and interpretations are sorely lacking, despite the presence of records from quite substantial numbers of investigated house sites by now in South Scandinavia. My concern has thus first and foremost been directed towards seeking new knowledge along hitherto largely unexplored paths and with the necessary methodological development still underway.

As it relates to the first systematic exploration of traces of daily life in comprehensive source materials stemming from house sites with sunken floors and other settlement constituents in a South Scandinavian region, many novel terms had to be developed. A new working term, "raw dimension", therefore had to be introduced to emphasize the point that the house ground plans outlined in our fieldwork may be quite different from the original outer or inner dimensions of the buildings. A new term, "floor-shadow", was likewise created with the intention of being able to make a fairly nuanced representation of the floors in the house sites by including certain soil traces, albeit with significant uncertainties. The observations gathered on house plots were systematized under the heading of "life-cycle biography" stages.

On relative chronology, by also including the secondary fills as part of the introduced expression "chronological entity", the varied pottery assemblages from the longhouses were able to form a significantly broader basis for the internal chronological ordering of these.

The new term "sunken-floor horizon" revealed strong potential, in a vitally important field, for the systematic scrutinizing of artefacts, plant remainders, soil patches, pits and floor layers, and it thus helped build a foundation on which to make suggestions regarding the highly varied activities from everyday life. When characterizing and discussing certain floor observations, the introduction of further new terms was necessary, namely "low zone", "scorched-stone patch", "mosaic patch", "activity space" and "free space". Moreover, the term "ground floor" was proposed as a replacement for negative expressions such as "unsunken floor" with regard to the western parts of the sunken-floor longhouses. In order to describe this particular and important property, the term "ground-floor longhouse" was suggested to denote a longhouse without a substantial sunken floor. Finally, the term "hill-edge residency" was presented in connection with the "Field/pasture hypothesis" which relates to strategies on where to place longhouses, where to pasture livestock, to deposit waste, to grow crops and so on.

This present study has clearly established that the selected house sites with sunken floors generally offer a richly-facetted source of information on certain fields of past human life. I consider the households as core units of production as well as units for the exchange of numerous different kinds of specialized products and services. This understanding is in contrast with earlier perceptions whereby people of the period were described as mainly focusing on ordinary agricultural activities and livestock. Moreover, I propose that communication and exchange, also including the seeking of marital partners, took place locally as well as widely within the region and beyond. In this way, connections and close networks could be established and maintained which, in my understanding, worked as a significant safeguard against war and, presumably, against political unrest and raids. The stabilizing role of plentiful acts of exchange would have thus been of paramount importance for households of the Limfjord region. The open settlements and the apparent absence of massive signs of warlike conflicts may likely sustain this view. The long and stable settlement, continuing generation after generation at Resengaard, is also an obvious indication of a high degree of stability.

From the onset of the Late Neolithic, novel and revolutionary ideas on production transformed everyday life in the Limfjord region. The new copper and copper-tin alloys became much appreciated and, where possible, local production was initiated. People now also learned how to benefit from sheep wool by weaving textiles. New methods of controlling fermentation processes may have been exploited for the making of foodstuffs such as cheese and yoghurt. Other fermentation processes were put to work for the making of alcoholic beverages. In certain instances, beer may even have been produced on an almost "industrial" scale, likely not least for use during varying kinds of gathering. Over this period, status – among other things – also became displayed in new fashions of delicately decorated pottery and in the manufacture of exquisite daggers, based on a local flint mining "industry" that was a hallmark of this region. As in certain other European regions, strong attention and consideration was at that time likely given to the sun, the moon, the planets, the stars and other phenomena of the sky, presumably as part of their religious beliefs. With regard to some of the above-mentioned novel and revolutionary ideas, for a limited time in the early Late Neolithic some areas of the region even functioned as gateway community to other parts of South Scandinavia for the introduction of Late Neolithic Culture, as well as Beaker traits. And yet why is it that the people of the Limfjord region seem to have been so open to new ideas and new knowledge on specialized production?

The existence of rather flexible households would, in my understanding, have been vital and I shall close by reflecting a little more on this. Some individuals within a household, or among those joining it, could have developed particular abilities for certain kinds of specialized work. Many different skills and competences could in this way have been achieved among household members. The composition of the individual households must therefore have been a deciding factor in terms of what the members would have been able to manage at any given time. Along with changes in household compositions – such as a rise or fall in the number of residents, changes in age and gender constellations, an increase or decline in the work capabilities represented, the health conditions of members and other traits – some new household strategies might thus, at times, have become desirable or necessary for the individual households. Perhaps new ways of cooperating with other households also had to be initiated. Transformations of the local ecology and changing needs in the communities could likewise have played a significant role and may have led to necessary adjustments in the kinds of specialized work to be carried out.

From the above perspective, it is actually quite interesting and conspicuous that the tradition for specialized flint tool production at Myrhøj, from my understanding, may appear to have been continued by the households over generations, assuming that the longhouses represent a chronological order. Correspondingly, at Glattrup IV, the tradition for establishing voluminous pits, cellars, sunken fireplaces and other interior arrangements, in my reading for beer production, is evidenced from the sites of all three sunken-floor longhouses which, in my understanding, may have succeeded each other. It appears, however, that dynamic changes took place from house to house as concerns pit size, pit placement and thereby probably also details of functioning, while still continuing to brew and store fermented beverages down three generations. Thereafter, the Glattrup IV settlement apparently came to an abrupt end.

It is plausible that, before building new longhouses, each generation at Resengaard had to assess their situation and make new choices as to how they wanted their dwelling and on what kinds of production in particular to concentrate their efforts. And yet, apart from extended cattle breeding, it has not been possible to point to any continued traditions of specialized household production for the long-established settlement covered by the provisional Resengaard chronology. The particular treatment of cereals thus only took place on any scale in two longhouses dated some time apart.

While I argue that numerous kinds of specialized production must have been carried out at the settlements of the Limfjord region, so far only comparatively few can be proposed as regards specific products related to specific houses. Exploring data on specialized production at concrete locations is hence an important area of future research. It would at first sight seem that, while some kinds of specialized production were perhaps of a seasonal or more occasional nature, others could have been carried out on a daily basis. The extraordinary venture into cattle breeding is a suggested specialized production that would inevitably have taken place every day.

This present study has attempted to introduce some ideas for interpreting the ancient vestiges of daily life, and plentiful traces of possible extinct working processes in relation to activity spaces have been presented from the deep floors of the longhouses in particular. Yet we are only at the beginning of how to approach and understand the vestiges of these buildings. Since excavation, my path has been a long one, from museum magazines and the massive accumulations of information in the reports, through planned selection of data and on to systematic analysis, interpretation, discussion and outlining of perspectives. For me, the study has meant that my earlier search, in particular, for common and general traits in the sites of the sunken-floor houses has now resulted in a marked change of focus, namely towards being increasingly aware of the individuality of the concrete dwellings and settlements.

My attention has also been on minute details, not least when considering the artefacts and soil patches of the sunken-floor horizons because it is precisely these particulars that provide vital information on daily life that would otherwise remain unexplored. I have also drawn attention to the difficulties in obtaining the proper information out of these settlement materials due to their complexity and the source-critical factors involved. And yet we should not let these difficulties govern us and should instead strive to learn how to break the codes of the sunken-floor longhouses from this ancient period. If we succeed, then a great deal of fresh new knowledge on everyday life will be obtained for a reflexive archaeology.

Appendix

Further detail on pottery relationships

This appendix provides via examples further background on the suggested chronological relationships between pottery assemblages (Ch. 3). Part A presents suggested relationships between the Resengaard pottery assemblages in detail. Part B presents the suggested affinities of seven "classic" pottery assemblages with those of Resengaard in detail. Part C presents the proposed affinities of two "new" pottery assemblages with those of Resengaard although only general comments will be made with regard to Kluborg II.

Part A. Resengaard, LN II/emerging Bronze Age

For all entries, the figure number given in Ch. 3 of this book is stated first. The affinities of the four reference assemblages from Houses 1, 2, 41, and 134 are indirectly presented through the numerous suggested relationships with ceramics from other pottery assemblages and no details are therefore proposed here with regard to these.

Fig. 3.9. House 13, affinities in detail

No rim profiles found in the sunken-floor horizon. Secondary fills: Two profiles have rims characteristically bent outwards. **RE272aa:** With the shoulder and rim forming a kind of slight furrow at the transition to the body and the rim top slightly tapering, it has very close affinities with the assemblage of House 1 (RE31aa, sunken-floor horizon) and close affinities with the assemblage of House 2 (RE135aa, sunken-floor horizon) as well as that of House 41 (RE419aa, secondary fills, and to some degree RE412aa, sunken-floor horizon). **RE655aa:** Having a very short, bent-out rim, it also supports some relationship to House 41 (RE406cb, secondary fills). **RE655ad:** The almost upright rim with thickened top has no direct counterpart in other Resengaard assemblages.

Fig. 3.10. House 14, affinities in detail

Sunken-floor horizon: **RE297aa:** With its convex belly, it seems related to the assemblage of House 2 (RE134aa, sunken-floor horizon) and that of House 41 (RE412aa, sunken-floor horizon). **RE298ab:** With its angularly out-turned rim, the profile is a parallel to RE258bi in the secondary fills. Both rims have affinities with pottery in the sunken-floor horizon and secondary fills of House 41 (RE406ce, RE406af, RE409aa, & RE420aa). These rim profiles are also related to profiles from the sunken-floor horizon and secondary fills of House 2 (RE7ae, RE92aa, RE161aa, RE179aa and other). **RE298aa:** This vessel fragment, from the sunken floor horizon, with a short horizontally projecting lug, is very important and shows a clear relationship to its parallel from House 1 (RE6ai, secondary fills).

Secondary fills: **RE258aq:** With convex outer rim and a very pronounced marking between rim and belly, it shows a relationship to the assemblage of House 41 (RE416aa, sunken-floor horizon) and that of House 2 (RE176aa, sunken-floor horizon). Further, the profile has a clear relationship to that of House 1 (RE31aa, sunken-floor horizon). **RE258bs** seems to some degree related to the assemblage of House 41 (RE406ab, secondary fills) and that of House 2 (RE119aa /121aa, sunken-floor horizon), as well as that of House 1 (RE153aa, sunken-floor horizon). **RE258ar:** It has no direct counterparts in the reference assemblages but exhibits some affinities with the assemblage of House 41 (e.g. RE406cb, secondary fills) and that of House 2 (RE135aa, sunken-floor horizon). **RE258am:** The very "upright" profile has some features in common with

429

RE258an from the same context. **RE258aa:** It has clear affinities with the assemblage of House 2 (RE102aa, sunken-floor horizon). **RE258ab:** The rim is supplied with a remarkable bent-out, voluminous rim top. Is has no clear counterpart in any of the house assemblages at Resengaard but shows some affinities with a rim top (RE976bd) from culture layer 293.

Fig. 3.11. House 42, affinities in detail

Sunken-floor horizon: **RE441aa:** Having a bent-out rim with a slightly convex outer side and a straight inner side combined with a furrow-like marking of the transition to the body on the outer side and a corresponding "knee" on the inner side, it has multiple relationships to other find materials. Among the reference assemblages, this first and foremost concerns the assemblages of House 41 (RE416aa, sunken-floor horizon), House 2 (RE92aa, when ignoring the absence of furrow, & RE176aa, having a furrow and an even more pronounced shaping, both rims from sunken-floor horizon) and House 1 (RE31aa, sunken-floor horizon).

Secondary fills: **RE654ab:** With the low horizontal cordon below the rim, it is related to the assemblage of House 134 (in particular 596ab with low cordon, sunken-floor horizon) and that of House 41 (RE422aa with low cordon, sunken-floor horizon). **RE654aa:** With its rather short, markedly out-turned rim, it has affinities with the assemblage of House 41 (RE406eb, secondary fills) and that of House 2 (RE135aa, sunken-floor horizon). Further, there are some affinities with the assemblage of House 13 (RE272aa, secondary fills) and that of House 200 (RE750bb, secondary fills).

Fig. 3.12. House 128, affinities in detail

Sunken-floor horizon: **RE561aa/540aa:** This rim is smoothly turned up, with a thickened, almost vertical rim top (RE 540aa is ascribed to the secondary fills but could originally have belonged to the sunken floor, see text). Its uncomplicated design offers little evidence of clear affinities of chronological value. **RE546aa:** At the transition to the rim, the horizontally-projecting lug has a different appearance to rims in the assemblages of House 200 (RE750cc, secondary fills), House 14 (RE298aa, sunken-floor horizon) and House 1 (RE6a1, secondary fills). Yet on a more general level it does have the projecting lug in common with only these three house assemblages.

Secondary fills: **RE540ac:** With its markedly bent-out rim, it may show some affinities with the assemblage of House 41 (RE406ca, secondary fills), House 14 (RE258an & RE258bg, both secondary fills), as well as those of House 130 (RE539ap, secondary fills) and House 240 (RE798bl, secondary fills). **RE540ba:** A slight, straight thickening on the outer side of the rim top is characteristic (this feature is observed in profile RE540ae as well). It shows affinities with the assemblage of House 2 (RE7ak, secondary fills). **RE540ad:** With its markedly turned-out rim, slender and simple shaping of the profile, it has affinities with the assemblages of House 41 (RE406aa, secondary fills), House 2 (RE191aa & RE7ag, both secondary fills) and, to some degree, to those of House 200 (RE794, secondary fills) and House 1 (RE153aa, sunken-floor horizon), in addition to House 240 (RE260ap, secondary fills), House 12 (RE250aj, secondary fills) and House RE183 (RE666ad, secondary fills). **RE552aa:** Having no preserved rim top but a marked shoulder and an indication of a somewhat out-turned rim, as well as no marked "knee" on the inner side, it shows affinities with the assemblages of Houses 41 and 2 although a profile from House 1 (RE31aa, sunken-floor horizon) seems to show the best match. **RE540ae:** It has some affinities with the assemblages of House 2 (RE7ak, secondary fills), House 14 (RE258am, secondary fills) and House 10 (RE260ak, secondary fills). **RE552ac:** It has no direct counterparts in any of the assemblages. However, with its marked thickening of the rim, it may show affinities with the assemblages of House 1 (RE58aa, the sunken-floor horizon), House 14 (RE258ao & RE258bm, both secondary fills), House 200 (RE792aa, RE790aa, both sunken-floor horizon, & RE750cd, secondary fills) and House 268 (RE824ac & RE824af, both secondary fills). It further appears to show affinities with the assemblage of House 41 (RE406ad, secondary fills). **RE552aj:** This profile, which could seem to be a kind of slim version of RE561aa/540aa, appears to represent a small bowl, having some affinities with the assemblage of House 2 (RE7ah, secondary fills).

Fig. 3.13. House 130, affinities in detail

Sunken-floor horizon: **RE580aa:** It is supplied with a relatively simple rim, albeit with a smoothly shaped narrowing below the rim, but no close relationships to specific assemblages are suggested.

Secondary fills: **RE539ab, RE539ac, & RE539bb**: With their relatively short, turned-out rims, they have some affinities with e.g. the assemblage of House 41 (RE406ab, secondary fills). **RE539aa**: Also having a turned-out rim and in addition a horizontal furrow-like marking at the transition between rim and shoulder, it seems, though less pronounced, related to the assemblage of House 41 (RE412aa, sunken-floor horizon, & RE419aa, secondary fills). Further, it shows some affinities with the assemblage of House 2 (RE176aa, sunken-floor horizon) and that of House 1 (RE31aa, sunken-floor horizon). **RE539ab**: With its out-turned rim, it has some affinities with the assemblage of House 41 (RE406aa, secondary fills) and House 2 (RE119aa/121aa, sunken-floor horizon). **RE539ad**: With its relatively thin, vertical rim it apparently has no direct counterparts in the other assemblages but a weak relationship might possibly exist to the profiles with a more sharply marked transition between the thin rim and the upper part of the vessel. This might apply to the assemblages of House 41 (RE406ai & RE406ah, both secondary fills) and House 2 (RE135aa, sunken-floor horizon). The thin rim may lead back to the House 41 assemblage. **RE539al**: Also having a turned-out, thin rim and a relatively swung profiling, it is clearly reminiscent of several House 134 forms (like RE564ab & RE564ba, both secondary fills). The thin rim finish is also reminiscent of the rim-top shaping of a clay pot in the assemblage of House 134 (RE594ac, sunken-floor horizon). With the kind of thickening of the outer rim top it is also, to some degree, associated with the assemblage of House 2 (RE7ak, secondary fills). **RE539ap**: Having a bent-out rim top, it shows some relationship with the assemblage of House 134 (RE594ac, sunken-floor horizon) and that of House 41 (RE406ca, secondary fills). **RE539at**: With its combination of thicker ware to the body and a marked transition to the body, it has affinities with the assemblage of House 41 (RE406ai & RE406ah, both secondary fills) and that of House 2 (RE135aa, sunken-floor horizon). **RE539bc**: Supplied with horizontal marking deviating somewhat from the early horizontal cordons, it has moderate affinities with the assemblage of House 197 (RE702ao). **RE539as**: The side fragment displays a rare combination of a horizontal cordon and a horizontal furrow-like appearance immediately below, having likely affinities with the assemblage of House 134 (RE564aa & RE564bb, both secondary fills) and that of House 41 (RE406as & RE406at, both secondary fills).

Fig. 3.14. House 138, affinities in detail

Sunken-floor horizon: **RE614aa**: It has a convex outer rim but a less concavely inner rim. At the transition to the fairly straight upper part of the body, the horizontal furrow-like marking on the outer side contrasts with a smooth outwards curving on the inner side. This rim profile has a relatively close match in the assemblage of House 2 (RE176aa, sunken-floor horizon). The latter is supplied with a somewhat more distinct "knee" on the inner side, though. It also has some affinities with the assemblage of House 1 (RE31aa, sunken-floor horizon) and that of House 41 (RE403aa/411aa & RE416aa, both shaped with more rounded bellies and both from the sunken-floor horizon). **RE614ab**: It likewise has many features in common with profile RE176aa immediately above, as it is supplied with a slightly concave outer as well as inner rim and, below the rim, a very pronounced "knee" drawn back into the inner of the clay pot, in contrast to an almost rectangular bending out of the outer side above the rounded upper part of the body. In Ch. 3, the design of RE176aa is called "dramatic" and this term would certainly apply to RE614ab, too. It ought to be noted that this rim profile also has traits in common with e.g. the assemblage of House 41 (RE416aa, sunken-floor horizon) but apparently less so. No rims represent the secondary fills.

Fig. 3.15. House 197, affinities in detail

Sunken-floor horizon: The pottery from pit F represents the floor finds. **RE702af**: With its moderate thickness and bent-out rim, it shows relationships on a general level to the assemblages of House 41 (RE406ap, secondary fills), House 2 (RE179aa, sunken-floor horizon) and House 1 (RE39aa, sunken-floor horizon). **RE702ba**: Having a markedly rounded upper belly (shoulder) and bent-out rim, it shows some relationship to the assemblage of House 41 (RE406aa, secondary fills) but in particular that of House 138 (RE614ab). **RE702ap**: Though somewhat fragmented, it appears to have a bent out rim and a slight indication of a thickening at the transition to the body. It shows a relationship to House 2 (RE92aa, sunken-floor horizon, & RE7ae, secondary fills) and it seemingly also has some affinities with the assemblage of House 41 (RE416aa, sunken-floor horizon). **RE702ag**: With its relatively short rim and "sliding" profile, it has a clear relationship to the House 41 assemblage (RE406ab, secondary fills, and RE404aa, sunken-floor horizon) and possibly also somewhat to the House 2 assemblage (RE119aa/ 121aa, sunken-floor horizon). **RE702aa:** Belonging to a large vessel with a relatively broad rim, it does not have direct counterparts in the four reference assemblages. However, due to the "sliding" profile, it resembles RE702ac, RE702ad, & RE702ag. It may also thereby share some of the relationships of these rims. In general, more or less "sliding" profiles are found in the assemblages of House 41 and House 2. **RE702ac:** It has more traits in common with RE702aa and may share the same relationships. **RE702ad:** Having a very distinct "sliding" profile with indication of rounded belly, almost vertical rim and no conspicuous marking of the transition to the rim shows a clear relationship to the assemblages of House 41 (RE410aa, sunken-floor horizon) and House 2 (RE133aa, sunken-floor horizon). RE702ao, supplied with a horizontal, slight cordon-like expansion at the transition to the body and relatively thin rim, does not appear to have direct counterparts among the reference assemblages.

Secondary fills: **RE700ab** & **RE700ac:** These profiles with bent-out rims merely show a relationship in general to assemblages from House 2 (RE161aa & RE179aa, sunken-floor horizon, besides RE7ab & RE7ae, secondary fills) and House 1 (RE39aa, sunken-floor horizon). Affinities with the House 41 assemblage (RE409aa, sunken-floor horizon, and RE406, secondary fills) also seem possible. **RE700aa:** With its characteristic thickening at the transition from rim to belly, this bent-out rim shows a clear relationship to the assemblage of House 2 (RE92aa, sunken-floor horizon & RE7ae, secondary fills). It might also have some affinities with that of House 41 (RE416aa, sunken-floor horizon). **RE278aa:** Having a thin, almost sharply bent-out rim, it shows clear relationships to House 41 (RE406ca, secondary fills) and some affinities also with House 134 (RE594ac, sunken-floor horizon). **RE700ai & 278ab:** It shows a waving outer side reminiscent of a horizontal cordon and may also be related to the assemblages of House 134 and House 41.

Fig. 3.16. House 200, affinities in detail

Sunken-floor horizon: **RE786aa** & **RE759ab:** Having out-turned rims, the profiles exhibit some affinities in general with House 41 (RE406ce, 406af & RE409aa, sunken-floor horizon). They further have affinities with the assemblage of House 2 (RE161 & RE179, both sunken-floor horizon). **RE792aa:** Also supplied with out-turned rim it seems to have the same relationships as the foregoing. The slightly waving outer rim side does not have the character of a horizontal cordon. **RE769aa:** With out-turned rim, its characteristic thickening at the transition from rim to belly has strong affinities with the assemblage of House 2 (RE92aa, sunken-floor horizon, & RE7ae, secondary fills) and possibly also to some degree that of House 41 (RE416aa, sunken-floor horizon). Comparable traits are observable in the assemblage of House 14 (RE284aa, sunken-floor horizon) and that of House 197 (RE700aa, secondary fills). **RE783aa:** Having out-turned rim and a slightly thickened part of the profile, it seemingly has no direct counterparts in the other assemblages but might only generally be related to some of the same assemblages as the other vessels with out-turned rims. **RE791aa:** With a convex outer rim side and a correspondingly concave inner rim, it has a narrow horizontal furrow-like marking on the outer side at the transition to the somewhat rounded upper part, which is in contrast to a smoothly out-curving contour on the inner side. The rim profile shows slight affinities with the assemblage of House 41 (RE403aa/411aa & RE416aa, both sunken-floor horizon) but relatively close relationships to the assemblage of House 2 (RE176aa, sunken-floor horizon) and also to some degree that of House 1 (RE31aa, sunken-floor horizon). **RE790aa:** It has a furrow at the transition to the body and a fairly short rim, which is convex on both outer and inner sides. The rim profile more or less shares affinities with the same assemblages as the foregoing specimen. **RE793aa:** It is also supplied with a furrow at the transition to the body and it has the same affinities as RE791aa. However, with its combination of convex outer side and straight inner side of the rim, it especially exhibits a relationship to the assemblage of House 1 (RE31aa, sunken-floor horizon). **RE760aa:** With a short, almost rectangular bent-out rim it has affinities to some degree with the assemblage of House 41 (RE406ca, secondary fills). Related profiles are also present in other materials, e.g. from House 128 (RE540ac, secondary fills) and House 197 (RE278aa, secondary fills). **RE759aa:** Having an almost vertical rim and a slim area below the rim, it possibly has some affinities with the assemblage of House 2 (RE102aa, sunken-floor horizon).

Secondary fills: **RE750ab, RE750ag, RE750bc, RE750bd, & RE750bh:** These rim profiles belong to classic open bowls without significant marks and are often difficult to assign to a specific stage in the pottery transformations The rim profiles **RE750af,**

RE750cd, **RE750am**, **RE750ap**, **RE765aa**: with out-turned rims, have relationships in general to the assemblages of House 41 (RE409aa, sunken-floor horizon, & RE406ce, RE406af & RE420aa, secondary fills) and House 2 (RE7ab, RE7ae, RE92aa, RE161aa, & RE179aa). **RE750cb:** Supplied with a bent-out and characteristically thickened rim, it apparently has no direct parallels but can only generally be ascribed the same relationships as the previous group. **RE750ak:** Having a bent-out and nearly lens-shaped contour, it seems to have some affinities with the assemblage of House 41 (RE406ap, secondary fills). **RE750bb:** With a short, out-turned rim, it shows a clear relationship to the assemblage of House 2 (RE119aa/121aa, sunken-floor horizon) and also some relationship to the assemblage of House 41 (RE406ab, secondary fills). **RE750ba:** Having a relatively short, almost vertical rim of less thickness than the body, it has clear relationships to the assemblages of House 41 (RE412aa, sunken-floor horizon) and House 2 (RE134aa, sunken-floor horizon). **RE820aa:** With its gently curved contour tapering off in a relatively pointed top at the rim, it has strong relationships to the assemblage of House 41 (RE409aa & RE408aa, sunken-floor horizon, & RE420aa, secondary fills). It appears further to have some relationship to the assemblage of House 2 (RE119aa/121aa), which also seems reflected in the tendency of specimens in both assemblages to be supplied with thin and tapering rims. **RE750ca** & **RE794aa:** These rim profiles have some resemblance to RE820aa, and thereby more or less share their affinities. **RE750ae:** Resembles RE769 (sunken-floor horizon) and, though less pronounced in outline, the same relationships to other assemblages must largely apply to it. **RE750aj:** With a rather weak indication of the transition to the rim, it might have a slight relationship to the assemblage of House 41 (RE406ai & 406ah, secondary fills) and that of House 2 (RE135aa, sunken-floor horizon). **RE750bm:** In the general shaping, with a rounded belly and almost vertical rim, it has some resemblance to the assemblages of House 41 (RE410aa, sunken-floor horizon) and House 2 (RE133aa, sunken-floor horizon), presumably strongest to the latter. However, the horizontal furrow at the transition to the rim is unique in this profile combination of RE750bm. **RE750cc:** It is supplied with a horizontally-projecting lug and it probably has some affinities with the assemblage of House 1 (RE6ai, secondary fills). Although the materials from House 41 and House 2 did not include any finds of such horizontally-projecting lugs it is nevertheless a possibility with its closeness to the time of the House 2 assemblage, since corresponding features were found in the assemblages of Houses 14 and 128. For comparison, the specimen in the assemblage of House 14 (RE298aa, sunken-floor horizon) is particularly interesting.

Fig. 3.17. House 202, affinities in detail

No rim profiles were found in the sunken-floor horizon. Secondary fills: **RE952aa:** Having a markedly bent-out rim with a slightly convex outer side combined with a straight inner side, it shows some affinities with the assemblage of House 41 (RE406ce, secondary fills). It further appears to have weak relationships to House 2 (RE7ad, secondary fills) and House 1 (RE6af, secondary fills). **RE752ac:** It seems without evident characteristics that might make it suitable for comparison with other rims.

Fig. 3.18. House 240, affinities in detail

Sunken-floor horizon: **RE876aa:** With bent-out, convex outer rim side above a marked horizontal furrow and a slightly convex inner side, it has close relationships to the assemblages of House 1 (RE31aa, sunken-floor horizon) and House 2 (RE176aa, sunken-floor horizon). The profile mentioned from House 1 is, not least, closely related. The rim further has some affinities with the assemblage of House 41 (RE403aa/411aa, sunken-floor horizon). **RE858aa:** With its convex, bent out outer rim side above a horizontal furrow and a flat inner rim side, it has relatively close affinities with the assemblages of House 1 (RE31aa, sunken-floor horizon) and House 2 (RE176aa, sunken-floor horizon) and, concerning the thickening of the inner rim side, it also displays some affinities with profiles such as RE92aa (sunken-floor horizon) and RE7ae (secondary fills). It also has some, possibly more distant, relationships to the assemblage of House 41 (RE416aa). **RE806aa:** Having a slightly convex outer rim side above a furrow-like marking and a straight inner rim side, combined with a relatively thick ware, the body generally seems to have affinities not least with the assemblages of House 1 and House 2, corresponding to the abovementioned affinities. **RE775aa:** With its almost straight inner rim side and its slender, relatively upturned shape, it has some affinities with the assemblages of House 1 (RE39aa, sunken-floor horizon, and RE6am, secondary fills) and House 2 (RE179aa, sunken-floor horizon, & RE7ab, secondary fills).

Secondary fills: **RE973ab**: With the bent-out rim and convex outer and inner rim side, it appears to have some affinities with the assemblages of House 41 (RE406ce, secondary fills), House 2 (RE119/121aa, sunken-floor horizon) and House 1 (RE6am, secondary fills). **RE860aa**: Having a bent-out, convex outer rim above a horizontal, furrow-like marking and a slightly convex inner rim, it shows close affinities with the assemblages of House 1 (RE31aa, sunken-floor horizon) and House 2 (RE176aa, sunken-floor horizon), as well as some affinities with the assemblage of House 41 (RE403aa/411aa, sunken-floor horizon). The design of this clay pot profile is even more dramatic than the profiling of RE176aa as it is supplied with a markedly drawn back base on the rim part, forming a shoulder. **RE798bg**: Though missing the rim top, it also indicates a very bold profiling and does presumably have more or less the same affinities as RE860aa with the reference assemblages. **RE798be**: It seems to have an upper profile created along the same lines as RE860aa, though obviously indicating a less marked design. It probably also, to some degree, has the same affinities. **RE799aa**: Having a convex outer rim side above a relatively sharp marking of the rim transition to the body and a concave inner rim side, it has clear affinities with the assemblage of House 2 (RE176aa, sunken-floor horizon, albeit without the horizontal furrow), and some affinities with the assemblage of House 41 (RE416aa, sunken-floor horizon), as well as weaker affinities with the assemblage of House 1 (RE31aa, sunken-floor horizon). **RE798ba**: Having a convex outer rim side above a furrow-like indication and a concave inner rim side, it has many features in common with RE799aa and seems to share more or less the same affinities. **RE798aa**: With a convex outer rim side above an only slightly sketched furrow and an almost flat inner rim side, and having a relatively slack profiling, it is shaped much like RE806aa and related in the same way to the reference assemblages. **RE804aa**: With an evenly turned-out rim, being convex on the outer rim side and almost flat on the inner rim side, it has affinities on a general level with the assemblages of House 134 (RE564aa, when ignoring the horizontal cordon, secondary fills), House 41 (RE406ce, secondary fills) and House 2 (RE191aa, secondary fills). **RE973ac**: With a bent-out rim it shows clear affinities with the assemblage of House 2 (RE135aa, sunken-floor horizon) and also somewhat with the assemblage of House 41 (RE406cb & RE406ah, secondary fills). The presence of this form in the House 2 context is underlined by the find of a jar with the same form elements in the pit immediately north of House 2 (RE81bb/85aa). **RE973aa**: With a drawn back base of the rim that presumably would have been curving outwards at the top it shows some relationship to the assemblage of House 2 (RE102aa, sunken-floor horizon & RE7ac, secondary fills). **RE798bm**: With a turned-out rim that has a convex outer rim side and almost straight inner rim side, combined with a considerable thickening of the rim top, it has no clear counterparts among the reference assemblages. However, in the shaping, some affinities with the assemblage of House 14 (RE258az, secondary fills) seem to be present. **RE798ae**: Having a somewhat out-turned rim, convex-concave outer and inner rim side with a significantly thinner rim top, it has some affinities with the assemblage of House 41 (RE406ad, secondary fills), whereas no clear relationships can be seen to the other reference assemblages. Some affinities with the assemblage of House 14 (RE258ba, secondary fills) do, however, seem recognizable. **RE798bd**: Having a bent-out rim with almost straight outer and inner sides as well as a significant thinning of the rim top, it must share the same affinities as RE798ae. **RE798bc**: Showing only a slight thinning of the rim top, it appears likewise to share some of the same affinities as RE798ae. **RE798bb**: With its slightly convex outer and inner rim sides combined with a significantly tapering profile, it has some affinities with the assemblages of House 41 (RE409aa, sunken-floor horizon) and House 2 (RE7ac & RE7ad, secondary fills). **RE798bk**: Being very fragmented with a cordon preserved and the inner side missing, it shows affinities with the assemblages of House 134 (RE564aa & RE564bb, secondary fills) and House 41 (RE406as & RE406at, secondary fills).

Fig. 3.19. House 289, affinities in detail

No rim profiles were found in the sunken-floor horizon. Secondary fills: **RE900bd:** It has a smoothly turned-out rim, gradually becoming slightly thicker upwards with concave outer side and convex inner side. When ignoring the cordon, it has affinities in general to the assemblages of House 134 (RE564aa, secondary fills) and House 41 (RE417aa, secondary fills). **RE1056aa:** With smoothly turned-out rim, it more or less has relationships matching those of RE900bd. **RE900ah:** With the rim powerfully bent outwards, it shows some relationship in general to the assemblages of House 41 (406ce, secondary fills) and House 2 (RE191aa, secondary fills). The particular feature of tapering rim top has affinities with the assemblages of House 41 (RE406af, secondary fills) and House 2 (RE191aa, secondary fills). **RE900aj:** It has a convex outer rim side and appears thickened, having an almost flat inner rim side. The rim is strongly bent outwards. Apart from the thickening, the affinities of the rim are in general similar to the assemblages of House 41 (406ce, secondary fills) and House 2 (RE191aa, secondary fills). **RE1058aa:** The rim is angularly bent outwards and has a convex outer side and an almost straight inner side. The relationship to other reference assemblages is more or less similar to that of RE900aj. **RE900aa:** The rim has a concave outer side and convex inner side. The rim top is turned out. The upper part of the body as a whole has a concave-convex profile contour and does not show clear affinities with any of the reference assemblages. The profile might have a limited affinity with the assemblage of House 41 (RE406ad, secondary fills). It shows some affinities with the assemblage of House 200 (RE783aa, sunken-floor horizon). **RE900ao:** Having a bent-out rim top and the outer rim side slightly convex, while on the inner side being obliquely bevelled and presenting a thin tapering rim top, it shows affinities with the assemblage of House 41 (RE420aa, secondary fills), as well as the assemblages of House 130 (RE539ac & RE539ab, secondary fills) and House 200 (RE760aa, sunken-floor horizon). **RE900ad:** With the upper part of the rim significantly turned out and tapering into a fairly thin end, and the rim top being obliquely bevelled, it appears to have almost the same affinities as RE900ao, due to the rim-top design in particular. **RE900ak:** It has out-turned rim, and almost straight outer and inner sides. The profile retains the same, relatively heavy thickness and is obliquely bevelled at the inner rim top. It does not show clear relationships to any of the reference assemblages but possibly has a weak relationship to the assemblage of House 42 (RE654ae, secondary fills). **RE900ag:** It has out-turned rim with concave outer side and convex inner side, retaining an almost equal rim thickness. On the outer side, it has a marked transition to the body with a smooth profiling of a low cordon-like feature on the inner side. It does not have close relationships to any of the reference assemblages but some moderate affinities with the assemblages of House 134 (RE596ab, sunken-floor horizon) and House 41 (RE422aa, sunken-floor horizon), while weakly also with that of House 130 (RE539bc, secondary fills).

Fig. 3.20. House 10, affinities in detail

Sunken-floor horizon: **RE310aa:** Supplied with a horizontal furrow below the broad rim, it has some relationship to the House 2 assemblage (RE176aa, sunken-floor horizon) and a relatively close relationship to the House 1 assemblage (RE31aa, sunken-floor horizon). **RE310ab:** With bent-out rim and evenly thickening at the transition to the belly, the profile has clear relationships to the assemblage of House 2 (RE92aa, sunken-floor horizon, and not least RE7ae, secondary fills), as well as some affinities with the assemblage of House 41 (RE416aa, sunken-floor horizon). **RE310ae:** With smooth profiling, having a turned out rim and a slight thickening at the transition to the rim, it shows clear affinities with the assemblages of House 41 (RE406af, secondary fills) and House 1 (RE153aa, sunken-floor horizon), as well as some affinities with the assemblage of House 2 (RE191aa, sunken-floor horizon). **RE310ad:** With its profiling reminiscent of RE310ae but being relatively thick at the transition to the rim and tapering towards the comparatively thin rim top, it may share more or less the same relationships as the foregoing specimen. **RE310ac:** Indicating a bent-out rim, it shows affinities in general with the reference assemblages of House 41, House 2, and House 1.

Secondary fills: **RE260aa:** With its combination of a furrow and bent-out rim, it seems to have affinities with the assemblages from House 2 (RE176aa, sunken-floor horizon) and House 1 (RE31aa, sunken-floor horizon). **RE260ae:** The evenly rounded shaping is that of an open bowl having affinities with the assemblages of House 134 (RE564ad & 564ba, secondary fills) House 41 (RE406cc & RE406cd, secondary fills) and House 2 (RE7ah, secondary fills). **RE206ai:** With a slightly thickened rim top, it belongs to the open bowl group and it has more or less the same relationships. **RE260ac & RE260am:** Having bent-out rims, they can be referred to more or less as having the same relationships as RE310ac. **RE260ak.** With an out-turned rim and an almost vertically bevelled rim top, it has affinities with the assemblage of House 2

(RE7ak, secondary fills). This special feature was also present in the assemblages of Houses 128 (RE540ae) and 130 (RE539al).

Fig. 3.21. House 12, affinities in detail

No rim profiles were found in the sunken-floor horizon. Secondary fills: **RE250af**: This profile, with its relatively thick rim top could almost similarly be found in the reference assemblages and cannot presently contribute to a closer dating. **RE250aj**: It has a curved profiling with much resemblance not least to the House 134 pottery assemblage (RE564ad & RE564ab, secondary fills) but also to some later assemblages. **RE250ag**, **RE250ah**, and **RE250ai**: These rims all have an almost straight outer side and a slightly curved inner side and all get thinner nearer the rim top. Rim profiles with some affinity are present in the assemblages of House 134 (RE564ac, secondary fills), House 41 (RE406cc & 406cd, secondary fills), House 2 (RE7an, secondary fills) and House 1 (RE28aa, sunken-floor horizon). These three profiles possibly represent classic open bowls.

Fig. 3.22. House 84, affinities in detail

No rim profiles were found in the sunken-floor horizon. Secondary fills: **RE485aa**: With its gently curved profile from the belly to the out-turned rim, which is somewhat thickened, it appears to have relatively strong affinities with the House 134 assemblage (RE564ab, secondary fills) and evidently also to other ceramics belonging to this assemblage.

Fig. 3.23. House 112, affinities in detail

No rim profiles were found in the sunken-floor horizon. Secondary fills: **RE513aa**: It has a smoothly turned-out profile that shows some relationship to the assemblage of House 134 (RE564ac, RE564ad, & RE564ba, secondary fills) and, to lesser degree, also to House 2 (RE7an, secondary fills) whereas no concrete profiles from House 41 show close relationships, except for the tendency to be supplied with relatively thin, turned-out rims. It is, however, precisely this feature that is rather characteristic of several clay pot profiles in the House 41 assemblage and there might well be a significant relationship. Some affinity with the assemblage of House 13 (RE655ag, secondary fills) can also be seen.

Fig. 3.24. House 158, affinities in detail

No rim profiles were found in the sunken-floor horizon. Secondary fills: **RE1040ab**: With its rim characteristically turned out, it shows clear affinities with the assemblage of House 134 (RE594ac, sunken-floor horizon, and not least RE564ba, secondary fills, as well as, when not taking into account the horizontal cordon, clear affinities also with RE564aa, secondary fills). The profile also shows some relationship to the assemblage of House 41 (RE408aa & RE404aa, sunken-floor horizon, & RE420aa, secondary fills). There is possibly also a weak relationship to the assemblage of House 2 (RE119aa/121aa, sunken-floor horizon). Among the materials that are not used as reference assemblages in this chronological analysis, a few have resembling profiles. It thus shows affinities with the assemblage of House 289 (RE900bd, secondary fills). **RE1040aa**: It resembles to some degree the previous profile and can be considered to have more or less the same affinities. **RE1040ac**: It has an almost straight inner rim side and the outer side is a little drawn back, so that the rim appears slightly thinner. It probably represents an open bowl. It may show affinities with the assemblage of House 134 (RE596aa & RE594ab, sunken-floor horizon). It shows affinities with the assemblage of House 41 (RE406cc, secondary fills) and also with the assemblage of House 2 (RE7ah).

Fig. 3.25. House 183, affinities in detail

No rim profiles were found in the sunken-floor horizon. Secondary fills: **RE666ad** & **RE666ae**: Both are rather short profiles with out-turned rims and show relationships to the assemblages of House 134 (RE564ah & RE564ad, secondary fills) and House 41 (RE417aa, secondary fills & RE404aa, sunken-floor horizon). They also appear to have affinities with the assemblage of House 2 (RE191aa, secondary fills). **RE666af**: With its bent-out profile and characteristic rim-top finish, it has no clear counterparts in any of the four reference materials. **RE666ab**, **RE666ac** & **RE666ag**: Having almost straight or only slightly curved inner and outer sides, these three profiles belong to the group of open bowls. They are probably related to the assemblages of House 134 (RE596aa & RE594ab, sunken-floor horizon), House 41 (RE406ad & RE406cc, secondary fills) and House 2 (RE7ah, secondary fills).

Fig. 3.26. House 193, affinities in detail

No rim profiles were found in the sunken-floor horizon or secondary fills. Two profiles stem from a posthole of the northern wall. **RE675aa**: The outer and inner rim sides are almost straight and retain almost the same thickness until near the bottom. The upper part resembles a classic open bowl which has affinities with, not least, the assemblage of House 134 (RE596aa, sunken-floor horizon). The lower part is – contrary to most simple bowls – supplied with a foot ring that has parallels in the assemblages of House 198 (RE678ag, secondary fills, not shown) and House 183 (RE666ah, not shown). The foot ring is quite slender with tapering end, while the specimen from 198 is more solid with an angular end. The foot ring from House 183 is relatively low and thin. **RE675ab**: The rim profile has almost straight outer and inner sides, slightly thickening towards the top. It represents an open bowl which has affinities with the assemblages of House 134 (RE596ac, sunken-floor horizon), House 41 (RE406cd, secondary fills) and House 2 (RE7ah, secondary fills).

Fig. 3.27. House 198, affinities in detail

No rim profiles were found in the sunken-floor horizon. Secondary fills: **RE678aa**: With the shape of a bowl with a characteristically bent-out rim, it shows a rather close relationship to the assemblage of House 41 (RE408aa, sunken-floor horizon) and a faint relationship to that of House 2 (RE119aa/RE121aa). **RE678ab**: With its short, bent-out rim, it displays some relationship to the assemblage of House 41 (RE420aa & RE406ca, secondary fills). **RE678ae & RE678aj**: With their relatively large, bent-out rims and straight or slightly convex outer rim sides, these profiles have some affinities with the assemblage of House 41 (RE406ce, secondary fills) but also generally with the assemblages of House 2 and House 1, both containing bent-out rim profiles of various kinds. **RE678ac**: It shows the same affinities as RE678ae. **RE1059aa**: With a gently curved upper part, it has some relationships to the assemblage of House 134 (RE564ba, RE564aa & RE564 bb, when ignoring the cordons, secondary fills) and some affinities with the assemblage of House 41 (RE417aa, secondary fills). The rim of RE1059aa is more marked and the curving less even than that of specimens in the assemblage of House 134. **RE634aa**: The rim-top finish shows affinities with the assemblage of House 183 (RE666af, secondary fills). **RE634ab**: Having a flat, horizontal rim top which is neither thickened nor thinned, it appears to have some affinities with the assemblage of House 41 (the uppermost part of RE410aa, sunken-floor horizon). As to the manner of finishing the uppermost part, it also displays some affinities with the assemblage of House 134 (RE564ba, secondary fills). **RE634ac**: When it comes to the rim-top finish, it may have the same affinities as RE634 ab.

Fig. 3.28. House 268, affinities in detail

Sunken-floor horizon: **RE849ac**: With its bent-out rim, having convex outer side above a relatively broad horizontal furrow and an almost flat inner rim side, it is very closely related to the assemblage of House 1 (RE31aa, sunken-floor horizon) and displays some relationships to the assemblage of House 2 (RE176aa, sunken-floor horizon). It furthermore shows fine affinities with the assemblages of House 200 (RE793aa, sunken-floor horizon) and House 14 (RE282aa, sunken-floor horizon). **RE849aa**: Having a bent-out rim with convex outer rim side and slightly concave inner rim side, and retaining almost the same profile thickness in the rim and body side, it has no direct counterparts in the reference assemblages but shows at least some affinities with the assemblage of House 2 (RE133aa, sunken-floor horizon). **RE844ab**: Supplied with a turned-out rim, having convex outer rim side and slightly convex inner rim side, it shows some affinities with the assemblages of House 1 (RE6af, secondary fills & RE39aa, sunken floor horizon) and House 2 (RE191aa & RE7ab, both secondary fills, & RE176aa, ignoring the horizontal furrow, sunken-floor horizon), besides a weak relationship to the assemblage of House 41 (RE409aa & RE416aa, both sunken-floor horizon). It furthermore shows a relationship to the assemblage of House 14 (RE298ab, sunken-floor horizon, & RE258aq, secondary fills). **RE843aa /846aa**: Having bent-out rim with slightly convex outer side, correspondingly slight concave inner side and, at the transition to the body, a marked thickening ("knee") on the inner side, it shows close affinities with the assemblage of House 2 (RE92aa, sunken-floor horizon, & RE7ae, secondary fills).

Secondary fills: **RE824af**: Having bent-out rim with convex outer side above a horizontal furrow and convex inner side, it shows very close relations to the assemblage of House 1 (RE31aa, sunken-floor horizon), as well as some affinities with the assemblage of House 2 (RE176aa, sunken-floor horizon). **RE833aa:** With bent-out rim, convex outer side and slightly concave inner side, it shares similar relationships to RE844ab. **RE824ae:** Having a turned-out rim with convex outer rim side and slightly convex inner rim side, it shares the same relationships as RE844 ab. **RE824ac:** With a turned-out rim, having pronounced convex outer rim side and almost straight inner rim side, it shows some weak relationship to the assemblages of House 1 (RE-6af, secondary fills) and House 2 (RE191aa, secondary fills). It displays some more specific affinities with the assemblages of House 14 (RE258ba, secondary fills), House 200 (RE791aa & RE790aa, sunken-floor horizon, both being also relatively thinner at the rim top) and House 240 (RE799aa, secondary fills, though not supplied with a "knee" on the inner side at the transition to the body). **RE840aa:** Having a bent-out rim with a convex outer side above a marked transition to the body and a concave-convex inner side, the profile does not have regular counterparts among the reference assemblages. However, the relatively low-positioned inner side bending at the transition to the body displays some affinity with the assemblages of House 14 (RE258bs, secondary fills) and House 200 (RE750ae, secondary fills). This low inner side bending can also be observed in another profile supplied with a horizontal furrow, being from the assemblage of House 200 (RE793aa, sunken-floor horizon) and that of House 240 (RE798aa, secondary fills). **RE824aa:** It has a relatively broad, bent-out rim with almost flat outer side and faintly convex inner side, thereby appearing as having almost the same thickness. It is worth remarking on the affinities with rims from the assemblages of House 14 (RE290aa & RE441aa, sunken-floor horizon), House 200 (750bh, secondary fills) and House 10 (RE310aa, sunken-floor horizon). **RE824ah:** The profile fragment stems from a rather massive clay pot. Missing the rim, the relatively thin uppermost part could perhaps be part of a broad horizontal furrow, and might in that case be shaped somewhat like RE824af. **RE837aa:** Supplied with a turned-out rim having a fairly concave outer side above a marked transition to the body and a correspondingly convex inner side, it does not seem to have clear affinities with any of the reference assemblages. The design of the clay pot likely indicates a relatively late chronological position. The inclination of the profile is not certain. **RE270aa:** Having a turned-out rim, a concave outer rim side with a low cordon-like feature and a convex-straight inner rim side, it does not have close relationships to profiles from the reference assemblages. The inclination of the profile is not certain. **RE824ab:** Supplied with a slightly turned-out rim that has a concave part and a low, somewhat cordon-like feature horizontally on the outer rim side. The inner rim side is rather straight. The profile does not display a close affinity with any of the reference assemblages but has elements of form in common with the above RE270aa. **RE257aa:** It is supplied with a relatively short rim, slightly drawn back with concave outer side and faintly convex inner side. The rim top is flattened and tapering towards the outer side. It shows no clear affinities with any of the reference assemblages. Concerning the flattened rim top, it has some relationship to the assemblage of House 128 (RE540ac, secondary fills). Further it has some weak affinities with the assemblages of House 197 (RE278aa, secondary fills) and, as regards the rim top tapering towards the outer side, House 200 (RE760aa, sunken-floor horizon) and House 289 (RE900ad, secondary fills).

Fig. 3.29. House 201, affinities in detail

No rim profiles were found in the sunken-floor horizon. Secondary fills: **RE972aa:** With a somewhat bent-out rim with a straight outer side and a convex inner side, it appears to have some affinities on a general level with the reference assemblages of House 41 (RE-406af, secondary fills & possibly also RE404aa, sunken-floor horizon) and House 2 (RE7ad, secondary fills), as well as with a number of other assemblages.

Fig. 3.31. Pit 160, affinities in detail

RE632ab: It has a smoothly turned-out rim with a marked concave outer side and a correspondingly convex inner side. It has close affinities with the assemblages of House 134 (RE564bb, when ignoring the horizontal cordon) and House 41 (RE417aa, secondary fills). It also has weak affinities with the assemblages of House 2 (RE191aa) and House 42 (RE445aa, sunken-floor horizon), as well as the assemblage from pit 161 (RE636ae, see below).

Fig. 3.32. Pit 161, affinities in detail

RE636aa: The smoothly out-turned rim with concave outer rim side and convex inner rim side and a slight thickening is closely related to the assemblage of House 134 (RE564bb, secondary fills, ignoring the horizontal cordon), and has some relationship to the assemblages of House 41 (RE417aa, secondary fills) and House 42 (RE445aa, sunken-floor horizon). **RE636ag:** The smoothly out-turned rim with concave outer side and convex inner side and a faint thickening has the same affinities as RE636aa. **RE636af:** The smoothly out-turned rim with concave outer rim side and convex inner rim side and a slight thickening of the rim has the same affinities as RE636aa. As to the bent-out rim top, the best affinities concern the assemblage of House 134 (RE564ba, secondary fills). **RE636ac:** The smoothly out-turned rim with concave outer rim side and convex inner rim side shares the same affinities as RE636af. **RE636ae:** The rim has almost straight, vertical outer and inner rim sides and the rim is thickened compared to the upper part of the body. As to the main pot form, it may have affinities with the assemblages of House 41 (RE410aa, sunken-floor horizon) and House 2 (RE133aa, sunken-floor horizon). **RE636ab**: The rim has a slightly convex outer side and almost straight inner side. It presumably represents a classic open bowl which, among the reference materials, has relationships to not least the assemblages of House 134 (RE596aa, sunken-floor horizon), House 41 (RE406cc, secondary fills) and House 2 (RE7ah, secondary fills). **RE636ax:** The rim has a faintly convex outer side and concave inner side, the rim top being slightly thickened. It seems to share the same relationships as the open bowl RE636ab. **RE636ay**: The outer and inner rim sides are almost straight with a slight thickening towards the rim top. It seems to share the same relationships as the open bowl RE636ab. **RE636ad:** The outer rim side and inner rim side are almost straight, although with the rim top slightly drawn inwards. It must more or less share the same relationships as RE636ab but the rim top feature is not known from the reference assemblages. **RE636ah:** The outer rim side is faintly convex and the inner rim side correspondingly concave, thereby retaining almost the same thickness. The rim top is obliquely bevelled. It probably represents an open bowl and seems to have the same relationships as RE636ab although the feature of the rim top is not known from the reference assemblages. **RE636as:** The rim has a slightly convex outer side and almost straight inner side. The rim top is drawn a little out at the outer side. It has no clear counterparts among the reference assemblages. **RE636an**: The concave outer side is supplied with a horizontal cordon (probably a little below the rim top) and the inner side is convex.

It displays clear relationships to the assemblages of House 134 (RE564bb, secondary fills) and House 41 (RE406as, secondary fills). **RE636au:** The rim is angularly bent outwards, having almost straight outer and inner sides combined with a slight thickening of the rim top. There are no clear counterparts among the reference assemblages.

Fig. 3.33. Pit 319, affinities in detail

RE693aa: The rim has a slightly convex outer and inner rim side. The rim top is almost evenly rounded. It represents a classic open bowl with relationships on a general level to, not least, the assemblages of House 134 (RE596aa, sunken-floor horizon), House 41 (RE406cc & 406cd, secondary fills) and possibly also, to some extent, the assemblage of House 2 (RE7ah, secondary fills). **RE693ab:** The rim has a slightly convex outer and inner side. The rim top is slightly turned more upright. **RE693ac:** The rim has a slightly convex outer and inner side. The rim top is evenly rounded. **RE693ad**: The rim has a slightly convex outer and inner rim side. The rim top is slightly prolonged inwards. **RE693ae**: The rim has a slightly convex outer and inner side. The rim top is slightly broadened. **RE693af**: The rim has a slightly convex outer and inner side. The rim top is faintly thinner. The five last specimens represent open bowls similar to RE693aa and have the same affinities.

Fig. 3.34. Pit 316, affinities in detail

RE694ac: The rim is convex on the outer side, retaining almost the same, modest thickness. It represents a classic open bowl. Among others, it has some affinities with the assemblages of House 134 (596aa, sunken-floor horizon), House 41 (406cc, secondary fills) and possibly House 2 (RE7ah, secondary fills). **RE694ae:** The rim is convex on the outer side, retaining almost same thickness. It represents an open bowl similar to RE694ac and has corresponding affinities. **RE694af:** The rim is convex on the outer side and concave on the inner side, retaining almost the same thickness. Like RE694ac it represents an open bowl and has corresponding affinities. **RE694ab:** The rim represents an open bowl. The rim top is relatively thin and might in this respect show some affinities with the assemblage of House 41 (RE406cd, secondary fills). It also has relationships corresponding to those of RE694ac in general. **RE694ad:** The rim represents an open bowl. It has relationships similar to RE694ac in general. The rim top is only slightly tapering and may not provide a basis for specific suggestions of affinities. **RE694aa:** The rim is convex on the outer side. It presumably represents a classic open bowl. It has relationships similar to RE694ac. The rim top is tapering above a slight, smoothly designed thickening of the profile but clear counterparts in the reference materials are not observable.

Fig. 3.35. Pit 317, affinities in detail

RE695af: The rim is convex on the outer side, retaining almost the same profile thickness. It represents a classic open bowl. Among the reference assemblages, the profile shows some relationship to the assemblages of House 134 (596aa, sunken-floor horizon), House 41 (406cc, secondary fills) and possibly House 2 (RE7ah, secondary fills). **RE695ai:** The rim is convex on the outer side and slightly convex-concave on the inner side. It represents an open bowl. The profile has the same relationships as RE695af. **RE695ah:** The rim is convex on the outer side and concave on the inner side. It represents an open bowl. The profile has the same relationships as RE695af. The rim top is markedly thinner than the body and appears to show some affinities with the assemblage of House 41 (RE406cd, secondary fills) although, in detail, the design is different. **RE695ad:** The rim is convex on the outer side. It represents a classic open bowl. The profile has the same relationships as RE695af. The upper part of the rim is slightly thickened but this feature is without parallel in the reference assemblages. **RE695aa:** The rim has almost straight outer and inner sides. It represents an open bowl, having affinities with the assemblage of House 134 (RE564ac, sunken-floor horizon). **RE695ab:** The rim has almost straight outer and inner rim sides. A slight thickening marks the rim top. It represents an open bowl. It probably shares the same affinities as RE695aa. **RE695ac:** The rim is smoothly turned out, having a faintly concave outer side and, correspondingly, a faintly convex inner side combined with a slight, gradual thickening of the rim. The profile displays close relationships to the assemblage of House 134 (564bb, secondary fills, ignoring the horizontal cordon) and to the assemblage of House 41 (RE417aa, secondary fills). Further it has some affinities with the assemblage of House 42 (RE445aa, sunken-floor horizon). **RE695aj:** The rim is turned out, having a concave outer rim side and a tapering rim top. The profile shows some relationship to the assemblage of House 134 (RE564ab, secondary fills), the assemblage of House 41 (RE420aa, secondary fills) and possibly also the assemblage of House 2 (RE119aa/121aa, sunken-floor horizon).

Fig. 3.36. Pit 89, affinities in detail

RE484aa: The rim has almost straight outer and inner sides. The rim top is faintly bent out from the body. It represents a classic open bowl which, among the reference assemblages, has affinities with the assemblage of House 134 (RE564ac, sunken-floor horizon). It also appears to have some affinity with the assemblage of House 2 (RE7an, secondary fills). **RE484ac:** The rim has almost straight outer and inner sides. The rim top of the open bowl is slightly bent out like RE484aa. **RE484ad:** The rim has almost straight outer and inner sides. Both of these last two profiles seem to share more or less the same relationships as RE484aa.

Fig. 3.37. Pit 278, affinities in detail

RE880aa: The rim has a convex outer side and a straight inner side. At the transition to the rounded upper part of the body, it has a narrow horizontal furrow on the outer side opposite a smooth bend on the inner side. The profile shows some affinity with the assemblages of House 41 (RE416aa, sunken-floor horizon), House 2 (RE176aa, sunken-floor horizon) and House 1 (RE31aa, sunken-floor horizon). It also has some affinities with the assemblages of House 14 (RE296aa, sunken-floor horizon), House 138 (RE614aa, sunken-floor horizon) and House 200 (RE791aa & RE793aa, sunken-floor horizon). Clear affinities with the assemblages of House X (RE260ab, secondary fills) and House 240 (RE858aa, sunken-floor horizon, & RE798ba & RE799aa, secondary fills) are also observable. In addition, it may have some weak affinities with the assemblage of House 42 (RE654aa, secondary fills). **RE880ab:** The major part of the rim is missing but the preserved part seems to indicate a slightly concave outer side and a straight or slightly convex inner side. On the outer side it has a rounded shoulder, while on the inner side it has a drawn back "knee" at the transition to the rim. It shows some affinities with the assemblages of House 1 (RE31aa, sunken-floor horizon), House 2 (RE176aa, sunken-floor horizon) and House 41 (RE403aa /411aa & RE416aa, sunken-floor horizon). It also has affinities with the assemblages of House 14 (RE290aa, sunken-floor horizon & RE258aq, secondary fills), House 42 (RE654ai, secondary fills), House 138 (RE614aa, sunken-floor horizon), House 200 (RE790aa, sunken-floor horizon), House 10 (RE310ab, sunken-floor horizon) and House 240 (RE876aa, sunken-floor horizon, and RE798bg, RE860aa & RE799aa, all secondary fills). In addition, it possibly also has weak affinities with the House 130 assemblage (RE539aa, secondary fills). **RE880ac:** The outer rim side is convex and the inner side concave. There is a slight indication of what might have been a horizontal furrow below the rim. In the assemblage of House 2 (RE176aa, sunken-floor horizon), there is probably a fairly close match to this rim which, in general, seems by and large to share the same relationships as RE880aa.

Fig. 3.38. Pit 310, affinities in detail

RE692ab: The rim and upper part of the body incline inwards, while the rim has a convex outer side. The rim top is smoothly turned out. The profiling clearly has a relationship to the assemblage of House 134 (RE564ab & RE564ba, secondary fills). **RE692aa:** The rim and upper part of the body incline inwards and the rim has a convex outer side. The rim top is smoothly turned out. The clay pot is supplied with a horizontal cordon and it is clearly reminiscent of rims from the House 134 material (RE564aa & RE564bb). To some degree, it also resembles profiles from the assemblage of House 41 (RE406as & RE406at, secondary fills) but, as only side fragments are preserved, the shaping of the rim tops cannot be compared. **RE692af:** The tapering rim is smoothly bent outwards and has a slightly convex outer side. It displays relationships to the assemblages of House 134 (RE564aa, secondary fills, ignoring the cordon) and possibly also to the assemblage of House 41 (RE406ce, secondary fills).

Fig. 3.39. Pit 311, affinities in detail

RE196ab: With its smoothly curved, convex inner side and correspondingly smooth shaping of the horizontal cordon, it has clear affinities with the assemblage of House 134 (RE564bb, secondary fills & RE596ab, sunken-floor horizon). Albeit less so, it also shows some affinities with the assemblage of House 41 (RE406as, secondary fills). However, the profile appears to have some affinities with a side profile from the assemblage of House 240 (RE798bk, secondary fills). **RE196ac:** The rim has out-turned, almost straight outer and inner sides with a faint decrease in thickening below the rim top, combined with a slight thickening of the rim top itself. It does not have a clear relationship with any of the four reference assemblages but shows perhaps some relationship to the assemblage of House 13 (RE655ad, secondary fills). **RE196ad:** The rim is turned out with a convex outer side, retaining almost the same profile thickness. It does not have any parallels in the reference assemblages.

Fig. 3.40. Pit 320, affinities in detail

RE81bb/RE85aa: The rim is drawn back and concave on its lower outer rim side above the marked transition to the body (shoulder). The inner rim side is smoothly shaped without a marked transition to the body. The rim has a relatively close counterpart in the assemblage of House 2 (RE135aa, sunken-floor horizon). Close parallels are not present in any of the other reference assemblages but a profile with some common traits (RE406cb, secondary fills) is present from the House 41 assemblage. The profile also displays some relationship to the assemblage of House 1 (RE31aa, sunken-floor horizon). **RE81aa:** Although missing the rim, the shaping of the side, with a marked transition to the body (shoulder), indicates that it possibly had about the same design as RE81bb/85aa and thereby also shares the same relationships.

Fig. 3.41. Pit 77, affinities in detail

RE469aa: The elegantly swayed outline of the profile has affinities with the assemblages of House 158 (RE1040aa, secondary fills) and House 198 (RE1059aa, secondary fills), as well as relationships of differing strength to e.g. the assemblages of House 200 (RE750ca, secondary fills), House 2 (RE119aa/121aa), House 84 (RE485aa), House 134 (RE564ba), (RE1059aa) and House 10 (RE310ae). The profile also has relationships to finds from early pits such as pit 322 (RE591aa) and pit 161 (RE636aa).

Fig. 3.42. Pit 80, affinities in detail

RE478aa: The rim has a concave outer side and gets gradually wider as it goes up. The rim top is smoothly and significantly bent out. The profile displays a relatively close relationship to the assemblage of House 41

(RE406ca, secondary fills) and also some relationship to the assemblage of House 134 (RE564ba, secondary fills). Concerning, in particular, the feature of the bent-out rim top, the profile has some affinities with the assemblages of House 128 (RE540ac, secondary fills), House 130 (RE539ap, secondary fills), House 197 (RE278aa, secondary fills) and House 198 (RE678ab, secondary fills).

Fig. 3.43. Pit 85, affinities in detail

RE486aa: The outer rim side as a whole forms a concave area above a marked transition to the convex outer side. The inner rim side is concave above a drawn back area, forming a "knee". The rim top is obliquely bevelled in a rounded fashion on the outer side. The profile exhibits affinities with the assemblage of House 41 (RE403aa/411aa, sunken-floor horizon, & to some degree also with RE406ac, secondary fills) and, weakly, also with the assemblage of House 2 (RE134aa, sunken-floor horizon). The profile shows very clear and strong affinities with the assemblage of House 130 (RE539ad, secondary fills).

Fig. 3.44. Pit 100, affinities in detail

RE504aa: The rim has a faintly convex outer and correspondingly concave inner side. It represents a classic open bowl, having affinities with the assemblage of House 134 (RE564ac, sunken-floor horizon) and other assemblages with open bowls. Perhaps some affinity with that of House 2 (RE7an, secondary fills).

Fig. 3.45. Pit 111, affinities in detail

RE520aa: The rim is missing. The body has considerable thickness but the profile appears to become considerably thinner just above the marked transition to the rim. A horizontal furrow there cannot be excluded. Profiles resembling more or less the preserved outline are observable in the assemblages of House 41 (RE403aa/411aa & RE412aa, sunken-floor horizon), House 2 (RE135aa, sunken-floor horizon) and House 1 (RE31aa, sunken-floor horizon). Further relationships seem present in the assemblages of House 13 (RE272aa, sunken-floor horizon), House 14 (RE296aa, sunken-floor horizon & RE258at, secondary fills), House 42 (RE441aa, sunken-floor horizon), House 130 (539at, secondary fills), House 138 (RE614aa, sunken-floor horizon), House 200 (RE791aa & RE793aa, sunken-floor horizon), House 10 (RE310aa, sunken-floor horizon), House 240 (RE793ac, secondary fills) and House 268 (RE849ac, sunken-floor horizon & RE824af, RE824ai & RE824ah, secondary fills).

Fig. 3.46. Pit 312, affinities in detail

RE225aa: The rim has a convex outer side of almost equal thickness. It represents a classic open bowl which, among the reference assemblages, has affinities with the assemblages of House 134 (RE596aa, sunken-floor horizon), House 41 (RE406 cc, secondary fills) and House 2 (RE7ah, secondary fills).

Fig. 3.47. Pit 313, affinities in detail

RE231aa: The rim has faintly convex outer and inner rim sides. The rim top is just faintly bent outwards from the body. It represents a classic open bowl which has some relationship to the assemblage of House 134 (RE564ac, secondary fills) and possibly that of House 2 (RE7an, secondary fills).

Fig. 3.48. Pit 315, affinities in detail

RE673aa: The rim is smoothly bent somewhat out. The upper part of the rim has almost straight sides. Below the rim, the body has a turned-out belly and the preserved clay pot profile exhibits a very pronounced curvature. The profile seems to display relatively close affinities with the assemblage of House 41 (RE406aa, secondary fills). The profile appears to have affinities with the assemblage of House 183 but the extent is difficult to evaluate (RE666ad & RE666ae, secondary fills).

Fig. 3.49-3.50. Culture layer 203, affinities in detail

RE1050aa: The rim with its convex outer side above a horizontal furrow and correspondingly concave inner side above a smoothly contoured "knee" shows relationships to the assemblages of House 2 (Re 176aa, sunken-floor horizon) and House 1 (RE31aa, sunken-floor horizon) and also weakly to the assemblage of House 41 (RE416aa, sunken-floor horizon). **RE1050ab:** The rim is smoothly out-turned with an almost straight outer rim side and slightly convex inner rim side. It has affinities with the assemblages of House 134 (RE564aa, secondary fills) and House 41 (RE417aa, secondary fills). **RE751cb:** The rim is turned out with slightly concave outer side and convex inner side. The somewhat upright, tapering rim (the thin rim top surface is missing) may, not least, indicate relationships to the assemblages of House 41 (RE406af, secondary fills) and House 2 (RE119aa/121aa & RE102aa, sunken-floor horizon). **RE1024ae:** The rim has convex outer and concave inner sides. The profile may share the same relationships as RE1050aa.

RE1024ab: The rim, having a convex outer side and a correspondingly concave inner side, may by and large share the same relationships as RE1050aa. **RE751ah:** The rim and the side lean outwards, having almost straight outer and inner rim sides with the rim top bent markedly out. The profile shows affinities with the assemblages of House 41 (RE406ad, secondary fills) and House 134 (RE594ac, sunken-floor horizon & RE564ba, secondary fills). **RE751ab:** The preserved part of the rim is concave with a marked transition (shoulder) to the body. Not least considering this transition, it might be related to the assemblages of House 41 (RE406ac, secondary fills), House 2 (RE134aa, sunken-floor horizon) and House 1 (RE134aa, sunken-floor horizon) although the straight body of RE751ab is not paralleled in these references. **RE1024aa:** The rim is out-turned with concave outer side and correspondingly convex inner side, retaining almost the same thickness. It has a markedly horizontal protrusion at the transition to the body opposite a slight recession on the inner side. The rim has no clear counterparts in the reference materials but may display affinities with the assemblages of House 14 (RE290aa, sunken-floor horizon) and House 268 (RE837aa & RE270aa, both secondary fills). **RE1000ad:** The rim is almost upright but shows a limited outwards bend with convex-concave outer and inner sides. The profile may show some affinities with the assemblage of House 2 (RE7ab, secondary fills), as well as the assemblages of House 130 (RE539ad, sunken-floor horizon) and House 200 (RE759aa, sunken-floor horizon). **RE653ac:** The rim is almost upright with concave outer side and convex inner side. The rim top is drawn somewhat outwards and may in this respect show some affinities with the assemblage of House 134 (RE594ac, sunken-floor horizon) although, considered as a whole, the profile does not seem to have clear counterparts in any of the house assemblages. A chronological position later than the reference assemblages should perhaps be considered. **RE1017ae:** Only the lower part of the rim is preserved. It indicates a concave outer rim side. The transition to the body ("shoulder"), also fragmentary, is marked similar to RE751ab and the profile presumably shares the same relationships. **RE751bc:** The out-turned rim has a concave outer side and a convex inner side combined with a thin, tapering rim top. It seems to share the same relationships as RE751cb. **RE751bj:** The rim has a convex outer side and seems to share the same relationships as RE1050aa. **RE751ae:** The rim has a convex outer side and correspondingly concave inner side above a marked "knee" at the transition to the body. A horizontal furrow was possibly present on the outer side. The profile seems to share the same relationships as RE1050aa. **RE751af:** The rim has a nearly upright, almost straight outer side above a horizontal furrow and concave-convex inner side. Apart from the details of the outer rim side design, the profile seems to have the same affinities as RE1050aa. **RE1017aa:** The rim is almost upright, being a little drawn back, with concave outer rim side above a marked transition to the body ("shoulder"). The inner rim side is smoothly convex. The profile has no clear parallels in any of the clay pot profiles from the settlement but some details show certain affinities. The concave outer rim side above the marked shoulder may, in its shaping, show some resemblance to the design of RE1024. In the combination of its concave outer rim side and almost upright position of the rim, it appears to display some resemblance to the assemblage of House 200 (RE750aj, secondary fills). **RE751bh:** The thin, tapering rim is almost upright with concave outer side and convex inner side. The small clay pot is supplied with a horizontally-projecting lug that has counterparts in the assemblages of House 200 (RE750cc, secondary fills), House 14 (RE298aa, sunken-floor horizon), House 240 (RE798bk, secondary fills), House 128 (RE546aa, sunken-floor horizon) and House 1 (RE6ai, secondary fills). Judged in isolation, the presence of the horizontally-projecting lug could point to a dating from somewhat before the time of House 2 to around the time of House 1, as the relative chronological positions of the other house assemblages mentioned are also placed within this frame. Yet, as the profile in question has no clear counterparts among the house assemblages, it might also be of a somewhat later date because it can be assumed that this kind of horizontally-projecting lug might have existed after the time of House 1.

Fig. 3.51. Culture layer 293, affinities in detail

RE910aa: The rim is somewhat bent outwards and has a convex outer side above a horizontal furrow and almost straight inner side with a smoothly contoured "knee" at the transition to the body. Among the reference assemblages it has relationships to that of House 2

(Re 176aa, sunken-floor horizon) and House 1 (RE31aa, sunken-floor horizon) and, to a lesser extent, the assemblage of House 41 (RE416aa, sunken-floor horizon). **RE976ap:** The rim has a convex outer side and likely shares about the same relationships as RE910aa. **RE976ae:** The rim is smoothly bent outwards. The outer rim side is slightly convex and the inner side correspondingly slightly concave above a slight "knee" at the transition to the body. It shows relationships to the assemblage of House 2 (RE92aa, sunken-floor horizon) and possibly also to the assemblage of House 41 (RE416aa, sunken-floor horizon). **RE976ab:** Above the marked transition to the body (shoulder), the upper part of the rim is gradually turned out. The rim has a concave outer side and correspondingly convex inner side, retaining almost the same thickness, with the rim top slightly marked. The profile has no parallels among the reference assemblages. **RE976be:** The almost upright rim has a concave outer rim side and, in some respects, resembles RE976ab although it has a relatively slack design. **RE976at:** The almost upright rim is slightly convex on the outer side above a low, horizontal furrow-like marking and fairly straight on the inner side. It seems to have some affinities with the assemblage of House 41 (RE412aa, sunken-floor horizon). It further seems to have some affinities with the assemblage of House 130 (RE539ad, secondary fills). **RE976bd:** The rim is supplied with a characteristic bent-out rim top combined with almost straight outer and inner rim sides. It has no affinities with any of the reference assemblages but some affinity with the assemblage of House 14 (RE258ab, secondary fills). **RE976bc:** The rim is almost straight on the outer and inner sides. It represents a classic open bowl. The profile has some relationship to the assemblages of House 134 (596aa, sunken-floor horizon), House 41 (406 cc, secondary fills) and others. **RE976af:** The smoothly out-turned rim with almost straight outer side and, when ignoring the cordon, slightly convex inner side has affinities with the assemblages of House 134 (RE564bb, secondary fills) and House 41 (RE417aa, secondary fills), and possibly House 2 (RE191aa, secondary fills). **RE976aa:** The rim is turned out and has slightly convex outer and inner sides. It has relationships with the assemblages of House 134 (RE564aa, ignoring the cordon, secondary fills) and House 41 (RE406ce, secondary fills). **RE976bb:** The out-turned rim has a slightly convex outer side. The profile shares the same relationships as RE976aa. **RE976ba:** The out-turned rim has almost straight outer and inner sides with the rim top tapering. The profile may, to some degree, share the same relationships as RE976aa. It also seems to have some weak affinities with the assemblage of House 2 (RE133aa, sunken-floor horizon).

Fig. 3.52. Culture layer 302, affinities in detail

RE1001aa: The rim, being turned out with concave outer side and correspondingly convex inner side, retains almost the same thickness throughout. When ignoring the horizontal cordon, it shows affinities with the assemblage of House 134 (RE564bb, secondary fills) and also that of House 41 (RE417aa, secondary fills). It may also have some weak affinities with the assemblage of House 2 (RE191aa, secondary fills). **RE1001ab:** The rim is out-turned with a concave outer side but fragmentary and it is not possible to state the general form. It seems likely that it represents almost the same shape as RE1001aa and thereby may share the same affinities.

Fig. 3.53. Culture layer 358, affinities in detail

RE577aa. The rim is bent outwards and has an almost straight outer side and slightly convex inner rim side. The rim does not have any clear counterparts in any of the house assemblages but shows some affinities with the assemblage of House 41 (RE408aa, sunken-floor horizon & RE406cb, secondary fills) and with the assemblage of House 2 (RE134aa, having a more marked profiling, secondary fills).

Part B. Classic sites, LN I or LN II/ emerging Bronze Age

Ceramics from the following seven locations are not illustrated in this work. Instead, references are given to figures in the original publications.

Myrhøj, some relationships

Several of the profile examples below are ornamented. When compared with the Resengaard assemblages, the following considerations seem relevant for the clay pot profiles (Figure references to Jensen 1973). **Fig. 28, 42, 47, 54, 62, 63, & 64:** Only vague affinities in general with some early pottery covered by the provisional Resengaard chronology. **Fig: 57, 59, 61, & 66.1:** No obvious affinities observed. Fig. **40:** Some affinities with the assemblage of House 134 (RE564aa, when ignoring the horizontal cordon). **Fig. 42 & 44:** No clear affinities observable. **Fig. 43:** Affinities with the assemblage of House 134 in general. As regards the thickening of the rim top, affinities with this assemblage, too (RE594ac). **Fig. 27:** Supplied with horizontal cordons. Affinities with the assemblage of House 134 (RE564aa & RE596ab, concerning proportion and cordon profile). **Fig. 65:** Some affinities with the assemblage of House 134 (RE564ba & RE596ab, when ignoring the cordon).

Tastum I, some relationships

When compared with the Resengaard assemblages, the following considerations seem relevant for the clay pot profiles (Figure references to Simonsen 1983, Figure 6, beginning with the profile to the left in the upper row being Fig. 6.1, the next one to the right being Fig. 6.2 and so forth). **Fig. 6.1:** The smooth turning of the profile has resemblances to the House 134 assemblage (RE564bb). The presence of horizontal cordons is also a feature in common but there is only a single cordon on the specimens from the House 134 assemblage (RE564ba & 564bb). The upright rim top is not present in the House 134 material. **Fig. 6.2:** As profile 6.1. **Fig. 6.3:** As profile 6.1, but presumably supplied with just one horizontal cordon similar to the profiles of the 134 assemblage. **Fig. 6.4:** The smooth bending out of the profile displays some affinities with the House 134 assemblage (RE564bb). The angular design of the cordon has no parallels in the 134 assemblage or other materials from Resengaard. **Fig. 6.5:** It has some relationship to the assemblages of House 41 (RE410aa) and House 2 (RE133aa). **Fig. 6.6:** As to the thickening of the rim top, it shows some affinities with the assemblage of House 134 (594ac). **Fig. 6.7:** It displays some affinities with the assemblages of House 134 (RE564ba & RE596ab, when ignoring the cordon) and House 41 (RE417aa). **Fig. 6.8:** Affinities with some Resengaard assemblages in general. **Fig. 6.9:** Probably the remains of a classic open bowl. Affinities with early Resengaard assemblages in general. **Fig. 7.1:** Some affinities with the assemblage of House 134 (RE564ab).

Egehøj, some relationships

When compared with the Resengaard assemblages, the following considerations seem relevant for the clay pot profiles (Figure references to Boas 1983). **Fig. 11:** Affinities in general (classic open bowls) with several of the Resengaard assemblages. **Fig. 10.7:** Some affinities with the House 128 assemblage (RE546aa) but the placement of the horizontal cordon fragment is somewhat lower in relation to the rim top. **Fig. 10.6:** Likewise some affinities with the House 128 assemblage (RE546aa) but, again, the placement of the horizontal cordon is lower. Some affinities with the assemblage of House 14 (RE258ac). **Fig. 10.8:** Some affinities with the assemblage of House 2 (RE102aa) as regards the combination of a very slim profile, the rim turned outwards and a furrow-like marking at the transition to the body. **Fig. 7:** Some affinities with the assemblages of House 2 (RE135aa & RE134aa) and House 14 (RE258bs). **Fig. 10.5:** Some affinities with the assemblage of House 14 (RE258ac, which also gradually thickens towards the rim top). **Fig. 10.4:** Some affinities as to the bevelling of the outer rim top with the assemblage of House 128 (RE540ae) and also weak affinities with the assemblage of House 10 (RE260ak). **Fig. 10.3:** Some affinities likewise concerning the bevelling of the outer rim top with the assemblages of House 128 (RE540ae) and House 10 (RE260ak). **Fig. 10.2:** Some weak affinities with the assemblages of House 14 (RE284aa), House 200 (RE790aa) and House 240 (RE798ba). **Fig. 10.1:** Weak affinities with the assemblage of House 138 (RE614ab). Some affinities with the assemblage of House 2 (RE176aa) and strong affinities with that of House 14 (RE258aq) and House 240 (RE799aa).

Torslev, some relationships

When compared with the Resengaard assemblages, the following considerations seem relevant for the clay pot profiles (Figure references to Rasmussen 1993). **Fig. 51.d:** Some affinities with the assemblage of House 268 (RE270aa, RE824ab, & RE837aa) as regards the accentuated transition to the body. From the waste area 203, a clay pot profile (RE1024aa) shows clearer affinities, having a marked protrusion at the transition to the body and a correspondingly small recession on the inner side. **Fig. 51.m:** The same affinities as the previous profile can, to some extent, be noted. **Fig. 51.c:** Only some general relationship with later Resengaard assemblages. **Fig. 51.k:** Some affinities with the assemblages of House 14 (RE258ao) and House 240 (RE798bd) regarding the thin, "squeezed" rim top. **Fig. 51.e:** The wavy contour of the in-turned profile seems rather unusual and does not have any clear affinities with the Resengaard ceramics. **Fig.**

50.a: No specific affinities observable. **Fig. 51.l:** No clear relationship but possible weak affinities with the assemblage of House 1 as regards the drawn back inner side, albeit without the marked shoulder. **Fig. 49.b:** Some affinities with the assemblages of House 1 (RE31aa), House 200 (RE793aa) and House 268 (RE824af). **Fig. 51.i:** Possibly some weak affinities with the assemblage of House 14 (RE297aa). **Fig. 49.e:** Some affinities with the assemblages of House 1 (RE31aa), House 200 (RE793aa) and House 268 (RE824af). **Fig. 51.g:** No clear affinities observed.

Vadgård Nord, some relationships

When compared with the Resengaard assemblages, the following considerations seem relevant for the clay pot profiles (Figure references to Rasmussen 1993). **Fig. 28.d:** Some fairly weak affinities with the House 268 assemblage (RE270aa, RE824ab, & RE837aa) as regards the accentuated transition to the body and with a profile from the dump area 203 (RE1024aa). **Fig. 28.c:** No clear affinities observed. **Fig. 26.b:** Only affinities in general (classic open bowls). **Fig. 27:** A profile representing a closed cup is e.g. present in the relatively late House 128 assemblage but, being so simple, it is not reasonable to refer to any specific resemblance apart from some affinities in general. **Fig. 28.b:** No clear affinities observed. **Fig. 28.a:** The thickening at the transition to the rim possibly has weak affinities with the assemblage of House 200 (RE783aa). **Fig. 30:** The thin tapering rim top, which is out-turned above a marked transition to the body, possibly seems to have some affinities with the assemblage of House 14 (RE258bj) and weak affinities with the assemblage of House 200 (RE750ba). **Fig. 28.e:** The markedly bellied form with slightly in-turned rim has some affinities with the assemblage of House 200 (RE750bm), if you ignore its "furrow" above the transition to the body.

Vadgård Syd, some relationships

When compared with the Resengaard assemblages, the following considerations seem relevant for the clay pot profiles (Figure references to Rasmussen 1993). **Fig. 39.d:** No clear affinities observed. **Fig. 39.b:** No clear affinities observed. **Fig. 39.c:** No clear affinities observed. **Fig. 38:** Only slight affinities of a general character. E: Fig. 39. A: No clear affinities observable in this extremely bellied profile.

Vejlby, some relationships

When compared with the Resengaard assemblages, the following considerations seem relevant for the clay pot profiles (Figure references to Jeppesen 1984). **Fig. 3.A:** The short, strongly turned-out rim top displays some affinities with the assemblages of House 41 (RE406ca), House 198 (RE678), House 200 (RE760aa) and House 128 (RE540ac). **Fig. 3.B:** The out-turned rim with convex outer side and concave inner side above a marked thickening, having a "knee" at the transition to the body, shows some affinities with the assemblages of House 41 (RE416aa), House 200 (RE769aa & RE791aa), House 2 (RE7ae), House 14 (RE799aa & 258aq) and House 10 (RE310 ad).

Part C. New sites, LN II/emerging Bronze Age

In both entries, the figure number in Ch. 3 of this book is given first.

Fig. 3.59. Gåsemose, House 1, some relationships

When compared with the Resengaard assemblages, the following considerations seem relevant for the clay pot profiles:

Excavation area I. **GÅ19:** Among the reference assemblages, close affinities with that of House 2 (RE176aa, with a convex outer rim side above a furrow-like transition to the body). Correspondingly, the rim side is slightly concave above a knee-like transition to the body. Some affinities also with the reference assemblages of House 1 (RE31aa) and House 41 (RE416aa). Furthermore, some affinities of varying degrees with the assemblages of House 14 (RE258bh), House 138 (RE614aa), House 200 (RE793aa), House 10 (RE310aa) and House 240 (RE858aa).

Excavation area II. **GÅ64:** Affinities similar to GÅ67, see below. **GÅ104:** Its strongly bent-out rim combined with slightly convex outer rim side, above a furrow-like transition to the body, and concave inner rim side above a faint, knee-like transition to the body (not illustrated in Ch. 3) corresponds to relationships much like those of the profile GÅ19. **GÅ108:** The gently curved profile with turned-out rim has affinities with the assemblage of House 41 (RE404aa, sunken-floor horizon).

Between excavation areas II and V: **GÅ67**: With its slightly convex outer rim side and correspondingly concave inner rim side above a distinct thickening ("knee") at the transition to the body, it displays affinities with the reference assemblages of House 2 (RE92aa) and House 41 (RE416aa). It further has some affinities with the assemblages of House 14 (RE284aa), House 138 (RE614) and House 200 (RE769aa), as well as relatively strong affinities with that of House 240 (RE799).

Excavation area V: **GÅ65**: The classic curved profile with turned-out rim has moderate affinities with the reference assemblages of House 41 (RE417aa) and House 2 (RE161aa & RE133a). **GÅ52**: Affinities much like GÅ65. **GÅ57**: Affinities to some degree like GÅ65. **GÅ111**: Affinities to some degree like GÅ65. **GÅ113**: Affinities to some degree like GÅ108.

Fig. 3.60. Kluborg II, House 5, some relationships

The clay pot profiles have some affinities with ceramics from Torslev and Vadgård Nord, as well as the youngest from Resengaard. See text. The inclination of the profiles belonging to KL25aa/38aa and KL16aa may have been slightly different.

Catalogue A

Ceramics at Resengaard

The catalogue concerns selected ceramics from Resengaard and is accompanied by profile drawings. The majority relate to parts of rims often also combined with upper parts of the bodies. In some instances, it has been possible to represent the entire clay pot profile, or most of it, while in others just some lower parts of the sides or bottom parts. The catalogue further includes clay items such as spoons, tubes and loom weights. The contexts of the ceramics are foremost sunken-floor house sites, but finds from culture layers and pits are also included.

The profiles have been drawn as meticulously as possible in order to also try to perceive rather minute details. It is not always an easy task, however, to make reconstruction drawings of the pottery from the period in question. Occurring lop-sidedness cannot be represented when only one or a few rim fragments are available, stemming from anywhere around the entire rim. Consequently, it has been my choice, when suggesting a two-dimensional reconstruction in drawing, to present the selected profile for the left side as well as for the right, thereby admitting that some of the possible asymmetries and individual "touches" of the ceramics will not come through. The profile considered most characteristic for the individual clay pot is, however, shown. Efforts have been made to assess the diameters and make reconstruction drawings showing opposite sides of as many clay pots as possible.

In all, these representations may provide fair impressions of the kinds of forms found. In many cases supporting materials such as for instance more rims are available and therefore can help to qualify the details of the profile. In a number of instances, it is possible that the suggested inclination of a clay pot part could have been different.

Some other kinds of information are given in the catalogue. This may relate to whether the diameter could have been different, whether the side is non-firm and crumbling, whether exposure to secondary burning is observable, whether soot or soot crust is present, whether certain clay pot parts belong together or whether ornaments, cordons or horizontally-projecting lugs are observable. Resources have not been available to make measurements of the tempering but many vessels have a coarse or even very coarse tempering, granite in particular, and do thus belong to coarse ware ceramics. Yet, when looking closer at the tempering, it very frequently appears that minor kinds of tempering are present in between the coarse grains. Even rather fine grains often seem present in the ware but might perhaps, at some scale, have been a natural component of the clay

One of the objectives of the above is clearly that the drawings should be instrumental in bringing about some idea of the pottery dimensions and forms of the centuries concerned. However, in some hundred cases, diameters could not safely be assessed and I have also therefore found it impossible to make symmetrical reconstruction drawings; their outer right side is therefore shown. It has been possible to state or suggest the total height for only a very small number of clay pots.

Generally, the pottery profiles are supported by measurements of the ware thickness at as many points (marked as round dots) as needed. These measurements are mentioned in the catalogue text in order, beginning with the uppermost measuring point on the concrete clay pot profile and working down (right to the bottom, when present). As it is not the intention in this present work to discuss terminology of forms, the neutral "clay pot" is therefore generally preferred.

The drawings are all made to full scale albeit here shown as a third of original size linearly (1:3).

Some of the clay pot profiles described and illustrated in the catalogue are highlighted in Chapter 3. In addition, many photos of the Resengaard pottery (Ch. 4 & 5), as well as some drawings of other burned clay items and a number of drawings of pottery from the Gåsemose settlement (Fig. 3.59) as a whole, help to give a broad impression of the local ceramics from LN II/emerging Bronze Age.

For the sake of legibility, the references to house contexts omit "site of". A catalogue number consists of the original serial number with the prefix "RE" (= Resengaard) added. This prefix replaces the longer museum number "SMS 449A". For this present work, a sub-number (two small letters) is added afterwards in order to ensure that the number is unique. The key entries state the main number of the ceramics as well as the context. The presentation follows the numerical order.

RE6

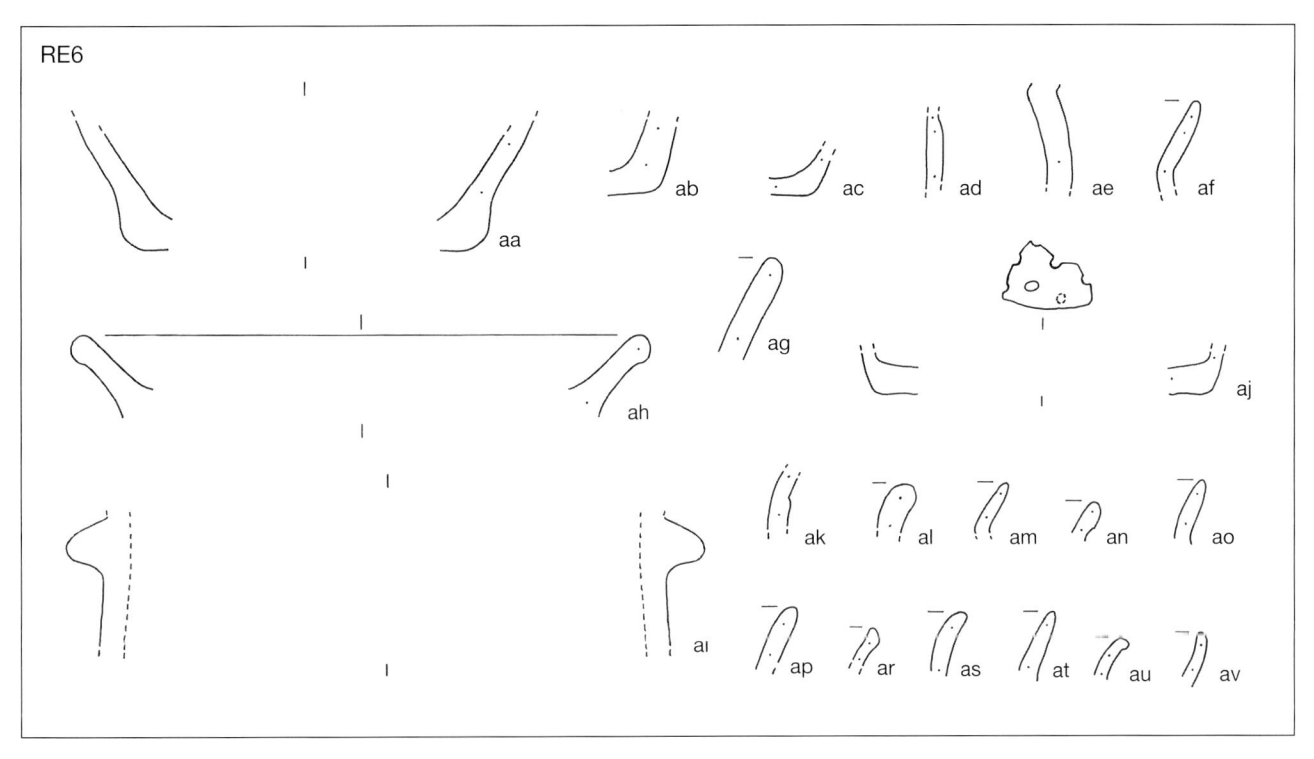

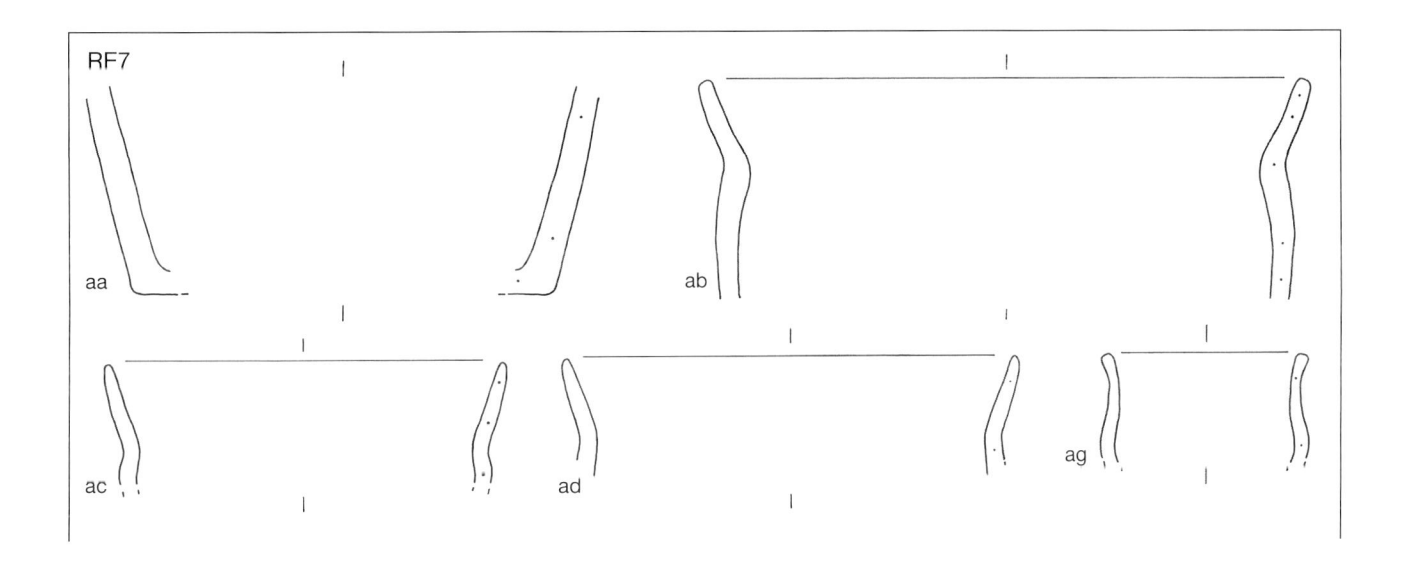

House 1, secondary fills
RE6aa. *Clay pot side & bottom. Calculation of outer bottom diameter: c. 15 cm. Ware thickness: 0.9-1.1 cm.*
RE6ab. *Clay pot side & bottom. Ware thickness: 1.2-1.5 cm. Relatively thick soot crust in a spot on the inner side near the bottom.*
RE6ac. *Clay pot side & bottom. Ware thickness: 0.6-0.7 cm. Tiny spot with thin soot crust on the inner side near the bottom.*
RE6ad. *Clay pot side. Ware thickness: 0.4-0.7-0.6 cm.*
RE6ae. *Clay pot side. Ware thickness: 1.0 cm.*
RE6af. *Clay pot rim & side. Ware thickness: 0.6-0.7-0.7 cm.*
RE6ag. *Clay pot rim. Ware thickness: 1.0-1.1 cm.*
RE6ah. *Clay pot rim. Calculation of outer rim diameter: c. 24 cm. Ware thickness: 1.2-2.1 cm. Appears to represent a kind of dish.*
RE6ai. *Clay pot side. Calculation of outer side diameter: c. 23 cm (ware thickness: c. 1.0 cm estimated). Supplied with a horizontally-projecting lug, length c. 5.4 cm. Inner side cracked.*
RE6aj. *Clay colander bottom. Calculation of outer bottom diameter: c. 14.5 cm. Ware thickness: 0.6-1.4 cm. The small colander fragment appears somewhat marked by wear but impact from the excavation process cannot be excluded.*
RE6ak. *Clay pot side. Ware thickness: 0.6-0.8 cm.*
RE6al. *Clay pot rim. Ware thickness: 1.1-1.0 cm.*
RE6am. *Clay pot rim & side. Ware thickness: 0.5-0.6 cm.*
RE6an. *Clay pot rim. Ware thickness: 0.7-0.6 cm.*
RE6ao. *Clay pot rim. Ware thickness: 0.6-0.7 cm.*
RE6ap. *Clay pot rim. Ware thickness: 0.8-0.8 cm.*
RE6ar. *Clay pot rim. Ware thickness: 0.5-0.4 cm.*
RE6as. *Clay pot rim. Ware thickness: 0.8-0.7 cm.*
RE6at. *Clay pot rim. Ware thickness: 0.6-0.8 cm.*
RE6au. *Clay pot rim. Ware thickness: 0.5-0.6 cm.*
RE6av. *Clay pot rim. Ware thickness: 0.4-0.5 cm.*

RF7

Ceramics at Resengaard **451**

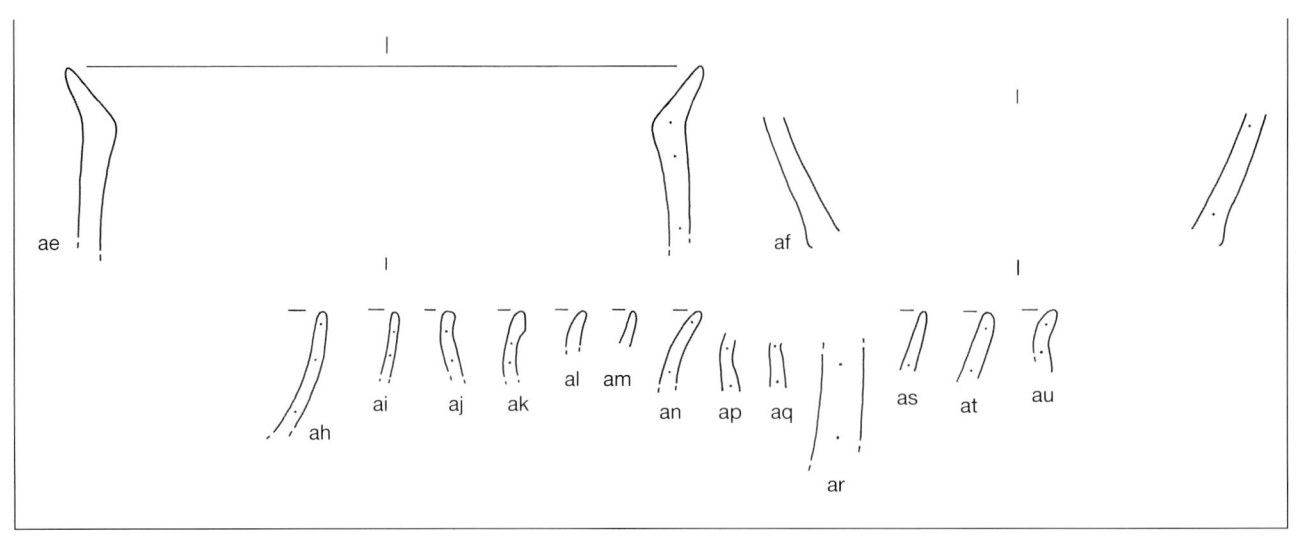

House 2, secondary fills
RE7aa. Clay pot side & bottom. Calculation of outer bottom diameter: c. 17 cm. Ware thickness: 1.2-1.3-1.0 cm. Soot crust on the side near the bottom but not present at the protruding spots. This might be due to rough cleaning in the prehistoric situation, which could have removed the soot crust there.
RE7ab. Clay pot rim & side. Calculation of outer rim diameter: c. 25 cm. Ware thickness: 0.8-0.8-1.1-0.9-0.8 cm.
RE7ac. Clay pot rim & side. Calculation of outer rim diameter: c. 16.5 cm. Ware thickness: 0.5-0.6-0.7 cm. The inclination may be slightly different.
RE7ad. Clay pot rim & side. Calculation of outer rim diameter: c. 19 cm. Ware thickness: 0.6-0.8 cm. The inclination may be slightly different.
RE7ae. Clay pot rim & side. Calculation of outer rim diameter: c. 26.5 cm. Ware thickness: 1.4-1.1-0.9 cm. Outer side faintly crumbling.
RE7af. Clay pot side & bottom. Calculation of outer bottom diameter: c. 17 cm. Ware thickness: 0.9-1.7 cm. Area with traces of soot crust.
RE7ag. Clay pot rim & side. Calculation of outer rim diameter: c. 8.5 cm. Ware thickness: 0.4-0.6 cm. Slightly thickened rim.
RE7ah. Clay pot rim & side. Ware thickness: 0.5-0.6-0.6 cm. Probably an open bowl with outer rim diameter approx. 20 cm.
RE7ai. Clay pot rim & side. Ware thickness: 0.4-0.4 cm.
RE7aj. Clay pot rim & side. Ware thickness: 0.5-0.6 cm.
RE7ak. Clay pot rim & side. Ware thickness: 0.6-0.6 cm.
RE7al. Clay pot rim.
RE7am. Clay pot rim.
RE7an. Clay pot rim & side. Ware thickness: 0.5-0.7 cm.
RE7ao. Clay pot side (not illustrated). Ware thickness: 0.6-0.8 cm.
RE7ap. Clay pot side. Ware thickness: 0.6-0.7 cm.
RE7aq. Clay pot side. Ware thickness: 0.5-0.7 cm.
RE7ar. Clay pot side. Ware thickness: 1.7-1.9 cm, being an example of very thick ware.
RE7as. Clay pot rim & side. Ware thickness: 0.6 cm.
RE7at. Clay pot rim & side. Ware thickness: 0.7-0.8 cm.
RE7au. Clay pot rim & side. Ware thickness: 0.6-0.6 cm.

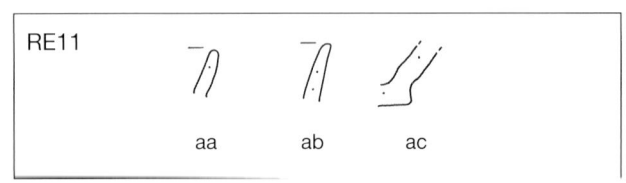

House 1, secondary fills
RE11aa. Clay pot rim. Ware thickness: 0.5 cm. RE11ab. Clay pot rim. Ware thickness: 0.6-0.7 cm. RE11ac. Clay pot side & bottom. Ware thickness: 0.9-0.8 cm. Thin soot crust on the inner side near the bottom.

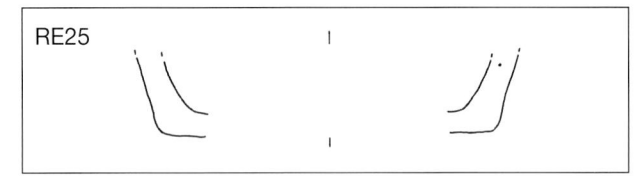

House 1, sunken-floor horizon
RE25aa. Clay pot side & bottom. Calculation of outer bottom diameter: c. 14 cm. Ware thickness: 1.1 cm. Thick soot crust (up to c. 1 mm) on the inner side near the bottom.

House 1, secondary fills
RE21aa Clay pot rim. Ware thickness: 0.3 cm.

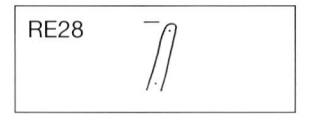

House 1, sunken-floor horizon
RE28aa. Clay pot rim & side. Ware thickness: 0.5-0.6 cm.

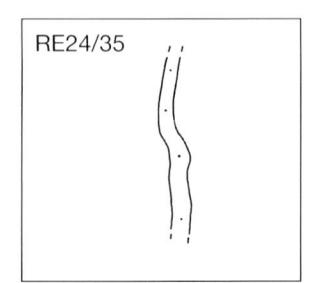

House 1, sunken-floor horizon
RE24aa/35aa. Clay pot side. Calculation of outer side diameter: c. 16.5 cm. Ware thickness: 0.6-0.7-0.9-0.8 cm. The ware appears unusual and burned reddish on inner & outer sides, while the inner parts are greyish. The outer surface more smoothed than usual.

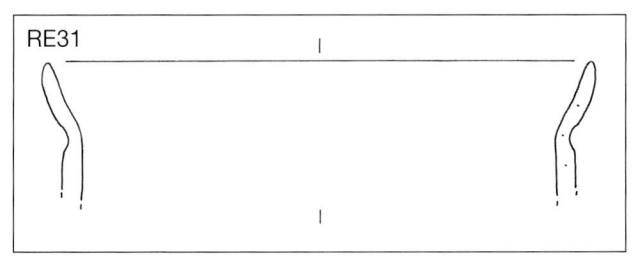

RE31

House 1, sunken-floor horizon
RE31aa. Clay pot rim & side. Calculation of outer rim diameter: c. 22.5 cm. Ware thickness: 0.7-0.6-0.8 cm.

RE35

RE35aa. Clay pot side. See RE24.

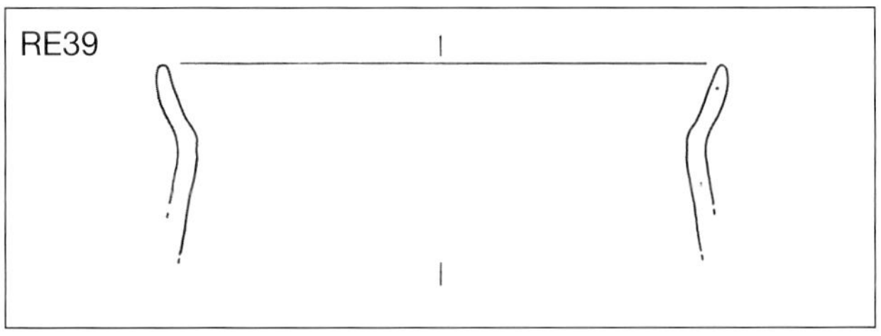

RE39

House 1, secondary fills
RE39aa. Clay pot rim & side. Calculation of outer rim diameter: c. 16.5 cm. Ware thickness: 0.5-0.5 cm. The inclination may be slightly different. Outer side faintly crumbling.

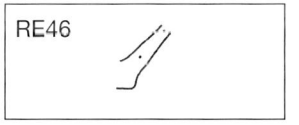

RE46

House 1, sunken-floor horizon
RE46aa. Clay pot side & bottom. Ware thickness: 0.5-0.8 cm.

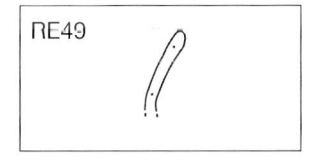

RE49

House 1, secondary fills
RE49aa. Clay pot rim & side. Ware thickness: 0.6-0.5 cm.

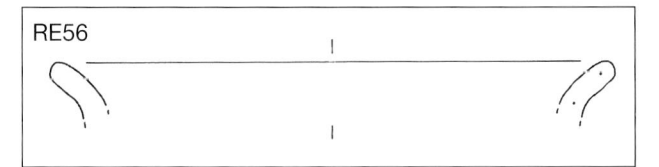

RE56

House 1, secondary fills
RE56aa. Clay pot rim. Calculation of outer rim diameter: c. 23 cm. Ware thickness: 0.9-1.0 cm.

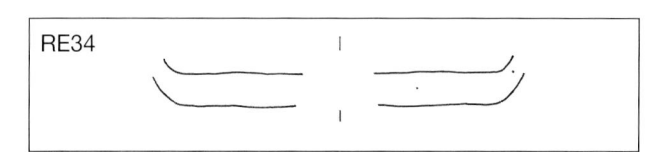

RE58

RE34

House 1, sunken-floor horizon
RE34aa. Clay pot side and bottom. Calculation of outer bottom diameter: c. 13 cm. Ware thickness: 0.8 -1.3 cm.

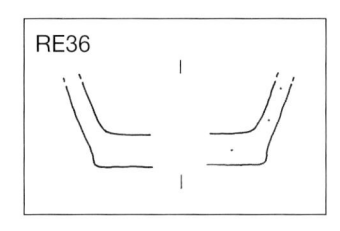

RE36

House 1, sunken-floor horizon
RE36aa. Clay pot side & bottom. Calculation of outer bottom diameter: c. 7 cm. Ware thickness: 0.7-0.7-1.2 cm. Relatively thick bottom.

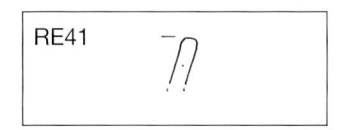

RE41

House 1, sunken-floor horizon
RE41aa. Clay pot rim. Ware thickness: 0.7 cm.

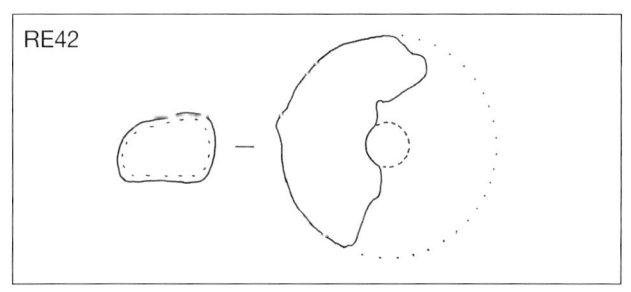

RE42

House 1, sunken-floor horizon
RE42aa. Loom Weight. Appears to have been almost regularly rounded. Outer diameter is calculated at c. 8.9 cm. It had a centrallyplaced, cylindrical hole, calculated diameter c. 1.7 cm. Medium-sized mineral tempering. Traces of organic tempering observable. More than a third of the loom weight preserved. The inner part is greyish, the outer part reddish. Presumably secondarily burned.

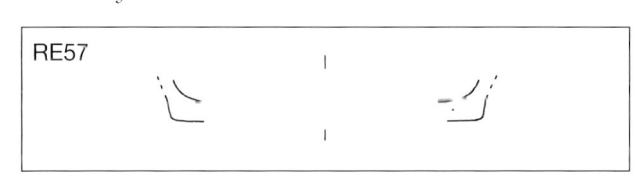

RE57

House 1, sunken-floor horizon
RE57aa. Clay pot side & bottom. Calculation of outer bottom diameter: c. 13 cm. Ware thickness: 0.8 cm.

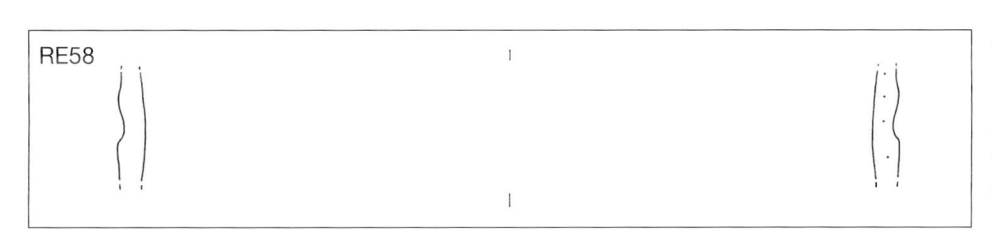

House 1, sunken-floor horizon
RE58aa. Clay pot side. Calculation of outer side diameter: c. 32 cm. Ware thickness: 0.9-1.1-0.9-1.1 cm. The diameter may have been slightly different.

Ceramics at Resengaard   **453**

House 1, sunken-floor horizon
RE60aa. Clay pot rim & side. Calculation of outer rim diameter: c. 28.5 cm. Ware thickness: 0.8-0.8-1.0 cm.

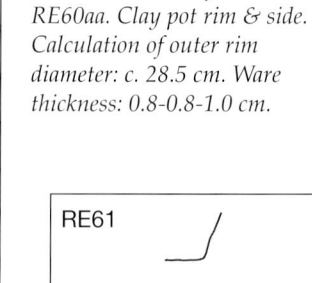

House 1, sunken-floor horizon
RE61aa. Clay pot side & bottom. Only outer contour preserved.

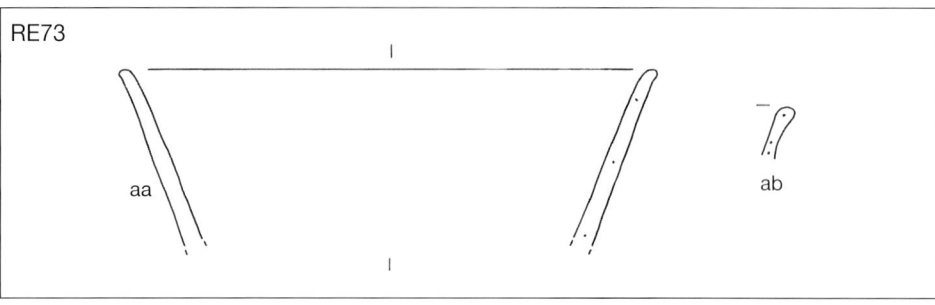

House 1, sunken-floor horizon
RE68aa. Clay pot rim. Ware thickness: 0.7-0.6 cm.

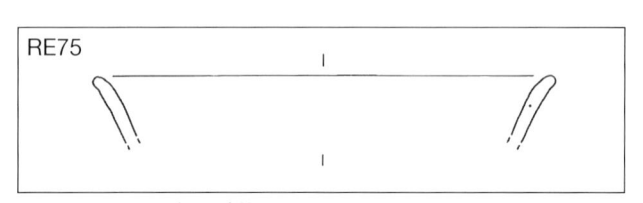

House 1, secondary fills
RE73aa. Clay pot rim & side. Calculation of outer rim diameter: c. 22 cm. Ware thickness: 0.6-0.7-0.8 cm. The inclination may be slightly different.
RE73ab. Clay pot rim & side. Ware thickness: 0.7-0.5-0.6 cm.

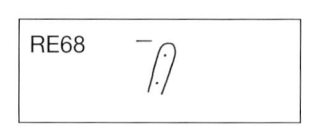

House 1, secondary fills
RE75aa. Clay pot rim & side. Calculation of outer rim diameter: c. 19 cm. Ware thickness: 0.6 cm.

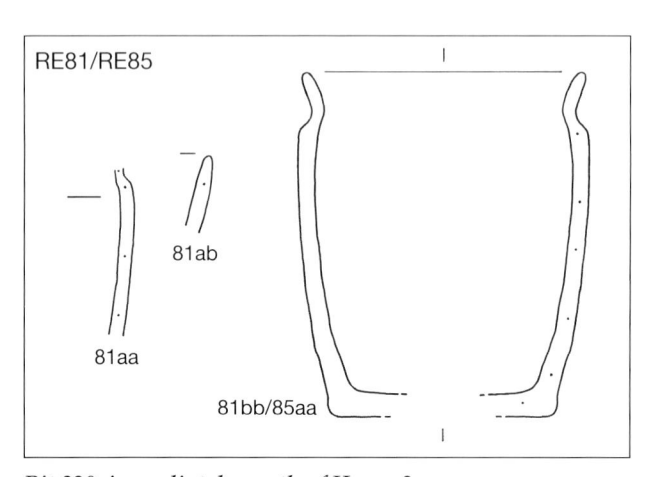

Pit 320, immediately north of House 2
RE85ab. Clay pot rim & side. Ware thickness: 0.8-0.8 cm.

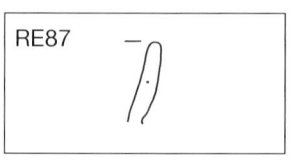

Pit 320, immediately north of House 2
RE81aa. Clay pot side. Ware thickness: 0.6-0.6-0.6 cm.
RE81ab. Clay pot rim & side. Ware thickness: 0.6 cm.
RE81bb/85aa. Clay pot rim, side & bottom. Calculation of outer rim diameter: c. 11.5 cm. Estimate of the original height: c. 14 cm. Ware thickness: 0.8-0.7-0.7-0.8-0.9-0.9 cm. A large part of the jar preserved.

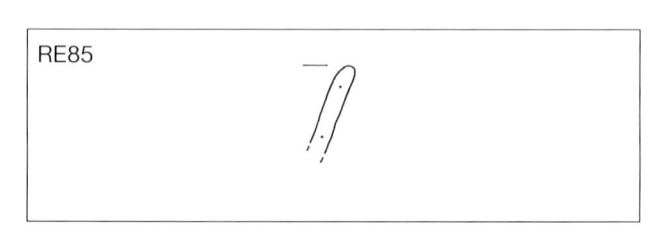

House 2, pit 9 west of the sunken-floor horizon
RE87aa. Clay pot rim. Ware thickness: 0.7 cm.

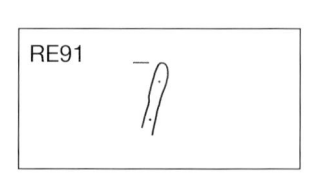

House 2, sunken-floor horizon
RE91aa. Clay pot rim & side. Ware thickness: 0.6-0.5 cm.

454 Catalogue A

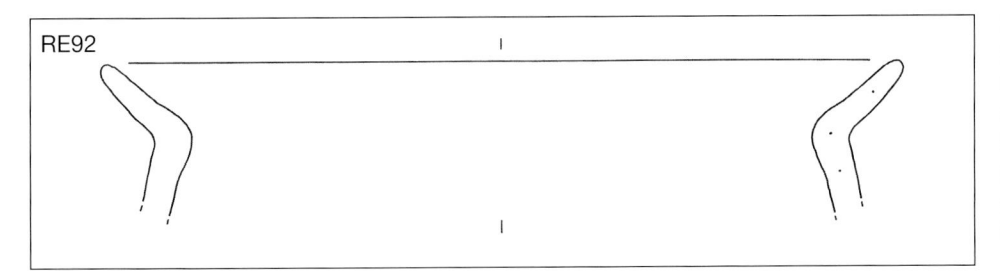

House 2, sunken-floor horizon
RE92aa. Clay pot rim & side. Calculation of outer rim diameter: c. 33 cm. Ware thickness: 1.0-1.5-1.3 cm. Several traces of soot on the outer side and the uppermost 2-3 cm on the inner side.

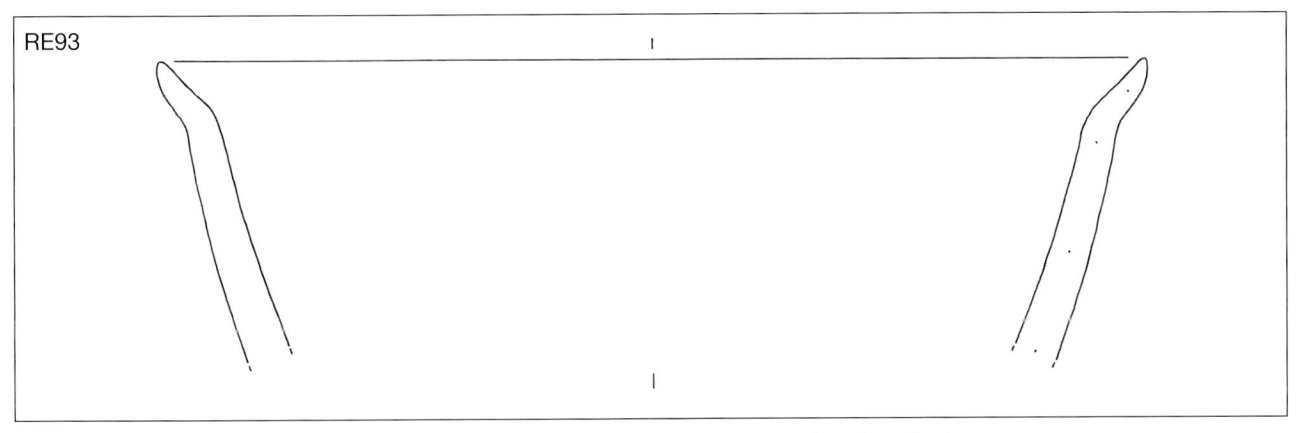

House 2, sunken-floor horizon
RE93aa. Clay pot rim & side. Calculation of outer rim diameter: c. 40.5 cm. Ware thickness: 1.0-1.5-1.7-1.9 cm.

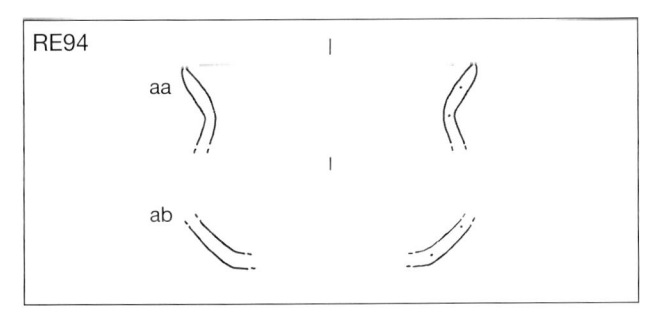

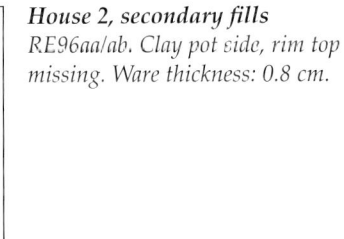

House 2, secondary fills
RE96aa/ab. Clay pot side, rim top missing. Ware thickness: 0.8 cm.

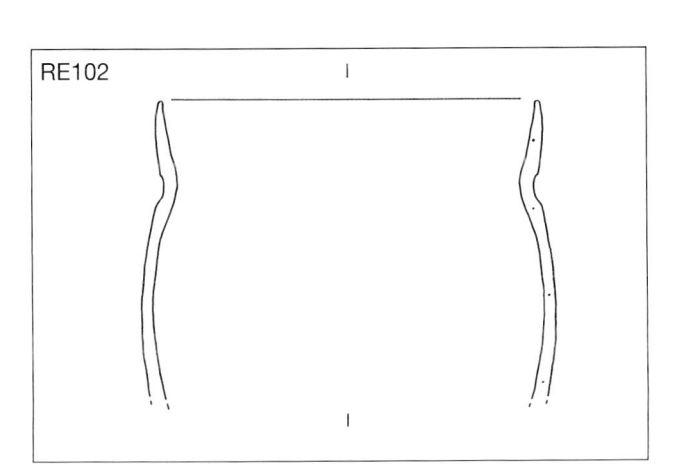

Pit immediately north of House 2.
RE94aa. Clay pot rim & side. Calculation of outer rim diameter: c. 12 cm. Ware thickness: 0.6-0.4 cm.
RE94ab. Clay pot bottom. Calculation of outer bottom diameter: c. 9 cm. Ware thickness: 0.5-0.6 cm.

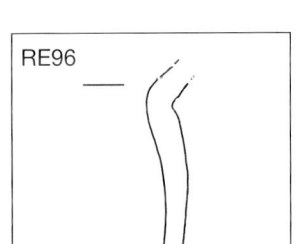

House 2, sunken-floor horizon
RE104aa. Clay pot rim. Calculation of outer rim diameter: c. 10.5 cm.
RE104ab. Clay pot rim. Ware thickness: 0.8 cm.
RE104ac. Clay pot rim.

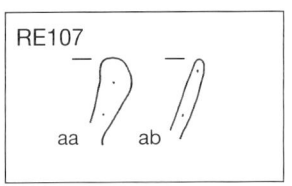

House 2, secondary fills
RE107aa. Clay pot rim. Ware thickness: 1.4-0.9 cm.
RE107ab. Clay pot rim. Ware thickness: 0.5-0.6 cm.

House 2, sunken-floor horizon
RE102aa. Clay pot rim & side. Calculation of outer rim diameter: c. 16 cm. Ware thickness: 0.5-0.6-0.6-0.5-0.7 cm.

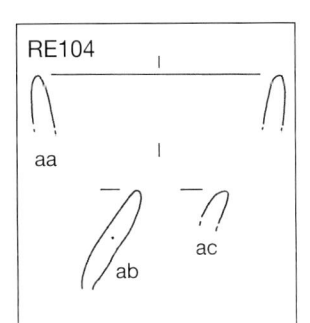

Ceramics at Resengaard

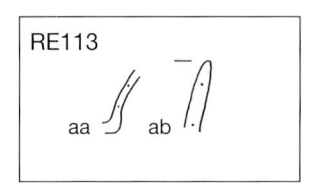

House 2, sunken-floor horizon
RE113aa. Clay pot side & bottom. Ware thickness: 0.3-0.3 cm.
RE113ab. Clay pot rim. Ware thickness: 0.6-0.7 cm.

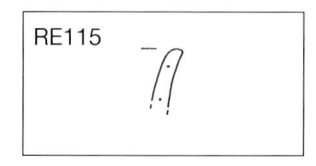

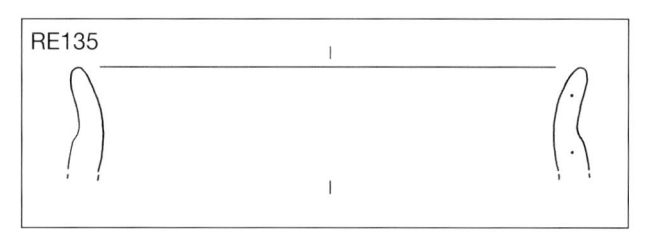

House 2, sunken-floor horizon
RE115aa. Clay pot rim. Ware thickness: 0.6-0.7 cm.

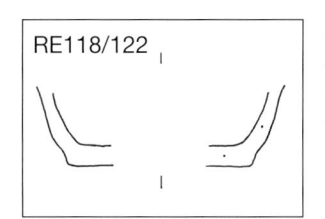

House 2, sunken-floor horizon
RE118aa/122aa. Clay pot side & bottom. Calculation of outer bottom diameter: c. 7.5 cm. Ware thickness: 0.7-0.8 cm.

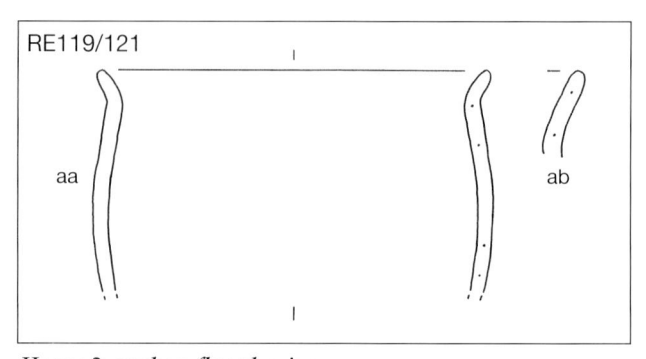

House 2, sunken-floor horizon
RE119aa/121aa. Clay pot rim & side. Calculation of outer rim diameter: c. 16 cm. Ware thickness: 0.7-0.7-0.7-0.7 cm.
RE121ab. Clay pot rim. Ware thickness: 0.7-0.7 cm.

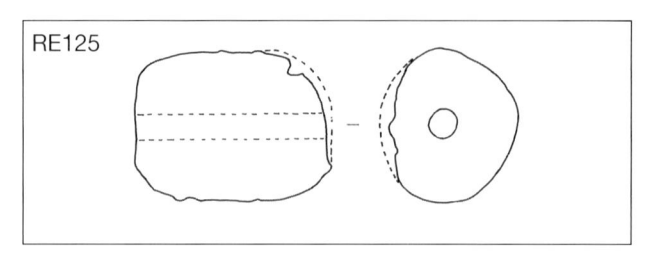

House 2, sunken-floor horizon
RE125aa. Clay tube. Almost complete. Length c. 8.2 cm. High content of mineral tempering. For further description, see the text, Ch. 4.

House 2, secondary fills
RE130aa. Clay pot side. Calculation of outer diameter above the "shoulder": c. 16 cm. Ware thickness: 0.6-0.7-0.8-0.7 cm.

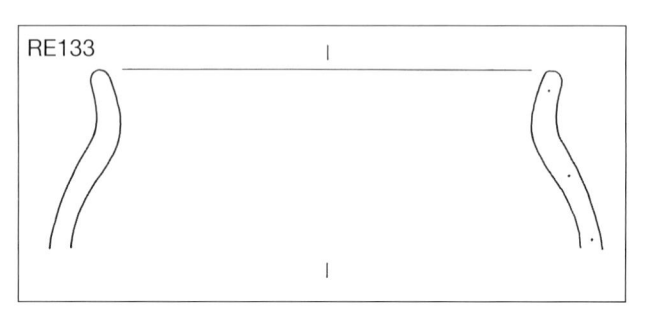

House 2, sunken-floor horizon
RE133aa. Clay pot rim & side. Calculation of outer rim diameter: c. 19.5 cm. Ware thickness: 0.9-10.-0.9 cm.

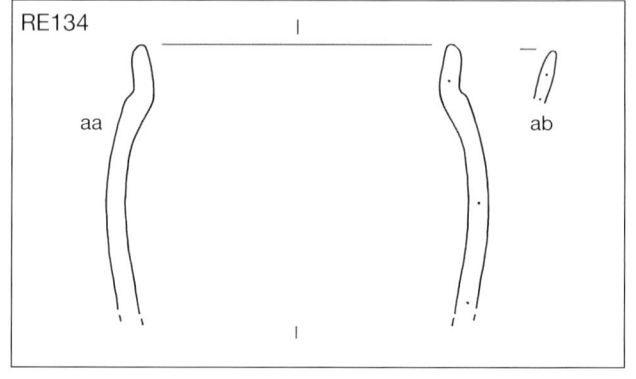

House 2, sunken-floor horizon
RE134aa. Clay pot rim & side. Calculation of outer rim diameter: c. 13.5 cm. Ware thickness: 0.9-0.8-0.9 cm. Thin soot crust on the inner side near the middle part of the body.
RE134ab. Clay pot rim. Ware thickness: 0.6-0.5 cm.

House 2, sunken-floor horizon
RE135aa. Clay pot rim & side. Calculation of outer rim diameter: c. 21.5 cm. Ware thickness: 0.9-1.3 cm. Some uncertainty regarding the diameter, as the rim is a little irregular.

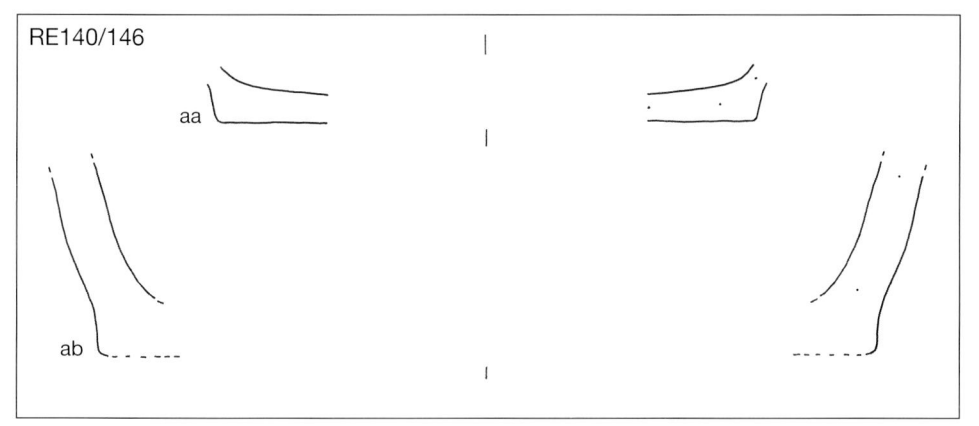

RE140/146

House 2, sunken-floor horizon
RE140aa. Clay pot bottom. Calculation of outer bottom diameter: c. 22 cm. Ware thickness: 1.0-1.4 cm.
RE140ab/146aa. Clay pot bottom. Calculation of outer bottom diameter: c. 32 cm. Ware thickness: 2.0-1.9 cm. Seems to stem from an extraordinarily large vessel.

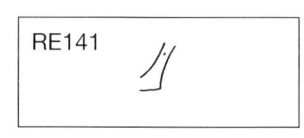

RE141

House 2, sunken-floor horizon
RE141aa. Clay pot bottom. Ware thickness: 0.5 cm.

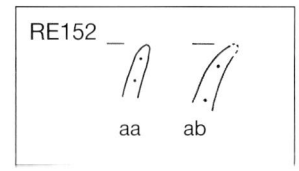

RE152

House 1, sunken-floor horizon
RE152aa. Clay pot rim. Ware thickness: 0.6-0.7 cm.
RE152ab. Clay pot rim. Ware thickness: 0.7-0.9 cm.

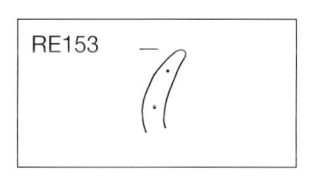

RE153

House 1, sunken-floor horizon
RE153aa. Clay pot rim & side. Ware thickness: 0.8-0.9 cm.

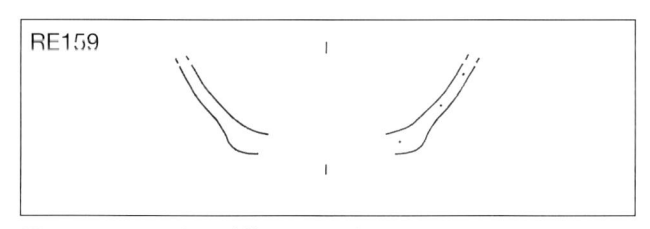

RE159

House 1, secondary fills
RE159aa. Clay pot rim & side. Calculation of outer bottom diameter: c. 8 cm. Ware thickness: 0.5-0.5-0.8 cm.

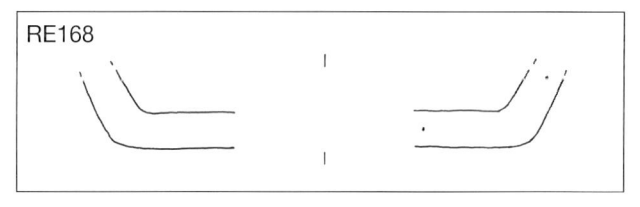

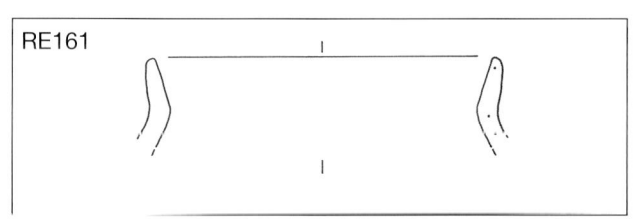

RE161

House 2, sunken-floor horizon
RE161aa. Clay pot rim & side. Calculation of outer rim diameter: c. 14.5 cm. Ware thickness: 0.6-0.9-0.8 cm.

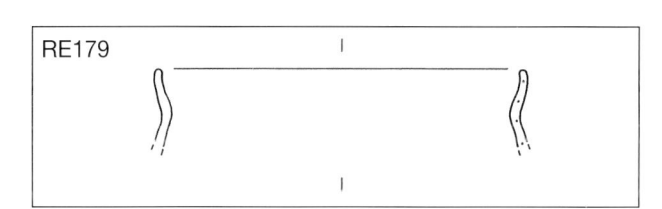

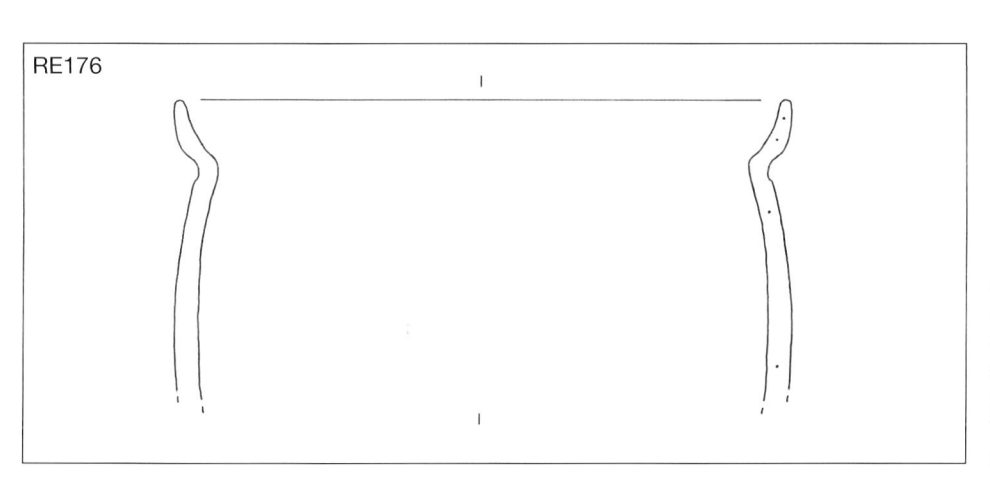

RE168

House 2, sunken-floor horizon
RE168aa. Clay pot bottom. Calculation of outer bottom diameter: c. 18 cm. Ware thickness: 1.4-1.5 cm. The diameter may have been somewhat different.

RE179

House 2, sunken-floor horizon
RE176aa. Clay pot rim & side. Calculation of outer rim diameter: c. 25 cm. Ware thickness: 0.7-0.8-0.8-0.9-1.0 cm. A small area with traces of soot on the inner side, upper part.

House 2, sunken-floor horizon
RE179aa. Clay pot rim & side. Calculation of outer rim diameter: c. 15.5 cm. Ware thickness: 0.4-0.5-0.4-0.5 cm. The diameter may have been slightly different.

RE176

Ceramics at Resengaard **457**

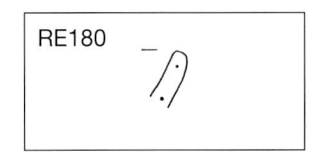

RE180

Find spot immediately north of House 2
RE180aa. Clay pot rim. Ware thickness: 0.8-0.9 cm. Context not clarified, see the text.

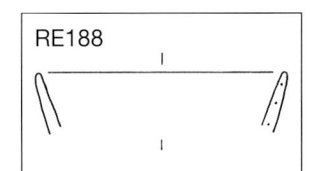

RE188

House 1, secondary fills
RE188aa. Clay pot rim & side. Calculation of outer rim diameter: c. 10.5 cm. Ware thickness: 0.4-0.5-0.6 cm.

RE196

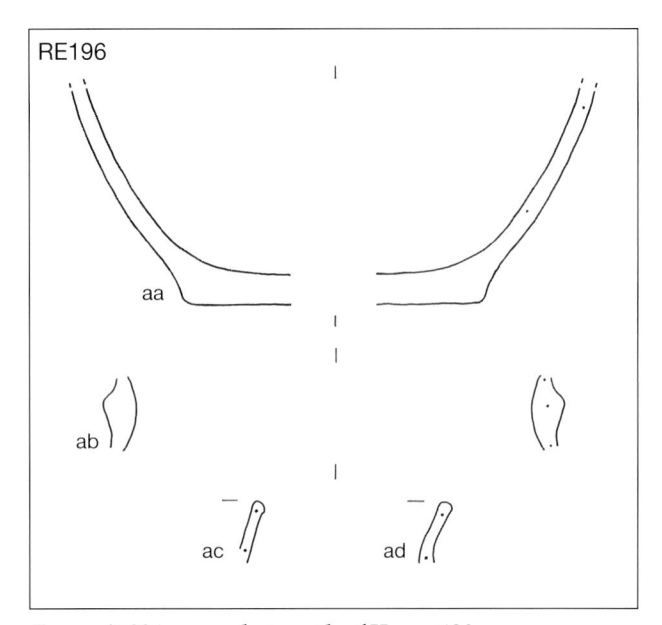

From pit 331 somewhat north of House 130
RE196aa. Clay pot side & bottom. Calculation of outer bottom diameter: c. 12.5 cm. Ware thickness: 0.7-0.8 cm.
RE196ab. Clay pot side. Calculation of diameter below the cordon: c. 18.5 cm, but may have been somewhat different. Ware thickness: 0.6-1.4-0.7 cm.
RE196ac. Clay pot rim. Ware thickness: 0.6-0.5 cm.
RE196ad. Clay pot rim & side. Ware thickness: 0.5-0.7 cm.

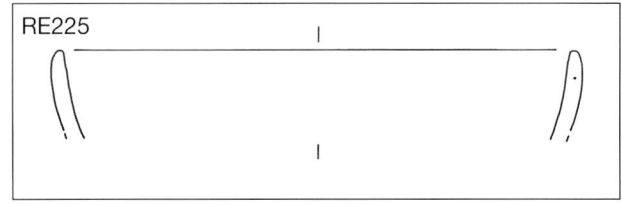

RE225

From pit 312, south of House 183
RE225aa. Clay pot rim & side. Calculation of outer rim diameter: c. 22 cm. Ware thickness: 0.7 cm.

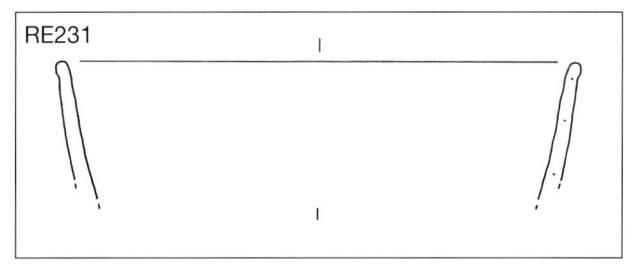

RE231

RE181

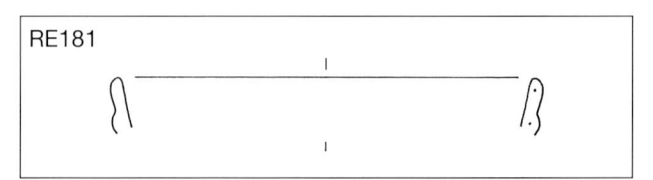

House 2, from a posthole.
RE181aa. Clay pot rim & side. Calculation of outer rim diameter: c. 18 cm. Ware thickness: 0.6-0.8 cm. The diameter may have been slightly different.

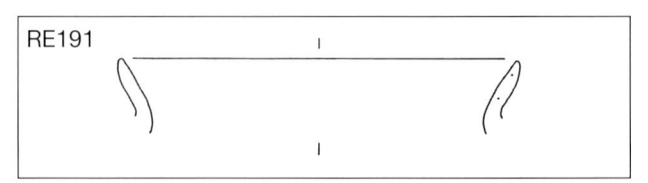

RE191

House 2, secondary fills
RE191aa. Clay pot rim & side. Calculation of outer rim diameter: c. 16.5 cm. Ware thickness: 0.5-0.6 cm. The inclination may be slightly different.

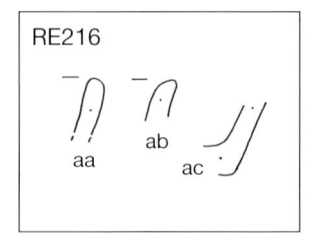

RE216

From a pit somewhat west House 112
RE216aa. Clay pot side & bottom. Ware thickness: 0.8 cm.
RE216ab. Clay pot rim. Ware thickness: 0.8 cm.
RE216ac. Clay pot side & bottom. Ware thickness: 0.8-1.2 cm.

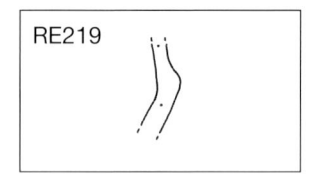

RE219

From a pit in an area west of House 112
RE219aa. Clay pot side. Ware thickness: 0.7-0.8 cm.

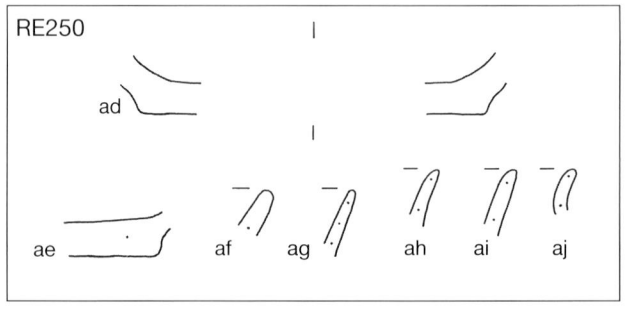

RE250

House 12, secondary fills
RE250ad. Clay pot bottom. Calculation of outer bottom diameter: c. 14 cm.
RE250ae. Clay pot bottom. Ware thickness: 1.4 cm.
RE250af. Clay pot rim. Ware thickness: 0.9 cm.
RE250ag. Clay pot rim & side. Ware thickness: 0.4-0.5-0.6 cm.
RE250ah. Clay pot rim. Ware thickness: 0.5-0.6 cm.
RE250ai. Clay pot rim & side. Ware thickness: 0.6-0.7 cm.
RE250aj. Clay pot rim. Ware thickness: 0.5-0.6 cm.

From pit 313, placed somewhat west of House 84
RE231aa. Clay pot rim & side. Calculation of outer rim diameter: c. 22 cm. Ware thickness: 0.5-0.6-0.7 cm.

458   Catalogue A

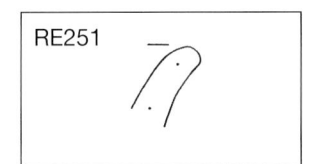

RE251

House 13, secondary fills
RE251ab. Clay pot rim. Ware thickness: 1.2-1.4 cm. The diameter seems to have been considerable.

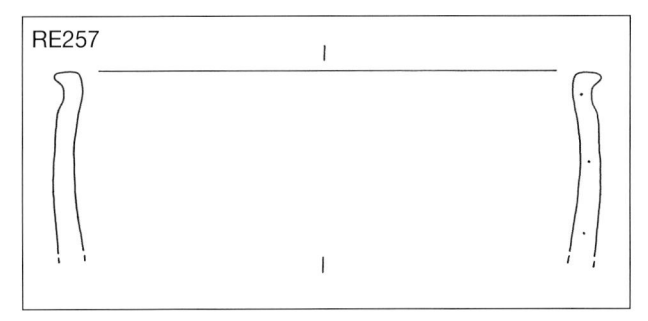

RE257

House 268, secondary fills
RE257aa. Clay pot rim & side. Calculation of outer rim diameter: c. 22.5 cm. Ware thickness: 0.8-0.9-1.0 cm.

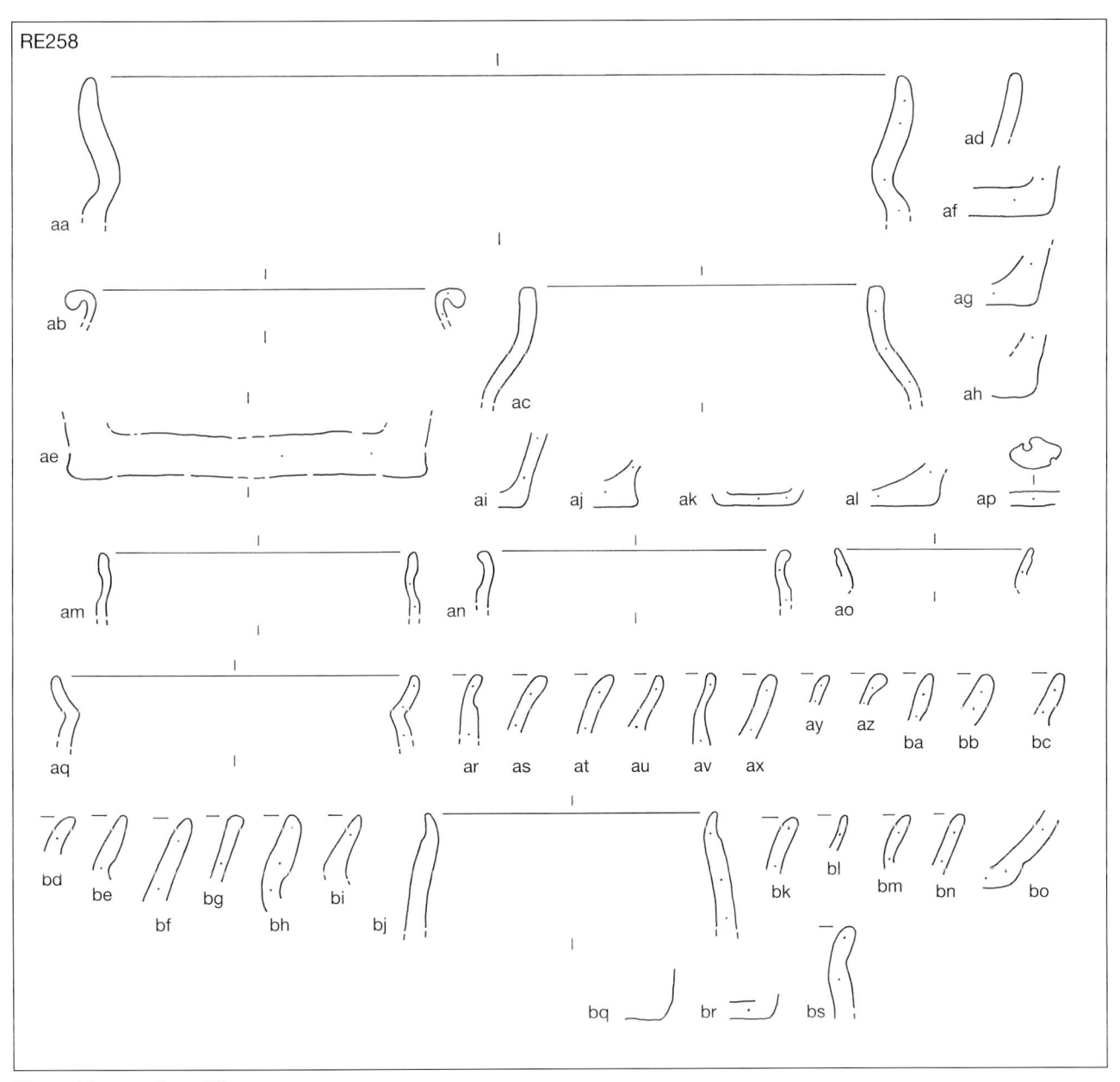

RE258

House 14, secondary fills
RE258aa. Clay pot rim & side. Calculation of outer rim diameter: c. 39.5 cm. Ware thickness: 0.9-1.1-1.0-1.1 cm.
RE258ab. Clay pot rim & side. Calculation of outer rim diameter: c. 19 cm. Ware thickness: 0.6-0.4 cm.
RE258ac. Clay pot rim & side. Calculation of outer rim diameter: c. 17.5 cm. Ware thickness: 0.8-0.7-0.7 cm.
RE258ad. Clay pot rim & side. Ware thickness: 1.0-0.8 cm.
RE258ae. Clay pot bottom. Calculation of outer bottom diameter: c. 17 cm. Ware thickness: 1.9-1.8 cm.
RE258af. Clay pot bottom. Ware thickness: 1.1-1.4 cm.
RE258ag. Clay pot side & bottom. Ware thickness: 1.3-1.1 cm.
RE258ah. Clay pot side & bottom. Ware thickness: 1.1 cm.
RE258ai. Clay pot side & bottom. Ware thickness: 0.6-1.3 cm.
RE258aj. Clay pot side & bottom. Ware thickness: 0.8-0.7-0.8 cm.
RE258ak. Clay pot bottom. Calculation of outer bottom diameter: c. 4.5 cm. Ware thickness: 0.6-0.5 cm.

Ceramics at Resengaard **459**

RE258al. Clay pot bottom. Ware thickness: 1.1-0.8 cm.
RE258am. Clay pot rim & side. Calculation of outer rim diameter: c. 15.5 cm. Ware thickness: 0.4-0.5 cm.
RE258an. Clay pot rim & side. Calculation of outer rim diameter: c. 15.0 cm. Ware thickness: 0.5-0.6 cm.
RE258ao. Clay pot rim & side. Calculation of outer rim diameter: c. 9.5 cm. Ware thickness: 0.5 cm.
RE258ap. Clay colander bottom. Fragment, a small piece. Ware thickness: 0.4 cm.
RE258aq. Clay pot rim & side. Calculation of outer rim diameter: c. 17.5 cm. Ware thickness: 0.5-0.5-0.6 cm.
RE258ar. Clay pot rim & side. Ware thickness: 0.5-0.9 cm.
RE258as. Clay pot rim & side. Ware thickness: 0.8-0.7 cm.
RE258at. Clay pot rim & side. Ware thickness: 0.8-0.7 cm.
RE258au. Clay pot rim. Ware thickness: 0.6-0.9 cm. Thin soot crust on the inner rim side.
RE258av. Clay pot rim & side. Ware thickness: 0.5-0.5-0.8 cm.
RE258ax. Clay pot rim & side. Ware thickness: 0.8-0.8 cm.
RE258ay. Clay pot rim. Ware thickness: 0.6-0.5 cm.
RE258az. Clay pot rim. Ware thickness: 0.6-0.4 cm.

RE258ba. Clay pot rim. Ware thickness: 0.7-0.6 cm.
RE258bb. Clay pot rim. Ware thickness: 1.1-1.1 cm.
RE258bc. Clay pot rim. Ware thickness: 0.8-0.8 cm.
RE258bd. Clay pot rim. Ware thickness: 0.8 cm.
RE258be. Clay pot rim & side. Ware thickness: 0.7-0.8 cm.
RE258bf. Clay pot rim & side. Ware thickness: 0.9-1.0 cm.
RE258bg. Clay pot rim & side. Ware thickness: 0.7-0.6 cm.
RE258bh. Clay pot rim & side. Ware thickness: 0.9-1.2-0.9 cm.
RE258bi. Clay pot rim. Ware thickness: 0.7 cm.
RE258bj. Clay pot rim & side. Calculation of outer rim diameter: c. 14 cm. Ware thickness: 0.6-0.9-1.0 cm.
RE258bk. Clay pot rim & side. Ware thickness: 0.8-0.7 cm.
RE258bl. Clay pot rim. Ware thickness: 0.4 cm.
RE258bm. Clay pot rim. Ware thickness: 0.6-0.4 cm.
RE258bn. Clay pot rim & side. Ware thickness: 0.7-0.7 cm.
RE258bo. Clay pot side & bottom. Ware thickness: 1.0-1.1-0.9 cm.
RE258bq. Clay pot side & bottom. Only a small piece of the outer side preserved.
RE258br. Clay pot bottom. Ware thickness: 0.9 cm.
RE258bs. Clay pot rim & side. Ware thickness: 0.8-1.1 cm.

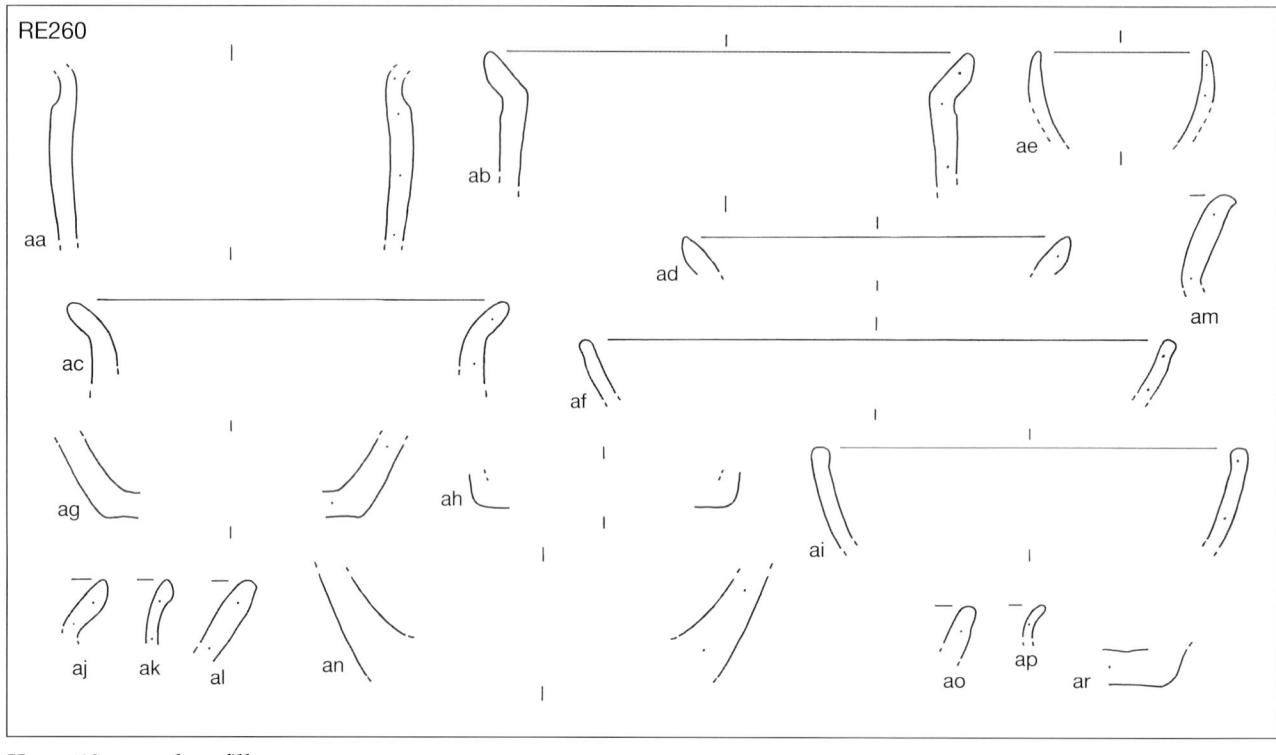

RE260

House 10, secondary fills

RE260aa. Clay pot side. Calculation of outer rim diameter: c. 15.5 cm. Ware thickness: 0.7-1.0-0.9-0.8 cm.
RE260ab. Clay pot rim & side. Calculation of outer rim diameter: c. 20 cm. Ware thickness: 0.9-1.0-0.8 cm.
RE260ac. Clay pot rim & side. Calculation of outer rim diameter: c. 18.5 cm. Ware thickness: 0.8-1.0 cm.
RE260ad. Clay pot rim. Calculation of outer rim diameter: c. 16 cm. Ware thickness: 0.8 cm.
RE260ae. Clay pot rim & side. Calculation of outer rim diameter: c. 7 cm. Ware thickness: 0.4-0.7 cm.
RE260af. Clay pot rim & side. Calculation of outer rim diameter: c. 24.5 cm. Ware thickness: 0.6-0.6 cm. The inclination may have been slightly different.
RE260ag. Clay pot side & bottom. Calculation of outer bottom diameter: c. 11 cm. Ware thickness: 1.1-1.0 cm.

RE260ah. Clay pot bottom. Calculation of outer bottom diameter: c. 11 cm.
RE260ai. Clay pot rim & side. Calculation of outer rim diameter: c. 18 cm. Ware thickness: 0.8-0.7 cm. Inner side faintly crumbling.
RE260aj. Clay pot rim. Ware thickness: 0.9-0.7 cm.
RE260ak. Clay pot rim. Ware thickness: 0.6-0.5 cm.
RE260al. Clay pot rim. Ware thickness: 1.1-0.9 cm.
RE260am. Clay pot rim. Ware thickness: 0.9-0.8 cm.
RE260an. Clay pot side & bottom. Calculation of outer bottom diameter: c. 14.5 cm. Ware thickness: 1.2-2.1 cm.
RE260ao. Clay pot rim. Ware thickness: 0.8 cm.
RE260ap. Clay pot rim. Ware thickness: 0.4 cm.
RE260ar. Clay pot rim. Ware thickness: 1.4 cm.

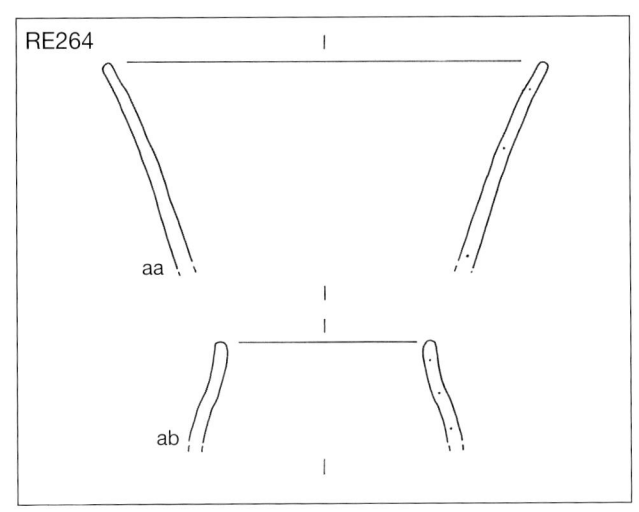

Pit 23, east of House 12
RE264aa. Clay pot rim & side. Ware thickness: 0.5-0.6-0.7 cm.
RE264ab. Clay pot rim & side. Calculation of outer rim diameter: c. 9 cm. Ware thickness: 0.6-0.6-0.6 cm. Ornamented with cardium impression.

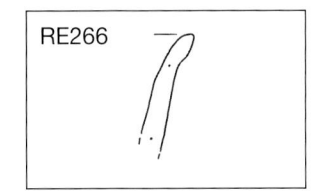

House 197, secondary fills
RE278aa. Clay pot rim & side. Calculation of outer rim diameter: c. 26 cm. Ware thickness: 0.8-0.8-1.0 cm.
RE278ab. Clay pot rim & side. Calculation of outer rim diameter: c. 22 cm. Ware thickness: 0.6-0.8-0.7 cm. The inclination may have been slightly different.
RE278ac. Clay pot side & bottom. Calculation of outer bottom diameter: c. 8 cm. Ware thickness: 1.1-1.3 cm. The bottom is rather thick in comparison to the diameter.
RE278ad. Clay pot rim & side. Calculation of outer rim diameter: c. 7 cm. Ware thickness: 0.4-0.4 cm. The preserved piece of the rim is somewhat irregular. The inclination may have been different.
RE278af. Clay pot rim & side. Ware thickness: 0.4-0.5 cm.
RE278ag. Clay pot rim. Ware thickness: 0.6-0.4 cm.

House 14, secondary fills
RE282aa. Clay pot rim. Calculation of outer rim diameter: c. 23 cm. Ware thickness: 0.7-0.9 cm.
RE282ab. Clay pot rim. Calculation of outer rim diameter: c. 22.5 cm. Ware thickness: 0.6-0.8 cm.

Stone-packed ditch
RE266aa. Clay pot rim & side. Ware thickness: 0.7-1.0 cm. The placement of the stone-packed ditch (no. 27) is not indicated on maps.

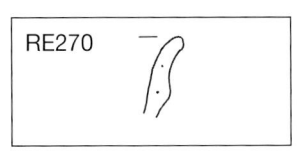

House 268, secondary fills
RE270aa. Clay pot rim & side. Ware thickness: 0.7-0.9 cm.

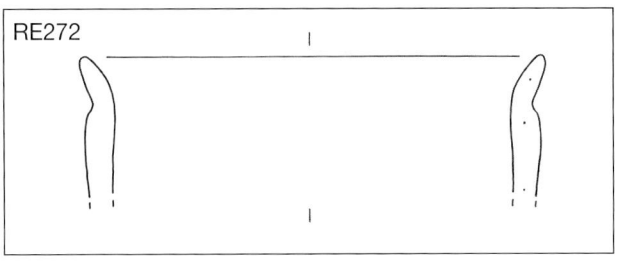

House 13, secondary fills
RE272aa. Clay pot rim & side. Calculation of outer rim diameter: c. 19.5 cm. Ware thickness: 0.8-1.2-1.0 cm. It presumably represents a younger addition to these fills.

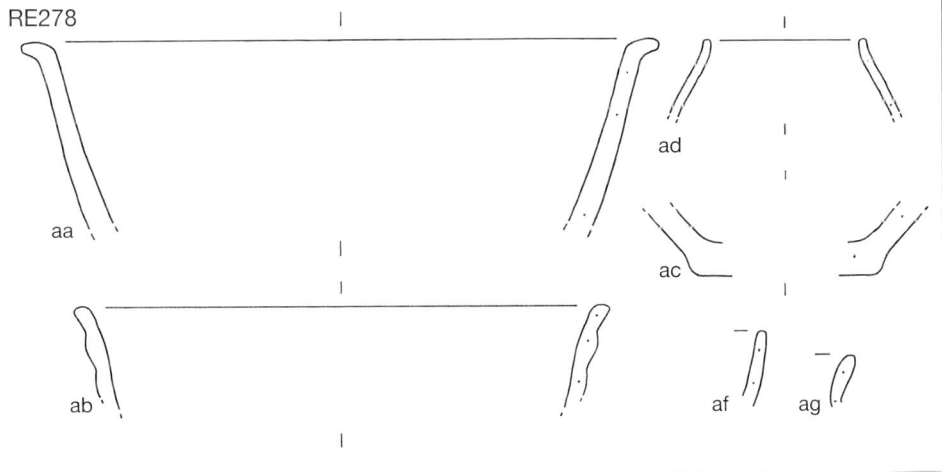

Feature 24, north of House 14
RE279aa. Clay pot bottom. Calculation of outer bottom diameter: c. 10.5 cm. Ware thickness: 0.8-0.7 cm.

Ceramics at Resengaard

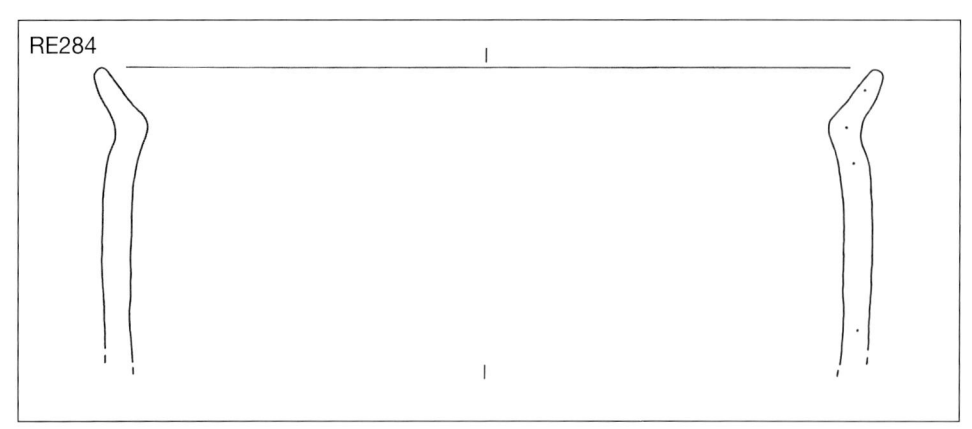

House 14, sunken-floor horizon
RE284aa. Clay pot rim & side. Calculation of outer rim diameter: c. 32.5 cm. Ware thickness: 0.9-1.3-1.2-1.1 cm.

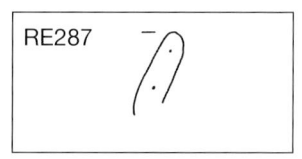

House 14, sunken-floor horizon
RE287aa. Clay pot rim. Ware thickness: 1.0-1.1 cm.

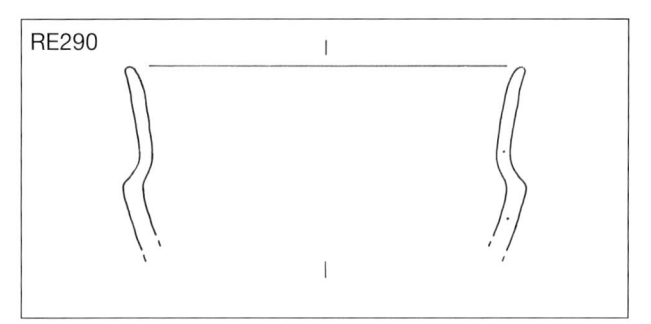

House 14, found at the limit of disturbing pit
RE290aa. Clay pot rim & side. Calculation of outer rim diameter: c. 16.5 cm. Ware thickness: 0.6-0.8 cm.

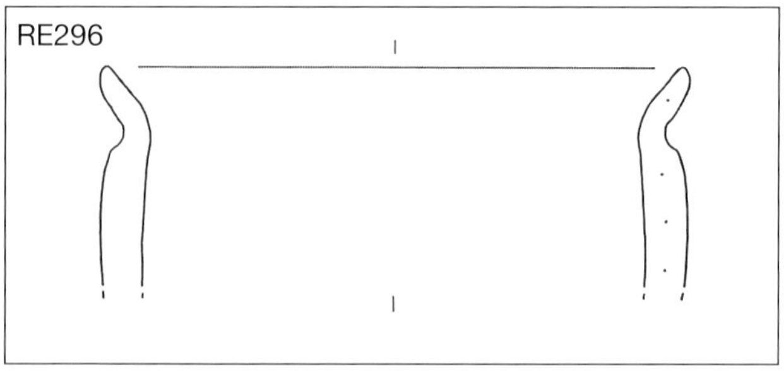

House 14, sunken-floor horizon
RE296aa. Clay pot rim & side. Calculation of outer rim diameter: c. 19 cm. Ware thickness: 0.8-1.4-1.4-1.3 cm. Rather thick-walled compared to the jar size.

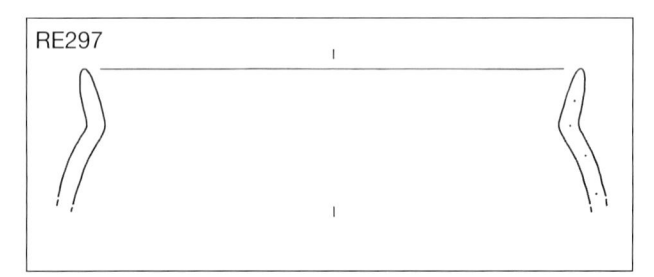

House 14, sunken-floor horizon
RE297aa. Clay pot rim & side. Calculation of outer rim diameter: c. 21 cm. Ware thickness: 0.8-0.8-0.8-0.7 cm.

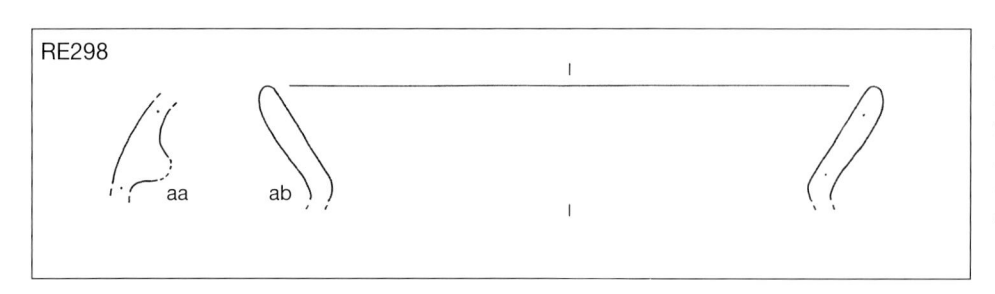

House 14, sunken-floor horizon
RE298aa. Clay pot side. Ware thickness: 0.8-0.8 cm. Supplied with a horizontally-projecting lug. RE298ab. Clay pot rim. Calculation of outer rim diameter: c. 26 cm. Ware thickness: 1.1-0.9 cm.

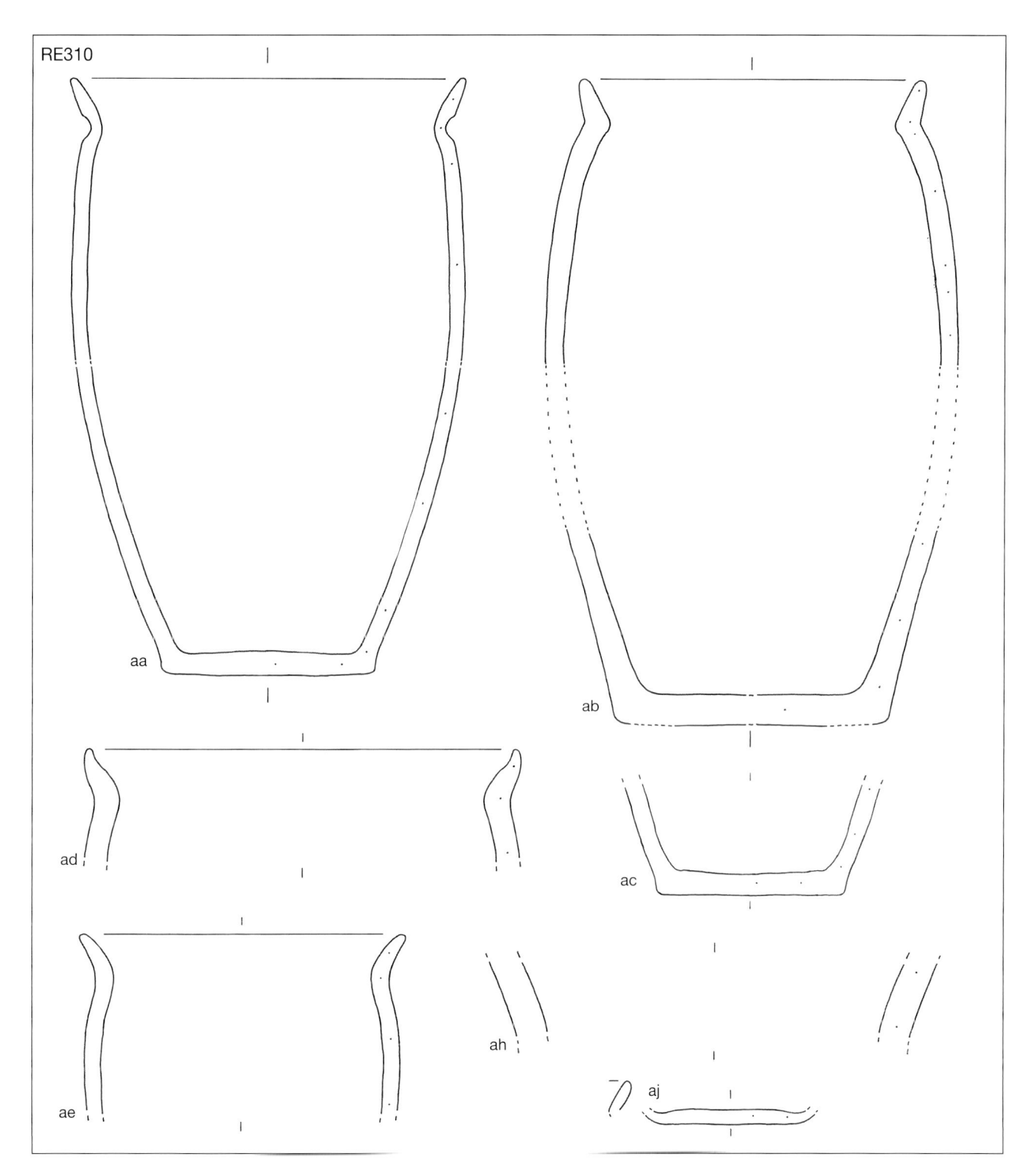

House 10, sunken-floor horizon

RE310aa. Clay pot rim, side & bottom. Calculation of outer rim diameter: c. 21 cm. Estimate of the original height: c. 31 cm. Ware thickness: 0.7-0.6-0.8-0.8-0.8-0.9-0.9-1.0-1.1-1.3 cm. A side from top to bottom may be conjoined. Soot observable on the inner side somewhat above the bottom.
RE310ab. Clay pot rim, side & bottom. Calculation of outer rim diameter: c. 19 cm. Estimate of the original height: c. 34 cm. Ware thickness: 0.8-1.3-1.2-1.2-1.2-1.0-0.8/1.2-1.4-1.7-1.7 cm. The height may have been a little different, possibly slightly taller. A spot with soot crust on the inner side above the belly middle, and further above a spot with just soot.

RE310ac. Clay pot side & bottom. Calculation of outer rim diameter: c. 10.5 cm. Ware thickness: 1.0-0.9-1.0-1.2-1.1 cm. The bottom almost complete. Rather flat underside.
RE310ad. Clay pot rim & side. Calculation of outer rim diameter: c. 23.5 cm. Ware thickness: 0.8-1.4-1.2 cm.
RE310ae. Clay pot rim & side. Calculation of outer rim diameter: c. 17.5 cm. Ware thickness: 0.8-1.0-0.9-0.9 cm.
RE310ah. Clay pot side. Calculation of outer side diameter: c. 21 cm. Ware thickness: 1.6-1.7 cm.
RE310aj. Clay pot rim & bottom. Ware thickness: (rim) 0.6-0.6 cm & (bottom) 0.7-0.8 cm. Outer bottom diameter c. 9 cm.

Ceramics at Resengaard

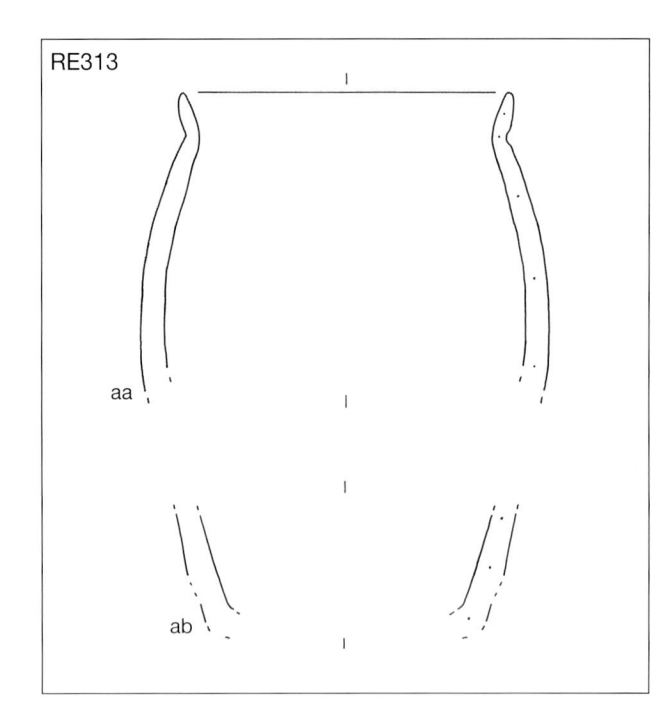

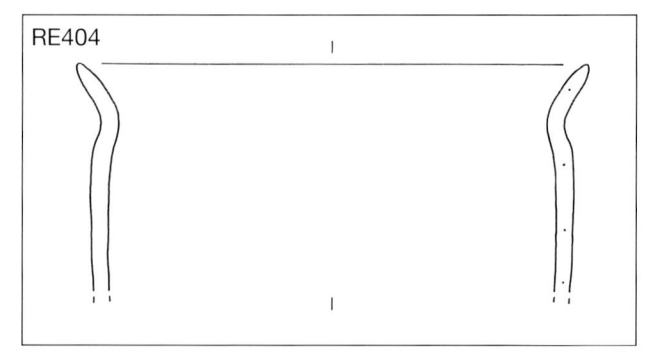

House 41, sunken-floor horizon
RE404aa. Clay pot rim & side. Calculation of outer rim diameter: c. 21 cm. Ware thickness: 0.6-0.8-0.7-0.6 cm.

House 41, secondary fills
RE313aa. Clay pot rim & side. Calculation of outer rim diameter: c. 14 cm. Ware thickness: 0.7-0.6-0.9-0.9-1.1 cm. The inclination may have been different.
RE313ab. Clay side & bottom. Calculation of outer bottom diameter: c. 11.5 cm. Ware thickness: 10.-1.2-1.3 cm. It may have been leaning more outwards. Very likely it belongs to RE313aa.

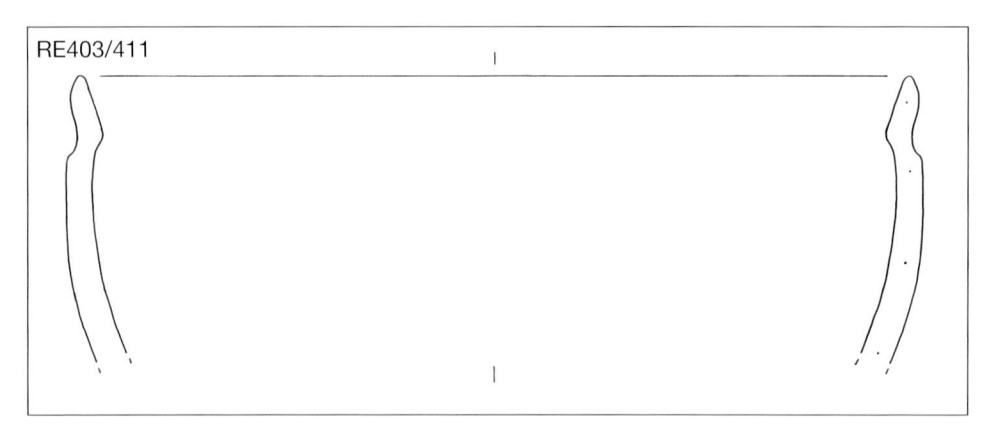

House 41, sunken-floor horizon
RE403aa/411aa. Clay pot rim & side. Calculation of outer rim diameter: c. 35 cm. Ware thickness: 1.0-1.2-1.3-1.4 cm.

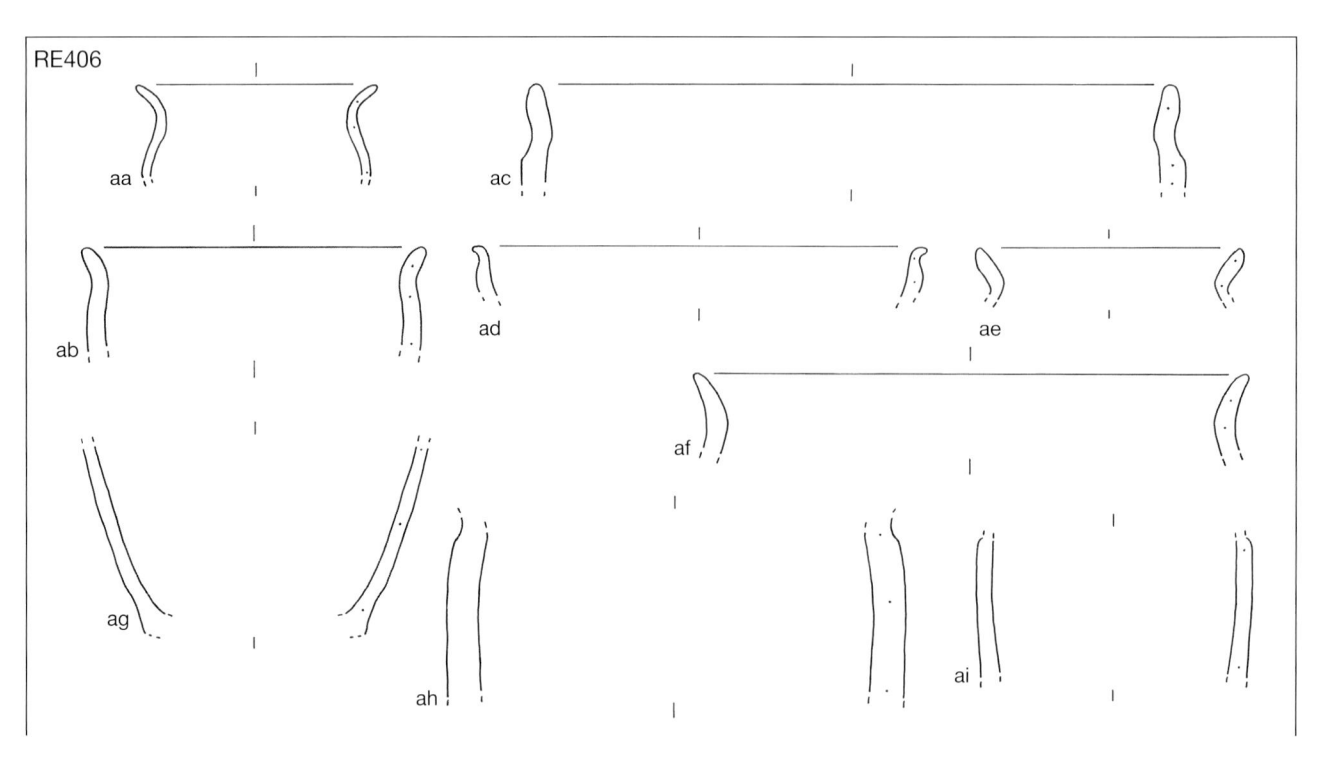

464 Catalogue A

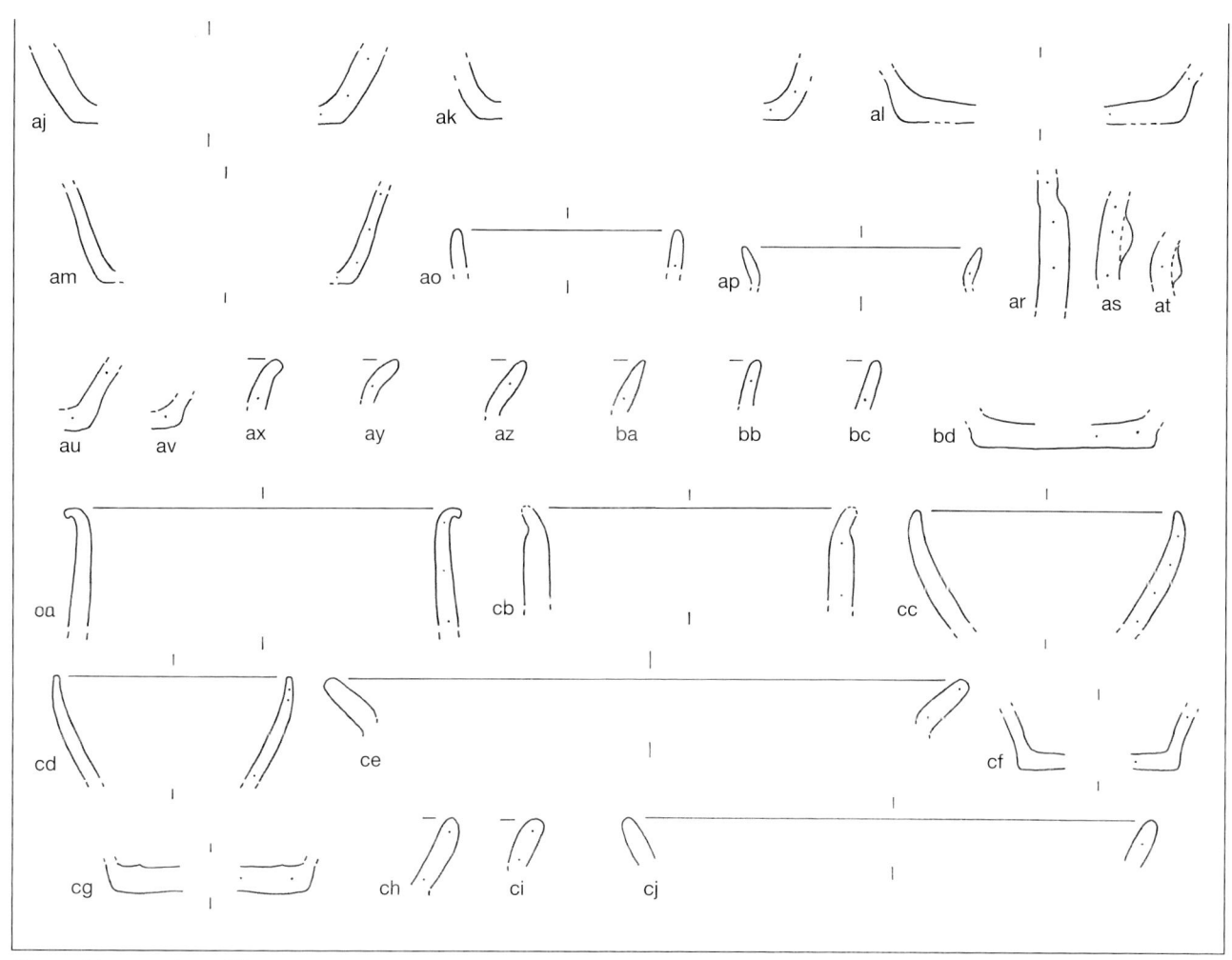

House 41, secondary fills

RE406aa. Clay pot rim & side. Calculation of outer rim diameter: c. 10 cm. Ware thickness: 0.4-0.5-0.3 cm.
RE406ab. Clay pot rim & side. Ware thickness: 0.7-0.8-0.8 cm.
RE406ac. Clay pot rim & side. Calculation of outer rim diameter: c. 26.5 cm. Ware thickness: 0.8-1.1-1.0 cm.
RE406ad. Clay pot rim & side. Calculation of outer rim diameter: c. 18.5 cm. Ware thickness: 0.4-0.6 cm. Two very thin incised lines offer very slight ornamentation.
RE406ae. Clay pot rim & side. Calculation of outer rim diameter: c. 11 cm. Ware thickness: 0.6-0.6 cm.
RE406af. Clay pot rim & side. Calculation of outer rim diameter: c. 23 cm. Ware thickness: 0.6-0.9 cm.
RE406ag. Clay pot side & bottom. Calculation of outer rim diameter: c. 9 cm. Ware thickness: 0.5-0.6-0.8 cm.
RE406ah. Clay pot side. Calculation of outer side diameter: c. 19 cm. Ware thickness: 1.1-1.3-1.4 cm. In comparison to its size, the jar was rather thick-walled.
RE406ai. Clay pot rim & side. Calculation of outer side diameter: c. 11 cm. Ware thickness: 0.7-0.8 cm.
RE406aj. Clay pot side & bottom. Calculation of outer bottom diameter: c. 12.5 cm. Ware thickness: 1.1-1.0 cm.
RE406ak. Clay pot side & bottom. Calculation of outer bottom diameter: c. 14.5 cm. Ware thickness: 0.9-0.7 cm.
RE406al. Clay pot side & bottom. Calculation of outer bottom diameter: c. 12 cm. Ware thickness: 0.6-0.7 cm.
RE406am. Clay pot side & bottom. Calculation of outer bottom diameter: c. 10.8 cm. Ware thickness: 0.5-0.6-0.7-0.4 cm.

RE406ao. Clay pot rim. Calculation of outer rim diameter: c. 10 cm. Ware thickness: 0.6 cm.
RE406ap. Clay pot rim. Calculation of outer rim diameter: c. 10.5 cm. Ware thickness: 0.4 cm.
RE406ar. Clay pot side. Ware thickness: 0.9-1.3-1.3 cm.
RE406as. Clay pot side with cordon. Ware thickness: 0.9-1.4-1.0 cm. Supplied with a horizontal cordon.
RE406at. Clay pot side with cordon. Ware thickness: 1.4 cm. Supplied with a horizontal cordon.
RE406au. Clay pot side & bottom. Ware thickness: 0.7-0.9 cm.
RE406av Clay pot side & bottom. Ware thickness: 0.8 cm.
RE406ax. Clay pot rim. Ware thickness: 0.8 cm.
RE406ay. Clay pot rim. Ware thickness: 0.6 cm.
RE406az. Clay pot rim. Ware thickness: 0.8 cm.
RE406ba. Clay pot rim. Ware thickness: 0.7 cm.
RE406bb. Clay pot rim. Ware thickness: 0.6 cm.
RE406bc. Clay pot rim. Ware thickness: 0.6 cm.
RE406bd. Clay pot bottom. Calculation of outer bottom diameter: c. 8 cm. Ware thickness: 1.2-1.0 cm.
RE406ca. Clay pot rim & side. Calculation of outer rim diameter: c. 17 cm. Ware thickness: 0.5-0.7-0.8 cm.
RE406cb. Clay pot rim & side. Calculation of outer rim diameter: c. 14.5 cm. Ware thickness: 1.0-1.1 cm. Rim top partly missing.
RE406cc. Clay pot rim & side. Calculation of outer rim diameter: c. 12 cm. Ware thickness: 0.7-0.8-0.9-0.8 cm.
RE406cd. Clay pot rim & side. Calculation of outer rim diameter: c. 10.5 cm. Ware thickness: 0.3-0.5-0.6 cm.

Ceramics at Resengaard

RE406ce. Clay pot rim. Calculation of outer rim diameter: c. 28 cm. Ware thickness: 0.7-0.9 cm.
RE406cf. Clay pot side & bottom. Calculation of outer bottom diameter: c. 7 cm. Ware thickness: 0.6-0.7 cm.
RE406cg. Clay pot bottom. Calculation of outer bottom diameter: c. 8.5 cm. Ware thickness: 1.1-1.1 cm.
RE406ch. Clay pot rim. Ware thickness: 0.8-0.8 cm.
RE406ci. Clay pot rim. Ware thickness: 0.8-0.8 cm.
RE406cj. Clay pot rim. Calculation of outer rim diameter: c. 23.5 cm. Ware thickness: 0.8 cm.

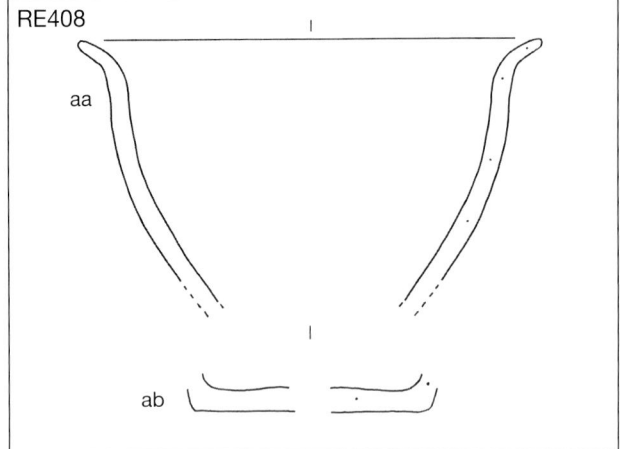

House 41, sunken-floor horizon
RE408aa. Clay pot rim & side. Calculation of outer rim diameter: c. 19 cm. Estimate of the original height: c. 12 cm. Ware thickness: 0.4-0.8-0.8-0.8 cm.
RE408ab. Clay pot bottom. Calculation of outer bottom diameter: c. 10 cm. Ware thickness: 0.8-0.9 cm.

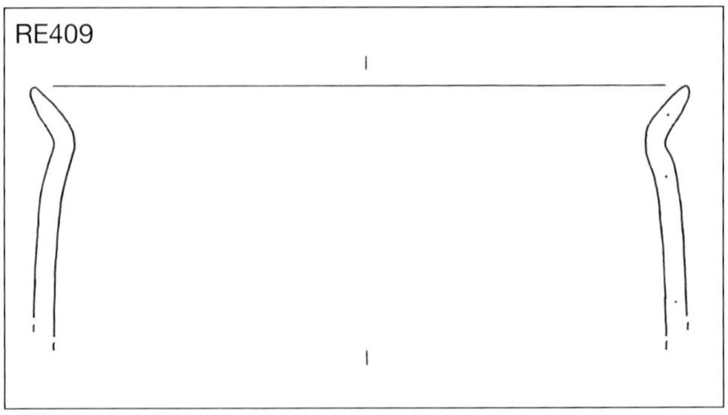

House 41, sunken-floor horizon
RE409aa. Clay pot rim. Calculation of outer rim diameter: c. 23 cm. Ware thickness: 0.7-0.8-0.8 cm.

House 41, sunken-floor horizon
RE410aa. Clay pot rim & side. Calculation of outer rim diameter: c. 16.5 cm. Ware thickness: 0.6-0.7-0.7-0.8 cm.

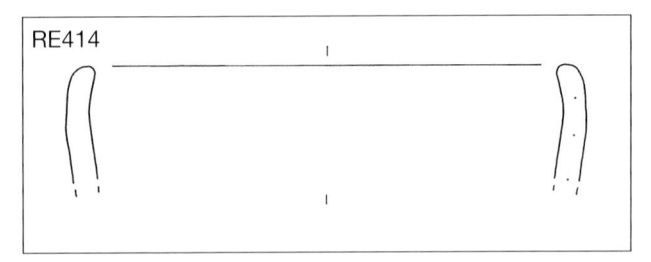

House 41, secondary fills
RE414aa. Clay pot rim & side. Calculation of outer rim diameter: c. 21 cm. Ware thickness: 0.9-1.0-1.0 cm.

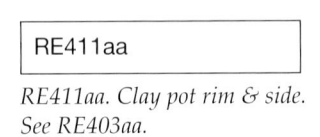

RE411aa. Clay pot rim & side. See RE403aa.

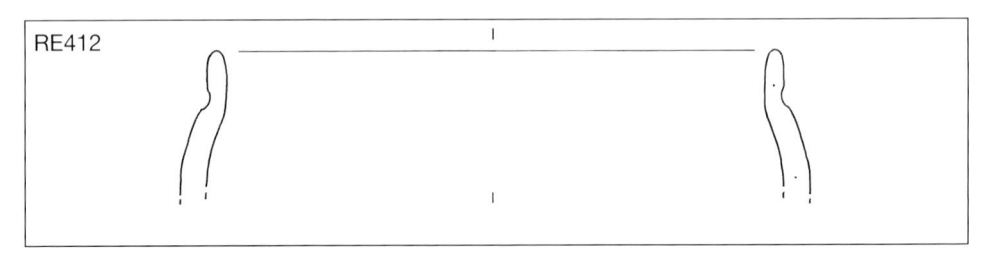

House 41, sunken-floor horizon
RE412aa. Clay pot rim & side. Calculation of outer rim diameter: c. 23.5 cm. Ware thickness: 0.8-1.1 cm.

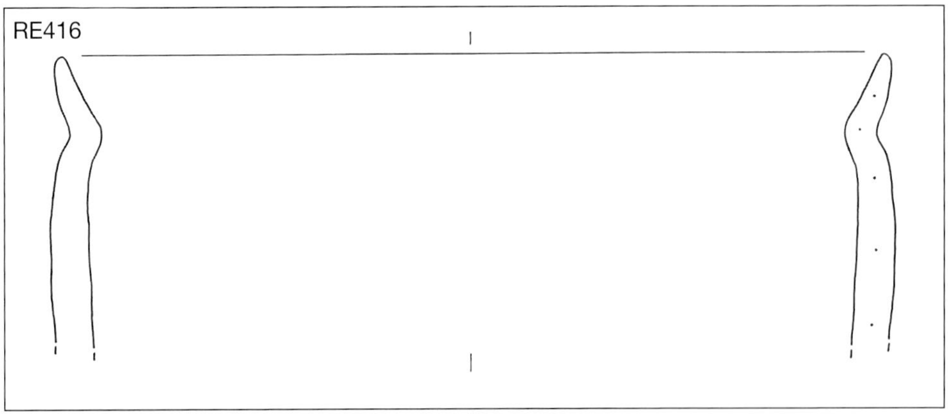

House 41, sunken-floor horizon
RE416aa. Clay pot rim & side. Calculation of outer rim diameter: c. 34.5 cm. Ware thickness: 1.0-1.3-1.4-1.5-1.6 cm.

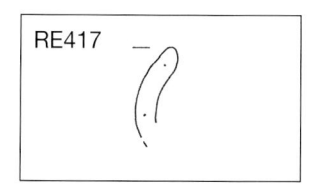

RE417

House 41, secondary fills
RE417aa. Clay pot rim. Ware thickness: 0.8-0.9 cm.

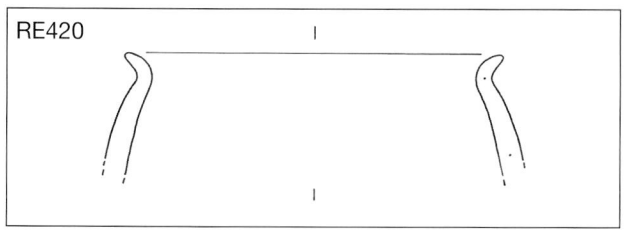

RE420

House 41, secondary fills
RE420aa. Clay pot rim & side. Ware thickness: 0.6-1.0 cm.

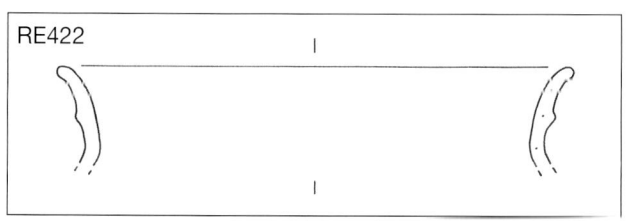

RE422

House 41, sunken-floor horizon
RE422aa. Clay pot rim & side. Calculation of outer rim diameter: c. 21 cm. Ware thickness: 0.6-0.8-0.6 cm. Supplied with horizontal cordon.

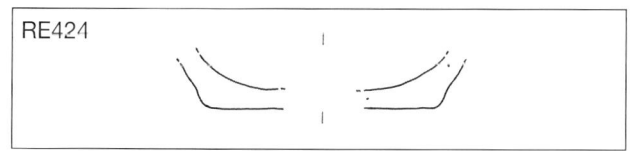

RE424

House 41, sunken-floor horizon
RE424aa. Clay pot side and bottom. Calculation of outer bottom diameter: c. 10 cm. Bottom thickness: 0.9-0.8 cm.

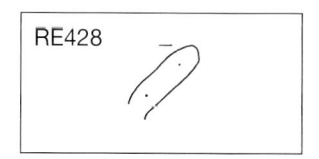

RE428

House 42, secondary fills
RE428aa. Clay pot rim. Ware thickness: 1.1-1.1 cm. The strong rim indicates a rather large diameter.

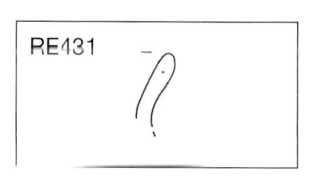

RE431

House 42, sunken-floor horizon
RE431aa. Clay pot rim. Ware thickness: 0.8 cm.

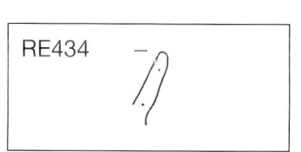

RE434

House 42, sunken-floor horizon
RE434aa. Clay pot rim. Ware thickness: 0.6-0.7 cm.

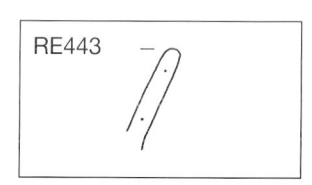

RE443

House 42, sunken-floor horizon
RE443aa. Clay pot rim. Ware thickness: 0.8-0.8 cm.

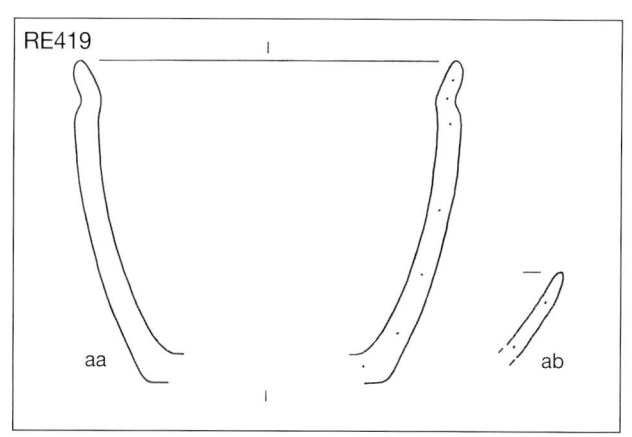

RE419 aa ab

House 41, secondary fills
RE419aa. Clay pot rim, side & bottom. Calculation of outer rim diameter: c. 16 cm. Ware thickness: 0.8-0.8-1.0-0.9.-1.0-1.1-1.2 cm. More than 30 potsherds belong.
RE419ab. Clay pot rim & side. Ware thickness: 0.6-0.7 cm.

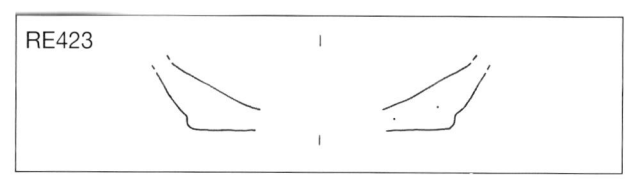

RE423

House 41, sunken-floor horizon
RE423aa. Clay pot side & bottom. Calculation of outer bottom diameter: c. 11 cm. Ware thickness: 1.9-0.8 cm.

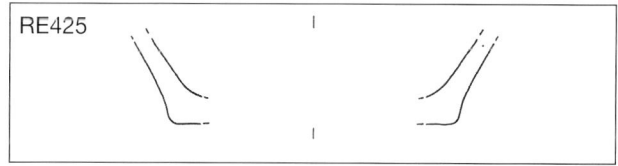

RE425

House 13, sunken-floor horizon
RE425aa. Clay pot side & bottom. Calculation of outer bottom diameter: c. 12 cm. Ware thickness: 0.8 cm.

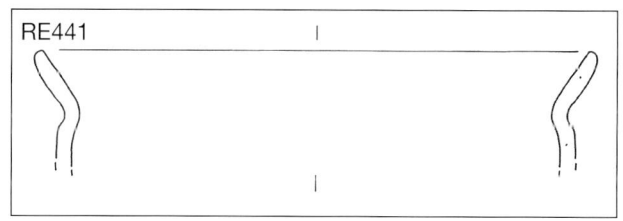

RE441

House 42, sunken-floor horizon
RE441aa. Clay pot rim & side. Calculation of outer rim diameter: c. 23.5 cm. Ware thickness: 0.6-0.6 cm.

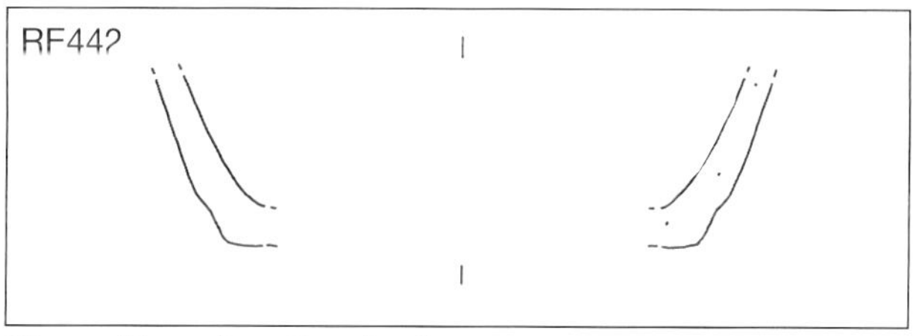

RE442

House 42, sunken-floor horizon
RE442aa. Clay pot side & bottom. Calculation of outer bottom diameter: c. 13.5 cm. Ware thickness: 0.8-1.0-0.9 cm. Soot crust on the inner side near the bottom.

Ceramics at Resengaard

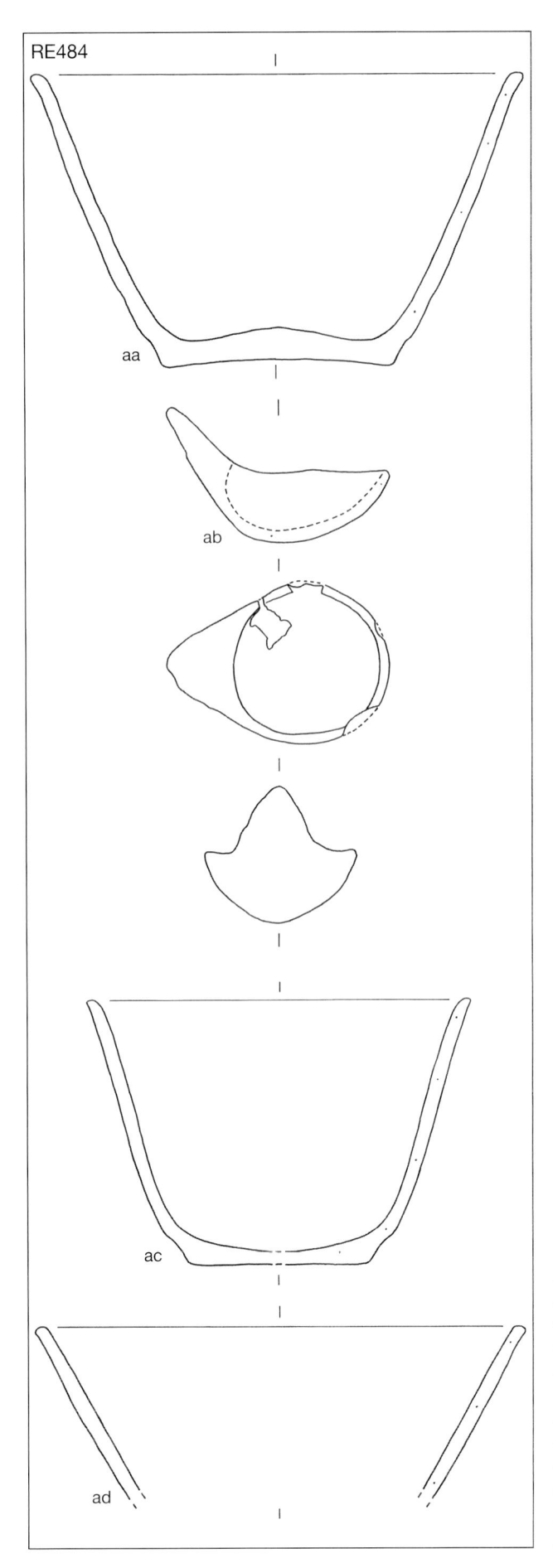

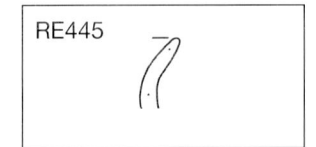

House 42, sunken-floor horizon
RE445aa. Clay pot rim & side. Ware thickness: 0.4-0.7 cm.

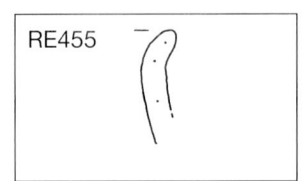

Pit 165, near House 193
RE455aa. Clay pot rim & side. Ware thickness: 0.8-1.0-1.0 cm.

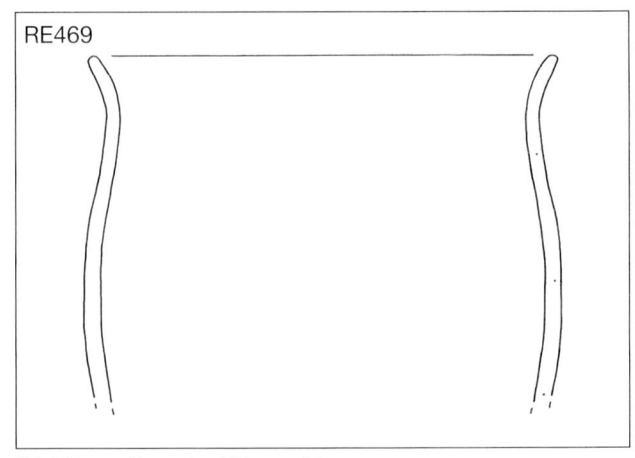

Pit 77, northwest of House 84
RE469aa. Clay pot rim & side. Calculation of outer rim diameter: c. 19 cm. Ware thickness: 0.6-0.7-0.7 cm.

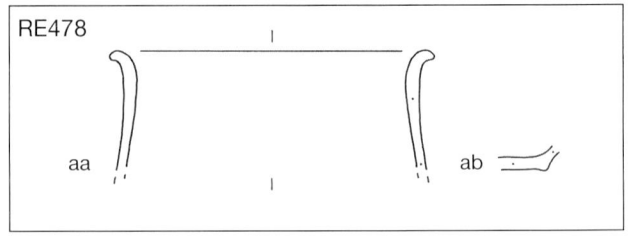

Pit 80, somewhat northeast of House 134
RE478aa. Clay pot rim & side. Calculation of outer rim diameter: c. 13.5 cm. Ware thickness: 0.6-0.4 cm.
RE478ab. Clay pot bottom (belongs probably to RE478aa). Ware thickness: 0.4-0.6 cm

Pit 89, west of House 84
RE484aa. Clay pot rim, side & bottom. Calculation of outer rim diameter: c. 24.5 cm. Estimate of original height: c. 14 cm. Ware thickness: 0.6-0.7-0.8-0.9 cm.
RE484ab. Clay spoon. Almost complete. Side thickness: c. 0.5 cm. The spoon has a total length of 11.1 cm.
RE484ac. Clay pot rim, side & bottom. Calculation of outer rim diameter: c. 19 cm. Original height: c. 13 cm. Ware thickness: 0.6-0.7-0.6-0.7-1.2 cm. The side a little irregular. Appears to have been markedly exposed to secondary burning.
RE484ad. Clay pot rim & side. Calculation of outer rim diameter: c. 24.5 cm. Ware thickness: 0.6-0.7-0.6 cm.

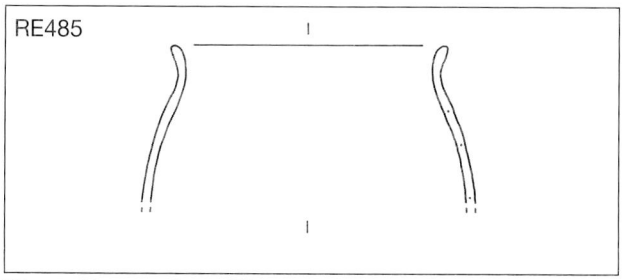

House 84, secondary fills
RE485aa. Clay pot rim & side. Calculation of outer rim diameter: c. 11.5 cm. Ware thickness: 0.5-0.4-0.4 cm.

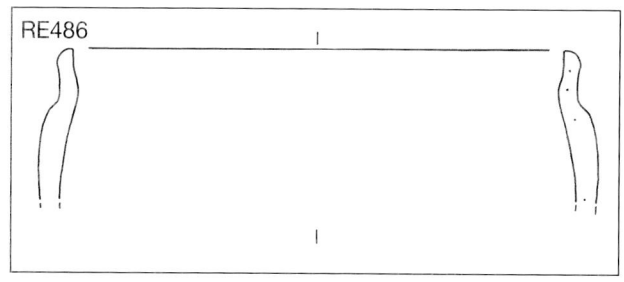

Pit 85, south of House 84
RE486aa. Clay pot rim & side. Calculation of outer rim diameter: c. 21.5 cm. Ware thickness: 0.8-0.7-1.1-0.8 cm. The inclination may have been slightly different.

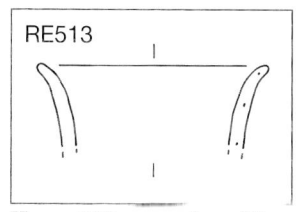

House 112, secondary fills
RE513aa. Clay pot rim & side. Ware thickness: 0.4-0.6-0.5 cm. Markedly exposed to secondary burning.

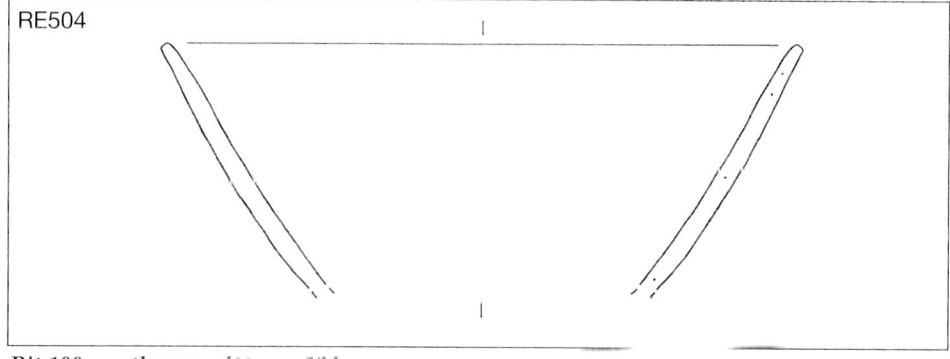

Pit 100, northwest of House 134
RE504aa. Clay pot rim & side. Calculation of outer rim diameter: c. 26.5 cm. Ware thickness: 0.6-0.7-0.7-0.7 cm.

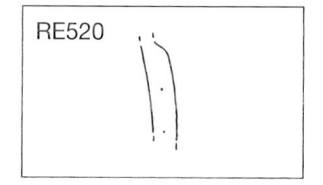

Pit 111, immediately south of House 112
RE520aa. Clay pot side. Ware thickness: 1.1-1.0 cm.

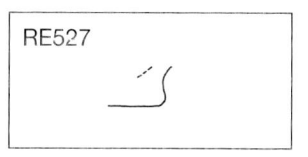

Pit 123, immediately east of House 112
RE527aa. Clay pot bottom. Only outer surface preserved.

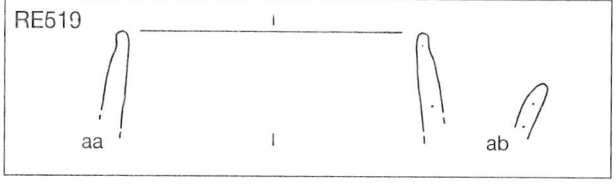

Pit 116, immediately west of House 112
RE519aa. Clay pot rim & side. Calculation of outer rim diameter: c. 13 cm. Ware thickness: 0.6-0.9 cm. RE519ab. Clay pot rim. Ware thickness: 0.8-0.7 cm.

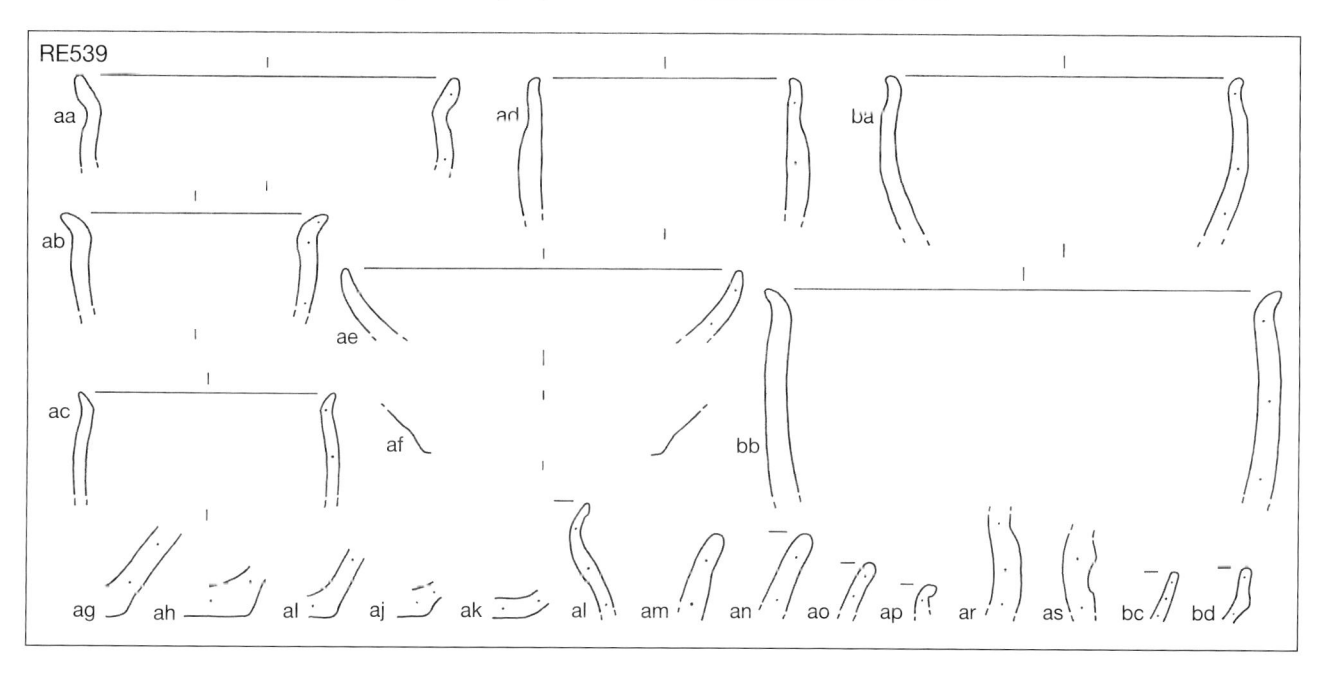

Ceramics at Resengaard   **469**

▲ *House 130, secondary fills (Page 469)*
RE539aa. Clay pot rim & side. Calculation of outer rim diameter: c. 16 cm. Ware thickness: 0.6 -0.7 cm. The inclination may have been slightly different. RE539ab. Clay pot rim & side. Calculation of outer rim diameter: c. 11 cm. Ware thickness: 0.6-0.8-0.7 cm. RE539ac. Clay pot rim & side. Calculation of outer rim diameter: c. 10.5 cm. Ware thickness: 0.5-0.6 cm. The inclination may have been slightly different. RE539ad. Clay pot rim & side. Calculation of outer rim diameter: c. 11 cm. Ware thickness: 0.6-1.0 cm. Traces of soot on the inner side near the rim. RE539ae. Clay pot rim & side. Calculation of outer rim diameter: c. 16.5 cm. Ware thickness: 0.6-0.7 cm. RE539af. Clay pot side & bottom. Calculation of outer bottom diameter: c. 10.5 cm. Only the outer surface preserved. RE539ag. Clay pot side & bottom. Ware thickness: 1.0-1.0 cm. RE539ah. Clay pot bottom. Ware thickness: 1.0-1.3 cm. RE539ai. Clay pot side & bottom. Ware thickness: 0.8-0.9 cm. RE539aj. Clay pot bottom. Ware thickness: 0.7-1.1 cm. RE539ak. Clay pot bottom. Ware thickness: 0.8-0.8 cm. RE539al. Clay pot rim & side. Ware thickness: 0.4-0.8-0.6 cm. RE539am. Clay pot rim & side. Ware thickness: 0.9-1.1 cm. RE539an. Clay pot rim & side. Ware thickness: 0.9-1.1 cm. RE539ao. Clay pot rim. Ware thickness: 0.6-0.6 cm. RE539ap. Clay pot rim. Ware thickness: 0.5 cm. RE539ar. Clay pot side. Ware thickness: 0.9-1.2-1.2 cm. RE539as. Clay pot rim & side. Ware thickness: 1.1-1.4 cm. Rim top missing. RE539ba. Clay pot rim & side. Calculation of outer rim diameter: c. 15 cm. Ware thickness: 0.6-0.7-0.9 cm. RE539bb. Clay pot rim & side. Calculation of outer rim diameter: c. 21.5 cm. Ware thickness: 0.8-1.0-1.1 cm. RE539bc. Clay pot rim. Ware thickness: 0.4-0.6 cm. RE539bd. Clay pot rim & side. Ware thickness: 0.5-0.5 cm.

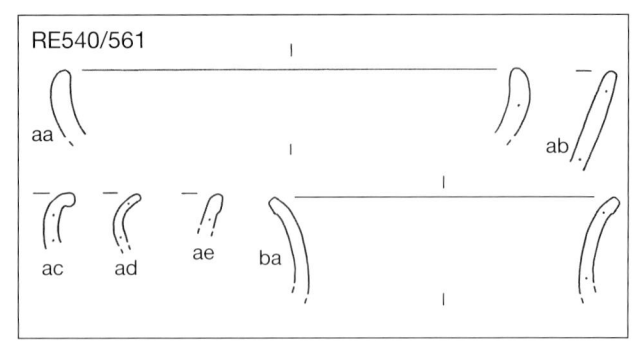

House 128, secondary fills & sunken-floor horizon
RE540aa/561aa. Clay pot rim & side. Calculation of outer rim diameter: c. 19.5 cm. Ware thickness: 0.9 cm. Markedly exposed to secondary burning. RE540 belongs to the secondary fills, RE561aa to the sunken-floor horizon.
RE540ab. Clay pot rim & side. Ware thickness: 0.6-0.7 cm.
RE540ac. Clay pot rim & side. Ware thickness: 0.6-0.6 cm.
RE540ad. Clay pot rim & side. Ware thickness: 0.4-0.4 cm.
RE540ae. Clay pot rim. Ware thickness: 0.5 cm.
RE540ba. Clay pot rim & side. Calculation of outer rim diameter: c. 14.5 cm. Ware thickness: 0.5-0.7 cm.

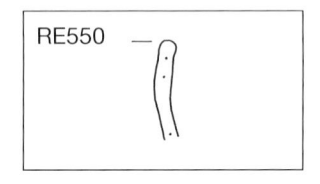

House 128, sunken-floor horizon
RE550aa. Clay pot rim & side. Ware thickness: 0.6-0.7-0.6 cm.

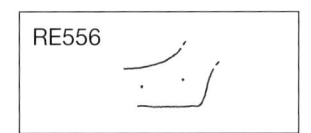

Pit 151, southeast of House 128
RE556aa. Clay pot bottom. Bottom thickness: 2.3-1.6 cm.

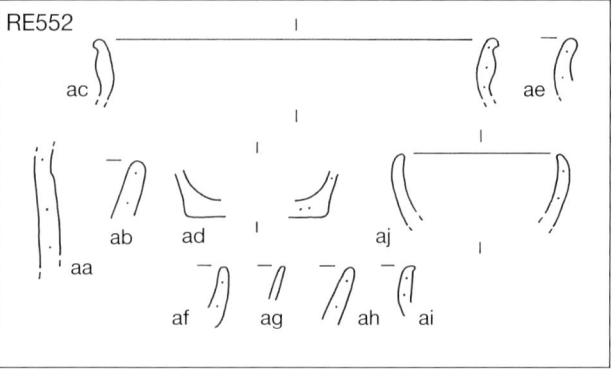

House 128, secondary fills
RE552aa. Clay pot side. Ware thickness: 0.7-0.9-0.9 cm.
RE552ab. Clay pot rim. Ware thickness: 0.8-0.9 cm.
RE552ac. Clay pot rim & side. Calculation of outer rim diameter: c. 16.5 cm. Ware thickness: 0.5-0.8-0.5 cm.
RE552ad. Clay pot side & bottom. Calculation of outer bottom diameter: c. 6 cm. Ware thickness: 0.4-0.9-0.8 cm.
RE552ae. Clay pot rim & side. Ware thickness: c. 0.6-0.8 cm.
RE552af. Clay pot rim & side. Ware thickness: 0.5-0.7 cm.
RE552ag. Clay pot rim (ware thickness: c. 0.3 cm).
RE552ah. Clay pot rim. Ware thickness: 0.6-0.7 cm.
RE552ai. Clay pot rim & side. Ware thickness: 0.5-0.6 cm.
RE552aj. Clay pot rim & side. Calculation of outer rim diameter: c. 7 cm. Ware thickness: 0.4-0.5 cm.

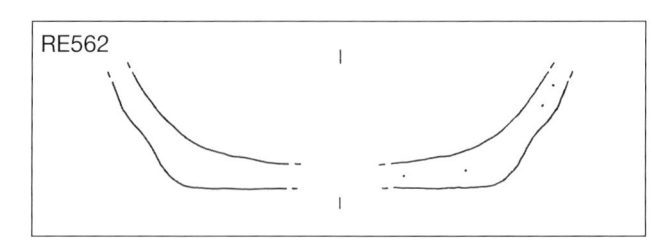

House 128, sunken-floor horizon
RE562aa. Clay pot side & bottom. Calculation of outer bottom diameter: c. 14 cm. Ware thickness: 1.0-1.2-1.4-0.9 cm. Traces of soot on the inner side near the bottom.

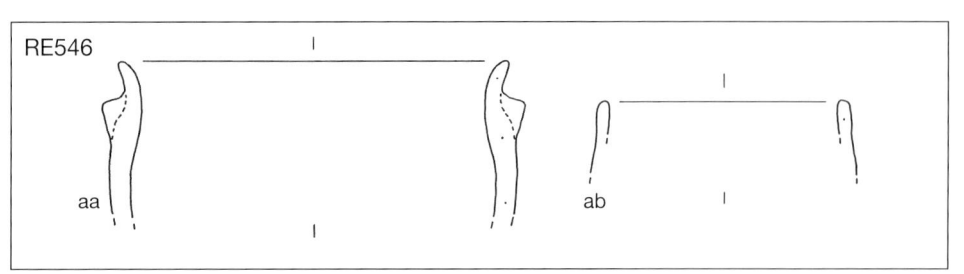

House 128, sunken-floor horizon
RE546aa. Clay pot rim & side. Calculation of outer rim diameter: c. 16.5 cm. Ware thickness: 0.7-1.0-0.9 cm. Supplied with a horizontally-projecting lug, original length assumed to be approx. 4 cm.
RE546ab. Clay pot rim & side. Calculation of outer rim diameter: c. 10.5 cm. Ware thickness: 0.5 cm.

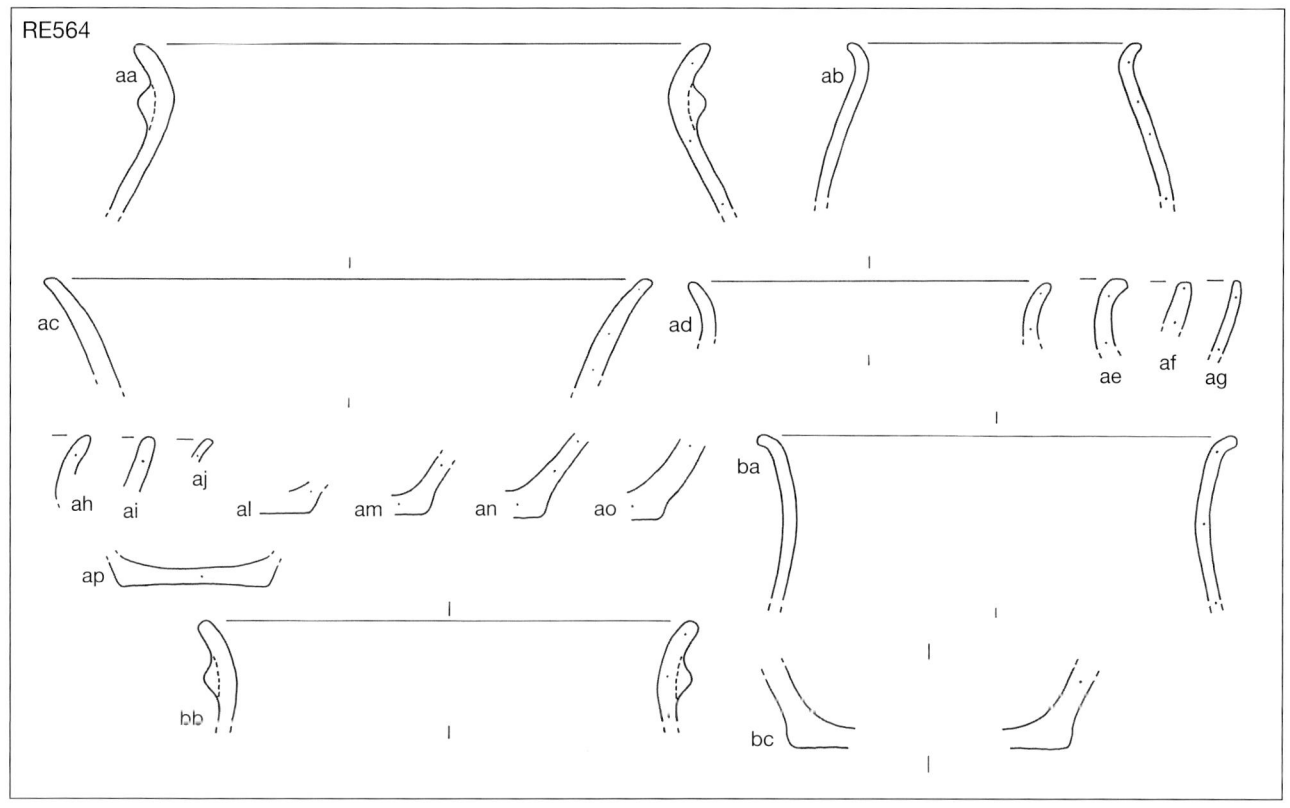

House 134, secondary fills

RE564aa. Clay pot rim & side. Calculation of outer rim diameter: c. 23.5 cm. Ware thickness: 0.7-0.6-0.6 cm. Supplied with a horizontal cordon.
RE564ab. Clay pot rim & side. Calculation of outer rim diameter: c. 12.5 cm. Ware thickness: 0.5-0.6-0.6-0.5 cm.
RE564ac. Clay pot rim & side. Calculation of outer rim diameter: c. 25 cm. Ware thickness: 0.6-0.9-0.8 cm.
RE564ad. Clay pot rim & side. Calculation of outer rim diameter: c. 15 cm. Ware thickness: 0.5-0.6 cm.
RE564ae. Clay pot rim & side. Ware thickness: 0.6-0.7 cm.
RE564af. Clay pot rim. Ware thickness: 0.6-0.8 cm.
RE564ag. Clay pot rim & side. Ware thickness: 0.4-0.5 cm.
RE564ah. Clay pot rim & side. Ware thickness: 0.6 cm.
RE564ai. Clay pot rim. Ware thickness: 0.7 cm.
RE564aj. Clay pot rim. Ware thickness: 0.4 cm.
RE564al. Clay pot bottom. Ware thickness: 0.7 cm.
RE564am. Clay pot side & bottom. Ware thickness: 0.7-0.8 cm.
RE564an. Clay pot side & bottom. Ware thickness: 0.7-0.8-1.1 cm.
RE564ao. Clay pot side & bottom. Ware thickness: 1.1-1.1 cm.
RE564ap. Clay pot side & bottom. Calculation of outer bottom diameter: c. 6.5 cm. Ware thickness: 0.8 cm.
RE564ba. Clay pot rim & side. Calculation of outer rim diameter: c. 20 cm. Ware thickness: 0.7-0.6-0.5 cm.
RE564bb. Clay pot rim & side. Calculation of outer rim diameter: c. 20.5 cm. Ware thickness: 0.7-1.4-0.6 cm. Supplied with a horizontal cordon.
RE564bc. Clay pot side & bottom. Calculation of outer bottom diameter: c. 12 cm. Ware thickness: 1.0 cm.

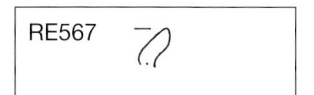

Pit 567, in the area of House 128

RE567aa. Clay pot rim. Ware thickness: 0.7 cm. From a soil feature in the top of the large pit west of the sunken floor. See text, House 128, Ch. 4.

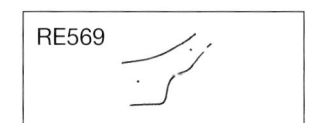

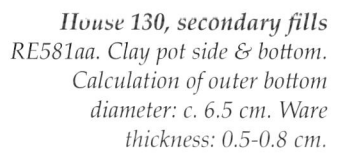

Pit 321, south of House 130

RE569aa. Clay pot side & bottom. Ware thickness: 0.9-1.8 cm.

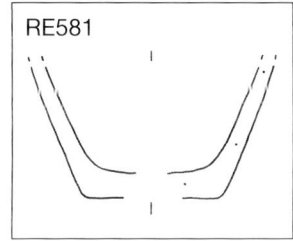

House 130, secondary fills

RE581aa. Clay pot side & bottom. Calculation of outer bottom diameter: c. 6.5 cm. Ware thickness: 0.5-0.8 cm.

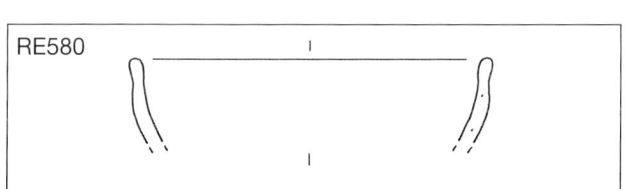

House 130, sunken-floor horizon

RE580aa. Clay pot rim & side. Calculation of outer rim diameter: c. 14.5 cm. Ware thickness: 0.5-0.6 cm.

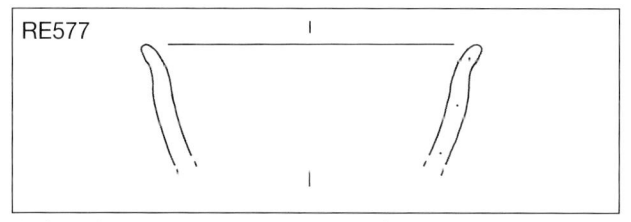

Culture layer 318, west-northwest of House 41

RE577aa. Clay pot rim & side. Calculation of outer rim diameter: c. 14 cm. Ware thickness: 0.6-0.8-0.8 cm.

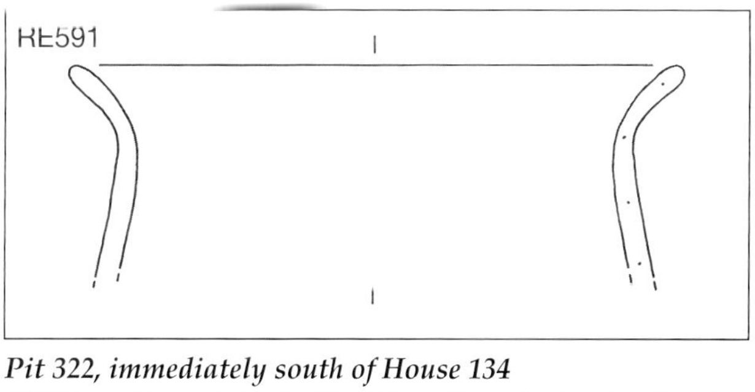

Pit 322, immediately south of House 134

RE591aa. Clay pot rim & side. Calculation of outer rim diameter: c. 21 cm. Ware thickness: 0.7-0.6-0.8-0.8 cm.

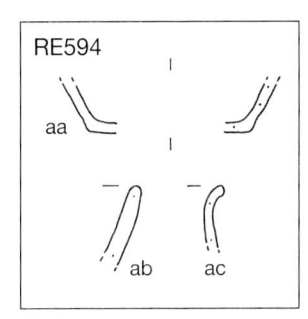

House 134, sunken-floor horizon
RE594aa. Clay pot side & bottom. Calculation of outer bottom diameter: c. 7 cm. Ware thickness: 0.5-0.4-0.4 cm.
RE594ab. Clay pot rim & side. Ware thickness: 0.6-0.8 cm.
RE594ac. Clay pot rim & side. Ware thickness: 0.4-0.5 cm.

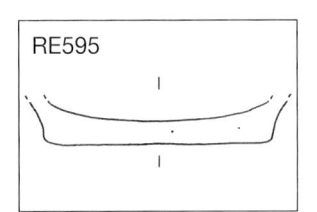

House 134, sunken-floor horizon
RE595aa. Clay pot side & bottom. Calculation of outer bottom diameter: c. 9.5 cm. Ware thickness: 1.2-1.0 cm. Underside of the bottom unusually flat.

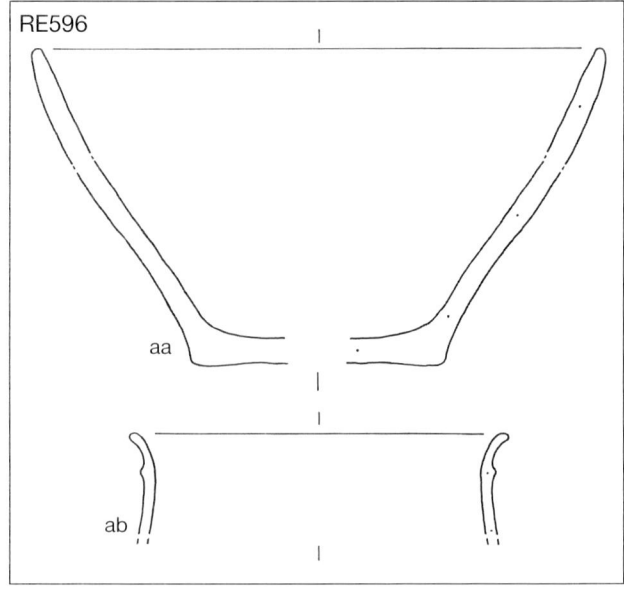

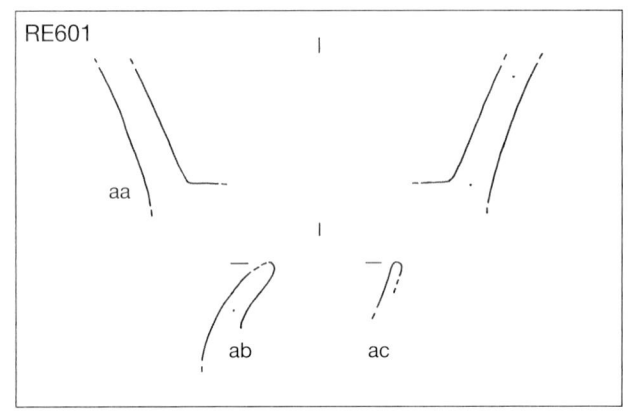

House 138, secondary fills
RE601aa. Clay pot side & bottom. Calculation of outer bottom diameter: c. 13.5 cm. Ware thickness: 1.3-1.7 cm.
RE601ab. Clay pot rim. Ware thickness: 1.0 cm.
RE601ac. Clay pot rim.

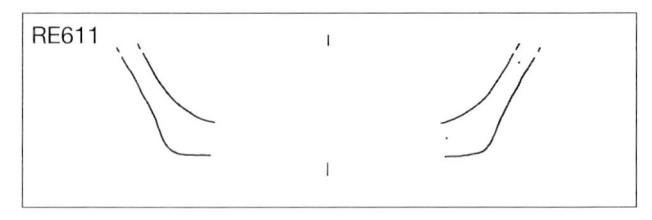

House 134, sunken-floor horizon
RE596aa. Clay pot rim, side & bottom. Calculation of outer rim diameter: c. 23.5 cm. Estimate of original height: c. 12.5 cm. Ware thickness: 0.9-0.7-0.9-1.0 cm. The height may have been slightly different.
RE596ab Clay pot rim & side. Calculation of outer rim diameter: c. 15.5 cm. Ware thickness: 0.6-0.4 cm. Supplied with low horizontal cordon.

Culture layer 309, north of House 198
RE611aa. Clay pot side & bottom. Calculation of outer bottom diameter: c. 13 cm. Ware thickness: 0.9-1.3 cm.

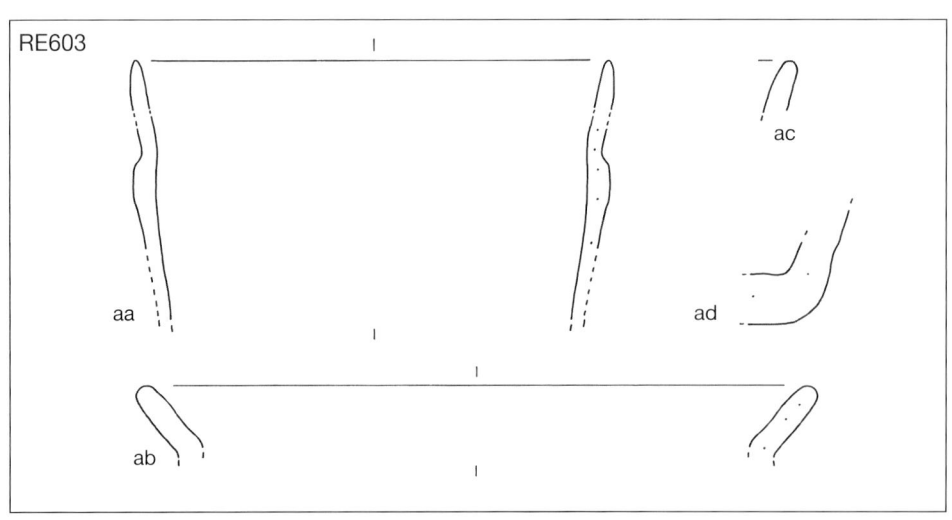

Culture layer 335, south of House 138
RE603aa. Clay pot rim & side. Calculation of outer rim diameter: c. 20 cm. Ware thickness: 0.7-0.6-1.0-0.9-0.7 cm. The outer side displays a somewhat smoothed surface. Some uncertainty as to the reconstruction and dating.
RE603ab. Clay pot rim. Calculation of outer rim diameter: c. 28 cm. Ware thickness: 1.0-1.0-1.1 cm.
RE603ac. Clay pot rim. Ware thickness: 0.7-0.9 cm.
RE603ad. Clay pot side & bottom. Ware thickness: 1.7-2.0 cm.

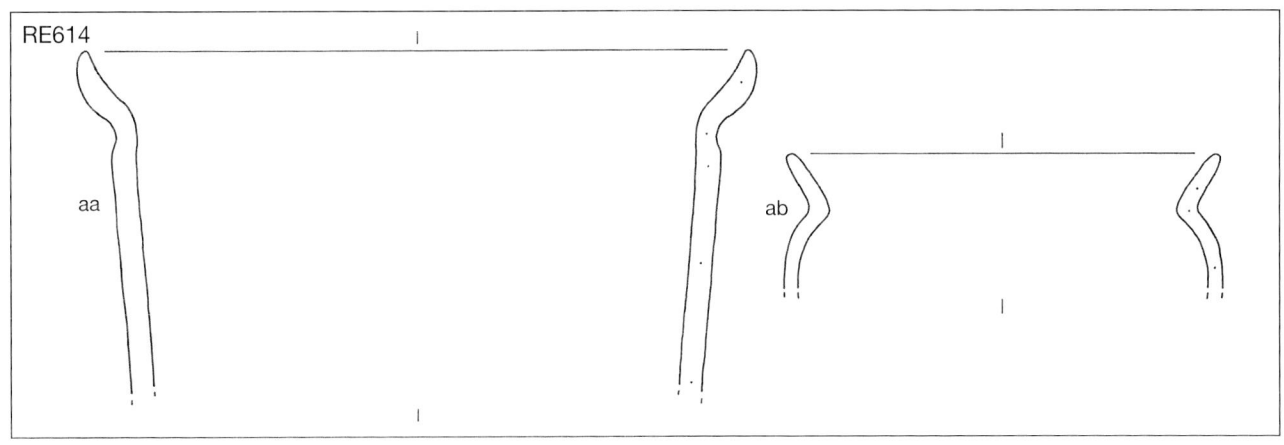

House 138, sunken-floor horizon
RE614aa. Clay pot rim & side. Calculation of outer rim diameter: c. 28 cm. Ware thickness: 1.0-0.9-1.0-1.0-1.0 cm.
RE614ab. Clay pot rim & side. Calculation of outer rim diameter: c. 18 cm. Ware thickness: 0.7-0.9-0.6 cm.

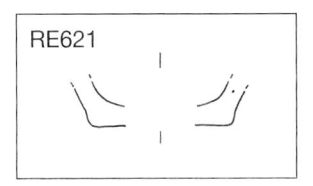

Pit 161, southwest of House 193
RE621aa. Clay pot side & bottom. Calculation of outer bottom diameter: c. 6 cm. Ware thickness: 0.8 cm

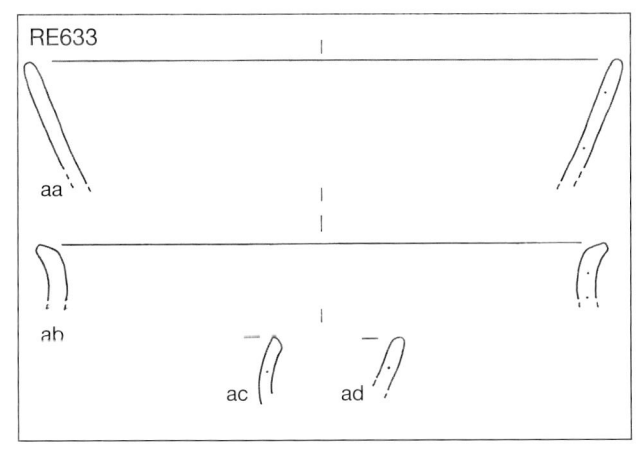

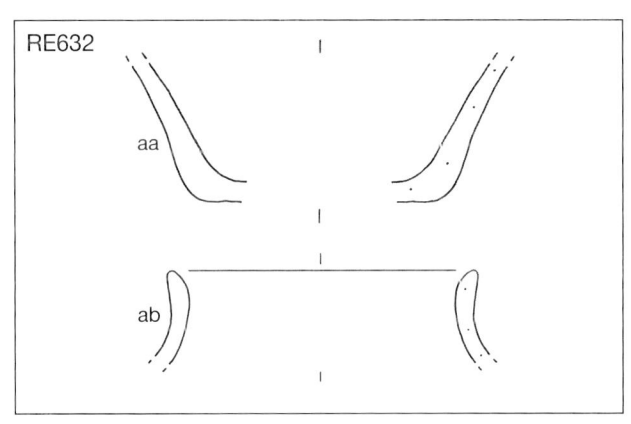

Pit 160, southwest of House 193
RE632aa. Clay pot side & bottom. Calculation of outer bottom diameter: c. 11 cm. Ware thickness: 0.7-0.8-1.2-0.9 cm. Somewhat unusual ware. Soot crust in an area on the inner side above the bottom.
RE632ab. Clay pot rim & side. Calculation of outer rim diameter: c. 13 cm. Ware thickness: 0.8-0.7-0.7 cm.

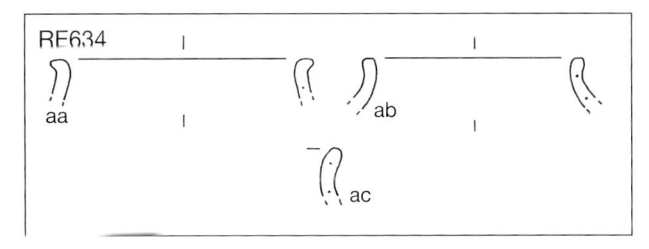

Pit 325, north of House 198
RE633aa. Clay pot rim & side. Calculation of outer rim diameter: c. 25 cm. Ware thickness: 0.6-0.6 cm.
RE633ab. Clay pot rim. Calculation of outer rim diameter: c. 23.5 cm. Ware thickness: 0.8-0.7 cm. Clay pot rim.
RE633ac. Ware thickness: 0.5 cm.
RE633ad. Clay pot rim. Ware thickness: 0.7 cm.

House 198, secondary fills
RE634aa. Clay pot rim & side. Calculation of outer rim diameter: c. 11 cm. Ware thickness: 0.5 cm.
RE634ab. Clay pot rim & side. Calculation of outer rim diameter: c. 9 cm. Ware thickness: 0.5-0.6 cm.
RE634ac. Clay pot rim. Ware thickness: 0.7-0.6 cm.

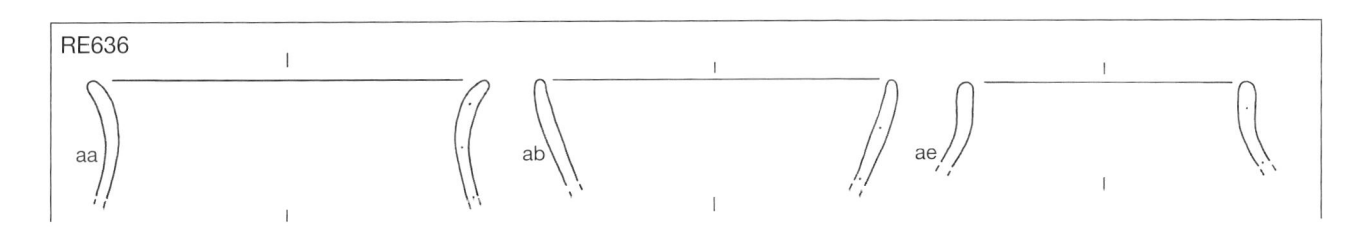

Ceramics at Resengaard

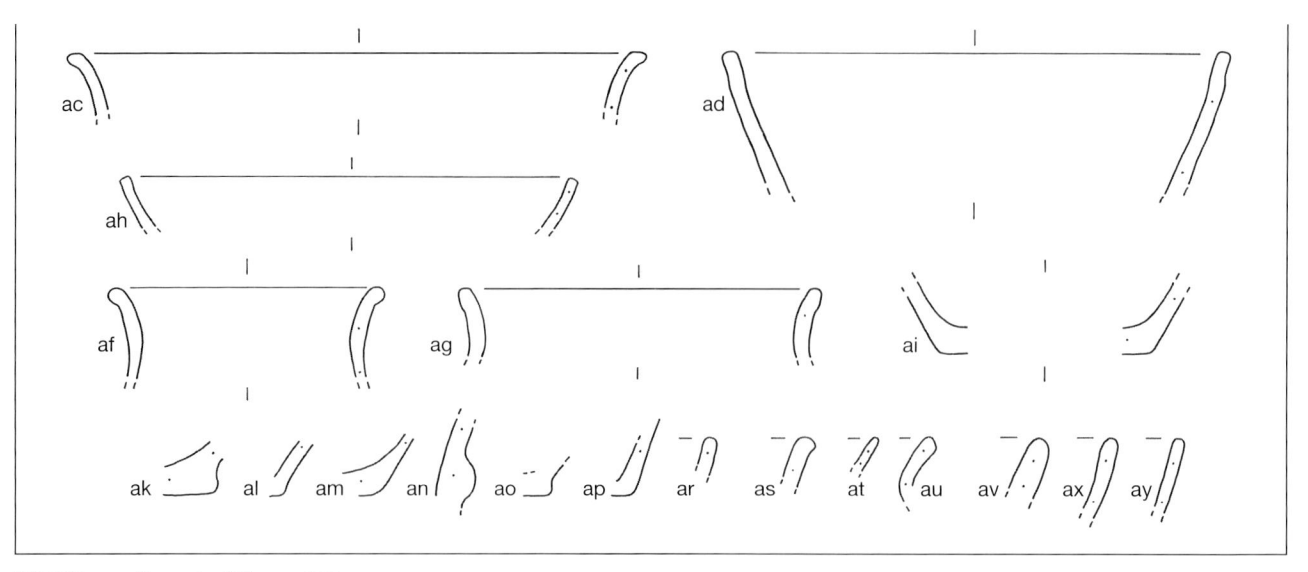

Pit 161, southwest of House 193

RE636aa. Clay pot rim & side. Calculation of outer rim diameter: c. 16.5 cm. Ware thickness: 0.7-0.6-0.4 cm.
RE636ab. Clay pot rim & side. Calculation of outer rim diameter: c. 15 cm. Ware thickness: 0.7-0.6 cm.
RE636ac. Clay pot rim & side. Calculation of outer rim diameter: c. 24 cm. Ware thickness: 0.5-0.6 cm. Ornamented with cardium impression.
RE636ad. Clay pot rim & side. Calculation of outer rim diameter: c. 20.5 cm. Ware thickness: 0.7-0.8 cm. The inclination may have been slightly different.
RE636ae. Clay pot rim & side. Calculation of outer rim diameter: c. 12.5 cm. Ware thickness: 0.7-0.5 cm.
RE636af. Clay pot rim & side. Calculation of outer rim diameter: c. 11.5 cm. Ware thickness: 0.6-0.4 cm. Ornamented with cardium impression.
RE636ag. Clay pot rim. Calculation of outer rim diameter: c. 15 cm. Ware thickness: 0.7 cm.
RE636ah. Clay pot rim. Calculation of outer rim diameter: c. 19 cm. Ware thickness: 0.5-0.5 cm. The inclination may have been somewhat different.

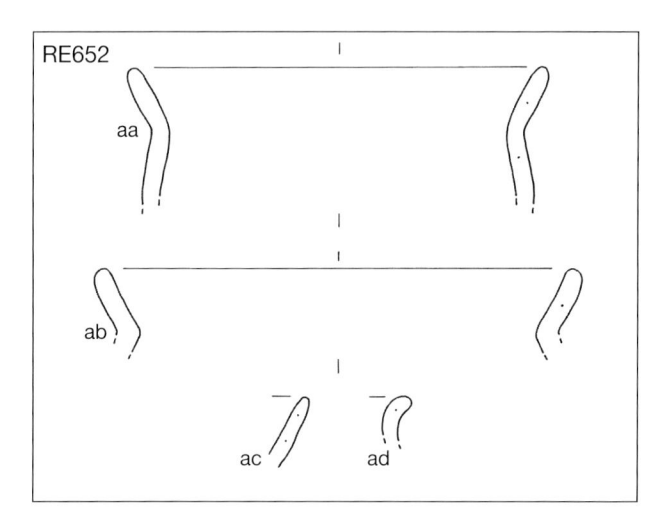

RE636ai. Clay pot side & bottom. Calculation of outer bottom diameter: c. 9 cm. Ware thickness: 0.7 cm.
RE636ak. Clay pot side & bottom. Ware thickness: 0.9-1.2 cm.
RE636al. Clay pot side & bottom. Only a bottom underside piece preserved. Ware thickness: 0.6 cm.
RE636am. Clay pot side & bottom. Ware thickness: 0.4-1.0 cm. The side becomes remarkably thin towards the top, in relation to the thick bottom.
RE636an. Clay pot side. Ware thickness: 0.8-1.5 cm. Supplied with a horizontal cordon.
RE636ao. Clay pot side & bottom. No inner side preserved.
RE636ap. Clay pot side & bottom. Ware thickness: 0.6 cm.
RE636ar. Clay pot rim. Ware thickness: 0.6 cm.
RE636as. Clay pot rim. Ware thickness: 0.7 cm.
RE636at. Clay pot rim. Ware thickness: 0.4-0.4 cm.
RE636au. Clay pot rim & side. Ware thickness: 0.6-0.5 cm.
RE636av. Clay pot rim. Ware thickness: 1.0-1.1 cm.
RE636ax. Clay pot rim & side. Ware thickness: 0.7-0.5 cm.
RE636ay. Clay pot rim & side. Ware thickness: 0.5-0.5 cm.

House 42, secondary fills

RE652aa. Clay pot rim & side. Calculation of outer rim diameter: c. 17.5 cm. Ware thickness: 0.8-0.8 cm.
RE652ab. Clay pot rim & side. Calculation of outer rim diameter: c. 20 cm. Ware thickness: 0.9 cm.
RE652ac. Clay pot rim & side. Ware thickness: 0.6-0.7 cm.
RE652ad. Clay pot rim. Ware thickness: 0.8 cm.

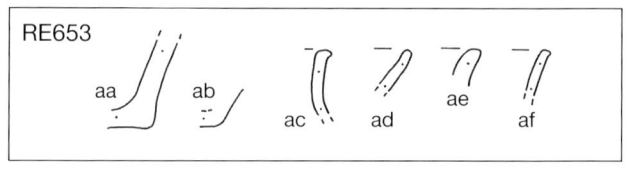

Culture layer 203, east of House 138

RE653aa. Clay pot side & bottom. Ware thickness: 0.9-0.8 cm.
RE653ab. Clay pot side & bottom. Ware thickness: 0.7 cm. Only outer side preserved.
RE653ac. Clay pot rim & side. Ware thickness: 0.5-0.4 cm.
RE653ad. Clay pot rim. Ware thickness: 0.5-0.5 cm.
RE653ae. Clay pot rim. Ware thickness: 0.7 cm.
RE653af. Clay pot rim & side. Ware thickness: 0.4-0.4 cm.

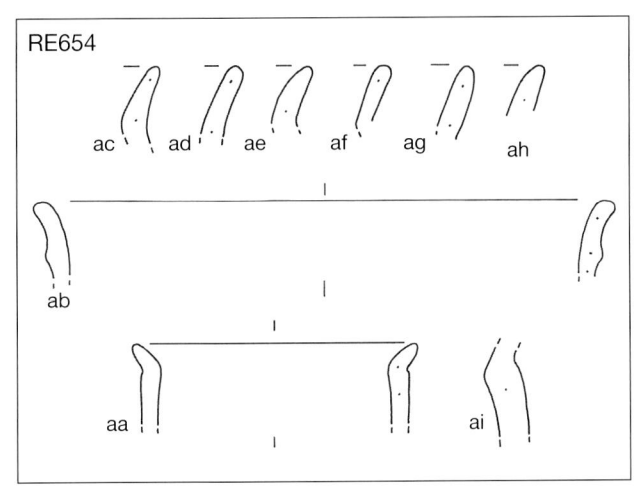

House 42, secondary fills
RE654aa. Clay pot rim & side. Calculation of outer rim diameter: c. 11.5 cm. Ware thickness: 0.7-0.7 cm.
RE654ab. Clay pot rim & side. Calculation of outer rim diameter: c. 24 cm. Ware thickness: 0.8-1.1-0.7 cm. Supplied with a low horizontal cordon.
RE654ac. Clay pot rim & side. Ware thickness: 0.6-1.0 cm.
RE654ad. Clay pot rim. Ware thickness: 0.8-0.9 cm.
RE654ae. Clay pot rim. Ware thickness: 1.0 cm.
RE654af. Clay pot rim & side. Ware thickness: 0.7 cm.
RE654ag. Clay pot side. Ware thickness: 0.9-0.9 cm.
RE654ah. Clay pot rim. Ware thickness: 1.0 cm.
RE654ai. Clay pot rim. Ware thickness: 1.3 cm.

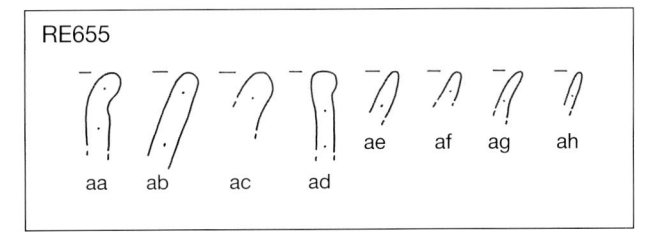

House 13, secondary fills
RE655aa. Clay pot rim & side. Ware thickness: 0.8-1.0 cm.
RE655ab. Clay pot rim. Ware thickness: 1.0-1.0 cm.
RE655ac. Clay pot rim. Ware thickness: 1.2 cm.
RE655ad. Clay pot rim & side. Ware thickness: 0.7-0.7 cm.
RE655ae. Clay pot rim. Ware thickness: 0.7 cm.
RE655af. Clay pot rim. Ware thickness: 0.6 cm.
RE655ag. Clay pot rim. Ware thickness: 0.5 cm.
RE655ah. Clay pot rim. Ware thickness: 0.4 cm.

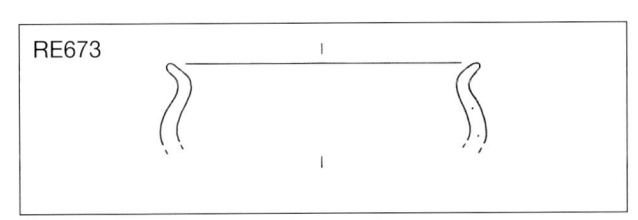

Pit 315, somewhat west of House 84
RE673aa. Clay pot rim & side. Calculation of outer rim diameter: c. 13 cm. Ware thickness: 0.5-0.6-0.7 cm.

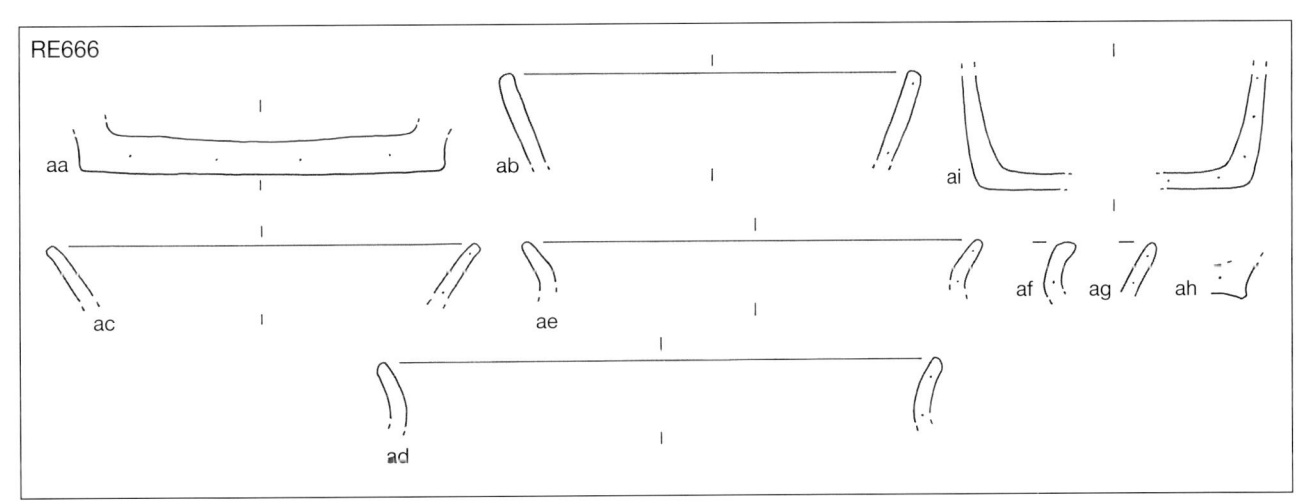

House 183, secondary fills
RE666aa. Clay pot bottom. Calculation of outer bottom diameter: c. 15 cm. Ware thickness: 1.5-1.3-1.3-1.4 cm.
RE666ab. Clay pot rim & side. Calculation of outer rim diameter: c. 17.5 cm. Ware thickness: 0.7-0.6 cm.
RE666ac. Clay pot rim & side. Calculation of outer rim diameter: c. 17.5 cm. Ware thickness: 0.5-0.6 cm. Shaping somewhat irregular.
RE666ad. Clay pot rim. Calculation of outer rim diameter: c. 28.5 cm. Ware thickness: 0.6-0.7 cm.
RE666ae. Clay pot rim. Calculation of outer rim diameter: c. 23 cm. Ware thickness: 0.6-0.7 cm.
RE666af Clay pot rim. Ware thickness: 0.8 cm.
RE666ag. Clay pot rim. Ware thickness: 0.6-0.6 cm.
RE666ah. Clay pot bottom. Ware thickness: 1.2 cm.
RE666ai. Clay pot side & bottom. Calculation of outer bottom diameter: c. 11.5 cm. Ware thickness: 0.5-0.7-1.0-0.8-0.6 cm.

Ceramics at Resengaard

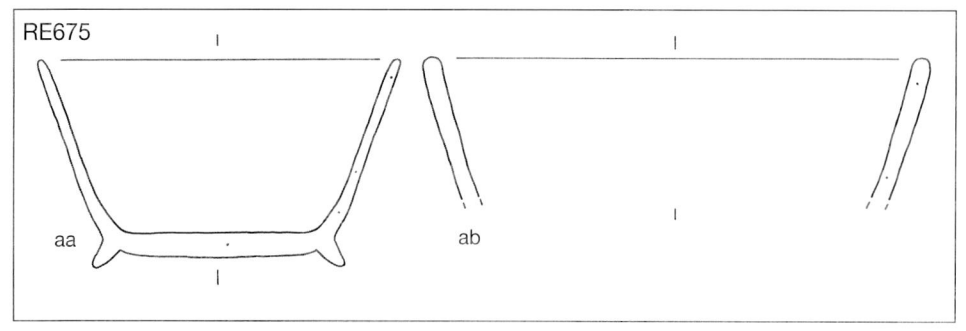

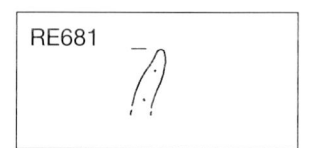

Pit 323, north of House 197
RE681ab. Clay pot rim. Ware thickness: 0.7-0.8 cm.

House 193, a wall posthole
RE675aa. Clay pot rim, side & bottom. Calculation of outer rim diameter: c. 15 cm. Original height: c. 8.5 cm. Ware thickness: 0.4-0.5-0.6 cm. Rather irregular shaping of the foot, mounted after finishing the bottom.
RE675ab. Clay pot rim & side. Calculation of outer rim diameter: c. 21 cm. Ware thickness: 0.8-0.7 cm.

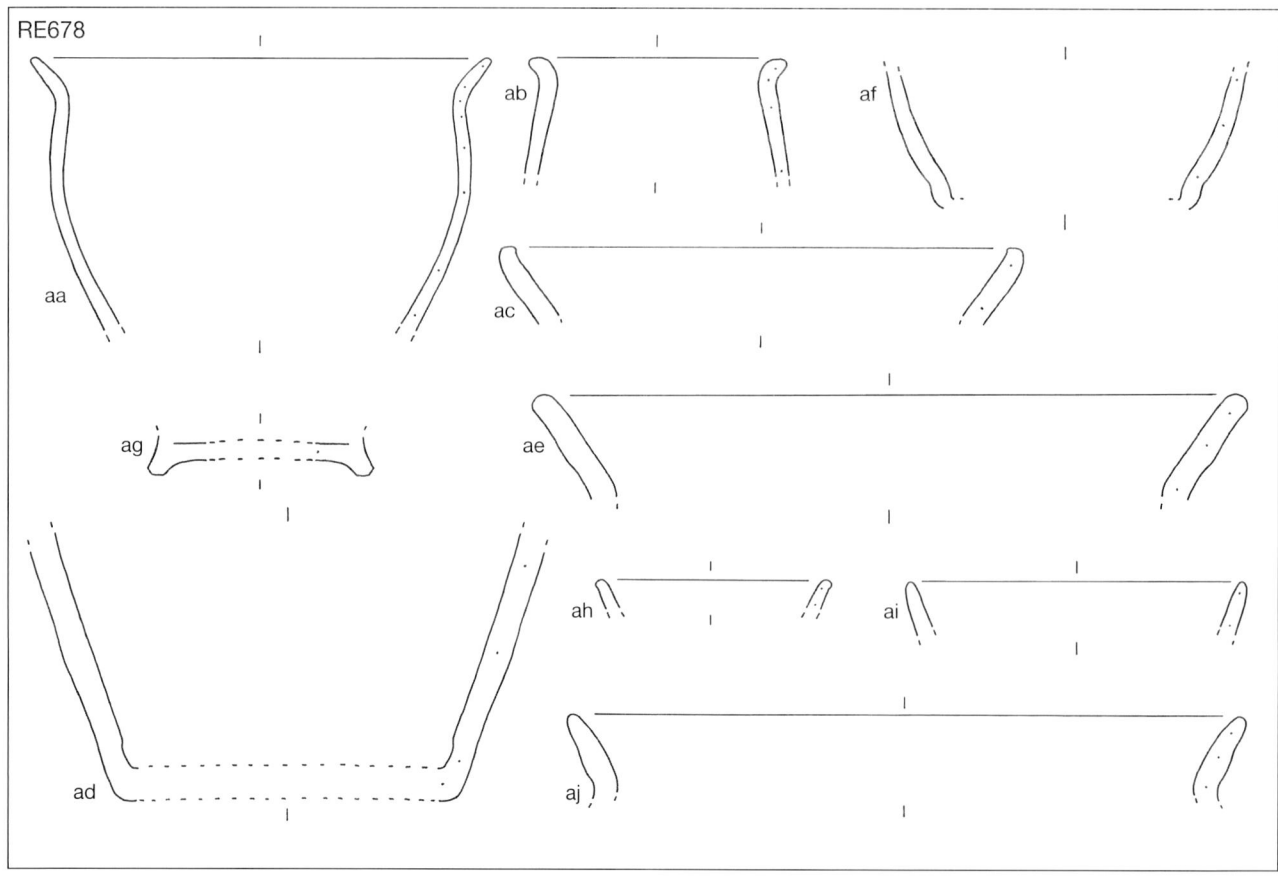

House 198, secondary fills
RE678aa. Clay pot rim & side. Calculation of outer rim diameter: c. 19 cm. Ware thickness: 0.5-0.6-0.5-0.6-0.6-0.5-0.5-0.7 cm.
RE678ab. Clay pot rim & side. Calculation of outer rim diameter: c. 10.5 cm. Ware thickness: 0.7-0.8-0.7-0.6 cm.
RE678ac. Clay pot rim. Calculation of outer rim diameter: c. 21.5 cm. Ware thickness: 0.8-0.7 cm.
RE678ad. Clay pot side & bottom. Calculation of outer bottom diameter: c. 15.5 cm. Ware thickness: 1.2-1.1-1.0-1.3 cm.
RE678ae. Clay pot rim. Calculation of outer rim diameter: c. 29.5 cm. Ware thickness: 1.0-1.1-1.1 cm. Soot & soot crust on the inner rim side.
RE678af. Clay pot side & bottom. Calculation of outer bottom diameter: c. 11 cm. Ware thickness: 0.6-0.7-0.8 cm. Only an indication of the bottom preserved.
RE678ag. Clay pot bottom. Calculation of outer bottom diameter: c. 9 cm. Ware thickness: 0.8 cm.
RE678ah. Clay pot rim. Calculation of outer rim diameter: c. 9.5 cm. Ware thickness: 0.5-0.6 cm.
RE678ai. Clay pot rim. Calculation of outer rim diameter: c. 14 cm. Ware thickness: 0.6-0.7 cm.
RE678aj. Clay pot rim & side. Calculation of outer rim diameter: c. 28 cm. Ware thickness: 0.7-1.0-1.1 cm.

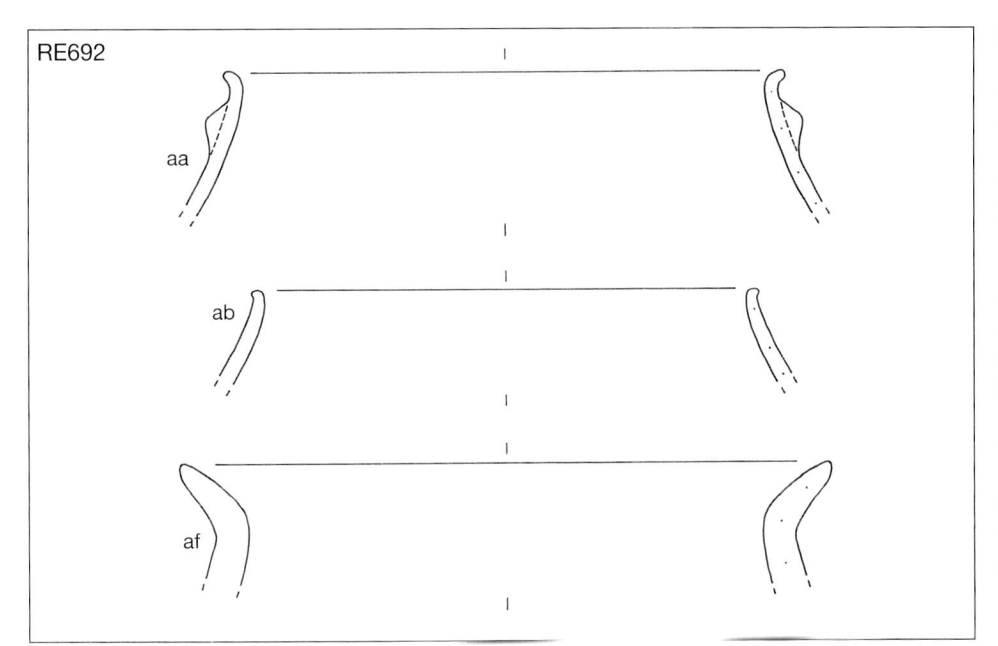

Pit 310, south of House 197
RE692aa. Clay pot rim & side. Calculation of outer rim diameter: c. 23 cm. Ware thickness: 0.5-0.6-0.6-0.5 cm. Supplied with horizontal cordon.
RE692ab. Clay pot rim & side. Calculation of outer rim diameter: c. 21 cm. Ware thickness: 0.5-0.6-0.6 cm. Spot with soot on the inner side below the rim top. A lower part of the inner body side with soot & indications of soot crust belongs to the clay pot. On the outer side, a spot with soot.
RE692af. Clay pot rim & side. Calculation of outer rim diameter: c. 27 cm. Ware thickness: 1.0-1.4-1.5 cm.

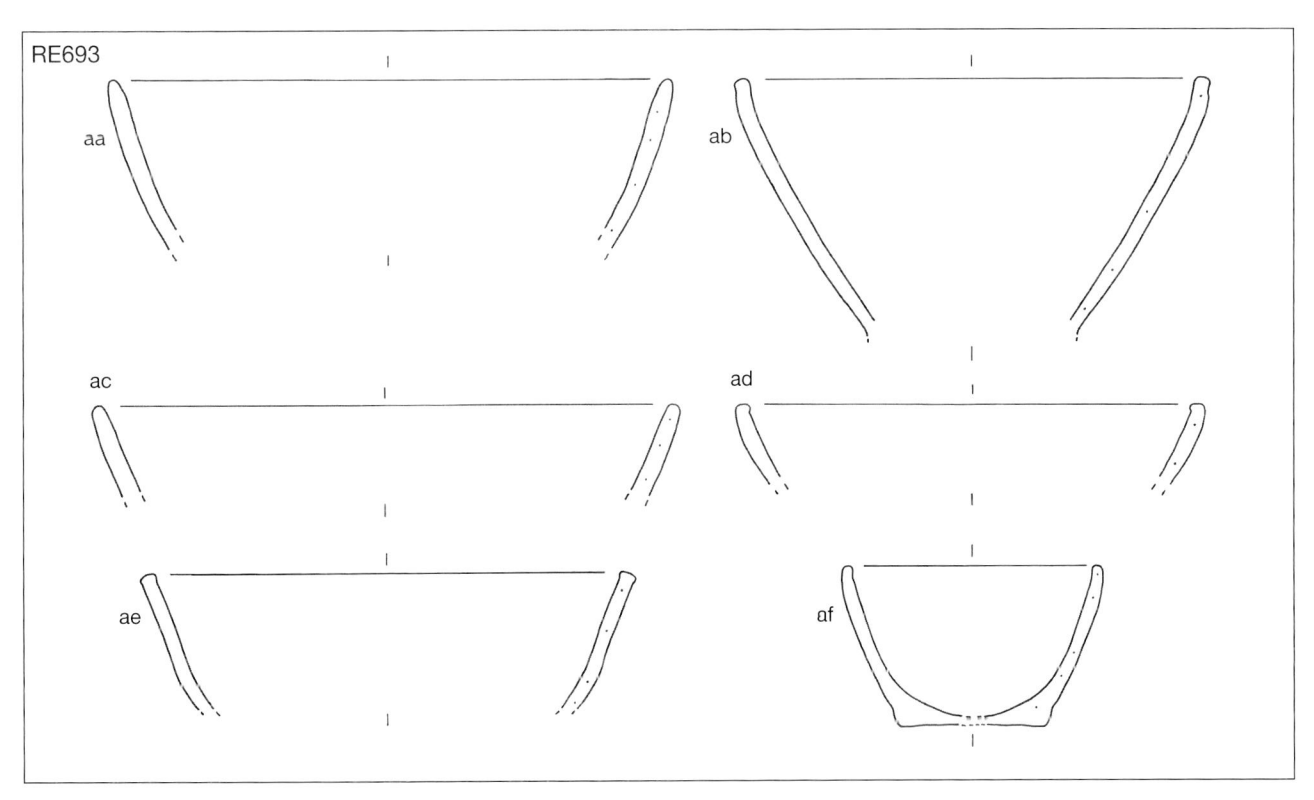

Pit 319 south of House 197
RE693aa. Clay pot rim & side. Calculation of outer rim diameter: c. 23 cm. Ware thickness: 0.8-0.8-0.7-0.7 cm.
RE693ab. Clay pot rim & side. Calculation of outer rim diameter: c. 20 cm. Estimate of original height: c. 11 cm. Ware thickness: 0.7-0.6-0.6-0.5 cm.
RE693ac. Clay pot rim & side. Calculation of outer rim diameter: c. 24 cm. Ware thickness: 0.7-0.8-0.8 cm.
RE693ad. Clay pot rim & side. Calculation of outer rim diameter: c. 19.5 cm. Ware thickness: 0.7-0.6 cm.

RE693ae. Clay pot rim & side. Calculation of outer rim diameter: c. 20 cm. Ware thickness: 0.6-0.6-0.6-0.5 cm. Ornamented with three horizontally-incised lines.
RE693af. Clay pot rim, side & bottom. Calculation of outer rim diameter: c. 6.5 cm. Estimate of original height: c. 6.5 cm. Ware thickness: 0.4-0.6-0.6-0.5-1.2 cm.

Ceramics at Resengaard

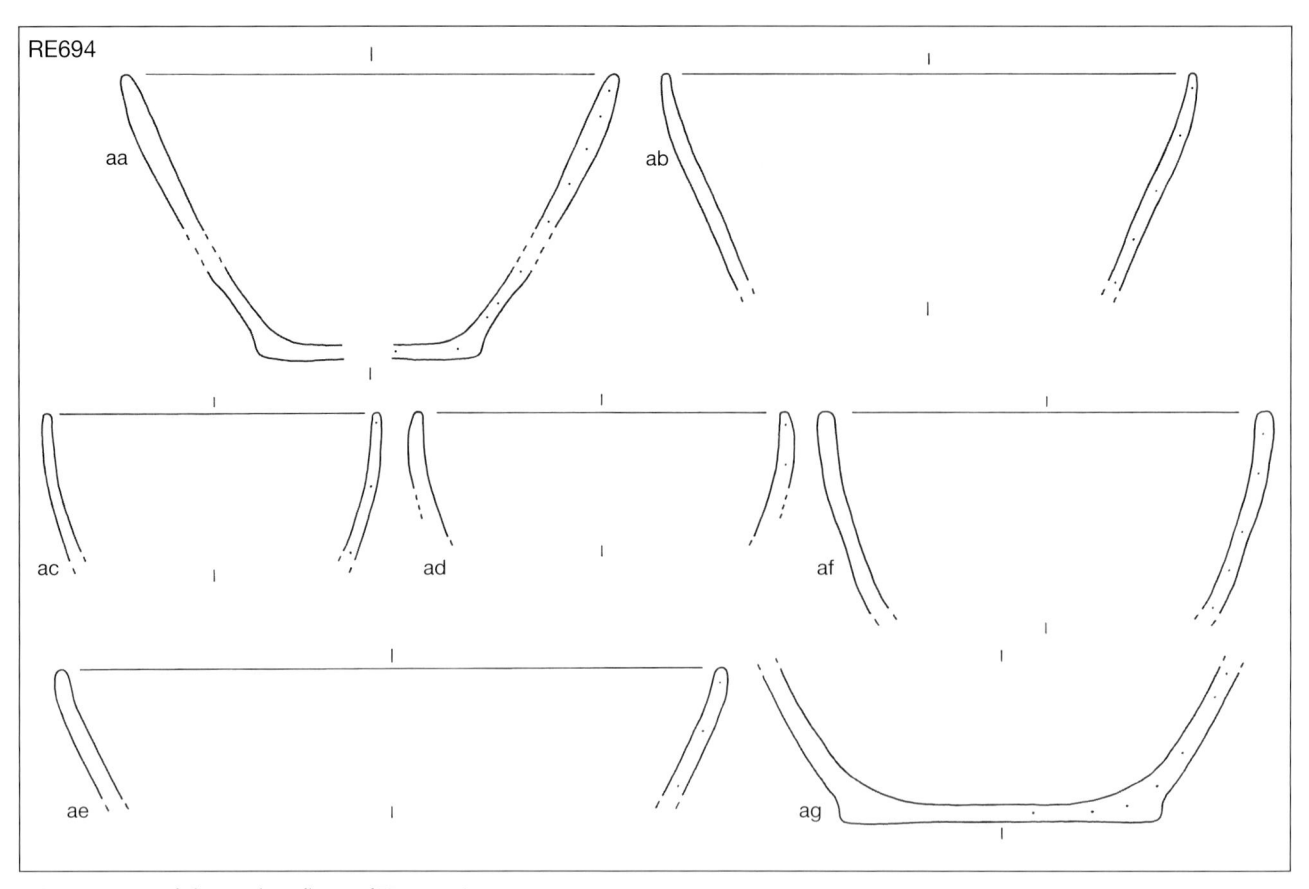

Pit 316 west of the sunken floor of House 197

RE694aa. Clay pot rim & side. Calculation of outer rim diameter: c. 20.5 cm. Estimate of original height: c. 11.5 cm. Ware thickness: 0.8-0.9-0.9-0.8-0.7/-0.7-0.6-0.7-0.8-0.6 cm. The tempering includes crushed pieces from other pottery.
RE694ab. Clay pot rim & side. Calculation of outer rim diameter: c. 22 cm. Ware thickness: 0.5-0.7-0.7-0.6-0.6 cm.
RE694ac. Clay pot rim & side. Calculation of outer rim diameter: c. 14 cm. Ware thickness: 0.4-0.5-0.6 cm.
RE694ad. Clay pot rim & side. Calculation of outer rim diameter: c. 16 cm. Ware thickness: 0.5-0.7 cm.
RE694ae. Clay pot rim & side. Calculation of outer rim diameter: c. 28 cm. Ware thickness: 0.6-0.7-0.7 cm.
RE694af. Clay pot rim & side. Calculation of outer rim diameter: c. 18.5 cm. Ware thickness: 0.7-0.7-0.6-0.7-0.7 cm.
RE694ag. Clay pot side & bottom. Calculation of outer bottom diameter: c. 13 cm. Ware thickness: 0.8-0.8-0.9-1.0-1.6-0.8-0.8 cm. Preserved potsherds belonging to the clay pot shows that it had a height of more than 10 cm. The tempering also includes crushed pieces from other pottery. With crumbling side and bottom, it seems to have been exposed to strong secondary burning. Soot on the inner side near the bottom.

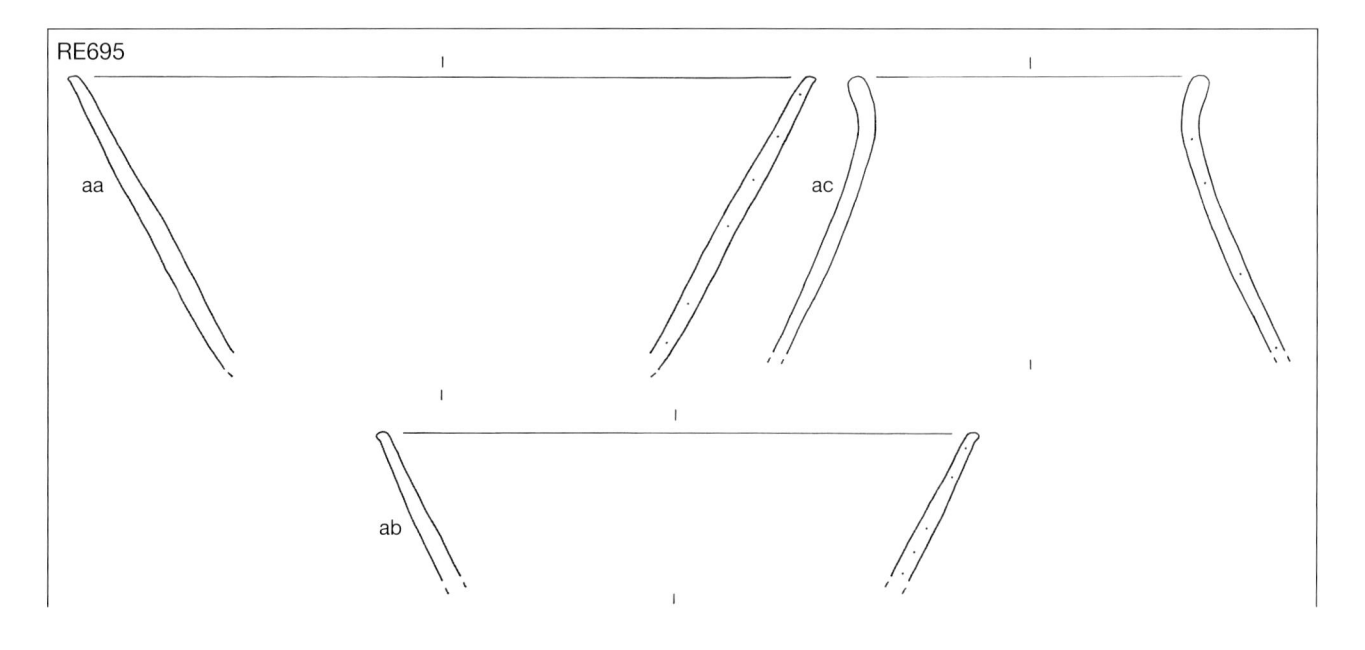

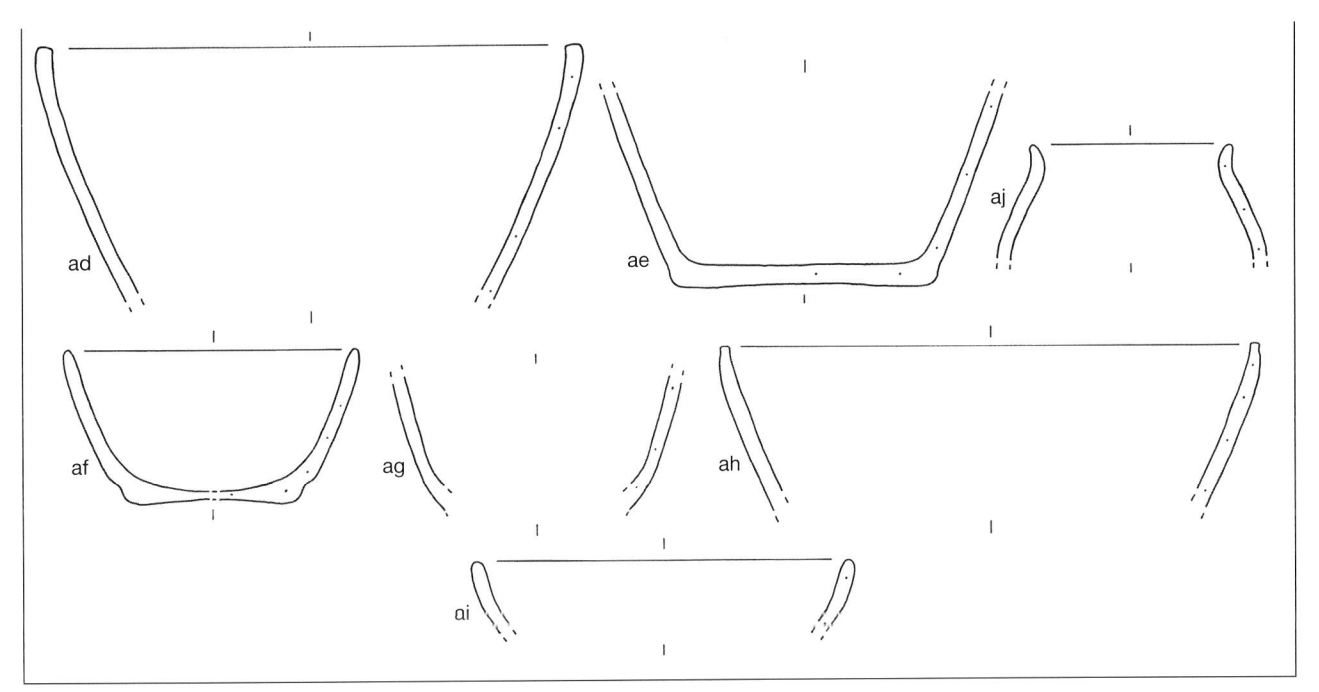

Pit 317 west of the sunken floor of House 197
RE695aa. Clay pot rim & side. Calculation of outer rim diameter: c. 31 cm. Estimate of original height: c. 12.5 cm. Ware thickness: 0.5-0.6-0.7-0.7-0.8-0.7 cm. With crumbling surface, it seems to have been markedly exposed to secondary burning.
RE695ab. Clay pot rim & side. Calculation of outer rim diameter: c. 25 cm. Ware thickness: 0.5-0.6-0.7-0.8-0.8 cm.
RE695ac. Clay pot rim & side. Calculation of outer rim diameter: c. 15 cm. Ware thickness: 0.7-0.6-0.6-0.5 cm.
RE695ad. Clay pot rim & side. Calculation of outer rim diameter: c. 22.5 cm. Ware thickness: 0.7-0.6-0.6-0.6 cm.
RE695ae. Clay pot side & bottom. Calculation of outer bottom diameter: c. 11 cm. Ware thickness: 0.6-0.6-0.7-0.9-0.8 cm. Soot on the inner side near the bottom & soot crust on the bottom.
RE695af. Clay pot, side & bottom. Measurement of outer rim diameter: c. 12.5 cm. Estimate of original height: c. 6 cm. Ware thickness: 0.6-0.5-0.7-1.0-0.4 cm. The surface is crumbling heavily. Seems markedly exposed to secondary burning.
RE695ag. Clay pot side. Calculation of outer bottom diameter: c. 7.5 cm. Ware thickness: 0.6-0.5-0.7 cm.
RE695ah. Clay pot rim & side. Calculation of outer rim diameter: c. 22.5 cm. Ware thickness: 0.6-0.7-0.7-0.7 cm.
RE695ai. Clay pot rim & side. Calculation of outer rim diameter: c. 15.5 cm. Ware thickness: 0.6-0.5 cm.
RE695aj. Clay pot rim & side. Calculation of outer rim diameter: c. 8.5 cm. Ware thickness: 0.6-0.6-0.5 cm. Surface crumbling. Seems to have been markedly exposed to secondary burning.

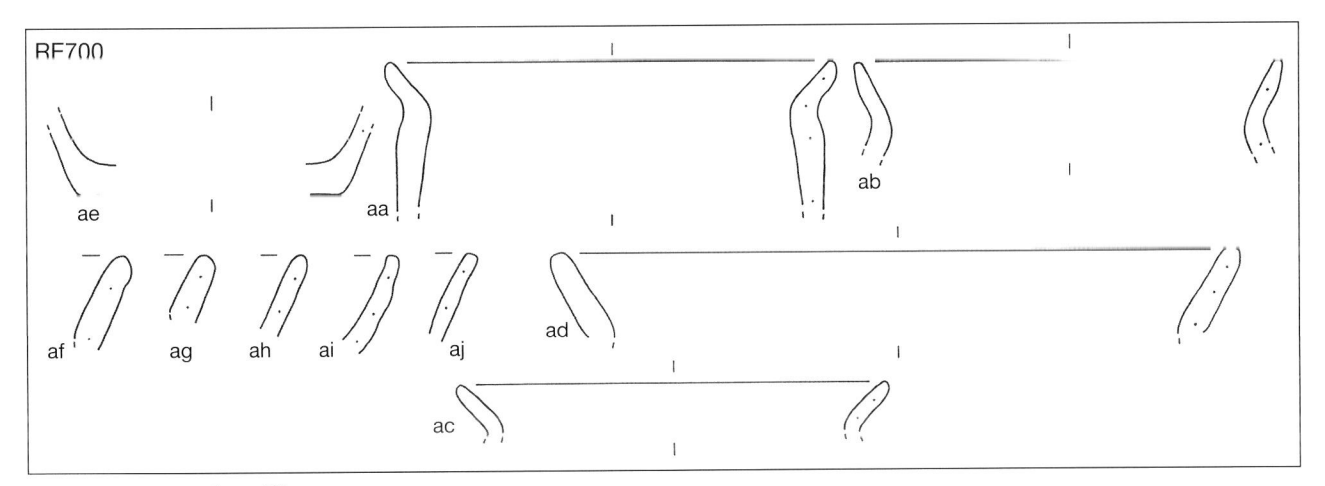

House 197, secondary fills
RE700aa. Clay pot rim & side. Calculation of outer rim diameter: c. 18.5 cm. Ware thickness: 0.8-1.1-1.2-0.9 cm.
RE700ab. Clay pot rim & side. Calculation of outer rim diameter: c. 18 cm. Ware thickness: 0.7-0.9 cm.
RE700ac. Clay pot rim. Calculation of outer rim diameter: c. 18 cm. Ware thickness: 0.6-0.6 cm.
RE700ad. Clay pot rim. Calculation of outer rim diameter: c. 28.5 cm. Ware thickness: 1.0-1.0-1.1 cm.
RE700ae. Clay pot side & bottom. Calculation of outer bottom diameter: c. 11.5 cm. Ware thickness: 0.9 cm.
RE700af. Clay pot rim. Ware thickness: 1.1-1.2 cm.
RE700ag. Clay pot rim. Ware thickness: 1.0-1.1 cm.
RE700ah. Clay pot rim & side. Ware thickness: 0.8-0.8 cm.
RE700ai. Clay pot rim & side. Ware thickness: 0.7-0.8-0.9 cm. The outer side is slightly wavy.
RE700aj. Clay pot rim & side. Ware thickness: 0.6-0.7 cm.

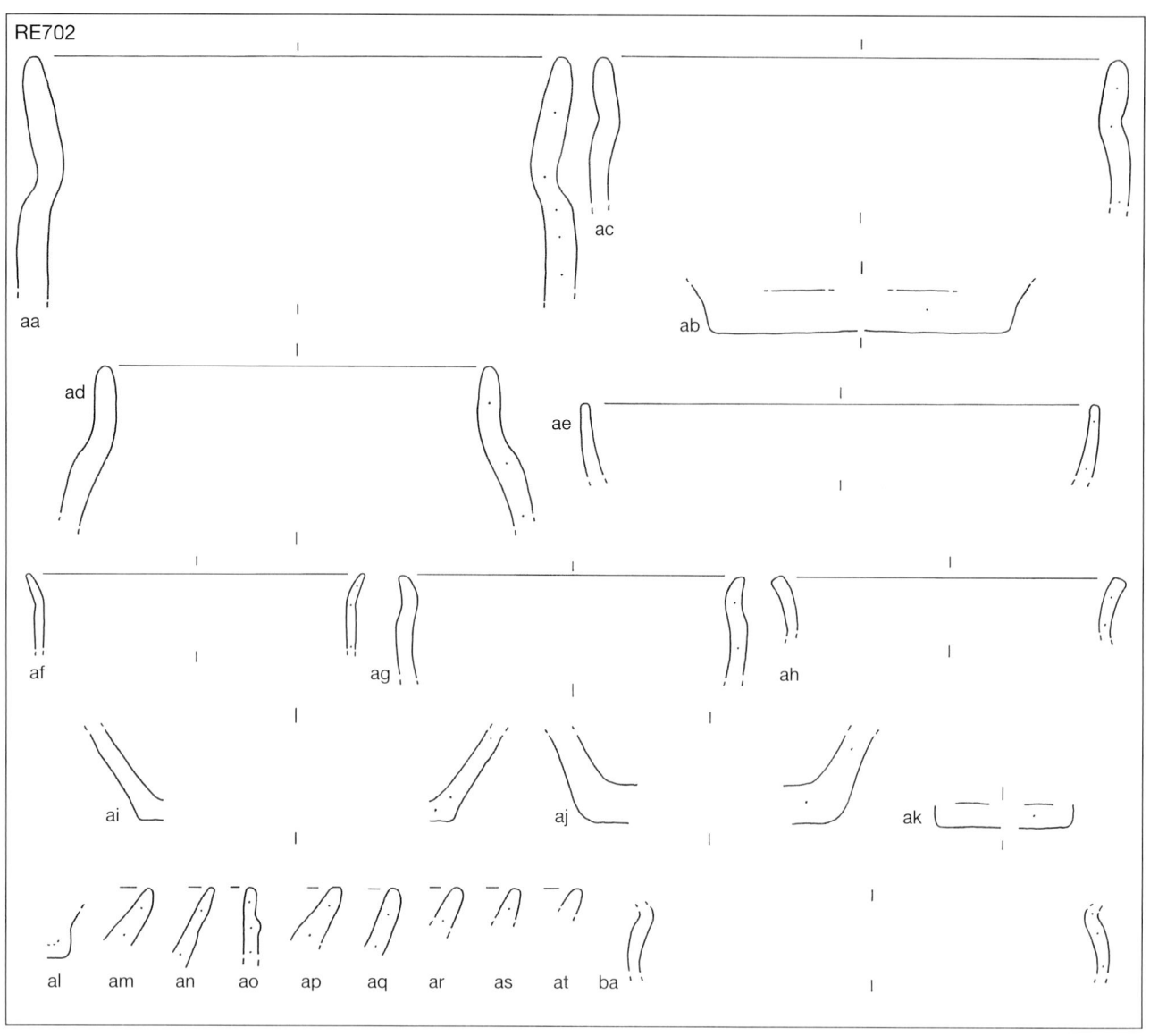

House 197, sunken-floor horizon

RE702aa. Clay pot rim & side. Calculation of outer rim diameter: c. 25 cm. Ware thickness: 1.3-1.2-1.4-1.5-1.5 cm.

RE702ab. Clay pot bottom. Calculation of outer bottom diameter: c. 14 cm. Ware thickness: 1.9 cm. It probably belongs to RE702aa.

RE702ac. Clay pot rim & side. Calculation of outer rim diameter: c. 24.5 cm. Ware thickness: 1.1-1.1-0.8 cm.

RE702ad. Clay pot rim & side. Calculation of outer rim diameter: c. 18.5 cm. Ware thickness: 1.0-1.3-1.1 cm.

RE702ae. Clay pot rim & side. Calculation of outer rim diameter: c. 24 cm. Ware thickness: 0.5-0.8 cm.

RE702af. Clay pot rim & side. Calculation of outer rim diameter: c. 16 cm. Ware thickness: 0.4-0.5-0.4 cm.

RE702ag. Clay pot rim & side. Calculation of outer rim diameter: c. 16 cm. Ware thickness: 0.8-0.8 cm.

RE702ah. Clay pot rim. Calculation of outer rim diameter: c. 16 cm. Ware thickness: 0.6-0.5 cm.

RE702ai. Clay pot side & bottom. Calculation of outer bottom diameter: c. 15 cm. Ware thickness: 0.8-1.0-0.9 cm. Soot crust on the inner side near the bottom.

RE702aj. Clay pot side & bottom. Calculation of outer bottom diameter: c. 12 cm. Ware thickness: 1.2-1.8 cm.

RE702ak. Clay pot bottom. Calculation of outer bottom diameter: c. 6.5 cm. Ware thickness: 1.1 cm.

RE702al. Clay pot side & bottom. Only outer side preserved.

RE702am. Clay pot rim. Ware thickness: 0.9-1.2 cm.

RE702an. Clay pot rim & side. Ware thickness: 0.6-0.9 cm.

RE702ao. Clay pot rim & side. Ware thickness: 0.5-0.7-0.6 cm. Beneath the rim a faint cordon-like marking.

RE702ap. Clay pot rim. Ware thickness: 1.3 cm.

RE702aq. Clay pot rim. Ware thickness: 0.9-0.9 cm.

RE702ar. Clay pot rim. Ware thickness: 1.0 cm.

RE702as. Clay pot rim. Ware thickness: 0.9 cm.

RE702at. Clay pot rim.

RE702ba. Clay pot side. Calculation of outer side diameter: c. 20 cm. Ware thickness: 0.6-0.7-0.5 cm. Basis of the rim preserved.

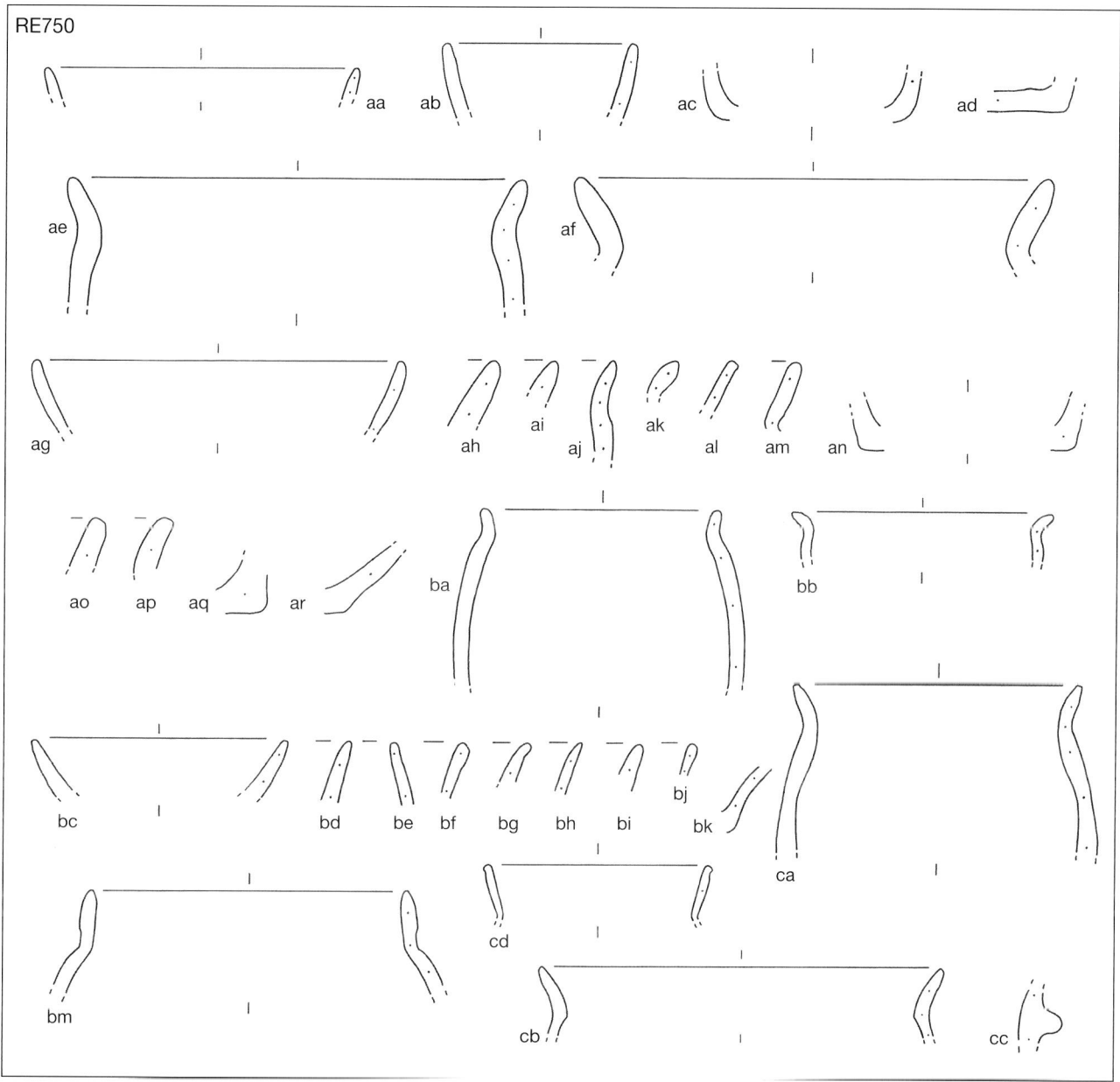

House 200, secondary fills

RE750aa. Clay pot rim. Calculation of outer rim diameter: c. 15 cm. Ware thickness: 0.4-0.5 cm.
RE750ab. Clay pot rim & side. Calculation of outer rim diameter: c. 9 cm. Ware thickness: 0.6-0.7 cm.
RE750ac. Clay pot side & bottom. Calculation of outer bottom diameter: c. 9.5 cm. Ware thickness: 0.8 cm.
RE750ad. Clay pot bottom. Ware thickness: 1.0 cm. A "finger" furrow round the bottom perimeter.
RE750ae. Clay pot rim & side. Calculation of outer rim diameter: c. 21.5 cm. Ware thickness: 0.9-1.1-1.2-0.9 cm.
RE750af. Clay pot rim. Calculation of outer rim diameter: c. 22.5 cm. Ware thickness: 1.1-1.1 cm.
RE750ag. Clay pot rim & side. Calculation of outer rim diameter: c. 17.5 cm. Ware thickness: 0.7-0.5 cm.
RE750ah. Clay pot rim. Ware thickness: 1.0-1.2 cm.
RE750ai. Clay pot rim. Ware thickness: 1.0 cm.
RE750aj. Clay pot rim & side. Ware thickness: 0.7-0.8-0.9-0.8 cm.
RE750ak. Clay pot rim. Ware thickness: 0.9-0.7 cm.
RE750al. Clay pot rim & side. Ware thickness: 0.6-0.6 cm.

RE750am. Clay pot rim. Ware thickness: 0.8-0.7 cm.
RE750an. Clay pot side & bottom. Calculation of outer bottom diameter: c. 10 cm. Ware thickness: 1.4 cm.
RE750ao. Clay pot rim. Ware thickness: 1.1 cm.
RE750ap. Clay pot rim. Ware thickness: 1.0 cm.
RE750aq. Clay pot bottom. Ware thickness: 2.1 cm.
RE750ar. Clay pot side & bottom. Ware thickness: 0.9 cm.
RE750ba. Clay pot rim & side. Calculation of outer rim diameter: c. 11 cm. Ware thickness: 0.6-0.8-0.7-0.7 cm.
RE750bb. Clay pot rim & side. Calculation of outer rim diameter: c. 12 cm. Ware thickness: 0.6-0.6 cm.
RE750bc. Clay pot rim & side. Calculation of outer rim diameter: c. 12 cm. Ware thickness: 0.5-0.7 cm.
RE750bd. Clay pot rim & side. Ware thickness: 0.6-0.8 cm.
RE750be. Clay pot rim & side. Ware thickness: 0.5-0.6 cm.
RE750bf. Clay pot rim & side. Ware thickness: 0.7-0.5 cm.
RE750bg. Clay pot rim. Ware thickness: 0.7 cm.
RE750bh. Clay pot rim & side. Ware thickness: 0.5-0.5 cm.
RE750bi. Clay pot rim. Ware thickness: 0.8 cm.

Ceramics at Resengaard **481**

RE750bj. Clay pot rim. Ware thickness: 0.5-0.4 cm.
RE750bk. Clay pot side & bottom. Ware thickness: 0.6-0.6 cm.
RE750bm. Clay pot rim & side. Calculation of outer rim diameter: c. 15.5 cm. Ware thickness: 0.7-0.6-0.7 cm.
RE750ca. Clay pot rim & side. Calculation of outer rim diameter: c. 13.5 cm. Ware thickness: 0.6-0.7-0.9-0.7-1.0 cm. Some uncertainty regarding the diameter, as the preserved potsherd is a little irregular.

RE750cb. Clay pot rim & side. Calculation of outer rim diameter: c. 19.0 cm. Ware thickness: 0.6-0.7-0.5 cm.
RE750cc. Clay pot side. Ware thickness: 0.8-0.9 cm. Judging by the inner side, it was probably of some width. Supplied with a horizontally-projecting lug.
RE750cd. Clay pot rim. Calculation of outer rim diameter: c. 10.5 cm. Ware thickness: 0.4 cm.

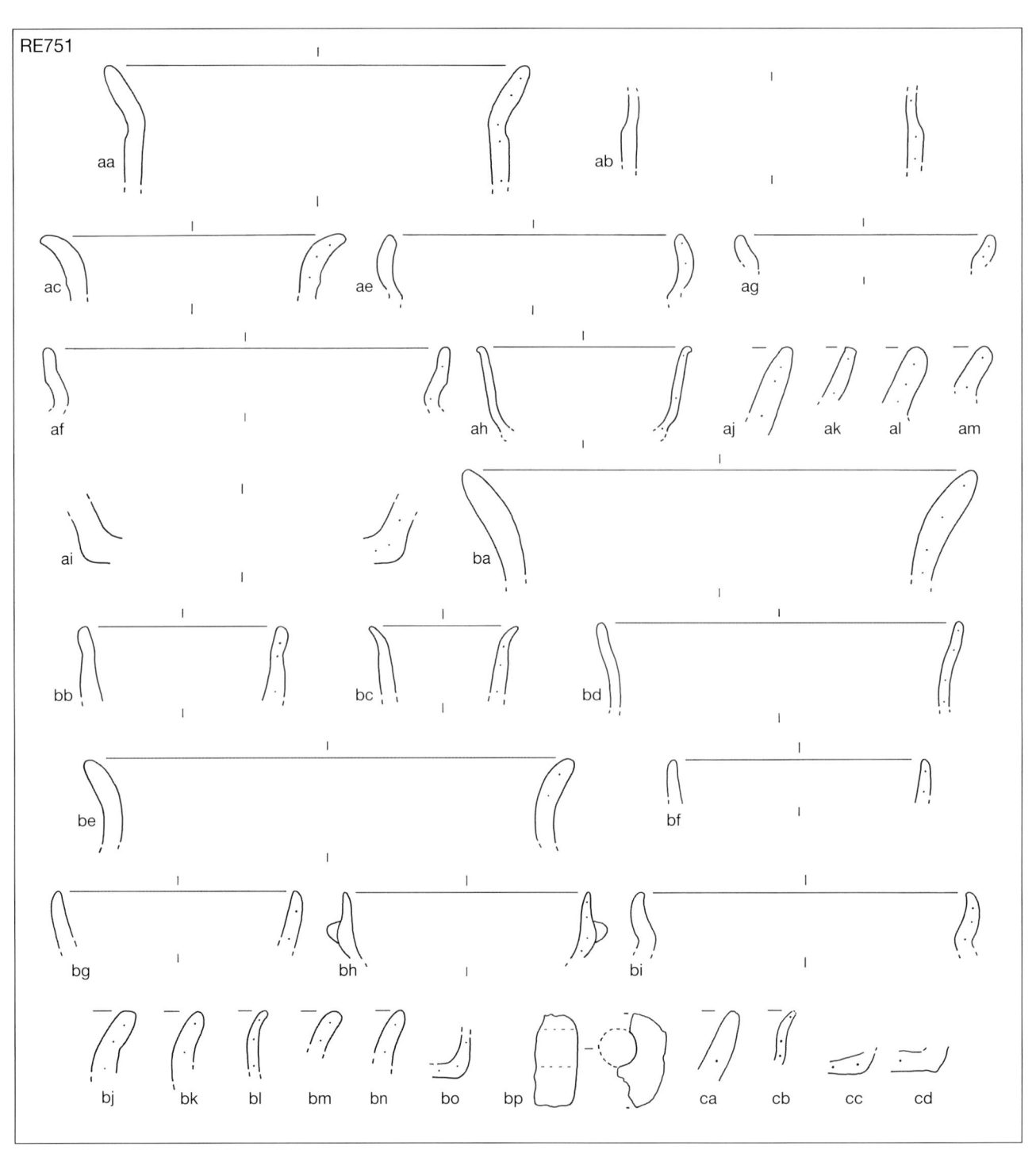

Culture layer 203 east of House 138

RE751aa. Clay pot rim & side. Calculation of outer rim diameter: c. 22 cm. Ware thickness: 0.8-1.0-0.9-0.9-0.9 cm.
RE751ab. Clay pot side. Calculation of outer side diameter: c. 15.5 cm. Ware thickness: 0.5-0.8-0.8 cm.

RE751ac. Clay pot rim & side. Calculation of outer rim diameter: c. 16 cm. Ware thickness: 0.7-1.0-1.0 cm. A low horizontal cordon-like marking on the outer side.
RE751ae. Clay pot rim. Calculation of outer rim diameter: c. 16.5 cm. Ware thickness: 0.7-0.8 cm.

RE751af. Clay pot rim & side. Calculation of outer rim diameter: c. 21 cm. Ware thickness: 0.6-0.7 cm.
RE751ag. Clay pot rim. Calculation of outer rim diameter: c. 13.5 cm. Ware thickness: 0.7-0.8 cm.
RE751ah. Clay pot rim, side & bottom. Calculation of outer rim diameter: c. 11 cm. Ware thickness: 0.4-0.4-0.5 cm. Only a tiny piece of the bottom preserved.
RE751ai. Clay pot side & bottom. Calculation of outer bottom diameter: c. 17 cm. Ware thickness: 1.3-1.7-1.4 cm.
RE751aj. Clay pot rim. Ware thickness: 1.1-1.3-1.4 cm.
RE751ak. Clay pot rim & side. Ware thickness: 0.7-0.8 cm.
RE751al. Clay pot rim. Ware thickness: 1.3-1.4-1.4 cm.
RE751am. Clay pot rim. Ware thickness: 1.0-1.2 cm.
RE751ba. Clay pot rim. Calculation of outer rim diameter: c. 27 cm. Ware thickness: 1.2-1.5-1.2-1.0 cm.
RE751bb. Clay pot rim & side. Calculation of outer rim diameter: c. 11 cm. Ware thickness: 0.7-0.6-0.8 cm.
RE751bc. Clay pot rim & side. Calculation of outer rim diameter: c. 8 cm. Ware thickness: 0.5-0.7-0.8 cm.
RE751bd. Clay pot rim & side. Calculation of outer rim diameter: c. 19 cm. Ware thickness: 0.5-0.6-0.5-0.5 cm.
RE751be. Clay pot rim. Calculation of outer rim diameter: c. 25.5 cm. Ware thickness: 1.0-1.1 cm.

RE751bf. Clay pot rim. Calculation of outer rim diameter: c. 13.5 cm. Ware thickness: 0.6-0.7 cm.
RE751bg. Clay pot rim & side. Calculation of outer rim diameter: c. 13 cm. Ware thickness: 0.7-0.8 cm.
RE751bh. Clay pot rim & side. Calculation of outer rim diameter: c. 13 cm. Ware thickness: 0.4-0.5-0.9-0.6 cm. Supplied with a horizontally-projecting lug.
RE751bi. Clay pot rim & side. Calculation of outer rim diameter: c. 17.5 cm. Ware thickness: 0.7-0.8-0.8 cm.
RE751bj. Clay pot rim. Ware thickness: 1.0-1.1-1.3 cm.
RE751bk. Clay pot rim. Ware thickness: 0.9-1.1 cm.
RE751bl. Clay pot rim & side. Ware thickness: 0.4-0.6-0.5 cm.
RE751bm. Clay pot rim. Ware thickness: 0.9-0.8 cm.
RE751bn. Clay pot rim. Ware thickness: 0.9-1.0 cm.
RE751bo. Clay pot side & bottom. Ware thickness: 0.5-0.9-0.7 cm.
RE751bp. Possibly a clay tube fragment. The ware is markedly red, perhaps due to secondary burning. Dating uncertain.
RE751ca. Clay pot rim & side. Ware thickness: 1.3 cm.
RE751cb. Clay pot rim & side. Ware thickness: 0.4-0.5-0.5 cm.
RE751cc. Clay pot bottom. Ware thickness: 1.0-0.7 cm.
RE751cd. Clay pot bottom. Ware thickness: 1.0 cm.

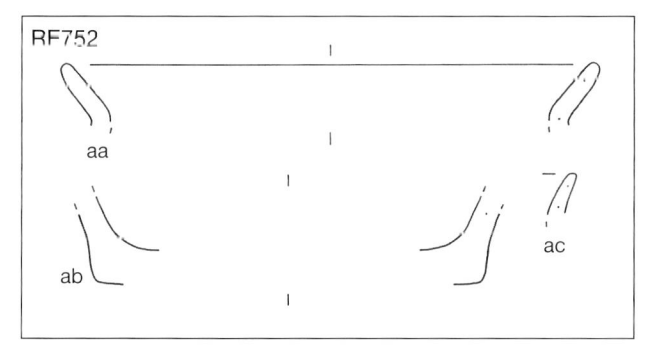

House 202, secondary fills
RE752aa. Clay pot rim. Fragment, irregular shaping. Calculation of possible outer rim diameter: c. 22 cm. Ware thickness: 0.7-0.8 cm.
RE752ab. Clay pot side & bottom. Calculation of outer bottom diameter: c. 16 cm. Ware thickness: 1.0 cm. Ware somewhat unusual.
RE752ac. Clay pot rim. Ware thickness: 0.6-0.7 cm.

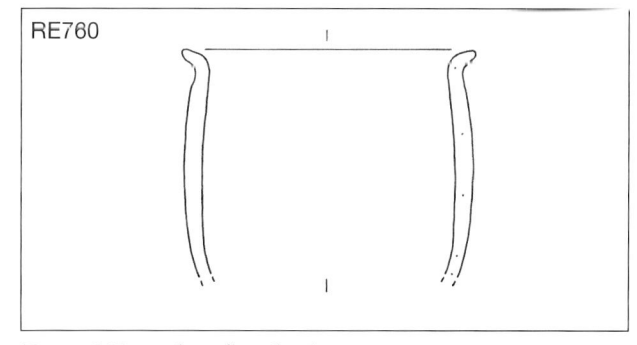

House 200, sunken-floor horizon
RE760aa. Clay pot rim & side. Calculation of outer rim diameter: c. 12 cm. Ware thickness: 0.6-0.7-0.7-0.5-0.4 cm.

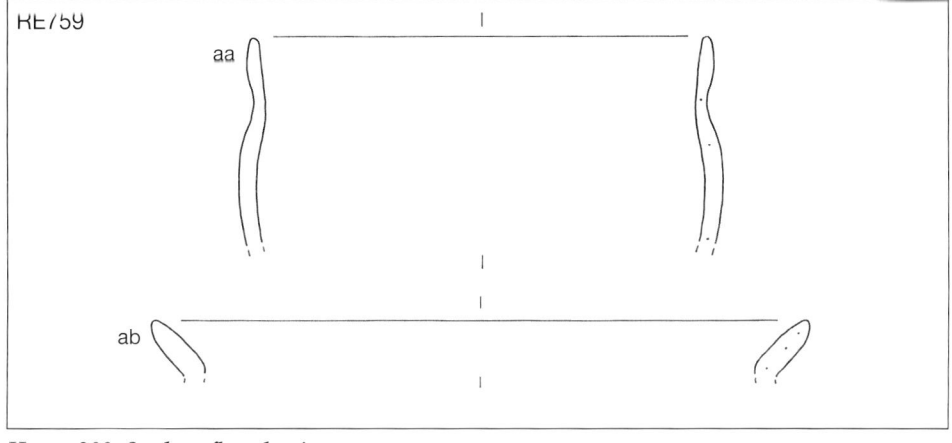

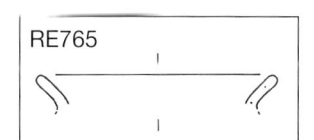

House 200, secondary fills
RE765aa. Clay pot rim. Calculation of outer rim diameter: c. 10 cm. Ware thickness: 0.5-0.5 cm.

House 200, Sunken-floor horizon
RE759aa. Clay pot rim & side. Calculation of outer rim diameter: c. 19 cm. Ware thickness: 0.5-0.8-0.7 cm.
RE759ab. Clay pot rim. Calculation of outer rim diameter: c. 24 cm. Ware thickness: 0.7-0.8-1.0 cm.

Ceramics at Resengaard

RE769

House 200, likely the sunken-floor horizon
Precise find spot not identified. RE769aa. Clay pot rim & side. Calculation of outer rim diameter: c. 35 cm. Ware thickness: 1.7-1.3-1.4 cm.

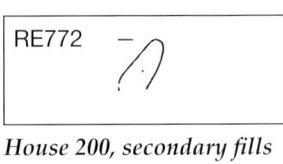

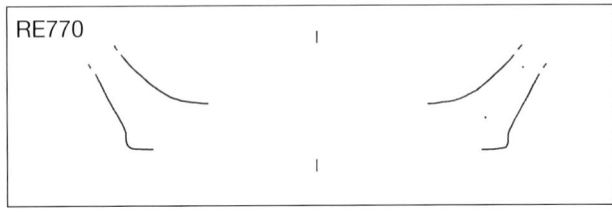

RE770

House 200, secondary fills
RE770aa. Clay pot side & bottom. Calculation of outer bottom diameter: c. 16 cm. Ware thickness: 1.3-2.6 cm.

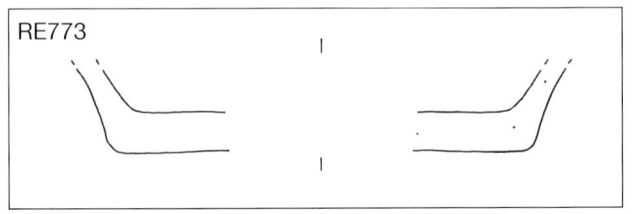

RE775

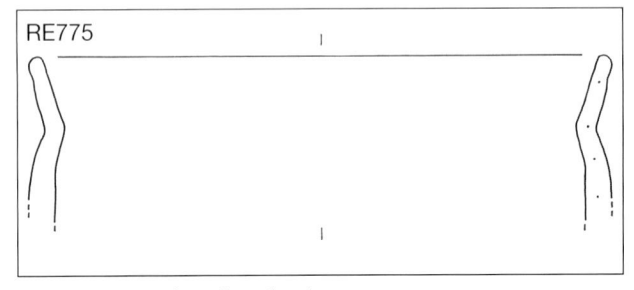

House 240, sunken-floor horizon
RE775aa. Clay pot rim & side. Calculation of outer rim diameter: c. 21 cm. Ware thickness: 0.7-0.8-1.0-1.1 cm.

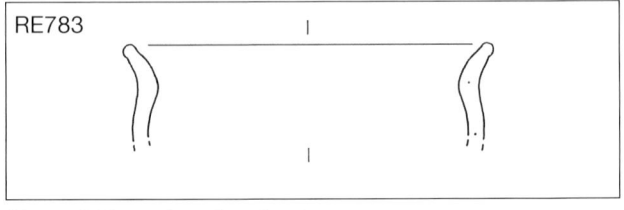

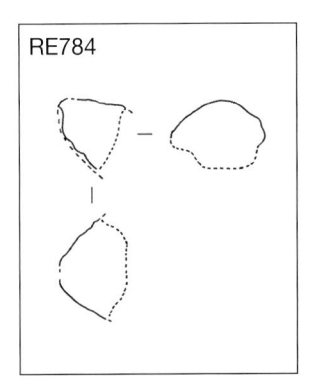

RE784

House 200, sunken-floor horizon
RE784aa. Clay spoon, handle. Width c. 4.0 cm. Seen from the side (uppermost, left), from the front (uppermost, right) and from above.

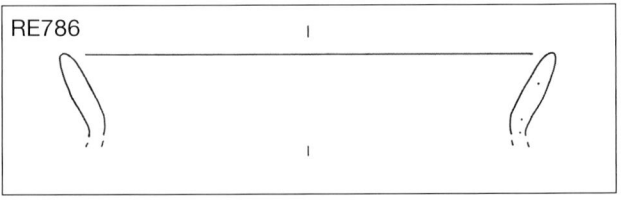

RE785

RE772

House 200, secondary fills
RE772aa. Clay pot rim. Ware thickness: 1.1 cm.

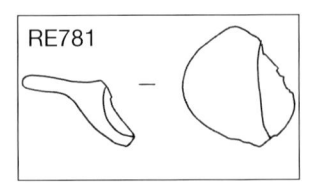

RE781

Pit 247
RE781aa. Clay spoon. Precise find spot not identified. Seen from the side (right) and from above.

RE773

House 200, secondary fills
RE773aa. Clay pot side & bottom. Calculation of outer bottom diameter: c. 17 cm. Ware thickness: 0.9-1.9-1.6 cm.

RE783

House 200, sunken-floor horizon
RE783aa. Clay pot rim & side. Calculation of outer rim diameter: c. 15 cm. Ware thickness: 0.6-0.8 cm.

RE786

House 200, sunken-floor horizon
RE786aa. Clay pot rim. Calculation of outer rim diameter: c. 20.5 cm. Ware thickness: 0.8-0.7-0.6 cm.

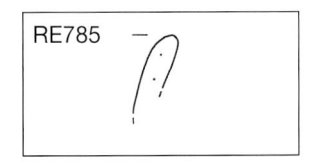

House 200, sunken-floor horizon
RE785aa. Clay pot rim. Ware thickness: 1.1-1.0 cm.

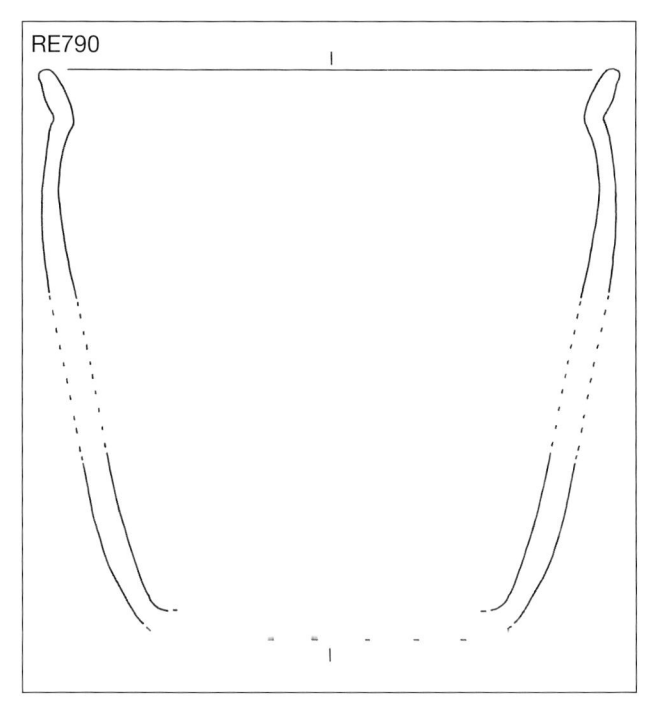

House 200, sunken-floor horizon
RE790aa. Clay pot rim, side & bottom. Calculation of outer rim diameter: c. 24 cm. Estimate of original height: c. 22 cm but possibly a little more. Ware thickness: 0.7-0.9-0.7-0.7-0.8-1.1-1.1-1.1-0.8 cm.

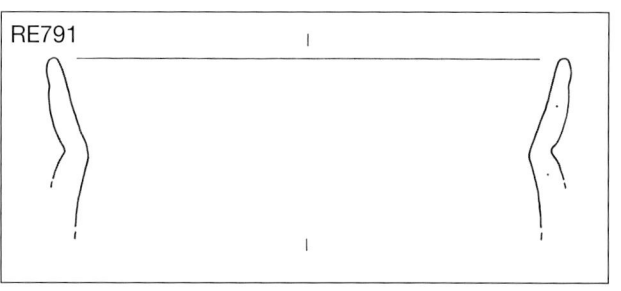

House 200, sunken-floor horizon
RE791aa. Clay pot rim & side. Calculation of outer rim diameter: c. 21.5 cm. Ware thickness: 0.9-1.1 cm.

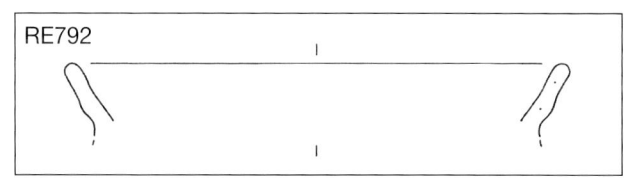

House 200, sunken-floor horizon
RE792aa. Clay pot rim. Calculation of outer rim diameter: c. 21 cm. Ware thickness: 0.7-0.8 cm.

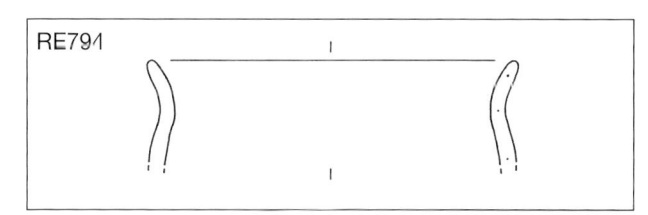

House 200, sunken-floor horizon
RE794aa. Clay pot rim & side. Calculation of outer rim diameter: c. 15 cm. Ware thickness: 0.6-0.7-0.7 cm.

House 200, sunken-floor horizon
RE793aa. Clay pot rim & side. Calculation of outer rim diameter: c. 25.5 cm. Ware thickness: 0.7-1.0-1.1-0.9 cm.

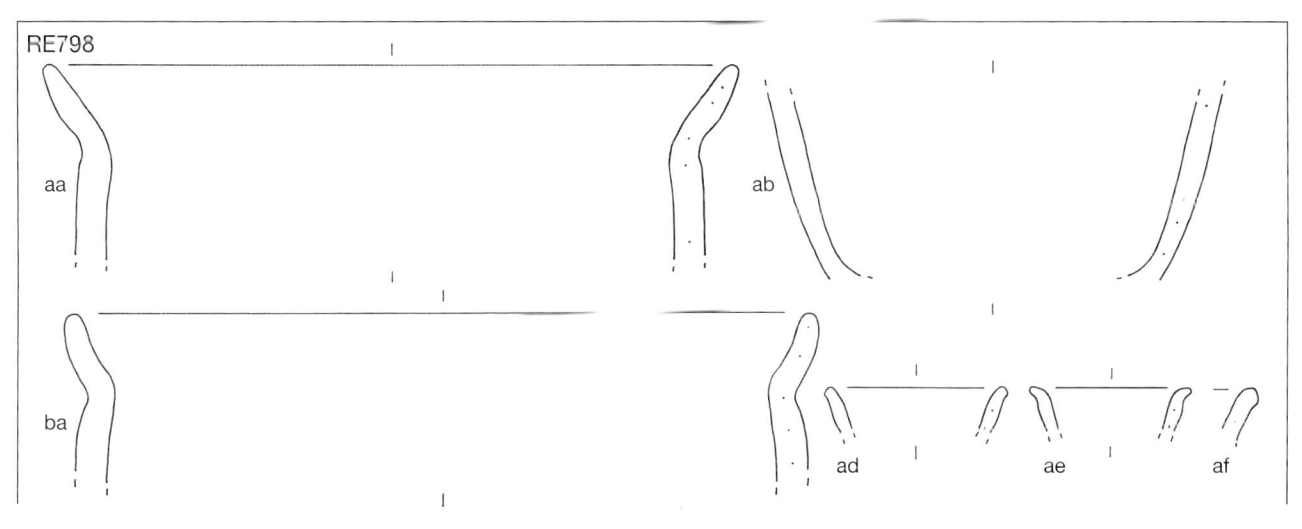

Ceramics at Resengaard

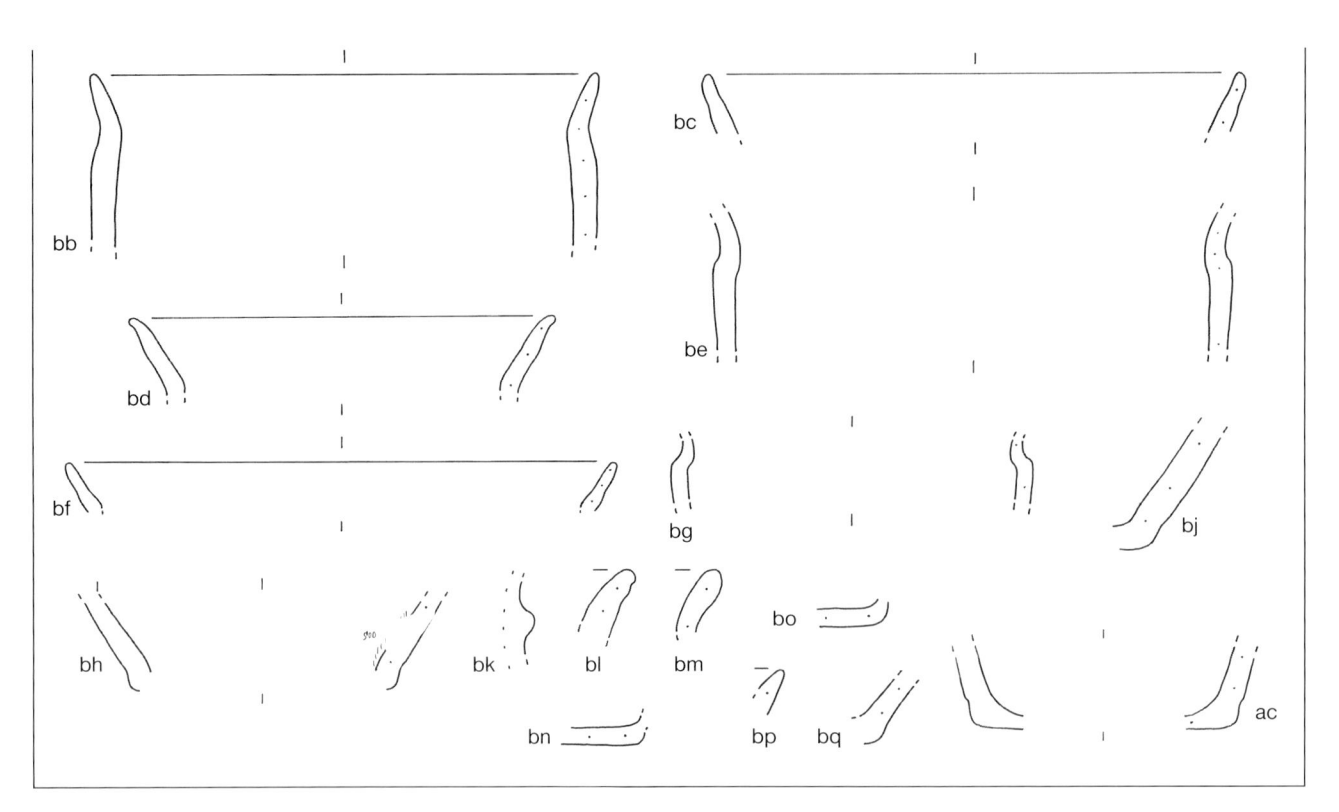

House 240, secondary fills
RE798aa. Clay pot rim & side. Calculation of outer rim diameter: c. 28.5 cm. Ware thickness: 0.9-1.0-1.0-1.2-1.3 cm.
RE798ab. Clay pot side & bottom. Calculation of outer bottom diameter: c. 13.5 cm. Ware thickness: 1.0-1.0-0.8-0.7 cm.
RE798ac. Clay pot side & bottom. Calculation of outer rim diameter: c. 11.0 cm. Ware thickness: 0.9-1.0-0.6 cm.
RE798ad. Clay pot rim & side. Calculation of outer rim diameter: c. 7.5 cm. Ware thickness: 0.6-0.5 cm.
RE798ae. Clay pot rim & side. Calculation of outer rim diameter: c. 6.5 cm. Ware thickness: 0.6-0.5 cm.
RE798af. Clay pot rim. Ware thickness: 0.8 cm.
RE798ba. Clay pot rim & side. Calculation of outer rim diameter: c. 31.5 cm. Ware thickness: 0.5-1.1-1.1-1.3-1.4 cm.
RE798bb. Clay pot rim & side. Calculation of outer rim diameter: c. 21 cm. Ware thickness: 0.7-0.9-1.1-1.0-1.0 cm.
RE798bc. Clay pot rim & side. Calculation of outer rim diameter: c. 22 cm. Ware thickness: 0.7-0.8 cm.
RE798bd. Clay pot rim & side. Calculation of outer rim diameter: c. 17.5 cm. Ware thickness: 0.5-0.7-0.8 cm.
RE798be. Clay pot side. Calculation of outer belly diameter: c. 21 cm. Ware thickness: 0.8-0.9-1.1-0.8 cm.
RE798bf. Clay pot rim. Calculation of outer rim diameter: c. 22.5 cm. Ware thickness: 0.4-0.6 cm.
RE798bg. Clay pot side. Calculation of outer side diameter: c. 15 cm. Ware thickness: 0.4-0.7 cm.
RE798bh. Clay pot side & bottom. Calculation of outer bottom diameter: c. 11 cm. Ware thickness: 0.8-0.9-0.9 cm. Soot on the inner side near the bottom.
RE798bj. Clay pot side & bottom. Ware thickness: 1.1-1.3-1.2 cm. Soot crust on the inner side near the bottom and, above that, some soot.
RE798bk. Clay pot side. Ware thickness: 0.5-0.8 cm, estimated. Supplied with a horizontal cordon. The inner side surface is split off and not preserved.
RE798bl. Clay pot rim. Ware thickness: 1.0-1.2 cm.
RE798bm. Clay pot rim. Ware thickness: 1.1-0.8 cm.
RE798bn. Clay pot bottom. Ware thickness: 0.8-0.7 cm.
RE798bo. Clay pot bottom. Ware thickness: 0.8-0.7 cm.
RE798bp. Clay pot rim. Ware thickness: 0.8 cm.
RE798bq. Clay pot side & bottom. Ware thickness: 0.8-0.9 cm.

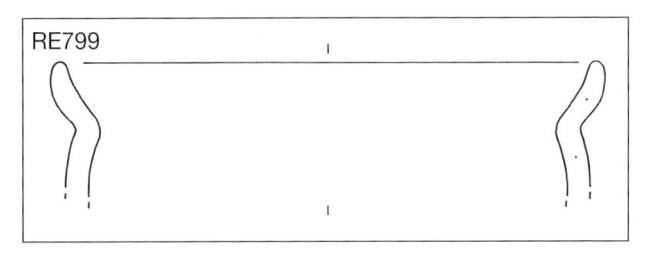

House 240, secondary fills
RE799aa. Clay pot rim & side. Calculation of outer rim diameter: c. 23 cm. Ware thickness: c. 0.9-1.1.

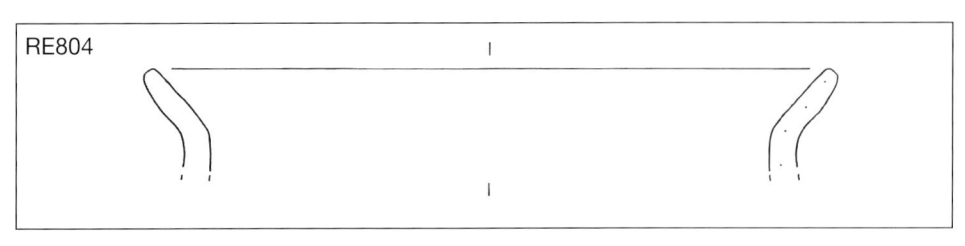

House 240, secondary fills
RE804aa. Clay pot rim & side. Calculation of outer rim diameter: c. 28.5 cm. Ware thickness: 0.8-1.0-1.0-1.2 cm.

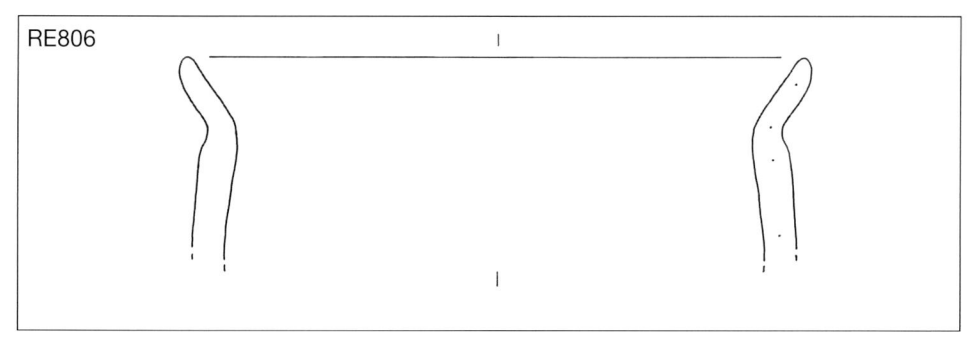

House 240, sunken-floor horizon
RE806aa. Clay pot rim & side. Calculation of outer rim diameter: c. 26 cm. Ware thickness: 1.0-1.2-1.5-1.4 cm.

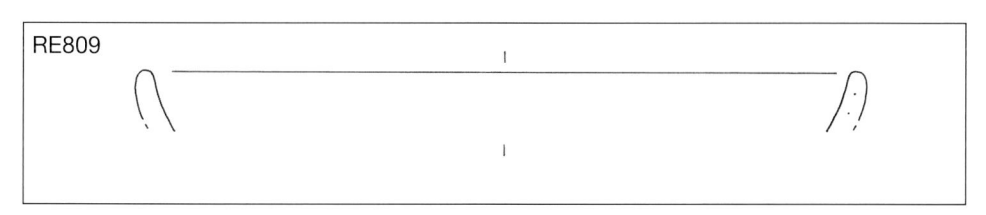

House 240, secondary fills
RE809aa. Clay pot rim. Calculation of outer rim diameter: c. 30 cm. Ware thickness: 0.9-1.0 cm.

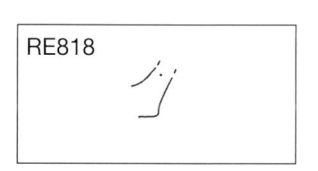

House 200, secondary fills
RE818aa. Clay pot bottom. Ware thickness: 0.8 cm.

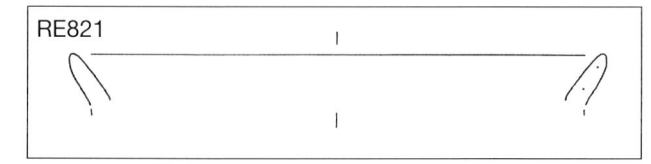

House 200, sunken-floor horizon
RE821aa. Clay pot rim. Calculation of outer rim diameter: c. 22 cm. Ware thickness: 0.7-0.8 cm.

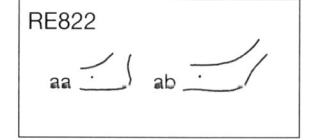

Pit 241, north of House 240
RE822aa. Clay pot bottom. Ware thickness: 0.8 cm.
RE822ab. Clay pot side & bottom. Ware thickness: 1.0 cm.

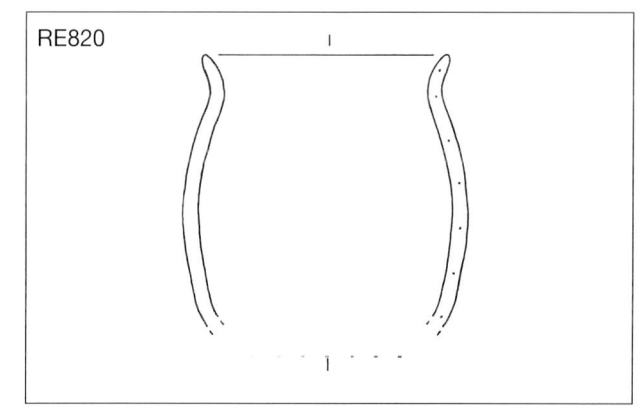

House 200, secondary fills
RE820aa. Clay pot rim & side. Calculation of outer rim diameter: c. 10.5 cm. Estimate of original height: c. 12 cm. Ware thickness: 0.5-0.6-0.7-0.6-0.7-0.7-0.6 cm.

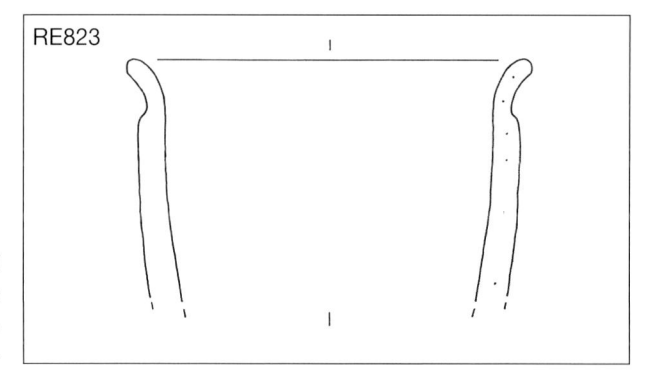

Pit 266
RE823aa. Clay pot rim & side. Calculation of outer rim diameter: c. 17 cm. Ware thickness: 0.8-0.7-1.1-1.1-1.2-1.3 cm. Precise find spot not identified.

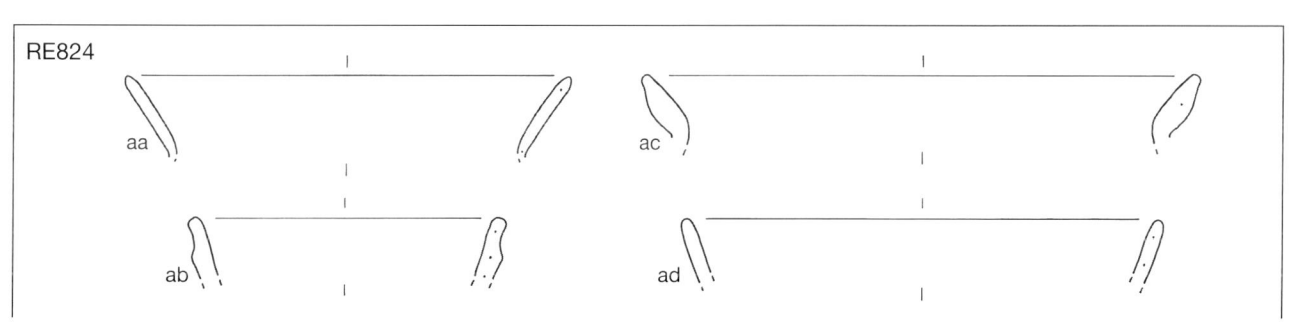

Ceramics at Resengaard   487

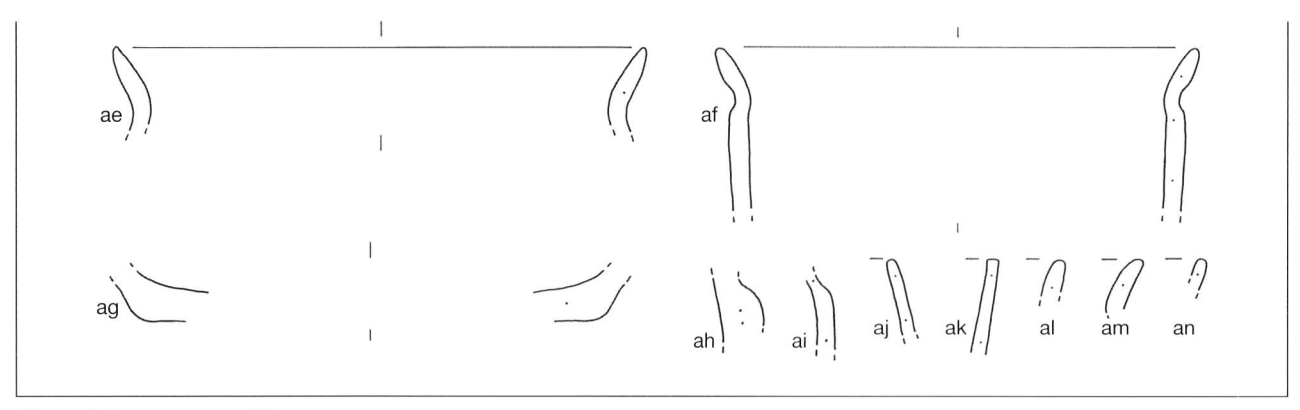

House 268, secondary fills
RE824aa. Clay pot rim. Calculation of outer rim diameter: c. 18.5 cm. Ware thickness: 0.6-0.4 cm.
RE824ab. Clay pot rim & side. Calculation of outer rim diameter: c. 13 cm. Ware thickness: 0.5-0.8-0.7 cm. The inclination may have been somewhat different.
RE824ac. Clay pot rim. Calculation of outer rim diameter: c. 23 cm. Ware thickness: 1.0 cm.
RE824ad. Clay pot rim & side. Calculation of outer rim diameter: c. 20 cm. Ware thickness: 0.6-0.6 cm.
RE824ae. Clay pot rim & side. Calculation of outer rim diameter: c. 22 cm. Ware thickness: 0.8 cm.
RE824af. Clay pot rim & side. Calculation of outer rim diameter: c. 19.5 cm. Ware thickness: 0.7-0.9-0.8 cm.
RE824ag. Clay pot side & bottom. Calculation of outer bottom diameter: c. 20 cm. Ware thickness: 1.5 cm.
RE824ah. Clay pot side. Ware thickness: 2.2-2.1 cm.
RE824ai. Clay pot rim & side. Ware thickness: 0.5-0.8 cm.
RE824aj. Clay pot rim & side. Ware thickness: 0.5-0.6 cm.
RE824ak. Clay pot rim & side. Ware thickness: 0.5-0.6 cm.
RE824al. Clay pot rim. Ware thickness: 0.8 cm.
RE824am. Clay pot rim. Ware thickness: 0.7 cm.
RE824an. Clay pot rim. Ware thickness: 0.5 cm.

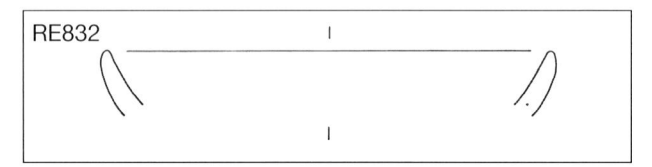

House 268, secondary fills
RE832aa. Clay pot rim. Calculation of outer rim diameter: c. 19 cm. Ware thickness: 0.9 cm.

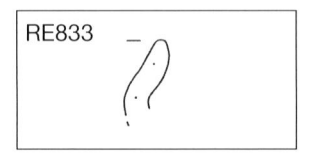

House 268, secondary fills
RE833aa. Clay pot rim & side. Ware thickness: 1.0-1.0 cm. Soot on the outer rim side.

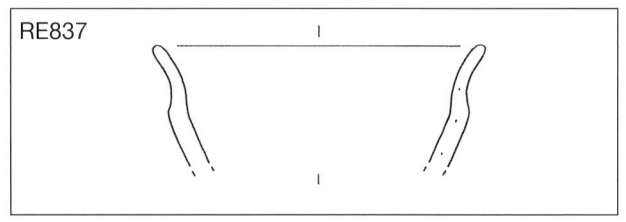

House 268, secondary fills
RE837aa. Clay pot rim & side. Calculation of outer rim diameter: c. 14 cm. Ware thickness: 0.6-0.8-0.8 cm. The inclination may have been somewhat different.

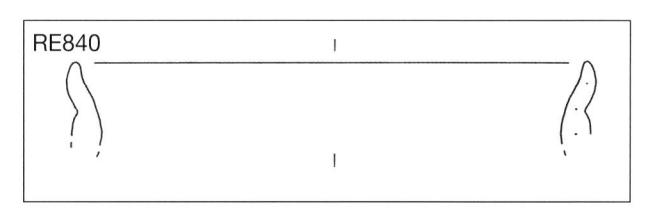

House 268, secondary fills
RE836aa. Loom weight fragment, about a quarter preserved. Sub-circular/oval shaping. Height 5.0 cm. Calculated length c. 12.2 cm & width c. 9.7 cm. Diameter of the central, cylindrical hole c. 1.6 cm. Tempering fine though with a few coarse grains. Outer surface reddish and the inner brownish. Possibly secondarily burned.

House 268, secondary fills
RE840aa. Clay pot rim & side. Calculation of outer rim diameter: c. 22 cm. Ware thickness: 0.7-0.8-1.2 cm.

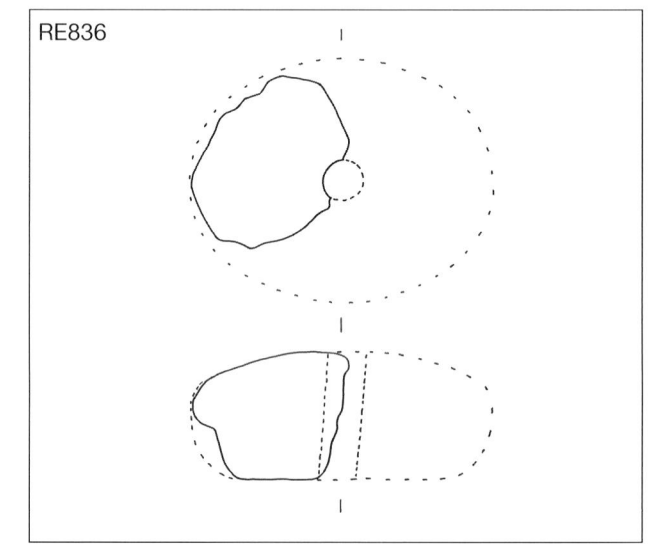

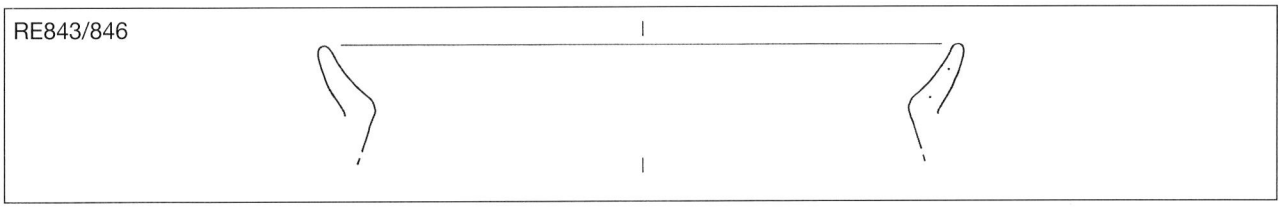

House 268, secondary fills/sunken-floor horizon
RE843aa. Clay pot rim & side. Calculation of outer rim diameter: c. 26.5 cm. Ware thickness: 0.8-1.1 cm. Secondary fills. The conjoining RE846aa belongs to the sunken-floor horizon.

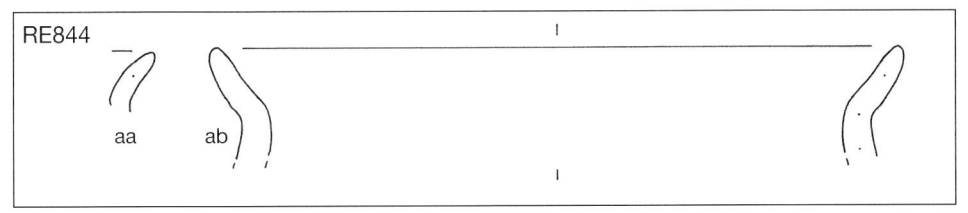

House 268, sunken-floor horizon
RE844aa. Clay pot rim. Ware thickness: 0.8 cm.
RE844ab. Clay pot rim & side. Calculation of outer rim diameter: c. 28.5 cm. Ware thickness: 0.9-1.1-1.2 cm.

RE846aa. Clay pot rim & side. See RE843.

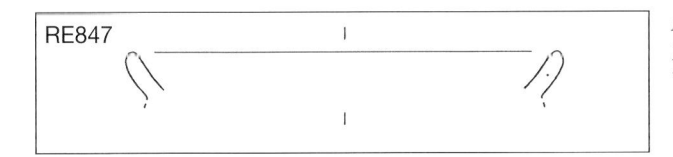

House 268, sunken-floor horizon
RE847aa. Clay pot rim. Calculation of outer rim diameter: c. 18 cm. Ware thickness: 0.8 cm.

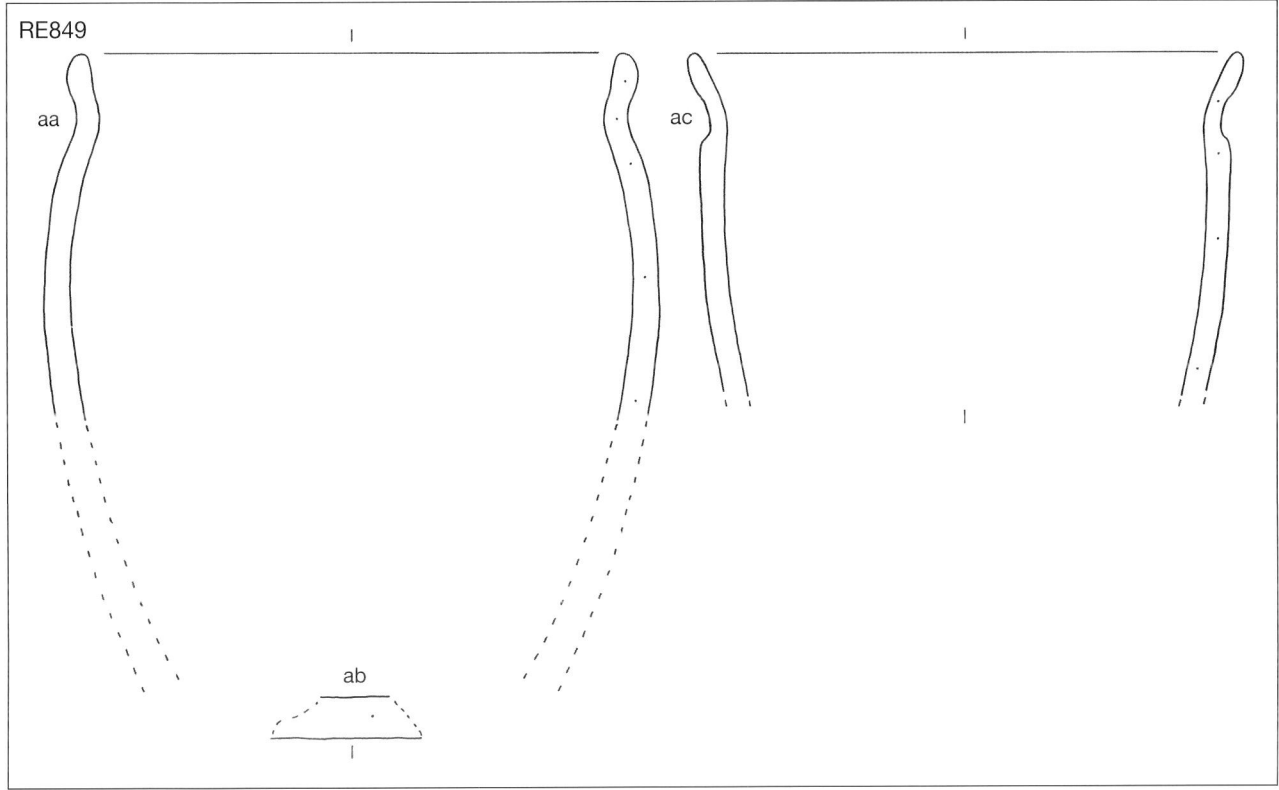

House 268, sunken-floor horizon
RE849aa. Clay pot rim & side. Calculation of outer rim diameter: c. 23 cm. Estimate of original height: c. 27.5 cm. Ware thickness: 1.0-0.9.-1.1-1.1-1.2 cm.

RE849ab. Bottom fragment. Ware thickness 1.7 cm. Belongs to RE849aa.
RE849ac. Clay pot rim & side. Calculation of outer rim diameter: c. 23 cm. Ware thickness: 0.7-10.-1.0-1.0 cm.

Ceramics at Resengaard

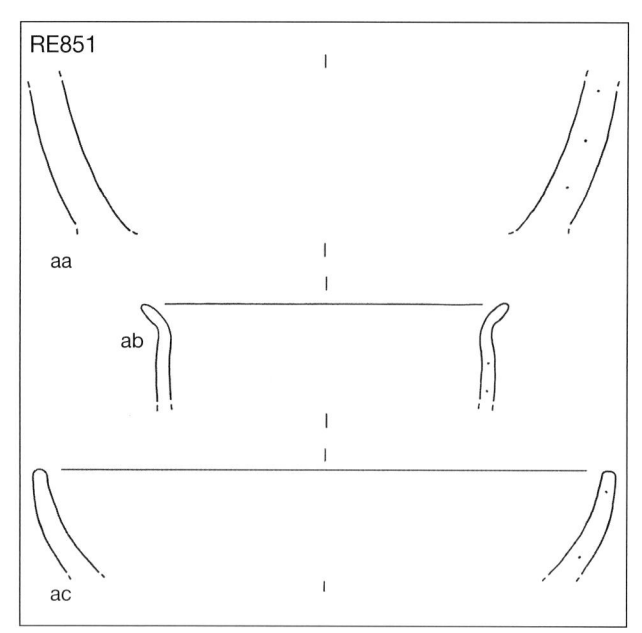

House 240, secondary fills
RE851aa. Clay pot side. Calculation of outer bottom diameter: c. 20 cm. Ware thickness: 1.5-1.7-1.6 cm.
RE851ab. Clay pot rim & side. Calculation of outer rim diameter: c. 15 cm. Ware thickness: 0.5-0.6 cm.
RE851ac. Clay pot rim & side. Calculation of outer rim diameter: c. 24 cm. Ware thickness: 0.7-1.0 cm. Secondarily burned.

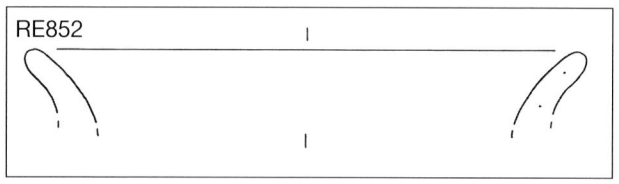

House 240, secondary fills
RE852aa. Clay pot rim. Calculation of outer rim diameter: c. 23.5 cm. Ware thickness: 0.9-1.2 cm.

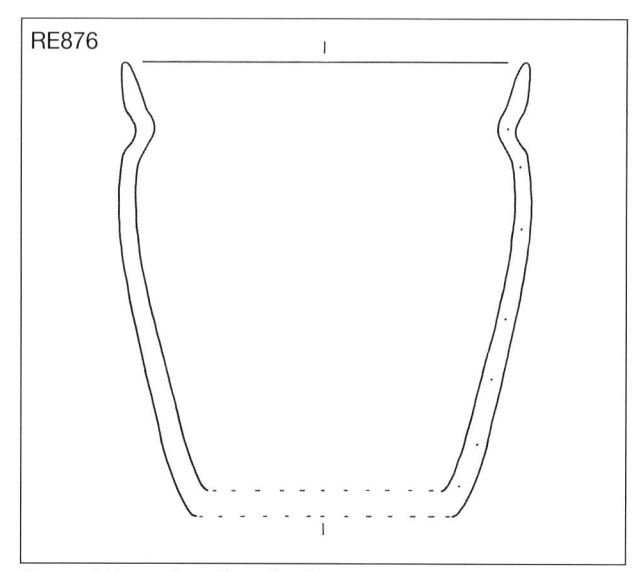

House 240, sunken-floor horizon
RE876aa. Clay pot rim, side & bottom. Calculation of outer rim diameter: c. 17 cm. Original height: c. 18 cm. Ware thickness: 0.7-0.7-0.7-0.8-0.9-0.9-1.0 cm.

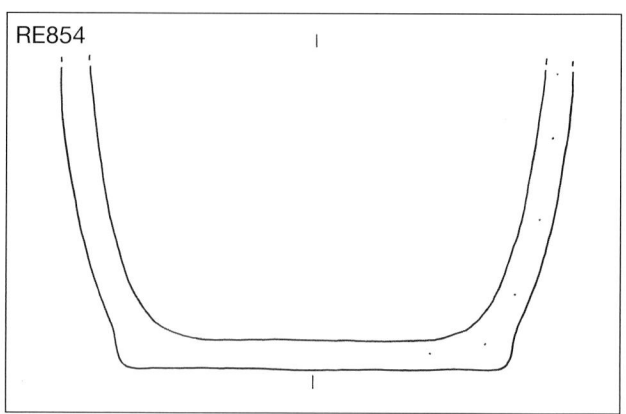

House 200, secondary fills
RE854aa. Clay pot side & bottom. Calculation of outer bottom diameter: c. 16 cm. Ware thickness: 1.2-1.3-1.3-1.3-2.1-1.2 cm. Soot & soot crust on the inner side near the bottom. Some soot above this area.

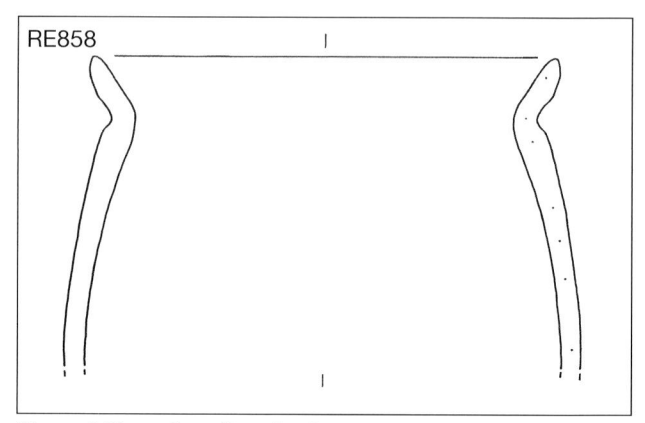

House 240, sunken-floor horizon
RE858aa. Clay pot rim & side. Calculation of outer rim diameter: c. 19 cm. Ware thickness: 0.8-1.0-1.3-1.0-0.9-0.9-0.8 cm. Soot crust on the inner side below the rim top. Soot & soot crust on the inner side, uppermost body part. Spot with soot on the outer side about the middle of the belly.

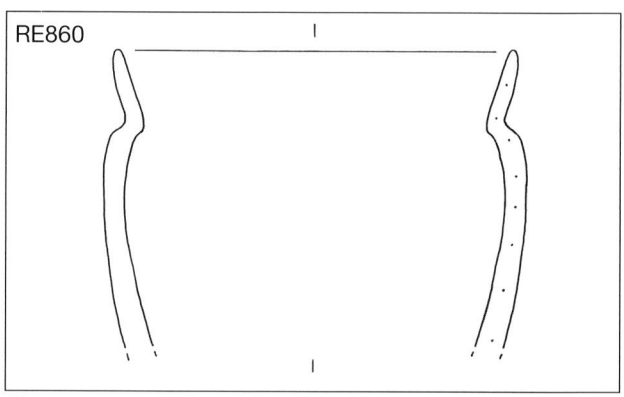

House 240, secondary fills
RE860aa. Clay pot rim & side. Calculation of outer rim diameter: c. 16.5 cm. Ware thickness: 0.7-0.8-1.0-0.9-0.9-1.0-1.1-1.1 cm.

RE880

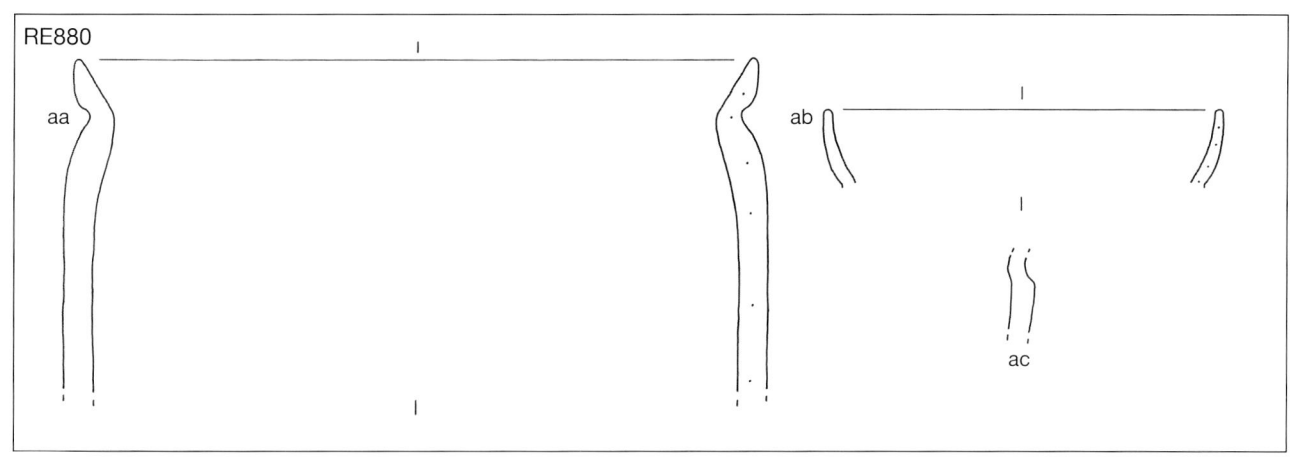

Pit 278, east-northeast of House 240
RE880aa. Clay pot rim & side. Calculation of outer rim diameter:
c. 28.5 cm. Ware thickness: 1.0-1.0-15.-1.3-1.2-1.2 cm.
RE880ab. Clay pot rim & side. Calculation of outer rim diameter:
c. 16.5 cm. Ware thickness: 0.4-0.5-0.6-0.6 cm.
RE880ac. Clay pot side. Ware thickness: 0.7-1.1-0.9 cm.

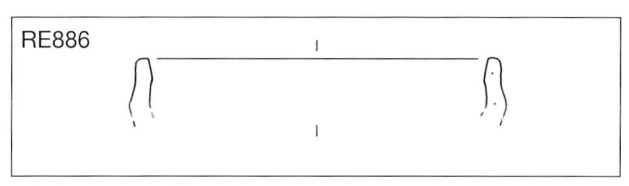

RE886

Pit 279, east of House 14
RE886aa. Clay pot rim & side. Calculation of outer rim diameter:
c. 15 cm. Ware thickness: 0.6-0.8 cm.

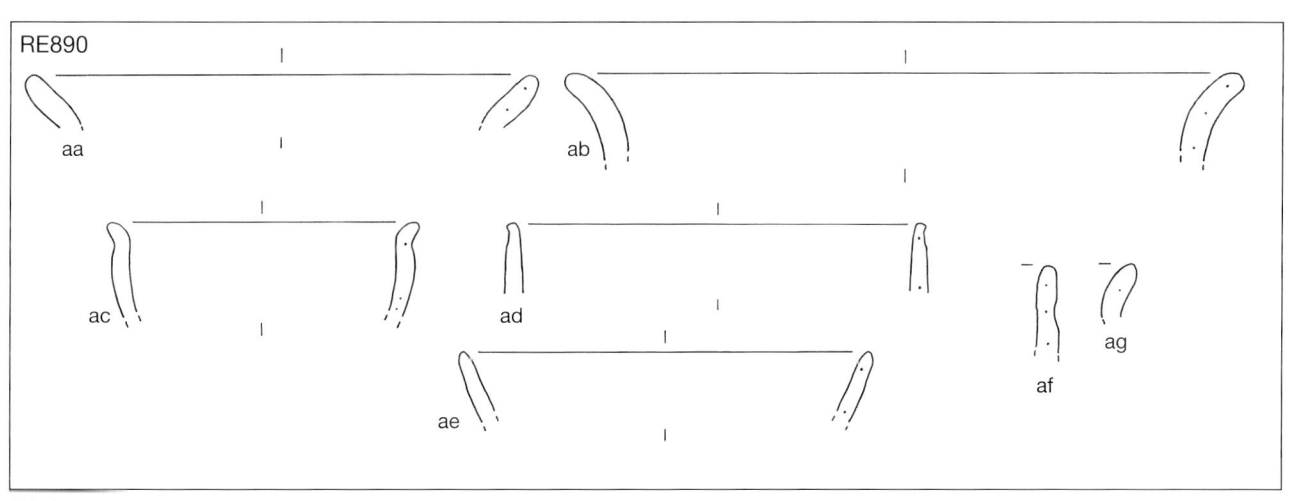

RE890

Pit 281
RE890aa. Clay pot rim. Calculation of outer rim diameter: c. 21 cm.
Ware thickness: 0.9-0.9 cm. Precise find spot not identified.
RE890ab. Clay pot rim. Calculation of outer rim diameter:
c. 28 cm. Ware thickness: 1.0-1.1-0.9 cm.
RE890ac. Clay pot rim & side. Calculation of outer rim diameter:
c. 13 cm. Ware thickness: 0.7-0.8-0.7 cm.

RE890ad. Clay pot rim & side. Calculation of outer rim diameter:
c. 17.5 cm. Ware thickness: 0.5-0.7 cm.
RE890ae. Clay pot rim & side. Calculation of outer rim diameter:
c. 17 cm. Ware thickness: 0.6-0.6 cm.
RE890af. Clay pot rim & side. Ware thickness: 0.8-0.7-0.9 cm.
RE890ag. Clay pot rim. Ware thickness: 0.9 cm.

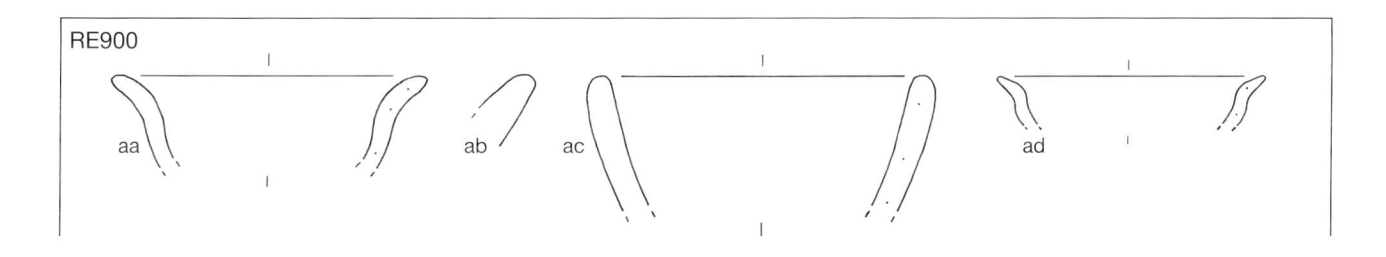

RE900

Ceramics at Resengaard 491

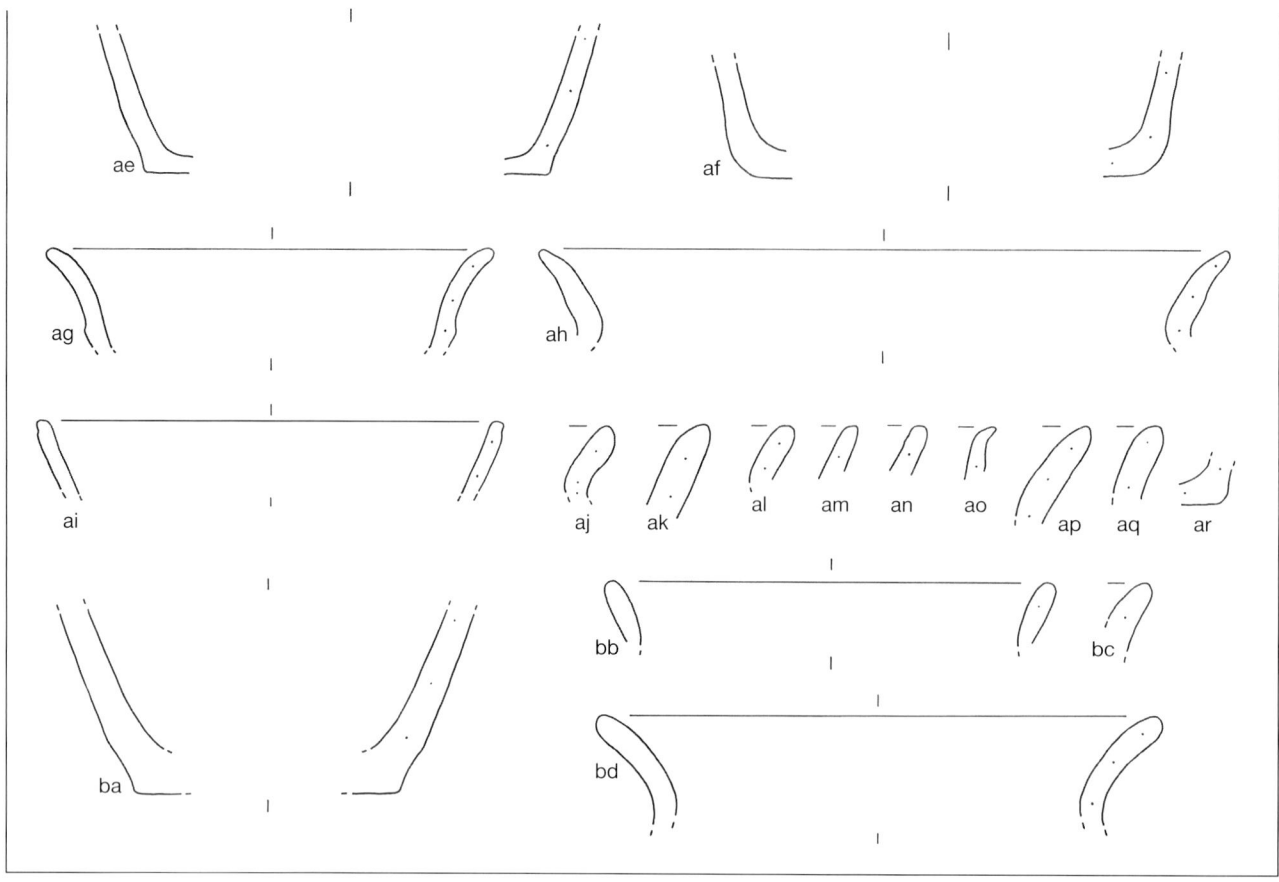

House 289, secondary fills

RE900aa. Clay pot rim & side. Calculation of outer rim diameter: c. 13 cm. Ware thickness: 0.8-0.7-0.7 cm.
RE900ab. Clay pot rim. Ware thickness: 1.1-1.6 cm. Judging by the strong rim, it likely concerns a rather large vessel.
RE900ac. Clay pot rim & side. Calculation of outer rim diameter: c. 14.5 cm. Ware thickness: 1.2-1.1-1.0 cm. Relatively thick-walled.
RE900ad. Clay pot rim & side. Calculation of outer rim diameter: c. 11.5 cm. Ware thickness: 0.5-0.6 cm.
RE900ae. Clay pot side & bottom. Calculation of outer bottom diameter: c. 17 cm. Ware thickness: 0.8-0.9-1.0 cm.
RE900af. Clay pot side & bottom. Calculation of outer bottom diameter: c. 17.5 cm. Ware thickness: 0.7-1.3-1.0 cm.
RE900ag. Clay pot rim & side. Calculation of outer rim diameter: c. 18.5 cm. Ware thickness: 0.7-0.7-0.8 cm. The potsherd is a little irregular. The inclination may have been somewhat different and the diameter may have been a little larger.
RE900ah. Clay pot rim. Calculation of outer rim diameter: c. 28.5 cm. Ware thickness: 0.7-1.0-1.0 cm.
RE900ai. Clay pot rim & side. Calculation of outer rim diameter: c. 20 cm. Ware thickness: 0.7-0.7 cm.
RE900aj. Clay pot rim. Ware thickness: 1.1-1.0-0.9 cm.
RE900ak. Clay pot rim. Ware thickness: 1.5-1.4 cm.
RE900al. Clay pot rim. Ware thickness: 1.0-1.0 cm.
RE900am. Clay pot rim. Ware thickness: 0.8 cm.
RE900an. Clay pot rim. Ware thickness: 0.8 cm.
RE900ao. Clay pot rim. Ware thickness: 0.8 cm.
RE900ap. Clay pot rim. Ware thickness: 1.1-1.3-1.1 cm.
RE900aq. Clay pot rim. Ware thickness: 1.2-1.2 cm.
RE900ar. Clay pot side & bottom. Ware thickness: 1.1 cm.
RE900ba. Clay pot side & bottom. Calculation of outer bottom diameter: c. 11 cm. Ware thickness: 1.2-1.4-1.5 cm. Soot crust on the inner side a little above the bottom.
RE900bb. Clay pot rim. Calculation of outer rim diameter: c. 18.5 cm. Ware thickness: 0.8 cm.
RE900bc. Clay pot rim. Ware thickness: 1.2 cm.
RE900bd. Clay pot rim & side. Calculation of outer rim diameter: c. 23 cm. Ware thickness: 1.1-1.0-0.9 cm.

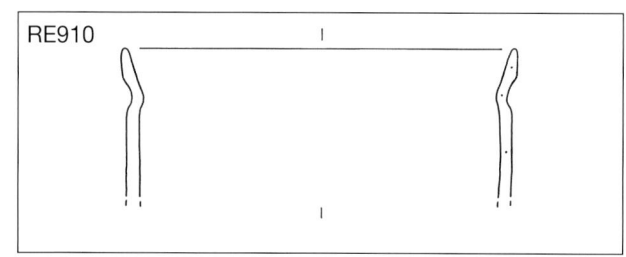

Pit 248, north of House 240

RE910aa. Clay pot rim & side. Calculation of outer rim diameter: c. 16.5 cm. Ware thickness: 0.5-0.5-0.6 cm.

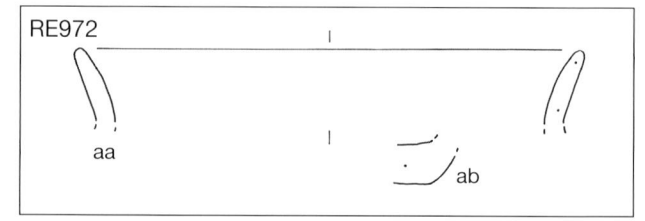

House 201, secondary fills

RE972aa. Clay pot rim. Calculation of outer rim diameter: c. 21 cm. Ware thickness: 0.6-0.8 cm.
RE972ab. Clay pot bottom. Ware thickness: 1.5 cm.

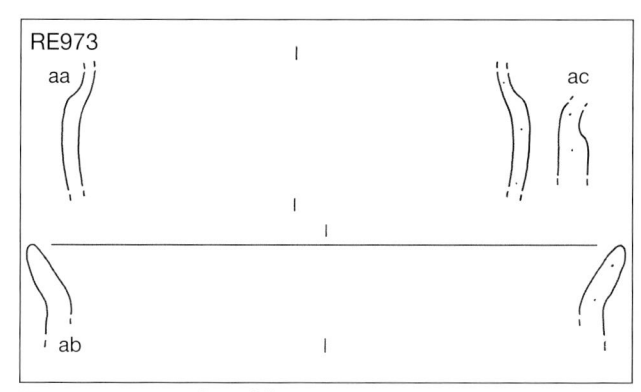

House 240, secondary fills
RE973aa. Clay pot side. Calculation of outer side diameter:
c. 19 cm. Ware thickness: 0.4-0.6-0.6 cm.
RE973ab. Clay pot rim & side. Calculation of outer rim diameter:
c. 25 cm. Ware thickness: 0.8-1.0 cm.
RE973ac. Clay pot side. Ware thickness: 0.8-1.3 cm.

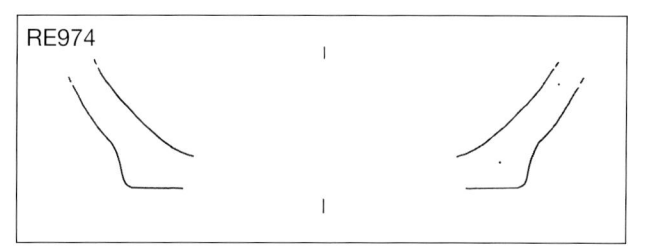

House 202, secondary fills
RE974aa. Clay pot side & bottom. Calculation of outer bottom diameter: c. 16.5 cm. Ware thickness: 1.2-2.3 cm.

Ceramics at Resengaard   **493**

▲ *Culture layer 293, southwest of House 14* (Page 493)
RE976aa. Clay pot rim & side. Calculation of outer rim diameter: c. 21 cm. Ware thickness: 0.9 cm. Diameter may have been somewhat different.
RE976ab. Clay pot rim & side. Ware thickness: 0.6-0.7 cm.
RE976ac. Clay pot rim & side. Calculation of outer rim diameter: c. 25.5 cm. Ware thickness: 0.8-0.7 cm. Perhaps secondary burning.
RE976ad. Clay pot rim. Calculation of outer rim diameter: c. 32 cm. Ware thickness: 1.2-0.9 cm.
RE976ae. Clay pot rim & side. Calculation of outer rim diameter: c. 19.5 cm. Ware thickness: 0.5-0.7 cm.
RE976af. Clay pot rim & side. Calculation of outer rim diameter: c. 29 cm. Ware thickness: 1.1-1.0 cm. The diameter may have been slightly different.
RE976ag. Clay pot side & bottom. Calculation of outer bottom diameter: c. 10 cm. Ware thickness: 1.0 cm.
RE976ah. Clay pot bottom. Ware thickness: 1.4 cm.
RE976ai. Clay pot bottom, outer surface preserved.
RE976aj. Clay pot side & bottom. Ware thickness: 1.0-2.0 cm.
RE976ak. Clay pot rim. Ware thickness: 0.4-0.5-0.6 cm.
RE976al. Clay pot rim. Ware thickness: 0.5-0.6 cm.
RE976am. Clay pot rim. Ware thickness: 0.5-0.7 cm.
RE976an. Clay pot rim. Ware thickness: 0.5-0.7 cm.

RE976ao. Clay pot rim & side. Ware thickness: 0.7-0.8 cm.
RE976ap. Clay pot rim & side. Ware thickness: 0.7-0.6 cm.
RE976aq. Clay pot rim. Ware thickness: 0.8-1.0 cm.
RE976ar. Clay pot rim. Ware thickness: 1.1 cm.
RE976as. Clay pot rim. Ware thickness: 1.3-1.2 cm.
RE976at. Clay pot rim & side. Ware thickness: 0.8-1.2 cm.
RE976au. Clay pot rim & side. Calculation of outer rim diameter: c. 18.5 cm. Ware thickness: 0.6-0.6-0.7-1.0 cm.
RE976av. Clay pot rim. Calculation of outer rim diameter: c. 12.5 cm. Ware thickness: 0.7-0.8 cm.
RE976ba. Clay pot rim & side. Calculation of outer rim diameter: c. 18 cm. Ware thickness: 1.0-1.0-1.2-0.9 cm.
RE976bb. Clay pot rim. Calculation of outer rim diameter: c. 30 cm. Ware thickness: 1.0-1.2-1.0-0.9 cm.
RE976bc. Clay pot rim & side. Calculation of outer rim diameter: c. 21 cm. Ware thickness: 0.8-0.9-0.8 cm.
RE976bd. Clay pot rim & side. Calculation of outer rim diameter: c. 26 cm. Ware thickness: 1.7-1.2-1.3-1.3 cm.
RE976be. Clay pot rim & side. Ware thickness: 0.6-0.8-0.6 cm.
RE976bf. Clay pot bottom. Ware thickness: 2.3-1.9-1.7 cm.
RE976bg. Clay pot rim. Ware thickness: 0.9-1.0 cm.

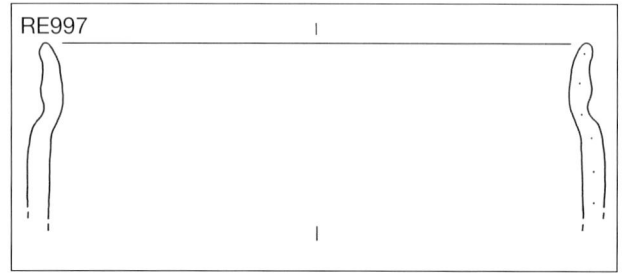

Pit 248
RE997aa. Clay pot rim & side. Calculation of outer rim diameter: c. 23 cm. Ware thickness: 0.7-1.0-0.8-0.9-1.0-0.9 cm. Precise find spot not identified.

Culture layer 203, east of House 138
RE1016aa. Clay pot bottom. Calculation of outer bottom diameter: c. 11.0 cm. Ware thickness: 1.1 cm.
RE1016ab. Clay pot side & bottom. Calculation of outer bottom diameter: c. 17.5 cm. Ware thickness: 1.6-1.5-1.6 cm.
RE1016ac. Clay pot bottom. Calculation of outer bottom diameter: c. 28 cm. Ware thickness: 2.1-2.4-2.1 cm. Probably stemming from an extraordinarily large jar, not dated.
RE1016ad. Clay pot rim. Ware thickness: 1.1-1.2 cm.

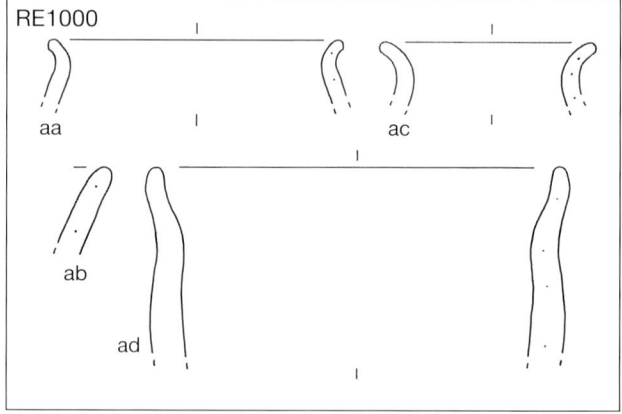

Culture layer 203, east of House 138
RE1000aa. Clay pot rim & side. Calculation of outer rim diameter: c. 12 cm. Ware thickness: 0.5-0.6 cm.
RE1000ab. Clay pot rim. Ware thickness: 0.9-1.0 cm.
RE1000ac. Clay pot rim & side. Calculation of outer rim diameter: c. 9 cm. Ware thickness: 0.6-0.7-0.7 cm.
RE1000ad. Clay pot rim & side. Calculation of outer rim diameter: c. 17 cm. Ware thickness: 0.8-1.1-1.1-1.3 cm.

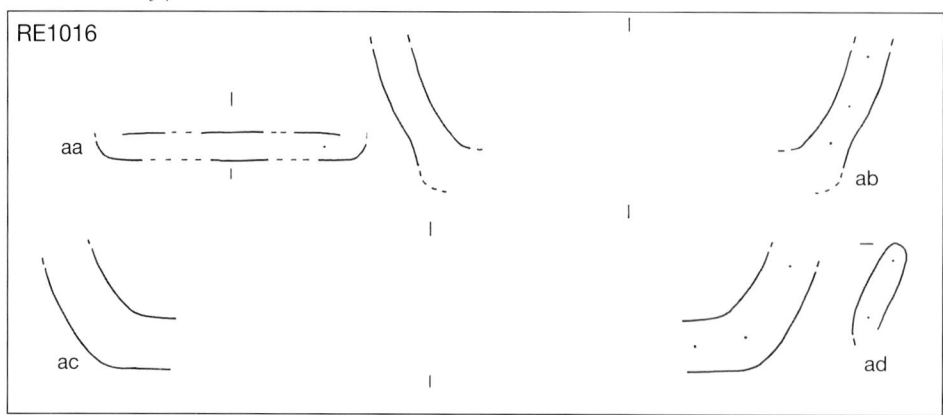

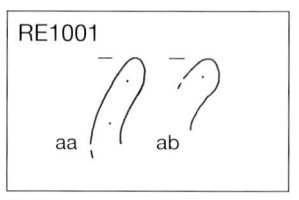

Culture layer 302, north-northeast of House 289
RE1001aa. Clay pot rim. Ware thickness: 1.1-1.2 cm.
RE1001ab. Clay pot rim. Ware thickness: 1.3 cm.

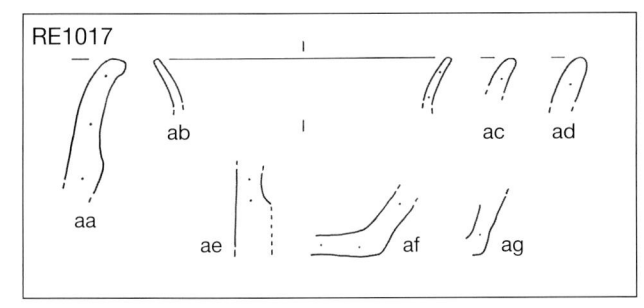

Culture layer 203, east of House 138
RE1017aa. Clay pot rim & side. Ware thickness: 0.9-1.0-1.3 cm.
RE1017ab. Clay pot rim. Calculation of outer rim diameter:
c. 12 cm. Ware thickness: 0.3-0.4 cm.
RE1017ac. Clay pot rim. Ware thickness: 0.7 cm.
RE1017ad. Clay pot rim. Ware thickness: 0.9 cm.
RE1017ae. Clay pot side. Ware thickness: 1.1-1.3 cm.
RE1017af. Clay pot side & bottom. Ware thickness: 1.0-0.9-0.8 cm.
RE1017ag. Clay pot side & bottom fragment. Ware thickness:
0.7 cm.

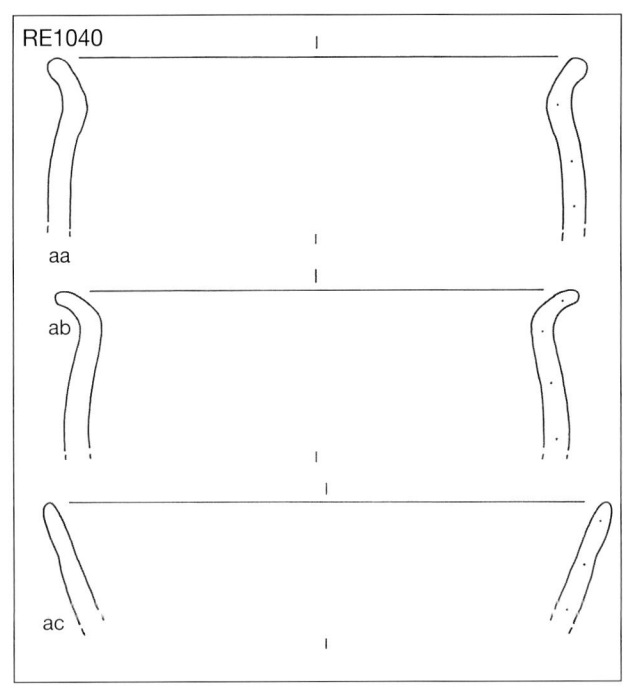

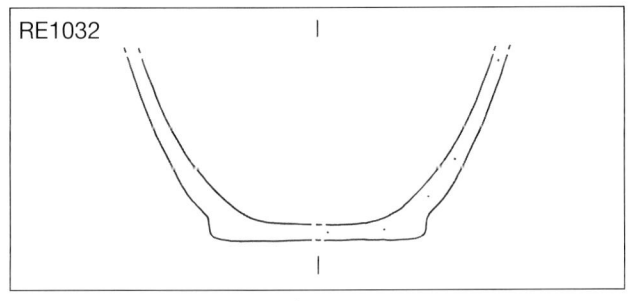

House 193, context uncertain
RE1032aa. Clay pot side & bottom. Calculation of outer bottom
diameter: 9 cm. Ware thickness: 0.6-0.7-1.0-0.8-1.7 cm.

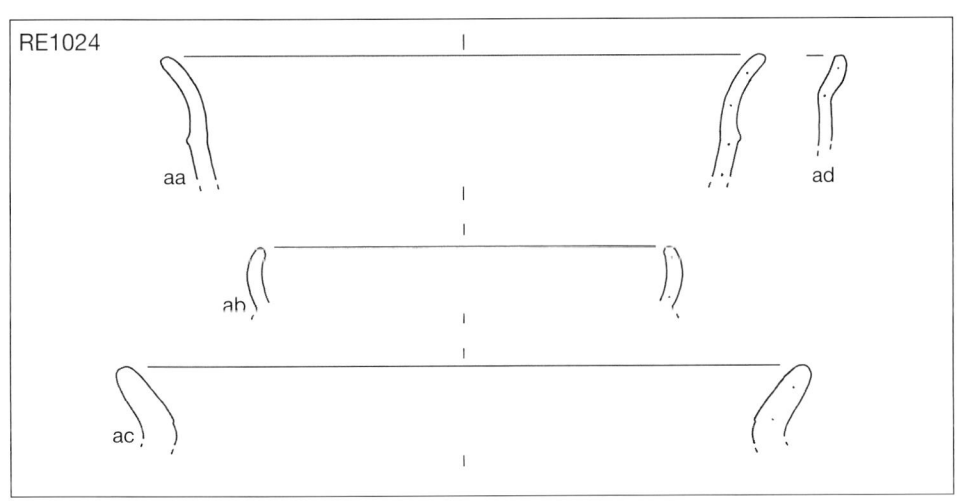

House 158, secondary fills
RE1040aa. Clay pot rim & side. Calculation of outer rim
diameter: c. 22.5 cm. Ware thickness: 1.2-0.9-0.9 cm.
RE1040ab. Clay pot rim & side. Calculation of outer rim
diameter: c. 21.5 cm. Ware thickness: 0.7-0.9-1.0-1.0 cm.
RE1040ac. Clay pot rim & side. Calculation of outer rim
diameter: c. 23.5 cm. Ware thickness: 0.7-0.8-1.0 cm.

Culture layer 203, east of House 138
RE1024aa. Clay pot rim & side. Calculation of outer rim diameter: c. 25 cm. Ware thickness:
0.6-0.6-0.8-0.7 cm.
RE1024ab. Clay pot rim. Calculation of outer rim diameter: c. 17.5 cm. Ware thickness: 0.5-0.6 cm.
RE1024ac. Clay pot rim. Calculation of outer rim diameter: c. 28.5 cm. Ware thickness: 1.1-1.3 cm.
RE1024ad. Clay pot rim. Calculation of outer rim diameter: c. 10 cm. Ware thickness: 0.6-0.6 cm.
RE1024ae. Clay pot rim & side (not illustrated). Ware thickness: 0.6-0.6-0.5 cm.

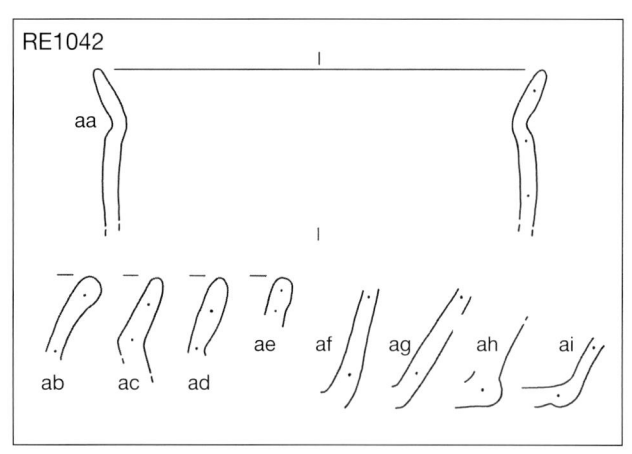

RE1042

House 158, secondary fills
RE1042aa. Clay pot rim & side. Calculation of outer rim diameter: c. 18.5 cm. Ware thickness: 0.6-0.7-0.6 cm.
RE1042ab. Clay pot rim. Ware thickness: 1.0-0.7 cm.
RE1042ac. Clay pot rim & side. Ware thickness: 0.9-1.1 cm.
RE1042ad. Clay pot rim. Ware thickness: 0.9-0.7 cm.
RE1042ae. Clay pot rim. Ware thickness: 0.9-0.9 cm.
RE1042af. Clay pot side & bottom. Ware thickness: 0.7-1.0 cm.
RE1042ag. Clay pot side & bottom. Ware thickness: 0.7-0.8 cm.
RE1042ah. Clay pot side & bottom. Ware thickness: 1.6 cm. Only the outer side preserved.
RE1042ai. Clay pot side & bottom. Ware thickness: 0.6-0.9 cm.

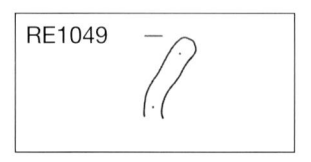

RE1049

Context not stated
RE1049aa. Clay pot rim. Ware thickness: 0.9-0.7 cm. The slightly protruding element at the outer rim side is unlike a cordon.

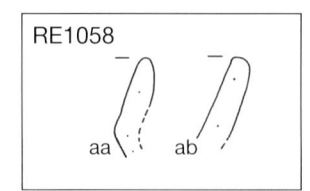

RE1058

House 289, secondary fills
RE1058aa. Clay pot rim & side. Ware thickness: 1.1-0.8-0.7 cm.
RE1058ab. Clay pot rim. Ware thickness: 1.0-1.2 cm.

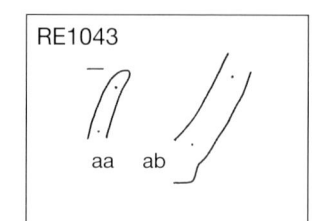

RE1043

House 240, secondary fills
RE1043aa. Clay pot rim & side. Ware thickness: 0.6-0.7 cm.
RE1043ab. Clay pot side & bottom. Ware thickness: 1.3-1.4 cm.

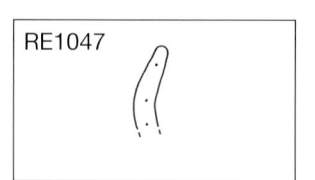

RE1047

House 197, secondary fills
RE1047aa. Clay pot rim & side. Ware thickness: 0.7-0.9-0.9 cm.

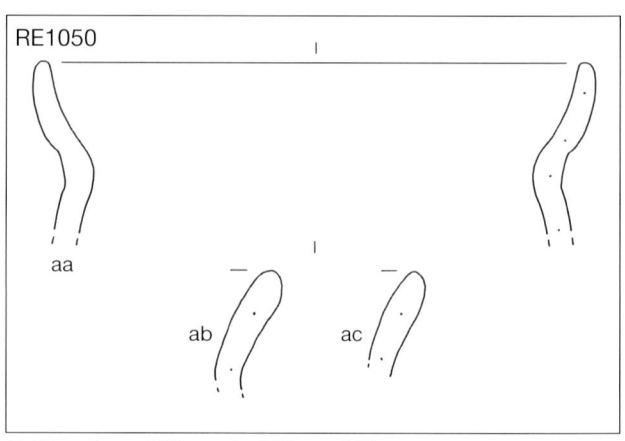

RE1050

Culture layer 203, east of House 138
RE1050aa. Clay pot rim & side. Calculation of outer rim diameter: c. 23 cm. Ware thickness: 0.9-1.0-1.1-1.0 cm. Soot on the inner rim side.
RE1050ab. Clay pot rim. Ware thickness: 1.3-1.1 cm.
RE1050ac. Clay pot bottom. Ware thickness: 1.3-1.1 cm.

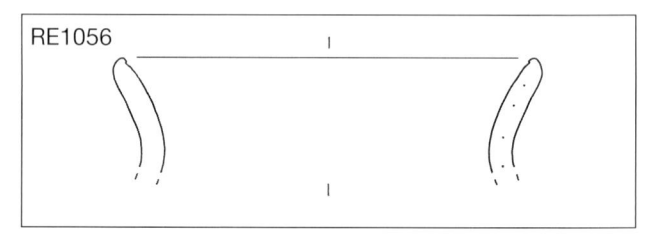

RE1056

House 289, secondary fills
RE1056aa. Clay pot rim. Calculation of outer rim diameter: c. 17.5 cm. Ware thickness: 0.9-1.0-1.0-0.9 cm.

RE1059

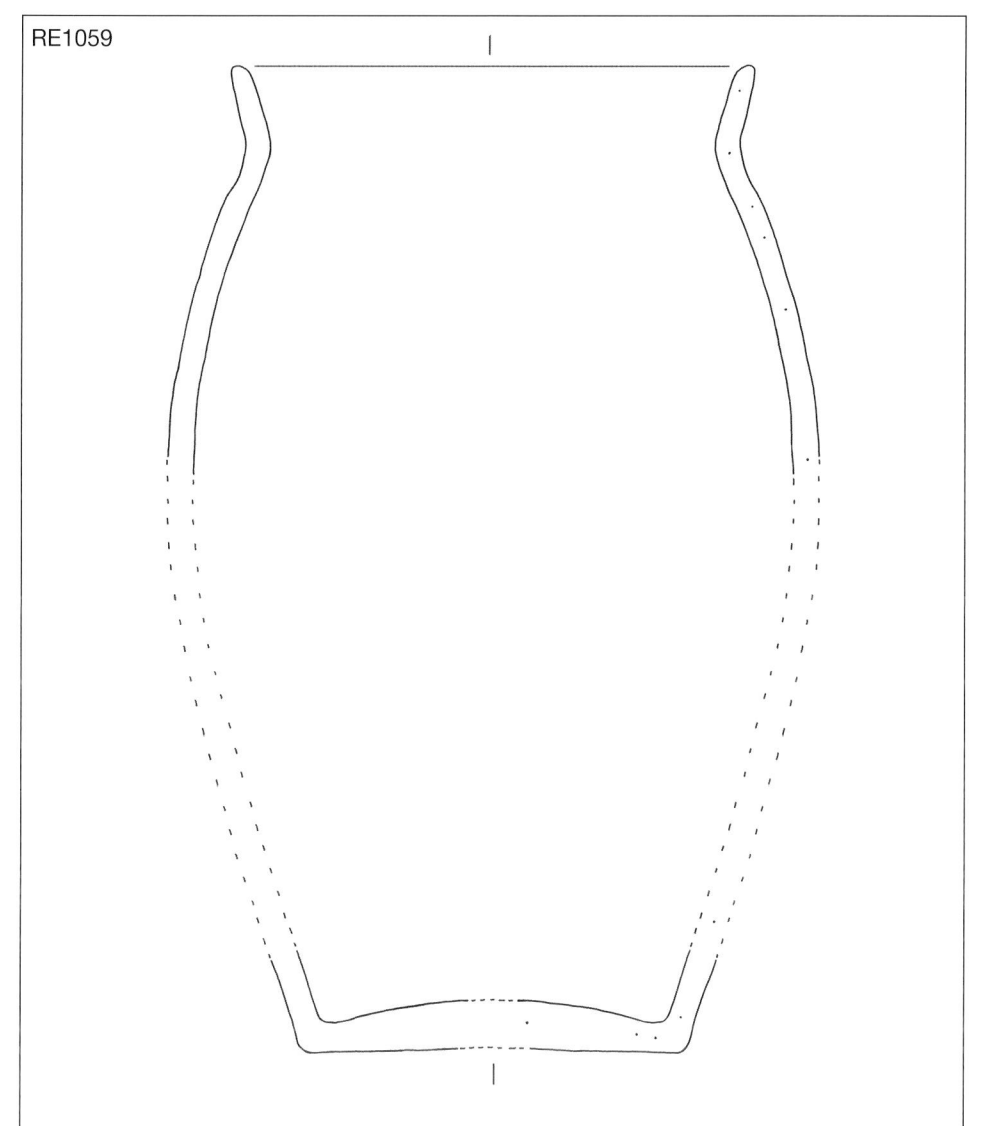

House 198, secondary fills
RE1059aa. Clay pot rim, side & bottom. Calculation of outer rim diameter: c. 21.5 cm. Estimate of original height: c. 39 cm (part of side missing). Ware thickness: 0.8-1.0-1.1-1.0-1.0-1.1-1.2-1.0-1.0-1.2-2.0 cm. A large area with soot on the upper part of the outer side. Spots with soot on the inner side near the bottom. A potsherd from near the bottom shows traces of secondary burning.

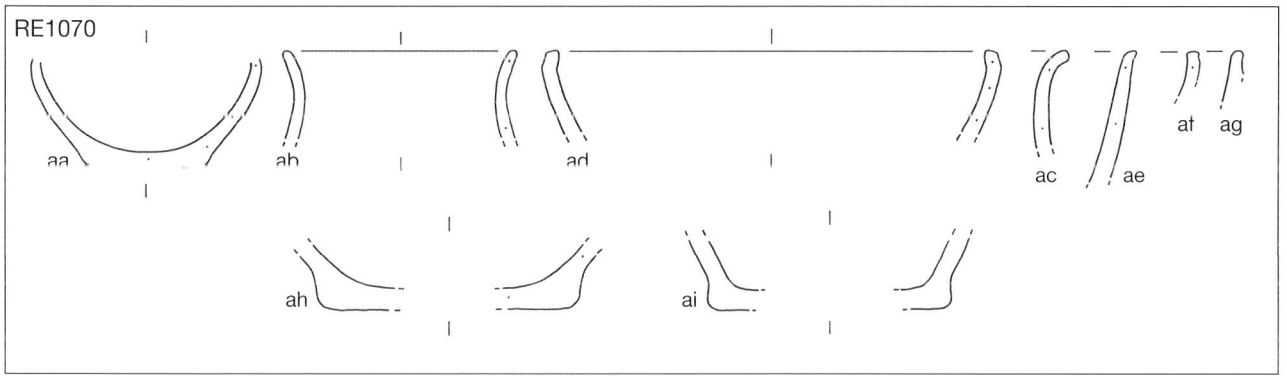

RE1070

aa ab ad ac ae at ag
ah ai

Context not stated
RE1070aa. Clay pot side & bottom. Calculation of outer rim diameter: c. 9.5 cm. Ware thickness: 04-0.5-0.9-0.6 cm.
RE1070ab. Clay pot rim & side. Calculation of outer rim diameter: c. 9.5 cm. Ware thickness: 04-0.5 cm.
RE1070ac. Clay pot rim & side. Ware thickness: 0.6-0.6 cm.
RE1070ad. Clay pot rim & side. Calculation of outer rim diameter: c. 18.5. Ware thickness: 0.6-0.6-0.7 cm.

RE1070ae. Clay pot rim & side. Ware thickness: 0.5-0.7 cm.
RE1070af. Clay pot rim. Ware thickness: 04-0.5-0.9-0.6 cm.
RE1070ag. Clay pot rim.
RE1070ah. Clay pot side & bottom. Calculation of outer bottom diameter: c. 10.5 cm. Ware thickness: 0.8-0.9 cm.
RE1070ai. Clay pot side & bottom. Calculation of outer bottom diameter: c. 10.0 cm. Ware thickness: 0.7-0.8-0.9 cm.

Ceramics at RESENGAARD **497**

Catalogue B

Stone artefacts at Resengaard

Presented in numerical order, the catalogue contains selected stone artefacts from Resengaard and among these are many bifacial flint items. Priority has been given in the selection to tools, roughouts and certain other items coming from the sunken-floor horizons, whereas those from the secondary fills above the sunken-floor horizons have been admitted on a more limited scale, and primarily when interesting in relation to the topics dealt with. Some items from other contexts such as pits are incorporated into the catalogue, as well as a few items that were already "antiques" in their observed prehistoric context. A few stray finds are included.

The flint tools of the catalogue include complete or fragmented specimens of daggers, spear-blades, axes, hammers, sickles, strike–a–lights, scrapers, knives, borers, pieces with notches, arrowheads (including roughouts for these) and an adze. In addition, some artefacts such as quern stones, smoothening stones, stone axes, stone hammers and whetstones are included.

The headings bring the raw materials to the fore. For instance, scrapers could have been made in several other materials such as bone, antler or wood but, in our case, the only preserved ones were made of flint. With regard to daggers and other flint items, the term "complete" refers to the observation that no significant parts have been broken off, even though they may have been reduced in size through resharpening. For flint daggers and fragments of these, grouping into type is often proposed (*cf.* Lomborg 1973a). When "greyish flint" is mentioned, the materials mostly appear to be Grey Danien. Dark, blackish flint seldom occurs.

Some of the remarks relate to micro wear analyses of flint tools and these concern examinations carried out by Claus Skriver (report S2004). In all, 126 pieces were analysed, and interesting results achieved for eight of them. Many pieces turned out to be rather patinated (smooth), unlike the appearance of freshly chipped flint. Nonetheless, all were scanned by microscope to check for the presence of plant polish.

From Resengaard, micro-wear analyses of two flint sickles and a flint dagger belonging to a three-aisled house site have been examined by Merete Christensen (Report S1991a). These finds are not included.

The flint tools most frequently found in the sunken-floor horizons are scrapers. Apart from the more or less atypical ones, I prefer to use the nomenclature from the plate book "The Late Stone Age" (1952) by Peter Vilhelm Glob. This work distinguishes between circular, long oval, pear-shaped and spoon-shaped scrapers. Some dimensions of their edges are accounted for. The minimum height of these is set as low as 1 mm because certain edges, probably intended for rather fine scraping purposes, would be at risk to fall outside the definition if 2 mm, for instance, were the criteria. The height of the scraper edge at, for instance, 2 mm from the edge is an expression of the steepness. The width of an edge is measured in a straight line between the end points. With regard to borers, the dimensions of the borer points are measured 5 mm from the ends.

The catalogue contains more than 250 items, presented in numerical order. For the composition of the catalogue numbers, see Catalogue A. Sub-numbers consisting of two small letters are added.

RE1ea. Flint spear-blade
Almost complete, the tip broken off. Length 7.7 cm, width 3.9 cm. Assessment of original length: c. 8.5-9.0 cm. Pressure-flaked. Greyish flint. Probably produced from the blade of a flint dagger. A notch for fixing it made at one side of the lower end. Stray find.

RE6ea. Flint dagger
Handle fragment. Length 2.0 cm & width 2.1 cm. Pressure-flaked. Presumably type VI. Greyish flint. Surface cracks due to heat. Another piece (RE6eb) is presumably also a burned fragment of a flint dagger. Context: House 1, secondary fills.

RE7ea. Fine-grained whetstone
Fragment. Length 8.2 cm & width 5.5 cm. Almost levelled surface, only vaguely convex. Context: House 2, secondary fills.

RE10ea. Flint scraper
Complete. Circular. Length 4.5 cm & width 4.1 cm. Scraper edge runs all around except for the bulb area. Height of scraper edge (0.5 cm from edge) c. 0.4 cm. Greyish flint. Much patinated. Micro-wear analysis. Context: House 1, sunken-floor horizon.

RE13ea. Flint scraper
Likely a spoon scraper handle. Length 3.5 cm, width 2.8 cm. Greyish flint. Context: House 1, sunken-floor horizon.

RE14ea. Flint nodule
Approx. length 4 cm, width 4 cm, & thickness 3 cm. Greyish flint. Small cortex area preserved. Context: House 1, sunken-floor horizon.

RE20ea. Flint axe
Fragmented, minor parts missing from the edge and the neck. Length 12.7 cm & width 5.6 cm. Partly polished on four sides. Greyish flint. Origin: Single Grave Culture. Context: House 1, sunken-floor horizon.

RE22ea. Stone hammer
Complete. Length 7.6 cm, width 4.8 cm, & thickness 3.6 cm. Crushing at both ends. Quartzite. Context: House 1, sunken-floor horizon.

RE29ea. Flint scraper
Fragment. Length 5.0 cm, width 4.5 cm, & thickness 2.1 cm. Atypical. Width of scraper edge 2.7 cm (originally presumably 3.5 cm). Height of scraper edge (0.5 cm from edge) c. 0.2 cm. Greyish flint. Cortex partly preserved. Much patinated. Micro-wear analysis. Context: House 1, sunken-floor horizon.

RE37ea. Flint nodule
Approx. length 7 cm, width 5.5 cm, & thickness 2.5 cm. Greyish flint., brownish-grey patina. Cortex partly preserved. Context: House 1, sunken-floor horizon.

RE38ea. Flint scraper
Almost complete. Pear-shaped. Length 4.0 cm, width 2.7 cm, & thickness 0.7 cm. Width of scraper edge 1.8 cm. Height of scraper edge (0.5 cm from edge) c. 0.3 cm. Greyish flint. Side blunted. Much patinated. Micro-wear analysis. Context: House 1, sunken-floor horizon.

RE40ea. Flint scraper
Fragment. Length 5.7 cm (original length: c. 6 cm) & thickness 2.1 cm. Atypical. Width of scraper edge 2.1 cm. Height of scraper edge (0.5 cm from edge) c. 0.4 cm. Greyish flint. Cortex partly preserved. Much patinated. Micro-wear analysis. Context: House 1, secondary fills.

RE44ea. Flint nodule
Greyish flint. Length 5.5 cm, width 4.0 cm, & thickness 3.3 cm Cortex partly preserved. Context: House 1, sunken-floor horizon.

RE45ea. Flint nodule
Greyish flint. Cortex partly preserved. Context: House 1, sunken-floor horizon.

RE51ea. Flint nodule
Approx. length 5.4 cm, width 5.1 cm, & thickness 4.6 cm. Greyish flint. Cortex partly preserved. Context: House 1, sunken-floor horizon.

RE52ea. Flint scraper
Fragment, only edge part preserved. Length 2.7 cm, width 3.3 cm, & thickness 1.1 cm. Width of scraper edge 3.3 cm. Height of scraper edge (0.5 cm from edge) 0.8 cm. Cracks in surface due to heat. Much patinated. Micro-wear analysis. Context: House 1, sunken-floor horizon.

RE53ea. Flint sickle
Fragment of crescent-shaped sickle. Length 3.1 cm, width 2.0 cm, & thickness 0.7 cm. Length of edge 3.1 cm. Possibly re-sharpened. Pressure-flaked. Greyish flint. Cracks in surface due to heat. Much patinated. Micro-wear analysis. Context: House 1, sunken-floor horizon.

RE63ea. Flint scraper
Fragment, edge part preserved. Length 2.8 cm, width 2.5 cm, & thickness 1.1 cm. Width of scraper edge 2.2 cm. Height of scraper edge (0.5 cm from edge) c. 0.4 cm. Greyish flint. Cracks in surface due to heat. Much patinated. Micro-wear analysis. Context: House 1, sunken-floor horizon.

RE65ea. Flint arrowhead
Complete. Tanged. Length 4.4 cm, width 2.4 cm, & thickness 0.7 cm. Pressure-flaked. Greyish flint. Much patinated. Micro-wear analysis. Context: House 1, sunken-floor horizon.

RE65eb. Flint nodule
Length 4.9 cm, width 3.4 cm, & thickness 2.7 cm. Greyish flint. Context: House 1, sunken-floor horizon.

RE66ea. Flint scraper
Complete. Atypical, "nosed". made on a large flake. Length 7.5 cm, width 5.5 cm & thickness 2.2 cm. Width of scraper edge 2.6 cm. Height of scraper edge (0.5 cm from edge) c. 0.4 cm. Greyish flint. Cortex partly preserved. Much patinated. Micro-wear analysis. Context: House 1, sunken-floor horizon.

RE69ea. Flint nodule
Length 6.5 cm, width 5.6 cm, & thickness 2.8 cm. Greyish flint. Context: House 1, sunken-floor horizon.

RE70ea. Flint nodule
Length 5.7 cm, width 4.5 cm, & thickness 2.4 cm. Greyish flint. Cortex partly preserved. Much patinated. Micro-wear analysis. Context: House 1, sunken-floor horizon.

RE72ea. Flint piece with notch
Presumably complete. Beside the notch, a blunting (scraper-like) retouch. Length 8.4 cm, width 3.8 cm, & thickness 2.1 cm. Greyish flint. Much patinated. Micro-wear analysis. Context: House 1, sunken-floor horizon.

RE80ea. Flint sickle
Complete. Crescent-shaped. Length 7.2 cm, width 4.3 cm, & thickness 1.3 cm. Length of edge 7.2 cm. Possibly re-sharpened. Pressure-flaked, cortex partly preserved. Greyish flint. Much patinated. Micro-wear analysis. Context: House 2, secondary fills.

RE81ea. Flint borer
Complete or almost complete, as a tiny bit is possibly broken off the borer point. Length 5.0 cm, width 2.5 cm, & thickness 0.9 cm. Borer point dimensions (0.5 cm from end) 0.6 × 0.4 cm. Greyish flint. Seems made on a flake. Much patinated. Micro-wear analysis. Context: Pit 320, immediately north of House 2.

RE81eb. Flint piece with notch
Complete. A blunting scraper-like retouch around the tool. Length 8.0 cm, width 5.0 cm, & thickness 1.2 cm. Greyish flint. Much patinated. Micro-wear analysis. Context: Pit 320, immediately north of House 2.

RE82ea. Flint scraper
Complete. Side scraper. Length 5.5 cm, width 2.6 cm, & thickness 1.0 cm. Width of scraper edge: convex part 5.1 cm, concave part 1.8 cm. Height of scraper edge (0.5 cm from edge) 0.6 cm. Greyish flint. Much patinated. Micro-wear analysis. Found north of House 2.

RE83ea. Flint arrowhead roughout
Complete. Probably re-shaped part of a pressure-flaked tool. Length 5.6 cm, width 3.5 cm, & thickness. Pressure-flaked. Greyish flint. Much patinated. Micro-wear analysis. Found north of House 2.

RE84ea. Flint scraper
Complete. Semi-circular. Width of scraper edge 5.0 cm. Height of scraper edge (0.5 cm from edge) c. 0.7 cm. Greyish flint. Cortex partly preserved. Much patinated. Micro-wear analysis. Found north of House 2.

RE86ea. Flint scraper
Complete. Spoon-shaped. Length 3.6 cm, width 2.8 cm, & thickness 1.3 cm. Width of scraper edge 2.8 cm. Height of scraper edge (0.5 cm from edge) 0.6 cm. Greyish flint. Cortex partly preserved. Much patinated. Micro-wear analysis. Context: House 2, sunken-floor horizon.

RE88ea. Flint scraper
Complete. Pear-shaped. Length 6.5 cm, width 4.3 cm, & thickness 2.2 cm. Width of scraper edge 3.6 cm. Height of scraper edge (0.5 cm from edge) 0.9 cm. Greyish flint. Cortex partly preserved. Much patinated. Micro-wear analysis. Context: House 2, sunken-floor horizon.

RE89ea/175ea. Flint dagger
Two pieces conjoined, almost complete. Only minor parts of the blade and the outmost end of the handle missing. Length 26.0 cm, width 7.2 cm. Parallel pressure-flaked. Type IV E. Greyish flint. Both dagger parts were found above the sunken-floor horizon (see the text, Ch. 3.2, 3.3, & Fig. 4.10). Context: House 2, secondary fills.

RE90ea. Flint dagger
Fragmented piece, transition to the handle. Length 7.0 cm & width 4.7 cm. Probably re-sharpened. Pressure-flaked. Type V B. This classification of the fragment (handle-blade transition) to sub-type V B is, in particular, based on the incipient enlargement of the width on one side of the lenticular handle towards its end (see text, Ch. 3.2 & Fig. 4.10). Greyish flint. Much patinated. Micro-wear analysis. Context: House 2, sunken-floor horizon. The dagger fragment was found in the northern part of the floor north of scorched-stone patch A.

RE95ea. Flint scraper
Fragment, presumably spoon-shaped. Length 3.9 cm, width 4.1 cm, & thickness 1.0 cm. Width of scraper edge 3.2 cm. Height of scraper edge (0.5 cm from edge) 0.4 cm. Greyish flint. Cortex partly preserved. Much patinated. Micro-wear analysis. Context: House 2, sunken-floor horizon.

RE96ea. Flint knife
Complete. Length 5.5 cm, width 2.1 cm, & thickness 0.7. Length of edge 4.0 cm. Greyish flint. Much patinated. Micro-wear analysis. Context: House 2, secondary fills.

RE99ea. Stone hammer
Fragment. Length cm 8.6 cm, width 8.7 cm, & thickness 4.9 cm. Circular spot of crushing, diameter 4.0 cm. Granite-like stone. Reddish due to heat. Context: House 2.

RE100ea. Flint nodule
Length 6.9 cm, width 5.3 cm, & thickness 2.5 cm. Greyish flint. Cortex partly preserved. Context: House 2, sunken-floor horizon.

RE101ea. Flint knife
Complete. Length 7.3 cm, width 3.4 cm, 0.9 cm. Edge length 5.6 cm. Greyish flint. Cortex partly preserved. No blunted back, but naturally smooth. Edge retouch probably stemming from use. Much patinated. Micro-wear analysis. Context: House 2, sunken-floor horizon.

RE108ea. Flint nodule
Length 6.9 cm, width 3.5 cm, & thickness 2.9 cm. Greyish flint. Cortex partly preserved. Context: House 2, sunken-floor horizon.

RE109ea. Stone hammer
Complete. Length 6.2 cm, width 4.4 cm, & thickness 3.7 cm. Surface crushing area of 1.2 x 1.5 cm, diffuse. Granite-like stone. Context: House 2, sunken-floor horizon.

RE109eb. Stone hammer
Complete. Length 4.9 cm, width 3.0 cm, & thickness 2.5 cm. Surface crushing area of 1.0 x 0.5 cm, diffuse. Granite-like stone. Context: House 2, sunken-floor horizon.

RE109ec. Stone hammer
Complete. Surface crushing area of 1.4 x 0.7 cm. Quartzite. Context: House 2, sunken-floor horizon.

RE109ed. Stone hammer
Complete. Length 6.1 cm, width 4.2 cm, & thickness 3.2 cm. Surface crushing area of 1.4 x 1.0 cm. Quartzite. Context: House 2, sunken-floor horizon.

RE109ee. Stone hammer
Complete. Length 5.4 cm, width 4.2 cm, & thickness 3.5 cm. Surface crushing area of 2.2 x 0.8 cm. Quartzite. Context: House 2, sunken-floor horizon.

RE110ea. Flint nodule
Length 8.2 cm, width 4.0 cm, & thickness 3.9 cm. Greyish flint. Context: House 2, sunken-floor horizon.

RE111ea. Flint scraper
Complete. Almost pear-shaped. Length 6.2 cm, width 4.4 cm, & thickness 1.4 cm. Width of scraper edge 2.5 cm. Height of scraper edge (0.5 cm from edge) 0.5 cm. Greyish flint. Much patinated. Micro-wear analysis. Context: House 2, sunken-floor horizon.

RE112ea. Flint nodule
Length 6.7 cm, width 5.3 cm, & thickness 3.5 cm. Greyish flint. Context: House 2, sunken-floor horizon.

RE114ea. Flint nodule
Length 7.3 cm, width 5.1 cm, & thickness 2.3 cm. Greyish flint. Context: House 2, sunken-floor horizon.

RE116ea. Flint scraper
Complete. Almost pear-shaped. Length 5.0 cm, width 3.9 cm, & thickness 1.3 cm. Width of scraper edge 3.8 cm. Height of scraper edge (0.5 cm from edge) 0.5 cm. Greyish flint. Cortex partly preserved. Much patinated. Micro-wear analysis. Context: House 2, sunken-floor horizon.

RE117ea. Flint nodule
Length 8.1 cm, width 6.1 cm, & thickness 3.1 cm. Blackish flint. Cortex partly preserved. Context: House 2, sunken-floor horizon.

RE120ea. Flint sickle
Almost complete, crescent-shaped sickle. Length 7.4 cm, width 3.4 cm, & thickness 0.8 cm. Assessment of original length 7.8 cm. Edge length 6.8 cm. Possibly re-sharpened. Pressure-flaked. Greyish flint. Micro-wear analysis revealed heavy traces from harvesting reeds. Fluted polishing (that derives from use) and absence of scratches (report S2004a). Context: House 2, sunken-floor horizon.

RE123ea. Flint nodule
Length 6.1 cm, width 4.2 cm, & thickness 2.7 cm. Greyish flint. Cortex partly preserved. Context: House 2, sunken-floor horizon.

RE129ea. Fossilized sea urchin
Fragment. Possibly used as hammer. Height 3.1 cm. Context: House 2, sunken-floor horizon.

RE138ea. Flint nodule
Length 6.1 cm, width 4.2 cm, & thickness 2.7 cm. Greyish flint. Cortex partly preserved. Context: House 2, sunken-floor horizon.

RE138eb. Stone hammer
Complete. Length 11.3 cm, width 8.1 cm, & thickness 6.0 cm. Surface crushing area of 2.4 x 1.2 cm. Quartzite. Context: House 2, sunken-floor horizon.

RE139ea. Flint nodule
Length 6.7 cm, width 5.2 cm, & thickness 2.6 cm. Greyish flint. Cortex partly preserved. Context: House 2, sunken-floor horizon.

RE143ea. Flint nodule
Length 5.7 cm, width 4.7 cm, & thickness 2.4 cm. Greyish flint. Context: House 1, secondary fills.

RE144ea. Flint nodule
Length 7.3 cm, width 4.3 cm, & thickness 2.6 cm. Greyish flint. Cortex partly preserved. Context: House 2, sunken-floor horizon.

RE145ea. Flint scraper
Fragment, presumed handle (with fine retouch) of a spoon scraper. Length 5.2 cm, width 2.5 cm, & thickness 0.5 cm. Greyish flint. Cortex partly preserved. Much patinated. Micro-wear analysis. Context: House 2, sunken-floor horizon.

RE147ea. Flint nodule
Length 5.7 cm, width 3.7 cm, & thickness 2.7 cm. Greyish flint. Cortex partly preserved. Context: House 2, sunken-floor horizon.

RE148ea. Smoothening stone
Only a minor fragment preserved. One side quite plane, the opposite side evenly curved. Length 5.0 cm, width 4.1 cm, & thickness 2.9 cm. Quartzite, almost white. Context: House 2, sunken-floor horizon.

RE155ea. Stone hammer
Complete. Surface crushing area at both ends and along most of the sides. May also have worked a smoothening stone, as one side is quite plane, while the opposite side is evenly curved. Length 8.9 cm, width 6.1 cm, & thickness 3.6 cm. Quartzite. Context: House 1, secondary fills.

RE162ea. Flint scraper
Complete. Atypical. Length 7.5 cm, width 4.7 cm, & thickness 1.8 cm. Width of scraper edge 2.5 cm. Height of scraper edge (0.5 cm from edge) 0.4 cm. Greyish flint. Cortex partly preserved. Much patinated. Micro-wear analysis. Context: House 2, sunken-floor horizon.

RE162eb. Flint nodule
Length 8.9 cm, width 4.9 cm, & thickness 4.3 cm. Greyish flint. Cortex partly preserved. Context: House 2, sunken-floor horizon.

RE163ea. Flint nodule
Length 6.9 cm, width 4.2 cm, & thickness 3.0 cm. Greyish flint. Cortex partly preserved. Context: House 2, secondary fills.

RE164ea. Flint nodule
Length 9.7 cm, width 5.0 cm, & thickness 3.3 cm. Greyish flint. Cortex partly preserved. Context: House 2, secondary fills.

RE167ea. Flint nodule
Length 6.3 cm, width 4.8 cm, & thickness 3.2 cm. Greyish flint. Cortex partly preserved. Two minor flint pieces at the same spot. Context: House 2, sunken-floor horizon.

RE169ea. Flint scraper
Fragment with scraper edge, presumably spoon scraper. Length 1.6 cm, width 4.6 cm, & thickness 1.0 cm. Width of scraper edge 3.5 cm. Height of scraper edge (0.2 cm from edge) 0.6 cm. Greyish flint. Much patinated. Micro-wear analysis. Context: House 2, precise find spot not identified.

RE175
See flint dagger RE89ea/175ea.

RE178ea. Flint arrowhead roughout
Complete. Length 4.2 cm, width 2.5 cm, & thickness 0.7 cm. Pressure-flaked. Greyish flint. Much patinated. Micro-wear analysis. Context: Find spot immediately north of House 2. Context not clarified, see the text.

RE189ea. Stone hammer
Complete. Length 14.0 cm, width 11.5 cm, & thickness 7.8 cm. Surface crushing area at one end c. 6.5 x 5.5 cm, at the opposite end 6.0 x 4.0 cm, and on the side 6.0 x 3.0 cm. Quartzite, grey-brownish. Context: House 1, secondary fills.

RE191ea. Flint scraper
Complete. Spoon scraper. Length 5.3 cm, width 4.1 cm, & thickness 1.0 cm. Width of scraper edge 4.0 cm. Height of scraper edge (0.5 cm from edge) 0.7 cm. Greyish flint. Cortex partly preserved. Much patinated. Micro-wear analysis. Context: House 2, secondary fills.

RE193ea. Flint scraper
Complete. Spoon scraper. Length 5.3 cm, width 4.2 cm, & thickness 1.0 cm. Width of scraper edge 4.0 cm. Height of scraper edge (0.5 cm from edge) 0.6 cm. Greyish flint. Micro-wear analysis, much patinated. Context: House 2, sunken-floor horizon.

RE194ea. Stone hammer
Complete. Length 17.1 cm, width 11.6 cm, & thickness 8.6 cm. Surface crushing area at one end 6.5 x 3.5 cm, at the opposite end 2.0 x 2.0 cm, diffuse. Grey-brownish quartzite. Context: Pit in the south wall area of House 1.

RE195ea. Flint scraper
Complete. Almost pear-shaped. Length 6.5 cm, width 3.2 cm, & thickness 1.3 cm. Width of scraper edge 3.1 cm. Height of scraper edge (0.5 cm from edge) 0.6 cm. Greyish flint. Much patinated. Context: House 1, soil feature.

RE196ea. Fine-grained whetstone

Three fragments, dimensions of the largest piece: Length 17.6 cm, width 10.4 cm, & thickness 2.7 cm. Dark, almost black stone with many tiny grains of a shiny nature. The surface is extremely smooth. There was a slight concavity in what used to be the middle of the stone, probably relating to use. Context: A pit somewhat north of House 130.

RE196eb. Quern stone

Three fragments of the upper part of a saddle quern. One side plane, the opposite side evenly curved. Dimensions of the largest piece: Length 19.1 cm, width 10.5cm, & thickness 9.0 cm. Dark-brownish sediment stone. Striations observable in the longitudinal direction. It was probably somewhat broader than the pieces together indicate. Context: A pit somewhat north of House 130.

RE220ea. Flint sickle

Complete. Length 12.9 cm, width 3.5 cm, & thickness 1.2 cm. Edge length.11.6 cm. Re-sharpened. Standard pressure-flaking. Greyish flint. Context: A pit west of House 134.

RE223ea. Flint dagger

Fragment, the blade point. Length 7.1 cm & width 2.9 cm. Pressure-flaked. Greyish flint. Much patinated. Micro-wear analysis. Context: A pit west of House 134.

RE225ea. Flint scraper

Complete, atypical. Length 5.2 cm, width 3.5 cm, & thickness 1.2 cm. Width of scraper edge 3.6 cm. Height of scraper edge (0.2 cm from edge) 0.4 cm. Greyish flint. Cortex partly preserved. Much patinated. Micro-wear analysis. Context: Pit 312, south of House 183.

RE250ea. Flint scraper

Complete. Spoon-shaped. Length 5.5 cm, width 3.1 cm, & thickness 0.9 cm. Width of scraper edge 3.1 cm. Height of scraper edge (0.2 cm from edge) 0.6 cm. Greyish flint. Cortex partly preserved. Context: House 12, secondary fills.

RE250eb. Flint axe

Fragment. Length 5.6 cm, width 4.9 cm, & thickness 2.0 cm. Greyish flint. Polished. Origin: Single Grave Culture judged by the "hanging" edge and other features. Context: see RE250ea.

RE250ec. Flint axe

Fragment. Polished. Length 7.1 cm, width 4.4 cm, & thickness 2.9 cm. Greyish flint. Origin: Presumably Funnel Beaker Culture. Context: see RE250ea.

RE251ea. Flint hammer

Fragment, about a third is broken off. Length 6.5 cm, width 6.2 cm, & thickness 4.8 cm. Surface crushing. Greyish flint. Context: House 13, secondary fills.

RE258ea. Flint piece with notches

Complete. Length 9.4 cm, width 5.9 cm, & thickness 1.5 cm. Greyish flint. Supplied with five notches but no blunting retouch in between. Much patinated. Micro-wear analysis. Context: House 14, secondary fills.

RE258eb. Flint sickle

Fragment, one end preserved. Crescent-shaped. Length 3.7 cm, width 2.7 cm, & thickness 0.7 cm. Possibly re-sharpened. Pressure-flaked. Greyish flint. Cracks in surface due to heat. Much patinated. Micro-wear analysis. Context: see RE258ea.

RE258ec. Flint scraper

Complete. Pear-shaped. Length 5.4 cm, width 3.2 cm, & thickness 1.3 cm. Width of scraper edge 2.8 cm. Height of scraper edge (0.2 cm from edge) 0.3 cm. Greyish flint. Cortex partly preserved. Much patinated. Micro-wear analysis. Context: see RE258ea.

RE258ed. Flint scraper

Complete. Spoon-shaped. Length 4 cm, width 2.7 cm, & thickness 1.2 cm. Width of scraper edge 2.6 cm. Height of scraper edge (0.2 cm from edge) 1.0 cm. Greyish flint. Much patinated. Micro-wear analysis. Context: see RE258ea.

RE258ef. Flint scraper

Complete. Atypical, "nosed". Length 6.1 cm, width 4.3 cm, & thickness 2.1 cm. Width of scraper edge 4.3 cm. Height of scraper edge (0.2 cm from edge) 0.6 cm. Greyish flint. Cortex partly preserved. Much patinated. Micro-wear analysis. Context: see RE258ea.

RE258eg. Flint scraper

Complete. Spoon-shaped, no blunting of the sides. Length 4.9 cm, width 2.6 cm, & thickness 0.7 cm. Width of scraper edge 2.6 cm. Height of scraper edge (0.2 cm from edge) 0.3 cm. Greyish flint. Context: see RE258ea.

RE258eh. Flint scraper

Complete. Spoon-shaped. Length 3.5 cm, width 3.1 cm, & thickness 0.7 cm. Width of scraper edge 3.0 cm. Height of scraper edge (0.2 cm from edge) 0.5 cm. Greyish flint. Much patinated. Micro-wear analysis. Context: see RE258ea.

RE258ei. Flint scraper

Complete. Atypical, wringed. Length 8.3 cm, width 3.1 cm, & thickness 1.8 cm. Width of scraper edge: one side 7.5 cm and the opposite side 3.5 cm. Height of scraper edge (0.2 cm from edge) 0.5 cm. Greyish flint. Much patinated state. Micro-wear analysis. Context: see RE258ea.

RE265ea. Flint dagger

Fragment, likely part of a handle. Length 5.3 cm, width 1.9 cm, & thickness 1.8 cm. Pressure-flaked. Greyish flint. In cross-section, the form is irregularly rhombic. On the two opposite sides there are small polished areas, which now and then occur on flint daggers (*cf.* Lomborg 1973a). Alternatively, this could be interpreted as a fragment of a chisel but the irregularity in the flaking and the observation that one of the "edges" in particular has a seam-like character gives priority to the interpretation of it belonging to a type III B/C handle. Context: House 197, secondary fills.

RE270ea. Flint scraper
Complete. Spoon-shaped. Length 6.1 cm, width 3.5 cm, & thickness 0.9 cm. Width of scraper edge 3.5 cm. Height of scraper edge (0.2 cm from edge) 0.9 cm. Greyish flint. Much patinated. Micro-wear analysis. Context: House 268, secondary fills.

RE271ea. Flint arrowhead
Complete. Triangular, with two lobes. Length 2.2 cm, width 1.0 cm, & thickness 0.2 cm. Pressure-flaked. Greyish flint. Context: House 13, secondary fills.

RE280ea. Flint scraper
Complete. Spoon-shaped. Length 6.1 cm, width 3.6 cm, & thickness 1.0 cm. Width of scraper edge 3.6 cm. Height of scraper edge (0.2 cm from edge) 0.8 cm. Greyish flint. Much patinated. Micro-wear analysis, report S2004a. Stray find east of House 14.

RE281ea. Flint arrowhead
Almost complete. Triangular, with two lobes, partly broken off. Length 2.3 cm, width 1.5 cm, & thickness 0.4 cm. Pressure-flaked. Greyish flint. Context: House 14, sunken-floor horizon.

RE283ea. Flint scraper
Fragment, central part of scraper edge broken. Probably pear-shaped. Length 6.0 cm, width 2.6 cm, & thickness 1.5 cm. Width of scraper edge 2.4 cm. Greyish flint. Context: House 14, sunken-floor horizon.

RE283eb. Flint scraper
Fragment, part of scraper edge broken off. Spoon-shaped. Length 4.0 cm, width 2.7 cm, & thickness 1.0 cm. Width of scraper edge 2.6 cm. Greyish flint. Context: House 14, sunken-floor horizon.

RE286ea. Flint hammer
Almost complete. Fossilized sea urchin used as hammer. Length 5.5 cm & width 5.0 cm. Crushing along the low edge all around. Greyish flint. Context: House 14, sunken-floor horizon.

RE291ea. Flint sickle
Fragment, one end preserved. Presumably crescent-shaped. Length 3.5 cm, width 3.4 cm, & thickness 1.2 cm. Coarse pressure-flaked. Possibly re-sharpened. Greyish flint. Much patinated. Micro-wear analysis. Context: House 14, sunken-floor horizon.

RE295ea. Flint scraper
Complete. Spoon-shaped. Length 6.7 cm, width 4.3 cm, & thickness 1.7 cm. Width of scraper edge 4.2 cm. Height of scraper edge (0.2 cm from edge) 0.9 cm. Greyish flint. Cortex partly preserved. Micro-wear analysis showed some patina, and at some spots it was possible to observe polishing that stemmed from scraping bone (report S2004a). Context: House 14, secondary fills.

RE299ea. Flint knife
Made on a blade. Blunted back. Length 5.4 cm, width 1.8 cm, & thickness 0.4 cm. Length of edge 3.7 cm. Greyish flint. It cannot be excluded that it might be an "antique". Much patinated. Micro-wear analysis. Context: House 14, sunken-floor horizon.

RE312ea. Flint spear-blade
Complete. Presumably a re-shaped dagger blade. Length 10.0 cm, width 2.8 cm, & thickness 0.8 cm. Pressure-flaked. Greyish flint. Cortex partly preserved on the lower part of the shaft. Much patinated. Micro-wear analysis. Context: House 41, secondary fills.

RE402ea. Flint spear-blade
Complete. Length 9.1 cm & width 3.3 cm. Pressure-flaked. Greyish flint. Context: Pit 44 but precise find spot not identified.

RE405ea. Flint dagger
Fragment, end of the handle, possibly type V A. Length 5.5 cm, & width 2.9 cm. Pressure-flaked. Greyish flint. Cortex partly preserved. Context: House 42, secondary fills.

RE405eb. Flint borer
Complete. Made on a flake. Length 3.1 cm, width 3.1 cm, & thickness 0.5 cm. Borer point dimensions (0.5 cm from end) 0.6 x 0.4 cm. Greyish flint. Much patinated. Micro-wear analysis. Context: see RE405ea.

RE405ec. Flint scraper
Almost complete. Pear-shaped. Length 6.1 cm, width 4.5 cm, & thickness 1.4 cm. Width of scraper edge 4.2 cm. Height of scraper edge (0.2 cm from edge) 0.6 cm. Greyish flint. evidently wind polished before shaping as roughout. Much patinated. Micro-wear analysis. Context: see RE405ea.

RE406ea. Flint piece with notches
Complete. A major flake with five notches and a scraper-like or blunting retouch. Length 10.9 cm, width 9.0 cm, & thickness 2.8 cm. Greyish flint. Much patinated. Micro-wear analysis. Context: House 41, secondary fills.

RE406eb. Flint knife
Complete. Length 7.2 cm & width 2.7 cm. Edge length 6.3 cm. Greyish flint. Cortex partly preserved. Micro-wear analysis showed patina, some polishing and some cracking

of the edge due to use but the material causing this could not be determined. Report S2004a. Context: see RE406ea.

RE406ec. Flint scraper
Complete. Pear-shaped. Length 4.2 cm, width 2.5 cm, & thickness 1.3 cm. Width of scraper edge 2.1 cm. Height of scraper edge (0.2 cm from edge) 0.7 cm. Blackish flint. Cortex partly preserved. Context: see RE406ea.

RE406ed. Flint scraper
Complete. Pear-shaped. Length 6.4 cm, width 3.6 cm, & thickness 1.2 cm. Width of scraper edge 3.1 cm. Height of scraper edge (0.2 cm from edge) 0.8 cm. Greyish flint. Cortex partly preserved. Much patinated. Micro-wear analysis. Context: see RE406ea

RE406ef. Flint knife
Complete. Length 7.0 cm & width 3.9 cm. Length of edge 4.3 cm. Greyish flint. Much patinated. Micro-wear analysis. Context: see RE406ea.

RE406eg. Flint piece with notch
Complete. Length 5.3 cm, width 3.1 cm, & thickness 0.9 cm. Greyish flint. Alongside the notches, a blunting retouch. Much patinated. Micro-wear analysis. Context: see RE406ea.

RE406eh. Flint piece with notches
Complete. Flake with three notches. Alongside the notches, scraper-like retouching (blunting) is visible. Length 6.8 cm, width 3.7 cm, & thickness 1.4 cm. Greyish flint. Much patinated. Micro-wear analysis. Context: see RE406ea.

RE413ea. Flint piece with notch
Complete. Polished, seemingly by wind, before the notch was shaped. Length 6.0 cm, width 3.7 cm, & thickness 1.4 cm. Greyish flint. Cortex partly preserved. Much patinated. Micro-wear analysis. Context: House 41, sunken-floor horizon.

RE415ea. Flint scraper
Complete. Spoon-shaped. Length 5.0 cm, width 4 cm, & thickness 1.4 cm. Width of scraper edge 4.0 cm. Height of scraper edge (0.2 cm from edge) 0.5 cm. Greyish flint. Cortex partly preserved. Micro-wear analysis, much patinated. Context: House 41, secondary fills.

RE417ea. Flint dagger
Fragment, end of the handle. Length 4.1 cm, width 2.3 cm, & thickness 1.3 cm. Pressure-flaked. Not determined but affinities with type II A. Greyish flint. Micro-wear analysis, much patinated. Micro-wear analysis. Context: House 41, secondary fills.

RE418ea. Flint borer
Complete. Length 6.8 cm, width 4.7 cm, & thickness 1.8 cm. Borer point 0.5 cm from end: 0.6 x 0.4 cm. Greyish flint. Cortex partly preserved. Micro-wear analysis, much patinated. Micro-wear analysis. Context: House 41, secondary fills.

RE428ea. Flint scraper
Complete. Pear-shaped. Length 4.3 cm, width 2.5 cm, & thickness 1.0 cm. Width of scraper edge 4.3 cm. Height of scraper edge (0.2 cm from edge) 0.6 cm. Greyish flint. Micro-wear analysis, much patinated. Micro-wear analysis. Context: House 42, secondary fills.

RE430ea. Flint dagger
Fragment, part of the handle. Length 3.8 cm, width 3.7 cm, & thickness 1.4 cm. Pressure-flaked. Possibly type V B. Greyish flint. Context: House 42, sunken-floor horizon.

RE432ea. Stone hammer
Complete. Surface crushing area at one end c. 3.2 x 2.0, the opposite end diffuse, slight crushing. Length 15.2 cm, width 8.4 cm, & thickness 8.0 cm. Grey-brownish quartzite. Context: House 42, sunken-floor horizon.

RE435ea. Flint arrowhead roughout
Complete. Based on a flake. Length 5.0 cm, width 3.0 cm, & thickness 0.6 cm. Pressure-flaked. Greyish flint. Cortex partly preserved. Context: House 42, secondary fills.

RE436ea. Flint, strike-a-light
Complete. Seems based on a wind-polished piece. Length 10.6 cm, width 2.8 cm, & thickness 1.9 cm. Length of "edge" c. 8 cm. Pressure-flaked. Greyish flint. Cortex partly preserved. Micro-wear analysis, much patinated. Context: House 42.

RE444ea. Flint arrowhead roughout
Fragment. Length 2.9 cm, width 3.0 cm, & thickness 0.7 cm. Pressure-flaked. Greyish flint. Context: House 42, sunken-floor horizon.

RE446ea. Flint scraper
Complete. Atypical, almost pear-shaped. Length 7.1 cm, width 5.1 cm, & thickness 1.6 cm. Width of scraper edge 2.6 cm. Height of scraper edge (0.2 cm from edge) 0.4 cm. Cortex partly preserved. Context: House 42, sunken-floor horizon.

RE448ea. Flint scraper
Almost complete. Pear-shaped, scraper edge at the proximal end. Length 7.0 cm, width 2.9 cm, & thickness 1.4 cm. Width of scraper edge 1.0 cm. Height of scraper edge (0.2 cm from edge) 0.5 cm. Greyish flint. Context: House 42, sunken-floor horizon.

RE484ea. Flint axe
Complete. Miniature axe. Traces of wear on the sides. Partly polished. Length 7.0 cm, width 3.3 cm, & thickness 1.5 cm. Seems re-sharpened. Pressure-flaked. Greyish flint. Context: Pit 89, west of House 84.

RE492ea. Flint sickle
Complete. Crescent-shaped. Length 9.8 cm, width 3.1 cm, & thickness 1.0 cm. Length of edge 8.5 cm. Re-sharpened. Pressure-flaked. Greyish flint. Micro-wear analysis, much patinated. Micro-wear analysis. Context: Pit 88, south-southwest of House 84.

RE500ea. Flint sickle
Almost complete. Crescent-shaped. Length 7.6 cm, width 2.3 cm, & thickness 0.7 cm. Length of edge 6.0 cm. Re-sharpened. Pressure-flaked. Greyish flint. Gloss on the sides resulting from use. Micro-wear analysis showed some patina. Strong traces of harvesting cereals were, however, observable on one lateral side. Some scratches in the polish revealed that the sickle must have been used in different working directions. Micro-wear analysis, report S2004a. Context: Pit 324 but precise find spot not identified.

RE539ea. Flint scraper
Complete. Pear-shaped. Length 5.1 cm, width 3.5 cm, & thickness 1.3 cm. Width of scraper edge 3.9 cm. Height of scraper edge (0.2 cm from edge) 0.8 cm. Greyish flint. Micro-wear analysis, much patinated. Context: House 130, secondary fills.

RE539eb. Flint scraper
Complete. Long oval. Length 4.6 cm, width 2.8 cm, & thickness 0.6 cm. Width of scraper edge 2.8 cm. Height of scraper edge (0.2 cm from edge) 0.3 cm. Greyish flint. Context: see RE539ea.

RE539ec. Flint dagger
Fragment, part of the handle. Length 5.3 cm, width 2.1 cm, & thickness 1.0 cm. Pressure-flaked. Not determined but affinities with type II A. Greyish flint. Micro-wear analysis, much patinated. Context: see RE539ea.

RE539ed. Flint hammer
Complete. Fossilized sea urchin used as a hammer. Length 5.8 cm, width 4.9 cm, & thickness 2.7 cm. Surface crushing area present. Greyish flint. Context: See RE539ea.

RE539ek. Whetstone
Almost complete. Length 22.1 cm, width 12.4 cm, & thickness 3.9 cm. Grey-brownish, fine-grained stone. Striations are clearly visible in the longitudinal direction. Context: see RE539ea.

RE542ea. Flint sickle
Complete. Crescent-shaped. Length 13.9 cm, width 3.6 cm, & thickness 0.9 cm. Length of edge 13.5 cm. Probably re-sharpened. Pressure-flaked. Greyish flint. Gloss on the sides resulting from heavy use of the sickle. Context: In the top of the shallow pit 135, east of House 128. In the pit fill 24 potsherds.

RE545ea. Flint arrowhead roughout
Fragment. Length 2.3 cm, width 2.3 cm, & thickness 0.4 cm. Pressure-flaked. Greyish flint. Context: A pit west of the sunken floor of House 128.

RE547ea. Flint dagger
Complete. Length 17.3 cm & width 3.4 cm. Seems heavily re-sharpened. Pressure-flaked. Type VI B. Due to the re-sharpening, the shape is less characteristic than originally but clear marking of the hand/blade transition still exists. Greyish flint. Micro-wear analysis, much patinated. Context: House 128, sunken-floor horizon.

RE548ea. Flint arrowhead
Fragment of transversal arrowhead. Length 2.7 cm & width 1.5 cm. Greyish flint. Possibly an "antique". Context: House 128, sunken-floor horizon.

RE549ea. Flint scraper with notch
Complete. Spoon-shaped with "nose" shaped centrally at the scraper edge. Length 7.2 cm, width 4.1 cm, & thickness 1.7 cm. Width of scraper edge 3.8 cm. Height of scraper edge (0.2 cm from edge) 0.5 cm. Greyish flint. A notch made on the side and, near that, a blunting scraper-like retouch. Cortex partly preserved. Micro-wear analysis, much patinated. Context: House 128, sunken-floor horizon.

RE551ea. Flint knife
Complete. Length 6.8 cm, width 3.8 cm, & thickness 0.8 cm. Length of edge 5.2 cm. Greyish flint. Traces of wear at the edge due to use. Cortex partly preserved at the back of the knife and a minor area in between with blunting retouch. Micro-wear analysis, much patinated. Context: House 128, sunken-floor horizon.

RE559ea. Whetstone
Fragment. Length 12.2 cm, width 14.8 cm, & thickness 7.2 cm. Transversal fracture of the fine-grained reddish stone. Striations expected in the longitudinal direction not clearly visible. Context: House 128, sunken-floor horizon.

RE563ea. Flint arrowhead roughout
Fragment. Length 2.9 cm, width 1.8 cm, & thickness 0.6 cm. Greyish flint. Context: House 128, sunken-floor horizon.

RE564ea. Flint borer
Complete. Made on a flake. Length 7.2 cm, width 3.6 cm, & thickness 0.8 cm. Borer point dimensions (0.5 cm from end) 0.9 x 0.3 cm. Greyish flint. Micro-wear analysis, much patinated. Context: House 134, secondary fills. Another borer (RE564eb) made on a flake likewise belongs to the secondary fills.

RE573ea. Flint hammer
Complete. Length 8.8 cm, width 6.0 cm, & thickness 5.3 cm. Surface crushing area at one end 4.5 x 3.8 cm and at the

opposite end 4.3 x 3.8 cm. Greyish flint. Context: House 128, secondary fills.

RE577ea. Flint scraper
Complete. Almost spoon-shaped. Length 8.5 cm, width 4.7 cm, & thickness 2.8 cm. Width of scraper edge 4.5 cm. Height of scraper edge (0.2 cm from edge) 1.0 cm. Greyish flint. Cortex partly preserved. Micro-wear analysis, much patinated. Context: Culture layer 318, west-northwest of House 41.

RE579ea. Flint scraper
Complete. Oval. Length 5.2 cm, width 3.1 cm, & thickness 0.8 cm. Width of scraper edge 2.4 cm. Greyish flint. Cortex partly preserved. Micro-wear analysis, much patinated. Context: House 130, sunken-floor horizon.

RE601ea. Flint sickle
Fragment. Crescent-shaped. Length 8.0 cm, width 4.3 cm, & thickness 1.0 cm. Possibly re-sharpened modestly. Pressure-flaked. Greyish flint. Micro-wear analysis showed patina. Traces of polishing from plants were not observed. The micro-wear report (S2004a) notes that, despite re-sharpening, plant polishing would normally be visible. Context: House 138, secondary fills.

RE602ea. Flint dagger
Fragment, pointed end of blade. Length 6.5 cm, width 2.2 cm, & thickness 0.9 cm. Possibly re-sharpened. Pressure-flaked. Greyish flint. Micro-wear analysis, much patinated. Context: House 138, secondary fills.

RE608ea. Flint arrowhead
Almost complete, outermost point broken off. Triangular, with two lobes. Length 3.0 cm, width 1.3 cm, 0.4 cm. Pressure-flaked. Greyish flint. Context: Culture layer 335, in this case found north of House 143.

RE609ea. Flint scraper & borer
Complete. Length 4.7 cm, width 3.5 cm, & thickness 0.5 cm. Width of scraper edge 3.5 cm. Height of scraper edge (0.2 cm from edge) 0.3 cm. Borer point (0.5 cm from end) 0.6 x 3.0 cm. Greyish flint. Micro-wear analysis, much patinated. Context: House 143, secondary fills.

RE610ea. Flint scraper
Almost complete. Almost pear-shaped. Length 6.0 cm & width 3.2 cm. Height of scraper edge (0.2 cm from edge) 0.8 cm. Greyish flint. Micro-wear analysis, much patinated. Context: Culture layer 335, in this case found north of House 143.

RE612ea. Flint strike-a-light
Complete, possibly re-shaped end of a flint dagger blade. Length 5.2 cm, width 1.8 cm, & thickness 0.9 cm. Length of "edge" 4.0 cm. Pressure-flaked. Greyish flint. The tool is of quite limited length, both ends are clearly characterized by specific traces of wear. Its edges appear marked by wear too. Micro-wear analysis, much patinated. Context: House 138, sunken-floor horizon.

RE613ea. Flint dagger
Fragment, pointed end of the blade. Length 6.6 cm, width 1.9 cm, & thickness 0.8 cm. Pressure-flaked. Re-sharpened. Greyish flint. Micro-wear analysis, much patinated. Context: House 138, sunken-floor horizon.

RE620eb. Flint axe
Almost complete, part of the neck broken off. Partly polished broad sides. Length 9.3 cm, width 4.7 cm, & thickness 1.8 cm. Edge width 4.7 cm. Seemingly not re-sharpened. Greyish flint. Context: House 158, sunken-floor horizon.

RE624ea. Flint dagger
Fragment, the handle broken at the transition to the blade. The fracture moderately re-shaped. Possibly used as a strike-a-light. Length 10.3 cm, width 2.9 cm, & thickness 1.2 cm. Pressure-flaked. Not determined but affinities with type II A and VI B. Greyish flint. Micro-wear analysis, much patinated. Context: A stone concentration north of House 200.

RE626ea. Flint scraper
Complete. Long oval, Length 6.5 cm, width 3.6 cm, & thickness 1.3 cm. Width of scraper edge 3.3 cm. Height of scraper edge (0.2 cm from edge) 0.7 cm. Greyish flint. Cortex partly preserved. Micro-wear analysis of the active edge showed a surface with varying degree of patina, from weak to strong. Some polishing and rounding of the edge indicates use of the tool for scraping of dry skin/hide (report S2004a). Context: From a cluster of postholes north of House 112.

RE634ea. Flint dagger
Minor fragment of blade. Length 3.8 cm, width 2.5 cm, & thickness 0.8 cm. Possibly re-sharpened. Pressure-flaked. Traces of polishing on one side. Greyish flint. Micro-wear analysis, much patinated. Context: House 198, secondary fills.

RE636ea. Flint piece with notches
Complete. Length 4.7 cm, width 2.5 cm, and thickness 1.5 cm. Greyish flint. Notches are made in both ends and have a scraper-like retouch. Between the notches, the sides have a blunting retouch. Cortex partly preserved. Micro-wear analysis, much patinated. Context: Pit 161, southwest of House 193.

RE638ea. Flint arrowhead roughout
Complete. Length 4.1 cm, width 3.1 cm, & thickness 1.0 cm. Coarsely pressure-flaked. Greyish flint. The surface whitened due to a natural chemical process. Consideration has been given as to whether the piece might originate from

a broken end of flint sickle. There is, however, no fracture to indicate this. Context: found immediately east of pit 160.

RE639ea. Flint dagger
Fragment, part of the blade. Length 9.6 cm, width 2.4 cm, & thickness 0.9 cm. Re-sharpened. Pressure-flaked. Micro-wear analysis, much patinated. Context: Pit 196, west of pit 160.

RE642ea. Flint arrowhead
Complete. Triangular, with two lobes. Length 2.9 cm, width 1.3 cm, & thickness 0.3 cm. Pressure-flaked. Greyish flint. Context: House 13, sunken-floor horizon.

RE674ea. Flint hammer
Complete. Length 11.5 cm, width 11.1 cm, & thickness 10.8 cm. Surface crushing over most of the surface. Greyish flint. Context: House 158, secondary fills.

RE692ea. Flint dagger
Fragment, pointed end of blade. Length 4.9 cm, width 1.4 cm, & thickness 0.6 cm. Heavily re-sharpened. Pressure-flaked. Greyish flint. Context: Pit 310, south of House 197.

RE695ea. Flint dagger
Complete. Length 14.0 cm, width 2.8 cm, & thickness 1.0 cm. Heavily re-sharpened. Pressure-flaked. Possibly type I. Greyish flint. Micro-wear analysis, much patinated. Context: Pit 317, east of House 13.

RE699ea. Flint arrowhead
Fragment. Triangular, with two lobes, but a lobe and the pointed end broken off. Length 4.2 cm, width 1.5 cm. Pressure-flaked. Greyish flint. Context: House 197, found immediately north of the sunken floor.

RE704ea. Flint arrowhead
Almost complete. Apparently made without side lobes. Length 3.2 cm, width 1.4 cm, & thickness 0.3 cm. Pressure-flaked. Greyish flint. Context: House 197, sunken-floor horizon.

RE750ea. Flint scraper
Complete. Pear-shaped. Length 7.8 cm, width 4.2 cm, & thickness 1.5 cm. Width of scraper edge 4.2 cm. Height of scraper edge (0.2 cm from edge) 1.5 cm. Greyish flint. Cortex partly preserved. Micro-wear analysis, much patinated. Context: House 200, secondary fills.

RE750eb. Flint scraper
Complete. Pear-shaped. Length 5.7 cm, width 2.9 cm, & thickness 0.6 cm. Width of scraper edge 2.7 cm. Height of scraper edge (0.2 cm from edge) 0.4 cm. Greyish flint. Cortex partly preserved. Micro-wear analysis, much patinated. Context: see RE750ea.

RE750ec. Flint scraper
Complete. Oval. Length 4.8 cm, width 4.2 cm, & thickness 1.1 cm. Height of scraper edge (0.2 cm from edge) 0.9 cm. Greyish flint. Cortex partly preserved. Micro-wear analysis, much patinated. Context: see RE750ea.

RE750ed. Flint axe
Fragment. Length 9.6 cm, width 6.0 cm, & thickness 3.5 cm. Greyish flint. Belonged originally to Funnel Beaker Culture. Context: see RE750ea.

RE750ee. Axe
Fragment. Length 8.2 cm, width 4.0 cm, & thickness 1.8 cm. Greyish flint. Belonged originally to Funnel Beaker Culture. Context: see RE750ea.

RE750ef. Flint arrowhead roughout
Complete. Presumably a failed roughout. Length 5.1 cm, width 1.7 cm, & thickness 0.6 cm. Pressure-flaked. Greyish flint. Micro-wear analysis, much patinated. Context: see RE750ea.

RE750eg. Flint dagger
Fragment, part of handle. Length 4.3 cm, width 3.3 cm, & thickness 1.3 cm. Pressure-flaked. Cortex partly preserved. Micro-wear analysis, much patinated. Greyish flint. Context: see RE750ea.

RE750eh. Flint dagger
Fragment, part of the handle. Length 5.0 cm, width 2.9 cm, & thickness 0.8 cm. Standard pressure-flaked. Not determined but affinities with type I. Greyish flint. Micro-wear analysis, much patinated. Context: see RE750ea.

RE750ei. Flint dagger
Fragment, part of the handle. Length 6.7 cm, width 2.6 cm, & thickness 2.0 cm. Pressure-flaked. Type III E (type III B might also be a possibility but the seam should, in that case, be in the middle). Greyish flint. Context: see RE750ea.

RE750ej. Stone hammer
Complete. Length 10.7 cm, width 7.3 cm, & thickness 5.8 cm. Surface crushing area at one end c. 2.8 x 2.2 cm, at opposite end c. 2.2x 2.0 cm. Grey-brownish quartzite. Context: see RE750ea.

RE751ea. Flint sickle
Made on a flint blade, one end preserved. Length 2.9 cm, width 2.8 cm, thickness 0.3 cm. Greyish flint. Micro-wear analysis, much patinated. Context: Culture layer 203.

RE751eb. Flint scraper
Complete. Pear-shaped. Length 4.1 cm, width 3.7 cm, & thickness 1.8 cm. Width of scraper edge 3.6 cm. Height of scraper edge (0.2 cm from edge) 1.3 cm. Greyish flint. Cor-

tex partly preserved. Micro-wear analysis, much patinated. Context: see RE751ea.

RE751ec. Flint scraper
Complete. Spoon-shaped. Length 7.9 cm, width 4.6 cm, & thickness 1.3 cm. Width of scraper edge 4.2 cm. Height of scraper edge (0.2 cm from edge) 0.5 cm. Greyish flint. Cortex partly preserved. Micro-wear analysis, much patinated. Context: see RE751ea.

RE751ed. Flint scraper
Complete. Pear-shaped. Length 4.6 cm, width 2.9 cm, & thickness 1.2 cm. Width of scraper edge 2.3 cm. Height of scraper edge (0.2 cm from edge) 0.5 cm. Greyish flint. Cortex partly preserved. Micro-wear analysis, much patinated. Context: see RE751ea.

RE751ee. Flint scraper
Complete. Atypical, some affinities with a spoon scraper. Length 3.8 cm, width 2.0 cm, & thickness 1.2 cm. Width of scraper edge 1.7 cm. Height of scraper edge (0.2 cm from edge) 0.3 cm. Greyish flint. Micro-wear analysis, much patinated. Context: see RE751ea.

RE751ef. Flint sickle
Almost complete, a tiny piece of one end broken off. Length 10.2 cm, width 3.4 cm, & 0.9 cm. Length of preserved edge 9.3 cm. Re-sharpened. Greyish flint. Context: see RE751ea.

RE753ea. Stone hammer
Complete. Length 9.6 cm, width 6.9 cm, & thickness 5.0 cm. Surface crushing area of 3.8 x 3.0 cm. Grey-brownish quartzite. Context: House 201, secondary fills.

RE756ea. Stone axe
Fragment of stone axe with shaft-hole. Shaft-hole cylindrical but not quite even. Hole diameter 3.0 cm. Length 6.2 cm, width 5.8 cm, & thickness 2.5 cm. Context: House 200, sunken-floor horizon.

RE757ea. Flint arrowhead
Fragment, triangular, with two lobes but the pointed end and most of the lobes broken off. Length 3.6 cm, width 1.1 cm, & thickness 0.4 cm. Pressure-flaked. Greyish flint. Context: House 200, sunken-floor horizon.

RE758ea. Flint scraper
Complete. Almost pear-shaped. Length 3.3 cm, width 2.0 cm, & thickness 0.7 cm. Width of scraper edge 1.8 cm. Height of scraper edge (0.2 cm from edge) 0.4 cm. Greyish flint. Micro-wear analysis, much patinated. Context: House 200, sunken-floor horizon.

RE761ea. Flint arrowhead
Fragment. Triangular, with two lobes, one of these broken off. Length 3.0 cm, width 1.2 cm, & thickness 0.3 cm. Pressure-flaked. Greyish flint. Context: House 200, sunken-floor horizon.

RE763ea. Stone hammer
Complete. Length 6.2 cm, width 5.3 cm, & thickness 3.1 cm. Surface crushing area of c. 2.5 x 2.0 cm at one end. Quartzite. Context: House 200, secondary fills.

RE764ea. Flint dagger
Fragment, part of blade. Length 4.5 cm, width 3.2 cm, & thickness 0.9 cm. Re-sharpened. Pressure-flaked. Greyish flint. Micro-wear analysis, much patinated. Context: House 200, sunken-floor horizon.

RE787ea. Flint scraper
Complete. Pear-shaped. Length 7.6 cm, width 3.8 cm, & thickness 1.3 cm. Width of scraper edge 2.2 cm. Height of scraper edge (0.2 cm from edge) 0.6 cm. Greyish flint. Micro-wear analysis, much patinated. Context: House 200, sunken-floor horizon.

RE789ea. Flint scraper
Complete. Spoon-shaped. Height of scraper 0.2 cm from edge. Greyish flint. Cortex partly preserved. Micro-wear analysis, much patinated. Context: House 200, sunken-floor horizon.

RE795ea. Whetstone
Complete. Length 10.5 cm, width 6.7 cm, & thickness 3.7 cm. The surface of upper side is quite plane. The fine-grained stone is reddish, maybe partly due to heat. Context: House 200, sunken-floor horizon.

RE796ea. Stone hammer
Complete. Length 8.2 cm, width 5.6 cm, & thickness 4.5 cm. Surface crushing area of c. 4.8 x 2.7 cm. Context: House 200, sunken-floor horizon.

RE798ea. Stone hammer
Complete. Length 5.0 cm, width 3.8 cm, & thickness 2.8 cm. Surface crushing area of c. 1.5 x 1.0 cm and 3.2 x 0.8 cm. Grey-brownish stone. Context: House 240, secondary fills.

RE801ea. Flint adze
Complete. Three sides. Length 6.4 cm, width 3.7 cm, & thickness 1.6 cm. Short adze, with a slightly hollow edge. Width of edge 3.6 cm. Possibly re-sharpened. Coarse pressure-flaked. Partly polished at the convex side opposite the slightly hollow edge. Greyish flint. Cortex partly preserved on one side. The adze possibly is an "antique" left in a new context. Context: House 240, secondary fills.

RE803ea. Flint scraper
Fragment. Atypical. Length 5.9 cm, width 2.3 cm, & thickness 1.5 cm. Width of scraper edge 3.8 cm. Height of scraper edge (0.2 cm from edge) 0.6 cm. Greyish flint. Micro-wear analysis, much patinated. Context: House 240.

RE805ea. Flint knife
Complete. Length 7.3 cm, width 4.1 cm, & thickness 0.8 cm. Length of edge 3.9 cm. Greyish flint. Traces of wear due to use. The blunted back of the knife may possibly have worked as a scraper. Micro-wear analysis, much patinated. Context: House 240, secondary fills.

RE810ea. Stone hammer
Complete. Length 11.7 cm, width 9.3 cm, & thickness 5.3 cm. Surface crushing area of c. 2.2 x 1.0 cm at one end and, at opposite end, c. 3.5 x 1.2 cm. Greyish to beige quartzite. Context: House 240, secondary fills.

RE812ea. Stone hammer
Complete. Length 5.2 cm, width 3.9 cm, & thickness 3.7 cm. Surface crushing area of c.1.5 x 1.5 cm at one end and, at opposite end, c.1.5 x 1.2 cm. Reddish quartzite. Context: House 240.

RE813ea. Flint scraper
Fragment. Pear-shaped Length 6.7 cm, width 3.5 cm, & thickness 1.4 cm. Probably a scraper. Width of scraper edge 3.5 cm. Height of scraper edge (0.2 cm from edge) 0.5 cm. Greyish flint. Cortex partly preserved. Micro-wear analysis, much patinated. Context: House 240, secondary fills.

RE814ea. Flint scraper
Complete. Atypical. Length 4.6 cm, width 4.2 cm, & thickness 1.2 cm. Width of scraper edge 4.3 cm. Height of scraper edge (0.2 cm from edge) 0.6 cm. Greyish flint. Cortex partly preserved. Micro-wear analysis, much patinated. Context: House 240, secondary fills.

RE821ea. Flint nodule
Length 6.6 cm, width 4.6 cm, & thickness 4.5 cm. Greyish flint. Cortex partly preserved. Context: House 240, secondary fills.

RE821eb. Flint nodule
Length 6.0 cm, width 4.4 cm, & thickness 2.4 cm. Greyish flint. Cortex partly preserved. Context: House 240, secondary fills.

RE853ea. Stone hammer
Complete. Length 12.2 cm, width 9.6 cm, & thickness 6.3 cm. Surface crushing area of c. 3.0 x 2.1 cm. Grey-brownish quartzite. Context: House 240, secondary fills.

RE877ea. Flint scraper
Complete. Made on irregular flake. Greyish flint. Micro-wear analysis, much patinated. Context: House 240, sunken-floor horizon.

RE976ea. Flint scraper
Complete. Almost spoon-shaped. Length 6.0 cm, width 3.3 cm, & thickness 1.2 cm. Width of scraper edge 3.3 cm. Height of scraper edge (0.2 cm from edge) 0.8 cm. Greyish flint. Cortex partly preserved. Micro-wear analysis, much patinated. Context: Culture layer 293.

RE976eb. Flint scraper
Complete. Almost spoon-shaped. Length 6.7 cm, width 2.9 cm, & thickness 1.4 cm. Width of scraper edge 2.1 cm. Height of scraper edge (0.2 cm from edge) 0.8 cm. Greyish flint. Cortex partly preserved. Micro-wear analysis, much patinated. Context: Culture layer 293.

RE976ec. Flint scraper
Complete. Pear-shaped. Length 6.6 cm, width 3.7 cm, & thickness 1.2 cm. Width of scraper edge 2.3 cm. Height of scraper edge (0.2 cm from edge) 0.6 cm. Greyish flint. Cortex partly preserved. Micro-wear analysis, much patinated. Context: Culture layer 293.

RE985ea. Flint dagger
Fragment. Length 7.5 cm, width 4.4 cm, & thickness 1.0 cm. Possibly re-sharpened. Pressure-flaked. Likely type V B. Consideration must, however, be given as to whether it might concern a dagger fragment of type VI B, although this is found to be less likely. In addition to the fine pressure-flaked surface, the considerable width of the lenticular handle indicates grouping with type V B daggers, although no end part with enlargement of the handle is preserved. Greyish flint. Cortex partly preserved on one side. Micro-wear analysis, much patinated. Context: belongs to a deep pit from the sunken-floor horizon of House 200.

RE985eb. Flint arrowhead
Fragment. Triangular, originally with two lobes but one lobe missing. Length 3.0 cm, width 1.1 cm. Pressure-flaked. Greyish flint. Context: see RE985ea.

RE1000ea. Flint dagger
Fragment, part of handle. Length 5.8 cm, width 2.8 cm, & thickness 1.8 cm. Coarsely pressure-flaked. Not determined but affinities with type VI A. Greyish flint. Cortex partly preserved. Micro-wear analysis, much patinated. Context: Culture layer 203.

RE1002ea. Flint scraper
Complete. Spoon-shaped. Length 5.9 cm, width 2.9 cm, & thickness 1.3 cm. Width of scraper edge 2.9 cm. Height of scraper edge (0.2 cm from edge) 0.8 cm. Greyish flint. Micro-wear analysis, much patinated. Context: Culture layer 303, not indicated on Fig. 5.7.

RE1003ea. Flint scraper
Almost complete, a tiny fragment near the edge broken off. Spoon-shaped. Length 5.0 cm, width 3.1 cm, & thickness 1.3 cm. Width of scraper edge 2.7 cm. Height of scraper edge (0.2 cm from edge) 0.4 cm. Greyish flint. Cortex partly preserved. Micro-wear analysis, much patinated. Context: House 198, sunken-floor horizon.

RE1018ea. Flint sickle
Fragment. Made on a blade. Length 2.7 cm, width 2.3 cm, & thickness 0.8 cm. Length of edge 3.8 cm. Probably re-sharpened. Coarsely pressure-flaked on dorsal side. Greyish flint. Traces of wear due to use. Micro-wear analysis revealed that one side of the tool had been used with a scraping movement (report S2004a). Context: Culture layer 203.

RE1020ea. Flint arrowhead roughout
End of a flint dagger, possible roughout. Length 6.5 cm, width 2.9 cm, & thickness 1.0 cm. Pressure-flaked. Greyish flint. Micro-wear analysis, much patinated. Context: Culture layer 203.

RE1021ea. Flint sickle
Fragment. Length 7.2 cm, width 4.0 cm, & thickness 1.1 cm. Length of edge 5.5 cm. Greyish flint. Micro-wear analysis, much patinated. Context: Culture layer 203.

RE 1022ea. Flint arrowhead roughout
Possibly a roughout for a triangular arrowhead. Seems based on a flint sickle Complete. Length 5.1 cm, width 4.0 cm, & thickness 1.0 cm. Pressure-flaked. Greyish flint. Micro-wear analysis, much patinated. Context: Culture layer 203.

RE1023ea. Flint dagger
Fragment, the handle preserved until transition to the blade. Length 8.8 cm & width 3.1 cm. Pressure-flaked. Type VI B. Greyish flint. Micro-wear analysis, much patinated. Context: Culture layer 203.

RE1040ea. Flint dagger
Fragment, handle. Length 5.7 cm, width 2.1 cm, & thickness 1.5 cm. Pressure-flaked. Type III A affinities but the thickness of the handle is no wider than the width and therefore it does not comply fully with the sub-type description. Greyish flint. Some cortex preserved. Micro-wear analysis, much patinated. Context: House 158, secondary fills.

RE1040eb. Stone hammer
Fragment. Length 6.5 cm, width 5.3 cm, & thickness 4.8 cm. The reddish stone may have become brittle due to heat impact. Context: House 158, secondary fills.

RE1041ea. Stone quern
Fragment, one side plane, the opposite side broken off. Upper part of a saddle quern. Length 15.2 cm, width 7.3 cm, & thickness 3.0 cm. Striations in longitudinal direction. Context: House 42, secondary fills.

RE 1042ea. Flint arrowhead
Complete. Triangular, with two lobes. Length 2.8 cm & width 1.6 cm. Pressure-flaked. Greyish flint. Context: House 158, probably from secondary fills.

RE1042eb. Flint sickle
Fragment. Crescent-shaped. Length 5.3 cm & width 5.0 cm. Possibly re-sharpened. Pressure-flaked. Greyish flint. Micro-wear analysis, some patina, but no traces of use observable. Context: see RE1042ea

RE1042ec. Flint scraper
Fragment. Long oval. Length 6.3 cm, width 3.1 cm, & thickness 0.6 cm. Width of scraper edge 2.9 cm. Height of scraper edge (0.2 cm from edge) 0.3 cm. Greyish flint. Cortex partly preserved. Context: see RE1042ea.

RE1042ed. Flint hammer
Complete. Length 6.7 cm, width 6.6 cm, & thickness 6.0 cm. Surface crushing over most of the surface, except two spots. Greyish flint. Context: see RE1042ea.

RE1042ee. Flint axe roughout
Complete. Length 12.8 cm, width 5.7 cm, & thickness 4.4 cm. Coarse flaking. Greyish flint. Context: see RE1042ea.

RE1045es. Flint axe
Almost complete, minor part of the edge broken off. Partly polished broad sides. Length 8.1 cm, width 3.8 cm, & thickness 2.0 cm. Edge width, estimated, c. 4.0-4.2 cm. Partly polished broad sides. Original edge polished, whereas the re-sharpened edge is unpolished. Greyish flint. Context: House 158, secondary fills. During excavation it was at first considered to belong to the sunken-floor horizon (see text).

RE1048ea. Flint sickle
Complete. Made on a blade. Length 8.6 cm, width 2.4 cm, & thickness 0.8 cm. Edge length 6.7 cm. Coarse retouch observable along the edge. Blunted back. Greyish flint. Micro-wear analysis, much patinated. Context: uncertain but presumably the sunken-floor horizon of House 41.

RE1061ea. Flint arrowhead
Fragment. Triangular, with two lobes, one lobe broken off. Length 3.6 cm & width 1.3 cm. Pressure-flaked. Greyish flint. Context: from faint, diffusely delimited culture layer immediately north of House 2.

RE1062ea. Flint dagger
Fragment, handle. Length 6.6 cm, width 2.0 cm, & thickness 1.8 cm. Pressure-flaked. Type III B. Greyish flint. Stray find.

Catalogue C

Charred plant remains at Resengaard

Presented in numerical order, the catalogue contains certain selected charred macrofossil remains from 40 samples taken at Resengaard. David Earle Robinson carried out the initial palaeo-botanical examinations of those needed for radiocarbon dating. Subsequently, Peter Steen Henriksen conducted the determinations for the greater part of the charred organic plant materials. For further information concerning the individual samples, see his report (S2001a). All entries below refer to it. See also Ch. 5.5, including note 18. The presence of charcoal is mentioned when presenting the floor patches (Ch. 4).

Many radiocarbon determinations were carried out on the charred material, see Ch. 2.4 and 3.3. Lis Højlund Pedersen examined 13 pollen samples from Resengaard. Most of these contained no or very little pollen (see the aforementioned report). Three samples however, were informative. Two stem from the site of House 2 (M61387 & M61388) and one from the site of House 138 (M61390). See Ch. 5.5 including notes 20-25.

Regarding the configuration of catalogue numbers, see Catalogue A. The added sub-number (ga) ensures that it is unique.

RE8ga. Charred cereals
Cereals: 1 naked barley, 1 wheat, 30 undetermined (100 % of the sample examined). Two radiocarbon determinations (AAR-6661.a & AAR-6661.b) available (see Ch. 2.4 & 3.3). Context: House 2, sunken-floor horizon.

RE25ga. Charred cereals, hazelnut, weeds
Cereals: 72 naked barley, 12 emmer/spelt wheat, 1,096 undetermined (52 % of the total sample examined). Other: Emmer rachis internode. Collected: Hazelnut. Weeds: Fat hen & knotweed. Context: House 1, sunken-floor horizon, sample area B (Fig. 5.16).

RE27ga. Charred cereals
Cereals: 140 naked barley, 21 emmer/spelt wheat, 1,180 undetermined (12 % of the total sample examined). Context: House 1, sunken-floor horizon, sample area A & B, together (fig. 5.16).

RE54ga. Charred cereals, weeds
Cereals: 182 naked barley, 15 emmer/spelt wheat, 590 undetermined (0.37 % of the total sample examined).
Weeds: Knotweed. A radiocarbon determination (K 5732) available (see Ch. 2.4 & 3.3). Context: House 1, sunken-floor horizon, sample area A (Fig. 5.16).

RE64ga. Charred cereals, heather, weeds
Cereals: 140 naked barley, 23 emmer/spelt wheat, 926 undetermined (1.4 % of the total sample examined). Other: Two sprigs of heather. Weeds: Knotweed & black mustard. A radiocarbon determination (K-5733) available (see Ch. 2.4 & 3.3). Context: House 1, sunken-floor horizon, sample area B (Fig. 5.16)

RE77ga. Charred cereals
Cereals: 103 naked barley, 25 emmer/spelt wheat, 1,030 undetermined (1.9 % of the total sample examined). A radiocarbon

determination (K-5734) available (see Ch. 2.4 & 3.3). Context: House 1, sunken-floor horizon, sample area D (Fig. 5.16).

RE78ga. Charred cereals, heather, weeds
Cereals: 56 naked barley, 29 emmer/spelt wheat, 695 undetermined (12 % of the total sample examined). Other: Three sprigs of heather. Weeds: Knotweed & false oat grass. Context: House 1, sunken-floor horizon, sample area C (Fig. 5.16).

RE79ga. Charred cereals, hazelnut
Cereals: 96 naked barley, 39 emmer/spelt wheat, 900 undetermined (18 % of the total sample examined). Collected: Hazelnut. Context: House 1, sunken-floor horizon, sample area E (Fig. 5.16).

RE136ga. Charred cereals, hazelnut
Cereals: 11 naked barley, 2 wheat, 1,000 undetermined (50 % of the total sample examined). Collected: Hazelnut. Context: House 1, sunken-floor horizon, patch B.

RE137ga. Charred cereals, hazelnut, weeds
Cereals: 2 barley, 28 naked barley, 6 emmer/spelt wheat, 180 undetermined (100 % of the sample examined). Collected: Hazelnut. Weeds: False oat grass, knotweed, & cleavers. Context: House 2, sunken-floor horizon (see Ch. 4.2).

RE198ga. Charred wheat, hazelnut, weeds
Emmer rachis internode. Collected: Hazelnut. Weeds: Fat hen & knotweed. Context: House 2 (Fig. 4.68). From a pollen sample (M61388) taken from the soil bench.

RE222ga. Charred cereals, heather, weeds
Cereals: 42 naked barley, 17 emmer/spelt wheat, 227 undetermined (100 % of the sample examined). Other: Sprigs of heather. Weeds: Knotweed. Context: House 2, sunken-floor horizon (see Ch. 4.2).

RE293ga. Charred cereals, hazelnut
Cereals: 3 undetermined (100 % of the sample examined). Collected: Hazelnut. Context: Feature 24 (north of House 14).

RE294ga. Charred cereals
Cereals: 51 naked barley, 25 emmer/spelt wheat, 1,315 undetermined (100 % of the sample examined). Other: 1 rachis internode. Context: House 197, from heavily ard-ploughed sunken floor.

RE305ga. Charred cereal
Cereals: ½ undetermined (100 % of the sample examined). Context: House 10, sample taken from the lower stratum in the northern part of the N-S-profile bench (not illustrated).

RE306ga. Charred cereals, hazelnut
Cereals: 1 naked barley, 1 wheat, 1 undetermined (100 % of the sample examined). Collected: Hazelnut. See report S2001a. Context: House 10, sample taken from the lower stratum of the southern part of the N-S-profile bench.

RE307ga. Charred cereals
Cereals: 2 undetermined (100 % of the sample examined). See report S2001a. Context: House 14, sample taken from the lower stratum of the northern part of the N-S-profile bench (not illustrated).

RE308ga. Charred cereals, weeds
Cereals: 3 undetermined (100 % of the sample examined). Weeds: Pansy. Context: House 14, sample taken from the lower stratum of the southern part of the N-S-profile bench (not illustrated).

RE309ga. Charred cereals, hazelnut, weeds
Cereals: 10 naked barley, 9 emmer/spelt wheat, 1,060 undetermined (49 % of the total sample examined). Collected: Hazelnut. Weeds: Fat hen & knotweed. Other: 1 emmer rachis internode & 1 spelt rachis internode. Context: House 197, sunken-floor horizon, sample from a heavily ard-ploughed area to the south.

RE433ga. Charred cereal, heather
Cereals: 1 undetermined. Other: Sprigs of heather. Context: House 41, sunken-floor horizon, sample taken from the floor layer.

RE565ga. Charred cereal, hazelnut
Cereals: 1 barley, 1 undetermined (100 % of the sample examined). Collected: Hazelnut. Two radiocarbon determinations (AAR-6663.a & AAR-6663.b) available (see Ch. 2.4 & 3.3). Context: House 128, sunken-floor horizon, pit I.

RE568ga. Charred cereal, hazelnut
Cereals: 1 undetermined (100 % of the sample examined). Collected: Hazelnut. Context: Pit 567 west of the sunken floor of House 128.

RE583ga. Charred cereals
Cereals: 25 naked barley, 1 hulled barley, 20 emmer/spelt wheat, 413 undetermined (51 % of the sample total examined). Two radiocarbon determinations (AAR-6660.a & AAR-6660.b) available (see Ch. 2.4 & 3.3). Context: House 106 (three-aisled), posthole belonging to the construction of the building.

RE584ga. Charred cereals
Cereals: 7 emmer/spelt wheat, 10 undetermined (100 % of the sample examined). Other: 1 rachis internode. Context: House 106 (the three-aisled), posthole belonging to the construction of the building.

RE585ga. Charred cereals
Cereals: 1 emmer/spelt wheat, 8 undetermined (100 % of the sample examined). Context: House 106 (three-aisled), posthole belonging to the construction of the building.

RE587ga. Charred cereal
Cereals: 1 wheat (100 % of the sample examined). Context: House 106 (three-aisled), posthole belonging to the construction of the building.

RE588ga. Charred cereals
Cereals: 1 barley, 1 emmer/spelt wheat, 3 undetermined (100 % of the sample examined). Context: House 106 (three-aisled), posthole belonging to the construction of the building.

RE589ga. Charred cereals
Cereals: 7 undetermined (100 % of the sample examined). Context: House 106 (three-aisled), posthole belonging to the building.

RE616ga. Charred cereal
Cereals: ½ undetermined. Context: House 138, on the sunken-floor bottom.

RE617ga. Charred cereals, weeds
Cereals: 4 undetermined (100 % of the sample examined). Weeds: Fat hen. Context: House 138, on the sunken-floor bottom.

RE627ga. Charred cereals
Cereals: 46 naked barley, 28 emmer/spelt wheat, 1,290 undetermined (6.3 % of the total sample examined). Context: House 197, from heavily ard-ploughed sunken floor.

RE631ga. Charred cereals
Cereals: 1 wheat, 14 undetermined (100 % of the sample examined). Two radiocarbon determinations (AAR-6659.a & AAR-6659.b) available (see Ch. 2.4 & 3.3). Context: House 13, sunken-floor horizon, patch H.

RE702ga. Charred cereals
Cereals: 25 naked barley, 17 emmer/spelt wheat, 1,090 undetermined (6.3 % of the total sample examined). Two radiocarbon determinations (AAR-6662.a & AAR-6662.b) available (see Ch. 2.4 & 3.3). Context: House 197, sunken-floor horizon, pit F.

RE705ga. Charred cereals
Cereals: 50 naked barley, 18 emmer/spelt wheat, 1,080 undetermined (0.75 % of the sample examined). Context: House 197, from heavily ard-ploughed sunken floor.

RE816ga. Charred cereals
Cereals: 1 naked barley, 1 undetermined. A radiocarbon determination (AAR-6664) available (see Ch. 2.4 & 3.3). Context: House 202, sunken-floor horizon, sample taken from the southern half of patch A.

RE904bga. Charred emmer
1 emmer rachis internode. For further information, see report S2001a. Context: House 200, sample taken from the cross-section.

RE962ga. Charred cereals
Cereals: ½ naked barley, 2 undetermined (100 % of the sample examined). Context: House 200, sample taken from the lower layer of the cross section.

RE967ga. Charred cereals, weeds
Cereals: 5 undetermined (100 % of the sample examined). Weeds: Knotweed . Other: 1 wheat rachis internode. Context: House 202, sunken-floor horizon, sample taken from the northern half of patch A.

RE1025ga. Charred cereals, hazelnut, weeds
Cereals: 1 naked barley, 2 emmer/spelt wheat, 1 wheat, 19 undetermined (100 % of the sample examined). Collected: Hazelnut. Weeds: Knotweed. See report S2001a. Context: Culture layer 203, sample taken from nearby subsoil level, near the ard-furrows.

RE1035ga. Charred cereal
Cereals: 1 naked barley. Context: House 138, sunken-floor horizon, patch C.

Illustration credits

Soil section drawings during fieldwork: Poul Mikkelsen, Kurt G. Overgaard & Jørn Bie

Plan drawings during fieldwork: Ole Jensen, Poul Mikkelsen, Kurt G. Overgaard & Jørn Bie

Photos during fieldwork at Glattrup I/III, Marienlyst Strand and Granlygård:
Poul Mikkelsen & the present author

Photos during fieldwork at Hellegård, Rosgårde, Glattrup IV, Tromgade and Kluborg II:
Kurt G. Overgaard & the present author

Photos during fieldwork at Resengaard: The present author

Survey mapping relating to Resengaard: Henny Lundsdorff & the present author

Digitizing of excavation plans, except Gåsemose: Terkel Brannet

Working of digitized plans in GIS: Henrik Vind Frimurer in cooperation with the present author

Studio photos of all artefacts: Ivan Andersen

Radiocarbon diagrams, based on determinations by Kaare Lund Rasmussen and Jan Heinemeier:
Marie Kanstrup & Jesper Olsen

Palaeobotanical tables and normalized diagrams, based on Peter Steen Henriksen's report:
Henrik Vind Frimurer

Accounts of house sites and finds in Excel: Henrik Vind Frimurer & the present author

Data and maps of find distributions, the Limfjord region: Kristine Stub Precht

Plan drawing during fieldwork at Lundvej 19: Martin Mikkelsen & Malene R. Beck

Hand drawing of contour lines (based on height measuring) for House 2 at Resengaard:
Søren Johnsen

Hand drawings of ceramics and flint items relating to Gåsemose: Henning Ørsnes

Final hand drawings of ceramics, soil sections and other from Resengaard and eight other settlements:
The present author

Krabbesholm photo: The present author

Graphics and working of largely all illustrations for publication: Lars Foged Thomsen

Literature

References to many small notes on concrete house sites in the yearly accounts *Archaeological excavations in Denmark (Arkæologiske udgravninger i Danmark, AUD)*, published for the years 1984–2005, are, as concerns the maps in Fig. 1.1 and 1.2, given in the list Fig. 1.3. The chapters refer to a following page (p.) and to following pages (pp.). Archaeological excavation reports and scientific examination reports are placed after the list of literature.

Aabo, C. 2001: Oldtidsagre i Svansø Plantage og en jernalderlandsby ved Siggård. In: Gormsen, G., Kristensen,: I. K., Mortensen, N. & Simonsen, J. (eds.) *Skive kommunes historie fra oldtid til 1880.* Skive, pp. 39-46.

Aaris-Sørensen, K. 1989: *Danmarks Forhistoriske Dyreverden. Fra Istid til Vikingetid.* Copenhagen.

Ahlberg, M. Akselsson, R. Forkman, B. & Rausing, G. 1976: Gold Traces on Wedge-shaped Artefacts from the Late Neolithic of southern Scandinavia analysed by proton-induced X-ray emission spectroscopy. *Archaeometry,* 18, 1, pp. 39-49.

Andersen, N.H. 1985: Neolithic. (AUD) *Arkæologiske udgravninger i Danmark,* 1984. Copenhagen, pp. 49-50.

Andersen, N.H. 1987: Neolithic. (AUD) *Arkæologiske udgravninger i Danmark,* 1986. Copenhagen, pp. 38-40.

Andersen, S.H. 1983: Kalvø – A Coastal Site of the Single Grave Culture. *Journal of Danish Archaeology,* 2 (1983), pp. 71-81.

Andersen, S.H. 1990: Limfjordens forhistorie – en oversigt. *Limfjordsprojektet. Rapport nr. 1.* Aarhus, pp. 29-65.

Andersen, S.H. 1998: Erhvervsspecialisering og ressourceudnyttelse i Limfjordsområdet i forhistorisk tid. In: Lund, J. & Ringtved, J. (eds.) *Variation og enhed omkring Limfjorden. Rapport nr.8, I. Rapport fra seminar afholdt 2.-3. november 1995 på Vitskøl Kloster.* Aarhus, pp. 97- 139.

Andersen, S.H. 2005: Køkkenmøddingerne ved Krabbesholm. Ny forskning i stenalderens kystbopladser. *Nationalmuseets arbejdsmark,* 2005. Copenhagen, pp. 151-171.

Andersen, S. Th. 1992a: Miljøhistorie og Kulturhistorie i det vestlige Limfjordsområde. In: *Kommunikation ved Limfjorden fra fortid til nutid. Rapport fra seminar afholdt 2.- 3.maj 1991 i Egense. Rapport,* 5. Aarhus, pp. 87-92.

Andersen, S. Th. 1992b: Pollenanalyser fra Bjerre Enge, Thy. In: Andersen, S. Th. & Rasmussen, P. (eds.) *Geobotaniske Undersøgelser af Kulturlandskabets Historie. Pollenanalyser fra Gravhøje og Søer 1991.* Danmarks Geologiske Undersøgelser. Copenhagen, pp. 4-19.

Andersen, S. Th. 1993: Early agriculture. In: Hvass, S. & Storgaard, B. (eds.). *Digging into the Past. 25 Years of Archaeology in Denmark.* The Royal Society of Northern Antiquaries/Jutland Archaeological Society. Copenhagen/Højbjerg, pp. 88-91.

Andersen, S. Th. 1995a: History of Vegetation and Agriculture at Hassing Mose, Thy, Northwest Denmark, since the Ice Age. *Journal of Danish Archaeology,* 11, 1992-93, pp. 57-79.

Andersen, S. Th. 1995b: Pollenanalyser fra Ove Sø, Thy. In: Andersen, S. Th. & Rasmussen, P. (eds.) *Geobotaniske Undersøgelser af Kulturlandskabets Historie. Pollenanalyser fra Gravhøje og Søer 1994.* Danmarks Geologiske Undersøgelser. Copenhagen, pp. 36-55.

Andersen, S. Th. 1999: Pollen analyses from Early Bronze Age barrows in Thy. *Journal of Danish Archaeology,* 13, pp. 7-17.

Andersson, K. Fagerlund, D. & Hamilton, J. 1990: Annelund – en senneolitisk bondegård. *Arkeologi i Sverige* (1987), pp. 15-44.

Andersson, K. & Hjarthner-Holder, E. 1989: Annelund – ett senneolitiskt bebyggelsekomplex i sydvästra Uppland. *Fornvännen (1988),* 3, pp. 209-215.

Andersson, M. & Thorn, A. 1996: Boplatslämninger från senneolitikum – järnålder. In: Svensson, M. & Karsten. P. (eds.) Skåne, Malmöhus Län, Järnvägen Västkustbanan, Delen Helsingborg-Kavlinge. Avsnittet Helsingborg- Landskrona (block 1-2). *Lund UV Syd, Rapport,* 1996:48, pp. 63-76.

Andreasen, M.H. 2005: Klejtrup Syd – en boplads fra sen yngre stenalder / tidlig ældre bronzealder. *Bygherrerapport, Viborg Stiftsmuseum,* nr. 6, pp. 1-16.

Andreasen, M.H. 2009: Agerbruget i enkeltgravskultur, senneolitikum og ældre bronzealder i Jylland – belyst ud fra plantemakrofossiler. *KUML* 2009. Årbog for Jysk Arkæologisk Selskab. Aarhus, pp. 9-55.

Anscher, T.T. 2000: Late Swifterbant/Early Funnel Beaker Houseplans from Schokland-PI4, Municipality of Noordoostpolder, The Netherlands. In: Kelm, R.(ed.) *Vom Phostenloch zum Steinzeithaus. Archäologische Forschung und Rekonstruktion jungsteinzeitlicher Haus- und Siedlungsbefunde im nordwestlichen Mitteleuropa.* Heide, Anscher 126-54.

Aner, E., Kersten, K., & Willroth, K.-H. 2008: *Die Funde der älteren Bronzezeit des nordischen Kreises in Dänemark,*

Schleswig-Holstein und Niedersachsen, Band XI, Viborg Amt. Mainz.

Apel, J. 2001: Daggers, Knowledge and Power. The Social Aspects of Flint-Dagger Technology in Scandinavia 2350-1500 cal. BC. *Coast to Coast,* 3. Uppsala.

Apel, J. 2004: From Marginalisation to Specialisation: Scandinavian Flint-Dagger Production during the Second Wave of Neolithisation, In: Knutsson, H.(ed.) *Coast to Coast – Arrival. Results and Reflections. Proceedings of the Final Coast to Coast Conference 1-5 October 2002 in Falköping, Sweden.* Uppsala, pp. 295-308.

Appadurai, A. [1986] 1992: Introduction: commodities and the politics of value. In: Appadurai, A. (ed.) *The social life of things. Commodities in cultural perspective.* Cambridge, pp. 3-63.

Artursson, M. (ed.) 2000: (med bidrag av Magnus Artursson, Thorbjörn Brorsson, Bo Knarrström, Patrik Lord och Lena Nilsson): Stångby stationssamhälle. Boplats- och bebyggelsemningar från senneolitikum till yngre järnålder. Skåne, Vallkärre sn., väg 930. *Riksantikvarieämbetet, UV Syd rapport, 2000:79.*

Artursson, M. 2005a : Byggnadstradition. In: Lagerås, P. & Strömberg, B. (eds.) *Bronsåldersbygd 2300-500 f. Kr. Skånska spår – arkeologi längs Västkustbanan.* Riksantikvarieämbetet. Stockholm, pp. 20-83.

Artursson, M. 2005b: Gårds- och bebyggelsesstruktur. In: Lagerås, P. & Strömberg, B. (eds.) *Bronsåldersbygd 2300-500 f. Kr. Skånska spår – arkeologi längs Västkustbanan.* Riksantikvarieämbetatet. Stockholm, pp. 84-159.

Artursson, M. 2005c: Bygnadstradition och bebyggelsesstruktur under senneolitikum och bronsålder. Västra Skåne i ett skandinavisk perspektiv. *Supplement till Skånska spår – arkeologi längs Västkustbanan.* Riksantikvarieämbetet.

Artursson, M. 2009: Bebyggelse och samhällsstruktur. Södra och mellersta Skandinavien under senneolitikum och bronsålder 2300-500 f. Kr. Riksantikvarieämbetet. *Riksantivarabetets Arkeologiska undersökningar. Skrifter* No 73. Göteborg University. Gotarc Serie B. Gothenburg Archaeological Thesis, No 52.

Artursson, M. 2010: Settlement Structure and Organisation. In: Earle, T. & Kristiansen, K. (eds.) *Organizing Bronze Age Societies. The Mediterranean, Central Europe, and Scandinavia Compared.* Cambridge, pp. 87-121.

Ashmore, P. 2005: Dating Barnhouse. In: Richards, C. (ed.) *Dwelling among the monuments: The Neolithic village of Barnhouse, Maeshowe passage grave and surrounding monuments at Stenness, Orkney.* McDonald Institute Monographs. Cambridge, pp. 385-388

Asingh, P. 1988: Diverhøj – A Complex Burial Mound and a Neolithic Settlement. *Journal of Danish Archaeology,* 6, 1987, pp. 130-154.

Assendorph, J.J. 1997: Die bronzezeitliche Siedlung in Hitzacker, Niedersachsen. In: Assendorp, J.J. (ed.) Forschungen zur bronzezeitlichen Besiedlung in Nord- und Mitteleuropa. Internationales Symposium vom 9.-11. Mai 1996 in Hitzacker. *Internationale Archaologie,* 38. Herausgegeben vom Institut zur Denkmalpflege im Niedersächsischen Landesverwaltungsamt und der Archaeologischen Kommission zur Niedersachsen e. V. Espelkamp, pp. 51-59.

Bailey, D.W. 1990: The Living House: Signifying Continuity. In: Samson, R. (ed.) *The Social Archaeology of Houses.* Edinburgh University Press, Edinburgh, pp. 9-48.

Bailey, D.W. 1996: The life, times and works of House 59, Tell Ovcharovo, Bulgaria. In: Darvill, T. & Thomas, J. (eds.) Neolithic Houses in Northwest Europe and Beyond. Neolithic Studies Group Seminar Papers 1. *Oxbow Monograph,* 57. Oxford, pp. 143-156.

Bakka, E. 1976: Fire vestnorske kystbuplassar från yngre steinalder. In Edgren, T. (ed.) Nordiska arkeologmötet i Helsingfors 1967. Berättelse over XII Nordiska Arkeologmötet i Helsingfors den 4-9. juni 1967. *ISKOS ,* I, pp. 35-39.

Bakkevig, S. 1982: Økologi og økonomi for deler av Sør-Jæren i sen-neolitikum. Del 2. Makrofossilanalyse. Saltvannsflotasjon av materiale fra Rugland på Jæren. *AmS-Skrifter.* Stavanger, pp. 33-40.

Bantelmann, N. 1975: Comments on The Flint Daggers of Denmark. *Norwegian Archaeological Review,* 8, 2, pp. 102-103.

Barber, E.J.W. 1991: *Prehistoric Textiles: The Development of Cloth in the Neolithic and Bronze Ages with Special Reference to the Aegean.* Princeton/Oxford.

Barclay, G.J. 1996: Neolithic buildings in Scotland. In: Darvill, T. & Thomas, J. (eds.) Neolithic Houses in Northwest Europe and Beyond. Neolithic Studies Group Seminar Papers 1. *Oxbow Monograph,* 57. Oxford, pp. 61-75.

Barker, G. 1999: Cattle-keeping in ancient Europe: to live together or apart? In: Fabech, C. & Ringtved, J. (eds.) *Settlement and Landscape. Proceedings of a conference in Århus, Denmark.* 1998. Aarhus, pp. 273-280.

Barrett, J.C. 1997: Defining Domestic Space in the Bronze Age of Southern Britain. In: Pearson, M. & Richards, C. (eds.). A*rchitecture and Order. Approaches to Social Space.* Routledge. London/New York, pp. 87-97.

Bartelheim, M. 1997: Einsatz der Korrespondenzanalyse zur chronologischen Gliederung der böhmischen Aunjetitzer Kultur. In: Müller, J. & Zimmermann, A. (eds.). Archäologie und Korrespondenzanalyse. Beispiele, Fragen, Perspektiven. *Internationale Archäologie 23.* Rahden, pp. 129-136.

Barth, F. 1967: Economic spheres in Darfur. In: Firth, R. (ed.) Themes in Economic Anthropology. *A.S.A Monograph 6.* Tavistock Publications, pp. 149-174.

Bech, J.-H. 1997: Bronze Age settlements on raised sea-beds at Bjerre, Thy, NW-Jutland. In: Assendorp, J.J. (ed.) Forschungen zur bronzezeitlichen Besiedlung in Nord- und Mitteleuropa. Internationales Symposium vom 9.-11. Mai 1996 in Hitzacker. *Internationale Archaologie,* 38. Herausgegeben vom Institut zur Denkmalpflege im Niedersächsischen Landesverwaltungsamt und der Archaeologischen Kommission zur Niedersachsen e. V. Espelkamp, pp. 3-15.

Bech, J.-H. & Mikkelsen, M. 1999: Landscapes, settlement and subsistence in Bronze Age Thy, NW Denamark. In: Fabech, C. & Ringtved, J. (eds.) *Settlement and Landscape. Proceedings of a conference in Århus, Denmark, 1998.* Aarhus, pp. 69-78.

Becker, C.J. 1951a: Flintgruberne ved Aalborg. *Nationalmuseets Arbejdsmark*, 1951, pp. 107-112.

Becker, C.J. 1951b: Late-Neolithic Flint Mines at Aalborg. *Acta Archaeologica*, 22, pp. 135-152.

Becker, C.J. 1952: Die Nordschwedischen Flintdepots. Ein Beitrag zur Geschichte des neolithischen Fernhandels in Skandinavien. *Acta Archaeologica*, 23, pp. 31-79.

Becker, C.J. 1954: A Segmented Faience Bead from Jutland. With Notes on Amber Beads from Bronze Age Denmark. *Acta Archaeologica*, 25, pp. 241-252.

Becker, C.J. 1954: Die Mittel-Neolithischen Kulturen in Südskandinavien. *Acta Archaeologica*, 25, pp. 49-150.

Becker, C.J. 1955: Coarse Beakers with "Short-wave Moulding". *Proceedings of the Prehistoric Society*, XXI, 65-71.

Becker, C.J. 1964: Sen-neolitikum i Norden. *Tor*, 10, pp. 121-134.

Becker, C.J. 1993: Flintminer og flintdistribution ved Limfjorden. In: Lund, J. & Ringtved, J. (eds.) Kort- og råstofstudier omkring Limfjorden. *Rapport fra seminarer afholdt 7.-8.november 1991 samt 23.-24. April 1992 i Aalborg. Rapport*, 6, pp. 111-134.

Bekmose, J. 1977: Megalitgrave og megalitbygder. *Antikvariske studier*, 1. Copenhagen, pp. 47-64.

Benjamin, D.N. [1996] 1998: Introduction. In: Benjamin, D. N. Stea, D. & Saile, D. (eds.). *The Home: Words, Interpretations, Meanings and Environments*. Aldershot, pp. 79-107.

Beran, J. 2000: Frühe Bronzezeit. Potsdam, Brandenburg, und Havelland. *Führer zu den archaeologischen Denkmälern in Deutschland*. Stuttgart, pp. 53-58.

Berglund, B.E. 1991: The projec – background, aims, and organization. In: Berglund, B.E. (ed.) The cultural landscape during 6000 years in southern Sweden – the Ystad Project. *Ecological Bulletins*, 41. Lund, pp. 13-27.

Bertelsen, J.B. 1996: Bronzealderbebyggelsen på Nordfur: In: Nielsen J. & Simonsen, J. (eds.) *Bronzealderens bopladser i Midt- og Nordvestjylland*. Skive, pp. 104-109.

Bican, J.F. 2012: Bulkister og bådgrav ved Bulbrogård – en senneolitisk gravplads ved vestbredden af Tissø. *Aarbøger for nordisk Oldkyndighed og Historie*, 2010, pp. 7-42.

Billig, G. 1958: Die Aunjetitzer Kultur in Sachsen. *Veröffentlichungen des Landesmuseums für Vorgeschichte, Dresden*, 7. Leipzig.

Billig, G. 1963: Frühbronzezeitliche Funde der Niederlausitz und ihre Stellung innerhalb der Aunjetitzer Kultur, Alt-Thüringen. *Jahresschrift des Museum für Ur- und Frühgeschichte Thuringens*, 16 (1962/63), pp. 247-273.

Binns, K.S. 1983: Et jernalders gårdsanlegg på Tussøy i Troms. Bygningsmessige og bosetningshistoriske aspekter, In: Olafsson, G (ed.). *Hus, Gård och Bebyggelse. Foredrag från det XVI nordiska arkeologmötet, Island 1982*. Reykjavik, pp. 43-50.

Biwall, A. Hernek, R. Kihlstedt, B. Larsson, M. & Torstensdotter Åhlin, I. 1997: Stenålderns hyddor och hus i Syd- och Mellansverige. In: Larsson, M. & Olsson, E. (eds.) Regionalt och interregionalt. Stenåldersundersokningar i Syd- och Mellansverige. Riksantikvarieämbetet, *Arkeologiska undersökningar, Skrifter*, 23, pp. 265-300.

Björhem, N. & Säfvestad, U. 1987: Stenåldershus. Rekonstruktion av ett 4000 år gammalt hus. *Rapport*, 2, Malmö Museer. Malmö.

Björhem, N. & Säfvestad, U. 1989: Byggnadstradition och bosättningsmönster under senneolitikum. *Malmöfynd* 5, Malmö Museer. Malmö.

Björhem, N. & Säfvestad, U. 1993: Fosie IV Bebyggelsen under brons- och järnålder. *Malmöfynd*, 6, Malmö Museer.

Boas, F. [1896; 1940] 1982: The Limitations of the Comparative Method of Anthropology. In: Boas, F. *Race, Language and Culture*. Chicago/London, pp. 270-280.

Boas, N.A. 1980: Egehøjbopladsen fra ældste bronzealder. In: Thrane, H. (ed.) Broncealderbebyggelse i Norden. *Odense Skrifter*, 28. Odense, pp. 102-111.

Boas, N.A. 1983: Egehøj. A settlement from the Early Bronze Age in East Jutland. *Journal of Danish Archaeology*, 2,: (1983), pp. 90-101.

Boas, N.A. 1986: Tidlige senneolitiske bosættelser på Djursland. In: Adamsen, C. & Ebbesen, K. (eds.) Stridsøksetid i Sydskandinavien. Beretning fra et symposium 28.-30. X. 1985 i Vejle. *Arkæologiske Skrifter*, 1. Copenhagen, pp. 318-324.

Boas, N.A. 1989: Bronze Age Houses at Hemmed Church, East Jutland. *Journal of Danish Archaeology*, 8, (1989), pp. 88-107.

Boas, N.A. 1993: Late Neolithic and Bronze Age Settlements at Hemmed Church and Hemmed Plantation, East Jutland. *Journal of Danish Archaeology*, 10, (1991), pp. 136-156.

Boas, N.A. 1997: Settlements and fields covered by sand drift in the Bronze Age, Djursland, East Jutland. In: Assendorp, J.J. (ed.) Forschungen zur bronzezeitlichen Besiedlung in Nord- und Mitteleuropa. Internationales Symposium vom 9.-11. Mai 1996 in Hitzacker. *Internationale Archaologie*, 38. Herausgegeben vom Institut zur Denkmalpflege im Niedersächsischen Landesverwaltungsamt und der Archaeologischen Kommission zur Niedersachsen e. V. Espelkamp, pp. 16-28.

Boddum, S. 2010: Møllegård, Klejtrup – boplads fra sen yngre stenalder og bronzealder. *Bygherrerapport, Viborg Stiftsmuseum*, nr. 44, pp. 1-14.

Boddum, S., Kieldsen, M., Larsen, L.A., & Terkildsen, K.F. 2015: Arkæologi i lange linjer. *Bygherrerapport, Viborg Stiftsmuseum*, nr. 80, pp. 1- 154.

Bohannan, P. 1955: Some Principles of Exchange and Investment among the Tiv. *American Anthropologist*, 57, 1, pp. 60-70.

Borup, P. (im manus.): (Article on Neolithic houses in the area of Horsens).

Bovin, M. 1965: Hvad øl betyder for mumuye stammen. *Jordens Folk*, 1, 3, pp. 85-91.

Brandt, E. 2006: 'Total War" and the Ethnography of New Guinea. In: Otto, T., Thrane, H. & Vandkilde, H. (eds.) *Warfare and Society. Archaeological and Social Anthropological Perspectives*. Aarhus, pp. 75-88.

Brink, K. 2013: Houses and Hierarchies: Economic and Social Relations in the Late Neolithic and Early Bronze Age of Southernmost Scandinavia. *European Journal of Archaeology*, vol. 16, issue 3, pp.433-458.

Bronk Ramsey, C., Dee, M., Lee, S., Nakagawa, T., & Staff, R. 2010: Developments in the calibration and modelling of radiocarbon dates. *Radiocarbon*, 52(3), 953-961.

Browne, K.E. 2009: Economics and Morality: Introduction. In: Browne, K. E. & Milgram, B. L. (eds.) *Economics and Morality. Anthropological Approaches*. Lanham/New York/Toronto/Plymouth, pp. 3-40.

Bruun, D. 1908: *Gammel Bygningsskik paa de islandske Gaarde: Arkæologiske Undersøgelser, 1-2*. Copenhagen.

Brøndsted, J. [1957] 1966a: *Danmarks Oldtid I. Stenalderen*. Copenhagen.

Brøndsted, J. [1957] 1966b: *Danmarks Oldtid II. Bronzealderen*. Copenhagen.

Burgess, C. & Shennan, S. 1976: The Beaker phenomenon: some suggestions. In: Burgess, C. & Miket, R. (eds.) Settlement and Economy in the Third and Second Millennia B.C. *British Archaeological Reports, British Series*, 33, pp. 309-325.

Burgess, C. 1980: *The Age of Stonehenge*. London.

Butler, J.J. 1975: Comments on The Flint Daggers of Denmark. Lomborg and Western Europe. *Norwegian Archaeological Review*, 8, 2, pp. 104-106.

Butler, J.J. & Van der Waals, J.D. 1966: Bell Beakers and early metal working in the Netherlands. *Palaeohistoria. Acta et Communicationes Instituti Bio-Acchaeologici Universitatis Groninganae*, XII. The Netherlands, pp. 41-139.

Buurman, J. 1990: Carbonised Plant Remains and Phosphate Analysis of two Roman period House Plans with sunken Byres at Oosterhout. *Berichten van de Rijksdienst voor het Oudheidkundig Bodemonderzoek*, 40 (1990), pp. 285-296.

Bönisch, E. 2001: Die ältesten Hornoer Häuser. Bronzezeitliche Gehöfte mit Speicherolatz auf der Hornoer Hochflache im Landkreis Spree-Neisse. *Archäologie in Berlin und Brandenburg*, 2001, pp. 59-63.

Callmer, J. 1973: Preliminary report on a complex of buildings from the Late Neolithic-Early Bronze Age at Norrvidinge, Scania. *Meddelanden från Lunds universitets historiska museum*, 1971-72. Lund, pp. 120-143.

Carrier, J.G. 2002: Exchange. In: Bamard, A. & Spencer, J. (eds.) *Encyclopedia of Social and Cultural Anthropology*. Routledge. London/New York, pp. 218-221.

Case, H. 2004: Beakers and the Beaker Culture. In: Czebreszuk, J. (ed.): *Similar but Different. Bell Beakers in Europe*. Poznań.

Cassau, A. 1935: Ein Feuersteindolch mit Holzgriff und und Lederscheide aus Wiepenkathen, Kreis Stade. *Mannus*, 37, pp. 199-209.

Champion, T.C. 1989: Introduction. In: Champion, T.C. (ed.) *Centre and periphery. Comparative Studies in Archaeology*. Cambridge, pp. 1-21.

Chapman, J. 1999: Deliberate house burning in the prehistory of Central and Eastern Europe. In: Gustafsson, A. & Karlsson, H. (eds.) *Glyfer och arkeologiska rum: en vänbok till Jarl Nordbladh*. Gothenburg, pp. 113-26.

Christensen, C. 1990: Stone Age Dug-out Boats in Denmark: Occurrence, Age, Form and Reconstruction. In: Robinson, D.E. (ed.) *Experimentation and Reconstruction in Environmental Archaeology*, pp. 119-141. Oxford.

Christensen, J.T., Cedhagen, T. & Hylleberg, J. 1998: Limfjordens naturforhold i fortiden – faunaændringer belyst ved subfossiler fra bjørnsholm Bugt. In: Lund, J. & Ringtved, J. (eds.) *Variation og enhed omkring Limfjorden. Rapport nr. 8. I. Rapport fra seminar afholdt 2.-3. november 1995 på Vitskøl Kloster*. Aarhus, pp. 223-234.

Christensen, M. 1996: Slid på flintredskaber fra bronzealderen. In: Nielsen J. & Simonsen, J. (eds.) *Bronzealderens bopladser i Midt- og Nordvestjylland*. Skive, pp. 76-89.

Clarke, D.V. 1976: Excavations at Skara Brae: a summary account. In: Burgess, C. & Miket, R. (eds.) Settlement and Economy in the Third and Second Millennia B.C. In: *British Archaeological Reports*, 33, pp. 233-249.

Clarke, D.V. & Sharples, N. 1990: Settlement and subsistence in the third millennium BC. In: Renfrew, C. (ed.): *The prehistory of Orkney*. Edinburgh, pp. 54-82.

Clastres, P. [1974] 1998: *Society against the State. Essays in Political Anthropology*. New York.

Coupland, G. & Banning, E.B. 1996: Introduction: The Archaeology of Big Houses. In: Coupland, G. & Banning, E.B. (eds*.)* People Who Lived in Big Houses. Archaeological Perspectives on Large Domestic Structures. *Monographs in World Archaeology*, 27. Wisconsin, pp. 1-9.

Craddock, P.T. 1995: *Early Metal Mining and Production*. Edinburgh, 1995.

Crumlin-Pedersen, O. 2003: The Hjortspring boat in a ship-archaeological context. In: Crumlin-Pedersen, O. & Trakades, A. (eds.) Hjortspring. A Pre-Roman Iron-Age Warship in Context. *Ships and Boats of the North,* 5. Roskilde, pp. 209-232.

Czebreszuk, J. 1996: *Społeczności Kujaw w początkach epoki brązu*. Poznań.

Czebreszuk, J. 1998: The North-eastern Borderland of the Bell Beakers. The Case of the Polish Lowland. In: Benz, M. & van Willingen, S. (eds.) Some New Approaches to The Bell Beaker "Phenomenon". Lost Paradise? Proceedings of the 2nd Meeting of the "Association Archéologie et Gobelets" Feldberg (Germany), 18th-20th

April 1997. *British Archaeological Reports, International Series*, 690, pp. 161-174.

Czebreszuk, J. 2001: *Schyłek neolitu i początki epoki brązu w strefie południowo-zachodniobałtyckiej (III i początki II tys. przed Chr.). Alternatywny model kultury.* Poznań.

Czebreszuk, J. & Szmyt, M. 2003: Introduction. In: Czebreszuk, J. & Szmyt, M. (eds.) *The Northeast Frontier of Bell Beakers. Proceedings of the symposium held at the Adam Mickiewicz University, Poznań (Poland), 26-29 May 2002.* Poznań, pp. 1-2.

Dalsgaard, K. 1985: Matrikelkortet fra 1844 anvendt til rekonstruktion af det udrænede landskab. En beskrivelse af terrænet omkring romertidsgravpladsen ved Himlingøje. *Aarbøger for nordisk Oldkyndighed og Historie,* 1984, pp. 283-302.

Dalton, G. 1981: Anthropological models in archaeological perspective. In: Hodder, I, Isaac, G. & Hammond, N. (eds.) *Pattern of the past. Studies in honour of David Clarke.* Cambridge, pp 17- 48.

Darvill, T. 1996: Neolithic buildings in England, Wales and the Isle of Man. In: Darvill, T. & Thomas, J. (eds.) *Neolithic Houses in Northwest Europe and Beyond. Neolithic Studies Group Seminar Papers,* 1. *Oxbow Monograph,* 57. Oxford, pp. 77-111.

Davidsen, K. 1982: Bronze Age Houses at Jegstrup, near Skive, Central Jutland. *Journal of Danish Archaeology,* 1, 1982, pp. 65-75.

Deetz, J. 1982: Households: A Structural Key to Archaeological Explanation. A*merican Behavioral Scientist* (special edition), 25, pp. 717-724.

Dilley, R. 1999: Introduction: The Problem of Context. In: Dilley, R.(ed.) *The Problem of Context.* New York/Oxford, pp. 1-46.

Dollar, S.R. 2013: Hustomter fra senneolitikum og tidligste bronzealder i Vejen Kommune. In: *Arkæologi i Slesvig / Archäologie in Schleswig* 14, 2012, pp. 39-49.

Douglas, M. [1975] 1984: Pollution. In: *Implicit meanings. Essays in Anthropology.* Oxford/New York, pp. 47-59.

Douglas, M. [1966] 2008: Introduction. In: *Purity and danger. An analysis of concept of pollution and taboo.* London/New York, pp. 1-35.

Downes, J. & Richards, C. 2000: Excavating the Neolithic and Early Bronze Age of Orkney: Recognition and Interpretation in the field. In: Richie, A. (ed.) *Neolithic Orkney in its European Context.* Cambridge, pp. 159-168.

Downes, J. & Richards, C. 2005: The Dwellings at Barnhouse. In: Colin Richards (ed.) Dwelling among the monuments: The Neolithic village of Barnhouse, Maeshowe passage grave and surrounding monuments at Stenness, Orkney. *McDonald Institute Monographs.* Cambridge, pp. 57-128.

Draiby, B. 1986: Fragtrup – en boplads fra yngre bronzealder i Vesthimmerland. *Aarbøger for nordisk Oldkyndighed og Historie,* 1985. Copenhagen, pp. 127-212.

Drenth. E. 2005: Het Laat-Neolithicum in Nederland. In: Deeben, J., Drenth, E., van Oorsouw, M.-F. & Verhart, L. (eds.). De Steentijd van Nederland. *Archeologie 11/12,* pp. 333-365.

Duncan, J.S. 1981: From Container of Women to Status Symbol: the Impact of Social Structure on the Meaning of the House. In: Duncan, J. S. (ed.): *Housing and Identity. Cross-Cultural Perspectives.* London, pp. 36-59.

Ebbesen, K. 1975: Comments on The Flint Daggers of Denmark. *Norwegian Archaeological Review,* 8, 2, pp. 107-111.

Ebbesen, K. 1978: Sikar og Klokkebægerkultur. *Holstebro Museum, Årsskrift* 1977, pp. 51-64.

Ebbesen, K. 1981: Klæstrup-fundet. Flintofre fra ældre bronzealder. V*endsysselske Årbøger,* 1981, pp. 41-46.

Ebbesen, K. 1984: Yngre neolitiske tap-stridsøkser. Nyt lys på enkeltgravtiden. *KUML 1982-1983. Årbog for Jysk Arkæologisk Selskab.* Aarhus, pp. 121-138.

Ebbesen, K. 1995: Spätneolithische Schmuckmode. *Acta Archaeologica,* 66. Copenhagen, pp. 219-279.

Ebbesen, K. 2004: En høj gruppen ved Kvindvad. Studier over senncolitisk tid. *KUML 2004. Årbog for Jysk Arkæologisk Selskab.* Aarhus, pp. 79-127.

Ebbesen, K. 2005: En senneolitisk stenkiste i Bjergby på Mors. *KUML* 2005. Årbog for Jysk Arkæologisk Selskab. Aarhus, pp. 61-74.

Emerson, R.M. 1976: Social Exchange Theory. *Annual Review of Sociology,* 2, pp. 335-62.

Ethelberg, P. 1987: Early Bronze Age Houses at Højgård, Southern Jutland. *Journal of Danish Archaeology,* 5, (1986), pp. 152-167.

Ethelberg, P. 1993a: Tre nye nordslesvigske fund fra ældre bronzealder. *Archaeologie in Schleswig,* 3, pp. 20-27.

Ethelberg, P. 1993b: Two more House Groups with Three-aisled long-houses from the Early Bronze Age at Højgård, South Jutland. *Journal of Danish Archaeology,* 10, 1991, pp. 136-156.

Ethelberg, P. 2000a: Bronzealderen. In: Ethelberg, P., Jørgensen, E., Meier, D., & Robinson, D.: Det sønderjyske landbrugs historie. Sten- og bronzealder. *Skrifter udgivet af Historisk Samfund for Sønderjylland,* 81. Haderslev, pp. 135-280.

Ethelberg, P. 2000b: Spätneolithische Häuser aus Schleswig. In: Kelm, R.(ed.) *Vom Phostenloch zum Steinzeithaus. Archäologische Forschung und Rekonstruktion jungsteinzeitlicher Haus- und Siedlungsbefunde im nordwestlichen Mitteleuropa.* Heide, 101-110.

Fenton, M.B. 1984: The nature of the source and the manufacture of Scottish battle-axes and axe-hammers. *Proceedings of the Prehistoric Society,* 50, pp. 217-243.

Ferguson, R.B. & Whitehead, N. 1992: The violent edge of empire. In: War in the Tribal Zone. *School of American Research Advanced Seminar Series.* Santa Fe, pp. 1-30.

Fokkens, H. 1999: Cattle and martiality: changing relations between man and landscape in the Late Neolithic and Bronze Age. In: Fabech, C. & Ringtved, J. (eds.) *Settlement and Landscape. Proceedings of a conference in Århus, Denmark, 1998*. Aarhus, pp. 35-45.

Fokkens, H. 2003: The Longhouse as a central element in Bronze Age daily life. In: Bourgeois, J. Bourgeois, I. & Cherretté, B. (eds.). *Bronze Age and Iron Age Communities in North-western Europe*. Brussel, pp. 9-38.

Forssander, J.E. 1936: *Der ostskandinavische Norden während der ältesten Metallzeit Europas*. Lund.

Fortes, M. [1958] 1971: Introduction. In: Goody, J. (ed.): *The Developmental Cycle in Domestic Groups*. Cambridge, pp. 1-14.

Frederiksen, E. 1976: *Skagafjorden og Glaumbær: En tørvegaard. Rejsestudier fra sommeren 1974*. Copenhagen.

Freeman, J.D. [1958] 1971: The Family System of the Iban of Borneo. In: Goody, J. (ed.): *The Developmental Cycle in Domestic Groups*. Cambridge, pp. 15-52.

Gerritsen, F. 1999: The Cultural biography of Iron Age houses and the long-term transformation of settlement patterns in the southern Netherlands. In: Fabech, C. & Ringtved, J. (eds.) *Settlement and Landscape. Proceedings of a conference in Århus, Denmark, May 4-7, 1998*. Jutland Archaeological Society. Aarhus, pp. 139-148.

Geertz, N. 2007: Nr. Uttrup – et langhus fra Senneolitikum. Årsberetning 2006. Nordjyllands Historiske Museum, pp. 32-34.

Gidlöf, K., Hammarstrand D.K., och Johansson, T. 2006: Almhov–Delområde 1. Rapport över arkeologisk slutundersökning. Senneolitikum och äldre bronsålder. *Citytunnelprojektet. Rapport nr.39*. Malmö, pp. 100-188.

Glob, P.V. 1945: Studier over den jyske Enkeltgravskultur. *Aarbøger for Nordisk Oldkyndighed og Historie*, 1944.

Glob, P.V. 1952: *Danish Antiquities II. Late Stone Age*. Mathiassen, T. (ed.). Compiled by the Staff of the National Museum. Nationalmuseet. Copenhagen.

Glob, P.V. 1971: *Højfolket*. Copenhagen.

Goody, J. [1958] 1971: The Fission of Domestic Groups among the Lodagaba. In: Goody, J. (ed.): *The Developmental Cycle in Domestic Groups*. Cambridge, pp. 53-91.

Greenfield, H.J. 1988: The Origins of Milk and Wool Production in the Old World. A Zooarchaeological Perspective from the Central Balkans. *Current Anthropology*, 29, 4, pp. 573-587.

Grierson, S. 1990: Traditional Scottish Dyestuffs and their Possible Identification from Archaeological Deposits. In Robinson, D.E. (ed.) Experimentation and Reconstruction in Environmental Archaeology. Symposia of the Association for Environmental Archaeology, No.9. Roskilde, Denmark 1988. *Oxbow Books*, Oxford, pp. 25-32.

Grundvad, L. 2014: *Beretning for større forundersøgelse af HBV 1220 Havgårdslund nær Gamst, Andst Sogn, Malt Herred, tidl. Ribe Amt, nu Region Syddanmark*. Museet på Sønderskov.

Grundvad, L. & Poulsen, M.E. 2013: Omvendte ofre. *Skalk*, 2013, 4, pp. 9-11.

Grundvad, L. & Poulsen, M.E. 2014: Nordens ældste væv. *Skalk*, 2014, 6, pp. 15-16.

Gräslund, B. 1973: Äring, näring, pest och salt. *TOR, Tidskrift för nordisk fornkunskap*, XV, 1973. Uppsala pp. 274-293.

Gräslund, B. 1974: Relativ datering. Om kronologisk metod i nordisk arkeologi. *TOR, Tidskrift för nordisk fornkunskap*, XVI, 1974. Uppsala.

Grøn, O. 2009: Analyse af flintspredninger på stenalderbopladser. In: Eriksen, B.V.(ed.) *Flintstudier. En håndbog i systematiske analyser af flintinventarer*. Aarhus, pp. 157-186.

Gyldion, Aa. 2004: Et hus fra slutningen af stenalderen, Dalsgaard II ca. 1880-1610 f. Kr. In: Gyldion, Aa., Jeppesen, J., & Lindholm, C. (eds.) *Oldtiden på Vej Mellem Riis & Ølholm. En række arkæologiske undersøgelser foretaget i forbindelse med Vejdirektoratets etablering af Riis-Ølholm Vejen*. Vejle, pp. 40-43.

Göthberg, H. Kyhlberg, O. & Vinberg, A. (eds.) 1995: Hus & gård i det förurbana samhället. Rapport från ett sektorsforskningsprojekt vid: Riksantikvarieämbetet. *Arkeologiska undersökningar. Skrifter*, 13. Stockholm.

Hagen, A. 1983: *Norges oldtid*. Oslo.

Hagen, A. 1985: Om ard, kornavl og bosetningsutvikling, *Viking*, 48. Oslo, pp. 44-69.

Hagen, A. 1987: Behov og vekst. Ekspansjon og arealbruk i Øst-Norge i neolitisk tid og bronsealder. *Viking*, 50. Oslo, pp. 37-64.

Halinen, P., Joensuu, J., Lavento, M., & Martio, L. 2002: House Pit Studies at Martinniemi in Kerimäki. In: Ranta, H. (ed.): *Huts and Houses. Stone Age and Early Metal Age Buildings in Finland*. Helsinki, pp. 201-210.

Hansen, H.-O. 1964: *Mand og hus*. Copenhagen.

Hansen, K.M. & Christiansen, D.V. 1997: Nymarksgård – Huse fra bondestenalderen og jordovne i hundredvis. *Kulturhistoriske studier*, 1997. Sydsjællands museum, pp. 60-79.

Hansen, M. & Rostholm, H. 1993: Single graves and Late Neolithic graves. In: Hvass, S. & Storgaard, B. (eds.), *Digging into the Past. 25 Years of Archaeology in Denmark*. The Royal Society of Northern Antiquaries/Jutland Archaeological Society. Copenhagen/Højbjerg, pp. 116-121.

Harrison, R.J. 1980: The Beaker Folk. Copper Age archaeology in Western Europe. *Ancient Peoples and Places*, 97. London.

Hastrup, F. 1964: Landsbyer med randbeliggenhed. Marskrandsbyer. In: Danske Landsbytyper. En geografisk analyse. *Skrifter fra Geografisk Institut ved Aarhus Universitet*, 14. Aarhus, pp. 214-237.

Hayden, B. & Cannon, A. 1982.: The Corporate Group as an Archaeological Unit. *Journal of Anthropological Archaeology*, 1. Washington, pp. 132-158.

Hayden, B.R. Gregory A. MacDonald, R. Holmberg, D. & Crellin, D. 1996: Space per Capita and the Optimal Size of Housepits. In: Coupland, Gary & Banning, E.B. (eds.)

People Who Lived in Big Houses: Archeological Perspectives on Large Domestic Structures. *Monographs in World Archaeology*, 27. Wisconsin, pp. 151-164.

Heinemeier, J. 2002: AMS ¹⁴C datings, Aarhus 2ool. (AUD) *Arkæologiske udgravninger i Danmark,* 2001. Copenhagen, pp. 263-292.

Helbling, J. 2006: War and Peace in Societies without Central Power: Theories and Perspectives. In: Otto, T., Thrane, H. & Vandkilde, H. (eds.) *Warfare and Society. Archaeological and Social Anthropological Perspectives.* Aarhus, pp. 113-139.

Hemdorff, O. 1993: Hus fra eldste bronsealder funnet på Talgje. *Fra haug ok heidni. Tidsskrift for Rogalands Arkæologiske Forening*, 4. Stavanger, pp. 24-26.

Henningsen, H. 2000: Middelalder i Fjald. *KUML* 2000. Årbog for Jysk Arkæologisk Selskab. Aarhus, pp. 151-198.

Henriksen, P.S. 1996: Oldtidens landbrug.- Forsøg med jernalderens agerbrug. In: Meldgaard, M. & Rasmussen, M. (eds.) *Arkæologiske eksperimenter i Lejre.* Lejre, pp. 65-72.

Hermanns-Audardóttir, M. 1989: Islands tidiga Bosättning. Studier med utgångspunkt i merovingertida-vikingatida gårdslåmningar i Herjólfsdalur, Vestmanaeyjar, Island. *Studia Archaeologica Universitatis Umensis, 1.* Umeå, pp. 1-184.

Hertz, E. 1997.: Vestervang-huset fra sen bondestenalder – et usædvanligt arkæologisk fund på motorvejen ved Vejen. *Mark og Montre* 1997, pp. 21-25.

Hesjedal, A., Damm, C., Olsen, B., & Storli, I. 1996: Tidlig metalltid. In: Arkeologi på Slettnes. Dokumentasjon av 11.000 års bosetning. *Tromsø Museums Skrifter,* XXVI. Tromsø, pp. 211-218.

Hill, J.D. 1995: 'Special', 'Structured' or 'Ritual' Deposition? In: Ritual and Rubbish in the Iron Age of Wessex. A study on the formation of a specific archaeological record. *British Archaeological Reports, British Series,* 242. Oxford.

Hingley, R. 1990: Domestic Organisation and Gender Relations in Iron Age and Romano-British Households. In: Samson, R. (ed.): *The Social Archaeology of Houses.* Edinburgh University Press, Edinburgh, pp. 125-148.

Hirsch, K. & Liversage, D. 1987: Ravforarbejdning i yngre stenalder. *Nationalmuseets Arbejdsmark,* 1987, pp. 193-200.

Hjärthner-Holdar 1977: Bennålar från yngre stenålder i Sverige. *TOR. Tidskrift för nordisk fornkunskap,* XVII, pp. 235-255.

Hodder, I. & Hutson, S. [1986] 1991: *Reading the past. Current approaches to interpretation in archaeology.* Cambridge.

Hodder, I. 2005: *Inhabiting Çatalhöyük – Reports from the 1995-99 Seasons.* Cambridge University. McDonald Institute for Archaeological Research. Cambridge.

Hodder, I. 2006: Çatalhöyük. *The Leopard's Tale – Revealing the Mysteries of Turkey's ancient 'town'.* London.

Hogestijn, J.W.H. & Drenth, E. 2000: The TRB culture 'house-plan' of Slootdorp-Bowlust and other known 'house plans' from the Dutch Middle and Late Neolithic, a review. In: Kelm, R.(ed.): *Vom Phostenloch zum Steinzeithaus. Archaeologische Forschung und Rekonstruktion jungsteinzeitlicher Haus- und Siedlungsbefunde im nordwestlichen Mitteleuropa.* Heide, pp. 126-154.

Hogestijn, J.W.H. & Drenth, E. 2001: In Slootdorp stond een Trechterbeker-huis? Over midden- en laat-neolitische huisplattengronden uit Nederland. *Archeologie,* 10, 2000/2001, pp. 42-79.

Hogestijn, J.W.H., Koudijs, W. & Bulten, E.E.B. 1994: Nieuwe Niedorp Zeewijk West en Zeewijk Oost, Nedersettingen van de Enkelgrafcultuur, Laat-neolithicum. *Rijkdienst voor het Oudheidkundig Bodemonderzoek,* (ROB), 1993, pp. 24-27.

Holm, J, Olsson, E. & Weiler, E. 1997: Kontinuität och förändring i senneolitikum. In: Larsson, M. & Olsson, E. Regionalt och interregionalt. Stenåldersundersökningar i Syd- och Mellansverige. Riksantikvarieämbetet. *Arkeologiska undersökningar. Skrifter,* 23, pp. 215-264.

Hornstrup, K.M., Overgaard, K.G., Andersen, S., Bennike, P., Mikkelsen, P.H. & Malmros, C. 2004: Hellegård – en gravplads fra omkring 500 f. Kr. *Aarbøger for Nordisk Oldkyndighed og Historie,* 2002. Copenhagen, pp. 83-162.

Hugh-Jones, C. 1995: Introduction: About the house – Levi-Strauss and Beyond. In: Carsten, J. & Hugh-Jones, S. (eds.). *About the House. Levi-Strauss and Beyond.* Cambridge, pp. 1-46.

Holsten, H. Kaphan-Herzfeld, R. Lucke, A. & Nikulka, F. 1991: Der Nachbau eines vorgeschichtlichen Langhauses am Hitzacker-See: archäologischer Befund und bauliche Rekonstruction. *Berichte zur Denkmalpflege in Niedersachsen,* 11, 2, pp. 64-67.

Holst, M.K. & Rasmussen, M. 2013: Herder Communities: Longhouses, Cattle and Landscape Organization in the Nordic Early and Middle Bronze Age. In: Bergerbrant, S. & Sabatini, S. (eds.) Counterpoint: Essays in Archaeology and Heritage Studies in Honour of Professor Kristian Kristiansen. *International Series 2508*, pp.99-110.

Hvass, S. 1978: A House of the Single- Grave Culture excavated at Vorbasse in Central Jutland. *Acta Archaeologica,* 48, pp. 219-232.

Hvass, S. 1985.: Hodde. Et vestjysk landsbysamfund fra ældre jernalder. *Arkæologiske Studier,* VII. Copenhagen.

Hübner, E. 2005: Jungneolithische Gräber auf der Jütischen Halbinsel. Typologische und chronologische Studien zur Einzelgrabkultur. *Nordiske fortidsminder, serie B,* 24: I-III. Det Kongelige Nordiske Oldskriftselskab. Copenhagen.

Højrup, o. 1980: *Landbokvinden. Rok og kærne. Grovbrød og vadmel.* Nationalmuseet. Copenhagen.

Ingold, T. 2000: The temporality of the landscape. In: The Perception of the Environment. Essays on livelihood, dwelling and skill. London, pp. 189-208.

Iversen, J. 1979: Yngre lindetid 3.000-500 f. Kr. Naturens udvikling siden sidste istid. In: Lundø, J. & Nørrevang, A. (eds.) *Danmarks Natur,* l, Copenhagen, (reprint 1979), pp. 407- 431.

Jaanusson, H. & Jaanusson, V. 1988: Sea-salts as a Commodity of Barter in the Bronze Age Trade of Northern Europe. In: Hårdh, B., Larsson, L., Olausson, D., & Petré (eds.) Trade and Exchange in Prehistory. Studies in Honor of Berta Stjernquist. *Acta Archaeologica Lundensia, Series in 8°*, 16. Lund, pp. 107-112.

Jensen, H.J. 1988: Plant Harvesting and Processing with Flint Implements in the Danish Stone Age. A View from the Microscope. *Acta Archaologica*, 59, pp. 131-142.

Jensen, H.J. 1990: Funktionsanalyse der bronzezeitlichen Flintmesser von Spjald und Stenild. *Acta Archaeologica*, 60. Copenhagen, pp. 209-214.

Jensen, H.J. 1994: *Flint tools and Plant Working. Hidden traces of Stone Age Economy*. Aarhus.

Jensen, H.J. 1996: En genvej til Danmarks ældste agerbrug.- Forsøg med kornsegle af flint. In: Meldgaard, M. & Rasmussen, M. (eds.) *Arkæologiske eksperimenter i Lejre*. Lejre, pp. 89-96.

Jensen, H.J. 2009: Slidsporsstudier – metoder til belysning af flintredskabers funktion. In: Eriksen, B. V. (ed.) *Flintstudier. En håndbog i systematiske analyser af flintinventarer*. Aarhus, pp. 207-218.

Jensen, J. 1979: Oldtidens samfund. Tiden indtil år 800. *Dansk social historie*, 1. Copenhagen.

Jensen, J. 1982: *The Prehistory of Denmark*. London/New York.

Jensen, J. [2001] 2006a: *Danmarks Oldtid. Stenalder 13.000-2.000 f. Kr*. Copenhagen.

Jensen, J. [2002] 2006b: *Danmarks oldtid. Bronzealder 2.000-500 f. Kr*. Copenhagen.

Jensen, J.A. 1973: Bopladsen Myrhøj. 3 hustomter med klokkebægerkeramik. *KUML* 1972, Årbog for Jysk Arkæologisk Selskab. Aarhus, pp. 61-122.

Jensen, J.A. 1984: Boplads under højen. En bronzealderhøj og en ny hustomt med klokkebægerkeramik. *FRAM – Fra Ringkøbing Amts Museer*. Ringkøbing, pp. 51-68.

Jensen, J.A. 1986: Bopladser fra enkeltgravskultur/senneolitikum på Ringkøbing-egnen. In: Adamsen, C. & Ebbesen, K. (eds.), Stridsøksetid i Sydskandinavien. Beretning fra et symposium 28.-30. X 1985 i Vejle, *Arkæologiske Skrifter*, 1. Copenhagen, pp. 169-174.

Jeppesen, J. 1984: A Late Neolithic/Early Bronze Age Settlement in Vejlby, East Jutland. *Journal of Danish Archaeology*, 3, (1984). Copenhagen, pp. 99-103.

Jespersen, S. 1961: Studier i Danmarks bønderbygninger (efter forfatterens død udgivet af Ester Andersen og Peter Michelsen). Nationalmuseet.

Jespersen, J.S. 1987: Et bidrag til bronzealderens byggeskik. In: Rigsantikvarens Arkæologiske Sekretariat (ed.) *Danmarks længste udgravning. Arkæologi på naturgassens vej 1979-86*. Nationalmuseet/de danske naturgasselskaber. Copenhagen, pp. 260-262.

Jessen, A. 1920: Stenalderhavets Udbredelse i det nordlige Jylland. *Danmarks geologiske Undersøgelse*, II, 35. Copenhagen.

Johansen, E. 1985: A Burial Mound with Culture Layers from the Early Bronze Age near Torslev, Northern Jutland. *Journal of Danish Archaeology*, 4. Copenhagen, pp. 115-120.

Johansen, E. 1986: Tre bosættelser fra sen enkeltgravskultur/tidlig senneolitikum ved Solbjerg, Østhimmerland. In: Adamsen, C. & Ebbesen, K. (eds.) Stridsøksetid i Sydskandinavien. Beretning fra et symposium 28.-30. X 1985 i Vejle. *Arkæologiske Skrifter*, 1. Copenhagen, pp. 280-285.

Johnson, T. & Prescott, C., 1993: Late Neolithic houses at Stokkset, Sande in Sunnmøre. *Arkeologiske Skrifter fra Historisk Museum, Universitetet i Bergen*. Bergen, pp. 70-89.

Johnson, M. 1990: The Englishman's Home and its Study. In: Samson, R. (ed.) *The Social Archaeology of Houses*. Edinburgh, pp. 245-258.

Jones, G. 1998: Distinguishing Food from Fodder in the Archaeobotanical Record. *Environmental Archaeology*, 1, (1998), pp. 95-98.

Jones, A. & Richards, C. 2005: Living in Barnhouse. In: Richards, C. (ed.) Dwelling among the monuments: The Neolithic village of Barnhouse, Maeshowe passage grave and surrounding monuments at Stenness, Orkney. *McDonald Institute Monographs Series*. Cambridge, pp. 23-52.

Jæger, A. & Laursen, J. 1983: Lindebjerg and Røjle Mose. Two Early Bronze Age Settlements on Fyn. *Journal of Danish Archaeology*, 2, (1983). Copenhagen, pp. 102-117.

Jørgensen, E. 1977: Hagebrogård – Vroue – Koldkur. Neolithische Gräber aus Nordwest-Jütland. *Arkæologiske Studier*, IV. Copenhagen.

Jørgensen, G. 1977: Fakta om korn. In: Dehn-Nielsen, H. (ed.) *Det Daglige Brød*. Nationalmuseet. Copenhagen, pp. 150-158.

Jørgensen, G. 1978: Acorns as a Food-Source in the Later Stone Age. *Acta Archaeologica*, 68. Copenhagen, pp. 233-238.

Jørgensen, L.B. 1992: *North European Textiles until AD 1000*. Aarhus University Press. Aarhus.: K: Kadrow, S. 1997: Korrespondenzanalyse und neue Aspekte der Chronologie der frühbronzezeitlichen Siedlung in Iwanowice bei Krakau (Polen). In: Müller, J. & Zimmermann, A. (eds.) Archaologie und Korrespondenzanalyse. Beispiele, Fragen, Perspektiven. *Internationale Archäologie*, 23. Rahden, pp. l37-146.

Kaelas, L. 1964: Senneolitikum i Norden. *TOR, Tidskrift för nordisk fornkunskap*, X. Uppsala, pp. l35-148.

Kamienska, J. & Kulczycka-Leciejewiczowa, A. 1970: The Bell Beaker Culture. In: Plater, K.(ed.): *The Neolithic in Poland*. Instytut Historii Kultury Materialnej Polskiej Akademii Nauk. Wroclaw/Warzawa/Kraków, pp. 366-382.

Kankaanpää, J. 2002: The House Pits at Kauvonkangas, Tervola. In: Ranta, H. (ed.): *Huts and Houses. Stone Age and Early Metal Age Buildings in Finland*. Helsinki, pp. 65-78.

Karsten, B. & Knarrström, B. 2000: En senneolitisk huslämning i Lilla Tvären. A*le, Historisk for Skåne, Halland och Blekinge*. Lund, pp. 23-29.

Katiskoski, K. 2002: The Semisubterranenan Dwelling at Kärmelahti in Puumala, Savo Province, Eastern Finland. In: Ranta, H. (ed.): *Huts and Houses. Stone Age and Early Metal Age Buildings in Finland*. Helsinki, pp. 171-200.

Kaul, F. 2004: Bronzealderens religion. Studier af den nordiske bronzealders ikonografi. *Nordiske Fortidsminder, Serie B*, 22. Copenhagen.

Keesing, R.M. & Strathern, A.J. 1998: *Cultural Anthropology: A Contemporary Perspective*. Orlando.

Khare, R.S 2010: Pollution and purity. In: Barnard, A. & Spencer, J. (eds.) *Enclyclopedia of social and cultural anthropology*. London/New York, pp. 437-439.

Kieldsen, M. 2010 : Løgstrup Nord – bebyggelse fra yngre stenalder til førromersk jernalder. *Bygherrerapport, Viborg Stiftsmuseum*, nr. 46, pp. 1-17.

Kieldsen, M. & Wåhlin, S. 2012: Bygdalgård – bebyggelse fra yngre stenalder til slutningen af bronzealderen. *Bygherrerapport, Viborg Stiftsmuseum*, nr. 62, pp. 1-16.

Klassen, L. 2005: Refshøjgård. Et bemærkelsesværdigt gravfund fra enkeltgravskulturen. *KUML* 2005. Årbog for Jysk Arkæologisk Selskab. Aarhus, pp. 17-59.

Koch, E. 1998: Neolithic Bog Pots from Zealand, Møn, Lolland and Falster. *Nordiske Fortidsminder. Serie B*, 16. Det Kongelige Nordiske Oldskriftselskab. Copenhagen.

Koch, E. 2001: Bijagt, biavl og biprodukter fra Nordeuropas bronzealder. *Aarbøger for Nordisk Oldkyndighed og Historie*, 2000. Copenhagen, pp. 7-54.

Kopytoff, I. [1986] 1992: The cultural biography of things: commoditization as process. In: Appadurai, A. (ed.) *The social life of things. Commodities in cultural perspective*. Cambridge.

Krause, R. 1997: Frühbronzezeitliche Grossbauten aus Bopfingen (Ostalpkreis, Baden- Wurttemberg). Ein Beitrag zu Hausbau und Siedlungsweise der Bronzezeit. In: Assendorp, J.J. (ed.) Forschungen zur bronzezeitlichen Besiedlung in Nord- und Mitteleuropa. Internationales Symposium vom 9.-11. Mai 1996 in Hitzacker. *Internationale Archaologie*, 38. Herausgegeben vom Institut zur Denkmalpflege im Niedersächsischen Landesverwaltungsamt und der Archaeologischen Kommission zur Niedersachsen e. V. Espelkamp, pp. 149-168.

Kristensson, A. Olson, C. & Welinder, S. 1996: Ecofacts Indicating Late Neolithic and Early Bronze Age Farming in Sweden. *TOR, Tidskrift för nordisk fornkunskap*, 28. Uppsala, pp. 53-67.

Kristiansen, K. 1974: En kildekritisk analyse af depotfund fra Danmarks yngre bronzealder (periode IV-V). Et bidrag til den arkæologiske kildekritik. *Aarbøger for Nordisk Oldkyndighed og Historie*, 1974. Copenhagen, pp. 119-160.

Kristiansen, K. 1978: The Application of Source Criticism to Archaeology. *Norwegian Archaeological Review*, 11, 1, pp. 1-5.

Kristiansen, K. 1985: Post-Depositional Formation Processes and the Archaeological Record. A Danish Perspective. In: Kristiansen, K (ed.) *Archaeological Formation Processes. The representativity of archaeological remains from Danish Prehistory*. Copenhagen, pp. 7-12.

Kristiansen, K. 1988: Landet åbnes. Den yngre bondestenalder 2800-1800 f. Kr. og bronzealderen 1800-500 f. Kr. In Bjørn, C. (ed.): *Det danske landbrugs historie*. Copenhagen.

Krzak, Z. 1976: *The Zlota Culture*. Wroclav/Warzawa/Kraków/Gdansk.

Kunwald, G. 1954: De ældste Vidnesbyrd om Ligbrænding i Danmarks Oldtid. *Dansk Ligbrændingsforening. Beretning for året 1954*. Copenhagen, pp. 71-109.

Kuhlmann, N. & Segschneider, M. 2004: Häuser, Gehofte und Siedlungen der Bronzezeit. In: Lehmann, T., von Schmettow, H. & Schmidt, J.-P. (eds.) Mythos und Magie. Archäologische Schätze der Bronzezeit aus Mecklenburg-Vorpommern. *Archäologie in Mecklenburg-Vorpommern*, 3, pp. 69-73.

Larsen, E.B. & Nielsen, S. 1987: Ædelt håndværk. Skalk 1987, 5. Aarhus, pp. 12-15.

Larsen, L.A. 2012: Abildal. En boplads fra sen yngre stenalder, samt brandgrave fra yngre bronzealder. *Bygherrerapport, Viborg Stiftsmuseum*, nr. 65, pp. 1-19.

Larsson, L. 1992: Settlement and environment during the Middle Neolithic and Late Neolithic. In: Larsson, L. Callmer, J. & Stjernquist, B. (eds.) The archaeology of the cultural landscape. Field work and research in a south Swedish rural region. *Acta Archaeologica Lundensia, Series in 4°*, 19. Lund, pp. 91- 159.

Larsson, M. 1991: The Neolithic. In: Berglund, B. E. (ed.) The cultural landscape during 6000 years in southern Sweden – the Ystad Project. *Ecological Bulletins*, 41. Lund, pp. 113-181.

Larsson, M. 1995: Förhistoriska och tidigmedeltida hus i sodra Sverige. In: Göthberg, H. Kyhlberg, O. & Vinberg, A. (eds.) Hus & gård i det förurbana samhället. Rapport från ett sektorsforskningsprojekt vid Riksantikvarieämbetet. *Arkeologiska undersökningar. Skrifter*, 13. Stockholm, pp. 23-64.

Larsson & Larsson 1984: Flintyxar, skoskav och massor av stolphål. Resultaten av arkeologisk inventering och undersökningsverksamhet under de två senaste åren i Ystadområdet. *Ystadiana*, 1984. Ystads Fornminnesförening, XXXI. Ystad.

Lekberg, P. 2000: The Lives and Lengths of Shaft-hole Axes. Social Daggers. In: Olausson, D. & Vandkilde. H. (eds.) Form, Function and Context. Material culture studies in Scandinavian archaeology. *Acta Archaeologica Lundensia*, Series in 8°, 31. Lund, pp. 155-161.

Lerche, G. & Steensberg, A. 1980: Agricultural Tools and Field Shapes. Twenty Five Years of Activity by the International Secretariat. *International Secretariat for Research on the History of Agricultural Implements. Publication*, 3. The National Museum. Copenhagen.

Leskinen, S. 2002: The Late Neolithic House at Rusavierto. In: Ranta, H. (ed.): *Huts and Houses. Stone Age and Early Metal Age Buildings in Finland*. Helsinki, pp. 147-170.

Liedgren, L. 1995: Förhistoriska bebyggelselämningar i Norrland. In: Göthberg, H. Kyhlberg, O. & Vinberg, A. (eds.): Hus & gård i det förurbana samhället. Rapport från ett sektorsforskningsprojekt vid Riksantikvarieämbetet. *Arkeologiska undersökningar. Skrifter,* 13. Stockholm, pp. 111-145.

Lindahl-Jensen, B. 1992: Valdemarsro – Från förundersökning till huvudundersökning, Arkeologi i Malmö. En presentation av ett antal undersökningar utförda under 1980-talet. *Stadsantikvariska avdelningen, Malmö Museer, rapport,* 4. Malmö, pp. 53-62.

Lindblom, I. 1982: Økologi og økonomi for deler av Sør-Jæren i sen-neolitikum. Del l. Rugland – en senneolitisk boplass på Jæren, Sørvest-Norge. A*mS-Skrifter* 9. Stavanger, pp. 15-31.

Lindman, G. 1988: Power and influence in the late Stone Age. A discussion of the interpretation of the flint dagger material. *Oxford Journal of Archaeology,* 2, 2. Oxford, pp. 121-138.

Liversage, D. 2003: Bell Beaker Pottery in Denmark – Its Typology and Internal Chronology. In: Czebreszuk, J. & Szmyt, M. (eds.) *The Northeast Frontier of Bell Beakers. Proceedings of the symposium held at the Adam Mickiewicz University, Poznań (Poland), May 26-29 2002,* pp. 39-50.

Liversage, D. & Robinson, D.E. 1995: Prehistoric Settlement and Landscape development in the Sandhill Belt of Southern Thy. *Journal of Danish Archaeology,* 11 (1992-93). Copenhagen, pp. 39-56.

Lomborg, E. 1969: Frühbronzezeitliche Trianguläre Metalldolche in Dänemark. *Acta Archaeologica,* 39. Copenhagen, pp. 219-239.

Lomborg, E. 1973a: Die Flintdolche Dänemarks. *Nordiske Fortidsminder. Serie B – in quarto,* l. Det Kongelige Nordiske Oldskriftselskab. Copenhagen.

Lomborg, E. 1973b: En landsby med huse og kultsted fra ældre bronzealder. *Nationalmuseets Arbejdsmark,* 1973. Copenhagen, pp. 5-14.

Lomborg, E. 1975a: The Flint Daggers of Denmark. Studies in Chronology and Cultural Relations of South Scandinavian Late Neolithic. *Norwegian Archaeological Review,* 8, 2, pp. 98-101.

Lomborg, E. 1975b: Reply to Comments. *Norwegian Archaeological Review,* 8, 2, pp. 115-124.

Lomborg, E. 1976: Vadgård. Ein Dorf mit Häusern und einer Kultstätte aus der älteren nordischen Bronzezeit. In: Mitcha-Märheim, H. (ed.) *Festschrift für Richard Pittioni. Archaeologica Austrica. Beiheft,* 13. Wien, pp. 414-432.

Lomborg, E. 1977: Klokkebæger- og senere Beaker-indflydelser i Danmark. Et bidrag til enkeltgravskulturens datering. *Aarbøger for Nordisk Oldkyndighed og Historie,* 1975. Copenhagen, pp. 20-41.

Lomborg, E. 1980: Bronzealderbopladserne ved Vadgård og Skamlebæk. In: Thrane, H. (ed.) Broncealderbebyggelse i Norden. *Odense Skrifter,* 28. Odense, pp. 122-126.

Lund, J. 1977: Overbygård – en jernalderlandsby med neddybede huse. *KUML* 1976. Årbog for Jysk Arkæologisk Selskab. Aarhus, pp. 129-150.

Lund, J. 1984: Nedgravede huse og kældre i ældre jernalder. *Hikuin,* 10. Højbjerg, pp. 57-82.

Lund, J. 1998: Oldtidsbebyggelsen i Limfjordsområdet. In: Lund, J. & Ringtved, J. (eds.) *Variation og enhed omkring Limfjorden. Rapport* nr. 8, I. Rapport fra seminar afholdt 2.-3.november 1995 på Vitskøl Kloster. Aarhus, pp. 141-188.

Lund, J. & Ringtved, J. (eds.): *Variation og enhed omkring Limfjorden. Rapport* nr.8, I-II. Rapport fra seminar afholdt 2.-3.november 1995 på Vitskøl Kloster. Aarhus.

Løken, T. 1998a: The longhouses of Western Norway from the Late Neolithic to the 10th Century AD: representatives of a common Scandinavian building tradition or a local development? In: Helge Schjelderup & Ola Storsletten (eds.) *Grindbygde hus i Vest-Norge. NIKU-seminar om grindbygde hus. Bryggens Museum 23-25.03.98.* Trondheim, pp. 52-61.

Løken, T. 1998b: Det forhistoriske huset i Rogaland – belyst ved flateavdekkende utgravninger. *Bebyggelseshistorisk tidsskrift,* 33, 1997, pp. 169-184.

Machnik, J. 1977: Frühbronzezeit Polens (Übersicht über die Kulturen und Kulturgruppen). *Polska Akademia Nauk – Odzial w Krakowi: Prace Komisji Archeologicznej,* 15. Wroclav/Warzawa/Kraków/Gdansk.

Madirazza, L. 1974: Undergrunden ved Mønsted. *MIV* 4, 1974. Museerne i Viborg amt. Viborg, pp. 12-15.

Madsen, T. 1978: Perioder og periodeovergange i neolitikum.- Om forskellige fundtypers egnethed til kronologiske opdelinger. *Hikuin* 4, 51-60.

Madsen, T. 1988: Determining priorities in archaeology – an introduction to a debate. (AUD) *Arkæologiske udgravninger i Danmark,* 1987. Copenhagen, pp. 24-27.

Madsen, T. 1989: Seriation – en grundlæggende arkæologisk arbejdsmetode. *KARK. Nyhedsbrev,* 3. Aarhus, pp. 8-19.

Madsen, B. 1993: Flint – extraction, manufacture and distribution. In: Hvass, S. & Storgaard, B. (eds.) *Digging into the Past. 25 Years of Archaeology in Denmark.* The Royal Society of Northern Antiquaries/Jutland Archaeological Society. Copenhagen/Højbjerg, pp. 126-129.

Magnus, B. & Myhre, B. 1976: Norges Historie. Oslo.

Magnusson, M. 1949: Wulstkeramik in skandinavischen Funden aus dem Spätneolithikum. Meddelanden från Lunds Universitets historiska Museum, 1949. Lund, pp. 269-278.

Makarowicz, P. 1998: Roła społeczności Kultury Iwieńskiej w genezie Trzcinieckiego Kręgu Kulturowego (2000-1600 BC). *Materialy do syntezy pradziejów Kujaw,* 8. Poznań.

Makarowicz, P. 1999: The emergence of the Trzciniec Cultural Circle in the western zone of the Polish lowlands (2000-1600 BC). In: Bátora, J. & Peška J. (eds.). Aktuelle Probleme der Erforschung der Frühbronzezeit in Böhmen und Mähren und in der Slowakei. *Nitra* (1999), pp. 75-85.

Makarowicz, P. 2000: Osadnictwo społeczności z wczesnej epoki brazu w Rybinach. Woj. Kujawsko-Pomorskie Stanowisko 17. *Sources for studies of prehistoric Kujaw,* 14. Poznań.

Makarowicz, P. 2003: Northern and Southern Bell Beakers in Poland. In: Czebreszuk, J. & Szmyt, M. (eds.) The Northeast Frontier of Bell Beakers. Proceedings of the symposium held at the Adam Mickiewicz University, Poznań (Poland), 26-29 May 2002. Poznań, pp. 137-154.

Makarowicz, P. 2005: Gesellschaftliche Strukturen der Glockenbecherkultur im Gebiet zwischen Weichsel und Oder. *EAZ, Ethnographische – Archäologische Zeitschrift,* 46, pp. 27-58.

Makarowicz, P. 2010: Trzciniecki krąg kulturowy – wspólnota pogranicza Wschodu i Zachodu Europy. Summary Trzciniec Cultural Circle. A community of the Borderland between the East and the West of Europe. *Archaeologia Bimaris. Monografie,* 3. Poznań.

Makarowicz, P. & Milecka, K. 1999: Society and environment: a case study of Early Bronze Age settlement complex from Rybiny, Kujawy, Poland. *Archaeologia Polona,* 37, pp. 49-70.

Malinowski, B. [1922] 1984: *Argonauts of the Western Pacific. An Account of Native Enterprise and Adventure in the Archipelagoes of Melanesian New Guinea.* Illinois.

Malmer, M.P. 1963: Metodproblem inom järnålderns konsthistoria. *Acta Archaeologica Lundensia. Series in 8°,* 3. Lund.

Malone, C. 2001: *Neolithic Britain and Ireland.* Gloucestershire.

Mannering, U. & Skals, I. 2013: Stenaldertekstilerne i Nationalmuseets Komparative Samling. *Nationalmuseets Arbejdsmark* 2013, pp. 80-95.

Mathiassen, Th. 1948: Studier over Vestjyllands Oldtidsbebyggelse. *Nationalmuseets Skrifter. Arkæologisk-Historisk Række,* 11. Copenhagen.

Matthias, W. 1976: Die Salzproduktion – ein bedeutender Faktor in der Wirtschaft der frühbronzezeitlichen Bevölkerung an der mittleren Saale. *Jahresschrift für mitteldeutsche Vorgeschichte,* 60. Halle, pp. 373-394.

Mauss, M. [1924 (French); 1950] 1997: *The gift. The form and reason for exchange in archaic societies* (with foreword by Mary Douglas). London.

McGrail, S. 1998: Ancient Boats in North-West Europe. The Archaeology of Water Transport to AD 1500. *Longman Archaeology Series.:* : Mertz, E.L. 1924: Oversigt over de sen- og postglaciale Niveauforandringer i Danmark. *Danmarks geologiske Undersøgelse,* II, 41. Copenhagen.

Michaelsen, K.K. 1989: En senneolitisk hustomt fra Vendsyssel. *KUML* 1987. Årbog for Jysk Arkæologisk Selskab. Aarhus, pp. 77-86.

Miettinen, M. 2002.: Investigations at the Madeneva Stone Age Site in Pihtipudas. In: Ranta, H. (ed.) *Huts and Houses. Stone Age and Early Metal Age Buildings in Finland.* Helsinki, pp. 137-146.

Mikkelsen, M. 1996a: De 3-skibede bronzealderhuse i Viborg Amt. In: Nielsen J. & Simonsen, J. (eds.) *Bronzealderens bopladser i Midt- og Nordvestjylland.* Skive, pp. 34-59.

Mikkelsen, M. 1996b: Bronzealderbosættelserne på Åshøjderyggen i Thy. In: Nielsen, J. & Simonsen, J. (eds.) *Bronzealderens bopladser i Midt- og Nordvestjylland.* Skive, pp. 110-123.

Mikkelsen, M. 2013: The topographical placing of the Late Neolithic and Bronze Age settlements and an introduction to a new interpretation of the layout of the individual farms in the Bronze Age. Siedlungen der älteren Bronzezeit. Beiträge zur Siedlungsarchäologie und Paläoökologie des zweiten vorchristlichen Jahrtausends in Südskandinavien, Norddeutschland und den Niederlanden. Workshop vom 7. Bis 9. April 2011 in Sankelmark herausgegeben von Karl-Heinz Willroth. *Studien zur nordeuropäischen Bronzezeit,* 1, pp. 33-66..

Mikkelsen, P. 1996: Gruber, fund samt aspekter af økonomien på bopladserne. In: Nielsen, J. & Simonsen, J. (eds.) *Bronzealderens bopladser i Midt- og Nordvestjylland.* Skive, pp. 64-75.

Mikkelsen, P. 1995: Tidlige bronzealderhuse ved Trængsel Holstebro Museum Årsskrift 1995. Holstebro, pp. 21-26.

Mikkelsen, M. & Simonsen, J. 1998: Projekt "Bronzealderbopladser i Viborg amt" – resultater og perspektiver. *Limfjordsprojektet, Rapport,* 8, Århus, pp. 261-269.

Mikkelsen, P. & Simonsen, J. 2000: Husene ved Resengaard. In: Steen Hvass & Det arkæologiske Nævn (eds.) *Vor skjulte kulturarv. Arkæologien under overfladen.* Det Kongelige Nordiske Oldskriftselskab/Jysk Arkæologisk Selskab. Copenhagen, pp. 64-65.

Mitchell, J.P. 2002: Ritual. In: Barnard, A. & Spencer, J. (eds.) *Encyclopaedia of social and cultural Anthropology.* London/New York, pp. 490-493.

Mouritsen, O.G. 2009: Tang – i menneskets tjeneste. *Aktuel Naturvidenskab. Biokemi og ernæring,* 6, pp. 6-11.

Müller, A. 1997: Die Anwendung der Korrespondenzanalyse anhand der Grabfunde der Glockenbecherkultur in Bayern. In: Müller, J. & Zimmermann, A. (eds.), Archäologie und Korrespondenzanalyse. Beispiele, Fragen, Perspektiven. *Internationale Archäologie,* 23. Rahden, pp. 115-128.

Müller, S. 1888: *Ordning af Danmarks Oldsager. Stenalderen.* Copenhagen.

Müller, S. 1897: *Vor Oldtid. Danmarks forhistoriske Archæologi.* Copenhagen.

Müller, S. 1902: Flintdolkene i den nordiske Stenalder. *Nordiske Fortidsminder,* I. Det Kongelige Nordiske Oldskriftselskab. Copenhagen.

Müller, S. 1918: *Stenalderens Kunst i Danmark.* Copenhagen.

Mydland, L. 1996: Resultater fra de arkeologiske utgravingene. Lok. 27, Rennesøy. In: Høgestøl, M. (ed.) Arkeologiske undersøkelser i Rennesøy Kommune, Rogaland, Sørvest-Norge. *AMS-Varia,* 23. Stavanger, pp. 125-132.

Myhre, B. 1999: Together or apart – the problem of nucleation and dispersal of settlements. In: Fabech, C. & Ringtved, J. (eds.) *Settlement and Landscape. Proceedings of a conference in Århus, Denmark, 1998.* Aarhus, pp. 125-130.

Møbjerg, T. & Mikkelsen, P.H. 2005: Enkehøj. En boplads med forkullet korn og klokkebægerkeramik i Midtjylland. *Herning Museum – Midtjyske fortællinger*, 2005. Herning, pp. 17-28.

Møbjerg, T., Jensen, P.M., & Mikkelsen, P.H. 2007: Enkehøj. En boplads med klokkebægerkeramik og korn. *KUML 2007. Årbog for Jysk Arkæologisk Selskab*. Aarhus, pp. 9-45.

Møller, J.T. 1982: Shoreline variations on a Danish North Sea Coast. *Geoskrifter*, 7. Aarhus, pp. 1-34.

Møllgaard, J. 1997: Bønder og handel i Salling 1680-1780. In: Poulsen, B. (ed.) Bonde og marked i 1700-tallet. *Bol og By. Landbohistorisk tidsskrift*, 2. Aarhus, pp. 48-77.

Nadler, M. 1997: Langhäuser der Frühbronzezeit in Süddeutschland. Endglieder neolithischer Bautradition? *Vorträge des 15. Niederbayerischen Archaeologentages in Deggendorf 1997*. Deggendorf, pp. 161-188.

Nadler, M. 2000: Aktuelles zur Frühbronzezeit und frühen Mittelbronzezeit im nordlichen Alpenvorland. Rundgespräch Hemmenhofen 6. Mai 2000. *Hemmenhofener Skripte*, 2. Schriften der Arbeitsstelle Hemmenhofen des Landesdenkmalamtes Baden-Württemberg. Freiburg, pp. 39- 46.

Nicolas, C. 2011: Artisanat spécialisés et inégalités sociales à l'aube de la métallurgie: les pointes de flèches de type armoricain dans le nord du Finistère. *Bulletin de la Société préhistorique française*, 108, 1, pp. 1-33.

Nielsen, B.T. & Rasmussen, L.W. 2013: Huse og høj ved Ørum Djurs. Årbog 2012 Museum Østjylland, pp. 38-45.

Nielsen, F.O. & Nielsen, P.-O. 1985: Middle and Late Neolithic Houses at Limensgård, Bornholm. A Preliminary Report. *Journal of Danish Archaeology*, 4 (1985). Copenhagen, pp. 101-114.

Nielsen, F.O. & Nielsen, P.-O. 1986: En boplads med hustomter fra mellem- og senneolitikum ved Limensgård, Bornholm. In: Adamsen, C. & Ebbesen, K. (eds.) Stridsøksetid i Sydskandinavien. Beretning fra et symposium 28.-30. X. 1985 i Vejle. *Arkæologiske Skrifter*, 1. Copenhagen, pp. 175-193.

Nielsen, J. 1996: Keramikken på bronzealderbopladserne. In: Nielsen, J. og Simonsen, J. (eds.) *Bronzealderens bopladser i Midt- og Nordvestjylland*. Skive, pp. 60-63.

Nielsen, J.N. 2000: Flintsmedens boplads. In: Steen Hvass & Det arkæologiske Nævn (eds.) *Vor skjulte kulturarv. Arkæologien under overfladen*. Det Kongelige Nordiske Oldskriftselskab & Jysk Arkæologisk Selskab. Copenhagen/Aarhus, pp. 6-47.

Nielsen, J.N. 2004: En bebyggelse fra stenalderens slutning. *Nordjyllands Historiske Museum, Årbog 2003*, pp. 16-18.

Nielsen, L.E. 2010: Ikeagrundens forhistorie. *Nordjyllands Historiske Museum, Årbog 2009*, pp. 45-50.

Nielsen, P.-O. 1998: De såkaldte 'madknive' af flint. *Aarbøger for nordisk Oldkyndighed og Historie*, 1974, pp. 104-118.

Nielsen, P.-O. 1998: De ældste langhuse. Fra toskibede til treskibede huse i Norden. Hus och tomt i Norden under förhistorisk tid. *Bebyggelseshistorisk tidskrift*, 33, (1997). Stockholm, pp. 9-30.

Nielsen, P.-O. 1999: Limensgård and Grødsbygård. Settlements with house remains from the Early, Middle and Late Neolithic on Bornholm. In: Fabech, C. & Ringtved, J. (eds.) *Settlement and Landscape. Proceedings of a Conference in Århus, Denmark, 1998*. Aarhus, pp. 149-165.

Nielsen, P.-O. 2000: Neolithic. (AUD) *Arkæologiske udgravninger i Danmark 1999*. Copenhagen, pp. 83-87.

Nielsen, P.-O. 2001: The Neolithic. (AUD) *Arkæologiske udgravninger i Danmark 2000*. Copenhagen, pp. 91-95.

Nielsen, S. 1977: En skibsformet grav fra den ældre bronzealder. *Antikvariske studier*, 1. Miljøministeriet, Skov- og Naturstyrelsen. Copenhagen, pp. 79-88.

Nielsen, S. 1987: Huller i jorden. In: Rigsantikvarens Arkæologiske Sekretariat (ed.) *Danmarks længste udgravning. Arkæologi på naturgassens vej 1979-86*. Nationalmuseet og de danske naturgasselskaber. Copenhagen, pp. 87-93.

Nielsen, S. 1999: The Domestic Mode of Production – and Beyond. An archaeological inquiry into urban trends in Denmark, Iceland and Predynastic Egypt. *Nordiske Fortidsminder, serie B*, 18. Det Kongelige Nordiske Oldskriftselskab. Copenhagen.

Nielsen, S. 2010: The Socio-economy of an Urban Site. Ribe Excavations 1970-76. Jutland Archaeological Society. Aarhus, pp. 161-262.

Nielsen, S. & Simonsen, J. 1987: Enkeltgravshøje. In: Ingrid Nielsen (red.) *Bevar din arv. 1937 – Danmarks fortidsminder – 1987*. Copenhagen, pp. 194-199.

Nielsen, T.B. 2012: Flintpladser ved Neden Skiden Enge. *Museum Østjylland, Randers Djursland. Årbog 2012*. Randers, pp. 21-29.

Nielsen, T.B. & Rasmussen, L.W. 2012: Huse og høj ved Ørum Djurs. *Museum Østjylland, Randers Djursland. Årbog 2012*. Randers, pp. 38-45.

Nielsen, V. 1993: *Jernalderens pløjning. Store Vildmose*. Vendsyssel historiske Museum. 1993

Nikulka, F. 1991: Drei Hausgrundrisse vom mehrphasigen Siedlungsplatz Hitzacker-See, Ldkr. Lüchow-Dannenberg. Vorbericht zu den Grabungskampagnen 1989 und 1990. *Nachrichten aus Niedersachsens Urgeschichte*, 60. Stuttgart, pp. 89-99.

Nyegaard, G. 1995: Animal Bones from an Early Bronze Age Midden Layer at Torslev, Northern Jutland. *Journal of Danish Archaeology*, 11 (1992-93). Copenhagen, pp. 108-110.

Odgaard, B.V. 1994: Vegetationshistorie i det nordlige Vestjylland siden sidste istid. (Danish summary of:) The Holocene vegetation history of northern West Jutland, Denmark. *Opera Botanica*, 123. Copenhagen, pp. 3-22.

Ojanlatva, E. & Alakärppä, J. 2002: Interpratation of the Peurasuo House Pit in Oulu. In: Ranta, H. (ed.) *Huts and Houses. Stone Age and Early Metal Age Buildings in Finland*. Helsinki, pp. 109-122.

Olausson, D. 1997: Craft Specialisation as an Agent of Social Power in the South Scandinavian Neolithic. In:

Schild, R. & Sulgostowska, Z. (eds.) *Man and Flint. Proceedings of the VIIth International Flint Symposium. Warszawa – Ostrowiec Swietokrzyski. September 1995.* Institute of Archaeology and Ethnology. Polish Academy of Sciences. Warszawa, pp. 269-277.

Olausson, D. 2000: Talking Axes. Social Daggers. In: Olausson, D. & Vandkilde. H. (eds.) Form, Function and Context. Material culture studies in Scandinavian archaeology. *Acta Archaeologica Lundensia*, Series in 8°, 31. Lund,: pp. 121-133.

Olesen, A.H. & Kjær, O.V. 1972: *Thverá – en islandsk tørvegård.* Efterord: Stefan Ørn Stefansson. Copenhagen.

Olesen, L.H. & Skov, T. 1989: *Oldtidsvejen fra Vesterhavet til Karup Å. En registrering af vejforløbets historie og nuværende tilstand.* Rapport udarbejdet af Holstebro Museum for Ringkøbing amtskommune (Teknik- og miljøforvaltningen). Ringkøbing.

Overgaard, K.G. 2003.: Lundbro – boplads gennem 10.000 år. Skivebogen 2003. *Historisk Aarbog for Skive og Omegn.* Skive, pp. 123-130.

Pearson, M.P. & Richards, C. [1994] 1997: Ordering the World: Perceptions of Architecture, Space and Time. In: Pearson, M. P. & Richards, C. (eds.) *Architecture and Order. Approaches to Social Space.* London/New York, pp. 87- 97.

Pedersen, V.J. 2006: Gilmosevej. Foreløbig analyse af bopladsspor fra yngre stenalder og bronzealder. *Herning Museum – Midtjyske fortællinger* 2006. Herning, pp. 27-34.

Penney, D. 1992: Sejlruter fra Limfjorden: forbindelser til Nordsøen i Holocænet belyst ved makrofossilanalyser. In: Kommunikation ved Limfjorden fra fortid til nutid. *Rapport fra seminar afholdt 2.- 3.maj 1991 i Egense. Rapport*, 5. Aarhus, pp. 31-44.

Pesonen, P. 2002: Semisubterranean Houses in Finland – a Revlew. In: Ranta, H. (ed.) *Huts and Houses. Stone Age and Early Metal Age Buildings in Finland.* Helsinki, pp. 9-41.

Petersen, K.S. 1992: Den yngre geologiske historie i det østlige Limfjordsområde. *Kommunikation ved Limfjorden fra fortid til nutid.* Rapport fra seminar afholdt 2.-3.maj 1991 i Egense. Rapport, nr. 5, Århus, 13-18.

Petersen, K.S. 1976: Om Limfjordens postglaciale marine udvikling og niveauforhold, belyst ved mollusk-faunaen og C-14 dateringer, *Danmarks Geologiske Undersøgelse. Årbog* 1975, pp. 75-103

Petersen, K.S. & Burfelt, K. 1998: Det naturgivne rum. In: Lund, J. & Ringtved, J. (eds.) *Variation og enhed omkring Limfjorden. Rapport nr. 8. II. Rapport fra seminar afholdt 2.-3.november 1995 på Vitskøl Kloster.* Aarhus, 189-197.

Petersen, P.V. 1999: Flint fra Danmarks oldtid. Copenhagen.

Pettersson, C.B. 2000.: I skuggan av Karaby Backar. Boplatslämningar från senneolitikum till folkvandringstid. Skåne, Västra Karaby sn, RAÄ 35, Västra Karaby 2:21. *Riksantikvarieämbetet, UV Syd Rapport,* 2000:103. Lund, pp. 5-67.

Poulsen, M.E. 2008: Kongehøj Etape II, Arkæologiske undersøgelser af bebyggelse fra bondestenalder og bronzealder. *Bygherrerapport for HBV,* j.nr. 1275. Museet på Sønderskov, pp. 1-7.

Poulsen, M.E. 2009: De monumentale midtsulehuse fra senneolitikum og tidligste bronzealder i Sydskandinavien. *Vitark 6: Acta archaeologica Nidrosiensia.* Det 10. nordiske bronsealder-symposium. Trondheim 5.-8- oktober 2006, pp. 156-168.

Poulsen, M.E. 2014: *Beretning for arkæologisk forundersøgelse af HBV j.nr. 1490 Kongeengen, Askov by matr.nr. 14a & 12i, Malt sogn, Malt herred, gl. Ribe amt, Region Syddanmark.* Museet på Sønderskov.: Poulsen, M.E. 2015: *Kulturhistorisk rapport for forundersøgelse af HBV 1466 Lille Tornumgård etape II.* Museet på Sønderskov, pp. 1-14.

Povlsen, K. 2014: Mølledalsgård, Korup. Boplads fra tidlig bondestenalder, sen bondestenalder og yngre middelalder. *Kulturhistoriske rapporter ved Nordjyllands Historiske Museum* 28, pp. 1-7.

Prieto-Martinez, M.P. 2008: Bell Beaker Communities in Thy: The First Bronze Age Society in Denmark. *Norwegian Archaeological Review,* 41, 2, pp. 115-158.

Prieto-Martinez, M.P. 2009: Reply to Comments from Marc Vander Linden, Helle Vandkilde, Premyslaw Makarowicz, Janusz Czebrezuk, Einar Østmo, and Christopher Prescott and Lene Melheim. *Norwegian Archaeological Review,* 42, 1, pp. 93-100.

Rahbek, U., Rasmussen, K.L. & Vandkilde, H. 1996.: Radiocarbon Dating and the Chronology of Bronze Age Southern Scandinavia. *Acta Archaeologica,* 67, pp. 183-198.

Randsborg, K. 1990: The Periods of Danish Antiquity. *Acta Archaeologica,* 60. Copenhagen, pp. 187-192.

Randsborg, K. 1996: The Nordic Bronze Age: Chronological Dimensions. *Acta Archaeologica,* 67. Copenhagen, pp. 61-72.

Rankama, T. 2002: Analyses of the Quartz Assemblages of Houses 34 and 35 at Kauvonkangas in Tervola. In: Ranta, H. (ed.) *Huts and Houses. Stone Age and Early Metal Age Buildings in Finland.* Helsinki, pp. 79-108.

Rapoport, A. 1969: Socio-cultural factors and house form. *House, Form and Culture.* New Jersey, 46-82.

Rasmussen, K.L. 1992: Danish radiocarbon datings of archaeological samples, Copenhagen 1991. (AUD) *Arkæologiske udgravninger i Danmark* 1991. Copenhagen, pp. 263-292.

Rasmussen, K.L. 1999: New archaeometric method for determining the provenance of pottery. (AUD) *Arkæologiske udgravninger i Danmark* 1998. Copenhagen, pp. 23-26.

Rasmussen, L.A. Bahnson, H. Mikkelsen, N., Nielsen, A.V. & Petersen, K.S. 1979.: Om den geologiske kortlægning af Fjendsområdet i 1978. *Danmarks Geologiske Undersøgelse.: Årbog,* 1978, pp. 105-118.

Rasmussen, L.A. & Petersen, K.S. 1980: Resultater fra DGU's genoptagne kvartærgeologiske kortlægning, *Dansk geologisk Forening. Årskrift for* 1979, pp. 47-54.

Rasmussen, L.W. 1990: Dolkproduktion og -distribution i senneolitikum. *Hikuin*, 16, pp. 31-42.

Rasmussen, M. & Adamsen, C. 1993: Settlement. In: Hvass, S. & Storgaard, B. (eds.) *Digging into the Past. 25 Years of Archaeology in Denmark*. The Royal Society of Northern Antiquaries & Jutland Archaeological Society. Copenhagen/Højbjerg, pp. 136-141.

Rasmussen, M. 1993a: Bopladskeramik i Ældre Bronzealder. *Jysk Arkæologisk Selskabs Skrifter*, XXIX. Højbjerg.

Rasmussen, M. 1993b: Bopladsstruktur og økonomisk variation i ældre bronzealder – set fra et par nordjyske bopladser. In: Forsberg, L. & Larsson, T. B. (eds.) Ekonomi och näringsformer i nordisk bronsålder. Rapport från det 6:e nordiska bronsålderssymposiet, Nämforsen 1990. *Studia archaeologica universitas Umensis*, 3. Umeå, pp. 11-26.

Rasmussen, M. 1995: Settlement Structure and Economic Variation in the Early Bronze Age. *Journal of Danish Archaeology*, 11, 1992-93, pp. 77-107.

Rasmussen, M. 1999: Livestock without bones. The longhouse as contributor to the interpretation of livestock management in the Southern Scandinavian Early Bronze Age. In: Fabech, C. & Ringtved, J. (eds.) *Settlement and Landscape. Proceedings of a Conference in Århus, Denmark 1998*. Højbjerg, pp. 281-290.

Rathje, W. & Murphy, C. [1992] 2001: *Rubbish! The Archaeology of Garbage*. With a new preface by the authors. Tucson.

Reimer, P.J., Bard, E., Bayliss, A., Beck, J.W., Blackwell, P.G., Bronk Ramsey, C., Buck, C.E., Cheng, H., Edwards, R.L., Friedrich, M., Grootes, P.M., Guilderson, T.P., Haflidason, H., Hajdas, I., Hatté, C., Heaton, T.J., Hoffmann, D.L., Hogg, A. G., Hughen, K.A., Kaiser, K.F., Kromer, B., Manning, S.W., Niu, M., Reimer, R.W., Richards, D. A., Scott, E.M., Southon, J.R., Staff, R.A., Turney, C.S.M., & Plicht, J. V. D. & Reimer, P.J. (ed.) 2013: IntCal13 and Marine13 Radiocarbon Age Calibration Curves 0–50,000 Years cal BP. *Radiocarbon*, 55, 4, pp. 1869-1887.

Reinhold, S. 1997: Zeit oder Sozialstruktur? Bemerkungen zur Anwendung von Korrespondenzanalysen bei der Untersuchung prähistorischer Grabfunde. In: Müller, J. & Zimmermann, A. (eds.) Archäologie und Korrespondenzanalyse. Beispiele, fragen, Perspektiven. *Internationale Archäologie*, 23. Rahden, pp. 161-174.

Renfrew, C. 1982: Explanation Revisited. In: Renfrew, C. Rowlands, M.J. & Sagraves, B.A. (eds.) *Theory and Explanation in Archaeology*. The Southampton Conference. New York & London, pp. 5-24.

Richards, C. 1990a: The Late Neolithic House in Orkney. In: Samson, R. (ed.) *The Social Archaeology of Houses*, Edinburgh, pp. 111-124.

Richards, C. 1990b: The Late Neolithic settlement complex at Barnhouse Farm, Stenness. In: Renfrew, C. (ed.) *The Prehistory of Orkney* (2nd edition), Edinburgh.

Richards, C. 1991.: Skara Brae: Revisiting a Neolithic village in Orkney. In: Hanson, W.S. & Slater, E.A. (eds.) *Scottish archaeology: New perceptions*. Aberdeen, 24-43.

Richards, C. 2005: The Neolithic Settlement of Orkney. In: Colin Richards (ed.) *Dwelling among the monuments: The Neolithic village of Barnhouse, Maeshowe passage grave and surrounding monuments at Stenness, Orkney*. McDonald Institute Monographs.

Richards, M.P. & Koch, E. 2001: Neolitisk Kost – Analyser af kvælstof-isotopen 15N i menneskeskeletter fra yngre stenalder. *Aarbøger for Nordisk Oldkyndighed og historie*, 1999. Copenhagen, 7-17.

Rieck, F. & Crumlin-Pedersen, O. 1988: *Både fra Danmarks oldtid*. Vikingeskibshallen, Roskilde.

Rindel, P.O. 1993: Bønder fra stenalder til middelalder ved Nørre Holsted – nye arkæologiske undersøgelser på den kommende motorvej mellem Vejen og Holsted. *Mark og Montre*, 29.årgang, 1993, pp. 19-27.

Roberts, B.K. 1996: *Landscapes of Settlement. Prehistory to the present*. London/New York.

Robinson, D.E. 2003.: Neolithic and Bronze Age Agriculture in Southern Scandinavia – Recent Archaeobotanical Evidence from Denmark. *Environmental Archeology* 8, pp. 145-165.

Robinson, D.E. 1994: Crop plants in Danish prehistory. (AUD) *Arkæologiske udgravninger i Danmark*, 1993. Copenhagen, pp. 36-39.

Rostholm, H. 1986: Naturgasundersøgelser i Herning Museums arbejdsområde 1983-86. *FRAM – Fra Ringkøbing Amts Museer*, 1986, 55p.

Rostholm, H. 1987: Vorgod, sb. 221. In: Rigsantikvarens Arkæologiske Sekretariat (ed.) *Danmarks længste udgravning. Arkæologi på naturgassens vej 1979-86*. Nationalmuseet/de danske naturgasselskaber. Copenhagen, p. 362.

Roymans, N. 1999: Man, cattle and the supernatural in the Northwest European plain. In: Fabech, C. & Ringtved, J. (eds.), *Settlement and Landscape. Proceedings of a conference in Århus, Denmark. 1998*. Højbjerg, pp. 291-300.

Russell, M. 2000: *Flintmines in Neolithic Britain*. Gloucestershire.

Rønne, P. 1996: Flydende bronze i digler og forme.- Forsøg med bronzealderens støbeteknik. In: Meldgaard, M. & Rasmussen, M. (eds.) *Arkæologiske eksperimenter i Lejre*. Lejre, pp. 97-112.

Sahlins, M. [1972] 1974: *Stone Age Economics*. London.

Sarauw, T. 2006: Bejsebakken. Late Neolithic Houses and Settlement Structure. *Nordiske Fortidsminder. Series C*, 4. Det Kongelige Nordiske Oldskriftselskab. Copenhagen.

Sarauw, T. 2007a: Male symbols or warrior identities? The 'archery burials' of the Danish Bell Beaker Culture. *Journal of Anthropological Archaeology*, 26/1, pp 65-87.

Sarauw, T. 2007b: On the Outskirts of the European Bell Beaker Phenomenon – the Danish Case. www.jungsteinsite.de, pp. 1-61.

Sarauw, T. 2007c: Early Late Neolithic dagger production in northern Jutland: marginalised production or source of wealth? *Bericht der Römisch-Germanischen Kommission*, 87 (2006), pp. 213-272.

Sarauw, T. 2008: On the Outskirts of the European Bell Beaker Phenomenon. The settlement of Bejsebakken and the social organisation of Late Neolithic societies. In: Dörfler, W. & Müller, J. (eds.) Umwelt – Wirtschaft – Siedlungen im dritten vorchristlichen Jahrtausend Mitteleuropas und Südskandinaviens. Internationale Tagung Kiel 4.-6. November 2005. *Offa Bücher*, 84, pp. 83-125.

Sarauw, T. 2009: Danish Bell Beaker Pottery and Flint Daggers – the Display of Social Identities? *European Journal of Archaeology*, 11, 1, pp. 23-47.

Schacke, A.T. 2003: Enkelt- og enestegårde på Fyn – i dyrkningsfællesskabets tid. *Landbohistorisk Selskabs Studieserie*.

Schauer, P. 1996: Hausgrundrisse und Siedelstrukturen der frühen und mittleren Bronzezeit Süddeutschlands. In: *Probleme der Bronze- und der frühen Eisenzeit in Mitteleuropa. Festschrift für Marek Gedl zum 60. Geburtstag und zum 40. Jahrestag der wissenschaftlichen Tätigkeit an der Jagiellonen-Universität*. Kraków, pp. 451-480.

Schefzik, M. 1995: Neuartige Funde und Befunde endneolitisch-älterfrühbronzezeitlicher Zeitstellung von Eching, Ldkr. Freising. *Bayerishe Vorgeschichteblätter*, 60, pp. 273-87.

Schefzik, M. 2001: Die bronze-und eisenzeitliche Besiedlungsgeschichte der Münchener Ebene. Eine Unterzuchung zu Gebäude- und Siedlungsformen im süddeutschen Raum. *Internationale Archäeologie*, 68. Rahden.

Schefzik, M. 2010: Siedlungen der Frühbronzezeit in Mitteleuropa – Eine Gegenüberstellung der Hausformen Süddeutschlands und des Aunjetizer Bereiches. *Tagungen des Landesmuseums für Vorgeschichte Halle*, 5, pp. 333-349.

Schiffer, M.B. 1987: Primary and Secondary Refuse. In: *Formation Processes of the Archaeological Record*. University of New Mexico Press. Albuquerque, pp. 58-64.

Schovsbo, P.O. 1987: *Oldtidens vogne i Norden. Arkæologiske undersøgelser af mose- og jordfundne vogndele af træ fra neolitikum til ældre middelalder*. Bangsbomuseet, Frederikshavn.

Segalen, M. 1988: *Historical anthropology of the family. Themes in the Social Sciences*. Cambridge.

Segerberg, A. 1978: Den enkla skafthålsyxan av sten. Fyndförhållanden och dateringar. *TOR, Tidskrift för nordisk fornkunskap*, 17, pp. 159-218.

Seymour-Smith, C. 1986.: Macmillan Dictionary of Anthropology. London.

Sherratt, A. 1983: The secondary exploitation of animals in the Old World. Transhumance and pastoralism. *World Archaeology*, 15, 1. Princeton, pp. 90-104.

Sherratt, A. 1987: Cups that cheered. In: Waldren, W.H. & Kennard, R.C. (eds.) Bell Beakers of the Western Mediterranean. Definition, Interpretation, Theory and New Site Data. The Oxford International Conference 1986. *British Archaeological Reports, International Series*, 331, pp. 81-106.

Siemen, P. 1993.: Mellem Ugvig og Tovrup – eller 3000 års bosættelser ved Grønnegård. *Mark og Montre*, 61-70.

Siemen, P. 2009: Sen yngre stenalder i Sydvestjylland. *Arkæologiske Rapporter fra Esbjerg Museum*, 4,1. Sydvestjyske Museer. Esbjerg 2009.

Simonsen, A., Lindblom, I., & Bakkevig, S. 1982 : Økologi og økonomi for deler av Sør-Jæren i senneolitikum. Del 3. Ruglandboplassen belyst ved ‹site-territory›-analyse. Arkeologisk museum i Stavanger. Stavanger, pp. 41-55.

Simonsen, J. 1979: Dolktidsgrave fra Vejby og Fjallerslev. *MIV* 8, 1978. Museerne i Viborg amt. Viborg, pp. 32-36.

Simonsen, J. 1982a: Bolig eller dødehus? *MIV* 11, 1981. Museerne i Viborg amt. Viborg, pp. 52-69.

Simonsen, J. 1982b: En analyse af geografisk repræsentativitet i fund fra enkeltgravskulturen i et jysk regionalområde. In: Thrane, H.(ed.) Om yngre stenalders bebyggelseshistorie. Beretning fra et symposium. Odense 30. April - 1.maj 1981. *Skrifter fra Historisk Institut, Odense Universitet*, 30, pp. 88-92a.

Simonsen, J. 1983: A Late Neolithic House Site at Tastum, Northwestern Jutland. *Journal of Danish Archaeology*, 2 (1983), pp. 81-89.

Simonsen, J. 1984: Dobbelt-åget fra Bredmose i Fjends herred. *Hikuin*, 10. Aarhus, pp. 137-143.

Simonsen, J. 1986: Nogle nordvestjyske bopladsfund fra enkeltgravskulturen og deres topografi. In: Adamsen, C. & Ebbesen, K. (eds.) Stridsøksetid i Sydskandinavien. Beretning fra et symposium 28.-30. X 1985 i Vejle. *Arkæologiske Skrifter*, 1. Copenhagen, pp. 292-300.

Simonsen, J. 1987: Settlements from the Single Grave Culture in North-West Jutland. A Preliminary Survey. *Journal of Danish Archaeology*, 5 (1986), pp. 135-151.

Simonsen, J. 1989a.: Fra oldtids-pottemagerens værksted. Skive.

Simonsen, J. 1989b: Eksotiske folk og arkæologiske rekonstruktioner. In: Højris, O. (ed.) *Dansk mental geografi. Danskernes syn på verden – og på sig selv*. Aarhus, pp. 162-172.

Simonsen, J. 1993a: Bronzealderhuset i Vile – og et dilemma. In: Bro-Jørgensen, M., Iversen, M., Jacobsen, B., Langballe, H., Nielsen, E.L. & Vellev, J. (eds.) *En hilsen til Peter Seeberg. Ps.* 1. Højbjerg, pp. 189-194.

Simonsen, J. 1993b: Resengaard, NV-Jylland. Bebyggelse fra tidlig bronzealder. In: *Kongresberetning: 19. Nordiske Arkæolog Kongres. Vejle 12.-19.september 1993*. Copenhagen, pp. 109-112.

Simonsen, J. 1996a: Inspiration, projektstart og arbejdsmåde. In: Nielsen, J. & Simonsen, J. (eds.) *Bronzealderens bopladser i Midt- og Nordvestjylland*. Skive, pp. 10-17.

Simonsen, J. 1996b: Bronzealderens bebyggelser i landskabet. In: Nielsen J. & Simonsen, J. (eds.) *Bronzealderens bopladser i Midt- og Nordvestjylland*. Skive, pp. 18-33.

Simonsen, J. 1996c: Bebyggelsen på Glattrup-næsset i ældre bronzealder. In: Nielsen, J. & Simonsen, J. (eds.) *Bronzealderens bopladser i Midt- og Nordvestjylland*. Skive, pp. 90-103.

Simonsen, J. 1999: Bronze Age settlements in Glattrup and around Lake Tastum, NW Jutland. In: Fabech, C. & Ringtved, J. (eds.) *Settlement and Landscape. Proceedings* of a Conference in Århus, Denmark. 1998. Aarhus, pp. 200-204.

Simonsen, J. 2001: Sjældne fund fra stenalderens sidste del. In: Gormsen, G., Kristensen, I.K., Mortensen, N. & Simonsen, J. (eds.) Skive kommunes historie fra oldtid til 1880. Skive, 39-46.

Simonsen, J. 2006: Strandet Hovedgaard. Children's graves of the late Single Grave Culture in North Jutland, and some social and cultural considerations. Journal of Danish Archaeology, 14, pp. 45-85.

Simonsen, J. (im manus.): (Article on the Rosgårde settlement, its topography and livelihood. Peer reviewed 2016).

Simonsen, J. (in prep.): (Article on the Glattrup Beaker settlements, beer production, gatherings, landscape settings, and other in the Limfjord archipelago).

Skak-Nielsen, N.V. 2009: Flint and metal daggers in Scandinavia and other parts of Europe. A re-interpretation of their function in the Late Neolithic and Early Copper and Bronze Age. Antiquity, 83, pp. 349-358.

Skjølsvold, A. 1977: Slettabøboplassen. Et bidrag til diskusjonen om forholdet mellom fangst- og bondesamfundet i yngre steinalder og bronsealder. AmS skrifter, 2. Arkeologisk museum i Stavanger. Stavanger.

Skousen, H. 1998: Rønbjerg Strandvolde – en kystboplads ved Limfjorden. KUML 1997-1998. Årbog for Jysk Arkæologisk Selskab. Aarhus, pp. 29-74.

Skov, T. 1978.: En hustomt med klokkebægerkeramik fra Stendis. Holstebro Museum. Årsskrift 1977. Holstebro, pp. 39-50.

Skov, T. 1982: A Late Neolithic House Site with Bell Beaker Pottery at Stendis, Northwestern Jutland. Journal of Danish Archaeology, 1, pp. 39-44.

Skårup, J. 1995: Stone Age burials in Boats. In: Crumlin-Petersen, O. & Munch Thye, B. (eds.) The ship as a symbol in Prehistoric and Medieval Scandinavia. Papers from an International Research Seminar at the Danish National Museum, Copenhagen, 5-7 May 1994. (PNM) Publications from the National Museum. Studies in Archaeology and History, 1. Copenhagen, pp. 51-58.

Stenberger, M. (ed.) 1943: Forntida gårdar i Island. Meddelanden från den nordiska arkeologiska undersökningen i Island sommaren 1939. Copenhagen.

Stenning, D.J. 1971: Household Viability among the Pastoral Fulani. In: Goody, J. (ed.) The Developmental Cycle in Domestic Groups. Cambridge, pp. 92-119.

Stoklund, B. 1972: Bondegård og byggeskik før 1850. Dansk Historisk Fællesforenings Håndbøger. Copenhagen.

Strandgaard, H.C. 1883: Om Bygningsforholdene i Salling, navnlig i ældre Tid. Samlinger til Jysk Historie og Topografi. IX, pp. 1882-83.

Strathern, M. 1985: Discovering 'Social Control'. Journal of Law and Society, 12, 2. Wiley/Cardiff University, pp. 111-134.

Strömberg, M. 1968: Et senneolitiskt grophus i Valleberga. Ale. Historisk tidskrift for Skåne, Halland och Blekinge, pp. 1-15.

Strömberg, M. 1971: Senneolitiska huslämningar i Skåne. Fornvännen 1971, pp. 237-254.

Strömberg, M. 1975: Comments on The Flint Daggers of Denmark. Norwegian Archaeological Review, 8, 2, pp. 112-114.

Strömberg, M. 1978: Hagestadsundersökningen som utgångspunkt for bebyggelseshistoriska metoder. In: Thrane, H. (ed.) Bebyggelseshistorisk metode og teknik. Beretning fra et symposium d. 19.-20.maj 1978 afholdt af Odense Universitet. Skrifter fra Historisk Institut, 23, Odense, pp. 4-13.

Strömberg, M. 1982: Ingelstorp. Zur Siedlungsentwicklung eines südschwedischen Dorfes. Acta Archaeologica Lundensia. Series in 4°, 14. Bonn/Lund.

Strömberg, M. 1992: A Concentration of Houses from the Late Neolithic/Early Bronze Age at Hagestad. Meddelanden från Lunds universitetets historiska museum, 1991-92. Lund, pp. 57-89.

Säfvestad, U. 1997: Husforskning i Sverige 1950 – 1994. In: Söderberg, B. Linderoth, T. & Knarrström, B. (eds.) Boplatslämningar från jäger- och bondestenålder samt bronsålder. Riksantikvarieämbetet, UV Syd Rapport, 1997:7. Lund.

Stäuble, H. 1997: Die frühbronzezeitliche Siedlung in Zwenkau, Landkreis Leipziger Land. In: Assendorp, J.J. (ed.) Forschungen zur bronzezeitlichen Besiedlung in Nord- und Mitteleuropa. Internationales Symposium vom 9.-11. Mai 1996 in Hitzacker. Internationale Archaologie, 38. Herausgegeben vom Institut zur Denkmalpflege im Niedersächsischen Landesverwaltungsamt und der Archaeologischen Kommission zur Niedersachsen e. V. Espelkamp, pp. 129-148.

Stäuble, H. & Huth, C. 1995: Wenn Sensationen Alltag werden: Die grossflachigen archäologischen Untersuchungen im Tagebau Zwenkau. Archäologie aktuell im Freistaat Sachsen, 3, pp. 10 -23.

Stäuble, H. & Huth, C. 1998: Ländliche Siedlungen der Bronzezeit und älteren Eisenzeit. Ein Zwischenbericht aus Zwenkau. Archäologische Forschungen in urgeschichtlichen Siedlungslandschaften. Festschrift für Georg Kossack zum 75. Geburtstag. Regensburger Beiträge zur Prähistorischen Archäologie, 5. Regensburg, pp. 185-230.

Streifert, J. 2004: Twå rum och kök – spår av rumsbildning i halländska boningshus under bronzålder och äldre järnålder. In: Carlie, L., Ryberg, E., Streifert, J., & Wranning, P. (eds.) Landskap i förändring. Hållplatser i det förgangna, 6, pp. 190-224.

Szczesiak, R. 1999: Eine bemerkenswerte frühbronzezeitliche Siedlung bei Neuenkirchen, Landkreis Mecklenburg-Strelitz. In: Budesheim, W. & Keiling, H. (eds.) Zur Bronzezeit in Norddeutschland. Freie Lauenburgische Akademie fur Wissenschaft und Kultur. Beitrage fur Wissenschaft und Kultur, 3. Neumünster, pp. 107-122.

Sørensen, M.L.S. 2010: Households. In: Earle T. & Kristiansen, K. (eds.) Organizing Bronze Age Societies. The Mediterranean, Central Europe, and Scandinavia Compared. Cambridge, pp. 122-154.

Terkildsen, N. 2006: Hustomter fra sen bondestenalder til yngre bronzealder. *Bygherrerapport for VMÅ* 2538. Vesthimmerlands Museum, pp. 1-11.

Terkildsen, K.N. & Mikkelsen, M. 2011 : Liseborg Høje II. Små treskibede huse fra y. stenalder? *Bygherrerapport, Viborg Stiftsmuseum*, nr. 59, pp. 1-19.

Thieme, W. 1997: Zu den Hausgrundrissen bei Daerstorf, Gemeinde Neu Wulmstorf, Landkreis Harburg. In: Assendorp, J.J. (ed.) Forschungen zur bronzezeitlichen Besiedlung in Nord- und Mitteleuropa. Internationales Symposium vom 9.-11. Mai 1996 in Hitzacker. *Internationale Archaologie*, 38. Herausgegeben vom Institut zur Denkmalpflege im Niedersächsischen Landesverwaltungsamt und der Archaeologischen Kommission zur Niedersachsen e. V. Espelkamp, pp. 29-39.

Thieme, H. & Maier, R. 1995: Aunjetitzer Kultur. In: Thieme, H. & Maier, R. (eds.) Archäologische Ausgrabungen im Braunkohlentagebau Schöningen, Landkreis Helmstedt. Hannover, pp. 166-175.

Thomas, J. 1996: Neolithic houses in Mainland Britain and Ireland – A sceptical view. In: Darvill, T. & Thomas, J. (eds.), Neolithic Houses in Northwest Europe and Beyond. Neolithic Studies Group Seminar Papers, 1. *Oxbow Monograph*, 57. Oxford, pp. 1-12.

Thorpe, I.J.N. 1997: From Settlements to Monuments: Site Succession in Late Neolithic and Early Bronze Age Jutland, East Denmark. In: Nash, G. (ed.) Semiotics of Landscape: Archaeology of Mind. *British Archaeological Reports, International Series*, 661. Oxford, pp. 71-79.

Thorpe, I.J.N. 2000: Bare but Bountiful: the later Neolithic Social and Physical Landscape of Thy, Jutland. In: Richie, A. (ed.) *Neolithic Orkney in its European Context*. Cambridge, pp. 71-78.

Thrane, H. 1976: Bebyggelseshistorie som arbejdsmetode. In: Thrane, H. (ed.) Bebyggelsesarkæologi. Beretning fra et symposium den 7-8 nov. 1975 afholdt af Odense universitet. *Skrifter fra Institut for historie og samfundsvidenskab*, 17. Odense, pp. 5-15.

Thrane, H. 1985: Bronze Age Settlements. In: Kristiansen, K. (ed.): Archaeological Formation Processes. The representativity of archaeological remains from Danish Prehistory. Copenhagen, pp. 142-151.

Thrane, H. 1989: Siedlungsarchäologische Untersuchungen in Dänemark. *Praehistorische Zeitschrift*, 47, pp. 5-47.

Thrane, H. 1991: Danish Plough-Marks from the Neolithic and Bronze Age. *Journal of Danish Archaeology*, 8 (1989), pp. 111-125.

Tilander, I. 1963: A Late Neolithic Settlement in Furulund, Scania. *Meddelanden från Lunds Universitetets Historiska Museum*, 1962-63, pp. 123-135.

Topping, P. 1996.: Structure and ritual in the Neolithic house: Some examples from Britain and Ireland. In: Darvill, T. & Thomas, J. (eds.) Neolithic Houses in Northwest Europe and Beyond. Neolithic Studies Group Seminar Papers, l. *Oxbow Monograph*, 57, Oxford, pp. 157-170.

Trigger, B.G. 1968: The Development of Settlement Patterns. In: Chang, K. C. (ed.) *Settlement Archaeology*. Washington D.C., pp. 53-78.

Tringham, R. 1995: Archaeological Houses, Households, Housework and the Home. In: Benjamin, D.N., Stea, D. & Saile, D. (eds.) *The Home: Words, Interpretations, Meanings and Environments*. Aldershot, pp. 79-107.

Turner, V. [1967] 2005: The Forest of Symbols; aspects of Ndembu Ritual. Ithaca.

Ullén, I. 1994: The power of case studies. Interpretation of a Late-Bronze-Age settlement in central Sweden. *Journal of European Archaeology*, 2.2 (1994), pp. 249-262.

van Gennep, A. [1909] 1975: The Rites of Passage. Chicago.

Vander Linden, M. 2001: Beer and Beakers: A Tentative Analysis. In: Gheroghiu, D. (ed.) Material, Virtual and Temporal Compositions: On the Relationships between Objects. *British Archaeological Reports, International Series*, 953, Oxford, pp. 45-51.

Vander Linden, M. 2007: What linked the Bell Beakers in third millenium BC Europe? *Antiquity*, 81 (312), pp. 343-352.

Vandkilde, H. 1989: Det ældste metalmiljø i Danmark. In: Poulsen, J. (ed.) Regionale forhold i Nordisk Bronzealder, 5. Nordiske symposium for Bronzealderforskning på Sandbjerg Slot 1987. *Jysk Arkæologisk Selskabs Skrifter*, XXIV, pp. 29-45.

Vandkilde, H. 1990a: Senneolitikum ved Limfjorden. Fra dominans til anonymitet. *Limfjordsprojektet. Rapport* nr. 1, Aarhus, pp. 109-122.

Vandkilde, H. 1990b: A Late Neolithic Hoard with Objects of Bronze and Gold from Central Jutland. *Journal of Danish Archaeology*, 7, 1988, pp. 115-135.

Vandkilde, H. 1993a: Aspekter af teknologi og samfund i overgangstiden mellem sten- og bronzealder i Danmark. In: Forsberg, L. & Larsson T.B (eds.) Ekonomi och näringsformer i nordisk bronsålder. Rapport från det 6:e nordiska bronsålderssymposiet, Nämforsen 1990. *Studia Archaeologica Universitatis Umensis*, 3, pp. 53-69.

Vandkilde, H. 1993b: The earliest metalwork. In: Hvass, S. & Storgaard, B. (eds.) *Digging into the Past. 25 Years of Archaeology in Denmark*. Det Kgl. Nordiske Oldskriftselskab/Jysk Arkæologisk Selskab. Copenhagen/Aarhus, pp. 145-151.

Vandkilde, H. 1996: From Stone to Bronze. The Metalwork of the Late Neolithic and Earliest Bronze Age in Denmark. *Jutland Archaeological Society Publications*, XXXII. Højbjerg.

Vandkilde, H. 2001: Beaker Representation in the Danish Late Neolithic. In: Nicolis, F. (ed.) *Bell Beakers today. Pottery, people, culture, symbols in prehistoric Europe*. Proceedings of the international colloquium, Riva del Garda, 11-16 May 1998. Ufficio Bene Archeologici. Trento, pp. 333-360.

Vandkilde, H. 2007: A Review of the Early Late Neolithic Period in Denmark: Practice, Identity and Connectivity. *Offa-Jahrbuch* 61/62 (2004/2005), pp. 75-109.

Vandkilde, H. 2009: Communities with Bell Beaker Transculture. *Norwegian Archaeological Review*, 42, 1 (2009), pp. 74-79.

Vandkilde, H. 2010: Et offerfund med tidlige metalsager fra Skeldal. In: *Danefæ. Skatte fra den danske muld*. Nationalmuseet. Copenhagen.

Vandkilde, H. Rahbek, U. & Rasmussen, K.L. 1996: Radiocarbon Dating and the Chronology of Bronze Age Southern Scandinavia. *Acta Archaeologica*, 57. Copenhagen, pp. 183-198.

Verhart, L.B.M. 1992: Settling or Trekking? The Late Neolithic House Plans of Haamstede-Brabers and their Counterparts. *Oudheidkundige mededelingen uit het Rijksmuseum van Oudheden te Leiden*, pp. 73-99.

Wetzel, G. 1979: Die Schönfelder Kultur. Veröffentlichungen des Landesmuseum zur Vorgeschichte in Halle, 31. Berlin.

Whittle, A.W.R., Keith-Lucas, M., Milles, A., Noddle, B., Rees, S., & Romans, J. 1986.: Scord of Brouster: an early agricultural settlement on Shetland. *Oxford University Committee for Archaeology. Monograph*, 9. Oxford.

Wilk, R.R. & Rathje, W. 1982: Archaeology of the Household: Building a Prehistory of Domestic Life. *American Behavioral Scientist*, 25, pp, 617-40.

Wilk, R.R. 1983: Little House in the Jungle: The Causes of Variation in House Size among Modern Kekchi Maya. *Journal of Anthropological Archaeology*, 2, pp. 99-116.

Wåhlin, S. & Mikkelsen, M. 2008: Randrup Mølle – et langhus med forsænket østende fra yngre stenalder. *Bygherrerapport, Viborg Stiftsmuseum*, nr. 25, pp. 1-8.

Zich, B. 1994: "In Flintbek stand ein Steinzeithaus ...". Ein Hausfund von der Wende des Neolithikums zur Bronzezeit aus Flintbek, Kreis Rendsburg-Eckernförde. A*rchaeologische Nachrichten aus Schleswig-Holstein. Mitteilungen der Archäologischen Gesellschaft Schleswig-Holstein* e. V., 4/5 (1993/1994). Schleswig, pp. 18-46.

Zich, B. 2000: Das spätneolithische Haus. Flintbek LA 20" und nord- und mitteleuropäische Entsprechungen. In: Kelm, R. (ed.): Vom Phostenloch zum Steinzeithaus. Archäologische Forschung und Rekonstruktion jungsteinzeitlicher Haus- und Siedlungsbefunde im nordwestlichen Mitteleuropa. Heide, pp. 88-100.

Zimmermann, A. 1997: Zur Anwendung der Korrespondenzanalyse in der Archäologie. In: Müller, J. & Zimmermann, A. (eds.) Archäologie und Korrespondenzanalyse. Beispiele, Fragen, Perspektiven. *Internationale Archäologie*, 23. Rahden, pp. 9-16.

Zimmermann, W. H. 2001: Phosphate analysis – an important tool in settlement archaeology. (AUD) *Arkæologiske udgravninger i Danmark* 2000, pp. 35-43.

Østmo, E. 1977: Schaftlochäxte und landwirtschaftliche Siedlung. Eine Fallstudie über Kulturverhältnisse im Südöstlichsten Norwegen im Spätneolithikum und in der älteren Bronzezeit. *Acta Archaeologica*, 48, 155-206.

Østmo, E. 2005: Over Skagerak i steinalderen: Noen refleksjoner om oppfinnelsen av havgående fartøyer i Norden. *Viking*, 68. Oslo, pp 55-82.

Østmo, E. 2009: The Northern Connection: Bell Beaker Culture Influences North of Skagerak. Norwegian Archaeological Review, 42, 1, (2009), pp. 86-89.

Årlin, C. 1999.: Under samma tak – Om "husstallets" uppkomst och betydelse under bronsåldern ur ett sydskandinaviskt perspektiv. In: Olausson, M. (ed.) *Spiralens Öga. Tjugo artiklar kring aktuell bronsåldersforskning*. Riksantikvarieämbetet, pp. 291-307.

Reports

Archaeological excavation reports and scientific examination reports referred to in the present work are listed below. The head of fieldwork usually also wrote the report. The reference numbers are only assigned to the reports for use in this work. The acronyms VSM, HOL and SMS relate to Viborg Museum, Holstebro Museum and Museum Salling (previously Skive Museum).

Besides those stated in the following, numerous excavation reports – in particular from the archives of The National Museum of Denmark and certain local museums – have been consulted in order to check on new information from fieldwork relating to the Late Neolithic and emerging Bronze Age settlements.

Archaological excavation reports

U1967a. Gåsemose: Report entitled: "Boplads fra yngre stenalder – ældre bronzealder". Gåsemose, Thise sogn, Salling Nørreherred, Viborg amt. Sb.nr.59. Journal number 1126/67. Year of excavation: 1967. Nationalmuseet, Copenhagen. The finds given an extra set of numbers are accounted for by Karsten Davidsen (1976) in: "Særnummereringsliste: GÅ 1-GÅ 426". Additional journal (Skive): SMS 1077A. Heads of fieldwork: Aino Kann Rasmussen & Jørn Bie.

U1983a. Glattrup I: Report entitled: "Beretning over arkæologisk undersøgelse af et bopladsområde med bebyggelsesspor fra (Maglemosekultur), tragtbægerkultur, enkeltgravskultur, dolktid, bronzealder og jernalder på Glattrup I, Skive sogn, Hindborg herred, Viborg amt". Year of investigation: 1983. File: SMS 270A. Head of fieldwork: John Simonsen.

Report U1990a. Glattrup III: Report entitled: "Beretning over arkæologisk undersøgelse af et bopladsområde med bebyggelsesspor fra (Maglemosekultur), tragtbægerkultur, enkeltgravskultur, dolktid, bronzealder og jernalder i Glattrup, Skive sogn, Hindborg herred, Viborg amt". Heading of this subpart: "Udgravningsrapport vedr.undersøgelse af tre felter med bebyggelsesspor, beliggende Lokesvej, Glattrup III, Skive Landsogn, Skive Kommune, Viborg amt. Year of investigation: 1990. File: SMS 270A. Head of fieldwork: Poul Mikkelsen. Comment: Glattrup III relates to a separate, later continuation of the excavation at Glattrup I.

Report U1992a. Marienlyst Strand: Report entitled: "Udgravningsberetning. Marienlyst Strand. Resen sogn, Hindborg herred". Year of investigation: 1992. File: SMS 519A. Head of fieldwork: Poul Mikkelsen.

Report U1994. Siggård: Report entitled: "SMS 557A Siggård, matr.20a og 18e, Dommerby sogn, Fjends herred, Viborg amt". Year of investigation: 1992. File: SMS 519A. Head of fieldwork: Christian Aabo Jørgensen.

Report U1995a. Granlygård: Report entitled: "Granlygård. Udgravningsberetning vedr. undersøgelse af bopladser fra Maglemosekultur, Dolktid, bronzealder og førromerskjernalder". Years of investigation: 1994-95. File: SMS 560A. Head of fieldwork: Poul Mikkelsen.

Report U1998a. Hellegård: Report entitled: "Rapport over arkæologisk undersøgelse ved Hellegård, Sæby sogn, Harre herred, Viborg amt." Year of investigation: 1998. File: SMS 654A. Head of fieldwork: Kurt G. Overgaard.

Report U1999a. Glattrup IV: Report entitled: "Beretning over arkæologisk undersøgelse ved Glattrup. IV, Skive og Dommerby s., Hindborg og Fjends h., Viborg a." Year of investigation: 1999. File: SMS 695A. Head of fieldwork: Kurt G. Overgaard.

Report U1999b. Drosselvej: Report entitled: "Drosselvej, Bremdal skole." Struer kommune. Year of investigation: 1999.: File: HOL 20.330. Head of fieldwork: Bo Steen.

Report U2000a. Kluborg II: Report entitled: "Rapport over udgravning af boplads spor fra MN A, ældre bronzealder og yngre bronzealder ved Kluborg II, Skive lands., Hindborg h., Viborg a" Year of investigation: 2000. File: SMS 722A. Head of fieldwork: Kurt G. Overgaard.

Report U2001a. Tromgade: Report entitled: "Beretning over arkæologisk undersøgelse af bopladsspor fra senneolitikum,: bronzealder og ældre jernalder ved Tromgade, Thise sogn, Salling Nørreherred, Viborg amt". Year of investigation: 2001. File: SMS 746A. Head of fieldwork: Kurt G. Overgaard.

Report U2001b. Kluborg II: Report entitled: "Rapport over udgravning af bopladsspor fra sen yngre bronzealder – tidlig førromersk jernalder ved Kluborg II, sb.nr. 146, Skive Ls., Hindborg h., Viborg a." Year of investigation: 2001. File: SMS 722A. Head of fieldwork: Kurt G. Overgaard.

Report U2001c. Rosgårde: Report entitled: "Beretning over arkæologisk undersøgelse af bopladsspor fra sten- og bronzealder ved Rosgårde, Mønsted s., Fjends h., Viborg a". Years of investigation: 2000-2001. File: SMS 731A. Head of fieldwork: Kurt G. Overgaard.

Report U2001d. Vindelsbæk I: Report entitled: "VSM 64G, Vindelsbæk, Elsborg sogn, Viborg amt ". Year of investigation: 2000. Museum: Viborg Stiftsmuseum. File: VSM G064. Head of fieldwork: Martin Mikkelsen.

Report U2002a. Kås Hovedgård II: Report entitled: "Udgravningsrapport over udgravningen af en hustomt fra ældre bronzealder og forsænkning fra sen-neolitikum". Lihme sogn, Rødding herred, Viborg amt. Year of investigation: 2002. Skive Museum. File: SMS 788A. Head of fieldwork: Inge Kjær Kristensen.

Report U2002b. Skringstrup øst: Report entitled: "VSM G290, Skringstrup Øst, Skals sogn, Rinds herred, Viborg amt". Year of investigation: 2002. Viborg Stiftsmuseum. File: VSM G290. Heads of fieldwork: Kurt G. Overgaard & Martin Mikkelsen.

Report U2004a. Hejlskov Hede: Report entitled: "Beretning over udgravning af bopladsspor fra GRK, SN/Æ-BRA ved Hejlskov,: Ørslevkloster sogn, Fjends Herred, Viborg amt." Years of investigation: 2003-2004. File: SMS 840A. Head of fieldwork: Kurt G. Overgaard.

Scientific examination reports

S1991a. Micro-wear analyses: Material: Flint artefacts from NW Jutland. Report entitled: "Slidsporsanalyse af redskaber fra Skive Museum, Museet for Thy og Vester Hanherred samt Fur Museum" Skive Museum 1991. Report by Merete Christensen.

S1999a. Archaeo-botanical examination: Material: Macrofossils from the Brd. Gram site. Report entitled: "Arkæobotaniske analyser af forkullede planterester fra sen-neolitikum og ældre bronzealder ved Brd. Gram, Vojens". Nationalmuseet, Copenhagen. Report number: NNU Rapport nr. 21. 1999. Report by David Earle Robinson & J. Harild.

S2000a. Archaeo-botanical examination: Material: Macrofossils and pollen from the Strandet Hovedgaard site. Report entitled: "Arkæobotaniske undersøgelser af materiale fra enkeltgravshustomter ved Strandet Hovedgaard". Nationalmuseet, Copenhagen. Report number: NNU Rapport nr .5. 2000. Report by David Earle Robinson & Ida Boldsen.

S2000b. Archaeo-botanical examination: Material: Macrofossils from Djursland. Report entitled: "Agerbrug i senneolitikum og bronzealderen på Djursland". Nationalmuseet, Copenhagen. Report number: NNU Rapport nr.7. 2000. Report by Peter Steen Henriksen.

S2001a. Archaeo-botanical examination: Material: Macrofossils from Resengaard, Glattrup (I/III, IV) & Kluborg II. Report entitled: "Arkæobotanisk undersøgelse af materiale fra fire bopladser fra dolktid til ældre bronzealder ved Skive". Nationalmuseet, Copenhagen. Report number: NNU Rapport nr. 11. 2001. Report by Peter Steen Henriksen.

S2004a. Micro-wear analyses: Material: Flint artefacts from Resengaard and other sites. Report entitled: " Slidsporsanalyse af redskaber fra Resengaard". Moesgård Museum, Aarhus. 2004. Report by Claus Skriver.

S2009a. Archaeo-botanical examination: Report entitled: "Makrofossilfund fra enkeltgravskultur, senneolitikum og ældre bronzealder. Arkæobotanisk analyse fra Rosgårde (SMS 731A), Hedevang (SMS 818A), Tinghøj Huse (SMS 871A), Sdr. Ørum (SMS 797A) and Lundbro II (SMS 785A)." Konserverings- og naturvidenskabelig afdeling, nr.4. Moesgård Museum, 2009. Report by Marianne Høyem Andreasen.